Also by Thomas Kessner

TODAY'S IMMIGRANTS, THEIR STORIES:
A New Look at the Latest Immigrants
with Betty Caroli

THE GOLDEN DOOR:
Italian and Jewish Immigrant Mobility in
New York City, 1880–1915

FIORELLO H. LA GUARDIA

FIORELLO H. LA GUARDIA
AND THE MAKING OF MODERN NEW YORK

Thomas Kessner

McGraw-Hill Publishing Company

New York   St. Louis   San Francisco
Hamburg   Mexico   Toronto

1 2 3 4 5 6 7 8 9 DOC DOC 8 9 2 1 0 9

ISBN 0-07-034244-X

Library of Congress Cataloging-in-Publication Data

Kessner, Thomas.
    Fiorello H. La Guardia and the making of modern New
York / Thomas Kessner.
      p. cm.
    Includes index.
    ISBN 0-07-034244-X
    1. La Guardia, Fiorello H. (Fiorello Henry), 1882–1947.
2. Mayors—New York (N.Y.)—Biography. 3. Legislators
—United States—Biography. 4. United States. Congress.
House—Biography. 5. New York (N.Y.)—Politics and
government—1898–1951. 6. United States—Politics and
government—1901–1953. I. Title.
E748.L23K47 1989
974.7'104'0924—dc19
  [B]   89-2293
                                            CIP

Book design by Mark Bergeron

B'ezras Hashem

for

Joseph, Hadassah, Sara, Yechezkel, Meir, David,
and always, Rachel

Contents

BOOK TWO: 1934–1947

FIORELLO H. LA GUARDIA AND THE MAKING OF MODERN NEW YORK

CONTENTS

Preface

*Dissatisfaction with the world in which we live
and determination to realize one that shall be
better, are the prevailing characteristics of the
modern spirit.*

Goldsworthy Lowes Dickinson,
The Greek View of Life, *1898*

More than forty years after he left office, Fiorello La Guardia stands today as one of the most striking political figures in recent American history, and one of the most important. Ascending to the mayoralty in dispirited times, he refreshed the faith of the people in their political institutions while implementing a reform agenda that laid the foundations of the modern metropolis. Adolf Berle, Jr., one of Franklin Roosevelt's brain trust and a close La Guardia adviser, once declared that La Guardia not only initiated but also closed the era of the modern creative mayoralty, that his successors would be reduced to managing the system that he had fastened upon the city. A half century later, what is remarkable is how apt Berle's comment remains.

The pat images that survive point to a unique character. The perspiring shirt-sleeved mayor dramatizing the comics into a radio microphone in his excited falsetto; the determined chief magistrate lifting a sledgehammer high to a pile of confiscated slot machines to purge his city of "tinhorn" gamblers; the bulky figure swathed in a fireman's raincoat directing firefighters at a dawn blaze. He thrived on the theatrical gesture—withdrawing a puny cut of meat from his pocket to illustrate the high cost of beef, mixing an intoxicating brew in the halls of Congress to ridicule Prohibition, walking the inflamed Harlem streets to cool tempers during a riot. These and hundreds of similar images were his moments of communion with New Yorkers, photo opportunities with the intent of parable, translating the abstract workings of government into immediate significance for the men, women, and children of his city.

In meeting the crises of his three terms in office La Guardia did not succumb to small enthusiasms. He was seldom ambivalent or subtle or diffident. This lent a clarity to his personality that might in others have produced a simple man. But he was not that. His breadth of character and his ability to balance a combustible righteousness with a keen political sense prevents a simple rendering of this fascinating and strangely vulnerable man. With rare panache he conveyed the magical ability of politics to instruct, care, and transform, and he attracted to the municipal service some of the best men and women of his time. He could be an inconsiderate, intolerant, even irascible man to work for, but he energized a generation of New Yorkers with bracing visions of urban possibility.

It had been different under Tammany. Before La Guardia the New York metropolis was a congeries of antiquated boroughs, dingily administered and divided into political and bureaucratic fiefdoms. It was a city riddled by corruption, run by politicians with a stake in every contract and no larger aspiration than to dispense patronage and perfect the practice of "honest graft." When the Depression hit, these good-time pols at first refused responsibility for the growing number of unemployed and then placed relief on a political basis. Before long, fiscal calamity forced the Empire City to sign over its independence in a humiliating Bankers Agreement that placed a consortium of moneylenders above its elected officials. A concurrent season of damaging scrutiny disclosed the corrosive deals and tawdry self-interest behind party machines, and New Yorkers finally lost patience with insouciant politics. Jimmy Walker was driven from office, but the colossal metropolis was left to grapple with what he had left behind, an eviscerated city without the soul of a commonwealth and without a plan to confront its most dangerous social and economic crisis in history.

La Guardia was one of a generation of extraordinarily gifted New Yorkers who helped usher in the liberal era in American history. Frances Perkins, Harry Hopkins, Adolf Berle, Henry Morgenthau, Herbert Lehman, Robert Moses, Al Smith, and of course Franklin and Eleanor Roosevelt, despite their disagreements, shared the sense that government must assume wider responsibility for those citizens who could not care for themselves. His election as New York's ninety-ninth mayor in 1933 touched off an immense transformation. La Guardia's fusion administration broke the hold of boss politics and secured the principle of a nonpolitical civil service. It helped replace an antiquated city charter, expanded relief and social services, and with its program for slum clearance, parks construction, public housing, and road and bridge building recast the physical city. Its fresh initiatives unified mass transit, expanded education, developed public health programs, and signaled a new labor policy. La Guardia made strong efforts to clean out the police and other departments while launching as vigorous an attack on organized crime and racketeering as has ever been attempted. He orchestrated a World's Fair dedicated to the World of Tomorrow, opened the City Center for Music and Drama, developed special schools for the talented, and fought successfully to bring New York its two international airports, all the while managing his diverse city's ethnic and racial tensions with reasonableness and a broad sympathy for its marginal populations.

Committed to a progressive agenda that represented the hopes of an entire generation of urban reformers, his administration was not geared merely to meeting crisis but to an audacious reshaping of the city. At a time when many were characterizing America's large cities as outdated dinosaurs his large original view of municipal possibility and his tangible achievements powerfully demonstrated that cities could be effectively run for the general good by gifted individuals who believed in public service.

La Guardia's election brought into office one of the most richly experienced politicans ever to assume the mayoralty. Throughout the 1920s La Guardia had served in Congress as leader of the House progressives, representing the working-class district of East Harlem, an area that enjoyed precious little of the ragtime decade's vaunted prosperity. Out of step with the dominant spirit of economic greed and political conservatism, he attended to the underside of American prosperity and triumphalism. The first Italian American elected to Congress, he lashed out at his colleagues for passing a racist immigration law. Speaking for the poor, before the Depression, when they were still a minority, he demanded that the business interests be regulated, insisting that laissez faire was an excuse for ignoring those least able to care for themselves. He fought a lonely fight trying to persuade a prosperity-drunk America that the poor deserved its attention, that a nation could not substitute a cash register for a heart and keep its moral balance. Conservative colleagues branded the perpetually bristling iconoclast a Socialist, but his assaults on privilege were motivated by moral indignation, not radical ideologies. Ironically, by the time his own ideas did achieve some prominence, with the coming of the New Deal, his constituents voted him out of office.

His coming to power in New York is the story of a fundamentally altered America in which reform came to power by way of the Depression. Experiment, New Deals, and the urban progressivism that La Guardia so forcefully represented in the twenties became the conventional politics of the thirties. His youth spent on the wide western plains shaped his personal credo: You did not complain about pain, you did not give in to fear, you carried on like a man; and his twenty years as an insurgent politician established his political style. He created a mayoralty suited to the times, his own aggressive character, and the lessons of his experience. Over an era that stretched from the depths of the Depression to the end of World War II, this abbreviated man of iron will and Brobdingnagian ambition forged a modern unified city, a humane city that assumed responsibility for the poor and dispossessed. He wanted New Yorkers to have a sense of ease and security, to be rid of debt, to live in decent quarters and hold regular jobs. And he conceived a government equal to the scope and complexity of these aims while achieving a degree of control over New York's complex urban machinery that remains unsurpassed.

To acquire the wherewithal to do this, La Guardia reconceived the relationships that governed municipal politics. Other mayors had dealt largely with local aldermen or state legislators. La Guardia argued that the Depression dictated new urban responsibilities for the federal government. Under him New York became a national city and the leader of a coalition of cities that thrust urban needs to the center of the New Deal's recovery policies. As president of the National Conference of Mayors, La Guardia shaped the lineaments of the federal-urban relationship; as mayor of New York in great favor with President Franklin Roosevelt, he won for his city a richly disproportionate share of federal largesse, while insisting on as much local autonomy as possible.

In La Guardia's New York the Roosevelt administration found an honest and well-managed testing place where New Deal experimental programs in pump priming and social welfare would have their best chance for success. Other mayors and governors would show up in Washington carrying vague proposals with larded budgets. La Guardia brought detailed plans and hard figures. During his first two administrations, before the World War put an end to large-scale domestic programs, New York became a vast demonstration project for federal assistance yielding hundreds of thousands of jobs for the unemployed and providing La Guardia with the "hammer and chisels" to reconstruct the physical city.

More than a half century after his successful Fusion campaign, candidates still wrap themselves in his mantle. Six-foot politicians squeeze themselves behind his desk to evoke the cleansing memory of his integrity, and facing a table full of his successors the incumbent mayor says of the Little Flower that "he set the standard of excellence for this office. He alone."

The comment is not an exaggeration. Along with his vast building program, his war on corruption, and his commitment to making New Yorkers good as well as happy, La Guardia refreshed the town with a conviction that the world could be changed, that political intelligence could actually create wonderful things. His ruthless optimism did have its sinister side, a moral complacency and dismissive arrogance, but despite his sporadic crudities he remained at one with the common folk of his city. They shared with him their needs and their hopes for their children. And by his final term he reported to them regularly on the radio in intimate chats that demonstrated the mayor's multifaceted predilection for minding the business of his fellow New Yorkers. His broadcasts would teach, exhort, and offer fatherly advice to his fellow citizens, providing the municipal government with a warm-hearted center to replace the boss and his machine.

The historical case for such figures sometimes crumbles under close scrutiny. They turn out to be less than nostalgia would have us remember. But that is not true about La Guardia. What the reader will notice is that he did much more than he is remembered for. And two more things: how much of contemporary urban life reflects his shaping hand and how much of his reform has been worn down through the decades by the racketeers and fixers (the "tinhorns," Fiorello used to call them) who have discovered the loopholes, compromised the safeguards, and dulled city government's luster.

We need to be reminded of a time when a thick, short man in a huge Stetson did not accept conventional limits and dared to look at urban politics anew. His later speeches with their appreciation of what cities must do have a contemporary ring, and yet he led in a time when he could walk into a welfare office unannounced and fire a handful of unsympathetic workers on the spot, when to make movie theaters safe for children theater owners were instructed to set aside special children's aisles with patrolling matrons, when the mayor had sanitation trucks confiscate salacious magazines from street vendors under his authority to collect garbage, when a willful little mayor who believed that politics must be not only fair and honest but also good and caring wrestled with the deadlocking forces of his time.

Money did not interest him, at least not for himself. Those stakes were too small. He was not interested in thousands or hundreds of thousands. He wanted hundreds of millions and billions. Only such sums could help rebuild the city and succor its distressed. He was interested in money for his people, his streets, his city. He delighted in expanding what the city could provide its citizens. There are mayors who build. They inspect the plans, sign the bills, and file the openings with their campaign literature. But they take no special pleasure in adding to the physical gifts of the city. La Guardia thrilled at every new opening. He attended as many of them as he could. The shovels, spades, and souvenirs of construction that others took home with them and then discarded became his most prized possessions. Once, because the gates were closed and he could not get close enough to inspect the newly completed Thomas Jefferson Park swimming pool, the excited magistrate pulled himself up on the border fence to poke his head over the spokes and gleefully take in the sight of one more pool for his city's children.

La Guardia felt deeply the hurt and pain of those not close to him—of common New Yorkers, whom he did not know—and this lent his leadership a rare human quality. He had a special sympathy for the afflicted. With his whiplash tongue he reminded self-satisfied Americans that the vulnerable too deserved their nation's concern. It was Yale University that in its honorary degree said that La Guardia had taken democracy from the politicians and restored it to the people. He embraced the people not as a single abstraction but as a multifarious group of individuals, and he was devoted to achieving decent treatment for them.

Alexander Herzen is supposed to have rejected bloody revolution by declaring to Mikhail Bakunin that "one must open men's eyes not tear them out." It was a sentiment with which La Guardia agreed. But when it came to opening men's eyes La Guardia was prepared to do it by yelling the most caustic terms into their ears. "People who love soft words and hate iniquity forget this," an acute observer once said, "that reform consists in taking a bone away from a dog. Philosophy will not do this." Fiorello La Guardia was prepared to take that fight as far as he had to, in order to wrest from the grafters their bone, whether it was patronage, "honest graft," or marvelous tin boxes that attracted untraceable wealth. And yes, his campaigns resorted to methods that would have made even the machine hesitate— ethnic appeals, demagogy, and the use of a private political apparatus known as the *Ghibboni*, who were not averse to lending a hand or a fist when necessary.

It is the fate of many men and women who wield political control to be seduced by power both for the good that it can do and for reasons having to do with causes more deeply embedded in individual personality. La Guardia shared with many strong-willed, capable individuals one open vice—he loved power. His lust for power colored his campaigns, his treatment of underlings, his aspirations for higher office, his use of the airwaves to extend his influence in ways no charter ever sanctioned, and ultimately it made an irascible, brittle, and deeply frustrated man of him. By his third term La Guardia desperately sought a way out of New York City and into the army. At one point the appointment seemed imminent. Fiorello ordered his uniform and waited, but the call never came. It was his greatest personal disappointment. Yet his personality was so large and his instinct for public service so powerful that he directed the Office of Civilian Defense, chaired the Joint U.S.-Canadian Permanent Defense Board, and furiously lobbied for a generalship, all while he was still mayor. After he left office in 1946 he served as director general of the United Nations Relief and Rehabilitation Administration, securing food and supplies for the millions of hungry left to suffer in the wake of World War II.

This complex, endlessly interesting, fiercely ambitious, intemperate man had grown up on the wide-open spaces of the West, where he acquired an admiration for directness and tough justice. He was fierce in the pursuit of his goals and he tended to concentrate control in his own hands. His government represented a dangerous style of personal rule hitched to transcendent purpose. Perhaps even in a democracy that sort of leadership is necessary to create the sweeping changes that La Guardia fashioned. This is of course the formula for demagogues and dictators, and the thirties were a time when they flourished. Yet it is very much a part of La Guardia's story that while he was criticized for using means that might be abused by bad leaders in bad times, he generally respected the prudent barriers that democracies place in the way of authoritarian leadership.

He recognized fewer limits, however, to his ideology of growth, open-fisted spending, and big government. By the time he left office the city had been transformed into the colossal metropolis; it was also saddled with debt, an infrastructure too expensive to maintain comfortably, dangerously expanding citizen expectations, and a snowballing bureaucracy.

He wanted to be president, to be a general, to feed the world after World War II. His aspirations represent the full range of the American dream. Yet few in 1882, when he was born in a lower-Manhattan apartment to immigrant parents, would have thought to frame such ambitions for a child so modestly born. His coming to office and power represents another important theme: the coming of age of immigrant America, an America that spoke with the accents and concerns of working-class Americans. In their hands the nation was remade. How much of their hearts, their loyalties, and their ambitions this young land claimed is amply demonstrated by La Guardia's life and hopes.

"He aspired greatly," Rexford Guy Tugwell wrote, "and we ought to find out all we can about such people. They make a vast difference in our lives."

Acknowledgments

How much this work is enriched by the work of others should be apparent from the extensive material cited in the footnotes. Many individuals took the time to share their recollections and thoughts with me. While it is not possible to mention each of them, I want to express my gratitude to Eugene Canudo, Anna Clark, Irving Ben Cooper, Elsie Fisher, Ira Hirschmann, Stanley Kreutzer, Goodhue Livingston, Jr., James Marshall, Morris Novik, Edmund Palmieri, Harold Seidman, Louis Yavner, and the late Marie La Guardia.

Many librarians and archivists provided me with assistance, and I want to thank especially Idilio Gracia-Pena and Kenneth Cobb of the New York Municipal Archives, the staffs of the New York Public Library Research Division, the Franklin D. Roosevelt Presidential Library, the Libraries of Harvard University, the Fiorello H. La Guardia Archives, the Columbia University Libraries, and my colleagues at the Kingsborough Community College Library. I wish also to acknowledge the cooperation of the FBI, the State Department, and the Department of the Army for providing me access to hitherto closed files.

It is my pleasure to recognize those generous sources that helped support the research that went into this book: the City University PSC-CUNY Award Program, the Rockefeller Foundation, the National Endowment for the Humanities, the Association for State and Local History, the FDR-Four Freedoms Foundation, and Kingsborough Community College's Program for Scholarly and Applied Research.

I began this book at the suggestion of Kenneth T. Jackson, and that is only a small hint of the debt that I owe this fine and generous man. Other friends and colleagues read parts of this manuscript at various stages and I have profited from their suggestions. I am grateful to Abraham Ascher, Betty Caroli, Timothy Gilfoyle, Cheryl Greenberg, Devorah Prag, Joel Schwartz, Leonard Schwartz and Frank Voss for their efforts. Tyler Anbinder, my research assistant for the past few years, deserves a salute for his reliable good work and I am grateful to Dan Weaver, for his sensitive editing, consistent support and for his weathering with good grace a crisis of my manufacture.

To my parents, my wife, and my children I owe a special debt.

THIS IS THE *new*
NEW YORK

The result of
La Guardia's honest and
efficient administration

KEEP IT—
RE-ELECT

LA GUARDIA
McGOLDRICK
MORRIS

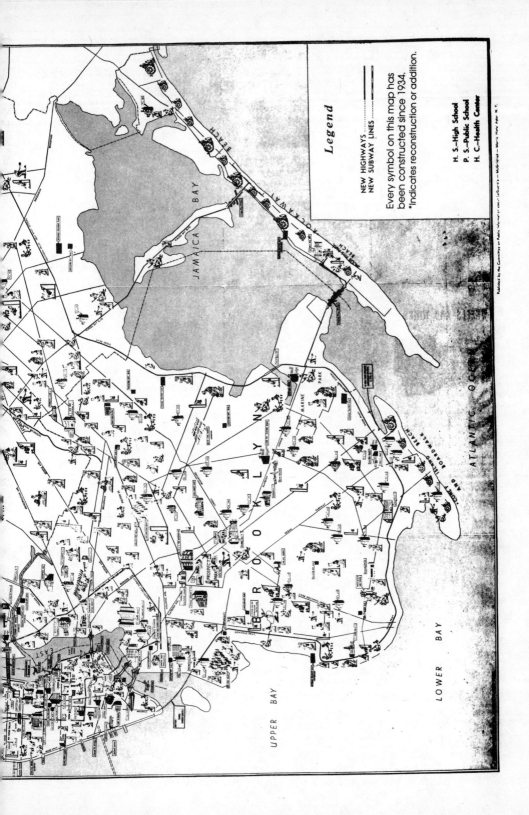

Published by the Committee on Public Information — Sources — McGraw-Hill — New York, N.Y.

Legend

NEW HIGHWAYS ....
NEW SUBWAY LINES ....

Every symbol on this map has
been constructed since 1934.
*Indicates reconstruction or addition.

H. S.—High School
P. S.—Public School
H. C.—Health Center

JAMAICA BAY

BEACH

ROCKAWAY

BEACH

BROOKLYN

MARINE PARK

PROSPECT PARK

EAST

BRIGHTON BEACH

BOARDWALK

ATLANTIC OCEAN

UPPER BAY

LOWER BAY

BOOK ONE: 1882–1933

The Making of Fiorello H. La Guardia

*What aim do you wish to achieve, where are
you going, what is in your soul? In a word,
who are you? What are you?*

Ivan Turgenev, Fathers and Sons, *1861*

CHAPTER 1

Foundations

1. Achille La Guardia

T HE small boy with the shock of black hair was unhappy. His father's army
unit, the Eleventh Regiment, had been shipped from the open plains of North
Dakota to the small town of Sackett's Harbor, New York. His accustomed
world of the wide frontier, of cowpunchers and Indians disappeared, to be replaced
with drab storefronts and unfamiliar indoor plumbing; and after his father finally
had enough of the boy's rambunctiousness, school. Once when the boy had built
a small rock fort smack in the middle of the parade grounds only to have it
demolished by an impatient officer, he grabbed one of the rocks and hurled it
through the window of the man's quarters. His father whipped him for doing it,
but that didn't seem to change him. He had a mind of his own. Let the school
handle him, thought his father.

And so, that morning in 1887, a surprised Miss Estelle Littlefield opened her
classroom door to a striking dark-skinned man in a crisp army uniform and full
beard, with a dark-eyed six-year-old in tow. This was his ''bad boy,'' army bandmaster Achille La Guardia told the teacher in a booming voice. She could beat the
child whenever necessary, the father said, although he doubted that it would do
much good. He continued to abuse Fiorello as he pulled him into the classroom.

Half a century later Estelle Littlefield still remembered the boy's response.
Little Fiorello La Guardia glared back at his father with a pair of the brightest black
eyes and with a willfullness she had never seen in a six-year-old; he tore away,
darted across the room, and unloosed a string of curses at his parent. Then, the
score having been settled, he calmly took a seat and turned to the task of becoming
the best student in the class. Decades later Miss Littlefield would recall: ''I never
saw one boy like him. He was phenomenal . . . a joy and a problem.'' The streak
of recalcitrant willfulness and fearless resentment that had taken Achille La Guardia

3

from the closed world of southern Italy to the American West had been passed on to his son. It would carry Fiorello even further.[1]

———

Achille La Guardia was born in 1849 in the coastal town of Foggia, just below the spur of Italy's boot-shaped perimeter. Here life was lived as it had been for centuries, a perpetual struggle against the elements, the government, and the local brigands. While the confluence of social and political movements known as the *Risorgimento* transformed the Northern Italian city-states, its effect was far more limited in the rural South, where enduring traditions held back the forces of modernization.[2]

Don Raffaele La Guardia, Achille's father, was a minor official with the municipal government. His post enabled him to provide his sons with an education, but Achille found the religion-bound curriculum stifling. He chafed at the forced respect, the joyless recitation of dogma, and the harsh discipline. Frustration led to mischief and, ultimately, trouble. Once, after Achille hid a tack under his teacher's seat, he was caught and pressed onto the ground to trace a large cross on the floor with his tongue. The humiliated teenager dashed home in tears. But when he complained to his parents, Don Raffaele sided with the teacher. Before long, Achille, bitter with school, church, and family, left home, vowing never again to step foot in the church of his father.

He took with him an interest in music and a developing skill as a cornetist. For all of his prankishness, Achille respected skill and beauty, and in music he found a way of creating something of his own. Pride in craft substituted for kin ties and church as he made the rounds of the small villages and towns of southern Italy playing at first for food and then for a fee. He traveled to northern Italy and Switzerland, and to the East Indies to perform. Eventually he signed on as a shipboard musician with the Hamburg Line.[3]

In 1878 Achille made his first trip to the New World, accompanying the celebrated diva Adelina Patti. The United States was a revelation, an energetic, bustling nation offering abundant freedom and opportunity. Who could say that about Italy, or, for that matter, about the many other places that he had seen? He returned to Europe carrying the idea of America with him. He had found a place where he could settle. In Trieste he found the person who would go with him.

Austrian-controlled Trieste, at the foot of the Istrian mountains, was a prosperous commercial city of Italians, Slovenes, Croats, Germans, and a small population of Jews who resided there in relative tolerance. To one of these Jewish families was born in 1859 Irene Luzzatto-Coen, the eldest of five children of Isacco Coen and Fiorina Luzzatto. Irene was raised in a liberal atmosphere, a young woman of Austrian citizenship and Italian culture who carried her religious identity lightly.

Achille met the twenty-one-year-old Irene at a chaperoned dance and was captivated by her quiet assurance and warm personality. Ten years her senior, the well-traveled Achille fascinated Irene with his stories of the world and his dreams of life in the United States. On June 3, 1880, a half year after they first met, they married in a civil ceremony. On the marriage documents, the bride gave her religion as "Israelite." The groom, true to a vow taken years before, declared his faith as "*nessuna*," nothing.[4]

By the middle of the nineteenth century, the ocean separating the New World from the Old no longer held the deep terror of the unknown. Millions, mostly from Great Britain, Ireland, and Germany, had already crossed its waters, and by 1880, the dislocating forces that had shaken them loose from northwestern Europe pushed east and south, spreading "immigration fever." Fewer than 150,000 immigrants arrived from Austria-Hungary, Russia, and Italy in the half century before 1880, but in the next thirty years the total skyrocketed to 8.4 million.

Shortly after their wedding, the La Guardia couple joined the waves of emigrants bound for the United States. No letters or diaries exist from Achille or Irene, but there is little mystery to their story. Unlike the thousands who left their wives and children back home, seeking only to gather some dollars and return in better circumstances, Achille brought with him his wife, his skills as a musician, a fluency in several languages, and his intention to lead an American life.

The La Guardias' destination was, in fact, a cosmopolitan subnation, the immigrant city of New York. By 1880 approximately 12,000 Italians lived in Manhattan's Five Points section. A reporter wandering amid this exotic community, with its peripatetic organ-grinders, unskilled day laborers, and gangs of ragpickers, characterized it as a group with "no intellectual capital but the primitive methods of farming handed down by their ancestors. . . ." She held little hope for their success, because "the idyllic life of an Italian hillside or of a dreaming medieval town is but poor preparation for the hand to hand struggle for bread of an over-crowded city."[5]

The La Guardias did not settle in the dilapidated tenements that lined Mulberry Street and the other thoroughfares of New York's Italian colony. Achille had little in common with the unskilled village men of limited experience. He had seen the world, he had rejected a future in the old villages of the *mezzogiorno*, and he did not adopt the narrow dreams of New York's Little Italy. He took an apartment in a comfortable four-story building on Varick Place between Sullivan and Bleecker Streets in Greenwich Village. This appositely named "American Ward" boasted a unique Bohemian community known for its art, fine restaurants, and diversity. Here immigrants from France, Germany, Scandinavia, and Ireland mixed comfortably with a small black population and some working-class native stock. There was only one other Italian family on the block.

On April 24, 1881, Irene gave birth to their first child, a daughter, Gemma, and nineteen months later, on December 11, 1882, their first son was delivered at home. Out of respect for Irene's mother, Fiorina Luzzatto-Coen, the couple named the baby Fiorello (Little Flower), adding Raffaele, for Achille's father, and Enrico, later Americanized to Henry.[6]

It was a fascinating, disquieted America that Fiorello La Guardia entered on that frosty December day. With the political reconstruction of the South ended, Americans, tired of causes and ideals, and wishing to be free of scarcity, sacrifice, and war, had rushed headlong into industrialization. Here was Mark Twain's Gilded Age, all brilliant surfaces and rich facade, and Yale sociology professor William Graham Sumner lecturing that social progress was drawn along by a competition in which only the fittest survived. "It's root, hog, or die," declared the respected professor.

Politics too had its iron laws. On the day Fiorello was born, a group of New York State Republicans went to Washington to remind the new president, Chester A. Arthur, that a successful administration must be founded on the tenets of party loyalty, and to lay their claims to a fair share of patronage. His predecessor, James A. Garfield, recently assassinated by a disappointed office seeker, had complained of similar delegations coming to the White House and taking up all his time. "I am considering all day whether A or B shall be appointed to this or that office. . . . I feel like crying out in the agony of my soul against the greed of office and its consumption of my time."[7]

That day's news columns reported on the civil service, tariffs, and the woman's suffrage movement, but the classified sections offered as penetrating an insight into the times as the front pages. Glimpse these advertisements and you understand New York City's ethnic hierarchy. "Situation Wanted" ads included the tag "good German girl" or "German Protestant." A few identified themselves as French or even "colored," but no one told of being Russian or Italian. Religion was important too. Thus a "respectable Protestant woman" applied for the job of cook, and another for housework. A "reliable Protestant" offered himself as a coachman and groom, while "Maurice Linquist's Office" advertised a select assortment of workers, "female and male; all positions; all Protestants." In its book review section the *New York Times* reported on the tome *Christianity and Progress* by Protestant churchman and reformer Charles Loring Brace, noting that it was wholesome Protestant teachings like those in Brace's book that would save the world from those "exposed to the Roman corruption." The point was simple and pervasive: Protestants from northwestern Europe carried the American seed.[8]

But America was becoming more diverse, especially in New York, where Jacob Riis, writing in the 1880s, remarked that a map of ethnic districts "would show more stripes than a zebra and more colors than any rainbow." The predominant hues would be "green for the Irish prevailing on the West Side . . . and blue for the Germans on the East Side." But there were others too:

The red of the Italian forcing its way northward along the line of Mulberry Street . . . and after a lapse of miles, in the "Little Italy" of Harlem. . . . On the West Side the red [is] overrunning the old Africa of Thompson Street, pushing the black of the negro rapidly uptown . . . occupying his home, his church, his trade. . . .

Hardly less aggressive than the Italian, the [gray of the] Russian and Polish Jew, having overrun the district between Rivington and Division Streets, east of the Bowery to the point of suffocation, is filling the tenements of the old Seventh Ward. . . .[9]

Irene La Guardia easily adjusted to her Greenwich Village surroundings. She made friends quickly, and together with Achille she tried to fit into their new surroundings as much as possible. Achille insisted that Gemma and Fiorello be raised as full-fledged Americans, without the ambivalence that marked other immigrant children. He forbade the use of Italian at home (Fiorello did not learn a passable Italian until he served as a consular agent in Europe), and he raised his children as Protestants.

Still, Achille found more difficulties than he had anticipated. Sometimes it seemed as if all the immigrant musicians in America were crowded into Manhattan, competing for the same few jobs, and Achille would go for many days between engagements. But La Guardia refused to take work as a day laborer, to accept the pick-and-shovel work that occupied so large a number of his countrymen. Not for that had he taken a twenty-one-year-old bride across the ocean, and not to raise his daughter to sew feathers on women's hats in the cramped rooms of Mulberry Street tenements and have his son go to work before he graduated elementary school. He had traveled the world alone, married outside his traditions, and did not need the immigrant ghetto to survive. He decided to try a stronger dose of America, without the comforting familiars of the immigrant city. In 1885 Achille La Guardia enlisted in the United States Army as a warrant officer, chief musician in the Eleventh Regiment of Infantry at Fort Sully, South Dakota.[10]

Under the great arch of the open western sky, the Dakota Territory offered a different America from the one the La Guardias had come to know in New York. Colorful pioneers and cowpunchers peopled its vast wilderness plains, which erupted periodically with the excitement of sporadic skirmishes with the Indians. It was a West as yet untamed, described by a visiting Theodore Roosevelt as "the west of the Indian and the buffalo hunter . . . of reckless riders who, unmoved looked in the eyes of life or death." It was a land whose plains shimmered in the summer sun, whose foliage bloomed in a breathtaking palette of colors and whose buffalo still outnumbered the hunters. Its winter blizzards were fierce and the cold could kill. It was land in its unspoiled natural state, a world apart from the man-made factories and cities of the Northeast. Life was rough and less reflective here, shaped by fewer rules and a raw justice that no settled community would tolerate. In the West, Teddy Roosevelt wrote, "we felt the beat of hardy life in our veins and the glory of work and the joy of living."[11]

Fort Sully's regimental commander assigned the La Guardias a hillside house in an area populated by Indians and apart from the straight row of homes in the fort. Daughter Gemma remembered her father's concern at the idea of having his young wife and the children among the mistrusted Indians, but Irene had no misgivings. She liked the house, and racial difference meant very little to this woman who had lived with Irish and Germans, Jews and Gentiles, blacks and whites. Before long, she and the Sioux women, who had picked up a Spanish dialect, were speaking to each other in their own special patois. The Indian women festooned the La Guardia home with handsome blankets, hand-sewn moccasins and multi-colored beads, and from the dark-haired, fair-skinned lady they received food staples in return. No one, recalled Gemma, was safer among them than Mrs. La Guardia. "The Indians would never have done her any harm."[12]

In 1887 Irene gave birth to her third child, Richard Dodge, named for the commanding officer at the fort. Shortly after Richard's birth, the Eleventh Infantry was ordered to Madison Barracks near Watertown, New York, where "Professor Achille La Guardia" became a popular figure, assembling a local band, tutoring students, and conducting the army orchestra in free community concerts. Locals tolerated his fiery disposition as a special combination of Latin and artistic temperaments and valued him for the cheer he brought through his music.[13]

Gemma and Fiorello were registered in the neighborhood school, where the dark-eyed boy quickly enchanted his elders with his recklessness. A neighbor remembered that while Fiorello liked to tease the girls and pull their hair, he always protected the children against local ruffians, no matter what the odds against him were. Small for his age, the lithe scrapper cursed like a drill sergeant, and he insisted always on being treated with respect. He "was such a quick, keen little fellow" one of his teachers later recalled.

One day a group of visitors were observing a lesson as the teacher began calling the roll of students, proceeding down the list to a string of pleasant "present"'s, until she called the young La Guardia's name. He refused to respond. "You're supposed to answer present," she scolded. "You haven't called my name yet," he shot back. His name, he made a point of instructing her, was not "Fie-o-rello," and with guests in the room he felt it was a particularly opportune time to let her know this.[14]

In 1889, after the La Guardias returned from a family vacation in Italy, the regiment was moved back out west, to Arizona's Fort Huachuca, a barren mudhole that was swept by dust and dullness. But within a few months the regiment moved again, to Whipple Barracks near Prescott, a breathtakingly beautiful area of pine-carpeted foothills dominated by huge mountain peaks. In this territory of jarring contrasts, of stark ranges and lush valleys, where violent men on the make mixed with settlers interested in laying the foundation for a decent start, the Indian, Mexican, and Yankee cultures rubbed against each other with combustible possibilities.

The territory's principal industry, mining, fed the rip-roaring boomtown atmosphere. More than 8000 active veins in the 1870s brought plenty of quick cash and hardworking men to the area, and they sought release in the traditional pleasures of drinking, gambling, and wenching. In 1875 there were ten saloons and a dozen gaming halls in Prescott, and they spread like ivy. "Last night," testified one visitor, "I was in a billiard saloon here, a game of monte was going on in one corner, brag poker in another, and a couple of dogs were having a free fight under the billiard table." It was not, he concluded, much like Boston.[15]

This frontier represented the rough edge between whites and Indians, a land of violent men and easy fortunes where the case for justifiable homicide might be made simply by saying, "He needed killing." Only ten years before the La Guardias arrived in the Arizona Territory, Tombstone had witnessed the gunfight at the OK corral. Three years later Geronimo and his band of Apaches, refusing to settle on the reservations, wreaked havoc on white settlements in the north of the Territory, prompting General George Crook to issue orders to shoot any "savage" found straying from their assigned territories. Only after the arrival of 5000 regular army troops the following year did the federal forces finally put down the resistance. In 1887 a range war between sheep men and cattle growers resulted in many deaths in the Tonto basin, south of Prescott. Two years after that, armed bandits ambushed the Wham payroll en route from Fort Graham to Fort Thomas, taking some $26,000; it was the same year that the Apache Kid became the most wanted man in the territory.[16]

"Prescott was really my hometown," Fiorello later told his friend and biographer, Lowell Limpus, and he remembered it as the most beautiful, most comfortable, and most wonderful city in the world, a place where social class had less salience and "playground was not measured in acres or city blocks, but in miles and miles." And the friendly soldiers taught Fiorello to fire a real six-shooter. As mayor of New York, La Guardia once told a group of corrections officials that when he was a boy he and his friends would spy a horse hitched to a post, "unhitch him and ride him around town and then return the horse." Was the mayor trying to say that he had been a horse thief as a child, asked a man in the audience. "No," he replied, "I'm just telling you that I was once a boy."[17]

The La Guardia children were registered in the town school rather than at the fort so that they would be taught by teachers instead of soldiers. Though he admired his teacher, Lena Coover, Fiorello never passed up a chance to needle her. When she returned a paper without correcting some of his arithmetic errors, he piped up: "Look here, you had better learn arithmetic if you are going to teach us." In her eightieth year Lena Coover would fly in for her most illustrious pupil's funeral to recall: "I knew he was bound to be someone important. He was not only stubborn about having his say, but he also knew what he was talking about. Everything interested him."[18]

One of his classmates described their Arizona days as "school, a few chores, a little play, light the kerosene lamp, a little homework and bed," but the days were filled with excitement. On the way to school the children would meet Indians, Chinese workers, and, "most glamorous of all," the cowboys. As they walked, occupied with their various games, Gemma remembered that Fiorello "would always play the leader. . . . Richard and I always had to follow him." In the summer they would borrow tents from the fort, pile them on donkeys, and ride off into the mountains to play among the bluffs and ridges, amidst the awesome boundlessness of the mountains. There were no city streets, industrial wastes, local police, or street merchants, and "the six years we spent in Arizona," Gemma would write, "were the happiest years of our youth."[19]

Fiorello La Guardia was essentially a product of the interplay between the free, open environment of the West that he came to love, the overbearing influence of his father, and a family tradition of continental culture. Achille La Guardia often complained to his children about a barracks pecking order that ranked him below enlisted men and West Pointers. He liked to remind them that he represented a richer, deeper tradition of civilized culture than the typical soldier, even if he wore fewer stripes. As a youth he may have felt constrained by the Old World's dogmas, but he valued its cultural traditions, its respect for discipline and beauty.[20]

Whipple Barracks houses were made of mud with a cover of whitewash, but the interior of the La Guardia home was decorated in an incongruously formal style. Flower-patterned carpet covered the floor, heavy brocade curtains hung above the doorway, and family pictures in elaborate gold metal frames lined the walls. Plants and flowers freshened the rooms that were filled with substantial pieces of furniture and musical instruments. A contemporary photograph of the La Guardia family is reminiscent of nothing so much as a museum setting of a middle-class European family. Each individual occupies a formal pose. Irene, by now a round, pudgy woman, has her hair simply piled atop her head. Erect, in a carefully pressed uniform buttoned to the top, Achille, with his neatly trimmed beard, is a handsome presence. Richard, Gemma, and Fiorello are all dressed in fancy children's clothing, the boys wearing knickers, boots, and large artist's bow ties and Gemma in gingham and ruffles. One face stands out distinctly from the dreamlike family pose: Eleven-year-old Fiorello, holding a cornet, fiercely stares out from under his dark, close-cropped hair directly into the camera.[21]

Aside from the motif of continental pretension that dominates this photograph, one is struck by all the musical instruments. "Father lived for music," Fiorello

10

recalled, ''and he began teaching Gemma and me as soon as we could distinguish one note from another.'' With a group put together from his students, Achille formed a musical club to present his original compositions at local functions; Fiorello would play the cornet, Gemma the violin, and Richard the piano.[22]

Their training, as all else about the stern taskmaster, was intense. Achille wanted Fiorello to follow in his own footsteps and become a musician, a composer, ''a second John Philip Sousa.'' Night after night he would make Fiorello and Gemma practice under his harshly critical eye, but Fiorello learned the trick of easing his relationship with his father, by internalizing Achille's perfectionism, actually thriving on the tough training. ''Keep on screaming Papa,'' he would say, ''in this way I'll learn.''[23]

Achille demanded much, criticized often, seldom acknowledged an error as his own, rarely offered a compliment, and showed approval only grudgingly. He instructed by means of criticism, and wielded authority with harsh confidence. And much as he resented Achille's austere discipline, Fiorello grew into a strong, resilient boy, with a generous streak of his father's forceful personality. From a young age Fiorello found it difficult to trust people, to show tenderness, or to accept criticism. Resentment and anger motivated him far more powerfully than affection or admiration, and he related to authority figures in a prickly, offensive fashion.

Growing to maturity in the special environment of the American West, Fiorello formed some of his strongest impressions and attitudes from his frontier experiences. The freewheeling gambling spirit was everywhere evident, in the exaggerated hopes of prospectors and the cunning deals of the land speculators, and in the games of sport and chance that fed the get-rich-quick frontier temper. After a fire tore through Prescott's main street, faro tables and roulette wheels were among the first objects salvaged, and with embers still smoldering the games continued on the streets. If such games were popular, they also brought with them swift sanction for those who were caught cheating, and, recalled Fiorello, ''there [were] no coroner's inquests.''[24]

When he found his mother playing a popular lottery that was crooked, Fiorello tried to persuade her to save her dimes and quarters, but like many of the women on the fort, she would not give up her dreams of quick wealth. From then on La Guardia could not pass one of these pretty gambling games without a powerful surge of anger at the ''tinhorns and sharpies'' who bilked the unsuspecting poor of their meager savings. As mayor of New York, La Guardia fought an unforgiving battle against gambling games and their crooked masterminds. And when, on occasion, the gaming industry found a legal loophole to continue fleecing the gullible, Fiorello would hark back nostalgically to his younger days on the frontier, where integrity was unambiguous, the air pure, and justice proceeded unhampered by lawyers to its proper end of clearing out the cheaters.

It was in his Arizona youth that Fiorello first encountered the ethnic prejudice that he fought against for much of his life. His lapsed Catholic father and Jewish mother paid religious and ethnic differences little heed in raising their children. "My father took pride in my mother's rich Jewish heritage," Gemma recalled, "and frequently . . . remind[ed] us that our grandmother, Fiorina was a Luzzatti —a member of one of Italy's most prominent Jewish families." Achille even taught the children some Jewish prayers, but the family did not consider itself Jewish. When, as mayor, Fiorello was asked about the extent of his Jewish heritage, he responded that there was hardly enough for him to boast about. For Achille, who viewed religion as a system of social and moral values rather than fixed theological principles, one church was about as good as another, and he enrolled Fiorello and Gemma in Prescott's Episcopal church.[25]

Despite their own insistence that they were exuberant westerners, not immigrants, the La Guardias were thought of as an Italian family, and Italians were held in low esteem in late nineteenth-century America. New York dockworkers denounced Italian longshoremen as racially inferior to "white men," while newspapers and street gossip connected them with the Black Hand and other secret criminal societies.

Fiorello was playing with friends one day near home when a strange-looking man came to town leading a red-capped monkey and carrying a hand organ. Passersby would flip pennies at the man as the kids gathered round, ridiculing the old Italian. "A dago with a monkey!" they screamed. "I can still hear their cries," La Guardia wrote a half century later. "Hey, Fiorello, you're a dago too. Where's your monkey?" To the vulnerable child, whose tough exterior never hardened against rejection, "it hurt." When Achille went over to the man and invited him to the La Guardia home for dinner, Fiorello was even more embarrassed. For some time thereafter Fiorello suffered the taunts of his friends. With millions of other equally puzzled, equally hurt, and equally vulnerable children of the second generation he was left to ponder the cruelties of prejudice. "What difference was there between us? Some of their families hadn't been in the country longer than mine."[26]

Early in his first administration as mayor, Fiorello would ban organ-grinders from the streets of New York. He explained that they interrupted the free movement of traffic, that they were exploited by work bosses, that they were beggars. But most important to this sensitive son of immigrants, they were an embarrassment that went back to a youngster's pain at being singled out by his friends. "I never did like organ grinders," he wrote, "ever since my days of ridicule in Prescott."[27]

Aware of his own distinctiveness, young Fiorello was touched by the plight of the Indians that he witnessed first hand. At Fort Whipple he saw troops march out to "round up renegades," but rather than share in the triumphal sense of taking the land, he felt sorry for the hapless natives who were labeled troublemakers for not acquiescing in their own humiliation. Why were so many of their children starving and begging for food? His own family had gotten along with the Indians. He did not see inhuman savages, only pinched hungry faces of red-skinned children who looked longingly at him when he munched an apple or ate a cookie. He witnessed the devastating "concentration" that gathered the tribes onto reservations to force them to "cease their wandering ways," as whites overran tribal lands, disturbing traditional arrangements. Succumbing to the inevitable, many tribes signed solemn treaties with the United States government, only to see these guarantees ignored.[28]

By the 1890s, the Bureau of Indian Affairs placed the infamous Indian agents over the reservations. Anthropologist George Bird Grinnell described the agent as holding "absolute control over affairs on his administration. . . . more nearly absolute than anything else that we in this country know of. . . . The courts protect citizens; but the Indian is not a citizen, and nothing protects him." Cut off from their sources of food, native Americans depended for sustenance, clothing, and shelter on a gang of political appointees who were interested solely in an easy fortune. These agents ruthlessly sold off government supplies meant for the Indians and systematically cheated them of their rights. The lesson impressed Fiorello with the danger of manipulative political appointees, and "from that day on," he told biographer M. R. Werner, "I think I have hated professional politicians."[29]

His respect for politicians scarcely grew when he got a glimpse of interest-group lobbying. Army bandleaders, Achille included, wanted their rank raised to commissioned officers. Each bandleader was asked to contribute a month's pay and an additional $50 to a fund for persuading Congress to pass the desired legislation. Even young Fiorello understood what all of this money was supposed to buy, and the crude effort to bribe Congress shocked him. "It's a fake," he cried to his father, persuading Achille to ignore the solicitation.[30]

In 1940 the *International Who's Who* asked La Guardia to check a draft biography entry for its 1941 edition. He sent it back with a stiff note. The newspapers were printing rumors about possible campaigns for higher office, but La Guardia insisted: "I do not want the word 'politician' used [in identifying his vocation]. . . . Its connotation . . . is such that I don't think it ought to be used except for politicians—and there are many of them around. I do not happen to be one of them." He insisted on substituting "municipal officer" for his job description. The crooked Indian agents, La Guardia once told Franklin D. Roosevelt, had soured him on "politicians" for life.[31]

The sensitive teenager also noticed the exploitation of low-paid immigrant labor as he caught sight of the railroad gangs working on the spur to connect Ashfork, Phoenix, and Prescott—men and draft animals side by side accorded the same rough treatment. Elsewhere in these years labor and capital clashed violently over the conditions and rights of workers, but the laborers Fiorello saw, in the main impoverished Italian and Mexican immigrants, were unable to band together to demand rights and higher pay on their own. When the 1893 depression threw many out of work, thousands of these displaced men lined the roadbeds or joined pools of roaming migrants. Fiorello witnessed their suffering firsthand, and his sympathies instinctively embraced these hurt people. It was confusing for the sensitive army

13

child to see soldiers drive the Indians into oblivion, support the corrupt Indian agents, and side with the railroads against its poor strikers, and it resulted in a lifelong ambivalence toward the military.[32]

As he grew older Fiorello discussed these and other issues with his contemporaries. Gemma recalled that she and her friends would be playing, when suddenly her brother would announce, "I am going to speak," jump on the nearest table, and start declaiming. He spoke about how teachers should teach, how parents should raise children, how workers and Indians should be treated, offering opinions on everything. More often than not, his friends listened, but if their interest wandered, recalled Gemma, "Oh my, it was terrible." In January 1898, Fiorello delivered the commencement address for his graduating elementary class. Instead of instructing his classmates to abjure greed, play fair, love mother, knowledge, and country, he spoke on the "Office Seeker's Platform."[33]

His boyhood was filled with more than issues and anger, but the mistreatment of the vulnerable reinforced Fiorello's own inclinations toward assertiveness. The Indians, workers, and other groups whom Fiorello observed being victimized shared one characteristic, they were weak and defenseless. In his own life he resolved not to be passive. His own sensitivities about being short (he grew to just over five feet tall), having a high-pitched voice, and being foreign-born led him to compensate with exaggerated combativeness. For young Fiorello the readiness to fight for one's rights became the measure of his manliness.

"I licked him every day," one of his classmates later boasted, "but Fiorello kept coming back for more." Once, as Fiorello was taking a real beating from a much taller boy whose face he could not even reach, he ran back into the school building to emerge with a chair, upon which he jumped, the better to swing at his opponent. In rejecting the hierarchy that placed enlisted officers above noncoms like his father, Fiorello struck for equality in the only way he knew: "I did not adhere to such rules. I would just as soon fight with an officer's kid as I would with anyone else." Each of his teachers, though certainly not all in admiration, called him a "real fighter."[34]

He reveled in the physical test, competing in dangerous matches, riding untamed burros and wild mustangs. In others too, he valued this tough fearlessness. In 1934 he recalled a fight that had taken place forty years earlier with vivid detail. "I still remember the fight . . . [two friends] had in Zora Morgan's barn! It was epic! It lasted from the time school was out until well after dark—and then it ended in a draw! I recall how I danced around them and egged them on and I was very disappointed the next day when they made up and failed to renew the fight according to agreement. I still think it was one of the best fights I ever saw."[35]

Many years later Fiorello La Guardia would admonish psychiatrists for their "mechanization of treatment," for making abstruse interpretations of childhood behavior when simple understanding went a long way. "Listen to me about children . . . ," he would say. "The most difficult child to handle is the ultra-sensitive child. Sometimes you think he's stubborn when he is only bashful. . . . I was a runt myself and a handful for my teacher.'' This sensitive, pint-sized, obstreperous child who was moved from army post to army post, who did not develop a strong sense of geographic place or confidence in the affections of his demanding father, learned early in life to substitute willfullness for trust and to make his mark with a conspicuous truculence. It was he who would dare to play on the regimental commander's porch, who would sass his teachers, who went around cursing like a soldier. ''Obstacles never seemed to faze him,'' his first teacher recalled with admiration; ''he was always ready to get into anything.''[36]

2. A Not So Splendid War and a Career in the Balkans

I N the spirit of the times, one test served as the truest measure of patriotism and physical courage, and the Cuban insurrection against Spain during the 1890s offered a gung ho America the opportunity to test itself in the crucible of idealistic war at the same time that it built a small empire. The cause, wrapped in the rhetoric of sacrifice and blood and guts, engaged the teenage La Guardia's imagination as it did much of the rest of the country.

Rebels determined to oust the Spanish from Cuba had been waging a guerilla war against the colonial government for several years, burning cane fields, blowing up industries, and sabotaging railway lines when, in 1896, Spain sent the ruthless General Valeriano Weyler to put down the insurrection. He implemented a savage policy of ''reconcentration,'' herding about half a million Cubans from the countryside into wretched camps to deprive the *insurrectos* of food and support. Sensational reports of ''Butcher'' Weyler's brutal program with estimates of perhaps 200,000 deaths stirred American demands for intervention. Part search for broader national influence, part personal quest for deeds of blood and valor, part America's desire to take its place by the side of older empires, and part American mission to protect the helpless and uplift the ''uncivilized,'' the momentum for intervention continued to grow.[37]

When the American battleship *Maine* blew up in Havana harbor on February 15, 1898, William Randolph Hearst's *New York Journal* reported what many Americans suspected, that the Spanish were responsible. There was no proof, but with 260 deaths and a destroyed battleship coming directly after the publication of a pilfered private letter in which the Spanish ambassador dismissed President McKinley in insulting terms, Americans blamed Spain. The yellow press stoked war fever with sensational, often fabricated, accounts. A *New York Herald* reporter counted more than 200 American correspondents, over 25 from Hearst papers alone, reporting on the Cuban situation. He recalled that "there was a factory out there for faking news."[38]

President McKinley refused to be rushed into an adventure. "I have been through war," he told a friend, "I have seen the dead piled up. I do not want to see another." But despite such misgivings, Congress and the president on April 25, 1898, authorized armed force. "The American people," declared Senator Albert Beveridge, "go forth in a warfare holier than liberty—holy as humanity."[39]

Back at Whipple Barracks there was great excitement; the army had one purpose for being, and the number of Indian renegades to put down was steadily dwindling. Few questioned the need to fight the Spanish. Prescott's admired reform mayor Bucky O'Neill told a huge rally that the United States had a moral obligation to rid the hemisphere of Spain's autocratic influence. Within ten days the Eleventh Infantry, experienced in protecting settlers, miners, and railroads, was called to foreign conflict. There would be guns and strategy and, inevitably, death. But the cause was liberty and the deck was stacked. Sherwood Anderson, not yet well known as an author, joked that it was "like robbing an old gypsy woman in a vacant lot at night after a fair," and U.S. Ambassador to England John Hay, thrilled at the prospect of a "splendid little war." Prescott's O'Neill, commissioned a captain, joined the "Rough Riders."[40]

Achille La Guardia's regiment was shipped to Jefferson Barracks in St. Louis and then to Mobile, Alabama, for training, while the women and children remained in St. Louis. Fiorello wanted badly to join the men and kept badgering his mother for permission to go off with the troops. When she refused, he pulled himself to his full height and presented himself to the recruiting officer as a volunteer. With thousands flocking to the colors, the officer was underwhelmed with the pint-sized rough rider. Maybe the next war.

He would not give up. A few days later Fiorello strode into the offices of the *St. Louis Post Dispatch* to apply for the post of war correspondent, offering his experience as a school journalist and amateur photographer for reference. He did not leave until he finally persuaded the editor to issue him a press card and a travel allowance, and he was off to war.[41]

With only 28,000 combat ready troops, the United States undertook the mobilization of some 200,000 more men. The initial euphoria filled recruiting quotas, but no amount of spirit could provide these enlistees with arms, uniforms, and decent food. Entire units lacked these essentials, while carloads of equipment lay abandoned on railroad sidings. Aggressive units like Teddy Roosevelt's Rough Riders elbowed others aside in the competition for supplies, but even they complained: "No words could describe . . . the confusion and lack of system and the general mismanagement of affairs here,'' Roosevelt griped. Men marching off for America's greater glory carried rifles that proved more dangerous to the soldiers who carried them than to their targets. Overwhelmed by the excitement, our young correspondent refused to allow the all too evident problems to dampen his jingo enthusiasm. "Everybody in fine spirits,'' reported "F. LaGuardi [*sic*],'' in his first dispatch, going on to describe the assembled troops as "a nice lot of spirited boys . . . the right sort of men to defend their country. . . . ready and anxious for orders to go to Cuba.''[42]

The cult of manly courage that so stirred Fiorello was amply represented in this war: "I freely sent the men for whom I cared the most to where death might smite them,'' Theodore Roosevelt wrote in his journal. One night, during a lull, Prescott's Bucky O'Neill spoke to TR of his dreams. He struck the future president as the only one of his men with "the soul and imagination'' to perceive the personal challenge of war with its opportunity for honor and renown, as well as death. "Who,'' Bucky once asked Roosevelt, "would not risk his life for a star?'' As O'Neill strutted about the encampment one evening, the sergeant warned him to keep low. "The Spanish bullet is not molded that will hit me,'' replied Bucky, catching a bullet full in the face as he completed his sentence and breathed his last.[43]

Fiorello joined Achille at Mobile but they never got to Cuba. The army's rampant disorganization and the cupidity of the war contractors proved even more dangerous in the mess than on the field. Achille had been scheduled to leave for Cuba to entertain the troops, but in Tampa, Florida, he fell victim to "embalmed beef.'' Theodore Roosevelt later compared the crooked "contractors who furnished the army with rotten food and shoddy materials'' to white slavers "in infamy.'' Nowhere was this infamy more in evidence than in the GI rations of diseased meat camouflaged with spices and chemicals. From this fare that claimed far more Americans than did Spanish guns, Achille La Guardia fell gravely ill with hepatitis complicated by malaria.[44]

The war with Spain ended on August 12, 1898, outfitting the United States with your basic small empire: the Philippines, Guam, Puerto Rico, and a special relationship with Cuba. For those like Hay the war was splendid; for TR it provided a hero's halo that shone on the rest of his political career. But for the La Guardias the denouement was disastrous. Achille was honorably discharged for "diseases of the stomach and bowels, catarrh of the head and throat and malarial poisoning.'' For this impressive list of damage the government three weeks later awarded him a pension of $8 a month.

The La Guardias had been an army family since 1885, assured a regular paycheck and a barracks home. Now they had nothing to return to. For a brief time the family moved to New York City, but the immigrant metropolis, crammed with hundreds of thousands competing for physically demanding, low-paying jobs, offered no attraction for Achille. He had never associated with the immigrant community, and it offered him little comfort now. The La Guardias discussed other possibilities, but Achille no longer wanted to live in the United States. A cultivated man of large pride and no little pretension, he was, at the age of fifty, broken, sick, and bitter. Fiorello wanted to remain and pursue his education, but the decision was taken without him. He packed his shelf of high school texts and his plans for an American future and, with the rest of his family, headed back to Trieste and grandmother Fiorina Coen. The family crowded into the old home in which Irene had been raised, and Achille leased a hotel near the seaside at Capodistria, which he built into a profitable business until his death in 1904.[45]

The change in family fortunes made it impossible for Fiorello to pursue an American education and an American career as he had hoped, but he had no intention of going into Achille's hotel business. Through Raymond Willey, a friend of his father's, eighteen-year-old Fiorello landed a clerical post with the American consul in Budapest in 1900. Despite the $9-a-month salary, Fiorello viewed the job as an opportunity for "learn[ing] useful things and gain[ing] valuable experience." The other clerks in the office lacked interest or inspiration. They were clerks who would always be clerks, filling out forms, interviewing immigrants, and filing tourist complaints, but Fiorello was different. Hair parted neatly in the middle, proud of holding a U.S. government appointment, ambitious for recognition and advancement, he displayed a genuine interest in helping people and a curiosity about everything. He read whatever he could lay his hands on, asked numerous questions, studied German, Italian, and Croatian, and kept his eyes open for every career opportunity.[46]

Frank Dyer Chester, consul general at Budapest, was a refined bachelor gentleman with a Harvard Ph.D. in Semitic languages and the strong support of Henry Cabot Lodge, senior senator from Massachusetts. The mildly eccentric Chester, with his puffed dignity and delicate features, was a revelation to La Guardia. He was a man without physical toughness, driven by no larger ambition than to be exactly what he was. He never married and later left the foreign service to teach in college and study his family genealogy. Fiorello could never appreciate the exaggerated regard for personal history. He was too modern to believe that the family crest made the man. Years later he would write to someone who inquired about his family tree, "The only member of our family who has a real pedigree is our little Scotch Terrier . . . but with all of that is only a son of a bitch." Intrigued by his senior officer's active dislike of women, Fiorello once handed Chester a revolver with the comment: "What do you have to live for?"[47]

Chester could not help but notice that his trim, good-looking young assistant was doing quite a bit of living, paying close attention to the pretty women who passed through the office. It is not clear whether Chester's primary concern was for the consular reputation or simply his own genteel morality, but he repeatedly warned La Guardia to stand clear of any extra-office involvements. Once when a woman whom Fiorello later described as a "bleached blonde entertainer" came to town, Chester cautioned his young colleague that it would cost him his job if he were so much as seen with the "entertainer." Fiorello called on the woman that very night, escorting her to the Folies Bergères. The consul was lying in wait, and fired him on the spot. It took all of Fiorello's persuasive powers to convince his dour superior of his sincere penitence.[48]

He kept his post, but he did not learn much of a lesson. Full of life, and with a pair of flashing dark eyes that won him a fair share of admirers, the self-confident, athletic young Fiorello headed the local soccer team and haunted the billiard parlors and local cafes. It was lotus-eating time and Fiorello made the most of it. Once it almost involved him in a sword duel, when a jealous suitor challenged him to offer satisfaction with long knives because Fiorello had captured his fiancée's interest. La Guardia had seen gunfighting and fistfighting back home in Prescott, but such civilized mayhem as swordplay was unfamiliar to him. It discomfited him to think that he might actually be skewered over this silliness. With no choice but to choose seconds or back down, however, La Guardia selected two rather interesting seconds, a well-heeled businessman to whom he had given lessons in German, and the Turkish consul, "a notorious roue [who] had married an ugly widow with plenty of money." Luckily for Fiorello, these wordly men arranged a written protocol that provided satisfaction short of swordplay.[49]

La Guardia's lively style disturbed Chester, who repeatedly badgered his young charge about his fun-loving ways and his lack of a college education. But Chester also displayed an appreciation for Fiorello's gifts and helped win his young clerk a promotion to consular agent in charge of the Budapest consulate's Fiume office, at a substantial raise in pay (to 6000 crowns, or about $66 a month), with responsibility for administering the day-to-day affairs of the Fiume outpost. Although the one-room consulate with the agent's bedroom adjoining and the shared hallway bathroom was far from imposing, all in all it represented an impressive rise for so young a man. (Fiorello actually had to wait a few weeks before assuming the duties of his new office until his twenty-first birthday in December.)

Fiume was Hungary's only seaport, a major point of embarkation for thousands of emigrants bound for the New World. The State Department had received reports that Hungarian officials were collaborating with the Cunard Lines to encourage emigration in violation of American laws. Their polite inquiries had elicited unconvincing denials, and nettled American officials, aware of Fiorello's reputation for irascibility, may have felt that a dose of La Guardia was just what Hungary deserved. If that was what they intended, they planned well. With his penchant for blunt indignation and his custom of issuing undiplomatic pronouncements "in the name of the United States," the young consular agent rattled the Central European government as no junior officer had before.[50]

19

Fiorello took the initiative to clear away outdated procedures and unnecessary obstacles that hindered the hundreds of emigrants who departed from the seaport on scheduled packets every two weeks. On his own authority he changed the process of certifying ships that carried immigration traffic to the United States. American law required local consuls to "certify the health of all passengers and crew" before granting clearance certificates to American-bound ships. In practice, however, consuls issued the document after a perfunctory check of the ship's papers and a quick glance at the departing crowd. Then, after the immigrants arrived at Ellis Island or another receiving station, they went through a battery of health examinations. Those who failed this test were denied entry and sent back home.

Fiorello saw these dispirited, often penniless rejects come back carrying only their dashed hopes and resolved to eliminate the uncertainties. There was no reason that the immigrants could not be put through a thorough health inspection before they left Europe, and if they proved unfit, at least they would be spared a harsh and pointless round trip. Fiorello decided to require a full medical check of each emigrant and make such exams a condition for issuing certificates of clearance to the transports.[51]

Consular certification had become a stylized diplomatic ceremony. The ship captain would invite the American consul for tea aboard ship, exchange some pleasantries over sweet cookies, and receive the required certificate of good health. When Fiorello showed up for his tea he had a local doctor in tow, and he insisted that each passenger be examined before he issued the clearance document. When surprised Cunard officials refused to cooperate, La Guardia left without anyone being examined. A few days later, as the departure date neared, shipping officials sent for the bill of good health, but La Guardia refused to sign it. There followed a series of stiff protests from both Cunard and the British consular officials, but Fiorello stubbornly held his ground, refusing to put the immigrants through games of sad chance for Cunard's convenience.

With no other choice, ship officials finally relented and the passengers were checked. Cunard paid the $5 fee for the certificate but refused to pay for the doctor. "I was not worried about that," Fiorello said later. "I knew that another ship was coming soon." This second time he presented Cunard with the outstanding bill and demanded a deposit for the next round of examinations. These health examinations that La Guardia adopted as a regular procedure dramatically reduced the number of immigrants from Fiume who were turned back at American ports of entry. More than twenty years later the U.S. Congress enacted legislation adopting a similar policy for all immigrants applying for a visa.[52]

La Guardia could usually manage to work with the State Department and even the ship companies, but he refused to pay European notions of class and nobility any respect. A notable example involved Archduchess Maria Josefa of Austria, who planned a visit to Fiume and made known her desire to view an immigrant ship boarding. These boardings offered picturesque scenes of the travelers in their assorted outfits bidding tearful adieu to friends and kin as they pushed sacks filled with all their worldly belongings aboard the ocean liners. The inspection process provided a rich tableau of intense emotions, street theater for the upper crust who filled the first-deck gallery to watch the scenes with much the same interest that blue-blooded ladies in eighteenth-century England toured the madhouses of Bedlam for diversion.

One morning a steamship official notified La Guardia that immigrants would be boarding the S.S. *Panonia* that afternoon, a few days earlier than scheduled, to accommodate Her Majesty's request. La Guardia objected that much as he regretted denying the archduchess her simple pleasures, once passengers were examined and placed aboard ship they could not leave the vessel. This meant that they would be forced to remain in their cramped quarters for three extra days if the boarding took place early, and he would not allow that.

Local officials pleaded with the twenty-two-year-old La Guardia to understand that Her Royal Highness's schedule left no option, but he refused. The last words that passed between Austrian officials and the American had to do with requesting the cheeky junior consul's recall after the port officer staged the ship boarding on his own. La Guardia warned that such a move would cost the ship its bill of health; the *Panonia* would not be able to deposit its passengers at an American port. Fiorello dismissed all pleas to understand the privileges of royalty and the obligations of commoners. "Tell the archduchess," La Guardia told sputtering local officials, "that she may boss her own immigrants, but she can't boss the American consul."

On the day of the visit a frantic port officer searched all over town for the young American consul, but La Guardia had become very scarce and the boarding performance had to be canceled. Later that evening La Guardia told his dinner companion, the British consul, that he had spent the day where no one would think to look for him, at the home of the port officer, sipping tea and chatting with the official's charming wife.[53]

On October 21, 1904, just before completing the purchase of the hotel that he was managing, Achille La Guardia died of a heart attack, and Fiorello's mother and sister came to live with him in Fiume. Irene La Guardia, convinced that her husband's death was a result of his military illness, applied for an army allowance. For months letters went back and forth between Fiume and Washington: Prove that you are indeed Achille's widow, that you have not remarried, that you are truly destitute and dependent upon this pension. Fiorello long remembered this lesson in bureaucratic insensitivity. More irksome than the questions was the difficulty of proving Irene's contention that Achille's heart attack was induced by pulmonary emphysema related to "hard labors." On October 11, 1906, almost two years after Achille's death, the case was settled with an award of $12.80, to the widow.[54]

21

The death of his father led La Guardia to think seriously about his own future course. In Fiume he had his soccer team, his friends, good music, good times, and at twenty-three a position that was interesting and paid well enough. But he was unsatisfied. Central European politics, with its ethnic hatreds, offended him, and he saw little future in the stifling corridors of junior diplomacy.

Fiorello knew five languages and was a crackerjack agent, but in the soft-toned circle of gentlemanly diplomacy he was an anomaly. He did not even have a high school diploma. In the hushed world of whispers and good breeding he was a strong-willed shouter who ignored channels, meddled in the affairs of other embassies, irritated superiors, and refused to defer to royalty, while insisting on "the respect due to this office." Ship companies complained that working with the willful young consul was "trying." Chester, disturbed by La Guardia's frequent clashes with Fiume officials, wrote Washington, asking officials to instruct Fiorello to deal courteously with foreign officials and to refrain from writing "any official letters . . . without first submitting them to me for examination and approval." Finally, after Fiorello ignored all suggestions for a quieter diplomacy, the exasperated Chester filed a report describing La Guardia as "detrimental to . . . good relations. . . ."[55]

La Guardia responded with demands of his own. Just a few months after his appointment as a consular agent, Fiorello asked Washington to raise the Fiume office to the level of a full consulate and that he—"the boy consul," as one official derisively referred to him—be promoted to full consul. Two years later, still unpromoted, he fired off another note, objecting that his office's "existence, . . . has been entirely forgotten by the Department of State." His counterparts in the other consulates consistently outranked him, La Guardia complained, and he was tired of being low man in the pecking order. He asked to be moved into the newly available position of consul general in Belgrade, Serbia. In tones little calculated to avoid offense, he then declared about himself: "If his . . . knowledge of the language and six years' service are not sufficient to counterbalance his total lack of political influence, there remains no doubt that the service is not the place for a young man to work up."[56]

Restless, bright, and energetic, Fiorello wanted to "work up." "I wanted more action, I didn't see any future for myself in diplomacy," he later wrote. He needed an education and a place open to large possibilities. "I am ambitious. I want to study and to get somewhere in my own country. I want to be somebody," he told his mother, as he informed her of his decision to leave Europe for New York. He did not ask her or Gemma to accompany him. He was leaving; it was as simple as that. Frank Chester asked Fiorello to hold off his resignation for a few weeks until he could find someone to fill the post, but, an angry Chester wired back to Washington, "Mr. La Guardia curtly refused."[57]

La Guardia was prepared to assume responsibility for his own future. In his partial autobiography, Fiorello devotes no more than a few cursory passages to his parents. The references are respectful, but opaque, betraying little affection and no sense of springing from strong stock. Later in his life when a distant cousin wrote asking him about his father, La Guardia admitted that he knew virtually nothing about his father's background. It was not important to him. Ultimately he was interested in his own possibilities. Like his father a generation before, Fiorello was leaving for America, and his own ambitions.[58]

3. A Spirited Unrest

In one of the most influential books of the early twentieth century, *The Education of Henry Adams*, the querulous autobiographer brooded about the impact of a spirit-crushing industrialism. "The cylinder had exploded," Adams wrote, "and thrown great masses of steam and stone against the sky," unleashing enormous power and prosperity and corresponding excitations of alarm and anger. For this terrible progress, the old leadership, the old men, the old *type* of men, his type, the "best men," had no answers. "All New York was demanding new men, and all the new forces . . . were demanding a new type of man—a man with ten times the endurance, energy, will and mind of the old type. . . . [T]he old one had plainly reached the end of his strength, and his failure had become catastrophic."[59]

Not quite twenty-four years old, ambitious for education, respect, and a career in handling just the type of forces that Adams brooded over, Fiorello landed in this "seething, sparkling, darkling" city. Without friends, without an education, and without a family to back him, he would have the opportunity that New York was so exceptional at offering, to make a success of himself or fail miserably. But at first he found little demand in New York for a contentious ex-consular official, knowledgeable in several languages, cutting red tape, and playing soccer. He took a job with the Haberson and Walker Co., who sent him to Portsmouth, Ohio, to produce fireproof bricks. But this was not the career that he had imagined, and Ohio was not the place he had dreamed about.[60]

He had come back to the United States to pursue a career he considered worthy of him. Since the days in Prescott, when he waited impatiently for the latest Sunday editions of the *New York World* to pore over its comic strips and tales of urban corruption, politics fascinated him, particularly New York politics, with its Tammany villains. More recently he had been moved by Jacob Riis's probe into the dark soul of slum life, *How the Other Half Lives*, to reaffirm his dream of a political career where he could make a difference in all of this.

23

He returned to New York City from Ohio and took a series of temporary jobs: the Society for the Prevention of Cruelty to Children paid him $10 a week to translate a section of the French Penal Code; he served as a clerk for a steamship company, clearing $15 a week; then he registered for a $7.50 course in stenography at the Pratt School, which equipped him for a better-paying clerkship at Abercrombie and Fitch. Within several months La Guardia had been to Ohio and back, moved up in three successive jobs, learned some new skills, and was earning $20 a week, a lot more than many New Yorkers in those times. His willingness to start anywhere, work hard, push ahead, and keep churning fit him for this city. It was not just his ambition, or even his belief in himself, though both of these were considerable. He adapted to the rhythm of the city. He understood that progress, growth, and change were key elements of life in this center of impermanence. And he was not satisfied with insignificant achievements.[61]

Larger goals than his daily bread and economic success animated him. After completing a preparatory course and acquiring a high school diploma, he applied for evening studies at New York University Law School, joined the local Republican Club, and took the Civil Service examination for interpreter of Croation for the Immigration Service. Earning the highest score of all applicants on the exam, he was appointed on November 6, 1907, as an interpreter of Croatian, Italian, and German at Ellis Island at a salary of $1200 a year.[62]

In these years American immigration reached historic peaks. Eight million newcomers streamed into the United States in the first ten years of the twentieth century. In 1907, the year Fiorello began working at Ellis Island, 1.3 million immigrants entered the country. Ellis, designed to process a maximum of 5000 individuals a day, jammed through as many as 12,000 on some days. If mass production of meat in Chicago could produce the kind of *Jungle* that Upton Sinclair would make famous, the mass processing of hundreds of thousands of human beings created its own harsh dramas. Some of the officials grew callous after repeatedly looking into the eyes of weary men and women afraid enough to lie; others took great pity on the masses who had been rendered so defenseless that even their own names and personal histories were altered to ease their chances to live free.

Early each morning Fiorello would take the subway to the Battery, board the 8:40 A.M. ferry, and set off for a day at the island. The unprecedented waves of immigration often forced interpreters to work seven days a week, and on each of these days La Guardia would witness the process brought to its critical point, where the tears and fears and hopes of vast numbers of people would be resolved by a series of questions and physical examinations. La Guardia had seen these people and thousands like them back in Europe. He had avoided the trap of looking away then, and he continued to offer care and concern for these vulnerable folk. "I suffered a great deal because I could not help these poor people," La Guardia would say. But if he could not prevent the breakup of a family because one of its members had a disqualifying disease, he worked to change the policy and have

24

immigrants examined overseas so that hopes were not raised and dashed unnecessarily. With his colleagues, Fiorello wrote to officials to change the law and ease the daily heartbreak that they witnessed.[63]

The entire process seemed to La Guardia unnecessarily harsh. He described for an acquaintance the anguish of a young girl from the northern Italian mountains whose obscure dialect made it difficult to communicate with her. Responding slowly to questions she barely understands, the child is observed closely to see if she is retarded or ill. This girl, perhaps never before alone with a man, is poked by a doctor, rapping her knees, checking her eyes, listening to her lungs, and turning her on her back, until finally she lets out a howl. "In two weeks she was a raving maniac." The famous legal scholar and Supreme Court justice, Felix Frankfurter, remembered first meeting Fiorello when he was "a gifted interpreter" at Ellis Island who fought for fair and humane immigration laws and policies.[64]

La Guardia encountered more lessons on the price of being vulnerable when he ferried young immigrant couples to City Hall to be married before they were formally admitted to the United States. As often as not, he would find an alderman sitting with a bunch of red-faced cronies in their cups, exchanging dirty jokes. Catching sight of the woman, the good-time pols would make some tasteless cracks, until one would bestir himself to perform the ceremony, often lacing it with lewd remarks and demands for an illegal gratuity. Here was nothing more than a petty, even insignificant, corruption, but it left him with a lasting impression about the character of New York's aldermen.[65]

In his last year of law school, La Guardia was assigned to night court duty so that he could complete his law classes by day. Night court dealt primarily with vice cases, and Fiorello was there to see if any of the detainees were immigrants who could be deported for such violations. In little time he became familiar with the system of payoffs at the heart of the city's commercial vice racket. Police would bring gangs of prostitutes, with whom they seemed to have a friendly relationship, before judges who pronounced light sentence, while lawyers arranged the deals on the sidelines. And running this game of sham arrests and sham punishments was the local political boss, whose protection kept the whores and pimps in business.[66]

La Guardia was not alone in witnessing this corruption, but his resentments were fresh. He had not grown up in the city taking such arrangements for granted. His notions of possibility had been nourished by frontier life, where government was simple enough to control and, if necessary, change.

But if change, how? That was too large a question for the moment, and La Guardia was still gathering impressions, still feeling his way toward some overall sense of the city and its operation. His savvy colleague Anthony Tedesco could not provide any answers to the large questions either, but he did offer La Guardia one important bit of advice. As chief inspector of the Immigration Service's white slave division, Tedesco worked close enough to the entrepreneurs of temptation to have been corrupted handsomely if he only wanted. But he was clean, and La

Guardia admired the unkempt and frequently harried chief inspector. Tedesco had seen too much to be shocked by corruption, or by how many legitimate interests were tied into the vice industry. He knew the hotels, the nightclubs, the politicians, the police, the liquor dealers, the lawyers, all of whom wanted to keep prostitution flourishing. Tedesco understood how temptation worked, and the rewards of graft. "You can get experience on this job," the hard-boiled inspector told Fiorello, "or you can make a great deal of money. I don't think you'll take the money. But remember, the test is if you hesitate. Unless you say 'no' right off, the first time an offer comes your way, you're gone." La Guardia carried the lesson with him all of his life.[67]

La Guardia was more than willing to foreswear illegal payoffs, but he did want to make more honest money than he was being paid, particularly after he learned that others with fewer responsibilities were paid more than him. He wrote Commissioner Robert Watchorn that as the "only interpreter you have who is a stenographer and the only stenographer who is a linguist," he deserved a raise. The commissioner transmitted La Guardia's request, adding his own endorsement of Fiorello's energy and initiative, although he noted that the little guy had an independent streak and tended to be argumentative.[68]

The raise came through in April of 1910, but by then La Guardia was completing his legal studies, just barely. Too much work at Ellis Island and with the local Republican Party had limited the attention he gave to his classes, and his transcript contained a generous sprinkling of Cs and Ds in such subjects as Contracts, Torts, and Property and Equity Jurisprudence. It did not much matter to him—he had no desire to be a legal scholar. The truth is that his was an education vulgar with ulterior purpose. The degree was going to be a way to get into politics, and while his grades may have been poor, one of his classmates recalled: "We all respected him."[69]

With diploma in hand and admission to the bar to come in the fall, La Guardia prepared to strike out as an attorney on his own. For just a moment, before leaving the Immigration Service, he hesitated, wondering if he should leave the security of his job, but Assistant Immigration Commissioner Byron Uhl took him by the arm and pointed out to him a number of elderly lawyers still working for the service. They had failed to make the move Fiorello was contemplating now, and they were dissatisfied, locked into closed careers, aware of roads not taken. Confirmed in his own inclination, La Guardia handed in his resignation at the end of the year to "practice law in this city."[70]

Two years short of thirty, with $65 in his pocket and a fresh law degree in need of a wall upon which to be hung, he bought a small bust of his hero Napoleon, and announced himself to the world as F. H. La Guardia, Attorney at Law. La

26

Guardia rented an office, a cubicle really, for $15 a month at 15 William Street, ordered letterheads and some secondhand furniture, and opened his doors. But for what? He had a legal education. He knew how to gather information from law books, but he had no respect for a profession that taught its practitioners to argue either side of a case. He would not think of joining the squad of eager attorneys seeking loopholes and technicalities to protect the profits and prerogatives of business. His first clients were immigrants threatened with deportation, referred to him by friends on Ellis Island. When they could they paid a fee of $10. No matter, at least these people knew he had helped them and he knew that he was not a hired mouthpiece for a soulless corporation.[71]

From the leavings of the profession he created a practice of street law for the destitute, servicing tenants with complaints against landlords, immigrants who needed help with the bureacracy, workers who were cheated by their bosses, and small storekeepers who ran afoul of one of the local ordinances. The modest practice promised to keep him poor, but it established his reputation as a "people's attorney," and the nickel-and-dime cases familiarized him with community problems. In 1912 he moved to a larger office and a partnership with Raimondo Canudo, servicing the immigrant trade with "opinions by mail ($2 each)" on areas of Italian or American law. Subsequent partnerships expanded the practice beyond Italians, but La Guardia's legal work remained essentially a ghetto practice among the needy and defenseless.[72]

This experience as a workingman's attorney familiarized him with the pervasive political favoritism of the courts. In one instance he had prepared a careful case and made a strong presentation in municipal court, only to lose the decision. Noticing the young attorney's dismay, the judge called La Guardia to the bench and quietly complimented him upon his arguments. Puzzled, Fiorello asked why then had he lost the case? The man in the robe just smiled down at him, and not without kindness, promised to give him a break next time. "What a hell of a way to dispense justice," Fiorello thought. He needed business "about as badly as any young lawyer in the game," La Guardia would write, but he refused to buy justice by cutting the deals and pursuing the political connections that greased lawyerly success. "The more I got to know about lawyers and their ethics," he later wrote, "the less respect I had for them."[73]

The only way to change all this, La Guardia became convinced, was through reforming government and politics. Fannie Hurst, an inexperienced young writer from St. Louis when she first met Fiorello (who went by the name of Frank in these years), remembered a "black haired, sloe eyed, fiery little fellow" hard at work at his ambition of making government fair and responsive to the needs of the common citizen.[74]

Studying for his postgraduate degree at Oxford University during these same years, another New Yorker, Robert Moses, presented a thesis paper that questioned the basis of the American system of elective politics: "We must decide," he wrote,

27

"how much encouragement we may honestly offer to those who expect to rise from the ranks without the almost essential early education of the university man." Like other idealistic young men and women who viewed city government as a political disaster area, Moses thought that the only solution to pervasive corruption and inefficiency was to hand over the management of city affairs to a corps of college-trained urban experts.[75]

No doubt Walter Lippmann fulfilled Moses' notion of the university man well qualified for the aristocracy of intelligent political leadership. And Lippmann had the desire to serve. While still a student at Harvard, he told a friend: "I long to . . . reach some small portion of the masses so that in the position not of a teacher but of a friend, I may lay open real happiness to them." But Lippmann understood another dimension to the problem: cerebral gifts were not enough. "For it is a fact that a man can't see the play and be in it too."[76]

While Lippmann was studying at Harvard with George Santayana and Henry James, Fiorello La Guardia was working at Ellis Island, completing an apprenticeship in human experience.

Accompanying La Guardia around town and joining him in investigating the corrupt courts, Fannie Hurst marveled at Fiorello's energy and drive and sense of outrage, his "magnificent unrest coupled with a desire to be a leader on his own terms." With his friends, drawn from a mix of educated professionals and artists, almost all of them Italian, Fiorello debated the issues of the day, and planned for the time that he would address these issues before a wider constituency.[77]

With this group of friends, he shared dinners, stories, and the excitement of New York in its years of fantastic possibility. One of the men, the artist Onorio Ruotolo, painted, did sculpture, wrote poetry, and edited an Italian-language magazine devoted to art and intelligent discussion. "Society will tolerate anything," Ruotolo was fond of saying, "but genius." The circle included Antonio Calitri, a former Catholic priest who wrote poetry; the syndicalist journalist-poet Arturo Giovannitti; Attilio Piccirilli, head of one of the leading commercial sculpting foundries in the United States; Giovanni Fabrizio, a New York Philharmonic flutist; Giuseppe Bellanca, who was caught up with developing airplanes; and his brother August, committed to organizing unions among New York's Italian garment workers. These were happy times, the last few years before the World War, when the environment seemed soft and pliable, amenable to all sorts of plans for improvement and the rehabilitation of evil. La Guardia's friends planned airplanes to bring people closer together and a robust labor movement to counterbalance the power of the corporations. While they debated radical theoretical principles, suffered for art, and made emotional commitments to the masses, Fiorello cast his eye toward practical politics.[78]

Fiorello's circle promoted his political plans. They assisted him in editing his speeches for the ethnic newspapers, ushered him around the local neighborhood, and introduced him to the fraternal associations. He spoke before meetings, helped with community legal work, and became an honorary member of the society of immigrants from his ancestral hometown of Foggia. In 1913 he was initiated into the Garibaldi Lodge of the Masonic Order. He also befriended several Roman Catholic clergymen. With no less attention to building personal bonds than a Tammany ward boss, Fiorello was preparing the scaffolding for his political career.

During the evenings his friends would drop by for food, wine, and to review his political progress. In their discussions some would advocate the dogmas of socialism, syndicalism, or anarchism, but Fiorello rejected arguments for European-style revolution. Among his radical friends he was the *Americano*, the lawyer, the system's advocate, but among his lawyer acquaintances he complained of the system's injustice. To Fannie Hurst he railed about the disgrace of the night courts, the shameful aldermen, and the comfortable smugness of men and women who accepted things as they were and limited their concern to doing their job. He deeply valued liberty and freedom, but he was grappling with the realization that in modern society the individual citizen was not always able to solve his own problems, that a modern politics required something more complex than laissez faire government.[79]

The role of labor in a rapidly industrializing economy offered one important example of the possibilities in cooperative efforts. Few today recall the tireless struggles, the intense idealism, the physical hardships, and the courage that went into the fight for decent working conditions. From friends and clients La Guardia learned firsthand the difficult conditions in the garment trade sweatshops that lined the immigrant neighborhoods. Some machine operators earned only $5 a week, and some weeks extended to over sixty hours during the busy season. But rather than address these issues, the owners tried to set the Italian and Jewish workers against each other by exploiting ethnic differences. In December 1912, when close to 60,000 garment workers in the men's clothing industry walked off their jobs, La Guardia joined the fight for better wages and improved factory conditions.

La Guardia's good friend August Bellanca headed the union's Italian section, and he put Fiorello to work helping on the legal issues, but La Guardia quickly became involved in other work, cajoling, convincing, recruiting, marching on picket lines, and making a difference. He spoke before Italian and Jewish workers, emphasizing their shared interest in better conditions, breaking down ethnic antagonisms. La Guardia immersed himself in the cause. "Night after night I spent my time with the union leaders . . . ," he recalled, "helping to organize their efforts. During the day I appeared in court to fight cases against the pickets and other cases. . . . I addressed literally hundreds of meetings." Other lawyers, fearful of antagonizing business interests, avoided such causes, but for Fiorello the opportunity to move into a larger sphere of activity was more important than well-heeled clients. Jacob Panken later recalled these early struggles as "days full of achievement and . . . satisfaction," filled with a sense of making history and extending the frontiers of labor rights, and La Guardia, said Panken, was never "just a friend. . . . He [was] . . . a participant in labor's struggle."[80]

It heartened the workers to know that this man without an accent, with the cowboy hat, string bow tie (conspicuous reminders of his western upbringing), and law degree thought enough of their struggle to devote to it his days and nights. For two months La Guardia worked at a frenetic pace, making Yiddish and Italian speeches, preparing court papers, and lifting the spirits of the strikers. Then, without consultation, the old-guard union leaders announced an agreement. An embittered La Guardia attacked the settlement as a sellout. The rank and file agreed, rejecting the dictated terms. Elated by the courage of the strikers, Fiorello once again made the rounds, papering over antagonisms, articulating goals, and taking a direct hand in the negotiations. With Meyer London, the future Socialist congressman, and Jacob Panken, the Socialist labor leader, he helped win a far more attractive settlement, which resulted in shorter hours and pay increases.[81]

Socialism played a large role in the garment trades labor unions, and La Guardia found sufficient common ground to work well with the labor ideologues. But while he refused to be charmed by the dream of a perfect society, the experience brought him close to the pioneering unionists who would build the Amalgamated Clothing Workers into one of the most influential unions in the country. For many of these men, the union movement represented an end in itself, a solution to the crucial problems of urban industrial life, and a path to a Socialist America. But La Guardia looked beyond the limited world of the ghetto and its homebred institutions; he saw unions as one of many means for redressing social imbalances in a democratic society, and he turned to electoral politics.

4. Into Politics

L A Guardia had come to New York in 1906 with politics on his mind. Within five months of his landing he had entered a subscription for the *Congressional Record* and joined the Madison Republican Club. While Republicans were not much of a force in the lower Manhattan neighborhoods familiar to Fiorello, he avoided the Democratic party and its Tammany Club. Since his days at Fort Whipple when he would race to the store for the Sunday edition of the *New York World* with its sensational accounts of a city besieged by venal corrupters, Tammany Hall smacked of unsavory men and unseemly politics. Not much had changed. In 1909 *McClure's Magazine* reported on the "Lawrence Mulligan Civic Ball," where Tammany leaders partied cheek by jowl with the city's notorious gangsters, prostitutes, and organized criminals. "Around him," wrote George Kibbe Turner of

Boss "Big Tim" Sullivan, "were a thousand pimps and thieves and prostitutes," his people. Big Tim was a traditional-style boss, hosting huge annual picnics and distributing gifts of shoes, coal, turkeys, and jobs to constituents who voted right. Politics in the districts Tammany controlled, a contemporary testified, was "frankly and boastfully corrupt."[82]

There were also practical impediments to joining Tammany. Fiorello was not Irish, and Tammany was still primarily a green machine. Some leaders did make grudging concessions to the new immigrant populations, but these were token gifts of minor consequence. Michael Rofrano's experience offered an instructive example. Rofrano had worked for Tammany boss Tim Foley, attracting support for Democrats among recently settled Italians. In return, Foley pushed city business to Rofrano's contracting firm and arranged a comfortable sinecure for him in the housing department. The *New York Times* described the two as "close personal friends." By 1912 Rofrano decided to cash in on his political work, and he asked Foley to arrange his nomination for Congress. Foley looked up at his Italian friend and laughed in his face. Within a few weeks Rofrano was bitterly telling acquaintances that he had been used by Tammany. The Democratic party was clearly not the place for an ambitious Italian politician.[83]

Moreover, this was a time when dramatic reform seemed possible. Growing awareness of the slums and wretched factory conditions drove reformers to fight for better housing and safer workplaces. Fear of the giant business combinations known as trusts spurred a movement to regulate and restrict monopolies, while muckraking journalists like Lincoln Steffens revealed how banal political corruption had become in the major cities. The relentless study and exposure of these and similar problems fueled a spirit of liberal reform that attracted La Guardia with its high-minded possibilities. "I had been storing up knowledge," he would write, "and I was eager to bring about better conditions . . . a more equitable economic condition and less favoritism." The opportunity for good works and dignity that La Guardia sought in politics, quid-pro-quo Tammany, with its sleaziness and corruption, could not hope to give him.[84]

Fiorello became active in the Madison Republican Club, which served a tangle of neighborhoods, including WASP Washington Square, a slice of the Irish and Italian West Side, and colorful Greenwich Village, with its sprinkling of nonconforming artists and intellectuals. The club itself was run by the type of men that Democratic boss George Washington Plunkitt disdainfully identified as "dudes who part their name in the middle." Of his own club, the Tammany pol had written: "We've got bookworms, too, in the organization. But we don't make them district leaders. We keep them for ornaments on parade days." Frederick Chauncey Tanner, the chief of the Madison Republicans, was the sort that Plunkitt would march out for parades. The son of a college president, with a sterling list of affiliations including the Order of Cincinnati and the Order of the Mayflower Descendants, Tanner viewed politics differently from the Plunkitts of this world. While the Tammany boss expressed his political philosophy as seein' his opportunities and takin' 'em, Tanner aspired to promote an intelligent government of civic virtue. Plunkitt might dismiss the "best men" as too highfalutin for operating a political club, but Republicans had done very nicely under Tanner, putting together a string of victories in a district that had been unwaveringly Democratic.[85]

The Republican county chairman, Samuel Koenig, a laconic, bespectacled veteran of Lower East Side politics, reflected a more pragmatic approach to politics. Much as he may have respected ideas and aspirations for social reform, Koenig was a political operator, whose practical function was to elect candidates. Shifting easily between the high-minded and the cynical, the committed and the hacks, Koenig steered a pragmatic politics, keeping his regular army of party workers at the business of gathering votes and rewarding loyal work with patronage and favors. He once described a fellow political leader in dismissive tones as "*clean* and almost idealistic," as if this violated the canons of the profession.

Whatever reformers might think of patronage, Koenig favored it. He worked amicably with Tammany, splitting up city jobs so that each party could protect its favored appointees regardless of who won the elections. "We Republicans and Democrats fight only one day a year," Koenig once whispered to a friend. The rest of the year they played patronage. The promise of jobs kept the troops working. Without this bundle of carrots and sticks parties would shrink into insignificance. Even the well-bred Republicans knew that. On September 15, 1911, Frederick Tanner took up his pen on behalf of "Mr. Fiorello La Guardia, who is a bright young lawyer, and has done good service in my district," recommending him for appointment to the attorney general's office.[86]

La Guardia had served the party for several years, working with families, clearing up local problems, learning the names of the voters, paying homage to their ethnic sensibilities, and competing with Tammany for their loyalty. As Boss Plunkitt had said: "You must study human nature and act accordin'." After several years of such work in the wards, La Guardia sought his reward. He sent the Republican district leader a letter outlining his experience and his service to the party and asked to be appointed a deputy attorney general, supporting his request with recommendations from four prominent Italian newspapers. The following week he sent another batch of endorsements asking Tanner to "please take the matter up with Mr. Koenig and get him sufficiently interested so that he will see [New York State attorney general] Mr. Whitman and procure the appointment." Both Koenig and Tanner encouraged Fiorello to plead his case personally before the attorney general, "for your personality will make a good impression on him."[87]

Whether it was his sparkling personality or some other reason, La Guardia did not get the post, but he understood precisely the rules of party etiquette. He bided his time, and continued making speeches and guarding the polls for the party. When William Chadbourne bolted the Republicans to back Theodore Roosevelt's Bull Moose ticket in 1912, Fiorello stood fast with Taft, proud of "being regular in every sense of the word." His regularity was immediately rewarded. He took Bill Chadbourne's place as district captain.[88]

The following year when Republican reformers supported John Purroy Mitchell's fusion campaign for nonpartisan municipal efficiency, La Guardia refused to join the insurgents. His reasons were thoroughly self-serving. The election of an attractive young Democrat might hurt Tammany, but it would do the Republicans no good. "I am thoroughly disgusted with the results brought about by the so-called Fusion Committee," he wrote to a friend. "While no doubt each of the 107 represents the other 106, I fail to see where any one of them is representative of any large body of voters." The GOP could not build a strong organization by electing idealistic Democrats, and he saw no reason to "play into the hands of a few disgruntled Republicans now classing themselves as 'Progressives.' "[89]

When the Madison Club nevertheless threw its support to Mitchell, La Guardia refused to campaign for the Democrat while working for the rest of the ticket. He was, at the age of thirty, still setting sure ground under his feet, hoping to open as many possibilities as he could for young Republicans like himself.

His Village friends and labor associates had oriented him in the wider issues of government and political ideas. Two new friends, Harry Andrews and Louis Espresso, helped La Guardia plant his politics firmly in the street issues of the district. Political technicians who understood voters, strategy, and wheeling and dealing far better than issues, these unschooled sons of the working class viewed politics as choosing up sides and then fighting to the end for a victory. From this colorful pair La Guardia learned a lot about how to play the game and how to win. Andrews and Espresso led Fiorello on a regular round of christenings, weddings, funerals, and social functions, the basic part of a fledgling politician's internship. They took him to the district captains, taught him to feign intimacy by calling people he barely knew by their first names, and they laid quiet plans for La Guardia's political future.[90]

———

In 1914 Fiorello's open interest in running for elective office won for him a rare opportunity. He liked to describe his first nomination as having been touched by serendipity. "One night [in late summer 1914] I happened to be in the club rooms of the 25th Assembly District . . . when the boys were filling in petitions for the nomination for Congress. . . ." Many of the offices were already assigned but no name had yet been inserted for the 14th C.D. race for the House of Representatives. The district leader poked his head out of his door, asking if anyone wanted to run for the seat. No Republican had ever been elected in the district so the nomination meant very little. For half an hour various names were bandied about, but the clubhouse caucus could not settle on a satisfactory candidate.[91]

Then, report La Guardia's biographers, Lowell Limpus and Burr W. Leyson, "somebody noticed the black-haired lawyer gesticulating in a corner of the room," and suggested to the assembled politicos that the nomination go to La Guardia. He at first hesitated, "knowing as well as they that the offer was meaningless. But," Limpus and Leyson write, "suddenly, he remembered that it was an opportunity to fight the Tiger. 'I'll take it,' he said simply," as he strode over to the corner where the petition was being filled out. "What's your first name?" the man asked. Fiorello answered him, but the harried cipher was in no mood for complicated foreign names. "Oh hell," he said, "let's get someone whose name we can spell." Not about to allow this opportunity to slip away, La Guardia proceeded to spell his name for the man very carefully. Nonetheless, he was listed as "Floullo" on the official manual of candidates for the State.[92]

Actually, Fiorello, who landed few jobs without having pursued them avidly, played a more active role than this account indicates. Republicans in the 14th C.D. regularly conceded the congressional seat to the Democrats, nominating loyal party supporters or obscure men of local stature to collect the ceremonial honors and go down to defeat. This year the designated candidate, Dr. Frederick Marshall, had withdrawn unexpectedly, and well before that clubhouse meeting that Fiorello recounted to his biographers, he began pursuing the opportunity with characteristic tenacity, writing Republican leader Tanner: "Dear Fred, I am out for the nomination for Congress in the Fourteenth District." He would not "dare dream of the nomination," La Guardia assured Tanner, "were it not for the fact that the District is absolutely against us and my only hope is in bringing up the Republican vote." The Irish population was declining and the new groups liked him. In the Italian districts he was confident of "unusually good support and will cut the Tammany vote considerably. . . ." And in that segment "mostly populated with Hebrews, I am well known . . . owing to my connections with the Garment Workers Union. . . . I can go down there and campaign in 'Yiddish' and put one over on Levy [the incumbent] . . . who, although a Jew, refrains from doing so." La Guardia insisted on his opportunity: "I want your O.K. I have spoken to some of the boys and as far as I know they are in sympathy with me."[93]

Between his own aggressive pursuit of the prize and the luck that graced his ambitions, Fiorello emerged with the nomination. But having secured it he could now ponder its insignificance. The 14th C.D. was Tammany territory. In the previous election the Republican had been buried by a three-to-one margin. Democrats, one wag noted, just kept enough Republicans around for sport and breeding purposes. La Guardia ignored all of this. He cast a cold eye on the district and waged a campaign to win.[94]

Very early in the contest La Guardia realized that he could count on little help from the party. At one of the campaign rallies Republican candidates were introduced and asked to say a few words, all except Fiorello. "I waited and waited for my turn." Every time a "young and exciting candidate was introduced" La Guardia prepared to rise, only to hear someone else's name. Finally the evening ended without his being introduced. When he complained to the district leader, he was told: "Why, Fiorello you haven't a chance of winning. We've never elected a Republican to Congress from this district."[95]

The message never penetrated. He was too flushed with possibility to accept the role of a scripted loser. From La Guardia headquarters in the Italian section, on Sixth Avenue and West Fourth Street, Fiorello, Andrews, and Espresso worked out a plan for each of the six assembly districts in the Fourteenth Congressional, and from here Espresso and Andrews ran La Guardia's campaign independently of the party. They plastered a beat-up model T Ford with posters and, recalled Fiorello, "went from corner to corner every night in that district . . . never miss[ing] a wedding, a funeral, a christening or any other kind of gathering. . . . I rang door-bells." And to take advantage of crowds brought together by other politicians, they would pull up in the aging roadster as other rallies were breaking up to present Fiorello before the gathered audience.[96]

Congressman Levy, whom Fiorello expected to oppose, was not renominated by Tammany. Instead his opponent was Michael Farley, the owner of a local bar and president of the National Liquor Dealers Association. The contest included both a Progressive and a Socialist, but La Guardia, uninterested in making this a philosophical debate, focused on his chief opponent, the Democrat. Out to win, not to pile up good works, he attacked Farley for being insufficiently anti-British, accused him of being unable to read or write, said that the Democrat refused his saloon customers' credit—in sum, all of the nonsense that is used in such campaigns. Only Fiorello did it better, offending even his own party. Tanner, used to the tradition of deep-pocketed, refined losers, warned Fiorello to lift the level of his campaign, but La Guardia was enjoying himself too much running against the "bartender" to take such advice. For his part, Farley ignored the bad-mouthing. Secure in his Democratic support, he chose to rely on the Tammany label and sit out the campaign.[97]

La Guardia failed to win, but his spirited effort attracted the attention of party veterans. By appealing separately to Italians, Jews, and even the Irish, exploiting such issues as the cost of food, the ill treatment of workers, and the hard life of the rentpayer while slashing at Tammany and its barkeep candidate, he came within a respectable 2000 votes of victory, with close to 15,000 cast.

The showing qualified him for a patronage appointment this time. La Guardia sought the post of appraiser. The $4000 salary would permit him to cut back on his private practice and prepare his campaign for 1916, but this post went to someone else. Instead La Guardia was placed in a lower-paying deputy attorney generalship. It was clear that this job was a political appointment and that Fiorello planned to use it to launch a more effective campaign for elective office. At the same time, however, La Guardia raised the position above the level of a spoils appointment by devoting himself to his duties and tackling a number of controversial and long-ignored problems.[98]

One of his cases dealt with the noxious fumes that regularly wafted over the Hudson from New Jersey factories. For years neighborhood associations had collected evidence and pressured officials to restrict the emission of foul pollutants. Finally, unable to ignore the issue, the attorney general undertook prosecution. Even La Guardia was surprised that someone as inexperienced as he should be assigned to so complex a case. Technical evidence had to be studied, the legal questions were knotty, and the implications for relations between the states and the influential industries involved all had to be sifted and weighed. Nonetheless, only eight weeks after his appointment on January 1, 1915, Fiorello was in Washington filing complaints against seven offending factories in the U.S. Supreme Court.[99]

Despite his quick work, his superiors appeared less than delighted, and Fiorello thought he understood why. "The party big shots were closely connected with this matter," La Guardia wrote. "The corporations had used their tremendous influence and I was given orders to take no action from now on," unless instructed by the attorney general. Other explanations for the squelching are possible. After all, the two states should have been able to negotiate a settlement out of court, but Fiorello immediately suspected that the "big interests" had reached into the attorney general's office to protect their dangerous practices.[100]

La Guardia also moved to enforce state conservation laws prohibiting the harvest of young scallops from the oceans and beaches, but despite strong evidence, he lost several of these cases. Long Island juries just refused to deliver a guilty finding. Fiorello learned that the local population resented the fact that this law was strictly used against the small fishermen, while the commercial fisheries always seemed to fill their quotas. La Guardia agreed that this was wrong and directed his staff to prosecute the larger offenders first. As the case was being prepared, however, the state legislature added an amendment to the law permitting scallop fishing on private beaches. The wealthier fisheries could afford to purchase these rights, while the smaller concerns were forced to continue breaking the law in order to compete. Disapproving of this inequity, La Guardia ordered his staff to drop any further prosecutions under this law.[101]

Another occasion brought him into court opposite "my neighbor in Greenwich Village, State Senator James J. Walker," in a case where the technical wording of a state consumer protection law was the central point of contention. Walker asked to address the court, advising that as author of the law under discussion he could testify that it was never intended for the particular situation before the court. The judge, whom La Guardia remembered as "an affable Tammany judge . . . went out of his way to be nice to Jimmy," and summarily dismissed the case. After the trial the judge, Walker, and La Guardia all went off for a drink. Fiorello, still upset by the verdict, pressed Walker, asking how he could defeat his own law. And La Guardia recalled that Jimmy, in his urbane way, said: "Fiorello, when are you going to get wise? Why do you suppose we introduce bills? We introduce them sometimes just to kill them. Other times we even have to pass a bill. Why are you in the Attorney General's office? You're not going to stay there all your life. You make your connections now, and later on you can pick up a lot of dough defending cases you are now prosecuting. . . . What are you in politics for, for love?"[102]

In 1913, while marching in one of the garment union picket lines, Fiorello met Thea Almerigotti, a young Catholic girl from Trieste. She was a pretty blond-haired woman—a contemporary spoke of her as "porcelainlike, frail, blond and willowy"—who was twelve years younger and several inches taller than he. With the quiet introverted Thea, La Guardia felt more comfortable than he did with any of the other women he had met. While, at least in theory, he believed that women had a right to compete with men, he personally was happier with a less assertive woman. With her reserved manner and her European influence, Thea represented a part of the old world that he remembered from his own mother. This simple working girl, a dress designer, removed from the charged world of politics that Fiorello thrived on, provided an enchanting contrast with his brash, conniving environment. For Fiorello the opportunity for a relationship built on more stable underpinnings than competitive politics was just fine. By late 1915 they were dating steadily. Louis Espresso was confident that they would marry, "as soon as Fiorello had the time."[103]

Politics still came first.

Much of La Guardia's spare time was spent with his advisers, Andrews and Espresso, planning for his next campaign. His nights were devoted to helping the garment unions and assisting local citizens. Harry Andrews told La Guardia biographer Arthur Mann that there was "not a meeting of five or ten people in that congressional district that Fiorello and I didn't attend for two solid years." Like a prizefighter in training, he insisted on remaining hungry. When a friendly congressman offered La Guardia a pass to the gallery of the House of Representatives in Washington, Fiorello refused the tickets. He would not enter the House of Representatives, he told his friend, until he could walk in as an elected Congressman.[104]

La Guardia was competing almost single-handedly with the Democratic machine, doing whatever he, Andrews, and Espresso could to build potential support. His mom-and-pop political apparatus could not provide patronage or deep connections, but it did tackle legal problems and difficulties with local government. "My law office was a regular Legal Aid Society," Fiorello remembered. Andrews, in particular provided additional help. As a secretary to Judge William H. Wadhams, the muscular Andrews would help minor offenders avoid punishment and win their allegiance. Later in his career La Guardia would criticize judges' secretaries for corrupting justice with their political work, but as a young politico on the make he used similar tactics to enhance his own chances.[105]

And La Guardia needed every bit of assistance that he could get, for he learned that he might not have party support for his candidacy in 1916. Clarence Fay, Republican district leader of the Twenty-fifth Assembly District, intended to nominate Hamilton Fish, Jr., from upstate Putnam County for the lower Manhattan congressional seat. Fish's friends and family were said to have pledged a hefty contribution to the party for the privilege of his making the race. La Guardia was told quietly that this was not his year, but he went right on with his plans. He had his petitions printed and, with Harry Andrews in tow, paid a visit to Frederick Chauncey Tanner, who had moved up to the post of Republican Party state chairman.

Tanner told Fiorello that the party had his best interests in mind. His good showing in 1914 predicted good things for him, but he must be patient and wait his turn. It did not pay to be pushy about these things; a political career had to develop slowly. But Fiorello would have none of it. He had already gone to considerable expense in publishing his campaign literature. Someone suggested that the party would take care of the bill. La Guardia exploded. He was not going to be bought off so that some rich upstater could take a shot at a lark. They could "go to hell." If the party did not designate him, he would enter the Republican primaries on his own and tear the carpetbagger apart. Tanner made one last effort to persuade Fiorello to back off. But he was talking to an impatient man. La Guardia pushed ahead, and the opposition quickly faded, as none proved willing to tangle with him. Fish dropped out even before the primaries, and Fiorello easily took the Republican nomination.[106]

In 1916, a presidential election year, American policy with regard to the Great War that had engulfed Europe became the principal issue, especially among the immigrant blocs that held the balance of voting power in the 14th C.D. Campaign politics turned into a mine field strewn with contending loyalties as the Irish, Germans, pro-British WASPS, Italians, and Jews all demanded comforting promises. The Irish craved England's defeat; Italians (Miss Thea Almerigotti included) wanted Trieste back from Austria-Hungary; Germans wanted continued American neutrality; and many Jews prayed for the breakup of the czarist government in Russia.

La Guardia handled these volatile issues with great care and more than a little cynicism. While President Wilson thundered against "hyphenism" and the balkanization of American loyalties, La Guardia celebrated each of the parochial positions in turn. It did not concern him that under the circumstances assertive nationalism was best kept muted. Instead he played on the sure theme of these emotions. To the Irish he charged that Farley was a paper Irishman who did not know the history of the Emerald Isle. Among the others, "I dismembered the

Hapsburg Empire and liberated all of the subjugated countries under that dynasty almost every night.''[107]

To the German community, which found itself increasingly isolated as the United States tilted toward England, he pandered shamelessly: ''German-Americans,'' he declared in a clear German tongue, ''have as much a right to be for Germany as the Plymouth Rockers have to be for England.'' La Guardia courted the influential Ridder brothers, publishers of the German-language *Stats-Zeitung*. When they commented on his fluent German, he responded, ''Nowadays every educated American should speak German.'' Since its founding in 1834, the *Stats-Zeitung* had consistently supported Democratic candidates. In 1916 it broke this tradition to support the ''son of an American soldier, out of the womb of an Austrian mother. . . .'' whose most important contribution was to emphasize that one American was as good as another regardless of his parents' nationality.[108]

Once again his Democratic opponent was Congressman Farley. Tammany toughs molested La Guardia's campaigners and denounced the Republican as a wop and a dago (failing to realize that these epithets would not necessarily hurt La Guardia in the 14th C.D.). Fiorello responded with his own gang of muscled campaign aides, who were sent out to give as well as receive. And then he took aim at Farley. If there was one thing that a local pol must do, Boss Plunkitt had warned, it was to avoid putting on airs. ''If you've got an achin' for style sit down on it till you have made your pile and landed a Supreme Court Justiceship with a fourteen-year term at $17,500 a year. . . . But before you have caught onto your life meal ticket, be simple. Live like your neighbors even if you have the means to live better. Make the poorest man in your district feel that he is your equal, or even a bit superior to you.'' But Farley seldom showed up at his bar, and ''forgot to treat the boys,'' and La Guardia denounced him for ''high hatting'' his old neighbors. The campaign freed Fiorello from all restraints. Even more unabashedly than in 1914, he baited Farley, calling him dumb, insensitive, disloyal to Ireland, a retailer of tainted whiskey, a man too ignorant to read a prepared speech. With the support of labor, the ethnic press, and his own hell-raising, La Guardia fought for each vote.[109]

Early on election day morning La Guardia dispatched ''school teachers, doctors, businessmen, longshoremen and some tough guys'' to make the rounds of the lodging hotels and flophouses waking the boarders, many deep in stupor. The La Guardia team offered coffee and doughnuts and, when necessary, even more, to encourage a proper vote. Later that morning the Democratic hacks making the same rounds were dumbfounded to discover that La Guardia had beaten them to the ''drunk'' vote.

After making sure that the good inebriated citizens of the metropolis had voted, the La Guardia workers went off to guard the polls. Fiorello himself stood watch in the roughest neighborhood, warning the Tammany crowd that they were not playing with a good little Republican. Few Republicans or gentlemen had acted this way before, but this was certainly no ordinary Republican. He was not in politics to impress with his manners and ability to lose gracefully. Of 18,670 ballots cast, Fiorello won by a margin of 357 votes. The flophouse vote and the close watch over the ballot boxes had surely made a difference.[110]

Friends and supporters were elated, and Fiorello savored the victory. He remarked to Espresso that it was a shame that his mother, who would have been so happy to see that his ambitions were finally paying off, had died of diabetes at the age of fifty-six, the year before. But for now introspection was swept aside. "My dream of a lifetime had come true."[111]

CHAPTER 2

The Politics of Liberal Ambition

1. Fiorello Goes to Congress

T HE Sixty-fifth Congress that welcomed Fiorello La Guardia in 1917 faced one of the gravest decisions in the history of the republic, certainly the most momentous since Abraham Lincoln's presidency. The German government's recent decision to resume unrestricted submarine attacks on all ships entering a broad trading zone represented a direct challenge to American rights on the high seas. On February 2, Germany torpedoed the SS *Housatonic*. Goods began to pile up in warehouses as shippers turned chary of the dangerous waters. On February 25, the president learned of a secret German proposal for an alliance with Mexico promising the United States' southern neighbor the return of her "lost territories" in Texas, Arizona, and New Mexico. This "Zimmerman Note" dispelled the notion that Germany's war plans were limited to the European continent and helped doom Wilson's policy of neutrality.

"It would be an irony of fate," Woodrow Wilson had said to a friend just before taking office in 1913, "if my administration had to deal chiefly with foreign affairs." Wilson, the austere son of a Presbyterian minister, had spent much of his life preparing for leadership. He had studied government and politics, had been a lawyer and a historian, and had served as president of Princeton University and governor of New Jersey. Elected to the White House in 1912, Wilson brought to Washington a broad, progressive vision for a modern America. In foreign affairs, however, he

41

was a provincial, unschooled in international relations and contemptuous of *real-politik*. Fate proved more than ironic, presenting Wilson with a series of the most agonizing foreign policy decisions in American history.[1]

After the Great War first broke out in Europe, Wilson, who had once described himself as an "idealist with the heart of a poet," called upon Americans to follow a policy of neutrality in word as well as in deed. Despite the German sinking of the British liner *Lusitania* in May of 1915, with the loss of 128 American lives, Wilson held fast to this policy, for which Theodore Roosevelt denounced him as an "abject creature" and a coward. Only after the German government reneged on its pledges to the United States and returned to its policy of torpedoing neutral ships early in 1917 did Wilson begin to think seriously of national armament and war. But as Wilson came to view neutrality as no longer tenable, a group of western progressives, led by Wisconsin Senator Robert La Follette, continued to oppose war preparations, charging that bankers, munitions makers, and speculators—the "merchants of death"—were manipulating public opinion toward unnecessary hostilities. Stung by their criticism and angered by the obstacles that they were placing in the path of his foreign policy, Wilson pilloried the "little group of willful men, representing no opinion but their own, [who] have rendered the great Government of the U.S. helpless and contemptible."[2]

Between the time of his election and the inaugural session of the Sixty-fifth Congress, a period of some four months, La Guardia visited Washington several times to prepare for the coming session. The House elections had resulted in a close division between regular Democrats and Republicans, spotlighting five congressmen whose votes could swing the election of the Speaker of the House and the distribution of committee assignments. La Guardia, who had run on both Republican and Progressive tickets, was one of the five whose vote was considered uncertain.

In many matters he found himself in agreement with the western Progressives. Like them, his sympathies favored the poor. He too thought that the country needed to carry forward the movement for reform and social justice even at the expense of business profits. He too heard the arguments of constituents who condemned war as a rich man's game for which the poor paid with their lives. Before taking up the issue of war, however, the Democrats and Republicans had to vote on organizing the sixty-fifth Congress, and La Guardia joined the regular Republicans on the votes for House Speaker, clerk, sergeant-at-arms, postmaster, and the other party positions; to little effect as it turned out, for the Grand Old Party was outvoted by the Democratic majority.[3]

Looking younger than his thirty-four years ("I am not in the habit of seeing youngsters here as Members," House Speaker Joseph Cannon told the freshman Representative), neatly dressed in a blue suit, with a bow tie and with his hair parted in the middle, the diminutive La Guardia strode down the aisle of the House, on the opening day of the session, to a seat in the front of the chamber and sat down. The first Italian American in Congress and the first Republican elected from his district, he had marched with labor on the Lower East Side and had offended monarchy in Europe. Most freshmen took a seat in the back rows, but La Guardia had already proven that he did not view politics as a spectator sport. He wanted to be recognized and to be reckoned with. He had never achieved anything by being diffident, and he wanted to speak for his working-class constituents from the front where he would be seen and heard.[4]

After Germany sank three ships with heavy loss of American life in March, President Wilson continued to agonize over war until finally the obligations of leadership overtook the hesitations of conscience. Composing both a war message and himself, Wilson called Congress to special session to receive his war address. Walter Lippmann wrote that in this speech Wilson summoned ''a power of decision unlike any he had shown before . . . ,'' placing American entry into the war on a higher ground than self-defense. American's war, said the president, would be a progressive war that would spread American liberty and democracy to the rest of the world.

Again the Progressives shouted their dissent: ''The poor, sir, who are the ones called upon to rot in the trenches, have no organized power,'' La Follette cried, ''but oh Mr. President at some time they will be heard.''[5]

La Guardia visited his district before the special congressional session called by the president convened, and he found a divided constituency. A considerable pacifist minority along with a vocal Socialist group opposed war. But La Guardia believed that Germany's disregard for international law and American life left the United States no choice. Germany had gambled that the United States would not be able to mobilize in time to make much of a difference, and it had to be proven wrong. With his mind made up, La Guardia toured his district waving the flag. ''These are days when we must renew our love for the land and the flag that flies over us.'' The war, he told the crowds, would liberate millions in Central Europe. It was just, it was necessary, and he supported it. We had been attacked. ''We've got to fight hard; we've got to take a man's part in this war.'' At numerous street rallies, accompanied by the strains of martial music, Fiorello stirred his listeners to war fever. Then he returned to Washington and voted for war. When one representative demanded to see those of his colleagues prepared to do more than vote others onto battlefields, La Guardia was one of a handful of legislators to indicate that he was prepared to join his constituents in the trenches.[6]

He had no reservations about voting for war, but his profound sense of grievance over his father's wartime poisoning led him to develop legislation to prevent its repetition. In an unusual step for a freshman congressman, La Guardia introduced his own proposal to make the sale of spoiled food or merchandise to the armed forces during war punishable by death. Newly elected members generally worked in the back halls agreeing to deals dictated by their seniors. But La Guardia was intent on taking a "man's part," in a hurry to do real work. His bill, born so brashly, was never passed.[7]

After the April vote for war, Congress turned to designing a plan for raising troops. In the spring of 1917 fewer Americans were in uniform than the number of French forces who perished at Verdun. The German high command had calculated that it would take the United States six months to make a difference in the war. The Allied cause absolutely depended upon a swifter mobilization, but with a standing army of no more than 128,000 the military would have to train hundreds of thousands and place them into action quickly. Before the vote on conscription, La Guardia polled his constituents on whether the United States should institute a forced draft or rely on a volunteer army. La Guardia offered a preemptive opinion: "I think conscription is needed and I am trying to educate the people up to it. It is up to you to respond; don't blame me if you do not like the way I vote." A majority of his constituents in fact rejected conscription, but La Guardia pressed for total mobilization. Even the physically handicapped and the conscientious objectors, he argued, should be called up to work behind the lines. It was only fair.[8]

Over the next few months, La Guardia displayed an aggressive disregard for traditions of fledgling diffidence by speaking out on a wide range of issues, insisting that government must do more for the protection of vulnerable classes. He demanded dignified and equal treatment for immigrants, railing at the "obnoxious and unwise" restrictions that Congress kept adding to its immigration laws. He put his colleagues on notice that Italians were no longer fair game on the floor of the House, dismissing insinuations that Italian nationals were hiding in America to dodge the draft at home. "I can vouch for the Italian residents of this country. . . . They are eager, willing, and anxious to fight . . . but they want to fight under the American flag." He forced the chief examiner of the New York Naturalization Bureau to retract insulting statements, reminding colleagues that "the first soldier in the service of the American Government in this war who gave his life for his adopted country was an Italian . . . John E. Epolucci," whose mother "takes her loss with resignation and fortitude and in a manner worthy of a true descendant of Rome, proud of the noble sacrifice of her boy."[9]

At the same time he demanded that aliens prove themselves worthy. In the days following the war vote, La Guardia told a crowd of a thousand Italian Americans in New York City: "I want to drive it home and impress it upon you . . . that we are in the midst of the most cruel war in the history of the world," and he expected them to show their loyalty to their adopted country. "Those," he told the immigrant assemblage, "who prefer Italy to America should return to Italy. I know there are some of you in my district who won't sacrifice themselves for any country—and if I thought that I owed my election to that sort I would resign."[10]

Many had feared that war would unleash illiberal emotions, and it did. While superpatriots hounded German Americans and others who fell under their broad suspicions, the White House proposed an espionage law that limited the right of citizens to criticize the government. La Guardia thought that so sweeping a limitation on press and speech freedoms would go well beyond guarding secrets to tamp dissent and hamper Americans in their legitimate right to debate government policy. He dismissed presidential assurances that the law would not be abused: "The law admittedly makes the President a despot, but with the comforting assurance that the despot about to be created has the present expectation to be a very lenient, benevolent despot. . . ."[11]

Americans, he argued, did not enjoy their liberties by sufferance, and national security was no excuse for denying basic rights. The war to make the world safe for democracy must not serve as the pretext for the curtailment of the most essential freedoms. Denouncing the proposal as "unAmerican and vicious legislation," he warned his colleagues that "if you pass this bill and if it is enacted into law you change all that our flag ever stood for and stands for." Loyal Americans had their heart and soul in this war, La Guardia declared, "but because we have our heart in it is no reason why we should lose our head."[12]

The bill passed over his objections, but La Guardia's warnings proved apt. Under the new law 2000 Americans were prosecuted and more than 800 imprisoned (including the respected Socialist Eugene V. Debs), not a single one for actual espionage. Under the new law, citizens could be prosecuted for opposing the sale of war bonds, discouraging enlistment in the armed forces, and even for expressing doubt about the eventual destination of stockings being knit for American soldiers. The government infiltrated suspected organizations, chilling liberties and freedom. "You can't even collect your thoughts," Max Eastman told an audience in July of 1917, "without getting arrested for unlawful assemblage. They give you ninety days for quoting the Declaration of Independence, six months for quoting the Bible, and pretty soon somebody is going to get a life sentence for quoting Woodrow Wilson in the wrong connection." Experience had taught La Guardia to suspect a government that could use espionage acts to insulate itself from criticism and expose a muzzled nation "to a domestic enemy who is willing to turn American blood into gold and sell rotten cornbeef, wormy beans, paper shoes, [and] defective arms for our American boys."[13]

While he did not trust the government to control speech, La Guardia trusted American businessmen even less to keep prices fair. As war inflation and shortages kept driving prices up, La Guardia demanded protection for the disadvantaged. Declaring that food prices had climbed as much as 50 percent since 1913, he told the House: "Gentlemen. The American people are not getting enough to eat." Businesses were pulling huge profits on war orders, warehouses were bulging with provisions headed for Europe, and in New York City the poor were rioting for food. Their right to the necessities of life took precedence over the right of speculators "seeking to amass . . . great fortunes at the expense of the health and happiness of the American people."[14]

45

The regulation of the production, conservation, and distribution of the necessities of life in wartime, La Guardia told Congress, "will do more to demoralize the enemy than anything we have enacted in this session. . . . The marshalling of our food supplies, control of export, this great getting together of the people, the taking of this drastic action will have a telling effect on the kaiser—and he will know that we mean business." (La Guardia added one caveat. The inspectors to be appointed must be placed under the civil service. Imagine, he winked, "7,000 men roaming . . . the country . . . preaching about hog cholera and incidentally extolling the virtues of the Democratic Party.") La Guardia wanted to extend this measure to peacetime as well. "After the war," he warned, "the speculators will be back to the old game." Like other La Guardia proposals, this one failed to pass. La Guardia was still more involved in being heard than getting things done.[15]

In his respected survey of modern American reform, *Rendezvous with Destiny*, Eric Goldman charges that La Guardia "skated the edge of demagoguery" with his attacks on inflation and his proposal for a constitutional amendment to limit profiteering. It is true that La Guardia's stands were popular in his liberal district, but his was far from a cynical or self-serving agenda. His congressional colleagues—lawyers and middle-class Americans of traditional stock—did not much trouble themselves with the foreign-born poor, his constituents. Congressmen weighed the impact of their legislation on people like themselves, loyal, satisfied, well-fed, and well-off Americans. They knew and cared little about the working class and its concerns. It was La Guardia's goal to bring precisely these concerns before Congress.[16]

His sharp language and brash manner were not calculated to ease controversial proposals through the legislative process, but the fact is that the softest-voiced representative could not have passed La Guardia's agenda of liberal legislation and constitutional reform. Insisting that the basic law must be interpreted in the light of the times and the needs of the people, he argued that a complex modern industrial society must assist its poor not out of some vague sense of pity but because no system was secure when it relegated a segment of its population to too harsh a life.

These considerations led him to oppose a war revenue bill that, by raising taxes across the board, claimed a proportionally larger slice out of laborers' paychecks. Working people had already made their contributions to the war effort by sending their sons to fight on far-off fields, La Guardia declared. The people who watched every penny should not also have to bear the burden of financing the war. "You tax his coffee, you tax his tea, you tax his soap, you tax his light, you tax his heat, you tax his insurance, you tax his amusements, and you tax his beer and his soda, and even his chewing gum for his children. . . ." Fiorello fought to take a larger bite out of the wealthy and business classes, but again he was in a small minority. All he could win was an amendment that placed a tax on opera boxes.[17]

On occasion, however, his dissenting voice proved not only prescient but also practical. The nation, faced with the momentous issue of world war, had to consider how much it was prepared to assist its allies. In considering a $3 billion foreign loan bill, Congress viewed the war in narrow, pinchpenny terms and tacked on a provision making the repayment of principal plus interest a condition for the loan. La Guardia rose to lecture his colleagues and offer realistic advice. If his colleagues judged the loan necessary, he said, then they should make bold and offer it without conditions. Congress cannot run the affairs of the nation with the soul of a bookkeeper. "I believe that a good portion [of the loan] will in due time be returned, but I am certain that some of it will have to be placed on the profit and loss column of Uncle Sam's books. Let us understand that clearly now," he asserted, quite prophetically, as it turned out, "and not be surprised later." If the loan "brings about a happy termination of the war, and a permanent peace for our own country," he declared, cutting to the heart of the issue, "it will have been a good investment."[18]

The loans would never be fully repaid. Throughout the twenties wrangling over their repayment would unnecessarily complicate relations between the United States and its former allies, and it would strengthen the hand of American isolationists during the thirties. After many years, following defaults and fruitless efforts at refunding, Congress in the early thirties would again speak of full principal plus interest and again Congressman La Guardia would insist on half a loaf. "Take it. Be lucky if you get it at all. I doubt if you will get even this much." And he was right again.[19]

The impertinent new voice, edged with suspicion and a sense of grievance, had in a very brief time made itself familiar in the halls of Congress. Fiorello La Guardia, the lone Italian-descended legislator, had come to Washington and made them take notice of him. Now it would be up to him to convert that attention into power, into an agenda for his constituents.[20]

2. Over There and Back

T HE United States was off to war, and the war captured La Guardia's interest as nothing else could. He still viewed battle as the strongest test of a citizen's loyalty and a man's courage. Few legislators sought to participate in actual combat—"SOLONS OF NATION CAN'T SEEM TO HEAR THE BUGLE CALLING" the *New York World* headlined—but La Guardia had pledged that he would join the armed forces even if it placed his congressional seat in jeopardy. By midsummer La Guardia was "eager to get into the action" and take "a man's part."[21]

Since well before the war, La Guardia had been fascinated by the subject of air flight and the possibilities that such travel opened up for trade, communication, and, most important, for defense. Withal, flying was also a flamboyant test of courage and derring-do. Years before coming to Washington, Fiorello had served as a director and attorney for Giuseppe Bellanca's airplane company. On Sunday mornings he would trek out to Bellanca's school in Mineola, Long Island, to take flying lessons and watch the other fliers. So when in July of 1917 Fiorello La Guardia marched down to the Southern Railway Building and joined a motley group of "acrobats and tumblers who thought that because they were good on a tightrope and a trapeze, they would be able to fly," to enlist in the army's aviation section, he was offered a lieutenant's commission, which he gratefully accepted.[22]

Two months before, La Guardia had introduced a measure requiring Washington "to continue the pay of employees in the service of the U.S. Government or Departments thereof" who enlisted for military service. But this was another of La Guardia's bills that did not make it out of the committee. For a while his congressional check, close to four times his army pay, was withheld. Unfazed, the flying representative assured his friends: "If the Germans don't get me, I'll get that pay." Characteristically, he did.[23]

By trading in his comfortable House seat for the battlefront, the freshman congressman who had little success in persuading his colleagues to enact any of his bills suddenly attracted the acclaim that other legislators work a lifetime to acquire. The "soldier statesman" was called before important committees, invited to receptions for visiting VIPs, and feted by the Republican party. The Italian community especially lionized him as their genuine American hero. Donning the mantle of ethnic tribune, he exhorted his ghetto constituents to "100 per cent Americanism," urging them to prove themselves through their patriotism. Then he bade them farewell and was off for Europe and a "man's part" in the Great War to make the world safe for democracy.[24]

By mid-October 1917, La Guardia, who had in the interim been promoted to captain, was Over There at the Eighth Aviation Center in Foggia, Italy, second in command to Major William Ord Ryan, a West Pointer. Ryan and La Guardia supervised the training of cadets by Italian flying aces and the preparing of recruits for combat. "Facilities for training are excellent," he wired back to headquarters, "and there is no reason in the world why we cannot turn out men as quickly and as efficiently as the most fastidious legislature would demand." Close-quartered army life provided him with more than the opportunity to command men; it also surrounded him with an exuberant male community, and he loved it. When one of the cadets decorated a ceiling with a nude drawing, La Guardia was so tickled that he brought in visiting Italian officers to inspect the artwork. During camp baseball games the captain would either umpire or serve as first base coach, keeping up a string of high-pitched profanity such that visitors were amused to learn that the foulmouthed officer was a U.S. congressman.[25]

Beyond the fun and games, La Guardia's sense of self-imposed duty to his men won their respect. Aware that many of the recruits were intimidated by the anti-American feelings in the region, La Guardia personally rushed off to Paris headquarters and brought back side arms for his fliers. When cadets suffered through a February snowstorm in unheated sheep sheds, Captain La Guardia boarded a train with a few soldiers and returned to the Foggia Center with three dozen oil heaters. Nobody knew where they came from and La Guardia would not tell, but all appreciated his concern. Foggia was different from Congress, where decisions were debated and reached collegially and freshman were ignored. Here he could take charge.[26]

Under the joint agreement between the Italian government and the United States Army, the host country was responsible for feeding as well as training the Americans, but La Guardia found the fare, larded macaroni paste infrequently supplemented with a sliver of meat, inadequate for American boys. He arranged with a local establishment for privately prepared "big well-balanced American meals." When an incredulous quartermaster received the bills for the catered suppers, he summoned La Guardia to Tours to explain his generosity at government expense to the judge advocate general. La Guardia offered no apologies. He declared that his men were entitled to decent food, and if regulations prevented that then he was prepared to use his congressional status to press the secretary of war to rewrite them. Indeed, his congressional position was put to more direct use in the army than on the floor of the House. When a colonel threatened to court-martial one of his cadets, La Guardia warned: "He's one of my boys. Lay off him," menacing the colonel with his congressional power.[27]

At Christmastime many of the cadets went off to Rome for holiday leave, and La Guardia, aware "that single men in barracks do not grow into plaster saints," devised a program for protecting them from venereal diseases that were infecting American troops at an alarming rate. In France Prime Minister Georges Clemenceau had offered to provide the Americans with prostitutes who had passed health examinations. General Pershing, unwilling to accept such an arrangement on his own authority, passed the offer along to the secretary of war, Newton Baker, who responded in horror, "Don't show this to the President or he'll stop the war." Captain La Guardia decided to tackle the problem in his own way. With Lieutenant O. B. Kiel he worked out a plan for portable prophylactic stations to be discreetly wheeled around the red-light district by a soldier pushing a baby carriage. When Foggia's chief medical officer protested that it was not the army's business to protect its men in the pursuit of vice, La Guardia had the medical man detained on a technicality and wheeled out the baby carriages. A discussion with the surgeon general subsequently resulted in praise for La Guardia's plan and a transfer for the straitlaced medical officer.[28]

Captain La Guardia's men repaid his concern with a blend of respect and admiration. Long after the war ended, A. D. Farquar wrote La Guardia: "You were a soldier (because we all had to be) but you were always a *friend*. There was not discipline for discipline's sake,—there was sympathy for the view point and feelings of the rest of us being in a strange land with unknown customs. And you *did* get things done! . . . but for you some of us would still be in Foggia entirely forgotten by the American Army. . . ." But while La Guardia looked after his men and cared about them—later in life he would always take the time to help any "Foggiani" in need—he also demanded a great deal, especially from those closest to him.[29]

Shortly after Fiorello decided to enlist, his good friend and barber from the Greenwich Village neighborhood, Frank ("Ciccio") Giordano, began pestering his congressman pal to help get him into the army. He would seek Fiorello out at his apartment and even journey to Washington to lobby for enlistment. "Everything was all right," noted Fiorello, "except that Frank was married, was over the age at which they were taking married men, had three children and flat feet." But what good was a friend in Congress if he could not deliver a favor once in a while? So La Guardia found an opening for his flat-footed barber and took him along to Foggia. All of this was brushed aside when one day the captain learned of a bar brawl between his cadets and some local folk. He demanded that Giordano identify the offending recruits. Ciccio refused. Despite Fiorello's insistence, he would not finger his colleagues. Finally, La Guardia clapped his friend in the guardhouse.[30]

Next morning La Guardia sent for Giordano for his morning shave. "Can't shave him today," Giordano told the messenger. "Can't shave him tomorrow. Jees he said stay in the guardhouse till I tell him. I won't tell. I'll stay here for the duration of the war. The cap'n can grow a beard." Tickled by the reply, La Guardia released Giordano, but it was clear to all that they were expected to obey the commanding officer in exactly the way he ordered.[31]

Rattling off a list of instructions on another occasion, La Guardia suddenly stopped when he noticed a subordinate taking careful notes. "What are you doing that for?" he challenged. "To insure against oversight," came the respectful reply. "Use your memory," La Guardia told the man. "Fix what I say in your mind. You won't forget. Or, if you do, you'll get hell, and you won't do it again. Anyway, what use is that bit of paper to you? If you're pinning your faith to that, you'll probably lose it, and then where will you be?" One of La Guardia's charges at Foggia was Albert Spalding, the renowned concert violinist who learned just how suffocatingly protective La Guardia's attitude toward his men could be. Spalding wanted very much to train for combat flight, but no matter how often he asked, La Guardia would simply not allow it. He was too old, said the captain; or he was too useful at what he was doing, or any of a number of different excuses that La Guardia could cook up to keep Spalding on the ground and protect his "fiddler's fingers." La Guardia, six years older than the violinist, allowed himself every dangerous exercise, but for this man, whom he eventually appointed his adjutant, he knew better. Only after La Guardia left Italy did the determined Spalding win approval for aviator training. And then he received a letter "affectionately and passionately profane," telling him that he was absolutely insane.[32]

It did not take La Guardia long to extend his interest beyond training fliers. In a pattern reminiscent of his early government days at Fiume when he drove Frank Chester to distraction by creating back channels to power, La Guardia used his congressional position and his local contacts to play a diplomatic and military role far beyond his captain's commission. Following Austria-Hungary's disastrous rout of Italian forces at Caporetto, disillusioned Italians were discussing a separate peace and even surrender, suggesting that the United States was an untrustworthy ally. Promised American troops and supplies were slow in arriving, and the Axis encouraged these frustrations by telling Italians that their homeland was being treated like the "forgotten ally," the stepsister of the Entente, while the United States provided the bulk of its assistance for England and France.

In December of 1917 La Guardia wrote to Paris describing the degree to which confidence in the United States had dropped. He offered to help fight the German propaganda by using his "personal acquaintance here and my standing as a member of the House . . . to bring about closer relations . . . as may be conducive to our common interest." Well liked and trusted by Italian military authorities and civilian officials, he developed close ties to such important officials as Francisco Nitti, the minister of the treasury, and Eugenio Chiesa, commissioner of aeronautics. Nitti, who would become prime minister in 1919, treated Fiorello like a trusted compatriot and plied him with sensitive information about Italian war policies. Shuttling between Foggia and Allied headquarters in Paris and Rome, La Guardia frequently delivered reports based on privileged conversations with Italian officials, once carrying a sensitive assessment of the military situation from General Armando Diaz to General John J. Pershing.[33]

American efforts to reassure Italy of its sincere commitment continued to flounder in the hands of the amateurish Committee on Public Information under George Creel. Albert Spalding painfully recalled how one of the representatives sent over by the CPI, an oafish member of the Royal Order of the Moose, told a large crowd studded with Italian dignitaries that America had never lost a war and that this great warrior nation had taken note of Italy's plight. Cuba, too, had been "down and out" and we had saved her; we would do it again for Italy. Walter Lippmann, then with the Military Intelligence Bureau, characterized Creel's operation as designed to "sell the war" by giving "shell shocked Europe to understand that a rich bumpkin had come to town."[34]

The American ambassador to Italy, the courtly novelist Thomas Nelson Page,

Sir Thomas of Shenandoah to his staff, concluded that the only way to reassure the Italian people and capture their trust was to link the war effort to something worthy of their sacrifice, and to do it in a way that did not insult their intelligence or sense of independence. He summoned Captain La Guardia to Rome for a frank discussion of the problem and to offer an unusual proposition. Page thought that La Guardia was one of the few Americans left with credibility in Italy. For the rest of them there "wasn't standing room in Hell" as far as the Italians were concerned. He asked Fiorello to give a series of talks designed to build Italian confidence in the United States and to steel local resolve. Page explained that the assignment was sensitive because the United States could not afford any more public relations setbacks. If anything went wrong, the embassy would disavow his words and La Guardia would be left to absorb the criticism alone, with possibly unfortunate consequences for his military and political future. If, however, all went as expected, the embassy would take credit for the speeches. Aware of the pitfalls, Fiorello readily accepted the challenge.[35]

The first of the talks was at the Genoese Bourse before a huge crowd. At first unsure of the tone and fumbling with the language, the short speaker in the captain's uniform seemed to shrink lower still. His awkwardness provoked laughter but it also concentrated his dramatic energies. He turned from platitudes to candor, chiding the audience for eating too much, drinking too much, and ignoring the fact that they were at war. They must extend themselves, he declared, and they must end the corruption that was undercutting American assistance. By mid-speech, an observer wrote, "he seemed to grow from a man into an Alp" as his delivery caught fire. He challenged his listeners to be true to their magnificent history. Italy had no need to be dependent on any nation, but it could and should be a trusted ally. Italy did not really want Americans to fight their fight, he said. What Italy wanted was for Americans to join them in a common cause and this the United States was eager to do. Washington was preparing troops as quickly as possible and providing other assistance as well. It had no interest, as the Germans claimed, in prolonging the dying; it wished only to help end the hostilities and, with its allies, to welcome a just peace. Relying on his formula of hanging "a speech on a handle you feel strongly about" and keeping it simple, he stirred the audience; and then going well beyond any authority that he had been given, the veteran of New York ethnic politics touched Italian national feeling by committing the United States to helping recover the "lost territories," Trentino Alto Adige, Trieste, and Fiume.[36]

La Guardia subsequently addressed audiences in Rome, Turin (where he met the touring undersecretary of the navy, Franklin Delano Roosevelt), Fiume, Florence, and Bari. In insistent, if broken, Italian phrases—to one sensitive listener it sounded like a mongrel mix of "Apulian, Neapolitan, and New Yorkese"—he roused the Italians to shouts of "Viva Wilson, Viva America." Crowed the *New York Times*: "President Wilson could not have chosen a better representative in

Italy than this brave soldier.'' The Italian newspaper *Giornale d'Italia* described the team of La Guardia and Spalding as ''harmonized, orchestrated, and harnessed in Uncle Sam's chariot in the vital and chief pursuit of today. . . .'' With uncharacteristic understatement, La Guardia later concluded, ''The Ambassador never had to repudiate me.'' Perhaps La Guardia also had occasion to savor the irony. As a youth he had been taunted as a ''dago''; now, in critical times, the United States was depending on him to help keep Italy in the war.[37]

As an honest broker La Guardia also took a real interest in Italy's needs. He peppered American headquarters in Paris with demands for urgent attention to the Italian front. In January, after he was designated the official army representative to the Joint Army and Navy Aircraft Committee, which made him the leading figure in American aviation in Italy, he repeatedly pressed officials to give his air cadets a larger role in the war, until finally, in June 1918, American fliers were assigned to combat against the Austrian enemy in the Dolomites.[38]

The swift rise of his fortunes encouraged La Guardia in his buccaneering style. His immediate superior, Major William Ryan, was by now chafing at La Guardia's favored status, and the orders he received from headquarters ''to collaborate with Captain La Guardia and advise him with reference to any questions which may come up . . .'' did not ease his resentment. Ryan complained to military officials that his colleague had forgotten who was Foggia's commanding officer, and accused La Guardia of conduct unbecoming an officer and a gentleman. Colonel De Siebert, the Italian officer in charge of cadet instruction at Foggia, reacted similarly to La Guardia's claim that ''to him are attributed functions of a representative of the United States Government in Italy, and therefore it is up to him and no one else to treat with Italian authorities for the better reciprocal relations in the preparation of the American pilots.'' The congressman clearly enjoyed carving a private path. But while La Guardia did tend to push hard at times beyond the limits of his authority, his cadets respected his courage and his concern for their safety.[39]

In the hectic effort to reach full mobilization from a standing start, the United States had contracted with the Italian manufacturer SIA for close to 1000 aircraft. Production problems had delayed delivery on the much-needed craft for some time, and the planes had just begun to arrive in early 1918 when La Guardia learned that they had not tested well; several had torn apart in midair, killing their test pilots. La Guardia became convinced that in spite of their advanced design these ''flying coffins'' had been rushed into production without sufficient concern for the men who would have to fly them. He reported on the plane's weaknesses to the air service in Tours. Yet no one was willing to cancel the order for the defective planes. Furious at the military's slowness to act, La Guardia, on his own authority, refused all deliveries on the SIA planes at Foggia.[40]

Again La Guardia was called to account, this time before the InterAllied Purchasing Commission. Fiorello explained what he had learned about the plane's defects, but, as he later told Lowell Limpus, "the Italian manufacturers had brought pressure to bear," and he feared that he would not be able to escape trouble this time. Fortunately, others backed La Guardia's story and came before the commission to testify about critical structural deficiencies that caused the craft to buckle and had resulted in several crashes of test vehicles. The hearing cleared La Guardia of any wrongdoing and led the commission to reach a settlement with SIA under which it accepted all planes that were ready for delivery for use under noncombat conditions and canceled the rest of the order. The free-form style had succeeded again.[41]

La Guardia's intrusive imagination was not limited to such issues as the SIA planes. One of his proposals, forwarded to Washington by Ambassador Thomas Page, suggested helping a band of Hungarian exiles stir a local revolution. Woodrow Wilson recoiled at so dangerous a plan that, the president sniffed, violated "the attitude of *honour* which it has been our pride to maintain in international affairs. . . ."[42]

Other La Guardia schemes proved more useful. Under German pressure, Spain had curtailed iron and steel shipments, hobbling the Ansaldo, Fiat, Isotta, Fraschini, and Caproni airplane factories. "Smuggling," La Guardia declared to aide Albert Spalding one day, "is an ancient art," as he proceeded to spin out his strategy for bringing out much-needed steel from Spain. He won enthusiastic approval from General Foulois at air service headquarters, but final approval from General Pershing could take a week or two. Too much time, Fiorello decided impatiently. He instructed Spalding to create the necessary documents. They would start immediately; approval would have to come after the fact. Spalding hurried off to buy clothing for the two of them. "I had to guess at La Guardia's measurements," Spalding later recalled, "but I was sure he was unconscious of anything short of the most outrageous misfit." In the meantime, La Guardia arranged for letters of credit for $5 million.[43]

As they traveled to Spain, La Guardia turned off his "galvanic energy" and relaxed. "The secret," Spalding explained, "is that it can be shut off at will. He rests as intensely as he works. . . ." He talked of his future after the war and his plans to marry. Reaching into his pocket, he took out a picture of his dear Thea, and his adjutant remembered thinking that he could not imagine two greater opposites than the pretty blond woman with the delicate features and the tough, explosive captain sitting next to him.[44]

When they arrived in Barcelona the energy started flowing again at high velocity. They would take in a bullfight, La Guardia said, and oh yes, Spalding was to check the newspaper clips. By now all tactics and ideas, Fiorello explained that they would need a steamship connection to bring whatever they could buy out of Spain, and he wanted Spalding to comb the papers for the name of a shipper who had suffered at the hands of the Germans. The violinist learned that not only had the Taja Line lost a fortune because of the Kaiser's armies but a German torpedo had also claimed the owner's only son. La Guardia arranged to meet with the shipper and won Taja's support for his plans. Taja helped La Guardia strike a deal for the steel, arranged for the necessary papers for port clearance, and assured the Americans that the materials would be delivered. He proved as good as his word, and ultimately this operation brought thousands of tons of critical raw materials to Italy.[45]

Upon returning to the Foggia base La Guardia went back to his own flight training. Like his old Prescott hero, Bucky O'Neill, Fiorello intended to be tested on the field of battle, to take a "man's part" in the fighting. After completing several hours of practice, he took up a Farman aircraft for a solo test. La Guardia remembered the experience as "a thrill that comes once in a lifetime . . . a great feeling. . . ." But Sandy Hand, who was on the ground, provided Lawrence Elliott with a more objective description:

> With only one man aboard the Farman trainer tended to climb, and you really had to throttle down for a landing. I guess La Guardia forgot that because he kept hitting the ground like a rock, with full flying speed and going straight up again. . . . Finally it got through to him that he couldn't stay up forever. But still he didn't throttle down—he just cut the switch and made a dead stick landing; the thump would have broken the bones of a skinnier man.[46]

Despite a style that relied more heavily on guts than skill, Fiorello was certified on December 12, 1917. Shortly thereafter, ignoring the warnings of his men, he took up a plane on a blustery day only to come hurtling down. He suffered a painful back injury that would plague him for the rest of his life. Dr. O. B. Kiel, who attended the injured captain, described the injuries as serious, but Fiorello refused to give up his dreams of combat flying.[47]

After he recovered, La Guardia returned to the main drama as the commander of the American Combat Division in Italy and as a pilot-bombardier. His flying technique was still pure hands and glands. "I can't take the buzzard off and I can't land him," he told one of his men, "but I can fly the son of a gun." He flew as part of a team composed of Major Pietro Negrotto, an experienced bomber and a member of the Italian Parliament, Captain Fred Zapeloni, and a rear gunner. On one mission Fiorello loosed the bombs just before Zapeloni veered sharply away. Unable to see what happened, La Guardia asked the pilot how he had done. "The best speech you ever made," shot back Zapeloni. More than once the three-motor Caproni returned riddled with enemy fire. On one occasion after "The Congressional Limited" returned with "more than two hundred holes in it," Lieutenant Donald Frost was amazed that the stocky captain "hadn't been blown to shreds." La Guardia's only comment was that the experience had been "very interesting," as he asked for another flight. "He was never a really finished pilot," concluded

Frost, "but boy how he loved to try! He flew by main strength and awkward-ness. . . . The Italians loved him for his guts." By August, the congressman was wearing the oak leaves of a major.[48]

At about this time King Victor Emmanuel III of Italy awarded Major La Guardia the Flying Cross at a ceremony in Padua and thereafter invited both La Guardia and Albert Spalding to dinner. Spalding would later write that Fiorello was perhaps the only person in the world who called him Al. The violinist was therefore less surprised than others who heard that after the amenities were over, La Guardia was calling the king "Manny."[49]

He had gone off to battle a vaguely known freshman congressman. In Foggia he became an experienced leader who commanded men, negotiated with foreign governments, served as a popular spokesman for the American cause, and earned a chestful of medals to boot. "The war," Arthur Mann has written, "made him." He came out of it a much admired "flying congressman." It sharpened his self-confidence and honed his administrative skills, but, more significant, he was no longer an outsider. If, before the war, he was sensitive about his Italian ancestry and the need to prove himself, he returned self-assured, fully accepted, even a hero, but surely an American. Foggia also broadened him. Since 1905 he had been a loner, away from mother and sister without any relationship resembling the closeness of family. In the army he learned the satisfaction of helping and looking out for others under dangerous circumstances. For the rest of his life he remained committed to these men, the "Foggiani," whom he had led. If ever they needed his help, or asked to meet him, or required his presence, he made himself available. "I hate to be a pest," he wrote to Congressman John Rankin in June 1940, "but the mother of one of my boys, and the wife of another who served with me . . . are actually in need." His "boys" remained intensely loyal to him. Decades later they lobbied President Roosevelt for cabinet posts for the major, describing the special type of leadership that he had demonstrated in Foggia.[50]

———

On September 17, 1917, as La Guardia had prepared to leave for the battlefield, he had written Republican state chairman Frederick Chauncey Tanner, "There is no danger of my seat being vacated for the time being—but they did stop my salary." The salary would be taken care of, but now, a year later, thousands of his constituents were restless over the idea that their congressman was off winning headlines and had left them without a proper voice in Congress.[51]

Before leaving for Europe La Guardia had arranged for Harry Andrews and his secretary, Marie Fisher, to handle the routine business of his congressional office. Constituent business that required official assistance was turned over to Harlem congressman Isaac Siegel. But some in the district regarded this as inad-equate for a neighborhood that wanted its unique point of view on war, mobilization, and the entire range of domestic issues forcefully articulated. As early as January 8, 1918, House Speaker Champ Clark received a petition with more than 3000 signatures demanding that the flying congressman's seat be declared vacant. If their representative wished to go off and make war, asserted the collection of pacifists, socialists, and reformers, then let the business of their representation be turned over to someone who wished to do it full time.

The *Philadelphia Record* upbraided the carpers: "Congressman La Guardia, absent to fight for his country, is absent little more than some Congressmen during the baseball season. Why raise a fuss over him?" La Guardia himself dismissed the effort with the back of his hand, suggesting that if any of his constituents were prepared to take his place in a Caproni biplane, he would be more than happy to return to "my upholstered seat in the House." Speaker Clark refused to introduce any recall resolution, nor would any member make such a motion. Instead, the House warmly endorsed La Guardia's overseas service, which "in our judgment entitles him to the loyal support of the constituents he now represents in his campaign for a return to Congress at the election this fall."[52]

La Guardia did not dismiss the complaints entirely. From Foggia he wrote Harlem colleague Siegel that he intended to come out fighting in the upcoming campaign, on an "anti-yellow, anti-socialistic, anti-German and true blood American platform." Caught up in the war spirit and his own fierce competitiveness, La Guardia planned a slashing "100 per cent American campaign," ripping at dissenters and pacifists.[53]

This tack brought him an astonishing dividend. Tammany boss Charlie Murphy, fearful of splitting the regular vote and strengthening antiwar candidates, decided to make the war the overriding issue of the 1918 campaign. Only patriots should be returned to Congress. The boss ordered his minions to form fusion campaigns against Socialists and antiwar elements. "I want you district leaders," Murphy commanded his Democrats, "to consult with the Republican district leaders and see if you cannot agree. . . . Pay particular attention to the doubtful districts where Socialists may prevail. We want only Americans—Americans whose loyalty is unquestioned—in Washington. . . . Sink all partisanship. . . . America first." La Guardia readily accepted the fusion arrangement and the support of the superpatriots. "Viva La Guardia," trumpeted *Financial America*. "Let Captain La Guardia be the unanimous choice of the two older parties as the nominee to Congress from the Fourteenth New York District. If any opponents contest, then let them be counted as vassals of the Kaiser, and turn their supporters over for internment or the chain gang."[54]

La Guardia was opposed in the campaign by Scott Nearing, a thirty-five-year-old economics professor, and a Socialist, who had been dismissed from two university positions for his unorthodox views, and indicted under the Espionage Act for publishing "The Great Madness," which denounced America's participation in the war. Nearing ran on a platform that called for transforming the United States into an "industrial cooperative commonwealth," and regarding the war the party declared provocatively, "The Socialist Party does not pretend to be 100 per cent loyal."[55]

The War Department did its share in the campaign, cabling General Pershing to ship the congressman home "for duty in connection with Caproni bombing instruction." It is impossible today to ascertain if any legitimate reason existed for La Guardia to return to the States (the Armistice ending World War I was just a few weeks off). There is little doubt, however, that his presence in New York certainly helped his reelection effort. Arriving in the city just one week before the election, La Guardia insisted that he would not campaign while still attached to the armed forces. Then he went out and campaigned like crazy, in a round of speeches and appearances.[56]

Indeed, the scene of his return from the European theater could not have been more effectively handled if it had been staged. Trim and tan in decoration-bedecked khaki, the congressman-major was greeted at the dock by the local press, anxious for word from the returning hero. Asked what he thought of Scott Nearing, he shot back with well-rehearsed puzzlement: "Who is Scott Nearing?" Reporters played along, telling the smiling Republican-Democratic candidate that this was his opponent. Feigning confusion, La Guardia asked if they were sure that it was not that other Socialist, Upton Sinclair. No, they reassured him, it was Nearing. Well, "If he is a young man," came the reply, "I shall ask him what regiment he comes from." No regiment, he was told. The man not only opposed the war but had been indicted under the very Espionage Act that La Guardia had so strenuously opposed the year before. La Guardia turned angelic: "The question of patriotism must not be introduced into this campaign," he preached, after having introduced it. "Scott Nearing must have a fighting chance, I did not know he was under indictment, but remember this . . . a man is innocent till he is proved guilty."[57]

While in Italy, La Guardia had written Harry Andrews that he did not want to make political capital of his service; "by no means use any picture of me in uniform. . . . I personally object to using the uniform for campaign purposes." La Guardia need not have said this to his political strategist unless he really meant it, but by the time he got back to New York his competitive instinct overtook him. It was simply too easy a shot for him to pass up. By the evening of his return he was going from corner to corner, speaking to crowds in his uniform, replete with wings and medals, converting his hero's welcome into political coin. "I went into this war because I wanted to stop all wars," he cried to the appreciative audiences, tearing into his opponent, calling him "a man without a country unless he stands for what the American flag stands for." By the end of this first round of appearances La Guardia was exploiting stark war emotions with gusto: "My remedy is better than the yellow dog Socialists."[58]

A few days before the election the two candidates jousted in more or less serious debate at the Cooper Union in lower Manhattan. The slender, fair-complected Nearing presented a social agenda for America, punctuating his solemn delivery with boyishly graceful gestures, in the manner of a bookish professor. He spoke of the new world aforming in the Soviet Union, condemned the Wall Street profiteers, and launched a Socialist critique of the American political economy. The short, swarthy La Guardia presented a sharp contrast. Terse and direct, his hands in perpetual motion, he refused to debate alternate visions of Utopia, directing the attention of his audience to the war. He denounced the Kaiser and the Socialists who were willing to let him have his way. Nearing remained the didactic lecturer, calm, boring, and fair, while La Guardia took every possible debater's advantage.[59]

He won overwhelming support in the press. The *New York Times* called him "a soldier . . . an orator and a patriot, an American by birth, but an Italian by origin and heart, who has shown himself to be the best mouthpiece of the White House's diplomacy. . . ." The *Herald* asked readers to compare La Guardia's record, "his valor won most of the decorations at the disposal of the king," with his "Socialist opponent [who] was indicted . . . and faces prosecution for persistent interference with American prosecution of the war."[60]

With the newspapers behind him, the Democratic and Republican parties working for his election, the Kaiser a convenient foil, and his opponent's patriotism the most contested issue of the campaign, La Guardia was confident. With good reason, it turned out, for the fusion strategy proved successful in each district where it was used, even defeating such popular East Side Socialists as Meyer London and Morris Hillquit. Heeding the *Times*'s call to thwart the "eminent friend of academic freedom and other kinds of freedom verging on sedition," the voters gave La Guardia a huge victory of 14,000 votes to Nearing's 6000.[61]

A week later, the Armistice, ending hostilities, was signed, and on November 21, 1918, Major La Guardia resigned his commission and returned to his upholstered seat in the House, to resume the main line of his career. And his life.

The delicate blond woman Thea Almerigotti was waiting. They had planned to marry as soon as her home state of Trieste was freed from Austrian control. It now was, thanks in part to her hero. In January Fiorello La Guardia and the immigrant dress designer whom he had first met while marching on the picket lines during the labor disputes of 1913 announced their engagement. Too much can be made of simple coincidence, but a number of interesting similarities hint at Achille La Guardia's enduring influence on his son. When Achille took Trieste-born Irene Coen for a wife, he had already traveled a good part of the world. He was an established musician with no real community roots and estranged from his family. Thirty-one years old, Achille married a woman more than ten years younger than he, whose religion was different from his, a woman who because of her youth, her minority faith, and his plans to leave Europe would be heavily dependent on her more experienced husband for everything but raising her children. Fiorello, now thirty-five, set in his ways, with a rich background and a promising career, was marrying a quietly reserved twenty-four-year-old woman who had no larger goal than helping him to be successful and raise his family. Like Irene, Thea valued nothing more than sharing her husband's private time and then receding into the background when he took a public stage. She was as withdrawn as he was outgoing, calm and frail as he was volcanic and unrelenting. Achille had taken a Jewish wife and made no point of pressing his religious views on his family. Fiorello, a tepid Episcopalian, limited in commitment to the religion of social gospel, gave little thought to Thea's Catholicism.

They were married in a Catholic ceremony on March 8, 1919, by Monsignor Gerardo Ferrante in the Cathedral College office of St. Patrick's before a handful of the couple's friends. The bride wore a stylish fur-trimmed suit; the groom, his army uniform with his soldier's cap rakishly tilted. They left after the ceremony for a brief honeymoon before settling into Fiorello's Charles Street apartment, and what was by all accounts a loving marriage.[62]

3. War's Aftermath and the Progressive Spirit

T HE United States had entered World War I after a critical French offensive had failed, ten divisions had mutinied, and dispirited Allies were talking of surrender. Italy verged on collapse after a stunning setback at Caporetto, and the separate treaty signed by the Bolsheviks in Russia had freed Germany's eastern front. The United States contributed more than 2 million fresh troops to the conflict. Measured against the losses of other countries American casualties were modest, but little else about its effort had been modest. As the *Rochester Post Express* observed, Germany found "itself running into extra innings . . . [with] no relief pitcher or pinchhitter" in sight, and the United States came off the bench to win the game for the Allies.

In addition to taking credit for the victory, the United States insisted on shaping the peace. President Wilson had set out an ambitious list of fourteen separate points that would make this a war to end all wars and usher in an era of global democracy and international cooperation. Once the war was over Wilson demanded that the peacemakers at Versailles draft a peace among equals, a peace without victors. He called for an agreement that would guarantee open seas and free trade, self-determination for national units, armament reduction, and an end to secret diplomacy. And to cap his new world order he proposed a League of Nations to secure world comity and democracy. Shattering precedent, he went personally to

Europe to shepherd his fourteen points past the boundary brokers, the conventional diplomats whom he privately derided as men of limited vision and narrow faith.[63]

The Allies, who had suffered fearfully in human and economic terms, did not share Wilson's idealistic vision. Determined to wring the last measure of revenge and reparations from Germany, they did not want Wilson to place his peace on their war. Wilson saw in his fourteen points the one possible justification for the bloodletting, but for the Europeans there was long-standing justification. They had not fought this as a special war but rather as the bloodiest and costliest in a progression of traditional wars sparked by parochial jealousies, economic rivalry, and imperial competition. Satisfied to be without noble goals, they wanted the traditional peace with spoils, reparations, and punishment. The Europeans and Americans, so recently allied, talked past each other at Versailles. And Wilson was denied his fruits of victory. Europe denied him everything but the League, and the U.S. Senate denied him that too.[64]

Although he was part of the Republican tide that swept into Washington following the 1918 elections, Fiorello La Guardia refused to join the opponents of the League. On March 3, 1919, he asked his colleagues to unite behind the president's plan for ending war. If this meant more involvement in foreign affairs than the United States was accustomed to, he considered it a proper price for guarding the peace. A month later, while accompanying a House Military Affairs Committee group investigating army camps, La Guardia stopped off in Paris to demand that Fiume, the Adriatic port where he had served some sixteen years before, be granted to Italy despite the 1915 Treaty of London (which Italy had also signed) promising the territory to Yugoslavia. Rejecting all arguments to the contrary, La Guardia insisted that he had promised the return of the disputed territories in his wartime speeches, and now he wanted his word to be "made good." His pleas, based on so personal a diplomacy, persuaded no one.[65]

His resolution denouncing the anti-Semitic pogroms that broke out in several of the newly formed Eastern European states won more support, resulting in a warning to Poland and its neighbors that the United States would not countenance "a people who desire liberty and self-government" for themselves but do not "exercise tolerance in religious worship and restraint and control over unnatural and inhuman hatred. . . ." Observers credited the cautionary resolution, which threatened to withhold all economic assistance, with quelling the anti-Semitic riots. "Some Poles in this country didn't like me after that," La Guardia later recalled, but he did win the gratitude of his Jewish constituents.[66]

It was with the controversy over the structuring of a peacetime military that La Guardia finally found an issue that attracted wide political support; it was also a position that later in life he would deeply regret. As Congress turned to designing a peacetime army, the Wilson administration, anticipating a more active foreign policy, proposed a 1-million-man force. But Americans were tired of war and

Versailles had been profoundly disillusioning. La Guardia spoke for many when he lectured the administration about the pointlessness of a large military. With their duty "gloriously done," he wanted the troops brought home. Let the Allies secure the peace in Europe. The United States would rely on the ocean as a buffer, and on its own proven ability to mobilize rapidly for protection. Anyway, there would be no more wars. La Guardia was certain of that.

Characteristically he detected an ulterior motive in the military's demands for preparedness—it had become a habit, a frame of mind, for him to see a villain behind every unpleasant fact. The generals, he assured his colleagues, were afraid of peace because it was their business to make war, and without troops there would be no wars. Then the men with the stars on their shoulders would have to do real work! La Guardia's proposal for a reduced military had everything to make a representative happy: It was broadly popular, it would result in lower taxes, and it was couched in a tough-sounding rallying cry: "The American Congress is going to run the War Department . . . the War Department is not going to run the Congress." And if this policy happened to be mistaken it would certainly not become apparent before the next election. The army was cut back to 200,000 troops.[67]

Many years later, after a second World War and the onset of a cold war with Russia, La Guardia wrote an unforgiving critique of his earlier stand, attacking it as one of the most unfortunate mistakes in his career. He regretted the mawkish legislative posturing and the "folly" of assuming that peace would care for itself. A strong deterrent force would have changed history, but he had led the wrong movement. At the time, however, flushed with certainty, he lectured the president and his advisers that the simple solution to war was to abolish armies.[68]

The Great War and the botched peace, and the cramped spirit of disillusion that followed it, so thoroughly wormed its way into the American psyche that it affected not only foreign policy but the entire mood and politics of the era, destroying the sense of innocence of an entire generation. Many returned from the battlefront with a new pessimism about human nature and the perfectability of human institutions. "He is more critical, less facile, and with . . . a deeper sense that you don't find truth by skimming milk," the English Socialist Harold Laski wrote about Walter Lippmann after the war. F. Scott Fitzgerald, just now graduating from college, surveyed the scene and found all "gods dead, . . . all wars fought, . . . all faiths shaken."[69]

Before the Great War, Progressives had forged a series of important social and economic reforms that aimed to protect the individual from such powerful forces as industrialization and big business. If there was to be monopoly, they argued, let it be checked through regulation. If there was a need for vast pools of industrial labor, let the workers be guaranteed a safer work environment with workmen's compensation, the regulation of maximum hours, minimum wages, and an end to the ugly exploitation of women and children. Enlightened businessmen, some of whom were themselves part of the progressive movement, knew that in the new scheme of things it was necessary to create order and predictability within the larger traditions of overall freedom. Other Progressives, social reformers, joined in a moral crusade to make America kinder and gentler by limiting the power of private interests and expanding the helping role of government.

These varied strains of reform shared a common way of viewing problems. While conservatives continued to insist that fault lay with the individual, whether he was earning a low wage, unemployed, or living in a slum, progressives viewed problems as systemic, as social or economic defects that were open to political discussion and solution. It was a settled belief with these men and women that the quality of national life could be improved through intelligent social engineering. More or less, La Guardia saw himself as a progressive. He might argue with some points, especially the racial assumptions of Anglo-Saxon superiority that ensnared a good number of these reformers, but he shared their suspicion of the business interests, supported the ignored classes, and was committed to grappling with the challenge of social and economic amelioration.

By the time he returned from Foggia, however, progressivism was in eclipse. The hostilities in Europe had helped unravel the precarious comity between American citizens of varied backgrounds. In the postwar atmosphere of a newly ascendant Ku Klux Klan, a rabid Red scare, and the wide popularity of such hero bigots as Henry Ford, the progressive spirit withered. Class peace, artificially enforced by no-strike pledges and War Industry Board control during the war, expired with the Armistice as labor demanded its fair share in American prosperity. The war had brought scarcity, meatless, wheatless, and heatless days; its end freed pent-up consumer demand and pushed off an era of materialist indulgence out of patience with conscience-bound reformers and Jeremiahs.

The war had also brought business and government closer, and it taught corporate America that there was little to fear from a government that believed that what was good for General Motors was good for America. Big Business was in the ascendant as marines went out to protect American industry south of the border, an adoring government offered businesses free research and assistance, and the Department of Commerce came to dominate the cabinet. The doctrine of laissez faire, of government's conscious disinterest in the economy, was raised to the level of republican dogma.[70]

Doubts about earlier commitments to expanding democracy further weakened the progressive mood. As boss politics and the low level of local political campaigns demonstrated some of the weaknesses in a politics of universal suffrage, the belief that democratic providence would bring forth wise government from the votes of uneducated workers and immigrants was shaken. Reformers backed away from their earlier agenda for expanding democracy through such proposals as the direct election of senators, the promotion of party primaries, referendum laws, and provisions for the recall of elected officials.

Walter Lippmann illustrates this retreat from progressive assumptions well. Like other liberals, he had initially assumed that majority rule was a moral principle derived from the equality of all human beings. By the mid-1920s his *The Phantom Public* denied the ethical superiority of majority rule. It was only a device for ratifying decisions, "a pacific substitute for civil war in which the opposing armies are counted and victory is awarded to the larger before any blood is spilled." In a letter to Judge Learned Hand he confessed that his "own mind has been getting steadily anti-democratic." The electorate was too large, too ignorant, and too fiercely superstitious for democracy. "For when the private man had lived through the romantic age in politics," he wrote, "and is no longer moved by the stale echoes of its hot cries, when he is sober," he abandons the "crusade to make the world something or other it did not become; he has been tantalized too often by the foam of events . . . seen the gas go out of it." Tired radicals, disaffected intellectuals, bitter idealists all gave up the progressive ghost. Those still inclined to seek solutions defined them in narrower terms, in personal revival and moral regeneration and the self-indulgent bohemianism of the "lost generation."[71]

La Guardia, however, remained essentially on course. The war had disturbed him, but it did not create the crippling disenchantment with politics and "the people" that it did for others. He had never been a true romantic—he was too cynical for that. His essential confidence in rational solutions and in the need to involve government in these solutions remained intact. He rejected the emerging spirit of postwar conservatism, identifying with those caught in the undertow of American prosperity. La Guardia saw politics as a number of things, including a career, but above all a practical exercise in a constituency-based politics of the American minority.

He was no ideologue or even a consistent thinker, and it is easier to describe what he did not favor than what he did. He was not a Socialist; he was not persuaded that capitalism had failed irretrievably or that a centrally directed economy was either feasible or an improvement. Socialist solutions to problems that were deeply imbedded in human nature he judged simplistic and dangerous. Who, he wondered, would protect the people from the bureaucrats, the "factory politicians," in a Socialist society?[72]

Like most young congressmen, he lacked a coherent agenda and often lapsed into inconsistency. While he opposed a large postwar army, La Guardia favored the expansion of America's fledgling air force. He favored national self-determination except when it came to Italy's claims to Fiume. While opposed to the Espionage Act as a limit on free expression, he attacked commissioner of immigration Frederick Howe for allowing radicals being held for deportation to receive Communist and IWW pamphlets, "that batch of anarchist literature," even going so far as to propose an amendment that would have cut off the commissioner's $6500 salary.[73]

La Guardia supported the Lever Act granting government unprecedented control over the economy, but with the war over, he approved the return of the railroads to private hands and backed limits on the regulatory power of the Interstate Commerce Commission. He opposed farm bloc efforts to raise food prices as detrimental to his urban constituents but ignored local prejudices to fight for black citizens' voting rights. And when the bill chartering the American Legion omitted black veterans, La Guardia attached an amendment, asking simply, "The Negro soldiers fought alongside us did they not?"[74]

La Guardia delivered opinions on as wide a range of subjects as any member of the House, undaunted by the complexity or political delicacy of the issues, attacking with abandon those who debated with him. After praising the March Revolution in Russia as a first step toward liberty, La Guardia offered a resolution sending greetings and good wishes to the Russian people and called for Americans to contribute needed foodstuffs. A few months later, in the hindsight of the Bolshevik takeover, he criticized American ambassador David Francis for supporting the regime of Alexander Kerensky rather than the White Russian officer General Kornilov, who he thought might have prevented the collapse of the Eastern front. Opposed in this analysis by Congressman Henry Flood of Virginia, La Guardia challenged Flood to demonstrate his expertise by naming the "Provinces of Russia and their capitals and their races, or explain recent changes there." But the long-range significance of the Revolution escaped the blustering La Guardia as much as it did most of his colleagues in the House.[75]

There was a larger theme to La Guardia than these positions would indicate. He was motivated by a large measure of idealism, by the pursuit of the good as he saw it. He knew the life of the poor, the immigrant, and the worker firsthand, and he wanted to ease it. And he wanted to make government fair and honest. Well before the Harding administration scandals were revealed, La Guardia was complaining of profiteers "buzzing around" the Capitol. He focused particularly on the food trust that was managing to keep $60 million of army surplus meat and supplies off the market. Greeting the director of government surplus sales, C. W. Hare, with characteristic warmth when he came before the Military Affairs Committee, La Guardia exclaimed, "Let's see what this $25,000 a year [Hare's salary] beauty says about meats. . . ." Hare said that his assistants had been combing Europe to find customers for 70,000 tons of canned meat. Why, La Guardia wanted to know, was this necessary? Hare replied that the meat companies had told him that Americans would not buy the six-pound tins. Appalled by the stupidity, La Guardia shouted at the director, "You couldn't find a can opener in all of Romania." Let the government make the inexpensive meat available to poor American workers, La Guardia declared, and the warehouses would be cleared quickly. Oh yes, the meat packers would not like that because it would force down their own prices, "but," La Guardia added, "I am not interested in that."[76]

Nor was he interested in allowing anyone to play Uncle Sam for a patsy, no matter how respected their reputation. After the war the YMCA and the Red Cross sent Washington bills asking for payment for the soldier clubhouses that they had erected on army bases. La Guardia railed at the nerve. "When the American people gave their donations to the Red Cross and the Young Men's Christian Association they did not give them to those organizations, but they gave the money to be spent for the American soldiers. . . . They are a direct gift of the American people to the soldier boys of this country."[77]

La Guardia's style of unrelieved resentment and protest seemed calculated not to leave any ego undamaged, and his social behavior proved no less assertive. His disdain for the Washington party circuit that linked those on the make with those on the take was tangible. The insipid talk and aggressive lobbying over canapes raised his hackles. Power brokers were not his people. Once, however, New York's senior senator, William Calder, persuaded Fiorello to join him at a Washington dinner party. Milling around among the guests, La Guardia struck up a conversation about Croatia and Dalmatia, delivering his outspoken opinions with the confidence of someone familiar with a region few Americans had ever visited. The man on the other side of the monologue disagreed with him, and La Guardia turned his scorn on the unfortunate individual. "I've lived in that part of the world for three years, and I know what I am talking about." What, the riled congressman wanted to know, did the other man know about this region? "I am the Serbian ambassador here," replied the indignant diplomat.

The guests were seated, and La Guardia turned to his left, initiating a conversation about the Liberty airplane engines manufactured for the army by General Motors. On the floor of Congress he had denounced these machines as a disaster foisted on the government by corrupt officials, and now he spoke at passionate length about the scandal to the woman at his side, denouncing the greedy transportation monopolies for their rapacity. She turned out to be the wife of a top GM executive.

Fiorello repaired to the men's room, where he met a gentleman who innocently asked how he was enjoying the party. "I never saw such a bunch of nuts before," he replied. "I'm going. Want to come along?" La Guardia asked. "I can't," said the man. "I'm your host."[78]

He had come back from Foggia with a chestful of medals and a bit of the glory, but in Congress, used far more to whispered tones in cloak rooms than to impassioned outbursts of righteous indignants, he remained a lone voice out on uncoordinated crusades. H. L. Mencken had characterized the postwar Congress as a "depressing gang of incompetents . . . petty lawyers and small town bankers," comparable in "intelligence, information and integrity . . . to a gang of bootleggers." His position in this august body provided La Guardia nothing more substantial than attention. He stood on the sidelines carping, but to little effect. Nor did his future in the House seem particularly promising. So insistent was he on his own ideas that he even failed to strike up a working relationship with those who shared his political bent, such progressives as William Borah, Robert La Follette, and

George Norris. The most critical of legislative skills, the ability to translate his sensibilities into law, he lacked.[79]

4. The Sidewalks of New York

L A Guardia had proved more adept at presenting his constituents' demands with Arizona directness than climbing the Washington power ladder. There was little that La Guardia could make happen in Congress. Every bill that he introduced died an administrative death in committee. At Foggia he had been at the center of things making decisions and having them implemented. In Congress he could only talk and do the political scut work that was expected of junior legislators. The seniority system concentrated real power in the hands of committee chairmen and party leaders. Gaining influence required patience, tact, and a willingness to pay dues; hoard your favors, become expert in some few areas, and build power slowly. What opportunity existed then for an impatient, street-smart, strutting independent type like La Guardia? His constituency was sharply different from the rest of America, and in representing them his goals conflicted with those of the other representatives. Caught between his people and the rules of his club, he had become his own most formidable obstacle, brandishing an unpopular opinion on everything with a grating insistence on being heard. A deliberative body promised few opportunities for a vitriolic insurgent off on an isolated tilt.

La Guardia's political friends began to suggest that perhaps Congress was not his best arena. Local politics might provide a better setting for his liberal themes and ambition to lead. Thea La Guardia in her quiet way made it plain that she too preferred having her husband at home in New York more than three days a week, especially since both of them were interested in building a family. Thus, when Republican boss Sam Koenig suggested that La Guardia run for the presidency of the New York City Board of Aldermen, to fill the unexpired term of Alfred E. Smith (who resigned to assume the state governorship), Fiorello listened. And when the Republican leader added the promise of a future mayoral nomination, he assented.[80]

The example of Smith, whose political trajectory pointed toward the White House, was not lost on La Guardia. Admittedly Smith was a Tammany man and that was an important difference, but Al Smith was a symbol of the self-made immigrant working-class politician who had made good. Born in 1873 over a barbershop at 174 South Street on the southern tip of the Irish East Side, he grew up in a neighborhood as distressed as any in the city. Before he reached thirteen his hardworking father became ill and died. The family was so poor that friends had to pay for the funeral, and on the following evening, with her two children in tow, Al's mother went to work in a neighborhood factory. Soon Al was forced to drop out of school to take jobs in turn as a newsboy, a "chaser" rounding up business for a trucking firm, a counter boy, a shipping clerk, and a fishmonger, supporting mother and sister on a salary that eventually rose to $12 a week in 1890.

There were two major institutions in Al Smith's neighborhood, the church and the local Tammany club, and he served both loyally. By 1896, at the age of twenty-two, he was working for the Democratic party, visiting the ill, calming the desperate, and offering whatever modest help he could in the name of the local Democratic machine. Boston's famous ward boss Michael Lomasney liked to tell his men, "There should be in every ward a guy that any bloke can go to when he's in trouble and get help—not justice and the law, but help." Smith's job was to guide the people to Tammany for help, and for this work he was rewarded with a position on the city payroll serving jury notices for $900 a year.[81]

In 1903, when Smith was just short of his thirtieth birthday, the party promoted him to a seat in the State Assembly. He made not a single speech that first year, secured not a single committee assignment. The language in many of the bills that came before the Assembly in Albany made no sense to the former fishmonger, with their subparagraphs and sections and convoluted legalese. In his entire life Smith had read only one book from cover to cover, *The Life of John L. Sullivan*. He simply voted as he was told. His votes counted just the same as anybody else's, but they counted for little because the Republicans held firm control of the state legislature. Upstate Representatives with not a shred of interest in the big city to the south would dictate its policies knowing full well that the less the state did for the metropolis, the lower the tax rate for their communities would remain.

Few city politicians who went up to Albany took with them any expectations beyond the Assembly. Smith was different. He was proud, determined to understand his work and to do it well. In his second term Smith still made no speeches, but this time he was carefully taking in everything going on around him, listening to the debates, developing his ideas on the issues and his grasp of legislative protocol. He taught himself to research the bills and to crack the law books and to analyze the transcripts of the sessions. By 1908 he was holding choice committee assignments. He also struck up a relationship with Robert F. Wagner, the son of a German immigrant tenement house janitor, and he finally was standing up to speak on the floor of the Assembly. By 1911 Smith was majority leader of the Assembly, continuing to work the boss's agenda, helping ram through a charter designed to throw thousands of jobs to the political machine.[82]

The Triangle Shirtwaist Company Fire of 1911, which resulted in the deaths of nearly 150 women because of unsafe work conditions, transformed Smith. The factory investigations that he led following this tragedy inspired Smith to change the miserable conditions that he and Robert Wagner discovered. They supported a program of labor rights that included old age pensions, decent pay, one day off a week, workmen's compensation, and prohibitions on child labor. While he steered these proposals through Albany, Smith never fought his party. Instead, he and a growing band of confederates persuaded Tammany that backing social welfare legislation paid practical political dividends. In 1918 Smith's loyalty was rewarded with the Democratic gubernatorial nomination. His victory in November symbolized the new possibilities for liberal politicians of ethnic background.[83]

Smith had launched his successful race for governor from the aldermanic presidency, and it was a chance at this office that Sam Koenig was offering Fiorello La Guardia. Koenig thought that the off-year special election to fill Smith's seat offered Republicans an excellent opportunity to make a friendly gesture to the large Italian community and build interest in the upcoming presidential contest. For his part, La Guardia saw Koenig's offer a bit differently. Stymied in Congress, he sought a local base from which he could move up in New York politics. Moreover, La Guardia had little to lose. If he did not win the election, he kept his seat in the House. If he won, he had every reason to expect his party's support for the mayoralty in 1922.[84]

The Republican machine stood solidly behind La Guardia. When William M. Bennet challenged him in the Republican primaries, Koenig saw to it that Bennet failed to garner a single vote in 100 election districts in lower Manhattan. The party also provided La Guardia with a campaign manager, an impeccably credentialed, thirty-four-year-old establishment Republican, Paul Windels. Windels admired La Guardia's energy and marveled at his special "temperament which went off in every direction, from extreme optimism to profound pessimism." In fact, Windels was one of the few who could rein in La Guardia's mercurial swings of mood. In addition, Windels's blue-chip connections provided La Guardia with the luxury of an adequate campaign chest for the first time in his career.[85]

Party assistance aside, La Guardia worked hard in his own behalf, making as many as sixteen appearances a night across the city. Fiorello's campaign manager stood in awe of his "inexhaustible mental and nervous energy and physical strength." Windels had never seen so driven a candidate, but that was only the half of it. La Guardia had honed his campaign tactics to a fine art, attacking his opponent, taking artful side steps on such controversial issues as the 5-cent transit fare, making carefully targeted promises to special groups, and appealing for—no, demanding—ethnic support. "Any Italo-American who votes the Democratic ticket this year," he announced in the Italian sections, "is an Austrian bastard." After a hard day's campaigning La Guardia would make sure to return to the Italian areas to fire up his enthusiasm for the next day. It was after one of these appearances

69

that La Guardia bragged to an aide, "I can outdemagogue the best of demagogues." At the same time that he pursued his natural constituency, La Guardia also attracted the backing of reform groups like the Citizens Union while winning the praise of the establishment press. The *New York Times* endorsed him as "that gallant aviator, that ardent American patriot . . . who has displayed . . . such keen, intelligent interest in economy and reduction of taxation," a politician who could be trusted "to protect the people's money. . . ."[86]

The election proved very close. La Guardia's Irish opponent, Robert Moran, an ailing florist, hardly campaigned at all, but Tammany helped arrange 142,000 votes, and the Socialist candidate drew 45,000 ballots. Not until two o'clock in the morning did Sam Koenig call with the message "F. H. you're in," with 145,000 votes. Were it not for the candidacy of a disgruntled Democrat, Michael Kelly, who siphoned off Irish votes (and according to some accounts was assisted in forming his independent Liberty Party by Sam Koenig), La Guardia would have had to go back to Washington. Still, no Republican in memory had put together such a victory, tenuous though it might be. He had succeeded in drawing the votes of the new immigrants and in winning the boroughs of Manhattan, Brooklyn, and Richmond. On December 31, 1919, La Guardia tended his resignation to the House of Representatives and prepared for his new career in local politics. He had been elected to preside over the Board of Aldermen. Serious politicians did not covet this job for long. He had been a congressman; he wanted to be mayor.[87]

For the while, however, he took office presiding over the same aldermen he had come to detest during his Ellis Island days—the pack of corrupt politicians of whom Boss Tweed had said with no little fondness that there "was never a time that you couldn't buy the Board of Aldermen." Aldermanic powers had been cut back by successive reforms, limiting the body to renaming streets and issuing innocuous resolutions, but for all their irrelevance they were still as ornery and argumentative a group as could be found in any municipality, carrying out their unimportant work with heated partisan passion. It did not take La Guardia long to catch the mood of the politically charged board, gaveling one alderman into his seat with the comment that "Every member present must behave as a gentleman and those who are not, must try to."[88]

Fiorello tussled most often with the Democratic comptroller, Charles Craig. He took an immediate dislike to the bullying Craig, who had been carrying on a barb-filled feud with the Democratic mayor, John H. Hylan. At the close of one letter to his nemesis that complained of a series of neglected payments, La Guardia wrote Craig: "Unfortunately, it would seem that these claimants have not that kind of political drag necessary to attain prompt attention from you." Another time he treated the paunchy comptroller like a recalcitrant child, telling him, "I am too busy with the work of the budget to play with you today."[89]

Before long, the two officials were villifying each other in the press, La Guardia charging Craig with billing the city for his private auto and Craig hitting back that La Guardia was making his private phone calls and mailing personal telegrams at city expense. Much of this was silly, which did nothing to dampen La Guardia's enthusiasm for the unbecoming repartee. "Nothing you could do," the press reported La Guardia telling Craig, "would make me mad. You're a complete official failure." At one meeting Craig became so enraged that he ordered the mayor to "hit that little wop over the head with the gavel." Another time, when La Guardia insisted on taking up a topic that Craig wished to delay, the Democrat threatened to give the aldermanic president "what you deserve." As La Guardia lunged at him, Craig's secretary ran over to hold him back.

"You try to start anything with me and you'll go out of that window, you bootlicking valet," he told the interloper.

"I'm no wop," answered the less-than-awed secretary.

This time it took a larger group to restrain La Guardia as he charged, screaming: "What's that you say? What's that you say? What's that you say?"

The Citizens Union was appalled by the "disgraceful brawls that featured the sessions of the Board," but city Republicans had not attracted so much attention in decades, and they were happy to see the spirited Fiorello on the attack.[90]

And on one occasion he actually landed a lucky punch.

Before La Guardia took office, the Board of Estimate approved plans for a new county courthouse, a project that promised bountiful Tammany patronage. When La Guardia came upon the scene, little could be done to cancel the Tammany-infested project, but he accomplished that little with great style. A public official could win headlines by charging corruption, and if a project was sufficiently large there was little doubt that some would turn up. Given the number of jobs and contracts that the courthouse project involved, the only question was how much scandal could be found and how high up it would go.[91]

In 1858 a rather modest courthouse had been approved by the city for a maximum cost of $250,000. William M. "Boss" Tweed, in a series of appeals, persuaded the city fathers to imagine a more fitting building than the bare-bones structure they had initially designed. A million dollars, then an additional $800,000, $300,000 more, and yet another $300,000, by 1871 fully $13 million had been spent, and still the courthouse was not completed. Not that it was all a waste, for the Tweed Ring had come to an arrangement with pliable contractors to split the take, 65–35, with the larger figure for the politicians. Thus the city paid $179,729.60 for three tables and forty chairs. The total cost of furnishings, close to $6 million, exceeded three times the cost of operating the U.S. diplomatic service for two years. "Plumbing and gas light fixtures" cost nearly $1.5 million, while each courthouse window was calculated to have cost $8000. Almost $2 million was billed for repairs, on a *spanking-new building*. The entry for brooms read $41,190.95, and for eleven thermometers, $7,500. And after all this had been spent, many floors were without carpets, some rooms without the roof completed and the plaster peeling.[92]

With this history as a guide, La Guardia was confident that Tammany had a share in the new courthouse contracts. He suggested that the new structure feature a tablet memorializing Comptroller Craig: "Sacred to the memory of a short but misspent public life." BlackGuardia, as Craig referred to his tormentor, studied every specification and every bid. He compared the price of limestone for the courthouse with the cost of similar materials for a building under construction in the same area, and he pored over the contracts, announcing finally that the new courthouse "out-Tweeded Tweed." The aldermanic president took his revelations to Mayor Hylan, who was genuinely shocked. To make sure that the Democratic mayor did not recover too quickly, La Guardia shared his findings with the *New York World*, which featured the scandal. Finally, Mayor Hylan, as honest as he was slow-witted, launched an investigation that led to the bringing of sixty-nine indictments.[93]

La Guardia refused to allow a small office to make an unimportant politician of him. As president of the Board of Aldermen he also sat on the Board of Estimate, which wielded power over the city's purse. Under the pretense of investigating budget items to insure honesty, La Guardia insinuated himself into every aspect of municipal operations, crowding the traditional prerogatives of the mayor and the comptroller. Meanwhile, he was learning the city, borough by borough, studying its issues, meeting its people, discovering its problems. Working twelve- and four-teen-hour days, taking lunch at a paper-strewn desk, often surrounded by reporters, whom he found it useful to take into his confidence, La Guardia arrogated for himself a full role in the city's politics. Evenings were devoted to speeches, explaining city government in the neighborhoods, and attending ceremonial functions. "You say you never eat," a friend wrote him; "the authorities have put it out of your power to drink. What do you do for sustenance?" He buried himself in his work. "What do you do, when you have no work to do?" the reporter asked. "Work," he replied. "I mean recreation," the correspondent explained. "That's it," he answered, "work. There is nothing I enjoy better than good hard work, and believe me, there is plenty of it around here."[94]

The hectic schedule took its toll. Shortly after the New Year in 1920, he addressed a dinner honoring the respected Episcopal clergyman and author Cyrus Townshend Brady. There was a special place in La Guardia's heart for established men of patrician mien, whose approval he sought almost as a son. The audience was distinguished, and a series of excellent speakers had preceded La Guardia. Usually this would not have daunted him, but his speech did not come off well. He had rushed all day and he had not eaten. After the speech he apologized to

Brady: "I made a rotten speech and I know it," he wrote. "Please forgive me." Brady began with a rather stiff rebuke, agreeing that La Guardia had missed a valuable opportunity, but then the tone turned fatherly. "Permit an old man who has accomplished little but who has spoken much . . . to give you a little advice. Don't attempt too much. . . ." Brady closed with a tender endorsement. "We all know you: we all know what you are, what you have been, what you can do." The letter meant a great deal to La Guardia, who preserved it for decades. Still he did not take the advice.[95]

He continued to run his office as no other aldermanic president had, under-taking a mayoral agenda despite his powerlessness to effect it. On municipal issues he applied the progressive attitudes that he had represented in Congress. He favored the direct primary, the development of public housing, women's rights, labor unions, civil liberties, and scrupulous integrity in office. When the New York Yankees sent him a season's pass for the 1920 season, a gratuity traditionally accepted by other city politicians, La Guardia wrote back: "Inasmuch as I have made it an ironclad rule not to accept any passes or favors of any kind, while in public office," he was returning the tickets. He closed his letter by telling the Yankees how much he liked baseball and that he would be attending as many games as his schedule allowed, but at his own expense.[96]

He insisted that New York's immigrants be treated with dignity. When an expert witness came to argue on behalf of a budget increase for city schools because they faced the impossible task of educating and assimilating the products of "the sewers of Europe," and for good measure added some disparaging remarks about immigrants from Italy, the aldermanic president bounded out of his chair to scold the woman "not [to] ever dare say that again before this Board." So long as he had anything to say in city politics, he assured the nonplussed "expert," she and her kind would "not get very far."[97]

During this period of Red scares and Palmer raids, La Guardia insisted that diversity was a safer policy than enforced loyalty. Jews in particular were often accused of Marxist machinations, and he defended the hundreds of thousands of Eastern European Jews residing in the city. These immigrants, La Guardia declared, fled czarism and all forms of oppression to seek the full promise of American liberty and opportunity. They had no love for revolution; they only wanted industrial justice. If they sometimes sounded bitter, it did not make them Bolsheviks, only Americans who wanted dearly to raise the standards of social decency in their adopted home-land.[98]

Popular evangelists like Billy Sunday were preaching the Red fever: "If I had my way with these ornery wild eyed Socialists and I.W.W.s I would stand them up before a firing squad. . . ." In Indiana a jury took two minutes to acquit a man who had shot and killed someone for yelling, "To hell with the United States." And New York City dismissed schoolteachers in a campaign aimed at learning "Who's Red and Who's True Blue," while the New York state legislature, led by upstate farmers and rural Republicans, voted on January 7, 1920, to unseat five elected Socialist assemblymen because they belonged to a "subversive and unpatriotic organization." In these fainthearted times La Guardia courageously fought the reactionaries in his own party. Debate the Socialists all you want, he said in a thoughtful interview with the *New York Times*. Reason may defeat them. But arbitrarily strip five elected representatives of their seats and you make a graver attack on liberty than any revolutionary. "If we are not careful we are going to build up a real anti-American, anti-government party in this country." The remedies for radicalism, he suggested, lay in a fair paycheck and an honest ballot, not oppression.[99]

By his second year in office, La Guardia was offering specific goals for making New York a more modern, more caring, more effectively governed town. He drew up proposals for a more progressive city tax, reorganizing the police force, expanding the Port of New York, installing a modern rubbish disposal system, unifying mass transit, and revising the city charter. Admittedly these plans added up to an improbable dream. But La Guardia took these dreams of a generous, happy New York very seriously. "The average citizen believes that the inherent right of life, liberty and happiness includes something more than a bite to eat and a place to sleep in," he declared. "It means a chance to play, a chance to educate himself and a chance to be happy. The day has passed when the man who is willing to work can be poverty stricken." A nation that crusaded to make the world safe for democracy, he said, had an obligation to make its society safe for poor and working people. When a family burned to death because the mother could not reach the fire department by phone, La Guardia charged the telephone company with murder. At public rent hearings he raised his thin voice to declare, "I come not to praise the landlord, but to bury him."[100]

In the conservative political climate of the twenties, La Guardia found it increasingly difficult to keep within the bounds of regular Republican politics. At first, when national Republican leaders emerged from their smoke-filled caucus with the prophet of normalcy, Warren Gamaliel Harding, as their candidate, La Guardia played the good soldier's role, stumping Italian districts in the autumn of 1920, rallying immigrants to the GOP standard. In New York State he helped unseat Al Smith in favor of a conservative business lawyer, Nathan Miller. The Republican victories heartened the ambitious Little Flower. But only briefly.[101]

Earlier in his career, La Guardia had worked with conservatives whom he respected; individuals who recognized the changed realities of American life but wished to address them more deliberately, with as much consideration for tradition and free enterprise as possible. The man he helped elect governor of New York State, however, was a conservative of different stripe. The upstate voters and the large business interests had put Miller into office to dismantle the social welfare programs established by Al Smith, and he complied, supporting a state Prohibition law, a loyalty pledge for teachers, and a full program of social retrenchment. Fearing for the spirit of American self-reliance, he decried such threats to freedom as city-financed health centers and milk stations. The immigrant proletariat made him particularly apprehensive with their sympathies for larger government and social welfare programs. To blunt the effect of their growing numbers, Miller won repeal of the direct primary system of nomination, bringing the selection back to the clubhouse, where he felt it belonged. Over this issue, finally, La Guardia broke with Miller, and the split became complete with a clash over mass transit policy for the city.[102]

When he first ran for the aldermanic presidency, La Guardia knew so little about mass transit that he avoided taking any position. After his election, however, he collected data from scores of urban systems around the country and concluded that the congeries of ill-coordinated lines, each operating under a different franchise arrangement with the city, should be replaced with a unified system under a city-operated board. Governor Miller had no intention of granting this kind of power to the city. Instead he backed a plan for state control. He specifically refused to offer any assurances that the 5-cent fare, an important symbol among city workers ("My policy," Mayor Hylan would say, "has been the preservation of democracy and decency and the retention of the five cent fare") would be maintained. Under Miller's proposal, districts that had never seen a street car would have more power over the city's subways than its riders. La Guardia warned the governor that this bill was not only unwise, but that it would also seal the fate of any Republican running for office downstate.[103]

When Miller refused to budge, an embittered La Guardia attacked the Republican governor. Storming about the city, carrying his message to the local political clubs, Fiorello denounced the leadership for catering to rural interests while abandoning the city. He called upon downstate Republicans to help him force the governor to change his mind, but the upstaters dominated the party and La Guardia lost his battle. By the time the bruising public fight was over he had also lost his party. Just a year before, he had been the bright hope of downstate Republicans. Now he was making strident attacks on GOP conservatives. The man who had campaigned the Northeast for Harding in 1920 sounded different just three months after the election, when he warned: "If . . . the reactionary spirit [continues] in control then I dread to think of what may happen. Not because of Bolshevism . . . but because of an honest and natural reaction to a policy of dishonesty."[104]

His fall from Republican grace was swift. Republican newspapers targeted the renegade. The publisher Frank Munsey, nursing a grudge from the time he praised La Guardia's efforts to raise the pay of police and firemen only to receive back a cutting note suggesting that he ought to raise the salaries of his own low-paid employees, now used his *Morning Herald* and the *Evening Sun* to portray La Guardia as a noisy, shallow, dangerous demagogue. In June, in the midst of La Guardia's fight with the party, the *Herald* printed a colorful piece under the headline "La Guardia Relative Granted a Divorce." The article told of Fiorello's sister-in-law's troubles with her husband. "Witnesses told of a raid . . . where . . . [Mr.] Stagliano was found in the company of an unnamed woman" and proceeded to menace the raiders with a pistol. The only name in this piece recognizable to most readers was of course that of the aldermanic president, who had nothing at all to do with the story. "La Guardia the petty and pitiful," taunted Munsey.[105]

By this time La Guardia had become a subject of honest pity in other quarters, and with good reason. He was living through an ordeal that makes one wonder how he had any mind for politics at all. But in a day when newspapers printed little about the private lives of politicians, not many New Yorkers could have surmised from the few oblique references in the news columns the personal tragedy that accompanied La Guardia's full-tilt campaign against the Old Guard Republicans.[106]

———

Following their marriage, Fiorello and Thea La Guardia had settled happily into their Greenwich Village apartment, enjoying a rewarding married life and friends with whom they shared a love for opera and music. Fiorello liked to don a large apron and direct kitchen operations while creating his special spaghetti sauce for such friends as Albert Spalding, Paul Windels, the artist Onorio Ruotolo, the sculptor Attilio Piccirilli, and the great operatic tenor Enrico Caruso. When the mood turned particularly jolly, Fiorello would take up his cornet and play for the group. In June of 1920, about a year after their marriage, Thea gave birth to a baby girl. The thirty-eight-year-old first-time father was delighted with his daughter and named her Fioretta Thea, for his maternal grandmother and his wife.

But from birth the baby was in delicate health, and there was an alarming change in Thea as well. Her color turned a pallid yellow, and she was very slow to recover her strength after the delivery. La Guardia scouted for a more healthful atmosphere than the congested tenement district in the Village. He borrowed money (this was the time when Craig accused him of passing his phone bills to the city) to buy a home in the Bronx, hoping that the fresh country air and higher altitude might strengthen the baby and restore Thea's health. He added a sun porch to the house. But she did not recover. By the end of the year he knew that his wife and daughter had the killing disease of the tenements, tuberculosis.

Trying to win back her own health while nursing her ill child drained the frail Thea. She had always appeared thin and delicate; now the strain overtaxed her and she suffered a breakdown. Fiorello rented a home in Huntington, Long Island, and placed Fioretta Thea in a hospital. Frantically running from his ill wife to his sick baby, Fiorello moved Thea to a sanitarium in Saranac Lake in the Adirondack Mountains. Then on May 3, 1921, the infant was rushed to Roosevelt Hospital. For five days doctors labored over her, but the disease had settled in the spine and the end closed in quickly. On May 8, 1921, Fioretta Thea died. Thea, by now deep in the grip of illness herself, proved too weak to accompany the baby to the cemetery. Fiorello went alone to bury his infant daughter and returned to nurse his dying wife. He sought the best medical help he could find, but her disease continued on its grim path, converting his beautiful bride into a shadow of herself, cruelly bending her smile into an agonized look of steady suffering.

All this occurred while La Guardia was presiding over the board of aldermen, clashing with Craig, and jousting with Miller. He continued to work at a high intensity, allowing himself no letup. With his endurance rubbed to the bone, La Guardia's rhetoric became sharper, more cutting. Adversity lent his politics a fierce focus. He denounced Miller for denying the city home rule, calling the governor's transit plan brazen, arrogant, and greedy. "Republicanism and Millerism are not convertible terms in this city. . . . Now that all the roads upstate have been built, most of the streams bridged, all public buildings constructed, . . . the greedy eyes of upstate political bosses are directed at New York City. The vicious traction bill is . . . what can be expected unless New York City defies this attitude and shows a united front this year." He accused Miller of taking orders from a coterie of politically connected money men and their lackeys.[107]

In March he had met with the Republican U.S. senator from New York, William Calder. After the meeting the respected senator announced that "if the Republican party does not make this little wop Mayor next fall, New York is going to Hell," but the clashes with Miller and the upstaters ("All you hear upstate," La Guardia told a meeting bitterly, "is 'We were born here, they were not' ") killed his chances in the party. By June, even Calder backed away from the "little wop," and in August 1921 the Republicans nominated Major Henry Curran, borough president of Manhattan, to run against Mayor Hylan.[108]

Thea was dying, but Fiorello could not forget politics. He wanted the mayoralty, and he wanted to deny it to the men who were cheating him out of an opportunity that he was promised in 1919. Although Miller had signed a repeal of the direct primaries, the system was still in effect for 1921, and Fiorello entered the Republican contest. Sam Koenig warned La Guardia that the party would destroy him if he went through with it. He should wait for a more opportune time. But with his responses coming from the extreme edge of his nerves, Fiorello wanted something he could fight. He could not combat the disease that took his daughter and was killing his wife, but he would fight the bosses. The city was not yet ready for an Italian mayor, Koenig told him. If he ran and lost he would be an outcast, unable to make even a bare living. "So long as I have five dollars in my pocket and some spaghetti, I'm all right, and if I can't get that, I've always got my army revolver," the overwrought La Guardia answered.[109]

La Guardia called his old crew together. But this time Andrews, Expresso, and Windels, convinced that he was making a mistake, refused the invitation. The party locked him out of its clubhouses. He could not get anyone with influence to back him. Desperately reaching for some victory in this season of loss, he turned as cynically political as any Tammany boss. He demanded support in the primaries from his appointed subordinates, purging from their city jobs those who refused to buckle under. Unfriendly newspapers denounced "our own little Stromboli" and "our little Garibaldi."[110]

The beleaguered La Guardia refused to give any quarter. He ran a lacerating campaign, calling attention to the outworn simplicities of the Millerite Republicans. He campaigned on his issues: home rule, efficient and honest government, modern mass transit, and public housing, appealing to Italians, Irish, Jews, and other ethnics for their support. The women were courted with promises of more appointments in a La Guardia administration. But when the votes were counted in September, the machine had won by more than three to one.[111]

The strain took its toll. By October his old army injury was causing excruciating pain. He could not even sit at his desk. Doctors advised him to have it operated on, but at first, too busy with his family and politics, he refused. Finally there was no choice; the abcess that had settled at the base of his spine forced him into the hospital and an operation. With Fiorello hospitalized and Thea in an upstate sanitarium, thieves broke into their University Avenue home, making off with the family silver and personal papers. His secretary, Marie Fisher, the one person who stuck by Fiorello no matter how erratic his behavior or his politics became, took over, handling the seemingly endless emergencies that kept cropping up.[112]

After he left the hospital, La Guardia cut his losses by falling in line behind the Republican nominee. Again he stumped the Italian districts, but this time there was an almost pathetic quality to the forced bravery of his appeals. "Good friends who have stood by me, don't worry about me; I'll get along. Just stand by me and vote the Republican ticket," he implored. He left Thea's sickbed upstate to campaign and make peace with the party. But the Republicans were routed in the mayoral election by the well-meaning, if somewhat befuddled, Mike Hylan.[113]

Death and dying continued to dominate these months. A few days after the election Fiorello's dear friend Enrico Caruso died in Naples. Representing Mrs. Caruso, La Guardia attended memorial services at the Metropolitan Opera House, where he presented a bust of the opera star by Onorio Ruotolo and spoke feelingly of the light that had gone out of their lives.

Two days later, on November 29, 1921, his own wife's flickering light gave out. The delicate woman who lent a softness and placidity to his life was dead.

"Ciccio" Giordano, who had been a friend for more than a decade, moved in with La Guardia during these last few weeks of Thea's life. Later he described the sight of the distraught La Guardia bent over the lifeless woman, sobbing pitifully, allowing the sorrow to work through him. Mayor Hylan brought some members of the City Hall staff to pay respects, but apparently accustomed to a more boisterous type of wake, the group offended Fiorello with their carefree style of commiseration. "What do you think this is," demanded a heartbroken La Guardia, flinging bottles across the room in a rage, "a German wedding?" For the second time that year he made the lonely trip back from the cemetery. M. R. Werner, who collaborated with Fiorello on his autobiography, wrote that this was "the greatest tragedy of La Guardia's life, one he was reluctant to mention even to his closest friends. Those who knew the couple . . . were always impressed with their deep love for each other and the gaiety of their enjoyment of it." Now, the soft joy was gone; what remained was the unrelieved sense of hard political purpose, but his career too had become unhinged.[114]

Enemies gloated. "La Guardia . . . wanted to be Mayor, and the people gave him their answer, now he is sore. He is," trilled his old nemesis Charles Craig, "the late lamented La Guardia." His losses overwhelmed him. Lowell Limpus writes that Fiorello paced the rooms of his house aimlessly, shutting himself off from friends. He picked up his cornet and then laid it aside, never to play it again. And according to some reports, in his melancholia he turned heavily to drink. "After ten years of lifting himself by his boot-straps," wrote J. F. Carter, "he was without ambition except to forget."*[115]

In a piquant symmetry, another exciting politician, this one tall, with a Harvard education and family wealth, also suffered a tragic derailment from a promising political career at this time. The former assistant secretary of the navy, who had served as a congressman from New York's Dutchess County and run for the vice presidency on the Democratic ticket in 1920, Franklin Delano Roosevelt, suffered a crushing blow when he was stricken with polio in August 1921 at Campobello. He sat lamely in a wheelchair unable to use his legs, with little hope that he would again capture the attention that once seemed so naturally to fall on his broad, handsome shoulders. Of three New York politicians born closely together, only one seemed still on track for a successful political career.

Short, slim, with electric blue eyes and black hair, James J. Walker cut a dashing figure in Albany. Garbed in custom shirts, made-to-order suits nipped at the waist to create the illusion of an athletic figure, silk cravats and matching overflow handkerchiefs, and pearl spats, and with an irrepressible twinkle in his eye, Walker enjoyed life with such insouciance and openness that others took pleasure in merely watching him. He delighted in sharing his exuberant good times with the public. Some thought of him as nothing more than a song-and-dance man who hit the Senate chamber "like a glad breeze." But this author of "In the Valley

---

* Some fifteen years after Thea's death, New York journalist J. F. Carter, writing under the pseudonym Jay Franklin, turned out a biography of La Guardia that alluded in two sentences to the boozing and brokenness of these years, asserting that La Guardia "drank heavily and was in danger of becoming a complete bum." When the book was published in 1937, Fiorello was mayor. Furious at the invasion of his private past, he fired off a telegram to the publisher, threatening a libel suit unless all books were withdrawn from circulation. The offending volumes were immediately recalled, and under La Guardia's watchful eye, clerks snipped out the sentences he objected to. Only then were they put back on the market.

Where My Sally Said Goodbye'' and "Will You Love Me in December as You Do in May,'' this hale fellow with the wonderful disposition and matching Irish wit, Beau James, clearly had a future. He had already caught the fancy of Governor Al Smith, who thought of him as mayoral material.[116]

It remained for Democratic Mayor Hylan to signal a future for La Guardia. "No more efficient, no fairer or more conscientious man ever held office in the City government,'' he said of the saddened Little Flower. Hylan wrote him a farewell letter, telling the departing aldermanic president, "There is no office in the gift of the people that is too good for you.'' In a fitting valedictory for the Italian band-leader's boy from Fort Whipple, Hylan welcomed La Guardia's Democratic successor as president of the Board of Aldermen by saying that he asked no more of him than that he live up to the honesty and efficiency of the round little man who had made his enemies respect him and his party disown him. As for Fiorello, he had tried politics and lost.[117]

CHAPTER 3

Times Are Changing: The Making of an Urban Progressive

---

1. "Men Can Be True to the People"

T HE battle between circumstance and will was fierce. Close to forty years old, his career sidelined and his family in the grave, La Guardia refused to dwell on his losses. Thea's death brought him a terrifying isolation. Acquaintances remarked upon the almost grim resolution with which he frolicked with the neighborhood children in his determination to squeeze some simple joy of human contact from this season of loss. He fought against depression and self-pity that would lock him into the past. Fioretta and Thea were shrouded in dignified silence. Even his private scrapbooks contain few remembrances of his wife and daughter and no mention of their tragic deaths. But their loss remained fresh pain for the rest of his life. Once, some twenty years after Thea's death, Fiorello, in the course of a private discussion with Charles C. Burlingham, turned to mimicking I. N. Phelps Stokes, a distinguished gentleman of exaggerated mannerisms. "Fiorello," Burlingham said slowly, "did you know that man's wife has been unable to recognize him, to know him, and he sat by her bedside for four or five years and he has never left her more than two or three hours at a time." Burlingham and La Guardia were very close, but it was the only time that Burlingham would hear about Thea. "That's the way it was with my wife," Fiorello said, and he always treated Stokes kindly after that. Most other friends never heard about her at all.[1]

Still, La Guardia was not a reflective man, and he found little comfort in the isolation of private thoughts. He had never been able to be alone. When he first became active in politics he would drag Cyd Bettelheim, Fannie Hurst, or some other young woman with him to strike meetings, political gatherings, or just to wander the city. It was not unusual for him to rouse a friend in the middle of the night to tour the streets with him. Even when he went shopping Fiorello wanted someone at his side. Lacking the introspective nature to reflect at length on the deeper meaning of his personal tragedy, he dealt with death and loss through action, not mourning, converting his private tragedy into a larger public purpose. Earlier in his life he had convinced himself that corrupt business interests had killed his father with their banal cupidity. Notwithstanding that this represented a highly exaggerated version of his father's army illness, for the rest of his life La Guardia took from this myth a powerful symbol for his fight against the profiteers. Even if it didn't happen, it very well could have because of the rotten way things operated. The twin deaths of Fioretta and Thea similarly became symbols of what could happen to the common people in a society too much concerned with the rich and mighty. A better society would have found a way of saving them.[2]

The passion and interest that other middle-aged men gave to their families he poured into his politics. "That man has a wife and three children," he would say of an opponent during a campaign. "I have no one left in all the world. If I am elected, I will devote myself solely to the job of . . . the people." The political defeat that so heartened his detractors steeled him in his insurgent instincts. He had spoken of "new politics" before, but such talk had been hedged about by the need to strike party deals. Now the party had abandoned him and he resolved to succeed on his own.[3]

Politics moved La Guardia beyond his sad season of loss. He was ambitious still to succeed in the important role he had defined for himself, more determined than ever to lead and serve on his own terms. His sense of civic possibility, never modest, took on an even larger scope. In a remarkable interview with Zoe Beckley of the *New York Evening Mail* shortly before retiring from the aldermanic presidency, La Guardia outlined his vision of a progressive New York. His words streaked with a new vulnerability, La Guardia spoke with a sad eloquence of the need to expand government.[4]

Beckley opened the interview by challenging La Guardia to tell if he could make more effective use of the city's million-dollar-a-day budget. "Could I! COULD I!" he boomed. "Say! First I would tear out about five square miles of filthy tenements, so that fewer would be infected with tuberculosis like that beautiful girl of mine, my wife, who died—and my baby—I would establish 'lungs' in crowded neighborhoods—a breathing park here, another there, based on the density of the population.

"Milk stations next! One wherever needed, where pure cheap milk could be bought for babies and mothers learn how to take care of them. . . . I would keep every child in school to the eighth grade at least, well fed and in health. Then we could provide widow's pensions and support enough schools for every child in New York on what we saved from reformatories and penal institutions." An active department of markets would check on the quality of food and merchandise sold in the city and post a list of fair prices protecting the consumer, squeezing out the profiteers.

He decried the censorship of films. "Why? Say, what do you suppose the men behind this censorship law care how long a kiss lasts or whether the villain uses a gun or an axe? . . . The motion picture is the most marvelous educator in the world today. And if films are shown that will teach people the truth about government, about war, about civics, about prisons and factories and tenements and every phase of life that touches their rights and their happiness there will be trouble," the kind of trouble that La Guardia welcomed.

He did not succumb to small enthusiasms. His reform agenda included more voting rights and a larger voice for the people, on the progressive assumption that the people's common sense would bring the good society. But he wanted more. He wanted a city, La Guardia told the interviewer, not only better run but happier, more beautiful. "I would provide more music and beauty for the people, more parks and more light and air and all the things the framers of the Constitution meant when they put in the phrase, 'Life, liberty and the pursuit of happiness.' "

Beckley wanted to know if all of this was possible. How could it be achieved within constitutional limits? "Nowadays," Fiorello replied, "we invoke the Constitution for the protection of the few and the destruction of the many. We protect the owner of the tenement, but we do not protect the man and woman and little child in that tenement whose lives are being taken by disease. They have no case, no chance for life," cried La Guardia. "There's money enough in this city for everybody in it to be well fed, housed, and clothed, educated and happy. A million a day spent on New York! And what do we buy with it *for the people*?" The need was for political will, intelligence, and honesty, not money. "I tell you, men can be true to the people and still hold public places . . . ," he declared. Why, decades earlier a proposal to establish municipal milk stations would have been greeted with howls that the radicals were trying to break up the home. Old fogies would have feared for the end of sacred mother-love, but milk stations strengthened the home and sweetened home life. Government must accommodate change; it cannot ignore progress. "Once landlords were not compelled to heat their tenements. In years to come it will be the law to refrigerate them in the summer . . . life depends upon it, for the 99 per cent who cannot go to Newport." Employing an analogy that would become popular in the New Deal, he compared the needs of urban Americans to those of a nation at war. The battle for decent social conditions, he suggested, deserved no less attention and affected no fewer people than the need to support troops on the battlefield. "For the price of a single military attack in battle all the babies in New York could be properly fed!"[4]

Even La Guardia, however, had to doubt whether his modern municipal community would ever get beyond the newspapers. For the moment he was the least attractive of all political commodities, an ambitious politician out of office, without party backing and with powerful enemies.

Before attending to his political future, La Guardia turned to the immediate problem of earning a living. He joined a new law firm named La Guardia, Sapinsky and Amster. His partners no doubt anticipated a large volume of political business from Fiorello's connections, and La Guardia did attract such clients as the Free State of Fiume, a newly formed Italian movie company, and some New York city business. More often than they would have wished, however, his associates found their partner with the connections and the broad cowboy hat accepting cases that did not bring in enough to keep them in pinstripes.[5]

Gradually he began to seek out old friends, bringing them home for meals and talk that invariably turned to politics. By March 1922, La Guardia was appearing before civic and political groups, making the rounds of neighborhoods, stirring the political waters with progressive programs and strong denunciation of both parties. But even he had no idea of what his next step would be. At Sam Koenig's urging and Thea's gentle prodding, he had left Congress for a different political track in city politics, but Thea was dead and Koenig no longer supported him. What was there for him in a party led by reactionaries like Governor Miller? And above all he knew that former aldermanic presidents had a short shelf life. Recognition faded rapidly. He had to get back in office quickly if he wanted to maintain his political momentum.[6]

While newspapers and reform clubs mentioned his gubernatorial possibilities or suggested a return to Congress, his party irregularity and his repeated clashes with Miller made the professionals wary. With troublesome Fiorello out of the way why should they bring him back? And without party backing, without the help of the network of canvassers and ward heelers a La Guardia race would probably be futile. Party workers arranged for the halls, publicized the speeches, provided the patronage, and above all delivered the votes. All well and good for La Guardia to paint a better future, but without a party to attend to the practical matters of a campaign, such a contest would be brutal and most likely quixotic.

Clearly, if he was to continue in politics, La Guardia needed a support base outside of the party, and he found it in the Italian immigrant community. While the population of Italians in the city had grown to well over 1 million, Italians held not a single district leadership in either party. If they wanted political power they would have to fight for it; they needed a leader, and La Guardia needed a following. Four days after Thea's death, on December 3, 1921, the Kings County League of Italian American clubs elected La Guardia honorary president. Similar clubs sprang up in the other boroughs, and even in a number of upstate communities that had significant Italian populations, all uniting behind La Guardia as their symbol of emerging political power. By March of 1922 these groups had banded together into the League of Italian-American Clubs, committed to reviving the political fortunes of their La Guardia, whom they hailed as their Napoleon preparing to return from exile.[7]

With these clubs as his base, La Guardia turned to the task of getting his message out to the electorate. Lacking party support, he had to appeal directly to the voters on the issues through the press. Since before the turn of the century daily newspaper circulation had grown steadily as aggressive new press lords avidly pursued increased readership through sensational exposés, revealing investigative reports, special women's pages, and comic strips. Newspapers became a daily staple in many households, a perfect vehicle for a politician with independent designs who sought a medium for his message. "The press, Watson, is a most valuable institution," Sherlock Holmes tells his companion in "The Adventure of the Six Napoleons," "if only you know how to use it."

Fiorello mastered its use by feeding the press's appetite for colorful stories and access to popular figures. No politician learned to exploit the press more effectively. Reporters called on him for an opinion or an interview at all hours, confident of good copy and trenchant commentary. He obliged their need for a show, throwing out charges of corruption and political chicanery, understanding well how the whiff of scandal and controversy was the common coin of the new journalism. If a reporter needed help writing a story, he pitched in with that too. And they reciprocated. Few politicians *in office* attracted as much press coverage as private citizen La Guardia. To appreciate the exaggerated dramatics, the willingness to appear faintly ridiculous, and the heated rhetoric that came to typify La Guardia, it helps to understand that very often he played to the balcony, aiming for the headlines.[8]

To the dismay of his new law partners, political planning increasingly absorbed Fiorello's time and interest. "Driving himself almost vindictively," wrote Lowell Limpus, La Guardia thrust himself into public attention. By the spring of 1922 newspapers were carrying La Guardia's opinions on almost everything. He championed the League of Women Voters, supported a bonus for soldiers, took a role in the Salvation Army drive, and delivered talks on a wide range of issues. The public must hear more symphony music. Jazz he judged "discordant, strident ear racking noises . . . typical of barbarous tendencies" that no normal person could enjoy. He called for higher wages for government-paid laborers, for the use of U.S. Army airplanes to deliver the mail, and for the municipal authorities to sell ice. Anywhere an audience could be gathered he would speak, attacking Republicans or enthusiastically pressing some new idea: municipal control over utilities, a new system of snow removal, milk stations, infant care centers, rent control.[9]

La Guardia made yet another adjustment before setting out anew on the electoral field. When he had been in Congress before, he had not coordinated his own crusades with the established reform elements in the legislature. This time he planned to play as part of a team, signaling his intentions by speaking in the name of "the progressive wing of the Republican Party and the new school of politics."[10]

Clearly La Guardia was preparing the ground for a campaign, but for which office? No one knew better than La Guardia that had he been elected mayor the year before, he would have been frustrated working with unsympathetic upstate legislators and a hostile governor. The New York State governorship was more inviting. Nothing would be sweeter than to defeat Miller and break his hold on the party. But how likely was it for a downstate Italian American with no party support to be elected? Congress was yet another possibility. While Washington reminded him of his earlier difficulties as a loner in a body governed by the will of contending groups, if he returned now he would work as part of the Progressive bloc. His old seat, however, was back under Tammany control, and it would take more than a short campaign to win it back.

Others also took an interest in La Guardia's career; the colorful press magnate and dabbler in reform politics, William Randolph Hearst, for one. The tall Californian, notorious already for the ego that Orson Welles would make famous in his classic portrayal of "Citizen Kane," had built a newspaper empire and owned a motion picture company, but he was known to hanker after political office, especially the governor's mansion. With his own power based in the Democratic party, Hearst had nothing to lose by advancing Republican La Guardia for the governorship in 1922. He respected the insurgent fireplug and anticipated benefits from roiling Republican waters and dividing the opposition party. La Guardia, sufficiently aware of Hearst's role in New York politics to enter this alliance with his eyes open, decided that a relationship with the powerful publisher could be useful.

Hearst's own plans for office encountered formidable obstacles, not the least of which was his long-standing political feud with Al Smith. The publisher had offended Smith back in 1917 by insulting the Tammany loyalist's political sponsor, "Big Tom" Foley. Smith and Foley in turn blocked Hearst's bid for the Democratic mayoral nomination in 1917, and in 1918 Smith himself took the governorship, again cutting short Hearst's hopes. Soon after Smith took office, the publisher attacked the governor for his Tammany ties and, although the connection was a bit strained, for contributing to the death of poor children through a rise in the price of milk. Denouncing Hearst's papers as "mud gutter gazettes," Smith called the publisher a man without "a drop of good, clean, pure red blood in his whole body," adding for good measure, "And I know the color of his liver, it is whiter . . . than the driven snow."

Now in 1922, Smith, who had been defeated in the Harding landslide of 1920, buried Hearst in the contest for the gubernatorial nomination. The publisher's supporters then confided that their candidate could be persuaded to accept the senatorial nomination. Smith trampled that one last hope by making it clear that he would not run on or support a ticket with Hearst on it. Exit Hearst.[11]

In the course of this enchanting political minuet, when Hearst still thought that he might be a candidate and benefit from a split Republican party, he offered La Guardia a regular column in his *Evening Journal*. We have seen what happened with Hearst in the fall of 1922, but Fiorello's fortunes were not tied to Hearst's. La Guardia was as calculating as the millionaire press lord. If Hearst wanted to weaken the Republicans, La Guardia wanted publicity and broad exposure. Threatening to oppose a "reactionary Republican platform" and contest Governor Miller's nomination, La Guardia, in late June, issued his own "Proposed Planks for the Republican State Platform." Then he elaborated on each of these ideas in the *Evening Journal* in a series of more than fifty articles developing the themes for his "new politics," beginning in July and stretching into the election season. The *New York Times* dubbed La Guardia's call for a "new politics" a "noble and Hearstian" program, but the jibe was unfair. La Guardia's program was woven from a combination of his own ideas about city life and traditional reform politics. And they were his own. Indeed, the ideas in these articles formed the basic La Guardia political text for the remainder of his life. The rest of his political career is commentary and tactics.[12]

The crusader in politics lives off his villains, and the columns begin with a set of villains: the old style of politics and the reactionaries who had captured the soul of the Republican party. The GOP, asserted La Guardia, had once been a party with principles that extended beyond attracting wealth and votes. It had once stood for something, with giants like Abraham Lincoln and Theodore Roosevelt; it was now embarrassed by the likes of Miller and Harding. He adopted Roosevelt's call for "social and industrial justice" as his progressive credo and quoted Lincoln as his source for industrial populism: "The state belongs to the people. Its resources, its business and its laws should be utilized, maintained or altered in whatever manner will best promote general interest. . . . [S]ome have labored, and others without labor enjoyed a large proportion of the fruits. This is wrong. . . ." These words, La Guardia puckishly instructed his readers, were not from some radical Russian or German but from the Great Emancipator. "Surely no one would deny the Americanism of Abraham Lincoln." But then, contemporary Republicans "know as much about the teachings of Abraham Lincoln," he zinged, "as Henry Ford [who gave wide circulation to the notorious anti-Semitic forgery, "The Protocols of the Elders of Zion"] knows about the Talmud."[13]

The matter of economic justice, La Guardia insisted, represented the most important political issue of the day. The political debate focusing on tariffs, contracts, and banks constituted a sideshow, a dangerous distraction from the main issues. "There are no more political issues," he wrote. The critical issues of the time were economic. "There must be an economic readjustment" to guarantee that the fruits of America's amazing prosperity were properly distributed. Quoting the "immortal Lincoln," he wrote: "Capital is the fruit of labor and could never have existed if labor had not existed. Labor is the superior of capital and deserves much higher consideration." The rights of people stood higher than the rights of property, "Only a well fed, well housed, well schooled people can enjoy the blessings of liberty."[14]

La Guardia argued that the wage earner must not be viewed as just another part of the production process. "Human labor cannot be treated like merchandise or chattels." Labor represented the workingman's investment in business, his human capital "of life devoted to work." This contribution was as important as the entrepreneur's and government had to guarantee it a fair return, but as between labor and capital, one side was reaping all the benefits. Moreover, while government did not prevent businesses from closing shop when they failed to make profits, it issued injunctions to prevent labor from striking for improvements. No society supporting so one-sided a system, La Guardia suggested provocatively, had the right to expect loyalty from its lower classes. Drawing on a network of social workers who fed him their special studies and reports, La Guardia showed that the exploitative mentality was not limited to the private sector. Thousands of government employees drew wages well below the poverty level, with some families earning no more than $840 a year. Laborers on the New York city payroll were bringing home $5 a day. The issue was not capital versus labor, but rather fairness and decency.[15]

La Guardia rooted these demands in the American political tradition. He ignored the work of such iconoclasts as Charles Beard, whose *Economic Interpretation of the Constitution* had been published close to a decade before. He had no interest in challenging the essential fairness of the Constitution itself or the private motives of its authors. Changing times and changing conditions, he said simply, required a fresh look at the Constitution, not a new constitution. The classic text written for an agricultural society where most families lived on easily acquirable property must be interpreted in the light of modern industrial and urban society whose needs for governmental protection were more extensive and complex than those of a string of rural communities. Legislators must construct from the basic law a broader authority for government and break free from the nation's conservative harness to create laws fit for the times.[16]

Several of La Guardia's columns provided deft little lectures on local government, offering readers a realistic picture of urban politics and the inner workings of the political process. He reminded city voters that misapportioned representation made an upstate vote twice as important as one from New York City. "Figure Mr. Voter, figure," he bade, foreshadowing a later Supreme Court decision, as he suggested that this violated the equal representation requirement of the Constitution. He exhorted voters to clean out corruption and the political machines upon which it throve. From this point forward he played the insurgent to the hilt, making his attacks not only on the issues and Tammany, but on the entire system of conventional politics. "Don't jeer boys," he scoffed, "the reactionaries are dying."[17]

As Americans prepared to banish poverty from their vocabulary amidst the prosperity of the Roaring Twenties, La Guardia went steadfastly against the grain of the times, calling attention to those who were not prospering. "The American people are having a hard time of it. The American breakfast of cereal, ham and eggs, potatoes, rolls and coffee has entirely disappeared from the breakfast table," he wrote. "Every daily paper contains recipes and advice on how to get along with less food. . . . The American workers are now almost on the meatless diet of the Russian peasant and if the monopolies of meat and grain and foods generally are continued, the American people will soon be on the rice diet of the Chinese coolie." His concerns painfully extracted from his own experience, he instructed his readers that "the first duty of the state is to the child." Dismissing the bogeyman of paternalism as shallow and cruel in a government that refused care for mothers and children while offering bounteous grants for farmers to create better breeds of cows and pigs, he urged citizens to demand infant health stations, free school lunches, low-priced government-certified milk, and municipally regulated terminal and retail markets. Families in distress must be offered state assistance. "In free America, big, rich, powerful, there should not be a hungry woman or child. . . . The greatness of a nation . . . will not be measured by . . . its cannons—but by the cheerfulness and ring of its children's laughter."[18]

And, he urged, give a care for beauty. Open the sky by tearing down the elevated railroad tracks and the old unsafe tenements. Replace the els with underground rapid transit and the tenements with government-assisted housing amidst cheerful environments. Offer open-air music concerts, create a music and arts center, scatter green parks and playgrounds among the cement streets. Remove discrimination. Make the Lower East Side as clean and healthful as the Upper West Side.

An ambitious, government-sponsored construction program to achieve these improvements would do more than provide the city with a spanking new infrastructure. By pouring money into these projects when unemployment was high and cutting allocations when the private sector was healthy, the government could exert some control over the economy, regulating swings of unemployment and economic unpredictability. A flexible construction program of new hospitals, public housing, bridges, parks, tunnels, and boulevards would buffer the demoralizing cycles of uncertainty that plagued urban workers. The city would be made spectacular and the people would live happily.

And the projects would pay for themselves over the years. New York would need fewer homes for the tubercular ill, fewer poorhouses, fewer jails. The lives of the aged and the indigent sick would be enriched. "Why is it that in times of war a shipping board will have thousands of ships bringing munitions . . . and carry men to kill and die at a cost of hundreds of millions and in times of peace

89

these same ships are permitted to rust and rot at anchor instead of carry food, clothes and supplies to the needy and hungry. Think!"[19]

Think indeed, but no thoughtful politician had yet devised the strategy for translating into reality the potpourri of deceptively simple proposals that La Guardia laid out. The *New York Times* wondered why La Guardia's program had not included "municipal ice cream sherbet at cost, or preferably, free." At best, his agenda represented an optimistic faith in the ability of government to forge a better life for the citizen, but contradictions abounded. He opposed government intrusiveness and yet he demanded greater government responsibility over a wide range of economic and social matters. But the key to La Guardia's program did not lie in the intellectual consistency of his ideas. He was a politician, an activist, not a political philosopher. He offered no elegant new weave of reform ideas. What he offered was a deep commitment to progressive politics in conservative times, and his ambition to project these ideas on the political stage.[20]

The *Journal* pieces, along with his many appearances before political clubs, and the growing number of Italian organizations that were pushing his candidacy all aroused interest in his intentions. For his part La Guardia did not yet know exactly what he wanted, but he began by threatening to fight for the Republican gubernatorial nomination if Miller was renominated. Plainly, he could not win the office, but if he carried out his threat to form insurgent Republican clubs throughout the state he could fragment the party and assure Miller's defeat. Party chief Koenig recognized La Guardia's strong cards. Bad enough to face a popular candidate like Smith; Republicans would only compound their handicap by dividing their own forces. Distasteful as it might be they would have to negotiate with the pesky progressive. In late August Koenig was dispatched to work out a deal with La Guardia and remove him from the gubernatorial stakes.

Fiorello emerged from the discussions with the Republican nomination for Isaac Siegel's East Harlem congressional seat (Siegel was awarded a judgeship) in the congested 20th C.D. The district was a run-down area with a large Italian and Jewish working-class population, a place where La Guardia's progressive politics could find comfortable nurture. Not one to trade away an advantage easily, La Guardia also extracted a pledge from Koenig that so long as he did not contest Miller's nomination he was free to run on his own platform. Not a bad deal for someone who just a few months back had been relegated to obscurity by his opponents. But it was transparently a deal, an agreement worked out by the bosses in the back rooms, leading the *New York Times* to write, "Some of our keenest lawyers hold that Mr. Koenig could be indicted under an old New York statute for the technical seduction of Mr. Hearst's apprentice."[21]

The *Times* again misread the relationship between the political insurgent and the sensationalist publisher. La Guardia was the one who stood for something in politics, and it was Hearst who dallied in causes as the mood hit him. Moreover, La Guardia had managed to make the best of the misalliance by coming back to politics in a district suited to his temperament and politics. He had played a delicate game well. If there was a shadow over all of this, it was his willingness to be bought off in the old style. For all the talk of a "new politics" without bosses, La Guardia wrangled his nomination from the party in a private room out of the sight of the populace on the basis of a deal with the machine. His supporters were left to reflect how close to the surface of La Guardia the progressive reformer stood La Guardia the political opportunist.

The nomination achieved, La Guardia faced a three-way race for the congressional seat against Tammany Democrat Henry Frank and Socialist labor lawyer William Karlin. In these circumstances he immediately disassociated himself from Miller and the rest of the party. "I don't fit in at all with the average so-called 'Republican' in the East. I am a Progressive."[22]

The three candidates differed little on the issues. Each favored modification of Prohibition, a minimum wage, old age pensions, the development of public utilities, expanded rights for labor, and a lower tariff. The strongest argument La Guardia could at first make for his candidacy was to tell the voters that Karlin, whom he respected, "would represent to the best of his ability some of the very ideas which I represent," but the Socialist would go to Washington as a lone voice. "I shall go there to work with the progressive group represented by such men as Senators Borah, Johnson, Brookhart and La Follette, all Republicans." Two weeks before the end of the campaign, La Guardia did not have a bad word to say about Frank either. And the worst Frank would say about his Republican opponent was to call him a "charming interloper." When Karlin issued a stiffly worded challenge to a debate, La Guardia sent back a disarming note: "My dear Bill, While it is true that we are both candidates for Congress I hardly see the necessity for making your letter so cold and formal. Why, bless your heart, of course I'll debate with you."[23]

Marked by gentle banter, the contest seemed limited to harvesting endorsements. Fiorello attracted the liberal press. Mayor Hylan crossed party lines to praise him, and Hiram Johnson, the respected California senator who ran with Theodore Roosevelt on the Progressive ticket in 1912, wired, "I know La Guardia and if I had a thousand votes in his district I would cast them all for him." For the Italian community, crowed the *Bolletino della Sera*, "Major La Guardia has no need of an expressed program." His appeal rested on different grounds.[24]

La Guardia's campaign was going well, so well that Tammany was driven to desperate tactics. On October 30, Jewish voters received a postcard signed by "The Jewish Committee."

The most important office in this country for Judaism is the Congressman. Our flesh and blood are united with our own on the other side of the ocean. Only through our Congressman can we go to their rescue.

There are three candidates who are seeking your vote: one is Karlin the atheist, the second is the Italian La Guardia, who is a pronounced anti-semite and Jew hater.

Be careful how you vote.

Our candidate is Henry Frank, who is a Jew with a Jewish heart, and who does good for us. Therefore it is up to you and your friends to vote for our friend and beloved one, Henry Frank for Congressman.[25]

Frank had already twitted La Guardia for making racial appeals to Italians, and it certainly would not have been out of character for the Little Flower to claim votes on ethnic grounds. But Frank's postcard campaign was different; it misrepresented La Guardia's position egregiously, attacking him on false charges. A few days later Frank turned over to police a letter purportedly from a secret Italian society warning him to stay out of La Guardia's way. Realizing that this set of attacks could cost him dearly, La Guardia resolved to slam back, sending a squad of carefully instructed speakers through the Jewish sections to deny the allegations. Then he personally swept through the district to refute Frank's charges and remind voters of his fight to punish anti-Semitism in Poland after the war. Curiously, he never considered disclosing his own Jewish ancestry. Instead he turned to an antic stratagem. The "Daughters of Italy" (led by Marie Fisher!) began passing out "An Open Letter to Henry Frank," printed in Yiddish. While Major La Guardia regretted the injection of the ethnic issue, it was too late for regrets. "Very well then. . . . I hereby challenge you to publicly and openly debate the issues of the campaign, THE DEBATE TO BE CONDUCTED BY YOU AND ME ENTIRELY IN THE YIDDISH LANGUAGE—the subject of the debate to be, 'Who is Best Qualified to Represent All the People of the Twentieth Congressional District.' "[26]

The unexpected response flummoxed Frank. He shot back a strident and unbecoming response. "A challenge from you with your well known anti-Semitic tendencies to debate in Yiddish is an insult and an affront to the Jewish electorate in our community. You are certainly not qualified to represent the people and you will know it on Election Day when the people send you back, bag and baggage, to your little cottage and sun-parlor on University Avenue in the Bronx." At the reference to the sun parlor that he had built for his beloved Thea, Fiorello flew into a rage. This "was as low, and unmanly an act as a man can resort to. I was compelled to move out of my district and purchase a house with a sun parlor in an effort to save the life of my poor wife." Frank had gone too far. His crude response offended many voters. This was only one of Frank's problems; another was the fact that he could not speak Yiddish.

92

He never showed up for the debate. Fiorello made a show of waiting for him. Then he dashed across the neighborhood giving speeches in quite passable Yiddish. "The rabbis themselves led the applause," wrote Lowell Limpus as the Little Flower ridiculed Frank's abuse and his claim to the Jewish vote as his birthright. "After all," he said, winking at the crowd, "is he looking for a job as a *shamas* [synagogue caretaker] or does he want to be elected Congressman?"[27]

The election was close. Tammany turned out the Democratic vote, and La Guardia later charged that it was assisted by disaffected Republicans. Determined to guard against irregularities, he scurried from poll to poll with a gang of supporters and a special detail of police assigned by Mayor Hylan, passing out boxes of candy to the women poll workers and checking on the balloting. It took two days to tabulate the final results. Karlin ran well behind previous Socialist totals, and he fell out of the race early. Frank decisively defeated La Guardia in the Jewish districts, but not by enough to offset Italian support, which provided the margin of victory.

La Guardia won by only a couple of hundred votes, and a postelection investigation narrowed the difference even more, but he had pulled another of his hairbreadth upsets. Frank filed an official protest charging that "bands of La Guardia's supporters intimidated the inspectors and were led by La Guardia himself. In one particular instance one of the watchers was threatened with bodily harm by Mr. La Guardia." It provided a charming turn, Tammany complaining of undue voting pressures! It was equally clear that La Guardia had fought for his political career by taking on Tammany at its own level and that in a very short time he had put together a remarkable personal organization and a hard-nosed victory.[28]

---

2. The Spirit of the Times

T HE difference between the tortured moralism of progressive Democrat Woodrow Wilson and the hearty superficiality of conservative Republican Warren Harding offers a measure of the changed atmosphere in the country as La Guardia prepared to return to Washington for the Sixty-eighth Congress. The changes that La Guardia himself had undergone did not relate well with the national trend. Nominally a Republican, he was held in suspicion by his own party, and he trusted Sam Koenig and the clubhouse boys even less. He had had his way with them and he had little respect for them. The fact that Nathan Miller had been thoroughly thrashed by Al Smith made La Guardia even more contemptuous of a group that had refused his advice and paid the price. He brought to Congress fresh personal wounds that placed a bitter filter before his perceptions of American good times. Like a surrealist painter he saw the same elements that other Americans saw but the scale and relationship were bizarrely different. While others boasted of the glittering dollar decade, he cried for attention to the underside of American prosperity. His constituents were poor. Their housing was uncomfortable. They opposed Prohibition. They carried a large sympathy for Socialist politics. And in this period of powerful American nativism and conformity, they were as exotic a mixture of races and nationalities as any neighborhood in the world.

This time, however, La Guardia was going to Congress as part of a group. A handful of western progressives like Robert La Follette, George Norris, Hiram Johnson, William Borah, and a few others shared the perception that all was not well in America. The only easterner among these "sons of the wild jackass," La Guardia told his constituents that these reformers "had not only the desire to do good but the absolute power to do it." Tired of carping on the sidelines, they had no intention of serving as some ignored voice of conscience. With the Sixty-eighth Congress closely split between Republicans and Democrats, the reformers hoped to control the balance. "How long," La Guardia asked an audience in the Institutional Synagogue of New York City, "will the people be satisfied by simply casting a protest vote to the party out of control as against the party in control?" The small farmers of the Midwest were already voting along progressive lines. He intended to add to this group the industrial workers of the East to mold a national party of the disaffected.[29]

Washington's progressive caucus was led by the lion-maned Wisconsin Senator Robert La Follette. Almost alone he had opposed the "war to make the world safe for democracy," and now with the same austere integrity he rejected the conservative ethos of the "new prosperity." Born in Primrose, Wisconsin, in 1855, "Battle Bob" served three terms as a Republican congressman before being elected governor of Wisconsin in 1900. Working closely with a group of university professors, he gave new meaning to the idea of the "state college," utilizing academic experts from the University of Wisconsin to develop a legislative reference library and craft modern policies in labor relations, political reform, railroad regulation, and tax policy. La Follette transformed Wisconsin into a national laboratory for social legislation and experimentation that was hailed around the nation as a model for progressive policy in the early years of the new century.

The flinty La Follette wielded the tools of his trade with a fine flair; he could mesmerize a crowd with a stem-winder, exploit his patronage powers, sometimes even ruthlessly, and oversimplify issues, at times shamelessly. Reflecting his prairie past, La Follette's progressivism was scaled to a rural vision of America. With other rural reformers he refused to consider that million-acre bonanza farms and centralized world agriculture markets were shrinking the role for the small farm entrepreneur. Elected to the Senate in 1905, he became a spokesman for easy solutions to complex systemic problems and frequently personalized the difficulties of modern life into a story of villains and good guys. Later, liberal historians would characterize La Follette as a man of "ruthless simplicities," but John Dos Passos, closer to the spirit of the twenties than commentators two score years removed, viewed La Follette's career in a different light. In his masterpiece trilogy, *U.S.A.*, Dos Passos, sharing La Follette's sense of an America divided between the exploiters and the exploited, wrote admiringly, in his uniquely styled prose, that after the bosses threatened to take care of the senator's career, "the farmers of Wisconsin and the young lawyers and businessmen just out of school

> *took care of him*
> *and elected him governor three times*
> *and then to the United States Senate,*
> *where he worked full time making long*
> *speeches full of statistics, struggling to save democratic government,*
> *to make a farmers' and small businessmen's commonwealth, lonely with*
> *his back to the wall, fighting corruption and big business and high*
> *finance and trusts and combinations of combinations and the miasmic*
> *lethargy of Washington.*[30]

Fiorello La Guardia was part of a corporal's guard of progressives drawn to the gallant senator with the glistening gray pompadour. He lauded the Wisconsin tribune's courage, gifted statesmanship, and large heart. Everybody was against him, La Guardia wrote, "except the voters." The rift over the Great War had healed and La Guardia was won over. "Pacifism is patriotism," he told a reporter. La Guardia went to Washington for the meeting of the Conference for Progressive Political Action in the winter of 1922. He joined some sixty-five legislators to shape an agenda for the coming congressional session and to weigh the advisability of forming a third party. These were not "wild-eyed radicals," La Guardia reported, "but serious minded men . . . with definite ideas of what shall be done."[31]

The simple solutions and the vivid villains of the rustic progressives completely won over the lone New York member of the conference. Before a Gotham audience he explained that the answer to unfair consumer prices lay in checking the infernal middlemen and profit seekers, the bankers, grain elevator operators, transporters, and investors. "Banks, loans, railroads, profiteering and speculating," he asserted, "we can abolish most of these." But the solution was unrealistic. Could the U.S. economy operate without middlemen? Could the farmers revert to a barter economy, forgoing borrowed money, storage facilities, and railroads? Were farmer businessmen who bought up property and seed in the hope of producing for profit any less speculators than the others? Once before, La Guardia had rejected the idea that farm prices should be artificially supported, because higher prices would come out of the pockets of urban consumers. This time he adopted the idea that profit should go to the prime producer, rather than the one determined by the

95

open market. His motivation was not socialism so much as sentimentalism, the idea that the sweating farmer deserved more and therefore the United States must reconstruct a simple economy that would distribute profits and benefits on the basis of the moral worth of the producer.[32]

Earlier Progressives had made strenuous efforts to study, analyze, and understand social complexity, but the new reformers settled upon simple solutions and La Guardia joined them. "Government," he told an audience "is simply housekeeping on a large scale. There isn't a mother in New York City trying to make both ends meet but can tell you all about government." With the Progressives he believed that a small ring of fine men and women would change the nation, and he poured his energies into the effort.[33]

In the months before taking his seat in the House, La Guardia helped the poor lead a meat strike in Harlem, went to Buffalo to fight for the Amalgamated Clothing Workers Union, organized a city hall demonstration for rent controls, and headed a committee to raise funds for the relief of fire victims. "So," he wrote to a Veteran's Bureau official in his unique style, "after much heralding and publicity of systematizing the work of the Veteran's Bureau, we find that it has been so scientifically systematized, as not to be able to find a veteran's papers! While I am writing you, and you are writing me, and the District Manager of District No. 2 is writing you, and a corps of clerks is looking for the papers, this veteran, unable to work, and on his reduced pension is not able to get enough to eat! It's a damn shame." So was the immigration bill being developed in the House, with quotas that were "solely for the purpose of excluding Italian and Jewish immigrants." And in an address at Erasmus Hall in Queens he tore into the telephone company for a disgraceful rate structure, bellowing, "You pay if you don't use and you pay if you do use, and the company gets it coming and going, and the public service commission is there to give it to them." His theoretical naivete notwithstanding, this was his most effective theme: an insistence on fairness and justice for the common citizen.[34]

When La Guardia learned that the United States Shipping Board invited a select list of VIPs to participate in the trial run of a refitted World War I troop ship, he commanded the board: "Invite the same number of persons who were passengers in 1917 and 1918 in dark crowded, uncomfortable holds of the ship and now permanently disabled and lingering in Walter Reed Hospital, but a few blocks from your offices in Washington, and in about the hospitals along the Adriatic coast. Make them the recipient of your engraved invitations and give them the opportunity for enjoying a bit of change from their dreary hospital life of the past five years and the benefit of the ocean air, while your experts are testing the engine." It was unfair to make such a commotion over a regular practice, but La Guardia bristled at the notion that VIPs were better citizens than soldiers just because they were rich.[35]

The Sixty-eighth Congress convened in December 1923, with the progressive bloc determined to liberalize House rules and loosen the seniority system. Controlling the balance of voting, they held up the election of a Republican Speaker until the leadership agreed to discuss their demands. But except for minor reforms, the discussions yielded no permanent changes, and La Guardia learned the cost of such challenges. Earlier, La Guardia had written a colleague, "I know you will look after me on the Committee on Committees. I want to make Judiciary." He was refused his request.[36]

This first contest was a good barometer of the rest of the session. As the United States celebrated its postwar economic prosperity, reformers' nagging demands for attention to those Americans who had been left out of the good times were viewed as an unwelcome damper on the festivities. With Congress passing a discriminatory immigration restriction law, the secretary of the treasury drawing up a tax bill that cut taxes on the rich, and the president vetoing a veteran's bonus bill, progressive reform was more out of place in the age of Warren Harding than ever.

The amiable former senator from Ohio, Warren G. Harding, who ushered in the era of "Republican Ascendancy," captured well the prevailing spirit of a retrenching America, even as he recognized his own inadequacies. He once confided to Nicholas Murray Butler, "I am not fit for this office and should never have been here." Although he was a genuinely charitable man, Harding's failings of character were monumental. Alice Roosevelt Longworth, who grew up in the White House during her father Theodore's tenure, could not contain her disgust at what Harding had done to the presidency. On one visit to the White House she found the study filled with the Ohioan's cronies, the table piled with cards and rows of poker chips, trays with tall glasses "and every imaginable brand of whiskey" (during Prohibition!), the air rancid with cigar smoke in a gambling den atmosphere of "waistcoat unbuttoned, feet on the desk, and spitoons alongside." Harding was not a bad man, she concluded. "He was just a slob." Perhaps only good breeding kept Mrs. Longworth from discussing Harding's penchant for adultery behind the back stairs.[37]

He was pitifully unprepared for the job. "Almost unbelievably ill-informed," wrote one journalist. Another newspaper reporter was struck dumb when the president tried to explain to him the logic behind the high protective tariff: "We should adopt a protective tariff of such a character as will help the struggling industries of Europe to get on their feet." "John," he once disclosed to a secretary, "I can't make a damn thing out of this tax problem. I listen to one side and they seem right and . . . I talk to the other side and they seem just as right, and here I am where I started. I know somewhere there is a book that will give me the truth, but hell, I couldn't read the book." Harding's know-nothing attitude extended to his administrative appointments. He brought into office individuals who proceeded to raid the Treasury with abandon. The Teapot Dome scam was only the most famous of the scandals that took place on his watch. Just before a shocked public learned of the squalidness that had overtaken the nation, Harding died on August 2, 1923. "Harding's story," concluded William Allen White, "is the story of his times . . . our democracy turned away from the things of the spirit, got its share of the patrimony ruthlessly and went out and lived riotously, and ended up by feeding among the swine."[38]

News of Harding's death reached Vice President Calvin Coolidge, at the family farm in Vermont, where his father, a justice of the peace, proceeded to swear in the fifty-one-year-old New Englander by the light of an oil lamp. Coolidge, the image of austere rectitude, with the perpetually worried look of a lonely bookkeeper (Alice Roosevelt Longworth thought that he must have been weaned on a pickle), restored respect and probity to the administration. And once the corrupters were cleaned out of the temple he handed it over to the businessmen.

Good-hearted Harding had been friendly to big business, but then he was friendly toward the Socialist Eugene Debs and corrupt officials as well. There was no ideological fervor behind his support for business beyond his easy acceptance of its role in assuring American prosperity. Coolidge fervently *believed* in a businessman's government. "The man who builds a factory builds a temple" said Coolidge, and government had no right to intrude in these holy halls. "We need a faith," he added, "that is broad enough to let the people make their own mistakes." After throwing out the political hacks whom Harding had installed, he kept the two key architects of Republican business policies, Herbert Hoover and Andrew Mellon, and sat back to fulfill his aspiration to become, in the words of Irving Stone, "the least President the country ever had."[39]

At the core of the new administration's business credo stood the principle that fusing government and business would usher in a period of unprecedented prosperity. Fusing business and government can mean bending business to the will of government. What Coolidge had in mind was quite the opposite. He filled regulatory agencies designed to patrol business with businessmen like William Humphrey, whom he selected to chair the Federal Trade Commission in 1925. The new chairman promptly denounced his own agency as "an instrument of oppression and disturbance and injury instead of help to business" and "a publicity bureau to spread socialistic propaganda." No wonder progressives bitterly concluded that the regulatory system they had fought to emplace was committing *hara kiri*. And off in the wings Woodrow Wilson's old nemesis, Henry Cabot Lodge, gloated, "We have torn up Wilsonism by the roots."[40]

Coolidge's minimalist presidency placed extraordinary confidence in Treasury Secretary Andrew Mellon, one of the richest men in the world, who presided over the Treasury with a natural regard for the prerogatives of wealth. Arguing that the high tax rates introduced during the war stifled business initiative, Mellon proposed to cut taxes on the wealthy while keeping them at their current level for those earning less than $66,000. Reduced revenues would be made up from economies in government and higher tariffs on imported goods. Mellon neglected to indicate that the cost of these tariffs would be borne by the American consumer. To critics who argued that a 66 percent reduction on the highest income levels favored the wealthy, he responded that the benefits would trickle down to all classes as business invested savings in factories and jobs. He neglected to mention that his plan rewarded the industrialist with a larger tax break for investing in machinery than for giving Americans jobs. He also neglected to consider that if industrialists chose to invest in stocks and high living instead of workers, the entire rationale fell apart.

On January 20, 1924, La Guardia sent Secretary Mellon a short letter asking him to consider including a veteran's bonus in the planned budget. The aloof millionaire, unaccustomed to receiving suggestions from meddling junior congressmen of unreliable party affiliation, had no desire to bicker with Fiorello over budgets. He responded curtly that unless the congressman "could present a comprehensive plan" for raising the funds for the bonus there really was not much to discuss. After hours of research in the congressional library, La Guardia designed an alternative to Mellon's "spare the rich" tax plan, with enough funds for a bonus. The taxes on highest incomes would be cut by 25 percent while he proposed slashing those on the lower ones by 63 percent. He forwarded the plan to the Treasury on February 20. The following day it was rejected. La Guardia exploded a withering attack on the secretary on the floor of the House, charging him with favoring the wealthy and reserving for the poor nothing but regal disdain.[41]

Prosperity created more than merely wealth; it captured the spirit of the times. "Wealth," President Coolidge preached, "is the chief end of man." The economist Stuart Chase wrote that in these years the businessman was "the dictator of our destinies," replacing the statesman, the priest, the philosopher "as the creator of standards of ethics and behavior." America's promise was narrowed to wealth and its pursuit.[42]

There is such a thing as ignoring a good thing too much. We should not dismiss the importance of prosperity in providing happiness and a higher level of life, but while Americans boasted of a "new era" many workers and farmers were suffering. It did not require much courage to speak for the businessman who wanted more freedom from government control. It did take boldness to demand that Americans take note of those who had stumbled along the way. This Coolidge did not see. This Mellon did not care to see. This La Guardia focused on almost exclusively. With their points of view so divergent, it was little wonder that La Guardia would respond to the rhetoric of the new era harshly. Their battles were not over facts but over ways of seeing and where to look, and whom to favor. And the battle could be sharp even if the answers were not always clear.

How one balanced the conflicting principles of individual rights with the desire to guarantee social welfare was a complex issue with many possible answers; or maybe none at all. "You see the dilemma in which I find myself," wrote social critic Vernon L. Parrington to a friend, "We must have a political state powerful enough to deal with corporate wealth, but how are we going to keep that state with its augmenting power from being captured by the force we want it to control?"

It should be recalled that a much-heralded contemporary alternative to Coolidge's diffident minimalism was the forceful statism of Italy's Benito Mussolini. When Coolidge retired from the presidency in 1928 he reflected on leaving behind the awesome powers of his office. "We draw our Presidents from the people," silent Cal said. "It is a wholesome thing for them to return back to the people. I came from them. I wish to be one of them again." Mussolini's exit was less peaceful and less quiet.[43]

Still, not all who wanted to address the problems of poverty and unfairness were either supporters of fascism or opposed to the American traditions of freedom. La Guardia was warning that government based on a close relationship with business was faulty at its foundation. Business should operate under government, not as a coequal or superior partner. Devoted to the pursuit of private profit, business could not take responsibility for public prosperity and welfare. The people's government must assume this responsibility. This was the message that La Guardia kept repeating. This, and the demand that the pursuit of social fairness play a central part in determining national policy. An administration that allowed such innovative tax breaks as oil depletion allowances should not reject the just argument of its veterans for a small bonus, or workers' request for decent housing. What, he demanded, was to be the position of the poor in a society where wealth was defined as the chief end of man?[44]

3. "I Would Rather Be Right Than Regular"

I T did not take the GOP long to tire of the barrage of criticism that their vocal House colleague kept raining upon them. Before long La Guardia was informed that his maverick politics could cost him the renomination. Early in the summer of 1924, a presidential election year, in which Republicans wanted to round up as much support for Coolidge as possible, Sam Koenig told La Guardia that there was talk of reading him out of the party and that the price of renomination for his seat was support for the national ticket. On June 15 La Guardia returned to New York to deliver one of his periodic reports to his constituents. East Harlemites jammed the Star Casino to hear their representative respond to the threats that he would be denied a place on the ticket.

"No one," he began "is going to read anyone out of the party. Any fool can antagonize the voters, but it takes a real man with ideas and courage, to get votes. . . . I believe that every individual who steals, grafts, or squanders money appropriated for disabled veterans, should be taken out and shot like a dog!" Raising the matter of the Harding scandals, La Guardia brusquely advised his party to get its house in order before demanding his unquestioning allegiance. "My country, right or wrong . . . but my party only when it is right." The crowd roared its approval. "Some people say I am as bad as La Follette," the diminutive representative beamed. "I only wish I were as good as La Follette." La Guardia came just short of rejecting Coolidge. "If a man does that which he knows is not right, he loses his soul; but if by doing right he becomes 'irregular' and loses the nomination, he really has not lost much. This is 1924. The world is progressing. Times are changing." Parties only demand regularity, he told the crowd, when they want an individual to do something that he knows is wrong. "I would rather be right than regular."[45]

He had come close, but the wily Little Flower was not prepared to renounce Republican support yet, and for its part, the party still wanted him. It was easier to try managing a recalcitrant La Guardia on the ticket than to fight him. Moreover as the *Brooklyn Eagle* pointed out: "nobody is anxious to chill La Guardia because in a pinch he's a great help in getting the Italian-American vote on Election Day." Already La Guardia was one of the best known congressmen in the country, garnering more notices in the *New York Times* than any other House member.[46]

Later that month La Guardia watched with interest as the Democrats convened in New York to choose their presidential slate. New York's Al Smith and Woodrow Wilson's son-in-law, the former secretary of the treasury, William Gibbs McAdoo, were the leading contenders. At the stifling Madison Square Garden convention the Democrats were badly divided. One wing of the party favored the fifty-one-year-old Catholic governor of New York for his new ideas and his vision of a polyglot, caring modern urban America. "The city," Arthur Schlesinger, Jr., has written, "was in his rolling walk, in the nattiness of his dress, in the nasal twang of his voice, in the tilt of his head and the breezy impudence of his wisecracks." Others objected to Smith's religion, his urban narrowness, his representation of new values, and his opposition to Prohibition. It was to a deeply split party that the partially recovered Franklin D. Roosevelt, leaning on his crutches, hailed Smith as "the 'Happy Warrior' of the political battlefield," and placed the governor's name before the convention.

More than any other issue, the two candidates battled over a platform plank condemning the Ku Klux Klan. By 1925 the hooded society claimed more than 5 million members devoted to keeping immigrants out and protecting the American flag from Catholics, Jews, atheists, and blacks. McAdoo refused to condemn the supremacist order by name. Instead he denounced Wall Street and New York City, while Smith favored a condemnation. In the end, the delegates voted down the proposal to denounce the Klan by name, 543$\frac{3}{20}$ to 542$\frac{3}{20}$.

The battle for the nomination was equally close, dragging on for more than a hundred ballots. Will Rogers implored the delegates: "This thing has got to come to an end. New York invited you here as guests, not to live." Finally, since neither of the front-runners could assemble the two-thirds required for nomination, the party turned to a compromise choice, John W. Davis, a leading corporate attorney. The delegates paired him with the brother of William Jennings Bryan, hoping to attract rural and reform votes. "A ticket that not even a brother could support," wired Fiorello La Guardia to a Progressive colleague. "No not even William Jennings Bryan can make it progressive, and how will he explain the impossible biology?"[47]

But what was the alternative to Coolidge and Davis? This was the question pondered by a "reunion of a generation of reform" that met in Cleveland on July 4. Most of the delegates were under forty, but the old-timers lent the meeting its special flair. Here was General Jacob Coxey, veteran of causes, who had led a protest march of the unemployed on Washington during the Depression of 1893; John Streeter, the New Jersey editor who had vowed not to shave until populism was victorious, sporting a flowing beard; the poet Edwin Markham, also bearded, who moved the audience with his spirited poem on Abe Lincoln; an assortment of labor leaders; old Progressives of both the "new nationalism" and "new freedom" persuasions; social gospelers, Socialists, and Nonpartisan Leaguers; and piping up with the enthusiastic refrain that he would rather be right than regular, Harlem's Fiorello H. La Guardia.[48]

"I rise," chirped the impassioned easterner, "to let you know that there are other streets and other attitudes in New York besides Wall Street, I speak for Avenue A and 116th Street, instead of Broad and Wall." And so he did. But few of those assembled really understood the special needs of his urban constituency. This varied mob of reformers was prepared to celebrate past crusades, voice a general suspicion of privilege, and shape these emotions into a presidential campaign that would pay homage to Robert La Follette. Few actually hoped to win the presidency; they pursued the contest more than the victory, relishing small debates over policy, fumbling with minor details, and failing to articulate a politics that reached beyond general protest for coherence. Even warm supporters of the third party presented only a weak case in its favor. Writing to Walter Lippmann, Felix Frankfurter lamely observed, "The forces that are struggling and groping behind La Follette are, at least, struggling and groping for a dream."[49]

Back in New York, La Guardia turned to his own campaign. He was hoping to be awarded the Republican nomination without committing himself to Coolidge, but Sam Koenig made it clear that GOP support hinged on support for the national ticket. In August La Guardia determined that if he was to be dismissed from the party he would make the best of it. He notified Koenig on the front page of the

New York Times that he did not want to be a Republican anymore. "The platform of the Republican Party as adopted at Cleveland makes no appeal to the hopes of the people I represent. . . . You are correct . . . that on many of the important bills that came before the House, such as the soldier's bonus, immigration, the Mellon tax plan, postal salary increase, prohibition, Cape Cod Canal, Henry Ford and Muscle Shoals, I did not support the reactionary attitude of the Republican majority. On these issues I am willing to go before the people of my district." Having dismissed the Republicans, La Guardia found convenient temporary shelter in the Socialist party. Two years before, La Guardia had clearly rejected the Socialist program, but he needed a line on the ballot and they made few demands. "With all my heart," Norman Thomas wrote, "I wish that you with your record of service . . . your political sagacity, and personal following were a Socialist. Since you are not, I am glad that you are so outspokenly progressive, and I trust that the non-partisan committee may simplify your cooperation with the Socialists. . . ." For La Guardia there was no agonizing; it was a ticket to run on. The formalities of politics and party allegiance did not mean that much to him. "Both old parties," he wrote to his constituents, "have degenerated into mere agencies to carry out the will of the privileged, and for the continuance of legalized exploitation."[50]

With his own campaign efficiently on its feet, La Guardia joined La Follette crony Gilbert Roe in directing the Progressive presidential campaign in the East. La Guardia genuinely respected La Follette, whom he called "my inspiration and ideal," and he took his campaign duties very seriously. Early in September La Guardia wrote the senator of "a splendid sentiment for you here" and went on to outline a list of practical steps for a serious campaign. He complimented La Follette for his courageous stand on the Ku Klux Klan and, despite his own open opposition to Prohibition, agreed that the issue was thorny. "Confronted with hypocritical New England, rummy New York, fanatical South and the dry West, our position nationally is delicate." La Guardia suggested a way to satisfy the wets without offending too many drys, by focusing on the problem of Prohibition-related corruption and the impossibility of enforcement. On one issue, however, La Guardia avoided offering La Follette "political" answers. "I am being pressed hard to get a statement from you on the immigration question. While we may stand for restriction in the highest sense of the word, the present discriminatory features of the bill are resented by hundreds of thousands of splendid citizens who want to protest against its enactment."[51]

Ultimately the La Follette campaign proved painfully frustrating. It took a very long time to pull together, and except for La Guardia and too few others, amateurs ran the campaign. While they focused on ideology and political theory, the chairman of the campaign, Representative John M. Nelson of Wisconsin, complained that it took him weeks to get letterheads and campaign literature. And La Follette's insistence on appointing Gilbert Roe to work with La Guardia proved disastrous. "I have your letter of September 4th," began a note from Fiorello to

John Nelson, "only the fact that I am dictating to a young lady who is not accustomed to my ways prevents me from adequately expressing my feelings." Roe and his incompetent band were crippling the campaign. They had mislaid or simply discarded lists of potential supporters, ignored the advice of professionals, and took unconscionably long to consider approving La Guardia's request for a $75-a-week organizer. These "five o'clock tea drinkers" botched every opportunity. While the other parties worked the ethnic zones to sharp advantage, Roe could not be persuaded to hire an Italian journalist for the campaign. "We cannot run a campaign in a city of six million people," La Guardia blasted, "by parlor discussions in the homes of amateur politicians," and closed by slapping a two-inch "Fiorello" at the bottom of the page. The campaign never solved these problems. "Fiorello La Guardia," John Nelson told a colleague, "could have been of great service to us. Now we have drawn him in, put his career in jeopardy and lost the benefits of his many points of contact and his large experience."[52]

The Republicans, following the dictum that any stigma was sufficient to beat a dogma, campaigned on the theme of "Coolidge or chaos," whispering that La Follette was a Communist. There were other obstacles too. The Progressive banner brought together so many different elements, united only in what they opposed, that its support was as thin as it was scattered. The coalition of farmers and workers that La Guardia and others had hoped for never materialized as each element focused on its own interest. No point more clearly showed the shallowness of the undertaking than when a fortuitous rise in hog and wheat prices after July quickly drove the farmers back to the traditional parties for their share of the vaunted New Era's prosperity. With ideology pocket-deep, the Progressive candidacy floated along on residual loyalties to the old rhetoric and the gallant La Follette's flinty honesty. William Allen White, who ran for governor of Kansas in this same year, discovered there were deeper fault lines than class. Though he had more sympathy for the workingman than Coolidge or Davis, he lost the labor vote, because "I was wrong on the Pope." He had denounced the Ku Klux Klan and it was enough to sink him.

La Follette garnered 5 million votes of some 29 million cast, an impressive, but in the end meaningless, number. The vote was a tribute to a man and an emotion, but when the fallen Progressives gathered in February 1925 in Chicago, Morris Hillquit remarked that the delegates had "come to bury Caesar not to praise him."[53]

La Guardia was out of his element with the western insurgents. Like a nagging aunt at a family get-together, he kept talking about the chores that had to be done while everyone else was out for a good time. These Progressives, La Guardia once told an interviewer, "were hardly the men to engage in complicated self-criticism." They were satisfied to pay homage to a symbol of insurgency, who within seven months would be dead, while La Guardia wanted to launch change not memorialize it. In April 1925, when John Nelson asked La Guardia to join a call for another progressive convention, Fiorello declined. This time he wanted to see some grass roots interest before becoming involved. "I am not in favor of the formation of the party from the top down," he wrote, with the La Follette campaign fresh in his memory. "[O]ur party should be built from the bottom up."[54]

His own campaign for reelection to Congress proceeded smoothly. The Republicans drafted Isaac Siegel from the bench to run for his old seat. ("Damnation," La Guardia's friend Siegel said to his wife. "You know I don't want to run against the Major but *someone* has to put up a fight against this confounded third party"), and the Democrats selected Henry Frank to try again. Speaking as often as twenty-five times a day, La Guardia conducted a strong, enthusiastic campaign. Friends found him more animated and involved than he had been in years. He relied mostly on his own group of supporters, a private party of "Ghibboni" (variously interpreted as apes, swashbucklers, or champions) now headed by a twenty-two-year-old local resident named Vito Marcantonio. The campaign featured a "La Guardia Exhibit" —a cut of meat, a piece of coal, and a beer mug—symbols of his fight for fair meat prices, against the fuel monopolies, and for an end to Prohibition.[55]

Mainstream Republicans attacked La Guardia as an insincere opportunist. "La Guardia," sneered Brooklyn regular William Simpson, "crawled in one tent, and came out at the other end a La Follette man! He has his finger in every pie and party." But East Harlem did not agree. He had represented them with a forceful voice, held regular meetings with the community, and ran one of the most helpful congressional offices in the city. They trusted him to back their issues. Contributions poured into his office; sincere $5 and $10 contributions from workers and common folk, eventually totalling $3764.25. The night before the election, the Ghibboni organized a great parade through the Harlem streets with red torches and fireworks, and on the following day the "lone Progressive from the East" achieved the most decisive victory of his career, sweeping six of seven assembly districts by substantial margins. Fiorello's younger brother, Richard, a school principal at the New Jersey Prison at Trenton, sent his congratulations. After complimenting Fiorello on his victory, Richard added a note that reminded his older brother how much a loner he really was, how unusual his politics seemed outside his district, even to his brother. "While none of us are personally in favor of the party which you are now a member of, we realize, however the special handicap you had in succeeding as well as you did."[56]

The solid victory did little to blunt the prickly congressman's resentments. In December he filed a suit against the *New York Tribune*, charging that the paper had held him up to ridicule and scorn during the campaign when it reported that La Guardia was electioneering in "a battered, rusty automobile" and was seen going around "without a collar." He sued for 6 cents and a million dollar's worth of satisfaction when he claimed damages from the *Tribune "to the extent of its limited circulation."* Another journal that referred sarcastically to the working-class representative as the "hobo plutocrat" was also sued for libel. Friends cheered La

Guardia on; after all, it wounded a man's dignity to be called a hobo. Fiorello set them straight. "I'm suing because they called me a plutocrat."[57]

When the Republican caucus convened in Washington in January 1925 to lay plans for the coming session, La Guardia and thirteen other progressives were left off the invitation list. Indiana's Representative Wood explained that the renegades would be welcome only if they "appeared as penitents." Despite protests the decision stood, barring the progressives from important committee assignments. La Guardia would not be humbled: "I serve notice now that they can keep me out of the caucus, but I can keep them out of the City Hall in New York City. We have our own conditions there, Mr. Floorleader." He offered no apology for supporting La Follette, whose record as "a legislator will stand out and live long after many inconspicuous and colorless representatives dragged into office by a party emblem will have been entirely forgotten." Listed in Congress as a Socialist, none laughed more heartily than La Guardia when the only other Socialist congressman, Milwaukee's Victor Berger, welcomed him by announcing that La Guardia would function as "my Whip."[58]

At the same time that his special constituency broke tradition by electing him on the Socialist ticket, most Americans voted along more conventional lines, resoundingly reapproving Calvin Coolidge. Across the board, Americans rejected the idea of a larger role for government in their lives and celebrated their self-satisfaction. "This country," Chief Justice and former President William Howard Taft mused, a few days after the election, "is no country for radicalism. I think it is the most conservative country in the world." Coolidge prosperity had captured the national spirit. Those propounding more radical visions found themselves a vanguard without a mass.[59]

———

F. Scott Fitzgerald remembered the twenties as "an age of miracles . . . an age of art . . . an age of excess . . . and . . . an age of satire." Caught between the pull of inherited ways of knowing and the push of revolutionary new knowledge, it was an age of flux and confusion. The twenties brought a new prosperity, a new woman, a new morality, a new openness in talk and dress, and the new language of Freud and Einstein and Hemingway. Converts to these new ways looked upon those denying the new knowledge with a perfect scorn. To H. L. Mencken the backward types were no better than animals. Why did he not leave a society so oppressively uncongenial, Mencken was asked. "Why do men go to zoos?" he shot back.[60]

More balanced observers than the fashionably caustic Mencken were equally concerned by what they saw as an age of snapping restraints. A conservative and disciplined society had corseted the liberal assumptions of American freedom in its early years. But as barriers to expression and individual choice crumbled, freedom, Walter Lippmann suggested in *A Preface to Morals*, had turned into a bewildering "dissolution of ancient habits," littering the trail between the old and the new with punctured values. The new wise men offered no truths, only skeptical wisdom. The noted biologist Virchow asserted that he had dissected over 250 bodies and found not a single soul. Science with its stark empiricism could not prove enough things to sustain a moral universe.

Any belief, Joseph Wood Krutch reasoned with unhappy irony, "required a temporary suspension of . . . disbelief." Krutch concluded his sad musings in *The Modern Temper* by calling the twenties a time "haunted by the ghost of a dead world . . . not yet home in its own." Modern man had changed his world irretrievably when he abandoned faith for science, yet he was tormented by the fear that he would be memorialized like Shelley's Ozymandias, as having been proud of yet another illusion. It was the philosopher C. E. Ayers who called science "superstition in another guise."[61]

Others found in the confusion of the times a mass dementia. Social critic Thorstein Veblen saw the twenties as a time of "derangement of mentality," evident "in a certain fearsome and feverish credulity with which a large proportion of the Americans are affected. . . . They are predisposed to believe in footless outrages and odious plots and machinations. . . . There is a visible lack of composure and logical coherence, both in what they will believe and what they are ready to do about it." Historian Paula Fass describes what they were "ready to do about it" as a "witch's brew of narrow, self righteous reaction," represented by the Ku Klux Klan, the Women's Christian Temperance Union, the Bible Belt Fundamentalists, the nativists, the Immigration Restriction Leagues, and the worshippers of laissez faire.[62]

La Guardia was a man of instinct, and by instinct he rejected the "witch's brew." Like his milieu he reflected the old and the new and sometimes a confused mix of the two. He was inconsistent in that his positions on related issues lacked intellectual consistency. His inclination rushed to the fresh visions of the period, but reality and expediency and his own nurture often held him back. He was a pacifist who fought war with courage, a practical man who trusted "the people" implicitly while not trusting individuals, a foe of boss politics with his own personal machine, a fighter for larger government who jealously guarded individual freedom, a defender of capitalism who did not trust and tried to limit business. While others argued about premises, he focused on conclusions.

Late in the twenties La Guardia wrote a short story titled "Tony Goes to Congress," a tale of the new politics. It was never polished beyond a second draft, and it was never published. It has no merit as a piece of fiction, but it interests us in other ways. A central part of the story has idealistic Clara Watkins joining a plan to overthrow the unscrupulous local political boss, who happens to be her husband. With other reformers she selects a young, squeaky-clean Italian American, Tony Scarbucco, to run against the machine candidate. Following the secret meeting, Clara is walking with Bert Clayton. She knows Bert from her college days. She is sorry now that she ignored him then in favor of her empty-headed football-hero husband. He is gentle and good, so different from the shallow, power-hungry man she married but has long since ceased to respect. How different it would have been. "They were both cultured. They both loved music. They both understood politics. . . . They both knew the tenements. They both knew what unemployment meant." Bert and Clara sit close by each other in the park and chance to overhear a sordid plan being masterminded by her husband, Hosea. They look at each other. "What's the use?" she asks. But they quickly decide that there is all the use in the world to fight the machine together. The scene closes with the two new partners walking arm in arm "silently, but better friends than they had ever been before."[63]

This is not literature, except of the most functional sort, but it does echo some of the loosening cultural values of the times. This couple who are about to break a marriage are on their way to political sainthood. This story would not have thrilled Achille and Irene La Guardia with its hint of adultery positively presented. Nor would it have gone over well in much of rural America. But Harlem's La Guardia saw this new freedom as part of the modern spirit of the decade.

Ernest Cuneo, who worked on La Guardia's congressional staff, tells the story of a weathered old Italian man who stepped into La Guardia's office one day, very agitated. He pulled out a court summons from his pocket, laid it before La Guardia, blurting: "My eighteen-year-old daughter got it against me. . . . For beating her." He had warned the girl not to go out with her young man, but she paid no heed, and when she returned "at *eleven o'clock, eleven o'clock* . . . what else could I do but hit her." He turned to La Guardia looking for some sympathetic understanding. Would the congressman call the judge and explain this?

La Guardia eyed the old man. Being a father was scant excuse for beating an eighteen-year-old. Parents were not medieval masters. He told the man that he would have to go to court. The old man slumped into a chair, looking desperately tired and confused. Back home he had learned different rules. A father's word was an order. Had he not been pummeled often enough by his own parent to know that? Children are told, not asked, to do their father's bidding. Even eighteen-year-olds. Had he not seen even married women reprimanded by their fathers. This was the way things were done. But who had ever seen or heard of a daughter going to a state magistrate against her own flesh and blood? And for the state to intervene in the family, was this right?

Too modern to be sympathetic to this point of view, Fiorello tried to explain that it was different here. But the old man did not understand. He knew only that his defeat had begun as soon as he left the village of his fathers to come to this new world, where *he* looked and sounded strange, and his word was rendered meaningless. The man lifted himself up slowly, shuffled to the door, his eyes glistening, defeated forever in his authority as a father. La Guardia went over to him, recognized the gulf between them, respected it, and whispered softly, "Funny country, isn't it, pop." The man made his way to leave, jerked himself around, and lifted a tight fist. "I wish," he choked, "I wish I had missed the boat!" Then he sagged out the door, bewildered by a system that required him to go to court to discuss how he was trying to raise his daughter. La Guardia turned to the younger Cuneo. "Our old people are good people. You youngsters just don't know. That's not funny at all." Cuneo was not laughing. It was the closest Fiorello could come to saying that he understood the old man and had a grudging sympathy for his confusion at a world that changed rules on him in midlife. Not without satisfaction did he consider the progress of a new world where men could not beat their teenage daughters. But there was also sympathy for a man forced to recognize the hardness of change.[64]

Some of the standards he absorbed as a youth La Guardia respected. When Fiorello said that jazz was a primitive, unpleasant form of music, he was honoring the careful beauty and disciplined craftsmanship that he learned at his father's knee. He had seen how assiduously Achille had worked at his craft and how much study it required to master the works of the great composers. This beauty of form La Guardia thought could not be matched by a freewheeling syncopation that celebrated improvised disorder. His attitude toward art was equally conservative, and ballet in particular seemed to him faintly offensive. All those young men tiptoeing in tights, he once told a friend, made him sick. On the subject of women's rights he wanted to be modern. He spoke of a woman's right to be treated equally, of her right to higher wages, and was an avid supporter of the suffrage amendment. But he still thought of women in traditional terms. He praised the League of Women Voters for applying "house cleaning methods to public affairs." And his sense of proper conduct ran to demanding that the women who worked for him forgo lipstick and makeup and always wear stockings. Women were still mothers and wives and dangerous playthings who must be properly toned down to keep them safe.[65]

So many in the twenties thought of him as a radical. Yet the most radical thing about La Guardia was his rebellious rhetoric. He honored too many of the attitudes of his past to be a radical. He could not articulate clearly any single political vision. Too many contending principles, old and new, were competing to allow that sort of clarity. He could not reason through the complex quagmire of the twenties on intellectual grounds alone. Instead he relied on his own feelings about what was politically fair and legitimate. In opposing unfairness, in suggesting that too many good men and women, in a fundamentally prosperous nation, were suffering while powerful monopolies had persuaded Congress to make the poor succor the rich, La Guardia offered a text for the spirit of the times: "To him that hath to him shall be given, and from he that hath not shall be taken even that which he hath." This finally was what he was clear about: that this spirit was false. In cauterizing tones he assailed the cultural narrowness, the comfortable rejection of insecurity and unemployment. A government could not focus all its energies on its successful members, he warned, and continue to demand the allegiance of its alienated; not when it passed hypocritical Prohibition laws, adopted a racist immigration policy, and despite 6 to 12 percent unemployment favored business over labor.[66]

---

4. "An Experiment Noble in Purpose"

F OR a brief moment in their history, Americans undertaking "an experiment noble in purpose" sought to create a sober society through legislative concord. They passed a law, intended in one clean act to rid the United States of the dread effects of alcohol, of the wife-beating husband, of the father who denied his children their food to support his drinking habit, of workers rendered undependable by their addiction to grogshops, of the immoral saloons where crimes and unsavory plans were hatched, of the corrupting influence of political bosses whose base was often in the bars that dotted the immigrant and working-class communities, of the sin of intemperance.

No issue engaged the Harlem congressman more intensely during the twenties than the fight over Prohibition. He resented Prohibition as a bill to control the intoxication of foreigners and workers, while others would find a way to enjoy their cocktails. Moreover, he personally opposed it. Like President Harding and many others in the government, he never let the law stand in the way of his drinking habits. Throughout the decade he jeered at his colleagues—some of whom barely wiped the whiskey from their lips to vote for enforced temperance—excoriating their moral posturing and documenting in unrelenting detail the failure of the "noble experiment."[67]

From the beginning he opposed Prohibition as ill conceived, clashing repeatedly with Congressman Andrew Volstead, the Prohibition law's author, warning in 1919, before it was enacted, that "this law will be almost impossible of enforcement. And if this law fails to be enforced—as it certainly will be as it is drawn—it will create contempt and disregard for the law all over the country. . . ." The bill was not honest, he sniggered at his colleagues. "You want to keep the lecture tours. You want to exploit the 'drunks.' . . . It has been profitable. It is a good thing for you and you want to keep it up." Serious efforts should begin with education, La Guardia argued, not legislation.[68]

He pointed his indignant finger at southern Congressmen in particular, telling Georgia's William Upshaw that the moonshiners down south "were very anxious to get this bill through because their business will increase." After the law passed, despite his opposition, La Guardia responded with sarcasm to charges that his hometown did not sufficiently enforce the federal law: "If the people from the dry states would keep out of New York City," he declared, "we would have no drunks there." Did the gentleman from New York mean that he did not want the trade of the glorious dry South, challenged Congressman Upshaw? "Absolutely," came the frosty reply. "It keeps our courts congested." La Guardia explained to a constituent why the "delegation from the southern states all vote dry and are strongly for prohibition" because it was only enforced "among the colored population but the white gentleman openly and freely can obtain and consume all the liquor he desires." On another occasion he again turned to Representative Upshaw, who was stressing the constitutional sanctity of the law. "May I remind the gentleman from Georgia that there is also a fourteenth amendment to the Constitution? The fourteenth amendment deals with human rights and human liberties and it is as dead as a doornail in certain sections of the country."[69]

"You are quoted in the press," began a letter to Congressman La Guardia from the chairman of the Senate Appropriations Committee, Wesley L. Jones, which went on to describe La Guardia's accusation that the Prohibition law was being violated in the state of Washington with the collusion of officials. Jones further understood that La Guardia, in charging that "a great statesman in the other body and one of the foremost champions of Prohibition pulled the Department of Justice off," had meant him. Senator Jones was therefore writing to advise his esteemed colleague that these charges were untrue. This, as far as he was concerned, closed the incident, leaving to La Guardia's sense of honor the question of an apology.

Rather than apologize, La Guardia tore right back at Jones. "Everyone knows that Puget Sound is the receiving point for wholesale liquor in such enormous quantities, and in daily shipments to such an extent that such conditions could not exist without the knowledge, if not the connivance of the very officials entrusted with the law." He then proceeded to spell out the basis of his charge and to refer the senior senator to the Justice Department for further elaboration. The newspapers had a field day.[70]

And so it went. La Guardia, by now well known for jumping out of his seat with a forceful "Will the gentleman yield?" interrupting Upshaw's denunciation of New York's wet governor, Al Smith, with an attack of his own: "The Governor of the gentleman's state permit[s] the manufacture of hooch and moonshine to be sent all over the country." When the stuffy Blanton of Texas yielded, La Guardia expressed the opinion that if everyone violating the law were jailed there would be no quorum in the House. A colleague disclosed that Prohibition agents were being appointed upon the recommendation of wet district leaders. What did he expect from the Treasury Department (which was entrusted with Prohibition enforcement), asked La Guardia; was not Secretary Mellon a former distiller himself? He combed the papers for any clues that could put him onto a good story. When a prominent attorney told a *New York Times* interviewer that he had "drunk liquor with Justices

111

of the United States Court. . . ,'' the wet warrior immediately fired off a letter demanding "full particulars," and the attorney paid the price for his indiscretion with a lot of squirming.[71]

Prohibition transformed the colorful congressman into a national figure. From all over the nation correspondents sent him notes of approval and encouragement, and information on the evasion of the law. These he filed in a bulky dossier that he shared often with his less than comfortable colleagues on the floor of the House. The primary line of attack was simply "It is impossible to tell whether Prohibition is a good thing or not. It has never been enforced in this country. . . ." La Guardia realized that it was futile to debate morality with the sides so far apart and so set in their ways. Instead he focused on the practical wisdom of the law. With opposition so widespread and so powerfully rooted in the wet areas, the only way to end drinking would be through an extraordinary commitment to enforcement. If there is a law, he challenged, let us enforce it. He demanded that his colleagues vote for huge appropriations for enforcement to prove that they were indeed serious about temperance. In 1926 he tried to amend a Prohibition enforcement law by increasing an appropriation from $2,686,760 to $102,686,760! Drys were forced into the embarrassed position of opposing the amendment, which would have made Prohibition the largest item in the national budget. Gleefully he pressed more and more money upon them and then regaled the press and the galleries as he converted congressional repartee into a blood sport, with stories of corruption, bootlegging, and hypocrisy.[72]

If he could not persuade the Congress to change the law, then he would shame the authorities into admitting its ineffectiveness. "I am seeking," he told his colleagues, "to carry on a campaign of education. I don't believe your folks back home know what's going on! And the people of this country don't know the farce, the crime, the hypocrisy, the graft, in the very department that is entrusted with the enforcement of this law. When they do, they will realize that there is something in the fight we are waging here." Infuriated by the chairman of the Committee on Alcoholic Liquor Traffic's statement that he did not know the Prohibition laws were being violated, Fiorello shouted at the innocent legislator, "Then go and learn something! You are probably the only man in the U.S. who would make such a statement." Rich bankers were doing it, honorable citizens were doing it, and he had a good mind to show the poor how to do it too! "Right in this room." The press was alerted. The congressman would create beer in the committee room of the Committee on Alcoholic Liquor Traffic![73]

On June 19, 1926, with two score journalists and photographers trailing behind him, Fiorello marched off to Room 150 in the House Office Building. Appearing in a bartender's apron—"He is," wrote his good friend, the journalist Ray Tucker, "the Belasco of politics"—he proceeded to mix two legal beverages, near beer and malt extract, to create 2 percent beer. Drys fumed that the roly-poly showman only did it because the House provided immunity from prosecution. And from Albany, New York State Prohibition enforcement headquarters, came the announcement that anyone caught making beer with the "La Guardia formula" would be arrested. The Little Flower required no further encouragement. On July 17, the *New York Times* announced that "Representative La Guardia will walk into a drug store at 95 Lenox Avenue," purchase the necessary ingredients, and mix his brew with a kick. "Then he will stand by and wait to be arrested."

He proceeded as promised to Kaufman's drugstore and exuberantly mixed the brew for the surrounding throng. No state Prohibition officer appeared to arrest him. The disappointed La Guardia called to a passing patrolman, asking to be taken in, but the officer wisely kept walking, telling the congressman that that was a job for a Prohibition agent. He couldn't make it into jail, but newspapers all over the country carried the story with a picture of the black-haired legislator waving a tall glass of foam-topped dark brew. The dedicated investigative reporters of the city press turned city rooms into laboratories to run their own tests. Wired one New York City editor: "Your beer a sensation. Whole staff trying experiment. Remarkable results."[74]

But it was not all antics and clever talk. These were an outlet for his deeper bitterness at a law that favored the rich with benign neglect and marked the immigrants and laborers as the primary violators when in fact they could least afford the illegal brew. "What is the use," he asked the House in February 1925, "of closing our eyes to the existing conditions? The importation of liquor into this country is of such magnitude, it comes in such enormous quantities, involving the use of a fleet of steamers, involving enormous banking operations, involving hundreds of millions of dollars, that it could not carry on without the knowledge if not the connivance of the authorities entrusted with the enforcement of the law."[75]

When an honorable member delighted his colleagues with tales of the latest shooting of a Prohibition law violator, La Guardia jumped up in white heat, denouncing the House for gloating at the shooting. The decade of opposition to Prohibition finally exploded in him. The whole thing was so ignoble. Didn't they know that the police were using such shootings to cover their own activities? Such powers did not belong "in the hands of every thieving, grasping, murderous police officer who spends half of his time hi-jacking and the other half of his time enforcing the prohibition law." But after a decade of his steady hectoring La Guardia could report nothing more than that "Politicians are ducking, candidates are hedging, the Anti-Saloon League prospering. People are being poisoned, bootleggers are being enriched, and government officials are being corrupted." Will Rogers cracked that "Prohibition is better than no liquor at all" and that Mississippi would vote dry as long as the voters could stagger to the polls, but to La Guardia this was serious business. More than anything else, bootlegging provided the powerful network of crime that grew in the twenties with its capital base and scarred the image of Italian Americans for decades.[76]

In Chicago, where brewers used hoodlums to distribute liquor, historian Humbert Nelli reports that "lush monetary opportunities [in bootlegging] . . . provided a powerful attraction for many qualified [Italian] young men who felt irresistibly drawn to this novel . . . economic enterprise." In 1920 Al Capone, a small-time hood from New York's Five Points section, moved to Chicago and registered as a secondhand furniture salesman, joining a criminal mob ruled by John Torrio. Less than eight years later he ran a $60 million business that bought police, politicians, and judges and boasted its own army of enforcers, an empire carved out of meeting the desires and demands of Americans for things that their government had declared illegal: alcohol, drugs, prostitution, gambling. And it was Prohibition that provided 60 percent of the syndicate's income during the twenties. Prohibition financed the take-off stage for large-scale organized crime in America.[77]

Prohibition so enraged La Guardia because it represented so perfectly the idea of misplaced government interest. He granted the need for some limit on the drinking of hard liquor, but the Prohibitionists would not moderate the law. They insisted that not only whiskey but wine and beer must be illegal. It was unreasonable, it was unenforceable, and it was aimed primarily at the people of the cities. There were poor people, there were sick people, there were needy people who could all benefit from the government's attention. Instead, an unconscionable amount of time and money was spent on a doomed crusade that was corrupting citizens, officials, and the very basis of their society. It was worse than bad, it was stupid and mean-spirited. It was not a sideshow; it was an alternative show that swallowed up energy and money and afforded a range of opportunities for corruption and criminal activity with potential rewards that lured so many into its rotten environment.[78]

La Guardia continued his fight into the thirties, mocking the law's intent, burlesquing its enforcement, and crying bloody murder at evidence of corruption. As "commanding officer of the Republican wet Forces," he planned attack after attack on the failed experiment. In 1930 newspapers headlined "Prof. La Guardia opens classes in winemaking," describing another of the wet warrior's zingers. Fiorello had discovered an Agriculture Department Bulletin (No. 1075) that provided instruction for home production of unfermented grape juice. The kicker was a warning at the end of the thirty-two-page pamphlet that extreme care must be taken in this process lest the juice ferment and produce—perish the thought—illegal wine. "Pending repeal of the obnoxious prohibition law," he wrote in the letter accompanying the government-produced wine-making booklet, "it is natural that citizens will continue to make home-made wine. . . . It is always a pleasure for me to be of service to you."[79]

5. "Keep on Protesting"

P ROHIBITION aroused La Guardia's opposition because of its stupidity and fakery and also because it treated his people differently. Indeed, La Guardia objected to much of the social program advocated by conservative America, which viewed the city, especially New York, as a threat to the staid élan of Protestant small-town America. With blacks far from integrated into the society and so many others, immigrants and natives, also standing outside the mainstream, it was delusionary to speak of a single American race held together by a cultural consensus. And yet as nativism settled on the heart of the country and held it in thrall, talk of Nordic America and its unique culture came to dominate national discourse. In this contrary age, with all evidence pointing in the opposite direction, an exceptionalist national identity was catching on. At first public policy circled around the issue, testing it, becoming comfortable with it, but in time it was set hard at the center of American policy.[80]

Fiorello La Guardia's own rise to political standing offers one cautionary note to the assumption that nativism pushed out other, even contradictory themes. The new immigrants, many of them into their second American generation, were reaching new levels of maturity and self-assurance in their urban communities. They were achieving economic power, making their way into local and state politics and gaining some acceptance. Fascinated intellectuals studied the immigrants and their special communities. Writers described their culture and life-style as more natural and earthy than veneered, genteel America. Realist novels portrayed the foreign-born as less spoiled by good manners and false facades; their struggles were for their daily bread not for degrees of relative leisure. While a striving for money and comfort among the native Americans struck some as Babbitry, the immigrants' pursuit of success was often portrayed as something noble and decent. And while American intellectuals might balk at the religions and folkways of the immigrants, they found in their plainness and piety a fascinating show and an exotic store of material.

At Harvard, George Santayana had bid adieu to the genteel tradition in American letters, focusing a skeptical eye on linear progress and aristocratic cultural hegemony. Theodore Dreiser, William E. B. DuBois, Thorstein Veblen, and Heywood Broun helped clear a path for a more diverse and inclusive perception of American culture that would transport it beyond the conventional. A young critic reviewing William Dean Howells's work wrote almost whimsically about this much-praised American author: "What if Howells be a native American of Anglo Saxon origin? Homer was blind. Coleridge was a slave to Opium. Poe drank.'' Being a WASP could also be overcome! And yet we understand that this sentiment for the foreigner was fashionable in small circles precisely because the commonplace perception was quite different.[81]

The scribbling of intellectuals held little sway with Main Street, which viewed both the writers and the exoticism they lionized with suspicion. As the new groups adapted to the American environment, moving into politics and toward economic security, nativist fears grew. Fearful of being displaced by foreign elements, nativists prepared to fight for the heart of America by seeking to impose ''a patriotic cult and [coerce] a sense of oneness.'' For these Americans the Constitution became a totem, more important as a symbol than for what it said or meant. ''Individualism?'' raged an American Legion commander. ''Down with all isms.'' In some quarters this emerged as a Bible-thumping Christ-and-Constitution campaign. Elsewhere it became a search for consecrated roots. ''Hyphens,'' Woodrow Wilson had muttered upon the demise of his peace plan, referring to the split loyalties of the foreign-born population, ''are the knives that are being stuck into this document.'' His ambassador to Great Britain, Walter Hines Page, could not be plainer: ''We Americans have got to . . . hang our Irish agitators and shoot our hyphenates and bring up our children with reverence for English history, and in the awe of English literature.''[82]

At about the time that Page issued his statement, Bagdasar K. Baghdigian was registering at a Kansas City school. A school official looked up from the complicated Armenian name on the form and advised: ''Oh, give that up and change your name to Smith, Jones or a name like that and become Americanized. Give up everything you brought with you from the Old Country. You did not bring anything worthwhile anyway.'' Baghdigian was not prepared to do that. ''The Turkish sword,'' he mused, ''did not succeed in making me become a Turk, and now this hare brained woman is trying to make an American out of me. I defy her to do it.''[83]

While some thought that the only way to become an American was to strip away all other experience, others understood the benefit of a rich national culture that included Baghdigian, Armenian loyalties and all. Randolph Bourne, for example. For whatever reason that lay deep in the making of his complex personality, Bourne, who could trace his generations back to those who originally disturbed the Indians, became a balladeer of generous pluralism. He rejected the notion of an exclusive American culture in favor of a kaleidoscopic vision, a culture in fascinating open process. ''Not a nationality,'' wrote Bourne, but a transnationality, a weaving back and forth, with the other lands, of many threads of all sizes and colors. Any movement which attempts to thwart this weaving, or to dye the fabric any one color, or disentangle the threads of the strands, is false to this cosmopolitan vision.''[84]

Few in Congress shared Bourne's liberal vision, but Fiorello La Guardia did.

His speeches suggest precisely the "transnational America" that Bourne sketched in his essay. And like Bagdasar Baghdigian he denounced the Americanizers for their sparse, false spirit. Those taken with Anglo superiority he taunted by telling them that it was his people, the Romans, who civilized England while the admired Nordics still roamed the land as barbarians. More important, he fought for fair and equal treatment for immigrants. In 1917, when Congress instituted literacy tests, freshman congressman La Guardia ruffled WASP sensibilities by insisting that selections taken from the King James Bible offended Catholics and must be struck from the exam.[85]

Shortly after his return to Congress in 1922, La Guardia made clear in a pointed if ungrammatical wire to Secretary of Labor James J. Davis, whose department administered the Bureau of Immigration, just how great a distance separated him from mainstream American policy:

> We may as well understand each other at once. You and your department cruel, inhuman, narrow minded, prejudiced. Attitude towards immigrants and unwarranted interpretation law been rebuked all over the country. . . .[86]

Although he had little power, La Guardia did not hesitate to press his unpopular position, and sometimes, against all odds, he even achieved results. While a boatload of some 300 East European Jews was on the seas en route to the United States, the quota for Russian immigrants became filled. The boatload of passengers would be turned back. A junior congressman in little favor with his party, La Guardia traced the whereabouts of President Harding, located him on a fishing vacation, and sent him a telegram demanding in the name of humanity that these individuals not be sent back. The president, showing the personal tolerance for which he was known, agreed to charge their slots against the next year's quota rather than refuse them entry.[87]

La Guardia's own ethnic identity was complicated. Had someone asked him, he would have insisted simply that he was an American. But in the tribal twenties being born in New York City and being raised on an army post were not sufficient to dispel a lingering sense of alienness. Swarthy complexion, jet-black hair, European parentage, uncertain religious persuasion (not to mention the un-American practice of having run on four or five party tickets, including that of the Socialists!), and a last name punctuated by no less than five vowels were enough to see to that. Moreover, even for La Guardia the answer was not so simple. His sense of being something other than simply American came not only from those who taunted him. Raised in a home steeped in European culture and traditions, he grew up with an awareness of being different. The organ-grinder that came calling to Prescott reminded Fiorello that like the disheveled hurdy-gurdy man with the monkey, he too could be called a dago.

He loved the West and marked this respect in the ten-gallon hats that made him the delight of his caricaturists. But when he returned to the United States from Europe in 1906, he settled in New York, not the Arizona of his youth. In New York, using the name Frank, as an anglicized version of Fiorello, he affiliated with the party of old line wealth and culture. In Congress, it was he, the one with the funny name, who along with a very few others left the safety of the legislature for the front lines when the Presbyterian Anglo president declared war to make the world safe for democracy.

After the war he joined the western Progressives hoping to shape a single voice for the immigrant slum and the rural farm communities, confident that such a merger could overcome the attitude of many rural citizens who thought that the best thing southern Italians and Russian Jews could do for America was to stay in Europe. He was "Fiorello" by now, for he had learned that it made little difference what your first name was in an era when Kansas City schoolteachers thought that it was un-American to be Baghdigian instead of Jones or Smith.

La Guardia also had a direct Jewish ancestry. Indeed, according to Talmudic law, which traces lines of descent through the mother, he would be considered a Jew. He never talked about this part of his background, although in 1933 when the subject came up in a number of news articles, he commented that he never thought he had enough Jewish blood to boast about. He did show respect for the needs of his Jewish constituents and vigorously defended them in an era when it was easier to join the anti-Semitic chorus. But then he represented East Harlem not Henry Ford.

Beneath the tough assertiveness and confident words lay anxieties. He resented the organ-grinders, and when the Lindbergh baby was kidnapped he told Ernest Cuneo, "I hope the bastard kidnapper doesn't turn out to be Italian." He hated to hear what an associate called "cheap Italian politicians," speaking in broken, heavily accented English, bragging about the glory that was Rome to immigrant audiences who couldn't care whether Da Vinci was a featherweight champion and Donatello a shortstop for the New York Yankees. He wanted all to know that he was born in this country. "I will tell you, gentlemen," he said on the floor of the Congress on April 8, 1924, "that he who steals my purse steals trash, but he who attempt to take my Americanism away from me takes all I have and all that is dear to me. Gentlemen, I was raised out in the big state of Arizona and anyone who seeks to question that Americanism, I do not care how big he is, will do so at his peril."[88]

He defended the immigrants because he believed they had a right to be here, not because he felt like one of them; and if he sounded personally involved it was because he felt that *others* thought of him that way.

No case portrayed more clearly the split between those welcoming new Americans and those fearing them as criminal rabble than the case of the "poor fish peddler and the fine shoemaker," Bartolomeo Vanzetti and Nicola Sacco. These two Italian immigrants were arrested in 1920 for murdering a payroll clerk and his guard in South Braintree, Massachusetts. Swarthy, with droopy mustaches, these penniless common laborers who professed an anarchist ideology barely spoke English. Their politics symbolized for many Americans all that seemed alien and terrifying about immigration.

In July 1921 Judge Webster Thayer sentenced the two to death after a trial criticized for inflammatory rhetoric and blatant prejudice. The judge was heard to speak privately of "those anarchist bastards." Many claimed that the verdict had more to do with Sacco and Vanzetti's politics and their Italian origins than their guilt. For six years Sacco and Vanzetti languished in jail while their cause attracted international attention. A commission appointed to investigate the case headed by A. Lawrence Lowell, the president of Harvard University, refused to criticize the finding. A member of the Harvard Corporation, at first impressed with Lowell's impartiality, later declared that the patrician educator "was incapable of seeing that two wops could be right and the Yankee judiciary wrong."[89]

With emotions so inflamed, La Guardia was asked to join the defense committee and he met with the imprisoned men. The meeting was a strange session. He later recalled that he could not move Vanzetti to discuss anything other than the class war that was victimizing him and his partner while Sacco just stood there gripping the bars of his cell, repeating again and again that the world would be cleansed with his blood. Unclear about their guilt, La Guardia was, however, convinced that they had not been treated fairly, and he assisted in preparing briefs asking for a new trial based on fresh evidence. His work in this instance, as in his last-minute efforts to have the governor, Alvin T. Fuller, commute the death sentence, failed.[90]

John Dos Passos' lines on the deaths of Sacco and Vanzetti, on August 23, 1927, capture the intensity of the feeling that the execution generated:

> *all right you have won you will kill the brave men our friends tonight. . . .*
> *all right we are two nations*[91]

But La Guardia's voice, usually the first to rise against slights both real and imagined, was unusually restrained.

If he could not save these two men whom he judged "demented," he wanted to keep the good name of their fellow nationals well burnished. One week before the execution, La Guardia published an article on Italian contributions to American society. He described the sculpting Piccirilli family, and Ruotolo, the poet, and an impressive catalog of vowel-punctuated surnames in the professions. He took special pride in Tony "Push em up" Lazzeri, the New York Yankees second baseman. As for those colorful street peddlers, La Guardia wanted his readers to know that while "many of the older immigrants are somewhat ashamed of the organ grinding and banana peddling Italian,'' it was different among those like him. ''We are quite proud of those honest and hard working immigrants.'' At this moment, concerned with counteracting the effects of the Sacco and Vanzetti trial, he wanted to focus attention on the positive accomplishments of a long list of fellow Italians, even if it meant making lemonade out of lemons. ''If the Italian went about grinding out music, his organ was in tune and its music good. He brought music to places where music was necessary. We are not ashamed of him today. . . .''[92]

But other Americans clearly wanted them and the whole exotic horde of new immigrants to remain on the other side of the ocean. In the passel of rural social reforms that commanded the political agenda of the twenties no issue engaged the prejudices of Nordic America more directly than the campaign to restrict American immigration on the basis of national origins.

Immigration had soared in the years between 1880 and 1920, when 23 million Europeans came to the United States. After France presented the American people with the Statue of Liberty, her call to the world's needy was phrased in global terms: America as world haven. Yet by the time Emma Lazarus's sonnet welcoming the poor huddled masses was bronzed and fastened to the statue's base in 1903, Congress had already begun to close the Golden Door.

The poet's concern for the weak, tired, and hurt gave way to a fear of being overrun by inferior men and women. A quickly expanding nation, it was argued, had to concern itself with the congestion, crime, and social disorder that marked the spreading immigrant slums. It had to prevent cutthroat competition for jobs and avoid clogging the cities with so many poor, uneducated, and needy immigrants. And Americans bolstered by a scientific racism that lent their prejudices the sanction of learning were insisting on a right to maintain the integrity of the dominant Anglo-Saxon culture. The United States, these citizens argued, could not in its maturity continue to absorb thieves, malcontents, adventurers, and dissidents with the equanimity of its colonial infancy.

It was impossible to decide the issue on high ground. Say that America had to be kept for Americans, and as little as that might mean to a philosopher, it packed an emotional charge. To oppose that, one had to speak of toleration, historical traditions, the long-range damage of shutting a modern nation off from the rest of the world, the international angers engendered by discriminatory policies against other nations. A five-page argument seldom defeats a two-word one in public debate. Polemics, not reasoned politics, typified the American dialogue on immigration. Collapsing sophisticated arguments into code words, the debate skidded on the issue's surface, drawn along by perceptions of private interest and public nativism.[93]

Clearly a nation with its frontier closing, its cities overflowing, and rampant cultural confusion had every reason to consider its immigration policies carefully. But the atmosphere of the times did not permit that. The debate did not turn on facts and statistics but on irrational fears and prejudices. Senator Albert Johnson, the author of the most restrictive of the immigration bills, argued that Americans had been too patient with immigration. ''The day of unalloyed welcome to all peoples, the day of indiscriminate acceptance of all races has ended.'' Americans must protect their own race and keep out the migrating hordes who threatened their jobs and institutions.[94]

Small wonder that the rhetoric was intense. No common ground existed. They were protecting flag and hearth from Jews and Italians, while La Guardia—against all odds—was staking his argument on a broader vision of America, one that included him. The Italian-American legislator could not accomplish much, but there was much that he wanted at least to say. The function of a reformer in contrary times, he often maintained, was to educate. Immigration, he lectured, was the nation's history. ''Whether you came over on the Aquitania or your ancestors came over on the Santa Maria, the Mayflower or the Half Moon, you are an immigrant or the descendant of immigrants. Bear that in mind.'' La Guardia noted sarcastically that in favoring British immigrants, the House apparently judged ''that this country is not in need of honest, hardworking laborers, but there seems to be a great desire for increasing the importations of butlers, valets and grooms.''[95]

The shame of it, declared La Guardia, was that the new immigrants, in seeking America, displayed the spirit that built this nation. Yet cows and sheep imported into the country received more consideration than did the immigrants. An importer could appeal decisions to a customs court and have his case considered by a judge, while the immigrants were processed by an ''overworked underpaid inspector of immigration at $1800 a year,'' who made final decisions on the ''fate of a human being and the destiny of his life.'' Why this pinched spirit in everything that touched the foreign born, including those already here, demanded La Guardia? ''A father who toils from morning to night to honestly support his family and keep his native American children in school, is entitled per se to American citizenship and a welcome helpful hand extended.'' This frontier land, he reminded those bent on invidious restrictions, was a child of Europe not England.[96]

On April, 8, 1924, La Guardia made his sharpest attack upon the immigration law being discussed by the Congress.

> Gentlemen: You cannot escape the responsibility for the vicious, cruel discrimination against Italians and Jews mainly. . . . Where will you find the average Jewish immigrant? . . . You will find him doing the most laborious work from the moment he lands until he is laid away. . . . to give his children the opportunity which was denied him and his ancestors for centuries. . . . The Italian too has made his contribution to this country. . . . with the pick and shovel, building our railroads, digging our canals, boring our subways, or in the depths of our mines. . . . You show me the house of an Italian laborer, no matter

121

how humble, and I will show every inch of his backyard cultivated as a garden. I will show you every place where there is space enough for one seed—a beautiful flower. . . .

"The spirit of the Ku Klux Klan," he said, "must not be permitted to become the policy of the American government."[97]

But it did. And for all of his fury the East Harlem congressman could do no more than assail the "fixed obsession on Anglo Saxon superiority." His exchange with Congressman J. N. Tincher of Kansas is typical:

MR. TINCHER: I think this chamber here is a place where we ought to think, act, and do real Americanism. (Applause) . . . [I]f you thrust open the gates the districts such as we have examples of here will keep increasing until finally when you get up and say "Mr. Speaker" you will have to speak in Italian or some other language. . . .

MR. LA GUARDIA: Will the gentleman yield?

MR. TINCHER: Oh hello, there you are, I knew you would come.

MR. LA GUARDIA: The gentleman doesn't know what he is talking about.

MR. TINCHER: I think the issue is fairly well drawn. On the one side is beer, bolshevism, unassimilating settlements and perhaps many flags—on the other side is constitutional government, one flag, stars and stripes; a government of, by and for the people; America our country.[98]

Throughout the decade La Guardia introduced amendments to liberalize the immigration quotas and jeer the narrow spirit behind America's racial policies. "I want to suggest to the gentleman," he said to Representative Busby of Mississippi on March 29, 1928, "that when the Constitution was amended, giving the Negroes citizenship and equal rights, that amendment carried with it an obligation to give Negroes an equal opportunity for education in this country. (Applause). . . ."

MR. BUSBY: Will the gentleman yield?

MR. LA GUARDIA: No, I have only a few minutes.

MR. BUSBY: I will give you the one minute you took away from me.

MR. LA GUARDIA: Oh. That's like giving the Negro the right to buy a Pullman car ticket in your State (Laughter).

MR. GREENE: [Florida] Can they ride with you?

MR. LA GUARDIA: Surely they can. . . . In New York City our colored boys can enter the City College of New York and the colored girls are entering Hunter College. We provide for their education whether they come from the South or elsewhere; and we believe in making the Fourteenth Amendment something real (Applause)."[99]

His role remained that of a gadfly creating disturbances, and warning officials that they would have to answer to his scorn and public attacks if they went too far. Early in the twenties, La Guardia had hoped the people would prove more generous than their officials, but by 1924 he could no longer delude himself into believing that nativism was the work of an ill-meaning few. It was the policy and the sense of the nation. La Guardia was almost alone. Conservatives and southerners opposed him and so did his Progressive colleagues. The Immigration Restriction law, which discriminated against Italians, Jews, and Asians, would protect "the race that believes in Christianity and has given us civilization," said California's Progressive Senator Hiram Johnson. The bill's sponsor, Senator Albert Johnson, addressed La Guardia in blunt terms. "I have no feeling of hatred toward any alien whatsoever, but I do have great contempt for alien-minded people in the United States who persist in airing their alien views, and I cannot agree with them, even if they sit in the House of Representatives."[100]

La Guardia was reduced to pointing out the inconsistencies in American immigration policy. As with Prohibition, the best he could do was flail at the law as it passed. On the losing side again, La Guardia resorted to symbolic sorties, firing off testy letters, demanding careful study of the credentials and financial security of assorted pretenders and princes who received easy welcome to the United States. "Perhaps it would be well to put an embargo in our immigration laws on impecunious, unemployed titleholders without visible means of support and to keep them out entirely. If we . . . establish the natural American abhorrence for fancy titles, perhaps fewer of the tarnished coronets of Europe will be imported for the sole purpose of being repolished and rehabilitated by American dollars." Was not Grand Duke Boris Vladimirovitch, cousin of the deposed Russian czar and on his way to American domicile, an "assisted alien," likely to become a public charge and therefore ineligible for a visa? La Guardia demanded in a letter to Secretary Davis. Was it not the plan of these "repudiated, unemployed and shiftless dukes and archdukes" to overthrow our republican government and introduce monarchy? Aghast at the *lèse majesté*, the duke's friends were nonetheless forced to traipse in with evidence of two well-filled bank accounts and a partial inventory of the dutchess's collection of Parisian couture to prove that this couple was unlikely to prove a financial burden to the United States. Other earls, dukes, counts, and even a queen were afforded the same treatment by this most insistent of commoners.[101]

What then did La Guardia accomplish on behalf of immigrant America? He kept their hopes up. He presented their resentments, and gave focus and voice to their demand for a more liberal United States as he pointed in the direction of a liberal transnationalism. And he lent shape to what would become one of the most potent elements of the New Deal coalition: ethnic Americans who would emerge from the nativist twenties with a stronger sense of their own right to political power. "The function of a progressive," he told an interviewer, was not to get things done by himself. It was "to keep on protesting until things get so bad that a reactionary demands reform."[102]

6. On the Watch: America's Congressman-at-Large

L a Guardia's agenda of objection achieved its biggest victory in the fight over the Muscle Shoals energy complex in Alabama. The Muscle Shoals controversy grew out of the government's wartime effort to construct synthetic nitrogen plants for producing explosives. World War I ended before the nitrogen works planned for Muscle Shoals, in Alabama's Tennessee Valley region, could be completed, and soon after the declaration of peace the secretary of war solicited proposals from the private sector for the plant, its resources (the not entirely completed Wilson Dam among them), and its associated properties. Before long the project drew the interest of the best-known American businessman of the times, Henry Ford.[103]

This lanky industrialist with the piercing, humorless eyes perhaps more than any other individual was responsible for ushering in an era of complexity and modernism. The automobile's broad impact on society and the ramifying effect of his innovations in management and production are impossible to exaggerate. Biographers Allan Nevins and Frank Ernest Hill tell us that many of Ford's contemporaries saw in him "a symbol of an all potent industrialism trampling down individuality, beauty and serenity and erecting machine altars to Mammon and Moloch." Yet, oblivious to his own true role, it was Ford who complained about powerful industrialists arrayed against the small businessman, Ford who saw himself as essentially a simple American, abused by the interests. "Do you want to know the cause of the war?" he once asked. "It is capitalism, greed, the dirty hunger for dollars."

Ford could be menacingly simple in nonindustrial matters. He believed in reincarnation, hated Jews, doctors, Catholics, bankers, and tobacco, and conducted his business with a "coarse tyranny." He carried a gun to ward off union organizers and fired workers who drove anything but a Ford car. In 1916, influenced by the European pacifist Rosika Schwimmer, he commissioned a "Peace Ship" to sail belligerent ports to persuade the warring powers to put down their arms. Allowing that "I don't like to read books; they muss up my mind" and claiming that "history is bunk,'' Ford published his own newspaper, the *Dearborn Independent*, which held Jews responsible for bolshevism, a decline in morality, Wall Street, Darwinism, women's makeup, jazz, and bootlegging. The motor magnate saw himself as a simple man, opposed to the Wall Street and banking interests. But his true role, historian Paul Carter suggests, is better glimpsed in the German silent film *Metropolis*, where, in a gripping scene, factory workers are pushed to work at a superhuman pace by a figure resembling Henry Ford, while those falling behind are fed to the machines they now serve.[104]

Now this singular American hero, this plain man of uncommon fortune, offered to buy the Muscle Shoals complex, including the nitrate factories, two steam electric plants, and the surrounding property, for $5 million. The proposal required the government to complete the Wilson Dam and one additional dam, as well as to install the hydroelectric plants, whereupon the auto mogul would lease the entire complex for 100 years, promising to pay 6 percent on the *additional expenses* involved in building the two dams, not to exceed $28 million. Ford would also pay something less than $100,000 for federal maintenance and repair and for the amortization of the equipment. While some welcomed Ford's involvement, others were quick to point out that the government had already spent more than $104 million on Muscle Shoals and that the value of the complex in scrap metal alone exceeded $12 million. Moreover, the amortization plan allowed Ford to extinguish $50 million in debt with payments of $4.5 million. No hard-driving ''banker'' could have arranged a more one-sided deal than the prophet of Dearborn. Nevertheless Commerce Secretary Herbert Hoover praised the offer, and Thomas Edison termed the offer generous. In the Senate one man, Nebraska Senator George Norris stood up to reveal that the emperor was without clothes. Had Ford made this offer to a minor, Norris declared, there was no ''court in Christendom but that would promptly set aside the conveyance as having been obtained for want of consideration.'' And standing alongside Norris in the fight against Ford was Fiorello La Guardia.[105]

The House began debate on the Ford offer on March 5, 1924. La Guardia immediately took the floor to tell his colleagues that ''Ford's proposal made Teapot Dome ''look like a petty larceny.'' Moreover, he wanted to know how the United States could rely on Ford for nitrogen during wartime. ''He might be on a ship with some Rosika petticoat trying to get the boys out of the trenches; and the only one Henry Ford ever got out of the trenches was his own son. . . .'' There was yet another reason, perhaps the strongest one as far as La Guardia was concerned, for rejecting the offer.

> Based on his ignorance of history, literature and religion . . . Henry Ford has done more, I will say, owing to his bigoted hatred, to create strife and hatred in this country among the races than any man in the United States. And I will say that the wealth and ignorance of Henry Ford combined has made it possible for vicious men to carry on a

nefarious warfare against the Jews, not only of America, but of the whole world. . . .[106]

More than bile and bitter sarcasm attended this conflict. As much as he hated Ford, La Guardia also thought that the government was making a rash decision in selling off a property so potentially important in the regional development of the Tennessee Valley as Muscle Shoals. La Guardia's opposition to the Hero of Dearborn aroused the usual enthusiasm that his plans attracted. Lieutenant R. Noble Esty, who had served under Fiorello in Foggia, wanted to know whether the old army injuries had finally caught up with the Major. Was he mad? Here Henry Ford was offering to do a job for the country and La Guardia did not have enough intelligence to get out of the way. "I don't want to believe of our Major that you are flying off half cocked," but Ford could guarantee cheap fertilizer, create jobs, and honestly adminster the Muscle Shoals plants. Had La Guardia gone over to the "other side"?

La Guardia responded with rare restraint. "You must know that if I did not stand for what was right some of you boys might not have been here today, but might have paid the price for selfish greed and rotten politics by having to fly in S.I.A. planes." He had not changed. "I refuse to be whipped into line, shut my eyes blindly and deliver my vote for measures that I know are wrong and against the best interests of the country." The Ford plan must be seen in its proper light. The battle was not over fertilizer and nitrogen but over possibilities that were "beyond ordinary vision," and he for one did not wish to leave the people of the Tennessee Valley to the tender mercies of the motorcar manufacturer.[107]

Despite La Guardia's attacks, the Ford bill passed the House by a large margin. But in the Senate George Norris by a series of adroit procedural maneuvers buried the bill in committee until finally Ford withdrew his offer.

Over the years the Muscle Shoals project evolved from fertilizer to power to even more. La Guardia's description of the project as "beyond ordinary vision" was not merely meant to calm criticism. He had in mind a plan for regional development, unprecedented in American history, that would include the revitalization of the Tennessee Valley, flood control, river navigation, rural electrification, and reasonably priced hydroelectric power, in addition to the production of fertilizer. Together with Senator Norris, La Guardia continued the watch, holding onto Muscle Shoals for the people of the Tennessee Valley and the United States even as the government and many of the farmers of the region continued to try to sell it off.[108]

Early in 1928, La Guardia and Senator Norris introduced a joint resolution in both houses of Congress calling for the government to take over the Muscle Shoals complex. "Let us be perfectly frank," the Harlem representative testified before the House Military Affairs Committee. "Why should the Government part with this priceless possession. . . . Whoever gets control of Muscle Shoals will have absolute control of the industry of that whole section of the country," and he did not feel that any one group of men should wield such power. As for the taboo against government enterprise:

> I am not afraid of this talk of the Government going into business, of the Government being paternalistic, and of the Government depriving private business of what they should have. There is nothing in that. I remember the time and you all do, when it was considered socialistic for a municipality to have its own water supply. . . . Gentlemen, times are changing. . . .[109]

When Congress finally passed a version of the Norris measure, the power and fertilizer interests persuaded the president to pocket veto the bill. La Guardia attacked these groups for tactics that he said only proved that "the world's oldest profession wasn't limited to one sex." He quoted one utilities executive instructing his subordinates to fight the Norris bill: "Don't be afraid of the expense. The public pays the expense." Drawing on a Federal Trade Commission investigation of the power lobby, La Guardia uncovered a secret utilities strategy for influencing opinion through the control of newspapers and inveigling such respected agencies as the General Federation of Women's Clubs and the Smithsonian Institution.

One day, as the Little Flower was speaking on the floor of the House, colleagues noticed him waving a fistful of papers, photocopies, he explained, of checks made out to educators and academic institutions from the National Electric Light Association. He quoted from an internal utilities lobby memorandum that someone had passed on to him: "The plan was put across in the usual way. We laid the groundwork circumspectly and with care so that the actual suggestions that such courses be started came from the faculties of the institutions themselves. The rest was routine." His own findings echoed other evidence pointing to unsavory tampering with university professors and textbook writers. "Why, this bribery in the form of subsidies," screeched the siren-voiced legislator, "this method of reaching the textbooks, would make a student an illegitimate alumnus of an immoral alma mater."[110]

Not until the next decade would the public fully grasp the possibilities that Norris and La Guardia had seen in Muscle Shoals, but their holding operation prevented the government from selling off this complex and made possible the greatest hydroelectric project in history, a project that harnessed the water resources of a 40,000 square mile area and brought affordable electrification to a severely disadvantaged region. In April of 1933, President Franklin D. Roosevelt would ask Congress to establish the Tennessee Valley Authority, "a corporation clothed with the power of government, but possessed of the flexibility and initiative of private enterprise," validating the vision of two stubborn men, one from the farm state of Nebraska and the other from an East Harlem district that had as little

127

awareness or concern for the farmers of the Tennessee Valley as anybody in the world.[111]

Put another way, it made sense for a farm senator like Norris to become involved in Muscle Shoals, but what was La Guardia doing there?

Aside from his own longtime interest in public control of energy, tracing back to his years as president of the New York City Board of Aldermen, the "thrilling" possibilities of so vast an undertaking entranced La Guardia with its promise of positive government. A nonpartisan public effort to harness nature and develop a region in a coordinated public effort carried responsible and caring government in the direction he favored. Thus far, only the largest corporations had been able to raise the money and commit the resources for such a project. Muscle Shoals would prove that social policy need not sit at the feet of private profit motives, that the nation could get those things done that it decided needed doing. It represented an experiment in more rational management of the nation's resources than merely throwing it open to the market.

His sense that there might be something more effective than the combination of America's captains of industry and the free market brought La Guardia into renewed conflict with the imperious secretary of the treasury, Andrew Mellon, over tax plans that favored the wealthy business interests. Many Americans, rich and poor alike, considered Mellon a great public servant, who either protected their prosperity or promised to bring it about. But to La Guardia, Mellon represented a distorted, self-serving, rich man's view of the American economy. Mellon had resigned from the boards of sixty corporations with a combined value of $60 billion in order to accept appointment to the cabinet. As far as Fiorello was concerned Mellon could resign from the boards, he could stash his money in blind trusts, but he could not cast aside the assumptions that accompanied his lofty position. "Any man of energy and initiative," Mellon liked to believe, "in this country can get what he wants out of life." La Guardia had seen too much of poverty *and* frustrated initiative to accept this complaisant reading. The son and representative of working-class immigrants demanded to know in what way the Mellons, Fords, and Rockefellers, were more brilliant than "Mrs. Marie Esposito, or Mrs. Rebecca Epstein, or Mrs. Maggie Flynn, while keeping house in a city tenement, raising six children on a weekly envelope containing $30, trying to send the children to school warmly and properly clad, paying exorbitant gas and electric light bills, and endeavoring to provide meat at least once a day for the family? *That's* financial genius of the highest order." If the United States was to continue to be a land of opportunity, La Guardia argued, it must prevent "the accumulation of enormous fortunes, and the control of industry and commerce that goes with such large fortunes. . . ."[112]

When a member of the Women's National Republican Club, a stenographer, attacked him for opposing Mellon's tax plan, La Guardia wrote back: "I can readily understand your anxiety and that of your co-workers on the taxes over $200,000 a year. I was a stenographer once and I remember how much I had to worry about my income over $200,000.'' Indeed, many Americans, stenographers and others, who thought not in terms of what they were but of what they might become, found La Guardia's unceasing criticism offensive, but he was more concerned about those who worked hard and could not make ends meet for their families. With many Americans in this position, no theory, trickle-down or otherwise, was working. ''I do not want to destroy wealth,'' he told critics, ''but I do want to abolish poverty.''[113]

So the decade found him supporting rent control in the national capital, a bonus for World War I veterans, and wage increases for low-paid postal workers. He left a sickbed to vote for the Child Labor Amendment and staunchly stood by the side of labor, denouncing the granting of injunctions to stop strikes, walking picket lines, and publicizing the poor conditions of working families. He even hatched a plan to unionize baseball and levy taxes on the sale of players from one club to another.[114]

The terrible plight of America's coal miners particularly attracted his interest. Numerous small operators in the bituminous coal industry competed in cutthroat fashion for the business of the large steel, railroad, and power monopolies, and owners periodically cut wages to make their prices more competitive. No industry was more volatile, and few laborers worked under more dismaying pressures. In 1925 La Guardia called upon the national government to take over the coal fields. Three years later, when the mine operators cut wages from an annual average of $1200 to $750 and even $600, miners struck and La Guardia rushed to their side.

With John L. Lewis he toured the Pennsylvania coal fields, where he found conditions so appalling that he immediately asked New York social workers to ship food and clothing. Then he gathered evidence of the poverty and shameful conditions to present to his colleagues so intoxicated with talk of the prosperous new era. ''Asbestos will not hold the statements I shall make on the floor of the House,'' he telegraphed Senator Hiram Johnson. Back in Washington he ripped into the mine operators for the miserable conditions, the private police forces, the black and Mexican scabs who were imported to break strikes and were themselves exploited in the worst way. If the owners could not pay better wages, La Guardia said, then the industry had no right to exist. The miners should not pay with their low wages for an industry whose owners extracted handsome profits.[115]

What so many Americans were willing to ignore in these high-flying times he gave his singular attention. In August 1925 the price of meat in New York City rose. His people could not afford to pay more for beef, and La Guardia organized a meat strike to force the price back down. He learned that retailers were barely meeting expenses. At the same time he surveyed his colleagues in Congress to check prices around the nation and to learn whether the cost of beef on the hoof had gone up. His western colleagues informed him that ranchers were having a hard time covering even the cost of feed. If the farmers and retailers were not getting the money, La Guardia wanted to know, where were all the profits going?

La Guardia flew to Chicago to confront the meat packers, the middlemen who formed the "Meat Trust," but these discussions led nowhere.

Finally, Fiorello asked the Department of Agriculture to investigate. The Secretary of Agriculture, William Jardine, declined, citing the expense of such an investigation as prohibitive. Instead he sent along a pamphlet on the economical uses of meat. "I asked for your help," La Guardia fulminated, "and you send me a bulletin. The people of New York City cannot feed their children on bulletins. They may be very interesting to amateur parlor reformers and to society cooking classes . . . but they are of no use to the tenement dwellers of this great city. The housewives of New York City have been trained by hard experience on the economical uses of meat."[116]

La Guardia did not forget the secretary's cavalier attitude. Several months later, when Congress discussed an appropriations bill for the Department of Agriculture, La Guardia took the floor. "Mr. Chairman and gentlemen, now that the House is engaged in its favorite indoor sport of fooling the farmer I want to take the opportunity to say just a few words for the consumer." He recounted his investigation of the meat industry, the price gouging, his unsuccessful meetings with the Armour Company and other packers, and his efforts to involve the Agriculture Department. "This," La Guardia shouted, waving a copy of "Lamb and Mutton and their Uses in the Diet," is the help I got. . . . Why 90 per cent of the people of New York City cannot afford to eat lamb chops." As he spoke, the congressman was going through his pockets. The other fine gentlemen of the House turned their attention to the momentarily discomfited La Guardia. "I have here with me now—where is it? Oh yes here it is in my vest pocket," and he pulled out a puny chop of meat, "30 cents' worth of lamb." From other pockets came a steak costing $1.75 and a more expensive roast. The issue was not how to make economical use of meat but how to get meat. "Gentlemen, we simply have to eat. We have formed the habit."[117]

Having given his colleagues a good show, he proceeded to give them an education in the flow of cattle across the United States, the various parts of the animal profitably sold off by the packers, the unconscionable increase in the price of meat between the time it arrived in Chicago and the time it was shipped out. The damned food trust—that same gang of profiteers who included the entrepreneurs who sold the army rotten goods in wartime—he charged, was making a decent meal impossible for many Americans. In another of his "show and tell" performances, he pulled out a loaf of bread, squeezed it down to half its size, and announced that the Bread Trust was feeding the people "pneumatic bread."[118]

He continued also to attend to the needs of America's servicemen, campaigning for veterans' bonuses and fair treatment for those in the army. In Foggia he had fought the brass to keep his men out of unsafe planes, and nothing infuriated him more than the disregard for the safety of American servicemen. On December 28, 1927, the American submarine S-4 sank after a collision and became stuck in a mudbank. Efforts to rescue the crew continued for an agonizingly long time, resulting in an outcry against the navy for sending out such a craft, for its ineffective rescue efforts, for everything connected with the tragedy. Probably the only representative at work at his desk on New Year's Day, La Guardia was prepared to assail the navy for its recklessness and join the chorus for restricting the construction and use of subs when he decided that he must check for himself.

He rushed to New London to the accident site and boarded the sunken sub's sister ship for thirty-six hours to investigate the rescue operations and the safety of the craft. Lowell Limpus writes that the observer sub suffered a six-hour breakdown, threatening those aboard with a fate similar to that of the *S-4* until the fault was finally repaired. Nonetheless, La Guardia concluded that the navy had done all it could to try to save the doomed ship. He reported his conclusions to the House that the accident was a freak occurrence and that navy divers had worked heroically to rescue the crew. He recommended continued support for the navy's program despite the tragedy. Twenty years later, Admiral Ernest J. King told Secretary of the Navy James Forrestal that La Guardia rescued the submarine program from the congressional budget cleaver by reassuring the nation about the reliability of the deep-water vessels.[119]

The causes continued, fueled by a tireless energy and a bottomless indignation. He stood in perpetual dissent against the prevailing sense of the majority, against the bluff, the live-for-today-and-hang-the-future spirit that carried over from the frenetic dance floor to the government's attitude toward such national treasures as the Muscle Shoals properties. The sense of indignation and resentment that he brought with him to Washington as a freshman congressman did not wane, although his impact remained small. More businesses merged in this decade than ever before in the history of the United States, creating more of the giant trusts that he so opposed. Mellon was cheered as the best secretary of treasury since Alexander Hamilton and Herbert Hoover promised to welcome the age of permanent materialism. The social program that marked Italians and Jews as inferior, outlawed the sale of beer and wine, and rejected as an oxymoron the idea of the deserving poor held strong sway.

It was a baffling, frustrating decade for reformers who remembered a time when social justice counted for more than the GNP. The liberal economist Stuart Chase recalled:

> Them was the days! When the muckrakers were best sellers, when trust busters were swinging their lariats over every state capitol, when ''privilege'' shook in its shoes, when . . . Utopia was just around the corner. . . .
>
> Now look at the damned thing. You could put the avowed Socialists into a roomy new house, Mr. Coolidge is compared favorably to Lin-

coln, . . . Mr. Eastman writes triolets in France, Mr. Steffens has brought him a castle in Italy, and Mr. Howe digs turnips in Nantucket.

Shall we lay a wreath on the Uplift Movement in America? I suppose we might as well.[120]

With his successes still in the future, La Guardia too despaired of moving America over to his point of view. "I am doomed to live in a hopeless minority for most of my legislative days," he told an interviewer, as he continued to raise his disapproving voice to fight for a more inclusive American politics.[121]

The Republican party, the party with which he occasionally consorted, he denounced as the "kept woman of big business," but he found no alternative to his liking. "The Democrats," he instructed on the floor of the House, "have a duty to fulfill. It is the duty of the minority party to check the ruthlessness of a majority." But there were no checkers, no one to speak for those who fell by the wayside in the race. "There is no party division in Congress," he said on another occasion, "on matters involving more than a million dollars."[122]

Clearly he represented more than the East Harlem population that had elected him, although he represented them well enough. The list of his interests and the causes he supported reads like the work of an entire party, not the opposition agenda of a single indefatigable representative from northern Manhattan. Little wonder that this supporter of coal strikers in Pennsylvania, blacks from the south, wets from all over the nation, urban immigrants and minorities, progressive reformers, veterans, farmers, workers, and consumers, who fought against the KKK, Henry Ford, Prohibition, the sale of Muscle Shoals, censorship, a "save the rich tax," and keeping cool with Coolidge, was known as America's congressman-at-large. Brought up in an aggressive home, where raised voices were not unknown in the course of a debate and where defiance won respect, he brought that same truculence to the floor of the House. "The Congress," he reported to his constituents at the Star Casino in July 1926, "has just passed through a crime wave. Ruled by the Ku Klux Klan and the trust bosses, the legislative body of the United States government is but a travesty of what it should be."[123]

Something else that he had brought with him from his Arizona youth made La Guardia unique. He disdained convention and fear. When an armed gunman stood up in the House gallery waving a pistol, demanding the right to speak, the horde of honorable gentlemen ripped the doors off the hinges in their haste to run from the chambers. One esteemed legislator crawled for cover with a cuspidor on his head. It was the roly-poly New Yorker who scrambled up the stairs to tackle the intruder. When Oscar De Priest, a black representative from Chicago, prepared to take his seat, a number of gentlemen in the House expressed their displeasure. La Guardia wired the Speaker of the House that he would be glad to have Mr. De Priest as his neighbor. In the course of his defense of Billy Mitchell's controversial campaign for a unified American Air Force, La Guardia testified against the establishment brass, taking Mitchell's side. "Are you quoted correctly in the newspapers, sir," asked an aggrieved general, "in calling me nothing but a beribboned dog-robber?" "No sir," responded the unchastened legislator. "I was not aware that you had any ribbons." "Beyond my powers of description," said the exasperated prosecutor, "thank heaven he is sui generis."[124]

The year 1928 seemed unusually auspicious to the Republican presidential candidate, Herbert Hoover. Accepting his party's nomination, he said, "We in America today are nearer the triumph over poverty than ever before in the history of any land." As the year drew to a close, Fiorello La Guardia toured New York's slums and admitted to an accompanying journalist that he had not expected the poverty and dreadful conditions that he found. The nation was preparing for its plateau of prosperity and there was La Guardia in his accustomed position, dissenting.[125]

In another context, Georg Brandes described a situation that he thought he discerned in some European countries. His description has an eerie relevance here. Self-satisfied, resting on their laurels, they lulled themselves to sleep. And while they dozed they dreamed that they were a very special race of people, fated for a separate destiny, mighty and free and rich, abundantly rich. When they woke up it was too late to grasp the emptiness of their dreams and the extent of their delusion. They lay amidst the ruins.[126]

CHAPTER 4

Between Two Americas

1. In the Community

JOHN Dos Passos wrote of two Americas. One was prosperous, confident, well-born; the other was the slum where everything flourished that prosperous America denied: poverty, illiteracy, decrepit housing, abundant disease, unemployment, drinking, organized crime, socialism, and an outspoken angry representative with his arm raised in perpetual objection. East Harlem, whose eastern perimeter was described by one historian as a perfect setting for an American version of Charles Dickens's *Hard Times*, stood at variance with the confident times, a core of decay surrounded by zones of plenty. Here stood the ugly offscourings of American industrialism, grimy factories amidst junkyards, warehouses, used-car lots, and repair shops. Coal yards and oil storage depots belching gaseous pollutants tinted the sky an ashen gray and raw sewage fouled the river. A transient population filled East Harlem's bars and whorehouses while its residents occupied seedy tenements and deteriorating housing.[1]

This environment shaped Fiorello La Guardia's ideas about opportunity in America. Here he contemplated the effrontery of Secretary of Treasury Andrew Mellon assuring the nation that any American could live the good rich life—so long as he wanted. It was a matter of will, insisted Mellon. Not in East Harlem, cried La Guardia.

Not in a district where as late as 1939 investigators would report that 84 percent of the housing lacked central heating and more than half of the apartments did not have private bathrooms. "Only demolition and reconstruction," concluded a post-World War I study of East Harlem, "could make it habitable." This district reported the lowest median level of education in the city. Educators complained not only of the expected lassitude of the uninterested school child but also the

134

disinterest and hostility of the parents. Even for the second generation the usual job was menial labor with little hope for advance.[2]

One overriding fact framed this district's politics: In good times, East Harlem was suffering a depression. Those of its inhabitants who achieved some success, who were able to put together enough savings to invest in a shop or send a child to college moved out to new sections in Brooklyn, the Bronx's Grand Concourse, or central Manhattan's West Side. Those who did not, gathered here; the uncomfortable, the unsuccessful, the uneducated, the defeated. So, while other politicians sat down to look at the cards that had been dealt their communities and demanded an adjustment here or there, a new post office, some jobs, a break for industry, La Guardia shaped a policy for a depression, demanding a new deal of the cards: sharp control over business, a redistribution of wealth, and an ambitious social program.

An East Harlem researcher in 1920 counted twenty-five different ethnic groups in this slum melting pot, with Jews and Italians dominating. However, the Jewish population dwindled from 125,000 in 1920 to fewer than 53,000 seven years later. It was commonly said that Jews were proletarians of only one generation, that factory workers raised doctors, lawyers, and college professors, and along with this advance up the status ladder they moved to more attractive neighborhoods. By 1932 fewer than 15,000 Jews could still be found in East Harlem. By then a new influx of Puerto Ricans again changed the character of the area.[3]

But mainly in these interwar years the neighborhood was dominated by some 80,000 Italians. On these streets gray-haired men played *bocci*, while kerchiefed women hung garlic around the necks of their grandchildren to ward off the evil eye and joined in the festive veneration of village saints. Here residents redrew Old World boundaries, dividing up the streets according to village origins and vendettas. "Outside the family group," recalled Leonard Covello, a perceptive student of East Harlem's Italians, "reigned indifference, often even hostility." Men who had worked hard to bring over their families raised their sons in the hope that they too would find work on the docks, in construction, or at day labor.[4]

Fiorello La Guardia was not raised in this way, and he saw little virtue in keeping the narrow peasant outlook. Learn the language, laws, and culture of the new society, he advised. He wanted Italians to move past the rim of American society, to win respect and make a better life by broadening their cultural milieu, as other groups had done. Blending a concern for modernizing the Italian community with his own interest in an expanded political base in the ethnic quarter, La Guardia undertook his first and only business venture in 1925. He withdrew all his savings, took a second mortgage on his Bronx home, and founded the La Guardia Publishing Company to develop an Italian-language magazine, called *L'Americolo*.

La Guardia sought to publish a sprightly, stylish journal, the "best damned Italian illustrated weekly that was ever gotten out in this country," that would compete with Generoso Pope's pro-Tammany and pro-Fascist *Il Progresso Italo-Americano* and *Corriere d'America*. If the venture came close to achieving his target circulation of 40,000, aside from all else, it would thrust the Little Flower to the forefront of the surging Italian-American community.[5]

L'Americolo absorbed all of La Guardia's savings and also much of his energy. He signed up the staff, secured the office space, and kept a tight watch on everything associated with the journal. He insisted that *L'Americolo* avoid the questionable practices of some ethnic journals that used their columns as a pretext for touting patent medicines, charm cures, submerged real estate, and the ubiquitous attorneys promising assistance with immigration, citizenship, and "all other aspects of the law." *L'Americolo* refused all advertising for easy cures and get-rich-quick schemes.

It featured articles on the home, travel pieces, critical essays on social issues, short fiction, and, of course, La Guardia on politics, manners, and anything that grabbed his fancy. Unfortunately for its poor editor, Andrea Luotto, the venture was so close to La Guardia's heart that he intruded into every aspect of the publication, peering over Luotto's shoulder from Washington to suggest layouts, photographs, features, ads, and anything else that came to mind. Once he sent a note asking for an article that would lift his spirits. Another message demanded "little more snap, little more pep, little more thought, little more ideas."[6]

The journal tried hard to shape community interests toward middle-class respectability, but it failed to attract a sufficient readership. Working-class Italians were not interested, and middle-class Italians could find better journals in English. More seriously, *L'Americolo* was not prepared to confront controversial issues within its own field of interest. In the same year that *L'Americolo* was launched, Count Ignazio Thaon di Revel founded the Fascist League of America to spread the "ideals of Fascism and the marvelous work of national reconstruction of the Fascist government in Italy." Organizations limning the praises of Italian dictatorship proliferated. Ronzi Abbondandola's Circolo Mario Morgantini on 116th Street distributed fascist propaganda and posted black-shirted young men at the front of its building to greet passers-by with the fascist salute. But La Guardia, who had little respect for Benito Mussolini and considered the dictator "a pitiful caricature of a man, a barbershop bully in a game far beyond his capacities," refused to address the issue in *L'Americolo* for fear of offending those who favored Italy's new assertiveness. Even in Congress, where he customarily skewered Great Britain for its Irish policy and voiced opinions on a wide range of topics, the blustering Flower warned colleagues that "It's none of our concern what kind of Government the Italian people have."[7]

The notion that an Italian-language magazine could interest an immigrant audience by speaking of Muscle Shoals, the Charleston, sports, and art while avoiding Mussolini and Capone in the end proved fatuous. *L'Americolo* was just too limited a magazine, a journal of La Guardia's opinion, an agent of his ambition. Every edition lost money, and a few months after the project's launching, the staff informed La Guardia, "We . . . already have a corpse at our feet." He cut costs, tried to drum up interest with promotions and prizes, but to no avail. The mortgage on the Bronx home that he had shared with his dying Thea was foreclosed. Fiorello lost more than $15,000 and learned to stick to politics. The failure of *L'Americolo* demonstrated the immigrant community's lack of interest in his cultural agenda, and it suggested that this was a gap he was not equipped to bridge. He did not appreciate this immediately, but *L'Americolo's* failure had a silver lining. It saved him from becoming exclusively identified with the Italian community and its internal development.[8]

With the folding of *L'Americolo*, La Guardia redoubled his attention to the other groups. The Yiddish-speaking "Italiainer" collaborated with a clutch of Jewish congressmen to fight anti-Jewish discrimination. For the Irish he offered his allegiance to the Free State and high praise for Eamon De Valera and the other revolutionists—"how I love that word." Few Filipinos lived in East Harlem or in the United States, but La Guardia supported revolution there too. He courted black Americans, Americans of Hungarian extraction, Germans, and, by the end of the decade, Puerto Ricans, who were filtering into East Harlem by the thousands.[9]

His congressional office helped the newly arrived islanders with housing and other needs, while Fiorello added stock denunciations of the American sugar interests to his speeches about the greedy trusts, and championed Puerto Rican independence. La Guardia also developed ties with Puerto Rican politicians on the island and would call upon them for help during his campaigns.[10]

In September 1928, after a hurricane hit Puerto Rico, Fiorello volunteered immediately to help with the emergency relief effort. "CAN START IMMEDIATELY," he wired both the White House and the Red Cross. "WILL GO EITHER BY BOAT OR PLANE ON ANY TASK ASSIGNED CAN COORDINATE WORK OR DO ANYTHING USEFUL STOP ANXIETY AMONG LARGE POPULATION PORTO RICANS IN NEW YORK CITY VERY GREAT CAN REACH ME AT MY OFFICE . . . OR MY HOME." Washington, unsure of what kind of political damage La Guardia could bring to such work, declined the offer. Three months later he led the fight for an $18 million appropriation to help disaster victims and coordinated a message center that kept mainland Puerto Ricans informed about their friends and relatives.[11]

———

His attitude toward the new group was one sign of his political sensitivity to his ever-changing constituency and its interests. It also demonstrated the effective work of a remarkable corps of second-generation Italian Americans who staffed his office, managed his campaigns, and served as his eyes and ears in the neighborhood. These

137

promising young lawyers, Al Scotti, Eddie Contento, Dominick Felitti, Nicholas Saldiveri, and Ernest Cuneo shared his victories and made him the godfather of their children. He treated them as surrogate sons, sharing with them the lessons of his experience, and taking quiet pleasure in their achievements. To be sure, he did not handle them tenderly. He dealt with them as his father had with him, demanding much, cheating them of deserved praise, plying them with unsolicited advice, burrowing into their private affairs, and caring about them deeply. And to them there was no greater praise than once in a while when the Major would call one of them into the office to meet a visitor and be introduced with "This is my son."[12]

La Guardia took special interest in a disheveled, sunken-faced young man, Vito Marcantonio, whom he first met at a high school graduation ceremony in 1921. After graduation Vito registered for law classes at New York University and worked for social uplift at Leonard Covello's Casa del Popolo, a neighborhood settlement house of leftist persuasion. Marc directed a Tenant's League, coordinated low-rent demonstrations, and apprenticed at Haarlem House, where he assisted immigrants, organized local peddlers, investigated political corruption, and pressured landlords to improve tenement conditions. Before long, Marc's full schedule of social activism got in the way of his legal studies. Still, despite failing grades, he refused to cut back on his commitments. Marcantonio paid as little attention to his appearance as he did to his legal studies, affecting the conventional shabbiness of the committed iconoclast. His rhetoric had a fine agitator's edge, and his ambition was a match for La Guardia's.[13]

When La Guardia was forced to run without Republican backing in 1924, twenty-two-year-old Marc converted his office at Haarlem House into a campaign bunker, pulling together a tribe of laborers, professionals, and local businessmen into the Fiorello H. La Guardia Political Association to create the Ghibboni. Lowell Limpus described them as a benign alternative to Tammany, a secret organization from the East Harlem tenements drawn to the sport of electing one of their own. Under Marcantonio, this battery of loyalists—numbering hundreds of volunteers—would sweep through the streets chanting slogans, passing out leaflets, and bringing out the crowds for La Guardia's rallies. When the campaign verged on insolvency, Marc cadged contributions from a local speakeasy, and on election day he borrowed hearses from a local mortician to deliver voters to the polls. Another of the Ghibboni, a professor, was put to work writing Italian leaflets, and if a strong arm or two was needed, Marc dispatched prizefighters Dominick Petrone and Tony Vacarelli to lend a hand. While Tammany denounced the Ghibboni as Mafia cut-throats, there is no evidence that they were connected to organized crime, as, for instance, some of Marcantonio's later supporters may have been.[14]

Following the 1924 campaign, Fiorello took his young acolyte under his wing. Marcantonio moved into La Guardia's home in the Bronx, where they would discuss politics and the law late into the night. When Fiorello joined the new law firm of Foster, La Guardia and Cutler, he asked for a $10,000-a-year salary, a promise that the firm would accept lower fees from immigrants and workers, that it would not defend gangsters or dope peddlers, and that Vito Marcantonio would be placed on the staff. "I want you to take this boy in," he wrote to his partners, "I want to make him my professional heir." In return he expected much from his young lieutenant:

My dear Boy:

Your conduct when I was in the city last was not at all what I had expected. You are young, you have a lot to learn, and a long way to go before you will be a lawyer in the real sense of the word.

I am fond of you and want to help you. Were I not interested I would not have planned as I did—looking far into the future.

You simply must learn that you don't know it all, and that others in this world have some brains. Both Mr. Cutler and Mr. Foster are splendid gentlemen and able lawyers, and I shall expect a courteous, respectful obedient attitude toward them at all times.

You have an opportunity presented to you as very few boys have, other than those who can step into their fathers' office, knowing that one day it will be theirs. That is what I am offering you. You must make up your mind and be fair with me. You either are going to be a politician, a social worker or a lawyer. If you are satisfied as I told you, to make a living from the Magistrate and Municipal Courts, with General Sessions as the possible limit, you can keep up your social and political activities.

But if you love your profession and want to be proficient, and intend to follow it, then you have got to change your attitude and your whole mode of living. You have to cut out your evening appointments, your dances, and your midnight philandering, for the next five years and devote yourself to the serious study of the Law. From 1907 to 1912 I did it. . . .[15]

His own freewheeling style notwithstanding, La Guardia offered Marc advice on making a conventional success. While La Guardia often referred to his own "shabby clothes and disproportionate figure," he encouraged Marc to "be careful of your personal appearance. Get a Gillette razor, and keep yourself well groomed at all times. Be always respectful and courteous to all—the humble as well as the high. And for goodness sake, keep your eyes and ears open, and keep your mouth closed for the next twenty years." Marc apparently took heed. He became a fastidious dresser and within six months settled down to marriage with a woman eleven years his senior from New Hampshire, whose lineage traced back to colonial Americans.[16]

He would not, however, give up his interest in politics, and La Guardia continued to hold him to impossible standards. He once upbraided Marcantonio so severely that the usually self-confident Marc whimpered like a wounded pup that he might have faults but La Guardia was unfair in making him out to be incompetent. He was attending to the political needs of the district while trying to prepare ten negligence cases and run an office, all at the same time.[17]

The tough training produced a skilled political manager who ran the congressional office and the La Guardia campaigns with zealous efficiency. Marc specialized in the rip-roaring political theater that lent La Guardia rallies their unique fervor. The lean, black-haired chief Ghibbone would get up on a flatbed truck, speaking slowly at first, bringing his heel down on the truck bed for emphasis. The pace quickened. The heel came down again and again, making a sharp noise each time, the words spilling out faster, louder. The heel was going down even more frequently, with each staccato bang accelerating the tempo and the decibel level. Finally Marc was shouting at the top of his lungs, stomping the floor as if he were a railroad caboose about to chug off, bringing the crowd to a frenzy. Once when Tammany bricks began to rain down on a La Guardia gathering, Ghibboni fanned out to find the source of the disturbance. Suddenly Marc spied the culprit. Without a care for safety, he lunged off the back of the truck onto the perpetrator. It was the kind of full-hearted style that Fiorello loved.[18]

Another of La Guardia's Italian American young men was put to the test on his very first interview. Ernest Cuneo, a recent law school graduate awaiting admission to the bar, worked as a reporter for the *New York Daily News*, and editor Lowell Limpus recommended him for a position with La Guardia's staff. Years later, Cuneo recalled his first interview with the congressman. He walked into an office on the sixteenth floor of 295 Madison Avenue and took a seat on a hard bench and waited. Determined-looking people carrying books and papers scurried about at a hectic pace, filtering in and out of a room at the far end of the office suite. Finally he was waved into the La Guardia sanctum, a medium-size room dominated by a huge desk with three plain chairs. At the desk a rumpled ball of a man in shirtsleeves slouched over a stack of papers, oblivious to the intruder. Behind him hung a painting of young street urchins playing on a vacant lot. Eventually the huddled figure moved, without quite looking up, and pointed a finger toward a chair. La Guardia spent another few minutes with his papers while Cuneo squirmed. Finally he pushed his glasses up on his forehead, looked up, and blurted, "What do you want?"

Why did Cuneo want to become a lawyer. "To live off the people? To take their earnings? When a decent world comes, there won't *be* any lawyers." He threw back his large head and laughed. Then he warned that he was an impossible boss. The job would be too much for such a tender young man. Why did Cuneo want such a job? Go out into the front office and ask Mimi Felitti what it was like to work here. "Then come back and we'll talk." Cuneo asked the haggard-looking Felitti his question. "I have worked for Major La Guardia for ten years," Felitti told him, "and all I have got out of it is a terrible inferiority complex." Cuneo stepped back in and revealed what he had learned to La Guardia, who roared with appreciation. "All right you can serve your clerkship here." Cuneo waited for details, but La Guardia turned back to his work. The interview had ended.[19]

Cuneo learned to suffer this behavior, along with the boss's moodiness and Vesuvian eruptions, with equanimity. Working for La Guardia was at once terrible and wonderful, hectic but exhilarating, since La Guardia took for his field the entire political arena. Every issue was a battle. The office was part of the infantry and their expected commitment to victory, total. Fiorello La Guardia's reactions were not balanced. His joy was unrestrained, his disgust monumental, his satisfaction extravagant, his denunciations explosive. Arguments based on precedent made him seethe—he wanted them based on good sense, preferably *his* good sense or something very close to it—while the notion of "progress" made him sparkle.

Always afraid that his staff might become complacent, La Guardia reminded them every once in a while of their bottomless stupidity. He might riffle through a freshly prepared report, exclaim his disappointment, and discard the paper. La Guardia thought this was necessary, explained Cuneo, to ward off the most evil of maladies, a swelled head. The staff tolerated the abuse in order to work for La Guardia. He was irascible but he had integrity, and he got more done in the name of unpopular causes than a battery of gentlemanly reformers. The affection of La Guardia's staff for him Cuneo compared to the love of the Old Guards for Napoleon. They were "happy to accept a minimum of security for a maximum of action." In which other office would a small band of young assistants be ordered to draw up a bill for the impeachment of a popular secretary of the treasury and have the particulars on the congressman's desk the following day? Where could they watch a possessed man who converted politics into a creative struggle with "the fury of a Michelangelo tearing a statue out of the living rock."[20]

The office staff tried to protect La Guardia from his rash behavior, but generally they could do no more than stand by with the gut-wrenching feeling that he was headed for disaster. He would make wild accusations. They would scamper all around to find supporting evidence. And then, after finding nothing, they would watch him stand up on the floor of the House perfectly calm, pulling documents out of his trouser pockets as if they had been filed there for years. Only later did they realize that almost nothing that La Guardia did was without calculation. He generally knew what he was doing and where every seemingly wild charge would lead. In the vast Congress, his was one of the voices that was truly exciting. John Peter Altgeld's philosophy of administration perfectly fit Fiorello's style. "The fact that you met with an accident or got your legs broken, your neck twisted and your head smashed is not equal to the delivery of the goods."[21]

One night during one of his congressional campaigns, Fiorello was preparing to speak before a street corner crowd when he noticed a Tammany group gathering less than a block away, preparing to disrupt the rally. A lone policeman stood between the two groups. "Ernest," Fiorello shouted to Cuneo, "go and tell that cop we were here first and we're staying. Tell him if the Law can't protect us, we can protect ourselves. . . . Get tough with him. And if you have to hit him don't hesitate. . . . Punch him in the eye, if he tries to finagle us." La Guardia was serious. Cuneo delivered the unappreciated message to the officer and received a tongue-lashing in return, but the officer then turned to the opposition crowd, shouting, "Beat it." Had the officer not dispersed the crowd, campaign workers were certain that Fiorello would have led a melee.[22]

In a campaign, victory was all. Ever vigilant against voting fraud by the other side, La Guardia had Cuneo deputized as an assistant attorney general to serve as a poll watcher on election day and put him through the La Guardia training course. What do you do if they try to steal the election? Why, arrest the culprit of course. No, no, said Fiorello. He had no interest in filling the jails; he wanted the election. If they rushed the machine, he expected Cuneo to place his body between the attackers and the goal and then "cast as many votes for me as they stole. . . . Vote until they knock you out." Cuneo had been a boxer in college, but he did not relish the prospect of hand-to-hand combat with Tammany. He would get a gun. Absolutely not, "I'd sooner see you dead," came the none too comforting bellow, "than tried for murder."

Cuneo reported for duty expecting the worst. As the very first citizen checked in and prepared to vote, Tammany's man walked over and moved the curtain aside to assist the man in the booth. Cuneo's complaint elicited a weary suggestion that he take it easy. Soon, Cuneo spied his antagonist passing bills out to a line of voters. Then Tammany raised the curtain to help yet another voter. Cuneo rushed the ward heeler and punched him in the jaw, throwing the stunned man back into the machine. Policemen rushed in, leading to a scuffle on the floor. A few minutes later a large limousine pulled up, discharging seven huge figures with La Guardia buttons in their lapels. They surrounded Cuneo and just stood there until another car roared up to the voting site. There was no mistaking the portly figure that rolled out shouting, "Attaboy Ernest." La Guardia ran over to the police to warn them that no more of this behavior would be tolerated. One more complaint and the congressman would take the pleasure of having them locked up.[23]

As a young boy, Joey Adams, the entertainer, worked for La Guardia as a gofer. Once, La Guardia sent him on an errand to deliver a message to an election poll watcher. A few minutes later Joey ducked back into headquarters. Tammany musclemen had kept him out of the polling place. La Guardia called for a driver and the pair went back to the site. La Guardia came to a door being blocked by a ruffian a good foot taller than him. "Get out of the way, you lousy bum," rasped La Guardia as he pushed his finger into the fellow's belly and threatened to lay him out on the floor unless he moved. The man pulled to the side. Later that day Adams came back with another story. This time it was about La Guardia's forces. They were stuffing ballots. It was wrong, said the tearful Adams, expecting Fiorello to put an end to it. Instead La Guardia laid his hand on the boy's shoulder and explained the facts of Harlem political life. "We must fight fire with fire—all is fair in love, war and politics. They are stealing, cheating, and murdering us, and we must fight them on their own grounds." Being good wouldn't make much difference if he was out of office, and being bad could keep him in power to help so many of the needy and the little people. Debate this rationalization all you wish, no doubts plagued La Guardia. He was better than Tammany and he had to win.[24]

And he really meant it. The little people he spoke of were not merely an excuse for taking liberties at election time. They were real and their problems of genuine concern to him. While others who came to Washington walked with the powerful lobbyists and their industrial sponsors, La Guardia remained loyal to the straitened East Harlem constituency that sent him, refusing to "descend to respectability" and abandon his people. It was his task, La Guardia liked to say, to serve the poor and afflict the comfortable, while comforting the afflicted.[25]

2. "When You Appeal to Me . . . I Will Respond"

As a congressman La Guardia mastered two jobs, doing the nation's business as a legislator and servicing the needs of his own district. La Guardia's office handled complaints about city services, immigration worries, problems with the law, citizenship papers, rent problems, school issues, and the full range of annoyances and difficulties with which citizens turn to friendly and helpful congressmen. Mistreatment or unfairness immediately set his blood to boiling. He would curse at the bureaucrats and the politicians, ready to make war with the government he himself represented, refusing to concede that there were insoluble problems.[26]

One day a simple laborer, barely clothed against the cold winter, came to the office complaining that his family was cold. The man explained that the gas had been turned off. Fiorello asked him how much money he needed for the company to turn it back on. A quarter. As he dug into his trousers for a few bills—obviously if the man did not have a quarter for gas, the children needed clothing—La Guardia started berating the fellow. He was a workingman, in overalls; why were his children cold and no doubt hungry? It was not right for a workingman to have to beg for money. The anger was so misplaced, directed as it was at the victim. Sometimes when he could not immediately find a target for his anger, La Guardia's frustration did fall on the wrong target. He gave the man the bills, warning him to use the money for the children and the gas bill. The man mumbled his gratitude and turned to leave. Wait, called Fiorello. Had the utility given notice? With the same pitiful resignation that had enraged La Guardia initially, the figure in overalls looked up at him. "No." The man had no fight in him. They just came in and turned it off. La Guardia marked down the family's name and address and warned him again to pay the bill and care for the children.

As soon as the door closed Fiorello's frustration turned to cathartic fury. There was a villain! The utility had no right to turn the gas off without giving the man notice. He dialed the governor's office, demanding the personal number of the public service commissioner. Now that he had a villain there was no stopping him. True, the villain was a mighty small part of the problem, but this was the part that he could deal with. It became the solution, the most important thing to do in the next few minutes. Nothing would deter him from having the gas turned back on. He reached the official, treating him to an opening salutation that seared his ears. He threatened to investigate him five generations back if he did not immediately clear up the injustice that had been done. A citizen had a right to be warned about such things even if he was poor and did not have money. The poor were not without rights! The commissioner had no opportunity to argue. He agreed to call the utility, and within a few hours the gas was reopened. (How important such victories were remained an open question. The next day the family would receive proper notice. They would not have the money to pay their bill, and within a short while the gas would be shut off for good.)[27]

Morris Diamond walked into La Guardia's office, introduced himself as "from Haarlem House," and asked La Guardia for a West Point appointment. The congressman jumped up from his desk, cupping his fists and raising them in a pugilist's stance, asking the visitor if he wanted to fight. "No," gulped the astonished Diamond. Then why was he interested in going to West Point? La Guardia recommended the young man, but not before he reassured himself that Diamond knew that officers were trained for combat, not empty glory.[28]

Some complaints he did not try to solve. About 2:30 one afternoon a young man with a daft look upon his face came into the office, took a seat, and refused to talk to anyone except La Guardia. At first Fiorello avoided the balmy-looking fellow, but by the end of the day the visitor was still there and La Guardia realized that he could not leave the office without passing him. So he came out and walked over to the visitor. "A dog bit me," the man said simply. Fiorello, grasping the purport of the situation, looked him in the eye. "He did? Did you get his name?" The constituent was taken aback. No, he hadn't, but, why yes, he could see that this was a mistake. Well then, said the solemn La Guardia, "How can I do anything about it if you don't know the dog's name?" Yes, the man understood. "I should have gotten his name." There was not a problem that the people of East Harlem did not bring to the office, whether it was over jobs, raising children, trouble with the law, or political corruption and shakedowns.[29]

His mail was a litany of the plagues of the poor and the displaced. Among the letters asking for help with veteran's benefits, jobs, and immigration papers were many with problems that had nothing to do with government at all. But then the people had come to look upon their congressman as more than a government official. For many he represented the only link to the new society and its strange rules. He was the Italian with American authority, the man of respect, the village chief, lord of the manor of East Harlem, the local sage-priest. "Fiorello La Guardia: Esq. Prominent, Honorable Name! Forgive me if I venture to recur to your high, powerful personality," began a letter from a local woman. Others inquired about dealing with a loutish husband, with children who demanded more freedom, with wives who were forced to work outside the home. La Guardia could not help very much with these problems. If they needed a lawyer he recommended Vito Marcantonio. If they needed advice he favored the modern way. With time they knew that he was freer with advice than with sympathy and that he could be curt when he was asked to bend a law. But if they were suffering from discrimination or rough treatment, no one was more effective than Fiorello.[30]

Many of the letters requested jobs. The requests for work, any work, came in heartbreaking torrents. He did his best, even with the difficult ones. On behalf of a young man who failed a teacher-licensing exam he wrote a sensitive letter of recommendation to a friendly attorney. The man's family "had invested everything in him," and Fiorello felt he deserved the chance for their sake. An immigrant, repeatedly turned down for a hack license, enlisted La Guardia, who pestered the police department for months until the man received his license. Other losers, some with prison records, turned to him as well.[31]

He refused to turn these requests away, even when there was more than sufficient cause. One constituent wrote, asking the congressman to testify in his behalf. La Guardia scrawled the Hapless Harry a note both sensitive and unforgiving. "You got yourself into this mess, and I say now what I have always said, that I think you are dumb, and that it was your stupidity and not your viciousness that got you into this mess." Moreover, the man was taking poor counsel. No character witness would clear him, no matter what the "politicians, fakirs, shysters and the rest of the bums whom you have always believed, and who have gotten you into the difficulty you are in" told him. But "when you appeal to me as you have, I will respond." La Guardia would leave Washington, Thursday midnight and arrive for his court appearance Friday morning. He insisted on only one condition. He did not want any coaching from any lawyers or to have anything at all to do with them.[32]

Other requests he rejected out of hand. An Italian law firm asked him to assist in bringing over an immigrant. It is a common enough practice for representatives to introduce personal bills that punch exceptions into the immigration quotas, and the letter hinted at future collaborations and payment for La Guardia's services—"several sons of the prospective immigrant, being today in prosperous conditions, are willing to sustain any legal expense." La Guardia simply quoted the letter of the law and sent his regrets. Another request from lobbyists resorted to a time-honored practice, offering La Guardia a contribution. Fiorello's offended response set them straight: "You must understand my dear boy, that money is not everything in this country. We have scoundrels here and there who accept money for doing their duty, but we also have a large number of splendid, decent, honest public officials who devote their time to their duties entirely—and nothing can influence them in any way."[33]

On the other hand, he could be disarmingly practical. A constituent once came to ask if a local Republican leader deserved support. Fiorello discussed the overall political picture and finally concluded that, all things considered, the Republican was the best that could be had in this election. As the man rose to leave, La Guardia remarked offhandedly that the politician was in the habit of passing out $10 bills to buy support. The voter should be sure to claim his money.[34]

The life of a politician is sustained by electoral victories. The story is familiar enough. A representative works hard, cajoles his way onto powerful committees, learns the issues, and builds a reputation among his colleagues. The newspapers quote the influential legislator's stand on the issues. The White House agonizes about the way he will vote, and the leaders of his party bargain for his support. In November he goes home for the election and wakes up the day after to learn that his constituents have put a rude end to his political career. In the newspapers, the White House, and the party caucus, all wonder at the vagaries of the political system, tsk tsk at how the mighty have fallen, and put in a call to congratulate the new congressman.

La Guardia knew that he had to divide his time between political issues and the politics of reelection. This was especially true of a political insurgent with an ambition to count for something in politics. In 1924, while the nation voted overwhelmingly for Coolidge, East Harlem elected him on the Socialist ticket. His party affiliation was of little consequence there. But in Congress he paid the price of his independence by being frozen out of the party caucus and off important committee assignments. Here, then, stood a very popular local candidate with a strong following, and there stood the party that could use such a figure and offer him the influence that independence could not. Politics being the dynamic field of forces that it is, it was likely that this situation, so inefficient in its distribution of power, would change. But who would move first, the party to haul in this useful if troublesome character or La Guardia to trade a bit of his independence for some decent committee assignments and influence in Washington?

"I have your letter of October 15, 1925 asking me to assist in electing your two local candidates," La Guardia wrote to Hugh Flaherty, president of the Federal Republican Club in Brooklyn. "You are doubtless unaware of the announcement made by national leaders of the Republican Party that they desire to elect their candidates without the aid of Progressives or persons outside of the Party. Also you must have forgotten that I was read out of the Party not very long ago." He was not prepared to make the wooing back easy.[35]

But he had become disillusioned with the Progressives. The debacle of 1924, with its homage to inexperience and disorder, cooled him on the politics of the heart. His letters to Progressives with plans generally ended by asking if they thought they had enough people to watch the polls and do the legwork necessary for a campaign. If not, they could hug their ideas and go play alone. He was a serious politician, not a dilettante. If they wanted to deliver a message, let them give a lecture or write a book. "Just because a man cannot get a job with one of the two old parties," La Guardia wearily wrote a friend, "does not necessarily make him a Progressive." Yet too many claimed the label for precisely this reason. "There are some fakirs in New York City calling themselves Progressives," he told a journalist, "whom I do not care to be embarrassed by any close contact with." Without a grass roots movement, La Guardia saw little purpose in a third party and broke off from the New York Progressive party.[36]

The rest of his political strategy was less plain. Supporters set off a boom for La Guardia as mayor in 1925. But after he cast a practiced eye on the situation, he decided against such a race. Republicans in New York were a small minority, and he was not even a Republican yet! Besides, the Democratic candidate, dashing Jimmy Walker, so well matched the high-flying times that La Guardia knew his candidacy would be futile. "[State] Senator Walker in all likelihood will be elected," the Little Flower forecast, and then he added a prediction. "The people of New York will receive a liberal education in public utilities ruling the City, favoritism in its basest sense and a real everybody-getting-his administration."[37]

Soon after Walker took the election by a large margin, La Guardia turned to his own upcoming congressional campaign in 1926, informing his constituents that he would run again as an independent. But he was talking for Sam Koenig's attention. True, La Guardia could not live in harmony with the Republicans, but he could not live without them. The glamor of being Socialist Whip had faded, and he accepted the Republican designation on the ticket.

It made all the difference in 1926 because he just managed to pull out the election by about 50 votes, another unique masterpiece put together with paste, mirrors, Ghibboni and, this time, Republicans. The only New York City Republican elected to Congress, he jokingly announced plans to call a caucus of city Republicans as soon as he found an empty telephone booth. Still it was better to joke about being a lone Republican than about being a lone Socialist.[38]

The Republican party caucus finally granted La Guardia his request for appointment to the Judiciary Committee. And he returned to the party a share of the victory. "Now this is the lay of the land," he confided to Samuel Koenig, going on to detail the congressional wheeling and dealing over the creation of additional judgeships for New York. "Besides these judges, hope to have several hundred jobs for you before long. Had a very satisfactory talk with Ogden [Mills, secretary of treasury] yesterday. Will tell you all about it when I see you." Cunning, tough, and ambitious, he made his alliances and kept his side of the bargain, but he warned Koenig that he "reserved the right" to fight "for the great masses of the people of the city who have confidence in me and who look to me to represent them. . . ." Koenig offered Fiorello a "friendly suggestion—not to take life so seriously!"[39]

In 1928 he ran again on the Republican line, with explicit reservations. As far back as 1920 he had denounced Herbert Hoover as "the most expensive luxury the war has produced. . . ." His respect for the golden boy of Republican politics had not appreciated since then. "Damn it all," he exclaimed to a Republican national committeeman, "I want to do what I can, but a lot of sons of female dogs in Washington are going out of their way to make things difficult for us here in New York." Still, he did refrain from going over to the Democrats and Al Smith. "Political totems and Republican presidents," wrote a friendly journalist, "mean nothing to him," but he respected the party's power and basked in the support of such GOP Brahmins as Nicholas Murray Butler, who said of Fiorello that "in this welter of unreason, intolerance, bigotry and hypocrisy through which we are passing, it is a pleasure to find a Republican candidate who will stand for American principles of government . . . and in favor of those truly progressive policies upon which the opportunity of the individual man and the lasting prosperity of the country can alone depend. I greatly hope that La Guardia will be elected by a substantial majority." He won by 1200 votes.[40]

But this victory, in La Guardia's sixth congressional election, left him unsatisfied. The desire to grow, to move up continued to frustrate any sense of finally settling into a comfortable niche and making the best of it. Impressed with the uses of radio in politics, he accepted the assignment of reporting on congressional business for one of the stations. He was attracting 150 press notices a year in the *New York Times*, far more than other congressmen. Yet he wanted a medium for his message to reach the "third House of Congress," as he referred to public opinion. *L'Americolo*'s costly failure cured him forever of the notion that a printing press, some ideas, and a staff were enough to make a successful magazine, but he continued

148

to seek a public forum. Soon after closing *L'Americolo* he signed on as a regular contributor to Bernarr McFadden's *New York Graphic*. "Journalism and politics," he told *Graphic* editor Emile Gauvreau, "make a great combination." He did not agonize over his writing. What words and sentences came to mind were quickly wrapped into an article and that was it. With his punchy, colloquial style, the regular column did not intrude upon his other activities. He just jammed it into his schedule.[41]

Still, the *Graphic* was a curious choice for La Guardia. McFadden's publishing formula involved some simplistic ideas on physical fitness and the "body beautiful," ample coverage of sex and scandal, and columns by Ed Sullivan, Walter Winchell, and "America's Most Liberal Congressman," Fiorello La Guardia. While Mc-Fadden did not much mind when New Yorkers took to calling his mass circulation tabloid the *Porno-Graphic*, La Guardia did not always agree with the paper's taste. Except for a few clashes over editorial interference, however, which La Guardia resolved by lecturing Gauvreau about "journalistic pimping" and threatening to "terminate my arrangement . . . and place my articles where I know they will be published under any and all conditions," the association served both sides perfectly adequately. McFadden got a zippy editorial page columnist and Fiorello secured a popular outlet for his views.[42]

———

By this time, Fiorello La Guardia was reaching a broad audience and attracting the amiable attention of the national press. Despite H. L. Mencken's penchant for tart dismissal and conspicuous pessimism—democracy he decried as the "worship of jackals by jackasses" and the notion that gentlemen should become involved in politics he compared to urging more virgins to work in brothels—his *American Mercury* magazine published an exceedingly complimentary feature on "La Guardia of Harlem." Prepared by Duff Gilfond, a personal friend of La Guardia's, the piece burnished the image of the "peppery gentleman" who lent "dash, color and temperament" to the gray Congress, a common man of the people who handed his engraved White House invitations to the neighborhood kids on 116th Street. Other legislators, even Democrats, displayed the dour visage of the president on their walls. La Guardia's office boasted one framed painting, of Rudolph Valentino. While his colleagues stretched a five-hour day over as little real work as possible in immaculate show offices, La Guardia ran a disheveled shop where honest labor took place. Gilfond found every surface in Fiorello's office piled with letters, news clippings, documents, unfinished articles, and reports. She watched him dispatch a stack of correspondence as he flipped through the letters, tossed half into the wastebasket, and replied to the rest with such comments as "bunk," "we appreciate his respect," and in response to a clergyman asking for special interest legislation, "Something for Jesus? Nice boy Jesus." He took extraordinary pleasure in re-

149

sponding to ministers who criticized his stand on Prohibition. To a Reverend Willis Ryder he wrote: "My Christian bringing-up has taught me humility. I am sure if you knew all the facts you would not write such an abusive letter. Of course I forgive you. In your spare moments do read St. Luke's Gospel. I am sure you will get a lot of comfort from it."[43]

Amidst the books, letters, and reports, La Guardia would talk heatedly to a constituent in Italian or Yiddish while scribbling an outline for his radio review of the day's congressional business. His ideas crowded upon each other and the syntax suffered, but the point, often modified with the word "lousy," remained razor-sharp. Even his secretary, Miss Fisher, differed from the other secretaries by working at the same frenetic pace he did.[44]

He prepared for daily House sessions by researching law and filling his pockets with props. Particularly complex legislation he laid over for the weekend, when he gathered expert opinion from his network of reform advisers and social workers. When the gong summoned the representatives to their desks, he would scamper to the House chamber and remain until close, munching on fistfuls of peanuts, as he kept guard, primed like a prizefighter, ready to pounce on any suspicious bills. A youngster who wrote La Guardia to ask whether he should go into politics or become a boxer was told to become a congressman and combine the two.[45]

His colleagues often disagreed with him on the issues, but they respected his mastery of the procedural rules and loopholes. When duty called other colleagues to a golf course or baseball game, they would trust him to look after their pet bills. Only the freshmen, reported one congressional observer, tried to match wits with La Guardia in debate. The others, conservatives as well as liberals, would come to Room 150 in the House Office Building to discuss their bills and smooth the ground for "personal bills" and pet measures for the folks back home. The House generally passed these bills unanimously with little debate, unless La Guardia stopped them with his pointed demurrals. He amazed his colleagues with detailed knowledge about fish dams in Salt Creek, Alabama, the relief of hay growers in rural Texas, river surveys in Mud Creek, Kentucky, and proposals to provide care for the insane in Alaska.

Perhaps the gentleman from New York should read a report on the condition of Brazoria County before voicing an opinion, suggested an honored colleague. Came the chilled reply: "I spent most of my Sunday reading this bill and the report." Few trifled with the Harlem petrel lightly. "He was just the best objector to these vicious little bills," his secretary recalled. And when he focused on a bill, "he remembered every comma." At first, his colleagues tried to deny him access to the floor, but he fended them off with "questions of personal privilege," "parliamentary inquiries," and "points of order." He could wrap an entire speech in a single point of order. It was no use to try to stop him.[46]

On February 4, 1929, as a new batch of consent bills came before Congress,

La Guardia immediately jumped to his feet to pepper sponsors with questions. One bill called for creating a bust of the "Late Lieutenant James Melville Gilliss" for presentation to the Chilean National Observatory. La Guardia asked to amend the bill "with the usual amendment that I offer to bills of this kind," that the art work be done by a U.S. citizen. The bill's author disagreed. True, Americans should be encouraged, but foreign artists, "some of whom have come from the country in which the gentleman from New York is, I think, much interested," did excellent work. La Guardia rejected the implication: "The gentleman from New York is only interested in one country, and that is the United States." The discussion continued for another few minutes, until finally La Guardia closed the point. "If we are to present a work of art to a foreign government it should be the work of an American artist. [Applause]."[47]

The House press corps voted La Guardia "the most effective, interesting, and picturesque member" of the lower house. In a book about contemporary progressives, Ray Tucker included only one House member among his profiles, the "Roistering Rebel" from New York who had become a respected national figure, receiving letters from citizens all over the nation complaining about government malfeasance and bureaucratic indifference. Oswald Garrison Villard, editor of the *Nation* magazine, called La Guardia "the most valuable member of Congress today, the most fearless, the most truthtelling."[48]

But for all of his correspondence and his many speeches, it was all so trivial, so ineffective. He had virtually no control, except to complain, to obstruct, to limit the work of others. "I tell you," he said to Ray Tucker, "it's damned discouraging trying to be a reformer in the wealthiest land in the world." Fighting alone and securing few real victories took its toll. A decade of fighting against the tide had left him discouraged.[49]

His relationship with his party remained prickly. "Desirous as I am of co-operating with you," went one letter to Koenig, "I must reserve the right to carry on the fight. . . ." Koenig was right when he wrote to Fiorello that he took everything too seriously. Everything remained a fight, an endless crusade. He worked harder than any congressman, and for all that, he acquired only a minimal influence. While others made economic and social policy, after six terms in office he had only captured control over pet bills. There is something corrosive about being a fiercely ambitious man doomed to small victories. La Guardia lacked the philosophical equanimity to live in peace with such frustration. Anger churned just beneath the surface. His staff feared his compulsion not only to win but to humiliate and to press his position no matter how petty the issue.[50]

Even his electoral victory in 1928 left him with a sense of unease. "It was a queer campaign with all sorts of defections," he wrote Oswald Garrison Villard, and in my section of the district, particularly so." The uncertainty reflected more than the influx of Puerto Ricans and the moving out of Jews, whom he had grown

151

comfortable with. He had built an amazing political machine, and yet every campaign demanded grueling work. The rapid turnover of East Harlem's population meant that he had to win his support over and over again, and all of this to go to Washington and be outvoted on all the important issues. He would have to turn, but the question was where.[51]

3. Marie

I N the years following the tragic deaths of his wife and daughter in 1921, Fiorello La Guardia became even more wrapped up in politics and public service than before and through his work came to appreciate a slight, plain-featured blond woman with a full-throated laugh and friendly manner who had worked alongside him since 1915. Marie Fisher left school as a young teenager after her father's untimely death in 1914 to support her mother and sister. She completed a few business courses and took a job with a law firm, where she first met and worked for the young La Guardia. When he ran for Congress in 1916 she volunteered to assist with his campaign, and after he won the election she became his New York secretary. From that time on they worked together in an interesting complement of contrasts. The mercurial La Guardia, with his range of highs and lows, and Marie, ever solid, well-mannered, and reliable. Hard work, few luxuries, and a strong sense of responsibility stamped her from early youth as an entirely predictable young woman, the kind of woman described in those times as knowing her place, doing her job, and minding her business.

Throughout his career Marie Fisher had worked by La Guardia's side, managing his office, orchestrating his campaigns, and when necessary stepping in to help run his life. She knew when to talk to her high-strung boss and when only to listen. She witnessed his tantrums and also his amazing energy, and she too was caught up in his political ambitions. When he went off to World War I she tended to the home front, answering voter mail, directing constituent requests to other congressional offices, and keeping Fiorello's name before the electorate. By the time La Guardia returned and married Thea Almerigotti, Marie Fisher had become much more than a secretary. When Thea and Fioretta fell ill, Marie looked after the La Guardia home and served as family spokesman while La Guardia cared for his sick wife and child.

During the twenties the small woman with the imperturbable disposition helped build the La Guardia political organization. She never took a forward position, leaving that to Vito Marcantonio and the other bright young men that La Guardia so enjoyed working with, but she could always be trusted to carry out the plans, type the speeches, and in her quiet way make order out of the havoc that attended his campaigns. Some thirty-six years after La Guardia's death, she would still respond with an emphatic "Oh my!" when asked if the congressman ever lost his temper. "Oh my! Did he!" And with her, as much as with anybody else. But he also trusted her totally. His bright men often took too much initiative, made too many decisions on their own, wrong decisions, unrealistic ones. Marie did as she was told and did it well.[52]

The staff relied on her too, checking with her about the congressman's mood before presenting him with a request or some bad news. Maurice Postley remembered her as "always the lady in the office, very cooperative, very responsive, friendly, aiming to . . . be helpful." She lent a tranquillity to the erratic environment that seemed always to follow in La Guardia's wake. While Lowell Limpus attributes too much to still waters in asserting that Marie directed La Guardia's campaigns, Fiorello did come to rely heavily on Marie's knowledge of the district, its problems, and his files. She did such a good job unspectacularly that he took her entirely for granted, while she became ever more devoted to him over the years. From the teenage girl who took stenography in the law office, she grew into a mature woman, single-mindedly committed to her boss. She was thirty-three years old and she had never married. When he had some prank to play, like his beer-brewing stunt, he took her along. Marie had become a fixture not only in the office but in his own mind, there whenever she was needed.[53]

The story is told of Marie working late one night during the Christmas recess of 1928—she not only worked late, she also worked weekends and any other time that Fiorello needed her—when he snapped at her about some papers that he needed. She smoothly retrieved the files and placed them before him. It was almost midnight, and it finally occurred to him to ask if she had eaten. She deflected the question, and he realized that he had claimed yet another of her nights without a second thought. "You go home right now," he said. "We'll finish this tomorrow." And then, writes Lowell Limpus, as she turned to leave, "Congressman La Guardia was really SEEING his secretary for the first time in fifteen years . . . as a woman not a machine." He ran out into the hall, caught her, and announced that she was fired. "How can I court a girl who works for me?"[54]

This rather fanciful version of the courtship aside, La Guardia was not one to suddenly fall head over heels for a woman he had known for fifteen years. For all his journalistic skill, Lowell Limpus could not convincingly make a lovestruck suitor of Fiorello. He was comfortable with Marie and knew how devoted she was to him. Certainly, Marie had been hoping for this for a long time. She had long before become attached to La Guardia. She worried about him, worked with him, and suffered his temper with calm grace. Now she would become his wife. On February 28, 1929, in a private ceremony, Reverend Ole J. Kvale, a representative from Minnesota, a Lutheran minister (Marie was Lutheran), and a friend of La Guardia's, married the couple in his Washington apartment. Following the ceremony the groom went directly to the floor of Congress.[55]

Marie accepted the priorities Fiorello placed on his political career. That came first, and he took all of the decisions alone. Many years later an interviewer asked Marie if her husband consulted her about any of his decisions. Did he check with her before running for an office or accepting an appointment? Had she ever told him to do things differently? She looked at the questioner with amazement. No, she never considered interfering in his prerogatives. It never even crossed her mind. "I wanted him to do what he wanted to do."[56]

She also wanted to do what he wanted *her* to do. Although she would have preferred to continue working with him in the office after they married, Fiorello immediately retired her as his secretary. He wanted Marie to run her household from home. And she dutifully stayed out of public view, refraining from speaking about public issues. Later he would quip that he had "lost a good secretary and gained a bum cook," but if the truth be told, what he did was promote his administrative assistant to wife.[57]

When Congress was in session they shared a tiny Washington apartment, returning for weekends to their modest East Harlem walk-up at 109th Street and Madison Avenue. Marriage did not break Fiorello of his obsession with his work. Often he would bring home two and three hours of reading and correspondence. On free nights Marie would join him for a music concert, or they would listen to the radio or play a game of cards. On Saturday nights friends would drop by for one of Fiorello's Italian dinners, described by Ray Tucker, Washington correspondent for the *World Telegram*: "Hustling from stove to door, creating a hollandaise sauce and conducting a conversational crusade, basting the stuffed capon and lambasting stuffed politicians . . . La Guardia directs and dominates with the artistry of a maestro, the tempo of good food, good cheer, good fellowship and stimulating argument."[58]

Fiorello's relationship with Marie was not tranquil. He brought the same demanding expectations, strong will, and volatile temper that typified his public life to his home. "The only time he was really reserved and quiet," Elsie Fisher, Marie's sister, would recall, "was with music." But Marie understood her husband well. She understood his frustrations, tolerated his explosions, and found fulfillment in his successes. At ease with her own purpose, a practical woman, she provided a calm, unruffled center to his hectic life.[59]

4. A City of Jimmy Walker and a City of Fiorello La Guardia

T wo weeks before his marriage, Fiorello outlined to Republican State Senator Courtlandt Nicoll his program for the upcoming mayoral campaign. Since 1919 La Guardia had coveted this office. In 1925 he had turned down suggestions that he run, predicting that Jimmy Walker would win hands down and introduce an "everybody getting his" administration, and he believed that Walker had proven him right. Now, in 1929, he hoped that New Yorkers, tired of the "night mayor's" devil-may-care life-style, would select substance over style. He was prepared to pursue the office in earnest, calling attention to the incumbent's insouciant inefficiency and offering instead his own platform of urban and social reform.

Perhaps there had always been two New Yorks. The sparkling mecca of the polished rich and the slum town of the struggling poor. A community blessed by education, ease, and style, and another of narrow loyalties and broad hatreds. A metropolis of joy and beauty and spirit, and a devouring, ruthless city of the scarred and desperate at rope's end. A city that after "making you rich in a week . . . ruins you in one morning." A city of Jimmy Walker and a city of Fiorello La Guardia.[60]

Jimmy Walker's city awed even the most cosmopolitan of observers. French scholar Andre Chevrillon called it the "first capital of the world," and historian Bernard Fay wrote that he did not understand ancient Rome until he saw modern New York. "New York dominates. . . . the only city in the world rich enough in money, vitality and men to build itself anew . . . the only city sufficiently wealthy to be modern." Visitors marveled at the furious energy and the vertical thrust of the city's growth. The New York skyline appeared to rise by twenty stories every decade. "Height" wrote a British journalist, "is the new destination of American architecture." The awesome skyscrapers struck Fay as a fitting token. "One cannot understand them . . . without first having tasted and enjoyed the thrill of counting or adding up enormous totals and of living in a gigantic, compact and brilliant world." The dazzlingly garish Great White Way offered an apt signature. "Night is abolished," declared an entranced European. Philipe de Rothschild limned the Broadway night as "a hundred Eiffel towers, a thousand Rue Pigalle . . . luminous epilepsy, incandescent hypnotism. Pity the sky," exclaimed the charmed guest, "with nothing but stars."[61]

Vast wealth sustained an urban economy of astonishing breadth and unmatched robustness. In 1929 New York shipped more than one-third of the entire nation's exports, brought in almost 50 percent of its imports, and accounted for close to one-fourth of its wholesale trade. Department stores raised merchandising to a science and profits to unprecedented heights. Retail shops provided elaborate opulence and easy credit, and the cresting stock market offered prosperity so effortless that few concerned themselves with particulars. You invested and got rich. That's all. Ever since the war, commented an envious European, money rolled into New York banks "as water down a hill." Seats on the stock exchange—the opportunity to collect a broker's fee on American dreams of quick wealth—went for as high as $625,000. The press of hasty investors forced the Exchange to schedule unprecedented Sunday shifts and night hours. Inexperienced speculators dismissed all warnings. "We are getting in too high," they would agree, "but tomorrow it will be higher." World financial capital and commerce center, New York also produced manufactured goods totaling nearly $6 billion. "Magnificence," wrote Sir Charles Cheers Wakefield, "is the first thing that strikes one in New York."

Another Briton sought to understand the effect of all of this prosperity and glamor. Looking into the city's soul, he found "a vast cash register" that "toils to amuse and charges accordingly." New Yorkers abandoned themselves to a crazy competition for getting and spending money, without asking why. Even those who admired the "gaiety" and "carelessness" of the city feared for its spirit of a "storming-party hurrying towards an unknown goal."[62]

Change and newness passed for creativity. Along Fifth Avenue the old robber-baron palaces made way for new buildings, "soaring masterpieces of stone and steel." One would have to go back to the lavish detail of medieval church architecture to find comparable ostentation, but New Yorkers did not build monuments to faith in the 1920s. Modern opulence was saved for entertainment palaces. The Roxy Theater was finished in 1926, at a cost of $15 million, with wide, thickly carpeted corridors, elaborate chandeliers, and appointments reminiscent of *ancien régime* castles.

Hotels, nightclubs, and theaters all contributed to the aura of fabulous spectacle, a city planted upon a cream puff. And entertainment's other half—the jazz clubs, cabarets, and speakeasies (some 20,000 according to a good estimate)—contributed to what struck Aldous Huxley as a "general atmosphere of hilarious inebriation." Life in Gotham was dashing, stylish, a bit racy, and great fun. "It is the City of the Good Time," Ford Maddox Ford wrote. "And the Good Time there is so sacred that you may be excused anything you do in searching for it."[63]

The wise student of American urban life Bayrd Still characterized the ethos of the pre-Crash city:

> New York was riding higher by the late twenties than ever before or
> since. . . . From the opening of the century New York, more than any
> other city, seemed to be scaled to the potential of the New World and

156

modern times. . . . The "magnum opus of modern material civilization."[64]

Dapper Jimmy Walker brilliantly symbolized a place in time, New York in
prosperity. Wearing New York in his lapel, he brought to office an insouciance
and a *joie de vivre* that captured that moment. No typical hungry pol on the make,
Walker had not even wanted a political career. He preferred sports, showgirls, and
Tin Pan Alley, but his father, a small-time Tammany assemblyman, insisted. After
considerable prodding Jimmy entered New York University Law School, where he
persuaded a friend to ease his studying by reading the law books aloud to him.
With his law degree in hand, Walker pursued his star as a writer of such popular
songs as "There's Music in the Rustle of a Skirt," "In the Valley Where My Sally
Said Goodbye," and "Kiss All the Girls for Me." He published "Will You Love
Me in December as You Do in May" in 1908 when he was 27, and its success
made him a reputation.[65]

"Time," writes Walker biographer Gene Fowler, "had Jimmy on its hands."
Only after he married vaudeville singer Janet Allen did he finally submit to his
father's will and pursue politics with the unhurried spirit that marked all of his half-
efforts. Charming and friendly, Jimmy attracted a wide circle of supporters, and
eventually he shook enough hands, told enough jokes, and showed enough good-
hearted fellowship to become Democratic floor leader in the State Senate. There
his outstanding achievements comprised the legalization of boxing and Sunday
baseball games. Early in his Albany days Walker became a friend of Al Smith's.
The two Tammany men shared a room in Albany, but while Smith took both politics
and his marriage vows seriously, Walker cultivated the loosest working habits and
dropped everything at the sight of a pretty woman. Still, Beau James was bright
and party-loyal, and Tammany decided to run him for mayor against independent-
minded John Hylan in 1925. Old roommate Governor Smith withheld his endorsement until Jimmy promised to be faithful to his wife; Walker's lack of administrative
experience and his laziness offended Smith much less.[66]

Tammany's hearty endorsement eased Walker's election, and on January 1,
1926, he took office. Despite a keen intelligence, Walker cared little about the
city's operations and confided to the city hall reporters that he had no patience for
books. An agile wisp of a man, weighing no more than 125 pounds on a five-foot-
eight-inch frame, the twinkling mayor lived in the style of a European dandy. He
designed his own clothes (including his bowler), changed as often as five times a
day, and generally did not arise until 10:00 in the morning. Thereupon, he would
spend three or four minutes perusing the morning papers and then fall back on his
pillow for a while until he was ready for tea, taken while still in bed. Then, propped
against the headboard, he would make a round of phone calls. Finally, he would
step into his dressing room, throw off his silk gown, select one of the suits laid
out for him by his valet, and prepare to meet the afternoon.

Walker's personal fastidiousness was the opposite of his slothful work habits. The mayor seldom replied to correspondence, shrugged off million-dollar errors in his budgets, and governed only when allowed no other option. Some things, however, were too serious to ignore. "There are a lot of things in life that we cannot do anything about," Walker once announced, "but a man's beard is his own fault." Walker tried to behave courteously at Board of Estimate meetings, but long speeches offended him and details bored him.[67]

New Yorkers admired Walker's openness and modesty. In the name of "good taste" he refused to have his name plastered over any improvements, parks, bridges, and hospitals undertaken during his tenure. He admitted that he knew little about urban problems. The commissioners, politicians, and bosses were supposed to take care of that. He saw his job as leading the cheers for the city and setting its style. He viewed good government types as too serious about other people's affairs, and he offered them his open contempt. A representative of one of these groups monitoring a Board of Estimate meeting rose to speak. The mayor asked him to identify his association.

"Citizens Union," replied the man.

"Did you say Citizen Union?" queried Jimmy.

"The *Citizens* Union," corrected the nettled reformer.

"Aha," exclaimed Walker, "then there are two of you."[68]

For those rare appointments that he did keep he came late. "I say so many yesses in a month . . . ," he once told a friend, "that it keeps me busy the other eleven months in the year apologizing for not being able to keep the engagement." The newspapers delighted in reporting on the meeting between the New York mayor and the dour Republican President Calvin Coolidge. The meeting actually went well—and Jimmy was forty minutes late.

In his first two years in office Jimmy took seven vacations, a total of 143 days. Overseas, crowds would follow him through the streets screaming, "Viva Jimmy," while the press lavished attention on his wisecracks and his appearance. After returning from one of his junkets to face a chaotic subway situation, Walker became involved in a series of negotiations. Before long, the mayor tired of the discussions, drew his papers together, piled them in his desk, and excused himself. All he wanted to do, said Jimmy, "was put on a pair of overalls and just fish. . . ." And with that the chief magistrate set off for Florida.[69]

Jimmy taught New Yorkers to relax and enjoy good times. He nightclubbed often, befriended the fight crowd, preened up the Great White Way in his tuxedo, fell in love with an actress, and joked his way into the heart of the city. Wrote one observer: "He loved like a woman; he played like a child; he hoped like a saint." City hall reporters appreciated the marvelous copy he afforded them, and in the spirit of good fellowship, they kept his racy comments off the record and ignored his indiscretions.

Welcoming Queen Marie of Romania to the city, he held a medal destined for Her buxom Majesty's coat. Fearing a mistargeted pin, Walker hesitated, whereupon the queen told him to proceed, "the risk is mine."

"And such a beautiful risk it is," twinkled Jimmy.

Another time, when the rumor that the mayor had been shot reached the just-arising Walker, he cracked, "Shot? Listen, I'm not even half shot."[70]

As for Walker's romantic liaisons, his long-suffering wife "Allie" could only hope that each was another of his passing fancies. After the forty-six-year-old Jimmy took up with a striking twenty-three-year-old Broadway actress named Betty Compton, however, he offered no apologies. He moved out of his home into a suite at the New York Ritz. Newspapers refused to print what they knew, and Jimmy continued to enjoy himself in the style to which he allowed himself to become accustomed, in part through the good graces of a number of wealthy benefactors who advanced him substantial sums of money with no expectation of being paid back, at least not from Walker's pockets.[71]

On a spring afternoon in 1929, Walker said to his police commissioner, Grover Whalen: "It is the custom of reluctant candidates to be drafted. They always hear the call of the people, even if it is only a whisper. Will you see to it that I receive this call?"

"You will hear the call," Whalen assured the mayor. He proceeded to compile a list of "forty praiseworthy points" and drafted philanthropist August Heckscher to head a list of distinguished citizens to draft Jimmy Walker for a second term. On July 18, 1929, Heckscher issued the call. "Mr. Mayor, your friends—and they are legion far and near—have been disturbed of late that after four years of brilliant effort in the service of the City of New York you may prefer to accept one of the many attractive business offers which have been made to you and retire to private life." Heckscher implored Walker to stave off urban calamity by accepting the people's call to carry out the "magnificent improvements under way and in contemplation." Walker responded graciously, "Who can say no?" although some thought that he seemed unfamiliar with Heckscher's list of planned improvements.[72]

Among Republicans, La Guardia claimed the exclusive right to oppose Walker. Returning from a tonsillectomy he said, "I feel in shape now for anything. . . . I'm even tempted to take on [heavyweight boxing champion] Max Schmeling." But for all his bravado, La Guardia attracted but a smattering of reformers and a small handful of real Republicans to his budding candidacy. Ogden Mills praised Fiorello's "capacity for indignation . . . the only possible antidote to the smiling complacency and cynical indifference" of the times, but most Republicans preferred to avoid a candidate of Fiorello's erratic political loyalties, particularly one who showed such concern for the poor over the propertied and who consorted with immigrants and Socialists. While he could not put these reservations to rest, Fiorello bullied his way to the nomination by threatening to further fragment the already outnumbered Republicans with a bruising primary fight.[73]

Thus, on August 1, the GOP gritted its teeth, fixed its smiles, and gave La Guardia what he wanted. Nominating speeches emphasized Walker's weaknesses but said little about the swarthy congressman whom they were reluctant to present to the world as their own alternative to the stylish Walker. Noted the *New Yorker* magazine: "The delegates told this maverick of the herd that he might go forth against Tammany Hall . . . but the respectables of Republicanism then asked themselves whether this Italian-American Congressman was not even more of a clown." They had little trouble controlling their enthusiasm.[74]

Fiorello had been able to force his nomination, but he could not force the Republicans to love him or to work for him, and the stalwarts made plain their unhappiness over being dragged into bed with the political streetfighter. Recalled Sam Koenig, "I was roundly abused for having nominated Mr. La Guardia." The Republican *Herald Tribune* spent its enthusiasm on the party platform while criticizing the candidate for his "unstable convictions" and for having "boxed the political compass in his efforts to win votes." Another Republican paper, the *Evening Sun*, went even further, backing Walker. Others defected to Socialist Norman Thomas. The gentle radical inspired little fear with his sermons on the rights of man, but La Guardia was dangerous. Had he been in business he might have been a ruthless robber baron. The Republicans recognized the type and feared the possibilities.[75]

Progressives did not all agree on La Guardia either. Each of the many reform groups still held out for its own version of the perfect candidate. Jimmy Walker did not fit their idea of a proper mayor, but he was not a catastrophe either. They did not trust La Guardia, especially after he made the mistake of appealing to regular Republicans by promising election captains, "I'll appreciate your work . . . and I'll see to it that you are recognized." They deplored his opportunism. No doubt, without his iron ambition La Guardia would have been a more attractive figure, overall. But unease with power presented more of a problem for the reformers than for La Guardia. Many who demanded change in government seemed drawn to candidates steeped in ambivalence and indecision, people guaranteed to fumble with power instead of utilizing it effectively. Reformers needed to be tough to bring change, but such strength was the thing they feared most. This is what made reformers so uncomfortable with La Guardia, a progressive who was not embarrassed by power, who made a career of seeking it. After calling La Guardia the best and most liberal congressman from New York, the *Nation* concluded that "with all due respect . . . he is not of the same stature as Norman Thomas." So the civic-minded reformers looked at La Guardia, decided that he was insufficiently good, and lemminged off to sea with the Socialist.[76]

At the same time, La Guardia roused a great deal of legitimate opposition. He had backed Democrat Hylan, had worked with Hearst, and was writing for

McFadden's rag. His ideals *did* seem a mite too flexible for a reformer. Who could deny that, forced to choose between victory and principle, the Little Flower would take the former in the name of the latter? He appealed to ethnic groups on provincial grounds, having nothing to do with civic betterment. "His is the keenest political mind that has been operating in many a day," Walker once said, "but he's a great showman too. His rivals talk English, good, bad, or indifferent. But Fiorello is the cosmopolite of this most cosmopolitan city. In the ghetto he talks Yiddish. . . . In Little Italy he talks Italian. . . . When he tells off the Germans, he can do so in their own language. Even when he speaks English, he speaks two kinds. . . . The Little Flower is no shrinking violet."[77]

In Harlem, La Guardia promised a black audience a "different deal." At a local church, he alluded to Walker's philandering by praising the Lord for the fact that at least some men went home to sleep with their own wives. "And that ain't so good neither," called a voice from the audience. He denounced anti-Semitism before the Jews and campaigned in Little Italy with a song featuring the lines

> *He's proud he's an American,*
> *And he's proud he's a Wop.*

Not every ethnic tack worked to his benefit. When Norman Thomas, who genuinely respected Fiorello, challenged him to renounce the American Fascists, La Guardia hesitated and then declined. A disappointed Thomas denounced Fiorello as a political chameleon and an opportunist.[78]

This unattractive side of Fiorello the campaigner was matched with a more appealing side of Fiorello the reform candidate who articulated for New Yorkers a program for modernization, public works, urban planning, and honest government. He promised low-cost housing, an end to tax breaks for business, new parks, playgrounds, and lower food prices. The campaign pitted La Guardia's New York, foreign-speaking, economically depressed, a community seeking change and reform, against Walker's glittering capital of good times and easy living.[79]

Delivering up to fifteen speeches a day, working with little support from the party, flailing at the Democrats, La Guardia could not capture the interest of the electorate. His issues were just not that important to them. As his campaign floundered, he began to attack the popular Walker personally. "Elect a full time Mayor," ran one of his slogans, "who will sleep at night and work in the daytime." Walker, preoccupied with Betty Compton's rehearsals for a Broadway-bound show and the renovation of the Central Park Casino, dismissed La Guardia's charges with a smile. The more Beau James ignored him, the more furious and unbalanced La Guardia's charges became, and Walker's cool campaign style easily outclassed La Guardia's hot hysteria.[80]

When the portly congressman assailed the mayor as an "English fop" and a loud dresser, Walker replied with delightful condescension: "If I . . . might serve the taxpayers better by appearing at City Hall clad in overalls, or even in a snood, I should do so. But until we have an ordinance to the contrary I shall bathe frequently, as is my custom; and change my linen often, as is my perhaps eccentric desire; and patronize the tailor of my own choice.'' After a barrage of criticism about the hours he kept, the women he loved, and the fact that he had recently approved a raise in his own salary to $40,000, Jimmy winked back: ''That's cheap! Think what it would cost if I worked full time.'' Attacked for perfidy to his race for holding an autographed picture of the Prince of Wales in his house, and assorted other indiscretions, Walker feigned exasperation with the unruly Fiorello: ''Can anyone expect me to keep my good nature in this campaign? I will go as far as the gutter to defend myself. I will not go down in the sewer.''[81]

La Guardia's scattershot charges buried a number of serious issues: Walker's inability to control Tammany greed, favoritism toward Walker cronies and a host of unsavory characters, Jimmy's unwillingness to mind the business of the city, and the apparent unwillingness of the police department to solve the Arnold Rothstein murder case for fear that it would expose a tangled connection between the underworld and Tammany.

The tall, suet-skinned, devilishly efficient Rothstein had built a multi-million-dollar crime empire that was accused of fixing the famous 1919 Black Sox World Series, counterfeited securities, bootlegged whiskey, ran a loan-sharking operation, and peddled drugs. Banker to the underworld, boss of a national bookmaking network, Rothstein also worked the political alleyways, assisting Tammany with elections, posting bail bonds for Tiger pols who had been arrested, and gathering tribute for assorted politicians. The amazingly diversified gangster also fixed night-club violations, acquired boxing licenses, and secured exemptions from local ordinances. Lawyer William J. Fallon characterized Rothstein as ''a man who dwells in doorways. A gray rat, waiting for his cheese.''[82]

On November 4, 1928, at the Park Central Hotel, Rothstein was shot; he died two days later. The district attorney seized his books and records. ''If those papers are ever made public,'' a Rothstein family attorney warned, ''there are going to be a lot of suicides in high places.'' What at first seemed like a strong case never developed. The police could find neither killer, nor witnesses, nor fingerprints on the murder weapon, nor any evidence in Rothstein's books to indict the dead man's many political protectors and clients. The police had managed to talk to Rothstein before he died; they had even taken a Park Central chambermaid into custody for several days. Yet, incredibly, they knew less after all of this than they did right after the murder. La Guardia suggested that this was less puzzling than it seemed. The police did not want to find the killer. They had persuaded the chambermaid to forget everything she had seen, he alleged, in order to cover up the link between Tammany and the underworld. The sensational magazines were saying this too, but La Guardia backed it up with evidence of a connection between Rothstein and Magistrate Albert Vitale, a trusted Walker operative. He released documents showing a $20,000 ''loan'' (since no evidence of repayment could ever be found others called it a ''payoff'') from Rothstein to Vitale and demonstrated ample reason for a police cover-up.[83]

Both La Guardia and Norman Thomas brought these allegations to Governor Franklin D. Roosevelt, calling on the newly installed governor to look into this case. But Roosevelt, already eyeing the White House and wary of offending Tammany, would not fish with La Guardia's bait. He demanded specific charges.[84]

Rather than concentrate on a few provable charges of consequence, La Guardia accused Walker of everything he could put into words. He floated so many allegations, many of them unsubstantiated and others frivolous, that the good-time mayor easily dismissed La Guardia as a reckless, petty pain. ''I must apologize,'' Walker said good-naturedly to an audience in the Bronx, ''for not taking the charges of my opponent seriously. If he wants to shout and scream while playing with his toys, let him. Sometimes I think, in speaking of toys, that the Little Flower, when but a child, played with stumbling blocks, and never recovered from the habit.'' On another occasion Walker waved aside La Guardia's accusations and insisted on his own question: ''Just why did Congressman La Guardia leave Bridgeport on June the first of this year?''

La Guardia was flustered. He had not been to Bridgeport in years. He had no idea what Walker might mean. The Democratic candidate worked Fiorello's exasperated denial into another piece of inspired nonsense. ''That's very interesting. You will note how carefully he denied having been in Bridgeport last June. And once again I ask, Why did he leave Bridgeport on that particularly significant day in his life, June the first of this year?'' After the election Fiorello asked Walker what this was all about. ''Nothing, nothing at all. . . . But it worked didn't it?''[85]

It worked like a charm. La Guardia was totally outgunned. His homegrown organization, adequate in East Harlem, proved no match for Tammany in a citywide contest. The Republican party sat on its hands and so did its large contributors, who flatly refused to help.

After all other points have been made, however, the simple fact is that this was no year for insurgents. The popular Walker melted criticism with a quip and a smile, especially when most New Yorkers were sated on good times and wanted more of the same. Few wanted to hear that the sky was going to fall. They would rather join with Jimmy in looking to a future that was more of the past, and if, as one wag noted, Jimmy took a few dimes, you could be sure that he passed around the pennies for others. It was a Democratic city; the times had treated them well; Walker presented a foxy, jaunty image of the city. Why change? Only La Guardia, it seemed, thought that he had a chance.

He did not even come close. He failed to carry a single assembly district. Even his home base in East Harlem voted for Walker. Throughout the city he drew no more than 26 percent of the vote. Of 1.5 million ballots cast, La Guardia lost by almost 500,000, the worst drubbing of a major party candidate in the history of the modern city. "If ever there was a foregone conclusion," commented the *New York Times*, "it was this one. The stars in their courses fought for Mr. Walker." Around 8:30 in the evening after reviewing the returns, La Guardia wired Jimmy Walker his congratulations, admonished his staff to go out of the headquarters smiling, and broke down and cried. The last word belonged to flinty old Sam Koenig: "We were too soon with the right man."[86]

A week before the election the stock market had crashed.

CHAPTER 5

La Guardia's New Deal

1. A Vast Transforming Depression

THE remarkable economic prosperity of the twenties redefined American aspirations. A spiraling stock market offered the grand gamble, on margin no less,
promising to break old barriers to widespread prosperity. Even laborers
dreamed of becoming fabulously wealthy. The market not only ruled the news,
John Kenneth Galbraith has remarked, "it also dominated the culture."[1]

The new era of economic prosperity knew no skepticism. The secret was out.
It was possible to make a fortune. All it took was nerve and good luck. As private
business gave way to the corporation, management was separated from ownership
and buying a piece of a company had much less to do with developing it than with
exploiting the rhythms and rumors of the stock market. Questions about price/
earnings ratios and other technical sobrieties were dismissed. Calculations of worth
based on demonstrated earnings were, experts explained, inherently conservative,
for they took inadequate account of the future. Spurred by such reasoning, Americans waved away prudence and put their money into the market. New industries
sprang up overnight on little more than an idea and a printing machine and the
security of limited liability statutes. Promise not performance determined stock
prices, and promise, in the atmosphere of pumped-up stock talk, was ubiquitous.
The market was a game of smoke and mirrors. You didn't look too closely and
you didn't ask questions, you just made money. Until one day the mirrors cracked,
a smoke machine was uncovered, and a generation of "prestigitation, double shuffling, honey-fugling, hornswaggling and skullduggery," in William Z. Ripley's
words, gave out. Within a few weeks in October 1929 the paper value of stocks
declined by some $26 billion, and the Great Crash ushered in the most radical
economic crisis in the history of the United States.[2]

Prosperity had been real but not deep. The great gains of the twenties were too narrowly distributed to sustain the massive production rolling off the assembly lines. Five percent of the population accounted for one-third of national income. As production efficiency grew and government policies, from favorable tax cuts to tariff protection, maximized industrial profits, too little was done to keep purchasing power healthy. Stability depended in the end upon distributing the product of this increased production, upon placing enough money in the hands of wage-earning consumers to buy all of the goods that were being mass-produced. Although the wide use of installment credit allowed a little to go much further, a dollar down and a dollar for the rest of your life was based on a wise use of credit, something the expansionist mood of the times made less likely.

Buoyant business-led growth had lifted the economy to a "plateau of permanent prosperity," and officials had shared a pervasive feeling that too close a scrutiny of business would inhibit it. The term "accepted business practices" hid a decade of swindles and sharp business dealings. Intricate holding companies ("a thing," cracked Will Rogers, "where you hand an accomplice the goods when the policeman searches you") and trusts recklessly wrung dividends from industries that required careful nurture and capital support. Banks blithely competed to loan out other people's money and collect the interest, with little control or regulation. They "provided everything for the customers," wrote one observer, "but a roulette wheel."[3]

In a free enterprise economy decisions about distribution, pricing, wages, hours of labor, and product development are made by individuals on the simple basis of personal profit motive. An "invisible hand" guided by supply and demand and competition is supposed to turn the pursuit of private gain into a dependable economic balance wheel for a robust economy. In such a system public perceptions create reality. Confidence leads to investments, purchases, the extension of credit, and in this way spurs economic growth. Banks can operate safely with only a portion of their savings on hand; industries hire workers and produce an output pegged to potential sales; consumers commit themselves to paying bills for which the money has not yet been earned; and workers, confident of next week's paycheck, spend on consumer goods instead of squirreling away their earnings. The crash shattered the sense of optimistic economic well-being that sustained so large a part of twenties prosperity, unleashing a wave of pessimism. An era that had known no skepticism now knew no rest. The billions lost on the market were not dollars that one man lost and another found. This money defied the law of conservation of mass and energy. It was altogether destroyed, and in a world of smoke and mirrors and honey-fugling it all happened with a swiftness that pulled the floor out from under the optimism-drunk prosperity of the twenties.

Like a dull fog moving in from the sea, the crash spread a cold mist of fear. The mighty had fallen and now all feared. The crash destroyed fortunes, wiped out holding companies, and ruined many banks, exposing the rotted core of the twenties economy. Decades later, learned economic scholars and historians patiently explain that the stock crash did not cause the Depression. And of course they are right. Well before that Black Tuesday in October 1929 when the market collapsed, Federal Reserve indices of industrial activity had begun to falter, inventories piled up alarmingly, and critical indicators in factory payrolls, freight car loadings, and department store sales declined. Construction and automobiles, the two key industries of the prosperity decade, had both slackened markedly by the summer of 1929. Many Americans were unemployed and agriculture was in terrible straits. But the booming stock market had hidden many of these weaknesses with its spectacular growth. Its collapse brought the rest of the economy tumbling after.[4]

Officials at first suggested that the setback would reduce expectations to realistic dimensions, that it would make the economy leaner and more resilient, but more rapidly than anyone could have suspected, the economy used up all the fat and continued consuming itself. No one had expected a depression and therefore few perceived the true dimensions of the crisis. Few experts believed that the damage was more than temporary. The Harvard Economic Society reported on November 10, almost two weeks after the crash, that a "serious depression like that of 1920–21 is outside the range of probability." In September, Professor Irving Fisher of Yale, had announced that securities "have reached a permanently high plateau." Now he looked out at an economic wasteland and babbled that "the price level of the market was unsoundly high . . . the fall in the market was very largely due to the psychology by which it went down because it went down." The initial response was limited by the hopes and experience of the twenties and the bewilderment of wise folk observing an unknown phenomenon. It was temporary; it would correct itself; it was a technical adjustment.[5]

But a calamitous fear lodged in the core of the economy, a disease rejecting all cures. The economy's distributive mechanism broke down, saddling the nation with the cruel paradox of want in the midst of plenty. With abundant coalfields, Americans were freezing; granaries overflowed with wheat while children hungered for more than a single meal a day; oranges and grapefruits hung heavy in orchard groves, as Americans forgot the taste of fresh fruit. In New York City, luxury apartments stood empty and foreclosed homes were without inhabitants, while the meanest housing was jammed with occupants and shantytowns sprawled out over empty lots and parks and into abandoned buildings. Industrialist Bernard Baruch bemoaned the irony: "In the presence of too much food, people are starving. Surrounded by vacant houses, they are homeless. And standing before unused bales of wool and cotton, they are dressed in rags." In 1929 three million were unemployed. A year after the crash 6 million prowled the streets seeking work and food. In 1931–1932 the number rose to 8 million and then to 13 million. The economy had turned anorexic, unable and unwilling to sustain itself.[6]

Urban children in day care centers played at a game called eviction, piling play furniture in one corner and then moving it to another with the comment "We ain't got no money so we's moved." Organizations laid plans for recycling food.

Someone placed baskets at New York City transit stations so that commuters could leave vegetables for the needy, while the *Brooklyn Eagle* suggested large central warehouses where families would send their leftovers for the unemployed. Breadlines—the "worm that walks like a man," wrote Heywood Broun—the symbol of Depression despair, coursed up the economic ladder reaching the middle class, a stake in the heart of American confidence. Well-known individuals got into the act. Among New York City's eighty-two breadlines, two were opened by William Randolph Hearst. And in Chicago Al Capone ran his own.[7]

Another symbol was the threadbare apple seller hawking fruits. Six thousand of these pitiful entrepreneurs, failed men drawn from all walks of life, plied New York's street corners. Each of the peddlers paid $1.75 for a crate of apples. If he sold the entire box of apples at a nickel apiece he stood to make a profit of $1.85 for the day's work. "Damn! I'm never going to forget this year 1930," muttered one of the apple vendors. "I can spit on it!" Crouching on the corners, with their roughly lettered signs advertising their fruit, these men were like "half remembered sins," remarked newspaper reporter Gene Fowler, "sitting upon the conscience of the town."[8]

On a trip to the mountains Eleanor Roosevelt saw a boy hide his pet rabbit. "He thinks we are not going to eat it," explained his sister, "but we are." The curse took on the dimensions of a biblical plague. No trace of the seven good years remained. The United Hospital Fund reported that donors were refusing to honor pledges and some were asking that previous contributions be returned to them. A teacher told a sickly youngster to go home for a meal. "I can't," said the pupil, "it's my sister's turn to eat." A clergyman touted the spartan benefits of adversity. Reformer Lillian Wald shot him an unbelieving retort: "Have you ever seen the uncontrollable trembling of parents," she demanded, "who have starved themselves for weeks so that their children might not go hungry?" In Pittsburgh a father stole a loaf of bread to feed his children and then hanged himself in shame. In Washington a debutante threw a lavish feast for $250,000. On the floor of the Senate George Norris said with deep pain, "I don't know how they had the heart to do it."[9]

Still it was hard to shake the sense of prosperity that hung over from the twenties. Many refused to believe that the crisis was real. Jimmy Walker asked New York theater operators to show only cheerful films; perhaps this would win back the gay spirit of prosperity. Officials offered bulletins predicting imminent recovery. But fear won out, and in the world turned around by depression, boosterism was worse than no talk at all. "Every time an administration official gives out an optimistic statement about business conditions," complained the Republican national chairman, Simeon Fess, "the market immediately drops."[10]

Americans were perhaps the most vulnerable citizens facing the depression in the world. No other modern nation had so few provisions for their needy. During the twenties the courts had wiped out much of the Progressive program for social justice. Appointed chief justice by Warren Harding in 1921, "to reverse a few decisions," the corpulent ex-president William Howard Taft led the court in trimming back federal responsibilities. Brandishing the doctrine of liberty of contract, the justices ruled against minimum wage guarantees and the outlawing of child labor. The census of 1920 counted more than 1 million children between the ages of ten and fifteen working. The real number can only be guessed, and an estimate of 7 million is not unrealistic, but reformers were reduced to a foundering campaign for a constitutional amendment. Neither the federal government nor the states had a program for old-age pensions at the time of the crash. Workers faced the Great Depression with no protection against unemployment, no relief, no insurance, no guarantee of even a minimal existence. The legacy of the good years was a system with no safeguards against the bad years now upon them.[11]

Little in the American experience prepared government for large-scale economic responsibility, and initially it rejected any real role for itself, keeping hands off and hoping that the slump would clear. "Liquidate labor, liquidate stocks, liquidate the farmers, liquidate real estate . . . ," urged Secretary of Treasury Andrew Mellon. "People will work harder, live a more moral life. Values will be adjusted, and enterprising people will pick up the wrecks from less competent people." Mellon was not an evil madman. He did what an entire lifetime prepared him to do: guard the free market. When it worked he had been heralded as the prophet of prosperity.[12]

President Herbert Hoover proved less dogmatic. He expanded programs for federal construction, cut taxes, and urged local governments to help their suffering citizens. He "jawboned" business leaders to maintain wages and payrolls. He worked very hard within the limits of his conception of the free enterprise system to mitigate suffering. From his own pocket he contributed thousands of dollars to help the poor, but he firmly opposed all proposals for direct public relief. A dole would unbalance the budget and vitiate the American character, robbing recipients of their initiative and self-respect.

As if there was still some self-respect left for the losers. Thomas Wolfe described the crowd of homeless men he found before a New York comfort station in his novel *You Can't Go Home Again*.

> Some were those shambling hulks that one sees everywhere. . . . But most . . . were just flotsam of the general ruin of the time—honest, decent, middle aged men with faces seamed by toil and want, and young men, many of them . . . boys in their teens. . . . They drifted across the land and gathered in the big cities when winter came, hungry, defeated, empty, hopeless, restless, driven by they knew not what . . . looking everywhere for work, for the bare crumbs to support their miserable lives, and finding neither work nor crumbs.[13]

Unable to pay rents and mortgages, families were cast out of their homes. At the edge of cities and in empty lots the homeless created ramshackle "Hoovervilles." In February 1931 the *New Yorker* recommended to anyone "wanting to see civilization creaking" that they visit the corner of West and Spring Streets in lower Manhattan. "There is a whole village of shacks and huts there, made of packing boxes, barrel staves, pieces of corrugated iron, and whatever else the junkman doesn't want, . . ." Central Park became a haven for the homeless. An unemployed carpenter, a man named Hollinan, lived with his wife in one of the caves for nearly a year; another occupied a baby buggy; an entire group built a shantytown in the Great Lawn and called it Hoover Valley. In December there were seven shacks in the Valley. The following year there were twenty-nine. By 1932 investigators estimated that between 1 and 2 million men, including several hundred thousand young boys, were aimlessly roaming the country. In the cities the poor dug through the garbage piles for food. "No one has starved," the president announced at one point, but even this minimalist boast was wrong. In New York in 1931, four local hospitals reported 95 deaths from starvation.[14]

New York City could not meet expenses from current revenues. While the president refused to unbalance the federal budget, he had urged upon the hard-pressed cities the task of providing relief for their unemployed. New York City had to borrow on anticipated tax receipts, piling up a debt almost equal to that of the forty-eight states combined. Construction of the Triborough Bridge ceased for lack of funds. The state legislature declared a moratorium on foreclosures, requiring only that taxes and the interest on mortgages be paid. Even this proved too much for many who could not hold onto their homes. Groucho Marx said he knew things were bad when he saw pigeons feeding the people in Central Park. The eminent critic and historian Carl Van Doren later recalled that he had one recurrent dream, "It was a dream of fear. . . ."[15]

Fiorello La Guardia had been warning about just this sort of calamity for much of the decade. Throughout the twenties he had lectured about the dangers of a lopsided economy and the need for proper assistance for the unfortunate, for public housing, unemployment insurance, old-age pensions. Louder and more consistently than any representative, he had complained about the rottenness, the swindle, the greed at the center of the Coolidge-Hoover business government. Skeptical about a government that preached laissez faire to the needy but assisted business with favorable tax rates and tariff policies, he had demanded economic principles concerned with something more than maximizing private profits. He had preached sensitivity toward the poor and the needy before the Depression, when they were still a minority. No one could stand by the side of the destruction visited by the economic crack-up and call out, "I told you so," with as much justice as the congressman from East Harlem.

"When more and more people are thrown out of work," intoned former

President Calvin Coolidge, "unemployment results." It came as a revelation. In 1928, when Coolidge was still president, Fiorello La Guardia had warned that "a great deal of . . . 'prosperity' is simply stock ticker prosperity, the fact remains that we have considerable unemployment." People listened more closely now.[16]

Even Calvin Coolidge was prepared to grant that business did not have all of the answers. "The final solution, to unemployment," said the dejected New Englander in 1931, with more meaning than the words seem to convey, "is work." On a cold December day in New York City, Coolidge unburdened himself to an old friend. "We are in a new era to which I do not belong and it would not be possible for me to adjust myself to it. These new ideas call for new men to develop them. That task is not for men who believe in the only kind of government I know anything about." Perhaps what he meant was not so much "new" men as different ones from those he had trusted. Some of these "new men" had been around for a while. And now the attention of a dispirited nation was upon them. In the Senate, George Norris and Robert F. Wagner were the "new men." In the House, it was the old insurgent from East Harlem, Other America's Congressman, Fiorello La Guardia.[17]

2. "The Word Dole Doesn't Scare Me"

THROUGHOUT the twenties La Guardia had warned that a modern economy could not rest on the workings of "invisible hands." He had insisted on economic reform in *good times*. In 1922, when national prosperity just began its phenomenal rise, La Guardia, in one of his articles for Hearst's *Evening Journal*, proposed a flexible reserve fund for large-scale public works to buffer economic downswings by infusing capital and providing jobs during recessions. Against objections about the cost of such a program, he calculated the savings in poorhouses, hospitals, and the enhanced quality of life and pronounced the plan a bargain. But it took the Depression for Americans to consider essential economic reforms.[18]

One month after the crash, in December of 1929, while the rest of the Republican party held to the false hope of a quick turnaround, La Guardia told the Eighteenth Assembly Republican Club that a "hands off" approach would only bring the skewed economy into deeper crisis. In other fields society used its new knowledge to exert increasing control over its environment. Economics too must be protected from the chaotic freedom of the uncontrolled market place. "Labor conditions, terms of employment, relations between employer and employee: these cannot stand still while science, mechanics, electricity, chemistry and education rapidly forge forward,'' he said. Purging was no longer an acceptable treatment in medicine, and government must not stand idly by while this primitive tactic convulsed the economy. In the face of a disabling depression, government had to respond. The modern national economy had been transformed from a simple ring of farms, shops, and artisans balanced by individual decisions and actions into an encompassing national system dominated by large corporations doing their best to control the market. This new economy required broader government involvement and responsibility in both good times and bad.[19]

President Hoover, meanwhile, would not surrender his faith in a free enterprise system that had taken a poor midwestern orphan, raised him to a millionaire, and then elected him president. If the people would only regain their confidence, he believed, the problems would be solved. ''Write a joke against these hoarders,'' Hoover appealed to Will Rogers. ''Humor might show 'em how foolish they are.'' Herbert Hoover, the world-renowned engineer, the organizer of postwar relief for starving Europe, the brilliant secretary of commerce who had promised once and for all to bring an end to poverty, was reduced to trying to make Americans smile. In the end it was all sadly laughable. ''I have no Wilsonian qualities,'' the Republican president lamented. But the most eloquent speaker could not make the Depression disappear. Exhortations to confidence snagged in the teeth of a declining economy. ''There has been more optimism talked and less practiced,'' Will Rogers announced, ''than at any time in our history.''[20]

By 1930, the ''Second Year of the Abolition of Poverty,'' in Elmer Davis's sardonic chronology, La Guardia was insisting that solutions must reach beyond jokes and boosterism. His calls for federal responsibility found a tenacious ally in the Democratic junior senator from New York, Robert F. Wagner. Wagner's father, who immigrated to the United States in 1878, had worked as a janitor, and Robert grew up among the working poor. ''Unless you have lived among these people,'' he later reminisced, ''you cannot know the haunting sense of insecurity which hangs over the home of the worker.'' By 1913 the florid-faced New Yorker was Democratic floor leader in Albany.[21]

The Triangle Shirt Waist fire ripened Wagner's social conscience, impressing upon this son of working-class immigrants that there were more important dangers than tampering with laissez faire. With Al Smith as his vice chairman, Wagner directed the New York State Factory Investigating Commission in an exhaustive study leading to a modern factory code with limits on work hours and child labor, and regulated health and safety conditions.

Elected to the U.S. Senate in 1926, Wagner began to gather information on unemployment, only to learn that no one had any idea of how many Americans were out of work. The government maintained figures on factory production, ''on

172

the traffic of our railroads, on bank loans, on the status of our wheat, prune, cherry and apricot crops; there were statistics on the cold storage holdings of cheese and pickled pork," but none on unemployment. In the Senate he fought for aid to the unemployed. "Bobby," he once told his son, "work is the only thing that matters."[22]

They made a strange match, recalled Lowell Limpus, "Wagner of the phlegmatic German temperament, the statesman and idealist,—strange product of Tammany Hall—. . . shoulder to shoulder with the excitable Harlem spitfire." Together, La Guardia and Wagner carried the fight in Washington for a positive government response to the Depression. By 1930 their program managed to break through the "hands-off" brigade and make some headway in the Senate, but in the lower house, where La Guardia's public works measures were invariably shunted to the judiciary committee, only to be deftly eviscerated by its reactionary chairman, Pennsylvania Republican George S. Graham, La Guardia was reduced to flaying his colleagues for their obstructionism and lecturing them about social justice.[23]

As the terrible winter of 1930–1931 progressed, unemployment climbed, but Hoover could not dislodge his nagging fear that relief to the unemployed would diminish individual dignity. Forced to choose between assisting the hungry and protecting the values of self-reliance, he treated the dilemma like a man forced to decide which of his arms should be cut off. He deliberated, suffered, delayed, hoping that a miracle would save him from losing either, but in the end lost both. When a friend asked New York Yankees slugger Babe Ruth why he was holding out for a salary much larger than the president's, the home run star responded: "So what, I had a better season than he had."

Throughout the decade Congress had worked closely with the Republican presidents in shaping the prosperity policies of the twenties, and at least initially, it agreed with Hoover, but finally it had to agree with the Babe. Over White House objections, the Congress enacted a national employment exchange pressed by Wagner and La Guardia. Hoover vetoed it. Instead, he established a modest employment division in the Labor Department. When the head of the president's in-house employment service addressed an American Legion conference in the fall of 1931, he promised to help find jobs for the unemployed veterans. Why, that very morning, he asserted with some satisfaction, "I found two of your men jobs . . . in one hour just using the telephone!" Replied a less than grateful Legion official: "Fine, I'll give you a list of 750,000 to place."[24]

In March 1931 a group of Allied Progressives, veterans of old social wars bound together by a conviction that the national economic catastrophe might serve as a historical turning point, met to shape a Depression program. The *New York Times*

173

offered them sardonic welcome: "It is good to know that eight Wisconsin Progressive Republicans in Congress are to call . . . a confabulation of themselves and six other statesmen, including our own La Guardia. . . . The fourteen . . . will lay down the policies that ought to be followed by the 72nd Congress. This is very kind of them and should be instructive to Congress." This confabulation represented something more significant than the *Times* suggested in its dismissive editorial. The major reform figures of the age, George Norris, Lillian Wald, Florence Kelley, Sidney Hillman, Harold Ickes, and Charles Beard, men and women who had sustained progressivism in unfriendly times, came together to tackle the Depression. The recurrence of his old war injury confined La Guardia to a hospital bed, but he followed the meeting carefully and sent a long letter to Senator George Norris suggesting several proposals.[25]

La Guardia encouraged the reformers to confront the central anomaly of the times. "We find ourselves with an unprecedented wealth, with warehouses full and millions of willing workers out of employment and large numbers dependent upon private charities," and a government reduced to praying for the crisis to clear, pronouncing itself too weak to deal with the situation. "Engineers," he scoffed, "apparently did not know what to do." He contraposed a set of liberating principles against those that had crippled the Great Engineer. Public assistance was preferable to private handouts. The government must guarantee every citizen willing to work a decent living and a share in the nation's economic progress in the form of shorter work hours, higher wages, and better conditions. Modern business cared for its machines in good times as well as bad; it must assume the same responsibility for its human toilers.[26]

When the Brooklyn Edison Company discharged 1600 employees in May of 1931, Fiorello raged that the company had passed a $57 million dividend to its shareholders, *a 20 percent increase over its 1929 distributions*. Utility companies, guaranteed a state monopoly, were collecting high rates and enriching stockholders while discharging workers. They could not do that. Why not? Because it was wrong. Because it failed to consider the laborers and their needs and their contributions. "The industrialists and financiers of this country have utterly failed in anticipating the inevitable, in preparing for depression by properly caring for the workers. . . ."[27]

The trickle-down theorists had promised that wealth would filter down, but the only thing that trickled down was misery. Forget trickle-down, said La Guardia. Safeguarding business profits would not restore prosperity. Recovery had to be built from the bottom up by restoring the "power to purchase rather than . . . curtail[ing] production." La Guardia told a Hearst representative soliciting his opinion on Depression solutions that he could not provide the "answer you would want and would publish. But of course I would rather be truthful than accommodating. . . . Yours for higher inheritance taxes, unemployment insurance, and a better distribution of the now hoarded and concentrated wealth of the Great Republic."[28]

Blocking any such efforts stood an idea that would not die, the notion with which most Americans had grown up, that in the United States a good, ambitious workingman had no need for assistance, that government aid came at the expense of liberty, dignity, and self-reliance. The spirit that had built America, went this thinking, accomplished as much as it did because no safety net stood ready to catch those who fell. Fear of failure and the possibility of unlimited success drew forth remarkable exertion, fueling America's unmatched economic power. Guarantee a man a dole if he fails and you compromise his vital urge to succeed.

"I do not give a damn, . . ." La Guardia wrote to a newspaper correspondent. "The word dole doesn't scare me." The Depression had thrown people out of work indiscriminately. Millions of Americans who tried and worked hard all their lives *"through no fault of their own"* were on breadlines. "The highest function of government," asserted La Guardia, "is the preservation of life," not profits or even intiative. This was not the time to consider the effect assistance would have on the fiber of the nation. What effect would it have to see all of these people suffer and bring up wounded children? If Hoover insisted on viewing employment insurance as a dole, let him, but as for La Guardia: "I do not hesitate to say that I would rather receive assistance as a matter of right from my government than be placed in line to appeal and beg from the fund created from private charity. . . ."

As the Seventy-second Congress convened in December of 1931, La Guardia, deluged with letters from his own district and from all over the nation indicating just how desperate the situation was, demanded his colleagues' attention. "We are not going to get out of this depression . . . by pep talks. . . . The present economic system is not adequate to meet the industrial age in which we are living . . . it may be necessary to go into the very fundamentals of our system and bring about an economic readjustment." Back in the twenties, La Guardia had talked as wildly as he wished, sometimes for effect and sometimes to relieve his own resentments. It did not much matter, there was no danger of his making any difference. Now his strategy was more complex because it was more practical. He still spoke about root and branch changes, but the proposals that followed this rhetoric were disarmingly moderate. They constituted a program designed for Democrats and Republicans. And within the next two years many of them would be passed into law by mainstream politicians interested only in preserving American institutions and domestic peace.[29]

La Guardia proposed direct relief aid to staunch misery, and a program of public works to steer the nation toward recovery. He recommended a list of public works that included highways, airfields, and an assortment of conventional expenditures, but also some new ideas that offered a foretaste of the New Deal to come. He suggested that the government take over some of the benign functions of the local ward boss by distributing clothing and shoes and coal. And with so many in the construction industry sidelined, he urged the consideration of another Progressive initiative that had been kicking around for a while, the construction of public housing. Such an undertaking would employ tens of thousands and offer the poor badly needed housing. In addition, he called for five regional Public Health-operated camps to care for transients, government-insured bank deposits, unemployment insurance, employment exchanges, and measures to spread the work through either curtailed hours or a shorter work week. "It will cost money, yes," said a solemn La Guardia, "but our country is worth saving and it will be a good investment." To those who interposed constitutional obstacles, La Guardia could not be more plain. "If the Constitution stands in the way, the Constitution will simply have to get out of the way."[30]

But Congress could not focus its many heads on any one program. "While millions of men, women and children in the country were suffering intense hardships," reported a December 18, 1931, dispatch from Washington, "the majority of the members of the House talks on everything but the only problem that they should discuss before they take up anything else [is]—how to get the people the things they need, and need RIGHT NOW." The legislators squandered the nation's time on narrow partisan issues. "After two days of this drivel," the dispatch continued, "a member from New York, La Guardia, noted for calling a spade a spade, strode on the stage and gave his fellow actors hell. The squat swarthy hell raiser is hated and feared by both Republican and Democratic machines." Again came the predictable objection about a dole. The paunchy New Yorker jumped to his feet. "I could go down to the market here in Washington and buy a parrot for two dollars and in one day I can teach it to say the word 'Dole, Dole, Dole.' " But no matter how carefully the present economic crisis was explained, the bird would never understand the issue. If Congress joined the president in failing to take action, La Guardia warned, all the talk about third parties would be academic. By 1932 "there will be only one party."[31]

———

For the moment, Washington preferred to create a dole for needy businesses. In December of 1931, Congress, carrying forward Hoover's trickle-down thinking, created the Reconstruction Finance Corporation to make loans to distressed industries and banks. Fine, remarked La Guardia, offer a subsidy to the "broken bankers" and "bankrupt institutions," but what had happened to concern about the effect of such handouts on initiative? Let the bankers experience the spiritual benefits of adversity and liquidation. This "millionaire's dole" would stimulate nothing more than the stock ticker.[32]

Bankers who had made speculative loans with other people's money and ruined millions of families were receiving federal help, fumed La Guardia, while decent folk were left to beg from private charities. Where he grew up in the West they would have found a better way of dealing with those horse-thieving bankers! A colleague interrupted Fiorello in mid-harangue asking, "Would the gentleman hang the bankers?'' He replied coolly: ''Yes; I would hang a banker who stole from the people.''[33]

Instead of a ''hospital for incurables,'' as he dubbed the RFC, he called for a deposit insurance system to protect the saver and force probity and prudence upon the banks. ''Anyone who deposits money in a bank has a right to sleep at night,'' he said. But his amendment failed. When he proposed a law taxing stock transfers, banks blamed the proposal for the decline in stock prices! ''Stocks and bonds listed on the New York Stock Exchange and owned by Life Insurance Companies, Savings Banks, Fire Insurance Companies, Banks and Individual Investors,'' charged the Harriman National Bank and Trust Company, ''have been deflated in value to the extent of more than $3,500,000,000 as a direct result of the La Guardia Tax Clause. . . .''[34]

But the banks could no longer deflect blame for their own failures. The chairman of the board of New York's Chase Bank, Albert H. Wiggin, received more than a quarter-of-a-million-dollar salary from Chase and also collected handsome retainers from fifty-nine other corporations, many of whom were Chase clients. Liberally assisted with Chase loans, these corporations played the market with a swashbuckler's daring and Chase's money. One series of deals on Chase stock with Chase money brought a Wiggins consortium a $4,008,538 profit. ''People of carping tendencies,'' writes John Kenneth Galbraith, ''might hold the profit was earned by the bank, whose stock it was, whose officer Wiggin was, and which had provided the money for the operation.'' But it was Wiggin who collected the remarkable profits. Wiggin might respond in his own defense that such loans to a bank's officer for speculation with its own stock made him even more interested in the institution's success; except that Wiggin made this munificent profit on selling short, betting on his own bank's stock to decline in value! As things became uncomfortable, Mr. Wiggin arranged an annual lifetime annuity of $100,000 for himself and retired from Chase in 1932.

Wiggin was a conservative banker in comparison with his counterpart at National City, Charles E. Mitchell. Mitchell too played the market on his own bank's stocks, but he got caught in the midst of the crash with a serious loss and a huge debt to the Morgan Company. To avoid a large tax liability, he entered into a series of transactions of sale and purchase with his wife. The upshot of these deals came on the evening of March 21, 1933, when Assistant U. S. District Attorney Thomas E. Dewey arrested him for evasion of taxes. Galbraith writes that this was not an unusual ploy in the Hoover era when tax avoidance strategies brought ''individuals of the highest respectability into extraordinary financial intercourse with their wives.''[35]

Fiorello jumped upon the disorder in the temples of native American business with undisguised glee. No other sector of the economy had achieved such elevated status or restricted WASP identity as the banks and the stock exchange, and he derived extra satisfaction from dragging these guardians of American prosperity over the coals. It should "take more than a pair of spats and a love nest on Park Avenue to make a banker," he wrote. Stripped of their polish and their civilized manners, the elegant "banketeers" were no better than the New Immigrant gangsters. "Now we have reached the stage," Fiorello said "where we have either to put some of our bankers in Atlanta or let Al Capone out."

He took in the scene of the foundering financial markets: "Look around you, a complete wreck," he wrote in 1933. "Marcus and Singer of the Bank of the United States are in Sing Sing; Mitchell of the National City Bank and Harriman of the Harriman National are under indictment; and numbers of others to escape the same fate are blowing out their brains or jumping from high windows." The banks, he declared, had failed the people. They had speculated on depositors' savings, rigged stocks, and dumped worthless securities on clients while costing the Treasury millions through tax evasion instruments that they designed for speculators. To ward off investigations, they threatened that full disclosure would result in panic. Then they repeated the threat of widespread bank failures to extort from Hoover the RFC. When bankers used the same sort of coercion on Woodrow Wilson, recalled La Guardia, he promised to hang them higher then Haman; Hoover had buckled under. "He's a naturally timid man," he wrote.[36]

Around the case of the Bank of the United States, La Guardia uncovered motives more vicious than greed. Its bankers, Messrs. Marcus and Singer and the other officers, were as guilty of the stock plugging and dishonesty as the others, but La Guardia was convinced that this bank and the savings of thousands of depositors "could have been saved." Instead "it was Hitlerized." La Guardia accused the banking fraternity of not wanting to save a "Jewish" bank, thereby sacrificing some 400,000 depositors "to anti-Semitic prejudice." Attacking the entire premise of free enterprise banking, he introduced a bill in 1932 to regulate interest rates.[37]

If La Guardia discovered rottenness surrounding the banking industry, he found it resting on the heart of the stock market. On November 30, 1929, just weeks after the crash, the governing committee of the New York Stock Exchange passed a resolution praising their acting president, Richard Whitney, for his labors during the crisis. Following the crash Whitney led the fight for retrenchment in government, calling for cuts in the salaries of federal employees and slashing veterans benefits. When New York University awarded Whitney an honorary degree for his wise leadership, La Guardia almost choked on the news. "Gentlemen: I note by today's newspapers that you have conferred an honorary degree upon Richard Whitney," he yelped. "Through what oversight did you overlook gangster Alphonse Capone of Chicago?"

It took several years to catch up with him, but in 1938 the United States government indicted Whitney for grand larceny. Unlike National City's Mitchell, Whitney's weakness was not merely between him and his tax man. "Theft," a shrewd student of the market has written, "was almost a minor incident pertaining to his business misfortunes"; not that he was averse to theft, as another observer notes: "He stole from his customers; he stole from his father-in-law; he stole from his yacht club." For starters. He also used stocks that individual customers had entrusted to his brokerage firm as collateral for his bad loans. The end came rather quickly.[38]

Not all leaders of business were indicted, but few escaped obloquy. Americans learned, for example, that J. P. Morgan and his nineteen partners paid no income taxes to the federal government for 1931 and 1932 and, even more disturbing, that the Morgan firm kept a list of insiders who bought stock at below market prices. Then in March 1932 Ivar Krueger took his own life in Paris. A painstaking audit of his accounts discovered that the Match King had also taken American investors for a quarter billion dollars. Scandal sheets had a field day that month as another of the world's great financiers came tumbling down. The utility empire of Samuel Insull fell like a house of cards, taking with it close to 700 million of investors' dollars. Company stock slid from 107½ in 1929 to 1⅓ in March 1932.[39]

Great hater that he was, these stories inspired La Guardia. ("I am horrified by the selfishness of our world," Henry Adams once wrote Muriel LaFarge. "We don't even curse each other heartily. A good hater is as rare as a good lover.") On April 26, 1932, he appeared before the Senate Banking Committee with two trunks of records and documents. From the trunks he presented in fascinating detail the peculations of the stock marketeers. La Guardia produced copies of checks drawn to financial reporters who had shilled securities in their newspaper columns. Always happy to provide the facts, just the facts, he calculated that 605 false stories had been circulated in 208 newspapers with a combined readership of 11 million in 157 cities. Honorary Doctor Richard Whitney's market had been rife with deception, deceit, and fraud, as La Guardia had charged in 1929, just weeks after the crash.[40]

In all of this La Guardia was still fighting against the tide of accepted political doctrine. The tireless acid complainer of American politics still had little effect and only a minority following. His charges were, after all, only diversions, venting his resentments against the larcenous core of twenties prosperity. The chief need remained relief and public works projects, and it all came down to money and the government's fear of spending it. "We cannot squander ourselves into prosperity," Herbert Hoover kept repeating. Budget deficits were too nasty a condition to even contemplate. But by the end of 1932, a growing number in Congress were listening more attentively as La Guardia insisted on turning the focus from the received economic wisdom of laissez faire to the needs of the unemployed and the poor.[41]

3. "The Bastards Broke the People's Back"

A FTER the stock market crashed in 1929, President Hoover had proposed a tax cut. Economists of a later era, writing from a Keynesian perspective, have judged this step his one correct move in advancing recovery. "Thereafter," writes John Galbraith, "policy was almost entirely on the side of making things worse." As Depression programs and declining tax receipts threatened a huge budget deficit, Hoover, conventional to the end, sought to increase revenues through a national sales tax. Fearful of appearing to oppose government solvency, Democrats folded their opposition to the regressive tax as Democratic House Speaker and presidential hopeful John Nance Garner announced that he would support a sales tax for the "financial salvation of my country." Passage of the tax appeared even more certain when the House Ways and Means Committee reported out a sales tax bill by a vote of twenty-four to one.[42]

La Guardia refused to go along with the tax. Rallying the Allied Progressives behind him, he fought against a policy of taxing the poor while reserving relief for business. He took aim first at the coldly aloof millionaire architect of Republican fiscal policy, Treasury Secretary Andrew Mellon.

La Guardia turned over the dossier that he had compiled on the imperious Treasury secretary to Ernest Cuneo, declaring simply: "I'm going to impeach Mellon. Get me a brief." Fiorello thought that Mellon, who owned a large portion of the outstanding stock in the Aluminum Corporation of America, was violating a law forbidding cabinet secretaries to serve as directors of private corporations. The nonplussed Cuneo was given a day to prepare. "I'm blasting at noon," trilled La Guardia. Try as he might, Cuneo could prove nothing more than that Mellon owned a lot of stock. Fiorello objected that the Treasury secretary controlled the directors, but these were very weak grounds indeed. No matter, he started firing at Mellon and did not stop until a few days later, when the president announced Mellon's resignation from the cabinet to accept appointment as ambassador to the Court of St. James's.[43]

Next, La Guardia turned to the tax plan. Unbalanced budgets were as inconceivable to La Guardia as to Hoover. "We must not pass on to future generations the burden of paying for the failures, the blunders, the mistakes of our present financial collapse," he told an NBC radio audience. In this he agreed with the rest of his party, but he opposed the president's sales tax. "There are three ways of paying for a sales tax," said La Guardia, and each of these placed the burden upon the least prosperous elements. The 1929 tax cut had favored those with higher incomes. This time the money must come from those who could take the bite. On March 10, 1932, La Guardia took the floor of the House denouncing a flat-rate tax in a nation where income was unevenly distributed and calling for a levy on luxuries instead. His cause seemed hopeless. But when a technicality delayed the vote Fiorello continued applying pressure, attacking the bill for taxing the few morsels of food still left to the poor. His staff prepared a well-reasoned study on the failure of similar tax plans for him to use during the floor debate, but La Guardia discarded it. "I am simply going to say, '*Soak the rich*,' " he declared. The distressed Cuneo feared so undignified and incendiary a response. "Wild and whirling words," commented an aghast *New York Times*. But La Guardia proceeded with his own proposal for higher taxes on luxury items and a graduated levy on incomes of $100,000 and above.[44]

Against all odds, La Guardia's growing forces blocked the administration steamroller in some of the stormiest sessions in the history of the Congress. Personal charges flew across the aisles, party discipline cracked, tempers flared, and at the center of the debate, munching on his peanuts and mocking the arraigned political batallions, stood the East Harlem insurgent, crying, "Soak the rich! Soak the rich!" The conservative press pounded him as a rabble-rouser and a demagogue, a Red and a foreigner, a party killer. The *Washington Star* fulminated: "He represents the wave of socialism, hatred and irresponsibility that sweeps Congress. . . ." But by the second week of the debate, representatives were abandoning their party leaders in droves to join the loud objector. "Congress . . . [has] in the last fortnight struck a harder blow against the stability and solvency of the United States," continued the *Star*, "than it has been called on to endure in its history." The *Chicago Tribune* wrote that the tax revolt confronted the nation with its gravest domestic crisis since Lincoln's assassination, and attacked La Guardia as "alien in mind and spirit from Americanism," disloyal to American principles. "Chaos reigns in Congress," raged the Sandusky, Ohio, *Register*, blaming "such men as La Guardia . . . a product of the steerage and Ellis Island a few years back," who "have dipped their fingers in the gore of confiscation and gone on an orgy which they themselves call 'soak the rich.' "[45]

Toward the end of March, the administration sought a compromise, but La Guardia, riding high in the saddle, refused even a partial sales tax. The working-class *New York Daily News* feared: "Soak Rockefeller 72 per cent of what he makes over $5,000,000 . . . and how can he go ahead with Radio City, not to mention his vast philanthropic activities all over the world?" Unmoved, La Guardia piloted the resistance, denouncing trickle-down favoritism from his front row seat. "He does not rise to speak," a correspondent wrote, "he bounces." Newspapers reported that the Major "tore to shreds the tax bill," routing his own party. But the *Brooklyn Eagle* saw more than congressional pandering in all of this: "To dismiss Mr. La Guardia's performance as mere perverse radicalism is to miss the point. The movement, in its deepest significance far from being a manifestation of communism, is an expression of resentment at the failure of the Congress to provide relief for the mass of the population, while billions have been appropriated for the relief of banks railroads and corporations.'' After the fight La Guardia exulted: ''They put Baruch alongside of me on the Congressional [railroad] that Friday and he talked my ear off all the way up. Boy they really wanted that Sales Tax. But they didn't get it. I showed them.''[46]

He showed them in a style that attracted national attention. After March 24, when Congress knocked out the sales tax by a vote of 211 to 178, *Time* magazine called La Guardia a politician who refused to accept any authority other than his conscience. ''Not within our time has an individual won such a striking legislative victory,'' gushed Heywood Broun. La Guardia had been offering the same message for a decade, but ''soak the rich'' never sounded so appropriate as it did now amidst tales of tax evasion and loopholes for the wealthy while the poor occupied paper villages on the outskirts of industrial towns. Congress substituted a series of levies on financial transactions and luxuries for the defeated measure, precisely what La Guardia had suggested. He knew that these would not be popular. ''I am going to get it coming and going,'' he muttered, but when a colleague told him that he deserved it, La Guardia replied that he accepted the price willingly for his role in defeating ''one of the most vicious pieces of legislation ever devised.''[47]

Finally achieving influence, he was offending conservatives not only with his rhetoric but with actual results. Gadfly in the advance army of social change, La Guardia had been proposing new ideas for years. His proposals occupied a sagging shelf of unpassed progressive measures. Now his time was at hand. This most ''insurgent of insurgents'' had taken on a president from his own party and won. Fearing that La Guardia's victory would ''strangle'' business, the *Evening Journal* wrote, ''Rep. La Guardia it is a shame you are classed as a Republican.'' A correspondent scrawled across the top of a newspaper clipping, ''next time you should run as a Red.''[48]

His power growing steadily, Fiorello attacked another presidential plan to cut expenditures by slashing public employee salaries and revamping administrative departments. Promising to ''fight to the last ditch,'' he refused to permit the budget to be balanced on the backs of the civil service. It was not *their* speculation that that had caused the Depression! He was not going to allow the president to use the fiscal emergency to wipe out decades of hard-won reform battles to erect regulatory agencies and raise the salaries of federal employees.[49]

With data gathered by a network of correspondents all over the country, La Guardia rewrote the bill, line by line. Yes, to cuts in the War Department. No, to reductions in the Children's Bureau, the Veteran's Bureau, the Office of Education, and a host of other monitoring agencies. If the ''shaky bankers, discredited stock brokers, nimble financiers, double dealing directors . . .'' who kept repeating the call for layoffs had any shame, La Guardia said, they would go off in a corner and hide. They had come begging to Congress for loans and gotten their RFC, and now they were pushing to cut congressional salaries. La Guardia denounced their congressional supporters for "one of the greatest grandstand plays—and I know something about grandstand plays. . . ." He polled his colleagues regarding their costs and expenses in Washington and concluded that they needed every penny of what they earned if Congress was to remain open to common citizens and afford them independence from the favor curriers. "It is hard work," he observed, "and those who do it earnestly, do not try to make themselves wealthy. . . ." By the time La Guardia finished, the $300 million economy measure had itself been pared to $30 million.[50]

Next he turned to Hoover's plan for federally guaranteed home mortgages. A "Bill to Bail out the Mortgage Bankers," La Guardia termed it, for under the terms that the mortgage holders had struck with the administration, the bill allowed them to pass uncollectable mortgages to the federal government. La Guardia would have none of it. With millions out of work, the government continued to worry about the bankers. "I'm not going to let them get away with it," he told his staff. The bastards broke the People's back with their usury. . . . Let them die, the People will survive."[51]

La Guardia tried to cripple the bill with amendments. "Mobilize your tank force to kill a mouse," a staffer told him in frustration at the picayune tactics. "Yeah," he replied. "And let me tell you something: I always get that mouse too." This time he did not, however. In its final form the law created twelve Home Owners Loan Banks across the country. La Guardia encouraged citizens to apply directly to the banks, insisting that the law made the HOLBs mortgage lenders of last resort. But bulging sacks of mail from all over the country advised him that trickle-down was still the reigning principle. Only banks could take advantage of the HOLBs, while private citizens were left to the mercy of the mortgage industry. Letters from towns as diverse as Michigan City, Indiana; Newbury, South Carolina; Tocca, Georgia; Los Cruces, New Mexico; and countless similar places informed La Guardia that it was still impossible for a workingman to get a loan, sell a house, or refinance a mortgage.[52]

It was spring 1932 and the national temper had hit bottom. A. N. Young, a Farmer's Union official testifying before a Senate committee, told the shaken congressmen: "I almost hate to express it, but I honestly believe that if some of them could buy airplanes they would come down here to Washington to blow you fellows all up. . . . I am as conservative as any man could be but any economic system that has in its power to set me and my wife on the streets, at my age—what can I see but red." Father John Ryan wished "we might double the number of communists" to put fear into the hearts of American leaders. Amtorg, the Soviet trade organization, advertised some 6000 jobs. More than 100,000 Americans applied for positions in Moscow.[53]

Congress finally made a token allocation of wheat and cotton for the poor, to be distributed through the Red Cross. This insistence on avoiding even the appearance of helping desperate Americans was bad enough, but then the Red Cross entered into its own hermeneutical analysis over whether it had a right to provide direct aid in the form of bread as opposed to giving it as unfinished flour. East Harlem's ombudsman for poor America flew into a rage: "Something spiritual seems to have been taken from us; something that we looked up to has been lost and lost forever. This great organization we all believed was always ready to succor any part of the country, any class of people . . . quibbled, talked constitutional law, talked about rugged individualism. . . . It was the greatest shock." He won an amendment for the wheat and cotton to be processed into food and clothing. And then finally it was given to the poor and hungry.[54]

Progressives wanted Washington to do more. They formed a caucus to develop relief legislation, but by May 1932, as they still wrestled with the issue, their colleagues began to speak of an early summer vacation. "Let us . . . go home and let the country have a rest," asserted Representative Blanton of Texas. No, said La Guardia, in the name of the progressives, there would be no adjournment until a "complete, constructive, effective" relief measure was passed. President Hoover took one look at the progressive proposals being cooked up and described the measures as the "most gigantic pork barrel ever proposed."[55]

After La Guardia's own proposal for a "small man's RFC" that would make direct government loans of up to $500 for food and necessities to individual families was throttled in committee, Progressives united behind a $2 billion relief program. Declaring that "there can be no compromise with hunger," La Guardia appealed to his fellow lawmakers to prevent "a tempest that will cost thousands of lives and hundreds of millions of dollars and write a page of everlasting shame in our country." La Guardia attacked the philosophy of stand-pat conservatism in some of the sharpest speeches of his career. "This is unAmerican. The old feudal days, where the tenants took the crumbs from the lord of the manor and awaited something to percolate down are gone and gone forever." If it took all summer, the Progressives would pass a relief law.[56]

It was a sweltering July, well past the Congress's usual vacation date, as the stubborn Progressives continued to stave off adjournment, until, finally, Congress passed an Omnibus Relief Bill. President Hoover, mourning for the American spirit, vetoed the measure on July 11, 1932, declaring, "Never before has so dangerous a suggestion been seriously made to our country." But La Guardia had warned that the Progressives would not leave Washington until there was a relief bill, and Hoover, fearing that the Progressives would push a veto override, did sign a less ambitious measure for assistance to strapped states and municipalities.[57]

Danger, like much else, was in the eye of the beholder. While Hoover feared for American vitality in the face of relief programs, La Guardia directed his colleagues' attention to the neighboring streets: "My colleagues need go no farther than a few blocks from the national Capitol to see human beings degraded to the extent of publicly sleeping in makeshift hovels, kennels and living off scraps of donated food. . . . that condition must not . . . continue!" He was referring to the encampment of some 20,000 army veterans who made up the ragtag "Bonus Expeditionary Force" that had first marched into Washington in the spring of 1932 to support Representative Wright Patman's call for the immediate redemption of veterans' bonus certificates, granted by Congress after World War I and scheduled to come due in 1945. In 1931 Congress voted to permit veterans to borrow against these "adjusted credit certificates," but now, with no end to the Depression in sight, the veterans were demanding immediate payment of their bonus. Threatening to stay in Washington until their demands were met, the bonus marchers camped on Anacostia Flats in shacks and in the unoccupied government buildings nearby. Will Rogers described them as "the best behaved hungry men assembled anywhere in the world. Just think of what 15,000 clubwomen would have done to Washington even if they weren't hungry. The Senate would have resigned and the President committed suicide."[58]

La Guardia had voted for the bonus and the special loan provision in 1931, but he now opposed the immediate payment of what added up to a $2.4 billion package. He testified before the House Ways and Means Committee that such a huge sum should be spent for the benefit of all, not just veterans. His stand won him few friends among the veterans' groups who had lined up behind him in the past. Still, his sympathies were with the ragged army of men and women milling on the torrid Washington streets. He urged that they be provided with food, shelter, and train fare to go back home with dignity.

By July 28 the president and his advisers had become uneasy with the marchers and decided to move them out of the vacant buildings along Pennsylvania Avenue. In a scuffle that marred the generally orderly dispersal, several District policemen were injured and two veterans were killed. Hoover panicked. Convinced that Communists had infiltrated the ranks, he called out the army. His political instincts, altogether inadequate to the challenge of the Depression, failed him again as he ordered Army Chief of Staff Douglas MacArthur to disband the BEF. In riding boots, spurs, flared whipcord breeches, eight rows of ribbons and medals, and waving a swagger stick, the imperious general led four troops of cavalry and four infantry companies equipped with machine guns, tanks, tear gas, sabers, and bayonets in dispersing the hungering veterans and their families. The general called the BEF a "mob . . . animated by the essence of revolution," capable of

185

"severely threatening the institutions of the government." Then the army burned their billets.

Nothing brought home the failure of the Hoover presidency and the degree to which it had lost touch with the American people more clearly than its panic in the face of a petitioning assortment of miserable army veterans. The loss of proportion and the Red-scaring appalled La Guardia, who had offered to act as a go-between in discussions between the government and the marchers. He wired Hoover that soup would have been cheaper than tear bombs and bread more effective than bullets in maintaining order.[59]

He was no longer speaking for effect. He spoke in behalf of a growing number of Americans disillusioned with Hoover and distraught over the calamity that Republican prosperity had wrought.

4. A Magna Carta for Labor and a Liberal Agenda for Congress

A T the same time that he struggled to make Congress meet the challenge of the Depression, La Guardia, together with Senator George Norris, erected a landmark labor law freeing unions from injunctive restraint by the government and outlawing the antilabor "yellow-dog" contract, which forced workers to foreswear unions. The Norris-La Guardia Act, aimed at redressing the imbalance between big business and labor, stands as the best-known monument to La Guardia's legislative career. And he accomplished its passage by fighting off the alligators as he drained the swamp.

Over the years few causes engaged La Guardia more intimately than the labor movement. From his days as a catchall people's lawyer mediating the daily difficulties that marred the life of the poor, he fought on labor's side in the competitive industrial economy. In the years before World War I, he picketed with Italian and Jewish workers, fought for labor rights in the courts, and entered into an enduring relationship with the early leaders of the garment workers' unions.

The World War and the Red scare sapped much of organized labor's strength, while prosperity fever drained the rest. In an era when porters, typists, and laborers worshipped Henry Ford and dreamed of becoming robber barons, labor consciousness proved a hard item to sell. Nonetheless, La Guardia saw no better solution to the routine exploitation of workers than building up the countervailing power of unions. In the abstract he understood that like any institution contending for power, unions could be as abusive as capital. But for the moment, workers were so weak that La Guardia focused on strengthening their hand. Disposed to suspecting the rich and agonizing over the poor, he laid aside his objections to the racketeers and hoodlums lurking behind some unions and became labor's chief spokesman in the Lower House.[60]

To businesses that tried to use the Depression as an excuse to bring down wages, La Guardia threw down the gauntlet: "They will find many of us . . . ready to meet them and show them that they cannot further exploit the poor and impoverish those who are earnest workers in this country." He supported legislation limiting the hours of work and reducing the workweek to spread scarce opportunities as widely as possible. And for the sad army of unemployed he sought job retraining, relief, unemployment insurance, and a right to the government's concern.[61]

While congressional colleagues commonly accepted large retainers from business interests, labor's man in Congress refused to strike similar deals, despite his often straitened circumstances. "I am absolutely hard up against it," he once wrote his law partners from Washington, asking for another advance. "Keeping my house in New York and living here is so high I didn't even have carfare to New York this weekend." But when he was invited to serve as a paid attorney for a union local he wrote indignantly: "For twenty years I have been helping Organized Labor without being retained in my professional capacity and I hope to be able to continue doing so."[62]

La Guardia worked closely with many unions, following their affairs, mediating disputes, advising on negotiating strategy and the other matters that exercise union locals. "It is your unfailing characteristic to be on the right side of every question from a workingman's point of view," wrote Sam Squibb, international president of the Stonecutters. In addition to coordinating union lobbying on the Hill, he kept a sharp eye peeled on the labor front across the nation. "AN INVOLVED LABOR SITUATION IS DEVELOPING IN YOUR CITY," La Guardia wired to Pennsylvania Congressman Patrick Boland. "BELIEVE YOU COULD BE HELPFUL STOP COULD YOU POSSIBLY COME TO NEW YORK TOMORROW . . . AT MY EXPENSE FOR A CONFERENCE UPON THE SUBJECT." Shippers, postal clerks, coal miners, railway laborers, longshoremen, garment workers, bricklayers, plasterers, masons, and countless others looked to the round little legislator as their champion. "Being a common ordinary working man," John Burke wrote to La Guardia, "I have always felt that I was getting very little direct representation in the national congress and always looked to you and Senator Norris as fighting single handed for the 'forgotten man' before that phrase was ever coined."[63]

"He was always working with Senator Norris," Marie La Guardia told an interviewer. And with the eminent midwestern Progressive, the East Harlem legislator led labor to its most significant victory before the New Deal.[64]

George Norris had learned poverty and tragedy firsthand, not from books or congressional studies, but from living the life. Norris's father died in 1864, when George was only three. A brother passed away in the same year and a sister one year later. His own wife did not survive a difficult childbirth and left him a widower with three little girls to raise on his own. In 1906 his second wife barely survived the stillbirth of twins. Tragedy spurs some men to success but it also hardens many of them to the disasters of others; in a few it molds a sensitive character, sympathetic, fearless, and devoted. Adversity made Norris common with the people he represented. He dedicated his successes to them and through the Progressive movement tried to root out favoritism and privilege. La Guardia admired the Nebraskan's integrity and his instinct for the people. As a freshman congressman La Guardia would trail over to the Senate after he had completed his own work to hear George Norris speak on the issues. Nominally a Republican, Norris shared little with the spirit of Harding and Coolidge, and Fiorello enjoyed listening to him rail against the Ragtime Decade's adoration of The Dollar. The plight of the Pennsylvania coal miners during the twenties attracted Norris's attention to the appalling labor conditions across the country and to the damaging use of antiunion injunctions.[65]

The injunction was a legal device created in English courts of equity to prevent damage to property while a suit was pending. Initially, courts issued injunctive relief as an extraordinary intervention to prevent damage that was both imminent and irretrievable. In the late nineteenth century American courts adapted this measure to labor law and applied it to *potential* loss, issuing injunctions against labor strikes that threatened to hurt business. During the hard-fought Pullman strike in 1894, on the pretext of protecting the flow of the mails, U.S. attorneys obtained blanket injunctive restrictions on all strike activities that might halt the movement of the trains. For ignoring this order that would have folded the strike, Eugene V. Debs was clapped in prison for six months.

The courts consistently viewed labor with suspicion. In 1922, walrus-shaped former president William H. Taft, sitting as chief justice of the Supreme Court, wrote concerning organized labor: "that faction we have to hit every little while." An Iowa Circuit Court judge asserted the prevailing legal philosophy: "There is, and can be, no such thing as peaceful picketing, any more than there can be lawful lynching." Few statutes governed the relationship between employer and employee; consequently, labor law was formed primarily in the courts where sympathetic judges offered injunctive relief at the drop of an expensive barrister's calling card. Corporate attorneys routinely marched into court claiming potential damage and marched out with orders halting all strike activities and the payment of strike benefits. In 1925 a New York judge prohibited the Amalgamated Clothing Workers from standing within ten blocks of the plaintiff's business, an area that included union headquarters![66]

Courts also recognized yellow-dog contracts as legally binding. "By the end of the twenties," writes labor historian Irving Bernstein, "the gulf between labor and the law had become perilously wide," and the reform-minded derided "judge-made law" as the enemy of labor and social progress. "Precedent," recalled a La Guardia associate, "how he hated that word." Frederick Lehman, who served as solicitor general under Chief Justice Taft, confided to a group including Felix Frankfurter that the "legal profession, . . . have been [the] meanest, most selfish force in resisting just reforms and perpetuating . . . abuse in administration of the laws." Added Frankfurter, "our courts . . . have failed and failed wretchedly because by training and selfish interests they are a conservative and timid body of the community."[67]

La Guardia had witnessed firsthand the injunction's crippling effects on the pre-World War I garment strikes, its use against the railroad workers in the Harding administration, and the relief it provided to the exploitative Pennsylvania coal producers during the Coolidge years. He had been a foe of judge-made labor law for many years. Each term, starting in 1924, La Guardia introduced anti-injunction legislation before the House, only to see it buried in committee. He could not even discuss the issue, wrote Lowell Limpus, "without flying into a red rage." By 1928 Senator Norris joined him in the crusade, together with a group of reform-minded labor lawyers and advisers, including Donald Richberg, Felix Frankfurter, and Francis Sayre, and they hammered out a new federal anti-injunction bill.[68]

This effort got caught in legal tangles for which the impetuous La Guardia had little patience. For more than a year and a half, Norris painstakingly worked on an anti-injunction measure that would satisfy both the law and various labor interests, while La Guardia continued to push the effort in the House. Finally, in 1932 the Senate, which had repeatedly rejected similar legislation in the past, approved Norris's measure. Just days before, La Guardia had engineered the defeat of the president's sales tax plan. The times were changing, and by a vote of 362 to 14 on March 8, 1932, the House passed the Norris-La Guardia Anti-Injunction Law.[69]

In the most far-reaching piece of labor legislation up to that time, this law placed specific restrictions upon the use of the injunction and rendered yellow-dog provisions unenforceable. Even more important, however, the law laid out a new policy with regard to labor, moving away from the strict construction of property rights and liberty of contract, toward recognition of the right of workers to unhampered collective bargaining. To A. Philip Randolph, leader of the most powerful black union in the nation, the bill's passage confirmed La Guardia's leadership of the liberal bloc in the House on behalf of "all the oppressed groups in America."[70]

Norris-La Guardia reflected a decade-long collaboration of kindred legislative spirits, each carrying the Progressive banner in his own house. "Dear La Guardia," Norris would write, "I wish you would read this and . . . interest yourself in this proposed legislation. I know without talking to you that it will appeal to you." And La Guardia would respond with equal economy. "Needless to say, I am in full accord and will do everything within my power to bring about consideration of this necessary legislation." Before Franklin Roosevelt's New Deal this partnership formed the keystone of Progressive forces as they pushed their liberal program through Congress.[71]

Designing reform legislation, speaking knowledgeably on dozens of national issues, and giving strong representation to his district, La Guardia pursued a range of issues that would have felled another man. In the records of the Seventy-first and Seventy-second Congress La Guardia is cited more than 4000 times, more than any other member of the House. "It was like he owned the U.S.," recalled his wife Marie. "Nobody should do anything to it." Not a few denounced him as a demagogue. He certainly had the equipment: a lust for power, a quick tactical mind, powers of denunciation, and clear dramatic language. But if he oversimplified, sometimes recklessly, he also took unpopular stands, risks that no mere opportunist would face. A young staffer recalled the intensity of those days: "The aura around him had more the clangor of arms and the camaraderie of a crack assault brigade than of an office force. . . . He was a seized man. The rage of creation was often upon him. . . ."[72]

Literally hundreds of issues landed on the desk of this "one-man grievance committee of the nation." None was shoved aside. Work expanded into the night, weekends, and holidays to keep up with everything. He gave up even his part-time lawyering as the volume of his obligations became too heavy; he never gave to his personal finances the careful attention that he reserved for the national pocketbook. His small staff was always swamped, and when he could not cajole a staffer to work on weekends he would draft Marie to do some typing.[73]

As the national mood swung toward La Guardia's positions on the sales tax and labor reform, his opposition to Prohibition gained new force. For more than a decade he had failed to dislodge the law, but now he prevailed. In the summer of 1932 Herbert Hoover finally accepted the inevitability of repeal. In December, as both Houses approved the Twenty-first Amendment repealing the Prohibition law, Fiorello hailed the end of an era: "Congress will now be able to give its undivided attention to economic matters, less controversial, but far more important."[74]

As he attracted more popularity La Guardia continued to assert his positions in the same untamed spirit that made him the most outspoken of insurgents. Favoring a relaxation of the immigration law to permit parents of American citizens to settle in the United States, La Guardia arranged for the postponement of an immigration bill until he could offer his amendment. Instead, late one day the bill was called up under a suspension of the rules. Enraged at the double cross, La Guardia bounded to his feet to block consideration, but it was useless. "All right, all right," he screamed at his colleagues, "you're out for blood and you're going to get it. . . . This bill deals with families that might be separated and you come in here with tactics that are a shame and a disgrace." The difference between La Guardia and others on immigration was always very clear. Franklin Roosevelt might chide the Daughters of the American Revolution by greeting them as fellow immigrants, but La Guardia hated the nativists. It was his parents they were talking about. He would not let them treat immigrants this way, and he won an adjustment in the bill.[75]

The idea of a forceful, dark-haired, rotund New Yorker prescribing a program for the United States offended some. "It goes against the grain of real Americans," clamored the *Denver Post*, "to have anybody by the name of La Guardia telling the American people how to run their government. If he doesn't like our laws, he ought to go back to the country whence his ancestors came. . . . No state but New York would disgrace itself by sending such a man as La Guardia to Congress. . . ." Another Republican wrote: "You are a little out of your class in presuming to criticize the President. . . . You should go back to where you belong and advise Mussolini how to make good honest citizens in Italy. The Italians are preponderantly our bootleggers and murderers." He was making a difference, so they hated him all the more for it.[76]

He sponsored a constitutional amendment for universal conscription of all manpower and materials. Under this measure, if war broke out the United States would take over all factories and seize all savings and would draft all citizens to prosecute the conflict. There would be no compensation, no currency, no private industry; everything would be provided on a ration basis. "If you are going to make a system that will take all profits out of war you must be ruthless about it"[77]

For weeks he tried to obtain reduced railroad fares for college students and slum dwellers. He supported a bill to protect the copyrights of composers and authors, led six separate investigations of federal judges charged with corruption, and masterminded the campaign to reduce the jurisdiction of federal courts. On New Year's Day in 1931 he collected affidavits from immigrant laborers who had been forced to pay kickbacks to secure work on War Department projects. He badgered the navy for jobs for needy constituents. And he continued to denounce the broken capitalists. When Martin Insull suggested that congressmen were hiding behind congressional immunity to attack honest businessmen, an indignant La Guardia escorted journalists to the street and there made an unimmune attack on the power trust.[78]

He introduced legislation to prohibit armed forces bands from playing for nonmilitary audiences—he did not want them competing with unemployed civilian musicians. He threatened the producers of the motion picture *Little Caesar* with a boycott for their portrayal of American Italians. When hospital workers notified La Guardia that the Veterans Administration was charging them for broken dishes, he polled hotels around the country about dishes broken by employees and insisted that the VA curb this pinchpenny practice. He upbraided another VA administrator for not going out of his way to hire veterans, and when the Navy Yard discharged several workers he demanded an explanation from the rear admiral of the navy.[79]

And no concern was too unpopular. Even the labor movement was ambivalent about organizing black workers, but La Guardia worked assiduously on behalf of this effort. Black leaders freely turned to him for help. In September 1931, after completing a round of impeachment hearings in Washington, La Guardia flew up to Utica, New York, to defend James Smith, a black railroad porter, indicted for assault. A local attorney had refused the case because Smith couldn't pay his fee, whereupon A. Philip Randolph, head of the Brotherhood of Sleeping Car Workers, drafted La Guardia to direct the defense. Despite a grueling schedule, including a hectic campaign for reelection, La Guardia took the case, pored over the evidence, and on September 26, won acquittal. He accepted no fee and paid all his own expenses.[80]

The list of bills that he introduced in the Seventy-second Congress fills six closely spaced typed pages. They represent the liberal agenda for the thirties. La Guardia's proposals ranged from investigating and preventing speculation in farm products and stocks to urging the governor of California to pardon Tom Mooney, to setting new dates for the inauguration of the president and Congress, to making it a federal crime to transport stolen goods over state boundaries, to creating a national holiday to commemorate Christopher Columbus. He worked indefatigably, huddling with colleagues, dramatizing for the press, and working late into the night studying the issues and planning strategies.

The Depression had made a prophet of him as the issues he had long been supporting won national assent, but he avoided contentment. He barely paused. He called for a new airport for New York, for the popular election of the governor of Puerto Rico, for regulating the securities markets, and for a fair retirement program for civil servants; for protecting newspaper reporters from being forced to disclose their sources, and a variety of unemployment bills; for the five-day week, a measure to guarantee bank deposits, and to slash interest on all outstanding debt by 29 percent; for bills providing individual relief and for a program of national planning.[81]

The Depression, Frederick Lewis Allen wrote, was hard to see with the naked eye. Even the most seasoned political observers could not fit it within available political or economic conceptions. Before the awesome breakdown, Walter Lippmann, perhaps the most magisterial of the commentators, reflected more drift than mastery. "We begin to know that we do not know," he wrote on New Year's Day of 1931. "We begin to see that we are not guaranteed an unending good fortune. . . . There are no phrases to save us. There are no miracles. There is only the courage to be intelligent and sober." It was not possible to make one's way through the crisis on intellectual grounds alone. There were so many possibilities and limited margin for error. The many sides all had some logic to their arguments—build confidence in the economy; step in and stir the people with bold steps; allow the crisis to clear itself; abandon the system. Each position could be supported with rational arguments. Good, smart men and women could ponder for a very long time and form no clear conclusions.[82]

La Guardia ignored the theoretical thickets; he smashed through the complexities by relying on his feelings. He did not suffer from the need to see the world whole. The thousands of letters that he exchanged with the needy and downtrodden contain the heart of his political thought and its process: Many were in desperate straits and they deserved assistance. Pre-Depression politics did not build from these assumptions, so it was difficult for conventional politicians to adapt to stark new realities. It took them longer to lay to rest the damaged persuasions of the ballyhoo years, and by that time they were reacting to an agenda that La Guardia had placed before them.[83]

As for La Guardia, he was fifty years old and still performing in one key: bristling, intense. Describing the leader of House Progressives, William Hand told an NBC audience about this "Napoleonic little man, . . . with a strongly muscled face and a broad commanding brow. Terrific energy. Wonderful instantaneousness. Doesn't seem to waste a moment of time. Mind is clicking every second . . . explosive, volcanic. When the technocrats get into power and start analyzing the public men of the United States, they will find more ergs in La Guardia than in almost anybody else."[84]

"Today," reported the *Pittsburgh Press*, "he is a public idol." The liberal journal *Nation* featured La Guardia on its honor roll for 1932, one of twelve public servants so honored. He had a large national following, and Heywood Broun credited him with holding the real leadership of the House. When he spoke to his constituents in September, the Star Casino was packed to overflowing. But to the people of East Harlem he was still a local congressman from whom they expected a lot. In November 1932 La Guardia ran for his sixth straight congressional term from the Twentieth District.[85]

He was defeated by James Lanzetta.

5. New Deal Casualty, Lame Duck Warrior

L A Guardia had anticipated a Democratic landslide in the presidential election year of 1932, even considering the possibility of running as a Democrat to make up for the tremendous burden of Hoover's name at the top of the Republican ticket. Senator Robert Wagner, William Green (president of the AFL), and John L. Lewis of the United Mineworkers supported the idea, and John McCooey, Brooklyn's Democratic party leader, found it intriguing. "Mr. La Guardia I would like to see you made Ambassador to Australia; but failing that I'll send you back to Washington. Anywhere just as long as you're kept out of New York City.'' But Tammany boss Jimmy Hines pronounced the last word, refusing to hand the Tammany nemesis such a gift. Instead, Democrats offered the nomination to a young local assemblyman, James Lanzetta. Tammany had finally learned in 1930 that the strongest candidate against La Guardia was another Italian. In that election Fiorello defeated Vincent Auletta, but only after a vigorous campaign, and by a cautionary margin.[86]

La Guardia biographers dismiss James Lanzetta as an obscure political tyro, pulled into office on Franklin Roosevelt's coattails. But Lanzetta was a bright and dynamic thirty-eight-year-old second-generation Italian, a graduate of Columbia University in nearby Morningside Heights, where he had studied engineering and law, and was an attractive, ethnic politician. Lanzetta won a seat on the Board of Aldermen in 1931 and his youthful good looks and becoming intelligence won for him the role of giant-killer.

La Guardia, playing the statesman in Washington, speaking out on issues of concern to farmers, miners, and Eskimos, provided Lanzetta with a convenient foil. The younger challenger charged that La Guardia's reputation had turned his head, that he was more interested in national issues than those of his own district. "La Guardia is always in Washington,'' went one Tammany complaint. "If you get arrested there is no one here to help you.'' Opposition to the veterans' bonus cost him. Moreover, he paid the price of his success. Sacks of mail requesting jobs or seeking assistance with immigration and redress from shabby treatment carpeted his office. By now Harlemites *expected* their congressman to settle all complaints.[87]

Giovanni Panza's family had supported La Guardia throughout the years. Now he wanted help with a life insurance policy. A lawyer would charge $75 to handle the problem and Mr. Panza wanted his congressman to do it. "My dear Mr. Panza,'' suggested Fiorello, "it would be a better idea to pay the $75.'' Replied Panza: "In my estimation, you did not go very far to befriend me in this instance. . . . Since you did not see fit to do this you may rest assured that my family will discontinue to support you. I might add there are six voters in my family.''

Perhaps other congressmen would have answered Panza with an opaque "happy to have heard from you'' letter. Not La Guardia. The tone hurt him. He wanted Panza to understand what his job was like and why it was important for him to do other things.

My time is entirely taken by my congressional duties . . . representing the interests and the welfare of the people who elect me. My official duties are such that I have been compelled to give up the practice of law. I devote all my time and my energy to my legislative duties. There are about 200,000 people residing in my district. Everyone is naturally affected by Federal laws. You will readily see that it is impossible to neglect the important and big task of legislation for individual and

private matters. That is the reason why I gave up the practice of law. . . .
I am quite willing to make the personal sacrifice and do a public service
of real value.[88]

But Panza "did not readily see," nor did others who thought that La Guardia's
main job was to help with heat complaints, rent strikes, work-related grievances,
uncollected garbage, and immigration papers, not federal legislation. In the end
many resented his commitments if they prevented him from relieving their immediate
problems.

Bad times made it hard on incumbents, even the best of them, and in early
October, La Guardia was writing a friend: "I have . . . one hell of a fight here."
He gathered endorsements from organized labor, assorted Progressives, prominent
blacks, and from Puerto Rican politicians and boxing star "Kid Chocolate," but
the Republican party maintained a discreet distance while Tammany went all out
for Lanzetta.[89]

On election day Franklin Roosevelt's party was victorious by a wide margin.
Voter turnout in the Twentieth Congressional District climbed from 18,000 in 1930
to more than 31,000 in 1932, and most of these votes were for the Democrats.
FDR routed Hoover by some 20,000 votes in this district alone, carrying Lanzetta
into office by 1200 votes. La Guardia suffered the first congressional defeat in his
life. He demanded a recount based on proven irregularities, but in the end the
House ratified the Tammany victory.[90]

He stood at the height of his political powers, finally at peace with the prevailing
spirit of the times. He had warned of impending disasters and they had come. He
had denounced the "banketeers," the "public utilities whores," and the "thieving
sons of bitches in robes," exposing corruption, pillorying the privileged, and demanding relief. He had been a lone drummer banging out his private beat until the
entire orchestra formed around him, and now the electorate had struck him from
the band.

Bitterness engulfed him. He blamed Tammany patronage. He blamed the
Puerto Rican vote. He blamed "floaters and repeaters." He blamed the people for
being fickle and disloyal. He felt sorry and cheated. "I so wanted to serve in the
next Congress," he wrote his friend Gilfond, "for I feel that many of the changes
for which we have been preparing will have come up for decision then." Politics
was his life and he felt the defeat keenly. "It's no use," he told a friend, "they
got me at last. I am too old to start over." He would retire to the country and raise
chickens.[91]

Then the unhorsed crusader pulled himself up to lead the most constructive
fight of his career.

The letters of regret and condolence poured in from political allies—Robert H. La Follette wrote of his "profound sorrow" that "the people have temporarily lost one of their most faithful servants"—and opponents, journalists, and labor leaders. William Green called the defeat "inexplicable." Hundreds of anonymous Americans expressed their grief over his fall—one man from Connecticut wrote that there were expressions of regret in every trolley car, at every newsstand, and a young girl from 110th street wrote that in her house, where it "looks as if there is a funeral," her father would not eat and the entire street was brokenhearted.[92]

By the time these letters reached him, La Guardia was again at his desk, planning his steps for the lame duck Congress that would introduce Franklin Roosevelt's historic New Deal, and busying himself with the needs of his constituents. "Naturally I will not have the influence I had when I was in office. I was in a position one time to do something for these people," he wrote sadly. "I am not in that position now." But he continued to do his best.[93]

Congress met in December (this was the last Congress to meet under rules that kept the outgoing legislature in office until March) for a lame duck session. La Guardia introduced a passel of bills for consideration. Representative Luce of Massachusetts objected that the proposals favored "minorities," prompting Fiorello to respond that past legislation had been enacted for "the minority that owns the wealth of the country [and] has ruined our country. . . ." In the new era this group would be "controlled instead of controlling." He joined the farm bloc to call for a domestic allotment plan of the sort that would later emerge as Roosevelt's Agricultural Adjustment Act, likening the extralegal revolt of midwestern farmers against foreclosures to the Boston Tea Party. He moved again to limit interest rates, designing the legislation in simple language "so that the bankers could understand it." Objections that investors would not put their money into low-interest mortgages brought little sympathy. "The capitalist, if he does not invest his money cannot eat it."[94]

During the twenties, before he returned to elective politics, Franklin Roosevelt periodically came to Washington to study legislation and keep in touch with Democratic leaders. Often he stayed at the Continental Hotel, where Congressman La Guardia had a room, and every once in a while the two would discuss legislative issues. Fiorello was drawn closer to the Roosevelt circle now through a brilliant young Columbia University economics professor, Adolf Berle, who with Gardiner Means had coauthored the influential *Modern Corporation and Private Property*. The book's central argument, that the rise of the modern corporation required new national policies to bring about a "collectivism without communism," was one that Progressives like La Guardia found congenial. Berle was brought into the Roosevelt "Brain Trust" and sent to Washington soon after the election to prepare with congressional Progressives for Roosevelt's New Deal.

House Speaker and newly elected vice president John Nance Garner suggested that Berle seek out the "good little wop" to work with, and Paul Kern, a former student of Berle's who worked in La Guardia's office, introduced the congressman to his former professor. Together with the man he would describe as "a pint of liquid dynamite," Berle went to work on legislation for the devastated debtor classes. La Guardia drew up measures to stop farm foreclosures, amend the national bankruptcy laws, and remove the reorganization of financially strapped railroads from a "receivership racket" in which corporate officials drained company resources through bankruptcy proceedings.[95]

La Guardia was working on borrowed time but it did not diminish his capacity for outrage. While everyone else focused on the total figure in an appropriation bill for the military, he chose to illustrate some of the allocations: $2500 to a family in Nicaragua for the killing of an unarmed father in the presence of his thirteen-year-old son by an intoxicated American marine; $2000 to a family in Chile whose daughter had been assaulted by a navy seaman; other appropriations for the relief of damaged property and pointless violence by American servicemen. Here was just one of the dangers of "sending troops to foreign lands at the request of the bankers" to collect their loans and shore up their investments. Americans must keep their money, investments, and troops at home, instructed the outgoing legislator.[96]

Finally, the last day came. He testified before a Maryland committee considering a state version of the Norris-La Guardia bill, conferred with Progressives on the program for the coming term, and heard himself praised as "the most remarkable Member of the House of Representatives" by Representative Howard of Nebraska, who expressed the "earnest hope that some day he will be back with us again. I do not care whether he shall come . . . as a Republican, as a Tammany brave or as an Independent. I want La Guardia back here again!" Then he joined Marie in packing their modest belongings, and as Franklin Roosevelt prepared to bring Americans a New Deal, one of its staunchest and earliest prophets, the person the *Nation* called "the one effective [Progressive] leader," left office, a man with a brilliant future behind him.

There was not really much that Fiorello La Guardia wanted to do besides politics. He turned down the post of assistant secretary of state in the incoming administration, explaining that at fifty he was "too old to take orders from anyone." He told journalist Raymond Clapper that he had put all of his energies into becoming an expert legislator. "I felt my services would be needed for the Seventy-third Congress. It is work that I like and wanted to do." Told that he could win again, La Guardia was not consoled. Even if he did win back his congressional seat, he would have to come back without his seniority. Another friend suggested that he could set up residence in Iowa and run for the Senate after two years. "I can't go to Iowa, Bob," he replied, "they have no symphony orchestras there." He had a law degree but hated the practice of law. Perhaps he would turn to teaching or maybe writing. But he was just kidding himself and his friends. From the time he had left his family behind in Fiume to pursue his calling in politics, nothing else would make him happy or provide the sense of large purpose and service that he craved.

On November 28, 1932, after his defeat, La Guardia had called a meeting at Town Hall to discuss election fraud. The turnout was disappointingly small, but in the course of the talk, La Guardia strayed from the topic to speak of future battles. "I say now, and I say it advisedly, that a fusion movement in this City would have a majority of 300,000 voters in a municipal election." Fiorello La Guardia was not prepared to go quietly into the ungentle night.[97]

CHAPTER 6

New York City Before
La Guardia

1. Jimmy Walker's Gotham: A City Without the
Soul of a Commonwealth

A FINE dusting of snow covered New York streets on the first Tuesday of November 1929 as voters strode to the polls to reelect the flamboyant mayor of New York City, Jimmy Walker, for a second term. Slim, touched by a stylish bit of the devil, the jaunty Tammany leprechaun exuded the Empire City's easy-living spirit. Shortly after the polls closed, assuring Walker's overwhelming victory, the forty-eight-year-old mayor dashed uptown to his twenty-five-year-old mistress, Betty (Monk) Compton, who was rehearsing dance routines for the play *Fifty Million Frenchmen*. A New York City policeman signaled the showgirl, threw a blanket over her skimpy outfit, and carried her out to a beaming Jimmy Walker. "I wanted you to be the first to congratulate me . . . I've been reelected." Compton wondered at the excitement. "Well it's no surprise, or is it?"

The campaign had filled Walker with ambivalence. Governing New York for another four years roused in him little joy or excitement. Years later he told his friend and biographer Gene Fowler, "I really was moving against my own desires most of the time, and the inner conflicts were great." The only personal satisfaction he took from the victory was in the adulation of the people close to him. Accustomed to politicians' glad hands, he wondered why Monk reacted so coolly to his victory. "Because," she said, "I believe you would be better off and happier if you quit politics."[1]

She was right. Before long, Walker's city of endless happiness turned its attention from the Great White Way and its playboy chief magistrate to the brooding, fearful, and hungry masses roaming the streets; the Roaring Twenties segueing into Depression, with no transitions, all jagged irregularities. Beau James had matched the happy-go-lucky ebullience of the twenties, but he was unsuited for managing a depressed city. Columnist Henry McLemore observed that Jimmy Walker had been created for brass bands, waving flags, parades, and bright lights. The frothy unconcern with policy and governing that he managed to make engaging before served him ill in tackling the formidable agenda now confronting his city. He was not fitted for hard times.

The new seriousness surfaced quickly. Shortly after the election, Patrick Cardinal Hayes summoned the errant Catholic mayor to his residence—popularly referred to as "The Power House"—to rebuke him for his adultery. A few weeks after *Fifty Million Frenchmen* opened, Betty Compton collapsed and had to withdraw from the show. The market was crashing, good times were dying, and Jimmy Walker could not concentrate on the task before him. The mayor looked more frail than ever. Even his specially tailored suits, designed to camouflage his small physique and emphasize his shoulders, could not hide his shocking weight loss and strain. His absences from city hall occurred even more frequently, with illnesses real and imagined, colds, heart flutters, stomachaches, infected wisdom teeth, lumbago, and "nervous exhaustion." He took another vacation, this time at John Ringling's Florida estate, followed by two weeks in Bermuda.

Factories were closing by the thousands. In December of 1930 the Bank of the United States, headquartered in New York, failed, wiping out the savings of hundreds of thousands. "Brother Can You Spare a Dime" became the beggar's anthem, as men of good background in threadbare jackets shambled through the streets peddling apples. And New Yorkers were starving. On a cold winter day in November, the *New York Times* reported that August Baumann, a fifty-three-year-old dishwasher out of a job, was found starved to death on a bench in Grand Central Station. Less than two miles from Grand Central, on East Eighty-first Street, William Columbo, a seventeen-year-old, collapsed from starvation; he had not eaten in five of the last eight days. So deep was the alarm, the sense of worse times impending, that working people were applying to assistance agencies *in anticipation* of unemployment. And natives in the Cameroons sent a contribution of $3.77 to feed "the starving" of Jimmy Walker's New York.[2]

An unemployed textile worker told Louis Adamic, "I wish there were war again." Steel tycoon Charles Schwab confessed, "I'm afraid. Every man is afraid." And Gan Kolski, an out-of-work artist from Greenwich Village, jumped off the George Washington Bridge, leaving a suicide note: "To All: If you cannot hear the cry of starving millions, listen to the dead, brothers. Your economic system is dead." An English visitor reported that the "dark undergrowth of horrid suffering" that she found in New York was "certainly more degraded and degrading than anything Britain or Germany knows."[3]

Will Rogers wondered about "those Rascals in Russia [who] along with their Cuckoo stuff have got some mighty good ideas. . . . Just think of everybody in a Country going to work." Norman Thomas refused to use the depression to "politicalize" workers for a Soviet-style revolution: "No men, still less their children, can live on the bread of Utopia. They hunger now. Cold and hungry children make for no constructive social revolution. They add to the needless weight of the world's woe." But others were growing impatient. John Dos Passos ridiculed socialism as "near beer" politics, and F. Scott Fitzgerald turned from the beautiful and the damned to consider social solutions. "To bring on the revolution it may be necessary to work inside the Communist Party," he suggested.[4]

The American Communist party, declaring an International Unemployment Day for March 6, 1930, scheduled protest meetings around the nation. In New York more than 35,000 demonstrators gathered at Union Square. Following the speeches the police refused permission for the crowd to march on city hall. Police Commissioner Grover Whalen offered instead to escort a small group of protest leaders to a meeting with the mayor. Communist leader William Z. Foster rejected the offer and urged the crowd to begin marching. In the worst street disturbance since the World War, the police tore into the crowd, clubbing and gouging the marchers, injuring as many as a hundred people. Many of the eyewitnesses were appalled by the violence and senseless overreaction. And when it was over the local Communist party secretary pronounced the riot "a great success."[5]

Jimmy Walker was not an insensitive man; the pain and suffering of the poor concerned him. When he was in town and feeling up to it, he hustled contributions for relief of the unemployed and contributed from his own pocket. But he was strangely out of touch with the broken spirit of the thirties. Soon after his election Walker signed into law a salary increase for himself and the Board of Aldermen. As the Depression worsened, Walker was overtaken by a consuming dolefulness. Doctors warned of a nervous breakdown. Always too full of himself and his search for a succession of good times, he began to sense the emptiness. On his fiftieth birthday he announced to a group of city workers that his reaching the half-century mark filled him with melancholy and was "the most difficult day" of his life since taking office.[6]

Walker kept striking the wrong notes. After five years in office he expressed shock at the vile conditions in the city. To solve gangsterism he suggested that strong young police be set on the villains to beat them up on the street before their neighbors. With unemployment climbing, Jimmy Walker barely escaped arrest on charges of high-stakes gambling on Long Island. At his mistress's elbow during a game of hazard, he dashed from the casino, donning a kitchen apron to avoid a raiding party. Miss Compton was not so lucky. Her evening out ended in night court. Later, she demanded to know why Jimmy had abandoned her. "Monk," he replied, "I knew you would get out all right. . . . But . . . it might be a good idea if I didn't tempt fate at this moment by showing up in the hoosegow." The time for lighthearted fun and audacious grabs was over. No rakish wink (or cheerful movie) could chase away the troubles. The *New York Times* reported that Mayor Walker, together with the Prince of Wales, had significantly influenced men's fashion, but who cared anymore? Jimmy Walker was out of his element, a shallow, fun-loving politician in the most trying times in the city's modern history. In March he went off for a monthlong vacation in Palm Springs. In August he took a six-week grand tour of European capitals and seashores.[7]

For Walker, politics had been an amiable diversion played by a hearty crew who contested for control over the large pot of municipal jobs; it did not represent for him the serious business of governing. The jobs he and his Tammany advisers dispensed with such cavalier grace had essential tasks assigned to them and represented the city's service to its citizens, a thought Jimmy Walker seldom bothered to contemplate. Nor had he wrestled with the implications of urban growth and development in any sustained or systematic fashion. Jimmy Walker was not Herbert Hoover, a competent politician agonizing over the course to take in dealing with the Depression. Jimmy Walker was Warren Harding, a sadly superficial man in the wrong profession, without the faintest sense of what he was doing there. Even without the economic crisis, his management of the city was bankrupt.

———

New York's continued growth masked a marked rearrangement of the city population. During the twenties the total population climbed by 1.3 million, filling in the outer boroughs with new neighborhoods. Brooklyn's Coney Island was transformed from a quiet resort community of some 33,000 in 1910 to a bustling neighborhood of 280,000 by 1930. East Tremont in the Bronx expanded over the same years from 50,000 to 264,000, and Queens's Jackson Heights more than tripled in number. But this growth at the periphery came at the expense of the center. In 1905 more than half of New York's residents lived within four miles of city hall. By the 1920s successful Manhattanites and even recently arrived immigrants were settling in fresher, less congested, less expensive areas of the city. In 1930 Brooklyn, with 2.5 million people, was the city's most populous borough, while Manhattan's population was declining; so was the number of its factories, the quality of its housing, and the temper of its community life.[8]

This new pattern dictated a reconsideration of municipal priorities, a change in the Manhattan-centered policy of the past. The shifting numbers suggested a Greater New York in which new roads and bridge connections, the infrastructure of a modern, well-articulated city had to be extended; a New York in which the outer boroughs should receive equal attention and services and major public works projects to match the resources expended on venerable Manhattan. This was the challenge of the new numbers. But a city government managed on a strictly partisan basis viewed these trends differently. Tammany Hall, the executive committee of the Manhattan Democratic party, had no reason to accommodate these shifts. Its traditional modes of organization in wards and blocks would be much more difficult in a dispersed City. The political machine could not handle the decentralization, so the Walker administration ignored it.

Growth accounted for one element of New York's transformation, diversity another. Here was the immigrant city *sui generis*, always open, ever changing. After a long absence, the French scholar André Chevrillon returned to Gotham in the 1920s, and he was struck by the change from what he remembered as a basically Anglo-Saxon city to one dominated by eastern and southern Europeans. Another visitor, Luigi Barzini, reported the conventional wisdom of the streets: "New York was built by the Italians, run by the Irish, and owned by the Jews." Of this city's 7 million inhabitants, more than 5 million were foreign stock and 2.3 million foreign-born. Despite immigration restrictions, between 1920 and 1930 New York's foreign-born population jumped by more than 330,000, mostly Italians and Eastern European Jews. These new national groups outpaced the Irish and Germans, who had been the largest groups before. In religious affiliation too, New York had become far more diverse. Protestants represented 37 percent of the total, only marginally out-numbering the Catholics, who were one-third. Jews accounted for much of the rest.[9]

Nicholas Murray Butler, the good-government eminence and president of Columbia University, saw in this diversity a troubling challenge:

> This city has a problem, or series of problems, more difficult, more many sided, more highly concentrated and more intense than have been presented to any city before in the history of the world. . . .

> It was the hope and purpose of ancient Rome to extend the rule of law, one conception of citizenship, one feeling of human solidarity over a vast variety of people, religions, languages, races spread over vast and widely distributed territory.

> That is our New York problem, with the distribution over widely distributed territory stricken out.[10]

The City had to mold a sense of civic unity out of this diverse population. Athens had been great because it shared the ideal of the general good. The challenge for modern New York was to bring its population together in a common civic identity. Lacking this, it would be no more than a place housing different groups, lacking the heart of a city.

More significant even than immigration in recasting the city's population was the massive cityward migration of southern blacks after World War I. "I sit on my stoop on Seventh Avenue," wrote a correspondent for the Negro paper the *Messenger*, "and gaze at the sunkissed folks strolling up and down and think that surely

Mississippi is here in New York, in Harlem, yes right on Seventh Avenue." From less than 3 percent of the population in 1920 (only slightly more than the total of New York's Hungarians), Manhattan's black population soared by 1930 to 12 percent. No other New York group grew so swiftly over these years. Moreover, they were all coming to one place. As 118,000 whites left Harlem during the twenties for better homes in better neighborhoods, nearly 170,000 newly arrived Afro-Americans replaced them. From 158th Street south to 126th between Fifth and Eighth Avenues, the population turned solidly black. The large numbers and the pervasive racism created a self-contained Negro neighborhood posing critical questions about the nature of a multiethnic and multiracial urban society.[11]

Here flourished an indigenous black urban culture that drew on everything that came before in the Afro-American experience, from African antecedents and slave spirituals to West Indian potions, southern farm habits, and urban adaptations. That is what James Weldon Johnson meant in referring to this section as the "greatest Negro city in the world." Harlem filled a special place in Jimmy Walker's New York, a place of menace and fun, and more importantly, a place outside the city's mainstream. Left alone to make a culture at a tangent to the establishment, Harlem developed a vitality and freshness that did not seek legitimacy in the eyes of the cultural mandarins; music, dance, and other forms of artistic expression flourished, apart and unique, as Harlem became a symbol and center of national black life.

But Harlem lacked the resources to be independent in other critical areas. Blacks had a hard time securing employment, and even on home turf they had to depend on others for jobs. Many in this essentially farm-oriented black community, from Virginia and the Carolinas primarily, but also from such deep south states as Tennessee, Georgia, and Mississippi, lacked critical skills for the industrial workplace and the urban milieu. By all accounts it was a difficult encounter. They moved into large apartments built for middle-class New Yorkers of some means and, to make rent affordable, subdivided the tenements and filled them to overflowing with lodgers and boarders. Remarked Negro educator Roscoe Conkling Bruce, "Sometimes even the bathtub is used to sleep on, two individuals taking turns." Within the decade "Harlem" became synonymous with unemployment, crime, and decay. And despite the awful housing, black residents paid high rents because other neighborhoods were closed to them. Judge John Davies of Harlem's municipal court testified, "It is common for colored tenants in Harlem to pay twice as much as white tenants for the same apartments."[12]

Rent was the least of the problem. Blacks could not get decent jobs. E. Franklin Frazier, the pioneering black sociologist, said there were two kinds of establishments in New York, "those that employ Negroes in menial positions and those that employ no Negroes at all." Blacks held the lowest-paying and least secure jobs in the city. In 1930, while approximately 18 percent of the white working class held unskilled dead-end jobs, fully 50 percent of the city's black population

THIS PHOTOGRAPH, taken in the 1890s, shows Achille La Guardia in his bandmaster's uniform with (*left to right*) Irene, Richard, Fiorello, and Gemma in their Whipple Barracks home. (*Fiorello H. La Guardia Archives, La Guardia Community College, CUNY*)

YOUNG FIORELLO, at about age thirteen, posed here with the cornet he played in his father's local music group. (*Fiorello H. La Guardia Archives, La Guardia Community College, CUNY*)

REPRESENTATIVE FIORELLO LA GUARDIA, wearing his flier's regalia, at Padua, Italy, after he left his congressional seat for the battlefront in the summer of 1917. (*Fiorello H. La Guardia Archives, La Guardia Community College, CUNY*)

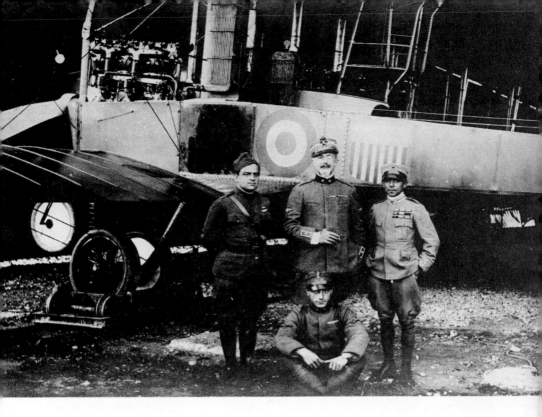

STANDING IN FRONT OF THE *Congressional Limited* in Foggia, Italy, in 1918 are *(left to right)* Major La Guardia, Major Cambiaso Negrotto, Captain Frederic Zapeloni, and *(seated)* Sergeant Mitragliere Firmani. The crew flew over enemy munitions depots and airfields. (*Fiorello H. La Guardia Archives, La Guardia Community College, CUNY*)

MAJOR LA GUARDIA as he appeared in his Fusion campaign for reelection to Congress against Socialist Scott Nearing in 1918. (*City of New York Municipal Archives*)

FIORELLO with his first wife, Thea Almerigotti. Married to Fiorello on March 8, 1919, Thea gave birth to a baby in June of the following year. Within two years both mother and child died. (*Parks Photo Archive*)

PRESIDENT OF THE BOARD OF ALDERMEN and Acting Mayor Fiorello La Guardia with (*left to right*) Secretary of State Bainbridge Colby, Mrs. William Randolph Hearst, and General John J. Pershing, on October 8, 1921, at a Loyalty Day celebration in New York's city hall. (*City of New York Municipal Archives*)

CONGRESSMAN LA GUARDIA at his overflowing desk in Room 150 of the House Office Building. (*Fiorello H. La Guardia Archives, La Guardia Community College, CUNY*)

ON JUNE 16, 1926, Representative La Guardia of the House Committee on Alcoholic Liquor Traffic responds to a colleague's doubts about the widespread circumvention of Prohibition by demonstrating how to make an intoxicating brew from malt tonic and near beer. (*Fiorello H. La Guardia Archives, La Guardia Community College, CUNY*)

ON FEBRUARY 16, 1931, La Guardia replies to the charge made by Chicago utilities executive Martin Insull that no congressman dared to allege the existence of a power trust outside the Congress (where their assertions were cloaked by immunity), by publicly assailing the power trust at a curbside press conference. (*Fiorello H. La Guardia Archives, La Guardia Community College, CUNY*)

DURING THE DEPRESSION La Guardia's programs took on a new prominence. He met frequently with the unemployed and the disaffected to develop new programs for social welfare and relief. (*Fiorello H. La Guardia Archives, La Guardia Community College, CUNY*)

FORMER NEW YORK MAYOR James J. Walker in 1936 with his second wife, the former Betty Compton, aboard the French liner *Normandie* as they sailed to Europe for a vacation. (*City of New York Municipal Archives*)

THE MAYORAL CANDIDATES meet under Citizens Budget Commission auspices on October 31, 1933. *Left to right*: Charles Solomon, Socialist party; unidentified man; Peter Grimm, chairman of CBC; Harold Riegelman, CBC counsel; Fiorello La Guardia, Fusion party; Robert Minor, Communist party; Samuel Untermyer, advisor to Democratic Mayor John P. O'Brien. John V. McKee, the Recovery party candidate, is before the microphone. (*City of New York Municipal Archives*)

FIORELLO on the campaign trail in the fall of 1933. The poster at his right reads, "Gabriel Over City Hall," and the handwritten inscription (from poster's creator) reads in part, "to the mastermind who will lead the people of New York back to decency." Marie La Guardia is at lower right. (*City of New York Municipal Archives*)

LA GUARDIA speaking before an enthusiastic group of Father Divine's followers in an election-eve campaign rally at the Rockland Palace in Harlem, November 6, 1933. (*New York Daily News*)

JUST BEFORE THIS PICTURE WAS SNAPPED, La Guardia had torn the badge off of a Tammany worker who was menacing voters on Election day, November 7, 1933. A policeman is separating them here. The *Daily News* photographer's camera was smashed, but he managed to save the film. (*New York Daily News*)

FIORELLO LA GUARDIA being sworn in as New York's ninety-ninth mayor by Justice Philip J. McCook a few minutes after midnight on January 1, 1934. Looking on proudly as the scene unfolds in his library is Samuel Seabury (*center*). Behind Seabury's right shoulder is Vito Marcantonio. Behind La Guardia stands Paul Windels. (*New York Daily News*)

MAYOR LA GUARDIA addressing citizens shortly after taking office on New Year's Day, 1934, pledging to turn over a city "far greater and more beautiful than it was transmitted to us." *Left to right*: Marie La Guardia, Paul Betters, Burdette Lewis, David Sarnoff, Richard Patterson, and Dr. John H. Finley. (*City of New York Municipal Archives*)

MAYOR LA GUARDIA dramatizes his war on tinhorns and gambling racketeers on October 13, 1934, by smashing confiscated slot machines destined for the bottom of Long Island Sound. (*New York Daily News*)

LA GUARDIA turning the key to the newly opened Central Park Picture Book Zoo, December 4, 1934. With him is Al Smith, appointed "Honorary Night Superintendent of the Central Park Zoo" by his dear friend, Parks Commissioner Robert Moses. (*Parks Photo Archive*)

IN THE SUMMER OF 1935, Robert Moses issued an ultimatum threatening to resign by noon of July 3 unless he was officially reappointed to his post as chairman of the Triborough Bridge Authority. La Guardia ignored the deadline and waited a week to swear in his strong-willed commissioner. Here, the two appear in good spirits for the benefit of photographers. (*City of New York Municipal Archives*)

LA GUARDIA, who presided over the U.S. Conference of Mayors from 1935 to 1945, addresses a regional meeting of the conference in San Francisco, April 20, 1936. (*City of New York Municipal Archives*)

WITH THE FINANCIAL ASSISTANCE of the federal government, La Guardia initiated the most ambitious public housing program in the nation. On the podium with La Guardia as he lays the cornerstone for Williamsburg Houses on October 15, 1936, are Housing Authority chairman Langdon Post (*bareheaded behind the mayor*) and (*at right*) Senator Robert Wagner, a crusader for federal housing legislation. (*New York City Housing Authority*)

IN JUNE OF 1937 La Guardia celebrates the completion of the foundation for Harlem River Houses, a housing project explicitly designed for Harlem's black community. (*New York City Housing Authority*)

LA GUARDIA being rushed to a fire in Woodside, Queens, 1939. (*City of New York Municipal Archives*)

were locked into these occupations and were unemployed at three times the proportion of whites.

"To touch most areas of Harlem life in the 1920s," Gilbert Osofsky, the scholar of modern Harlem, has written, "is to touch tragedy." The vital statistics were shocking. Twice as many Harlem women died in childbirth as other New York women, and infant mortality was equally disproportionate. Tuberculosis, pneumonia, heart disease, cancer, and venereal and other infectious diseases were all alarmingly higher here than in the rest of the city; so were statistics on murder, juvenile delinquency, vice, drug crime, and gambling. "Speakeasies downtown," noted one reporter, "are usually carefully camouflaged. In Harlem they can be spotted a hundred yards off." Cocaine, heroin, and morphine were readily available, and numbers runners abounded.[13]

Officials viewed the city's black neighborhood as one large red light district. A Committee of Fourteen, which conducted an investigation during the twenties, lamented, "Harlem has become a slumming ground for certain classes of whites who are looking for . . . 'thrills' . . . and for a convenient place to go on moral vacation." The committee indicted the city's easy attitude toward Harlem vice. But the report ignored the root of the problem. It was not only Harlem vice with which the city was unconcerned but the entire issue of the special plight of the poor and the black. Police, school administrators, park officials, and health commissioners all stood by as the pathology took root. Nor did they do much to combat the discrimination upon which this process fed.

The Depression only made things worse. "Negroes had been in the Depression all the time," said black journalist George Schuyler. Unemployment, crime, narcotics, loan sharks, a slew of abhorrent diseases, noxious streets, crumbling houses, people crammed into tight quarters with no way out, this Harlem tragedy was made in the 1920s, when a city administration bent on good times refused to take responsibility for what had become a difficult, troubling, and troubled symbol of Balkanized New York.[14]

———

The physical city reflected a similar unconcern. New York's parks, hospitals, and schools were badly outdated. Its 322 square miles represented one of the most densely packed areas in the world. Its factories, shops, department stores, service industries, and pedestrian traffic all depended upon the smooth flow of its people. But its mass transit network was fragmented into an uncoordinated, uneconomic set of competing systems. Under Walker, an ambitious effort to replace the elevated tracks with eighteen miles of subway was halted as funds ran out.

Modern New York was rapidly turning into an automobile city. But it was never planned that way. It had been laid out to accommodate homes, factories, shops, even a bit of urban leisure, but no one foresaw the car. Business and passenger traffic clogged its arteries with fume-spewing autos all headed in different directions and in each other's way, strangling the city on its own traffic. In 1932 close to 800,000 autos traveled the same street system that had existed in 1918. Construction of a West Side Highway from the Battery to Seventy-second street, initiated in the late twenties, stopped, and the highway stood idle and unusable for lack of entrance and exit ramps. Brooklyn, growing at a faster pace than Manhattan, had not a single major thoroughfare. The four East River bridges linking Manhattan to Brooklyn and Queens had been completed by 1910, when horses not cars were the major vehicular carriers.

In 1933, on average, 238,000 cars and trucks rode across these East River spans. The twenty-seven-year-old Queensborough Bridge still did not have lane markers. A 1931 police department study showed that during rush hours the average driver spent forty-three minutes making his way across the 1182-foot roadway. In 1921 the city began work on a great narrows tube to link Brooklyn with Staten Island. After $7 million the project was stopped in 1923 in its very first stages. Another project begun in the twenties, a Triborough Bridge to connect the Bronx, Queens, and Manhattan, stood incomplete, with only its seventeen bare masonry piers in the East River offering a faint hint of the span that was supposed to link these piers.[15]

New York City did not even have an airport for incoming flights. Its single municipal airfield, the commercially unsuccessful Floyd Bennett, was primarily for thrill seekers who wanted to see the city from the air. International traffic landed at Newark International airfield in New Jersey. New York's docks, once world-famous and busy around the clock, were rotted and ramshackle. Its surrounding waters, which had provided magnificent bathing areas for leisure and recreation, had been fouled with discarded refuse and sewage, forcing neighboring New Jersey to bring suit in the Supreme Court to curb the city's noisome practices.

New Yorkers could not even be certain that their supply of drinking water would last. A decision by the Supreme Court, this time in the city's favor, allowed a brief reprieve by permitting the daily diversion of 440,000 gallons of water from the Delaware River, but engineers predicted a dangerous water shortage unless the city upgraded its outdated and overtaxed water supply system that, while managing to transport water a hundred miles overland through aqueducts, beneath a mountain, over one river, and under another, allowed one-third of it to leak away through archaic plumbing and faulty controls.[16]

One of the fondest hopes of the urban reformers was to make the city more livable by setting aside "breathing spaces," green parks to offer respite from pollution, filth, and concrete. But as bricks, stucco, and industrial smoke rapidly covered the woodlands and farms of the outer boroughs, the municipal government did little to guarantee adequate parks and recreation grounds. During the summers when schools closed and the tenements turned forbiddingly hot, children roamed the streets, learning its language and suffering its dangers. In 1933 street accidents injured more than 12,000 children and killed 249 in mishaps. City officials liked to point out that in the four years after 1929, New York added 2440 acres of parks. They failed to mention that almost all of this land was in the less populated districts of Richmond and Queens.

Under the outdated city charter, management of the parks, the city's "lungs," rested with the local boroughs. A different political appointee in each county supervised his piece of the city's domain. In Brooklyn, the parks department built a large restaurant which it then turned over to a private businessman for $10 a year. The agreement allowed the businessman to keep all of the profits from the restaurant's operation. A brick manufacturer who needed storage space rented ten acres of park land for $2.50 a year. The Brooklyn Park Commissioner, less generous with his favors than it at first seemed, banked $1,071,713 during his tenure. Elsewhere some of the choicest beach property was removed from public use and rented to political insiders.

In 1932 most parks department vehicles were still horse-drawn, and the staff largely unskilled. "You couldn't tell the difference between a park employee and the bums hanging out in the park," recalled an old-timer. Park comfort stations were supervised by a corps of Tammany-selected female attendants, many of them the widows of loyal members of the tribe. "Some of the aged biddies," wrote *Fortune* magazine, actually "curtained off all but, say, two of the eight toilet compartments, had imported chairs, tables and hangings into the cozy space, and frequently had their friends in for afternoon tea."[17]

Women bringing their children to city beaches taught them another of those rules with which parents plied city kids: *Never go near the first aid stations*. Here gangs of prostitutes ("some of the ugliest women I have ever seen," recalled Samuel White, who later took charge of the lifeguards) rested from their exertions with the lifeguards. This explained why the lifeguards were often tired, but then again they were out of shape to begin with. A special examination of 100 recently appointed lifeguards in the early thirties found that fourteen patrolling the beach waters could not swim; another eighteen refused to show up for the test.

The green parks had themselves become a decaying compost of dying trees, scabby, moth-eaten grass, and rotting fences. The wading pools where city children were supposed to cool off in the summer flowed with filth, and the grounds were dilapidated. One survey found not a single structure in any of the city's parks that did not require repair. Central Park, the Olmsted-designed jewel of New York's park system, had deteriorated into an unattractive patchwork of rutted walks, broken benches, and untended fields, its zoo filled with elderly and diseased animals.[18]

Jimmy Walker was not oblivious to the charm of pastoral settings so long as they were reserved for his cronies. During his first term he had insisted on a place in the city where he and New Yorkers of similar mien might "entertain visitors without being molested." One of the mayor's circle of friends, restaurateur Sidney

Solomon, offered to build just such a place in Central Park. The enchanted Walker promised his mistress, "The Casino will be our place, Monk." He personally approved each of the sketches, devoting himself to every detail of the new casino. The result was a swank dining place, some 400 yards beyond the Sixty-fifth Street transverse road, dappled with silver, maroon, gold, and black glass. So taken was the mayor with the casino that insiders whispered that he spent more time in the park than at city hall, transacting official business in a private office with green moiré walls and gold leaf ceiling. And for a bit of diversion Tammany favorites would be entertained by Broadway chorus lines in an upstairs duplex closed to the public.[19]

The poor lived a world away from Walker's good-time casino in wretched slums that approximated the Hobbesian condition described in his *Leviathan*: "No arts; no letters; no society and, which is worst of all, continual fear and danger of violent death; and the life of man, solitary, nasty, brutish and short." A 1927 report to Walker found "A third of the city's population—over two million people . . . in unsatisfactory conditions, many under distressful conditions, some under disgraceful conditions." Intolerable during much of the year, in the summer the tenements where many of New York's working-class families lived became "an inferno of torture to little children, the sick, and the weak."

Life in the slum was in its rawest form—no privacy, shared bathrooms, shared water sources, shared firetraps. In the 1880s Jacob Riis had warned New Yorkers of the terrifying price of the slums, of the half-crazed "man with the knife," who would leap from the shadows slashing in anarchic rage at a society tolerant of the daily abuse of his loved ones. Almost fifty years after Riis's work, New York's slums remained the most conspicuous tenement hellholes in the world, repeatedly condemned as a menace to health, safety, and morals.[20]

In its business districts the city projected a titanic quality. The 56-story Chanin Building and the 77-story Chrysler, both completed in 1929, prepared the midtown skyline for the 102-story Empire State. The view from these soaring masterpieces was breathtaking, but the point is that the skyline reflected bold *private* visions. The huge structures, the Chrysler, Woolworth, Equitable, Astor, and Chanin, overwhelmed the city with massive private landmarks. No municipal intelligence shaped this growth. Yet the city had to deal with the results. It had to get the working masses to these monster buildings. It had to direct street traffic and safety amidst the new congestion that they brought on. Like the four-foot parent whose authority is mocked by the six-and-a-half-foot youngster smiling skeptically down on him, the skyscrapers offended the idea of civic control merely by being.

Jimmy Walker's New York lacked freshness, vision, and expertise; its leaders failed to conceive the city in ways appropriate to its size and complexity. Archaic, corrupt, and inefficient, New York's politics was needle-narrow, a field for political spoils instead of social policy and civic betterment. Walker's crew of genial grafters eviscerated the tradition of civic virtue. The closest they came to discussions of moral tone was in the analysis of "honest graft," and then, as if having uncovered a magical powder whose dust made sharp dealing ethical, they turned all efforts to its practice. The highest ground for city politics, it seemed, was the consideration of what was not absolutely illegal. In the base atmosphere of sachems and ward heelers the notion of politics as service had evaporated.

The metropolis lacked a communal imperative to bring public New York to scale with its private magnificence. No great new bridges, tunnels, statues, or public housing matched the bold achievements of the private builders. In New York, civic pride focused on the achievements of what Walt Whitman called "the simple, separate, person." This then was the *critique réçue* of Walker's New York: It lacked the soul of a commonwealth.

2. The Price of Boss Politics:
An Esteem for Backwardness

I N 1927, as a first step toward constructing inexpensive working-class apartments, New York City acquired for close to $16 million a two-block stretch of property known as the Chrystie-Forsyth Street parcel. For the next few years the land stood unused. Finally, in May of 1933 the city solicited plans for low-cost housing on this site. A "Thomas Plan," acceptable to the city's chief engineer, offered a design for $8.31 a room, per month, but the Walker administration settled on another plan submitted by the Sloan Robertson architectural firm, which worked out to $10.75 per room. One clue to the decision favoring the more expensive plan lay in the identity of the architectural company that promulgated the plan.

For years Sloan Robertson enjoyed a fine reputation as respected professionals who submitted solid designs at competitive cost, only to lose out to other, less gifted firms. In 1928 the company changed its policy and distributed political contributions with a careful eye on upcoming contract competitions. As more than $20,000 went to Tammany candidates over a two-year period, city business suddenly found its way to their office. No longer did Sloan Robertson bother to boil down their bids to the lowest price as in the past; friends in important places proved far more helpful than efficient cost.

Very helpful indeed. After Jimmy Walker promised a Rikers Island project to another firm, he received the following message from Tammany bigwig George Olvany through the city commissioner of corrections: "GWO [Olvany] telephoned

me that Sloan and Robertson were to be the Architects for the new penitentiary. . . ." Walker obeyed the command. Sloan Robertson's books showed a
$10,000 entry for political expenses contributed to feed the Tiger, charged to the
city as an expense item! Outside analysts estimated the actual cost of the Rikers
project, which brought Sloan Robertson $90,000, at no more than $22,000. Little
wonder that they were contributing so loyally. Little wonder that the State Board
of Housing disapproved their plan for Chrystie-Forsythe and left the city with no
plan for low-income housing in the area. Walker's metropolis stood so far behind
in planning for low-cost housing that after the New Deal came to power and
introduced its heavily subsidized works projects, New York did not submit a single
acceptable plan while other cities collected handsome grants.[21]

In other ways as well, boss politics tied the city to a mode of operations
rooted in the past. The bosses preferred an essentially unskilled, labor-intensive
system of municipal service made up of political hacks who did loyal party work
in return for their patronage appointments. Any upgrading in service or introduction
of merit-based government would deprive the bosses of their patronage power.
Equally sound reasons led the machine to oppose budget allocations for costly
equipment that reduced the funds available for hiring clubhouse favorites. Thus it
was more than the boss's conservative esteem for backwardness that made the
ragged old system attractive; it represented the very real basis of his control.

Over the years reformers had managed to pass civil service laws requiring
competitive examinations and objective criteria for municipal appointments, but
Tammany erected a host of subterfuges, from creating "exempt" positions to
neglecting to make public the lists of openings and rewarding favorites with inside
information. The magistrate and municipal courts, long a hive of political patronage,
appointed clerks without reference to the civil service lists. More than 10,000
workers appointed under emergency relief provisions also stood outside the civil
service. Another 6000 jobs on the city-operated IND subway and 12,000 in the
Sanitation Department were assigned with no examinations. In 1933 no more than
55 percent of the municipal work force was chosen by competitive examination.[22]

Instead of creating jobs around function, New York created functions for
individuals. Since it was not what you did but why you were appointed that was
important, identical job titles often paid very different salaries even in the same
department. One stenographer in the Department of Education earned $4640, an-
other $1170. One man appointed to the city Markets Department was assigned the
title "Statistician and Market Reporter." When this was disallowed by the New
York State Civil Service Commission, his title was changed to "Director of Statistics
and Market Reports." Again the commission demurred. This time the statistician
was made a "General Inspector of the Department of Public Markets" and then
"Confidential Inspector, Examining Engineer-(refrigeration) in-charge." It took
awhile for the state civil service to find this versatile fellow, but when it did, the

commission finally insisted that his position required an examination, which he took and failed.

So many city jobs required "special skill and training," the basis for exemption from civil service requirements, that New York should have boasted one of the most skilled staffs in the nation. Alas, these special skills had more to do with machine politics than municipal service. The Civil Service Reform Association in 1932 found ninety Democratic district leaders and their relatives, together with sixteen Republican district leaders, on the city payroll. Not one of these individuals had passed a civil service examination.[23]

Sinecures abounded. The city paid a crew of custodians to guard the 4225 voting machines used in city elections and stored in bonded warehouses for safekeeping. Despite the bond and a regular police guard, you can never be too careful, so the Walker administration paid twenty custodians $2810 a year to protect the invaluable machines. Curious about the work done by these custodians, a *World Telegram* reporter visited the warehouse.

In a corner of the tenth floor a patrolman was seated before an opened window . . . feet comfortably resting on the sill.

"Voting machine inspectors?" he repeated. "They're gone."

"How many are assigned here?"

"Four, I guess. Maybe two. You see two are on their vacations. They get four weeks off. Then when they come back the others go. We got to stay here though. Three eight hour shifts for us.

"But when can I find the custodians?"

"Try between 10 and 12. They're pretty near always here then.

"Couldn't I find them some afternoon?"

"You'd better make it from 10 to 12."[24]

Vested interest in inefficiency made competent municipal service impossible. The Department of Sanitation had not much improved on the nineteenth-century practice of setting scavenging animals loose to pick at discarded trash. Its force of 13,700 old trucks with overflowing open tops rattled down 4000 miles of streets to collect the refuse of New York's 7 million. While one man lifted the garbage over the truck's high sides six or seven feet off the ground, his partner would stand in the heaping pile, knee-deep in offal, shoveling the stuff around. Many of the trucks—not to mention the men—never made it through the day. As for snow removal, it was done by special crews (hired on the recommendation of the district leader) who broke the ice and scooped up the slush by the shovelful into the trash trucks. Heavy snowfalls tied up the city for days.

The sanitation fleet included a number of decrepit wooden scows for carrying the garbage to sea. The cost of repairs for one of the 1904-vintage hulks came to $37,409; modern steel barges of far larger capacity could be had for under $50,000, but that would eliminate the need for crews of repairers and yield less patronage. The debris was unloaded at sea. Simple and primitive. In 1933 New York was ordered by the Supreme Court to find a safer system of disposal or pay a $5000 fine.[25]

Walker's New York showed a shocking insensitivity in the treatment of the ill and helpless. The hospital system was outdated, inadequate to its purpose, and cynically mismanaged. After building Queens General Hospital for $4 million, the city could not open its doors for lack of equipment. The Department of Health's important Division of Preventable Diseases, a bureau with critical epidemiological responsibilities, was administered by a part-time chief physician. Statistics on maternal death rate, a measure of adequate preventive medicine and careful work during the rather routine medical procedure of delivering a baby, were shockingly high, much higher than they had been in 1905 when most New York babies were delivered at home.[26]

The hospital department operated a City Home for Dependents on Welfare Island under Tammany loyalist Louis J. McNally as director. McNally regularly assigned the unfortunates under his care duties as laborers, gardeners, and maids, for which they collected salaries from the municipal treasury. The idea behind this apparently enlightened policy was a cover for fraud and extortion in which McNally forced the inmates to deposit their earnings in trust accounts for his relatives. And McNally made sure he got what was left over by having the home residents name him in their wills. One woman in the home had saved some $6000 after almost twenty years of waiting on tables and making beds. This was supplemented by a $4500 Civil War widow's pension. When she died, her savings had dwindled to $190.01. During the eight years of his directorship McNally salted away $84,686.51 in his bank accounts, mulcted from the people entrusted to his care.

Conditions in the home were an abomination. Filth abounded. McNally sold food meant for the enfeebled inmates for his own private profit. Ignorant orderlies leaned on drugs as a cure-all for demanding or difficult patients, and medical treatment was free-form. Charles Johnson had served as a cook on sailing ships before coming to the home as an inmate. "Dr. Johnson" saw stomach patients in his "ulcer clinic," where he prepared his own treatments and performed surgery with a pocketknife sterilized by dipping it into an alcohol lamp's reservoir.[27]

The list of backward departments and city problems seemed endless. The fire department was fighting larger, more dangerous fires with the same junk and lack of knowledge that their grandfathers used, and they relied on the same old connections for promotion. The school system was rife with patronage. Hardly a municipal department could stand close scrutiny.[28]

"Get yourself a 'Rabbi,' " the well-built young Irishman with the open face, flat nose, and no-nonsense eyes was told upon joining the police force in 1903. Thirty years later, cops were still assuring their careers by hooking up with a political patron. Lewis Valentine, uncomfortable about mixing politics with his police work, never followed the advice, and he paid for his stubbornness with a checkered police career. From patrolman the bull-necked Irishman moved up to sergeant in due time, but lacking a protector, his career showed little promise of taking off. Then one day in 1914, Inspector Dan Costigan offered Valentine a new position. "This new Fusion administration has some ideas about cleaning up the Department," "Honest Dan" explained, inviting his friend to become his assistant on a special anticorruption squad.

The confidential unit shook up the department. But senior officers bided their time and waited for John Purroy Mitchell's reform administration to leave office. Once it did, the succeeding administration quickly disbanded the special squad and assigned Valentine and his commander to the city's least desirable precincts.

When Jimmy Walker came into office, he appointed George McLaughlin, a tough professional, to head the police department and promised the commissioner a free hand in running it. McLaughlin sought out Valentine and placed him at the head of a new confidential investigative unit that eventually grew to more than forty police officers. Valentine began by attacking Times Square gyp joints, illegal abortion clinics, and high-stakes gamblers. His gambling raids forced the card sharps to institute floating games, every day at a different hotel or apartment, but Valentine kept up the pressure. When the gamblers equipped their dens with steel doors, Valentine issued his men sledgehammers. Finally, the gamblers moved their games to the political clubhouses, giving the local bosses the house cut.

Valentine's men sledgehammered some of the most powerful doors in the city. Of course, by the time the police could walk through, the gamers pulled out the chessboards and threw some pieces on the table. Convictions were impossible but the idea was pretty audacious. Dozens of such raids on Democratic clubhouses turned a discomfiting spotlight on the politicos, but Tammany friends in the courts did their best to help out. Of 278 gambling-associated arrests at Boss Jimmy Hines's club, not a single one resulted in a penalty.

In 1927 Commissioner McLaughlin resigned and Walker brought in Joseph Warren. The mayor explained to his new appointee that some of the district leaders were unhappy "about the supervision that their clubs were receiving." The commissioner conveyed the message to Valentine and then promptly ordered him to ignore it. Before long, Warren too had resigned, and this time Walker chose more carefully, bringing in the debonair Wanamaker department store executive Grover Whalen. The stylish Whalen, "famous for his gardenia and well trained mustache," understood the mayor perfectly. He disbanded the confidential squad, demoted Valentine to captain, and banished him to an obscure command in Queens. The example of a broken Valentine delivered the message with crystal clarity: Do not mess with Tammany.[29]

The failures of Walker's administration were matched by a failure of design. New York's city charter, adopted in 1901, after the consolidation of the boroughs into the greater city, grafted a city government on top of the existing county governments to produce a hideous snarl. Drafted in great haste, the 400,000-word document, eighty times as long as the Constitution of the United States, was an undigested mass of laws, many of them outdated, stitched together with hundreds of special acts and statutes. Dividing power between a loose confederation of semi-independent borough governments and a mayor resulted in 140 different departments, agencies, and boards in 1933. The cumbersome scheme yielded redundancy, confusion, missed connections, waste, overlapping powers, unclear lines of authority, and a Manhattan-centered city government. The city was straitjacketed into a system designed for the turn of the century, while the county governments became nests for political spoils with their rosters of unnecessary sheriffs, registers, clerks, and record keepers.[30]

This system also carried forward the singularly inept legislative body known as the Board of Aldermen. Their weekly meetings lasting about twenty minutes were devoted to renaming streets, changing the numbers on buildings, regulating theaters, authorizing parades, and designating play streets. The board failed conspicuously in doing the job it was created for: fixing New York City to an appropriate legislative compass and a prudent budget. The board customarily approved budgets of more than half a billion dollars that filled 370 pages with figures, after no more than a perfunctory discussion of twelve minutes. Not that more time would help much. "Of the fifty eight Tammany Hall aldermen in 1928," one observer noted, "it is doubtful if five could, if they would, read an annual report of the services obtained from tax money." The aldermen did have some help with their voting. "Don't fret about it," one of the illustrious group told a colleague. "They had a lot of experts go over this budget. . . . Why worry?" By "they" he meant the political bosses who gave the aldermen their marching orders.[31]

In 1931 a committee of architects, engineers, and urban experts drafted a new building code for the city. The Board of Aldermen studied the document and was preparing to pass it when a hint of Tammany's opposition was received. Building contractors, fearful that the code could be changed in the middle of a project, suspended construction, idling thousands. The chairman of the Committee on Buildings explained that with the county leaders on vacation in Florida he had not yet received his instructions, and the aldermen would have to wait for guidance.

Outraged by this control of "an invisible government," the president of the City Club fired back a suggestion: "Take a long breath and pass the code anyway! Just as if you were grown men! Just as if the Capitol of the city were located at City Hall. Just as if you were paid $5,000 a year for taking such responsibilities! Just as if you had minds! Just as if you had guts!" This proved too much to ask of a body described by a contemporary as a gathering of second-raters "who cannot get their feet into the main trough."[32]

The Regional Plan Association of New York focused ten years of work and study and a million dollars on developing an agenda of growth and planned development for the "New York Region and Its Environs." This landmark study, which served as a model for other community planners, suggested a policy to protect harbors, zone industrial use, plan airports, subways, highways, playgrounds, parkways, beaches, public housing, pollution control, and transportation management, while demonstrating some concern for civic beauty and aesthetic grace. The planners called for an enlightened political leadership that would bend private wishes before the needs of the greater city. Admittedly this would require courage and intelligence and skillful political helmsmanship. Even for an honest politician with ability and commitment the job was of heroic proportions. And New York had only Jimmy Walker.[33]

3. All Drift and No Mastery

New York is colossal, astonishing, fascinating.
But politically New York is a failure. As a
municipality it is corrupt, and sluttish to the
last degree.

Alva M. Johnson, 1931[34]

W HAT could a good-time mayor do in bad times? Was there anything else that Jimmy Walker could do but beg the theater owners to show happy movies? A career in government had not visibly broadened his understanding of municipal responsibility beyond the guiding principle of his political career: People want to be happy, and the politician who can sell them that illusion will be forgiven all else. He was almost right. But empty stomachs, wailing babies, and crippling unemployment made happiness impossible for too many. And there stood Jimmy Walker, his bag emptied of the one big trick he had mastered.

It fell to private initiative to address the economic crisis. In the fall of 1930, after the police completed a census of jobless, they joined other city employees and set up a fund to help the unemployed. Public school teachers established another fund for the Depression's children. Private efforts mushroomed, but lacking central coordination they remained sporadic, haphazard, disorganized, and insufficient.[35]

In August of 1930 the Association for Improving the Condition of the Poor and the Charity Organization Society jointly created an Emergency Work Bureau, offering work relief for the unemployed. In September the committee, chaired by Seward Prosser of Banker's Trust, established an initial target of $4 million to provide 10,000 jobs at $15 a week for six months. Even before this amount was fully subscribed the goal climbed to 6 and then $8 million. The Prosser Committee exceeded even this figure. From December 1930 to April 1931, they assigned 37,531 individuals to community and government projects, paving roads, surfacing playgrounds, repairing fences, fixing water fountains, cleaning hospitals, renovating city properties, and clearing vacant lots.

But the problem dwarfed all efforts at private solution. Social workers demanded a $10 million program to put the rest of the poor to work. City officials responded that the New York city charter prohibited it. Walker waited for the state legislature to take the lead, and then allocated a wholly inadequate $2 million. Another private group, this one headed by Harvey D. Gibson, carried forward the work of the Prosser Committee, but its millions dried up within a month. By the Spring of 1932, private philanthropy had exhausted itself on the ever-growing Depression. Since 1929 nearly 400 private social service institutions, one-third of the agencies in the city, had closed their doors. "We have to beg for money now," an associate of the Henry Street Nurses wrote Lieutenant Governor Lehman. The head of the Emergency Work Bureau compared private efforts to using a fire hose on a forest fire. Leadership passed from the philanthropists and social workers to the politicians.[36]

Governor Franklin Roosevelt had moved deliberately at first. But he heeded the reformers in his own administration as well as such forceful spokesmen as New York City Welfare Council Director William Hodson, who demanded state-funded public assistance. In August of 1931, Roosevelt summoned the state legislature to a special session on relief. Asserting the state's responsibility to the needy "not as a matter of charity but as a matter of social duty," he proposed a $20 million Temporary Emergency Relief Administration to underwrite municipal aid for the distressed, the money to come from a 50 percent hike in the graduated income tax. Within a month, on September 23, 1931, Roosevelt signed the TERA into law.

From Washington, Fiorello La Guardia lauded Roosevelt's initiative: "CONGRAT-
ULATIONS. . . . YOUR COURAGEOUS STAND ON PROVIDING REVENUE FROM TAXATION
TO CARRY OUT PROGRAM IS INDEED TO BE COMMENDED IN THESE DAYS OF TIMIDITY
TO FACE ISSUE AND PASS THE BUCK TO REDCROSS AND SALVATION. . . . IN THE
NAME OF THOUSANDS OF INNOCENT VICTIMS OF PRESENT DEPRESSION WITH WHOM
I AM IN CONTACT THANKS"[37]

Roosevelt initially outlined a $20 million dollar program, but TERA's director,
Harry Hopkins, expanded the program to cover every tenth family in the state. By
winter of 1935, TERA was disbursing funds at the rate of a billion dollars a year.
Despite the quick buildup, Hopkins insisted that these funds be invested in carefully
supervised projects and that local administrative agencies be staffed by professionals. "Social workers are at the bat," he exclaimed. And by keeping TERA free of
the taint of favoritism and inefficiency that compromised other relief programs, he
proved that relief could be administered on a professional basis.[38]

How different from the Walker record! Under the Tammany mayor, New
York City's relief effort grew by 1932 to a $10 million operation. But like much
else in the Gotham government it was riddled with corruption and political favoritism. Political connections and considerations of ethnic and religious background
reduced New York's relief coffers to a special fund for needy Democrats. In Staten
Island enrolled Democrats accounted for nine of ten relief recipients, and many of
these were not needy. One recipient owned four automobiles (though to be fair,
others had only two cars in their garages). City workers already on the payroll were
double-dipping from the poor pot. Women with maids and political connections
gained assistance while legitimate applicants got nothing. Through the good offices
of the Democratic bosses one man was assisted in reclaiming a share of the taxes
he paid on $60,000 worth of real estate by being certified for relief. In Manhattan,
the borough president's office took the straightforward approach of distributing
batches of preapproved relief applications to the district clubs to be handed out to
the loyal membership. Thus were the poor "humbugged, swindled, and betrayed,"
cheated out of the meager assistance that their misery entitled them to.[39]

The misappropriation was understandable in a way. At least it served some
purpose. But the cruel inefficiency of the system served no one. City relief, William
Hodson sadly concluded in 1932, failed to meet even "the minimum needs of large
numbers of unemployed." The Department of Public Welfare featured eight different types of assistance, each with its own rules and application. Bureaucratic
confusion reigned. Veterans qualified for one program, the blind another, yet another
served solely the aged and the dependent. The unemployed applied to a special
agency, mothers of dependent children to yet another. Play your story right and
you could collect several times. If you knew nothing more than that you needed
help you might spend a good part of your time going round and round.

In March of 1933 social workers resigned en masse, protesting the disgraceful way the city disbursed relief assistance. Only a state investigation and growing public indignation finally forced the mayor to salvage relief from a total loss of credibility by appointing a nonpolitical panel to oversee its operation.[40]

———

No such blue-ribbon front could rescue the city's fiscal veracity. In good times the city had squandered its treasure unwisely. "If we are to have Staten Island docks, Bronx Terminal Markets, overlapping bureaus, excessive salaries, political sinecures, an out of date classification [system], a worn out charter and an extravagant pension system, I suppose," wrote a *New York Times* editorialist, "we must pay for them." Realty values were sinking, relief expenses rising, and the decline in tax receipts accompanying the Depression brought the city to the brink of receivership.[41]

New York City budgets perfectly illustrated the story of the committee appointed to design a cow and producing a camel. Executive departments would submit their requests, which the Board of Estimate translated into budget allocations and passed on to the Board of Aldermen for final approval. The budget makers scarcely paid any attention to projected income or overall expenditures, and the mayor, who did ultimately have to concern himself with these troubling matters, was denied any role in the process by the charter. Without anyone to restrain them, the politicians, who viewed expenditures in terms of jobs per dollar, cobbled together their various programs into exceedingly padded budgets. Those with a less analytical turn of mind found more practical shortcomings. Republican Alderman Joseph C. Baldwin identified some $60 million in graft laced through the 1931 budget, and William H. Allen of the Institute for Public Service discovered that a city employee four years buried and definitely dead was still being issued a paycheck.[42]

Half of the 1931 budget of $620,000,000 went for salaries and wages, much of it unwisely spent. Another third of the budget, $196,000,000, close to the combined debt of all the forty-eight states, serviced the municipal debt, which was growing at the rate of $300,000 a day. By 1931 the *New York Times* warned of impending bankruptcy. Walker refused to believe any of this. New York, he would say, was not some small village that had to watch its pennies. It—not to mention the horde of Tammany sinecurists—had a style of life to support, Walker said, as he rejected all but symbolic economies.[43]

Came the reckoning in January 1932. Tax receipts plummeted. Scared off by Gotham's undaunted prodigality, lenders avoided city paper and New York faced the real possibility of defaulting on its debts. By pulling together its reserves and delaying payment on outstanding bills, New York had managed to scrape by 1931, but only barely. Now in January 1932, Controller Charles Berry announced that the financial capital of the world was living "from hand to mouth." Finally, even Jimmy Walker could not avoid the fact that plunging tax income and skyrocketing relief costs were leading to fiscal catastrophe. There remained only one source for the money to pay salaries, bills, relief, and the cost of municipal services, and Walker had no choice but to go there to get it.[44]

With his royal blue chapeau in hand and advisers in tow, a forlorn Beau James trooped to the home of Charles Mitchell, chairman of the board of the First National City Bank, to plead for loans to bail out the city. The financial satraps had never been happy with Walker's irresponsible spending and exuberant inefficiency. Now they had a solid stick with which to thwack the Tammany crowd. The bankers brought in Price Waterhouse accountants to audit city books and, after receiving a report on the municipality's true condition, shook their heads gravely and pondered long before offering the mayor their help, so long of course, as they did not put their investors' capital at undue risk. In brief, New York would have to accept their control if it wanted their dollars.

Thomas Lamont, of the J. P. Morgan Co., Charles Mitchell, and their fellow paladins of prudence were not disposed to be brief or deferential as they lectured the hapless mayor on what it would take for them to accept New York as a ward of the banks. "Mayor Walker and his associates undoubtedly realize," they announced, "that New York City like the National Government and other large governmental bodies and public corporations must undertake measures of strict economy and, especially in these times, must proceed on a more restrained and orderly development of its construction program; must make every effort, wherever possible, to transform existing enterprises which today are not self supporting into ones that carry themselves and thus take a heavy burden off the city's budget." With no choice, the city agreed to terms, marking an end to the happy spending of the twenties, and to its own fiscal independence.[45]

On the city's promise of retrenchment, a consortium of thirty-four banks put together a $350,000,000 package to resuscitate the city treasury. While the banks had worn bare the path to Washington to beg the federal government to help them out with low-interest loans, they treated New York with professional dispassion, applying the banker's rule of thumb: The more you needed the money, the more it cost you. New York was in trouble and it would pay dearly. New York State paid 4 percent interest on its loans, but with the city over a barrel, the bankers forced it to sign for 5¾ percent and 6 percent, with most of the loans in short-term notes, so that they could be denied if the city did not follow precisely the dictates of the moneylenders.[46]

Walker had by this time been forced to resign as a result of a state investigation, and the acting mayor, former aldermanic president Joseph V. McKee, articulated the new constraints. "I got $17,000,000 recently to last us until October 1. We won't get any more," he warned, "unless we put through a definite retrenchment program. The bankers want results and I'm determined to see that they get them."[47]

Things continued to get worse. The city budgets had allowed for approximately $7 million in defaulted tax receipts, but more than $211 million in 1932 taxes could not be collected. In October Charles Mitchell and W. W. Aldrich of Chase refused any more loans until municipal salaries were slashed. Keeping city workers happy had always been a Tammany priority. This was the way they made loyal Democrats who pitched in at election time. The chief representative of civil service workers, Frank Prial, exerted great influence in Democratic circles. The last thing the machine wanted to do was to cut salaries. The Board of Estimate desperately tried to avoid this, manipulating the budget, canceling large-ticket capital-improvement items (something that virtually guaranteed the decay of city properties), shuffling accounts, and delaying obligations to pension funds. But the bankers knew all about honeyfugling and cooking books, many were experts at it, and they would not stand for it from the politicians. They reviewed each budget item, dictating adjustments and demanding cuts in worker salaries.[48]

Even this, however, could not bring the wildly unbalanced books into shape. Hundreds of millions of short-term note obligations were coming due in early 1933, and with more than $200 million in uncollectable taxes there was no hope of meeting the deadline. Between December 5 and December 13 some $235 million in banker's maturities fell due. The city had cash for the December 5 and 6 payments, but it was short $12.5 million of a $40 million payment due at three o'clock on December 7. Unless the bankers advanced the funds, New York would default on these notes and bankruptcy would follow. At the last minute (and only after Democratic boss John Curry assented to the agreement) the city finally threw up its hands and surrendered the last bit of financial independence that it still had. Salaries were cut from 6 to 33 percent, and the already approved budget was rescinded and rewritten to please the bankers.[49]

While Depression and fiscal crisis pounded the city, nothing so stunned its citizens and so broke their spirit as a series of sweeping disclosures about where so much of this money had gone and the type of people who controlled it. The end of New York's innocence came not with the Depression but with a trio of investigations that uncovered a comprehensive system of payoffs, bribes, rotten deals, and insider favoritism that left government corruption nakedly revealed. Botched municipal government was not as artlessly inefficient as had been imagined. There was a design to the madness. Police, judges, inspectors, and department bureaucrats were not all graduates of the Alphonse and Gaston school of government; they were skillfully raking off a bundle and leaving the city to pay the price.

When Jimmy Walker was first elected to office in 1925, Fiorello La Guardia predicted that the new administration would be an "everybody getting his" administration. Opposing Walker in the 1929 mayoral campaign, La Guardia charged Walker with establishing a rogue regime built on boss-connected political arrangements. "A temporary bus permit," he bellowed over and over again, "is to Tammany what a horse and a six shooter were to the James Brothers.'' Drawing on information from Dr. William H. Allen's Institute for Public Service, he hammered away at the theme of rascality and corruption, taunting that except for Al Smith ''there was not a Tammany politician that would dare to have his bank account examined.'' La Guardia made dramatic charges about the Arnold Rothstein murder, Justice Albert Vitale's unsecured $20,000 loan, and the short line that led from Tammany to the underworld. But it all sounded too fantastic, and so much of it was self-serving speculation.[50]

Four weeks after the 1929 mayoral election, the Tepecano Democratic Club tendered a dinner to Justice Vitale at the Roman Gardens in the Bronx. The festive testimonial featured a gaggle of politicos and outstanding individuals drawn from allied fields of public service. Representing the food industry was Ciro Terranova, familiarly known as the ''artichoke king'' for his stranglehold on the import of these vegetables through his underworld enforcers. Other equally esteemed gangsters were joined in honoring their friend and paragon, Magistrate Vitale, when suddenly pistol-wielding bandits burst into the hall and stripped the guests of jewelry and cash. A city detective handed over his pistol (the wily Vitale quickly slipped his ring into his pants). The motive for the holdup is unclear, although police speculated that Terranova used the incident as a cover to retrieve a murder contract from one of the guests.

After the dinner the guest of honor dashed over to the Democratic clubhouse for a little discussion. Shortly thereafter, the stolen goods, including the service revolver, were gallantly returned. Clearly the judge was well connected. New Yorkers could not avoid wondering, however, whether these were the right associations for a sitting judge. An investigation discovered that in his four years on the bench the magistrate had managed to accumulate $165,000 on a salary of $48,000, and by March Vitale was a former justice. After his retirement, Vitale's well-intentioned colleagues, perhaps interested in setting an example for the decent treatment of dismissed justices, plied the disbarred judge with lucrative receiverships and other offices of trust and profit.[51]

In August the courts were in the news again. Supreme Court Justice Joseph Force Crater stepped into a taxi and waved good-bye to two friends on West Forty-fifth Street. He was never seen again. In the course of the quarter-million-dollar search for the jurist it was learned that Crater had played the Ziegfeld chorus line at the same time that he played the loyal husband to his wife and paramour to his mistress. One naturally wondered where the money for this high life was coming from, and this led to revelations of personal finances as twisted as Crater's love life.

The magistrate's court screened all felony arrests in the city. After hearing evidence, magistrates decided if a case should be forwarded to a grand jury or quashed at this point for insufficient evidence. With the power to turn men free, this court attracted an incredible array of sharpers whose business it was to reach the judges and their clerks. Payoffs and bribes coursed the entire system. J. Richard Davis, gangland attorney nonpareil, estimated that the bail racket alone netted $100 million a year. This racket guaranteed bootleggers, pimps, numbers runners, and assorted racketeers that arrested underlings would be sprung from court swiftly, before they could give testimony against higher-ups. Low-salaried court officers salted away thousands of dollars, even hundreds of thousands, in shoe boxes and the bank accounts of trusted relatives. In this court flourished the rankest atmosphere where everyone had a price and none had shame.

"It is open gossip in every political club in New York," Fiorello La Guardia wrote, "that appointments have been pretty generally peddled or paid for." In 1929 La Guardia had asked Governor Franklin Roosevelt to investigate city corruption, but he could offer no facts when Roosevelt demanded specifics. This time Governor Roosevelt understood that there was nothing to be gained by delaying what was an inevitable investigation. Beating La Guardia to the punch, he instructed the Appellate Division of the First Judicial District to appoint a referee and carry out a proper investigation of New York City's magistrate courts.[52]

---

4. Tammany's Biographer

The three things that a Tammany leader most dreaded were, in ascending order of repulsiveness, the penitentiary, honest industry and biography.

Edwin L. Godkin[53]

S HORTLY before midnight on August 26, 1930, Samuel Seabury took a transatlantic call in his London hotel suite. In his hands was a rare first edition of *The Just Lawyer*, printed in 1631. He had just recently added this much-coveted volume to his elegant library of rare legal books and manuscripts. The caller, a newspaper reporter, desired a statement on Seabury's new assignment to investigate the magistrate's courts. It was fitting for Seabury to learn of his appointment from a journalist, for unlikely as it seemed, this impeccably credentialed lawyer of aristocratic mien would serve as a 1930s version of the ink-stained reporter-muck-raker who revealed to the public the extent of municipal corruption around the turn of the century.

Tall, heavy-set, and ramrod-straight, with a stern bearing that seemed to forbid intimacy while exuding civic rectitude, the fifty-seven-year-old Seabury was descended from American stock that traced back to the founding days of the Republic. His ancestors were lawyers, doctors, professors, and mainly men of the cloth, American nobility. Five generations of Seaburys had served as Episcopal ministers, and his great-great-grandfather, his namesake, was the first bishop of the Protestant episcopate in the United States. The Seabury family crest carried the motto *Supera Alta Tenere*, Hold to the Most High.

The Seaburys viewed life as a calling, and their men were judged not only by what they accomplished but also by how they accomplished it. "I will not be exceeded in courtesy," he liked to say. Raised in modest circumstances, young Sam was imbued with the Seabury regard for virtue, morality, and hard work. As a student he studied diligently. As a young man trained in the law he committed himself with equal pertinacity to reforming the political system. Appalled by the tangled embrace between politics and vice and the general air of vileness surrounding urban government, Seabury joined other reformers to campaign for the restoration of civic dignity and political integrity. He was deeply influenced by Henry George's *Progress and Poverty*, with its search for root causes and its radical advocacy of a "single tax" on land.

In 1897 Seabury dropped out of his own race for alderman to devote himself to George's campaign for the New York mayoralty. The combination of patrician pedigree and radical politics struck some as unusual, but those who knew young Sam Seabury knew that social justice concerned him far more than class tradition. Seabury took from his brief relationship with the prophet of the "single tax" a firm belief that the selfless individual could redeem municipal politics. He became a crusading lawyer, fighting for labor rights in the courts, excoriating the Supreme Court decision granting an injunction in *United States vs. Debs*, as "the most extreme case of judicial usurpation and tyranny. . . ."[54]

At the age of 28, in 1901, Seabury won election to the bench of the city court of New York. The youngest judge in the city, he offended conservatives with his activist judicial philosophy. "Judge Seabury, the boy judge on the City Court and also of the Henry George Society," jeered the *New York Sun*, "does not act on the theory that persons holding judicial office should either be reticent or inactive in political matters." He refused to tolerate legal loopholing and technical evasions before his court. In a jury-fixing case he ordered the district attorney, William Travers Jerome, to pursue a particular line of inquiry that the prosecutor seemed quite intent on ignoring. Jerome stalked from the courtroom demanding Seabury's impeachment. Years later Jerome himself was arraigned on charges of misconduct and Seabury was called as a witness. "Mr. Justice, will you be good enough to

223

express your honest opinion of me," asked Jerome. Seabury wanted to be sure. "Do you really want my honest opinion?" "I do," answered the tainted politican. Seabury looked straight at the man and said, "I find it impossible to raise you to the level of my contempt."[55]

After Seabury won a fourteen-year appointment to the state court of appeals in 1914, Theodore Roosevelt invited him to come out to Sagamore Hill for a political powwow. The former Republican president told Seabury that he was unhappy with the incumbent Republican governor, Charles Whitman. "The truth is not in [Charles] Whitman," he told his guest. Then he told the Democratic judge that he wanted him to run in 1916 and was prepared to support him, despite his party affiliation. The Democratic Roosevelt, Franklin, also supported Seabury and helped him secure the party nomination. But when it came to delivering the Progressive support that he had promised, Teddy backed down. Learning of TR's change of heart, Seabury charged out to Oyster Bay to tell him, "Mr. President you are a blaitherskite," striding out of the room before the surprised cowboy statesman could respond. "The truth," Seabury liked to tell his relatives after the ill-fated election, "is not in Roosevelt." Tammany also abandoned him in this election, and in his later years when he spoke of this campaign he always recalled the twin treacheries of the reformer and the bosses.[56]

Seabury turned to private practice, where his gifts for scrupulous analysis and broad interpretation won handsome reward. Million-dollar fees supported him in the comfortable life-style of an English gentleman barrister, but he never gave up the social awareness of his younger years. Periodically he mounted the public stage to defend unpopular causes, to denounce Tammany, and to offer prescriptions for municipal betterment.

Seabury accepted his assignment to investigate the courts as an opportunity to win attention for the kinds of reforms that had always interested him. On its face the assignment was a narrow one, but Henry George had taught him to look for root causes and his own training had taught him the importance of inspired digging.[57]

Seabury assembled a staff of hungry young Turks (average age: twenty-eight), many of them straight out of law school and out to rip Tammany. "Old heads for counsel," the gray-haired investigator liked to say, "young heads for war." These driven men worked around the clock for little pay and with an elan few prosecuting staffs could match. They were prepared to dramatize for the public the evil that the crooked courts had made so banal. Of one thing they were certain, their work would count. This was not going to be a quiet investigation ending with a staid committee report for the files. Seabury was bent on laying bare the corruption of the Old Guard and they wanted a part of the action.

Seabury began hearings in October of 1930, gathering private testimony from more than 1000 individuals. His manner was nothing if not thorough. He demanded bank records, stock transactions, income tax returns. The staff waded through more than 15,000 pages of initial testimony to match testimony with evidence. From the discrepancies Seabury constructed his inquiry strategies. Then he recalled the witnesses to answer questions, this time in public. When the subpoenaed officials refused to testify, cloaking themselves in constitutional immunities against self-incrimination, Governor Roosevelt ordered that all "pleading of immunity by public officials in regard to public acts shall cease."[58]

Chile Mapocha Acuna, nicknamed the "human spitoona" (the Seabury team was acutely skilled in selecting memorable figures for the stand), was brought before the inquiry to explain his work as a vice squad stool pigeon. Acuna testified that he furnished information on brothels for about $150 a week, ah, that was $150 a week, plus a share of the "take." On slow days he would join the vice police on forays into Harlem, where they would raid some flats indiscriminately and round up women, holding the threat of arrest over them to shake them down.

The human spitoona's primary duty was to entrap women into offering sex for a fee. Then the vice squad would step in to make an arrest. These arrests formed the basis of a lucrative business for bail bondsmen, court clerks, police, prosecutors, and local political clubs, who traded justice for a price. One could buy influence, an easy sentence, a dismissal with fine, altered testimony, lost records, the list went on. John C. Weston, a prosecutor in the women's court, for example, collected $20,000 for going easy on 600 vice cases involving 900 individuals.[59]

Acuna's most shocking disclosures dealt with the guiltless women caught in these traps. He told of passing marked money to innocent women and then beginning to undress, enough for the swooping vice squad to make an arrest. Then the woman would either pay off or be brought to court to stand trial as a prostitute. Seabury located innocent women still languishing in prison on trumped-up charges. A medical report on one of these innocent women declared that the arresting officer had blackened the woman's eye, bruised her thigh and belly, and left marks around her breast that "resembled teeth marks." Mayor Walker confessed that he was "more or less shocked by the reports of the framing of innocent women." Heywood Broun parsed the mayor's sentence: "In this duel between 'less' and 'more' the former has won the day, for the city's chief executive is about to take a vacation of three or four weeks at Palm Springs. . . ."[60]

For this small part of his inquiry, regarding the stool pigeons and police payoffs, Seabury's staff checked 2000 records in banks and brokerage houses to learn who held accounts and under what names. In other instances, the staff found policemen, bondsmen, clerks, court attendants, and assistant district attorneys who had stashed hundreds of thousands of dollars from the traffic in justice. No such system of comprehensive graft could exist for even one day, Seabury concluded, without the knowledge and approval of the sitting magistrates.

He turned to a close study of *each* magistrate. Several immediately resigned, complaining of ill health. The others were challenged to explain their huge bank accounts, their erratic actions on the bench, and their conflicts of interest. Then

Seabury moved the probe into the way that magistrates secured their appointments. Most, he found, came by their lofty positions through the political club. Did this mean that they owed the boss? One magistrate acknowledged that the Democratic leader interceded some forty times in cases before him. District leader James W. Brown proudly remarked that such influence peddling on behalf of his constituents was a "civic duty." "That," Brown testified, "is how we make Democrats." Referee Seabury unmasked the meretricious deals, the hack personnel, and the ethnic favoritism that pervaded the courts, concluding his inquiry on October 26, 1931, with a recommendation for creating a nonpolitical court system.[61]

By this time, Seabury was already busy with another state investigation. New Yorkers had begun to wonder, as they learned of the corruption in the courts, where the district attorney had been during all of this nefarious business. The City Club and the City Affairs Committee had already blasted the prosecutor's timidity and ineffectiveness in dealing with the racketeers and grafters. On March 10, 1931, in the midst of the magistrates' investigation, Governor Roosevelt asked Seabury to launch a separate inquiry into the conduct of Thomas C. T. Crain, district attorney in New York County.

Again the Seabury team burrowed through voluminous evidence, combing through carts of grand jury transcripts. Seabury's racketeering investigations disclosed that scarcely a business in New York failed to pay tribute for protection and labor peace. In the Fulton fish market Joseph "Socks" Lanza handled labor negotiations for the United Sea Food Workers local. Employers were taxed a specified amount per worker to be able to carry on their business. Unionized businesses paid off Lanza for sweetheart contracts while nonunion plants paid him to keep the union out. Seabury documented just how far Lanza's grasp reached:

> Every fisherman bringing his haul into New York had to pay tribute to dock his boat, and in default of payment he was unable to unload his cargo; the wholesaler had to pay tribute to get his fish from the dock to his counter in the market and if he failed to pay, no amount of money could secure him the necessary porterage; the retailer had to pay to have the fish carried from the wholesale counter to his wagon. If he failed to do so, he was not only unable to hire labor, but his stock was sprayed with kerosene oil and ruined. Moreover, while he was arranging to have his fish carried from the wholesaler's counter to his wagon, he [paid] to prevent his wagon from being destroyed or disabled.[62]

Seabury uncovered similar patterns in the grocery, meat, vegetable, and milk industries.

Yet District Attorney Crain had done nothing to disturb any of this, or the extensive corruption in the magistrate courts. Crane could not even pin a conviction on a grafting assistant district attorney, much less on a gifted veterinarian named

William F. Doyle, who served as a horse doctor for the fire department and thereby established a number of valuable political connections that led to his dealing with the Bureau of Standards and Appeals. Among its other responsibilities, this bureau granted variances on real estate that could increase the value of a piece of property by allowing it to be used for multiple dwellings or for commercial purposes. This was the kind of power safely trusted to saints. After a New Jersey woman declared bankruptcy, and an investigation of her accounts revealed payments to a Doctor Doyle, it came out that the good doctor practiced therapeutic zoning as a sideline.

Over the years Dr. Doyle had used his offices on behalf of this woman and a host of other clients to convert $5 million of residential properties into commercial holdings worth twice the amount. Doyle's own records indicated that he was paying off officials. When all of this information was turned over to Crain, he wrote to the veterinarian asking him to come and testify. When Doyle refused Crain dropped the matter.

Seabury's analysis of Crain's indictments showed that most defendants with serious offenses often pleaded guilty to misdemeanors. Of 1279 indictments for grand larceny in 1930, 623 resulted in conviction but only 72 for the crime charged, all the rest for lesser crimes. Although he could not prove any criminal malfeasance, Seabury concluded in his report on August 31, 1931, that the DA was thoroughly incompetent, which under the circumstances was just as bad for the city.[63]

The clamor for a more comprehensive probe of New York's municipal government snowballed. Unable any longer to dismiss these demands, Governor Roosevelt approved a $250,000 allocation and the designation of investigator extraordinaire Samuel Seabury to serve as counsel to the Joint Legislative Committee to Investigate the Affairs of the City of New York, chaired by State Senator Samuel H. Hofstadter. Early in the hearings a Democratic member of the committee turned to Seabury and asked whether it was true that he had once collected a million-dollar fee. "Yes," Seabury answered, "over a ten year period." The legislator noted incredulously, "*I* never got such a fee." The dignified Seabury replied gravely, "Senator the reason is obvious. You were never worth that much to anybody." In any event, Seabury was doing his investigative work *pro bono*, and clearly he was worth much more than he was being paid. His team interviewed more than 2260 individuals in private, gathering more than 47,000 pages of testimony. In thirty-seven public hearings he called upon 175 witnesses, adding another 5000 pages to the record.

Seabury first pursued the case of Dr. Doyle, learning that the veterinarian had secured 244 variances for building garages, 52 approvals for gas stations where they had previously been forbidden, 187 assorted modifications of state labor and tenement house laws and numerous permits for alterations routinely denied to unconnected citizens. The record also showed Dr. Doyle to be an extraordinarily persuasive man who got the Board of Standards and Appeals to reverse itself in numerous instances on behalf of his clients. Initially, Doyle refused to answer direct questions about bribery and influence peddling for fear of incriminating himself. Granted immunity and ordered to answer Seabury's questions, Doyle refused again and was cited for contempt.

Tammany did not yet understand the effect the revelations were having; the bosses thought that this was just another of the periodic good government jaunts through darkling politics. They would tough it out. Sentenced to thirty days, Doyle won a quick pardon from a Tammany appellate judge. Seabury called on Manhattan's Democratic boss, John F. Curry, to tell the committee whether he had intervened with a sympathetic judge in upstate New York on Doyle's behalf. Curry admitted that he had made a call and would do all in his power to prevent the committee from carrying out "a crucification [sic], if it can be had, of the Democratic Party." The committee strengthened Seabury's hand and beckoned him to proceed.

The inquiry turned to the administration of relief, exposing a dense political hive around the multi-million-dollar honey pot. Rotten deals in Staten Island's transportation system came under scrutiny next, and then Queens, the domain of Democratic county boss John Theofel. The county leader had been appointed chief clerk of the surrogate's court, but under oath he showed great difficulty in defining his duties beyond "walk around the office and keep them on their job." More to the point, the surrogate who appointed Theofel owed the boss his own job; so did the district attorney, a supreme court judge, and assorted other officials. Theofel saw to it that Queens officials drove fancy cars, Pierce Arrows, only Pierce Arrows purchased from Wilson Bros. Inc., owed by Dudley Wilson and his father-in-law. Dudley Wilson was John Theofel's son-in-law. In six years as Democratic leader this huge-bellied high school dropout increased his net worth from $28,650 to $201,300.[64]

In Bronx County, William J. Flynn (no relation to county leader Edward J. Flynn), a former coroner, served as commissioner of public works for the borough (under the charter, such operations were handled by each borough separately). When Bronx businessman Louis Willard tried to buy a piece of Bronx property to erect a parking garage, Flynn blocked this move as a "detriment to our people." Instead, Flynn built his own garage directly across the street! Because Willard did not have the grace to accept this as the price of doing business in the Bronx and complained loudly, Flynn harassed him by obstructing other ventures. Willard lost his business, his property, and his home. His wife killed herself and finally he too tried suicide. Flynn was far more successful. His real estate holdings approximated $400,000 and his savings accounts held another $650,000. It was, after all, bad times, and Flynn explained that the Depression had substantially *decreased* his private fortune.

In Brooklyn the county boss John H. McCooey saw to it that his son John H. McCooey, Jr., ran unopposed for a supreme court judgeship. In this borough, Seabury learned, judgeships were regularly split between the Democratic and Republican bosses through cross endorsements and unopposed candidates. If one had ambitions for such a position and did not have as influential a father as the inexperienced thirty-year-old Jack McCooey, Jr., it cost several thousand dollars.[65]

The borough of Brooklyn was coterminous with Kings County and the county register was the Hon. James A. McQuade, surely one of the kindest and most loyal family supporters in Brooklyn. The short, stocky, and bespectacled coleader of the Greenpoint district was all humility and sweetness before the committee. On a $12,000 annual salary, was it really possible to accumulate $510,000 in six years? he was asked. Truth be told, the humble pol declared that he had borrowed to feed the "other thirty three McQuades," the ones that the press took to calling the "starving McQuades." He would start from the beginning. Guardedly he bared his soul to Seabury. "I unfortunately went into politics. . . ."

"You don't base that on the deposit, do you?" wondered Seabury.

Ah, back to the deposit. Well, after a family business was brought low by an untrustworthy associate and all "thirty four McQuades [the number did change] were placed on my back," Jim McQuade, "to keep life in their body, sustenance," went out and borrowed money. "I felt it my duty, being that they were my flesh and blood, part and parcel of me, to help them." Things were improving "when my mother, Lord have mercy on her, dropped dead." Then his brother dropped dead, Lord have mercy, willing him some more McQuades. This explained the money; he needed it. But Seabury insisted this did not really explain how he got the money. Could he for instance tell the committee from whom he borrowed the hundreds of thousands of dollars?

"Oh, Judge, offhand I could not," replied the Hon. Mr. McQuade. It was all very complex and over and done with so he just forgot the whole thing. It had all been paid back. The evasions continued. McQuade blessed the Lord, declared that McQuades had pride, and tested Seabury's patience. "Mr. McQuade, what are you worth?" asked Assemblyman Cuvillier.

"I got enough to do the rest of my life if I die today."

Cuvillier persisted: "What's that?

"Nothing. You can't be worth much when you have thirty four in the family."

McQuade was similarly lucid about illegal gambling in the Democratic clubhouse. "We have a good library there, . . ." began his answer and meandered from there. After leaving the hearing room, a smiling McQuade inquired of a group of reporters, "How did my story go over?" Apparently quite well. Boss McCooey approved McQuade's candidacy for a higher office with a salary increase to ease the burden of the "thirty four."[66]

The mystery persisted. Try as he might, Seabury was outfoxed. It was like pinning down mercury; he never learned where the money came from. McQuade's coleader, an admiring Peter J. McGuiness, dubbed his slippery cohort "Payroll Jim the Jesse James of Greenpoint."

McGuiness was next. When he had retired from the Board of Alderman to the higher office of party leader, McGuiness delivered a speech detailing all of the benefits he had brought his constituents: clean streets, millions in paving contracts, three playgrounds, subway connections, and bridges. The proud leader closed his talk by saying "I done good. I thank you." What Seabury wanted to know about was the illegal bookmaking in his club, and how such records came to be in the safe marked "Peter J. McGuiness." It was a mistake, the leader assured Seabury. "I never put a toothpick in that safe," although he did admit that his club's Christmas basket fund and charity carnival fund were freely mixed with his personal savings.[67]

Thomas M. Farley (no relation to James M. Farley, Franklin Roosevelt's political adviser), sheriff of New York County and head of the Thomas M. Farley Association Democratic Club, was a jolly fat man who proved the equal of his colleagues. Asked by Seabury to explain why well-known gamblers stood around a crap table in his club at two o'clock in the morning, Farley remembered the incident well. "The members that was there was busy packing baseball bats, skipping ropes and rubber balls," for a May Day children's party. Skeptical, Seabury inquired if anything else might have been in evidence. Well, yes, replied the sheriff, "There were canopies and Maypoles."

Testimony turned to money, as it inevitably did with these successful, self-made men. Seabury too had climbed up from humble surroundings and he was fascinated by the techniques employed by his contemporaries. Politely he asked Farley to explain, please, how he had deposited some $400,000 on an annual salary of $8500.

These deposits "represented moneys I had saved. I took the money out of a safe deposit box at home." A tin box.

SEABURY: Is it the type of tin boxes that are specially manufactured and designed to serve as a receptacle for cash?

FARLEY: It is.

SEABURY: Giving you the benefit of every doubt on sums from your official vocation and other gainful pursuits, the eighty three thousand dollars extra you deposited in 1929 came from the same source that the other money came from?

FARLEY: It did.

SEABURY: Same tin box. Is that right.

FARLEY: That is right.

SEABURY: Now in 1930, where did the extra cash come from, Sheriff?

FARLEY: Well, that is—. My salary check is in there.

SEABURY: No, Sheriff, your salary checks are exclusive of cash deposits which during the year you deposited in those three banks.

FARLEY: Well, that came from the good box I had. [Laughter]

SEABURY: Kind of a magic box.

FARLEY: It was a wonderful box.

SEABURY: A wonderful box. [Laughter] What did you have to do—rub the lock with a little gold and open it to find more money?

In the midst of his examination Seabury wrote Governor Roosevelt that Tammany held sway in all five boroughs of the city. The quality of this style of government was apparent from the testimony. It was up to the governor to take "prompt executive action." Sheriff Farley was called to Albany. Charging him with having failed to provide "a reasonable or credible explanation" for his income, Roosevelt removed Farley from office. The tin box became the symbol for Tammany graft.[68]

There were plenty of tin boxes in Manhattan, where everything seemed to carry special surcharges. Couples applying for marriage licenses customarily paid the city $2 and dropped an equivalent sum into deputy City Clerk James McCormick's open desk drawer. Ultimately McCormick's thirty bank accounts held close to $400,000. "I'll get it at home for holding out," he groaned, apparently no more forthcoming with his wife than with the city of New York.

Similarly, after the North German Steamship Company was unable to rent a city pier for more than nine years, they hired a lawyer with strong Tammany ties, delivered a $50,000 fee, and picked up the lease. The single most effective law firm for such work boasted no Ivy League degrees, but it did have as its senior partner the Hon. George Olvany, former leader of Tammany Hall. Olvany, Eisner and Donnelly provided a list of services that just could not be duplicated. They could get land condemned, official policy altered, laws modified, licenses granted, and administrative decisions rendered. Even the medical profession found its way into Seabury's ambit. He discovered a group of doctors who bought the monopoly on workmen's compensation examinations by delivering generous kickbacks to Dr. William Walker, the mayor's brother.[69]

The steady parade of genial grafters and shameless sachems revealed a pervasive crookedness. Burly hacks were banking fortunes on marvelous tin boxes, anonymous gifts, and casual loans by broad-hearted benefactors who apparently did not much care to be paid back; persons entrusted with public duties could not account for hundreds of thousands of dollars. Here was Tammany in the glare of public lights, unable to cut the small deals that had saved them in the past. Their stories were the key. These officials had displayed rapacity on a grand scale and cared so little for civic probity that they larked the defense. They still believed that they were beyond the reach of regular rules. They would bluff on.

And what in fact would all of this exposure of corruption lead to? Muck sold newspapers. Did it remake cities? The *Nation* wanted to know if Seabury was "thinking of . . . further and permanent aims in the midst of . . . unearthing official misconduct? If not, you are merely wasting time." The point was well taken. In due time Seabury would pay it proper heed, but he was not yet finished with his investigation.[70]

CHAPTER 7

La Guardia Comes to Power

1. A Juggler Missing All of His Tricks

A reformer is a guy who rides through a sewer
in a glass bottomed boat.

James J. Walker[1]

J IMMY Walker thought that Seabury's investigations had taken on a pinched focus. "This is the day for the critic of little things. . . . I have little sympathy," he continued, "for those who see little things to the exclusion of big things done in this greatest city in the world." The inquiry, he thought, was feeding off the frustrations of the Depression. "We are like the sick man in bed who is annoyed by a fly." He waxed philosophical about the turn of events that was bringing the spotlight ever closer. "We are a sort of snap judgment people and we are not bound by any traditions, that's why I am Mayor." When balance returned and New Yorkers looked back on these days more calmly, Walker thought they would say, "Life is a circus and there must be a clown in every circus, and we'll say 'New York had its clown.' " "Will You Love Me in December as You Do in May" had won Jimmy Walker some fame as a Broadway songwriter. Now in May of 1932 he was preparing to be the clown before the Hofstadter Committee. The questions were

233

bound to be thorny, though Seabury, ever chivalrous, would avoid Walker's dalliance with Betty Compton.[2]

Would Walker still be around in December? Seabury was determined to bring more than general accusations against Walker; he wanted to find Jimmy Walker's tin box. Seabury accountants and law clerks sifted through thousands of records searching for illegal cash. "A sense of humor is life's fire escape," said Walker. "The man who has a real sense of humor is . . . the fellow who is onto himself and can still laugh. I take the bow." He would need all the personal resources he could muster, for one day a bank employee suggested to Seabury's researchers that they had failed to look at letters of credit. Following this tip, the team emerged with a folder containing drafts with Jimmy Walker's signature.

Some of these letters were endorsed by a consortium of speculators called the Equitable Bus Company. Mayor Walker had rammed their application for a bus franchise through the Board of Estimate. What made this award so suspicious was that Equitable did not own a single bus. They won the franchise and several extensions *in anticipation* of putting together a company, while bona fide bidders offering better terms were ignored.[3]

Another "beneficence," as Walker took to calling these gifts, came from J. A. Sisto, who had $26,000 in bonds delivered to the mayor at city hall as his share in a stock deal, for which Walker had not put up a penny. Sisto's large interest in the Checker Cab Corporation, with its favored position in the regulated taxi business, may have accounted for his generosity. Newspaper publisher Paul Block was another generous patron. He opened a joint brokerage account with the mayor into which Walker never deposited anything, but still "earned" $246,693. Perhaps the fact that Block owned a company that wanted to sell tiles to the New York City subways explained his regard for Walker, or maybe, as he suggested, his son's concern that the mayor could not live on his meager salary prompted him to "make a little money for him."[4]

Then a senior official in a brokerage firm told Seabury of a secret account opened by Russell T. Sherwood, Jimmy Walker's financial agent. There was no signature card on file for this "investment trustee account" to hide the fact that Jimmy Walker withdrew from it regularly. From January 1, 1926, to August 5, 1931, Sherwood deposited close to a million dollars in this account, three-quarters of it in cash. Seabury wanted very much to speak with Sherwood, but he fled to Mexico before Seabury could serve the papers.[5]

Came the day of reckoning. Scrupulous, with a deep regard for virtue and dignity in government, upright Samuel Seabury prepared to do battle with flip, loud, fast-living, unserious, theatrical Jimmy Walker, to call the brash Tammany politician to account for abusing the people's trust.

May 25, 1932. The crowd in front of the county courthouse near Foley Square had begun to gather at six in the morning. A lucky few held tickets that would allow them to be seated inside the courthouse for the confrontation. It was a Walker crowd waiting to cheer the beleaguered mayor and to wish him well. "Good luck, Jimmy," "Atta boy, Jimmy." They knew he was no angel, just a boy, a fifty-year-old boy, running around with Monk Compton and the fast crowd. They admired his spirit and his style. As for the reformers who were attacking Walker, many doubted whether they were up to the challenge of governing. They would appeal to man's goodness and all that weak stuff and be robbed blind. Better a professional who knows how far he can go than some bright-eyed college grad who could be bluffed out of the whole treasury. With Tammany you had people who knew the basic needs of people. Besides many in the crowd felt that the match was unfair. The inquiry had inquisitional powers. It hauled in witnesses, interrogated them in secret, showered Tammany with subpoenas after offering immunity, and threatened contempt charges to loosen reticent tongues. It had zealously riffled through maybe a ton of people's private papers. All Jimmy Walker had was his charm.[6]

Finally the mayor appeared, dressed in blue from head to toe. An elderly woman sprang from the crowd and threw her arms around him; others reached out to touch him. And finally Walker took the stand. "Don't look him straight in the eye," a friend had warned Seabury, and indeed he stood at Walker's side when he interrogated him. Walker outpointed Seabury in showmanship. He ridiculed the ponderous questions and deftly parried damaging queries with tears, humor, and indignation. When all else failed he charged that the Communists were after him. But like Lady Macbeth's damned spot, Walker could not erase his "beneficences." He shared secret accounts with a $3000-a-year accountant who managed to fill these accounts with a million dollars harvested during Walker's mayoralty. These gratuities came from individuals who had business dealings with the city. The evidence was circumstantial but persuasive; still, a divided joint committee refused to call for Walker's removal.

Seabury went out on a limb. Acting as a private citizen, he sent the governor his report on June 8, 1932, detailing Walker's "gross improprieties" and appending a list of fifteen specific accusations. Then he threw the entire issue in Roosevelt's lap by failing to make a recommendation and leaving it up to the governor to decide whether Walker was fit to continue to serve as mayor.

The drama took a break as New York Democrats took off for Chicago at this juncture to nominate a presidential candidate to oppose Herbert Hoover. In an act of courage, folly, or sheer spleen, Walker declared for Al Smith ("good old Jimsie!" exclaimed Smith. "Blood is thicker than water"). For a brief moment Seabury actually took his own candidacy seriously, leading to hard feelings between the investigator and the governor, but Franklin D. Roosevelt came back from the convention a presidential candidate with a decision to make. Whither Jimmy?[7]

For three weeks in late summer the scene shifted to a cherry-paneled hearing office at the governor's mansion in Albany. Seabury, Walker, and Roosevelt joined to bring the drama to its conclusion. Delaying the start of his presidential campaign, FDR would listen to the charges, to Walker's defense and decide whether to remove him from office. "The old gay mayor ain't what he used to be," cracked a columnist. Walker even brought his wife, Allie, in a staged show of domestic cheer. FDR was tough and impartial, in full command of the process, exclaiming about Walker's beneficence from Paul Block: "The most extraordinary business proposition I ever heard of." Roosevelt was leaning toward removal after weeks of Walker's determined evasions, and Jimmy knew it. "I think Roosevelt is going to remove me," Walker fretted to a friend on September 1.

W. C. Fields had once told Walker that "a juggler fears the day when he will miss not one trick but *all* of them." This was the day. Al Smith turned to his longtime colleague and sadly delivered his own judgment. "Jim, you're through. You must resign for the good of the party." That night James J. Walker addressed an official message to the city clerk: "I hereby resign as Mayor of the City of New York, the same to take effect immediately." Caught between May and December, the fifty-one-year-old mayor's song and dance was over. To Judge Seabury, who had managed the most intensive investigation of municipal politics in the city's history, Walker's resignation marked the beginning of a new era. "The elimination of Mr. Walker as Mayor is a distinct victory for higher standards of public life. . . ."[8]

———

For a year and a half Seabury had played the role of Tammany biographer with rare virtuosity. Every day brought another revelation, some new indictment, or new trial. He masterfully riveted the city's attention to a problem it had too long ignored: New York's leaders reserved their most imaginative strategies for defrauding the government they were pledged to serve. And the municipal authority was as inefficient as it was corrupt, wasting as much as it stole, managing to destroy the credit of the richest city in the nation. In the smallest and the largest points it was a city without intelligence. It polluted its bathing beaches with raw sewage. It hired lifeguards who could not swim. It spent unconscionable sums to construct piers that were inaccessible. It paid cost-plus for many of its purchases, the plus representing assorted payments to line official pockets. And it jailed innocent girls to force their parents to bail them out before judges who were literally the best that money could buy.

What it was supposed to do it did poorly or not at all, providing services haphazardly and taking little responsibility for the massive relief needs of its people. What it did well it did exceedingly well, but unfortunately this meant taking bribes, selling official favors, corrupting politics, and leaving New Yorkers vulnerable to an assortment of bloodless racketeers. So well, in fact, was this accomplished that after all the investigations were over not a single major political figure was jailed. If nothing else, the methods of honest graft, trading insider information, making cash payoffs, selling political influence under the guise of legal fees, disguising bribes, short-circuiting paper trails, and making evidence vanish had been artfully perfected.

So pervasive was the perception of graft that many city employees thought that they could only secure a promotion by making payoffs. Con men shook down ambitious policemen, who paid $600 and more to secure a sergeant's badge. The city's licensing process, created to guarantee some control over pushcarts and newsstands, led to the disgrace of blind men and disabled veterans being shaken down for $1000 to $7000 for the certificates. Licenses for plumbers, stationary engineers, and motion picture operators all required payoffs under the table.

What Lord Bryce had called the "august dynasty of the bosses" had systematically sacked the city, entrenching a politics of selfishness. Individuals went into government with their eyes wide open, calculating their incomes on the basis of salary plus a great deal more. This government, in which every man had his price, had destroyed the delicate fabric of civic virtue that underlies all good government.[9]

---

2. "I Promise You Will Never Regret This"

FOLLOWING Walker's forced abdication from office, Joseph V. McKee, the president of the Board of Aldermen, became acting mayor. The handsome Bronx-born son of Scotch immigrants, McKee was a devout Catholic ("Holy Joe," his colleagues called him) who had taught in the New York City schools, published several articles, collaborated on a history textbook, and boasted a Fordham law degree. After his election to the State Assembly in 1918, the Citizens Union pronounced the twenty-nine-year-old freshman an "alert recruit who did himself and his constituency credit." McKee rose rapidly with the backing of Democratic leader Ed Flynn. In his first citywide race, in 1925, for the aldermanic presidency, McKee drew almost as many votes as Walker did for mayor. By 1929 he attracted even more votes than the then fabulously popular mayor.[10]

Touted as a representative of the "new Tammany," McKee exerted a brisk, no-nonsense authority over the Board of Aldermen. He developed plans to modernize the city's mass transportation, hospitals and bridges and spoke with an engaging sensitivity about municipal responsibility: "Out of the depression has come more than pain and suffering and the loss of material things; . . . We are . . . evolving a new feeling and finer realization of our communal obligations." His conservative personal habits, grasp of entangled city finances, and disciplined leadership contrasted with his discredited predecessor. Happily married, without the burden of Walker's life-style and administrative slovenliness, he directed the city with authority, impressing even reformers with his seriousness and independence.[11]

The Democratic bosses, fearing that McKee was too close to Bronx boss Edward J. Flynn (who had broken with the machine to endorse Franklin Roosevelt for the presidency despite his role in the Walker hearings), conspired to pull the rug out from under him by demanding an election to fill Walker's unexpired term. McKee countered with a suit to keep his office until the next regularly scheduled mayoral election in November 1933. On September 9, 1932, the courts found in his favor. The next day Tammany appealed the decision, and in October the court of appeals reversed the lower court, resulting in a one-month campaign for the remaining year of Walker's term. Tammany dumped McKee and backed surrogate court justice John P. O'Brien as the regular Democratic candidate. The judge, a huge man with a prominent brow, large jaw, and protruding lip, was less experienced in municipal administration than McKee, and far less bright. He had been an organization loyalist for thirty years; he was a devoted Catholic and family man who made boring speeches about religious morality. He would do.[12]

Meanwhile, a raft of good government committees cast about for mayoral possibilities. These anti-Tammany forces—the City Club, City Affairs Committee, Citizens Union, Citizens Budget Committee, Women's City Club, United Neighborhood Houses, and assorted committees of ten, seventeen, and one thousand—wanted to make a contest of it, but in the brief time available they could not lift a campaign off the ground. Every candidate to whom they offered the nomination refused it. Only one candidate could effectively bring together the diverse groups on such short notice, but Samuel Seabury refused to run. Nor did anyone think that there was much hope for anyone opposing the Democratic ticket in this year of FDR. Better to gather forces and plan for 1933. The Republicans nominated an elderly gentleman, Lewis Pounds, who proceeded to lose by the predicted margin of more than half a million votes.

Still, Tammany could take little satisfaction from the returns. The *World Telegram* had asked New Yorkers to write in Joseph McKee's name as a protest, and although the former acting mayor did not campaign and his name did not appear on the ballot, more than a quarter million New Yorkers penciled his name in. His appeal was even more widespread. Tens of thousands of voters wrote in such versions as Okee and McKoo, and even McKee in Yiddish. Their ballots were disqualified, but clearly the machine was vincible.[13]

The same Democratic landslide that swept John P. O'Brien into the mayoralty forced Fiorello La Guardia's retirement from Congress. He brooded, telling friends he was through with politics. He would practice law, teach, write a book. While still in Congress he had written a short novel, which he now sent to publishers. Grenville Vernon of the Dial Press encouraged La Guardia after reading the manuscript of "Tony Goes to Washington," burbling that the superficial tale of a progressive Italian legislator in Washington "hits me as an idea between the eyes." On the margin of this letter La Guardia already began to calculate royalties, but with his defeat, interest waned.[14]

La Guardia took a position as an impartial arbitrator for the Associated Dress Industries of America, spending three days a week at his office and the rest at home writing magazine pieces. But he was unhappy. The Seabury revelations proved many of the charges he had leveled against Walker in 1929. "It is widely recognized . . . that your campaign begat the Seabury Inquiry," William H. Allen, director of the Institute for Public Service, wrote La Guardia. And the *New York Times* suggested that La Guardia was the only one with the right "to stand up in New York City today and say 'I told you so.' " All of this, however, meant very little. More than to be proven right he wanted to be back in politics. He wanted to be mayor.[15]

Shortly after his congressional defeat in 1932, La Guardia invited reformers, civic leaders, and all those interested in combating corruption to a meeting at Manhattan's Town Hall, where he delivered an impassioned attack on boss politics. He called for a "sincere Fusion movement" to reclaim city politics from the machine. He was available. But while fusion was clearly the idea of the moment and Republican state chairman W. Kingsland Macy asked former governor Charles Whitman to work with reformers and anti-Tammany Democrats to seek an acceptable fusion candidate, La Guardia was not high on any lists.[16]

Few denied La Guardia's commitment to fair government or his documented ability to bloody Tammany, but reformers feared his unpredictable politics, his loud mouth, and the crude style that had made him the number one reform roughneck in New York politics. There was also the matter of pedigree. Reformers viewed La Guardia as "Half Wop, Half American, Half Republican," said Fiorello's friend Edward Corsi, and they wanted full breeds. Moreover, it was widely believed that Republicans were looking for an independent Democrat to support, someone like McKee.[17]

News of Republican support for McKee made La Guardia more than a little irascible. When insurgent Republicans asked him to join their revolt against Old Guard leader Samuel Koenig, La Guardia snapped that he was not interested in reforming the Republican party. He was prepared to trade support for help with his candidacy, but he was not giving anything away. Instead, he pressed his own cause on radio, before civic organizations, with various reform clubs, to any group that would listen. But he could not dislodge McKee. Early in April La Guardia bowed to reality and agreed to back McKee if he declared his fusion candidacy before May.[18]

On May 3 McKee startled fusionists with a bombshell announcement, withdrawing from the race in order to pursue a private career in banking. La Guardia could hardly contain himself. He lectured moping reformers to pick up their chins and look around; surely the hopes of millions of New Yorkers need not "be deflated because one individual has voluntarily removed himself from the fight." He joined other reformers in a pro forma bid to Al Smith, but Fiorello did not expect the former presidential contender to run for city hall. So he advised that if Smith could not be had, he was available.[19]

But few were interested in him. The nominating coalition approached Seabury. Fiorello endorsed the impossible candidacy, meanwhile releasing an eight-point program that might serve as a fusion platform. After a parade of candidates were boomed in the press one day only to be shot down the next, La Guardia continued with his own plans. On May 21 he appeared before Dr. C. F. Reisner's Broadway Temple of Applied Christianity to speak sensitively on the needs of "The American Boy," proposing a balanced progressive agenda of child labor laws, slum clearance, school lunches, and more playgrounds to protect the sweet "democracy of child-hood." At Yale University he delivered a thoughtful address on labor legislation, and he spoke about financial reporting at the Columbia School of Journalism. In another address he denounced the rise of Hitler, leaving no doubt with each of these well-reported appearances that he was running hard for the mayoralty.[20]

Roosevelt brain truster Adolph Berle, committed to a La Guardia candidacy, helped with several important introductions, first to Samuel Seabury. ("Tell me," Seabury asked of Berle, "You're in the new national administration. What do they think of the candidates for mayor?" Berle assured him that La Guardia was a valued New Dealer). Next, Berle brought Fiorello before reform's first circle, and finally to the *éminence grise* of anti-Tammany reform, seventy-five-year-old Charles Culp Burlingham. When Newbold Morris, another of the socialite Republican reformers, met La Guardia, he was completely won over and invited La Guardia to speak before his upper-crust Republican club. These were the men and women who looked upon the Little Flower as a proletarian rabble-rouser of alien sympathies, the ones who had assured his defeat by withholding support in 1929.[21]

The evening did not begin well. The punctilious crowd had begun to shift in their seats when the speaker rushed in ten minutes late and strode to the podium. The huge audience expected a night of excessive language delivered in an undis-ciplined soprano. Instead, they had to strain to catch the opening explanation for the guest's tardiness. "I apologize for being late. Marie, my wife, sent my suit out to be pressed and it didn't come back until a few minutes ago. I couldn't leave the house until it was returned." The line went over well. A poor politician couldn't be all bad. The next one won them over. "I'm very proud to be here tonight. But I don't know whether you ladies and gentlemen have decided to admit me to the social register, or whether you just wanted to go slumming with me." His words on Tammany corruption and his prescription for a modern, honest, and caring New York drew a standing ovation. Then he modestly proposed Samuel Seabury for the mayoralty. La Guardia knew that Seabury was no more interested now than he had been before, but his good form impressed the crowd.[22]

While La Guardia went about making friends, Vito Marcantonio whipped the

Ghibboni into an instrument of Fiorello's ambition, sending them around the city to collect petitions, which were sent to Seabury. But the Fusion Conference Committee refused to be persuaded, passing the nomination around to anyone but Fiorello. These fusionists valued respectability more than anything: "I want to defeat Tammany," Sally Peters wrote to Richard Welling, a fusion lawyer who had devoted his life to causes, "but I feel . . . that a crude, brawling loud-mouthed person like La Guardia is the surest way to defeat that end."[23]

The nomination was becoming ragged from the many hands through which it passed. Raymond Ingersoll, a wealthy social worker who had served as Al Smith's campaign manager in 1924, was not healthy enough for a campaign; Richard C. Patterson, Jr., a broadcast executive refused for career reasons; Nathan Straus, Jr., feared that in the aroused atmosphere of the thirties his candidacy would bring one Jew too many into political office (New York's governor, Herbert Lehman, was Jewish). Other names included John D. Rockefeller, Jr., John H. Hylan, Samuel Untermyer, Langdon Post, and Bainbridge Colby. In all, the committee sounded out more than a dozen men, and each turned them down. La Guardia would meet Maurice P. Davidson, one of the committee regulars, and ask, "How are you getting on? . . . Well who's your latest mayor?" At Davidson's mention of some name, Fiorello would jump up and down and pound his fist. "Well there's only one man going to be the candidate, and I'm the man. I'm going to run. I want to be mayor." More than any candidate, La Guardia wanted to be mayor, and the desperation and intensity of that desire was becoming clear. Nothing would be allowed to stand in the way of that candidacy, even the cause of reform itself. It was a game of he who dares wins, and La Guardia was telling the fusion power brokers that La Guardia dared.[24]

"He wanted the nomination, . . ." Davidson recalled. "Nobody else wanted it! They were afraid of it—afraid of being licked, afraid they couldn't carry it through. But . . . he wanted it!" But he could not get it on his own, and the one man who could get it for him, The Bishop, as Samuel Seabury's friends had taken to calling the great investigator (behind his back), had not yet decided on whom he would support.[25]

Meanwhile the Fusion Committee finally decided that they wanted Robert Moses, the brilliant and phenomenally effective state parks commissioner. Moses' reform roots were familiar to many fusionists and they trusted him far more than La Guardia. He had fought for many of their issues, held a large view of political possibility, and boasted a daunting record of getting things done, quickly, cleanly, and on cost; and he was closely connected with the one Tammany politician whom reformers could respect, Al Smith. But Seabury had clashed with Moses in 1932 over charter reform. He also feared that Moses' close relationship with Smith would make a fusion victory ambiguous. Tammany would still hang on, for certainly Smith's patronage requests would be honored and his counsel followed. Not for this had he stalked the Tiger. Seabury, the beau ideal of fusion (columnist Heywood

241

Broun wrote, "I would have my son know Seabury instead of Cicero"), did not want Moses, and fusion needed Seabury.[26]

But if not Moses, then who? Seabury finally decided on La Guardia. He could get along with the peppery insurgent and respected his considerable political experience. La Guardia's Washington career, constituent service, and experience as president of the Board of Aldermen made him the best prepared of the candidates. He was honest, cared deeply about the city, and would dramatize the fight against Tammany. For all his cockiness and temper, he could meet the challenge of making the municipal government honest and the city modern. But every time Seabury suggested La Guardia the name was greeted with open hostility.

On July 26, Joseph M. Price, a wealthy dress manufacturer and chairman of the City Club Board of Trustees, polled the committee by phone, counting eighteen votes for Moses and five for La Guardia. He argued for nominating Moses and presenting The Bishop with a *fait accompli*. Many of the members agreed and directed Price to draw up the announcement. The next day Seabury met Maurice Davidson for lunch, just three hours before the Moses nomination was to be released to the press. Presented with the committee's decision, the dignified Seabury turned livid. He slammed the table at the Bankers Club so hard that dishes rattled and the room turned still. "You sold out to Tammany Hall," Seabury cried. "You sold out the movement to Tammany Hall." Davidson chased after the departing Seabury, who refused to be mollified. "You sold out. Good-bye."

Seabury strode back to his office and denounced the choice to the press as a sellout, warning that he reserved "all personal liberty of action." He would not accept Moses, under any circumstances, hinting that he might oppose this ticket with another candidate. Meanwhile, Moses was meeting with Smith, who despite his high personal regard for him told Moses that he would not support him against the Democrats. Between Seabury's opposition and Smith's rejection, Moses saw only a greatly complicated campaign. He called Price to withdraw.[27]

The reformers, still bent on avoiding La Guardia, looked for fresh faces. Henry Bruere, cofounder of the Bureau of Municipal Research, alumnus of the last fusion administration, and president of the Bowery Savings Bank, stated the new position. "We have a population now quite different . . . with millions of women, flappers and young City College philosophers excercising an influence based upon cynicism regarding the morals of the politicians. . . . Isn't there some real fellow who could be got for the job with the least possible political experience?"[28]

Charles Whitman, the man whom Seabury opposed in the 1916 gubernatorial election and the chairman of the Republican mayoral nominating committee, and one of La Guardia's chief detractors ("He hated anybody of *that* type," recalled La Guardia advisor Paul Windels), proposed just such a candidate, General John F. O'Ryan, vice chairman of the City Fusion party. O'Ryan, a distinguished lawyer, had little political experience beyond a stint on the City Transit Commission. O'Ryan's fresh presence appealed to some, but Seabury, now bent on La Guardia, insisted on someone who could lead a reform crusade and pin Tammany's ears back, someone who would make a lasting influence on city politics. Seabury had not been so politically aroused since his days with Henry George. He dropped his judicial reserve. In bold letters on its front page the *Herald Tribune* proclaimed: SEABURY TELLS ORYAN HE CANT WIN.[29]

Now it was O'Ryan who was characterized as a front for the machine, as Seabury joined La Guardia in threatening to split the party if the nomination went to another. "What a pity it is about Seabury," muttered R. Fulton Cutting, former head of the Citizens Union and another of the fusion elite. "I do not understand how La Guardia can have captured him." The explanation is simple. Seabury had concluded that O'Ryan's narrow coalition of mostly Republicans could not assure victory and that the general could not stop La Guardia in a primary. While the committee held back its final decision, trying to bring Seabury around, La Guardia, in his best Olympian tones, announced that the "issue is between the judgment, sincerity, vision, unselfishness of Mr. Charles Whitman and Judge Samuel Seabury." The real issue was who would survive this battle strong enough to carry the day.[30]

Like Moses, O'Ryan understood that a fusion nomination without Seabury was an empty honor. Hurt by the judge's strong opposition, he began to reconsider his candidacy. On August 2 the various fusion groups formed a "harmony committee" chaired by the grand old man of good government, C. C. Burlingham. "It is unseemly that an old codger like me should be going through all these motions which belong to youth," he wrote an associate, but Burlingham would work with the energy of a thirty-year-old for the next few weeks to pull fusion forces together.

C.C. was, like Seabury, a minister's son. Educated at Harvard and Columbia, he became a respected specialist in what he called "the close preserve" of admiralty law. One of his noted cases involved defending the owners of the *Titanic* from liability. Twice elected president of the New York Bar and showered with honorary degrees from the most prestigious schools, he succeeded such notables as J. P. Morgan and George Wickersham as senior warden of St. George's Protestant Episcopal Church. Representing the best of New York's best men, the tall, slightly stooped CCB addressed presidents and governors in familiar terms and was recognized as the power behind every reform mayor in Greater New York's history. He still had the gift, as Robert Caro writes, "of making men forget their differences and remember their common cause."[31]

With feeling among the various elements running high and the real possibility that the entire fusion idea might collapse, Burlingham went to work. Kenneth Dayton telegraphed Burlingham in desperation about The Bishop. "CAN'T ANYONE MAKE HIM SEE NEED OF TEAMPLAY AND SURRENDER HIS OWN VIEWS." Burlingham was too old a hand to try to move a determined Seabury; there were other ways. On the same day that he took the chairmanship of the harmony committee, Burlingham wrote a private note to the chief editorial writer of the *Herald Tribune*, the most influential Republican newspaper in the country, offering "a suggestion or two" before the journal expressed its opinion on "the fusionist mess." He thought that Republicans should reject the Whitman committee's proposal of O'Ryan and join the fusion harmony group to chart a course out of the impasse. "I think the H[erald] T[ribune] is in a position to affect that committee by its statement."

Next morning's editorial, "Let's Fuse," repeated many of Burlingham's points and concluded by calling for Charles Whitman to step aside "with his candidate" and for the Republicans to form a new subcommittee to confer with the fusion harmony committee headed by Burlingham.[32]

La Guardia feared that he too would be asked to withdraw like O'Ryan to make way for a fresh name. That was the way these genteel folk made compromises. "Why is it," he complained to Berle, "that every time you get to a point where you can do some good the *nice people* move in and block you? That's what drives a man like me to be a demagogue, smacking into things." Close to desperation, La Guardia feared that he had been compromised out of consideration.

Berle reassured him that he still had his support and that of both Seabury and Burlingham.[33]

On August 3 the Republican Mayoralty Committee met to make its decision. Chairman Charles Whitman held fast behind O'Ryan. But Vito Marcantonio and Ed Corsi, supported by Stanley Isaacs and Charles Tuttle, stymied Whitman. The meeting ended inconclusively, and both Tuttle and Republican state chairman W. Kingsland Macy dashed off for a meeting of C. C. Burlingham's harmony group at six that evening at the Bar Association. This meeting had to produce a candidate before the whole effort unraveled. Seabury was asked to run. He refused. Price again proposed Moses. Others pushed O'Ryan, who had support among many of those in attendance. Seabury remained adamant. He kept popping up to announce that he would not work with O'Ryan. Burlingham shocked the younger confreres when he finally shouted at Seabury, "Sit down, Sam, sit down!" though it is unclear whether the notion of ordering The Bishop into his chair or addressing him with such familiarity was the greater surprise. Another voice screamed, "If it's La Guardia or bust, I say bust."

By midnight, nerves frazzled and defenses worn down, the committee reached its conclusion. Options were as clear as they were limited; Seabury would stand by his choice. The price of harmony was La Guardia. Berle, whose close relationship with the White House was well known, told the group that in 1933 when he was sent to Washington to develop a law to protect stockholders, he had worked with La Guardia and he respected him. "Now a man like that is needed to clean up the New York situation."[34]

Faced with deadlock, O'Ryan withdrew, throwing his support to La Guardia. And when the game was done, no one was left but the chunky former congressman from East Harlem. Seabury called La Guardia at home with the good news. "I promise you faithfully you will never regret this," the nominee assured The Bishop.

The next day, Seabury released a statement praising La Guardia's selection as New Yorkers' ''opportunity to express their indignation and disgust with Tammany Hall and its methods, by the election of an honest, fearless and capable anti-Tammany mayor . . . who will put an end to the squandering and wasting of the people's money . . . and restore it to unemployment relief, schools, hospitals, and the other purposes for which it was intended.''

Burlingham wrote with more reserve to Bailey Burritt: "La G. is okay, and I can prove it. We got down nearly to the bottom of the barrel and he was the best there. . . . It was a mad business.''[35]

---

3. The Election of 1933

FIORELLO La Guardia lived to the age of sixty-five. If he had died at fifty-one, it would have been as a defeated man with only a fraction of his ambitions achieved. Since 1921 he had actively coveted the mayoralty, a job he considered second only to the presidency in significance. Now it was a mere matter of campaigning. The contest would be in the classic La Guardia style: liberal in principle, studded with strident ethnic appeals, and scaffolded by an exquisitely diverse coalition of New Yorkers.

Fusion selected a distinctive four-leaf-clover emblem, set up headquarters at the Paramount Building on Times Square, and fashioned the first New York ticket balanced with Italian, Irish, Jewish, and WASP candidates. For comptroller they selected *Croix de Guerre*-decorated Major W. Arthur Cunningham from Queens. Forty-nine-year-old Bernard S. Deutsch, former president of the Bronx County Bar Association and president of the American Jewish Congress, ran for president of the Board of Aldermen. Jacob Gould Schurman, Jr., the token upper cruster, was the nominee for district attorney. Candidates for borough president were chosen with equal care: Reform Democrat Langdon Post for Manhattan; Raymond Ingersoll, cofounder of the City Fusion party for Brooklyn; George U. Harvey, born in Galway, Ireland, for Queens; Charles Barry, New York University professor of government, for the Bronx; and Staten Island-born secret service agent Joseph A. Palma for the borough presidency of Richmond.[36]

Burlingham, Seabury, Berle, and *World Telegram* publisher Roy Howard, together with Paul Windels and fusion veteran William M. Chadbourne, formed La Guardia's campaign brain trust. Over eggs and coffee, and sometimes joined by Walter Lippmann, Kingsland Macy, and Maurice Davidson, this group hammered out the fusion strategy and attracted a clutch of good-government types to the effort. General O'Ryan signaled his satisfaction with La Guardia by accepting an important post in the campaign, and fusion seemed launched on a harmonious path. While Burlingham complained to Felix Frankfurter about Chadbourne, that "WMC's little gray cells have been washed out. . . . his thoughts are . . . unrelated and unsequential," the group generally got along well and proved an important steadying influence on their mercurial candidate.[37]

The Democrats renominated cherubic sixty-year-old John Patrick O'Brien, characterized by Alva Johnson as belonging to the "Organization's upper ten percent in character and upper fifty per cent in ability." Facing some of the largest problems in the city's history, he had sought to muddle through. Other mayors had done no better, but the times demanded more. Moreover, the press did O'Brien the disservice, as Arthur Mann writes, "of quoting him accurately." To a ladies club he remarked: "During the week I have momentous matters to attend to. I must meet great people and I must go here and there to make up the addenda that goes with being Mayor of the City. Therefore, when I come here . . . and see before me flowers and buds, ladies, girls, and widows, emotion is just running riot with me." His careening syntax was matched by a generous disposition for foot in mouth. Before a Jewish audience he spoke reverently about that "scientist of scientists, Albert Weinstein." He announced to a black group that Harlem was the "garden spot of New York," and told a gathering of Greek Americans that he had excelled in college in translating that "great Greek poet, Horace." The errors were less important for their indication that the man had his facts balled up than for the fact that he failed so pitiably every time he tried to sound knowledgeable.[38]

O'Brien was not an idiot. He was a kindly, likable man, intelligent and even witty in private company. He cleared out some redundant city offices, streamlined the Sanitation Commission, and consolidated several municipal agencies, but he did nothing to clean out the city's patronage nest, and he so closely fit the caricature of the fatuous Tammany politician that few took him seriously. He wanted to be a journalist, he declared to the city hall press corps, again reaching for approval through extravagant praise, "because I love the classics and I love good literature," which he presumably read in the newspapers. Work for Tammany Hall, he instructed New York's young men and women because—and here one must remember that O'Brien came into office behind a trail of tin boxes and starving McQuades— because "Reward will come." While his supporters were denying that he was a creature of Tammany Hall, a reporter asked whom he intended to appoint police commissioner. The mayor blurted, "I don't know. I haven't got the word yet."[39]

On September 19 the Democratic primary handed Tammany's "wooden Indian" the mayoral designation, but the returns were anything but heartening for the bosses. A sample of virtual unknowns polled more than 130,000 protest votes, and the voters defeated Tammany's candidate for comptroller while toppling three district leaders. Early in September oddsmakers had laid two to one against La

Guardia, but by the end of the month fusion pulled ahead in the polls. La Guardia was ecstatic.[40]

It was all premature. The day after the Democratic primary Bronx boss and New Deal adviser Ed Flynn journeyed to Washington for a meeting with the president and Postmaster General James Farley. Roosevelt feared that a Democratic defeat in New York would strengthen the local Republican party, threatening Democratic Governor Herbert Lehman's chances in 1934 and clouding the president's own reelection prospects in 1936. At the same time, FDR wanted to reduce Tammany's local control and expand his own influence with New York City Democrats. O'Brien's candidacy presented FDR Democrats with two disagreeable possibilities: If O'Brien lost, patronage and power passed to fusion; if he won, it stayed with Tammany. The three plotted a new option. Recalled Flynn, "He [Roosevelt] asked me to urge McKee to become a candidate for Mayor." Flynn returned to New York to coax McKee back into politics with assurances of White House support and a full campaign chest.[41]

As McKee pondered his next move, the *World Telegram*, which had promised to support him in the early months of 1933, warned against a belated candidacy: "We would gladly have gone with Mr. McKee through the main gate. But we cannot condone . . . the present effort to boost him over the back fence," wrote Roy Howard. "You did not want to make this fight in August, when it looked tough," he added. "You will not attempt to chisel in on the fight in September when it looks soft."[42]

Well yes, in fact, he would. Reformers, disillusioned with O'Brien and unhappy with La Guardia, encouraged McKee, recalling one pundit's observation that any Democrat personally honest and able to walk without tripping over his tongue looked like a miracle of nature compared with the rest of Tammany. McKee put together a respectable ticket balanced for Irish, Italian, and Jewish representation and declared his availability. While the White House's position in all of this remained hidden, businessmen, anti-Tammany Democrats, and disaffected Republicans flocked to the new candidate, changing the race from an incipient rout to a heated three-cornered contest. Earlier, the simple strategy of tarring O'Brien with Tammany and feathering him with his own quotes had seemed an adequate campaign strategy for La Guardia. McKee's entry threw these plans into turmoil. It also saddled fusion with a severely depressed La Guardia.[43]

The turn of events badly shook Fiorello. The roller coaster of the past year, which had brought him from a startling congressional defeat to a roughly contested Fusion nomination and what seemed like a simple campaign against Tammany, was going swiftly downward again. He could not shake his depression until he was able to come up with a rationale against McKee. First he persuaded himself that McKee was not independent. He was Flynn's boy. And he had not run in the primaries. Fiorello would ignore the bumbling O'Brien and attack McKee as a paler shade of Tammany. Presented in the excessive rhetoric of political campaigns, this became the line against McKee. Elect the man from the Bronx and the "tin box brigade" would march back to power, with Ed Flynn pulling the strings this time.

The threat of a real contest also forced La Guardia to define a program. Promising honest government with intelligence was no longer enough to get elected. The press of a real contest sharpened his own thinking on the city. In a dozen or more appearances a day, frequently with Seabury at his side, he crisscrossed the city promising a government with a heart. "We want . . . to make our city . . . a great big beautiful, kind New York." He bundled his programs into a progressive urban agenda, calling for adequate relief, transit unification, slum clearance, low-cost public housing, and a modern charter. And he pledged a municipal civil service based on excellence, not spoils. "On January 1, when I enter City Hall," he announced, "I go out of politics for four years." He had no intention of being a good fellow, he warned repeatedly, only a good mayor. "La Guardia, with his social progressivism, could make out of New York a gigantic laboratory for civic reconstruction," wrote a clearly impressed *Nation* magazine.[44]

Encouraged by such support and reassured by his own line of attack against McKee, La Guardia resumed a frenzied campaign schedule. Delivering four speeches to each of his opponents' one, arms flung akimbo, rumpled double-breasted jacket flying ("Do not appear in public to speak before anybody," a distraught adviser implored after seeing a picture of him in the newspaper, "unless you are dressed in a suit that has been pressed that day"), shirt unbuttoned, tie askew, hair dropping over his brow, and his voice at its highest screech, Fiorello tore into the opposition. "He was a magnificent campaigner," C. C. Burlingham recalled with admiration. He would come to the hall where he was scheduled to speak, but he would not go on immediately. First he would stand unseen, behind a curtain or a post, listening to the crowd. Then after two or three minutes he would go on. "He got something from that before he started." Burlingham marveled at his ability to capture the spirit of the crowd and incorporate it into his talk.[45]

With McKee speaking about the need for structural reform, La Guardia emphasizing expanded social services, and O'Brien providing comic relief, the campaign became a real contest. More than 2.3 million New Yorkers registered to vote, the highest figure in a nonpresidential election in history. McKee, catching the campaign spirit, attacked La Guardia as an unprincipled demagogue, "a communist at heart," a volatile, ambitious, dangerous, man, a liege of "boss" Seabury. Unfortunately for McKee, his criticism seldom rose above name-calling to a sustained argument against La Guardia's policies. One day he denounced the Little Flower as a Red for advocating American recognition of the USSR. The very next day he called him a tool of the conservatives, an enemy of the New Deal.[46]

This last point Berle and Seabury contested at the highest levels. On September 24 Berle, aware of talk at the White House about supporting McKee, telegraphed the President:

Joe McKee is telephoning you tonight to confirm your part in the following arrangement: Joe had been promised by Ed Flynn that if he will run for mayor . . . you will furnish enough patronage to buy Tammany leaders sufficient to assure election. . . . All of us feel strongly you ought to stop this unauthorized use of your name and prestige in a situation which can result in nothing but harm to you with probable effect of exchanging a premier moral position for reputation of second grade politician. [Roy] Howard puts it even more strongly. Better . . . steer clear of being in the position of rehabilitating Tammany.

A month later Berle complained that McKee was claiming White House support again. This time Berle demanded reassurances that Roosevelt would stay out of the race and he got them. This achieved, the campaign turned to fighting the opposition. Samuel Seabury attacked McKee as the "pliant, subservient and vacillating tool" of the "sinister" Bronx bosses, ridiculing his claim to New Deal support as a sign of Tammany duplicity.[47]

It was, of course, Roosevelt who was playing the cynical game. McKee had entered the race only after White House assurances—"They really twisted McKee's arm," recalled Paul Windels—but Roosevelt either never intended to go public with his support or caved in to Berle and the other fusionists, and in Windels's words, "ran out on the promise." Meanwhile, Flynn's increasingly panicky calls for White House support met only artful evasions.[48]

With the issue of presidential endorsement laid to rest, the campaign barely resumed its high ground before stumbling again, this time on an exchange of specious charges keyed to ethnic sensitivities. Past master at ethnic politics, La Guardia appealed to Italian, Jewish, and Irish groups, each on their own terms. He promised special consideration to Puerto Ricans, Norwegians, Turks, Croats, and all the long list of New York nationality groups in the earnest tones reserved for campaigns. During one trip through Harlem he ran into a church during services long enough to shout: "Peace, Father Divine, peace be with you all! I say, Father Divine, no matter what you want, I will support you. I am going to clean up this city. And I come here tonight to ask Father Divine's help and counsel." Then he sped off to another appearance. The old pro had it over the bosses. He could campaign in five languages and on a hundred ancestral hatreds. Robert Moses recalled that "in exploiting racial and religious prejudices La Guardia could run circles around the bosses he despised and derided. . . ."

Seabury too warmed to his assigned task as a campaigner, speaking on the stump with an abandon that he had not allowed himself as the Jovian investigator. When thirteen Brooklyn leaders came out for McKee, Seabury flung a muddy line with aplomb, calling the bolt the "parade of the tin box brigade." Paul Windels said of Seabury that the aristocratic barrister was "a great fellow when he got into a campaign to take a swipe at everybody he didn't like," and he did not like Governor Herbert Lehman, whom he planned to oppose in the 1934 gubernatorial election. He took the opportunity in one of his speeches to make a gratuitous attack on Lehman as a do-nothing governor who allowed the crooked Tammany men to control his party.[49]

Jewish voters, who represented more than one-quarter of the city's total, idolized Lehman, the first Jewish governor of the state. Jews were particularly sensitive in these years of spreading anti-Semitism, and La Guardia feared that Seabury's attack could backfire. "Judge, you're ruining me," he told Seabury in private. "Stop attacking Governor Lehman." McKee siezed the opportunity to make La Guardia even more uncomfortable, hinting that the patrician Seabury just could not tolerate the idea of a Jew in the State House. He challenged La Guardia to repudiate the wayward Saint of Fusion. McKee's challenge so shook La Guardia that he prepared a statement backing away from the man who had won the nomination for him.[50]

Paul Windels stopped Fiorello from issuing the statement. Since at least 1929, reformers knew that McKee had published an essay in a Catholic journal many years before that was said to criticize Jews. Now La Guardia's staff set out to find it. Democrats had long ago shredded all the copies they could lay their hands on, and it took a while to locate a copy in Washington. They finally found the article, written in 1915 when McKee was a young teacher. Published in the *Catholic World* magazine, the essay decried the wide practice among Catholic parents of withdrawing their children from school at an early age. By sending their children out to work, they were abandoning the future leadership of the city to the Jews, who accounted for only one-fourth of the city population but made up three-fourths of the high school student body. He feared the world that these Jews, who, he declared, were abandoning religious faith in favor of materialism and socialism, would make. "Surely," Holy Joe thundered, "we cannot look for ideal results from such material."[51]

With article in hand, La Guardia, who once told Joey Adams, "I invented the low blow," gleefully thrust back at McKee. "Are you trying to draw a red herring across the cowardly, contemptible and unjust attack that you have made and published against a great race so gloriously represented by our Governor?" Almost jumping for sheer joy, Fiorello closed by jousting, "Answer that, Mr. McKee, and think twice before sending me another telegram."[52]

It worked. Samuel Untermeyer, a wealthy McKee supporter, thought he detected a "reverberation of Hitler" in McKee's article and dropped the candidate cold. McKee explained lamely that the quotes were out of context. He had not attacked Judaism. His words represented the feelings of a religious man facing the decline of faith and his hopes for a more educated Catholic youth. Poor McKee could not defend himself; the language was unfortunate and sounded even more alarming in the bias-shaded thirties. He secured endorsements from Jewish friends but the bloom was off the rose. Many Jews resented being pulled back and forth by their deepest emotions, but they could not help it; the doubts had been shrewdly planted.[53]

Flynn pleaded again with Roosevelt for his support but it never came. With both Roosevelt and the anti-Semitism issues neutralized, Paul Windels collected endorsements from the powerful and respected. Robert Moses skewered the opposition. Consider, he urged the voters, the mayors that Tammany had sent to office: John Hylan, "the ranting Bozo of Bushwick"; Jimmy Walker, "half Beau Brummel, half guttersnipe"; and the latest, John O'Brien, "a winded bull in a municipal China shop." These men and dozens like them had destroyed good government, and the "pious fraud . . . Holy Joe McKee" promised more of "the most ruthless political and patronage machine this country has ever seen and one with exceedingly low standards." He endorsed La Guardia in ringing terms. "You have no strings on you. You are not engaged in an obscure struggle for the control of a rotten political machine. You are free to work for New York City. Go to it." It was an important endorsement—straight to the front pages—coming from a man known to be tough-minded, independent, and close to Al Smith.[54]

By the end of October La Guardia reached full stride. His talks were fresh and carefully documented, based on thorough research by former City Affairs Committee director Paul Blanshard, who now headed the fusion research team. Picking deftly through Tammany deals and budgets, painstakingly sifting through the civil service, Blanshard gathered new evidence on Tammany's continued baneful influence during the O'Brien administration. Only cash was in short supply. Toward the end of October most of the $180,000 that had been raised by the La Guardia campaign was spent. There was no money left for radio announcements or even posters. Large donors shied away. "The few Wall Street men who did give money," Burlingham wrote to Felix Frankfurter, "hid their names."[55]

Inspired volunteers compensated for the reticent fat cats. Young men and women, especially from the Jewish and Italian sections, many direct from Socialist or Reform clubs, pitched in, anxious to join a campaign of liberals, intellectuals, and reformers. Mature men like Louis Yavner and Stanley Kreutzer still recall, fifty years later, the singular thrill of the 1933 campaign, the La Guardia crusade. They knocked on doors, distributed literature, licked envelopes, helped with light research, spread the word through the neighborhoods, and, when necessary, were joined by the Ghibboni to clear streets, protect speakers, and retaliate against Tammany's dirty tricks, all in the name of bringing New York a just government. According to Edward Corsi and Ed Flynn, Italian gangsters (Corsi insists without Fiorello's knowledge) also pitched in to help place an Italian American in the mayor's office.[56]

The campaign reached its climax on the night of November 2. From a dozen sections of the city, thousands led by torch-bearing marchers converged on Madison Square Garden. Every seat in the Garden was filled and an estimated overflow of

50,000 clogged the surrounding streets. As Samuel Seabury came on stage, the fusion crowd jumped to its feet, stomping and whistling. The dignified Seabury smiled, adjusted his pince-nez and delivered a stem-winder, announcing: "The whole country looks to New York City to promote the cause of good government. The hour is ripe for action. I ask you . . . strike the blow that will make the city free." Finally, the candidate himself appeared. For ten minutes the Garden was in pandemonium. And he promised them victory.[57]

Walter Lippmann supported him. So did the *New York Times, Herald Tribune, World Telegram*, and *Evening Post*. The more popular newspapers with a far larger combined readership, the *Daily News, Daily Mirror, Evening Journal, American*, and *Sun*, fell in line behind McKee. John O'Brien, *hors de combat*, could not attract a single major journal.[58]

Tuesday, November 7, proved a busy day for the police. Democratic ruffians decked out in identical pearl-gray fedoras marched on polling booths to "assist" voters with their balloting. Bill Chadbourne protested to police that in Boss Albert Marinelli's district 200 unauthorized persons—he called them gangsters—upheld the Tammany cause; the agitated Chadbourne was arrested for disorderly conduct. Others complained of blackjacks, brass knuckles, and lead pipes in plain view. But La Guardia was ready. The veteran of half a dozen brawling campaigns against Tammany sent out the well-muscled "Fusioneers" to tame the Tiger.

The Little Flower went to the toughest precincts. On East 113th Street he barreled through the crowd, strode over to a bulky man with a Tammany badge. "You're a thug," he growled, tearing the badge off his lapel. "Now get out of here and keep away." He turned to the rest of the machine's election squad: "I know you. You're thugs. You get out of here and keep moving." The little man's fearlessness urged the others on. "These fellows are yellow," he told his lieutenants. "They're a lot of punks, and I'm going to run them out of the city." One day of his belligerent poll-watching left few doubts that he would do just that.[59]

La Guardia retired to Seabury's elegant East Sixty-third Street mansion to wait for the returns. Early in the night he was well ahead. By ten o'clock he walked over to Paramount Building headquarters, where the delirious crowds threatened to create an immediate leadership crisis by crushing the little man, until a police wedge finally got him through the mob intact. He stepped out onto the hotel marquee to address the cheering Times Square throng, but he could not be heard above the din. At Tammany headquarters on East Seventeenth Street, O'Brien, a gentleman to the end, came to sit with his supporters. At eleven o'clock he wrote his successor a note of congratulations and then, to show that his gift for sounding stupid had not failed him, turned to the reporters to say: "The man who takes over the City Hall will have an easier job. . . . I ironed out the worst problems."

La Guardia polled 868,522 votes; McKee 609,053; O'Brien, 586,672. If there was a consoling thought for those who hated him, it was that the Democrats had drawn the majority of the votes. They could also speculate that if McKee or O'Brien had withdrawn, La Guardia might have been defeated. But above all, they were left to ponder the implications of the election of New York's first fusion mayor since World War I.[60]

It was a stunning victory for one whose political obituary had been pronounced so unequivocally just a year before. After the victory Fiorello and Marie left for Panama for a vacation, leaving the postelection analysis to others. Actually the best analysis of the election was not completed until 1965, when Arthur Mann published *La Guardia Comes to Power*, a fine-grained study of the election returns. Mann disagreed with those who viewed the 1933 election as a mandate for fundamental social change. La Guardia did not attract strong support in the poorest sections, the ones with the large populations of unemployed. These poor remained hitched to the bosses. Either they did not understand better or they knew all too well that a benign and corrupt Tammany promised more immediate benefit than an honest administration committed to good and impartial government.

About half of La Guardia's votes came on the Republican line from comfortable New Yorkers convinced that La Guardia would bring efficiency, honesty, prudent financial management, and lower real estate taxes. He also attracted the votes of liberals and those who were fed up with Tammany's corrupt and archaic city government and its Irish-dominated spoils. Protestants, Jews, and Italians all supported him, but it was the Italians who swung the election with 80, 90, and in some districts even higher percentages of their vote. They had voted heavily for Tammany before. Poor O'Brien, in his own way, understood the importance of this community for Tammany. Repeatedly during the campaign he appeared in New York's Little Italies to remind Italian Americans of their traditional tie to the machine, but he was fighting an emotion that wrung Italians free from their traditional Democratic moorings. Exulted *Il Progresso* following the election: "Finally the greatest city in the world has an Italian Mayor. *Viva Il Nostro Fiorello La Guardia!*" For recognition, as symbol, to achieve entree, the ethnic group marched behind its own. It would not find it necessary perhaps ever again to vote with such decisive unanimity, but he was the first, and they wanted a first.[61]

A few days after the election C. C. Burlingham wrote Felix Frankfurter: "I know of no campaign which has cost so little, and the management was inefficient beyond words. It was almost impossible to find a Democrat of importance who would speak for us. We had no general committee of *stuffs*." All they had was a cause, La Guardia, and the Italians. From that combination, New York's ninety-ninth mayor and first to be drawn from among the "new immigrants" would alone have the opportunity to translate the election into more than victory.[62]

Fiorello H. La Guardia and the Making of Modern New York

For the first time in sixteen years the city awakes this morning to find its public destinies in the hands of new men filled with a fresh energy and a fresh sense of public responsibility. It is a new year so singular for this community as to be somewhat difficult to take it all in at once; its implications may prove so far-reaching in the lives of all residents of the city that no one would attempt to foresee them.

Herald Tribune,
"Passing of an Old Regime," January 1, 1934

CHAPTER 8

Now We Have a Mayor

---

1. "In This Administration, I'm the Majority"

A FEW minutes after midnight, January 1, 1934. The light snows offer a seasonal backdrop for merrymakers celebrating the New Year. Throngs of revelers spill out of theaters and restaurants onto the streets, momentarily reprieved from the sad business of unemployment and depression. With Prohibition just ended the exuberant crowd can make proper libations. Not in fifteen years has the Great White Way seen so tumultuous a celebration. They bury their fears in this night of beginnings. Ah, to be an optimist, or drunk, or both!

While the streets ring with the din of desperate merriment, an intimate group of Fiorello La Guardia's friends, including his loyal barber Cheech Giordano ("The Brahmins and the Wops," cracked one wag), gather soberly in Judge Samuel Seabury's leather-and-oak library. The stocky mayor-elect, wearing a dark business suit freshly pressed for the occasion, contrasts with the elegantly attired guests surrounding him. La Guardia in a tuxedo could best be compared to a besatined fireplug, but more than fashion sense dictates his choice of raiment. Among Seabury, Burlingham, Brahmins, and power brokers, Fiorello La Guardia wears the clothes of the common man.

In this elegant study Samuel Seabury had painstakingly plotted Tammany's biography. Now he looks on with satisfaction as Justice Philip J. McCook swears an unsmiling Fiorello H. La Guardia into office as New York's ninety-ninth mayor. La Guardia had ruled out a public inaugural as unseemly in hard times. No parades, no bands, no reviewing stands. "I never heard of a receiver taking possession of a business with a brass band," he tells a news reporter. The ceremony is carried out without the use of a Bible, prompting the newspaper of record to check with the rector of St. Edmund's Episcopal Church before reassuring its readers that this omission does not offend the reverend clergy.[1]

257

As if La Guardia cares. He believes that the clergy, like the political bosses, have one proper place in politics: blessing parades and lending their dignity to celebrations. But right now it was time to rebuild the city; celebrations would follow accomplishment. In a modest speech La Guardia simply declares his commitment to honest, nonpartisan government; urban management through experts instead of party hacks. He closes by taking the classic "Oath of Athens," pledging to avoid dishonesty and cowardice, to keep ideals high, to foster respect for municipal law and civic virtue, and to make the city greater and more beautiful. Seabury, a broad smile setting his ruddy face aglow, pumps Fiorello La Guardia's hand and exclaims: "Now we have a Mayor in the City of New York."[2]

The new mayor brought into office a fascinating, many-sided personality. He was an idealist who was shrewd and tough, a compassionate man driven by resentments and high ambitions, a progressive politician of strength and guile who skirted the edge of scruple to win elections. Five foot two and tub-round, he carried a seven-foot ego and a gigantic self-confidence that bordered on recklessness. In politics as in challenges purely physical, La Guardia would not bow to convention or odds. He fought Tammany, the Republican party, drys, big business, and such certified American heroes as Henry Ford and Andrew Mellon and prevailed. By his final term in Washington the brash East Harlem congressman represented the maturing voice of liberal America, working furiously at the difficult center of American politics, fighting powerful men, potent interests, and dangerous foes and giving a fair account of himself, immigrant surname and all.

He had watched power carefully and had learned to use it. Even as an outsider in Congress he had manipulated the mirrors and blown the smoke to make his lone voice count. And he had taught the fine Republican gentlemen who had wanted a more "proper" fusion candidate for the New York mayoralty a thing or two about guerilla politics. If he was calm and sober in Newbold's club and at Harvard had presented a polished speech on the economy, he had also made a mudslinger out of the judicious Seabury. And no politician eviscerated a troublesome opponent more deftly than Fiorello had carved up Holy Joe Mckee.

Indeed, some feared the ascendancy of so forceful a personality in these unsettled times. Across the ocean in Italy and Germany, the dread of ruin and disorder had given rise to dictators. Closer to home, the New Deal concentrated power in the central government as never before. And in Louisiana, the "Kingfish," Huey Long, demonstrated how despotic a politician could become, even in a democratic society.

As governor of Louisiana, Long had pilloried some of the same enemies as La Guardia: the utilities, the large corporations, Henry Ford, and the Ku Klux Klan. Once when the Imperial Wizard of the KKK threatened to come to his state to campaign against him, Long warned, "That Imperial bastard will never set foot in Louisiana" unless he was prepared to leave with "his toes turned up." The wise Wizard stayed away.

In his penetrating study, *Voices of Protest*, Alan Brinkley describes how the Kingfish built his extraordinary power within democratic forms. He "terrorized the legislature into doing his bidding . . . intimidated the courts . . . dominated the state bureaucracy so totally that even the lower level of government employees served only at his pleasure." He controlled virtually every government appointment in Louisiana from agency head to janitor. And then he piled the power of money and graft on top of iron-fisted patronage. "Louisiana is crawling," Treasury agents reported. "Long and his gang are stealing everything in the state."[3]

Fiorello La Guardia wanted power as well, but he accepted different limits and different goals. Ill-gotten money repulsed him. Whether in campaigns or even to bail out his failing journal *L'Americolo*, he wanted no tainted funds, and he never overcame an early revulsion for "honest graft." He had worked in Congress at passing laws, not building power. His political organization existed for the purpose of getting him elected and serving his constituents, not for terrorizing the opposition and collecting kickbacks. And his sense of outrage bound him to a larger purpose. A half century later, Supreme Court Justice Irving Ben Cooper, an outstanding member of the Seabury investigating team and an early La Guardia appointee, thinks back to 1934 and still smarts from the tempestuous mayor's frequent denunciations; but he also remembers willingly suffering the abuse to work with La Guardia in attacking unfairness. "He was selfless. Any hurt to a human being, unjustified or unfair was enough to throw him into a . . . rage. . . . His outrage saturated every molecule of his being, shook him. I can still see him throwing away his sandwich, shouting, COOPER GET HIM!" He sought power to GET THEM.[4]

———

"I don't expect to have too much to do with La Guardia," C. C. Burlingham wrote to Felix Frankfurter soon after the election. For those who did not retire so gracefully after the campaign, La Guardia announced that whatever debts he owed for help with his election were personal, and he had no intention of paying for them with city jobs. "You simply can't be grateful to the people who worked for you," he declared, as he began to stitch together his new administration, ignoring the advice of friends and power brokers. He took counsel from a small coterie of Berle, Seabury, and Windels, jealously guarding his independence to shape a government free from established parties.[5]

Past master at courting the public, La Guardia used the month and a half before taking office to nourish anticipations of new possibility. The glare of public exposure had wilted the maladroit Mayor O'Brien, but La Guardia displayed a tropism toward the public stage's warming light. H. L. Mencken joked that "it distresses me greatly to see my excellent friend La Guardia on so hot a seat. If he is well advised he will make his will, get a shave and a haircut, burn all of the letters he has ever received from women and jump off the Al Smith [Empire State] building." But La Guardia had hankered after this job for a long time and he had a good idea of what he intended to do in it. Drawing the desperate populace around him for the "long and tedious repair job," he promised a "vital new type of government . . . for the benefit of all the people; . . . an administration, tender hearted toward the weak and unfortunate and hardhearted toward the wrongdoer and the grafter. . . ." Franklin Roosevelt had proven that a decisive, involved leader pursuing new solutions could mobilize the support of the people. La Guardia sought to rouse the same prospect of fresh possibility.

In the six weeks before his inauguration La Guardia assembled his agenda for modern New York. He traveled to Washington, pitched projects to congressmen and administration officials, met with national experts, and dispelled any notions that he intended merely to steer the city clear of its fiscal crisis. While everyone else seemed preoccupied with the question of whether New York could avoid bankruptcy, La Guardia trumpeted plans to transform his city into a fresh, caring, honest metropolis with a new city planning commission, unified transit, adequate relief aid, municipal beer gardens, low-cost public housing, reformed courts, a modern charter, slum clearance, improved schools, and assistance for the unemployed. Looking past the fears of the moment, a confident La Guardia beckoned New Yorkers to dream of a bold new future.[6]

On January 1 La Guardia took office, and suddenly, somebody said, the city was overrun by fat little men in big hats. First La Guardia, "wearing a blue serge suit that clung to his stocky figure with the affection of years of companionship," stopped at police headquarters to swear in the police commissioner and announce a new policy to 250 commanding officers. Since the turn of the century, police had divided the city into informal zones of preferential enforcement. "I have been told that Fulton Street is considered the deadline for crooks," La Guardia said. "That deadline," he bellowed, "is now removed. It is replaced by the Hudson River on the west, the Atlantic Ocean on the south, the Westchester County line on the north and the Nassau County line on the east." Until now, organized crime had bought benign neglect. "We are removing that protection. Now see that that kind of crime is ably handled. If not—get out!" The acceptance of "even a dime" would result in dismissal. To make sure that his crisp message penetrated, La Guardia appointed "Honest Cop" Lewis J. Valentine chief inspector. "Be good or begone."[7]

Then he was off to swear in Paul Blanshard as commissioner of accounts. In the past this office did the routine tracing of departmental paperwork and fiscal accounts. No longer. La Guardia charged Blanshard with building a tough department of municipal investigations. "You are the eyes and ears of my administration," he said, ". . . you will not be interfered with." Next, La Guardia swore in the new commissioner of taxes and assessments, telling him: "There is something wrong in the tax department. I don't know what it is. . . . find out!" Paul Windels, installed as the new corporation counsel, was ordered to avoid "pettifogging opinions" and create the best law department in the country. La Guardia welcomed Austin McCormick to his post as commissioner of corrections by commanding him to fire every deputy in his corrupt department and start from scratch.[8]

Then, bounding past some 1000 persons who had braved the snow to welcome him on his first day, La Guardia went into his office at city hall. (Later in the day La Guardia learned a lesson only mayors appreciate. He had to scrape together an extra $1 million to pay for snow removal.) Robert Moses witnessed the sawed-off dynamo at work at his desk on this first day and he never forgot it: "The mayor was tossing letters at a pint sized secretary and shouting 'say yes, say no, throw it away, tell him to go to hell. . . .' The fusion regime was warming up." The push-button telephones on his desk got in his way and La Guardia ordered them removed; he liked to work face-to-face. And he ordered a huge wastebasket.[9]

At eleven o'clock La Guardia hastened from his office to the NBC radio studios for a national broadcast. He briskly introduced his department chiefs and the new "golden rule" of his administration: "Do after the election as you said you would do before the election." For all the talk of La Guardia's unpredictability and mercurial character, his career had been one massive consistency. For decades he had harbored a progressive vision of New York City, and he relished the opportunity to bring that idea to life. He closed his speech with the Oath of the young men of Athens:

> We will never bring disgrace to this our city by any act of dishonesty or cowardice . . . we will fight for our ideals and sacred things of the city both alone and with many; we will revere and obey the city's laws . . . we will strive unceasingly to quicken the public sense of civic duty. Thus in all these ways, we will transmit this city not only not less, but far greater and more beautiful than it was transmitted to us.[10]

Following his radio speech, La Guardia marched over to the Tammany-dominated Board of Aldermen. After fellow fusionist and aldermanic president Bernard Deutsch ruffled the honorables by referring to them as an "assemblage of district errand boys," La Guardia demanded their support for his financial program. Warning that he would push ahead "whether I have your cooperation or not," he presented a measure to eliminate unnecessary city and county offices, slash wages, and order payless furloughs for city employees. "That's the only way to do it," La Guardia explained about his autocratic approach. Registering a protest, a Democratic alderman asserted the Tammany majority's right to lead. "That all depends on who the majority is,'' La Guardia replied. ''In this administration, I'm the majority.''[11]

He needed the power of the majority to deal with a city whose fiscal profile had been twisted grotesquely out of shape by previous administrations. La Guardia inherited an economic mess of daunting proportions. The reckless spending of the twenties had saddled the city with huge debts. In good times, rising tax receipts had allowed the city to carry this debt comfortably, but with the Depression and the need to provide relief, the mushrooming debt had pushed New York to the edge of bankruptcy. In 1932 alone, tax delinquencies reached $79 million or 15 percent of all taxes owed. The financial squeeze that had sent Jimmy Walker running to the bankers confronted the city with its time of reckoning. It had always been an agreeable task to appoint friends and supporters to city jobs, but cutting workers was painful and politically dangerous. In 1933, with the city teetering on the brink of financial disaster, the Board of Aldermen refused to part with eleven superfluous sergeants-at-arms, one for every six aldermen on the board, while powerful political coalitions defeated every proposed economy. With $236 million in short-term securities due in June 1933, New York City, in the throes of its most extreme financial crisis in modern history, pondered the example of Chicago, which had already defaulted and then buckled under the civil service pressure to raise pensions and adopt an expensive three-platoon system for the fire department.[12]

With no solution in sight and an election coming in November, City Controller Charles Berry brought in Samuel Untermyer, a respected financial expert, to tackle the problem. Mayor O'Brien was only too happy to dump the thorny crisis in Untermyer's lap, but in the end the administration lacked the spine to carry out the recommended spending cuts and tax increases. When Governor Herbert Lehman called an extraordinary session of the state legislature in the summer of 1933 to design a retrenchment plan, O'Brien brought to Albany nothing but vague hopes for assistance. Rebuffed in his pleas for a state bailout, the hapless mayor belatedly turned to a consideration of new taxes, only to withdraw each of his proposals in the face of opposition. The stock exchange killed a proposed stock transfer tax by threatening to move to New Jersey. Labor, merchant, and consumer groups beat back a sales tax, and the courts disallowed a taxi surcharge.

Each time, as notes came due, the city in a *Perils of Pauline* scenario, would just manage to cheat disaster with the help of the banks, but each such rescue came at the expense of more of the city's independence (as well as usurious rates of interest). ''The way in which our Tammany rulers have played ducks and drakes with our municipal finances,'' wrote the *New York Times* in June 1933, ''is now common knowledge everywhere.'' By September the city owed upwards of $330 million, with $227 million coming due before the end of the year. Again O'Brien begged for more loans, but this time the banks insisted on a formal four-year agreement binding the city to a dictated program for financing its budget, restoring municipal credit, and funding unemployment assistance.[13]

The plan, known as the "Bankers Agreement," committed city tax revenues to paying off the bank loans before meeting any other obligations and obliged the city to set aside a $50 million reserve fund to cover the loans in case tax income proved insufficient. The bankers also commanded—Corporation Counsel Arthur Hilly emphatically recalled later that no member of the administration approved this; the bankers forced it upon the city—a 10 percent penalty for late tax payments. To remove the possibility that they would have to engage in an unpopular competition with the unemployed for the same tax pie, the bankers dictated a new tax on utilities together with a special issue of serial bonds to raise $70 million earmarked for unemployment relief. (Recognizing its new restraints, the city quietly dropped a planned tax on savings banks and insurance companies and agreed to the demands of real estate interests to freeze property taxes at their 1933 levels for the next four years.)

"The bankers," noted the *New York Times*, "had taken ample precaution to safeguard the money they had already lent as well as the funds they proposed to lend." Having taken care of themselves, the bankers and real estate interests did nothing about the rest of the fiscal problem. How the city would pay its salaries, pensions, and expenses remained unclear, leaving open the possibility of payless paydays, forced furloughs, cutbacks on relief, extensive layoffs, and the deterioration of its physical plant. The aldermen, bewildered by all this serious business and anxious to have the disagreeable task done with, voted as they were told. But if the politicians worked in a fog, the bankers knew very well what they were doing. On the same day that the Bankers Agreement was adopted, city bond prices rose from 2 to 5½ points on the market.[14]

During his campaign for the mayoralty, La Guardia had pledged to live up to the Bankers Agreement. He also promised to avoid new taxes and avoid firing civil servants while cutting costs. In short, he made promises with little thought about what he would really do once in office. City finances were not particularly complicated, he had said in one speech, so long as you had the courage to make the hard decisions. As he stepped into office he confronted those hard decisions for the first time.[15]

Special city financial counselor Untermyer had proposed bold financial reforms, new taxes, 8500 layoffs, and the abolition of the Board of Aldermen, Board of Assessors, and city chamberlain. Otherwise, he warned, New York would not meet its four-year fiscal agreement. Untermyer did acknowledge one rather imposing obstacle: The steps he outlined required revisions of the city charter and "earnest . . . not politically minded" support from the aldermen. How quixotic! Merely ask the Board of Aldermen to eliminate itself, and curtail the patronage power of its big brother the Board of Estimate! Even Untermyer understood that this would require that "the city be relieved from legislative restrictions and given a free hand." But how to be rid of legislative restrictions? It would require almost dictatorial powers to be vested in the mayor.[16]

On January 1 La Guardia would inherit a city shoehorned into a narrow set of fiscal restraints, lacking a policy for anything but paying back bankers. How ragged the city situation had become was made painfully clear to La Guardia when he was in Washington shopping for public funds a few weeks before. "Go home and balance your budget," public works administrator Harold Ickes had told him; "your credit is no good."[17]

In Congress La Guardia could put on fine shows railing against injustice and unfairness, but as mayor he had to do more than criticize; he had to assume executive responsibilities and govern. And the situation was grim. The 1934 budget of $551 million was unbalanced; ravaged sinking funds, disputed taxes, delinquent revenues, growing transit fare subsidies, unrecorded expenditures and obligations all made it unclear by just how much. So much, however, was agreed by all: At the very least the deficit stood at $30 million and perhaps double that. In the immediate future loomed the threat that relief funds might be exhausted. Thereafter the city would not be able to meet its payrolls. The federal PWA would withdraw its financing from projects. And then the banks would pull the plug. No longer could La Guardia vent frustration by making some lurid disclosure or some rabble-rousing speech. He had to act.

On December 28 La Guardia completed the finishing touches on an emergency fiscal plan that he had developed with Adolf Berle. The measure resembled the economic legislation with which Franklin Roosevelt kicked off the New Deal, when he warned, "Too often in recent history liberal governments have been wrecked on the rocks of loose fiscal policy." Congress had granted FDR sweeping executive powers over the federal budget and the bureaucracy. Faced with the staggering challenge of New York's financial reconstruction, La Guardia demanded similar unobstructed powers. It was either this, the new mayor said, "or chaos."[18]

More than any other measure introduced in the first 100 days of his administration, La Guardia's economy bill demonstrated his intention to assume the necessary power to carry out his programs for recovery. On his very first day in office La Guardia asked the Board of Aldermen for a resolution to the state legislature in favor of an emergency economy bill to "effect economies in, and to increase the efficiency of the operation of the government" of the city. Specifically, he requested unchecked authority for a period of two years to merge bureaus, reduce salaries, reorganize pension funds, order payless furloughs for a maximum of one month a year, eliminate city and county departments, and slash as many as 10,000 employees from city work rolls through executive order.[19]

On the next day an amendment limiting the emergency powers to nine months instead of two years helped the resolution sail through the Board of Estimate by a comfortable margin of twelve to four. "You aren't Roosevelt," old-guard Bronx borough president James J. Lyons vainly objected to the day-old mayor. "Your job is quite different. I am opposed to this highhanded attempt at dictatorship." But La Guardia made no excuses for the broad powers he demanded. Tammany had dallied for years. Even Samuel Untermyer, O'Brien's financial adviser, had called for bold steps. "Gentlemen we would be sitting here until next summer," if the Board of Estimate tried to do the job. Committees had debated and discussed endlessly. Now it was time to clear out the deadwood and the sinecures and reform a style of financing that was just one step ahead of the penitentiary. And such action required a strong single hand.[20]

La Guardia had shown his bill to several officials, including the governor, and he expected swift action from the Albany legislature, whose approval was required. But the bill received a wary reception upstate. The *Albany Times Union* characterized it as a "smashing drive to gain single handed control" of the city government. Municipal employee groups, seeking to avoid cuts in salaries and personnel, vigorously fought the bill and they quickly gained the support of the Democrats. Much of this was expected. Governor Herbert Lehman's response, however, was not. He was aghast. "My reservations go very deep into the roots of governmental policies and principles," he wrote to La Guardia. These were the most temperate and conciliatory words in a scathing twelve-page message which Lehman released shortly after receiving the economy bill.[21]

While expressing sympathy for the mayor's economic burden, Lehman deplored the solution that La Guardia had settled upon. "No man in this country has ever asked for or received the dictatorial powers which would be yours through the enactment of this bill." Lehman charged the mayor with exaggerating the fiscal emergency in order to grab extraordinary powers. He recommended that La Guardia use his existing executive authority to adjust official salaries and work out the necessary personnel cuts with his Board of Estimate.

With banks failing and institutions crumbling, the fear for the collapse of American freedoms was palpable. Senator William E. Borah, Idaho's veteran Republican Progressive, lauded Democrat Lehman for his sharp words. "It was timely; it was patriotic; it was statesmanlike. It is distinctly a matter of congratulations to the whole country that the governor of a great state in these days of wild grasping for power and the utter disregard for personal rights should say for once and for all that such things are un-American." (Curiously, Borah was on excellent terms with two of the most feared demagogues of the thirties, Huey Long and Father Charles Coughlin.)[22]

Lehman's advisers had hoped that the governor would avoid incendiary language, but he was genuinely shocked by the power grab. He sternly rebuked La Guardia for "ruthlessly" seeking to strip city officials of their proper powers. "This bill," he chided, "will obviously afford you the means of completely scrapping the present city charter and give you the authority, single handed and with full dictatorial powers, to set up another charter." With contemporary visions of strong men who had ridden unstable economics into power, Lehman admonished his controversial colleague: "I regard it as not only entirely unnecessary but as essentially unAmerican. . . . Representative and Democratic government, bestowed upon us by centuries of human struggle, should not be so hastily scuttled."[23]

La Guardia hit back at Lehman, calling the governor a banker and a politician who had helped foist a "financial dictatorship" on the city and wanted to protect the "ward heelers and payroll parasites" from La Guardia's cuts. But despite his aggressive tone, La Guardia closed his letter with assurances that he remained Lehman's "humble servant." The *New York Times* commented with some relief that though robustly written, the letter "was without a touch of violence," and advisers in both camps arranged a meeting between the two executives for January 10 in Albany. Still smarting from Lehman's rebuke, La Guardia told a press conference that the "humble mayor of New York City, a city of seven million is crawling up to Albany, hat in hand to beg the right to go to our own legislature . . . for a bill in keeping with the Governor's own view of Constitutional democracy."[24]

The humble mayor brought to Albany detailed reports demonstrating the financial emergency and, after eliminating some of the bill's more provocative features, arrived at a workable compromise with Lehman. La Guardia returned to the city praising the governor, confident that he had cleared the largest hurdle. From Washington, the Roosevelt administration pitched in its support for the mayor's efforts and pressured the legislature by threatening to cut off $23 million in federal transit assistance if the budget was not balanced soon. Charles Burlingham wrote Felix Frankfurter with some satisfaction that La Guardia had played his game well, emerging with a viable bill and Lehman's support.[25]

Burlingham's sanguine analysis was as premature as the activities of the city hall staff, who, equally certain of the bill's passage, began planning specific steps under its new powers. But La Guardia knew that the fight was far from over. On January 25 he left a sickbed to travel up to Albany to testify and lobby for the bill—"Wear your rubbers Mr. Mayor," the *New York Daily News* gently prodded. "You're turning out to be too good a mayor to lose." He was met by a massive demonstration against the bill led by civil service employees and their backers. And when the votes were counted the bill was defeated.[26]

The old saw about a man with a grievance being worth ten with a principle proved true. The mayor could talk principle with Lehman and compromise, but there was no compromising with Tammany, which understood the threat to its own existence in this bill. Give La Guardia the power to trim the municipal work force and eliminate redundant county government, and they were finished. Assemblyman Millard Theodore put it plainly: "I would be against this bill even if the City of

New York went bankrupt or the United States went bankrupt.'' What was government for if not to fuel the party with jobs?[27]

La Guardia pressed on. He delivered a fighting radio address in favor of the economy bill. If Albany was serious about helping New York clean house and avoid fiscal chaos, he said, it must grant the city the power to heal itself. ''Let us have home rule for saving as we had home rule for looting,'' he demanded. Local Republicans who would not support his economy bill he denounced as bosses with only patronage on their minds, signaling an early split with his most recent party. Only after the bill won the unexpected support of the postmaster general of the United States and overlord of New Deal patronage, James Farley, and Bronx boss Ed Flynn did La Guardia relax a bit. With the most powerful national Democrats behind his measure he felt confident that it would pass on a second vote. He sent it up to Albany again. And on February 14 the Democrats voted it down again.

La Guardia called them reactionaries, they called him worse, and he went back home to sort out the situation. Two days after the bill failed, the Transit Commission payroll was not met for lack of available funds.[28]

It did not take La Guardia long to figure out that Farley and Flynn had played a sharp game, speaking for the bill publicly while conspiring to kill it in private. All seven Democrats from Flynn's Bronx voted against the bill, and all but seven other Democrats from the rest of the state, politicians beholden to job-master Farley, did the same thing. Such unanimous disobedience usually followed only after a political boss was safely buried. If the Albany legislators voted against the bill, important voices were whispering in their ears.[29]

La Guardia continued his fight through the winter, rising before dawn to board the train for Albany to testify, dispatching Berle and Windels to bring pressure, while publishing a list of the superfluous jobs that drained meager city resources. No mayor had fought so tenaciously before. ''We did not support La Guardia for Mayor,'' editorialized the *Daily News*, ''but we are glad he won. What a fire he is building under the chair warmers and the parasites.'' Even his rhetoric was catching on! During a meeting with Democratic assemblymen, the new mayor mentioned that he had been in office only a few weeks. One of the members whispered that ''you'd swear it was a year the way things have been turned upside down.''[30]

Finally La Guardia realized that he would have to negotiate. He conceded guarantees to civil service workers and a few other changes, and on March 6 the economy bill was brought up for a third vote in the state legislature. By seven votes it failed again.[31]

That night, before a Bronx Board of Trade dinner, with Postmaster General Farley sharing the dais, La Guardia departed from his prepared speech and, turning directly toward Farley, accused him of surreptitiously killing the bill. With the business leaders cheering, the mayor told a reddening Farley that ''his boys'' would never have voted against the economy bill unless Farley wanted them to. The postmaster general, by now a deep crimson, rose to offer lame excuses about his inability to control grown men. La Guardia, puffing on his cigar, looked up at the six-foot Farley and laughed in his face.[32]

The image of a tough mayor going to Flynn's Bronx to tell the Democrats that he understood the duplicity of double-crossing bosses and would hold them to account appealed to New Yorkers. "Tammany tactics have allowed him to get his case to the people," the *Daily News* wrote approvingly. "The people know he is doing the best he can. . . ." These were, after all, preliminary skirmishes early in the administration. La Guardia was going to be mayor for at least four years, and his first job was to rouse the public's support. The more protracted the fight with Tammany, the more publicity his attack against waste, corruption, and favoritism sparked. Newspapers printed enemy lists of assemblymen who voted against the mayor, ordering their defeat. He was building his forces for the long-term fight against the old guard.[33]

The exchange with Farley placed additional pressure on both Lehman and Roosevelt to shore up Democratic credibility. Assembly leaders were summoned to Washington to have their arms twisted by the president and the governor. It was almost spring, with the city still fighting for control over its finances, and few were blaming La Guardia. City representatives finally hammered out a new understanding with the upstate leadership as La Guardia agreed to drop most cuts in the county offices and limited other economies to city workers earning more than $1200.[34]

On March 28, with Lehman herding the Democratic votes and La Guardia's corporation counsel, Paul Windels, directing the friendly forces, Assemblyman Abbot Low Moffat of New York City called up the economy bill for a fourth time. It was late in the day, and in an unscripted move, Democratic Assembly Minority Leader Steingut asked for a recess to caucus his Democrats. Windels, fearing that his own forces might disappear in the late hour, signaled Moffat to deny Steingut's request despite Lehman's urgent plea that it be granted. Declaring that he was tired of the Democrats' "chiseling," Moffat ordered the assemblymen to consider the issue with no further delay. At this, the Democrats roared back that all deals were canceled and voted the measure down by a wide margin.[35]

Fearful of losing everything, La Guardia personally rushed to Albany to warn of a catastrophic economic meltdown as money ran out, the federal government closed its Civil Works Administration operations, and withheld $130 million in grants until the city balanced its books. To bring the point home La Guardia sent out four hundred pink slips to city transit workers, whose jobs depended on federal grants. The resulting public pressure brought the Democrats back to the bargaining table.[36]

Finally, on April 5 the State Assembly passed a gutted version of the original economy bill, and five days later, in the early hours of the morning, the State Senate voted its assent. Precisely 100 days after taking office, La Guardia had his bill. "I feel like a father expecting his first-born," the chastened mayor told reporters. "I awaited a big, healthy bouncing child, and find a small, puny, anemic, undernourished, undersized baby. . . . I love the little brat, but I am disappointed. I will try to nourish it into something useful." La Guardia was hardly exaggerating. The twelve amendments tacked on to win passage left the bosses with their much-maligned county offices intact. The emergency powers he had sought were trimmed back and the civil service was protected from deep cuts. Despite these limitations, La Guardia managed to use the new law to chip away more than a thousand jobs from the payroll, while salaries above $3000, including the mayor's own, were reduced.[37]

La Guardia had not achieved half of what he had wanted, and much remained to be done before the city won back its independence from the bankers. But the new administration had demonstrated its determination to take charge of the city's pocketbook. On the day that the economy bill was finally signed into law, New York City bond prices jumped to their highest levels since autumn 1931. In June Controller McGoldrick sold an issue of sixty-day revenue bonds for three-quarters of 1 percent, an all-time low for short-term city paper. And with the city's improved credit, Washington prepared to funnel millions to La Guardia's New York.[38]

By late autumn, however, despite the economies and tax increases, fiscal disaster threatened anew. The La Guardia economy cuts had pared $14 million from the budget, and increased business taxes raised some more money, but with the ranks of the unemployed and the assisted already in excess of 400,000, the banks were again refusing to advance any more money without new taxes. La Guardia and Berle passed through the few options available and cobbled together a package of increased public utilities taxes, an inheritance tax, and a tax that only a year before East Harlem's insurgent congressman had ripped to pieces when it had been proposed by President Hoover. But the financial crisis did not afford him the luxury of a consistent tax philosophy. The city needed a high-return tax, and La Guardia, quipping that a tax in hand was worth two in committee, swallowed hard and signed a 2 percent sales tax on all commodities except foods and medicines for a period lasting until the end of 1935.[39]

Norman Thomas called the regressive tax a "disaster," which "taxed the poor to support the poorer." La Guardia knew the clever lines. He had used them himself. He refused to be pictured signing the law, admitting that he was ashamed of the tax. He betrayed the tough-guy gracelessness that he occasionally substituted for reflection by lashing out at a nearby reporter, "You can tell that big fathead, your editor that it was his opposition to the sales tax that decided me in its favor." Operating at the center instead of the sidelines he could no longer carp; he had to

269

settle for what was possible. He was uncomfortable as a target rather than a biting critic, but he needed the money, and as soon as the taxes were passed, the banks delivered a $15 million loan.[40]

The O'Brien administration had also tried to impose new taxes, but there was a difference and New Yorkers recognized it. Tammany had tried to raise taxes without cutting patronage, and it ran into a firestorm of protests. This time, New Yorkers knew that La Guardia had looked at every reasonable alternative first. And if he had to tax the poor, he was also prepared to stand up against the bankers.[41]

In July New York City put $72 million in securities on the market after receiving assurances from banks that it could expect to pay around 3.9 percent interest on the long-term notes. When the comptroller opened the sealed bids he turned pale. There were no bids below 4 percent. Others were gloomy but the mayor simply refused the deal. For the first time in history New York City rejected all bids and demanded better terms. And unless it received such terms, La Guardia asserted menacingly, *he* would deal with the banks. "The banks know exactly what I am talking about. They know that I know them." Jesse Jones, Roosevelt's director of the Reconstruction Finance Corporation, hastened from Washington to mediate, and La Guardia walked away with a 3.8 percent rate. Soon after the securities issue was placed on the market it was quickly oversubscribed. "The City of New York has credit!" Adolf Berle exulted to FDR.[42]

With city finances under control, creditors accepted major modifications in the Bankers Agreement. O'Brien's commitment to set aside $50 million as a reserve against uncollected taxes for four years had tied up millions in inactive accounts while the city was forced to borrow on the money markets. Under La Guardia, with many more New Yorkers paying their taxes, the banks consented to cut the reserve requirement in half. La Guardia extracted further concessions, reducing the previously set interest rate by a full percentage point. In just one year this partial rollback of the O'Brien agreements saved more than $5 million. In December the city returned to the banks for a short-term loan to fund unemployment relief, and the recently wary bankers offered a rate of 1.75 percent.[43]

Taking office after the Depression had delivered the city to the bankers, La Guardia managed through the 100-day battle over the economy bill to return control over the city purse—and ultimately municipal priorities—back into the hands of elected officials. He had, of course, intended to do much more, and his errant overreaching in this uncertain time of emerging strongmen around the world proved unnecessarily provocative. Prepared to govern in the most efficient way possible, by taking power to himself, he had threatened democratic traditions in the name of sustaining them, a familiar irony for audacious insurgents. But he had also shown a pragmatic flexibility in the pursuit of his program. He swallowed hard and accepted a sales tax, compromised on county offices, and refused to accept repeated legislative setbacks as final, emerging with a bill that placed control over the city's fiscal future in his hands.

2. "Get the Hell Out of Here. This Is My Case."

S HORTLY after his inauguration, La Guardia expressed to a friend his dream for the city he had inherited:

> I think I know its potentialities. . . . It is the greatest and most daring experiment in social and political democracy. . . . Its capital of wealth and material resources, of humanity and spiritual resources, is such as no other great city has ever commanded. I shall not rest until my native city is the first not only in population but also in wholesome housing; not only in commerce but also in public health; until it is not only out of debt but abounding in happiness. . . . What an opportunity lies before the new administration![44]

Eager to convert these opportunities into solid achievements, La Guardia wasted little time taking charge. "Perhaps never before," wrote the *New York Times* after La Guardia's first day in office, "did a mayor of New York begin his term with such an air of getting down to business and enforcing industry and honesty on the part of every city employee." Two days later the paper reported incredulously that commissioners were actually "spending a full day at their desks."[45]

To guarantee that civil servants did not revert to habits of old, La Guardia made unannounced personal inspections at city offices to check on the service and the conditions. On one such visit to the municipal courthouse at 30 West Thirty-fifth Street, he found such filth ("the toilet, was in a condition that would not have been permitted by the Army even at the front") that he threatened to close it down. His first weeks were filled with plans and action and a sense of urgency about helping the unemployed. "We are making jobs as fast as we can," La Guardia called out to demonstrators asking for more relief. He was doing everything as fast as he could, in the spirit of government driven to confronting its toughest problems head on. "Aggressive, dynamic little Fiorello La Guardia had brought a new spirit into the conduct of municipal affairs," proclaimed the *World Telegram*.[46]

You can't get people excited about a sewer, La Guardia once observed. Mayors had to create the momentum for reform by dramatizing city government and creating a tempo of change. "BREATHTAKING ACTIVITY REPLACES TAMMANY SOMNOLENCE," ran a *World Telegram* headline. By month's end there could be no ignoring the fat little man with the big black sombrero as he dashed about town instructing the citizenry, denouncing the gangsters, scalping

271

Tammany, and settling into a style of frenetic personal leadership. In the smallest things he craved for excellence. La Guardia rode past a private food market reputed to be the best in the city with a journalist. Why, La Guardia demanded to know, did no *municipal* market have such a reputation?[47]

He had wanted for these many years to make the city good, beautiful, and healthy, and now he wanted to do it all at once. Newbold Morris once sat alongside La Guardia enjoying a musical performance at Radio City Music Hall, when Fiorello gestured toward the organist. "Newbold," he whispered, "that's how our city must be run. Like that organist, you must keep both hands on the keyboard and both feet on the pedals and *never let go.*" The city became his obsession. Being mayor, he said, was a twenty-four-hour responsibility, and at times it seemed that he was on call for each of them, opening the day with a proclamation at the Hunt's Point Market before daybreak and not closing it until he completed haggling with labor negotiators and entrepreneurs past midnight. After two weeks in office La Guardia told a reporter that he intended to limit his nights out with Marie to perhaps once a month. He wanted to conserve his energy so that he could serve the city properly.[48]

In the first weeks he established the pattern for the rest of his tenure in office. He would start working at breakfast in his East Harlem tenement, studying reports, or meeting with a department head or a trusted adviser over toast and eggs. Breakfast ended abruptly at eight o'clock as La Guardia sprang up from the table, reached for his tall hat, and scampered out the door to the elevator and down to a waiting car. The official car was equipped with a folding table for the mayor to write or mull over reports on his way to the office when he did not have a meeting going on in the backseat. A police radio kept him in touch with all emergencies so that he could rush to hot spots to supervise his cops and firefighters. A bit later into his term, a pistol was packed into his seat to free the men assigned to guard him for other duties.

He often changed the route from his East Harlem apartment downtown to city hall to enable him to survey the different parts of his realm. One day it was down the East Side to check on construction projects, another time through the median streets to observe snow removal and federally assisted work projects. La Guardia would often order his driver to pull over as he dashed out to interview a patrolman about his "beat," or ask a street cleaner what he thought of the trucks that the city was using, or call out to children to ask them about school. "Running a city resembles running a house," he would say, and "if the servants are honest . . . then the house can be managed well and economically run." He meant to see that the servants were well supervised.[49]

He took in everything. "Dear Sir," he wrote to a certain Clement Stone. "You were very careless . . . when driving across Park Avenue. The pavement was wet and you had a very heavy load. The City of New York is making special efforts to lessen the number of accidents and save lives. . . . I am giving you this warning, and because you are a young man I do not want to cause you any trouble at this time but . . . you must be careful in driving." Another time, the mayor flagged down a speeding taxi and started berating the driver. A policeman arrived, hastily pulling out his book to write a ticket, only to be pushed aside as La Guardia growled: "Get the hell out of here. This is my case."[50]

Everything was his case.

One morning Lowell Limpus accompanied La Guardia to a Lower East Side relief station. Parking the car a block away, they joined a line of jobless waiting to apply for assistance. The queue moved with infuriating slowness as one or two staffers interviewed the applicants, while others lounged around their idle typewriters. It took La Guardia but a few minutes to reach his boiling point. Then he pushed through the line to the front, knocking an unknowing attendant back into the crowd. Another came to his colleague's assistance and went the same way. Responding to the noise, a natty supervisor with a derby hat and a cigar in his mouth came rushing over.

It was a mistake. Before he had a chance to understand, his cigar and hat were on the ground. "Take your hat off, when you speak to a citizen," ordered the pint-sized disrupter. The mayor was recognized too late. La Guardia marched over to the director's office only to learn that he was not in. He ordered a secretary to summon the welfare commissioner at once. In the meantime, he took out his watch and perched on a stool near the front of the line, rasping, "Now let me see how fast you can clear up the applicants." La Guardia had walked in at 9:15, by 9:37 many in the crowd had been interviewed and hustled on their way. When the commissioner arrived, La Guardia ordered him to "wait here . . . until your director gets here," and to fire him unless he produced a doctor's note. Others were singled out for discipline. As he strode out, the mayor paused, pointed to the man with the derby, and called back, "Oh yes. . . . There's another SOB that has no job."[51]

Arriving at city hall, he bounds up the steps and strides off toward his office, barely nodding in response to the chorus of "Hello Mayor." Impatiently pulling off his coat, he calls for two stenographers (sometimes as many as four worked simultaneously), as he hangs the coat on a hook, slips on his horn-rims, and falls into a chair, his short legs not quite reaching the ground. On particularly busy days the secretaries work in relays to help him attack the piles of correspondence before him. His eyes dart across the letters as he shuffles through them, simultaneously dictating his answers. He routes complaints, addresses requests and jabs back at critics. One stenographer works exclusively at recording the mayor's terse replies, which are to be shaped into full letters by a correspondence secretary. Another takes memos to department heads directing them to follow up on information in the letters. Special problems are noted for discussion with the cabinet, and charges of corruption go to Commissioner Blanshard.

Suddenly the darting eyes halt. He rereads a letter and sputters at the stenographer: "My dear _____," begins the indignant message to a prominent congressman, "Pull plays no role in this administration. . . ." Rushing through the batches in record time, La Guardia snaps off decisions instantly. "Speed," writes a fascinated observer, "is the order of the day," the object being to get through the piles as quickly as possible, with no points awarded for elegant style or deep thought. At first it seems that everyone in New York is responding to La Guardia's promise to act upon complaints. In 1934 thousands of grievances come in for the Department of Accounts alone, but by 1936, after two years of La Guardia, the number drops by 90 percent. The mail is usually done in less than an hour. Then the mayor begins a round of commissioner discussions, civic group meetings, Board of Estimate sessions, and a long day conducting the city's business until evening.[52]

The change from congressional tribune to executive of the largest city in the nation required new managerial and administrative skills, but even La Guardia's enemies granted that he was eager to grapple with the largest challenges of his office, to wrap his thick, short arms around the problems and wrestle with realistic solutions. The reign of passive government, of gloomy drift was over. He came into office anxious to *govern*. "We have had years of 'don't rock the boat,' " Will Rogers wrote after Franklin Roosevelt's first week in Washington. "Go and sink if you want to. We just as well be swimming as like we are." It was Westbrook Pegler who, six weeks into Fiorello's term, first called La Guardia a "lower case Frank Roosevelt."[53]

3. Creating the Technocratic Order: The Chasing of the Green

L A Guardia had intended through the original economy bill to trim the patronage-heavy municipal service and clean out the grafters and Tammany hacks. The final version of the bill, however, lacked the reorganization powers La Guardia had requested. But there was more than one way to skin a Tiger. To carry out his fight against the boss rule that he termed a "cancer on the heart of the city," La Guardia launched a series of investigations that revealed just how routine municipal graft and favoritism had become under the bosses. "The bosses are going to fight for their lives," he told an acquaintance, "but I am going to fight for the life of the city." Before the end of January more than twenty major investigations were under way, damagingly scrutinizing such Tammany legacies as cronyism in the patronage system, the use of insider knowledge to guide real estate investments, corruption in bus franchises and tax assessments, favoritism in Riker's Island construction contracts, and graft in the Triborough Bridge Authority. The resulting public outrage afforded La Guardia the support for comprehensive reforms and a new administrative order in the city.[54]

"I have sought high and low for men who could effectively do the job," La Guardia told New Yorkers, and more than any mayor in New York's history, he meant it. The newspapers at first suggested that he would name at least one woman to a high post. In the end it remained a cabinet of men, but men of an unusually high caliber. La Guardia appointed his chief challenger for the fusion nomination, General John F. O'Ryan, to the post of police commissioner. A graduate of the City College of New York, the fifty-eight-year-old O'Ryan was a respected lawyer with a sparkling military background who immediately reassured New Yorkers that he knew the difference between the army and the police. "In the police department we are dealing with our own people, not an enemy," he said. Liberals were impressed and Acting U.S. Attorney General Thomas Dewey hailed the appointment as "incomparably fine."[55]

La Guardia installed impeccably credentialed Paul Windels as corporation counsel. The forty-eight-year-old Windels wisely extracted assurances of exclusive control over his department before accepting La Guardia's offer, and within a year he converted a department that habitually retained expensive outside counsel for every nonroutine matter into one of the best legal staffs in the country.

To head the Department of Markets, La Guardia selected William Fellowes Morgan, Jr. The "Social Register Commissioner" came from an old New York family that ran a very successful frozen-fish business. Morgan had learned firsthand the baneful effects of the racketeers and courageously testified against mob dock boss "Socks" Lanza during the Seabury trials. The new market chief, who had never met La Guardia until after the election, neglected to secure the kind of guarantees of independence that Windels had demanded. One weekend he picked up the newspapers to read that Matthew DeSerio had been appointed his deputy. He telegraphed La Guardia that he did not even know the man. La Guardia sent back a note advising his commissioner not to worry. DeSerio's name could be found on page 55 of the *Social Register*. An hour later came a second note from His Honor. Sorry, page 55 was correct, but it was in the Bronx telephone book, not the *Social Register*. But DeSerio would prove invaluable in attacking the gangsters who had taken hold of New York's food industry.[56]

The new commissioner of public welfare did not come from the ranks of defeated assemblymen or bosses' relatives as he might have in the past. William Hodson, the kindly visaged, jug-eared, prematurely bald relief expert, looked like the neighborhood pharmacist; he also happened to head the largest private welfare agency in the United States. In 1931 Hodson had turned down Governor Franklin Roosevelt's invitation to take control of New York State's relief program, but La Guardia succeeded in bringing the exceedingly respected social work professional into his administration. Hodson's first speech dispelled the appearance of diffidence.

"Bureaucratic attitudes" were *verboten* and politicans were warned away. "I've had no political experience," Hodson announced, "and will accept no political dictation from any politician, whatever his shade of color or previous condition of servitude."[57]

During the campaign La Guardia had ridiculed the New York City charter as an antiquated museum piece studded with such quaint offices as city chamberlain. But with the city in economic crisis, La Guardia named his erudite friend Adolf A. Berle, Jr., city chamberlain and assigned him responsibility for restoring financial stability. Berle agreed to serve as administration troubleshooter in Washington and Albany until the city's finances were cleared up but pledged to abolish his office before he left it. He also asked for a reduction in salary.[58]

Tammany traditionally awarded the fire department commissionership to organization hacks with no fire safety training. "The new commissioner," announced La Guardia, "will be a firefighting commissioner . . . not a swivel chair commissioner," as he raised John J. McElligot, a twenty-eight-year veteran of the department from chief of the uniformed ranks to the post of commissioner. A former assemblyman, mayoral hopeful, and recently defeated candidate for Manhattan borough president, Langdon Post, was brought in to head the Tenement House Commission and coordinate the program for public housing.[59]

La Guardia lured away the eminent New York University authority on municipal purchasing, Russell Forbes, from the ivory tower to put his theories to work as commissioner of purchase. Rufus McGahen, the Citizens Union financial whiz, was installed as budget director, and Frederick Kracke, carrying a strong recommendation from the state Republican chairman, assumed control of plants and structures, while O'Brien's dock commissioner was held over. Maurice P. Davidson's service as one of the leading fusionists was recognized with an appointment to head the Department of Water Supply, Gas and Electricity.[60]

Previous New York mayors had drawn their appointees from the pool of loyal party men. They sought neither inspired work nor national reputations, having no desire to be outshone by some crackerjack administrator. La Guardia had the self-confidence and passion for excellence to seek the best. In searching for a health commissioner he addressed a simple inquiry to the U.S. Health Service. Which city had the best public health record in the United States? Then he coaxed Dr. John L. Rice, who had won that honor for New Haven, to take over New York's Department of Health. His national search for a commissioner of corrections to clean out the corrupt prisons and return them to their original purpose of rehabilitation was equally well rewarded. He offered the position to the foremost penologist in the country, Sanford Bates, director of the Bureau of Prisons. Mr. Bates declined, but his exemplary assistant director, Austin McCormick, accepted the challenge.[61]

Dr. Sigismund S. Goldwater, an outstanding authority on hospitals, became hospitals commissioner, while Robert Moses brought his worldwide prominence as a planner and builder to the parks department. Bristling with plans for a comprehensive system of roads, parkways, and recreational parks, the stormy forty-five-year-old president of the Long Island State Parks Commission conditioned his acceptance on the right to retain his state positions. He got it.[62]

Fiorello La Guardia romanced the best with the persistence of a collector. "I can't afford to have such an intelligent person on the outside," he would explain as he pursued another expert. Once he wooed a Queens lawyer who twice turned down a magistrate's post by pleading with him and sending over a liveried messenger at five o'clock in the morning with a lavishly embellishment telegram ordering the attorney to come to city hall at noon to be sworn in. La Guardia got his man. "Everybody seems to agree," Commissioner Goldwater wrote the mayor, "that you not only make an effort to surround yourself with the very best type of men, but that you display genius in finding them." Felix Frankfurter wrote C. C. Burlingham that La Guardia's cabinet, with the exception of Fred Kracke, whom he considered a hack, was a "remarkably good lot . . . extraordinarily fine and . . . devoted."[63]

But Al Smith thought not. He met Reuben Lazarus shortly after the appointments were announced. "It doesn't make any difference does it Rube?" the former governor needled. "Democrat picks Democrat and Fusion picks Fusion." But even Smith had to acknowledge that there *was* a difference. Yes, some of the new department heads were fusionists, but the least of them was competent and the best were strikingly qualified. Few presidential cabinets in the nation's history could match the stature or political diversity of La Guardia's circle of department heads. The fusion administration included Socialists, Democrats, Republicans, and nonpolitical professionals, all arrayed under the banner of good government.[64]

An old pro listening to La Guardia thank fusion workers after the election heard him conclude with a characteristically brash flourish. "You're not going to get a thing—no jobs no favors." He owed them nothing. "Ain't he cute," scoffed the pol. "The papers will eat it up." More than anybody really expected, he meant it. Within weeks, after Republicans and Fusionists submitted their lists and he ignored them, they were grumbling at his ingratitude. No boss dared march into city hall brandishing his job quota. Samuel Seabury and C. C. Burlingham might suggest or offer their opinion on a name but La Guardia made the decisions, and largely those decisions were based on objective criteria. He really did believe that there was no Republican or Democratic way of cleaning streets or distributing relief. There was only a good, honest way and a wrong way.[65]

La Guardia brought important personal gifts to the task of city management. He had a clear, uncluttered mind, and while he lacked the depth and patience for nuanced intellectual thought, in his ability to concentrate quickly and powerfully on complex problems, to absorb details and draw on his large practical experience, he was brilliant. He could "summon up his whole background," Nathan Frankel of the New York Industrial Relations Bureau said, "to meet the problem of the minute. . . . an artist, not a scientist." He had a zest for governing and a flair for leadership. "What a dramatic sense La Guardia has," wrote a beguiled Felix Frankfurter. Critics called him a fanatic. Even his admirers were sure that he was in control of himself only most of the time. "There is no doubt," Ernest Cuneo allows, "that Fiorello was a seized man." He had an immense power to overwhelm, to fill his surroundings with the largeness of his will; a creative, tense, impatient will. After bringing together his uncommonly gifted cabinet, La Guardia proceeded to harass, browbeat, scold, berate, hector, and abuse these accomplished men and pummel them into a whole that was even better than its parts.[66]

La Guardia also brought into office an unassailable personal honesty. Even his enemies granted that the "little guy was honest." The opportunity to make money did not entice him. When he won the election for mayor, Marie celebrated privately that they would now be able to afford a new rug for her living room. Then once he came into office he cut his salary, twice. Said an admiring associate, "I don't think he was interested in a second pair of pajamas." He wore his impecuniousness like the badge of an honest man in politics, just as his rumpled clothing meant that he was too busy working for the people to have tailors fussing over him. "No use my putting on the dog," he would say. "They didn't elect me for my looks," he told Eric Goldman. "They wanted things done and they knew damn well I'd do them."[67]

In Congress he had charged forth on the basis of his wildest suspicions and improbably was often proved right. In 1929 his charges against Walker were outrageous, wilder arguably than he himself actually believed—and again they proved correct. Experience had rewarded his chary nature and now he was more suspicious than ever. He trusted very few people explicitly and none completely. He could believe the worst about even his closest advisers, and on the flimsiest rumor or chance impression accuse long-trusted associates of gross improprieties. It was an altogether unattractive characteristic, but this extreme distrust equipped him to guide a corrupt metropolis embarking on a giant cleanup.[68]

La Guardia brought a fair share of the well-born and the wealthy into his administration. Some found this a curious departure from his antiprivilege forays. But while he mocked their pedigrees and their pretensions, he respected their integrity. Too many of the first-generation *arrivistes* were still on the make, more shrewd than honest, and he trusted these established folk who by inheriting their wealth had not had to compromise themselves to get it.

The new administration established an unbending standard of integrity; anything even faintly questionable was forbidden. On his very first day in office La Guardia warned city workers that accepting so much as a nickel from a citizen was cause for dismissal. And with everything else to do, he ordered Corporation Counsel Windels to check through the ads in the police department magazine *SPring 51000*. Perhaps advertisers were buying more than ad space. Neither of them had even had time to sit at their desks, but La Guardia was impatient to clear out all possible improprieties *on the very first day*.[69]

278

For moral responsibility to be effective it has to be incorporated in adequate social mechanisms. Under La Guardia, lapses in integrity were swiftly punished. There were no mitigating circumstances. "The age of these employees or the length of service in the city," he wrote to a commissioner recommending mercy, "makes no impression upon me. In fact it aggravates the case and would indicate they have been too long in the city service. The fact that the value of property was not very great likewise does not detract from the moral turpitude involved." In another instance a friend and longtime supporter of the mayor, with a fine record in his post as a deputy commissioner as well as an outstanding record of community service, had four truckloads of dirt (worth approximately $65) delivered without authorization to a camp that he had purchased from his own funds for the Boy Scouts. La Guardia dismissed the offender and handed the case over to the district attorney.[70]

In the early days of his administration La Guardia was naturally on the prowl for wrongdoing, but after he had been mayor for years and lapses reflected on him and not his predecessors, he remained unyielding. By 1941 he had spent numerous early-morning hours alongside Fire Commissioner McElligot, meddling in his operations, seeing enough of the thirty-five-year veteran firefighter to know his honesty and devotion. In May of that year, a number of oil service inspectors working for the fire department were accused of accepting gratuities. They were tried internally before Deputy Fire Commissioner George L. McKenna, who found one of the inspectors guilty of the reduced charge of "conduct unbecoming an officer," rather than extortion. When Commissioner McElligot accepted McKenna's verdict, La Guardia summarily dismissed both the deputy and the commissioner for being soft on petty graft.[71]

There was no sympathy, no letup. "Beware of the nickel cigar," he warned motor vehicle inspectors in the last months of his second administration. "Accept no favors. . . . Oh they will want to know if you're interested in fights or ball games. Look out. That's the preliminary necking. If you succumb to the preliminary necking you're gone." Repeatedly he handed down strict punishments for the least indiscretion, with the message: "No relenting for anyone at anytime."[72]

In 1873, in the wake of the Tweed scandals, New York set up a Department of Accounts to ferret out municipal graft. The commissioner of accounts was given wide powers of investigation to subpoena city officials, compel testimony under oath, and pry into the personal bank accounts of any New Yorker doing city business, but successive Democratic administrations had curbed this department into insignificance. As Tammany avidly pursued honest graft, the Department of Accounts withered into a tiny group of paper chasers, checking the records and accounts of various departments for clumsy, overt larceny.

La Guardia revived "Accounts" as a key department (later changing its title to Department of Investigations), assigning it vigil over municipal integrity. He appointed as commissioner the forty-two-year-old Socialist reformer Paul Blanshard, who had coauthored with Norman Thomas a trenchant study entitled *What's the Matter with New York* and charged him with keeping that question fresh, by probing into every department for evidence of graft, incompetence, or favoritism. The counsel to the commissioner of accounts, the young star of the Seabury investigative team, Irving Ben Cooper, was assigned to investigate criminal racketeering.

Blanshard initiated a score of investigations within weeks of taking office. From a racket that forced the crippled and disabled to fork over up to $7000 for newsstand licenses, to the Welfare Home for the Aged, where inmates were robbed and miserably abused, to evidence of defective construction work on city projects, Blanshard carried forward the fusion tradition of deftly detailed disclosure, forcing Tammany into the open in order to tear it out by its roots. Blanshard disclosed irregularities in the Department of Purchase and corruption in the courts. He discovered one city employee who had not shown up at work for eleven years. In both the Sanitation Department and the medical examiner's office, investigators discovered a schedule of "fees" collected by city employees for services that were supposed to be free. (After he dealt with the crooks, La Guardia had these illegal charges fixed as city fees and began collecting them for the city treasury.)[73]

Other inquiries showed that residential builders in Queens had regularly bought exemptions from city code requirements, with the result that entire developments were built with unsound lumber and stiff mud instead of concrete; fire hazards were rampant. The exposure of drug use in the city, dangerous foster care facilities, a new bail bond racket, and the swapping of relief for votes sent corrupt holdovers scurrying from office. Some ran almost as soon as they heard that Blanshard was on their trail; others waited for the evidence and resigned. The rest were either removed or brought to trial on criminal charges. In the first three years, his department alone forced 122 officials from office.[74]

La Guardia enlisted others in his cleanup. Hospitals Commissioner Sigismund Goldwater fired forty-nine physicians whose good-natured superintendent admitted selecting his medical staff from a list provided by the district leader. On a rainy Wednesday morning, January 24, the commissioner of corrections moving with military precision, led a raiding party on Welfare Island, and found there a prison ruled by the inmates, divided between Irish and Italian chieftains who held the other criminals in terror and sent the warden out on errands. Narcotics, weapons, private gardens, and hospital suites instead of prison cells for the criminal elite characterized this "gangster's paradise." Following the raid, sixty-eight racketeer inmates were moved behind bars for the first time and the deputy warden was placed under military arrest.[75]

The chief medical examiner completed a study of New York's public school faculties and concluded that as many as 1500 of the teachers were mentally un-balanced, with half the number actually insane. Hospitals Commissioner Goldwater reported that under Tammany, city surgeons had acquired the habit of accepting gratuities from patients and actually refusing to deliver critical medical services unless they were tipped.[76]

Those who had the bad fortune to come under fusion's searching light were quickly disposed of, but it was not enough to clear out the grafters. La Guardia insisted on a new spirit of civic responsibility. "For doing your duty," La Guardia told municipal workers, "you deserve no special thanks; that's what we pay you for. Your excellences are taken for granted; they will not offset your negative characteristics." To those who supervised municipal employees his instructions were equally direct: "You men cannot relax, you cannot get chummy with your subordinates and you cannot expect them to buy you a drink when the day's work is done. You cannot accept any favors, even a cigar from those who work under you." Executives were expected to "get your coats off and pitch in."[77]

"Again you whine," he wrote to a commissioner who insisted that he was shorthanded, a bit too strenuously. Commissioners were repeatedly chided to pro-duce results, "not alibis." When one department head suggested that the city adopt President Roosevelt's example and give the civil service several days off around Christmastime, the mayor responded characteristically:

I have yet to receive a message from you indicating how greater service could be obtained from employees to the city. It is always more employees and less work. It so happens that the Mayor has a slight knowledge of the Nativity and also of the Gregorian calendar, and perhaps if you devoted more time to your duties, the Mayor might be depended upon to take appropriate action on matters that are entirely within his province and none of your business.[78]

Vacations he found particularly irksome. "I don't see how you can conscientiously go on a vacation at this time," he wrote budget director Kenneth Dayton. "You may stay away permanently if you do." A commissioner might come back from a two-week sojourn to find that his department had been reorganized. To one such administrator who sought an appointment with the mayor in a panic to discuss the changes that greeted him, La Guardia wired back: "THE MAYOR IS ON DUTY EVERY DAY OF THE WEEK AND EVERY HOUR OF THE DAY STOP COMMISSIONERS DO NOT HAVE TO MAKE AN APPOINTMENT. . . . PERHAPS IF YOU HAD BEEN IN THE CITY YOU WOULD KNOW WHAT IS GOING ON IN YOUR DEPARTMENT."[79]

Even medical leaves he found faintly offensive. He could not avoid the suspicion that some advantage was being taken. A recuperating Commissioner McElligot received an order in his hospital bed: "Resume the duties of Commissioner to the extent of your physical capabilities. This can be done from the hospital.'' When Commissioner McCormick required a period of convalescence, the mayor wished him a quick recovery and ordered him to cut out all speeches, and cancel all appointments so that he could at least give the city the benefit of "your limited energy and time." Another commissioner was told that it was a good thing that he was in the hospital. "I hope that they will do a good repair job because you are going to find a new office—no more loafing and you will have to work for a living. I mean business and you will have to get down to work when you come back."[80]

Supervisors were expected to be at La Guardia's beck and call. After he tried to reach the police commissioner and could not locate him, La Guardia wrote to the official, "I fear you have not quite fully understood my policy that a city official is on duty all of the time." Reuben Lazarus was at city hall one Saturday when the mayor looked up from a letter that he was reading to punch at his buzzer and order that a commissioner be located. Several hours later the man appeared, having driven back from his weekend home in another state. The mayor asked some trivial questions and sent the hapless fellow on his way, all to Lazarus's puzzlement. With the door closed, La Guardia turned to his legislative assistant and grinned sheepishly. "Wrong commissioner." He had misread the name on the letter. "Once he put the phone in his car," said one of his advisers, "it was impossible to be away from him. He would get ideas in his car and call up . . . [on] that horrible radio telephone."[81]

While most mayors went weeks without speaking to their commissioners, La Guardia met with them regularly to remind them that *this* administration demanded excellence. After Police Officer John J. Quigley was brought to departmental trial for turning over his revolver under duress, the inquest recommended leniency. La Guardia denounced the finding. "The Indians had a very effective punishment for men of this kind," he wrote to the police commissioner. "They dressed them up in squaw's clothing and compelled them to work in the camp as squaws. . . . This man cannot be trusted with the possession of a gun, if we cannot tell when he will be seized with the yellow jitters again." His intrusive presence at fires was legendary, and the other department heads felt his steady gaze over their shoulders too. Once after the city took delivery of three ferryboats, La Guardia refused to approve payment until he rode in the engine room of the new ferries for several hours, took careful note of all imperfections, and called in representatives of the shipbuilders. He handed them a detailed list of shortcomings and negotiated a large reduction in the price. He wanted more appealing interiors for the airport, criticized the door designs on the House of Detention for Women, checked into the material used for police blouses, and called his own emergency drills.[82]

At 4:13 P.M. on a quiet April Saturday, an emergency alarm brought thirty police radio cars shrieking into the Wall Street area, followed by six emergency trucks, each carrying ten men and one sergeant, fifty mounted officers, ten patrol wagons with as many patrolmen as they had been able to pick up along the way, and seventy-five motorcycle cops, some with machine guns, filling the downtown canyons with a sea of dark blue. They quickly located the emergency. There stood the bulky mayor piping, "Keep the crowd moving but leave the Congressmen alone."

The riot call was the mayor's dramatic response to congressional arguments that Governor's Island must be reserved as a garrison to protect lower New York's financial district and the federal subtreasury. He wanted the island converted into a modern airport for international plane traffic and chose this way to prove that the city police could handle any emergency quickly. The legislators were duly impressed, confiding to reporters that the army could not have turned out that kind of response in twice the time.[83]

Looking into the medical examiner's office, which limited its work with the most sophisticated pathology cases to discovering issues of fact, La Guardia insisted that this office's incomparable experience be put to more significant use in a pioneering research laboratory specializing in forensic medicine. At three o'clock one morning, William Carey, the independently wealthy industrialist who had accepted the commissionership of the Sanitation Department, picked up his phone to hear a familiar soprano: Did Carey have a snow alarm plan, Fiorello wanted to know? "Sure, I'm called as soon as the first flake falls." "Wonderful," piped the irascible caller. "Stick your head out the window," and hung up. Several weeks later, Assistant Commissioner of Markets Carl W. Kimball arrived late for a ceremony attended by the mayor. Within a few days Kimball received a newspaper clipping in the mail. It described how a Japanese official who had been tardy for a public function had committed *hara-kiri*. "That," the mayor scrawled in the margin, "is what I call class."[84]

The volcanic temperament never mellowed. "Murderer," he shouted at Hospitals Commissioner Goldwater, after reading a letter from an indigent father complaining that his son had died untended in a city hospital. Goldwater hastened to check the records and learned that every possible medical assistance had been provided. "And for this you call me a murderer?" he asked. "What do you expect from a grieving father?" the mayor replied, with no hint of an apology for his outburst.

He berated commissioners with abandon. Four different commissioners received notes during the 1939 World's Fair denouncing them for staffing department exhibits with "lazy, sloppy, fat and indifferent" representatives. "If that is typical of your department I want you to know it because I will make an investigation that will be a real investigation." Such lassitude, he scolded, "permeates from the top" (of the department, not the administration!). The commissioners were summoned. "Come prepared to give me a personal report, name and record, of each division head in your department and I expect you to know the name of every employee in your department and all about them." This was no minor matter, the mayor continued. "If there is anything I hate, it is indifference, or a let-up of a stroke of every second of the minute, every minute in the hour, every hour in the day and every day of the week. Personal attention to details should be given by the Commissioner."[85]

The take-you-out-to-the-woodshed tone was typical. When La Guardia asked for something, he meant immediately. His most desultory suggestion was to be observed as a crisis order. So many tell the same story: He asked an aide to prepare a report. The assistant put the assignment on his list and proceeded with other work. Called in two days later and asked for the report, the staffer answered lamely that it would be ready soon. The thick head would snap forward, the hair would fall over the brow, and the glasses would fly off all in one terrifying motion as the mayor cut through the unfortunate laggard's ego with a hot knife, raving about stupid, irresponsible asses. His impatience was sulfuric. Once the municipal radio station WNYC was supposed to broadcast a mayoral speech, but the engineer arrived too late to set up the audio equipment. The enraged mayor suspended the tardy worker on the spot before the large audience. "Punctuality is one of the most important rules of this administration," he told the crowd of onlookers. "That's how we do business."[86]

La Guardia liked to think that his outbursts were calculated to keep officials on their toes. He boasted that he never lost his temper unless he had planned to the day before. And few politicians were more adept at the creative use of interpersonal terror. But this was a tricky business and it could deteriorate into abuse for the sheer pleasure of it. His commissioners would come to city hall for appointments only to be forced to cool their heels, sometimes for hours. Robert Moses and Sigismund Goldwater refused to be intimidated, but most were, and wasted hours on a hard-backed bench waiting outside the mayor's door for no good reason.[87]

At the weekly meetings of his commissioners, Fiorello would make a ceremony of presenting a shiny sheep shankbone in a fancy box done up with ribbons to the commissioner who had pulled the week's worst "boner." Paul Moss, city license commissioner, claimed the prize for seating the mayor next to a well-known racketeer at a public function; the police commissioner got his bone for suggesting that a man found murdered in the park had committed suicide; Fire Commissioner McElligot received the municipal dunce cap after proclaiming that Fourth of July celebrations must be safe and sane and then burning himself with a Roman candle.[88]

The humiliations were not always lighthearted. There was something compulsive about La Guardia's bullying. For if part of him was ever untrusting, another needed to dominate. The "mayor . . . does not mind a little hard feelings among commissioners. He'd rather they didn't get together too much," Rexford G. Tugwell recorded in his diary. If any of his commissioners upstaged him or won too many headlines, he could fly into a violent temper tantrum. Some speculated that this obsession had something to do with La Guardia's physical size. In one memorable instance, Maurice Davidson, the commissioner of water supply and electricity, rejected a man that La Guardia suggested for the post of inspector: "He won't do,"

Davidson said unthinkingly; "he's too small." He would prefer to appoint a tall, husky man to work the tough neighborhood. La Guardia lost his head. Jumping up and down he screeched at the hapless official: "WHAT'S THE MATTER WITH A LITTLE GUY? WHAT'S THE MATTER WITH A LITTLE GUY? WHAT'S THE MATTER WITH A LITTLE GUY?"[89]

He bore other resentments as well. At an Inner Circle skit La Guardia played the part of an editor trading unpleasantries over the phone with the mayor. At the end of the conversation he slammed down the phone and ad libbed, "that dirty little wop." The line brought down the house. It also bared the mayor's own insecurity about how others thought about him. Later in his career, when La Guardia toured the country to test presidential waters, he finished a rousing speech and, turning to one of his handsome WASP assistants, said, "If I had a face and a name like yours they might think of me as a presidential candidate."[90]

His resentments made him a tough, demanding boss, sparing with thanks and incapable of expressing gratitude. He approached his exceptional administration with the attitude of a reformatory supervisor, always sniffing for indiscretions, constantly reproving, unable to mind his own considerable business. He constantly reminded these men of uncommon integrity and intelligence that nothing must be done without his approval. Even now that he *was* the administration, his identification with the underdog prevented him from fully respecting his own expert administrators without giving them some grief. An insurgent even against his own government, he went on protesting not on principle but on raw temperament; the outsider even now.

Of course there were limits. He tended to humiliate those who did not fight back, cutting very deeply where he found no backbone. These he would engage in *mano a mano* sideshows of office politics. Once he called in a stenographer only to shout at her before a mortified department head, "If you were any dumber, I would make you a commissioner." Reminded that these were human beings with feelings, he responded unconvincingly that he was loyal to "principles not men," as if human kindness itself was not a principle. "He liked to see people . . . cringe," recalls Justice Frances Bloustein.[91]

Paul Windels had traipsed around the city with La Guardia, campaigning with him for various election contests since 1919, yet their official correspondence was just that, official and often quite brusque. Windels finally became fed up. After receiving three imperious commands from city hall he returned one letter with the note: "I must decline to accept communications such as the one enclosed. I would appreciate it if messages sent to me are sent in the language appropriate to official communications to the Corporation Counsel." Commissioner Goldwater, after being treated to La Guardia's rare powers of invective, challenged the mayor's manners and warned him that he would resign if La Guardia spoke to him that way again. But few others stood up to him.[92]

La Guardia went right on with his blistering style, offending abundantly while he bridled at even the most unintentional slight. "I have repeatedly informed you," he wrote to a young favorite, "that the mayor issues orders to his departments and does not receive orders." Commissioners were regularly reminded in a form letter: "The mayor decides the policy of this City." And in the first few weeks of his administration he took care to inform his cabinet that the La Guardia administration would speak with one voice. No commissioner would appear before the Board of Estimate or contact state, federal, or other municipal governments without his permission. Perhaps La Guardia remembered a young consul in Fiume who built his private power base by developing independent contacts within the State Department. If he did, he obviously wanted no troublesome Frank La Guardias in his administration.[93]

Even imagined challenges were brushed back forcefully. James Marshall, one of the Board of Education's most devoted presidents, crossed La Guardia by demanding more funding for the schools, and La Guardia refused to speak to him for a year and a half, discussing business only through an intermediary. When they were on *good* terms, Fiorello wrote to Marshall: "This smacks of petty spite work. If anything such as this is attempted know that it is contrary to my policy. . . . Whoever conceived this idea to hit at the Mayor is a pretty low type mentality and I know just how to handle such people. I hope I have made myself clear." As a rule those administrators who disagreed with La Guardia were fired "absolutely and permanently." No one he cared enough about to argue with escaped being fired dozens of times, only to have a secretary call the next day to assign them some work as if nothing had happened. "You're fired" was just another of the many colorful epithets that Fiorello used to let off steam.[94]

But he could mean it as well. And when he did he did not permit personal feelings to stand in the way. Just as having little money was his badge of honesty, he was proud to put integrity and high standards of efficiency ahead of personal considerations. Under Tammany, integrity had lost its good name. It was viewed as a form of mild insanity. When everyone was out getting his, only a fool or a pollyanna spouted moral arguments to the looters. La Guardia rebuilt municipal integrity in a tough cast. His righteousness was hard-centered, a ruthless righteousness, able to do hard battle in the name of its goals. "There are very few people in government who are capable of firing," a later mayor of New York, Edward I. Koch, has written. "And there are especially few who are capable of firing their friends." La Guardia did not agonize over the decision; he would just go ahead and do it. "I like you! I like you a lot but you just can't do the job," and it was over.[95]

There were excesses. He rode roughshod over his administrators, always looking for some better way to do their work. "As you know," Fiorello wrote to a commissioner, "the motto of my administration is 'progress.' Perfection is never reached. What may be the last word today is obsolete tomorrow." But the meddlesome temper was tied to a large sense of responsibility. "A mayor who cannot look fifty or seventy-five years ahead is not worthy of being in City Hall," he would say. In his audacious effort to shape a modern service from a corrupt, inertia-ridden bureaucracy, he refused to speak softly. Authority in a man of La Guardia's powerful resentments was bound to prove problematic, but a politician less driven, less suspicious, less truculent, less vituperative could not have cleared out the bosses, the hacks, and the grafters to prepare New York for its modern government.[96]

When La Guardia came into office, New York's civil service was supervised by a sclerotic hierarchy that had closed its deals with Tammany. It betrayed little interest in the city's welfare or pride in accomplishment, honing its one skill of obstructing reform to protect its jobs. La Guardia understood the challenge that stood before him. He could not take the reins of the city until he took control over the municipal work force. He told a meeting of NYU alumni that he intended to shape a bureaucracy fit to manage the modern metropolis. This, he said, would be the crowning achievement of his fusion mayoralty.

The key, Charles Burlingham wrote La Guardia, was to create a Civil Service Commission that was "first chop, and [to] watch the departments like a lynx."[97]

La Guardia selected James Finegan, a respected Brooklyn attorney with a background in fusion politics, to head the Civil Service Commission and directed him to develop a systematic personnel policy for appointments and promotions. The commission threw out the old subjective essay-type exams that left discretion with friendly or corrupted exam-graders, redrew promotion lists that rewarded connections more than competence, and undertook the task of defining criteria for thousands of municipal positions, job classifications, and salary levels. The new regime developed career ladders in which promotions followed an orderly pattern, removing personnel management from the black arts of pull, connections, and political favors.[98]

La Guardia extended commission jurisdiction into new areas. Bypassing the hopelessly corrupt Board of Examining Plumbers, La Guardia ordered Finegan to institute a new exam series for plumbers. At first uncertain of his powers, Finegan wanted to wait for a corporation counsel ruling, but La Guardia informed his diffident appointee that his administration did not intend to have good policy wait upon lawyer's decisions. "It is my opinion that this can legally be done. Therefore I see no necessity of referring the matter to the Corporation Counsel." When Finegan hesitated about another La Guardia proposal, the taping of all oral examinations conducted by the commission to guard against favoritism, the impatient mayor simply told the Civil Service Commission president, "I insist. If you cannot agree with my policy, you know the honorable thing to do."[99]

La Guardia allowed little of the commission's work to escape his meddlesome scrutiny. He reviewed examination questions himself, consulting outside experts to gauge their fairness and appropriateness. (He once had an expert review the exam for statisticians, presenting the man's technical critique of the exam as his own, leaving commission members to marvel at their broadly informed mayor.) La Guardia's pet plan to develop a merit ladder for judges never won sufficient support, but he pushed his progressive belief in a nonpolitical meritocracy quite far. The commission increased sixfold the number of jobs that were filled through competitive examination. Appointments to the catchall "laborer" classification, which in the old days covered a myriad of favors and spoils, dropped markedly. From 1933 to 1940 the number of New York civil servants holding unclassified positions was reduced from 15,000 to 1500. It did not take long for the message to reach the public. Under Tammany, in 1933, 6327 individuals had applied for civil service positions. Six years later more than a quarter million of the best educated and motivated young men and women in the city were applying for posts with the municipal service.[100]

The new civil service was also better trained. Departments developed in-service courses. Others instituted requirements of a high school diploma, while offering every possible accommodation for those who registered for college work. "I have ten firemen going to college now," La Guardia told a group with evident pride.

La Guardia's commitment to a tightly managed civil service even led him to hedge his long-held support for labor unions. He had worked in Congress to extend collective bargaining to both public and private employees. But as mayor he suggested that public employees were different. In industry, where private profits were viewed as the highest good and exploitation was rife, labor required union protection, but civil servants were the *people's workers*, and he wanted no careerist mentality among them. Depression-era New York could not afford to provide liberal benefits and salaries. "We cannot afford to be sentimental. . . . I do not want any of the pinochle club atmosphere to take hold," he said. When it came to public monies, La Guardia talked of cutting jobs with the fervor of the tightest personnel manager: "I want to cut clerical, stenographic, and all ink slinging jobs."

He insisted that, even in their private lives, public workers should be held to a higher standard. They had to be "of good moral character, law abiding and living in accordance with the law, customs and conventions of this country." Under La Guardia, employees involved in extramarital affairs were disciplined for conduct "prejudicial to the good name and interest" of the city.[101]

Tammany had trained New Yorkers to bring their problems to the club, to apply for jobs at the club, to pick up relief checks at the club. More effectively than any would have dared predict, La Guardia broke the connection between the machine and the civil service to establish an honest and effective bureacracy of unusually high competence.[102]

The reform of the civil service had a direct impact on New York's Irish, who had derived the largest benefit from Tammany's appointive powers and were now rudely pushed aside. Under Tammany, New York's police, fire, and sanitation departments spoke with the lilt of Erin, while other departments were almost as deep green. Information about jobs passed through a Gaelic network and subjective civil service examinations were benignly graded by the extended clan. Tammany's Hon. George Olvany thought that nature had selected the Irish for political dominance: "The Irish are natural leaders. The strain of limerick keeps them at the top. They have the ability to handle men. Even the Jewish districts have Irish leaders. The Jews want to be ruled by them." But by the thirties, when Jews and Italians outnumbered the Irish, they were itching for their own chance at city jobs and "handling men."[103]

Under La Guardia the civil service lost its brogue as the proportion of Irish department heads decreased from between 25 and 40 percent, under previous administrations, to 5 percent. Al Smith caught the drift early. Addressing a dinner benefit for German Jewry, Smith, with tongue only partly in cheek, cracked: "All my life I've been hearing about the plight of poor Jews some place in the world. . . . As I look around the room tonight, I see the Governor here, Herby Lehman. He's Jewish. Take the Mayor. He's half Jewish. The President of the Board of Aldermen, my old job, Bernie Deutsch, he's Jewish, and so is Sam Levy the Borough President of Manhattan. I'm beginning to wonder if someone shouldn't do something for the poor Irish, here in New York."

Other Irish took the change with less good humor. When La Guardia appointed a Protestant Italian, Dr. Charles Fama, who had written dismissively about the Irish, as medical examiner for the Employee Retirement System, Hibernian groups protested that the appointment indicated how "little regard for the opinions of people of Irish blood" the mayor had. While La Guardia had nothing against the Irish, he was certainly pleased by the Democratic machine's discomfort with the new order.[104]

As La Guardia appointed Jews and Italians in unprecedented numbers and broke long-standing barriers to the assignment of blacks to supervisory positions, the Irish began to protest in earnest, not about an appointment or two, but about far broader changes in the makeup of city government. Daniel Danaher, of the Federation of Irish Societies, objected that the Irish "as a race are . . . being pushed aside to make room for other more aggressive and better organized races. . . ." By the time La Guardia left office, writes Warren Moscow, "county offices and county government had been wiped out or placed on a civil service basis. . . . [and] there was not . . . a single person outside of the state and county courts who owed his job . . . to Tammany."[105]

La Guardia's Tammany-bashing initiated an ironic train of events. Once the machine was stripped of its powers to skim and graft, its fortunes declined so precipitously by the 1940s that the bank holding the mortgage on Tammany's $1 million wigwam on Union Square and Seventeenth Street (built in 1928) sold it to the International Ladies Garment Workers Union. "I never thought I'd live to see the Tiger skinned," lamented Jimmy Walker. To avert Tammany's disappearance, the club delivered itself over to the underworld, and ironically paid with its Irish identity. In its heyday Tammany had sold organized crime protection, but by the 1940s the gangster Frank Costello called the shots, and before he was through Tammany spoke with an Italian accent.[106]

La Guardia took over when the city's morale had fallen lower than its credit. Its government was run by people with a private interest in each decision, a share in every contract. His assault on corruption and favoritism raised civic morale and won back for New Yorkers not only the respect of the nation but their own self-respect. By recapturing the charmed capacity of politics to instruct, care, and transform, he attracted to it some of the best-intentioned individuals of his times. By his own account he was "an inconsiderate, arbitrary, authoritative, difficult, complicated, intolerant and sometimes theatrical" boss, but in the words of a man stung often by the mayor's intemperate tongue: "his was the most exciting show in town. I wouldn't have missed it for the world." For the first time in a very long while, individuals of goodwill felt that by their efforts, the commonwealth, their city, could be changed for the better, that the good fight had a powerful, decisive leader.[107]

And in this they were correct. "His impulses," Robert Moses has written, "were generous and to a remarkable degree, unselfish." La Guardia's feelings for the vulnerable were gentle and protective. An elderly man wrote to the mayor that he was being intimidated into selling his property. La Guardia commanded Investigations Counsel Irving Ben Cooper: "Please send one of your courteous assistants. . . . As you will see the gentleman is 71 years of age. First ascertain if he has anything else to complain of, and secondly reassure him that anything the city can do to protect his rights will be done. . . ." Again and again he informed his commissioners that their departments would be judged not for their ability to follow rules but for delivering humane and competent service. The more needy, the more vulnerable, the greater his sympathies. Naturally, his favorite constituency was the city's children. "If the children of this city were its electors," said one of his chief assistants, "the mayor could be reelected by their votes alone."[108]

"FH," as those close to the mayor, but not old enough to remember him as "Major," tended to call him, did not apportion his time wisely. He was jealous of his administrators, and he intruded into their affairs shamelessly. He got bogged down in trivia, and his wary and austere nature prevented him from delegating authority. But this unorthodox executive overpowered these shortcomings. It is probably impossible to reconcile the imperatives of the bureaucratic form and its necessary regimentation with warm personal service. Making decisions based on judgment is an executive responsibility. Bureaucrats are supposed to execute directives and avoid bending rules to their own convictions. Yet La Guardia demanded "critical bureacracy," rules, *and* humane judgment, arguing that institutions were not worthwhile in themselves but only as they affected the lives of the people of the city. Open as this principle of humane pragmatism was to abuse and inconsistency, La Guardia made it work, not in principle but in fact. Through his unrelenting criticism and by his own example of prodigious service, he came as close as any mayor has to squaring that circle. In the words of Felix Frankfurter, he "translated the complicated conduct of the City's vast government into warm significance for every man, woman and child."[109]

His administrative style could no more be outlined in a manual than he could pass along his almost tactile sense of civic integrity. But by devoting an awesome amount of time and energy to his job and relying on his razor-sharp political skills, he was able to make it work and put on a thrilling show to boot. It was a tense game, and it took its toll. "I am so tired," he confided to Robert Wagner, Sr., after the first 100 days. "At times I can hardly stand it." Only when fatigue reminded him of each of his fifty-two years and slowed him to a normal pace did the precariousness of so personal a government become apparent. "The devil is easy to identify," he mused. "He appears as your best friend when you're terribly tired and makes a very reasonable request, which you know you shouldn't grant."[110]

Within a few weeks of taking office La Guardia fell into the comforting habit of sharing his burdens with Charles Culp Burlingham. The elderly patrician had a world of experience, and mature wisdom to match. His judgment was as sound as could be had; he coveted no office, was entirely self-sufficient, and had received all the honors he needed in his full life. He enjoyed Fiorello but did not need him. From this remarkable man, and from almost no one else, La Guardia would take criticism and even sometimes be diverted from ill-considered plans. One of the wise old man's letters softly lectured the mayor that he was doing too much. "You are a very tired man," it went on, "and must get some rest. When I drive through the vast reaches of the Bronx and see the swarming myriads, I say to myself: 'Can it be that one man is responsible for the welfare of these people?' "[111]

CHAPTER 9

New Deal City

1. Extending the Locus: New York Goes to Washington

T HE responsibility for those millions that Burlingham feared rested on the mayor's shoulders alone was, of course, too much for one man. La Guardia recognized that it was also too much for one city, even the grand Queen of Cities along the Hudson. For more than a century the imperial municipality had swallowed up outlying regions, annexing them to the greater city. It threw bridges over rivers and tunneled under them, reached 200 miles away to bring fresh water, and built an extensive hospital and educational system. It erected the largest subway system in the world and cleared a world-class park to adorn its midsection. The colossal city accomplished this and considerably more without federal or state assistance. Indeed, its robust economy produced generous surpluses for Washington and Albany. But modern times had put an end to the self-sufficient city.

The U.S. Constitution makes no mention of a federal responsibility for the cities. Traditionally, municipalities were treated as wards of their states, as an Iowa court decision stated in 1868: "Municipal corporations owe their origins to, and derive their powers and rights wholly from, the [state] legislature. It breathes into them . . . life. . . . As it creates, so may it destroy. Municipal corporations are the mere tenants at the will of the legislature." In another decision, this one after the turn of the century, the Supreme Court concurred, announcing that "the State . . . at its pleasure may modify or withdraw all . . . [city] powers . . . expand or contract the territorial area, unite the whole or a part with another municipality, repeal the

292

charter and destroy the corporation. All this may be done . . . without the consent of the [city's] citizens, or even against their protest.''

In his 1925 state of the union address, President Calvin Coolidge cautioned against federal intervention in local matters. ''It does not at all follow that because abuses exist it is the concern of the Federal Government to attempt their reform.'' And ignore them he did, with an assiduousness that made a virtue of neglect. At the International Conference of Cities in 1931, the U.S. delegation was the only one to report that its government took no direct responsibility for its cities. Three years later C. A. Dykstra, a student of the American city, looked out at urban America with its unemployed masses and chaotic finances and wrote, ''At this moment the city trembles,'' while the federal government continued to do nothing.[1]

Franklin Roosevelt brought into office the mixed feelings about cities of a Dutchess County squire raised on the expansive acres of rural property. As governor he had devoted his energies to countryside issues, and the Jimmy Walker scandals did little to endear the downtown districts to him. Nor was he particularly comfortable on the sidewalks of New York. ''Al Smith,'' he admitted to Raymond Moley, ''knows these city people better. He can move them. I can't.''[2]

But big-city mayors did their best to try to move Roosevelt. In May of 1933, pleading that their resources were exhausted, they implored Washington to reverse its policy of fastidious neglect to rescue strapped American municipalities. Although the scion of Hyde Park hesitated to add urban debts to the staggering federal budget, headlines detailing the imminent financial collapse of Detroit, Chicago, and New York changed his mind. He directed the Reconstruction Finance Corporation (RFC) to make millions available in the form of loans to imperiled cities, and he initiated a vast public works program under Interior Secretary Harold Ickes. Unfortunately, the supercautious Ickes tied up the billions entrusted to him in bureaucratic red tape.

Meanwhile unemployment was rising, cities were broke, and people were starving. ''What this relief business needs,'' one newspaper remarked ''is less RFC and more PDQ.'' Reformers pleaded for openhanded assistance with a sense of urgency. One night Harry Hopkins, New York State's temporary emergency relief administrator, together with his friend William Hodson, cornered Secretary of Labor Frances Perkins at the Women's University Club in a cramped space under the stairs. They asked for her support for an ambitious program of direct federal relief. Miss Perkins brought the two reformers to the White House, where they persuaded the president to create a $500 million Federal Emergency Relief Administration (FERA) to distribute assistance grants through the states. ''It is socialism,'' bellowed Representative Robert Luce, but amidst the crying need of the times the epithet had lost its sting. Too many real radicals were running around for the New Deal Congress to worry about another Roosevelt reform. The bill passed by a comfortable margin.[3]

Hopkins went to Washington to head the new agency. ''For a social worker,''

William E. Leuchtenburg has written about the new relief czar, "he was an odd sort. He belonged to no church, had been divorced and analyzed, liked race horses and women, was given to profanity and wisecracking, and had little patience with moralists." Shrewd, cynical, and brusque, Hopkins was tactless with senators but tender with the distressed. He spent money with zest and brought with him a sweeping commitment to the rights of the poor. Harold Ickes was still searching for the perfect program while Hopkins, a half hour after accepting his appointment, set up a temporary desk in a federal building hallway to distribute federal largesse immediately. In his first two hours, working amidst discarded crates and packing boxes, chain-smoking and gulping coffee, assisted by a staff that he threw together on the way, he handed out $5 million and continued to spend with a sense of mission. He had little patience with the penny-pinchers and the dispensers of long-term solutions. "People have to eat in the short run," he would say. He insulted the bureaucratic pashas, bent conventions that hindered quick action, and was fully prepared to be sent packing within a few months, "so I'll do as I please."[4]

And as the 1933 Depression winter approached, Hopkins argued for even more relief for the unemployed. Handing out relief checks was not enough. In an industrial society work was the key to a person's identity, and relief without work corroded a man's spirit. Instead of doles he wanted the government to create projects that would yield jobs for the unemployed. Such work relief might be more expensive but, Hopkins declared, it "preserves a man's morale. . . . saves his skill . . . [and] gives him a chance to do something useful." He won Roosevelt's approval for a Civil Works Administration that would make work for 4 million unemployed by funding federal improvements. But while previous assistance programs had been administered through the states, the new CWA offered outright grants directly to municipalities.

In November 1933 Hopkins invited mayor-elect Fiorello La Guardia to help plan the new CWA. La Guardia had been a familiar and passionate friend of the unemployed, and he would soon be managing the nation's largest city. Hopkins wanted his support for any program designed for the cities. Thus, weeks before he actually took office, La Guardia was called upon to assist in designing the most significant program of urban assistance in the nation's history.[5]

La Guardia also cast an interested eye in the direction of Interior Secretary Harold Ickes's PWA, which was finally beginning to make large-ticket public works allocations. In the past, New York City had failed to claim its portion of federal grants. Its applications were invariably weak, thrown together by hacks who inspired little confidence in Washington. La Guardia changed that. Teaming the best public planner in the nation with one of the brightest experts on public finance, he dispatched Robert Moses and Adolf Berle to Washington to deliver the message that New York was prepared to compete for federal projects and prove that it could manage them with integrity and efficiency.

Then La Guardia himself came to the capital. The Washington press corps turned out to greet their old friend and as usual he had a story for them. He was here, he declared, to claim New York's fair share of public allotments. He happened to have in his pocket—veteran journalists knew about *that* pocket—a few proposals for the secretary of the interior, for subways, bridges, slum clearance, street repair, airfields. . . . The list was long, but each of the requests was carefully laid out, with a firm price tag and a prudent projection of labor needs; and each of the projects promised to leave a large permanent public monument to the New Deal upon its completion.

Ickes was impressed with the tough, knowledgeable New Yorker. This was someone with whom he could do business. He felt assured that any money that would go to a La Guardia administration would be spent carefully and honestly. "I liked his appearance," the secretary confided to his diary on November 23. "He is short and quite stocky and apparently full of vigor. His career in Congress shows that he has real ability and high courage. . . . [H]e ought to give New York a great administration."[6]

What Ickes might not have realized was how critical a part La Guardia actually intended for Washington to play in his administration. For La Guardia was determined to bring New York under the economic umbrella of the New Deal. Shortly after assuming office he told Congress that the crash had "put every municipality to the wall," and the states were not able or willing to help much. The federal government would have to step in, and La Guardia intended to make New York City a model for federal-urban cooperation. "What I want to do," La Guardia's adviser, Adolf Berle, wrote President Roosevelt, "is to navigate New York City into a friendly cooperative basis with both the state and the National Administrations, and if there is any line to be taken here I should be glad of a steer."[7]

Back in New York City, La Guardia assembled planning groups of engineers, architects, and other experts and put them to work on proposals for CWA grants. "I come to you," he told the pleased professionals, "because I want . . . help from people who know something . . . rather than from the politicians." No longer would New York projects be developed with rewarding a small clique of favored Democratic friends in mind. He instructed the planners to design projects that could be completed swiftly because the entire CWA program would last only a few months. And because CWA would pay for workers but required a municipal contribution for the cost of materials, he asked for labor-intensive projects.

Three weeks after his election and more than a month before taking office, La Guardia signed deals with contractors to furnish equipment and completed detailed plans for the useful employment of some 200,000 CWA workers to construct covered municipal markets, clean and refurbish the city's parks, reclaim its rotting docks, set up temporary shelters for the homeless, and repair public buildings. One shrewd two-stage plan applied for CWA labor to clear slums and then

295

asked CWA for money to build low-cost public housing on the cleared sites. By the time La Guardia took office, New York had captured 20 percent of all job slots allocated by the CWA.[8]

At La Guardia's suggestion, Hopkins appointed Travis Harvard Whitney as New York's CWA administrator. The fifty-eight-year-old attorney, a member of the Banker's Club, left a partnership with a prestigious Wall Street law firm to assume the CWA post on December 2, 1933. The task of creating jobs for New York's unemployed consumed him. He drove himself unsparingly to help the hundreds of thousands wandering the streets. He called newspaper columnist Heywood Broun one day. If Broun could provide a list of unemployed reporters, he could place them in one of the CWA projects. When should he come, asked Broun? Now, said Whitney.

Broun walked into the office and faced a remarkably intense man behind a plain desk. Whitney asked him for the list. Broun (list-less) had expected a lunch and some talk and a bureaucratic turnaround of several weeks. "That won't do at all," rebuked the fired-up administrator. "You don't understand. This is a rush job, every day counts." Carrying on his shoulders the suffering of every New Yorker who needed a job, in less than a month Whitney placed 200,000 unemployed New Yorkers in the slots that La Guardia had won for the city. On January 8 an exhausted Whitney collapsed at his desk. He was rushed to a hospital, but it was too late. "Killed in action," wrote Heywood Broun. Little wonder that Ickes and Hopkins took La Guardia's word seriously. His men were cut of different cloth from the Tammany crowd.[9]

The coming of the CWA to the city, wrote one social worker, "sounded like the opening of the gates of Heaven to the unemployed." For months the needy had been forced through ego-smashing means tests to qualify for assistance. Now there were real jobs for them with salary checks. During its brief few months—roughly coinciding with the first 100 days of the La Guardia administration—CWA contributed more than $50 million to the city's needy, tiding hundreds of thousands of families over one of the bitterest winters in New York history. And its 4000 separate projects put a fresh new face on the streets, parks, and public buildings of the metropolis.[10]

In this first major test handling a federal program, La Guardia demonstrated how much New York had changed. Hundreds of relief suggestions and requests from the mayor's friends, supporters, and relatives were passed to the Department of Welfare, to be evaluated on their merits with all of the rest of the applications. On one of his first unannounced site visits La Guardia found a crowd of park workers "resting" during hours. He walked over and fired sixty of them for "loitering."[11]

In other cities federal programs were being filtered through the political machine, or frittered away on useless projects. In Chicago, Harry F. Gosnell, the respected Negro leader, charged that blacks were threatened with a cutoff of relief funds if they voted Republican during the 1933 elections. San Francisco Mayor Edmond O. Hansen stated flatly that it was "necessary to register as a Democrat" to qualify for relief in some parts of his home state. In Boston, the relief administrator refused to accept any direction from Washington; he wanted the federal authorities to drop off the money and disappear. So completely did Massachusetts State Treasurer Charles Hurley control CWA appointments through the State Relief Board that the press referred to CWA as "Charlie's Workers Administration." The administration would suffer no such embarrassments in La Guardia's New York. A few weeks into the new municipal administration, national studies singled out New York for the most honest and effective CWA in the country, and state investigators reported that "New York City . . . is remarkably free from political control or influence."[12]

The New Deal feared something else besides corruption. Lorena Hickok traveled around the country to sample the mood of the people for the White House. She informed Harry Hopkins that Communists were finding a receptive audience around the nation. It did not take much, she suggested, to make a hungry man with a starving family into a revolutionary. Communities like Aberdeen, South Dakota, which could not have been more conservative in their natural tendencies, were turning Red. The jobless, she reported, were "right on the edge." Another investigator, Martha Gellhorn, reported on the pervasive fear, the demoralization, the sense of foreboding and collapse, "each family in its own miserable home going to pieces." In the late 1880s Jacob Riis had warned about the man with the knife, half crazed by the suffering of his family, lashing out in nihilist rage, destroying all in his path. To quiet that man, and calm the impoverished cities that were multiplying his number, Roosevelt had to demonstrate that reform could bring recovery, and he trusted La Guardia to give the New Deal programs their best possible shot at success.[13]

Of course, Roosevelt's commitment to spending his way to recovery was, like many of his commitments, limited. As the Depression continued and business critics argued that work relief competed with private enterprise, rugged individualists like Henry Ford were suggesting that adversity had its benefits. Even reformers worried that welfare programs would create a class of "gimmes," leading Roosevelt to allow the expensive CWA program to expire after three months. In year number five of a protracted collapse he was still seeking cheap, easy solutions.[14]

In New York City, as winter temperatures dropped below zero, La Guardia opened armories and shelters to feed the hungry. Ten thousand gathered at St. John's Cathedral to protest the closing of the CWA, and to hear La Guardia declare that with a national economy, national market, national unions, and a national depression, the solution to depression and unemployment must also come from the central government. The municipalities had exhausted themselves on relief. Without federal assistance they would soon be heaped on the national doorstep. As a congressman, La Guardia might have spoken more forcefully, but Mayor La Guardia explained simply that the city would try its best to make up the difference and keep the cuts humane.[15]

When 1500 demonstrators descended on city hall, threatening "to do something about" the CWA cutoff, La Guardia, more in pity than in anger, met with the agitated leaders of the march and asked what they intended to do about it. They continued to spout the threatening rhetoric of the day, about being sick and tired and about the responsibility not being theirs for what was going to happen. He understood their pain. He refused to be curt. He explained again the limits on his power and the city's pocketbook. But they wanted jobs, not explanations. "We have force out there," barked one of the demonstrators. And because he knew how little there was behind that threat, La Guardia tried again to explain the distasteful realities. The protesters went out and exhorted the crowd to force the continuation of relief. "We'll throw La Guardia out and we'll go into city hall ourselves," one marcher shouted.

After a few hours the crowd broke up and left singing the "Internationale." "It's a lucky thing for them that I have a sweet, calm, Nordic disposition", La Guardia joked to the city hall reporters. His humor was his shield, but he knew that in the past he too might have made the same threats in the name of suffering masses, only now La Guardia was calculating what was possible. He still hoped to convince Roosevelt of the need to be generous to the cities where a majority of Americans now lived and worked.[16]

Roosevelt needed to be educated about the Depression in the cities. "Nobody," Roosevelt had declared rather offhandedly, "is going to starve in the warm weather." Perhaps this was true on the farms, where at least something could be gotten from the ground, but on urban concrete the number of destitute continued to mount. With factories still closing, construction anemic for several years already, trade and shipping in poor health, and banks and investment firms in the doldrums, New York's principal economic supports had been knocked out. By late summer of 1934 one family in seven was dependent on relief, and 1200 new cases were being processed daily. Welfare offices reported that the "highest" type of applicants ever, doctors, lawyers, and engineers, were applying for relief.[17]

"What else can we do, but dig into our pockets?" La Guardia asked New Yorkers after the CWA was closed down. "Surely we can't leave these people to their fate." And he insisted that relief be stripped of any stigma. At a party for a children's assistance project he was asked to pose with one of the boys. "What's that?" he asked. "This is the boy from the charity," the man explained. The mayor's eyes flashed. "Sorry," he huffed, "there is no such word as charity in my administration. This is the first time anybody has used such a word to me." Four men accused of illegally bootblacking on city streets were brought before La Guardia, who was trying court cases in his role as chief magistrate. They begged to explain that they were out of work and relied on this street trade to bring some pennies into the house. He found them guilty, with an explanation. They did not have to shine shoes to earn a living. There was a perfectly honorable alternative: "Apply for relief. You'll get it."[18]

But even this no longer seemed certain. In August the city ran out of relief money. Opposed to pushing the cost of relief onto future generations through bonded debt, the mayor insisted on new taxes. "I fully realize how heavy and burdensome this additional tax will be," he asserted. "It is nevertheless, nothing compared to the sorrow and hardship suffered by hundreds of thousands of our own people in this city." When the Board of Aldermen tried to block his plans, he halted all relief checks for four days, wreaking havoc on the poor, until the Board of Aldermen turned more agreeable. La Guardia took a deserved blast for playing with the emotions of the poor, but he got his taxes, including the previously discussed sales tax (a "drastic remedy for a desperate condition," he called it), and placed relief on a solid basis for another two years. With this accomplished, he turned to bringing Washington's public works bounty to the sidewalks of New York.[19]

---

2. Building with Relief

HISTORIAN Bernard Fay had remarked in the twenties that New York was the only city wealthy enough to rebuild itself every ten years and rich enough to be modern. It was no longer rich enough, but La Guardia wanted to keep building. He envisioned a grand program of new bridges, airports, playgrounds, roadways, schools, parks, parkways, public housing projects, health stations, and beaches; and his plans were not limited to functional necessities. He wanted to make New York more beautiful and through public art and sculpture to lift the spirit of the fallen city. "Too often," he told an acquaintance, "life in New York is merely a squalid succession of days; whereas in fact it can be a great living adventure." It was the middle of the 1930s, tough times, when most mayors were begging to get a school or a bridge, and he insisted that he was serious about art. So the engineers and architects to whom he described his dreams smiled. But he was serious. "I do not mean to be funny," he scolded them. "The city could use quite a little beautifying." He wanted to bring to New York's cold, sad canyons the grand aesthetic spirit of the European cities that he had known as a youth.

On Sundays Paul Kern would drive La Guardia around town as he surveyed the city "to think of new things that should be built," to make it more beautiful and more humane. "You know," La Guardia mused, "I am in the position of an artist or a sculptor. . . . I can see New York as it should be and as it can be. . . .

But now I am in the position of a man who has a conception that he wishes to carve or to paint, who has the model before him, but hasn't a chisel or a brush.'' Interior Secretary Ickes held the chisels and brushes in the form of a $3.3 billion public works budget, and La Guardia sought a gifted builder to translate his dreams for a modern graceful city into projects that would attract Ickes's funding.[20]

Not another lawyer; he hated them. Lawyers, he once said, had done more to harm civilization than smallpox and cancer. They were the ''semi-colon boys'' always finding some new wrinkle in a plain English sentence, squeezing forth another technicality. They always had hundreds of reasons why the city could not do something while they sprang another criminal free from justice; prostitutes selling their services to the highest bidder. Architects and engineers he respected. They built. ''He stood like a child before the simplest engineering feat,'' recalled Paul Kern. And public builders he respected most of all.[21]

To manage New York's public works he wanted the Man Who Could Get Things Done, president of the State Parks Commission, Robert Moses. La Guardia was awed by the job that Robert Moses had accomplished with the New York State parks. He once told Paul Windels that he liked to drive along the Long Island parkways that Moses had built, for inspiration. And they were inspiring! For Moses thought in terms that few other public officials had even dared to dream: huge public undertakings that changed not only the physical landscape but the terms of social reference by which entire communities related to their surroundings.

In the early 1920s Moses had fixed his thoughts on Long Island and dreamed of a state park on Jones Beach, another on Fire Island, and three more state parks on the south shore of Long Island, and four parks on the Sound, and two more at the island's center. In fact, he dreamed of tens of thousands of acres of new parks. And parkways connecting them, so that a family driving from New York City could drive up to the island parks and beaches along beautiful roads. He had dreamed, in fact, of 124 miles of parkways, carefully landscaped to form ''ribbon parks.'' In the summer of 1924 Moses took Governor Al Smith for a tour of his dream. ''Why don't I make you President of the Long Island State Park Commission,'' asked Governor Smith. Why, yes, he would take the job, said Moses. And then he went out and converted his dream into real grass.

In the process he had learned how to use the law to get things done, to drive men to get things done, to find the best engineers and architects and back them to the hilt to get things done, to reward executives who worked under him with power and perquisites in order to cement their loyalty and spur their devotion to get things done; to use every bit of information and shrewdness to cow legislators into getting things done, to curry favor with the powerful and the press to get things done. And over all of this to spin the gossamer of higher purpose. Moses was ready for new dreams. The challenge of equipping New York with modern physical surroundings and parks offered a proper scale for his interests.

La Guardia wanted this uniquely gifted Man Who Could Get Things Done to manage his public works program.

However, before he would accept the post of city parks commissioner, Moses laid down a set of conditions: The five separate borough parks departments must be consolidated under his single hand; he must retain his presidency over the State Parks Commission, to enable him to exert "unified control of the whole metropolitan system of parks and parkway development"; and he insisted on control of the Triborough Bridge Authority and over another authority not even yet in existence, the Marine Parkway Bridge Authority that he planned to establish to construct a bridge to the Rockaways. La Guardia agreed to everything, exulting, "I'm appointing the best man in the United States."[22]

The state legislature had to approve a state official's appointment to a city job, and La Guardia entrusted Moses, "the best bill drafter in Albany," with preparing the enabling legislation. What the best bill drafter did was to create a bill with enough hidden possibilities to allow him to hold as many jobs as La Guardia might ever want to send in his direction. Responding to the complaint that no one man could serve two masters faithfully, La Guardia explained that the two were really one master: "New York City is the only geographical and political unit in the State of New York, not part of a state park region. . . . Obviously, if the state wished it could use the city Park Commissioner as its agent for state park and parkway work . . . just as it is using County Park Commissioners in Westchester and Erie." There could be no possible conflict. Governor Lehman and Al Smith endorsed the appointment, and reformers from all over the state rallied behind the man they counted as one of their own. On January 19, 1934, a day after the governor signed the "Moses bill," Mayor La Guardia swore in his new parks commissioner.[23]

The CWA had put some 68,000 men to work on parks and other refurbishing projects around the city before Moses took office. But many of the workers and supervisors carried out their tasks halfheartedly, as if this work was only an excuse to pay the unemployed. Inspectors touring Marine Park in Brooklyn found most of the 5000 CWA workers assigned there keeping themselves warm around small fires and passing the bottle. The few who were working would rake the frozen ground or build part of a fence here and there. The whole thing was undirected and aimless.

Pronouncing the existing staff "undisciplined, untrained, and unskilled," Moses fired all five borough park commissioners, their deputies, and their entire staffs on his very first day in office. He brought in a corps of "Moses men," handpicked and hard-trained to weed out those who had managed to take the beauty and excitement out of the parks under Tammany. Personnel covered by civil service could not be fired summarily. They were reassigned as far from their homes as possible, at tasks calculated to make them quit. Robert Caro tells the story of an old woman who refused to go on her own: "One ancient biddy, accustomed to spending her days at the Arsenal (Department Headquarters in Central Park) knitting in a rocking chair, refused to admit she was over retirement age and gracefully accept a pension. When a search failed to produce a birth certificate to disprove her story, she was ordered to work overtime—all night. Every time she tried to rest, she was ordered to keep working. She retired at 2 A.M.''

La Guardia backed Moses even when the commissioner insisted on breaking rules. He wanted to hire architects at wages above the maximums set by the CWA. He wanted more generous allotments for materials and planning than the CWA would approve. But La Guardia knew that Moses could convert these special allowances into savings many times over the outlays and he supported him. Every once in a while when Moses did not get his way he would simply deliver his single most powerful argument: "I quit." At $13,000 a year he was the city's largest bargain, and La Guardia knew it. The argument was invariably persuasive.[24]

On January 28 the Parks Department began hiring architects and engineers, who flocked by the thousands to apply for 600 openings that were announced. Those hired were handed assignments and put to work immediately. On the very first day they were initiated into the frenetic work pace of the new team. As the men laid down their pencils and began to go home at the end of eight hours, a number of them were told that they were needed to complete plans. If they went home tonight, they need not report tomorrow. Cots were set up outside the offices for them to nap and work through the night.

Laborers were treated even more harshly. Moses brought in the toughest "ramrods," unsparing construction foremen, that he could find to whip the CWA crews into shape. Workers who were too slow or undependable were fired on the spot. Moses offered no apologies. "The government and the taxpayers have a right to demand an adequate return in good work, faithfully performed, for the money that is being spent. . . . We inherited men who were working without plan and without supervision. The plans have now been made, the supervision is being supplied, *and we expect the men to work*."

Teams of engineers and park experts were sent out to survey the parks. They returned with lists of thousands of renovation projects. Others drove around the city with Moses, brainstorming new construction programs: a West Side Highway, Riverside Park, a modern and enlarged Orchard Beach.

Hidden out behind Pelham Bay Park, Orchard was not much of a beach when Moses found it. It was a low spit of sand that linked Hunter's Island and Rodman Neck near the Bronx–Westchester line. The small site had become a private playground for several hundred well-connected families who rented the 625 bungalows surrounding the beach. Moses ordered the bungalows torn down, and with them the ill-constructed bathhouses and poorly designed sand bar that cut the beach in two. His planners designed a fresh, light, and large beach by filling in the water between Rodman and Hunter's with landfill to create a mile of crescent-shaped beach-playground with picnic and game areas, a curved boardwalk, and ample parking. "He just decides what he's going to do", marveled one of the park engineers, "and it's done."[25]

As the sight of Moses' men building parks and beaches quickly became routine, the mayor and his builder went to work on another project that fit the monumental scale of the new administration's aspirations. Years before, New York City had created the Triborough Bridge Authority to negotiate a federal loan and issue bonds for a Triborough Bridge project, pledging bridge toll collections to their retirement. The project called for a colossal complex of four bridges linking together three boroughs and two East River islands to provide efficient car transportation across the coastal waters. One span, vaulting over the Harlem River to connect Manhattan with Randall's Island, would itself be the largest vertical lift bridge in the world. Linking Randall's to the Bronx would be an eight-lane, triple-truss structure across the Bronx Kills. Yet a third arch, a half-mile-long suspension bridge, would join Ward's Island and Queens. Into the anchorages of this single span would go enough cable wire to circle the globe twice around. A causeway between Randall's and Ward's Islands would complete the bridge complex.

In the midst of a depression this $50 million project promised employment to thousands. One estimate calculated that Triborough construction would generate 31 million man-hours of work in 134 cities in twenty states. But when La Guardia took office, the quasi-independent agency responsible for this immense project was controlled by three Tammany incompetents.

By the end of January one of the commissioners resigned after being indicted for violations ranging from conflict of interest to political favoritism, and another was removed for cause along with the authority's general counsel. On February 4 La Guardia appointed Robert Moses commissioner, secretary, and chief executive officer of the Triborough Bridge Authority and filled the second vacancy with George V. McLaughlin, a Moses admirer. Soon thereafter, La Guardia sent a bill up to Albany creating the Marine Parkway Authority. In this instance the authority had only one member, Commissioner Moses. Seven agencies were entrusted with power over parks and parkways in New York State, and Robert Moses ran them all.[26]

La Guardia and Moses were alike in many respects, in their audacious sense of urban possibility, their dedication to the large job, and the fear and grudging admiration that they inspired among those who worked for them. In Moses, La Guardia found a man at least as driven, ambitious, and work-addicted as he. La Guardia once wrote his parks commissioner that he had sponsored Moses for membership in the Circus of Saints and Sinners. "It is quite an affair and I am sure it will be in keeping with your high and exalted position." Moses wrote back, thanking the mayor, but "if you don't mind there is so much to do that I am going to forego all parties, luncheons, speaking engagements, etc., except those of a strictly official nature. I cut them all out some time ago as a matter of fact."

Between the two power-driven men it was like a famous marriage: They could hardly stand to be with each other and they could not at all stand to be without each other. "There were moments," Paul Kern recalled, "when you could swear they were going to come to blows. . . ." Moses refused to do commissioner duty waiting outside La Guardia's office; instead he would send a deputy or a potted plant. He would sometimes come out of Fiorello's office, after one of their confrontations, livid. "Someday I'm going to hit that son-of-a-bitch and knock him through the door!" he once sputtered to Reuben Lazarus. Privately he would refer to the mayor as "that dago," "wop," or "guinea son of a bitch," or more tenderly he would speak of "that little organ grinder, Rigoletto," and La Guardia would refer to his arrogant commissioner as "His Grace." Moses never allowed the mayor to threaten to fire *him*. Instead, he was always ready to resign at the first sign of disagreement. "I must insist," he would insist, that this or that project be approved, money be made available, or some rule be bent, "otherwise I cannot assume further responsibility for this work." The tactic would usually shake La Guardia and win Moses his demand.[27]

Tired of this reversal, the mayor tried sarcasm: "Enclosed are last five or six resignations; I'm starting a new file." His Grace was not amused, so naturally La Guardia pressed further, producing a batch of preprinted resignation forms: "I, Robert Moses do hereby resign as _____ effective _____." The next time Moses raised his threats, La Guardia pulled out the pad. "Here, just fill in the blanks." Moses glanced at the form and flung it across the room. But despite his arrogance, La Guardia trusted Moses to accomplish the broad modernization that he envisioned. "No law, no regulation, no budget stops Bob Moses in his appointed task," he once remarked admiringly. The man was impossible, and he crunched the ego of anyone he worked with, but his projects were awesome. La Guardia gave him as free a rein as he gave anyone who ever worked for him. Theirs would be a great, painful, tempestuous, and ultimately effective collaboration.[28]

───────

Robert Moses looked at the plans for the Triborough Bridge and shuddered. These were the kind of unimaginative, incomplete, patronage-larded plans that were typical of Tammany. The design made inadequate provision for approach roads in Queens and the Bronx. In Manhattan the bridge terminus was inexplicably placed at 125th Street, when as much as 85 percent of the interborough traffic would be headed for destinations below 100th Street. With 100th Street directly across from the Queens boundary, it would have made all the sense in the world to have placed the terminus there. Moses suspected that the exit was twenty-five blocks out of the way because Democratic newspaper magnate William Randolph Hearst owned real estate in that area and wanted to sell it to the city for a handsome return. Moses studied the plans—he absorbed them—and he concluded that the initial proposal for a two-deck, sixteen-lane, granite-covered bridge was too bulky and too expensive. Everything on the bridge seemed to be covered with costly granite to enrich Tammany pols who owned the quarries.

He did not challenge Hearst, leaving the terminus where it was planned, but he got rid of the granite, trimmed the size of the bridge, and packed off the holdover Tammany chief engineer and his crew with a hail of dismissals and resignations. As new chief, Moses selected the designer of the George Washington Bridge, Othmar Hermann Ammann, and paired him with a tough-as-nails administrator, retired brigadier general Paul Loesser. Working with experienced bridge builders, the new team created fresh plans, chipping more than $20 million off the estimated cost of the project.

Moses had no intention of returning the savings to the Public Works Administration. With this money he wanted to build approach roads and a system of connecting streets, none of which had been adequately provided for in the original plans. While, strictly speaking, PWA money was only for the bridge and entry ramps, he argued that new streets were a necessary part of the project and he won Ickes's approval. In fact, the usually parsimonious PWA chief kicked in an extra $2 million for this part of the project. Moses saved some more money by listing much of the construction along the Triborough passages as park work and utilizing CWA workers, saving the PWA allocations for materials and land.

The price of labor was nothing compared to what would have to be paid for the land. The city had the power to condemn through legal proceedings, but it would have to pay a fair price. Even on a depression market the miles and miles of real estate needed for these connecting roads were valued at more than the entire project. Moses discovered that many of the old deeds for property along the East River included a covenant reserving waterfront footage for the city in the event that it ever built there. More land came from local businesses who traded property for concessions from the city. Where it was possible, new land was created. In Flushing Bay two miles were filled in, connecting the Grand Central Parkway to the bridge, and in Manhattan a ten-foot-wide concrete extension was hung over the East River above Ninety-second Street. After the city panhandled some more money from Ickes, La Guardia kicked in another $1.3 million to build a six-lane East River Drive with a tree-lined riverfront park.

At the time, the two islands that were part of the Triborough ring, Randall's and Ward's, were being used for the disposal of refuse and housing the disabled and unfortunate. Moses wanted to build parks here. In Manhattan he could only nibble small chunks of property out of the most expensive real estate in the world. Here, just a few miles from midtown, a drive over the Triborough away from three boroughs, it was possible to plan in terms of acres rather than feet; to plan tennis courts, baseball, football, and soccer fields, boat basins, benches, trees, playgrounds, and parks; and a sports stadium to hold 70,000. Materials costs would not exceed $300,000, and Moses would assign CWA workers to the project, passing the cost of labor to the federal government. Under Moses, the Triborough became New York City's brood mare of public works projects.[29]

Then suddenly the federal money stopped coming, and in late February 1934 it was put to a stunned La Guardia that he would have to choose between his master builder and the president who held the money for the chisels.

Years before, when Bob Moses was a very powerful member of Al Smith's cabinet and Franklin Roosevelt was a recently paralyzed man with a wonderful future behind him, the two men fixed their none-too-tender attitudes about each other. FDR was just beginning to coax his legs back to strength and to reinvolve himself in politics when Al Smith persuaded him to accept the chairmanship of the Taconic State Park Commission. Roosevelt accepted on the condition that his pet project, a Taconic Parkway through the scenic Hudson region, be approved. He also wanted a place for his personal secretary and political adviser Louis Howe with the Taconic Commission. Moses, president of the State Parks Commission, nixed Howe's appointment, declaring snidely that if Roosevelt wanted a secretary and personal valet, he would have to pay him himself.

Moses, by then the second most powerful man in the state, several times blocked approval of the Taconic Parkway that had become Roosevelt's passion. After repeated assurances and broken promises, Roosevelt, in November of 1926, unburdened himself to Smith: "I wasn't born yesterday. . . . You know, just as well as I do, that Bob has skinned us alive this year. . . . I am sorry to say it as a fact that Bob Moses has played fast and loose with the Taconic State Park Commission since the beginning."

The letter was as plain as two years of frustration and pent-up anger could make it. Roosevelt was tired of Bob Moses' lies and he submitted his resignation. Smith apologized profusely and the resignation was withdrawn but Roosevelt never forgot Moses' cavalier disregard. When Al Smith, bitten by the presidential bug, went off to chase the presidency, he passed over Secretary of State Robert Moses and nominated Roosevelt to succeed him to the governorship. Moses did not hide his disappointment. Pity that Al set his heart on such an empty man, he told acquaintances; all Roosevelt had going for him was a smile and a name. The Dutchess County gentleman was not up to the job, Moses confided to Mrs. Smith. He would be a poor governor. Moses' private comments about Roosevelt were even more vicious. The crippled patrician, he would taunt, was a poor excuse for a man, and Eleanor a gawky caricature of a woman. When Roosevelt learned what Bob Moses was saying he hated him even more.[30]

La Guardia knew none of this when he appointed Moses. He had even sent Moses, together with Adolf Berle, to Washington to represent the new administration in critical discussions regarding federal assistance to the city. It did not particularly disturb the mayor when his parks commissioner criticized Washington for a "virtual breakdown" in the CWA and voiced frustrations with directing "carpenters who have no wood, painters who have no paint and cleaners who have no mops and brooms." A bit of Moses criticism would keep Washington on its toes.[31]

Then on February 22 La Guardia learned that he had made a mistake. "Jesus Christ," the mayor yodeled to Paul Windels, "of all the people in the City of New York I had to pick the one man who Roosevelt won't stand for and he won't give me any more money unless I get rid of him." Alternately shaking, cursing, and screaming, La Guardia was in a panic. Jealous of every minute that municipal workers owed the city, he had nonetheless ordered New York offices to close early on January 30, to celebrate Roosevelt's birthday. He took his relationship with the president very seriously. And now all his plans were jeopardized. Damn![32]

La Guardia's enlightenment was rapid and crystal-clear. Summoned to Washington by the secretary of the interior, La Guardia was informed by Ickes that "Moses was a bitter personal enemy of the President's. The President and such friends as Jim Farley and Louis Howe think that Moses would leave nothing undone to hurt the President." Ickes then told La Guardia, "We don't want to do any business with Moses." A shaken La Guardia regretted that he had not known before. He voiced the highest respect for the president and asked for a few days to work it out. It did not have to be pointed out to the mayor that he was waiting for some $65 million in loans from Ickes's PWA, and that his economy bill was being raked over the coals by New York State Democrats who would have to be persuaded to change their votes.[33]

Windels and Berle both advised La Guardia to stand fast. Give in to the feds and "your name is going to be mud," the corporation counsel advised. And Berle, who just a month before had written that he "would be glad of a steer" from the White House in navigating the City and the federal government toward a friendly relationship, wired Roosevelt: "MOSES MATTER WILL PROBABLY BECOME A NATIONAL INCIDENT WITHIN A FEW DAYS SINCE TRIBOROUGH FUNDS ARE STILL HELD UP STOP THINK THIS IS ONE OF THE THINGS YOU CANNOT DO." If Moses was pressured into resigning from the Triborough, the city chamberlain wrote, then he would resign from all of his other posts, calling attention to the president's heavy hand. "I HARDLY KNOW MOSES BUT SUGGEST THERE MIGHT BE MORE REAL DEVILS TO FIGHT STOP REMEMBER THE EXECUTION OF THE DUKE D'ENGHIEN BROKE NAPOLEON." Roosevelt wrote back the next day, making excuses that members of an independent "authority must be divorced from any other public agency." This was the rationale for deposing "your friend, the duc. . . . I think you will see the point." The president was confident that on this principle he would be able to drive back any public outcry.[34]

Berle tried to reason with Roosevelt. It would look awful for Washington to dictate Moses' firing by threatening to cut off federal funds. "We can defend . . . a ruling of general application," Berle wrote, but an order so obviously singling

307

out Moses "FH could not defend without wrecking his administration and alienate both for him and you, progressives everywhere." Ickes, uncomfortable at being forced to play the heavy, would have liked to back off, but Roosevelt refused. "The President has a feeling of dislike of [Moses] that I haven't seen him express with respect to any other person," Ickes confided to his diary.[35]

La Guardia did the only thing he could do. He kept on putting Ickes off with one excuse after another, hoping that the issue would die down. And after a few weeks the troublesome noises from Washington did indeed cease. There seemed to be no hard feelings as Democrats helped pass the economy bill and Ickes's PWA awarded New York a $7.6 million grant for extending the West Side Highway. Other grants for the Sixth Avenue subway, new school buildings and hospitals totaling more than $92 million were approved before the summer, assuring thousands of jobs for city workers. La Guardia kept sending Adolf Berle back to the well for more, and the chamberlain proved remarkably effective. The Holland Tunnel, public housing, pier construction and parks were all added to the list of high-ticket PWA grants to the city.

Moses, using PWA funds and CWA workers and whatever he could squeeze out of the mayor, meanwhile carried out his own ambitious park agenda, oblivious to the behind-the-scenes controversy about him. Despite a fierce winter, laborers who just a short while back had spent their workdays looking for a place to warm up, were put on double and triple shifts. On February 23 New York had eighteen inches of snow on the ground. Offices closed, cars could not pass through many streets, but the Parks Department did not stop working *outdoors*. Through ice and snow and below-zero cold, the refurbishing of the parks never halted. An atmosphere of excitement took hold of the architects and engineers who saw their plans almost immediately turned into finished improvements. In one feverish sixteen-day stretch, working with one eye pitched out the windows of their Arsenal headquarters, a team of fifteen architects completed plans for a new Central Park zoo.[36]

La Guardia could not be happier with the operation. "Please go easy on me today, boys," he called out to city hall reporters as he sank into his chair and gathered them round his desk. The press corps knew the tone. The mayor was going to enjoy himself. "I've just had a terrible shock. I visited two work relief projects and I found every single, solitary man on them working, and working hard." He had poked around the two sites, one in Central Park and the other at the Columbus Circle monument, and, boys, the crew was really doing a job. Stonecutters, carpenters, electricians, and laborers "were all working—and when I say working I mean working." Over the years, Attilio Piccirilli's monument to those who had died in the explosion of the U.S.S. *Maine* had become encrusted with grime, and vandals had snapped pieces off. La Guardia had taken Piccirilli with him to view the restoration and cleaning of the huge monument. When his sculptor friend saw the repairs, "tears streamed down his face."[37]

After the CWA was phased out in March, half the parks laborers were dismissed, but Moses' ramrods kept the rest working, and when on the first balmy Saturday of the new spring New Yorkers visited their parks, they were amazed. Seventeen hundred renovation projects had been completed; everything in the parks had been repainted, every lawn reseeded, and every tennis court resurfaced. Miles of walks, bridle paths, and playing surfaces had been refinished. Hundreds of comfort stations, drinking fountains, wading pools and park benches were repaired, thousands of dead trees uprooted, sandboxes refilled and nineteen miles of fences put up. Moses put uniforms on park employees, including the relief workers assigned to the parks. When the welfare commissioner protested that they were not Parks Department personnel, Moses told him, "I won't have them slopping around in any old clothes." Parks were meant to be fun, not grave reminders of down-and-out reliefers in their sackcloth.[38]

From empty plots that had for the longest time been strewn with the refuse of careless New Yorkers bloomed colorful flowers. Seven new municipal golf courses were opened. Central Park was brought back to life. The roaming rat packs were exterminated. Squatters who had taken up residence from Hoover's days in the dry reservoir bed were evicted, making way for a Great Lawn. Play areas, pools, sports courts and a Tavern-on-the-Green were all added. Moses had spent $26 million on parks, all of it, he assured New Yorkers, "judiciously." The biblical Moses had smitten the rock and brought forth water; La Guardia's Moses, joked wags, smote the rock and brought forth water, flowers, trees, and playing fields. And he did it while cutting administrative costs to half what they had been under Tammany.

He made new parks as well. La Guardia had no money for parks, so Moses did it without money. Every strip of public land that was not being put to use was fair game, as the Parks Department surveyed the city record for idle property and La Guardia instructed the Sinking Fund Commission, which held control over much of this property, to turn it over. By May sixty-nine new small parks and play areas had been developed. In 1918 the city had raised through public subscription more than $200,000 for a war memorial. It was never enough for the elaborate arch that had been contemplated, and the money remained in a city account for all these years. Now it was put to use in a war memorial playground for each borough.

On the Lower East Side, where from Jimmy Walker's time the city had dawdled with the huge Chrystie-Forsyth tract, the new administration created a fine playground for the slum children. Even Arnold Rothstein's estate was converted to public use. The murdered gambler had died with tax arrears of $334,000. The bill was cleared by forgiving the back taxes in return for a seventy-four-acre chunk of Rothstein's estate in middle Queens.

There had been 119 playgrounds in New York in the summer of 1933. In the summer of 1934 there were 179.[39]

3. Administrative Order 129

I N November 1934 the new Central Park zoo was completed. The old menagerie was replaced with a sprightly "picture-book zoo," standing several hundred feet behind the old Arsenal. With only $500,000 to spend, it had not been possible to create a world-class zoo. Instead the designers aimed for something significant and fresh on a smaller scale, an amusing collection of animals for New York's children.

Trumpeteers blew their horns as polka-dot and candy-striped paper wrapping was ripped away to reveal a huge picture book with a door. And there, happy as a kid on vacation, stood a bulky five-foot-two figure with a huge gold key. Unlocking the picture-book door, Fiorello La Guardia led 1200 invited guests through a narrow corridor covered with cheerful six-foot-high paintings of animals inscribed "A is for ape," "L is for llama," "Z is for zebra." Where the old wooden animal sheds had been stood new low-slung single-story brick buildings grouped around a landscaped quadrangle with a pool of barking seals. The walls of the cage buildings were decorated with bright drawings and carvings. That day more than 32,000 people came to visit the new zoo. Within months, 100,000 New Yorkers came by every Sunday; another Moses success story.

The parks commissioner had his critics as well. When Moses demolished a reproduction of Washington's Mount Vernon homestead to clear land in Brooklyn's Prospect Park, they denounced his high-handed tactics. Moses had given notice that if any groups were interested in preserving the faux presidential home they must take it down and move it elsewhere. Accustomed to Tammany efficiency they dallied; he bulldozed. He liked to tell his staff that you can't make omelets without cracking eggs. The complaints of his most dangerous critic, however, did not appear in the newspapers. He did not even know about it, but the Parks Commissioner and Triborough Authority Member was about to be part of an omelet prepared by the president.[40]

The White House effort to dump Moses had not been dropped, only set aside for a while as the president turned his full attention to bringing about an elusive economic recovery and to the fall congressional elections. Every time La Guardia went to Washington he received a warm reception and another grant that he brought back and often as not handed to his superbuilder, Robert Moses.

Meanwhile, Robert Moses had caught the electoral bug, challenging Governor Herbert Lehman on the 1934 Republican ticket. Without bothering to ask for it, Moses announced La Guardia's backing and ran his campaign as if it were a prelude to a coronation. There is very little that a candidate can hide in a modern campaign, and what came through most clearly during this one was Moses' consuming arrogance and incivility. Lehman invariably treated him with respect (on the night of his election victory Lehman assured Al Smith that he would not remove Moses from his state park posts), but Moses resorted to name-calling—"liar," "puppet," "stupid," "miserable, snivelling . . . contemptible," being a few examples. His rough treatment of the respected incumbent governor further alienated Washington. "The bitterness displayed by Farley and the whole gang . . . against Moses," a friend later wrote to La Guardia, "was vitriolic." But it also protected him. With a campaign under way, the administration was wary of appearing heavy-handed and partisan. Ickes approved tens of millions in New York City PWA proposals.[41]

Gifted in everything but the common touch, Moses went on to a thorough trouncing in the election. With the returns in, Fiorello began hearing from Ickes again. More than $8 million in Triborough requisitions were on his desk. If Moses stays, they don't move. There would be no new allocations for *any* New York projects; those already approved might also be held up. But, sputtered Fiorello, he could not dismiss Moses without preferring charges. Ickes was unmoved. He told the distraught mayor to do as he wished. It was "his funeral and not mine," Ickes confided to his diary. The entire idea of a city–federal partnership seemed to be foundering on the silliest of obstacles. FDR's hatred for Moses was forcing La Guardia to either wound his own credibility or give up thousands of jobs for New York's unemployed as well as untold millions in public works.

On November 21, 1934, as the PWA board met to review submissions, Ickes struck all New York City proposals off the list. Out of patience with La Guardia's excuses, Ickes wanted action. He even offered La Guardia the choice of simply assuring him that Moses would not be reappointed when he came up for renewal in June.[42]

La Guardia's closest advisers warned against knuckling under. "There is only one course to pursue," tough old Burlingham wrote him, "and that is to stand like a rock against Ickes and all the rest. It is none of their d____ business. . . . Nothing would do your administration more harm than to have one of the very best men in it crowded out. . . . R.M. is a dangerous nettle to fool around with." La Guardia also had to consider the fusion coalition upon which his election had been built. He had not been their first choice. For many that first choice had been Moses. To dismiss RM would shake more than Fiorello's image. La Guardia finally had an answer for Ickes. Moses might be a bastard, but he was his bastard and he would have to reappoint him as Triborough commissioner in June.[43]

Ickes sent investigators ferreting into Triborough operations, looking for some cause to remove Moses on charges, but they came up with nothing. If the White House wanted Moses fired, it would have to come out in the open and say so. On the day after Christmas 1934 it said so loud and clear. Ickes sent La Guardia a new order, PWA Administrative General Order No. 129:

311

Hereafter no funds shall be advanced to any authority, board or commission constituting an independent corporation or entity created for a specific project wholly within the confines of a municipality, any of the members of the governing body of which authority, board or commission holds any public office under said municipality.

This general order was aimed, Ickes confided to La Guardia, specifically and solely at Moses. Roosevelt personally helped Ickes draft the order and personally told La Guardia that he wanted Moses out. FH promised to send Ickes a letter that he would not reappoint Moses in June. Then he said he would bring it. Then he came to Washington and he didn't have it, again promising to send it. Stalemate.[44]

Back at home, La Guardia was suffering over the order. A strong New York-Washington relationship was the cornerstone of both his unemployment and reconstruction policies for the city. He was preparing to announce a bouquet of plans for $310 million in additional PWA monies, and he was going to argue for these loans at the rate of one-eighth of 1 percent interest. There were more plans for another $100 million. These were not pie-in-the-sky proposals. He had good reason to believe that many of them would be approved, except that Moses was now in the way. Could he endanger the city for the principle of protecting Moses? But he did not want to lose Moses from the parks commissionership; nor did he want to remove him from Triborough without giving him a chance to resign. To give Moses some appreciation of the pressure he was under, La Guardia showed him a copy of the general order and the private letter that Ickes had written to him, spelling out the intent of the order.[45]

Moses moved the stalemate off center in a way that was painful for La Guardia and embarrassing for Ickes, in a way no politician who had to weigh the larger consequences would have done. All of this maneuvering had been going on more or less in secret for close to a year. To the public, General Order No. 129 seemed like one more bureaucratic policy. It had no idea that the order was aimed only at Moses. Of all the participants in this tug-of-war, only Moses had nothing to lose by going public, and he did, leaking the story to the press.

Berle had warned the president that it would not look good in the papers and Moses made sure that it did not, taking full advantage of his position as the wronged party. Here he was, he explained, doing the best job he knew how, and the politicians were working behind his back for shabby motives to get rid of him. He was willing to resign, he said, but if he left the Triborough he was not going to stick around to run parks in an administration that would not back him on the bridges.

The administration had managed to give Moses a way back into the public heart so shortly after his huge drubbing at the polls. He was on the right side this time, and the public drew around him as the underdog. The papers were roaring their wrath and Ickes couldn't much blame them, except for his discomfort at being the one "left holding the bag."

312

He was not alone. Not alone. Stepping off the train from Washington, La Guardia was met by a bevy of reporters. This was his first serious clash with Washington. How would it be handled? "Are you going to get rid of Commissioner Moses?" He had not known that the story was out until just a few minutes before. He had no idea how Ickes would be answering the same questions. Years of experience with the press had taught Fiorello to answer such questions at an angle.

"I am the Mayor of the city am I not?"

"What are you going to do?"

"I'll think it over."

"Did they ask that the Parks Commissioner quit?"

They actually had not asked Moses to quit his Parks Department position, only the commissionership of the Triborough, so again La Guardia replied to the question in the narrowest sense.

"They have nothing to do with a city job."

But would this contretemps cost the city its PWA funding? La Guardia reassured the journalists that the relationship with Washington could not be more harmonious, "in every respect and every detail."[46]

Meanwhile, although the president had tried to make his policy fit Moses alone, Order 129 caught one more official in its web, New York City's Tenement House commissioner and Housing Authority chairman, Langdon Post, who was out of the country. "At least Post is on the high seas," cracked the embattled mayor at a news conference on January 4, "and he can't issue any statements."[47]

Aldermanic president Bernard Deutsch saw no choice for Fiorello but to back Moses. Burlingham had reassured FH that the Triborough funds could not legally be halted, and that Ickes himself might not last in Washington for other reasons. Perhaps the PWA would be taken out of his hands. Stand pat. But La Guardia could not be so sanguine. It reminded him, he wrote Burlingham, of the lawyer who told his client that he could not be put in jail for what he had done when the client was *in* jail. "I can't build on litigation; I need steel girders and brick, mortar and labor to build." Burlingham disagreed. He felt that La Guardia had played weak. He should have stopped Ickes earlier. If he fired Moses now he would lose the trust of the entire fusion coalition. "I told him last night," Burlingham wrote Felix Frankfurter, "that if he did not look out the guns now directed against Washington would be turned on him. It is intolerable that personal spleen should affect laws."[48]

The editorial writers added their advice: The mayor must reject so contemptible and extraordinary a *ukase*; resign rather than give in; stand up to them, and let them take their contracts; "backbone," urged another; "Bureaucracy! Patronage! Politics!" exclaimed one paper, with the slimiest imprecations it could find. Civic associations and citizens councils all over the city announced their indignant support of Moses. And the letters poured in to the newspapers. "Our Mayor has repeatedly crawled on his belly before Washington in abject supplication," one Edward Chase

313

wrote to the *Herald Tribune*. "Are we, as citizens of the sovereign State of New York, to have a political mongrel from the Middle West [Ickes] instruct us as to who shall build our bridges and who shall plant our gardens?"[49]

Ickes too blamed Fiorello for following "a crooked course during the whole proceeding." The interior secretary felt that his confidential letters should not have been shown to Moses. "I had felt that La Guardia was a man of real courage and substance, but in this matter he has acted like the cheapest kind of double crossing politician." But Ickes's great preoccupation with how all of this affected Harold Ickes distorted his perceptions. While holding New York hostage for millions of dollars to satisfy presidential spite, Ickes wanted La Guardia to act the gentleman, but La Guardia could not afford to cave in to presidential bullying. He was far from heroic in this, but it was Ickes who was dealing the harsh hand. "My action in the Moses case is at utter variance with any other act of mine," Ickes admitted to himself in his diary. Fiorello had no options but to try to survive on his own sly moves.[50]

Moses was enjoying himself too much to give up the initiative. He kept issuing press releases about the dwindling Triborough funds, drawing attention to the administration's refusal to release allocated dollars. Among the hundreds of letters to the White House concerning Moses was a wire from C. C. Burlingham urging compromise. "Kindly tell Skipper," read the message to presidential Secretary Louis Howe, "universal sentiment here pro Moses. Hope he will develop face-saving formula for secretarial retreat from order 129."[51]

Ickes, who had been having problems getting in to see the president, finally met him on Thursday, January 10, for the first time since the story hit the press. The meeting began on a cordial note. Then Ickes brought up Moses. The president turned to steel; this was no mere grudge, there was true hatred at the bottom of this. Yes, he still wanted the order to stand and he did not mind if Ickes passed responsibility for it directly to him. Other New York projects would receive their money—and the papers would soon report loans and grants to New York that added up to a billion-dollar works program—but Ickes was to hold back every penny from the Triborough until Moses was retired. Two weeks later Roosevelt repeated the same thing.[52]

Returning from the capital on January 18, La Guardia told the press that nothing would be permitted to disturb relations between Washington and the city. Too much was involved on both sides. Ickes, when asked what would happen if Moses sat tight and refused to resign, replied: "That makes two of us. It will become a popular indoor sport. I've issued an order and that's all I've got to say about it." Entrail readers were again predicting that Moses' days were numbered. Some papers reported that La Guardia had decided to fire Moses to break the deadlock. "We . . . depend on him," FH said about Ickes. "We simply must have close cooperation and understanding with Washington."[53]

Again Burlingham sent Fiorello some strong advice. "You have told me that you did not think one man should be permitted to obstruct or imperil the relief of hundreds of thousands.'' But that one man had become too important to abandon. ''Washington has taken the position the English Kings took toward the American colonies.'' La Guardia represented every municipality in the nation, and the issue was no longer merely Moses but the nature of the emerging federal-urban relationship. La Guardia must reject ''the unreasonable and tyrannical order'' to show that the cities would not sell their independence for federal lucre. ''The sentiment in New York is so strong that as our representative you must respect it. . . . Public sentiment at all points . . . is unanimous. Even those who dislike Moses for his bad manners and rough stuff agree that it would be far better to let the work on the Triborough cease than to yield to order 129.''

One hundred and forty-seven of New York's most prominent social, civic, and business groups representing a wide range of responsible public opinion echoed Burlingham. They told La Guardia to find other money rather than pay for the federal loan with the head of a duly appointed public official.[54]

Meanwhile, Roosevelt was running into opposition on other fronts. The Senate saddled his public works appropriations request with unwelcome amendments and soundly rejected his proposal for American entry into the World Court. The solid New Deal Congress was developing cracks, and some legislators thought that Congress should investigate the entire issue surrounding General Order 129. The Moses matter was causing too much damage. Ickes's tone in his diary changed from self-righteous to rueful. ''My action . . . was entirely out of keeping with my whole record and with my political philosophy,'' and for the first time he intimated that the president too would ''welcome a way out of this cul-de-sac. . . .'' To a visitor who asked him to back off, Roosevelt asked whether the president of the United States was ''not entitled to one personal grudge,'' but he was ready to deal.[55]

Late in February Roosevelt asked La Guardia to join him on the train as he rode from Philadelphia to Cambridge and then on to Hyde Park. He wanted to discuss Moses again, but this time, wrote Ickes, ''the President and I came to the conclusion that a retreat was in order.'' La Guardia handed Roosevelt a draft of a letter that he thought might allow a graceful solution, along with a note that he had written at home:

My dear Mr. President,

I submit the enclosed proposed draft in the course of a pourparler looking to an exchange of communiques. After reading the enclosed draft I admit it is a sort of cross between Gertrude Stein's poems, the Einstein theory, and a Mrs. Sanger essay on birth control. That ought to qualify it as a political document.

For much of the train ride Roosevelt and Ickes worked with him on the two-page draft, and on the response that was to come from Ickes. The drafts were left

315

with Ickes to polish. Characteristically, Ickes polished and polished and days went by without release of the correspondence. All the while, Triborough money languished in Washington as the self-absorbed curmudgeon sharpened the part of the letter that attacked Moses. "I put a lot more teeth in this portion of the President's letter in my redraft. In fact I made it quite savage." Then it went back to the president. Washington seemed intent on delaying. Maybe something would come up and they could still get rid of Moses.[56]

On February 27 Al Smith broke into the headlines. Many had been surprised that he had kept quiet this long. But he made up for it now, blasting Roosevelt and Ickes for jeopardizing the Triborough project. Moses was absolutely critical for its effective completion, Smith declared, but Washington was too caught up in its "narrow, political and vindictive" games to notice. La Guardia must insist that the federal commitment be honored. On the very next day the president released the correspondence.[57]

First came a copy of La Guardia's letter to Secretary of the Interior Ickes, dated February 23, 1935, emphasizing the mayor's interest in maintaining cordial relations. Order 129, it said, had caused him a serious problem. A commissioner whose term of office was expiring held both an authority position and a city commissionership in technical violation of 129, but the secretary was no doubt familiar with this individual's "splendid work" and special expertise. He would be impossible to replace. "What is more, he is enthusiastic, zealous and energetic in his work. It would be a pity to displace him at this time." The mayor offered every assurance that New York would comply with 129 in the future but asked that the order be applied only henceforth and not retroactively. This would allow Langdon Post, chairman of the Municipal Housing Authority, to keep his critical post as Tenement House commissioner of New York.

It was a bit cute, and more than a bit disingenuous, but disarmingly deft also, to frame the solution around Post, and to deal with Moses in a single-sentence postscript: "P.S. The only other case in the City covered by Order 129 is that of Robert Moses who is a member of the Tri-Borough Bridge Authority and Park Commissioner of the City of New York." La Guardia had suggested the soft touch in a handwritten note added to the draft that he had handed to Roosevelt in Philadelphia:

> It occurred to me that inasmuch as so many "serious minded" persons have talked on this subject in such a ponderous manner that the Moses end of it might well be treated in a lighter vein.
>
> *Fiorello*[58]

To give the impression that the entire matter was solved before Smith's comments, Ickes predated his own response to La Guardia to February 26, 1935.

316

He agreed not to apply 129 retroactively and, except for a few tepid parting shots at Moses, put the debacle to rest. "The whole thing," Ickes confided to his diary rather sadly, "was a mistake from the start."[59]

It was a large personal victory for Moses, who had only recently suffered ignominiously at the polls, but it was also a huge victory for La Guardia, not in the sense of attracting public acclaim but because he had worked constructively with the federal administration to find a solution to a prickly problem, building a good relationship with Roosevelt, despite refusing to accede to him, and striking a fine pose as a city leader spelling out the limits of federal intervention in this new age of federal loans and handouts.

"The Mayor Wins," celebrated the *New York Times*. The paper congratulated him for fording the narrow straits between New York's needs and its dignity. "By persistence and persuasion he at last won his point." His note to Ickes, continued the *Times*, "is a little masterpiece, fairly exuding good nature and the desire to cooperate, but throughout maintaining his point of view and never losing sight of his object." So expert was the artifice that although everyone understood that Moses was the issue, no one was offended by Fiorello's switch. Those who knew only La Guardia the radical shouter who toughed his way around Congress and the Board of Aldermen were pleasantly surprised to see that the Mayor had kept calm, and won. A check for $1.6 million was issued to the Triborough Authority forthwith.

Ever sensitive, La Guardia's friend CCB turned to buck up the man whose goodwill was still the key to New York's future. "Dear Governor," old Burlingham wrote to FDR, "Thank you for the *magna pars* in settling the Ickes-Moses row. R.M.'s tongue is an unruly member. Indeed he is quite a blackguard, sparing neither friend nor foe. . . . However, he is one of the most efficient persons extant, and in my opinion Order 129 was what B. Franklin would call an *erratum*."[60]

There is a coda to this story. In *The Power Broker*, Moses biographer Robert Caro closes his chapter on the Triborough contretemps with an account of the bridge opening, furthering the image of a brilliant, if obnoxious, Moses getting the last word again. A year before the opening, however, La Guardia repaid Moses for having put him in such a delicate position. In another part of his book Caro tells of Moses' loyalty to Al Smith and his touching appointment of the former governor and old animal lover as "night superintendant of Central Park" after the picture-book zoo was opened. The bright opening ceremony is recounted in detail.

A similar celebration was planned for Brooklyn's Prospect Park zoo on July 3, 1935. Moses, who had been forced to miss the Central Park zoo opening because of illness, was feeling fine and planned to come to this one. He even dreamed up another honorific title for his patron, Smith, and expected to enjoy the festivities. The only problem was a small technicality. La Guardia had not formally reappointed him to the Triborough Authority when his term was up for renewal on June 30, 1935. And he was mad.

For a few weeks before this date, the press teased New Yorkers wondering whether Moses would be reappointed. The mayor enjoyed the game and played coy. Moses, however, fumed at the *lèse majesté*. His Grace did not like his job prospects becoming the common talk of the hoi polloi, and he threatened to resign from all of his city posts if La Guardia did not reappoint him formally to a three-year term on the Triborough Authority Commission by noon of July 1. "Baby talk," La Guardia shot back. "He's talking big but all it amounts to is baby talk." The mayor's office announced that incumbent commissioners are automatically extended unless they are dismissed. Returning from a Washington conference on July 1, La Guardia turned back all questions about Moses' tenure and referred all queries to Corporation Counsel Windels.

La Guardia had been less than thrilled with Moses' behavior during the Ickes affair, especially the tactic of releasing Ickes's private letters, and he did not mind having some fun at His Grace's expense. There was more than symbolism, however, in Moses' demand. While he might be continued in office without it, Moses knew that unless he had a formal reappointment he could be dismissed at any time, and RM did not want his tenure dependent on the goodwill of his friend the "dago son-of-a-bitch." On July 2 Moses delivered an ultimatum, threatening to resign from both his city positions and to boycott the Prospect Park dedication if he was not officially reappointed to his Triborough commissionership by noon of July 3.

In the next scene of this *opéra bouffe* Corporation Counsel Windels promised to study the issue and to deliver an "opinion" on whether a formal reappointment was necessary. On July 3 Moses waited in his office for word from La Guardia, expecting to join the mayor, after he was sworn in, for the three o'clock Prospect Park ceremonies. Noon came and passed, but the corporation counsel released no opinion, and there was no word from La Guardia.[61]

The Prospect Park festivities began shortly after three in the afternoon. A thirty-four piece band played and the park and zoo sparkled in the summer sun. The zoo, built in a huge arc on eight acres just off Flatbush Avenue, centered around a great sea lion pool. From the pool wide flagstone paths radiated out to animal and bird houses, where red brick and gray concrete floors mixed with the natural colors of the plumed birds and the exotic animals. Behind the cages animal range areas allowed the creatures to lope and drink from the moats that separated them from twenty-foot-high walls, above which fascinated children and adults looked down. Directly behind the seals was a great elephant house, its two front towers and bas-relief tablets adding the touches for which the parks commissioner had become well known.

The celebration had other signature touches as well: corsages for the lady guests, attendants in pressed khaki, and Al Smith in a place of honor. The night superintendent of Central Park was being appointed "rental agent for the zoo," another of the commissioner's drolleries. With the seals barking in the background,

Smith, deeply tanned and dressed in gray, smiled, but only briefly. He spoke of the great gift that the city was making to its children, and then, as his voice turned less lilting, he congratulated the absent parks commissioner: "Bob Moses stands in my estimation today as the most forward-looking and most energetic and most intelligent public servant I have ever met." But Smith was peeved. "I believe that he [Moses] is to be congratulated because he, after all, had the master mind to think it all out. And it would be a regretful thing for the people of the City of New York if any back alley politics would interfere with the progress of the work under the direction of Commissioner Moses."

At 4:30 P.M., after the park ceremonies were over, Counsel Windels's opinion was ready. "Being sworn in twice is like being vaccinated twice," the corporation counsel decided. "It won't do any harm. On the other hand it might reduce the temperature. It is therefore recommended in the case of Commissioner Moses." Accepting the recommendation, La Guardia, who had denounced the tempest as "childishness" and then carried on like a perfect eleven-year-old, set eleven o'clock on July 10 for the formal swearing-in. Moses walked in eighteen minutes late, but the two men, of whom Marie La Guardia said that "they were two men with almost similar temperaments and clashed . . . and worked well together," smiled, shook hands, and proceeded with the swearing-in. "Now Mr. Moses could you put your arm around the Mayor's shoulder," begged the photographers as they put the two different-size men next to each other. "Nothing doing," piped up the foot-shorter magistrate. But Moses, in a white suit, draped a loping arm around Fiorello and said with a big smile, "If the mayor can stand it, I guess I can."[62]

On July 11, 1936, exactly one year later, New York was in the midst of a heat wave, with the temperature reaching 117 degrees. The cool breeze blowing over the central span of the Triborough Bridge made it only slightly more comfortable. Secretary Ickes was there. He had received only a general spectator invitation to the opening ceremonies. "That is the doing of Robert Moses . . . very small indeed," Ickes told his diary, but Fiorello fixed that, even arranging a five-minute speaker's slot to go with the special guest ticket that he had secured.

The president was there too. At first he had been "too busy," but after receiving assurances that La Guardia and not Moses would introduce him, he agreed to attend. And, of course, the mayor was there, together with his parks commissioner. A charming time was had, and finally Ickes told his dear diary: "The Triborough Bridge is a wonderful affair. From the engineering point of view, it is one of the greatest in the world as it is the biggest." The bridge that had threatened for a while to rend this remarkable partnership of talent, money, initiative, foresight, force, and truculence was holding them all, and despite all the strains, this grand alliance of mayor, master builder, and presidential patron brought the city many, many more benefits.[63]

4. Getting Public Housing Off the Ground

H OUSING historian Peter Marcuse has summed up the history of the past fifty years of American public housing policy in a single scathing sentence: "The United States started building social housing later, has built less of it, of poorer quality, maintained it more parsimoniously, charged more for its occupancy, and accorded it less status than almost any other Western industrialized country." Quite an indictment for a program that had hoped to provide fresh air, sunshine, ample space, and healthful environments at a reasonable price. And yet, who, looking at today's public housing projects in New York City, would deny that after billions of dollars and a surfeit of good intentions, the high rise projects in the slums serve as a housing of last resort for the poor and the left-out; fresh slums with new bricks, high crime, graffitoed walls, and the air of defeat that the reformers had hoped to eradicate.[64]

Class segregation and racism, crime, fear, high density, and awful environments all preceded the experiment in public housing, but this was what slum clearance and low-cost public housing were supposed to cure. Public housing was supposed to provide jobs, create stability, reinforce the values of sobriety, thrift, cleanliness, and municipal virtue. Along the way it got sidetracked into a dumping ground for the unemployed and the racial minorities.

This was not the way La Guardia had planned it.

To say today that New York City was a pioneer in public housing recalls little of the boldness that went into this effort in the thirties. We must look away from the contemporary situation and conjecture upon a different time, when to clear the slums was a battle that seemed promising, the key to changing not only a lugubrious environment, but the crime, disease, and defeat that it produced. To fight the warehousing of the poor in dangerous firetraps, New York City hitched its municipal agenda to a free-spending federal government and proposed a vast program of slum clearance and low-cost public housing that would create a model environment for the decent, deserving poor. It was a special time when the Depression spread poverty broadly and thereby removed its stigma. With mass unemployment, blame fell on the system instead of the individual, creating a new openness toward social welfare projects. For decades housing reformers had called upon the United States to take a lesson from the European democracies and construct subsidized public housing. Now it seemed that these hopes might become a reality.

For a brief moment in the thirties, then, housing represented a different dream. Yes, Robert Moses, with his breathtaking parkways and imaginative playgrounds,

320

engaged the civic reformers who valued the touch of country expanse in the pell-mell crush of the city. Places to relax, play, and enjoy made city life more pleasurable. But the crux of any program for urban betterment had to do with the places where people lived and raised their families. No bold city of the future was possible without eradicating the blighted slums and providing decent accommodations for those who could not buy it at market prices.[65]

La Guardia knew firsthand the life in America's downtown hovels. For a decade he had worked with no little frustration to try to help his poor constitutents in East Harlem with their housing difficulties. He was more familiar than most with slum landlords and deteriorating conditions, and he remembered how he had had to transport his first wife all the way to the Bronx to find a healthful environment away from the tenement sickness that eventually took her life. La Guardia announced that New York would sweep away its slums and replace unsafe rookeries with reasonably priced housing and ''more air, more playgrounds. A window in every room—maybe two windows, and cross ventilation wherever possible. What I'm seeking is to proceed on the type of tenement remodeling that has been so successful in Berlin. The architecture must receive as well as reflect beauty.'' Public housing would work a reform not only on the cityscape but on the lives of its inhabitants, reinforcing sobriety, thrift, cleanliness, and civic virtue. It would reduce crime, uplift the poor, and provide jobs.[66]

Not in that order.

The Mayor would have to fetch the chisel in Washington to sculpt his new housing. While Paris, Glasgow, Vienna, Amsterdam, London, and Berlin had a tradition of public housing, and many European democracies had built full-scale public or ''social'' housing for their workers dating from after World War I, the United States had not. New York Senator William Calder stated the traditional position at the end of the twenties: ''The Government is an organization to govern, not to build houses or operate mines or run railroads or banks.''[67]

The New Deal changed some of these assumptions, but there by the Potomac, clearing the East Side or Harlem was much less of a priority than jobs. Perhaps public housing deserved to be treated as a reform on its own, but Depression politics dictated that the only lever for large-scale federal funds was the promise of jobs, and so the housing program, like so many others, developed backwards out of a search for places to spend money. The goal was jobs, not houses. For the moment this would not make that much of a difference, except that it would be impossible to stake long-range plans for housing on such foundations. As soon as unemployment went back to normal levels, the federal housing program might end.

Before the turn of the century some ninety thousand tenements—flammable, dark, ill ventilated, and unsanitary, with no central heat or water, and shared toilets either outside the premises or in the hallway—had been put up in New York City. These were the tenements that led Jacob Riis to write: "The most pitiful victim of city life is not the slum child who dies, but the slum child who lives. Every time a child dies, the nation loses a prospective citizen, but in every slum child who lives the nation has a probable consumptive and possible criminal. You cannot let people live like pigs and expect them to be good citizens." Reporting on an investigation of slum conditions in the city in 1900, an upstate commissioner delivered this terse recommendation: "New York should be abolished."[68]

After a successful campaign for reform led by Lawrence Veiller, New York City enacted landmark legislation in 1901 to regulate the construction of tenement housing. Existing "old-law" tenements were permitted to stand, however. Not until 1929 was there any real effort made at upgrading them. But even then, builders and real estate interests riddled the multiple dwelling law with 200 separate amendments and exceptions. More than 350,000 of these old units existed in 1934 when La Guardia was sworn in. In that year 1300 tenements still had outhouses in the yard, 23,000 still had toilets in the hall, and 30,000 had no bathing facilities. Between 1918 and 1929 there were four times as many fires and eight times as many deaths in these old-law tenements as in the ones built after 1901. The incidence of diseases such as tuberculosis was similarly disproportionate. And crime festered here.[69]

With the Depression these slums also became unprofitable. Tenants were unable to pay rents at the same time that new safety laws went into effect requiring expensive renovations. As tax arrears piled up, landlords abandoned their properties. The slums were soon scarred with thousands of vacated houses, symbols of the decomposition of New York's working-class districts. In these decaying areas those unable to afford better fought to make a life and raise a family. Confronted with this sorry situation, even free-enterprisers abandoned their free-market assumptions. Admitting that he had once thought that the solution to slums was asking 500 men of means to contribute $500,000 each to wipe out the blight and raise decent housing in the city, financier August Heckscher now called upon the government to get involved.[70]

Even before La Guardia could put his slum clearance plan into effect, a rash of fatal fires dramatized the dangers of substandard housing. The story was almost always the same: A winding spit of flame suddenly swept up the open stairway shaft, spreading to the tinder of the banisters and walls. Again and again screaming headlines described the dead and the crippled, sacrificed to the disgrace of New York's firetrap housing. The tragedies lent the crusade against the slums an urgency that only the scorched bodies of perished children being carried from burned tenements could generate. After one of these fires killed three children, five adults, and a dog, the Tenement House commissioner said, "When I went down to that fire this morning I thought of the appalling fact that 75 per cent of the multiple dwellings on Manhattan Island are old-law tenements, built just as that building was built.'' How that building was built was without any protection against fire, with few openings to the outside for egress in emergency, and with materials that fed the flames hurrying the fire along its deadly course.[71]

What sort of city brags about its skyscrapers, demanded La Guardia, while its lower-class neighborhoods were honeycombed with firetraps? The problem with low-rent housing was that it was substandard housing. He demanded and got a law to force owners to bring their old-law tenements up to minimum safety or board them up. In the past the city had passed tough apartment safety laws, only to cave in to the threats of the landlords and issue moratoriums on enforcement. Armed with fresh data indicating that New York's population was no longer growing and that there was actually a housing surplus in the city, La Guardia determined to scrap all of these exemptions.

Those landlords unwilling to make improvements were ordered to make way for the bulldozers. As for the slum landlord who would have to spend thousands to upgrade his housing, La Guardia declared, ''I have no sympathy for him.'' He had allowed his property to run down and he had no one to blame for that but himself. Moreover, many of these homes were just too old. They could never be made into decent housing. ''The only ultimate cure for them,'' said Tenement Commissioner Langdon Post, ''is dynamite.''[72]

In the next two years the new policy resulted in the boarding up of approximately 10,000 decrepit tenements, removing some 40,000 units from the market. Other landlords complied with the new requirements and upgraded their buildings to medium-priced apartments, removing another 30,000 units from the low-rent category. As a consequence, inexpensive housing stock in the city declined rapidly. But if the dangerous tenements were removed, the slums cleared, and the blight pressed back, what would happen with New York's poor, who could afford only low-rent housing or nothing at all?

In February 1934 New York City passed a law to carry out ''the clearance, replanning, and reconstruction of the areas in which unsanitary or substandard housing conditions exist,'' establishing a New York City Housing Authority (NY-CHA) to direct this public housing. Mayor La Guardia appointed Tenement House Commissioner Langdon Post chairman of the semiautonomous authority. He also named Louis H. Pink, Mary K. Simkhovitch, Rev. E. Roberts Moore, and B. Charney Vladeck to the authority. ''Where can you find a housing board to equal it,'' La Guardia would say, ''an idealist on housing, a social worker, a Catholic priest and a Socialist.'' The new authority sent out 5000 CWA canvassers to conduct a real property inventory of the city from which to create a policy for slum clearance and housing construction.[73]

As with so many of his intiatives, La Guardia put together an excellent team around a goal and a reform vision, dramatized its needs, and sent it off to do work good enough to win federal funding. La Guardia himself had prepared the ground for such funding, persuading Harold Ickes to include slum clearance and low-cost public housing in his budget plans. On January 3, 1934, the third day of La Guardia's tenure, Ickes earmarked $25 million, one-fourth of the total PWA housing allocation, toward the development of a low-cost housing project in New York. What precisely this money was to be used for, under what conditions it was being allocated, who would be spending it, and who would finally be responsible for the housing erected with it were all left unclear by the brief telegram notifying the elated mayor of the grant.

These questions surfaced very soon after the hastily delivered $25 million commitment reached La Guardia's desk. The complications and hesitations for which Ickes's staff was so often criticized cropped up. While NYCHA proceeded with its real property inventory, sponsored an architectural competition for low-cost housing designs, and cleared dilapidated homes from vast tracts in Manhattan and Brooklyn, Ickes's representatives demanded plans. They received eight alternate proposals from Post, none of which were perfectly acceptable, in part because the PWA Housing Division did not yet have its own clear policy. While agriculture or industry were recognized as ends in themselves, housing was only a means to stimulate the construction industry and provide jobs, and it was difficult to fix a policy on the shifting sands of the latest pump-priming theory. Three months after the initial commitment, Ickes still clutched the millions in his tight fist, while NYCHA was reduced to panhandling from the Board of Estimate and raising money by selling material salvaged from its slum demolitions.[74]

Preliminary results from the property survey reported that New York's 17 square miles of slums held 516,000 families. Ten of these slum miles were pronounced "unfit for human habitation" and unprofitable for their owners. Of these worst areas, 4.4 square miles were in Manhattan and 5.3 in Brooklyn. Occupant families earned an estimated income of $700 a year, which meant that according to prevailing formulas they could afford only $7 a room per month for rent. Since new housing could not be built privately for anything close to that figure, NYCHA decided to attack the problem by developing subsidized low-rent housing for the working poor.[75]

A number of city housing groups clamored for the rehabilitation of existing slum housing instead of wholesale demolition and new construction. But the opportunity to redesign an entire neighborhood and lay it out anew offered greater promise of wiping out the slums. Moreover, La Guardia wanted striking demonstration projects that would cast national attention on the city. Rehabilitation projects would not do that.

Too many of the old tenements, in any event, were structurally unable to support modernization, and in most cases renovation would prove more costly than new construction. Others thought NYCHA should separate public housing from slum clearance and build on the city outskirts. It would be cheaper, it would not have the slum surroundings to contend with, and it would not bail out the slum landlords by paying them for their wretched properties. But settlement house reformers and ethnic leaders supported NYCHA's decision to build where the poor already lived. The *land* cost might be lower far from the city center, but this meant drawing working-class families away from their intensively developed sources of industrial employment. It meant developing new sewers, water connections, hospitals, schools, settlement houses, everything. And it would destroy the web of existing social attachments.

The ideal site for a demonstration project was the best-known slum in the world, Manhattan's Lower East Side, where more than 90 percent of the residential buildings were at least thirty-five years old, more than half lacked central heating and private toilets, and one in six had no running hot water. But the price of assembling the property here proved prohibitive. Land below Third Street and east of the Bowery was assessed in 1934 for $6.12 a square foot, with an additional $4.15 per square foot for the buildings. It would not be possible to buy property at such prices and still build apartments to rent at $7 per room, even with subsidies. Other Manhattan areas were even costlier.[76]

NYCHA therefore decided to initiate its projects in the outer boroughs. The worst slum it could find for its money was in Brooklyn's Williamsburg section. ("There are no worse slums anywhere, at the price," said NYCHA technical director Frederick L. Ackerman.) The working-class tract offered fine transportation connections, long rows of buckling tinder houses, and "every evil condition requiring remedy." All of this misery at less than $1 per square foot for the land![77]

With an actual site on which to test the exciting new experiment in worker housing and neighborhood rehabilitation, NYCHA asked Ickes for its promised funding. At the end of March the check was still "in the mail." PWA assured Post that the check would arrive within a week. The Williamsburg proposal was approved a month later. PWA agreed that it would buy the various tracts, assemble them, and then convey title to NYCHA to carry out the rest of the project and manage the housing once it was rented. The money would be there soon.

A month later a shakeup in the PWA produced a raft of meetings and modifications of the original agreement. Sorry for the holdup, but the money would be coming. By June NYCHA had gathered options for the land in Williamsburg. Still no money. Another shakeup. This time Ickes discarded his first plan to work through local authorities. Under his new policy the federal government would exert detailed control over local housing programs from Washington, reducing NYCHA to the role of rental agent after construction was completed. City representatives objected that it was their city, their slums, and their poor who were at stake. PWA reminded them that all of this was true, except that the city was not paying the bills, and since feds were paying the piper, they were going to call the tune. Either New York would agree to allow Washington to buy, build, and manage the projects or PWA would take its gifts elsewhere.[78]

When La Guardia accepted the initial promise of $25 million he knew that this was not enough for more than a demonstration of what could be done with federal assistance. The first projects, in the words of NYCHA counsel Charles Abrams, would "serve as the priming factors in the initiation and construction of other projects. . . ." With so much riding on the Williamsburg project, La Guardia did not intend to allow Ickes to mess it up through his bureaucratic muddling. Nor would he permit control over this important municipal initiative to rest with a distant and plodding federal agency. After the money ran out, the only ones with continued interest in the houses would be the people of New York, and he meant to protect their interest.

Meanwhile, NYCHA proceeded with its collection of option agreements for the Williamsburg properties. It soon discovered that PWA's housing division was surreptitiously doing the same thing, signing a reported $6 million of its own options. When NYCHA complained to Ickes that his people were undercutting them, the interior secretary denied that Williamsburg had even been agreed upon. He seemed paralyzed by the fear that once the money was out of his hands he would lose control. If he could, he would have demanded to see the housing built and bringing in the rent before he delivered the funds.[79]

In a lead article titled "Confusion Attends the New York Housing Program," the authoritative *Real Estate Record and Builder's Guide* took the feds to task for playing at public housing. After months of false starts, assurances of commitment, and repeated reference to the phantom $25 million, not one brick had been disturbed on account of public housing. La Guardia too was apprehensive. Unless the project began soon, it might be canceled completely. He wired Ickes: "MUCH WORRIED OVER DELAY IN PROCEEDING WITH SLUM CLEARANCE AND ACTUAL CONSTRUCTION OF HOUSING STOP THE CITY HOUSING AUTHORITY IS PROGRESSING RAPIDLY AND THEY FEAR BEING SLOWED UP AND RETARDED UNLESS YOUR DEPARTMENT SYNCHRONIZES WITH THEM " The Williamsburg options were running out, and he feared that speculators would enter the field and drive prices up. "I WILL GO NINETY-NINE PERCENT OF THE WAY TO MEET YOU IN EVERY POSSIBLE MANNER IN ORDER THAT WE MAY GET ACTION IN STARTING BUILDING"[80]

Ickes tucked his chin into his chest, hurt looks being his speciality, and wrote *Nation* editor Oswald Garrison Villard, denying that he had promised to give New York $25 million. Too many bad experiences, he explained, had forced PWA to demand full control over all housing projects. "Moreover we cannot very well adopt one policy for New York and a different one for Chicago or St. Louis." The note was meant for La Guardia's eyes, and the mayor wrote back, begging to differ. New York, with its long experience with housing reform, *was* different. It had set up a financially responsible authority with the statutory power to borrow money and issue bonds to guarantee repayment, and unlike other cities, NYCHA personnel were "of the very highest calibre. It is absolutely non-political, non-partisan and every member is an expert on the subject. It has appointed a staff of technicians and experts and is doing a real job." Next day La Guardia sent the secretary a longer letter refining his point: "You will recall that . . . you advised me to finance as many [public works projects] as I could, taking the federal grants out of such amounts as may be allocated to my city. . . . In pressing this kind of work, we surely have demonstrated our unselfishness and willingness to cooperate with the administration for the benefit of the entire country."[81]

With Post in tow, La Guardia hastened to Washington to tell Ickes that if New York was to become the national laboratory for public housing, it must have both the money and the freedom to operate. Ickes came to the meeting poorly briefed but willing to deal. The first thing that he agreed to was a special New York housing liaison to work out a comprehensive plan. Willy-nilly New York *was* different, with its own special pleader and expediter. On September 5, 1934, with New York's housing plans still bottled up, La Guardia met with President Roosevelt to tell him that PWA was suffering from a severe case of faintheartedness. An agency with billions in its budget was holding pennies to its breast and agonizing over each and every one of them as if it were an only child. PWA had a more ambitious purpose than merely to guard its funds, and Ickes's chronic phobia about possible abuses was crippling the housing program. La Guardia suggested that the president inject his interior secretary with a dose of his own courage and willingness to take chances for the larger purpose.[82]

Within days a newly energized Ickes resolved all outstanding issues. The government would buy the land and lease it to NYCHA, pay 30 percent of the labor and material costs, and provide a forty-five-year mortgage at 4 percent for the rest of the outlay. In return, the city would provide services, land, and subsidies in the form of tax exemptions. Control would be wielded jointly. Backed against the wall, Ickes turned gracious, complimenting NYCHA for its excellent work. Finally, on October 13, after Ickes conferred once more with Post and with some more prodding from La Guardia, PWA exercised the first of a series of options on Williamsburg properties, opening a new chapter in federal-urban cooperation.[83]

By this time, however, New York had already begun a public housing project on its own. In the developing relationship with Washington, La Guardia wanted to demonstrate the city's capacity to carry out its own policy if it felt hampered by an unreliable federal partner.

Early in 1934 NYCHA learned that Vincent Astor was interested in unloading lower Manhattan real estate that was owned by his family. Anxious to locate a housing project so close by the historic immigrant slum quarter, NYCHA quickly closed an agreement with Astor for the parcel between Avenue A and Second Avenue at a cut rate and drew up a plan combining the rehabilitation of the aging tenements with limited new construction designed to fit in with the scale and layout of the neighborhood.[84]

Two obstacles, however, had to be overcome: The sale of used bricks from demolition projects, which represented NYCHA's principle source of income, could not raise enough to pay Astor or the costs of construction, and Andrew Muller, who owned two houses that separated the Astor properties, refused to sell to the authority at a reasonable price.

NYCHA easily hurdled the first obstruction, persuading Astor to finance the transaction himself by accepting full payment in sixty-five-year bonds, with a mortgage paying 1½ percent interest for the first year and 3½ percent interest per annum thereafter (a rate lower than that being charged by PWA). Then NYCHA went to Washington to pay for the labor and supplies. To avoid the nitpicking, turtle-paced Harold Ickes, NYCHA described its project as a renovation rather than new construction. This brought it under the jurisdiction of Harry Hopkins's Federal Emergency Relief Administration (FERA). Langdon Post met with Hopkins and told him how taken he was with the FERA-financed Central Park zoo that Robert Moses had built recently. Housing people, he pleaded to Harry Hopkins, was as important as housing monkeys. Hopkins agreed to have FERA buy materials and pay the costs of construction from work relief.[85]

Continuing its resourceful shoestring operations, NYCHA negotiated a loan from Bernard Baruch to purchase the Muller properties, but Muller continued to hold out for a windfall, threatening to hold up the project indefinitely.

Meanwhile Ickes's policy of hands-on federal control of public housing construction sustained a fatal blow. In January 1935 Justice Charles I. Dawson of the Louisville, Kentucky, circuit court ruled that the federal government did not have the authority to condemn local property for public housing development. The decision, one of a handful that for a while threatened to send the New Deal back to the drawing board, strictly limited federal power: "[Low cost housing] is certainly not a public use," pronounced the court, "in the sense that the property is to be used by the federal government for performing any of the legitimate functions of the government itself." The construction of housing for needy individuals, no matter how commendable, held the court, was unconstitutional. Upheld on appeal, this ruling quashed Ickes's plan for federally directed public construction. So long as PWA could not condemn land for government use, any group of property holders would be able to hold the government up for exorbitant prices, the same problem confronting NYCHA in the Muller instance.[86]

On March 4, 1935, NYCHA went to court to force Muller to sell to the city at a fair price. The landlord urged that the Louisville precedent regarding limits on eminent domain be applied to NYCHA. Muller argued that the city did not have the right to take property from one group to aid "others in acquiring a home, whose temperament, environment or habits have heretofore prevented them from attaining a like position." In a landmark decision by New York State Supreme Court Justice Charles R. McLaughlin, the court rejected the Louisville precedent and found in favor of New York City on the grounds of public health and the general welfare of the citizens.

Slums, the jurist argued, breed disease, crime, and family breakdown; they subvert order, destroy the normal bonds of municipal life, and claim a burdensome portion of city resources. They represent a present danger to the life of the municipality. "Juvenile delinquency, crime and immorality are there born, find protection and flourish," declared the oft-quoted court decision. This public menace warranted government action to demolish and replace these diseased zones, "and only where there is power to deal *in invitum* with the occasional greedy owner seeking excessive profit by holding out" can this be carried out. "The cure," said the decision, is to be wrought, "not through the regulated ownership of the individual, but through the ownership and operation by or under direct control of the public itself." Justice McLaughlin closed his demurral from the Kentucky precedent with a flourish: " 'The law of each age is ultimately what that age thinks should be the law.' . . . It is difficult to conceive of a law, the purposes of which are more for the public good than the one under discussion."

The judge ordered NYCHA to pay Muller $26,000 for his parcels, $10,000 less than NYCHA had initially offered. Public housing, it was affirmed, was an eminently public issue, but only for municipalities. Taken together, the restrictive Louisville decision and the affirmative Muller action made local implementation the only viable way to proceed with a federally assisted public housing program, settling a debate that had held up New York's $25 million for a year.[87]

Legalities settled, financing in place, the modest project called First Houses proceeded. Every third building was torn down, driving shafts of fresh air and sunlight between the renovated tenements. Courts, gardens, and imaginatively landscaped playgrounds replaced the demolished rookeries.

Critics objected that the city was "putting a new finish and equipment into a poorly oriented and rotten shell of ancient tenement houses." But carpers failed to take note of the symbolic breakthrough First Houses represented and the resourcefulness that the La Guardia administration had demonstrated. Making decisions on the run, maneuvering First Houses toward the sympathetic and generous Hopkins, creating funding out of promises, and pile-driving in place a powerful precedent, First Houses handsomely fulfilled the hopes of its planners.[88]

Moreover, First Houses was far more than a renovation. Five of the eight buildings were built fresh from the ground up, and except for a few walls and foundations, the remaining three structures were also practically new. The result was welcomed by the neighborhood as an outstanding improvement, providing 122 modern, new, centrally heated, fireproof apartments at an average rental of $6 a room per month. Each unit had a laundry for the cooperative use of the tenants. In addition to the play areas and playgrounds, the site boasted indoor recreation rooms and large common meeting halls.

Decent, healthful, modern, low-cost housing for the poor was no longer a figment of the chubby mayor's rhetoric. There it stood in the heart of the most notorious slum in the Western world, offering, in the words of a clearly impressed

New York Times, "garden suites of modern type with conveniences equivalent to those offered in some of the more exclusive Manhattan neighborhoods." And in the middle of the complex stood a city health center. Crowds jammed the NYCHA office to apply for the apartments, forcing it to open First Houses on January 15, 1935, earlier than planned. Despite efforts to limit applications, NYCHA received 3800 applications for the 122 units.[89]

Setting rents at a level to pay off incurred debt and operating costs, the authority did not accept the unemployed or those on relief into its new apartments. Five of the families selected for First Houses were headed by professionals, seventy-six household heads were skilled laborers, clerical workers, or proprietors, and only forty-two held lower-level unskilled jobs. Tenants were expected to hold modest insurance policies, show at least $100 in the bank, and hold membership in a fraternal society. After sifting through thousands of applications, the selection committee awarded apartments to those whom historian Joel Schwartz calls "the heroic poor," those who overcame trying circumstances to raise decent families and nourish middle-class aspirations.[90]

———

It was a cold day in December 1935 when a delighted Fiorello La Guardia swept his arms expansively, indicating the eight new structures that he was now officially opening: "This is boondogling exhibit A and we're proud of it." Here, he declared, was the *real* system of rehabilitation. Compare it with the old system, the breadlines. (Earlier that day Herbert Bayard Swope introduced the mayor to a crowd of housing reformers as "a pretty good all around roly-poly sort of a fellow who usually is in the right and who always assumes himself to be.") Pointing to a group of children, La Guardia offered his reading of the Constitution: "There is the Constitution, those school children, and there is nothing in the Constitution that says the Federal Government cannot do anything to promote the health, happiness and welfare of the American child."

Glancing at the guests, Governor Herbert Lehman and Mrs. Eleanor Roosevelt among them, bundling their coats against the frosty December weather, La Guardia indulged himself. "A great constitutional lawyer two years ago told me it would be a cold day when the government builds houses. Well," the smiling mayor declared after a pause, "he was right that time—the first time a constitutional lawyer has been right in the past three years."[91]

5. The Limits of Housing Reform

I N February of 1935, buoyed by the completion of First Houses, La Guardia went to Washington to get the long-delayed $25 million. The controversy over Moses was as yet unresolved, and the interior secretary was telling the press that he would not be happy with anything less than Moses' scalp. Yet he was so impressed with New York's public projects that he enthusiastically approved a batch of new proposals, saying, "I think that New York can use $150 million for low-cost housing." La Guardia had plainly won the trust of this singularly distrustful man. By this time Fiorello was bringing home one-seventh of the total federal outlay for relief, and federal officials assured reporters that the Empire City would continue to "be properly taken care of."[92]

Following the Louisville decision that upset Ickes's plans for a detailed federal control over housing, the PWA chief made La Guardia a sporting proposal: If the mayor could complete option negotiations on the Williamsburg project within a month, PWA would release the funds and transfer control to NYCHA.

As La Guardia moved to secure the options, a new obstacle rose. Justice Department lawyers reviewing the agreements began to speak of waiting for court decisions and initiated cumbersome reviews of the land titles. La Guardia was in no mood for any more of this. He blasted the "semi-colon boys" for their obstructionism. "We can't move a family into a court decision," he bellowed. Testifying before Congress, he scored the mindless legal technicians for their nitpicking focus on punctuation when the poor needed homes. His spirited testimony made all the papers, winning more attention and support for PWA's housing program than Ickes's own statements before the same committee. Again Washington took note: Allied on its side, La Guardia was a powerful weapon; opposed, he could sting a program to death.

Meanwhile, the city completed all Williamsburg options in record time. "If Mayor La Guardia delivers satisfactory titles for the Williamsburg land it indicates what he can do with other projects," remarked an openly impressed Secretary Ickes.[93]

First Houses had been a miniature demonstration project. Williamsburg represented the most comprehensive slum clearance and low-rent housing project ever attempted in the United States; "a $12,500,000 laboratory," boasted NYCHA, "in which the Federal Government is learning how such housing should be built." It represented the La Guardia administration's showpiece for the possibilities of urban regeneration. "You may state to the Public Works Administrator," La Guardia wrote to Langdon Post, "that I personally am eager and anxious to . . . make this first unit . . . a model for the whole country." PWA prepared a handsome booklet on the story of Williamsburg Houses to serve as a public housing primer for other cities.

After relocating the displaced tenants, NYCHA demolished 565 row houses and shoddy worker cottages slung across the Williamsburg tract, clearing twenty-five acres for development. First Houses had been built with relief labor, but PWA policies called for hiring craftsmen and paying prevailing union wages. The project was initially planned for eight blocks, but Ickes agreed to four more blocks when La Guardia pledged to locate a large public school on the site. The housing complex was planned by chief architect R. H. Shreve, whose firm had designed the Empire State Building. Less than a third of the available acreage was built up (as compared with 90 percent for the old housing) to allow ample open spaces, and each of the twenty buildings was set at a slight angle to afford the apartments maximum sunlight and fresh air. Almost every apartment overlooked a garden or play area.[94]

Two years after the bulldozers cleared the land, on September 30, 1937, six of the twenty buildings were opened for occupancy. Rents were set at about $7 a room per month, half the cost of comparable housing on the private market. As with First Houses, thousands of applicants were carefully screened, and only those with solid jobs, an insurance policy, a bank account, and tidy householding habits were selected. And before they moved in all their belongings were fumigated.

At the heart of NYCHA beat the spirit of the settlement house and its ethos of social uplift. Williamsburg aimed to do more than house tenants; it sought to educate and train them into personal and civic responsibility. On the grounds was a kindergarten, a nursery (where new mothers were given lessons in baby care), a day care center, and communal meeting rooms. Like other social reformers who wanted to make people good, NYCHA sometimes became too involved. The young women sent to collect the rent every week or two (NYCHA did not want to take the chance that the rent money might be gone come month's end) were instructed to chat with the families and gently ascertain if they needed any help. They were also to note whether the tenants were taking proper care of their apartments. NYCHA intended to use public housing to build a proper, responsible community life for its inhabitants. It selected the best and the safest, and after a year and a half of operations it was able to boast that "no tenant at anytime has been in arrears."[95]

But others questioned whether NYCHA's experiment was not too limited. If public housing was supposed to clean out the slums and rehabilitate the poor, could it do so through such contrived selections? Chairman Post had thundered that the slums bred crime. "The boys and girls living under such conditions . . . must get out. It is not just the pangs of hunger that urge them on. It is the dirty rotten, stinking, life which surges all around them. . . . From their early life the ordinary canons of morals and decency are . . . denied them." But NYCHA was not welcoming troubled families, or even those on relief, into its demonstration apartments.

How the new housing would help precisely those, the already wounded, whose cause was summoned with such facile rhetoric in the campaign to win funding and support for public housing remained a vexing challenge.[96]

There was another criticism: Williamsburg was racially segregated. It was for whites only.

NYCHA upheld the essential conventions of American middle-class life. Instead of burdening the experiment in public housing with the added aim of racial equality, it planned a separate project for about 500 black families to be located in Harlem.

Harlem property holders were demanding high prices—"just crazy," complained La Guardia—so once again the authority made an offer to a mogul with underused real estate. In 1928 John D. Rockefeller, Jr., had built the Dunbar Apartments, well-designed homes for the "better element" of the Harlem community at a reasonable rental, immediately below 150th Street. But the investment proved unprofitable and Rockefeller was looking to sell. He offered the Dunbar together with a stretch of largely vacant Harlem territory running from 151st Street to 153rd, between Macombs Place and the Harlem River. While this was not, strictly speaking, slum territory, it was close enough, and NYCHA was interested, but only in the vacant land.

Spurred to action by racial disturbances that broke out in March 1935, Post told a local rally, "We won't get that land without a fight, but," he promised, "we'll get it." Three months later, on July 25, 1935, the city acquired title through condemnation and proceeded with an impressive 572-unit complex that arranged four- and five-story red-brick buildings around a spacious plaza that included two playgrounds, abundant plantings, and a children's wading pool. Harlem River Houses featured the signatures of NYCHA's early period: generous open plazas providing air, light, and play spaces, as well as a nursery school, health clinic, laundry, social hall, and children's playrooms. At one end of the project stood a black John Henry pounding a large hammer, and at the other a sculpted Negro woman with her child. Overlooking the Harlem River stood an amphitheater.

Thousands of applicants for the $7-a-room-per-month apartments, advertised as being "of particular significance to Negroes," were carefully reviewed according to NYCHA's established criteria. How carefully is apparent from the conservatism of the Harlem Houses tenants. Throughout the thirties, while Harlem activists formed tenant organizations to foment rentpayer radicalism, Harlem River tenants avoided all such movements. They had been selected well.[97]

With these projects under way, NYCHA turned to its long-range agenda of clearing out the worst slums and replacing them with modern housing to spur a far-reaching urban renewal. Post tried to enlist his friend Franklin Roosevelt for this project, outlining a $2 billion ten-year federally funded New York City program for a "real new deal" in urban housing. Post made no apologies for the price tag. No one spoke of "safe returns" on police, parks, sewers, or any other government services. Housing too must be reckoned on a social standard, he argued. Low-rent housing would bring social justice and raise the standard of living for millions of Americans, while producing savings in expenditures for police, courts, prisons, and hospitals.[98]

Post took a great deal for granted in this pitch to Roosevelt. Many planners were criticizing the effort to reclaim the big old cities. Lewis Mumford, for example, maintained that the dying megacities were not worth saving. Too large and distant from the "sources of life," the cities were collapsing. This natural course of urban entropy, Mumford argued, should not be interfered with. Redevelopment programs would only allow the urban dinosaurs to "run badly a little longer." Before long, predicted Mumford, the giant cities would be "cemeteries for the dead." Better to start all over and build afresh.[99]

Rexford Guy Tugwell, a close Roosevelt adviser, told the president the same thing. If the federal government was going to take a hand in housing, Tugwell thought that it should build fresh towns, away from the suppurating cities, and relocate the urban poor in these new towns. The president, whom historian William Leuchtenburg describes as "a man with little love for the city and less for housing reformers, with their cold calculations about plumbing requirements and unit costs," preferred single-family homes on rural land to city high-rises; cities in any event he was inclined to think of as rather hopeless. Post's multi-billion-dollar program for urban housing did not interest him. Between 1934 and 1937, PWA accounted for no more than 2 percent of all new housing in the nation. While the administration was "spending money . . . like drunken sailors" to build the rural town of Arthurdale, Ickes complained, his own housing budget was being squeezed into insignificance. Writes Mark Gelfand, a scholar of New Deal urban policies: "Having entered through the back door, public housing had by the end of 1935, exhausted the New Deal's lukewarm hospitality."[100]

Fiorello La Guardia's commitment to "decent, modern, cheerful houses in place of the present tenements" went much deeper than the president's. Thus, when he asked special New York Housing Commissioner Nathan Straus before the summer of 1935 to make a study of the European experience with public housing, some thought that he was prepared to launch his own new initiative.

Straus brought back a report advocating an approach even more radical in concept than Post's. Looking back at New York's housing policies during the twenties, Straus wrote that the city had spent more money on subsidies and had less to show for it than any other municipality in the world. After World War I, with housing in short supply, New York dangled $200 million in tax exemptions before developers to spur new construction. Any building. Anywhere. With no strings attached to these exemptions, the developers "disfigured great portions of our city with shoddy ill-designed ramshackle buildings without central plan, without adequate space for recreation and with no thought of anything except profit to the individual engaged in the building operations.'' The contrast with London, Paris, Amsterdam, Zurich, Leeds, Manchester, Edinburgh, and Glasgow could not be more striking. The European cities used their subsidies as incentives for good low-rental housing while in New York it "line[d] the pockets of speculative builders."

Straus opposed rebuilding slum areas. The new houses would only be swallowed up by their loathsome environment. He advocated quarantining entire city sections, declaring the old housing unfit and therefore unrentable. After realty values plummeted, the city could buy these cut-rate properties and replace them with parks and playgrounds. To prevent the further spread of blight, he recommended strong zoning laws limiting height and density and prescribing adequate light, ventilation, and space for adornment and play.

One could easily imagine Congressman La Guardia delivering a version of the Straus plan on the floor of the House, speaking forcefully in favor of government assistance for the slum dweller at the expense of the landlords, calling for panoramic planning and massive allocations. Only Straus did not pass the entire burden onto the federal government. New York City had to become seriously involved as well, he suggested, beyond its current piecemeal planning if it was to rebuild itself; and it must contribute its share of dollars.

La Guardia received the report and praised Straus for the "unstinted effort and intelligent observance." Then, apologizing for not being able to give it proper consideration, he placed it on the shelf and never removed it. The old reform warrior had become skeptical of single-barrel cures.[101]

The scourge of congressional stand-pattism, who lanced Andrew Mellon, Henry Ford, the power interests, bankers, brokers, and coupon clippers, had become a very practical mayor. Piecemeal was better than no meal at all, especially when he had no money to pay for comprehensive programs to rehouse the city's poor. He allowed the housing reformers their enthusiasms, accepting their memoranda and listening to their pleas for billions. He exploited their commitments to build First Houses and Williamsburg, picked their brains for proposals, and then scaled these down before submitting them to the kindred spirit in Washington.

It was not only Franklin Roosevelt who saw housing as primarily a way to dispense money. For La Guardia too the first priority was finding programs to assist New York with relief and unemployment. More sensitive to the need for slum clearance and new housing than Roosevelt, he also recognized that the problem was more thorny than throwing bridge spans across the water or finding some land and money to wedge a playground into an overcrowded neighborhood. The scale of social engineering and the level of funding necessary was daunting, and it prevented him from taking seriously the possibilities trumpeted by the housing reformers.

La Guardia took the hopeful experiment in large-scale planning that excited the housing reformers and reduced it to the scale of the politically possible, a few housing developments and several thousand families in better surroundings than they had ever dreamed possible. But so long as only the "heroic poor" were rehoused, the entire premise of rehabilitating the socially unfit through sunshine and private toilets was never really tried. Moreover, even if it had been, a billion-dollar investment in upgrading living conditions without addressing such related issues as appropriate and plentiful employment, effective schooling, and adequate health care would probably have disappointed even the most optimistic reformer.

---

6. Urban Spokesman

T HE Depression persisted into its sixth winter. Legions of the poor and desperate continued to stalk the city streets, warmed only by their resentments. Federal investigators who regularly dipped into the mood of the people found a harder edge to these New Yorkers. There was a disquieting desperation, a willingness to follow a leader, any leader. City Welfare Commissioner William Hodson feared that unless jobs were made available soon the masses might pursue "a new social order," and Communists were making gains through their unemployment councils. "The next idol," warned another social worker, "is likely to be someone who has a promise. . . ." Months earlier, La Guardia had led a delegation of mayors to Roosevelt's beloved Hyde Park and, there among the autumnally bare fruit trees and generous lawns, delivered his message: "stripped of all pretty phrases and stock quotations," the cities could no longer care for their own.[102]

In early April Congress, in its single largest appropriation ever, allocated $4.8 billion, for a Works Projects Administration, and Roosevelt placed open-fisted Hopkins at its helm. "Boys . . ." proclaimed Harry Hopkins, "[w]e've got to get everything we want—a works program, social security, wages and hours, everything—now or never." This was no guarded Ickes program, and La Guardia expressed its generous spirit: "Will some of these billions be wasted? Sure. In such a gigantic undertaking there's bound to be a small percentage of waste. But I am sure that when the history of these trying times is written it will not begrudge one penny to aid the hungry and the jobless."[103]

The mayor would come to the capital on the Potomac, alone without any advisers, and drop in to discuss projects with Roosevelt. "Our Mayor is probably the most appealing person I know," Roosevelt once said. "He comes to Washington and tells me a sad story. The tears run down my cheeks and tears run down his

cheeks and the first thing I know, he was wangled another fifty million dollars."
While cabinet members were having trouble getting on the calendar, La Guardia
would slip into Washington on short notice and in a half hour complete plans for
yet another batch of projects. Together the protean mayor and his indulgent patron
forged programs for a modern New York, worth hundreds of millions of dollars.
"He has a confidential relationship with President Roosevelt enjoyed by no Democrat," wrote *Albany Times Union* political columnist John Heffernan. "The doors
of the White House open at his radiant approach, and the President is never too
busy to sit down and have a chat with him." Heffernan thought that it had something
to do with Roosevelt's determination to destroy Tammany. But there was much
more to this relationship, as Heffernan himself sensed: "New York's Mayor has
boxed the political compass as capriciously as Franklin Roosevelt, who can be
Right today, and Left tomorrow and when he's in the middle, boys, he's neither
up nor down." Liberal pragmatists both, the president and the mayor respected
each other.[104]

Trustworthy, articulate, loyal, and savvy, La Guardia also had the uncanny
ability to take the heat off the president when a fresh program with a mind-boggling
price tag came down the pike. After Roosevelt introduced his four billions-plus
relief agenda in 1935, even before conservatives had a chance to express their
anguish for the Republic and its free institutions, there came the chunky New
Yorker bounding into Washington demanding more. Straightaway, the president's
proposal appeared moderate by comparison. "The Mayor took his program to
Washington to lay it before the President personally," reported the papers, regarding
La Guardia's request for a cool $1 billion for his city. "It was understood here,"
stage-whispered one correspondent, that the administration welcomed the mayor's
excessive proposals, which made their requests seem modest, considering the level
of need.[105]

When the inevitable chorus of complaints rose to criticize this or that New
Deal program, Washington's favorite rasp attacked the "fault-finders and whiners"
who called on the government to keep out of the people's business as an excuse
for ignoring the people's starvation. Fiorello went down South to respond to Pulitzer
Prize-winning Robert E. Lee biographer Douglass Southall Freeman's charge that
the New Deal was a threat to American liberties: "I admire the vision and courage
of a Federal government that reaches out and gives succor to localities in time of
dire need." "MAYOR DEFENDS NEW DEAL" ran the headlines.[106]

By May 1935 New York had rented a three-room D.C. flat for its peripatetic
mayor, who flew into Washington for meetings with the president, Ickes, Hopkins,
or Secretary of the Treasury Henry Morgenthau as often as twice a week (generally
planning to return to his city hall office by afternoon), wisecracking to reporters
that the District of Columbia was "no further than the Bronx," anyway.[107]

In the same month Roosevelt finally acknowledged that the cities deserved a significant voice in planning national economic recovery. He created a mayor's chair on the Allotment Advisory Committee that controlled public works allocations. To no one's surprise, the administration selected its favorite mayor for the committee. For a few days it seemed that the president had overburdened La Guardia by half. Citing a New York City charter provision prohibiting chief magistrates from holding a concurrent office, Kingston Associates, a New York City real estate firm, brought a taxpayer's suit in July "to restrain the Controller of the City of New York from paying any money to the defendant, Fiorello La Guardia as salary for the office of Mayor of the City of New York," and disqualifying him from office.

La Guardia and Roosevelt exchanged several notes, with Fiorello voicing an old frustration. There always seemed to be a law available to obstruct some good intention or other. "Wouldn't it be fine if you had the power to declare a moratorium on all lawyers, legal opinions and perhaps decisions [?]" But the New York State Supreme Court freed the hero's neck from the tracks in time and he took his seat on the advisory committee, developing policy guidelines and awarding grants for public works to feed the hungry and jobless, while Roosevelt cheered heartily.[108]

But which hungry and jobless were going to receive the hundreds of millions being allocated? La Guardia feared that the overwhelmingly rustic Congress would funnel public works billions toward rural programs and blue-collar projects, short-changing the cities, with their large proportion of white-collar unemployed. In New York City, for example, one-fourth of the unemployed came from white-collar occupations. La Guardia's lobbying brought immediate results as Harry Hopkins announced that the lion's share of the newly won relief monies would fund projects in large cities where the "great bulk of the unemployed were to be found."[109]

Through his influence on the Allotment Advisory Committee, La Guardia also managed to steer one-fourth of all federal highway allocations toward the cities, even if the technical definition of "highway" had to be stretched to include avenues and parkways. Of the more than twenty members on the committee, La Guardia was the only one aside from the president to attend each of the twenty-two meetings. He had learned in his congressional days the value of doing the detailed drudge work. While others worked for the spotlight, he worked for results and often as not got them.

PWA grants had become expensive gift horses, paying outright for 30 percent of labor and material costs on approved projects while making the rest of the money available as loans at 4 percent interest. La Guardia, complaining that cities could not absorb such debt, persuaded President Roosevelt to change the formula to 45 percent outright gift and 55 percent loan, at 3 percent. Crowed La Guardia: For the "first time the conditions of cities have been considered by the Federal Government in any general plan for the whole country." Secretary of Treasury Morgenthau prodded the president to rescind the interest rate reduction, but La Guardia and the cities were becoming a formidable power in national councils. A few weeks later La Guardia was named to a special committee that awarded reductions in the rate of interest that Washington charged on loans.[110]

Recognizing La Guardia's special role, the cities also singled him out to lead them. For years, power had lagged behind demographics, as rural interests continued to dominate state legislatures and national congresses, while population flowed into the cities. The United States had changed from a nation of farms to one of cities, and spurred by the Depression, mayors from across the nation joined together in a national organization to articulate their needs and demand their fair share. In November of 1935 they selected New York's tart-tongued chief magistrate and the New Deal's favorite municipal officer as president of the U.S. Conference of Mayors, an office that he continued to hold for the next ten years. New York did not suffer for Fiorello's larger enthusiasms. Even before his municipal colleagues digested his confidential memos detailing new WPA programs, La Guardia was developing plans for more than $300 million in new projects for New York. By October 1935 New York had won 200,000 WPA job slots while other cities were still reading the fine print on the applications.

In leading the cities' fight for direct access to federal assistance without going through their states, La Guardia had the Conference of Mayors petition Harry Hopkins to create independent WPA units for the twenty-five largest cities on an equal level with the forty-eight state-directed operations. On June 26, 1936, Hopkins announced his decision. WPA would award the privilege of administering its own federal relief operation to only one of the twenty-five municipalities, La Guardia's New York. The Empire City would be treated as the "forty-ninth state." New York had won Hopkins's confidence by developing a wide range of WPA projects and administering them with integrity. The decision represented a personal victory for a tireless mayor who had developed the trust and power to place his city at the forefront of the emerging partnership between Washington and the cities.[111]

On La Guardia's advice Hopkins named General Hugh Johnson to administer the New York City WPA. The cagey former director of the National Recovery Administration smoked too much, drank too much, and tangled too much with real and imagined enemies, but he had outstanding managerial abilities and important friends in Washington. FH knew that such a man would wrestle for his programs and he wanted him in New York. Johnson did not take long to prove La Guardia right.

When the national administration set WPA pay schedules substantially below prevailing wages, and in a number of instances below the accepted living needs for a family, First Houses construction workers walked off their jobs in protest. Explained one building tradesman: As a union man he had earned $1.40 an hour and WPA paid about half for the same work. "Union rates don't come from sitting down and asking pretty. They was fought for. . . . I'd rather work any time than sit home and rot. But if I am going to follow my trade, it's got to be at union rates. I can't scab can I?'' La Guardia agreed. And after only two days in office General Johnson used his discretionary power to raise wages. Within a few weeks Johnson, along with Hopkins, Roosevelt and La Guardia, worked out a compromise formula that served as a national model for maintaining wage levels that labor had fought decades to achieve, even if meant fewer total projects.[112]

After its initial shakedown period, WPA became the most dynamic economic force in the city, hiring and assigning as many as 7000 people a day, from park laborers to artists. But the programs raised new questions, and Robert Moses, in his gentle fashion, managed to trample the delicate turf of partnered responsibility. When Hugh Johnson decided on a stagger system to pass the limited number of jobs around, he temporarily suspended some 1600 parks workers to give work to others. The imperious parks czar, unwilling to play worker roulette with his parks, countermanded the order with a gratuitous swipe at out-of-towners who had the cheek to tell him how to build and administer parks (conveniently ignoring who had paid for his parks and bridges).

A few weeks later Moses again rebuked the WPA for assigning his department ''bums, jailbirds and rifraff.'' These ''vagrants'' would not ''work on any project of mine.'' The mayor and General Johnson reacted with forbearance, patiently explaining that the federal government was prepared to provide relief but it was not prepared to have its workers pass Mr. Moses' personal test. ''We don't call them rifraff . . .,'' scolded Johnson, ''we call them unemployed.'' The mayor suggested that RM would have to make do even if the workers did not wear tuxedoes to work.[113]

Ten days later La Guardia advised all city departments, ''The purpose of federal relief projects is to give employment.'' While it was the responsibility of city officials to weed out laggards and incompetents, the new workers must be trained. ''Before arbitrarily rejecting workers and sending them back, give them a chance to make good.'' The mayor understood, even if his brilliant parks commissioner did not, that the federal government had to be accommodated if it was to continue with its help, and that the federal government was more interested in occupying the unemployed than in Moses' parks. With intelligence and tact, federal work relief would result in parks, bridges, and schools, but it did not pay to bully the process.[114]

In all of this, in taking the federal money and translating it into projects, in maintaining a good trusting relationship with Washington while insisting on his city's prerogatives, in setting a model and speaking for urban America, La Guardia proved nimble and adept. His relationship with Moses symbolizes the balancing act that he had to engage in. Gathering the best men around him did not make life easy. And Moses' temperament was the hardest of all. ''I don't have to praise Bob Moses. His work speaks for itself,'' a sobered Fiorello told S. J. Woolf of the *New*

York Times. "But I wish that some of the people who accuse me of having no restraint would know what I went through when we were having trouble with the federal government. And while . . . on that subject, let me say that I do not like to think what would have happened if the Federal government had not come to the aid of the country during the emergency."

Cities were no longer as free and easy as before. Slow-paced laissez faire was as out of place as Jimmy Walker's old insouciance. Fastening upon his city a broad conception of municipal responsibility, La Guardia understood that the new lineaments of a large, salient, serious city government depended on federal assistance. And no other mayor harvested federal opportunities for fruitful cooperation with more persistence or imagination. Mastering what historian Henry Graff has called "the art of spending public money, before that skill became commonplace," the first La Guardia administration brought to New York City a list of grants, loans, and WPA projects that fills pages: the East River Drive, the Triborough, First Houses, Williamsburg Projects, Marine Parkway, the Lincoln Tunnel, the Queens Midtown Tunnel, piers, public schools, libraries, hospitals, sewage disposal plants, prisons, Hunter and Brooklyn colleges, public baths, subway extensions, health centers, garbage treatment plants, water mains, boardwalks, swimming pools, beaches, zoos, health centers, parks, parkways, the Public Health Research Institute, huge indoor market areas, and miles and miles of repaved city streets. The city was rebuilt with a promise of even more to come. And behind all of these projects a plump man kept his feet on the pedals and pumped furiously, flooding the Great Dispenser in Washington with insistent demands for more and more. "I wish you would keep your shirt on," Harry Hopkins once shouted at the mayor in exasperation. "You and I can talk to each other without having snappy wires going back and forth."[115]

Just a couple of years back New Yorkers applied for relief by promising ward heelers that they would vote Democratic on election day. This relief offered narrow, private benefits, for Tammany and the lucky recipient, but the city was atrophying. Fiorello La Guardia seized the opportunity of the Depression unemployment crisis to transform construction from a private to a public enterprise and cities from neglected wards of the state to wards of a more bountiful federal government. At the start of his administration La Guardia had to beg for home rule from Albany to straighten out a $30 million budget crisis. Two years later he was negotiating directly with Washington for ten times that amount. The massive new works that he brought to New York supplied jobs, stimulated dormant industries, and enriched the public and private life of the region; they also symbolized the possibilities for a creative federal partnership in creating the modern city.

CHAPTER 10

To Preserve and Protect

1. "I Am Like the Boys in the Trenches at Zero Hour"

H E had come into office demanding authority to steer the city clear of disaster only to spur an outraged defense against municipal dictatorship. He brushed aside the defeat and wove together grants and park openings, investigations and dramatics, to fashion an exuberant mastery before which all opposition folded. With a daunting display of municipal leadership, La Guardia siezed control of the city as no mayor had in modern memory. He met its emergencies, shored up its faltering finances, opened the federal relief tap, and laid out New York's modern infrastructure with a panache that made good government exciting and immediate. And in the end he held the power he had sought.

He was in control, prodigiously involved in the "big job" that he had pursued for much of his adult life. By the end of his long days he would be exhausted, scarcely able, recalls Edmund Palmieri, to drag one foot a few inches ahead of the other. But he was fulfilled, roaming the streets like a latter-day Haroun-el-Raschid dispensing personal justice and rousing dread in the servants of his realm. And as he expanded his control over the city, he kept the populist outlook of the outsider, ever suspicious, ever resentful of corrupted power.

Awake at five o'clock this winter morning in 1936, he bounded out the doors of his East Harlem tenement followed by a flock of reporters to make unannounced rounds of police precincts. Bursting into the 126th Street station before dawn, he asked for Captain Quirk, announcing, the "mayor is present." The captain was out. A scowling La Guardia turned to the bleary-eyed reporters: "The captain is in bed." He left a message for Quirk to get in touch with the commissioner. At another station he sat as a magistrate to hear a disorderly conduct charge. Wending his way downtown, he stopped in several more precincts, inquiring of commanding officers about the peace and safety of his realm. After a last check at the city hall station house he was ready for a day's work.[1]

Hollywood producer Leo Carrillo suggested that the mayor, a "great little 'Wop,' should be immortalized" on the silver screen. In breathless producer-talk he outlined the immortality that he planned: "His life, his loves, his women, his political enemies . . . fearless aggression for the good of the common people." Told that there would be little of "his loves, his women" to focus on, the producer wired back a bit flagged, "LACK OF WOMAN INTEREST HAS SORT OF HAMPERED IT   "

His women, it turned out, were no different from his men, New Yorkers in need. La Guardia learned that a neighbor's daughter had applied for a surgical residency at New York's Bellevue Hospital and had been turned down by the all-male department. The mayor intervened and saw to it that the city hospital brought its first woman surgeon on staff. He delighted feminists by removing from City Hall Park a huge statue of a male "Civic Virtue" trampling female-figured vices underfoot. Too loutish, offered the mayor in explanation. He appointed more women to responsible city posts than other mayors, although his reasons appear less advanced than his motives: "City government is just housekeeping," he would say, and women knew all about that. He named the first black city magistrate, a man who held degrees from both Harvard and Columbia, leaving carpers little margin for complaint.[2]

Extending his pursuit of a "new normal" to labor policy, La Guardia placed city government foursquare on the side of organized labor in industrial relations. He used his good offices to settle strikes among elevator operators, hotel employees, taxi drivers, fur tailors, and sundry garment trades workers. During a laundry strike, he threatened to turn off water to the businesses unless they made concessions. When hotels refused to honor a compromise labor agreement, health and safety inspectors paid them surprise visits, and he warned the taxi industry that he would send in receivers to seize collected taxes if they did not reach a proper adjustment with their drivers.[3]

La Guardia used similar pressures against milk distributors, selling milk at city-operated baby health stations for cut rates and threatening to introduce municipal milk depots if prices were not kept reasonable. He climaxed his decade-long campaign against high utility costs with a plan to finance, build, and operate a municipal power plant with Washington money. No one knew if this was feasible, but no one doubted that the mayor would do it either, least of all the utilities companies, who took the message to heart and cut their rates by $2 million. FH refused to be grateful. "That's all right but Mrs. O'Flaherty, Mrs. Epstein and Mrs. La Guardia will hardly notice it on their bills." What Mrs. La Guardia could hardly fail to notice was the baby alligator that her famous husband accepted from the mayor of Palm Beach and brought home "for the kids." What he would not accept was the gift of a gun for his young son Eric.[4]

343

Briefly confined to the hospital with sciatica, he kept his staff cracking with scribbled orders. Windels: "PLEASE TAKE ALL PRELIMINARY STEPS TO REMOVE TRACKS FROM QUEENS BOULEVARD." Carr: "What is happening to re-employment plan. I do not want this to sleep. I want action and plenty of it." Valentine: "How come Vera Stretz had a pistol permit? Assuming it was issued in 1932, how about 1934 and 1935?" His relationship with the governor who had denounced him as a dictator in the early days was repaired to the point of charming repartee: "My standing here at the hospital went up immediately when you phoned, and it helped quite a bit." The two were now working together smoothly. "I hope to be out in a day or so, and am going to Washington. I will not take up the matter . . . unless I get instructions from you." Even in bed the mayor kept his feet on the pedals.[5]

He refused to mellow, offending profusely, especially powerful groups who placed their own interests ahead of the public good. So harshly did he take the New York City Bar Association to task for suggesting judicial appointments drawn from old-boy establishment lawyers that even his close friend the venerable C. C. Burlingham was offended. A year later, however, when La Guardia withdrew from the American Bar Association with a public blast at the group for devoting "its efforts to special interests rather than to the uplift and welfare of the profession," CCB praised the move. FH scolded doctors for their preoccupation with profits and "stubborn resistance to [such] new ideas" as group health treatment and expanded public health services, offended knee-jerk patriots by vetoing a bill compelling the display of an American flag at indoor gatherings of fifteen or more persons, and irked New York Firsters by opposing the Lyons Bill, requiring municipal employees to reside within the city limits, as inappropriate for a modern cosmopolis.[6]

When the fire department received thirteen identical bids for rubber-lined water hosing, the mayor, old trust-bashing juices splashing, orchestrated a national campaign against the "Fire Hose Trust." At one point he drafted a bill to put the city into the business of manufacturing its own tubing. Between guffaws and denunciations of incipient bolshevism in the state's southern district, Albany quashed the bill, but the Federal Trade Commission took note. Its investigation resulted in antitrust proceedings against the companies. Six months later the delinquent monopolists signed a consent agreement to cease fixing prices.[7]

La Guardia would not calm down. He railed against "raw magazines," drunk drivers (commanding the police commissioner not to allow "technicalities, nor lack of evidence" to stand in the way!), water pollution, high city insurance rates, inefficient sanitation disposal. To modernize the city's streets he ripped out trolley tracks and tore down the elevated train platforms. He pressed the police to move against the "tinhorns and horse thieves" responsible for street gambling and made an annual pageant of sledgehammering confiscated slot machines and roulette wheels before dumping them into Long Island Sound.[8]

Once he discovered his statutory authority to sit as a magistrate, he would drop in on a local police precinct to hold court and pronounce swift judgment against the "punks." (City Magistrate Rudich once dismissed a woman's complaint that she had been defamed by a gentleman who referred to her as a "punk" by ruling that the mayor had a copyright on that word.) He did accept certain limits on his involvements. After Ernest Cuneo wrote him from Washington that it would be a good idea to extend daylight saving time, La Guardia wrote back: "The last time I saw you, you were rewriting the Constitution. Now I see that you are adjusting our solar system." He passed on the opportunity to fiddle with the calendar.[9]

A luckless bus driver drove through a red light when the patrolling sultan happened to be on the watch. La Guardia copied down his license, had him brought to trial before Magistrate La Guardia, pronounced judgment, and collected a $2 fine. Visiting the Bronx Terminal Market, La Guardia found private guards carrying billy clubs. He personally confiscated the weapons. He did not want his markets to look like a patrolled danger zone. Little wonder that New Yorkers imagined an army of stout little men in big black sombreros scampering about the city![10]

A creature of his enthusiasms, Fiorello was always looking for some new way to roll back the price of urban life, for reclaiming the rural placidity of his beloved Arizona youth. The city was a hard enough place to enjoy, he decided one day, without the dissonant clamor of honking, screaming, jackhammering, screeching, reveling, tooting, and pedestrian noise-making that filled the air. Like all big cities, New York City's decibel level arched toward the nerve-jangling and Fiorello wanted it brought down. Committees were formed, school children enlisted, newspapers inundated with mayoral pronouncements, and the billboards papered with a doddering Father Knickerbocker urging quiet in half a dozen languages. The mayor launched his war on noise with a list of prohibited clatter and gave the new program its proper sendoff by having the police issue 172 summonses for unnecessary horn tooting, loud radio playing, unlicensed use of loudspeakers, and disturbing caroling. The Borden Company contributed to the campaign by covering the hoofs of its delivery horses with rubber shoes (Borden's held a special place in the mayor's heart. Once he told a group that he had grown up on Borden's Eagle Brand condensed milk. Then he caught himself. "Gee I should not be putting in a plug . . . perhaps that is why I did not grow.")[11]

Some noises, however, made the glandular Fiorello's spirits soar. His appreciation for music extended to a wholehearted belief in its spiritual power to calm, uplift, and inspire. When he got the chance, he would steal away from his desk to accompany his young friend Ira Hirschmann to Philharmonic rehearsal performances. He conducted as many orchestras as would respond to his baton, offhandedly commanding one in Carnegie Hall to "just treat me like Toscanini." Although the *New York Times* critic failed to point out the similarity between the two conductors, he did allow that the mayor offered a serenely workmanlike interpretation. "In the pianissimi patches he lifted his left hand and delicately signaled

345

for just the proper volume and in the more spirited bars his right arm moved vigorously in up and down vertical strokes.''[12]

Seeking for New York a level of art worthy of a great international cosmopolis, La Guardia created a Municipal Arts Comittee, instructing one of the appointees, the writer John Erskine, that the committee should ''endeavor through art to increase the grace, happiness, and beauty of our municipal life.'' He directed the committee to develop low-priced symphony concerts, plan a special public school for music and art, design a music and art center, and establish a municipal symphony orchestra. When New York opened the first municipal art gallery in the United States, La Guardia called it one of his best contributions as mayor. He personally led the effort to underwrite free summer concerts at Lewisohn Stadium.[13]

''Can One Spunky Little Mayor Show the World?'' the *Brooklyn Eagle* headline asked.

He wants to spend some of the people's money in ways calculated to increase the public's taste, enrich its mentality and encourage its esthetic impulses. What a cockeyed idea for a Mayor.

The little man with the dark double chin is a curious anomaly. He cares more about art than the crease in his pants. He had rather give the city a municipal art center than to get somehow, by ways politicians know, the money it would cost in his own pocket. He'd rather give the people of New York the opportunity to listen cheaply to a symphony by Beethoven than to hear them sing in his honor ''The Sidewalks of New York.'' He actually considers Wagner better music than ''Will You Love Me in December As You Do in May.'' I guess the man is crazy.

In 1936, as he opened the High School of Music and Art, a beaming La Guardia told friends that he now understood how Senator George Norris felt when Muscle Shoals was opened.[14]

He remembered the singular vulnerability of children. They held a special place in his government. He hired sixteen high school students to serve as city hall interns, to teach them how the government works firsthand, and to plant in them a feeling for government service. One group of youngsters went off to class one day only to be met by a pudgy man with a forceful falsetto giving a lesson in city government. Children, he believed, needed space and recreation. He was happiest opening a park, playground, or community health center. These, he said, did more to combat juvenile delinquency than hundreds of jails.

And he made sure that Brooklyn kids got their circus after License Commissioner Paul Moss, heeding the complaints of Flatbush residents that the big top disrupted their quiet neighborhood, refused Ringling Brothers a permit for a tent in Brooklyn. La Guardia thought of all the unhappy children and ruled that ''the circus under canvas is an American institution," canceling Moss's injunction. He also opened the movies to the kids. With many films inappropriate and the mid-afternoon crowds often unwholesome, the city prohibited theaters from admitting unaccompanied children. To avoid the ban, kids would often ask strangers to bring them into the theaters as their own, opening them to danger and abuse. La Guardia had new legislation introduced permitting children into the movie houses after school hours so long as the theaters showed proper fare and placed a uniformed matron on guard at a specially marked children's section. Then he personally led police inspections to see that the proper safeguards had been taken. To assure children wide futures, he refused to allow budget-minded reformers to institute tuition at the city colleges.[15]

His hatred of "punks" and various troublemakers ran deep, but for children he had a special tolerance. "Suppose he does break a window or hook an apple," La Guardia would say; this was no reason to bring a court case. He remembered his own youthful pranks in Arizona and asked judges to temper their treatment of young offenders with wise mercy. "Nothing," he told an audience of jurists at the induction of Jacob Panken to the Domestic Relations Court, "has such a tendency to make a boy a criminal as to arrest him and lock him up." Juvenile delinquency, he said, was too complex to be solved with a narrow mind. "Remember we are dealing with human beings. Give these kids a chance to be born right. See that they get proper nourishment in their infancy. . . . See that their families have decent homes in which to live." What society offered today's youth, he brooded, was four years of college followed by a relief application for $21 a week. A graduating class from the Central Needle Trades High School heard La Guardia's own vocational counsel: "a first class tailor is worth more than a third class lawyer." He opened health centers, swimming pools, recreation fields, and baby-care centers with the exuberant joy of a medieval patron, happy to frame better lives in caring government.[16]

He continued to operate at full throttle. While his city automobile was being repaired, La Guardia rode about in a police sidecar, squealing, "I ain't no sissy." The *New York Times* responded to the remark with a tender paean to the spunky mayor, contrasting his commitment to work, even when ill and in pain, with that of previous mayors who cruised about the world, pleasure-bent, at the people's expense. When an aide mentioned that he planned several rounds of golf for the coming Sunday afternoon, La Guardia eyed him incredulously. "I thought you did that *last* week." Invited with Marie to accompany Billy Rose and Arthur Garfield Hays to an opening night, FH replied with thanks and a demurral: "We never attend first nights. They are for the social registerites. We will go along with the common people some time later on."[17]

C. C. Burlingham recoiled in mock horror at the rumor that the mayor planned to cover city hall's patrician marble with plebian linoleum, pleading that the "desecration" of a pavement worn down "by the faithful Tammany men like pilgrims at St. Peters,'' be avoided at all costs. If that was tongue in cheek, Fiorello's refusal to consider an official mayoral residence was quite real. When the City Council contemplated making Gracie Mansion into mayoral quarters, La Guardia suggested that it be used for a museum. East Harlem tenement life was just fine for the La Guardias. There was no telephone in the lobby from which to announce visitors, but the elevator operator could always come upstairs to check before bringing guests up in the old iron cage. The *New York Times* agreed with him. Imagine the mayor coming home from one of his hands-on fires, oil slicker dripping water, traipsing through Gracie Mansion's art-bedecked halls and brushing up against a painting by Velasquez.[18]

Fiorello had his own ideas about moving. For all his efforts at centralizing the city government, La Guardia took notice of more than Manhattan. When Brooklyn (Kings County) celebrated its centenary he relocated the city government, mayor's office, and Board of Estimate—lock, stock, and barrel—to the Kings County borough hall for five days. With Marie and the children he moved into a Brooklyn hotel for the stay. Later he took the government to the Bronx and Queens. "This is a big city," he said as he worked at knitting its parts together. How were you going to get the people to abandon their trust in local bosses unless you showed them that the government was willing to come closer? After his weeklong sojourn in Brooklyn, a local newspaper wrote: "It makes us in Brooklyn feel, Mr. Mayor, that you consider our interests, that you are solicitous for our welfare, that we mean something more than a taxable asset to the government." Seventy-four residents of northern New York were asked in a boundary dispute between the city and Westchester County to vote in a referendum on their preference. When the vote was announced in favor of the city, a grateful La Guardia sent the police department band to serenade the seventy-four loyalists.[19]

And always his schedule was punctuated with unplanned trips to city emergencies. In Greece it was said that a store could not open or even a door to a new apartment without the priest coming with his holy water to bless the new enterprise. In New York there could not be a roof collapse, railroad wreck, or tenement blaze without the little figure in the big sombrero rushing up to the scene. In he would go among the emergency workers to keep an eye on operations, lend an often unwelcome hand, or voice some important urging. Those who inquired were told that as boss he should be there; those who did not believed that he had never outgrown his adolescent urge to pit physical courage against danger. After a few tense hours he would emerge covered with soot, water dripping from his big slicker, and pleased with the knowledge that his city servicemen were doing a good job.

One day, just after he had settled into a seat at Radio City Music Hall, a note was slipped into his hand alerting La Guardia to a fire nearby. Leaping from his seat, the mayor rushed down the aisle to the closest exit and from there to Fifty-first street, where smoke was pouring out of a restaurant. Then he disappeared. Only a couple of hours later, as firemen were coming out of the building muttering,

"Will someone get the mayor out of there," did his companion learn where he was. As the last firefighter emerged with no mayor in sight, there was new concern, until finally the familiar figure appeared, explaining: "I gave the refrigeration system a personal going over. I wanted to find out whether the building code had been violated." New Yorkers came to expect his presence at every major emergency and to respect his fearlessness and concern for others. When a Bronx building collapsed, La Guardia climbed an unsteady ladder to comfort a man pinned by the beams as rescuers worked around him for two hours.[20]

Much of his time and correspondence was spent fending off job seekers, from the down-and-out seeking work to congressmen pressuring on behalf of constituents. "I have nothing to do with the selection or appointment of anyone in the [Queens College] Department of History," he wrote to a congressman. It would be "improper for me to make any recommendation. . . . Very truly yours." But every once in a while he gave in. Matthew DeSerio reminded La Guardia of his family's loyal work on his behalf and although he was turned down for the first position that he requested, Fiorello did finally appoint him to his staff.

One busy day, personal secretary Stanley Howe darted into the office from a back entrance, whispering that there was a man outside "on his uppers," saying he had served with the American flying forces during the Great War and claiming that he had met Major La Guardia at the Italian front. "Do you remember him, Major?" Of course not, he says, waving Howe out. The man, Howe goes on, is on relief. By now La Guardia is bent over his papers and Howe is heading for the same back door through which he slipped in. Housing officials are being ushered in. As an afterthought the mayor calls over his shoulder without turning, "Is he a flier or a mechanic?" Howe, with one foot out the door, calls back, "Mechanic." "Okay, we need mechanics in the Department of Sanitation."[21]

For the poor he offered good intentions and sympathy, and sometimes it proved insufficient. "A family of three cannot exist, cannot live on forty-five dollars a month," a representative of the Worker's Alliance was saying. "Boys, don't forget, I am not a sovereign state," he replied softly. "It's hell the way you pound in on me." There had been demonstrations, harsh denunciations, and even calls for his impeachment by the more radical of the unemployed worker groups. "You crush me because I am decent," La Guardia complained. "We've been crushed some too," came the response. For this he had no answer, except his good intentions. "I am more interested in your cases than anybody else and you ride me."[22]

There was little time for reflection. He worked on instinct from the sympathies and principles he developed in the twenties: "I am like the boys in the trenches at zero hour," he would say. "It is not time to hesitate or reflect. It is not time to consider one's self. I am going over the top because it is my duty. If I succumb it will be in a worthy cause." The exaggerated sense of his own self-sacrifice and his lonely battle for honesty in government became a familiar, somewhat grating, refrain. "It is a most discouraging feeling," he would confide with false intimacy to a number of interviewers, "to be at the head of the largest and richest city in the world and find yourself helpless just because you want to clean the city, and it would be so easy if you could only eliminate the selfish greed of politicians." Hundreds who wrote the mayor their congratulations or good wishes read a similar message: "There are few compensations in public life to offset the sacrifice, the unjust criticisms and the daily anxieties, but occasionally there are compensations and one of them is to receive such a fine letter as yours."[23]

He did not mean a word of it. Doing the "big job" was compensation enough.

2. Coddling Pickets and Mussing Criminals

NEW York got to know its mayor at his best and at his worst. "He has been," declared the *Nation*, "courageous, choleric, threatening, dilatory, rash, and always interesting." Gathering power and attracting admiration were a beginning, but he aimed to do more. Life was not yet safe or bearable for too many New Yorkers, even with relief and Lewisohn Stadium concerts. He wanted to make New York a model for labor union power, to ease blacks into the mainstream, to fight the spread of international anti-Semitism and to draw the difficult line between recklessness and fairness on the treatment of Communists. One hundred different days were the happiest in his life. Scores of events represented his single proudest achievement. And all of these goals were his top priority. La Guardia was like that. Another of his first priorities was to shape the police department into an effective extension of his own progressive policies.[24]

La Guardia had chosen the man he defeated for the fusion nomination to head the New York police department, but slow-talking General John O'Ryan never won La Guardia's respect. The ramrod-postured martinet was the type of leader who measured performance by degrees of spit and polish. One of his first orders, in the frosty days of January, commanded police not to remove their heavy wool jackets in the summer. He wanted the force "sharp and smart," even if uncomfortable. "Every member of the department," O'Ryan declared with a seriousness more wisely reserved for thornier issues, "will have to stand up like he-men and take it, and like it." Right off he won the resentment of his men. The general instituted a crisp, military-style command and planned to renew the practice of full-dress police pageants with brass bands, whipping flags, and immaculate officers.[25]

Perhaps the police commissioner should have caught the drift when the decidedly informal mayor announced that he expected less strutting and more policing from his peace officers, or when La Guardia declared that there would not be any police parades until all the criminals were taken care of. Certainly the commissioner might have taken pause when the mayor told him that he thought it was ridiculous to enforce dress codes on the beaches: "I would rather catch a burglar with a bullet-proof shirt than a bather without any shirt." La Guardia had little patience with spit and polish, and a great deal of sympathy for sweating patrolmen. He saw no reason, he announced before the summer, why they should not be permitted to remove their jackets.[26]

La Guardia's meddling temper involved him in more than sartorial controversies. In the first week of his administration he sent O'Ryan a confidential memo: "Will you be good enough to personally look into the records and present activities of the following persons who I understand are openly and flagrantly violating the law." There followed more than a dozen names and addresses of high-stakes gamblers and policy bosses. Clearly La Guardia intended to keep an active hand in the police department.

Often as not, however, La Guardia passed his commands on to the department through the first deputy inspector and not the commissioner. For this post La Guardia picked "honest cop" Lewis Valentine, the bluff Irishman who had been kicked around by Tammany for doing his job too well. La Guardia had become familiar with Valentine during the 1933 campaign when the two met to discuss the need for reform in the police force, and he respected his direct, unadorned style. La Guardia had paid his political debt by appointing O'Ryan, but he made sure that the capable Valentine ran operations, and issued most of his own directions through the first inspector, a situation scarcely conducive to good departmental relations.[27]

———

"Here's a boob, with kids that are hungry. Does he use his last two bucks to buy them food? No. This boob pays it over to some tinhorn bookie because his honor—his honor, if you please—is involved. Huh! Some honor. Some boob." It was to protect these boobs and, yes, even their honor, if you please, that La Guardia undertook a crusade that preoccupied him for all the years of his mayoralty. Curious as it might seem for an inveterate opponent of enforced temperance, La Guardia could not abide public gambling, and he did all in his power as mayor to wipe it out.

New York's gambling business was no small nickel-and-dime operation of the type that had swallowed up his mother's change in Arizona. In the 1930s gambling surpassed bootlegging as the principal source of underworld profits. In the five boroughs alone, an estimated 25,000 slot machines in mom-and-pop store-fronts collected $500,000 a day. In 1932 Frank Costello, the acknowledged kingpin of the slots, together with his partner Phil Kastel, took in $37 million from these one-armed bandits, while "Dutch Shultz" Flegenheimer's policy racket pulled in

$20 million more. These small-change games inveigled the young, leeched the poor, and corrupted the police and the politicians.[28]

La Guardia commanded Valentine to clear numbers, policy, slot machines, horse wagering, and high-stakes poker and craps off the streets and out of the storefronts. The wet warrior had ridiculed the national frenzy over Prohibition, but gambling was different. It was evil, pure and simple. Out west, he remembered, the crooked tinhorns were treated to the rough justice he so admired, and city cowboy Fiorello wanted them varmints out of his town.

Early in 1934 he ordered Valentine to raid the True Mint Company at 1860 Broadway, where 460 crooked machines were found, along with a set of books that revealed in detail the scale of the racket's operations. Valentine continued to round up sharpers by the bushelful. In one two-week stretch police arrested 714 slot machine racketeers together with hundreds of craps shooters, policy and numbers runners, and bookmakers. To put off the police, the resourceful Costello converted 15,000 of his mechanical bandits into "candy machines" and won a court injunction against further police action. La Guardia ordered Corporation Counsel Windels to take an appeal to the Supreme Court, but even before that was done, he directed the police to confiscate the machines and notify him as soon as the first arrest was made. He would show them how to deal with the gangsters and their injunctions.

Before long, uptown police arrested a woman proprietor on whose premises they found one of the altered slot machines, brought her to the West 100th Street precinct, and notified the mayor. Slipping a large green law book under his arm, La Guardia rode out to the station house to try the case under his powers as a magistrate.

Anna Jurovaty proved a rather meek culprit. In broken English she stammered that a tough-looking man had installed the machine in her diner with strict orders to not dare disturb it, telling her "that it is all right now," in light of the court injunction. And here she was now, standing before the mayor, in trouble. Fiorello pronounced her "respectable and hardworking," but no, it was not all right at all. The recent decision of the court notwithstanding, "Section 982 of the Penal Act is so clear that there can be no mistake as to its intent and meaning. People's exhibit Number 1 is clearly a slot machine. The machine speaks for itself[!] . . . It is not a vending machine, and not even a federal judge can make it a vending machine. It is a gambling machine. A slot machine." Mrs. Jurovaty was guilty. She must never allow such a machine on her premises again. The police, he promised, would protect her against any more threats.[29]

To teach New Yorkers all about the crooked machines, La Guardia put on a gambling fair. An assortment of confiscated one-armed bandits and mechanical games of chance were set up in the lobby of Radio City Music Hall, and New Yorkers were invited to come play and convince themselves that "You Can't Win." They flocked to the gambling arcade, absorbing Fiorello's gentle message that gambling rewarded only the racketeers. The police proceeded to confiscate thousands of the rigged devices and remove them from circulation by sinking them in Long Island Sound. Within a few months Costello and Kastel relocated their business to Huey Long's Louisiana and set up their machines as charitable games. On profits of close to a million dollars they distributed $600 to charities. (Long's organization, of course, received a more generous share of the proceeds.)[30]

The campaign against gambling was the last thing that the police commissioner and the mayor agreed upon. La Guardia's frequent intrusions and his habit of working through Valentine, even taking the chief inspector on personal raids of suspected gambling dens without informing his superior, wreaked havoc on O'Ryan's line of command. La Guardia had originally promised no interference in the "regular performance of police duty by anyone, anywhere, anytime." But then, Fiorello was always an exception to any rule that he made. After a month he butted in at will. One afternoon, amused visitors found the mayor at his desk fingering swatches of material and button samples. He was studying changes in the police uniform! Two months after his promise to keep hands off the police department La Guardia was making his own investigations in the department.[31]

O'Ryan especially resented the mayor's interference into the handling of strikers and pickets. La Guardia's sympathy for labor ran deep. In a 1933 speech at Yale University he stated flatly, "If the right to live interferes with profits, profits must necessarily give way to that right." In the past, police had often waded into picketers on the slightest provocation. Now the cosponsor of the Norris-La Guardia Act declared unequivocal support for labor's right to strike and demonstrate. This policy made O'Ryan, who feared the working classes for their subversive possibilities, intensely uncomfortable. A city taxi strike brought the simmering disagreement into the open.[32]

Under the O'Brien administration the city had enacted a taxi excise that was recently overturned by the courts. By the time this decision was handed down, monies had already been collected. The city had no right to these funds, but since it was impossible to return the money to the passengers, the question was, who did have claims on this windfall? This question led to a dispute between the drivers and owners in an industry already riven over unionization. Early in February, discussions broke down, leading to a deeper conflict over union recognition. The drivers walked out and set up picket lines around the fleet company garages.

La Guardia reminded police of the new policy regarding peaceful picketing and ordered O'Ryan not to disturb strikers gathered in front of the garages, even if it meant redirecting traffic. Warning that the pummeling of pickets would no longer be tolerated, La Guardia took away police billy clubs to prevent any abuses. He hoped that his solicitous treatment of the strikers and his good-natured request that they avoid the "rough work" would keep the heated atmosphere calm. But he was wrong.[33]

On February 7, 1934, after an initial agreement fell through, an angry mob of 500 striking drivers rampaged through mid-Manhattan, stopping more than a dozen hacks driven by independent taxi owners and scabs, smashing windows, ripping off doors, and manhandling drivers. The police waited more than fifteen minutes to stop the disorder and rein in the roving mobs.

Over the next few days drivers began to return to their hacks as the smaller companies agreed to terms. The 5000-driver Parmelee system, however, installed its own company union and refused to deal with the striking drivers. Other fleets soon followed with their own house unions and refused to negotiate. On March 17 taxi drivers voted a second general strike.[34]

O'Ryan wanted to respond to unruly picketing firmly this time. "My background has been military," he later told a grand jury, "and my training hasn't much to do with liberalism. I don't believe in times of emergency in letting crowds collect." But the mayor again ordered police to permit strikers and picketers a wide berth. O'Ryan later testified that the mayor told him that "he felt very strongly in principle as to the right of assemblage and as to the right of speech." La Guardia blamed the previous violence on the companies' violent exploitation of the drivers through starvation wages, strong-arm tactics, and sham unions. These "Chicago-style tactics," he declared, would not be allowed to serve as a pretext for limiting the pickets.[35]

Unfortunately, the demonstrations got out of hand again. "Cab Strikers Curbed After Riots; Scores Injured," trumpeted the *Herald Tribune*. In one series of incidents, strikers attacked more than 150 cabs, smashing windows, slashing tires, setting fires, overturning vehicles, and injuring more than a score of "scab cabbies." Again the police were restrained by the mayor. Only after receiving reports of independent drivers being stoned and stabbed did La Guardia allow a full police response to try to restore order during what the *New York Journal* called "one of the worst disturbances New York has seen for years."[36]

La Guardia still refused to come down on the workers. "The companies are paying starvation wages and there is no question about that." The reports of violence were "exaggerated," and he insisted that the police had the situation well controlled, even after film evidence showed police standing by as violent strikers attacked nonstriking drivers and turned over taxicabs.

A grand jury, convened a few weeks later to investigate the disorders, disagreed. It criticized the police for losing control of the mobs and considered charging both the mayor and the police commissioner as accessories in the riots. A deeply offended O'Ryan passed the blame to his superior, agreeing with the jurors that the situation had been mishandled and warning that if La Guardia interefered with him again he would insist on his own authority or resign. Jurors charged La Guardia with unduly hampering the police with "a special obligation of consideration" for strikers and the "unusual privileges" that he had granted picketers.[37]

Owing to the mayor's habit of working through Valentine and the public disagreements over the handling of picketers, O'Ryan lost the respect of his men. "We got so we were afraid to open a closet door for fear some general or major or corporal would tumble out and give us orders," said one bitter patrolman. "When the Mayor meddles from City Hall," said another, "it is bound to be dangerous for the morale of the police."[38]

By August La Guardia and his PC were again at loggerheads over the man-handling of pickets, this time during a garment strike. O'Ryan managed to make matters worse by announcing a new policy requiring union officers to register their credentials and photographs so that the police could keep track of agitators. Labor upset turned to outrage when news leaked out about a new "rifle squad" reportedly being trained for strike duty. With union leaders attacking O'Ryan for his "bitter opposition to organized labor," and his "Fascist policies and inclinations," La Guardia lost whatever remaining confidence he had in him. The mayor called a meeting of police on crowd control, without inviting his commissioner; a few weeks later he planned police details for the upcoming primaries, again ignoring O'Ryan. Finally, the humiliated commissioner had had enough. With a parting blast at a mayor he had come to loathe for encouraging "Communists and the vicious elements of the city," he resigned.[39]

La Guardia did not look far for a replacement. Lew Valentine had stood up to Tammany in the twenties as the "Honest Cop," and he knew that the racketeers and criminals were a graver threat than striking workers. La Guardia had worked with the savvy veteran and valued his judgment and his straight talk. To Valentine criminals were "mugs and bums." He called in his officers for "turkey talk," to discuss serious business, and emphasized tough police work instead of dress codes. This was the kind of down-to-earth police leadership that La Guardia respected. Valentine warned superior officers that he considered "highhatting," the emphasis on rank and command honor, offensive. He dismantled the tightly centralized system that O'Ryan had instituted and invited patrolmen to bring their gripes directly to the commissioner, setting aside specific hours when he was available for just this purpose. At the same time the new top cop assured New Yorkers that every single complaint against the police would be investigated.[40]

An early test of Valentine's command came in the September primaries. Shortly after his own election in a campaign marred by frequent violence, La Guardia had promised that the very first contest under his administration would be so peaceful that children would be able to skip rope outside the polling booths. Valentine assigned his chief of staff to the task of policing the polls and then invited the state attorney general and every political party in the city from Tammany Hall to the Communists to send representatives to the central command office and see what happened. They could hear every complaint that came through the office and judge the adequacy of the police response. And outside the polls children played their games, oblivious to the citizens streaming around them to carry out their civic duties.[41]

La Guardia carried with him a rather simple view of old-fashioned justice. "Out where I was raised," he told a police Holy Name Society gathering, "we didn't have much of a police department. We had a Sheriff and a few deputies. We kept no locks on our doors, but robberies were unknown. Our Sheriff was quick on the trigger, if you know what I mean. Roughnecks call you cops and me a wop. . . . If gangsters speak well of the Police Department it's a sign there is something wrong in the department." Like the lawman of old, he was ordering the gangsters to leave town or be put out by his police. While the tone discomfited some liberals, many were willing to forgive the mayor for cheering the police on, since he had shown a willingness to hold them back as well.[42]

Career police officials, however, had not banked the same trust. Civil libertarians, already on edge from some of O'Ryan's moves, were dismayed when Valentine revived the "strong-arm squad," with a rhapsodic tribute to the third degree: "There will be promotions for the men who kick those gorillas around and bring them in" and loosen their tongues to lead to the higher-ups. A few weeks later Valentine made headlines again. After performing the most trying duty of the police commissioner, visiting a dying patrolman shot in the line of duty, he returned to a lineup of suspects who were being questioned for the shooting.

On the platform, among the accused and the decoys, stood a young hoodlum arrested for the murder of a garage employee. His record showed eighteen arrests for serious crimes including murder, yet the thug was swaggering about in a smart Chesterfield coat, a pearl-gray fedora, and a cocky disregard. The stylish tough had been freed on each of the previous arrests; the law held no terror for him. Valentine's gaze fell on the line for a minute, and then, catching sight of the weapons cache that had been found in this man's possession, he thought of the six recent police deaths and he exploded. Turning to his men, he told them to handle suspects with less care. "When you meet such men draw quickly and shoot accurately," he snarled. "Don't be afraid to muss them up. . . . Blood should be smeared all over that velvet collar. . . . He looks as though he just came out of a barber shop." His frustrations plain, the PC promised to back his men: "Make them fear you. . . . Make the thugs learn that this town is not a place for muscle men or racketeers."[43]

News of Valentine's words spread quickly. By the time he returned to his office, it was buzzing with journalists on a headline hunt. And he accommodated them: "It will be the crooks who are carried out in boxes, not the cops. . . . With the criminals, racketeers and gangsters the sky is the limit." Across the country hundreds of editorials pilloried the indiscreet language. Even police chiefs were aghast. "No one is justified," said San Francisco Police Commissioner Theodore J. Roche, "in giving such an order." From Los Angeles, Houston, Cleveland, and even crime capital Chicago, police professionals all criticized the intemperate remarks. Charles Burlingham urged La Guardia to reprove his commissioner for the "brutal, foolish. . . . offensive outburst" and forwarded to La Guardia a sharp letter from Felix Frankfurter. Oswald Garrison Villard, editor of the *Nation*, wired that the PC's words were an "incitement to crime. . . indefensible." Unless Valentine withdrew the statement, he warned, "your administration will forfeit liberal support."[44]

La Guardia, however, was more concerned with routing gangsters. He felt that the judges were just not up to the task. Six police officers had been shot, three were critically wounded, and the courts played their petty games of "search for the technicality" and freed hardened criminals. The time had come to strike a more favorable balance between self-defense and civil liberties, to prevent the criminals from taking over, a situation in which, he told Burlingham, "You and Dr. Frankfurter and the rest of the respectable people would be the first to suffer and complain and properly so."

Valentine continued his unbuttoned rhetoric. When gangster Dutch Shultz was arrested, he declared that he would have been happier had the notorious gangster come down "in a box," rather than on the arm of a policeman. Again the fine folk responded in an uproar. All citizens deserved decent treatment and the presumption of their innocence. But La Guardia had to deal with the police as well as the criminals, and he understood that there were limits to controlling them. He had been tough on the police, clearing out some of the old Tammany crowd, cracking down on those caught drinking, and forcing an unaccustomed restraint upon them during labor demonstrations. "It is not an easy job," he wrote Burlingham. "You do not know how I have labored to prevail upon the officers of the department to create a spirit of understanding and patience on the part of the police." Police were used to whacking insulting picketers and unruly demonstrators and swinging clubs into crowds that strained their lines. His orders stopping this did not win him any friends on the force. Now he wanted to show the cops that when they faced real dangers he was on their side in spades. If he demanded full respect for the rights of the "victims of economic forces," he was willing to ignore overzealousness at the expense of gangsters. Moreover, he was not going to "coddle crooks."[45]

A few days after these remarks, police brought in a twenty-year-old armed robbery suspect, James Toomey, in awful shape. The arresting officers took him directly to the hospital, where a few hours later he died, according to police, from "ulcers." But the multiple scalp lacerations, fractured ribs, and open rumors that police had jumped up and down on Toomey's abdomen while colleagues pounded him on the head suggested that he represented exhibit A in the new era of "muss 'em up." Valentine further upset liberals when he declared, "Just another dead criminal . . . a small loss." Then he appeared before the Association of Grand Jurors of New York County to advocate tough new "public enemy" laws, which would allow the police to remove the "barbarians and savages walking the streets today." The mayor followed this speech with his own tough words, urging New Yorkers to avoid "sentimentality." Later in the year, six jewel thieves arrived at headquarters looking as if their faces had been used to drill the hole through the wall leading to the heist. The mayor cheered on: "When six gangsters meet six policemen and the gangsters are mussed up it's just too bad for them. We have no room in the Police Department for sissies." After a series of syndicate-connected shootings, La Guardia and Valentine played the by now familiar refrain directing any patrolman who got his hands on Johnny Torrio, Lucky Luciano, Buggsy Siegel, Meyer Lansky, Lepke Buchalter, or any of the rest to "muss 'em up."[46]

The problem with all of this was that it left the impression that a tough police department would scare away the gangsters, and that a resolute little mayor, invoking the memory of cowboy sheriffs, need only order the bad men out of town. The campaign itself became the too-simple message. But unlike the people he was used to dealing with, the gangsters and racketeers would not run even if the mayor screamed and threatened.

---

3. Organized Crime and the Limits of Urban Reform

NEW York became a center of underworld criminal activity during the twenties when Prohibition was a rags-to-riches industry. Salvatore Lucania, better known as "Lucky Luciano," recalled that in those years a case of "processed" booze could bring $1000 from eager imbibers. "I'll bet," he told his amanuensis, "in the days when me and my guys got our whiskey business together, we had a bigger company than Henry Ford. We controlled plants, warehouses, all kinds of manufacturin'; we had a fantastic shipping business, and our drivers hadda drive good and shoot straight. We had bookkeepers . . . exporters and importers, all kinds of help that any corporation needs only we had more. And we had lawyers by the carload, and they was on call twenty-four hours a day."

By the mid-twenties, Luciano's liquor business was doing $12 million annually and contributing liberally to the support of the local police. "Hell," Luciano allowed, "we shoveled out ten thousand a week every week like clockwork to the top brass of the Police Department, and that was only a small part of it. We hadda take care of the precincts too, the captains, the lieutenants, and the sergeants; they all had their hands out." Then he went higher, creating a huge "Buy-Bank" bribe chest to purchase protection from the commissioner's office. If Luciano is to be believed, by the late twenties mob underling Joe "The Coon" Cooney was dropping off an envelope with $20,000 every week at police headquarters in lower Manhattan.[47]

Following Arnold Rothstein's murder in 1928, veteran crime boss John Torrio took his organizational genius from Chicago and set himself up, in the words of crime scholar Humbert Nelli, as "banker and financier for underworld enterprise in New York." The diminutive, gentle-looking Torrio had muscled competing bootlegging gangs into one centrally directed syndicate in Chicago, and he replicated the feat in Gotham, combining the seven major northeastern liquor smugglers into a massive crime organization that carried out its activities with impunity and enforced discipline through untempered terror.

The secret of this underworld's strength was the fact that ultimately it battened off public demand. During Prohibition it was liquor, but even after that law was repealed, the mob offered gambling, narcotics, illicit sex, and usurious loans, ample range for its "service of outlawed desires" that "convention may condemn and the law prohibit, but which nevertheless, human appetites crave." Writing in the early thirties, Walter Lippmann put the large problem in simple words: "We find ourselves revolving in a circle of impotence in which we outlaw intolerantly the satisfaction of certain persistent human desires and then tolerate what we have prohibited . . . having in the end to deal not only with all the vices we intended to abolish but with the additional dangers which arise from having turned over their exploitations to the underworld."[48]

It did not take the mob long to extend beyond trafficking in illegal pleasures. It diversified into conventional money-makers like bank robbery, extortion, blackmail, murder for hire, and industrial racketeering. In the late twenties the *Unione Siciliano* was being run by men set in their old Sicilian habits. Vendettas against each other and fear of outsiders prevented them from creating a modern, comprehensive crime organization. Lucky Luciano and his generation of American-raised crime figures bridled at the conservatism of the leaders and bided their time. "All us younger guys hated the old 'mustaches.' . . . We was tryin' to build a business that'd move with the times and they was still livin' a hundred years ago. . . . The old guys and their ideas hadda go. . . . For us rubbin' out a mustache was just like makin' way for a new buildin', like we was in the construction business." Luciano masterminded the elimination of two old-style bosses, Joe "The Boss" Masseria and the more elegant but equally backward Salvatore Maranzano.

In place of the "mustaches" he constructed a holding company directed by a board of six, each heading his own major crime enterprise. Luciano ruled as chairman but disavowed the old boss title, *capo di tutti capi*, and the feudal practices. When Maranzano was crowned in April 1931, more than 500 crime chieftains jammed into a large Grand Concourse banquet hall in the Bronx to pledge fealty and pay tribute. On the stage the gang boss sat in a thronelike sofa that had been rented from a theatrical prop outlet, delivering a Sicilian-flavored speech emphasizing rigid control along family lines. After he finished, each guest marched past, demonstrating loyalty by laying cash-stuffed envelopes before him.

Luciano spoke English, refused the traditional gift of tribute, and looked immediately to broaden organized crime horizons. He insisted on opening the *Unione Siciliano* to such non-Sicilians as Meyer Lansky, "Longie" Zwillman, and Benjamin "Buggsy" Siegel. Vaulting the twin obstacles of Depression and Prohibition repeal, the new regime carried organized crime to unprecedented prosperity and influence. The bootleg veterans nimbly diversified into legitimate whiskey distribution and a gambling network that replaced the dollars from hootch with a hundredfold take in nickels, dimes, and small bills from policy, numbers and off-track horse betting. Vito Genovese nurtured a trade in dope, and Luciano served as New York's premiere whoremaster.

The *Unione* also honed industrial racketeering to a fine art. "Dopey Benny" Fein, Louis "Lepke" Buchalter, and Jake "Gurrah" Shapiro sold industrial-strength muscle to fend off competition and stymie unionization. They and their associates also worked the other side, servicing unions that wanted to wipe out competition or create industrial havoc. Lepke, for instance, was said by authorities to "maintain complete domination over the city's garment industry," under threat of "destruction, acid throwing, mayhem, or murder." The underworld laid similar control on the baked goods, kosher poultry, motion picture, millinery, taxi, handbag, and shoe industries. The versatile Dutch Shultz headed a racket that collected protection money from such well-known restaurants as Lindy's and the Brass Rail, while Socks Lanza controlled the Fulton Fish market, and Joe Adonis and Albert Anastasia dominated the Brooklyn longshoreman's unions and ran the hijacking and theft of goods on the piers. Brooklyn was also the home of a corps of cold-blooded killers for hire known as Murder Incorporated.[49]

Against this chillingly effective combination of the criminally experienced and the ruthless, the old traditions of slogging police work were useless. Seventeen times before 1934, Socks Lanza was arrested without once being convicted. And there is good reason to believe that Tammany Tom Farley's wonderful tin box was kept full not only from his share of gambling receipts in the local Democratic club but also from handsome payoffs contributed by gangsters Lepke Buchalter and Gurrah Shapiro.

The most powerful of the political protectors, the burly former blacksmith James J. Hines, serviced a stable of syndicate kingpins including Lucky Luciano, Joe Adonis, and Frank Costello. When the NYPD Sixth Division, responsible for much of Harlem, began a sweep of gamblers, Hines had the drive halted. With his assistance, the white-run syndicate took over local black and Hispanic gambling operations from Jose Miro, Wilfred Brunder, and Joseph Ison. And when Jimmy could not shoo away the police, he would have hotshot cops transferred or broken in rank and route major gambling cases to friendly magistrates Francis Erwin and

Hulon Capshaw, who resided comfortably in his pocket. The lesson was not lost on the mob: Crooked politicians were worth every penny. In 1933 the mob contributed $30,000 to the campaign of Jimmy Hines's favorite lawman, William Copeland Dodge, in his race for district attorney of Manhattan.[50]

Fusion had promised to end the corrupt bargains between gangsters and their protectors, but the same election that brought La Guardia into office saddled the city with Dodge as the Manhattan district attorney. Accounts Commissioner Blanshard could investigate and expose, but it was up to the DA to prosecute. And in all the boroughs except the Bronx, these offices remained, in the words of a clearly frustrated Blanshard, ''nests of the spoils system, reeking with incompetence and favoritism, expensively operated by gentlemen of obvious unfitness.'' A 1934 American Bar Association survey of district attorney offices around the country reported that Manhattan's ''prosecutor's office has not been functioning satisfactorily for over ten years.''[51]

In all of this the mayor's tough talk counted for little. ''Instead of shutting up and working quietly until they could obtain indictments against the real culprits . . . they go into the thing with brass band tactics,'' complained Samuel Marcus, a veteran anticrime crusader and counsel for the Society for the Prevention of Crime. Incantations against tinhorns and punks won headlines, and La Guardia's support for abusing known criminals encouraged the police, but the fireworks did not significantly impede the growth of underworld racketeering. The simple fact was that while his investigations department studied scores of abuses of public trust, it had no criminal jurisdiction. When Commissioner Blanshard uncovered a bail bond racket tied directly to organized crime, he had to bring the information to the district attorney, who sat on it.[52]

Still, once in a while La Guardia did make a difference. The mayor had emphasized his interest in providing New York food merchants with safe, clean municipal markets, where pushcart peddlers and street vendors would be brought under a roof and protected from street toughs and gangsters. ''I found you pushcart peddlers,'' he once told a group of vendors, ''I have made you merchants.'' La Guardia appointed ''Big Mike'' Fiaschetti, a former New York detective with a reputation as a tough battler against the Italian underworld, deputy commissioner of markets and charged him with clearing the rackets out of food distribution. Fiaschetti's investigations revealed that the notorious hoodlum Ciro Terranova ran a mob monopoly that was forcing retailers to pay double the normal price for all small artichokes that came into New York City.

One predawn December day in 1935 the mayor, accompanied by assistants and a press entourage, set out from his uptown apartment for the Bronx Terminal Market. On this bitterly cold day, as retailers were walking around the market swinging buckets of burning coals to keep warm, La Guardia swung out of his car with a huge furled document under his arm and clambered up onto the tailboard of a truck. A pair of police buglers played a trumpet fanfare (one of the horns actually froze on a sour note!), and the compact magistrate read a mayoral proclamation banning the "sale, display, and possession" of artichokes in all public markets. "I want it clearly understood that no bunch of racketeers, thugs and punks are going to intimidate you as long as I am the Mayor of the City of New York." To those who wondered under what authority La Guardia was doing this, La Guardia referred to his powers to suppress disorder and quell riots!

At first some retailers dismissed the ban as "another publicity stunt." The racketeers would just move into another vegetable for a while, but La Guardia proceeded to negotiate with West Coast importers of the artichokes, and within a week the distributors signed an agreement in his office pledging to sell the thistly vegetable directly to retailers and market dealers. Terranova's Union Pacific Company closed its doors.[53]

Too often, however, there was less in these victories than met the eye. Immediately after his appointment as commissioner of markets, William Fellowes Morgan moved to flush the rackets from the Fulton Fish Market. As president of the Brooklyn Bridge Freezing and Storage Company, Morgan had been victimized by the gangsters, and he passed names, dates, and evidence to the DA in 1931. In retaliation, one of his warehouse was torched, his trucks were sabotaged, and his business was crippled. Then "Socks" Lanza walked into his office with a new labor contract, the precise thing that Morgan had been fighting against, but this time he signed, defeated for the while. As commissioner, Morgan was committed to fighting these rackets, and Lanza was first on the list. He managed to have Lanza indicted under federal statutes for restraint of trade, resulting in a $10,000 fine and a two-year jail sentence. But from his prison cell in Flint, Michigan, the semiliterate fish king continued to run his rackets, with benign assistance from Tammany mob liaison Albert Marinelli.[54]

La Guardia's frequent police shake-ups and tough talk of training X-men and G-men against the rackets were all severely limited tactics in a major war. In trying to change the atmosphere of city politics, to break up the cozy alliance between gangsters and politicians, there were no magic bullets, no comprehensive solutions. Periodically La Guardia would announce with great fanfare that the crooks were on the run, but reality kept intruding in the form of more arrests, more raids, more drives, and more crime. If they were on the run, the track seemed to be a circle that soon brought them back after this particular attack had spent itself.

There were gratifying victories to be sure. Jimmy Hines was convicted of protecting Dutch Shultz's racket, Frank Costello took his slot machines to Louisiana, and Albert Marinelli was exposed as Lucky Luciano's favorite political leader. But the stubborn problems of crime and the police proved the limits of good intentions to correct certain problems. The La Guardia prescription—investigate here, shake up there, apply pressure here, dramatize gangsterism there, and douse with invective all around—discomfited the criminals as much as any mayor in modern times has managed to do, but the problems persisted.[55]

Fighting crime was complicated. No Robert Moses could take over the problem and single-handedly shape a solution. It was not like building a bridge or opening a swimming pool. Once the pool was completed you marched out the band, snipped the ribbons, and the physical improvement would endure as a monument to good intentions. But crime did not yield to permanent solutions. After La Guardia cleaned out the slots in 1935 the gangs introduced pinball games in their place. In 1941 an Investigations Commission report revealed that 11,000 of these machines were each taking in between $35 and $40 daily.[56]

La Guardia's pressure and dramatics did publicize the issue. His talk of "making fur fly" and tearing out the corrupt police by their roots, and all the shake-ups—as often as two and three a year in the first administration—had an impact, but while the fight went on he was never able to make the police an effective instrument of his own priorities.[57]

Every once in a while La Guardia just got fed up and ordered raids on prostitutes and gamblers, but the plain fact was that the police could fill the jails to overflowing with streetwalkers and numbers runners on any given night. And sometimes Valentine did just that. A generally friendly court of special sessions complained that its time was taken up with the prosecution of low-level gambling-connected infractions. "These arrests of everybody having these [policy] slips in their possession . . . is a very easy way to make a great show of activity against this particular evil." But, complained the court, "cases against the real backers of games have been few and far between."[58]

Frustration would eat at him. La Guardia would pass on to Valentine citizen complaints about open prostitution and gambling that could not continue without police cooperation. The commissioner would send his men out to investigate the charge and receive routine excuses and explanations, which he would pass back to La Guardia. The mayor returned one of Valentine's regular "everything has been checked and found to be in order" letters with a sharp rejoinder: "I consider this one of the most serious cases of neglect of duty that has come before me. . . . Not one, not a dozen, but at least one hundred individuals including ministers, doctors, lawyers, men and women, have reported conditions existing where officers absolutely refuse to see and recognize flagrant violations of law, prostitution, selling of dope, and do absolutely nothing about it." But despite this and despite his remarkable doggedness, keeping at the issue year after year, the problem persisted.[59]

Periodically the mayor would blow his top at the police department's lackadaisical efforts to investigate itself. La Guardia passed an anonymous complaint regarding three drug dealers and low-level racketeers to Valentine, who returned a report to La Guardia. The commissioner received it right back with a scathing reply:

> Fortunately the report is on the letterhead of the Police Department, written in great big black letters. Otherwise I would be at a loss to know whether such a report came from the boy scouts or from some student

of a correspondence school on How To Be A Detective. It is the most idiotic, incomplete, stupid investigation that I have seen and I have seen a great many along the same line. . . .

It is this kind of conduct that brings scorn upon the whole department. A known crook is pointed out to the police and he is called in and says he is a good man and that is all there is to it. . . .

Hereafter you will be good enough to read the reports before submitting any such drivel and rot to the Mayor. I am too busy to read such stupid writings, but I am not too busy to go over to headquarters and take hold of the department if that is necessary.[60]

Unfortunately, he *was* too busy to do that. Hundreds of complaints would come in indicating police collusion with criminals, and the best he could do was send them out to the field for verification, where as often as not they were quashed. Again and again La Guardia would rail at Valentine about the poor quality of police work—"in the name of all of the Saints that you have been told about, in addition to those that you have forgotten about, don't send such a routine communication"—but he could not do much more. Valentine, too, had to admit that the racketeers reached into his department with relative ease. Unless La Guardia was willing to uproot the entire department and ignore much of the rest of the job of governing the city while converting the police into a tightly organized antimob army, they would remain poorly matched to fight a decisive, flexible, secretive, rich, and powerful underworld. New York was much bigger and more complicated than the Arizona badlands, and La Guardia could not simply order the mob out of town.[61]

Lucky Luciano's ghosted memoirs are hardly the last word, but he makes an important point. While La Guardia remained honest—"I just couldn't understand the guy. . . . When we offered to make him rich he wouldn't even listen"—Luciano knew that there were other weak points. "So I figured what the hell, let him keep City Hall, we got all the rest—the D. A. the cops, everythin'."[62]

In the tradition of former Manhattan DA Thomas C. T. Crain, whose grace toward the criminal element attracted Samuel Seabury's withering attention, Manhattan District Attorney William Copeland Dodge proved broadly solicitous of the men with the funny nicknames. But when Dodge failed to investigate a bail bond racket, Blanshard did, revealing a conspiracy involving property owners, a gambling syndicate, and local government officials. Disclosure of corruption in the DA's office and La Guardia's strong attacks on lax justice had aroused the public, and after Dodge dragged his feet on these rather broad clues, a runaway grand jury completed

LA GUARDIA leaving the site of a fire on Cherry Street on January 1, 1939, where he helped rescue a firefighter pinned under a beam during a blaze. (*Brown Brothers*)

THE MAYOR, who once said that he refused to "descend to dignity," photographed in his bathrobe playing cards with his second wife and former secretary, Marie, in their modest East Harlem apartment. (*Fiorello H. La Guardia Archives, La Guardia Community College, CUNY*)

THE LA GUARDIA FAMILY at home in East Harlem. *Left to right*: Marie, Jean, Fiorello, and Eric. Not until May of 1942 did the La Guardias move into Gracie Mansion, which was designated the official mayoral residence. (*Fiorello H. La Guardia Archives, La Guardia Community College, CUNY*)

TO ESCAPE THE SWELTERING MANHATTAN HEAT during the summers, City Hall would be moved out to one of the boroughs, while the La Guardia family vacationed at the beachfront. La Guardia is shown here rowing at Asharoken Beach on Long Island in the summer of 1937 with his son Eric (*left*), his daughter Jean (*third from right*), and their friends. (*Fiorello H. La Guardia Archives, La Guardia Community College, CUNY*)

FIORELLO LA GUARDIA slashing the ribbon to the airport of his dreams at North Beach in Queens, October 15, 1939. The airfield was soon renamed for the mayor. Robert Moses holds the ribbon. Comptroller Joseph McGoldrick stands behind Moses' right shoulder. (*Parks Photo Archive*)

LA GUARDIA (*right*) with master builder Robert Moses (*left*) and president of the 1939 World of Tomorrow Fair, Grover Whalen, review plans for the fair as it rises from the ashes of the reclaimed Flushing Meadows. (*Fiorello H. La Guardia Archives, La Guardia Community College, CUNY*)

O'DWYER CAMPAIGN cartoon from the 1941 mayoral contest.

O'DWYER CAMPAIGN cartoon from the 1941 mayoral contest.

FRANKLIN ROOSEVELT and Fiorello La Guardia developed a strong, mutually respectful relationship during the New Deal years. Here La Guardia pays the president an informal visit at his Hyde Park estate, August 27, 1938. (*Franklin D. Roosevelt Library*)

LA GUARDIA, who made a habit of not breaking his regular office routine to celebrate election victories, at his desk on the day following his reelection to an unprecedented third term as mayor, November 4, 1941. Just a few hours before, he had told a reporter that the election meant ''four more years of hell.'' (*City of New York Municipal Archives*)

AFTER HIS APPOINTMENT in the spring of 1941 as director of the Office of Civilian Defense, Fiorello asked the president to make the First Lady his codirector. Eleanor Roosevelt, shown here at her swearing-in on September 29, 1941, did not always appreciate working with the imperious mayor. (*Franklin D. Roosevelt Library*)

AS PART OF HIS DUTIES AT OCD, La Guardia traveled across the nation to plan for home-front emergencies, rouse Americans against the Axis, and organize campaigns such as this one, devoted to collecting scrap metal. (*City of New York Municipal Archives*)

THE ARCHITECTS OF NEW YORK'S NEW DEAL, Franklin Roosevelt, Herbert Lehman, and Fiorello La Guardia, driving to inspect the Red Hook Houses on October 28, 1940. (*Fiorello H. La Guardia Archives, La Guardia Community College, CUNY*)

LA GUARDIA with Secretary of Agriculture Henry Wallace at the Brooklyn Academy of Music, dramatizing the federal Food Stamp Plan, August 16, 1940. (*City of New York Municipal Archives*)

LA GUARDIA with Thomas Dewey, the gangbusting prosecutor and later Republican governor of New York. The two Republicans shared presidential aspirations and after a while little else. (*City of New York Municipal Archives*)

LA GUARDIA with Senator Robert Wagner after testifying before a congressional committee in favor of the senator's slum clearance bill on June 6, 1935. The two men collaborated on New Deal legislation when La Guardia was in Congress, and they developed an abiding respect for each other. (*City of New York Municipal Archives*)

LA GUARDIA with former mayor James J. Walker, whom he brought back into municipal government in 1939. Here, on June 12, 1940, the two men listen to a broadcast of war-front news after halting a municipal conference on transit unification to tune in. (*City of New York Municipal Archives*)

LA GUARDIA with President Harry S Truman (*right*) on October 27, 1945, at the commissioning of the USS *Franklin Roosevelt*. Also present were (*left to right*) Mrs. Woodrow Wilson, Secretary of the Navy James Forrestal, Mrs. Truman, Admiral Jonas Ingram, and Admiral William Leahy. (*Franklin D. Roosevelt Library*)

ON JUNE 19, 1945, millions of New Yorkers turned out to give war hero General Dwight David Eisenhower a rousing welcome. La Guardia, accompanying the popular military hero, knew that Eisenhower had helped keep him from receiving the military appointment he so craved. (*Fiorello H. La Guardia Archives, La Guardia Community College, CUNY*)

WHEN A STRIKE deprived New York City children of their Sunday comics, the mayor went on the air to read them the adventures of "Dick Tracy," "Orphan Annie," and others of their favorites over municipal station WNYC. (*Museum of the City of New York*)

THE LA GUARDIAS bid farewell to city hall on December 31, 1945. (*Fiorello H. La Guardia Archives, La Guardia Community College, CUNY*)

ON HIS FIRST DAY as a private citizen, La Guardia at his desk prepares for his broadcasts and articles, January 1, 1946. (*Parks Photo Archive*)

WITHIN THREE MONTHS of his retirement from city hall, La Guardia returned to public service as head of UNRRA, accepting the challenge of feeding the world's hungry and stateless. (*Fiorello H. La Guardia Archives, La Guardia Community College, CUNY*)

DR. EDWARD BENES,
president of Czechoslovakia,
presents UNRRA Director
General La Guardia with the
Order of the White Lion,
First Class, his country's
highest national honor,
August 11, 1946, in Prague.
(*Fiorello H. La Guardia
Archives, La Guardia
Community College, CUNY*)

IN JULY OF 1946, UNRRA
director La Guardia arrived
in Italy and paid a visit to
the Villaggio del Fanciullo
and its ''shoeshine boys''—
youths who had been
separated from their families
and had stayed alive during
the war by relying on their
wits. (*Fiorello H. La
Guardia Archives, La
Guardia Community
College, CUNY*)

MARIE LA GUARDIA and Newbold Morris viewing a bust of Fiorello La Guardia that was dedicated in front of the La Guardia Houses housing project in lower Manhattan on September 9, 1957. (*Parks Photo Archive*)

its own investigation in the summer of 1935 by asking Governor Herbert Lehman to supersede Dodge with a special prosecutor.

Despite initial reluctance to be drawn into what promised to be an embarrassing probe into Democratic ties to the underworld, Governor Lehman finally turned the job over to the young crime-busting former federal prosecutor, Thomas Dewey. Dewey assembled a crew of handpicked police detectives, private investigators, and young attorneys with no connections to business or politics to investigate industrial rackets. His prostitution racket probe revealed the connection between Lucky Luciano and Tammany boss Albert Marinelli, whom Dewey linked to the most powerful gangsters of the time. In one case that Dewey studied, he learned that while Manhattan DA Dodge creaked along slowly carrying out an investigation, a mobster accused of murder was allowed to disappear for two months, while witnesses were intimidated. The defense attorney who coordinated the strategy of flight, intimidation, and then defense was an assistant district attorney who was privy to the prosecution's case.[63]

Dewey investigators looked into racketeering in more than 100 industries. "There is a vast field to cover," wrote the *New York Times* in 1936; "almost the entire racket structure in New York is so far impregnable to assault." But La Guardia had aroused the public with his attacks on crime, and this strengthened Dewey's hand. The young prosecutor uncovered a protection scheme that involved the restaurant waiters union, the cafeteria workers union, and a bogus employers association known as the Manhattan Restaurant and Cafeteria Association.

Lucky Luciano had responded with disdain to La Guardia's order that he be arrested on sight, but Dewey was able to dislocate the gangster from his elegant Waldorf-Astoria suite, collecting testimony from more than seventy prostitutes about the existence of a vice system entirely controlled by Luciano. The underworld tried to offer huge bribes and positions on the state supreme court bench to investigators, but on June 6, 1936, the "whoremaster of Gotham" became the first racketeer to be convicted on charges other than tax evasion. He was found guilty of sixty-one counts of compulsory prostitution and sentenced by Justice Philip J. McCook, the man who had sworn La Guardia into office in 1934, to a term of thirty to fifty years in prison.[64]

Dewey divulged the control that Lepke Buchalter and his gang of cutthroats had over the garment, baking, and flour industries and traced Dutch Shultz's gambling payoffs to Jimmy Hines, "the most powerful Democratic politician in the state." Six months of digging into the loan-sharking business resulted in three dozen prosecutions of usurers, some of whom charged more than 1000 percent interest. By the summer of 1937 Dewey had won seventy-one convictions on seventy-three indictments. His investigations led to the arrests of Tootsie Herbert, James Plumeri, Johnny "Dio" Dioguardi, J. Richard "Dixie" Davis, Anthony "Binge" Curcio, Lepke Buchalter, and Jake "Gurrah" Shapiro on charges of prostitution, industrial rackets, narcotics trade, labor and business extortion, union embezzlement, and policy. But the new generation of crime leaders had built well. The machine they created endured despite the arrests. The vicious muscle necessary for enforcing underworld crime remained in place, as did the internecine turf conflicts, and the sordid conquest of innocent businesses and labor unions.[65]

The intimate tie between organized crime and the district attorney's office that had brought Dewey onto the scene was even worse in Brooklyn, where, under the benign eye of Democratic District Attorney William F. X. Geoghan, murder, rackets, and gangsterism flourished. "Murder is safe in Brooklyn," Tom Dewey declared in November of 1938. "Two out of every three murders remain unsolved. Two out of every three murderers are never indicted . . . walking the street, free men."[66]

On March 3, 1935, Brooklyn police responded to reports of a disturbance in a garage at 225 Moore Street in Williamsburg. They found a man slumped over a pool of blood. He had been bludgeoned and garrotted. Nearby the police found murder weapons and three men with fresh blood on their hands and clothes. The dead man was Samuel Druckman. He had worked for a mob-connected trucking firm from which he had lately been embezzling funds to cover heavy gambling losses. Two of the three suspects picked up at the scene of the murder were Meyer and Harry Luckman, owners of the trucking firm. The district attorney presented the case to a grand jury, which found insufficient cause for indictment. The men were freed and their bloodstained clothes and all other evidence was immediately returned to them. Another case successfully concluded in the files of Kings County District Attorney William F. X. Geoghan.[67]

The case was too flagrant to pass. Rumors about payoffs and police collaboration were rife. La Guardia had discussed the notorious Brooklyn police department many times with Valentine, demanding shake-ups and improvements, but the problem went far deeper than either realized. After studying grand jury records of the Druckman case, Valentine became convinced that police officers had destroyed evidence and delivered bribes to the grand jury. He notified Geoghan that "Acting Detective Sergeant Charles Hemendinger . . . was the go-between for members of the Police Department in the collection of money paid to the police in the Druckman case," and he described for the DA the involvement of syndicate figures and the detailed arrangements for distributing the money. "What kind of a crime do you have to commit in Brooklyn," snapped Valentine, "to obtain an indictment?" He pressed the DA to reinvestigate the murder, bribery, and police complicity, but Geoghan refused to resubmit the case. "I urged him, I pleaded with him," Valentine later testified, "I threatened him, I did everything but physically assault him."[68]

Finally, in December the furor forced Governor Lehman to appoint a special prosecutor, Hiram Todd, to supersede Geoghan. Within six weeks Todd had a murder trial under way, leading to convictions. Todd also indicted the son of one of Geoghan's assistant DAs for influencing the first grand jury; other indictments were brought against the chief of the clerical staff of the State Assembly and a former assistant U.S. attorney. By the time all indictments dealing with the bribery were handed down, another eight individuals were implicated, including the assistant DA whose son had already been charged, a detective, and a number of mob members. The jury went further, demanding Geoghan's removal from office for incompetence, negligence, and association with known hoodlums, but Lehman refused to act on what he called insufficient evidence.

In the spring of 1938 Geoghan, still in good humor, joked that his office did not have much work; Brooklyn's criminals were just not committing serious crimes. He spoke too soon. A special Citizen's Committee on the Control of Crime in New York City, formed at La Guardia's behest, presented the mayor with a damning report on the continued malfeasance of the Brooklyn DAs office. They had followed 14,000 cases through the courts and discovered widespread irregularities. This time Lehman had to act. Superseding Geoghan for the second time, he appointed former President Grover Cleveland's son-in-law, John Harlan Amen, to look into official corruption in Brooklyn. Amen bared a crooked braid knotting together police, magistrates, appellate court judges, gamblers, loan sharks, and such powerful racketeers as Abe "Kid Twist" Reles and Lepke Buchalter. He handed up indictments against a new batch of tainted assistant district attorneys and police. Within the year he won a total of 193 racket convictions.[69]

After William O'Dwyer took over from the discredited Geoghan, a new series of indictments illustrated the continued salience of the rackets. Focusing largely on the notorious desperadoes associated with Murder Incorporated, O'Dwyer indicted and sent to prison Joe Adonis, Lepke Buchalter, Mendy Weiss, Abe Reles, Frank Abbadando, Dukey Maffetore, Harry Maione, Louis Capone, and Albert Anastasia. Yet, despite the recurring crackdowns and sweeps and intiatives, not even La Guardia could believe that New York was winning anything but a few skirmishes in the war against organized crime. The killing, the sordid turf battles, the inveigling of innocent business and vulnerable labor all continued. And in the late 1940s, when the spectacular prosecutions of O'Dwyer were tainted with charges that they purposely ignored industrial racketeering, gambling, and narcotics because of O'Dwyer's own connection with mob figures, the difficulty of destroying the underground behemoth became sadly clearer.[70]

His first order to the police in 1934 was to pursue the gangsters mercilessly to the borders of the city. Twelve years later, when La Guardia was completing his third

367

administration, he was still ordering police to "Go out and act. . . . Snap into it clean them out." It is at once a statement of his devotedness and his inability to solve the single knottiest problem of his tenure.[71]

To fight organized crime La Guardia would have had to take on union gang-sterism, industrial racketeering, and the entire organized network. But he could not carry on a disruptive, consuming war on crime while trying to battle a Depression, build a modern city, and maintain a delicate relationship with Washington.

The police remained an imperfect weapon. Valentine feared making great waves among his men. He held their confidence and paid the price by not upsetting too much their established practices. It is unlikely that any commissioner could, without creating tremendous disorder, attempt to lay strong control on a paramilitary organization like the police. Just how difficult became clear in a badly handled disturbance in Harlem that highlighted the complex relationship involving police, crime, and other deep urban problems like racism and poverty.

4. Harlem Erupts

ON March 19, 1935, a young boy caught stealing a penknife from a Harlem five-and-dime on 125th Street set off a disturbance that demonstrated the devastating anger that lay on the heart of this unique black community. The stunted sixteen-year-old Puerto Rican youth, Lino Rivera, had spent the earlier part of the day in Brooklyn unsuccessfully looking for a job. He returned uptown, took in a movie, and at about 3:30 in the afternoon started for home, cutting through the Kress store on West 125th Street. Rivera had no money in his pocket, but as he passed one of the counters, he noticed a knife that matched his fountain pen set. As Rivera later admitted, "I wanted it and so I took it." A floor guard saw the youth take the knife and, along with another worker, grabbed him. The boy bit both his captors before they managed to subdue him and summon a policeman, who led the youth to the back of the store for questioning.

By this time a crowd of curious onlookers had formed and various versions of the incident were going back and forth. One woman started shouting that they "were taking the boy to the basement to beat him up." An ambulance pulled up to the front of the store shortly thereafter, adding to the panicky mood. When it left empty, some in the crowd mumbled that the cops had killed another one. The rumor spread like a fire in a match factory. It's "just like down South where they lynch us,'' cried another black woman. The police gruffly turned back all questions, ordering the crowd to mind their business and keep moving.[72]

It did not matter that the Kress manager had decided against bringing a complaint for the pilferage of the 10-cent penknife. By the time the crowd was confronting a growing squad of police, the wiry Spanish youth had been freed from a downstairs exit, on the other side from the milling mob. When the ambulance pulled up to treat the bitten and scratched guards, Lino Rivera was on his way home. It mattered little that he was safe and that the only ones requiring medical treatment were those injured scuffling with him. It mattered little because the opposite was plausible. Black women and men believed that a nonwhite child arrested for a minor charge could be billy-clubbed to death in a back room. And that was what they believed had happened.

Feelings between white Harlem storekeepers and neighborhood residents had been strained for many months after a series of efforts to force local stores to hire blacks. Now the rumored injustice to a neighborhood child stirred the pent-up rage. The crowd started overturning counters, spilling merchandise onto the floors. It took police more than an hour to clear the store and lock its doors. By then Kress had become a focal point. The Young Liberators set up a picket line in front of the store, waving freshly painted placards protesting the brutal beating of a Negro child and passing out handbills proclaiming: ''The boy is near death. . . . A Negro woman had her arm broken.'' The Young Communist League inflamed the community further:

> The brutal beating of the 12 year old boy . . . by the Kresses' special guard . . . again proves the increasing terror against the Negro people of Harlem. Bosses, who deny the most immediate necessities . . . who throw workers out of employment, who pay not enough to live on, are protecting their so-called property rights with brutal beatings. . . . They lynch Negro people in the South on framed up charges.[73]

By sundown the crowd, grown large from the streams of homecoming workers, milled around the picketers, joining the protest, while a small group of outnumbered police, themselves terrified, tried to keep order. A man named Daniel Miller urged the crowd on with his tales of brutality and discrimination. Suddenly a bottle flew through the air. Then another. Kress's huge plate glass windows shattered and the crowd charged the store. Looters swarmed into the aisles, grabbing whatever they could from the showcases and wall racks. Word spread instantly. Residents poured out of the multistory apartment houses onto the streets, as their confederates heaved bricks, bottles, bats, and spare building parts from two and three stories high at the almost uniformly white contingent of patrolmen below. A black station wagon appeared and a woman shrilled, ''There's the hearse come to take the boy's body." As if on signal, looters smashed dozens of plate glass storefronts, rampaging through neighboring shops, sweeping merchandise off shelves, setting fires, feeding the riot with their rage.

At some point it occurred to the police to bring the Rivera boy back to show that he was alive and well. A frantic search finally turned him up at two o'clock in the morning. Rivera was brought to the front of the looted Kress store to prove that he was unharmed, but the riot had progressed beyond its initial cause. Few were interested anymore in this one particular youth, pretext no longer being relevant. Resentment had found its outlet. Black merchants put up signs identifying their shops as "Run by COLORED People," while several white-owned establishments announced, "This store employs Negro workers."[74]

Whites who happened to be in the area were pummeled for being the wrong color on the wrong night. Snipers took positions on rooftops and squeezed off ammunition rounds into the street. Police were rushed in and charged the mobs in phalanxes, bringing their gun butts down on the rioters. It took all night to restore peace and clear the streets. Next morning's casualty count tallied more than 100 persons stabbed, beaten, or shot, 250 shop windows smashed, 125 men arrested, most of them young and black, for disorderly conduct, inciting to riot, and burglary. And 3 were dead. Like most of the casualties, the dead were black, shot by the police.[75]

But what did it all mean? District Attorney Dodge felt certain that the Communists were behind this disruption. "We have evidence," the Manhattan district attorney said, "that two hours after the boy stole that knife the Reds had placed inflammatory leaflets on the streets." Many of the rioters, the DA continued, were reliefers and immigrants. He announced a grand jury investigation and in the same breath announced his conclusions: "My purpose is to let the Communists know that they cannot come into this country and upset our laws." The Communists were as quick to pronounce their own conclusions: "Negro Harlem Terrorized," blazed the *Daily Worker* headline.[76]

Others looked deeper for the roots of the rage. Wrote the *Herald Tribune*: "Every night Harlem has its petty stabbings and fistfights. But yesterday the air crackled with animosity and the policemen who stood every 100 feet throughout the section received passively the jibes and insults of belligerent Negroes rather than provoke a new war. The factors lying behind this situation are rooted in the economic problems of a poverty stricken area within which a vast population is squeezed." To Dr. Adam Clayton Powell, Jr., assistant pastor of the Abyssinian Baptist Church, the factors were more than impersonal economic distress. "Continued exploitation of the Negro is at the bottom of all the trouble," he said, "exploitation as regards wages, jobs, working conditions." Local businesses, utilities, even government assistance programs, he declared, discriminated against Harlem's population while taking its money and votes. And the people were finally fed up.[77]

La Guardia was taken aback by the disorder. He had tried to respond to New York's shut-out groups, and in particular he had shown sympathy for blacks. Back in 1931 the respected black daily, the *Amsterdam News*, praised La Guardia as "one of the most fearless friends the Negro has ever had in or out of Congress." Once in office, La Guardia named blacks to important posts in his administration, treating Tax Commissioner Hubert T. Delaney as an unofficial ombudsman for the black community. A year before the riot La Guardia responded to complaints about discrimination in the Board of Transportation by summoning the chairman of the board and directing him to end all bias in job assignments. His relations with leaders of such organizations as the NAACP, the Urban League, and black churches were cordial and warm, and he generally took liberal positions on racial issues, challenging established biases and urging Americans to greater tolerance.[78]

But he had focused on some issues more than others, and his commitment to correcting the plight of blacks was circumscribed. The problems seemed so intractable. He pitied the poor and their troubled children. He wanted better housing, worked well with black leaders, and bridled at thrill seekers who went slumming in Harlem to see the dives and exploit the opportunity for easy sex, fast jazz, and policy games. But there was a distance between him and the black community that was not there in his relations with Jews, Italians, and Irish. This very conventional family man did not know what to make of the open prostitution, broken families, and social problems rampant in this black mecca. He was sure that it had something to do with the poverty and limited opportunities enforced by the environment, but he was unsure how much of it had to do with a culture that he had no basis for understanding.[79]

La Guardia *spoke* feelingly of the plight of urban blacks, but their pain was strange to him, far more distant than that of the other ethnics with more familiar backgrounds. When he spoke of the heroism of the housewives, he would mention Mrs. Epstein or Sullivan or La Guardia, but never a Mrs. Jones or a Mrs. Robinson. The adversity of the immigrants he understood out of a common background with them. There was no such shared experience with blacks. His New York, the New York for which he took abundant credit and worked himself to the edge of exhaustion, was the New York of ethnic slums, schools, playgrounds, and bridges; of fighting rackets, winning relief, and preaching uplift. It was a New York that was Irish and German and Polish, Slav, Jewish, and Italian, composed of workers, labor union leaders, worthy folk ruggedly making do with reality. That these same groups were often the shopkeepers, union leaders, and landlords in Harlem, the ones singled out as exploiters and oppressors of the community, made it even more difficult for La Guardia to appreciate the black perspective. He offered no special program to single out this black ghetto and treat its unique problems; brought little sense of urgency to its extraordinary need.

Just six months after his inauguration, La Guardia had received an insistent appeal from the presiding justice of the city's domestic court, Justice Edward Boyle.

371

Alarmed by the disproportionate crime rate among Negro children, Boyle had commissioned a study of "The Negro Problem as Reflected in the Functioning of the Domestic Relations Court of the City of New York." The study reported that childhood crime among blacks had risen over the past thirteen years by more than 240 percent. In Manhattan fully 25 percent of all juveniles arraigned in children's court were Negroes. More than one-fourth of all nonsupport cases in the city involved black families. The problem was staggering. "The court has not been able for some years satisfactorily to function in cases involving Negro children," the report concluded.

Boyle rushed publication of the report to win public attention for a problem that he warned was too pressing for lengthy deliberation. Delay would only exacerbate a situation already made acute by the Depression. La Guardia received the report with Judge Boyle's impassioned letter and passed it on to his assistant, Louis Dunham, who recommended "further study."[80]

Harlem faced its unique problems alone. The national economic crisis had sent the already depressed ghetto economy into a tailspin. Last hired and first fired, blacks suffered from a level of unemployment two and three times the rate for whites. The migration of blacks from southern regions to New York brought in large numbers who competed for the shrinking number of low-skilled occupations that were by and large the only ones open to blacks. The influx also placed added pressure on the housing market. In 1935 eight Harlem blocks were jammed with more than 3000 residents each; one block held close to 4000. No other block in the city held even 3000 people.[81]

Men, unable to secure jobs, abandoned their families, while women were forced to go out to work and leave the young children to fend for themselves. A September 1935 report disclosed that 43 percent of Harlem's black families depended upon relief for their daily bread. And things were worse than they seemed. Programs designed to help the poor openly discriminated against blacks. La Guardia's close friend Edward Corsi, director of the Home Relief Bureau, was described by a former relief worker as "the most vicious Negro hater in the Bureau." The federal CWA program initially required blacks to come to Harlem to register regardless of where they lived and consistently placed them in positions that were below their skill level. The State Employment Service listed only menial jobs in its Harlem offices. Women applying for relief, one Harlem resident testified, were met by reception clerks asking, "Have you tried the streets?"[82]

Entire industries were kept lily-white even for menial employment. The Metropolitan Insurance Company, with over 100,000 policyholders in Harlem alone, hired no blacks. The Fifth Avenue Coach Company would not even discuss its hiring policies with mayoral investigators. With regard to businesses and stores outside Harlem, a mayoral commission reported that they "may be divided into two classes: . . . those that employ Negroes in menial positions and those that employ no Negroes at all." An example of the first type was Macy's, which used blacks to clean its floors and for routine maintenance; Gimbels had no blacks at all. New York Edison listed 65 black employees (porters or janitors) among its 10,000 workers; New York Telephone had not one Negro operator; subway and surface carriers sprinkled a very few blacks among their janitorial staffs but closed them out from any middle-level jobs and kept them all in Harlem.[83]

A New York Telephone vice president explained the biased hiring as "customary practice." Other employers were more direct, stating that blacks were inferior, or that the public would not stand for integration, or that it would harm employee relations. And unions helped secure the invisible line. Twenty-four unions explicitly barred Negro membership. "Negroes," an Emergency Relief Bureau official commented, "have one half a bad chance."[84]

In this grim environment, with only themselves to rely on, blacks increasingly turned to racial solidarity as a shield. The clergy, already involved in assistance projects, helped lead "Don't Buy Where You Can't Work" programs. The energetic young minister Adam Clayton Powell, Jr., said proudly of his parishioners that they were "as much at home on the picket line as they are in church." Growing militancy brought them into abrasive contact with the one New York agency that they trusted least, the NYPD. A March 1934 demonstration deteriorated into an hourlong melee after police hurled tear gas into a Lenox Avenue crowd of more than 5000 who had gathered to honor Mrs. Ada Wright, mother of two of the Scottsboro Boys (nine black youths who were found guilty of raping two white women and sentenced to seventy-year terms in Alabama on very questionable evidence). When Police Commissioner Lewis Valentine called in the cop who had thrown the gas to ask if he regretted such rash use of force, the officer responded: "I can't say I do. It was the only way of dispersing them without injuring them." While Valentine found the use of the gas unjustified, he took no disciplinary action.[85]

Such incidents only hinted at prevailing attitudes. A Housing Department survey of juvenile delinquency reported that police bias was one of the foremost obstacles to a healthy relationship between young blacks and city authorities. The report suggested that the police assigned to Harlem, all from outside the community, took no real interest in the residents. So strained were relations between the community and their protectors that critics likened the NYPD to a racist army of occupation. Residents complained of police breaking into apartments without warrants, conducting illegal searches of persons and property, referring to them as "black bastards," and using gratuitous violence in ways that they did not dare to do with whites. Traditionally the department did not discipline police upon the charges or complaints of Negroes. Perhaps the least justifiable practice was Valentine's custom of banishing cops with bad judgment or poor records uptown to Harlem.[86]

Poor judgment by the police helped ignite the Harlem riot. On the afternoon of March 19, when the primary concern of the crowd was still for the safety of the arrested youth, individuals came over to police officers to inquire about the Rivera boy. Instead of providing a civil answer, the police brushed aside queries, snapping that it was "none of your damned business," shoving questioners toward the door. "Can't you tell us what happened?" one of the women pleaded. She was ordered to move on "if you know what's good for you." Later, when a mayoral commission took local testimony regarding the police in Harlem, the feelings were so intense that the hearings were continually interrupted with jeering, bitter language, and open hostility.[87]

On the night of the riot two high school boys, Lloyd Hobbs and his brother Russell, were walking home from a movie theater when, attracted by the pandemonium, they joined a crowd forming before an auto supply store. A police car with two officers pulled up and Patrolman John Heineray swung out of his car with gun drawn. Everyone began to run. Heineray fired, hitting Lloyd Hobbs. According to witnesses, he had neither called upon the boy to halt nor fired a warning shot. The youth died a few nights later, leaving the impression that life in Harlem was cheap. Few were reassured when Commissioner Valentine praised his force for its "discipline, tact and courage. . . ."[88]

Little of this occupied La Guardia's thoughts before March 19. Other emergencies and other interests filled his day, and frankly, other problems seemed more promising of solution. Just the week before he had brought the Moses-Ickes contretemps to a close, and he did not have Harlem on his mind. The riot changed that. Other white leaders were prepared to dismiss the incident as an isolated breakdown of law and order, a night of vicious release by the city's lower elements. But La Guardia, after reflexively placing blame on "a few irresponsible individuals" who spread false rumors of race discrimination, thought again and concluded that the events following the Kress incident could not be dismissed as some Communist plot. He admitted that Harlem's grim conditions had contributed to the disturbance and established an eleven-member biracial commission to study the causes of the rage that this night had laid bare, and for the first time to ask blacks what it was like to live in Harlem.[89]

Chaired by a black dentist, Dr. Charles Roberts, the Commission on Conditions in Harlem appointed the famed Negro sociologist E. Franklin Frazier to conduct the actual research. The commission held twenty-five hearings, collected testimony from 160 witnesses, and after more than a year of deliberations issued "The Negro in Harlem: A Report on Social and Economic Conditions Responsible for the Outbreak of March 19, 1935." The commission described the riot as Harlem's inarticulate response to racism and unemployment and made an impassioned plea for municipal action to combat job discrimination, build decent affordable housing, and address the tangled problem of crime and insensitive police. The report called for improved health care, more schools and parks, and an earnest effort to root out the prejudice that touched all municipal services from relief to medical assistance and poisoned black-white relations.

The report criticized some of La Guardia's most trusted and best qualified commissioners for insensitivity and worse. Moreover, the commission operated outside the constraints of budgets and politics. It could recommend without the burden of finding the funds or wherewithal to implement its suggestions. La Guardia had once said: "It is much easier to tell the other fellow how to do it than to do it yourself. I know—I used to be a congressman myself." He was now in the position of the other fellow and it was not pleasant. For example, the commission correctly pointed out that even after the city completed the Harlem River Houses, and even if rents were reduced throughout the neighborhood and the housing code was strictly enforced—all elements of a very ambitious housing reform agenda— "the fundamental problems will not have changed." Nothing less than a large-scale subsidized housing program for the 56,000 depressed families in Harlem would make a real impact on the effects of poverty, racism, and slum conditions. La Guardia knew it, but he also knew that there were limits to what he could do and that comprehensive solutions were impossible. He told a conference of Negro church leaders that he carried "no illusion about the difficulties facing your people in New York," but as he admitted before another delegation, "I am as helpless in handling large scale economic problems as the League of Nations was in preventing the war between Italy and Ethiopia."[90]

Moreover, he knew only too well that many of the commission's criticisms would be aimed at entrenched practices that he could not easily change. He had to weigh the price he was willing to pay. The commission came down very hard on the police, accusing them of "shocking barbarity," declaring, "It is a grave state of affairs when the inhabitants of a large section of the city have come to look at the . . . police . . . as lawless oppressors who stop at no brutality or at the taking of human life." The commission recommended establishing a biracial citizens' committee to regularly investigate complaints against the police. But such a step would cost him heavily with an already demoralized force. It would weaken his efforts to attack the rackets, including those based in Harlem, and it would bring him in conflict with Valentine, whom the commission faulted for being "too busy, unsympathetic or uninterested" to cooperate with them. There was little room for a prudent path between his police department and the commission's conclusion that the police did not have respect for black life.[91]

Precisely because the recommendations were so sweeping, La Guardia did not release the report. It was too ambitious and too critical of his administration, and he did not want its prescriptions to establish the standard by which his good faith toward blacks would be judged. At the same time, he sincerely wanted to address some of the issues raised by the report. He asked his department heads for their response to the criticisms. A number of commissioners disputed some of the facts and conclusions. Instead of using this as an excuse to drop the report, La Guardia turned to Howard University professor Alain Locke, famous for his study of the "New Negro," and asked him to consider the commission report in the light of its critics' comments. After a full review of all the material, Locke agreed with most of the initial report's conclusions and urged La Guardia to publish the document so that it could become the basis of a new program of sweeping reform in Harlem.[92]

While La Guardia refused to adopt Locke's list of prescriptions in its entirety, he did commit the city to allocating more resources to Harlem than ever before. He was not prepared to place Harlem at the center of his agenda, as Locke and the commissioners were demanding, but he did place it far higher on his list of priorities than before.

Over the next four years New York City built Harlem River Houses, erected the Central Harlem Health Center, added a new Women's Pavilion for Harlem Hospital, and built two new schools for the area. La Guardia pressed for these improvements despite strong resistance. He also tackled long-standing prejudices, integrating the all-white staffs of city hospitals and expanding civil service opportunities for blacks. He attacked discrimination in relief, establishing at the least an official demand for fair treatment, and he toppled long-standing barriers by appointing blacks to the Emergency Relief Board, to supervisory posts in the fire and sanitation departments, and in such offices as the City Marshall, District Attorney, and Corporation Counsel.[93]

In June 1935 he asked his one-man personnel screening committee, C. C. Burlingham, to test reaction in judicial circles to the appointment of a Negro magistrate. CCB reported back that, except for the opposition of Presiding Justice Frank Martin, such an appointment would cause no undue ruckus. Despite his frequent denials—"I have never appointed and never will appoint a man to office because of his color," he said in 1935—Fiorello played the game of ethnic appointments with rare flair. He understood the impact of a carefully selected token. As he swore in Myles A. Paige as the city's first Negro magsitrate in 1936, he stared up at the the six-foot-two former football star and Columbia University graduate and told him, "You just have to make good because the attention of the city will be focused on you." A few years later he appointed another token, the first black woman judge. But tokens establish precedents, and it took courage in the thirties to make such symbolic breakthroughs.[94]

If there was not much that he was prepared to do to improve police relations within the community, he took careful note of the incendiary possibilities. On a summer night in 1936 La Guardia was being driven to an evening concert when the police radio broadcast an alarm about a murder in Harlem. He ordered his driver to rush uptown, where he took charge and helped calm the situation. A few days later he responded to a robbery call. No longer was the mayor oblivious to Harlem or to the impact of racism. He resisted sweeping indictments of his commissioners and refused to commit himself to large promises, but within a year after the riot, New York's "suffering struggling race" had been brought into his progressive focus. The *Amsterdam News* lauded La Guardia for appointing "more Negroes to big, responsible jobs in city government . . . than all other mayors of the city combined,'' and these appointments educated New Yorkers to wider possibilities for integration than they had allowed themselves to expect before. By 1940 Walter White, executive secretary of the NAACP, wrote La Guardia that his forward-looking policies on civil rights were influencing officials across the country.[95]

CHAPTER 11

"He Likes the Feel of the Driver's Seat. He Wants to Stay There"

1. Issues for the Opposition

"N EW York has just passed through some twenty-nine months of disorder, violence, and chaos in addition to the traditional inefficiencies of a Reform administration," wrote *New York Sun* reporter George Ritchie in the summer of 1936, heralding the new mayoral election season. "Strikes, riots, mass picketing and countless radical 'demonstrations' all spurred on by countless sheafs of cheer and good will to malcontents, ground out by the Mayor's mimeograph battery at City Hall have resulted in thousands of injuries, widespread personal hardship, and vast property damage. Businessmen, property owners and orderly citizens have been given little protection." As Fiorello La Guardia moved energetically forward on his own agenda of progressive modernization, critics were labeling him the most dangerous inhabitant of city hall in decades. Reformers were supposed to respect traditions of limited power, but from his very first moves with the economy bill La Guardia sought power without apologies.

In Congress he had railed, proposed, and attacked with abandon, and to little avail. Eunuch in the harem, he took great but unconsummated liberties, all the while nursing larger plans. As mayor, no longer limited to tilting forays, he aimed to make a difference quickly, directly, powerfully.[1]

One of the reasons La Guardia made politicians uncomfortable was that he drew his model for leadership from outside politics. For all of his formal regard for Abraham Lincoln and Theodore Roosevelt, La Guardia was not very familiar with their ideas and had not even supported Roosevelt in his Bull Moose campaign of 1912. Nor did he take much of a lesson from Congress. This large deliberative body with its hundreds of members and dozens of minor fiefdoms, diffused power as deals, debates, and inordinate stretches of time gradually inched things along to effect.

Fiorello took his ideas of leadership from a man he knew intimately and admired, often through gritted teeth, the hardheaded army bandmaster, his father Achille. Fiorello had witnessed firsthand how this steel-willed immigrant *maestro* pulled together a group of performers and trained, conducted, shaped, *led*. Achille was harsh and uncomplimentary but, above all, demanding in the name of his art. When Achille La Guardia held the baton, every eye was peeled for his signal, every instrument bent to his order. That was the unambiguous style that Fiorello respected. Blending the virtuoso's meticulous attention to art with the prima donna's preening temper and contempt for criticism, he formed his closest relationship with his art, his politics of practical competent idealism. He used people or abandoned them in its service and, like other artists, experienced a tension between highlighting his work and promoting himself. Achille was "the maestro," he "the mayor." From his first day in office he referred to himself in third person, as in "When the Mayor talks to you [as he curtly instructed a woman who neglected to answer one of his questions], you answer."[2]

The first economy bill fight taught La Guardia that his liberty of action was more circumscribed than he had anticipated. He had to acknowledge the role of others—state legislators, the governor, the president—but for the rest of his tenure he fought the idea that politics was a team sport. He persisted in drawing on private talents, compromising only grudgingly and only with those more powerful than he. If he could not ram his bills through then he looked for a hook, a power base, a connection, a weakness in the opposition. "Come, let us reason together" was not his style. Maestros did not lead by consensus.

La Guardia liked to speak frequently of having introduced a scientific politics. By this he meant systematic, rational, enlightened policies. But he did not come to his policies through rational analysis. He relied on a blend of intuition, resentment, suspicion, and liberal inclination gathered into a dramatic whole. His commissioners often found it impossible to predict how he would decide on matters, and the more timid feared his considerable wrath. "The other day," reported the *New York Sun*, "the Mayor attacked his friend Edgar Bromberger . . . for planning a recreational field for the Sanitation Department employees. 'The next time you plan anything like this, let us in on the secret,' he stormed angrily." Commissioners and department supervisors would delay making decisions until receiving his explicit instruction, reduced to figureheads in a government where, caviled the *American*

Mercury, "His Honor holds in his own hands most of the portfolios of government; a one man autocracy with no if or buts, now rules New York."[3]

Even his supporters knew that La Guardia could be very prickly about incursions into his spotlight. Mrs. Bea Blanshard, who worked for, and later married, La Guardia's investigations chief, remembers: "He was a petty man in those things. He couldn't stand his commissioners getting the headlines. . . . Reports had to come through his office. . . . We had to be so cautious because if we breathed a single word he'd go into mad tantrums." By the end of the first term the reserved Blanshard, who seldom raised his voice in public, found it impossible to continue working alongside the tempestuous magistrate.[4]

Naturally officious, La Guardia was made even more insistent by the powers and responsibilities of office. State Supreme Court Justice Lockwood described the Little Flower as "a man who wants what he wants exactly when he wants it, whether right or wrong and when he does not get it exhibits an ungovernable temper and lets loose an unbridled tongue, seeing red, stirring up trouble, throwing black mud around, bespattering the record or reputation and the family of friend or foe."[5]

After several years of La Guardia even some of Tammany's most stalwart foes were questioning what had been gained by switching to La Guardia. The Tiger had taken every opportunity it had seen, but it was interested only in money and jobs. Buffoons with magical boxes they may have been, but when it came to the pursuit of power in its own right, they paled next to this fusion mayor with the Roosevelt rhetoric and the Mussolini style. The staunchly Republican *New York Sun* concluded after almost two years of La Guardia that "New York has never been nearer a one man government than today. No one of the Mayor's commissioners dares to decide anything more than a routine matter without consulting him for his O.K. . ." Louis Yavner who joined the administration in 1934 and worked at La Guardia's side on the mayor's last day in city hall concedes, "He could be cynical, churlish, hot-headed, petty and just plain wrong." And then he would brag that this was his way of keeping his people on their toes. Government by tantrum, others called it.[6]

New York had been placed on a private track. And not all enjoyed the ride along the "Manhattan Messiah's" personal agenda. His on-again, off-again campaign for municipal ownership of electric utilities offended all sides. Supporters of municipal control resented his vacillating, while others objected to the mayor's demagogic attacks on an easy target. The *New York Times* was not amused. "He . . . has unfortunately too often given the impression of being a restless and undecided man, fond of toying with haphazard proposals that may be benevolent in intention but . . . dangerous or impossible in practice. He seems always to want to have in hand some socialistic plaything or other. Just now it is a municipal power plant."[7]

All agreed that his energies might have been better invested, but few dared deliver such advice. (To La Guardia, a city hall reporter wrote, "the word advice is like a red flag to a bull.") When he closed the artichoke business by proclamation or asked the police to shoot first and ask questions later, only the more dedicated civil libertarians complained, but when La Guardia cut off relief payments to 300,000 families to pressure Democratic aldermen into voting for the sales tax, ordered a benign policy toward violent strikers, and closed the burlesque theaters because *he* considered the skin shows immoral, or when a police lieutenant was forced to humbly apologize for having called La Guardia a left-winger and then was assigned to wait upon the mayor at city hall and carry his mail before being transferred to switchboard duty in Harlem, others too began to carp. Officers within earshot of the lieutenant's *lèse majesté* were hounded for failing to report their superior's remarks. Five of them, who claimed not to have heard the remark, were mirthlessly sent to the chief police surgeon to have their hearing checked. Treating gangsters as public enemies was one thing, but using power so casually and so brusquely scared people.[8]

"Little Napoleon" they took to calling the sawed-off political warrior behind his back. "Dictator," proclaimed Frank Taylor, Tammany's candidate for comptroller, when he heard of La Guardia's cutoff of relief checks. "The dictator is at work again. . . . 'Pass my tax program or I'll set the hungry and unfortunate upon your trail.' " The *American Mercury*, which had run a complimentary profile of Congressman La Guardia a few years back, now published a slashing attack by *New York Sun* columnist George Ritchie, blasting the "Midget Mussolini" for embracing radical schemes at the expense of New Yorkers' comforts, rights, and decencies. "What," the *New York Post* begged to know, "induces him to think that New York can be ruled by Proclamation?"[9]

The outspoken Ritchie (La Guardia once refused to deliver an address before the Citizens Budget Commission until Ritchie left the room) pulled together a comprehensive negative accounting of the mayor's first term. Granting what was obvious—the peerless zest for governing, and unequaled personal honesty—Ritchie went on to attack La Guardia for breaking his promises of economy, for introducing new taxes, and for encouraging labor violence. He also questioned the claims of greatly improved efficiency. The simple job of snow removal had proven so beyond the capacity of the fusion government that after three years, more than $21 million, and a raft of plans, winter snows continued to throw the central city into frozen chaos, while vast sections of the outer boroughs resembled nothing so much as unserviced arctic tundras. In the days of the Tiger the pols would put hundreds of friends and relatives on the payrolls and clear the streets. "Some of the boys, of course, appeared on the payroll under three different names—but they shoveled snow. And traffic moved. And business went ahead. And sidewalks were cleared. Good old Tammany!"[10]

The misdirected spring action of a "jack-in-the-box gone haywire," wrote Ritchie, was a poor substitute for intelligent government. Add to this "a belligerency born of an inferiority complex, toss in a persecution mania and a fillip

of Napoleonic grandeur, mix in a scrupulous personal honesty . . . and you have"
a perennial officeholder with a polished skill at self-promotion dragging New York
through the higher disorder. By appealing to the thoughtless rabble, the "Little
Corporal" was delivering the Empire City over to its least stable, least desirable
elements.[11]

More serious and ultimately more damaging than the splenetic attacks of disaffected
journalists was La Guardia's problem with the city's relief system. The vast programs were simply not run well, or honestly, just the sort of thing La Guardia had
promised would never happen under his fusion administration. Relief raised hackles
among the more rigid individualists about the limits of government responsibility,
but the problems that the mayor faced had little to do with ideological controversies
about how you made hardier citizens. It had to do with recognizing that a program
quickly slapped together to dispense great amounts of money, under loose guidelines, had to be watched very carefully and policed ruthlessly. Diverted by the
challenge of winning funding and planning diverse relief projects, La Guardia had
left the operation of the department to Welfare Commissioner Hodson, whose
background in social work made him a perfect pleader but provided little experience
for the massive administrative tasks involved with the relief programs.

By the spring of 1935, New Yorkers were reading about aldermanic investigations of relief that uncovered enough waste, chicanery, and lavishly funded
projects of dubious value to run the tabloids into special editions. Equally plain
was evidence that New York was playing national patsy. Needy Americans from
all over the nation were tramping to New York to feed at its generous trough, at
an estimated cost to the city of $20 million, while New Yorkers struggled with
emergency taxes to pay for the soaring relief bill. And to top it off, the Welfare
Department was ladling out large pay raises to its managers. Challenged to explain
the raises, administration officials defended the increases as necessary to keep the
staff from leaving.[12]

"Miss Gosselin," asked Lloyd Stryker, counsel for the Aldermanic Investigating Committee, "did you ask for the raise?"

"No. But I was glad to get it."

"Did you threaten to leave if you did not get it?"

"I certainly did not."

It appeared that public funds were being squandered with little thought or
care. Police, firemen, and other civil servants who had absorbed pay cuts in the
name of greater municipal economy were furious, and La Guardia was unprepared.
He claimed not to have known about the raises. To a series of direct questions
from the aldermanic investigators, Welfare Commissioner Hodson answered that
he had informed the mayor. What he had meant, explained the discomfited Fiorello,

was that, ah, was, ah, that he had not studied the details carefully. Aldermanic President Deutsch, appalled by the lack of candor, charged a "racket."[13]

Shades of Tammany!

Unwilling to defend the raises, as some of the Welfare Department officials insisted he do, a less than masterful La Guardia had them rescinded. Colonel William Wilgus, the world-famous engineer who headed the works relief division, disappointed by the lack of support, resigned, leaving Hodson with an even bigger headache and La Guardia with a fiasco. Many years later Robert Moses called La Guardia's buckling under to the Stryker investigation one of his weakest moments. He criticized La Guardia for showing gross "indifference to personal loyalty" by failing to stand behind his municipal workers against Stryker's badgering and witch-hunting.[14]

La Guardia had no choice. There was much to criticize in the city's relief operations, and the aldermen were only too happy to do the job. La Guardia had supported ruthless inquiry throughout his career, and there was little he could do to cut it short now that it was focused on his administration, no matter how uncomfortable it made him and his administrators.

Aldermanic investigators next turned to analyzing the millions of dollars allocated for white-collar works projects. New Yorkers learned that their tax dollars had funded a scholarly translation of a Russian-language study of ancient Roman trade relations, the development of maps illustrating temperature and rainfall in Italy, charts tracing early Chinese history, and scale drawings of Pompeian and Diocletian baths.

"You also made a map of the 'Geographical Distribution of Greek dialects,' " accused aldermanic counsel Stryker. One could imagine Congressman La Guardia indignantly pulling one of these studies from his pocket and puffing, "In a city with these terrific taxes and the Great Depression, I was wondering how much a distribution of Greek dialects would help us here," only now it was Stryker on a roll. Another study, "Archeological Evidence for Chief Bronze Age Culture: A Geographical Distribution of Chief Type of Fibulae," aroused his interest.

"What's that? Bones in the leg?"

"No, . . . safety pins."[15]

The investigators turned from scholarship to white-collar work relief. Mr. Weintraub was called upon to explain his work: "We get a list of addresses and we call at each. We ask the lady her name and all about her family, but that's a lead up you might say. Finally we get around to the point: how many ducks and how many chickens and how many eggs the lady and her family have eaten that week . . . to find out how many ducks and chickens are eaten. And eggs."

One hundred men were employed on this unusual census. Mr. Weintraub confessed that the results were less than comprehensive because most women, thinking him crazy, slammed the door in his face. And what did he think of his job?

"I think," said Mr. Weintraub, "that this is ridiculous. I'd like to have a real job."[16]

La Guardia could only squirm as Stryker continued his interviews. Mrs. Myra Wilcoxon testified that New York City paid her to teach eurythmic dancing ("a natural type, simple form of dancing"). Mr. Robert Marshall trained teachers of "boondoggling" ("collecting odds and ends and making things out of them"). Mr. Henry Dresser explained his functions as a hobby guide. "I talk hobbies and pretty soon I get other people talking hobbies." Worse than the careless spending of the funds was the seemingly programmatic commitment to waste. The aldermen learned that real estate surveys available from private firms for $1639 a year were being funded by the city for a staggering $2,239,683. Scores of ineligibles were found not merely on the relief rolls and work lists but in supervisory positions.

Blue-collar work did not come off much better, serving as the butt of endless jokes: A foreman had sent in a requisition for shovels. "No shovels available," came the reply. "Let the men lean on each other."[17]

In the effort to get relief out to as many as possible, La Guardia had lost sight of the need to keep it honest and sensible if it was to retain public support. Several months later a chastened La Guardia was paying more attention to relief proposals, disapproving forty-six of forty-eight white-collar projects as not "worthwhile." He also superseded the overwhelmed Hodson with a succession of "relief czars," each chosen to blunt the sharpest public criticism of the moment. The first, at C. C. Burlingham's suggestion, was Oswald Knauth, a tough-talking Harvard graduate and former Macy's executive, who admitted that he did not know "the first thing about relief or the ramifications of the situation. . . . I don't know a darn thing about boondoggling, hornswaggling or any other sort of babytalk." He was going to put relief on an honest, businesslike basis and clear the rolls of chiselers.[18]

In less then two months changed guidelines in Washington brought a new czar, Hugh Johnson. La Guardia had helped choose the rough-hewn, hard-drinking general to impose order on the chaotic relief situation. Johnson lasted little longer than Knauth, and as he departed for blessed private life, he put into words what was bothering La Guardia and many others: "You've got to find something better [than existing relief procedures] for two reasons—you can't afford this and it isn't doing any good if you could." For La Guardia and the national administration this remained the central relief dilemma.[19]

A more fundamental question plagued all involved in relief: Just what was relief supposed to be? Was it municipal charity to which the recipient had no more than a moral claim or was it an absolute public responsibility for which the municipality must strain its resources to the limits? What about the work to which reliefers were assigned? Must it be useful and important in its own right or was it only an excuse for funding the unemployed, for maintaining their dignity and keeping them occupied? If that was so, then what was wrong with supporting professors in examining the fascinating social orders of ancient Kish or Italian temperature changes during the Middle Ages? Scholars had as much right to dignity and food as blue-collar workers. Clearly *they* thought that these questions were important. How sturdy a building could such a man put up, anyway, even if he were added to a construction crew?

In the land of Horatio Alger, being on the dole forced reliefers to wrestle with their own insecurities as well. Gratitude gave way to discomfort at being forced to rely on handouts, and finally to anger at a system that could not care in a dignified way for its own. The unemployed banded together in "unemployed councils" of the jobless, to protect their interest in government generosity. When federal allocations were chopped in the first months of 1936, resulting in local cuts, New York's unemployed turned to direct action, picketing WPA headquarters and, on March 20, invading Welfare Department offices.

The event galvanized Victor Ridder, relief czar III. He bridled at the ingratitude and blamed the protests on Communists. Ridder dismissed the strikes as insincere radical hell-raising. In a round of speeches during the summer he labeled demonstrators "rats" and "vermin," vowing to fire any WPA employee involved in a demonstration. Clubs were distributed around WPA headquarters with instructions to "use 'em on anybody who gets tough," while pistol-toting guards patrolled the corridors against leftists. Comics might joke that striking reliefers were playing "Mutiny on the Bounty," but Ridder and many other New Yorkers feared that the protests were part of a coordinated plan of disruption. Tammany aldermen, only too anxious to call attention to the troubles, demanded tighter controls on every aspect of relief, and the Board of Estimate passed a stringent residency requirement.[20]

It had taken some time, but by the fall of 1936 La Guardia knew what he wanted from relief and what he did not want. Reminding his colleagues that much of the money they were so interested in hoarding came from Washington, where a "fortress New York" policy would not be looked upon kindly, he vetoed the residency bill, only to have the board override his veto. Then, in another of those moves that caused civil libertarians to curse him for his high-handedness and bless him for the results, he ordered the bill suspended, arguing that it conflicted with state policies. Bronx Borough President Lyons, the bill's sponsor, thought that the state's threat to withhold $6 million if the bill was implemented was only a bluff. "That I do not know," Fiorello declared. "I do know I will not play poker with home relief."[21]

Nor would he join his friend Ridder in his Red fears. Even as Ridder claimed that Communists were using relief expenditures as a "$9,000,000 campaign fund every month," and former police chief O'Ryan accused him of encouraging disorder to win support for his relief budget and pander to the "vicious elements of the city," La Guardia refused to have police put down welfare demonstrations, insisting

385

that the poor and the unemployed had a right to be heard even if the message was unwelcome. "Don't you see the state of his mind?" La Guardia pleaded to a police audience. "Don't you see how easy it is for him to accept half truths? Don't you see how easy it is for him to be misled when he knows he hasn't enough for his family?"[22]

When the economy turned up slightly in late 1936, La Guardia warned Roosevelt and Hopkins not to rush to cut relief. They ignored him, and the cuts set off further violent demonstrations in New York. La Guardia, convinced that their optimism was premature, scraped together funds from his own budget to compensate for the federal cuts. The next quarter proved La Guardia's fears all too accurate as the nation dipped into the "Roosevelt recession" in the fall of 1937 and Fiorello resumed his old post in Washington, begging for jobs and assistance.[23]

La Guardia foes detected a single motive in all of this: a marked indulgence for left-wing solutions. Never mind that the Communists themselves abused La Guardia as a pseudoreformer, a "bourgeois politician parading as a progressive," a fascist, a servant of Wall Street bankers, and a progressive who had sold out. Never mind La Guardia's continued use of the police "Red Squad" to keep tabs on aliens and radicals. Never mind his bristling lectures to Red marchers in front of city hall reminding them that "if they came within the same distance of the City Hall of Leningrad or some other city in control of the Soviet government they would be put up before a firing squad." Never mind La Guardia's own record as an unideological pragmatist, or even the fact that he ordered police to use all necessary force "not only to protect themselves but to suppress violence and unlawful conduct" when taming *radical* protesters. Notwithstanding all of this, La Guardia was smeared as a Communist or, at the very least, a mighty good friend of this enemy that the Hearst papers described as "poison carriers filled with hate of all that Americans respect and venerate . . . subsidized from mysterious and foreign centers of enmity to the United States." The *New York Daily Mirror* called Communist demonstrators "the scum of the city fattening on human destitution and suffering . . . skulking rats," and announced that "the time for forbearance has passed."[24]

Tammany finally found an issue with which to flog La Guardia, denouncing its old nemesis as "the town's . . . rabble-rouser in chief, and its shrewdest political radical in a day when the rabble in the streets were responding to such appeals." State Assemblyman Edward S. Moran sought an investigation of the mayor for "fomenting disputes between capital and labor." Having repeated the charge often enough, the Tiger at least convinced itself. When John J. McNaboe's Committee on Communist Influence in the Schools was phased out of existence, the silver-haired McNaboe blamed the radical in city hall who, McNaboe intimated, was linked to the Soviet industrial arm, Amtorg. It did not dawn on the conspiracy-drunk legislator that the fact that he had not called his committee into meeting even once, had not spent a farthing of his allocation, and had issued not a single line of findings might have had more to do with the committee's demise than the Communist in city hall.[25]

Many Catholic New Yorkers, influenced by the church's strong stand against international communism, also turned critical. Patrick Scanlan, editor of the Catholic weekly *Brooklyn Tablet*, reported that his study of the relief lists convinced him that Catholics were systematically discriminated against and that the distribution of relief in New York City was honeycombed with Red connections. Communists, he complained, were creating Welfare Department policy, serving as case workers, and disposing the unemployed toward revolution. Speaking before some 4000 Catholics in April of 1937, Alfred E. Smith declared that there was no room in a Christian country for godless social philosophies. Communism was the enemy of the church and of human liberty. After Smith, Bronx Borough President George U. Harvey told the cheering crowd that, had he been mayor, he would have provided police with "three feet of rubber hose" to clear the streets of radicals "within two weeks." Father Edward Lodge Curran, who organized the rally, followed, assuring the faithful that the Commies would be defeated, by peaceful means if possible, but "if they wanted it the way it was in Spain, we'll let them have it." Mayor La Guardia's name brought forth loud booing from the audience, who wanted to know why he was not using the tactics that he had so dramatically employed against the gamblers and racketeers against atheistic Communists.[26]

La Guardia responded that he refused to attack philosophies with weapons reserved for criminals and that he would guarantee First Amendment rights. Communist-hunters perceived further proof of La Guardia's Commie coddling in his relationship with protégé Vito Marcantonio. Marc had been elected congressman from Fiorello's former district and turned out to be quite a firebrand, telling followers that "American labor must go to the left," militantly representing the unemployed councils and winning a reputation as the mouthpiece of the Communist party in Congress. The relationship between La Guardia and Marcantonio had cooled somewhat since the days when Marc had directed La Guardia's campaigns and ran his congressional office, but the mayor loyally supported the congressman and continued to speak of him as "my son," although he would add "my erring son." When Police Commissioner Valentine denounced the youthful Marcantonio as a boy on a man's errand, "a publicity seeking demagogue who would love to don a martyr's crown even to the extent of creating grave disorder in order to crash into the headlines," he received a note from La Guardia rebuking him for his "unbecoming and entirely uncalled for . . . lack of restraint. . . . You will be good enough to refrain from such conduct in the future."[27]

———

La Guardia's autocratic leadership, his sympathy for the unemployed, and his loose rein on relief and Communists could have been predicted by those familiar with his record. Less anticipated was La Guardia's abandonment of careful economies that he had painstakingly erected to solve the city's financial crisis. In 1933 La Guardia had run on a platform of retrenchment, promising to cut $50 million, by draconian measures if need be, to bring the budget into balance.

La Guardia's forceful program of investigation was supposed to save even more through the elimination of corruption and the introduction of efficient modern management, but the investigations produced disappointingly modest economies. While the Department of Accounts uncovered many cases of minor corruption, short weight, $500 bribes, $10 shakedowns, payoffs, swindles, incompetence, and graft, in the end, the ninety-eight actions brought against private citizens by the department resulted only in modest fines, token prison terms of under three months, or suspended sentences.[28]

Take the investigation of the county sheriffs. In August 1936 La Guardia, with customary fanfare, made public the results of a nineteen-month inquiry into the operation of the five sheriff's offices (still under Tammany control), laying bare waste and graft. But the sheriff's office represented less than one-half of 1 percent of the total city payroll. It took close to two years to complete the study, which represented the only systematic audit of a departmental payroll carried out by the Department of Accounts. To place municipal administration on an efficient basis would have meant auditing each department with equal precision to determine the most practical basis for its functioning. Studies, no matter how accurate and pains-taking, that wanted mostly to prove how bad Tammany had been could not achieve the efficiency and economies that La Guardia had promised.[29]

Moreover, government by investigation is by its nature limiting, inhibiting the freedom to expand and build. It focuses on honing a relatively static system to perfection. In the end, investigation-driven government is small government. But La Guardia was committed to vigorous growth. He wanted to keep the government as honest as he could, but he would not slow its pace to the point where every department and its operations could be kept under careful scrutiny. That was what he could not tolerate about Harold Ickes. Blanshard would have to catch whatever he could; La Guardia was not going to abandon dynamic government to guarantee that it was penny-perfect or inexpensive.

The promise of ruthless efficiency also fell by the wayside. La Guardia had promised, for example, to modernize the police department, to bring large savings by introducing new technologies and more efficient service. He replaced traffic police with mechanical traffic signals, expanded the use of radio cars, and imple-mented other expensive innovations to yield efficiencies that would result in per-sonnel cuts. But despite all the new technology the number of police kept growing and the bureaucracy kept swallowing them up and asking for more.

La Guardia had another pet program that was going to make the NYPD more effective. The department regularly used full-fledged officers to do routine office work, answer phones, file data, and do light research. This practice limited the number of officers that could be deployed on patrol. It made little sense, and La Guardia had pledged to free the desk-bound cops and replace them with lower-paid civil servants, but the long-standing practice was not so easily halted.

For years the availability of uniformed desk jobs had permitted commanders to transfer ineffective, aging, or untrusted police off patrol, and they were not ready to give up this flexibility. Only a single-minded focus on such wasteful practices could end them, but here was another study that Blanshard did not make! After no more than a handful of police were moved out from behind their desks, close to 2000 continued doing clerical work that could just as easily have been carried out by civil service personnel at half the cost.[30]

As for the much-heralded benefits of scientific management, the results were mixed. La Guardia prided himself in having appointed a police commissioner from the ranks, his proof of scientific nonpolitical government. But the appointment of a "real professional" like Valentine meant that inbred practices like the ones just described would not be questioned. A cop's cop, Valentine demanded honest police work, but he did not challenge the department's entrenched weaknesses, whether the inefficient use of police time or such deep-rooted problems as departmental racism. For the cost of running the entire city of San Francisco, New York supported a police force that was still inefficient, corrupt, racist, and unable to promise New Yorkers the safe streets they so desperately demanded.[31]

In his first few months in office, La Guardia trimmed the civil service, slashed salaries, and curtailed expenditures. Had the legislature not blocked his economy bill, the cuts would have reached even deeper, but before long La Guardia abandoned his promise of lean, economy-focused government in favor of sculpting a modern, humane New York. With time, fewer and fewer of La Guardia's priorities centered on savings and more and more on building and spending. The cut-rate salaries were raised. The fire department adopted a three-platoon system, adding hundreds to the payroll. (The mayor had vetoed the idea in his first week in office as too expensive.) Staffs were expanded and restraints loosened as the sense of strapped sacrifice made way for spending-fueled modernization. After fusion's third year the city had 9609 more workers than were on the rolls in 1934 when La Guardia took office (excluding the temporary relief workers in WPA jobs).[32]

Those who had taken his campaign pledges of cuts and limited government seriously viewed the easy spending policies as a broken promise. "The present Fusion administration has piddled away more of the taxpayers dollars on fantastic folderols than even the most artful Tammany Robin Hoods could ever secrete in their black tin boxes," complained one critic. Tammany had stolen and misman-aged, but the cost of its government would never approach the price of La Guardia's ambitions for New York. Millions in loans would have to be paid back, dozens of new structures would have to be maintained, and the city would never again be able to ignore the needy. La Guardia of course considered this a good thing and, in any event, absolutely necessary, but while gearing up for a prodigal city he continued to talk economy and bare-bones budgets.[33]

Robert Moses, never shy about rattling skeletons in others' closets, appeared before the city budget director to testify about the Parks Department requests for 1936 and provided a clue into the difficult bookkeeping arrangements that the mayor had to devise to maintain the appearance of economy while supporting high-expense projects. Moses told how he had been ordered to submit a show budget of $5,097,078, a mere $1000 increase over the previous year's appropriation, despite the fact that he intended to spend much more. Actual expenditures, he said, would be $7,964,971, with the rest of the outlays coming from a separate allocation. "The whole thing should have been in the budget," Moses remarked offhandedly, dropping a bombshell. "The budget isn't a true budget. It is a sham . . . it does not reflect the demands of the department."[34]

To support the illusion of higher tax income and camouflage the true cost of city government, the administration was forced to resort to a series of misleading policies. It kept on the tax rolls property that had been taken over by the city, despite the fact that this real estate would never yield a dollar in taxes. It deliberately delayed the adjudication of contested assessments to maximize tax income, drawing a sharp rebuke from State Supreme Court Justice Joseph M. Callahan, who called it a threat and a "disaster" for democratic government. It courted the outrage of property holders, who threatened tax strikes if the city did not roll back assessment increases, higher water rates, and tax penalties that had been raised during the fiscal emergency. William H. Allen, director of the Institute for Public Service, brought suit to impeach the mayor for deliberate tax misassessments, and others warned that the undue burdens on real estate would lead to more blight as landlords abandoned marginal properties. La Guardia paid them no heed. Higher taxes were the necessary price for the modern government he wanted.[35]

When La Guardia first came into office he persuaded the state legislature to grant the city an emergency sales tax to fund unemployment relief for a two-year period ending in January 1936. La Guardia had called the sales tax a bad tax. In Congress he had hounded President Hoover and the Republican party for proposing such taxes, and he frankly admitted his embarrassment at having to rely on them as mayor. But by mid-1935, after New York City budgets had begun to show modest surpluses, La Guardia petitioned the state legislature to renew the emergency tax power for another two years. The city could have absorbed some of the relief burden into the regular budget and shaved the regressive sales tax, but La Guardia would not give up the $46 million in extra income. Indeed, he asked the legislature to remove statutory restrictions that limited the use of these funds to unemployment relief. When Governor Lehman objected that the emergency had passed, La Guardia blasted "The Governor's . . . pawnshop system of city finances" with the spirited tantrum of a youngster about to lose his allowance.[36]

Fusion had hoped that La Guardia would educate the public to municipal responsibility. But he kept much of the real price of his agenda hidden from the public. He preferred to conceal the expense of bringing New York to a higher standard by beefing up his regular budgets with supplementary allocations, a style of budget writing that a succession of New York mayors would adopt with multiple variations until it got so out of hand that the official budget masked much more than it showed.[37]

But if La Guardia was not forthright about his plans for ambitious, expensive government, his critics were not even close to understanding what he was doing. Foes charged him with being a Communist, a dictator, giving away the city to the reliefers, destroying real estate, destroying civil liberties. Each of the faults was exaggerated into parody. Nitpickers complained that the mayor spent too much time on the road. Others examined his expenditures on telegrams, telephone bills, travel expenses, and accommodations. It took little to understand that comparing Fiorello's expenses with those of Jimmy Walker, who never brought back hundreds of millions from Washington or led the nation's mayors in expanding the influence of cities, made no sense. And while John O'Brien kept costs down, he did not give the city new parks, bridges, vast relief programs, and music concerts. That La Guardia spent a few hundred dollars more on travel and phone calls was just fine with most New Yorkers.

That he was a powerful leader did not seem to bother them too much either. Few New Yorkers really trembled for their liberties under La Guardia. Even the most fervid civil libertarians found it difficult to scare up much opposition on the basis of a few examples of La Guardian excess.[38]

It was his insistence on the large city, with broad services and the continued growth of metropolitan government, that could be fashioned into a real campaign issue. Here the problems of powerful leadership, expensive government, responsibilities for citizen welfare, and implications for the style and standard of urban life were joined. But so long as his critics also promised new buildings, money for the unemployed, larger police forces, and grants from Washington, their effect was limited. He was doing *that job* as well as it could be done.

That the rackets were still in bloom, Harlem suffering, and the unemployed dissatisfied, that the emphasis on progress produced a distorting emphasis on change, on headlines that heralded ground breakings and ribbon cuttings while older structures deteriorated, provided ample opportunity for a real alternative agenda, if a candidate could be found to articulate these issues and take on La Guardia on new ground.

There were social reformers who called for downplanning and contraction, conceiving of ways to scale down the vast metropolis to reasonable size where the individual spirit could flourish and government, business, and social institutions be kept in safe balance with the powers of the people. Critics attacked the mega-city in unequivocal terms. "Even if Robert Moses rebuilt New York from end to end in the fashion he has already followed," declared Lewis Mumford, "it would still be a doomed city . . . its rebuilding [hastening] . . . its doom." Frank Lloyd Wright characterized the modern metropolis as a vast, soulless catastrophe, "an insatiable maw devouring quantity, instead of protecting quality. . . . [T]he city is inhabited only because we have it, feel we must use it and cannot yet afford to throw it away." The contemporary metropolis, he said, "devoured" freedom, ground down individuality and spontaneity, and exaggerated natural imbalances. It operated on a level monstrously out of human scale and proportion. Said Wright, "The soul, properly citified, is so far gone as to mistake exaggeration for greatness. . . ." In Gotham—"Some thriving little village port driven insane by excess"—Wright found all evils harshly magnified. "Here is a volcanic crater of blind confused, human forces pushing together and grinding upon each other, moved by greed in common exploitation, forcing anxiety upon all life. No noble expression of life this. . . . This Moloch knows no god but 'More.' . . . And it is nothing more than much more of much too much already."[39]

If a serious politician opposed La Guardia by calling for shrinking New York, the mayor would respond by celebrating its savage energy and vehement silhouettes as signs of possibility rather than of decay. He would share with them the mood of a visiting Le Corbusier, who saw New York in 1936 and was impressed to exclaim: "This is architecture's hour. . . . today it is possible for the city of modern times, the happy city, the radiant city, to be born. . . ." But this challenge of casting a scientific modern city through the art of municipal reconstruction was open to debate if anyone dared to tackle the issue.

"He likes the feel of the driver's seat," wrote George L. Ritchie. "He wants to stay there." Anyone who wanted to take over would have to consider how far along La Guardia's agenda of growth the city had already come and whether it was realistic to consider reversing this. If not, then the debate would be fought on La Guardia's grounds, unless he could not put together the magical coalition that had elected him in 1933.

There was growing reason to suspect that he might not; that, in other words, the next election might be contested not on the high grounds of policy but on what political support the prickly Little Flower could assemble; that politics and not issues would determine the election of 1937 as it had so many others; that he had not educated the electorate sufficiently to run a campaign on matters of real substance; that his 1933 victory had not changed things all that much.[40]

2. A Giant Beech Tree . . .
Nothing Grows Underneath

As a new mayoral election drew closer La Guardia's foes took consolation in history. No previous reform administration had lasted longer than one term (When Seth Low, the one-term reform mayor from 1901 to 1903, first ran for election, he campaigned on an antivice platform. "Everyone is interested in vice," he said. But when he ran for reelection on a platform of pro-virtue, he lost. "No one," he quipped, "is interested in virtue."). An unusual combination of events had brought La Guardia into office: revelations of widespread corruption, the city treasury poised on the edge of default, a wave of revulsion with Tammany, and a bitter split between national and local Democrats. It was unlikely that the situation would be the same this time, or that there would be another three-way race.

"In the 271 years of its existence as a chartered community," crowed George Ritchie, "no chief executive elected on a Holier Than Thou platform has survived to enjoy a second four year term. . . . Normally Democratic by a landslide, the Metropolis has a habit of swiftly soothing its outraged civic virtue, whipped to momentary heat by rambunctious reformers, and resuming its incorrigible ways, under the smooth functioning, if reprehensible tutelage of Tammany." Reformers were just not able to wield power and be good at the same time.[41]

The fusion coalition had been worn down too. W. Arthur Cunningham, elected comptroller with Fiorello in 1933, died in the very first year of his term. La Guardia replaced him with owlish Columbia University professor Joseph P. McGoldrick, but when reformer McGoldrick ran for office in a special election in November 1934, La Guardia offered little support. Unable to overcome both La Guardia's lack of interest and the heavy Democratic turnout generated by the Lehman-Moses contest, McGoldrick lost. One year into the fusion era, Tammany won back the second most important elective office in the city and with it the comptroller's three votes on the Board of Estimate. Fusion's thirteen-to-three majority was down to ten to six.

The following year McGoldrick ran for district attorney of Brooklyn against the discredited William F. X. Geoghan. Playing up the scandal-ridden Druckman murder case, he attacked Tiger justice, promising to bring reform to Brooklyn. Again the mayor proved unable to rouse that marvelous instinct for the jugular on behalf of his erstwhile colleague. The baffled McGoldrick could not understand

393

why until La Guardia called him in for a talk one day. The press was giving President Roosevelt a hard time and Geoghan's defeat could hurt FDR nationally, La Guardia explained. This intelligence was being passed on for more than the professor's files. Nevertheless, McGoldrick refused to withdraw, and with a less than pleased La Guardia doling out only perfunctory support, Geoghan easily won reelection.

The machine also took the 1935 aldermanic elections, sweeping thirteen fusionists from office by huge pluralities, to capture sixty-two of the board's sixty-five seats. As Democrats hailed a "return to normalcy," downcast reformers fumed over the mayor's lack of interest in fusion candidates. "We're Republicans from now on," declared one disenchanted coalitionist, adding that in the coming mayoral election, "it's every man for himself." Angered by La Guardia's refusal to campaign for them the defeated fusion aldermen used the lame-duck session to block the mayor's budget, leaving Tammany to pull his chestnuts out of the fire.[42]

La Guardia scarcely helped matters when he suggested that the setback did not mean all that much since he was still at the helm and that was all that mattered. In a statement studded with more "I" s than Argus, he said in part: "The kind of government I am giving the people of the City is such that I have no worries, misgivings or anxieties in having the Board of Aldermen majority ostensibly against the administration. I've had it for two years." Supporters winced and enemies were gleeful at the turn of events. "With Republican support disappearing and his friends more and more questioning his motives," wrote the *New York Sun*, "New York . . . [stands] more than ever alone today—a one man government headed, it would seem, for the limbo of forgotten fusion mayors."[43]

Before the new Tammany-dominated board was even sworn in, fusion took yet another blow. Aldermanic President Bernard Deutsch, a loyal advocate of progressive city government, died suddenly at fifty-one years of age and the vice chairman of the Board of Aldermen, Timothy J. Sullivan, Tammany leader of the Eighteenth Assembly District, ascended to the aldermanic presidency. From controlling thirteen votes when La Guardia was inaugurated on January 1, 1934, fusion's share of the Board of Estimate had dwindled to a minority of seven. Halfway into La Guardia's term the mayor was back in his accustomed—and, some intimated, preferred—role of lone political wolf. Looking out at the wreckage of what had been his majority, La Guardia exclaimed shortly after Deutsch's death, "I am lonely," adding wistfully, "but I refuse to be discouraged."[44]

In the special election to complete the remainder of Deutsch's term scheduled for fall 1936, the Democrats nominated a little-known sheriff from Queens. Republican leaders suggested a number of candidates to La Guardia, seeking his advice and support. But they could not capture his attention. Posed in his disdain for temporal politics, La Guardia offered only a maddening list of requirements that had to be met before he would lend his support to any candidate. There being no

Fiorello clone available, and out of patience with the mayor, exasperated Republican leaders named Newbold Morris, a Republican from the silk-stocking district who traced his lineage back to the *Mayflower* and his political philosophy to the urban progressivism espoused by the Little Flower. Here was a progressive Republican that even the unpredictable La Guardia would have trouble rejecting.

The Republicans had not counted on the mayor's perversity (or his thin skin; Morris, of whom friends cracked that he was born with a silver foot in his mouth, the year before had criticized the mayor for "cheap politics"). Fiorello reacted to the news of Morris's nomination like a wine connoisseur holding a bottle of dubious vintage. He held it up to the light, sniffed it, slowly decanted a few drops, and finally took a sip. He announced that Morris was a good enough man, but inexperienced. New York needed a politician with more body, more aroma, more character. A bottle of Adolf A. Berle, please![45]

Fiorello's edgy, arrogant friend and confidant had been a boy prodigy, graduating Harvard College at eighteen and the law school at twenty-one. Three years later he joined the staff sent to the Paris Peace Conference. An observer described the brilliant coauthor of *The Modern Corporation and Private Property* as "small, quick, he walks like a wrestler about the ring. . . . he talks at a lightning-like rate. It seems his mind works too fast for his tongue, that he fears life will be too short for him, to say—and do—all the things he wants to." But despite Berle's qualifications, Fiorello's was an impossible suggestion. Berle was a registered Democrat and a New Deal braintruster. Republicans had supported La Guardia in the hopes that he would bring their party some badly needed victories. If they backed Berle, New York Republicans would demonstrate that they had not a single acceptable progressive in their ranks for the relatively unimportant job of aldermanic president. And it would keep the patronage tap firmly shut.

Why would La Guardia push such a plan? He was evidently quite serious in his recommendation, going so far as to enlist President Roosevelt's support. The answer goes beyond the mayor's orneriness and earnest desire to have pal Berle at his side. For several years now he had been talking of a national realignment of parties along an ideological axis. He had no respect for existing parties. They stood for nothing. He wanted parties that debated liberal and conservative policies, not two centrist globs of mush. While Morris might draw support from Republican progressives, only a liberal like Berle would be able to articulate and help bring about the realignment that La Guardia envisioned.

There remained one obstacle: La Guardia had not checked with the gun-shy Berle, who was out of the country. Adolf, as it turned out, had no stomach for electoral politics. Having crippled Morris by withholding his support when it might have meant something, La Guardia finally fell in behind the Morris candidacy. The undistinguished Tammany sheriff trounced the hapless Morris by 900,000 votes.[46]

395

In three successive contests the machine had clobbered fusion and La Guardia had done little to prevent it. He poised himself above the fray, preaching the purer statecraft of nonpolitical reform. "New York City cannot afford a political administration," he remarked to an audience of engineers. "It may have one more, but if it does it will be the last because the City will go broke and bankrupt. . . . That time [when you could pick the head of a department from a political clubhouse] is gone forever." Then, to dramatize his commitment, he called engineer Andrew Hudson to come up from the audience and swore him in on the spot as deputy commissioner of plants and structures. "If a civil service man is going to do the work, he might as well get the position, the responsibility, the honor and the salary. But [the mayor turned to Hudson] you remember that your job is purely engineering."[47]

To make sure that his appointees remembered, La Guardia issued an order prohibiting commissioners and high-ranking officials from holding party posts. Members of his administration, from commissioners on down, were commanded to sever party ties and resign their county, state, and district offices.

Republicans fumed at being placed in the same category with Tammany in an administration that they had helped elect. But the real casualty was the fledgling Fusion party. Fusion had contributed its best and brightest to the administration, and now La Guardia ordered these very individuals to drop their party work. By denying the party the benefit of its most gifted members, La Guardia cut the party off at its stem. La Guardia did not care. He was now against all parties, not just Tammany. "I want no 'yes' party behind me and backing me up in all I may do," he declared rather unctuously. "I don't place any value on organization in municipal politics."[48]

Fusion had never limited its agenda to La Guardia's election. It had sought to spark a movement for municipal renewal by bringing competent nonpartisan experts into government. Fusionists were as revolted as La Guardia by the meretricious trading in favors that accounted for the low caliber of the New York civil service. But if fusion was to succeed, it needed loyal troops, an organization, some clout, and some patronage. All that they were asking for was a hand in helping suggest good and capable appointees who could help the party along, but La Guardia rejected their requests as the special pleading of just another party. As it lost the comptrollership, aldermanic presidency, and Board of Estimate majority, fusion's 1933 victory was narrowed to La Guardia, and that was not enough. He was their "giant beech tree . . . magnificent to look at . . . but nothing grows underneath."[49]

La Guardia's unwillingness to help fusion went beyond denying patronage and ordering his administrators to sever political ties. It went to the point of gracelessly ignoring them. "Your repeated failure to either attend any of the meetings or say anything in behalf of the City Fusion Party is doing us an irreparable injury," a nettled Charles Belous, head of the Fusion party in Queens, wrote to the mayor. Two years later the fusionist wrote again, this time more bitterly, that the mayor had broken his spirit. "For more than two years I have struggled . . . sacrificing my time, my money, my effort and even my reputation trying to keep alive those ideals which brought the Party into existence, without aid or encouragement from those who have profited most from efforts such as my own."[50]

Belous made the mistake of expecting gratitude. It was a mark of pride with La Guardia that he gave none. Each rejected request for spoils represented a moral victory for him, proving that he was unbought and unbossed. He delighted in instructing congressmen, political leaders, friends, and fusionists, one and all, that under his "new philosophy of government," no one got any favors. It was La Guardia at his most sanctimonious. Instead of thanks from "the great infallible," Belous muttered, the mayor kept throwing "the bugaboo of 'patronage' . . . into my teeth on the slightest pretext." Holding La Guardia directly responsible for fusion's losses, too tired and discouraged "to fight both my enemies and my supposed friends," Belous resigned his chairmanship, costing fusion the services of an experienced and dedicated reformer. "I have been endeavoring since your election [one year ago] to have a satisfactory talk with you," Ben Howe, the chairman of the Fusion party, wrote to La Guardia, "but after cooling my heels in your office for a month, I gave up. . . ."[51]

By May of 1935, shortly before he died, a dejected aldermanic president Bernard S. Deutsch, joined the chorus of lament: "I cannot conceive a dream more completely shattered," he cried. "There is no close and consistent co-operation between members of the Fusion administration in respect to plans and policy . . . ," and he blamed La Guardia for failing to work with the Fusion aldermen. Judge Jonah J. Goldstein understood why. "He wanted to do everything himself," he remarked about La Guardia. "He couldn't be part of a team. He'd want to be the whole nine players in baseball . . . in football all eleven." He worked as the star, not as part of a team, and so he destroyed the team. La Guardia simply lacked all the elements of a faithful, dutiful party builder, from selflessness to joy in common achievement. By 1937 the city Fusion party was no more than a relic.[52]

His other party, the Republicans, he treated as his kept woman, refusing to appear with them in public while demanding their unfaltering loyalty in private. "I realize, my friends, that the New York Republicans are just as handicapped by the lack of patronage today," the state GOP chairman moaned, "as they would be were a Democratic administration in control of the city." Bronx Borough President James J. Lyons, a Democrat, joyfully concurred, introducing a resolution in the Board of Estimate "respectfully requesting the mayor" to continue treating the Grand Old Party in his "usual courteous manner."[53]

By late 1936, as La Guardia's thoughts turned to reelection, he had to consider new sources of support upon which to base a campaign. But while La Guardia made no deals with fusion, he had no reservations about courting that special coalition of labor, new immigrants, and good-government reformers that had formed the backbone of the fusion movement. While he rejected parties that presumed to speak in the name of this coalition, La Guardia continued to pursue these groups, which were his natural constituency.

"More workers are paid more wages for producing more goods in more manufacturing establishments here," boasted the *New York Panorama Guidebook*, "than in any other American City." More than a half million workers were employed in some 26,000 factories, and nearly a million more were unemployed. Previous administrations had viewed New York as a business, financial, and commercial city. La Guardia was the first to recognize that above all else it was a worker's city. Other mayors considered labor strikes, at best, a nuisance bordering on incivility and, at worst, the opening moves for a worldwide insurrection. But La Guardia cheered on strikers. "I am criticized by cheap politicians," he told a labor audience, "because they say I favor labor. I do. I am charged with encouraging labor organizations. I do." Attacking the notion that strikes were subversive, he saw them as a legitimate weapon in the war between labor and capital. His first police commissioner paid with his job for disagreeing with him.[54]

La Guardia took a direct hand in labor negotiations by threatening to harass uncooperative managements with his municipal powers unless they made fair concessions. He established an arbitration panel staffed with alert progressives to mediate labor disputes and prevent damaging strikes where possible. "Mayor La Guardia is fast making a reputation as an industrial conciliator," the *New York Times* wrote approvingly. "One strike after another in this city has been averted through his good offices," often because businesses fearing La Guardia's wrath made concessions. On occasion, the mayor himself would pull both sides into his office and demand that they come to terms, keeping them there for hours, sometimes even turning off the heat to spur concessions. More often than not the parties arrived at an agreement. By bringing labor to the same table with capital, La Guardia forced a presumption for collective bargaining, something that many businesses were still fighting in the early thirties.[55]

Labor unions, he said in a 1934 Labor Day address at the Chicago Exposition, had won the right to collective bargaining "without seeking the destruction of our form of government." It was capital that had leeched the economy into depression. By eliminating inequities the unions were strengthening the capitalist system, and he celebrated their victories. "I see," he told a mass rally of garment trades unions, "you have grown into a mighty and powerful organization of self-respecting workers

. . . with your own health department and clinic and such a fine research department that when you go into negotiations you know more about the business than the employers." By 1937 he was pledging to make New York a "100 percent union city," declaring his unequivocal support of the controversial closed shop. As for those businesses that threatened to leave town, he warned that he would blacklist them in the city.[56]

By placing the bulk of the civil service on the merit system, La Guardia, in one clean act, managed to destroy the basis of Tammany's hegemony, the Irish patronage system. Its elimination opened up city posts to younger, better educated, and often non-Irish New Yorkers. By insisting on an ethnically balanced slate in 1934, La Guardia broke forever the tradition of the straight Green ticket in both parties, and by reaching into the newer ethnic neighborhoods for appointees, he gave these new groups the recognition that they craved.

This spirit of inclusion, of reaching out beyond the Irish, was carried forward after the election into the administration. "I was amused," Charles Burlingham wrote Fiorello, "at the religious character of the Housing Authority." It was an example of exquisite cultural symmetry: Jewish Socialist, Catholic priest, woman social reformer, and housing reform evangelist, all under a WASP chairman. Considerations of ethnic balance played an important part in many La Guardia appointments. "I have a new Aryan for you," the wizened CCB wrote playfully, "a grand young fellow. . . . also I have a fine bunch of Semites. . . . but I forgot you want a Lutheran don't you?" On another occasion, La Guardia's administrative secretary, Stanley Howe, asked him: "Have you thought of _____ in connection with Italian judicial potentialities?" Again and again Burlingham would file his appointment suggestions by religious or ethnic background. Once in a while La Guardia's advisers reminded him not to overdo it: "A Gentile or two on that staff would be a good idea," chided A. A. Berle.[57]

Of the newer immigrant groups, the Jews had achieved quick success, moving out of blue-collar occupations in one generation and pushing their children ahead of them. Many had invested small sums, scrimped from their meager earnings, and done well in business, achieving substantial wealth through real estate, the film industry, garment manufacturing, and commerce. Others made slower progress through their occupations, building unions to improve the conditions of labor and increase their own benefits. Children of these "proletarians of a single generation" flooded the professions, completing a cycle of rapid ethnic mobility perhaps unmatched in modern American history.

So widely was Jewish economic achievement perceived as extraordinary that *Fortune* magazine undertook a close occupational study of Jews to test the notion that this small group had seized control of the entire economy. "There is no basis whatsoever," *Fortune* concluded, "for the suggestion that the Jews monopolize United States business and industry." Written about any other recently arrived immigrant group this would have sounded ridiculous, but the impression that the Jews had indeed somehow managed to capture the American economy was so widely held that the point was worth making. Reviewing the WPA Federal Writers Project study of "The Jews of New York," Harriet Schneiderman addressed a related point. Other Writers Project studies of ethnic groups emphasized economic achievements; the Jewish study concentrated on what the Jews *did not* control. "What it amounts to," Schneiderman complained, "is challenging the right of the Jews to succeed in the economic field. Basically that right is challenged because in the minds of non-Jews there is a subconscious idea that Jews somehow do not belong, and therefore have no right to play important roles."[58]

The Jews were an anomaly. Despite their obvious economic achievements, they felt the least secure of the immigrant groups. The elite universities that played so important a role in educating their children were initiating quotas to keep them out; banks, insurance companies, and Wall Street law firms barred them from employment; by the late 1930s the American Jewish Congress reported that want ads specified non-Jewish applicants in unprecedented numbers; and such movements as Charles Coughlin's Movement for Social Justice, the Ku Klux Klan, the Nazi Bund, and Charles Pelley's White Shirts were carrying on anti-Jewish campaigns dismayingly similar to those of the German Nazis.

Despite, and in a curious way because of, their economic success, Jews felt particularly vulnerable, a vincibility intensified by the victimization of their European coreligionists. For all the talk of their control, discrimination lapped at them, unprovoked violence threatened their neighborhoods, and they could not bring the United States to intervene in behalf of Europe's Jews or grant them generous refuge. This ironic blend of power and peril helped explain the commitment of so well-to-do a community to a politics of moral justice.

The Jews' substantial economic power, together with their numbers of close to 2 million and their heightened political involvement, made them the most potent new political force in the city. "La Guardia," recalled Paul Windels, "was always very conscious of any group influence. Specifically he never forgot the Jewish vote." He involved Jews in his government, articulated their concerns, and shielded them from the sense of isolation.[59]

La Guardia's foes liked to portray him as an opportunist, and his denunciation of Hitler in 1937 as a sop to Jewish voters. They forgot that he had fought American racism and immigration restrictions in Congress and that La Guardia was one of the first to warn Americans about Hitler in 1933. In that year, calling Hitler "a perverted maniac," La Guardia joined the National Conference Against Racial Persecution. "Civil strife is usually a domestic affair," he said, "but when the internal affairs of one country affects the peace of the world, then it is time to protest." He asked Americans to boycott German imports, "let them know that we will no longer do business with them while the present situation is tolerated."[60]

On March 7, 1934, noting that an American citizen who was Jewish had been advised by the American consul that his safety could no longer be assured in Germany, La Guardia called upon the State Department to abrogate its Treaty of Friendship with Germany. Few paid any attention. Mayors were notorious for interfering in State Department business for local consumption. But La Guardia did not forget. More than a year later Paul Kless, a German citizen living in New York City, applied for a masseur's license. Under the Treaty of Friendship the two countries were supposed to recognize each other's professional licenses. Corporation Counsel Windels directed License Commissioner Moss to grant Mr. Kless his license.

Windels had not consulted higher opinion. Informed of the matter, His Honor overruled corporation counsel for issuing another of those technical decisions devoid of intelligent judgment. But what about the international treaty? reporters wanted to know. Elementary! Treaties are based upon reciprocity and "it is well known that American citizens of the Jewish faith have been discriminated against in Germany." Nazi sympathizers jeered and Friends of New Germany threatened that German Americans would see him at the polls, but La Guardia refused to limit himself to running New York City. Protocol had never stopped him before; there was a vacuum in Cordell Hull's State Department and he meant to fill it.[61]

The impact on New York's embattled Jewish community was riveting. Torn between the desire to strike back at Germany and the fear of hurting the chances of European Jewry (and also fearful of attracting too much attention at home), they were pulled in so many different directions that they had become paralyzed before the great hazard confronting their coreligionists. They had no solutions. But in the absence of solutions, the outraged voice of a firm supporter lent them comfort. The fact that he was technically part Jewish had little to do with it. La Guardia did not speak as a Jew. He spoke as a defender of humanity in a diplomatic world in which veiled language and practiced circumlocutions were the norm. In the mannered speech of ambassadors even an international killer was an esteemed gentleman; to La Guardia he was a punk tinhorn murderer, and the Jews loved him for it.

The State Department made its lame apologies, but La Guardia refused to stop grabbing headlines—"MAYOR BANS JEW BAITERS FROM JOBS"—and winning hearts. When a Yiddish speaker ended his address by referring to Stalin, Mussolini, and Hitler as three madmen running the world, the mayor piped up in Yiddish, *"Ich ken die drei menschen, die schlag zoll zei trefen."**[62]

By month's end more than 6000 New York Germans met to denounce La

---

*I know these three men, the Devil take them.

Guardia and promise to send him back to his slime pit come next election. He enjoyed every expletive. Laid up in New York's Mount Sinai Hospital in November of 1935, he nevertheless carried on his economic war with *Der Fuehrer*. For a Triborough underpass in Queens, the Bridge Authority had ordered 500 tons of German sheet steel. La Guardia dictated a curt telegram to Robert Moses advising the Triborough chairman that he did not want "the damned steel." Although the authority was independent and could order its own materials, La Guardia said, he was responsible for the safety of the city's inhabitants, and German steel was, in his learned opinion, unsafe. "I cannot be certain of its safety unless I have had every bit and piece of German steel tested before used. *Verstehen Sie*?" Triborough understood very well. A domestic replacement for the imported steel was found. La Guardia managed to spotlight the boycott and sting the Nazis. It was more than anyone else was doing.[63]

Next he turned to their domestic allies.

Robert Edward Edmonson had scrambled from one small-time journalism position to another without achieving any lasting success, until he discovered the existence of an international conspiracy of "sinister Jewish leadership forces" bent upon undermining the American economy. The Edmonson Economic Service discovered its cause in detailing the dangers of Jewish conspiracy. His findings included such eye-openers as the "esoteric meaning of the six pointed star." It symbolized the half dozen ominous forces in Roosevelt's "Jew Deal" bent upon undermining the United States. The proof was plain. This star appeared in synagogues, on U.S. Army helmets, on dead-letter envelopes that had not been delivered by the post office, and on dollar bills. (La Guardia responded to a letter with similar reasoning by referring his correspondent to "Dr. Karl Bowman. I think he might understand. . . . He is in charge of the psychopathic Department of Bellevue Hospital, 29th Street and Fifth Avenue.") Edmonson's articles listed as prominent members of the Jewish cabal Louis Brandeis, Henry Morgenthau, Frances Perkins, Bernard Baruch, and Fiorello La Guardia, and promoted the formation of "Gentile vigilante groups" to deal with them. By 1936 Edmonson was purveying 5 million pieces of hate mail a year, stirring hostility and threatening to rend the delicate civic bonds that held New York's diverse community together.

Invoking a rarely used mayoral power, La Guardia issued a summons charging Edmonson with malicious criminal libel, informing the district attorney that "unless checked, this type of agitation may incite to a breach of the peace and public order." It was flimsy legal doctrine but La Guardia was a pragmatist. In law, as in politics, he believed that if it worked you used it, and if it didn't you screamed louder. "While generally the wild utterances of a bigot may be ignored, when the diffusion and circulation is organized and the literature itself . . . suggests violence, it is time that those in responsible authority take notice."[64]

Again and again he took notice.

In March 1937, with preparations under way for a New York World's Fair,

La Guardia told the women's division of the American Jewish Congress that the New York World's Fair should include a "Chamber of Horrors" for "that brown shirted fanatic who is now menacing the peace of the world." A furious German government protested to the State Department, and the Nazi press caricatured the New Yorker as the prototypical *untermensch*: of mixed racial background with imperfect features, apelike posture, and Jewish ancestry; a "dirty Talmud Jew," a "well poisoner," "war profiteer," and all-around gangster. (One German press photograph, showing a squat little man patting scantily dressed women on the behind, described La Guardia as a pervert and a pimp. The man turned out to be entertainer Billy Rose testing showgirls and not the more reserved Little Flower.)[65]

Secretary of State Cordell Hull apologized for the mayor's words and complained to the president that La Guardia was making his life difficult. Roosevelt agreed to chastise the errant mayor. Tapping his wrist lightly with two fingers, he told Hull, "We will chastise him like that." Soon after the incident La Guardia came to a White House meeting. As he entered the office, President Roosevelt raised his arm in a Hitler salute. "Heil Fiorello," snapped the president. "Heil Franklin," the mayor called back, and that was all the president said about it.[66]

"There is one great American," said Rabbi Stephen Wise, referring to the crisis of German Jewry, "who lifted up his voice and spoke the truth. His name is Fiorello H. La Guardia." By serving as a powerful spokesman for their interests in these trying times, La Guardia cemented his relationship with New York's Jews. There were New Yorkers who were not happy to see their mayor take such a position. Some had their own reservations about the Jews, others resented what they saw as an unacceptable intrusion into the affairs of a sovereign state by a vote-hungry politician. New Yorkers were used to city hall flaying the British, but this was something new. Commented Johnny Crews, Republican leader of Brooklyn: "As the Chief Executive of a great City he ought to keep his tongue in check. . . . [Critical statements] can only bring discord among friendly nations."

But among Jews there was only gratitude and admiration. The *American Hebrew* awarded La Guardia a medal of honor, proclaiming that "so long as his vigorous cleansing will prevails, New York will be ruled in a wholesome spirit. The influence of such a man is not only through what he says and does, but above all else, through what he is and, thereby, what he radiates." Jews were looking for friends in these years, and La Guardia, speaking their piece, mitigating their sense of isolation, was a friend they considered true and dear.[67]

Italians were equally fond of their La Guardia. They had lionized him in Congress and now gloried in New York's first Italian mayor. Their share in his success went beyond symbolism to the real rewards of easier access and a fair share of city appointments. But La Guardia remained careful with his compatriots. He feared losing their support if he spoke as forthrightly about Italian fascism as he did on German Nazism. And while a case might be made for distinguishing *Il Duce* from the *Fuehrer*, it was a case that La Guardia had no heart for making. He simply kept his distance.

Still, ethnic politics being the thorny thicket that it is, Fiorello got properly nicked. Late in 1935, as tensions between blacks and Italians grew worse over the Ethiopian conflict, La Guardia agreed to attend a Madison Square rally for Italian war relief. Anti-Fascists blazed with indignation. "He can't have one foot in the camp of Mussolini," protested Norman Thomas, "and one foot in the camp of the progressives." Thomas tried to persuade La Guardia to stay home, but the mayor had got his dander up and he wasn't going to be told that he couldn't go to a "meeting of mercy," even if the police had to clear away almost 4000 protesters.

La Guardia walked in to a rousing ovation from 25,000 supporters of Italy, insisting that he did not understand what all the commotion was about. But the words of Justice Salvatore Cotillo conveyed the sense of the meeting. The war between Italy and Ethiopia, said Cotillo, was "for the cause of civilization. . . . a fight to free the backward and untutored people of Africa and at the same time permit Italy's legitimate expansion. . . ." Chided Norman Thomas, "If you said to Justice Cotillo, 'Yes I stole but . . . I needed it . . . and all those other fellows took more . . . and that Negro fellow I stole from—he isn't civilized like I am,' " then he might understand the limits of his own reasoning.[68]

Except for such rare lapses, La Guardia generally struck a balance between principle and political expediency, but his fear of offending the single most valuable group of supporters that he had forced him to be quiet about Mussolini. Some might criticize that "the Mayor has got to stop posing as a great liberal and progressive in this city and backing Mussolini in Europe and keeping the Italians here in back of him." But that was precisely what he intended to do. Norman Thomas might say that "it was not one of his most heroic efforts," but it was pretty good politics.[69]

Like any other politician La Guardia lived on votes. But rather than bargaining for votes with the power brokers in the clubhouse, he based his support in a broad popular coalition of labor, the new ethnics and good-government reformers. If he let down the reformers by failing to stand openly against Mussolini, he did support their program for charter reform, a program dear to the heart of every progressive who believed that it was possible to craft structural changes that would keep the rascals out and make a modern centralized New York from a congeries of tribal sinecures.

The campaign for charter reform was not limited to reformers. Al Smith had said of New York's unwieldy 400,000-word document that it was as big as a telephone book and made just about as much sense. The basic text was a hodgepodge of conflicting, overlapping, and outdated laws. Hundreds of amendments had been sloppily grafted on without weeding out what was irrelevant or contradictory. Its 1700 sections and thousands of statutes included provisions forbidding New Yorkers to lodge their sheep and goats in boardinghouses. A dead horse left in the street was supposed to have a light attached to it after dark, and businesses with more than ten employees were required to have one cuspidor for every two persons. And anyone caught incinerating bones in Manhattan was to be banished.[70]

Reformers wanted the charter updated and streamlined. La Guardia criticized the cumbersome old hulk for making each borough president "a Polish Corridor in himself." But the Charter Commission that he assembled in 1934 was overstocked with twenty-eight commissioners who could not arrive at a consensus. La Guardia's second commission under former solicitor general Thomas Thacher proved more effective. By April 1936 it had completed its proposals, replacing the unwieldy sixty-five-member Board of Aldermen with a City Council of twenty-nine. The proposed charter also strengthened the Board of Estimate and trimmed back borough autonomy, while calling for a powerful City Planning Commission to direct future growth within a master plan.[71]

At first La Guardia was disappointed, calling the proposal a "Caesarian delivery out of the belly of the old charter, with a bit of inscientific plastic surgery applied. What a mess!" But he quickly got over his quibbles. No plebiscite would ratify the centralized powers he coveted. The impediments to power that the new proposal kept were wholesome obstacles, placed there by design to serve as benign barriers. And after getting off a few good lines about the protected "Borough President's Union," La Guardia joined the campaign for the only available new charter.

As the vote neared, he campaigned alongside New York's blue-chip reformers, asserting that "the new Charter represents very substantial gains for the citizens. . . ." He supported the effort to modify Manhattan's dominance and enhance the power of the city's minorities through a complicated system of proportional representation, which replaced district races between paired opposition candidates with a boroughwide slate of candidates. "Proportional representation," declared La Guardia, "is in my judgment, the greatest progressive step for labor and minority groups of all types that has ever been offered to the citizens of New York." Most New Yorkers agreed with their popular mayor and approved the new charter. "You seem to have a way of getting the impossible done," exulted William Chadbourne.[72]

He had promised to throw out the old politics and the old power bases. He was so bent on proving his independence that he would not work with or even assist the Fusion party that had helped elect him. But while they called him a beautiful beech tree under which nothing grew, his benevolent interest nourished a new political coalition. Unlike the old clubhouse where the few were favored and the rest were charmed, La Guardia's constituency was made up of new groups, some of whom had never before achieved power and others that had rejected politics as corrupt and corrupting. Labor, the new immigrants, and the good-government reformers had elected him. He repaid their trust by creating a respect for their legitimate role in New York's politics and courting their support for the next step in his own political career.

3. A Great Shuffling About

L A Guardia had come to view the major political parties as organizations of job hunters who drafted platforms to grab votes so that they could take office and distribute spoils. They stood for nothing, and he refused to give them his respect or loyalty. For years he had spoken of his hopes for a more meaningful party system that was divided along ideological lines, like the European parties that stood or fell on the principles they espoused. During the twenties he had participated in the ill-fated effort to build a Progressive party. Now with the Depression, he discerned a "great shuffling about" of political alignments along precisely those lines that he favored. It was an issue in which he was intensely interested. Indeed, his hopes for future office depended on it.

In May of 1935, 10,000 supporters of Robert La Follette's son and Wisconsin's governor, Phil La Follette, listened to La Guardia call upon President Roosevelt to cast off soulless Democratic politics for a new party of farmers and workers. A week after La Guardia's talk, the United States Supreme Court invalidated the National Industrial Recovery Act, tumbling the foundations of Roosevelt's economic program. "Americans Stunned," ran a London *Daily Express* headline, "Roosevelt's Two Years Work Killed in Twenty Minutes." With the New Deal forced to make a new start, La Guardia repeated his call to Roosevelt for a forthright progressive program instead of the centrist policies of the early New Deal. Confident that a turning point had been reached, an expectant Fiorello announced, "The fight is on—Progressives stand by."[73]

As La Guardia and progressives around the nation stood by, events conspired to give Roosevelt a shove in their direction. The big-business-led Liberty League launched a fierce attack on Roosevelt making obvious that no centrist recovery program would satisfy these conservatives. Meanwhile, splinter movements on both the right and the left were eroding the president's popular support, and the Supreme Court continued to dismantle the New Deal on narrow constitutional grounds, forcing the administration back to the drawing boards for a new recovery program.

Displaying the bold political instinct for which he was so well known, Roosevelt seized control of events by staking out a new recovery policy. If business and laissez faire advocates refused to cooperate in moderate reforms that were designed to shore up the free enterprise system, then he would waste no efforts on placating them. Roosevelt would concentrate on those more concerned with food and rent than laissez faire. He offered a comprehensive new policy, a Second New Deal, that featured the Social Security Act, the Wagner Labor Act, a law to break up giant holding companies, new relief legislation, and a path-breaking "soak the rich" income tax. Over the torrid summer of 1935 a newly energized president drove Congress to pass each measure on his agenda. "Pat Harrison [conservative Democratic chairman of the Senate Finance Committee] is going to be so impressed," Roosevelt chuckled to Raymond Moley, "he'll have kittens on the spot."

Progressives were impressed. Justice Louis Brandeis, the architect of Woodrow Wilson's reform presidency, told friends approvingly that Roosevelt had finally settled on a liberal compass for his administration. And through the banks and the clubs, the brokerage offices, boardrooms, and Park Avenue salons coursed a hot fury at the traitor in the White House. They denounced him as a syphilitic, a liar, and a Bolshevik. "Come along," says one doddering blue blood to his friend in the famous Peter Arno cartoon, "we're going to the Trans Lux to hiss Roosevelt." Having "earned the hatred of entrenched greed," FDR announced in his annual message, he was proud of it and proceeded to open the 1936 presidential campaign with a salvo at "economic royalists" who with "other people's money, were seeking to impose a new industrial dictatorship."[74]

Moving the New Deal into the gap between needy citizens and a decent life, offering a system of pensions for the aged, assistance to the handicapped, a helping hand to unions, relief for the unemployed, and restraints on big business, Roosevelt was shifting precisely in the leftward direction that La Guardia had proposed. Appearing before a capacity crowd in New York's Madison Square Garden, Roosevelt roared, "The forces of organized money are unanimous in their hate for me," then, with the great big Roosevelt teeth glinting in the lights, he grinned in magnificent defiance, "and I welcome their hatred."

To oppose Roosevelt in 1936, the Republicans nominated a moderate conservative, Governor Alfred Landon of Kansas. Landon attracted a passel of rightwing Democrats discomfited by Roosevelt's new activism, including Al Smith. If the New Deal wanted to don the mask of Lenin and Marx, or even Norman Thomas, bellowed the old Tammany wheelhorse, that was okay, "but what I won't stand for is allowing them to march under the banner of Jefferson, Jackson and Cleveland." The old Democratic party, he cried, had been captured by strangers. "Who," the former Happy Warrior demanded, "is Ickes? Who is Wallace? Who is Hopkins, and who in the name of all that is good and holy, is Tugwell, and where did he blow in from?" Al Smith embracing the Liberty League while FDR pounded economic royalists confirmed La Guardia in his hopes for a "great shuffling about" and a new progressive movement.[75]

In September of 1936 progressives from all over the nation came together in Chicago to decide on a presidential candidate. Adolf Berle wrote to his father, who attended the meeting as a New York delegate: "It comes down to two men, Phil La Follette . . . and Fiorello. These two men between them with Sidney Hillman of the labor crowd have got to carry the ball." Others agreed that the New York mayor bore watching. "I came all the way from San Antonio for this meeting," gushed Texas congressman Maury Maverick. "And why not? I'd go half way around the world to sit down in conference with such men as . . . Norris, . . . La Follette and . . . La Guardia." Then, with La Guardia, La Follette, and Hillman carrying the ball, the convention endorsed Roosevelt.[76]

Having decided on a candidate, the progressives went home to build state parties that would translate their dreams into votes come November. In New York the work was carried forward primarily by a handful of garment union leaders: Sidney Hillman, David Dubinsky, Alex Rose, and Luigi Antonini. For years Joseph P. Ryan, president of the International Longshoreman's Union and head of the Central Trades and Labor Council, had delivered labor's vote to Tammany and reaped private rewards. The garment leaders were fed up with being taken for granted by a machine that had scant sympathy for their cause, and a local Democratic party that accepted papal encyclicals as the farthest border of permissible social thought and party policy. They formed the American Labor Party to offer progressive New Yorkers an opportunity to take FDR without Farley and Flynn. Coincidentally, the new party would provide a ticket for their progressive friend in city hall, who at this moment had no party support and a campaign contest coming up in fifteen months.[77]

Both James Farley and Ed Flynn tried to talk FDR out of accepting the ALP nomination. It offered him nothing that he did not already have. Progressives were not about to vote for Landon. On the other hand, if Roosevelt ran on the ALP line, the new party would probably secure enough votes to become a permanent anti-regular force in New York politics. What this party would do is serve La Guardia, not Roosevelt. "I told Mr. Roosevelt," Farley later recalled, "[that La Guardia] was going to use it as a vehicle for his own nomination, because the Republicans weren't going to nominate him and certainly the Democrats wouldn't, and unless he had a party of his own, he might have difficulty getting into the race for mayor." The *New York Times* perceived even larger possibilities: "By a year from now plans are afoot greatly to enlarge [the Labor party] and in fact to make it the nucleus of a national Labor Party. . . . [La Guardia] is looking ahead further than 1937. A Labor party organized throughout the whole country and entering the presidential campaign would have an irresistible attraction for Mayor La Guardia."

Such possibilities bothered Roosevelt far less than Farley and Flynn. Persuaded by La Guardia, Hillman, and Mrs. Roosevelt that the ALP nomination could bring 75,000 new voters to the polls who would otherwise stay home, Roosevelt heeded their advice and accepted the ALP nomination.[78]

Compare La Guardia's behavior in two 1936 campaigns, fusion candidate Newbold Morris's bid for the aldermanic presidency, and Franklin Roosevelt's campaign for reelection. He plodded through the local election, offering Morris little but perfunctory backing. But the presidential contest set his adrenaline pumping. He traveled through the major cities bringing word of the New Deal's importance for urban America. Placing his reedy falsetto at the president's service, he hammered at blinkered conservatives who feared to be fair. It was vintage La Guardia running through his best lines: A nation that revered scientists and inventors for their new knowledge must not reject fresh-thinking politicians as radicals; only a nation open to modern change could meet the challenges of growth; no rule that called for ignoring suffering was worth enforcing; no politician advocating such policies was worth electing.

If La Guardia wanted to be taken seriously, one observer wrote, he had to persuade the nation that he was more than a colorful "little half Jewish wop" from New York. Speaking on behalf of the reform president across the country in the company of Western progressives, La Guardia accomplished that at the same time that he labored to bring about the political realignment so critical to his political future.[79]

———

"As things stand now," Berle wrote to Roosevelt early in 1937, after La Guardia turned down an offer to join the new cabinet, "he has a better than even chance of being [re]elected. Anyhow we would rather be defeated trying to do something we believe in than throwing up the sponge." Berle added his hope that if La Guardia did run, Roosevelt would not help the opposition. "As in 1933 there is nothing in it for you; the alleged Democratic machine includes the very people who tried to cut you. . . . In return they are apparently asking you to give them the City."[80]

La Guardia was going to run for mayor. But on which ticket? He could count on the ALP. They had pledged their support early, with extravagant praise. What precisely such backing might mean remained an open question. The ALP was no substitute for the broad fusion coalition that had brought La Guardia into office in 1933, and then just barely. It did not even represent the bulk of New York's laborers. The Labor party was largely built by the Eastern European Jews who had been exposed to the radical milieu of labor politics overseas and nurtured these sensibilities into their garment unions. It was a paradox, this development of labor power through moderate movements built on radical beliefs, but by the mid-thirties many of the labor leaders from the Jewish needle trades had abandoned an ideology of class in favor of a pragmatic policy of worker self-interest. Party rhetoric drew on the image of toilers united in the name of civic betterment and economic justice, but many of the ALP's members had toiled over books, not sewing machines. "The

409

ALP was not . . . even closely associated with indices of economic class or status,''
writes Kenneth Waltzer in his history of this movement.[81]

Welcome as this support might be, it was too narrowly based on the political
culture of the immigrant garment unions to carry an election. The ALP favored
municipal ownership of electric power and transit, regulation of essential commodities like milk, and as a general principle, ''where private enterprise and capital
have failed to meet public necessities adequately the people must rely upon their
cooperative power, exercised through government agencies.'' This third party that
Mike Quill addressed familiarly as ''Socialists, Communists and refugees from the
Republican and Democratic parties'' could bring together the disaffected, but it
could not carry La Guardia into office unaided.[82]

Republicans who had helped elect him in 1933 were still fuming at his support
of FDR in 1936. Party chiefs Warren Ashmead in Queens, Johnny Crews in Brooklyn, and John Knewitz in the Bronx opposed a second term for the mayor. They
were tired of being denounced for expecting his support and patronage. Republican
partymen, he wrote to a friend, are ''interested only in patronage. . . . Their philosophy of government is no different than that of Tammany Hall.'' Those few for
whom he did shake the plum tree were, in Warren Moscow's words, made to ''jump
through hoops for their tidbits.''[83]

Frederick J. H. Kracke, an old party hand, could have been a big help rounding
up party support, But after Fiorello appointed the former Kings County Republican
leader commissioner of plant and structures, he had ordered the ''Foxy Grandpa''
of Republican politics to surrender his political party post. Belatedly, as Fiorello
turned to courting Republicans, Kracke was sent out on political errands, but
his connections were rusty and the leaders were insisting on ''anybody but La
Guardia.''[84]

Fiorello had only one response to all of this. He was the only Republican
who could defeat Tammany. The message had a certain charm for the newly installed
New York County Republican leader Kenneth F. Simpson. Yale graduate, ''Skull
and Bones'' man, and member in good standing of the social register, the debonair
Simpson inherited a badly battered organization that had won precious few elections
in New York City. Simpson understood that a party so starved should perhaps listen
to its most consistent vote getter, even if he was difficult; besides, he had a grudging
respect for La Guardia's flair and political style.

Simpson and La Guardia met several times to discuss the upcoming election.
On one occasion, after the Republican leader accompanied the mayor to a Lewisohn
Stadium concert, the two men retired to Simpson's graceful home on East Ninety-
first Street for nightcaps and negotiations. When La Guardia declared that he expected the Republican nomination, Simpson suggested that the New Deal's favorite
mayor might feel uncomfortable in the company of real Republicans. Preliminary
sparring gave way to substance, and Simpson did not rule out a nomination. But
the political leader was thinking of a larger strategy. As he later explained to Charles

Burlingham, "Owing to four years of bitter hostility between the Mayor and all elements of the Republican Organization, together with the fear . . . that he will use the Mayoralty . . . to destroy the Republican Party and turn the country over to Moscow, it becomes imperative in my opinion, to give the 'rest of the ticket' a strong Republican flavor and this can only be done by building it up from the bottom."

The Republican leader was prepared to back La Guardia, but only if he could name the rest of the ticket. Simpson could not hope to control La Guardia, but he wanted to use Fiorello's coattails to bring into office loyal Republicans who would help build the party into the future.[85]

The two men said good-night with no deal having been struck. Fiorello could not help but admire Simpson's strategy. But La Guardia wanted Berle for his comptroller, and Simpson would not accept that. Then, before La Guardia made any decision, the wily Simpson removed the choice from La Guardia's hands by announcing Joseph P. McGoldrick as his nominee for comptroller, and Newbold Morris for City Council president (the office created by the new charter to replace the aldermanic presidency), while withholding any endorsement for mayor.[86]

Simpson had played a crafty game well. If La Guardia wanted the Republican nomination he would have to accept Simpson's men on the ticket. But the Republican county head wanted even more. He wanted La Guardia to promise to behave like a proper Republican and stop offering "aid and comfort to our political enemies," but Fiorello refused to be bound. He considered himself a "Lincoln Republican," a progressive who made "Americans of Communists," while the reactionaries were driving needy Americans to radical schemes. "He is an s.o.b.," muttered the Republican boss, "but he is our s.o.b. and we must stick with him for the good of the Party." Now Simpson had to take his s.o.b. and sell him to the rest of what was plainly a reluctant Republican party.

Then, suddenly, the entire premise of La Guardia's campaign for the nomination was shaken by an old nemesis. His strongest point in asking for Republican support was his claim that he was the best they could hope for. One Republican could blast that argument to bits. And it seemed that Robert Moses just might.[87]

———

Robert Moses had changed a good deal from the idealistic urban reformer of the early twenties. The lordly power broker of the thirties still carried a vision of shaping the environment to public needs, but he went about it with an imperiousness that brooked no opposition, that viewed labor as a lowly commodity and affirmed his belief in fixed class and racial distinctions. He charged those who opposed him with the basest motives, of planning insurrection and fomenting disorder. Like a good many individuals far less intelligent than he, Moses was uncomfortable amidst changing ideological currents and was quick to denounce New Dealers, urban

411

planners, and nouveau architects as pinkos, Bolshies, and Commies. Rexford Tugwell he branded the "Planning Red," Frank Lloyd Wright he put down as "regarded in Russia as our greatest builder," and social planners he assailed as the Socialists and revolutionaries whom true Americans must fear. "They teach the teachers. They reach people in high places . . . influence the press. . . ."

Conservatives admired Moses' tough rhetoric and his uncompromising treatment of labor. Here was a tough man who could get things done cheaply, effectively, and forcefully and yet create the largest and most imaginative city structures in the world. And he shared their hatred of Roosevelt to boot.

The disputatious commissioner made this plain in his gratuitous skirmishes with the New Deal, lately refusing to post federal insignias on park work done with WPA funds, calling the signs "cheap, grotesque, . . . political advertising for the administration. . . . I had the same difficulty with Mayor La Guardia," he added, to show that no one put his signature on a Moses park. "He wanted to plaster the parks with signs with his own name in huge letters. I wouldn't let him do it, and I won't permit anyone else to do it." (Yes, he admitted reluctantly, his own name could be found there, but only on "small directional signals.") To some, the noise coming from the Arsenal signaled that Moses was playing with the notion of running for city hall.[88]

His tussle with the mayor over a ferry slip did little to put such fears to rest. With the completion of the Triborough Bridge in the spring of 1936, the Astoria ferry that ran from East Ninetieth Street across the East River to Queens became obsolete. La Guardia agreed to phase out the marine shuttle over the summer and to turn over the Queens ferry slip to Moses' Triborough Authority. Once this was accomplished, Moses, as ever pleading a higher need, demanded the Manhattan docks too. The mayor said he would think about it. One fine summer day, after the ferry pulled off for Queens, a Parks Department demolition crew began demolishing the Manhattan slip with its approaches. "I have a ferryload of people in the middle of the river and Bob Moses is tearing down the dock. What can I do?" shouted a frantic docks commissioner over the phone to Assistant Corporation Counsel Frederick van Pelt Bryan. Knowing Bob Moses, the counsel gave the only reply he could: "Send them back to Queens."

A fuming La Guardia, informed of Moses' latest insurrection, dispatched a command of fifteen police to drive off the demolition crew. Within twenty-four hours the half-dismantled slip was built right back up again, commuters were being ferried across the river under the protective gaze of a squad of patrolmen, and the mayor reported that "all was quiet on the Eastern Front." But La Guardia did not enjoy the foolish public spectacle of dispatching his police to protect city docks from the parks commissioner. At a beach opening a few days later he referred obliquely to the incident and to his rambunctious commissioner, who shot back, "I haven't any patience with people who can't stand up under criticism . . . if you don't like it you ought to get out and do something else."[89]

Moses was the one person who could take the Republican nomination away from La Guardia, and now it seemed that he might want to do just that. He grabbed headlines by denouncing WPA personnel as loafers, chiselers, and ne'er-do-wells. Every WPA project, he remarked, cost double the normal amount to cover for the red tape, the mistakes, and the boondogglers, but when Colonel Brehon Sommervell removed 5000 WPA workers from the parks in a series of economy moves, RM lashed out at the relief czar, calling him another of the "birds of passage. . . . [W]e get a new administrator about every four months." Then he padlocked 142 parks and playgrounds and sat back to wait for the inevitable cry of the mothers.

La Guardia, en route to a Conference of Mayors meeting in Los Angeles, was forced to call out the constabulary again. The parks, he said, belonged to the children, and they had not ordered them closed. The police were ordered to cut the locks and open the parks. Meanwhile, Moses threatened more closings unless his request for larger city allocations was met. By the time the mayor returned to city hall, scores of protesting mothers had papered city hall with petitions and letters. Wrote one, "As a mother of three children I ask you to take your party squabbles out of the parks and give Mr. Moses enough dollars to run the playgrounds." With the Democratic Board of Estimate against him and Moses' mothers creating a storm in the newspapers, La Guardia capitulated, and Parks got its increased budget. "Treachery in our own ranks," scribbled Berle in his diary, convinced that the prickly commissioner was plotting to bring together Republican conservatives with Al Smith's band of Democratic irreconcilables to mount his own campaign for mayor at the least sign of La Guardia's stumbling.[90]

While La Guardia tried to rein in his parks commissioner and put on a show of detachment, Republicans were forming ABL clubs, "Anybody But La Guardia." "His administration," sniffed Bronson Trevor, "is one of the most extravagant the city has ever had. He has done nothing to stop the spread of communism in relief agencies and schools. He has given insufficient police protection during riots and strikes. . . . His policies and appointments have favored the growth of the American Labor Party at the expense of the Republican Party." The rank and file kept coming back to their single most telling reservation—he was not a "true Republican." "Everyone I met who voted for him in 1933," Mrs. Hylda Goldsmith declared, "says *positively* that they will not vote for him again."

The Republican president of a Manhattan real estate firm found the little mayor "too impulsive," too pro-labor, too slow in putting down the Harlem riots, too free with the taxpayers funds. "He will be supported by all radical groups in the city and may feel he has a mandate to carry out some of their plans," feared Lincoln Cromwell. Lawrence Ellman of Pease and Ellman Real Estate, Inc., thought that the problem went deeper than merely spending. "Mr. La Guardia unfortunately has a background which should have been overcome by his residence in New York, but he still has the European continental idea of paternalism deeply embedded in his makeup and what we need is someone who believes in the old fashioned homely principles of economy, thrift and self help.''

There was something faintly un-American about La Guardia, these good Republicans feared. That was why he was so occupied with the needs of other foreigners. His ''evident bid for the Hebrew support in his attack on the head of the German government,'' Lindley Vinton wrote to Goodhue Livingston, just showed his pandering tendencies. Suggested another party regular, ''Mr. La Guardia is unfit to continue in office except as Mayor of a 100% Jewish City.''[91]

On July 29 Paul Windels learned that Kings County Republicans were holding a massive rally to block La Guardia's nomination. He rushed to the meeting and won a delay in the vote. Then he reasoned with Brooklyn boss Johnny Crews, warning the politico, ''You may whip us but you'll split the Republican Party and wreck your own organization in the battle.'' Slowly, point by point, in his dispassionate lawyerly style, Windels made his case. Simpson had already declared his choice. It was a question of going along or splitting the ticket, which would render the massively outnumbered GOP (Democrats enjoyed a more than five-to-one registration advantage) irrelevant. It was La Guardia or nothing at all, and finally Johnny Crews agreed. With the two most important boroughs tied down, La Guardia was assured the Republican nomination. He could breathe easier and ignore Moses.[92]

Much as he resented the process of having his name bandied about by the dear respectables, La Guardia made a show of cool detachment while he had his administration prepare for the campaign by pulling together press clippings and preparing campaign versions of departmental accomplishments. Paul Windels noticed a letup in the rules against patronage, especially for ALP loyalists. ''He . . . play[ed] politics right up to the hilt with them in order to build them up,'' recalled Windels, ''because he looked upon them as a personal ace in the hole. . . .'' City workers received significant salary increases. The *Sun* noted that the workers had at first been promised nothing but pay cuts. ''But economy in a campaign year is —well, it's not.'' Municipal radio station WNYC began offering the mayor's ''nonpartisan'' lessons on scientific government under the theme of ''New York Advancing,'' while election strategists cluttered his outer office to plan the campaign against the Democrats.[93]

For the moment, thoughts of progressive reshuffling and political reconstruction were set aside. La Guardia assumed his campaign mode, struck the necessary deals, and made ready to clobber anyone the Democrats put up against him.

Meanwhile, the Democrats were having trouble agreeing on a candidate to oppose La Guardia. After former police commissioner and business spokesman Grover Whalen's campaign died abornin', the five dueling Democratic county leaders came together briefly to ask Senator Robert F. Wagner to make the race. But Wagner would not run against La Guardia. Four of the leaders then turned to State Supreme Court Justice Jeremiah T. Mahoney, a distinguished-looking judge and a moderate New Dealer with a good record on labor and an outspoken critic of Adolf Hitler. Al Smith, however, refused to back Mahoney. He hated Roosevelt now, and he wanted to humiliate the president by running an anti-New Deal Democrat in his home state.[94]

Something had changed in Smith, Robert Wagner told Harold Ickes. The "big fellows" had taken care of Al, he said. The poor Irish boy who had worked as a fishmonger to keep his family together now lived on Fifth Avenue, and his politics had congealed into pro-business conservatism. Smith persuaded Manhattan Democrats to back New York's Democratic U. S. senator, Dr. Royal S. Copeland, in a primary fight for the nomination. A former health commissioner who had become well known through his medical advice columns and as Randolph Hearst's horse doctor (he would have been a good doctor, quipped Max Lerner, if he had not become a quack senator), Copeland also challenged La Guardia in the Republican primaries.

Carrying Smith's anti-Roosevelt banner, the aging senator denounced the New Deal, Mahoney, La Guardia, the social engineers, and all the newfangled ideas that robbed Americans of the right to fight the Depression bare-handed. Copeland managed to poll some 280,000 votes in favor of limited government, but he was roundly defeated in both primaries, and the November contest narrowed to the moderate judge and the mercurial mayor.[95]

La Guardia adopted an incumbent's strategy, using his office to win headlines and remind New Yorkers how much their town had improved over the past four years. For electoral insurance, he played on the divided loyalties of New Yorkers. "I can out-demagogue any candidate I have met yet," he told Republican women, and proceeded to appeal to the divided soul of the city. "In 1917, when British influence was all powerful in this country," proclaimed the Irish American Non-Partisan Committee for Mayor La Guardia, "when Americans were fighting for the freedom of all small nations except Ireland—when it was dangerous and almost seditious to speak up for Ireland's cause, Congressman Fiorello La Guardia was a champion of that cause and a friend of all who were working for it." Years later Robert Moses, with ample reason to envy the mayor his unerring sense of New Yorkers' riveleted loyalties, recalled the La Guardia touch: "The Mayor adopted a Lincolnesque approach to Harlem, made broad his phylacteries in East New York, emphasized his ancestral links with and unquestionable respect for the Roman Catholic Church, and attended an occasional Church of England service at St. John's Cathedral." Had the city a "solid group of Chinese Mohammedans, he would doubtless have discovered strong ties with them."[96]

It fell to Mahoney to try to pin La Guardia down to a debate on the real issues, but the feckless Democrat proved incapable of defining a set of clear policy differences. Instead, he fell into the trap of fighting the Little Flower on his own terms, with devastating results.

Panting after the Jewish vote, estimated at close to 30 percent of the total, Mahoney attacked La Guardia for waffling on anti-Semitism. It did not help him that the Jewish community had a memory. Then he selected Max J. Schneider, president of the United Synagogues of the Bronx, as his candidate for presidency of the City Council, but this sort of recognition was no longer enough to tie up support. Mahoney next turned to senseless racial pandering. Referring to his law partnership with Robert F. Wagner, he said: "Robert Wagner and I would not have gotten anywhere by ourselves. We saw that the only successful legal firms in New York City were those that had one or more Jewish partners. So we added the eminent attorney N. Taylor Phillips and from that day to this, oh boy! what prosperity we have had." The next step was to smear La Guardia for having failed to reappoint several prominent Jews to office.[97]

In a contest with few policy issues, the right of Nazi sympathizers to march through the city streets became for a while the most explosive question of the campaign. Shortly before the election, members of the German-American Bund applied for a parade permit. La Guardia's feelings about Nazis were well known, but he would not refuse them their constitutional rights. He stood up to both the public outcry and the Mahoney-inspired press barrage by taking a sensible approach, issuing the permit but curtailing the line of march and prohibiting the paraders from wearing their provocative brown-shirted uniforms. Try as he might, Mahoney could not drive a wedge between La Guardia and his Jewish supporters. Charles Burlingham, whom Felix Frankfurter called the "Madame Pompadour, the *Eminence Grise*, the Col. House, and the Jim Farley all rolled into one of the Little Flower," had correctly advised La Guardia early in the campaign: There was no need for concern, "the Jews are yours, for this election. . . ."[98]

Mahoney's problems went deeper than this or that false step. He had no issue. He too supported the New Deal. He too supported relief and the entire menu of progressive services that La Guardia had introduced. Mahoney's own campaign platform demonstrated precisely how extensive was the transformation that La Guardia had worked. Within four years his innovative extensions of municipal responsibility had become the "new normal" that he had advocated, and no serious candidate, least of all the moderate Mahoney, dared attack it. All the judge could do was to promise "me too, only better." But when he criticized expanded budgets and higher taxes and then in the same breath promised to extend city services further, he offered no reason to believe that he could pull it off.[99]

Even his campaign strategy was La Guardian. He competed for votes by appealing to each of New York's many constituencies—Jews, Irish, laborers, Catholics, real estate interests—even rigging up a Trades Union party to contest with the ALP for union votes. Thoughtful critics had decried the "corruption of organized minority pressure groups," the fracturing of the *polis* to satisfy an array of interest claques, each pursuing its own narrow cause. But the thoroughly conventional Mahoney had no more unifying vision to offer.

Without a real hope of securing any major blocs and lacking a central issue, Mahoney turned in desperation to smearing La Guardia as a Communist. Not long before, the Communist party had denounced La Guardia as a "banker's mayor," but the party had recently adopted its "popular front" policy of backing progressives and gave La Guardia its endorsement, from which the mayor tried his best to distance himself. Labeling the ALP an "active adjunct of the Communist party" and La Guardia a "coddler" of radicals, Mahoney charged that under La Guardia the godless elements had converted a happy, placid municipality into "a city of strife, a haven for red agitators." Former police commissioner O'Ryan chimed in by characterizing the mayor as an "emotionally abnormal" individual who had destroyed a "magnificent Police department" in order to satisfy the "red fringe." Mahoney then focused his ire on Commissioner Blanshard, "exposing" him as La Guardia's in-house Bolshie, a "notorious red . . . head of the Mayor's OGPU." Right there in his hand, Mahoney held yellowing documents more than a decade old that "implicated" the socialist reformer in radical politics![100]

It didn't work. La Guardia refused to be riled.

"I was talking to [a blue-chipper] the other day," he told an audience of Republican Women,

> and he was telling me, "Mayor, you know, I like some of the things that you do but, on the other hand we can't tolerate some of your views."
>
> Of course I was talking to a great big financier, so I said, "You big bum! Didn't you tell me along in '34 that you had a half million dollars of city securities?"
>
> He said, "Sure I did."
>
> "Well," I said, "what were they quoted at the time?"
>
> "Oh," he said, "they were down below 77."
>
> I said, "What are they now?"
>
> "They are running between 110 and 116."[101]

Early in the campaign Adolf Berle had asked President Roosevelt not to take sides in the coming election. FDR did better than that. He liked La Guardia, respected the job he had done in New York, and recalled his loyal service in the 1936 presidential contest. While Roosevelt's own liege, James Farley, worked furiously for La Guardia's defeat, the president adopted a stance of benevolent neutrality. With Mahoney in need of every bit of public attention, FDR brought

La Guardia to the White House for well-publicized discussions, highlighting Fiorello's importance as a national urban spokesman. Farley recalled that he "used to argue with [Roosevelt] about La Guardia all the time," but the president just seemed comfortable with keeping the New Deal's favorite city in La Guardia's capable hands.

Shortly before the election Harold Ickes told Roosevelt that La Guardia had invited him to New York to dedicate a federally assisted municipal sewage plant. If Ickes went he would be expected to bring some kind words with him. Should he go? Roosevelt's response surprised Ickes. The president seemed eager for him to go, despite the tantrums he could expect from Farley. A week before the election, the interior secretary appeared alongside the mayor and praised his leadership, adding, "I may say that I have always found it difficult to say no to your eloquent and persuasive mayor." At a cabinet meeting just a few days later, Farley accused Roosevelt of supporting La Guardia "against the Democratic nominee in the City of New York."[102]

Who could blame Farley for his frustration? The hapless Mahoney was attacking La Guardia as a myth, while the mayor pointed to the $60 million Triborough Bridge, slum clearance projects for 3000 families, 18 miles of new subways, 235 new playgrounds, a drop of 38 percent in street accidents, a 40 percent decline in fire-related losses, city bonds at par or better, and much of this paid for with federal funds.

Enemies and friends agreed that the flamboyant Flower, who had brought New Yorkers bread and circuses, was the most popular mayor in recent history. The arch-Republican *Herald Tribune* and the communist *Daily Worker* both lauded him as the best. Even The *Sun*'s George Ritchie was forced to admit that "the great masses of the citizenry . . . love him," while the *New Republic* explained why. "New York's 440,000 Italians love him because he is one of them. The 1,765,000 Jews love him for his criticism of Hitler. Half a dozen other groups have an affection for him because he speaks their languages. . . . In his incessant public activity, his ease before the camera and his ability to say the right thing 99 percent of the time, he had been matched by no one since the first Theodore Roosevelt." A *New York Post* reporter assigned to Mahoney during the campaign switched to covering La Guardia for one night, and he understood why Mahoney hadn't a prayer: "After the political prose of Jeremiah Mahoney, Fiorello La Guardia gives the feeling of poetry. He does things so smoothly. His entrance at Madison Square Garden last night was a calculated triumph. Like a flowing black spot he stepped down the long aisle to the pulsing of the Marine's Hymn played by 20 pieces. . . . The Garden became bedlam. His gestures had the effect of poetry; a sweep of the forearm dismissing with total contempt the world of the regular politician. . . ."[103]

The campaign had by this time taken on a larger dimension. "Do not forget one thing," James G. Gerard, Mahoney's campaign manager, admonished the president. "If La Guardia wins he will be a candidate for President and carefully coached . . . may prove a formidable contender.'' As the campaign was drawing to a close, La Guardia showed Paul Windels a letter from Roosevelt that could be used as an endorsement. Should he release it? Windels thought no, and La Guardia agreed. He wanted victory with few obligations, and presidents with IOUs, no matter how late they join the bandwagon, are not so easily dismissed as a pack of fusionists.[104]

With the ALP providing the balance of his voting strength, La Guardia went on to a resounding triumph, smashing the tradition of single-term reform. He drew 1,344,016 votes to Mahoney's 889,591, carrying most of his ticket with him. The night after the election cheering crowds gathered before his home, and a procession passed by with ''pallbearers'' carrying a long black-draped box marked ''Tammany Rests in Peace.''

Before ten o'clock that night the president called with his congratulations, wasting no time, Berle thought, because ''he proposes to annex this if he can.'' The great shuffling about that La Guardia had predicted had brought him and the president closer than ever before; it also encouraged La Guardia in his true ambition.[105]

He wanted to follow Roosevelt into the White House.

CHAPTER 12

The Wider Field

1. Ambition's Tempering Forge

ADOLF Berle interpreted La Guardia's overwhelming victory as "a political revolution," signaling an interest in more than cleaning house. The people had reelected the smart, tough, incorruptible Fiorello La Guardia because they wanted real reform, and for the long haul. "Congratulations," beamed First Mother Sara Roosevelt at a private celebration of the mayor's triumph held in the president's East Sixty-ninth Street town house, "I knew your victory was assured long before election. Nevertheless I am pleased that you have won." Her son, reduced to a postelection endorsement by the crafty mayor, was equally gracious and friendly.

For the second time La Guardia won the opportunity to provide New York with a modern urban government, while he, in Robert Moses' wonderfully eclectic portrait, was

> . . . rushing to fires, reading the comics, leading the band, helping Grover Whalen to greet trained seals fresh from swimming the English Channel, jeering at stuffy tycoons knee deep in soft rugs in Park and Fifth Avenue clubs or at "tinhorns" in the less elegant bistros, crucifying a market inspector for accepting a cheap necktie from a pushcart peddler, acting as a committing magistrate to pillory a welfare inspector who did a favor for somebody on relief . . . firing a faithful if sometimes sappy secretary for getting tight, driving the gay hurdy gurdies from the streets, . . . [and] proposing with impish glee to hang the wet wash in the back of Gracie Mansion where everyone . . . could see the short and simple flannels of the ruling family. . . .[1]

420

New Yorkers considered him, on balance, not merely a good but a spectacularly great mayor. Plain folk who never dreamed of writing to a "politician" took
out their pencils and lined pads and poured their hearts out to him, convinced that
his sympathy was genuine, without ulterior purpose. Their crudely phrased letters
shared intimate concerns, begged for help, or simply related how proud he made
them and how much they trusted him. Simple citizens cut out stories about him
and pressed them in velvet-bound books next to those of Franklin Roosevelt as they
anticipated his larger destiny.

New York Times reporter S. J. Woolf had spent a full day with Fiorello when
he first came into office in 1934. Four years later he began a follow-up piece by
marveling at the undiminished pace. The orders were still crisp, the sense of work
to be accomplished still urgent, the energy churning. As they rode around the city
taking inventory of the changes that La Guardia had wrought, the mayoral limousine
broke down. It was all Fiorello could do to restrain himself from getting out to
help two men push the crippled auto to a service station.

What *had* changed was the attitude of the common people toward their city.
Citizens no longer dismissed it as an employment bureau for corrupt politicians.
They looked to it as a source of help, a soft ally in hard times. For two weeks
Brooklyn WPA worker Robert Lee had not been paid. The grocer was owed $12
and there was no food in his winter-frosted apartment, not even a drop of milk for
the baby. Mrs. Lee was frantic with concern for her family. Black men like her
husband were having a particularly hard time finding work. She turned to the only
place she knew: "Will you please help me, I have no food for my children," she
pleaded to La Guardia. "Tomorrow is Christmas, and we are starving." The mayor
sent a food package for which he paid personally. "There is a Santa Claus,"
beamed the oldest child.[2]

When he learned that black boxing great "Boston Tar Baby" Sam Langford
had recently been struck by an automobile on a Harlem street, La Guardia invited
him downtown. At forty-nine years of age the former ring champion was destitute
and almost blind. He still wore the coat in which he had been taken to the hospital,
joking that the doctors couldn't do much for the ragged garment. The mayor
promised him a job. When it turned out that the job could not begin for two weeks,
FH quietly laid out two weeks' salary for Langford from his own pocket.[3]

He took as much pleasure tweaking the privileged as he did helping the poor.
A. G. Newmeyer, a Hearst newspaper executive, wrote the mayor one of those
hearty letters that drop a few names, deliver regards from a mutual friend, and ask
for a special favor: His chauffeur would often take the Mrs. shopping in mid-
Manhattan and then have a hell of a time finding parking space for the limousine.
Would the mayor be so kind as to provide a "parking courtesy card," of the sort
that the Newmeyers received in other cities? "It would facilitate things a bit" if
the mayor would be a good chap and help out. Newmeyer received back a brisk

note: "Mrs. La Guardia, Mrs. Vanderbilt and Mrs. O'Flaherty" and their chauffeurs all receive equal privileges in this administration. The only courtesy card available was for rolling baby carriages through city playgrounds. "How many such cards can I send you?"[4]

He had won election twice, dispelling the reform jinx. But would the mayoralty, traditional graveyard of political ambitions, prevent him from ever becoming senator, governor, or even president? The summer before, William Allen White, piqued by a hidebound Republican leadership, suggested that the Grand Old Party could do worse than nominate New York's swart Italian mayor for president. White's suggestion was no longer being dismissed as the odd ramblings of a midwest editor in high dudgeon. "Mayor La Guardia," pronounced the New York Times, "has become an outstanding national figure." Another article by columnist William Conklin gushed, "He has accomplished the seemingly impossible in the past, and there is no telling what he might accomplish in the future." News of his decisive mayoral victory was carried in Rome, Berlin, and London. Everyone seemed interested in the Little Flower's blooming possibilities.[5]

As a young man he had aspired to make a difference. He had. The question now was how much of a difference did he want to make? He enjoyed the crowds, the competition, the decisions and power of politics. No one attacked problems with more gusto. Some politicians savored the big issues and the high moments; La Guardia took satisfaction out of tackling the nuts and bolts as well as the blueprints. He would lock himself into a room with budget estimates and slash away for days, emerging only for food and rest. The people's work. All day long he scampered from hearings to openings, to office meetings, dropping papers and notes into his black "diplomatic pouch." At night when he left city hall, he carried it with him to complete the day's work undisturbed in his East Harlem apartment. "Nature," Rexford Guy Tugwell once said, "made politicians love what politicians have to do, just as she made mothers love the caring of children." When a citizen carped about the mayor's rumpled appearance, La Guardia did not merely ignore the taunt. He replied with pride that the mayor of New York was just too busy to be fashionable.[6]

The political fanfare that converted American politics from the purposeful work of anonymous men into the spotlighted activity of political stars he loved most of all. He thrived on leading the fire department band; inspecting underground tunnels in a sandhog uniform; stepping off the pitching rubber in Yankee stadium, cap photogenically askew, to fire a high hard one at the catcher; biting into a hot dog with a circle of laughing children about him; looking endearingly quizzical in academic robes while accepting an honorary degree. Daffy as he might appear, these were his moments of communion with New Yorkers. What made all of this interesting was not that a middle-aged man could carry on, but how far he was willing to go to put New Yorkers at ease with his power. No regular guy like this one, citizens were to conclude from this, could be suspected of overweening ambition.

Beneath the impish character of the news pictures, however, was the Italian bandmaster's abbreviated son still fighting for approval as a full-fledged, full-sized American. Again and again he would tell acquaintances that no man with his name could aspire to higher office. And the more he said it, the less he accepted it. He had never accepted limits on his personal ambition before, and the political profession itself impelled him forward. Which politician worth his campaign manager wants anything but the next highest office? Which successful politician does not entertain thoughts of being president? Radical, insurgent, or simply ornery La Guardia may have been, but his goals were as conventional as those of any other member of the guild. In him too the impatient notion that the best position was the one you did not yet hold made the future exciting. Reelection brought him a fresh realization. He wanted to be president.

Politics is a curious profession, demanding an image of mature reasonableness, while keeping its men and women playing at sport, competing for adulation and acceptance. Little wonder so much of the child prevails in these perennial contestants, and so much of the uncertainty of childhood. Politics is one of the few professions where a man at fifty-five still thinks of what he wants to *be* in four years. For Fiorello, it all depended on the winds. If he got in front of a good one he could end up president: if a third party developed, if Roosevelt kept to tradition and did not run again, if circumstances made Americans forget that short politicians of Italian ancestry who came from New York City were not your stock-in-trade presidential timber. Fate now held him in suspension, uncertain of what his next job would be. And as with many who carry a young man's interest into later years, his mature years proved more turbulent for it.

Mentally he was in top form. The swift, agile, retentive, issue-oriented mind still skimmed reports rapidly, grasped the basics of abstract issues, and made clean judgments with no looking back; a good, strong, pragmatic politician's mind, drawing on humane social insights and a righteous passion for relieving suffering. While these instincts did not cohere into an orderly framework, they were enough of a ''political philosophy'' to hang a political career on, even a presidency. In fact, it passed for brilliance in a nation whose political tradition lacked the old Hebrews' reverence for scholar statesmen. (Often as not, the few scholars who did fall into politics found that their cerebral style hampered the hasty action that Americans demanded from their executives.)

Physically, his deceptively delicate constitution did not escape the strain of his overwork. ''The fellow . . . interested in his job,'' he liked to say, ''is on a continual vacation. Do commanding officers take vacation during war? How can I?'' But rheumatism, arthritis, kidney ailments, mild diabetes, and his old war injuries frequently acted up. His doctor, George Baehr, repeatedly warned Fiorello to vacation *before* he became exhausted. It did little good. Like so much else, he saw illness as something to be overcome, and he took a perverse pride in neglecting his health. "I agree with what you say," he wrote to a correspondent who warned that he must slow down, "but I really do not think that there is anything I can do about it."[7]

He was still proving his courage. When a ticking suitcase was found in Pennsylvania Station, the mayor positioned himself recklessly close to the bomb crew working on the suspicious baggage. Dr. John White, responding to an emergency call, found a man gruesomely pinned by a subway car. All around were frozen except a boxy man in a wide-brimmed Stetson shouting that they must amputate. It was the mayor. He was right. "Brains, nerve and energy make men," the impressed doctor wrote La Guardia. "This event proves you have all three." When, just before Christmas of 1938, a deranged man attacked him from behind, La Guardia instinctively grabbed his attacker and began pummeling him. He had to be dragged off the younger and larger man. Well into his fifties, Fiorello was still reacting with his guts first, refusing to flinch, swinging at men much bigger than he. "I cannot rid myself of the notion that the Mayor is supposed to be on the spot in time of trouble, to do what he can," he explained to a friend inquiring why he continued to hasten to all emergencies. It was all part of the credo that he had learned out west as a boy. You did not complain about pain, you did not give in to fear, you carried on like a man.[8]

In the winter of 1935 an attack of sciatica forced him into Mount Sinai Hospital for a week (but only after the budget had been completed), and it would not be his last visit. Sometimes even he admitted to the toll that his work was taking. "This job has made changes in me," La Guardia told William Conklin. "It has aged me, and I think that every year a man puts into this office takes five years off his life." But a man did not give in to weakness. Harold Ickes remarked just before the 1937 election that La Guardia was close to exhaustion but working like a horse. All polls predicted a landslide victory; why was he campaigning so hard? Because, the mayor said, having been an underdog so long he did not know how to run differently.

Or to relax. Adolf Berle once brought Tennessee Valley Authority administrator David Lilienthal to the mayor's office for a visit. The federal official found there a man "terribly high strung and on edge—no repose whatsoever." By all rules his energy should have flagged. In that inverse relation marking age, his hair was thinning and his waist thickening. His jowls grew more prominent and his eyes receded deeper into the huge head. But he did not allow his vigor to decline.[9]

He ran on adrenaline much of the time. With age, his impatient nature became even more brittle, more short-tempered, less considerate not only of himself but of those around him. Journalists seeking a simple key attributed his fire to a Latin temperament. Not at all. The bubbling impatience, the ambition to see results and see them right, to be rid of evil and inefficiency were quintessentially American. Who but a western progressive would, after a generation in politics, still chafe at the bad guys. When he could—and at times he could magnificently—bend his impatience to the service of his goals, he put on one of the best performances in American politics. But no matter how often he told friends that it was all a show, that he did not lose his temper unless he had planned to, there was no kidding anybody. His intensity was on his sleeve, like the ambition that would keep him forever one job away from his goal.

Fiorello had already won two elections in New York; he was thinking of bigger things. Even before the votes had been counted in 1937, La Guardia was discussing higher office, including the governorship and the vice presidency, with Adolf Berle. A week after his smashing victory in New York, the secretary of the interior suggested at a press conference that if Franklin Roosevelt did not run in 1940, Fiorello La Guardia would make a fine leader. Harold Ickes was not alone. A year-end *Fortune* magazine survey showed that many Americans, intrigued by the successful urban politician from the East, were prepared to vote for him in 1940.[10]

The message found its medium in a national press weary of speculating about whether or not FDR would run again. La Guardia's relationship with city hall reporters was often prickly, as it must be for any executive who finds close scrutiny suffocating and abhors criticism, but the upper echelons of the press guild, the editorial writers and feature columnists, were taken with the colorful political figure. After complimenting Fiorello's design of a gown for little Eleanor Flanigan to wear as she christened a fireboat, the city's newspaper of record waxed eloquent on the qualities of the reelected burgomeister. "What a man! Today the Pol Poiret of Baghdad-on-the-Hudson. Tomorrow something else. Who but our good caliph can bust a bronc. . . . Art critic, lawyer, soldier, flyer, steam shovel operator, assistant to surgeons, statesman—and none of it done with mirrors, either, but easily, gracefully and in five languages if necessary." The *Times* went on to laud the mayor's steady leadership, his persistence and flexibility. If the rumors of his *drang nach* Washington proved true, concluded the charmed editors, then "New York will lose more than his prismatic color. But the country will recognize what a vigorous catalyst the Latin temperament becomes in the sturdy fiber of Americanism." Most local politicians were buried before a respectable newspaper would run so enchanted a eulogy.[11]

By 1938 La Guardia reportage had become a cottage industry. Journals of opinion, newsmagazines, and newspapers from all over the country offered quick-study profiles of the political maverick who had turned Tammany out and New York around. Journalists who asked for interviews were challenged to spend the day, if they had the stamina. Invariably they left charmed. He dazzled with his energy and frenetic pace; the variously coded buzzer buttons on his desk; the telephone that wasn't (it wasted too much time, he would tell interviewers); the mayoral chariot rigged with a desk, police radio, and pistol; his shirtsleeve lunches. They were used to politicians who enjoyed their perquisites and watched their tongues; he gave them a man of simple tastes, obsessed with work and speaking in a pungent idiom. They took this for candor and honesty. He dazzled them so that they forgot to ask their questions.

They just took notes on what he did and wrote glowing pieces on the new star rising on the Hudson. "He is a heavy duty mechanism," wrote political scientist Karl Shriftsgiesser for the *Atlantic Monthly*, "whirring away at a tremendous rate of speed, every cylinder hitting." "The busiest man in the world," began the opening paragraph of a *Movie and Radio Guide* article. William Allen White dubbed him the "Lincoln of the Ghetto." *Newsweek* ran his face on its cover. So did *Time*. The *New York Times Magazine* announced in bold headlines, "The Mayor Has Become a National Figure by His Vigorous Handling of Local Affairs." "At work," stated another piece, "he is one of the sights of the City." Yet another *New York Times Magazine* number continued the image of a man with only selfless service on his mind. "What's the next appointment on your calendar?" asks the interviewer of the man already described as a "marvel . . . [who] every waking minute of every day . . . is busy." Fiorello, bone-weary, but his political instincts perfectly sharp, answers that he is going home to sleep. "And how can I sleep? I dream! But my dreams rest me. Sometimes I see the City of Tomorrow, with marvelous parks and buildings, finer hospitals, safer and more beautiful streets, better schools, more playgrounds, more swimming pools, greater markets. There are fewer prisons too, because in the city of tomorrow there will be less incentive to crime. I see a city with no slums and little poverty. It will be a reality some day."[12]

American Magazine, Current History, Esquire, the *New Yorker, Collier's*, and the *Yale Review* all published their own features on the mayor, all very flattering, emphasizing the same points about his melting-pot background, western youth, hatred of chiselers, and congressional service to underdog America; many credited him with supporting the New Deal before there was such a term, and all were impressed with the amount of work he squeezed out of his abbreviated frame. The dozen or so profiles that appeared were all similar. Not one made a stab at criticism or probing analysis, a testament to La Guardia's mastery over the interview process as much as to his fresh political personality. They spoke of his integrity and his parks, but not one article weighed the implications of his modernization agenda or its cost. One way or another they all posed the question that was on his mind: Could the mayoralty contain this man?

Yale University awarded him an honorary degree. "The mayor is an expert in nerves" proclaimed the citation.

He knows how to explode them to the public advantage, how to control them. Coming in contact not only with nervous politicians but also with politicians who have nerve, he rides in the whirlwind and directs the storm. He recognizes the familiar symptoms of every variety of crank and extremist, and steers a safe course between Scylla and Charybdis, aided by his hereditary knowledge of the channel. He has taken democracy away from the politicians and restored it to the people.

The citation went on to laud every aspect of La Guardia's leadership, courage, and commitment to his constituents. "YOU WILL FROM NOW ON MAKE GREAT PROGRESS BY DEGREES," wired a less than cryptic Samuel Seabury. Charles Burlingham telegraphed simply: "YOU CAN'T IMAGINE HOW HAPPY YALE HAS MADE ME TODAY." Not nearly as happy as it made the Italian bandleader's son with the long last name. If the Ivy League could offer him a degree with a 500-word adulation, perhaps the presidency was possible.[13]

But first he had to be mayor.

In addition to electing the first fusion administration in New York history to succeed itself, the voters had adopted a new charter. The old aldermen were replaced with a City Council based on proportional representation. The complicated process elected the most diverse, best educated, and least controlled council in New York history. Here on one side sits Joseph Clark Baldwin, Jr., impeccably credentialed Harvard man, with a Park Avenue address and membership in the Racquet and Tennis Club. Directly behind him is the scholarly manager of the *Jewish Daily Forward*, Baruch Charney Vladeck, whose liberal politics were annealed in the Czar's Russian prisons and emerged on the streets of the Lower East Side as a benign socialism. To his side is the council's only woman member, redoubtable reform battle-ax Genevieve Earle, waving her cigarette in its long holder, insisting on better government. Union executive, newspaper reporter, real estate executive, Yale man, Sicilian-born labor organizer, Cambridge University graduate, boilermaker, Tammany sinecurist, these and their like made the council New York's most representatively diverse voice in history. The debates were often raw with the emotion of the streets, and New Yorkers were often shocked by their crudeness. It remained to be seen if the new council could govern. "It is a good show," remarked the *New York Times*, adding hopefully, "it may be constructive."

To free the mayor from burdensome detail, the charter created the office of deputy mayor. La Guardia was not the sort to delegate power, however, and before long his avuncular deputy, Henry H. Curran (who in 1921 had defeated La Guardia for the Republican mayoral nomination), was reduced to silly humor in his frustration with his ever-declining responsibilities. Even Fiorello twitted Curran to be more dignified: "Why do you do it? I understand the attempt to bring levity and humor . . . but remember there are several millions in New York who do not understand."[14]

427

The charter also established a City Planning Commission to shape the long-range development of the city, its power second only to the mayor's. La Guardia intended to make this commission the keystone of his new administration and he proceeded to stock it with excellent appointees. To chair the commission he thought first of his most effective planner and builder, Robert Moses. RM was willing, but only if he was granted absolute control over the commission and its staff. It was an offer La Guardia wanted to refuse, and Burlingham steeled his resolve: "I have my doubts," confided CCB, "about his ability to look ahead 50 years as Andrew H. Green, who was the begetter of not only Central Park, but all the Bronx parks, did." Finally, FH decided against giving so powerful an office to a man whose ambition dwarfed even his own. Adolf Berle took the helm for an interim period. When Berle left to accept a post as assistant secretary of state, FDR brain truster Rexford G. Tugwell took over the chairmanship.[15]

Other new appointments were equally good. Investigations Commissioner Blanshard was replaced by the brilliant and relentless hotshot of the Thomas Dewey prosecution team, thirty-two-year-old William Herlands. Paul Kern, La Guardia's gifted protégé, was promoted to the head of the Civil Service Commission, and Paul Windels left the job of corporation counsel in William Chanler's capable hands. (Before accepting his appointment, Chanler insisted that Fiorello see a sharp anti-La Guardia letter he had written on behalf of Joe McKee in the 1933 election. He wanted no surprises from La Guardia later. The mayor read it, commenting, "Damn good political letter," and appointed him.) But there was a new wrinkle in the second La Guardia administration. When his top advisers recommended candidates, they no longer noted objective qualities alone. "He served us loyally in the campaign" now appeared more often in the recommendations submitted to La Guardia for his consideration. This time he was looking for a team that would work with and *for* him. With his new appointments he sought to control such semi-independent agencies as the Transit Commission, the Board of Education, the Housing Authority, and the courts. He also campaigned in Albany for greater municipal autonomy, for New York's right to raise funds without being forced to beg permission from the state legislature.[16]

This last issue involved him in another of his imbroglios with Governor Lehman. After the city passed a 3 percent sales tax on utilities, the state legislature superseded 2 percent of the tax with its own impost. Fiorello huffed at the outrage of the state "carrying off bodily" money intended for city relief. Lehman shot back that the mayor's reasoning was as faulty as his administration of city taxes. Were both carried out properly, there would be no shortage. "I wrote a letter to a statesman," La Guardia retorted, "and received a reply from a politician." The mayor asked the City Council to pass a list of nuisance taxes, "Lehman taxes," he told the reporters, "not La Guardia taxes." He was becoming impatient with the periodic struggles that were a regular part of a big-city mayor's life.[17]

His clash with Lehman could be attributed to the pressures of state-city politics; his guillotining of the administration of the New York Housing Authority appeared more unusual. Franklin Roosevelt had chosen Nathan Straus, who had written a special study on European public housing for La Guardia in 1935, to head the Federal Housing Administration. Shortly after assuming office, Straus called a national conference of housing administrators to develop a comprehensive housing policy and placed all pending applications, including those submitted by New York, on hold. The idea of a new round of talks infuriated La Guardia. "For ten years," the Little Flower howled, "we have had nothing but conferences. The law is clear. . . . We are long past this stage. The thing to do is get architects and engineers" and start building houses, not plans. The homeless needed action, not "stargazing conferences, [and] silly discussions on definitions." The mayor ordered NYCHA to ignore the invitation and boycott the Washington housing conference.

Irate at La Guardia's interference, NYCHA counsel Charles Abrams resigned in protest. When chairman Langdon Post agreed to send a delegation to a follow-up conference, La Guardia accepted his resignation too. Post lamely pointed out that he had not offered it and that he intended to hold the office until a replacement was appointed. "Well . . . ," said La Guardia, turning to his secretary, "[Lester] Stone raise your right hand," and swore him in as temporary chairman. The chairman of an authority, which is a quasi-independent body, the mayor was reminded, is supposed to be selected by its members. La Guardia's response was a warning to the remaining members that they better not oppose him.[18]

To those who did not understand the depth of La Guardia's disaffection with unrealistic reform schemes, the firing of Langdon Post and the high-handed treatment of the authority seemed bizarre. The confrontation, however, had its roots in a more tangled problem than the Straus contretemps. Indeed, the mayor quickly patched up his relationship with Straus and got housing back on track, but he held Post responsible for bringing New York to the brink of a crisis that he could not hope to solve.

When Post's Tenement House Commission began condemning large tracts of slum property, the city still had an excess of apartments. Reformers, settlement houses, community groups all contributed to a clearance mania, each pushing for the demolition of its own favorite hovel. In Depression times, fewer people were getting married, and those who were often doubled up with their families. But after a few years of razing and boarding up tenements, and the feverish clearance activity attending Robert Moses' many construction projects, the city's low-rent housing stock was reduced by the tens of thousands. By 1937 New York faced imminent

429

housing shortages, as improved times placed more renters on the market and the influx of blacks from the South and the West Indies further reduced low-rental vacancies. In 1933 80 percent of New York's low-rent housing had been occupied; by the end of the decade the figure stood at 97 percent.[19]

La Guardia wanted to modify slum demolitions and other policies that reduced the city's housing stock, but Post paid this situation little heed. In the past, banks and other large property-holders had warded off new safety requirements by threatening to board up their old tenements, and Post was determined not to give in to such threats. In the winter of 1936 he proceeded with a set of tough new guidelines requiring owners to upgrade their tenements immediately. Precisely as they had promised, the major realty holders issued thousands of dispossess notices rather than comply with the expensive new requirements. Only a frantic program of public housing construction could avoid a disastrous shortage. Post lobbied the president, tried to arouse the public, and pressured the mayor, expecting that these steps would produce the new housing that was needed.

Several times before, La Guardia had warned Post not to overdo the "ballyhoo and dramatics, the situation is too critical for anything like that." In December 1936 NYCHA counsel Charles Abrams orchestrated a series of hearings, focusing on the greed of landlords. In the circumstances the result was predictable: a public outcry against the realty interests and a demand that they comply with tough new tenement laws or close down. La Guardia was taken aback by the rabble-rousing. It was not possible to move families "into briefs, court decisions, or even blueprints," or even public outrage. And yet NYCHA seemed content to raise hell rather than houses. The situation demanded prudence and some compromise until there was enough new housing to accommodate the families that would be displaced by the new policy. But Post's stubborn insistence on implementing the new codes pushed the administration into a cul-de-sac.[20]

With a comprehensive public housing program out of the question and an apartment shortage looming, the administration was reduced to backing off from its threats. La Guardia finally came out for a compromise, the same sort of exemption from code enforcement that the realty interests had won time and again in the past. Tenant groups, whose expectations had been raised by Post, reacted with bitterness and disappointment. This was the kind of predicament that La Guardia expected intelligent commissioners to avoid.

By February, correspondence from the mayor no longer began with a friendly "My dear Langdon." It was now "Dear Sir:" and by the following month La Guardia was ordering Post not to "interfere in this matter," while he worked out the details of a compromise agreement. In September 1937, several weeks before the mayoral election, Post managed to get into more hot water by calling a housing conference in Washington that competed with one arranged by Harold Ickes. "I have no use for Post," confided Interior's curmudgeon. "I consider him a stuffed shirt without any stuffing." Ickes's letter to La Guardia, who could not be at the federal conference, was of an entirely different tone: "I am sorry that you cannot come . . . but you know that you can always sit down at my desk and tell me in your own eloquent and forceful way what to do and what not to do."[21]

Between a commissioner whom he considered increasingly unrealistic and his excellent friends in Washington, La Guardia chose to sack Post. He had little tolerance for reformers pushing their own agenda at his expense. Attendance at the Straus conference was an irritant. He had supported Straus's appointment and he just wanted to get moving on New York's applications. FH used the disagreement over the Washington conference to get rid of Post and to make the point that his administrators were entitled only to one opinion in this administration, La Guardia's.[22]

Post's departure signaled a new emphasis on practical politics in La Guardia's second term. Easing himself away from the warm campaign language of caring, dreaming, and hoping, La Guardia steered toward the political mainstream and plans that placed a priority on what was reasonable.

He turned for Post's successor to the pool of realistic administrative types that he now favored over the crusading visionaries. Housing, he said, was too important to leave to the reformers; it had become a "big business proposition." He suggested that John D. Rockefeller, Jr., take the NYCHA chairmanship, and when that did not work out he appointed Alfred Rheinstein, a noted city builder, to the position. After paying his respects to Post and his band of dreamers, the new commissioner dismissed their work as primarily "a propaganda bureau" for dangerous expectations. "The enthusiasm they have engendered, has . . . outstripped their leadership. . . . People are now hoping that the slums will crumble like a lump of sugar in a spoonful of coffee, and in their place will arise a sort of magical Maxfield Parrish castle where weariness and worry will be checked at the entrance." Builder Rheinstein insisted that only private enterprise could produce the volume of construction needed by the city. NYCHA could fill some gaps, create some innovative models, and provide a "few apartments," but it could never solve the city housing problem alone. The new tone brought NYCHA in line with the limited promises of the national government.[23]

It also marked a new border for La Guardia's dream for his city. He did not reject the underlying environmentalism of housing reform—telling Red Hook tenants that "given the proper housing, you know how to live in them. The people are all right; the houses are rotten." But he rejected the disillusion of those who, having sought perfect results, greeted failure with a complacent bitterness: "Once upon a time," one of these burned-out reformers told *Fortune* magazine, "we thought that if we could only get our problem families out of those dreadful slums, then papa would stop taking dope, mama would stop chasing around, and Junior would stop carrying a knife. Well, we've got them in nice apartments with modern kitchens and a recreation center. And they're the same bunch of bastards they always were.'' La Guardia did not lose faith in the idea of public housing or in the people; he scaled it down to the level at which he felt it could be supported.

His first administration had chased possibilities, the second was making concessions to gain what was possible. Over the next three years NYCHA made 10,000 new units available. It did not replace the entire stock of dilapidated dwellings; it didn't even aim to, but it made more than 40,000 individuals' lives more comfortable with fresh housing. For La Guardia such an approach was sensible and possible, and therefore enough.[24]

2. The Airport of the New World and the World of Tomorrow

REALISM won out over more ambitious visions in housing because a comprehensive housing solution carried an astronomical price tag and a forty-year completion cycle. La Guardia acknowledged no similar barriers to boosting New York to preeminence in the emerging field of air transportation. FH had been fascinated with air travel since before World War I. For him, passengers flying through the air in man-made chariots held aloft by the equations of physicists symbolized the majesty of science and modern progress. As a congressman he had fought for a separate air defense force. And from the very first day that he became mayor he argued that the key to New York's continued prominence was a first-class airfield.

In 1934 La Guardia boarded a flight from Chicago carrying a ticket for ''New York.'' The plane landed at Newark airport, as all similar ''New York'' flights did. But this balky passenger refused to disembark, insisting that the terms of his ticket be carried out. His ticket read ''Chicago to New York,'' not Newark. Next day's newspapers ran pictures of an empty airplane but for a lone round figure, with the look of a cat having polished off the canary, being shuttled to Floyd Bennett Field in Brooklyn. ''And remember,'' he remarked as he deplaned, ''Newark is not New York.''[25]

La Guardia began badgering the post office to switch its mail flights from landing at Newark to Floyd Bennett. From detailed records that he kept on all flights that were diverted from Newark because of poor weather he would send postal authorities telegrams, reminding them that flying was better in Gotham. But

Postmaster General James Farley had no interest in polishing Fiorello's Big Apple, and La Guardia proved no more successful in winning the feds over to the idea of converting Governor's Island into a landing field.[26]

During the twenties the old Glenn Curtiss Airport at North Beach in Queens had served as an airpark for wealthy sports flyers, but the Depression put a damper on such entertainment, and La Guardia turned his attention to this converted amusement park. Existing neighborhood housing was constructed close to the ground and the low terrain had no large obstructions. The surrounding marshlands could be filled and made into runways, and once the Triborough Bridge was completed, it would link the area to Manhattan, the Bronx, and Queens. He envisioned the creation of a vast air- and seaplane complex that would serve the Northeast and assure New York dominance over regional air commerce. "When our program is completed," he was saying by the end of 1934, "New York City will have a ring of airports within a few minutes distance of the business and commercial center. Aviation is established. Nothing can stop it."[27]

In the midst of the Depression when every municipal dollar being spent competed with relief, La Guardia continued to plan air bases for the future. As president of the Conference of Mayors he had himself warned colleagues that airports were extremely costly symbols of urban pride. It's all very fine to make glorious speeches about beautiful silver ships bringing the city within hours of the entire world, he declared, "but just find out how much the airport is going to cost . . . then find out what your revenue is going to be. . . . It is purely a business proposition." Except, of course, in New York City, where the airport became the mayor's pet project. Robert Moses could build the bridges and parks, Hodson would disburse relief, and Valentine would lead La Guardia's attack on the gamblers, but Fiorello alone planned and put together the financing for his dreamport by convincing federal officials that air travel and transport were now a critical part of modern urban life.[28]

Critics grumbled about the cost. Fiorello's Folly, they called it. But the federal government eventually contributed $27 million to the $40 million project, underwriting the conversion of hundreds of acres of dismal wetlands into 90 acres of new runways and 53 acres of apron space. Tons of refuse hauled from Riker's Island and elsewhere were used to fill in 357 acres of marshes. A thousand carloads of cement, 3 million gallons of asphalt, 200 miles of cable, 25 miles of underground piping, 20,000 tons of steel, and enough electrical power to provide street lighting for 14,000 city streets went into the project. Five thousand men worked three shifts six days a week for close to two years to complete the massive undertaking. So great was Fiorello's haste that the work was pushed forward even when plans were not yet ready, resulting in a noticeable difference between the blueprints and the actual structure of the airport hangars.

When the field was formally dedicated on October 15, 1939, a crowd of 325,000 joined the delighted mayor in celebrating the completion of his modern marvel. The airfield boasted a 6000-foot runway, the longest in the world, engineered to tolerate a load of 25 tons per square foot. The rotating beacon above the tower projected a 13 ½-million-candlepower shaft of light, the brightest anywhere. The administration building dwarfed most railroad terminals and the hangars could hold Madison Square Garden, with room to spare. The scope of this achievement put to rest forever the notion that WPA workers were only good at moving leaves from one end of a dirty street to another. And overseeing it all, from the raising of hundreds of acres of tidal flats to the erection of the giant terminals, had been Fiorello La Guardia.

He would take every distinguished guest—to some it seemed every visiting fireman—on a personal tour of his North Beach. So often did the little mayor rush out to the Queens lagoon that the workers took to handing him their tools, and when it was done he proudly described it to President Roosevelt as "the greatest, the best, the most up-to-date and the most perfect airport in the U.S. It is " 'the' airport of the New World."[29]

Then, after completing the superport he had promised, he went after business with the spirit of the old robber barons. He undercut Newark to attract the largest air carriers, only to raise prices once renters began vying for space. "La Chargia," the concessionaires took to calling the new airport. But they no longer had a choice. John Rockefeller would have been proud. La Guardia put another Rockefeller, old John's grandson David, to work securing tenants for North Beach. Before long a florist shop, drugstore, bank, post office, haberdashery, jewelry shop, beauty salon, and brokerage office converted the terminal into a bustling section of the metropolis it served. The terminal promenade, designed to accommodate 5000 visitors watching planes come and go, was offered as a concession for $12,000 a year. There were no takers, so the city operated the "Sky Walk" itself and within a year brought in $100,000.

By then the new airfield was the busiest in the world, handling 200 flights a day. Across the nation New York's achievement stirred envy and praise. "We observe that the city of New York is casting about for a name for its new municipal airport," wrote the *Oklahoma City Times*. "The dynamic mayor's name and his works are known from coast to coast." Name it "La Guardia Field" suggested the western journal, along with hundreds of others. No one had fought La Guardia more fiercely throughout his mayoralty than Bronx Borough President James J. Lyons, but Lyons agreed. He introduced a resolution that the new airport be named "La Guardia Field," as a testimonial "to the Mayor of our city who conceived the idea . . . and who was solely responsible for its development." Proclaimed the *New York Herald Tribune*, "Never was there a more fitting tribute to a man than La Guardia Field."[30]

The city paid a price for the hasty planning and accelerated construction schedules. As the field's volume of activity outstripped even La Guardia's most optimistic projections, the incessant landing of heavily loaded aircraft, combined

434

with the weight of the busy buildings, literally dropped the airport into the ground as the landfill gradually gave way. The difference between the architect's renderings and the actual buildings made repairs more difficult. One popular story told of an engineer looking for a broken pipe and fixing a rutted section of brass, only to discover that it was part of the landfill foundation. A decade after the airport's completion, it was easy for all to tell where nature had left off and Fiorello took over with landfill. Surfaces were cracked, hangar aprons had sunk an average six inches a year, in some areas to a full six-foot drop. La Guardia Field won a reputation among professionals as the only airport built on high tide, with its shoreline steadily eroding and its long line of shore lights disappearing into the sea.

None of this was irreparable. And none denied that La Guardia's plunge into the future had a galvanizing impact on air travel. His reputation as a tough-minded administrator recasting the modern metropolis continued to shine. Barely was the new air terminal for the Northeast region operational when the mayor pushed through the Board of Estimate the purchase of a polluted bathing beach at Idlewild Point in Queens. This time the goal was to turn the barren territory into an even larger international airport that would fix for decades the place of New York City as America's entrepot for North American travel.[31]

The physical transformation of the city, of which ultramodern airfields were a part, injected a new spirit of growth and fresh possibility into a community that had been brought low by the Depression. Providing relief and improved services and cleaning out corruption were all responses to problems and breakdown, attacks on negatives. But there is more to great cities than essential services, and the imperative of urban grandeur had been ignored for too long. By 1939 La Guardia's New York craved something positive that went beyond survival, a celebration of itself and for what it stood.

New York was scheduled to put on a world's fair in 1939. Initially, the fair's board drew plans for a commercial pageant that would celebrate American technology. But reformers and civic leaders wanted to use the opportunity to make a serious statement about the renascent city and about the perils of uncharted mechanical progress that was transforming society. Said Michael Meredith Hare, secretary of the Municipal Art League: "We are . . . choked by that very progress. The world is in chaos struggling to master its own inventions. We are in danger of being annihilated by forces which we ourselves have set up. The world calls for an answer to this problem of mastering our own inventions."

The idea of a fair with a message caught up distinguished social planners, architects, designers, sociologists, and civic reformers in the challenge of designing a coherent theme about urban life and its future. Lewis Mumford urged planners to "project a pattern that will fulfill itself in the future of the whole civilization."

Take care, he warned, to avoid the dangerous delight in machinery's brute force so characteristic of other fairs. Emphasize instead the harnessing of modern inventions to create positive "environments . . . industry . . . civilization." New York's fair would celebrate the end of laissez faire in the World of Tomorrow.[32]

The idea of a progressive fair charmed La Guardia. He was awed by the scale of the undertaking, the engineering, the ambition to define a culture of commitment and community responsibility. The fairground itself, reclaimed from a noisome garbage dump, symbolized the possibilities of a technological future. F. Scott Fitzgerald had characterized the Flushing Meadows in memorable terms:

> a valley of ashes—a fantastic farm where ashes grow like wheat into ridges and hills and grotesque gardens; where ashes take the forms of houses and chimneys and rising smoke and, finally, with a transcendent effort, of men who move dimly and already crumbling through the powdery air.

Parks Commissioner Moses converted this Valley of Ashes into an immense sparkling fair site. Amidst the lingering shadow of depression and disturbing international trends, the fair projected an audacious optimism in a perfectible future. In the words of cultural historian Warren Susman, "No more self conscious 'document' ever existed to demonstrate forcefully the effort to create a culture on the basis of the Great Technology than the World's Fair that opened in Flushing Meadows in 1939."[33]

With the fair's designers, the Little Flower believed that the primary challenge of the future was not to make it work but to make it good. The scientists and engineers would see to it that it would work, but only an aware citizenry could make it good. It was precisely to this citizenry that the fair offered, in the words of Robert D. Kohn, chairman of the Fair Committee on Theme and a member of the board of design, "some of the serious thought of the day." The didactic carnival replaced the traditional categories of science, art, agriculture, and manufacturing with practical themes like food, transportation, and housing, to make "dynamic" connections with the daily affairs of the citizen. No previous fair arranged itself so expressly to inform the common man. "The fair," declared World's Fair Corporation president Grover Whalen, "was built for and dedicated to the people . . . to delight and instruct them." And bounding through this futuristic world of sculpted communities, advanced mechanics, and perfectly balanced cityscapes was an enchanted mayor stirred by this vision of a democratic tomorrow.[34]

La Guardia showered himself with fair attention. He set up his summer city hall amidst the construction noise and debris as the fair was being erected on the Flushing Meadows landfill. At his signal on December 28, 1938, lights in 200 Fifth Avenue store windows simultaneously went on to reveal displays on the world's fair theme. "While other nations of the world are wondering what the spring will bring,'' La Guardia declared, ''we will be dedicating a fair to the hope of the people of the world. The contrast must be striking to everyone. While other countries are in the twilight of an unhappy age, we are approaching the dawn of a new day.''[35]

Once the fair opened the proud mayor roamed his Flushing Meadows domain with lordly aplomb, inspecting exhibits, conducting orchestras, hosting foreign royalty, welcoming visiting fleets, dedicating Freedom Plaza, conferring with President Roosevelt, accepting the borrowed Magna Carta, greeting heads of state, rushing to fair emergencies, parading in western costume, spewing outrage at a nude-miss contest, acting as a reporter on press day, and scurrying from one pavilion to the next to keep within reasonable bounds of a frenetic speaking schedule. Against the striking backdrop of ''Tomorrow's'' Trylon and Perisphere he addressed issues that transcended municipal politics: the national economy, religious freedom, pan-Americanism, international politics, all natural topics for a world's fair with a message. To promote the fair and its version of the World of Tomorrow he traveled across the nation and to South America.

Some City Council members were outraged that the city subsidized the fair at the same time that it was cutting department budgets. One councilman criticized the fair as a shill for business, a ''great con game.'' Another, Bronx labor representative Salvatore Ninfo, charged that the Fair Corporation was forcing the city into hock to ensure lavish private profits. La Guardia ignored the critics. The city, like the birds who flocked to Flushing Meadows, required food and necessities, but it needed to soar too. It needed the gaiety and resurgent joy that the fair brought. ''Bands of strolling players—singers, dancers, musicians, acrobats, clowns . . . roamed about the Fair . . . strumming banjoes, singing popular songs, giving out swing music . . . surrounded by crowds wherever they went,'' wrote the *New York Times*. The World of Tomorrow on Flushing Meadows represented his city's festive island celebrating a bright future of peace and abundance and a sense of ease with the new technology.

Not all birds soar. Some are captured and caged, limited to a few square feet of freedom. Others also trapped may maintain illusions of freedom if the confining walls are farther apart, less perceptibly limiting. Fair planners had promised a solution to the modern world's dilemma of mastering its own inventions. The central theme exhibit, ''Democracity,'' was put on display in the architecturally clean geometric shapes of the Trylon and Perisphere. It was the perfectly planned community, with optimal population, symmetrical layout for business, social, and cultural activity, linked by futuristic autobahns.[36]

After only a brief period the fair's original premise slipped away. Everyman's Fair with lessons in interdependence and progress turned into a festival of light entertainment. Its subtle themes glided by the audience. The mayor too was entranced by the glitter. Insistently plebian in 1934, he had stood alone in a business suit while all around him wore tails for his inauguration. But at the fair opening he insisted that his commissioners come in formal clothes and his own tailcoat developed a shine from overuse. "Nancy and I have been enjoying your pictures," wrote Charles Burlingham, "hobnobbing with Royalties, top-hatting with F.D. and E. R, Eddie Flynn, et al." Highmindedness gave way to carnival. Mummers, marchers, giant square dances with country fiddlers, and a steady train of celebrities floated the fair above its self-conscious seriousness. And while it cost a quarter to get into Democracity, the sophisticated industrial exhibits were free.

Joseph Wood Krutch reviewed the lesson-laden themes of the fair and suggested to visitors that they avoid the themes and enjoy the entertainment that combined the snazziest of science with acrobats and trained seals. La Guardia had railed against nudity and strip shows. Not at his fair. No sir. "Democracity," declared Krutch, was a bore, but the Crystal Lassies, "nude dancers . . . deliriously multiplied" by reflected mirrors, were a thrill.

Industry and showmanship won out over the civic planners. Of the hundreds of films shown at the fair, only a handful were not in one way or another designed to sell a product. The World of Tomorrow was a showcase for "Tomorrow's Propaganda," chided the *New York Times*. Small shops, farmers, and common folk could not afford exhibit space in the striking Trylon and Perisphere. Inevitably, their message was not there. At the fair for the common people the World of Tomorrow was interpreted by General Motors, the Edison Co., Eastman Kodak, and AT&T, by the polished hawkers of a consumer society. And they knew something that the planners did not. Given a choice between themes and spectacle, the masses would opt for a good time.

General Motors' futuristic paean to the automobile in modern life, not Democracity, was the fair's most popular exhibit—rank commercialism dressed up in the shiny idiom of "American progress." The great car companies put on the best exhibits and captured the heart of the fair, convincing Americans that the auto meant comfort and freedom. "Americans live in their cars," wrote Gerald Wendt, science director of the fair and author of *Science in the World of Tomorrow* (1939). "Here they attain temporary privacy, an isolation from pressing neighbors. Here they enjoy the sensation of motion, of action and progress, even though it be vicarious and futile. Here they feel too the sense of power and of control over their course and destiny which is otherwise lost in their dependence on society. Here they escape from monotony and often from squalor."[37]

The Norman Bel Geddes GM "Futurama" exhibit took the visitor for a fifteen-minute ride past crisscrossing expressways that arched over spectacular country and mountains, past lakes and rivers, steel foundries and play parks, to the city of the future. Here traffic ingeniously slid into beautifully intricate patterns of undisturbed motion. Automobile Utopia. Commented Walter Lippmann, "GM has spent a small fortune to convince the American public that if it wishes to enjoy the full benefit of *private* enterprise in motor manufacturing, it will have to rebuild its cities and its highways by *public* enterprise."

The earlier La Guardia would not have been smitten so entirely. He would never have trusted the business interests so fully. But the opportunity to project New York as the world capital of social thought, art, culture, and technology beguiled him with the promise of dual dividends for the city and for its mayor. Many of the fair's shimmering goals proved ephemeral: The fair never achieved its projected profits. It failed to attract the number of visitors that had been expected, and it fell short of provoking the broad public to a new awareness of technology and planning. "I imagine that the Fair site will make a lovely park once the salesrooms are cleared away," declared Bruce Bliven in the *New Republic*. But the nation and the world now knew New York and its mayor better than it ever had before.

"I hope you will get down to lentissimo for awhile now," clucked Charles C. Burlingham after reviewing the mayor's fair activities. "There's a limit even to your capacity."[38]

3. Beyond Office: Family and Friend

THE Oral History Collection at Columbia University holds a fifty-eight-page transcript entitled "The Reminiscences of Marie La Guardia." It is a disappointingly empty document, a skein of random recollections strung together with no particular insight for having lived with a remarkable public man for close to forty years. Marie La Guardia was not trying to hide anything in her reminiscences. On the contrary, this bluff, open woman was remarkably candid about most things. The reminiscences are full of his public achievements, but there is nothing at all in these recollections about what made Fiorello run. Truth is, Marie was often the last to know whether he would run and for what.

La Guardia once described for policemen's wives his idea of good family life. "A good husband . . . will not complain or even discuss the sordid things he sees. . . ." A good wife provides a cheerful, positive environment. "Sometimes your husband will come home tired or disappointed. Perhaps he has tried to do a good job and has been discouraged. . . ." Provide soothing support, never nag, never inquire. It is a good description of Marie's role. She avoided city hall, cultivated none of her own causes, cared for her husband and children, and asked no nagging questions.[39]

"Any people," Fiorello once said at a preview of Irish art, "that insist on progressive government and maintain conservative art are pretty well balanced." He felt the same way about conservative family values. "Mrs. La Guardia devotes all her time to the children," he wrote proudly to a constituent, "and we are trying to do a good job of it." When Health Commissioner John Rice suggested that Mrs. La Guardia wield the symbolic trowel at a cornerstone ceremony, the mayor muttered, "John, her name is Marie not Eleanor." He was the only public figure in the family. "I'm very fortunate at home," La Guardia confided to *Collier's* magazine. "There's no strain. Mrs. La Guardia has no social ambitions." She fussed over his diet, his smoking (Rabbi Stephen Wise once promised to bring him tobacco "unless Marie kills me first"), and overwork, dressed in black, shunned makeup, and stayed completely out of his professional life. He respected and honored her and was faithful. But no one shared his life. Together they attended the symphony, listened to the radio, played Russian Bank, and shared the margins of his interest.[40]

When "Fiorello . . . started to build La Guardia Airport," Marie recalled for an interviewer, "I think he spent every Saturday and Sunday out there watching every bit of sand that was put in. Just nurtured that like a plant." It was the sort of attention that he never gave to her, but she understood. She was perfectly satisfied, she would say, to adjust her life to his needs. After Vice President John Nance Garner retired to his Texas home, Mrs. Garner wrote Fiorello: "You would be glad to see how happy Jno. N. [sic] is in his private life . . . has enough real business to engage hours of his day, & the balance is spent in activities over [at] our place." "Here," wrote Fiorello to Marie sarcastically, "is the happiness which comes with retirement."[41]

Marie might have viewed it differently, but as usual she was not asked and she would not presume to say. "Did you want him to retire from office?" an interviewer asked many years later. "No, we wanted him to do what he wanted to do," she said with no apparent irony. Did he appreciate such devotion? she was asked. "You'd never know it. He took it for granted. . . . Only thing you'd know is if you did something wrong." What was he like? "Volatile . . . mercurial. . . ." If he was displeased did he let you know? "Did he ever!" Yet, lest these words leave a misleading impression, none of this was said in anger; much of it was with a smile and a warm recollection of the special man being discussed.

Their home was private and modest. Harold Ickes described the apartment as a tenement "in one of the humble sections of New York." In 1937 reporter S. J. Woolf found the same "mission furniture" there that he had seen on a visit four years earlier. Neighbors included pushcart peddlers, blue-collar workers, and a sprinkling of professionals.[42]

Marie could not have children so they adopted a girl and a boy. Jean, a dark-haired five-year-old of Italian extraction, was the daughter of Fiorello's first wife's sister. Her mother, unable to care for the child, gave her up for adoption on the condition that she be brought up in the Catholic faith. (Many assumed that La Guardia was a Catholic. Harold Ickes once heard La Guardia vehemently abuse the church hierarchy and expressed surprise only to discover that the mayor was a Protestant.) Despite their own casual Protestantism, the La Guardias tried to honor the pledge and were displeased when in later life Jean joined the Episcopalian church. The second child, Eric, a fair-haired boy of Scandinavian parentage, was selected through the city adoption bureau when he was three years old. The boy had been in another home for a while and grew up with a painful shyness that Fiorello tried with only partial success to dispel.[43]

It is hard to appreciate today the extent of privacy that was still available to public figures in the late thirties, and La Guardia insisted that the children's background be kept quiet. When a *Who's Who* profile in an Italian-American publication disclosed the information, he scolded its editor, Giovanni Schiavo. "I am not concerned at all in what you say and what you print," began his letter, but "I do resent, that characterization of my children [as adopted] and I insist such characterization be stricken from anything you print." Schiavo, who had been a friend, knew that Fiorello meant it. In 1937, after Fiorello threatened a libel suit over two mildly critical sentences from Jay Franklin's favorable campaign biography, Modern Age Books snipped the two offending passages (one dealing with his depression after his first wife's death and the other stating that some of his clients complained about his service as a young attorney) from each of 100,000 books that they had printed.[44]

La Guardia did not want Jean and Eric to grow up as "special kids." They were brought up in a strict, though not austere, home environment. Fiorello played with them as often as he could when they were young, taking them on his lap, listening intently to their stories, surprising them on their birthdays, cooking weekend suppers, and creating elaborate plays with scripted parts for all members. Years later Jean also remembered the official part of being a mayor's daughter. "How many of my childhood Saturdays were spent (in addition to parade viewing) at the dedication of a remote public school in Queens, in a trip to the City Sewage Disposal Plant or in the austere precincts of City Hall." Father Fiorello would quake in mock fear of how "your mother will be mad at us" if, as they inevitably did, they returned late. "He was lovely with his two adopted children," Secretary Ickes noted in his diary after visiting with the La Guardias.[45]

During the summers the La Guardias would gather up some children from friends and relatives and move out to the country. In 1938 they vacationed at Northport and brought along a nephew, Richard, a neighbor's daughter, and the son of their housekeeper, Jessie. This melange caused a small ruckus when the La Guardias went calling on the Roosevelts at Hyde Park and brought along the black housekeeper's son to visit the president. Local gentry were outraged at the *lèse majesté*, giving the puckish visitor no end of pleasure, especially when the president urged Hyde Park's finest to try to persuade the mayor to buy a farm in the county and become a neighbor.[46]

Summer weekends were reserved for the brood. Barking orders in his excited falsetto, Fiorello would muster the local children into a mock army, instructing them in close-order drill, Sousa marches, and the survival skills designed to keep them alive in the wilds of Long Island beachfront. Jean proved stubbornly unable to get the art of flag raising down pat. Once she raised the flag upside down, inadvertently giving the sign for distress, and it took Fiorello a full day to calm down. Drills were often followed by a trip to sea by rowboat (led by Admiral La Guardia). On weekend nights the kids invariably demanded to hear Edgar Bergen speaking through his dummy Charlie McCarthy on the radio, while Fiorello argued for the Lewisohn Stadium concerts. They compromised: It was Charlie McCarthy until 8:30, Brahms and Beethoven thereafter. But as the years went by he was increasingly preoccupied, and the children had to insist on their time in order to get it.

Fiorello liked to think of children as inhabitants of a special world, where rule breaking was limited to harmless pranks and rehabilitation endlessly possible. Children needed to test themselves and vent their emotions, just as he had done on the boundless plains of Arizona. But he could not offer his own children the carefree, easy world that he remembered so fondly. He would romp, roughhouse, and hatch wonderful conspiracies with them, but underlying it all was a sense of serious purpose. Everything, recalled daughter Jean, was bent "by my father to teach something, whether a specific skill, a love of art or a moral lesson." Her father's "educational impulse . . . almost a compulsion," wrote Jean, led to a childhood organized into a series of lessons on citizenship, proper behavior, art and music, and how-to's: how to ride a horse, how to organize an army, how to live a moral life. The children were graded for their behavior on the West Point system. When they gathered enough points they reaped rewards. If they misbehaved they lost points, and the accountant was strict.

He did not foster in his own children the sense of frivolous freedom that he so often advocated in others. "It was very thoughtful of you to send the little package of needles for Jean," Fiorello wrote a friend. "I hope it will inspire her to get acquainted with a needle," and it might make her forget her preoccupation with hockey sticks, roller skates, and baseball bats. To another correspondent who inquired about his family he complained that Jean was too lazy in her studies. "We are trying to make a scientist out of her, but the prospects are not very good just now. Eric is a typical boy and prefers baseball to mathematics and swimming to music."[47]

Fun and games and pranks on the open plains were fine for nostalgic mind trips, but father Fiorello tended to be didactic, overbearing, a champion of early maturity. Each year on the Fourth of July he would sit Eric and Jean down and

442

read to them the Declaration of Independence. He was always concerned "lest we grow too blasé too soon," Jean recalled. Fun activities like the circus, ship christenings, baseball games, and movies were as carefully rationed as sweets. "You see we do not permit them to see more than two performances a year," Fiorello wrote to John D. Rockefeller in response to a charming note complimenting his daughter's behavior at a Radio City Music Hall performance. Jean adapted far better to Fiorello's demands than her brother, who often retreated into a private world that even his father could not pierce.[48]

Much as Achille La Guardia had prescribed rigorous musical training for his own son, Fiorello wanted his children to study music seriously. Jean tried but Eric refused. He hated concerts and rebelled at practicing. This withdrawn boy was overwhelmed by the large shoes he was expected to fill. "My son!" Fiorello exclaimed to a friend, clasping his hand to his head in disbelief at the thought of a La Guardia untutored in harmonics. He might refer to Eric as an insurgent, "just like me," but Fiorello wanted this insurgent tamed. When little Eric demanded a play gun, his father refused. There was a limit to the amount of Wild West that he allowed into his own home.[49]

Later, as a high school student, the boy was sent out west during summer vacation to work on a Texas ranch with the McCrary family. "The change will do him a world of good," Fiorello hoped. He wanted Eric exposed to a "good and wholesome" alternative to the city that would "make a man" of the "timid" and "sheltered child. . . . in many respects . . . very young for his age." The public limelight and his strong-willed parent had taken their toll, and La Guardia asked that the youngster be protected as much as possible from references to his father.

But there was no protection from parental manipulation. "The first thing," he instructed Mr. McCrary, was to "impress on him that he must get up in the morning at a designated hour and be ready for a day's work." Fiorello's long and carefully detailed instructions to the McCrarys warned that Eric must be held to firm restrictions and a tough discipline. For someone who spoke of childhood as a time to gather experience, Fiorello was much more concerned with responsibility than with experimentation. "Anytime he is off the beam . . . ," he wrote to McCrary about Eric, "he is to be called to task . . . sternly and sharply."[50]

The summer before, La Guardia had taken his son with him on a trip to Europe where Eric was supposed to assist him with some minor chores (even overseas vacations had to include some duties!). Fiorello drew up an agreement, which he asked his secretary to type and send to Eric. The tone was so businesslike—no doubt Fiorello hoped by this to impress Eric with the no-nonsense detail of his duties—that the secretary was embarrassed to send it. "Look at what the boss made me write today!" she confided to his sister-in-law, Elsie Fisher. The letter closed: "Trusting you will have a successful trip and knowing that you will attend to your duties carefully, I am/ Very truly yours." It contributed little to the boy's self-confidence. Not long thereafter, Eric disappointed his father again. A

United Nations staffer informed Fiorello that the boy had ignored all requests for repayment of a small loan.

Fiorello so much wanted to see his son succeed, but he wanted to personally mold that success. Eric could have used more of the freedom that Fiorello himself so often prescribed for other youngsters. La Guardia prized a caricature of himself dreaming about the North Beach airfield titled "The Dreamer and Doer." The artist had given it to him, and the father touchingly reinscribed it: "Eric: To my boy of whom I often dream—that some day—he may dream and build, Daddy." It is a tender glimpse of Fiorello's vulnerability as a parent and of how badly he wanted Eric to succeed, but it also demonstrates how much more he valued his son's success than his freedom. One understands why the youngster ofttimes found life too constricting.[51]

If La Guardia's relationship with his wife was conventional and with his children demanding, it was almost nonexistent with the rest of his family. He had left his mother and his sister, Gemma, behind in Europe to pursue his career, and for the rest of his life career came first. He and his younger brother, Richard, were not especially close. Richard was involved in church and social work in Trenton, New Jersey, and died unexpectedly of a heart attack in 1935. But for all the condolence letters that emphasized the shared sympathies of the two brothers, they were not similar. Richard, says Fiorello's sister-in-law, Elsie Fisher, with a big laugh, "was a *real* Republican."[52]

When his mother, Irene, died in 1915, La Guardia asked Gemma several times to join him in the United States. She chose to remain in Europe, where she supported herself by teaching English. Over her brother's objections she married an older man, a Jewish bank clerk who had studied in one of her classes, and with him settled down in Budapest, and for a while brother and sister fell completely out of touch.

Then, shortly after Fiorello was inaugurated for his first term, *The Day*, a Yiddish newspaper, ran a story detailing the mayor's Jewish ancestry, based on an interview with Gemma and her husband. For a few days the revelation caused a flurry in the city. At first the mayor refused to talk about it. But when his silence was taken as an effort to deny or ignore his background, La Guardia called in a Yiddish press reporter and dictated a carefully worded statement, acknowledging his mother's Jewish background and that his sister was "married not to a rich [Jewish] banker, but only to a bank clerk in Budapest. . . ." He told another Jewish reporter that he did not really understand the furor.

The hullabaloo over his ancestry made him intensely uncomfortable. Like his father he had put religion behind him. Perhaps he held Gemma responsible for this story, since she was prominently mentioned in the report. The estrangement between the two left a painful void. "Uncle Fiorello and Marie, auntie dear," reads a letter from Gemma's daughter Yolanda, "do write a line now and then to dear mama. She always says she would be so happy if she would hear from you." The girl described her mother—"a great deal of grey hair but . . . still fresh and young looking"—and promised to make Jean a dress. There is no record of a reply, or of a contact between brother and sister, until some years later when Gemma's Jewishness and kinship with the old Nazi nemesis from New York caught her in the net of Hitler's persecution. Only then would the two resume contact.[53]

Relations with family have a fixed tradition. They carry expectations and kinship ties. Friendship is looser, more freely defined. There is either trust or nothing. Fiorello's inability to set aside his suspicious nature and suspend his assumptions of low motive for even those close to him made friendships very difficult. The same suspicious reserve that kept him from sharing confidences with his wife and led him to expect the worst from his children kept him from forming close relationships with others. Sometimes his fear of taint was carried to ridiculous ends. When La Guardia's license commissioner, Paul Moss, a man he trusted sufficiently to bring into his administration in a sensitive position, invited him to an opening night at the opera as a guest of a friend of his, La Guardia responded with wooden integrity, "I very much appreciate your thoughtfulness but we are adhering strictly to a rule which we adopted after my election, not to accept any social invitations of any kind from anyone with whom we did not associate socially before election." Rexford Tugwell, who respected La Guardia and served as the mayor's appointed chairman of the City Planning Commission, said of him that he was more incapable of real friendship than almost anyone he knew.[54]

The group with which he associated for fun and occasional Saturday night dinners at his house consisted of political associates, journalists who had become part of his coterie, some musicians, and a few of the men who still remembered the old Greenwich Village days. These friendships were for casual diversion, not sharing confidences or plans. A number of these friendly journalists tried their hand at writing articles about him, and Lowell Limpus did a full-length biography. What is interesting about all of these pieces is how shallow they are, how little below this man's surface his friends actually got. Their work could have been about a long-dead historical figure for all that their closeness to their subject edified their work. They saw only what he chose to show.

Yet La Guardia needed people around him, if not as close friends then to fill his space with comfortable talk, to be there for him to perform. "I will tell you something," a relative who knew him well remarks, pleased with the sudden revelation, "he never wanted to be alone." After he left the office at the end of the day he would take one of his aides, or the commissioner with whom he had last met, or one of his newspaper friends to join him for a drink. When Marie and the kids were out of town, he would invite his sister-in-law, or take one of his assistants to accompany him to a play or a concert. The private life of calm thought eluded him. He needed action, an audience, reactions.[55]

Aristocratic gentlemen who bent class loyalties to social fairness evinced in him a special regard. He enjoyed the wellborn presence around him, and the upper crust was well represented among his appointees. Newbold Morris might joke about the *Mayflower* and the Little Flower, and Fiorello might write a constituent that the only member of his household with a family genealogy was his terrier, but old ancestry and new wealth were well represented on his staff. There was even a Rockefeller.

One patrician, however, was very special, and with him La Guardia developed the sort of relationship that Emerson must have meant when he called true friendship a masterpiece of nature. They were alike in so very little, and yet La Guardia very deeply respected and loved Charles Culp Burlingham. With this gentleman of the old school he shared his secrets. To him he turned for advice, and from him he took a measure of civility and calm that mitigated somewhat his tempestuous nature. "He is my spiritual salvation army and always sees to it that I get a hand out when he knows I am down dejected and nearly out," La Guardia wrote to an acquaintance. And although he often put people through his childish tests to see if they could be trusted, he never descended from gentility when with this grand old man of patrician reform, never even entering a door before Burlingham. When he respected someone, he knew all the rules and followed them; it was only with those for whom he had disdain that he resorted to brutalities. Unfortunately, there were a great many of these. He cared a great deal, though, about CCB, like a loving son for a wise, tactful, and tolerant father who provided the perspective and calm wisdom that he so much needed.[56]

"I was alive during the Civil War," Charles Burlingham wrote to Samuel Seabury, recalling the dreadful days of the New York draft riots, and he retained in memory almost everything that he saw after that. A Harvard graduate, member of the select circle of admiralty counselors, CCB enjoyed a career that brought him influence and regard at the highest levels of American government. He practiced before the Supreme Court, presided over the Bar of the City of New York, and served as senior warden of St. George's Protestant Episcopal Church. Throughout his long life—he lived to be an extraordinarily acute 101 years old—Burlingham carried the caste mark of the American establishment with ease and humane concern for the "lower third."[57]

He championed the cause of Sacco and Vanzetti, supported Margaret Sanger in her crusade for birth control, helped open the New York Bar to blacks and women, served as the Warwick of New York fusion, and fought for a broad public welfare program during the Depression. Ninety-five years old in 1953, deaf and close to blind, he continued his support for unpopular issues, vainly petitioning President Dwight David Eisenhower to stay Julius and Ethel Rosenberg's death penalty.

An intimate of presidents, power behind judges from the Supreme Court down, adviser to governors, Burlingham developed a warm regard for the salty, ambitious "Eyetalian" who ran New York City. La Guardia fought with each one of his advisers except the distinguished old man with the flashing eyes and remarkable enthusiasm; Charles Burlingham never fell from grace. On the contrary, it was the mayor who looked to him and continued to look to him for approval, counsel, a calming influence, and the wisdom of fine, elegantly aged intelligence.

"Please, please," pleaded La Guardia, "accept my apology," after he had missed an appointment with CCB. "There is no excuse for it—except that I am an ass. . . . I had a hard and trying day. . . . Visiting the injured patrolman upset me. He was in such bad condition. When I reached the Garden I was handed a slip that Jesse Jones was waiting in Wash. to get me on the phone. Well—like the dumbbell that I am I did not see the memo on the other side of the slip that you had called. . . . Please C.C.," he wrote, anguished, "forgive me." La Guardia's executive secretary, Goodhue Livingston, recalls that "Burlingham was God to La Guardia."[58]

Burlingham would pepper the mayor with suggestions, often as many as nine in a letter, particularly regarding judicial appointments and legal matters. These letters were often studded with learned references, phrases in three and even four languages, and a style so becomingly direct that they provided La Guardia (as well as the modern reader) with a welcome break from the long-winded ambiguities of less confident advisers. "I heard a rumor . . . of your appointing Gus Hartman to the Domestic Relations Court. I denied it. . . . Yours, with a passion against Gus' service." Hartman was not appointed. "I wish I were Commissioner of Accounts," came another brief note, "I'd begin to investigate the Fire Dept. [triple underline] & when His Honor the Mayor got wind of it & began to raise Hell I'd go right ahead until removed." After License Commissioner Paul Moss arbitrarily limited city advertising to five newspapers, Burlingham complained, "This is preposterous and worthy of Hitler." When Fiorello attacked the courts in harsh terms, Burlingham sent him a parody of his own outburst and signed it "Franco H. La Guardia, Mayor and Generalissimo" *and* "F. Hitler La Guardia, der Fuehrer."[59]

Generally the exchange between La Guardia and his eminent adviser took place face-to-face. Fiorello would pick Burlingham up at his home at 860 Park Avenue for the trip to his downtown law office. On the way they would review the state of the city and its politics, and Burlingham would deliver his opinions in the unfalteringly liberal political idiom that marked his own career and now helped guide another.

Burlingham's most important function, as in the Moses-Ickes controversy and with La Guardia's support for the "mussing up" of criminals, was to keep reminding Fiorello of first principles. Their correspondence is studded with closing sentences that say in one way or another what CCB wrote to La Guardia when he told him to veto a bill requiring any assembly of fifteen or more New Yorkers to display the flag. "Declare your independence. . . . Veto the bill and state the true principle." Fiorello followed this advice, as he generally did, and received a letter from CCB congratulating him and taking absolutely no credit for having led him to the decision.

When the mayor's staff tried to protect His Honor from some mistake but feared to approach him, they would turn to Burlingham. La Guardia too would rely on his well-connected and trusted adviser: "Will you please tap all various sources of information," he would ask CCB, before deciding on an appointment to his administration. Justice Edmund Palmieri, who served as La Guardia's counsel, recalls that the mayor would not go to a White House meeting without having discussed the issues with Burlingham first. If Burlingham thought that the mayor was working too long, he would march into the office, place Fiorello's Stetson on his head, and march him off for a drink and ship him home. No one else would dream of taking such liberties with the fiery magistrate.[60]

"Your letters," La Guardia once wrote his friend, "are an elixir of cheerfulness," and it was to Burlingham that the mayor would unburden himself with full candor. "The recent decisions of the Court of Appeals have been nothing short of disgraceful. Not mistakes of law, not misunderstanding of the facts, not novel points to be first established, but deliberate abuse and misuse of judicial power. . . . I get so darned mad when I think of their miserable conduct that I cannot even type right—much less calmly talk about it." When Burlingham was out of town Fiorello missed him: "I think the best thing for you to do is to come right back to New York. The weather is cool. Then you would be here and I would have the benefit of your wise counsel and advice from time to time."[61]

Most of their substantive exchanges were saved for their limousine rides downtown, but during the sweltering summers, when the mayor and his staff moved to a summer city hall outside the city and La Guardia spent his Saturdays away from the office, he would write warm, discursive letters to his mentor. "So happy to have found your letter," begins one dated August 23, 1938. "This is the first time for many years that I have used the typewriter. Had to search the whole house for paper and these scraps were given to me by Eric. [One of the sheets is lined and the typing is studded with wonderful mistakes.] He said he had them hidden where the other kids could not find his supply." La Guardia delivers the latest political gossip from Washington. "The other day I found just two who were not candidates for the Presidency—one was waiting the return of the President for the restoration of citizenship, and the other was on his way to Atlanta [federal penitentiary]." He writes of back-home "skulduggery," jokes about the Republicans, and promises to "tell you all about" his conversations with the president as soon as they get together.

With Burlingham, Fiorello was even able to laugh at himself. "Here is a good one. I was supposed to fly to Bennett Field to take part in a . . . celebration." Informed by the coast guard commandant that the weather was too bad to risk the flight, FH responded in "my usual boastful manner . . . that I did not mind and to send the plane along anyway as I was willing to take the chance, and thanking him for his solicitude. The Admiral replied 'We don't mind you taking a chance, Mr. Mayor, for mayors are plentiful, but we just cannot take a chance with the plane for good planes are scarce and hard to get in the Coast Guard.' So I phoned a poor message and the C.G. is one plane to the good.'' A bit of business: Please suggest some good people for several city openings. Then the mayor takes up a point that Burlingham had raised about growing deaf. ''What is this you say about your hearing? Are you spoofing . . . ? I . . . will invoke all the habits of my Italian father and Jewish mother—surely we will get enough action out of that. But what will you do with your soft voiced Union League Club friends? . . . Let me come some afternoon to visit.'' Scrawled at the bottom in bold red crayon was the sign-off: ''fiorello the red.''[62]

Next week: ''I hasten to show off the fancy letterhead Marie bought after seeing what I was using last week.'' There follows news about the children, why he did not accept a Seabury invitation to the judge's home (''to tell the truth I don't shave on Sundays.''), the president's private grumblings about how difficult it was finding a real progressive for the Supreme Court vacancy, ''I am telling you this because—well because I get a little comfort out of it—after some of the things you say about my judges.''

The following week: After reviewing the exploits of Douglas ''Wrong Way'' Corrigan, who without maps, radio, or even adequate instrumentation set out for California and landed at the Dublin, Ireland, Baldonnel Airport, Fiorello discussed the latest moves of Republican Chairman Simpson, who ''would make an ass of himself, if nature had not already attended to that little matter.'' And so this rewarding correspondence continued throughout the summer, with Fiorello dashing off weekly reviews of his activities and the political buzz. Then, as they both moved back to the city, the two reverted to their backseat parleys.[63]

As soon as the La Guardia family settled the following summer at Asharoken, Long Island, the long letters started again. Seated before the radio, listening to the Lewisohn Stadium concerts that he so enjoyed (''during the first part of the letter I was listening to Beethoven's delightful ''Seventh'' and then Sibelius' Finlandia''), La Guardia apologized that he would have written earlier but Marie had hidden the typewriter! She did not want him working on Sunday and relented only for ''CC.'' The tone of the letters, so special, diffident, solicitous, respectful, and loving—by this time Fiorello was signing his letters to Burlingham ''Love, Fiorello''—provided La Guardia the fatherly comfort he never received from his own dad.

By this time, however, Fiorello was paying increasing attention to events that would claim much of his time over the next two years: the impending war in Europe and fresh designs on national office.[64]

4. La Guardia II

I n February of 1938 Fiorello La Guardia delivered a thoughtful address before a select audience that included Samuel Seabury, John Haynes Holmes, and other City Affairs Committee Brahmins. La Guardia biographer August Heckscher calls this "one of the best speeches of [La Guardia's] career . . . witty and defiant . . . a man completely in control. . . ." Perhaps, but it is hard to fathom what is so impressive in this long, caustic, complaining speech. The speech is an incumbent's speech—a reverential tour of the "La Guardia achievement" combined with a demand for more power while signaling empty pockets. This incumbent being La Guardia, it is a well-delivered speech, deftly skewering such "obstacles to greater efficiency" as the Transit Commission, the state legislature, and the courts.

If this speech is important, it is for what it does not say. Before this audience of reform leaders, the fusion mayor reviewed his past achievements and the few loose ends that he intended to tie up. The address contains no new agenda for the future, only a paean to the past. It marks an end to the exciting era of positive reform and creative leadership.

La Guardia's big job was over.

Fiorello's confidant and reform strategist, Adolf Berle, said as much a while later when he told La Guardia that he had accomplished the "last big job that could be done in" New York City "within the existing rules of finance." He had brought the city as far along the path to modernity as possible. His successor would be confined "merely to managing" what Fiorello "had set up for him." La Guardia concurred, confiding to Berle that "most likely the next mayor of New York City would be nothing to speak of." This was true not only of the next mayor but of La Guardia himself. La Guardia II had little more to do than preserve and manage what La Guardia I had established.[65]

He had set the model for a progressive mayor, throwing out boodlers, winning a modern charter, cleaning out the slot machines, creating a hospitable atmosphere for the new immigrants, building parks for children, providing low-cost housing, defining a "new normal" for urban welfare programs, and seizing control over a runaway budget. When the job of running New York required the sensitive timing and sharp intelligence of a progressive politician at the peak of his art, he had been magnificent, smothering the many problems with energy and concern. He dashed to Washington, Albany, Harlem, fires, wherever he was welcome, to make the city fresh and new, fulfilling the long positive agenda that he had brought into office. His plans had required excellent officials and generous help from Washington. He secured both.

But with much of that original agenda achieved, La Guardia would be reduced to managing the system. That this could be a difficult job was evident from the intractability of police problems, the racial and ethnic antagonisms that continued to divide the city, the impossibility even of guaranteeing that snow could be removed with speed and efficiency. There remained embarrassing conflicts over housing and painful budget choices between competing necessities. These vexing issues were not amenable to broad-stroked political artistry. Social welfare services, ambitious building projects, and the battening bureaucracy of growing municipal government meant that taxes had to be raised. He saw no solution to the stubborn dilemma of progressive urban government confronting limited budgets. The city had reached a modern impasse: big government pitted against its cost. Fiorello was not prepared to devote the rest of his career to plugging budget gaps and keeping officeholders efficient and honest.[66]

As an administrator he had certain gifts. Forcefulness, integrity, and decisiveness were all pluses. But he lacked system, was chronically incapable of delegating authority, and refused to accept the possibility that criticism could be well motivated. He had little tolerance for routine. Dealing with sewers, squeezing revenue out of strapped sources, trying to weed out corruption more subtle than the sort Tammany tolerated, these were jobs that no longer engaged his full attention. The single-minded, uncompromising visionary of 1934 had transformed the city. In 1938 he had little more to do, he muttered, than to clean the streets and collect the garbage. The positive mayoralty for which he won fame all over the country was over. From this point forward he was a caretaker of his own government. He was bored. The source of much of his energy, the burning zeal to change things, was curbed.[67]

There were diversions, and periodically they could be spectacular. The world's fair challenged his sense of grandeur. The airport offered another of those huge building projects that thrilled him. But he needed more to keep his restless energy focused. His speeches no longer spoke of things to do. Like the one before the City Affairs Committee, they spoke of what had been done. He was working in his own shadow, preparing the finishing touches on his mayoralty and looking elsewhere.

Robert Moses was one of the first to sense that Fiorello was distracted, and to try to bend the situation to his own advantage. Washington's relief dollars that had funded his immense construction projects in the first administration were being cut, putting an end to New York's bonanza years of bridge and parkway construction. The next great frontier for federal funding, he saw, would be public housing, and with the single-minded immersion for which he was held in awe, Moses aimed to make housing his new field.

In the late spring of 1938 he sent La Guardia a memorandum, dismissing the present city housing program as inept and chaotic, declaring that "neither the City Housing Authority nor the State Housing Commission are properly constituted for any major construction." He went on to suggest that La Guardia "put all the city work under one man, which is really the only effective way of carrying out a program of this kind." Moses volunteered to serve on a committee to formulate "a program for the remaining years of this administration." Or, if necessary, he would even accept a position as housing czar. When New York State voters approved a constitutional amendment creating an ample budget for public housing construction, Moses became even more intent on capturing control over housing.

By the fall of 1938 Moses had a team of his own architects quietly designing a comprehensive new public housing program, while he developed a secret plan for reorganizing the New York City Housing Authority under his own control. Then, in a style that had become all too characteristic of the mature Moses, he took aim at Alfred Rheinstein, chairman of the NYCHA.

It was not difficult for Moses to nettle the much more deliberate Rheinstein. The housing chairman would write Moses a letter exploring some possible cooperation between the Housing Authority and the Parks Department only to receive in return an abusive lecture on how to run his department. At the same time that he was complaining about Rheinstein behind his back, Moses would also blast him directly. "If I knew as little about the Constitution, statutes, and procedures of the State of New York as you do . . . I should first study them before indulging in any more correspondence," Moses wrote to Rheinstein in November. Other Moses letters were equally insulting, calculated to embarrass and shake the executive. They included such salutations as "The weather has gotten to you," "What you say makes no sense at all, and indicates again how inexperienced you are," and "Much as I like you personally, I don't know what the hell you are talking about." The condescending tone wounded Rheinstein, but he plugged on, earnestly carrying on his painful dialogue with the parks commissioner, oblivious to Moses' true intentions. For his part, Rheinstein kept pleading with Moses to treat him better. Late in the year, when he learned that Moses planned to make a speech on housing, he asked for an advance copy. Moses just ignored him.[68]

On November 22 the reasons for Moses' disconcerting behavior became crystal-clear. Before an invited audience of housing reformers, realtors, and builders, Moses delivered what had been billed as a talk on "housing and recreation." The mysterious care that went into the preparations for this talk suggested its importance. Moses and his backers rented a wing of the Museum of Natural History, invited the friendly press, and arranged for municipal radio station WNYC to carry the broadcast live. Just before Moses strode to the microphones, his men passed out beautifully printed four-color brochures spelling out a $245 million program for ten specified housing projects. This was to be no mere talk!

It was a bold move to usurp the city housing program, befitting a man of Moses' consuming arrogance and ambition. After attacking housing professionals as inefficient bureaucrats who had frittered away millions with little to show for it, Moses offered his fresh alternative, a comprehensive system based on carefully laid out principles of selection, clearance, construction, and financing. The proposal was detailed down to the exact dimensions of the houses, their location, and their precise costs. It was a deliberately aimed, sharply focused power grab. Now he set out to make his case to the audience and, most importantly, the thousands listening on radio.

An oracular Moses looked down at his well-heeled audience and at the WNYC microphones in front of him. Two WNYC technicians gave him the thumbs-up sign. All was ready. He started his speech, aiming it at the tens of thousands of WNYC listeners whose support would force La Guardia to appoint him housing czar. But no one listening to WNYC that night heard Moses. In fact, they heard nothing at all.

Someone had tipped off La Guardia. Distracted though he might be, he was not crazy. He was not about to allow his power-hungry parks commissioner to launch a coup for control over city housing. He might have his problems with Rheinstein, but they were as nothing compared with the difficulties he would have with Moses, who had a dozen powerful enemies in Washington, with the president heading the list.

So he pulled the plug on Moses.

"Early in the evening, Mr. Novik [director of WNYC] phoned me stating that he had doubts that whether the meeting in question was a park department matter," Fiorello later explained. "I advised Novik, 'Get your money or discontinue the broadcast.' He took me literally," deadpanned the Mayor. Nor did Novik bother to tell Moses or any of his men to cough up $81 if they wanted to use the microphones. As to why the studio technicians had misled Moses: They used "good judgment in refusing to disturb the equilibrium of the speakers by informing them that they were not on the air."

As for Moses' housing plan, La Guardia dismissed it as "a beautiful printing job" that displayed more imagination and public relations than familiarity with housing. After shooting down every point in the proposal, FH made certain that his special Housing Committee failed to act on even one of Moses' ideas. La Guardia stopped Moses from expanding his domain for the while, but that domain was already quite ample.[69]

Robert Moses had built that domain by using the institution of the "public authority." An authority was empowered to float bonds for building specified public projects like bridges and tunnels and to collect tolls to pay off debts. Once the debts were paid, most authorities faded out of existence and the government took over the management of the public improvement. Moses' bridges, however, were bringing in far more money than he or anybody had envisioned, and he saw no reason for folding them. By 1938 the Triborough was earning $1.3 million a year, net, creating hefty surpluses.

With the $4.5 million that his authorities were bringing in annually, Moses realized that by trading in the old bonds he could float new ones for $81 million and continue to extend his influence by building other works. So long as profits were good and the bondholders confident, his authorities could go on building forever, utilizing powers of eminent domain and exempted by their semipublic status from taxes and other normal business obligations. (The courts found that authorities were even shielded from inspection of their books.)

By the time Moses finished pyramiding his authorities, he had integrated some dozen of these semipublic entities into what political scientist Marshall Berman describes as "an immensely powerful machine, a machine with innumerable wheels within wheels, transforming its cogs into millionaires, incorporating thousands of businessmen and politicians into its production line, drawing millions of New Yorkers inexorably into its widening gyre." While the city's resources for building the beautiful new metropolis that La Guardia envisioned were dwindling (the 1940 capital budget was limited to a symbolic $1), Moses' authorities were bringing in large surpluses.[70]

Fiorello had developed a wary respect for Moses' way with power and a deep admiration for what he could accomplish. When it came to roads, highways, or bridges there was no one he trusted more to ram them through. Much of what he had done in New York would have been impossible without Moses, and he continued to rely on his peerless builder to finish that job. But he had no intention of giving him more power. Yet it was difficult for La Guardia, with one eye on new political possibilities and traveling all over the country, to keep Moses under rein.

Long before, RM had won La Guardia over to his plans for a coherent road system that wove "together the loose strands and frayed edges of the New York metropolitan arterial tapestry." Moses had built a marvelous parkway along Manhattan's shoreline, and he wanted to build one for Brooklyn and Staten Island and connect it all, in one sweeping peripheral *Ringstrasse* that drew traffic away from the congested inner-city streets. This plan included a tunnel across the mouth of the East River, an elevated highway to pick up traffic from the tunnel, lift it above the dense Brooklyn streets, and swing it over to a "circumferential parkway" along the borough's edge, sending out connective links leading to Nassau, Westchester, and the Rockaways. The cost was estimated at $105 million. La Guardia went shopping in Washington, gathering pledges for $55 million, but the city, so strapped that it was slashing departmental budgets, could not complete the financing.[71]

Only Robert Moses, with the surfeited coffers of the Triborough Authority at his disposal, could provide the money. Moses was as anxious as La Guardia to build the circumferential road system, and he was willing to trade money for power. "Some people," an acquaintance of RM's once said, "aren't satisfied unless they have a career. Moses would have been happy with a ham sandwich—and power." In 1936 La Guardia had instructed Reuben Lazarus to "leave the son-of-a-bitch off" the Tunnel Authority that Lazarus helped design. Now Moses wanted on. In return for Moses' capitalizing the profits of the Triborough Bridge to finance the new road system, La Guardia agreed to make Moses czar over all intracity water crossings, tunnels as well as bridges.

By the autumn of 1938, Comptroller Joseph McGoldrick decided that the entire plan for a circumferential highway system was ill-advised. Moses projects had already swallowed up an inordinate portion of city resources. Over the past four years city development had proceeded in a thoroughly unbalanced fashion, because a powerful Moses had pushed his roads, bridges, and parks at the expense of hospitals, schools, mass transportation, libraries, police stations, and health centers. McGoldrick believed that another "stupendous investment" in a Moses roadway was wrong. The city had already been forced to delay large-ticket maintenance expenses for two years because of its budget crunch. The new project, McGoldrick argued, would exhaust the city's "debt incurring capacity, with no margin remaining for normal capital growth of its existing facilities. . . ." It made no sense to build more at this point while existing structures rotted for lack of maintenance. Council President Newbold Morris and Manhattan Borough President Stanley Isaacs joined McGoldrick in opposing any new road program until the budget picture brightened.

Moses responded by threatening that if his highway plan was delayed he would keep it "dead for a long long time." The debate involved fundamental issues, but La Guardia, with other fish to fry, was in no mood for an extended analysis of urban priorities. There was $55 million from Washington available, but it could be spent only if Moses released the rest and got his highway.

With the 1940 presidential contest already on his mind, La Guardia welcomed a heavy-duty construction project that would brighten his luster as the can-do administrator. Moreover, he wanted to avoid another damaging fight within his administration. Appearing personally before the Board of Estimate on October 15, 1938, La Guardia pressed its fusion members "to go along with me on this," and they caved in. Years later McGoldrick gave a simple explanation for the vote. "We changed because—you know La Guardia was very intolerant of differences. . . . it would have thrown the entire administration into chaos."[72]

Three months after La Guardia pushed through the vote, Moses announced a minor alteration in the plans. On January 22, 1939, the Triborough chairman announced that the Brooklyn Battery crossing would be a bridge and not a tunnel. He had decided that a tunnel would be more expensive to construct, more costly to maintain and operate, carry less traffic, and take longer to complete. He also had esthetic reservations. A tunnel was nothing more than a hole in the ground, "a tiled vehicular bathroom smelling faintly of carbon monoxide," Moses would say. It did not compare with the majesty of sky-cast arches towering over the waters. Moses wanted his monuments displayed for all to see. La Guardia understood. It would be a bridge.

A powerful coalition of wealthy civic-minded New Yorkers quickly united to oppose this bridge, however. They argued that such a structure, with its massive anchorage, outsized approach ramps, and immense pier supports, would irreparably alter the local ecology of the riverside area. Lower Manhattan would lose sunlight, fresh air, the magnificent river view of New York harbor, and the few blocks of serene Battery Park that were left. The bridge would send real estate values plummeting. According to one calculation, lost property taxes for two decades alone came to $30 million, and the cost in terms of diminished quality of life in the overfull southern Manhattan district was incalculable.

In the past, reformers had simply accepted Moses' projections on his word. They were more skeptical this time, and his figures and mock-ups did not stand up to their scrutiny. His sketches misleadingly minimized the effect of the bridge. When tunnel designer Ole Singstad checked Moses' figures he discovered that they were false. On the basis of real costs and relevant economic factors, a tunnel was far cheaper than the Moses bridge. Citizens groups independently looked into Singstad's charges and they too found that some of Moses' figures were dubious. Others were complete fabrications.

Opponents of the bridge raised an outcry much louder than ever before. The new plans did not affect some ethnic neighborhood in one of the outer boroughs. It threatened the environment that many of New York's best men knew intimately. The Fine Arts Federation of New York, speaking for eighteen leading arts societies, issued a statement declaring that the bridge would "disfigure perhaps the most thrillingly beautiful and world renowned feature of this great city." "The same old tripe," replied Moses confidently. He was the only one who had the money to get anything done and he wanted a bridge. The pieces were in place, the plans ready, the money available. La Guardia had no choice. The project was submitted for formal approval to the War Department, which had jurisdiction over all structures built in navigable waters.

Secretary of Labor Frances Perkins, who admired Moses, understood what had transformed the idealistic reformer into an arrogant power broker. "It used to shock me because he was doing all these things for the welfare of the people. . . . [But] to him they were lousy, dirty people, throwing bottles all over [his] Jones

Beach. . . . He loves the public but not as people. The public is a great amorphous mass to him. It needs to be bathed, it needs to be aired, it needs recreation, but not for personal reasons—just to make it a better public.'' Dostoievsky had warned about political idealists who loved the people in the abstract but could not tolerate them in person. They tended to become totalitarians of the spirit.[73]

The City Council scheduled hearings on the bridge plan and invited the civic groups and Moses to testify. After a few hours of testimony bringing much of Moses' case into doubt, gallant old George McAneny, president of the Regional Plan Association, spoke before the council, and in his gentle way pleaded for some alternative or at least an impartial study of the possibilities. Then Moses himself rose to speak. Opponents who could fight back were hit with low blows; those who could not were demolished. Looking directly at George McAneny, Moses dismissed the dignified old man as ''an extinct volcano . . . , an exhumed mummy.'' Then with a broad smile on his face he snatched up his notes and stalked out of the room. Others took a long while to get up, shocked at the indecency. But La Guardia, still convinced that the bridge was the only crossing he could have, bludgeoned the City Council into passing the necessary legislation and continued to support his commissioner.

Charles Burlingham, appalled at Moses' behavior and outraged by his plans, did not. He suggested to antibridge confederate Paul Windels that he get in touch with Eleanor Roosevelt. On April 5, 1939, the First Lady's newspaper column, ''My Day,'' turned from a discussion of her family to a deft paragraph exhorting New Yorkers to give a care for beauty and serenity and not disturb what was left of lower Manhattan's natural grace. A few days later the *Herald Tribune* printed Mr. Burlingham's three-column letter to the editor reiterating the First Lady's point and, ''at the risk of being called an extinct firecracker,'' demanding to know the justification for hasty decisions in favor of a bridge that would destroy one of New York's rare places of history and beauty.

Then Burlingham wrote ''in graveyard confidence'' to his friend Franklin Roosevelt. ''Nobody fit to have an opinion wants the Battery Bridge.'' This was no time to spend millions for a scenic motorway for Bob Moses. ''It should have been stopped by the Planning Commission. It might be stopped even now by the Art Commission. It can easily be stopped by the War Department. . . . The channel of the East River should be widened, not narrowed or obstructed. . . . *Verb. suf. sap.* [a word to the wise is sufficient] especially when the sapient being is a lover of New York, as well as President of the United States and Commander in Chief of the Army.'' Within a few days the president asked for alternate proposals from other reformers. La Guardia, preoccupied with his own national ambitions, was unaware of all of this, still taking Moses' word for what was possible.[74]

Secretary Ickes tried to help La Guardia by supporting the bridge at cabinet meetings, but the president kept evading the issue. It took the interior secretary a while to remember the players before he caught on. ''The President is going to kill this," he told Labor Secretary Frances Perkins. "I wish you would argue this out with him. . . . He's getting the military to . . . say that it interferes with navigable streams and it doesn't—not at all. . . . It's just that he so hates that Moses." Perkins raised the issue with the president, who replied that he was "reliably informed" that such a bridge was a "very great hazard to navigation. In case of war we can't have any bridges around there. They'll drop bombs and so forth." Perkins went back to Ickes and told him that there were plenty of other projects that did not have Moses' name on them. He should focus on those.

By May the president knew that the secretary of war would reject the bridge. Two months later Secretary Woodring announced the decision publicly. Because the "proposed bridge is seaward of a vital Navy establishment," the Brooklyn Navy Yard, it "creates additional hazard and obstructions to the already congested water traffic at the locality." In the event of war a bridge could be tumbled to block the harbor. It was fortunate, the secretary went on to say, that other feasible alternatives existed.

Moses was enraged and La Guardia disappointed. To supporters it seemed that he had gone down with Moses and the bridge. The president, who had always been so helpful in the past, was using a farfetched technicality (air force experts estimated the odds of the bridge being knocked down and blocking harbor passage at 100,000 to 1) to deny New York the bridge.[75]

Moses lashed out at the decision, suggesting that it be "immortalized by a new Gilbert and a new Sullivan." He understood the "higher strategy" involved in the rejection. "No doubt this squares up accounts as far as the Triborough Bridge Authority is concerned. The effort to . . . force the resignation of its chief executive officer" several years before, he reminded the public, "failed because public opinion would not stand for it." But this time the public was on the other side. And this time a foxy Roosevelt left no tracks of his own involvement.

Moses turned to La Guardia for help but got none. La Guardia had no desire to get between Moses and Roosevelt. He wrote Burlingham that he felt obliged to apologize to FDR for Moses' intemperate outburst, and to Moses he said simply, "We must go on to the next thing." While Moses seldom considered the consequences that his actions might have for La Guardia or the city, he pouted, as long as a decade after La Guardia's death, that Fiorello lacked the "bred in the bone personal loyalty of leaders like Governor Smith to old friends and followers."

Moses nursed his wounds, but La Guardia regained his balance quickly. With the help of friends in the White House the tunnel option was revived. Adolf Berle lunched with the head of the Reconstruction Finance Corporation and came away with a supplementary allocation for the tunnel plan. Others too took up the cause.[76]

At the ceremony marking the completion of Moses' circumferential highway (renamed the Belt Parkway) in the spring of 1940, La Guardia announced that the city was accepting an RFC loan of $57 million at a favorable rate of interest for a tunnel linking Manhattan to Brooklyn. It was a bittersweet day for the man La

Guardia called His Grace. He had dreamed of a peripheral parkway system linking the boroughs since 1927 and it was now a reality, but the link that he had hoped would be "the biggest most beautiful bridge in the world" would be a functional underground traffic tube. He regarded it as his greatest defeat.

And La Guardia, who had not enjoyed the experience of serving as Moses' battering ram, took the opportunity to teach him a small lesson. At a meeting following the decision to make a tunnel he told Moses that there was only enough money to complete the tunnel and the Manhattan approaches, but not for the Brooklyn approaches. What, Moses asked, had happened to the Owl's Head Highway that had been planned to hook up the Battery crossing with the Belt? There just wasn't enough funding, replied the mayor, *and given the feelings in Washington*, he could not ask for more money there. Without the highway, Moses' Belt system would have a five-mile gap. Moses offered to have the Triborough Authority build the connecting road if it could impose a toll to finance the construction. No, said La Guardia, knowing how badly Moses wanted the Belt system completed, he did not like the idea of tolls on highways. Outmaneuvered, the "Master Builder" agreed to pick up the $12 million tab for the highway.[77]

By the end of 1939 there remained one more piece of unfinished business from La Guardia's 1934 agenda, the unification of the city's transit system. New York City was served by a number of surface transit lines and three rapid transit companies, the Interborough Rapid Transit or IRT, Brooklyn Manhattan Transit (BMT), and the city-owned Independent line (IND). Together these lines, consisting of both elevated and subway routes, covered more than 815 miles, the most extensive system in the world. Soon after taking office La Guardia had put together a committee under Samuel Seabury and Adolf Berle to bring the welter of transit lines under a single central system to improve service and reduce costs.

In 1913, in return for the franchise and city financing for their subway tubes, the BMT and IRT companies had agreed that the railroads would charge "the sum of five (5) cents for a single fare, but not more." This same agreement assigned the companies a "preferential" for fixed costs and profits before the municipality claimed its share of the receipts. Over the years corporate preferentials invariably consumed all revenues, forcing the city to use tax levy funds to cover the interest on its transit bonds. Thus, at the same time that the IRT and BMT took in $514 million between 1919 and 1940, New York laid out $461 million on transit-related costs.

The 5-cent fare brought handsome profits at first. Interborough stockholders in the prewar years realized a 187 percent return on their investment. But as inflation undermined the assumptions that had gone into the agreements, the fixed fare resulted in what Clifton Hood, the historian of New York City Rapid Transit, calls

459

"the San Francisco earthquake of municipal fiscal calamities." The 5-cent fare pushed the IRT into receivership, and the BMT into the red. On the city's own IND line, which was far more expensive to build and maintain because it was entirely a subway system, the 5-cent fare meant that by the 1930s the IND was losing 3 or 4 cents for each rider it carried.[78]

The 5-cent fare had become a political shibboleth by the early twenties. Every time a good-government type spoke of efficiency, the pols charged that he meant to raise the fare. La Guardia himself, as president of the Board of Aldermen in 1921, had denounced even the consideration of any fare increase. Now in 1934, twenty years after it had been adopted, the 5-cent fare remained more firmly entrenched than ever. Unification would not necessarily raise the fare, but it would streamline operations and yield efficiencies that might reverse declines in ridership.

The city had actually been kicking around a unification plan since 1921, but the idea made little headway under Mayors John H. Hylan and Jimmy Walker. La Guardia pledged that it would be different under him. He formed a Unification Committee to negotiate with the companies for the "combination, rehabilitation, improvement and extension of existing railroads." But the four-way discussions with the two companies and the State Transit Commission proved complicated and rancorous. After Seabury and Berle finally hammered out an agreement acceptable to the two companies in 1935, the commission took ten months to review it and announce its disapproval in caustic, personal terms. New discussions lagged on until after the 1937 election.[79]

Early in 1938, with Berle and Seabury retired from the negotiations, La Guardia pressed for a settlement with renewed urgency. The 1935 proposal had been too closely tied to him and his advisers, attracting the fire of both Tammany and state officials. Now, La Guardia appointed elected officials Comptroller McGoldrick and Council President Morris to work with the state transit commissioners. He wanted to complete his 1934 agenda before he left office, and his new attitude helped avoid the backbiting that had killed the first agreement.

Within a few months New York completed the single largest transaction in municipal history and the largest railroad merger ever. For $326 million (the 1937 recession had set transit securities tumbling, reducing the sale price by $110 million from the figure agreed to by Berle and Seabury in 1935) the city purchased the IRT and BMT and Manhattan trolley bus lines, taking charge over a system that serviced 2 billion passengers a year, the most extensive transit network in the world.

The unexamined implications of the municipality's new role as transit manager and entrepreneur surfaced quickly. On May 16, 1940, the Board of Estimate approved a plan of operations for the unified transit system, keeping the fare at 5 cents. In the past, at least, the companies had pressed for higher fares. Now, with control in the hands of elected officials, no one dared make that case for fear of voter disapproval. It was easier to hide the cost by dipping into taxpayer levies.

Once the trains were mixed in with other city services, who cared if the transit system brought in a profit anymore? Only the transit workers, who needed a higher fare to increase their bargaining power, cared, but the existence of the Transport Workers Union was placed in jeopardy by the takeover.[80]

Throughout the years the transport workers had borne much of the burden of the 5-cent fare. When the companies were forced to cut corners it was the workers' lives that were put in danger. On the IRT, work-related fatalities averaged 18.1 deaths per year from 1914 through 1934. Pressed by the low profit margin, traction companies would chop their labor force and use yellow-dog contracts to keep out unions. Under such adversity the hardiest workers formed a militant labor organization, and they elected the CIO-affiliated Transport Workers Union to represent them in collective bargaining. By the late 1930s the TWU signed eleven contracts with the traction companies, successfully insisting on a closed shop.

With unification looming, union leaders demanded assurances that their traditional rights would be protected. La Guardia promised that there would be no immediate changes in labor policy, except one: "No employees' status will depend upon his affiliation with any labor union organization." The city would not tolerate the closed shop. La Guardia also explicitly rejected the right of transit workers to strike.[81]

In the past the pro-labor mayor had spoken in favor of the closed shop. Now he distinguished between private industry and the municipal work force. While many unionists accepted such a distinction, they argued that the city as the proprietor of what had been a private enterprise, as in the case of the trains, should be viewed as different from the city as provider of traditional government service, as with the police. Perhaps the early La Guardia would have seen this difference; perhaps he would have said that strikes cause hardship and a transit strike would no doubt cause much of it, but that did not justify taking away the basic right of workers to strike. But this La Guardia was working under other pressures. "I am somewhat worried," he wrote to Franklin Roosevelt in March 1940, "that you are under the impression that I have changed my attitude as to a 'closed shop' in Government service. . . . I feel exactly the same as I did when we discussed the subject [before] . . . and that is that a right to strike is not recognized and a closed shop cannot be had among Civil Service employees." La Guardia wanted to show how tough he was on such matters. When FDR answered back, "The papers had you all wrong. Use my 1937 letter if it will help. . . ," that is just what he did.

His actions were now under broader review than before. "If I have not made myself clear," Fiorello wrote back to FDR, "please let me know and I will be only too happy to amplify." Motivated by his interest in national office, La Guardia was moving closer to the mainstream, replacing the blunderbuss rhetoric with a more nuanced style focused on a national constituency and the man in the White House.[82]

461

5. Eyes on the Prize: The Common Man Who Would Be President

T wo weeks after his reelection in 1937, La Guardia met with Harold Ickes to discuss national politics and the future role the two of them, progressive Republicans associated with the New Deal, might play within the existing party system. A few months later, when New York's U.S. Senator Royal Copeland died unexpectedly, La Guardia rejected pleas that he run for the Senate. He would love to return to Washington, he said, but he could not abandon New York so soon after having been reelected; and the Senate was not quite what he was aiming for. Biding his time, La Guardia did not want to be pressured into anything prematurely. Even his old dream of a new party was placed on hold.

Wisconsin Governor Philip La Follette, however, was ready, even if La Guardia was not. Declaring that "the old last is outworn," La Follette called a meeting of progressives in Madison, Wisconsin, in the spring of 1938, to proceed with plans for a national third party. La Guardia declined the invitation and sent Adolf Berle in his stead, instructing his adviser not to go further than to declare support for the New Deal and a general statement about the need for fundamental adjustments, but he was to "decline to join a third party at this time."[83]

La Follette went on to incorporate a Progressive party after the April meeting and La Guardia continued to ignore it. As between La Follette's amateurs (and worse: Berle was amazed at how similar La Follette's party was to fascism, without knowing it) and the big leaguers in Washington, he would rather play on Roosevelt's team. In Guthrie, Oklahoma, decked out in a ten-gallon hat and cowboy togs, he announced before a local crowd that "there will be no third party." There were too many radicals of the left and right already, he said, and the foreign situation required a united nation. He told Berle that he felt comfortable as a man of the Rooseveltian middle, an alternative to the Liberty Leaguers, Charles Coughlin, and Huey Long.

By 1939 La Guardia was informing the City Affairs group, the same audience that he took for a tour of his past accomplishments in 1938, that he felt like a "glorified janitor" in New York and that Americans needed to stop thinking of presidents as personalities. The speech was not particularly well focused, but it left the distinct impression of a man trying to decide where he fit in the picture he was painting.[84]

His possibilities were real. No other candidate, wrote George Britt in *Collier's*, with the exception of the incumbent, who would presumably not run for an unprecedented third term in 1940, matched the fiery New Yorker's political experience and proven ability to stir the electorate. One major obstacle stood in his way. The people might vote for him, but as things stood, no party convention would nominate him. He would have to piece together his own coalition and be ready, in John Chamberlain's words, "to ride the lightning when it is about to strike."[85]

The lightning increasingly appeared to Fiorello as a crippled man in a wheelchair with a huge smile, a powerful office, and the most effective political imagination in modern American history. Only FDR could help La Guardia secure his shot at the presidency. The Republicans were not going to give it to him and the third party was not going to make it off the ground. There were no scenarios, only possibilities, and every one of them involved the man in the White House putting his huge arm around Fiorello.

His Republican party affiliation had never meant much to La Guardia, but now he actually undertook political work for the Democratic president. In July 1938 La Guardia called in one of his political aides and instructed him to carry out a political errand for Roosevelt to help dump Lower Manhattan Democratic Congressman John O'Connor, who was a consistent opponent of the New Deal. The president was also relying on La Guardia for political intelligence. "Recalling our talk of a few days ago," La Guardia wrote in a personal note to the president, "I sent out feelers and spoke to several people concerning the gubernatorial situation in our state. I am sending along the reaction. . . ." While Roosevelt was considering other possibilities, Fiorello advised him not to dismiss Herbert Lehman too quickly. The American Labor Party was going to support Lehman, and he still might be the best the Democrats had.

He turned out to be right about Lehman. Unable to agree on a strong alternative, the Democrats settled on the incumbent while Republicans chose the highly regarded mob-buster, Thomas E. Dewey, to oppose him. Both the Dewey and Lehman camps sought Fiorello's endorsement but he refused to become involved. His relationship with the Democratic governor, though generally correct, had been punctuated by spectacular clashes, and his personal link with Tom Dewey, never warm, had cooled a great deal, especially now that Dewey was nursing his own presidential plans.[86]

As the election neared, state Republicans pressed La Guardia to take a hand in the Dewey effort, but he wasn't interested in them now. He loosed a withering personal blast at Republican State Chairman William S. Murray and once again broke off from his party. Meanwhile, Roosevelt, anxious for both Lehman and Senator Wagner, who was also running for reelection, asked Berle to bring La Guardia into the campaign. After Berle extracted assurances that the president would "protect" Fiorello in return, he had a talk with the Little Flower.[87]

La Guardia was more than willing to be of assistance, adding his own flourish to make the next step a pure political mugging. The economically conservative

Lehman, whose family had made its fortune in investment banking, was a reluctant New Dealer at best. He had maintained an independent mien, just recently having criticized the president for his ill-fated court-packing scheme. It was no secret that Roosevelt had looked around quite a while before settling on Lehman, but once he did he had to back him to the hilt to avoid a Dewey victory and a Republican resurgence in his home state. La Guardia labored under no such limitations. After calling on the president, for what he candidly described as a "political discussion," the mayor announced that he was prepared to back Lehman, if the governor would make an unequivocal statement in support of the New Deal. With newspapers speculating that his endorsement could be worth 200,000 votes, La Guardia assumed the position of New Deal enforcer. After the governor finally met his approval, La Guardia spoke warmly of "our great Governor," in time to take a share of the credit for Lehman's reelection.[88]

With his travels, the fair, his political work, and the National Conference of Mayors, Fiorello was running the city on half time. The national press was reporting the mayor's incessant work and grueling schedule, but the truth is that by 1939 La Guardia was out of city hall as often as Jimmy Walker had been. To keep up with his work when he did find himself in the office, he put in his marathon days, and these were the occasions when the journalists were invited in to spend a day with the human dynamo.

Franklin Roosevelt had advanced his national reputation while serving as governor of New York State by attending governors' conferences and speaking around the country. Similarly, La Guardia used his presidency of the U. S. Conference of Mayors to spotlight his ideas and to speak out on national issues. Americans met a La Guardia who did not seem as wild-eyed and obstreperous as he had during the twenties. The Depression had moved the nation to the left and he had moved toward the center. He was hoping that they would meet somewhere close by each other by November 1940.

La Guardia's thoughtful addresses on national issues won attention across the country. A well-crafted philippic on dictators drew the praise of an expert, Cuban strongman Fulgencio Batista. While in San Francisco, drumming up business for the fair, he was asked to discuss the situation in Germany. Avoiding the gingerly talk that passed for diplomacy in querulous times, he delivered a forthright tirade that won wide praise. "They are burning the books of the sages and the philosophers," he said of the Fascist regimes, "but they must know that we are writing the history of their miserable deeds. . . . Oh, yes the dictators are now in the limelight, but they are in the light of a setting sun; they are in a light that cannot endure. . . ." Another address called for the United States to ensure the economic welfare of the Central and South American commonwealths to forestall Fascist expansion and protect American markets. Fiorello was so proud of this speech that he sent a copy to the White House with the note: "Here is my bedtime story for the President this evening. . . ."[89]

La Guardia's renewed interest in the American farmer was another sure sign of his new intentions. After publishing an article in *Survey Graphic* calling for expanded agricultural assistance programs, he appeared in New Orleans to warn that the government must help the farmers lest "we . . . all go down together." In Springfield, Illinois, local newspapers reported that the visiting New Yorker "stopped the show" with a sandwich pulled from his pocket to illustrate agriculture's raw deal. He delighted a cheering Oklahoma crowd by introducing himself as a westerner who had lost his innocence in the East. Next stop was Wichita Falls to discuss national relief policy. On the West Coast, wearing two watches, one to tell local time and the other to remind him of what time it was in New York, he urged a government relief plan well into the next decade.[90]

The further he got from New York and his "janitorial" functions, the more undivided seemed the esteem. On a three-week fall tour of the West, overflowing audiences turned out to greet "America's No. 1 Mayor." "Mayor La Guardia has set us the example," praised the mayor of Los Angeles, "and has shown that an honest man can overcome corrupt government, and that a reform government can also be efficient and economical. . . ." Upon his visit to hometown Prescott, Arizona, he was hailed by U.S. Senator Henry Ashurst as the American politician with the brightest future in the country. "The American people," declared the senator, "are seeking leaders with his qualifications. Men of his courage and vision will always be in the forefront of American public life." When the townsfolk of Muenster, Texas, learned that the New York maverick was passing through their region, they dispatched automobile patrols to flag down the motorcade and bring it through their town. Wherever he went La Guardia managed to grab headlines. In San Francisco the papers reported that the liberal mayor refused to cross a picket line set up by hotel strikers and was staying with a local family in their apartment.[91]

La Guardia was discussing his possibilities in earnest now with Tugwell, Ickes, and Berle, but Tugwell, for one, thought that all plans were useless. Roosevelt would break tradition and run again. La Guardia knew that it could happen, but he refused to believe it. So he would dash off on another trip to harvest the adulation of the crowds and persuade himself that there was real support for his candidacy. Even when he refused to travel he generated news, declining an invitation to a conference of the International Union of Local Authorities that was held in Berlin. Local government, he declared, had "been obliterated in Berlin."[92]

Back home, city councilmen, especially Democrats who had never missed the mayor's presence before, were complaining about his absences. Councilman Kinsley plotted the flying magistrate's travels while in office. The result, he said, was "little short of amazing." He counted twenty-four separate trips, including a half dozen transcontinental ventures, covering more than 38,000 miles; and the tempo was increasing every week, keeping La Guardia out of town for days at a time.

He did not rush back for crises anymore. When seventy-mile-an-hour winds hit New York in September of 1938, resulting in power failures and some 462 deaths, Fiorello allowed Acting Mayor Newbold Morris to deal with the emergency. But when he did return to the metropolis, he could with one clever act of political artistry remind New Yorkers why they tolerated his liberties. A trucking strike had developed during one of his tours, and when he returned he tried to settle the impasse. Industry negotiators stubbornly held their ground, trying the mayor's delicate patience. He called the parties together one last time to offer a compromise proposal, but before allowing any response he pulled aside his curtain to reveal a platoon of a thousand city trucks lined up in City Hall Park (many of them, as only he knew, obsolete junk piles), with drivers standing alongside at the ready. Sign the contract within a few minutes, FH warned, or the city will be in the business of delivering food, medicine, and other necessary items forthwith. He got the signatures.[93]

Most New Yorkers understood Fiorello's arching ambitions and were willing to grant him his fling with higher office. "He deserves all the fun he has had," suggested an indulgent *New York Times*, "and the occasional discharge of political speeches was another relief to his system. He was far away from his troubles." Local headlines crowed: "MAYOR'S VIEWS HAVE RECEIVED ATTENTION AS THOSE OF A NATIONAL FIGURE."[94]

As La Guardia was about to board a train for Shreveport, Louisiana, a reporter called out to ask about his plans for election year 1940. He replied with no apparent irony that he was too busy running New York City to worry about that. "The man in office who has his eye on another office," he would say with a wink, "is like the automobile driver with a pretty girl at his side—he can't keep his mind on his work." But observers continued to match him up with that pretty girl and his protests grew ever more faint. Said one political leader in Shreveport, "If you had forced me to name the five most prominent men in public life today, La Guardia would not be worse than third, and he would be second in the minds of many people." A month after returning from his western tour he darted out again, this time to speak in several midwestern cities, pitching New York's fair and the vision of tomorrow that had become a symbol for his social agenda. Helen Harris, who headed the National Youth Administration office in New York and worked with La Guardia on related matters, recalls that she was surprised that this plain man had a real ambition to be president. But then, she says, that was Fiorello, the common man who would be president.[95]

He was seeing the president a lot these days, and their talks often veered from city issues to politics. La Guardia continued to come away with the impression that Roosevelt was not interested in a third term. Privately, Fiorello believed that the people would not tolerate it. But in dealing with Roosevelt, La Guardia was meeting more than his match. Huey Long was supposed to have put the difference between Roosevelt and his predecessor this way: "Hoover is a hoot owl and Roosevelt is a scrootch owl. A hoot owl bangs into the nest and knocks the hen clean off and catches her while she's falling. But a scrootch owl slips into the roost and scrootches up to the hen and talks softly to her. And the hen just falls in love with him, and the next thing that you know there ain't no hen." The president's endless resources of charm, his willingness to agree with all sides of an argument while he threaded his own pragmatic course, his ability to keep clearly in mind his own intentions, and to mean sincerely, at least for the moment, the ideas that he expressed made him the sleekest of scrootch owls.

FDR liked Fiorello, often remarking to Berle that he could use him in the cabinet. La Guardia, of course hoped that he could win Roosevelt's support for something more than that. But while Roosevelt believed that La Guardia was a genuine progressive and "the ablest of the lot," he would not back him for president. First, he did not believe he could win. "As a practical matter," Berle recorded the president's reasoning, "although he had been brought up in the west and was a Mason and a Protestant, the country was not prepared to elect an Italian whose mother was partly Jewish as President of the United States, and his language and accent were those of New York. This would not go over well in the farm belt." Roosevelt told Ickes the same thing: Fiorello was a crusader, and would make a fine president but his candidacy would be hopeless. Moreover, Roosevelt was not booming anyone for president, although he hinted that La Guardia might make a good vice presidential selection.[96]

By this time, however, the deteriorating international situation was casting its shadow over presidential politics and directly affecting La Guardia's candidacy. Much of the New Yorker's appeal rested on his advocacy of a progressive vision of a future that integrated scientific advance with a humane social policy. The World of Tomorrow.

The giant Trylon and Perisphere that dominated the Flushing Meadows fair with its dazzling white symbolism of clean modernity was supposed to represent that confident, abundant tomorrow. But by the time the fair closed in the fall of 1940, its season had passed. Europe was crashing into the news. On the fair's final night a double-talk expert mounted the stage at the Court of Peace, proclaiming: "In this vast amphitheater millions from all the Americas and from all corners of the world have heard addresses by statesmen, Whalen, graisnas, . . . cabishon, Gibson, forbine and nobility. Here was the pledge of peace which might well have been the . . . goodle of this expedition. Now that pledge is forgotten. Sleedment, twainst, and broint forbish the doldrum all over the world. Alas." It made no sense, except for the sighing "Alas," but its undercurrent of acute sadness rang true. The pledge of peace had been dashed against the "sleedment, twainst and . . . doldrum" of war again. The Trylon and Perisphere, 4000 tons of symbolic steel, were melted down and fashioned into bombs to help fill the cemeteries of tomorrow. By its close, the pageant had become a prewar fair, the theme of interdependence making way for vigorous Americanism, and La Guardia had become a strident warrior.[97]

Fiorello La Guardia took the war very seriously. What makes La Guardia interesting, and ultimately more than a colorful wrapper around a bundle of outsized ambitions, is the sense of private duty that impelled him to tackle the large issues of his time. The impending disaster of a crumbling international order engaged him profoundly. For two decades he had been an avowed pacifist, warning that modern technology would make the next war infinitely more devastating. "The civilian population in large and industrial centers and distant from the battle line will suffer more than the military forces in actual conflict. Long-distance guns, aerial bombardments and poisonous gases will recognize no pact, treaty, symbol or person."

With such horrible consequences to ponder, "The thing to do is to work for universal peace." He had railed against the warmakers in Congress, warning the United States to guard against imperial instincts. In 1936 he implored American women to keep the men out of war, and in 1938 he wrote Roosevelt that he was having nightmares from the president's "daring foreign policy" with "bugles calling and drums beating and cannon shots all night." As late as 1939 he was still telling the AFL convention that "the workers want no part of this war," that all they would do in it was the dying and they would rather pass.[98]

Shortly after this speech La Guardia became convinced that the United States must confront the possibility of war. His pacifism had always had a hard time keeping an aggressive Americanism in tow. When he thought the United States was right he had nothing against sending in the Marines, and his hatred for the band of Fascist dictators stalking international politics was visceral. He was perhaps the most outspoken American politician to denounce Hitler. "Secretary Hull and I have an agreement," Fiorello liked to say. "He attends to foreign affairs and I attend to cleaning the streets of New York; and when it concerns relations with a certain gentleman in Europe, we're both dealing with the same commodity." When a jittery German consul demanded that Secretary Hull guarantee the safety of German officials and mission property in New York City, the rattled secretary asked New York Governor Herbert Lehman to instruct the mayor. "I CAN REALIZE THE ANXIETY OF THE GERMAN GOVERNMENT AFTER THE OUTRAGES COMMITTED BY THEM—SUCH ANXIETY BEING THE RESULT OF A GUILTY CONSCIENCE THEIR PLEA . . . IS TYPICAL OF THE BULLY WHO . . . CRINGES LIKE THE COWARD . . . WHEN HE IS IN A MINORITY," replied Fiorello.[99]

Most Americans, however, were preoccupied with their own economic problems and with a consuming sense of past betrayal at Versailles. If the peace treaty marking the end of World War I was now seen as a huge injustice, the war itself was viewed equally darkly. Senator Gerald P. Nye's investigation on the causes of the World War left many Americans with the impression that money interest, symbolized by the arms manufacturers, the "merchants of death," had dragged an unwilling nation into an avoidable war. As the dictators became more aggressive, Americans drew more deeply into a politics of detachment, passing a series of laws that prevented the sale of arms and equipment to any belligerent, friend or foe. In a 1937 survey, with the deteriorating situation in Europe making headlines, fully 94 percent of the population thought that American policy should be directed at keeping out of all foreign wars rather than trying to prevent them from breaking out. In that same year Roosevelt condemned the aggressive nations for creating a state of international anarchy that isolation and neutrality were insufficient to halt. He proposed quarantining the aggressors, but despite the moderate tone of his criticism his suggestions were met by an outpouring of protest that saddened and sobered him. "It's a terrible thing," he said, "to look over your shoulder when you are trying to lead—and to find no one there."

By late 1939 the president could count on at least one fat little man marching resolutely behind him. Even before Hitler attacked Poland, La Guardia supported an end to the restrictive neutrality laws that outlawed the sale of planes to France and Britain, only to have the Senate Foreign Relations Committee reject the proposal by a twelve-to-eleven vote. An infuriated Roosevelt suggested that the Congress allocate funds to erect statues of Senators "Austin, Vandenberg, Lodge and Taft in Berlin and put the swastika on them."[100]

After Germany occupied Czechoslovakia, La Guardia attacked American supporters of Germany as "international cooties" and broke with the midwestern progressives who had been his closest allies and were now the leading isolationists. The president, convinced that resisting aggression was more important than keeping out of war, launched his "secret war" on the side of the Allies, and Fiorello enlisted in the cause. As the president became more reclusive to protect himself from criticism and close scrutiny, Fiorello said the things that the national executive could not say, carrying the message to such conservative venues as Little Rock, Arkansas, where he told a local group, over a serving of chitlins, that the United States could not avoid taking sides. By the end of the speech the peppery New Yorker was drawing spirited applause.

On the West Coast he said that the United States was obliged to respond when another state turns into a menacing international outlaw. Roosevelt could hardly keep a straight face when, as part of a Conference of Mayors resolution, La Guardia publicly pledged that mayors would not interfere in foreign affairs. The press reported that the president, "shaking with suppressed laughter," pointed to his New York ally and grinned. "Fiorello that . . . applies to you too." Roosevelt meant not a word of it as he continued to make good use of La Guardia as his tough proxy.[101]

Increasingly La Guardia came to be isolated from the progressives and the Republicans, who saw their possibilities in running a peace candidate. Even the

Democrats were seeking a standard-bearer who would lull rather than arouse. For a time many considered Cordell Hull, the tight-lipped, passionless WASP secretary of state, a strong contender, sweeping aside all the talk about a La Guardia candidacy. Just a year before, universities were showering the Little Flower with adulation. In the spring of 1940, Charles Burlingham sounded out Harvard University trustees about presenting Fiorello with an honorary law degree. They "looked him over," Adolf Berle recounts with some anger, "and decided he would not do."[102]

In 1938 Rexford Tugwell had infuriated La Guardia by suggesting that Roosevelt might run for a third term. "He berated me savagely . . . for being un-American." Fiorello had not wanted to hear that. Increasingly, however, it seemed that the president might do just that, as he discounted this and then that candidate, allowing the notion to sink in that there was no candidate with the credentials, experience, and leadership qualities to compare with the incumbent; that between ignoring the two-term precedent and losing Roosevelt, the former was far more desirable.[103]

As for La Guardia, while he dismissed talk about national office as "a midwinter's day dream," he had closed too many options and staked too many hopes to give up yet. Franklin Roosevelt still held the key to Fiorello La Guardia's future.[104]

CHAPTER 13

The Lost Leader

1. Just for the Riband to Stick in His Coat

Just for a handful of silver he left us
    Just for the riband to stick in his coat . . .
How all our copper had gone for his service!
    Rags—were they purple, his heart had been proud
We that had loved him so, followed him, honored him,
    Lived in his mild and magnificent eye. . . .
He alone breaks from the van and the freemen,
    He alone sinks to the rear and the slaves! . . .
Deeds will be done while he boasts his quiescence
    Still bidding crouch, whom the rest bade aspire;
Blot out his name, then record one lost soul more. . . .
Life's night begins: Let him never come back to us!
    There would be doubt hesitation and pain, . . .
Best fight on well, for we taught him,—strike gallantly,
    Menace our heart ere we master his own;
Then let him receive the new knowledge and wait us,
    Pardoned in Heaven the first by the throne!

            Robert Browning,
            "The Lost Leader"

"How could a man stand four more years in this office?" La Guardia asked Marquis Childs in February of 1940. But New York City still expected and needed his services, and his desertion of mayoral duties to pursue the excitement of higher office disillusioned his supporters.[1]

Critics noted the mayor's new tendency to "check with the Chief" before making decisions. Bad enough that Jimmy Walker, a less than disinterested character witness, as it turned out, was calling La Guardia "the greatest mayor New York ever had." Much worse, Fiorello soon enough delivered a rather generous quid pro quo, appointing Beau James to a $20,000-a-year post to mediate labor disputes as the "impartial chairman" of the Women's Cloak Industry. Many regarded this as FDR's errand, a sop to local Democrats and new national party chairman Ed Flynn. The move so disappointed Samuel Seabury that he wrote a sad attack on his backsliding fusion colleague, applying the words that Robert Browning had penned in the "Lost Leader" upon Wordsworth's acceptance of the laureateship: "Just for a handful of silver he left us, just for the riband to stick in his coat." When the mayor appointed twenty-four-year-old oil heir David Rockefeller to a municipal post, he neglected to announce it to the press and forbade any pictures, prompting this *Daily Worker* headline: "His Honor, Eye on the Vice Presidency, Figures a Good 'In' with the Rockefeller Clan Won't Hurt Him One Little Bit."[2]

In the twenties the flaming representative from East Harlem welcomed visiting royalty with the back of his hand, insulting touring dignitaries with abandon, regaling all with the dirty linen of the highborn and high-handed. No longer. When Dominican dictator Trujillo came calling, Fiorello acted the part of the perfect diplomat, twitting Burlingham, who admonished him for consorting with strongmen: "Strange how some people confuse a situation. . . . It is not necessary to be rude to be a liberal—but bad manners are often used as the expression of liberalism." Equally disturbing was La Guardia's new evenhandedness on issues that had moved him to fiery rhetoric in the past. In the struggle between the industrial unions that had banded together as the CIO, and the more conservative AFL, La Guardia sided with the AFL. His voice was hardly heard on the Wagner Labor Act, and the once active supporter of collective bargaining for federal employees was positively hostile toward municipal labor unions. Little wonder that the *New York Sun*, which used to revile the "sawed off Mussolini," no longer found much to criticize.[3]

Nothing had fueled La Guardia's resentments more in his radical days than the thought of defense contractors making profits off the world's misery. The first bill he introduced as a freshman congressman threatened unscrupulous war profiteers with death. Now with war imminent and the prospect of hundreds of millions of dollars in defense allocations an urgent possibility, Rexford Tugwell was telling La Guardia that he was disgusted by the sight of the arms dealers negotiating their fat contracts. The government, he told La Guardia, ought to do something, perhaps nationalize the industries essential for war preparation. Tugwell was taken aback by the mayor's reaction:

> He became furious. Said that present machinery had to be used and that we were a lot of dreamers. . . . I recalled the cost plus scandals of the previous war and pointed out that even the business minded press every day was illustrative of what was going on. La Guardia said I was crazy, that only businessmen could run this show. . . . He has been talking with the Generals.[4]

For the riband in his coat he had changed more than just his ideas. When Housing Commissioner Alfred Rheinstein became involved in a public dispute with Federal Housing Administrator Straus over where to build new public housing, La Guardia failed to back his commissioner. Instead, he told Rheinstein that he wanted results, not analyses, and ordered him to work it out. Rheinstein, who found the mayor out of town every time he tried to meet with him, wrote back a curt note, for which he was reprimanded and told to go back to his desk and get some work done. Finally, with no one at city hall to turn to, the commissioner poured out his frustrations in a *Harper's Magazine* article titled "Why Slum Clearance May Fail," berating Straus for sabotaging the program. Straus retaliated by canceling his approval for a housing project in Bedford Stuyvesant.[5]

La Guardia was not prepared to scuffle with Washington again. One commissioner with enemies in Washington was enough, and Rheinstein did not have Robert Moses' saving brilliance. La Guardia apologized publicly for the article. Rheinstein's resignation reached the mayor while he was attending the Yankee-Cincinnati World Series, and it was accepted with cold alacrity. The housing chairman had been foolish, even stupid, but he had been forced to deal with a difficult problem with little mayoral guidance, and La Guardia showed little of the buccaneering nerve that had in the past wrestled Washington into new policies. And he was not satisfied with forcing Rheinstein out; he wanted to humiliate him. In a move calculated to create the impression of malfeasance, La Guardia ordered the Department of Investigations to seal off Rheinstein's office.[6]

Within the week came the announcement from Washington that the Bedford Stuyvesant project would now be approved. In almost perfect tandem, La Guardia reached into the higher echelons of the business community for his next housing commissioner, former General Electric chairman Gerard Swope. No one was surprised to learn that Swope was highly thought of in Washington.

Rheinstein's parting shot rang true. "The Mayor is playing politics in Washington and doing somersaults to every one in the national administration." Fiorello's old pal Ickes knew it too. "I told him that I was now certain that he was a candidate for something, otherwise he would not have supported Straus at the expense of Rheinstein."[7]

In the spring of 1940, the City College of New York offered the famed philosopher Bertrand Russell a chair in philosophy. A man of immense intellectual ability, Russell, who had been awarded a British peerage, possessed a prodigiously restless mind that led him to unorthodox positions on a wide range of subjects. One of the most uninhibited men, certainly in scholarly circles, he was reticent only about that closeted Cambridgian company that Lytton Strachey once styled the "higher Sodomy," while he trumpeted his contempt for conventional social views: "I am quite indifferent to the mass of human creatures," he once wrote,

> though I wish as a purely intellectual problem, to discover some way in which they might all be happy. I wouldn't sacrifice myself to them, though their unhappiness, at moments, about once in three months, gives me a feeling of discomfort. . . . I believe emotionally in Democracy, though I see no reason to do so. . . . I believe in several definite measures (e.g. infanticide) by which society could be improved. . . . I live most for myself. . . . I care for very few people, and have several enemies—two or three at least whose pain is delightful to me. I often wish to give pain, and when I do, I find it pleasant for the moment. . . . Logically I can find no meaning for the word Sin.[8]

When City College offered Russell its philosophy appointment New York's reverend clergy were not amused. In his book *Marriage and Morals*, published a decade before, Russell had advocated "temporary childless marriages" for university students, removing the state from regulating sexual norms, and suggested that adultery might not be a bad idea; Christianity he dismissed as a "force tending toward mental disorders and unwholesome views of life." Episcopal Bishop William T. Manning kept a file on the suspect peer, and when CCNY made its offer to the seventy-year-old philosopher, Manning delivered a scathing attack on the noble earl, a "recognized propagandist against religion and morality who specifically defends adultery."

After the Catholic clergy joined the fray, a frustrated La Guardia wrote to the chairman of the Board of Higher Education: "Why is it that we always select someone with a boil on his neck or a blister on his fanny? I don't think we ought to get a collection of damaged goods." Mail poured into city hall denouncing the white-haired philosopher's baneful influence on college youth. With the good citizens of Gotham screaming for a posse to ride Russell out of town, or at least off campus, old Burlingham dashed off a note to steady his agitated friend: "I'm sure you won't let our anachronistic cinquecento Bishop or the Tammany Enquirer press you to press the Board of Higher Education to press the adulterous Peer out of his post."[9]

For the moment La Guardia was rescued from the need to make a decision because a public-minded citizen, fearing for the good reputation of the city, its college, and its youth, petitioned the state supreme court to order the appointment rescinded on the grounds that Russell was "lecherous, libidinous, lustful, venerous, erotomaniac, aphrodisiac, irreverent, narrow minded, untruthful and bereft of moral fibre"; besides, the complainant had it on good authority that Russell approved of homosexuality. The brief added that Russell was unfit for the position because he was a sophist whose "alleged doctrines which he calls philosophy are just cheap tawdry worn out, patched up fetishes."

The case was brought before a Roman Catholic jurist who had previously distinguished himself by having tried vainly to have a portrait of Martin Luther removed from a courthouse mural. With equal detachment, Justice John E. McGeehan offered multiple grounds for denying the appointment: Russell was not an American citizen, had not passed a competitive exam for the position, advocated illegal sexual practices, threatened the purity of young women. McGeehan upbraided the college for "in effect establishing a chair in indecency," and voided the appointment as a "direct violation of the public health, safety and morals of the people and of the petitioner's rights herein." Burlingham called the opinion "one of the worst I have ever read."[10]

Russell's supporters, confident that so flawed a decision would easily be overturned, awaited the corporation council's appeal on behalf of the Board of Higher Education. They also asked La Guardia—who had in the past spoken unequivocally in favor of First Amendment rights even when the views expressed were personally distasteful to him—to make his own position clear. Any university worthy of the name, they argued, must have the right to select its faculty without benefit of clergy. University groups and intellectuals compared the McGeehan decision with "the persecution of Socrates and Galileo" and they waited for La Guardia to join them.

But La Guardia was different now. He was afraid of offending public sentiment. With an alacrity worthy of a better cause, he pulled the rug out from under any attempted appeal by striking from the annual budget the $8800 appropriation for the City College chair in philosophy. No chair, no Russell. Then the mayor advised the corporation council in very clear language to forget about any appeal.

John Dewey howled with dismay: "I have regarded you as a person who could be counted on to do the straightforward thing independent of political pressure. . . ." But as usual Burlingham put it best: "Why should a man with your record in a free country do to the CCNY what the Nazis have done to Heidelberg and Bonn? . . . Your attempts to dispose of the case while it was in the courts was bad enough; but to prevent the Board appealing to higher courts is far worse. It is not like *you*."[11]

But it was more and more like him. Tugwell noted that the mayor was busily

475

patching things up with the local Democratic organization, with both working toward the same goal: He wanted their help to leave New York and they wanted him out. Borrowing a page or two from Tammany, he stocked a number of discretionary municipal positions with friends and fired some of his more liberal-minded advisers. He was denouncing "Communists" more often now, siding with positions that in the old days he dismissed as "lousy."[12]

In aiming to bolster his popularity with conservatives, La Guardia ordered officials to furnish Dun and Bradstreet with the names of all patrons found in gambling places during police raids, whether they were involved in illegal activities or merely standing around. At the behest of church groups, La Guardia ordered sexy magazines removed from the newsstands. "There is no question of freedom of the press involved here," he insisted tendentiously. "It isn't censorship I am seeking to invoke. The Mayor has no such power. But you know the Mayor has power of sewage disposal . . . ," he said as he ordered a fleet of twenty-four garbage trucks to seize the indecent literature.[13]

So used to having his way had La Guardia become that when Board of Education chairman James Marshall refused to knuckle under to mayoral orders and insisted correctly that the schools were a quasi-independent body, he refused even to speak to Marshall for more than a year. And shortly after the Bertrand Russell affair, Professor Morris Raphael Cohen, one of City College of New York's most illustrious faculty members, complained to Burlingham that La Guardia was interfering in the selection of a new president for CCNY. Even Tammany had never done that. "Already the rumors of the Mayor's peculiar attitude are beginning to spread," wrote Cohen.[14]

Observers noted even more worrisome lapses. Paul Blanshard had built the Office of Investigations into a powerful, independent agency of municipal government by standing up to the mayor when he had to. The bright and efficient investigations commissioner, William Herlands, who replaced Blanshard, lacked his predecessor's backbone. He took the mayor's personal abuse and buckled under when La Guardia ordered him to investigate individuals for no better reason than that they had made themselves unpopular with city hall. He allowed La Guardia to order investigations personnel to seal off the offices of resigned officials to create the impression of wrongdoing where none existed. One former investigator offers a chilling view of his investigative technique under La Guardia, an approach that La Guardia rewarded with generous promotions.

> I would tell people [who fell under his suspicion] that ordinarily people live, and no one bothers them. . . . They do things that are bad, but no one knows about it and no one cares, but every so often in a minority of cases government happens to stumble upon them and decides to make an example of them.

476

Government is a great big thing that includes every agency from cleaning the streets to prosecuting . . . to judges. When government decides to go after someone it has unlimited resources, it can do anything and ultimately they will find out everything. And you are one of those unfortunate people and government is going to get you.[15]

Unhappy about his own blocked ambitions, La Guardia played cruel games with people, dangling promotions in front of them, forcing them to jump through hoops to show their personal loyalty. Even more than before, he humiliated his commissioners. In the presence of one of his deputies, the investigations commissioner was told that "you let them shit all over you and pee all over you and you like it so much you lick it up." Newbold Morris was told, "You're so stupid it's an art."[16]

When he was away on his frequent absences, he wanted city hall to hum. But the burden fell on his staff. They had to work twice as hard and there was hell to pay if things did not work out neatly, while he galavanted all over the nation in search of larger political thrills. At least one member of La Guardia's official family (who will not speak for attribution) says that the mayor's desire to keep everything calm and clean led him to ignore rumors that a commissioner was involved in narcotics, associating with known racketeers, and interfering in the judicial system. When an investigator advised La Guardia of these charges, La Guardia said to him, "I don't want to hear about it," and then took the investigator off the case.[17]

La Guardia had once viewed investigations as the way government kept itself clean, holding a spotlight to internal processes as well as the general deportment of its personnel. Now, he wrote the publisher of the *Daily News* that too many investigations were politically motivated, too expensive, and too disruptive of the regular patterns of government. His aspect had changed from the suspicious outsider to the insider with a reputation to protect.

Burlingham was disturbed by the changes. Increasingly, La Guardia's public forays were motivated by the search for headlines, particularly his offensive against the courts of appeals. "In my opinion your attacks, so often repeated, accomplish no good, and do great harm. It is to the Courts of last resort in this country that we must and do look for the preservation of our civil rights. It is to these high courts that Labor owes much. No one knows this better than you. And yet deliberately and not in passion, you have been playing a role that I think unworthy of you, and I am truly grieved."[18]

La Guardia's personal behavior turned even more irascible than usual. Secretary Mitzi Somach sent Burlingham a confidential note remarking, as many others were, on La Guardia's erratic behavior. "It seems incredible," Geoffrey Parsons, of the *Herald Tribune*, wrote Burlingham, that [La Guardia] could do the outrageous things that he has done to decent unoffending folk, subordinates, large and small. 'Calculated explosions' he calls them. No doubt the fact that his word is regarded as valueless both inside and outside his official family would be defended by him on a similar basis of calculated treachery for the public good. . . . But I am frank to admit . . . that I am becoming a little weary of this latest model of reformer, who because he is money honest and his aims are high, feels under no obligation to live up to the ordinary standards of courtesy and fidelity to a promise.[19]

An anxious Burlingham discussed Fiorello's behavior with the mayor's personal physician, Dr. George Baehr, who was equally troubled by La Guardia's frazzled nerves. In the past, Fiorello had deployed his temper as a marvelous tool, bullying recalcitrant administrators into line, raging into the headlines with his zealous anger, and cowing political opponents. Now, overwork and frustration threatened to push him out of control. Baehr wanted to hospitalize the mayor for a rest.

To help persuade Fiorello that others agreed with his diagnosis, Dr. Baehr showed him Burlingham's letter, but La Guardia had no intention of fueling reports that he was close to a breakdown by entering a hospital. Instead, he wrote CCB a sarcastic note mimicking the old man's disquiet. "I feel I must write you because I am so worried that you are not taking care of yourself. Here you are when you should be resting, in so many activities and giving so much of yourself to each of them, from the eugenics of Bertrand Russell to the breeding of horses of Herbert Swope, and then jumping to the military strategy of parachute invasion. . . . That is simply too much. . . . Take it easy for a while and be guided entirely by your friends."

Burlingham responded in doggerel:

This medico's name is George Baehr
*   He's supposed to control the Lord Mayor*
But that's all in your eye,
*   He might as well try*
To tame a wild man-eating beast

There is a foolish old man called C. C.
*   Who is awfully fond of La G.,*
He wrote Baehr a letter—
*   He should have known better—*
And urged him to tell
*   His patient august*
That he'd better pipe down
*   Or he'd certainly bust.*

Forgetting his oath Hippocratic . . .
The letter Baehr showed to La G.
Whereupon Fiorello . . .
Turned the tables on C,
And Said: "Dr. B.
You've got the wrong party,
Myself I am hearty,
The man you should see
Is that ancient C. C. . . .

FH kept up the teasing exchange, suggesting that he might have to cancel a Harvard Club dinner that the gnarled advocate had asked him to attend. He wired CCB at his Park Avenue home:

"DR GEORGE BAEHR ABSOLUTELY FORBIDS ME GOING ANYWHERE AT NIGHT STOP DOES NOT WANT ME TO SPEAK AT DINNER TOMORROW NIGHT AT HARVARD CLUB STOP WHAT SHALL I DO"

Next morning came the response:

"FIRE GEORGE AND HIRE BUGS [a popular newspaper humorist] BAER"

And finally, Fiorello's coup de grace:

"GEORGE FIRED BUGS HIRED FIORELLO INSPIRED"[20]

Despite the banter there was ample cause for concern. James Kieran, the mayor's press secretary, resigned after a row with La Guardia, and a short while thereafter Mitzi Somach, also fed up with the abuse, resigned her $1-a-year post as La Guardia's confidential secretary. Lapsing into his tough-guy gracelessness, the mayor declared, "It has lasted six years and we got a lot out of her during that period."

While his administration was beset by a plethora of problems, governmental as well as internal, he could not chase images of the White House from his head. To a member of his cabinet who wanted to schedule him for a speech several months ahead, he said, "There is only one date I can think about and that's January 1, 1941." He continued to pursue national attention, but as FDR's intentions began to emerge, his own hopes shriveled. Sadly, Berle understood: "And that was all it came to, save for the pleasure of seeing a man who has done a magnificent job, and is entitled to the next step forward, which lesser people are prepared to take away from him if they can, and perhaps they can." The game was up for 1940,

La Guardia told Berle, adding bitterly that he might give a thought to the "fun of running on a third ticket." The war had overtaken his ambitions.[21]

At dawn on April 9, 1940, Nazi troops poured across the Danish border in a lightning attack. Within hours Denmark fell. Norway followed. On May 10 the *Fuehrer*'s armies struck the Low Countries. Holland surrendered after five days; Belgium was lost in eighteen days; and on June 22, in the same railway car in the Compiegne forest where Germany had signed the armistice ending World War I, the French Republic capitulated. The national mood in the United States changed overnight. What had been a distant threat became awesomely real. What America's precise role would be remained uncertain, but the blinkered neutrality of the past seemed suddenly misguided and worse. Between the United States and Hitler stood only England. The president inaugurated a program of swift preparation, throwing together defense policies with the same flair that had produced the New Deal. Then, declaring that "On this tenth day of June, 1940, the hand that held the dagger has struck it into the back of its neighbor," he announced a new policy of assistance to the opponents of force.

The presidential campaign took on a new character. For Democrats a third term for Roosevelt was no longer held out as a possibility; it was imperative. Among Republicans there was talk of running Tom Dewey, of whom Harold Ickes would say, "he threw his diaper into the ring." Wendell Willkie, who was eventually nominated, had even less governmental experience than Dewey.[22]

With the presidency out of reach, La Guardia channeled his energies into a campaign for preparedness. He wrote Burlingham in June that "everything seems so trivial in the face of world conditions." Two weeks later he sent Roosevelt a message of strong personal commitment: "You have now assumed the most difficult task and a responsibility of greater importance to the future of our country than ever before confronted any man or candidate in our entire history. You are now facing one of the hardest campaigns ever waged in our time and you require all the strength, courage and fortitude God can give you, which is the wish of your sincere friend, Fiorello."

According to some observers, Willkie would have liked to ask La Guardia to run as his vice president, but the Republican candidate decided against such an offer for fear that the erratic Flower might take the occasion to decline publicly and announce his support for Roosevelt. While Willkie did not give him the chance to make quite so spectacular an endorsement, La Guardia did forsake the Republicans again. "Roosevelt has made America the hope of the world," La Guardia declared, and joined Senator George Norris to form Independents for Roosevelt.[23]

The campaign to reelect Roosevelt afforded the mayor an excuse to leave New York again. The graduate of night school law classes even went to Harvard to plead on behalf of its illustrious alumnus, prepared to chide the men of Cambridge for the disdain with which they treated their Roosevelts, both Theodore and Franklin. But before Fiorello was introduced, another speaker, a former law partner of FDR's, complained at length about just this, knocking out his speech. La Guardia quickly recast his text, presenting an abridged version: "Harvard has always been most generous to its sons, recognizing them in all possible ways—unless they're Presidents of the United States." Then he sat down. The president thanked Fiorello for "restoring my speaking acquaintance with my fellow graduates."[24]

If La Guardia showed that he could still keep his wits about him and win any audience that he set his mind to charming, he also unsheathed the lethal, and at times unprincipled, campaign fury that marred many of his past campaigns. Politics—the contest between contending parties for the power to shape national destiny—that he had so often denounced as an anachronism in the age of "scientific government" now preoccupied him. Despite Willkie's open honor and integrity, La Guardia unjustly berated him as a heartless pawn of capitalist forces, an untrustworthy hypocrite trying to buy the election and intimidate voters. All the bad feeling that his frustrated hopes had welled up in him found convenient release in the campaign.

Many among fusion's first line, including Samuel Seabury, and others who had worked with La Guardia broke with the mayor over his support for Roosevelt. They charged Fiorello with abandoning first principles to make a pact with bosses Flynn, Hague, Crump, Kelley, Pendergast, and "the remains of the Huey Long boodle organization in New Orleans." There was no denying the important role of the machines and the reward they would reap from a Roosevelt victory, but La Guardia offered his own defense. "Hitler," he would tell audiences, "understands the language of Roosevelt."[25]

In dozens of appearances around the country as Roosevelt's spear-carrier, La Guardia attacked Republicans as the kept party of business and Willkie as the polished front for this shameful enterprise. Words like "whore" and "pimp" and others equally opprobrious rolled freely off his tongue. "It was simply incredible," recalled Paul Windels, "how he spoke against Willkie—personally vituperative. . . . I suppose he wanted to make a big hit with Roosevelt." His old fusion mentor Samuel Seabury he denounced for bearing an "obsessive hatred of Roosevelt." "By that time," continued Windels, "he wasn't the FH he used to be. The job was beginning to tell on him."[26]

This was obvious in Detroit, where a heckler drew blood by asking Fiorello if he was taking orders from Boss Flynn. La Guardia wheeled toward the fifty-one-year-old man and grabbed him by the neck, tearing his collar and shirt buttons before being dragged off. Barely in control of his emotions, La Guardia was pushing himself nonstop. Some said that he would collect his reward in a cabinet post; others feared he would not last long enough to enjoy it.[27]

In fact, FDR had decided to make La Guardia secretary of war after the election. Fiorello's "hopes were so high and his eagerness so apparent," recalled Tugwell. He asked his advisers what they thought of Robert Moses, or perhaps Adolf Berle, as his replacement.[28]

Just before election day, Roosevelt delivered the assurances that many Americans had been waiting for. "Your President says this country is not going to war," he said. Voters overwhelmingly returned him to office for an unprecedented third term. Then, shortly after the election, Roosevelt announced that the United States was prepared to serve as the "arsenal for Democracy." The quick about-face scared many who had voted for him on the strength of his promises. William Allen White, who led the Committee to Defend America by Aiding the Allies, now feared that aiding the allies was shading into active American participation. He attacked plans to convoy military equipment to Britain as "a silly thing, for convoys, unless you shoot, are confetti and it's not time to shoot, not now or ever. . . . If I were making a motto," declared the Kansan, "it would be the Yanks are not coming."

But La Guardia remained resolute in his support of "The Chief" and in taking an increasingly hawkish stand on the war. "Strange," he scolded White,

> when the going was good for the Allies, you and others were strong in saying what you would do. Now that the going is bad, you are doing a typical Laval [the hated leader of Vichy France who willingly delivered his nation to Germany].
>
> It occurred to me that the Committee had better divide. You would continue as Chairman of the Committee to Defend America by Aiding the Allies with Words and the rest of us would join a Committee to Defend America by Aiding the Allies with Deeds.[29]

After the campaign was over, La Guardia left a trail of besmirched reputations, but it was he who refused to forgive those who attacked him for siding with the bosses during the campaign. He hit back at his tormentors with a provocative open letter to the fusionists, including Seabury. He denounced their "filthy" charges. Let them accept the responsibility for keeping New York clean and honest. They were the backsliders, supporting a utilities man like Willkie over Roosevelt's record of proven reform. He was a free man; he had the right to work for the best candidate. He had done the job in New York, a job that with all of their goodwill they had never managed to have done before him. They had done "irreparable damage" to the cause, but he found comfort in 2 Timothy 4:7: "I have fought the good fight. I have finished my course. I have kept the faith." He would not run for mayor again.

It was a bitter, stupid, cantankerous letter from a man with a shockingly weak hold over his emotions. "I wish," Burlingham wrote with more than a touch of sadness, "you had a secretary or a friend who had the courage to tell you not to send a letter which you should destroy before you sign it." But he did not, and it was all too clear that no subordinate or friend would survive such candor.

Burlingham offered one more suggestion. In his effort to show the reformers how much more they needed him than he needed them, La Guardia had said that he would not run again for mayor. La Guardia had time to burn his bridges.

> No one knows what the situation will be in New York or the USA six or eight months from now. You may be needed in New York as much as FDR was and is in the USA. Next to the Presidency, the Mayoralty of New York is the most important office in the USA—certainly far more important than any Cabinet post, even the highest. So I beg you to keep your shirt on and give out no statements. The less talk, the more do, Your old friend.[30]

The shame of it was that he did not take the advice. Instead he laid plans to move to Washington. "Rex," he said to Tugwell, "what shall we do? I can't stay here with the world falling to pieces."[31]

"My husband had an affection for him and a great admiration for his qualities of leadership," Eleanor Roosevelt wrote of La Guardia. There was little doubt about that. "I will be in Washington," he would write. "There are several things I would like to listen to the President about." Other mayors would receive short, perfunctory notes from a secretary, but La Guardia invariably got the president's ear. "How about giving the City of New York a small experimental contract to transport . . . mail . . . via City owned subway," advised a presidential memo to Postmaster General Farley. "The mayor is very anxious to have this."[32]

Roosevelt was not alone in his regard for La Guardia. Across the country many who remembered the candid, tough-talking mayor they had read so much about the previous year were writing to the White House suggesting that he be brought to Washington. Unaware that the president had already decided on bringing him into the cabinet as war secretary, many thought that he would make an excellent secretary of labor. Black Americans spoke of their confidence in La Guardia and praised him for his fairness. Others lauded his courage, take-charge attitude, and outstanding war record. "If he were chosen Secretary of War," wrote Dr. O. B. Kiel, who had served under Major La Guardia in Foggia, "he would visit every state in the union, every training center, and he would inspire these soldier boys and make them realize it is an honor to wear the uniform of the American soldier."[33]

But Roosevelt changed his plans. On the day of FDR's resounding reelection victory, Adolf Berle visited La Guardia at a deserted city hall. Something had happened. La Guardia was no longer certain of his appointment, and Berle was struck by the pathos: "The Administration owes him a good deal in this campaign. I hope they know it and recognize it—but you can never tell." From the tough independent spirit of early fusion days, La Guardia was now a man fully dependent on reward for political work well done to define his future in politics. That was what his ambition had done to him. It was sad.[34]

2. Drifting Toward Washington

B URLINGHAM had cautioned La Guardia against burning his bridges in New York City, and now Roosevelt had heeded those warning him that the outspoken La Guardia was temperamentally unsuited for a cabinet post. But La Guardia also had himself to blame for the disappointment.

In August 1940 Roosevelt appointed him chairman of the American side of the U.S.-Canadian Joint Permanent Defense Board. The challenge of planning the coordinated defense of the North American continent engaged Fiorello in a way that he had not been stimulated since the early days of cleaning out the boodlers. Home with a cold when the appointment was announced, he literally jumped out of a sickbed, flew down to Washington for briefings, picked up a military attache, and hurried off to Ottawa for the founding conference.

There he took charge in his own style. "In exactly six and one-half minutes all the formalities were cleared and all the courtesies were accomplished. The board decided from the outset to use plain, everyday understandable English and to dispense with the complexities involved in diplomatic usage and in legalisms." La Guardia made no modest claims. Having been given the ball, he ran with it. "We are considering all phases of defense, including the economic phase." La Guardia's take-charge leadership on the Joint Permanent Defense Board won praise from both sides of the border, but it also demonstrated the difficulty he would have serving as part of a cabinet. He insisted on his own rules, bullied his way toward solutions, and paid scant attention to the niceties of a diplomatic process that had purposely built safeguards and delays into language, procedures, and frequent demands for consultative cooperation.[35]

There was talk of other offices. "Dear Mr. P.," Frederick M. Davenport, chairman of the Council of Personnel Administration, wrote Roosevelt, "Couldn't we use Fiorello down here to blast holes in resistances governmental and extragovernmental. Might he not save you valuable time and energy?" "Dear Fred," came the reply, "Not at all a bad idea. I hope I can make it bear fruit. FDR." But every time the president floated a trial balloon it fell to the ground. By year's end

Roosevelt and La Guardia were discussing the post of presidential assistant to coordinate a newly established Defense Council. "If he is to go to Washington at all," the *New York Daily News* wrote in an editorial titled "Is Butch Quitting?" "he rates a bigger post than that. He is Cabinet size, mentally, politically and every other way."[36]

But La Guardia was now dealing with a man at least as power-wise as himself. "He has met his nemesis now," prophesied Rexford Tugwell. "He will have to take little or nothing." What worried Tugwell and others was that because he was so excited by the war, he would leave New York and "take the little."[37]

Months before, Burlingham had written Seabury what he thought of La Guardia's pursuit of national portfolio: "I hope he will not be such an ass as to go into Roosevelt's cabinet. He would only be a tool." Now he told La Guardia the same thing. "It is extraordinary how impossible it seems to resist the blandishments of our Good and Great Friend. You won't get anything by cuddling up to Franklin. He doesn't give a damn for you. I'm perfectly sure of that, and he would chuck you out in a minute." The harsh analysis was not entirely correct, but it would have saved La Guardia much grief and frustration had he taken it to heart.[38]

Instead, the drama of where Fiorello's name would be raised next was played out openly for all to speculate upon. The exposure of his aspirations and their many blind alleys made him all the more irascible, but he would not give up. Talk of a special undersecretariat in the War Department dealing with aviation was quickly shot down. "I would never take any damned undersecretaryship, I'd rather have a soapbox," he said.[39]

While La Guardia pursued his reward in Washington, many in New York were convinced that the city could not survive without him. The *New Republic* spoke for many when it wrote, "There should be a Cabinet place for Mr. La Guardia, and there should be two La Guardias, so one could stay in New York." They feared the return of Tammany. The trouble, Berle wrote, was with "the second string man, Newbold Morris." Few were confident that Morris could do the job. Robert Moses made them scarcely more comfortable, although for different reasons.[40]

"We don't . . . want Butch to get a Cabinet job," editorialized the *Daily News*. We want him to stay right on as Mayor of New York City. . . . La Guardia has been and is, in our estimation, the greatest Mayor New York City ever had. . . . He is the ideal Mayor for a time like this, when the war across the ocean is pulling the various racial groups' heartstrings every whichway." Governor Herbert Lehman told the president privately that no one could handle the anticipated problems of war, espionage, fifth column activity, and New York's radical elements like La Guardia. Even Harold Ickes, La Guardia's friend, and aware of how achingly the mayor wanted to leave city hall, suggested that it was important to keep La Guardia in New York. With his liberal record he would be able to go further than anyone else to crack down on suspected subversives "without too much criticism." Clearly, if La Guardia's powerful friends had thought he belonged in Washington, they could have brought him there. They wanted him in New York.[41]

Even with only half his mind on the job he was a better mayor than any of his predecessors. His instincts were still excellent. He pushed against corruption, and he tolerated little of the shoddiness that crept into other administrations. But he no longer liked his job. In 1934 he had come in full of fight and goals. Everything was open to question, nothing sacred. The more that was discovered as being out of shape, the happier he was. Uncovering corruption or inefficiency in 1940, however, was a bit more painful. It reflected on him directly. He had been in office too long to fight his predecessor; now he was forced to limn the progress that had been made. It was an awkward position for an insurgent. His principles had changed only a bit, but the entire axis of his mayoralty had changed an awful lot. There was no comfortable solution other than moving on. In this sense it was not merely an egotistical urge to more power, but a positive step that he had to take, to move on before he got stuck defending his past record instead of making a new one.

Rexford Tugwell understood the problem:

> He had to give up so much, contrive so constantly, submit to such demanding disciplines! And for what? So that at the peak of power, he could go on with the same regime, grown now more taut and routinized, knowing that every month and every year he grew less rather than more effective, being thus the victim, as others were the beneficiaries, of his sacrifices and efforts. And yet, confined as he was he had always to find new resources of imagination, to invent new devices, and to exert exhaustingly the magic of public persuasion.

> The trappings and routines of power, after a while, are not the compensation that they were at first. Gradually they become bindings and ties; finally they become something submitted to and undergone with apathy, even with resentment. The horrible fatigues of the ceremonial, fiercely resented as they often are, finally have their way and are no longer even evaded. The man has become the prisoner of the office. The small nagging urge that started him off has landed him in a padded cell—a cell padded with plush, it is true, but one in which he must perform, it seems for him, as an animal does on his treadmill, routines prescribed by tradition and circumstances.[42]

Berle met the La Guardias shortly before Christmas and he was troubled by Fiorello's uncertain future. "Marie does not want him to run for a third term in New York and neither does he." He got no argument when he told them that the place for Fiorello was Washington. But in February 1941 Berle was saying, "He will have to take the third term himself, just as the President had to." Then on April 23, Fiorello was summoned to Washington, after a session of the U.S.-Canadian Joint Defense Board, to meet with the president.[43]

Fiorello La Guardia had promised himself and his wife that he would not put them both through another campaign and another mayoral term. "It takes more than a human body to take eight years of that kind of punishment," he had remarked. He had worked harder than any mayor in memory, and he was glad to fling the mayoralty back at the best men, who had criticized him for supporting the New Deal, and to challenge Seabury and his friends to find someone better.

The problem with all of this was that La Guardia had nowhere else to go. He could not even be certain of reelection. The ALP, so important in his 1937 victory, was hopelessly split between Communists and Socialists. Republicans were only too happy to take him at his word that he would not run. "Why don't you round the circle and turn Democrat like me?" wrote Burlingham. But that remained unlikely, at least at the local level. In fact, the Democrat-dominated City Council had finally got hold of an issue that was sure to wound La Guardia, perhaps critically.[44]

Paul J. Kern, tall, well educated, and brilliant, was one of the "junior brain trust" that La Guardia brought with him into city hall in 1934. Kern had impressed La Guardia with his brash intelligence while still a twenty-three-year-old law student clerking on Capitol Hill, and La Guardia put him to work in his congressional office on what eventually became the Norris-La Guardia Act. Appointed the mayor's law clerk after the fusion election, Kern became a personal favorite, welcome at the La Guardia home, often spending Sundays with the mayor touring the city to plan new projects. In 1936 La Guardia appointed the twenty-seven-year-old Kern to the Civil Service Commission, and in 1938 he eased out commission president James Finegan and replaced him with Kern.

It was not one of his happiest appointments. Kern's arbitrariness and abrasive arrogance produced a succession of explosive confrontations. His affiliations also proved unnecessarily provocative. As head of the Civil Service Commission, Kern was charged with eliminating partisanship in municipal appointments. In this sensitive position Kern was supposed to rise above any suspicion of partisanship or political favoritism. Yet he was an outspoken advocate of liberal politics and held a prominent political post in the ALP. His membership in organizations that were often described as "of Communist complexion," his subscription to radical publications, and his ownership of Soviet bonds all had nothing to do with how good a job he did, but again they ruffled a large part of the population that was supposed to trust him to be politically neutral. His open support of the Loyalist forces in the Spanish Civil War offended Catholics, a group that had already expressed its doubts

487

about fusion's evenhandedness. Before long, even the Civil Service Reform Administration, which praised Kern's accomplishments in office, censured him for his partisan activities and his insolence toward other officials.[45]

Kern's brash style was calculated to offend friends and multiply enemies. He did not advise, he demanded. He did not discuss, he sledgehammered his way through the bureacracy, and he had the unfortunate tendency to humiliate those in the administration with whom he did not see eye to eye. He charged Housing Commissioner Rheinstein with maintaining "one of the last bulwarks of the old spoils era," publicly accusing his colleague of juggling titles to avoid the intent of civil service laws.[46]

If it was unbefitting to clash with Rheinstein, it was absolutely suicidal to take on Robert Moses. But Kern set out to bring the Parks Department under rein and teach the imperious Moses that parks workers were not his private slaves. He also wanted to put a stop to Moses' practice of rewarding favorites with bonuses from the public pot. But taking on Moses was begging for trouble. RM had brought more powerful individuals to heel and for much less. He was not about to allow the "boy commissioner" to cramp his style.

Nor was Kern's public support strong enough to carry out his intentions. Kern himself would later admit that he had been a "sucker for causes," and Moses took full advantage, attacking Kern for his liberal politics and radical affiliations. From a large investigative file on public officials that he kept, the parks commissioner leaked material calculated to smear Kern as a Communist. When Kern initiated a program awarding points toward promotion for municipal employees who reported instances of official venality and corruption, Moses denounced the plan as "un-American," suggesting that Kern "send this communication to the OGPU" in Russia, "whose American representative you seem to be." Father Charles Coughlin, the anti-Semitic demagogue-priest, followed suit, characterizing Kern's civil service plan for the police as a plot to "place over the Cops of New York . . . 90 percent of them good Christians, *a group of Reds*, an OGPU! . . . who could not tell a nightstick from a streak of salami."[47]

Democrats in the City Council gleefully rallied to the cause. In May of 1940 Councilman Al Smith, Jr., son of Moses' patron and mentor, initiated a comprehensive investigation of Kern to learn whether the Civil Service commissioner was a Communist, whether he had favored fusionists in city appointments, and whether he was responsible for establishing "an alien espionage system" to spy on workers. Everything from Kern's sex life to the magazines that he read, the causes he supported, the associations he developed as a teen, and his political ideology was scrutinized.

Again La Guardia was forced to deal with a personnel issue in which the appointee had a "boil on his fanny," but unlike the case of the noble earl, La Guardia chose to reappoint Kern, whose term was due to run out in June, without waiting for the results of the council's investigation.

Meanwhile, the Smith committee came up with a number of damaging revelations about fusion's "scientific" civil service. They discovered instances of departments changing position titles and resorting to other subterfuges to circumvent civil service requirements. Then there was the case of the Sanitation Department's scowmen. After advertising openings for the position of sanitation scowman, the department received a total of 993 applications, all but 8 from individuals who carried "able-bodied scowman's certificates," understood signals, lights, tides, winds, and all of the other things that went with the position. Amazingly, the 8 applicants without any qualifications were selected. Not so amazingly, it turned out, for these men were excellent baseball players, and Commissioner Carey, looking to build a superior team for his department, was more interested in fine athletes than able scowmen.[48]

The committee also uncovered cases of direct mayoral interference in appointments. A former Civil Service Commission member testified that Kern himself had told another commissioner that he ought to resign if "he could not conform to the Mayor's wishes." To be sure, there were far fewer such indiscretions than in the past, but that was a weak defense for an administration committed to the highest ethical standards in government. As the committee began to dig deeper, La Guardia adopted the tactic of withholding records under a claim of executive privilege. His own friend Justice Philip M. McCook threw the claim out of court, in a decision that was unanimously upheld on appeal.[49]

Kern called the investigation a witch-hunt, which is what such investigations tend to become, but that did not excuse his own flagrant lapses of judgment. He allowed himself to be baited into arguing the relative evils of nazism (bad) and communism (no clear opinion), moving the *New York Times* to call Kern's testimony "an extraordinary tale of astonishing blind spots." His hysterical comparison of the inquiry to the work of "Himmler, Hess and Goebbels" did him little good, and his refusal to cooperate with the investigation resulted in several citations for contempt; more than once he was nearly jailed. While Kern may have been justified in complaining that the committee was making very much out of very little, that there had been wrongdoing was indisputable. And the administration's heavy-handed effort to retaliate by having Commissioner Herlands dig into the financial records of committee personnel resulted in a court order directing Herlands to end his harassment.[50]

The investigation resulted in a 120-page report condemning both the mayor and his Civil Service Commission president for fostering favoritism and discrimination in the city work force. Noting that Commissioner Kern himself was unwilling to testify as to what was absolutely a rule and what was not, the report scored the chaotic state of La Guardia's "scientific and nonpolitical" civil service. The absence of clear-cut regulations was blamed on a preoccupied mayor "too busy" to approve a revised set of laws that had been submitted to him in 1938! It was further proof of La Guardia's disturbing distraction from the city's business.[51]

He was interested in Washington; New York was only a place to hang his hat until Franklin Roosevelt came through, but the President had not come up with a position of comparable worth for the feisty Flower, and those in a position to know were saying that FDR had decided to keep La Guardia at the helm of the Empire City. "Mr. La Guardia," it was reported in the press, "is understood to have been informed of the way the President feels about the situation through a third person." Even the bosses seemed to support a third-term run for La Guardia. Speaking at Chapel Hill, North Carolina, Democratic boss Edward Flynn called La Guardia "one of the best mayors that New York ever had."[52]

In April La Guardia backed away from his categorical statements of the past: "In these days no one can say with any degree of certainty just what he will or will not do . . . [although] I prefer not to run again for Mayor of the City of New York." He was, in short, willing to be persuaded by good citizens making the proper noises about his indispensability. On cue, the Citizens Non-Partisan Movement to Draft La Guardia for Mayor was established, with Marshall Field, Fannie Hurst, James MacGregor Burns, Bennet Cerf, Irving Berlin, Jacob K. Javits, and assorted lawyers of impeccable reputation as members. After all, declared John Haynes Holmes, Franklin Roosevelt had already proven that two good terms deserve a third.

Holmes said much more, turning the mayor's head with the praise of a fine man: "I would be the first to proclaim you a great man, who, through an extraordinary combination of genius, character and sheer devotion has fitted himself with unique success to the exigencies of the [second] most important single political office in this country." La Guardia was not offended by the obeisance of this man and his fellow reformers, who just a short while back had been denouncing his intemperate tongue. In fact, he quite enjoyed it.[53]

La Guardia submitted to the good Reverend's plea. A third term was all right in the case of the president, and, he allowed, "it would be all right in my case," so long as "we do not get into the habit of perpetuity in office." An overwrought Holmes responded to the welcome news: "I rejoice in your joy in your job. I admire your ceaseless energy and inexhaustible vitality. I adore your early morning and late at night fidelity to your multitudinous duties. I reverence your integrity, your courage, your pride in the city, your confidence in its citizens." Holmes continued his peroration. "I love it when you race to a fire, like the unquenchable boy within you; I love it equally when you take your horn spectacles and lock yourself in for a week on bread and water with your budget like a saint doing devotions before the altar of his faith." If this was an apology for reform criticism of his mudslinging at Willkie, then the mayor was disposed to accept it.[54]

In January the president had written La Guardia about some policing problems that were plaguing the capital and asked to borrow Commissioner Lewis Valentine for a few days. Roosevelt had more than local police work in mind. The president wanted to know more about La Guardia's defense operation in New York City from Valentine, who was its coordinator. Roosevelt was still thinking about an appointment for La Guardia, and lately Fiorello had been thinking about defense more than almost anything else, encouraging his mayoral colleagues to follow him in drawing up plans to protect their cities against the threat of a home-front war. In New York City, La Guardia developed a comprehensive emergency defense plan and established a defense board that met behind barred doors in a spirit of driven urgency.[55]

In February 1941 La Guardia testified before Congress, in support of the president's Lend-Lease Bill "with all my soul." England, he said, was America's first line of defense. "War between Mayor La Guardia and the Axis," wrote columnist Dave Boone, "is as good as declared, and it ain't a half bad idea . . . it will startle the enemy as nothing else has so far." As La Guardia delivered his testimony before the Foreign Relations Committee hearings, Senator Barkley asked what the mayor thought of New York domestic relations court judge Herbert O'Brien's prediction that the passage of lend-lease would so stir ethnic hatreds in New York that it would lead to a civil war. "If I had known the Committee wanted that kind of testimony," replied the mayor, "I could have given you better ones from the psychopathic ward." But, queried Senator Clark of Missouri, was it not true that the jurist in question had been appointed by La Guardia? Why, yes, answered Fiorello without pause, "I have made some excellent appointments in my time and I think I am good, but Senator, when I make a mistake it's a beaut."[56]

President Roosevelt was still thinking of La Guardia, but he did not want to commit one of Fiorello's "beauts." Roosevelt tried to pacify him with small favors. When Fiorello asked that his elderly friend John Morin be reappointed as director of the Federal Compensation Board despite his advanced age, the president responded in Italian, "The old are happy when protected by the good," and scrawled, "All right Fiorello, you win," at the bottom of the note. But he knew that Fiorello was still aching for a meaningful job in Washington.[57]

At the same time, Roosevelt was having difficulty finding someone to fill the post of presidential assistant for defense. Those to whom he offered the post, including La Guardia, had turned down the thankless task of defending the civilian population in the event of a home-front war. Convinced that Fiorello had the broad experience and sense of drama that the job required, Roosevelt offered it to La Guardia again in the spring of 1941. Roosevelt knew that Fiorello would consider such an appointment seriously if it was at a sufficiently high administrative rank, and if he could keep his city hall office concurrently. On April 21, just before flying off for a U.S.-Canadian Permanent Joint Board on Defense meeting, La Guardia told Roosevelt that he would prepare a proposal for the civil defense post, and he asked the president to hold off signing the Home Defense Plan until he had a chance to discuss it with him.[58]

Upon his return, La Guardia presented the president with a detailed blueprint for a cabinet-rank director of civil defense. "Now, Mr. President," he wrote, "as I see it, what is needed is something more than just another Board, Bureau, Commission, Committee of Volunteer Firemen's Association. . . . The new technique of war has created the necessity for developing a new technique of civilian defense. . . . It is not just community singing, sweater knitting and basket weaving that is needed. . . . What is needed is to create a home defense among the civilian population, to be trained to meet any possibility of an air or naval attack in any of our cities." He had in mind a program for education, panic control, defense drills, and sabotage deterrence. La Guardia outlined a bureaucracy as large as a branch of the armed forces, with extraordinary powers, including the authority to direct all state and local public health agencies and, in case of attack, to control virtually every agency outside the military. This office would also direct home-front propaganda and domestic intelligence.[59]

The old civil libertarian had become a real fan of covert government operations. In New York City he had formed a supersecret "sabotage squad," whose existence was unknown even to the FBI and army intelligence, composed of 180 specially trained police officers selected to infiltrate and report on potentially subversive groups. In addition, he worked with the FBI, coordinating surveillance activities in New York's Italian and German communities. Sometimes, as in his suggestion of labor union infiltration, it was the FBI that had to remind him of the legal limits on undercover work.[60]

La Guardia closed his four-page single-spaced job description for a civil defense czar by telling the president, "If you approve the plan in general I shall be very glad to cooperate and help. . . ." A week later Anna Rosenberg, who was carrying messages between city hall and the White House, advised Roosevelt that La Guardia would accept the appointment even without cabinet rank so long as he could sit in on cabinet meetings. "Fiorello . . . wanted some assurance," Ickes wrote in his diary, "that the new job really ranked him."[61]

On May 18, after hosting an immense preparedness rally of close to 700,000 New Yorkers, La Guardia flew to Washington to accept the unpaid position of director of civilian defense. As Ernest K. Lindley pointed out in the *Washington Post*, the job of preparing the national defenses amidst the threats of war was big enough. "It embraces everything from protecting civilians from bomb raids that may never come to seeing that babies get proper food, and includes the amorphous assignment of improving civilian morale." The administrative structure alone would take four months to fashion. And La Guardia would be running New York at the same time.[62]

Why at the age of 60 was he still interested in career insurance? Ego and comfort with the power and perquisites of the New York office had something to do with it, but even La Guardia realized that holding two full-time jobs would limit his success in each. The answer is that La Guardia still dreamed of being president, and while the office of Director of Civilian Defense might in fact become one of the most important in the nation, that depended upon whether there would be a home-front war. Anything short of that would reduce the job to behind-the-scenes work, coordinating air raids, filing plans, collecting useful information, and making speeches. If he did only that, then La Guardia would lose his spotlight, violating rule number one for designing politicians: Never give up a highly visible office except for one of at least equal wattage.

Tactically this made sense. It remained to be seen if it was humanly possible to carry out the two sets of responsibilities. Harold Ickes thought that coupling "morale" with other defense activities was already too much. "Here are two very big jobs, each of which will take all the time and resources that any man possesses. Yet Fiorello is to run these two jobs, continue as Mayor of New York, campaign for reelection, and at the same time operate as chairman of the Joint United States-Canadian Defense Board. It is absurd on the face of it. . . . No one . . . is better qualified to head Civilian Defense, but . . . he has to eat and sleep like other human beings." It was quite in character for Ickes to be jealous of La Guardia's expanding press kit, but he was more right than envious. No person could do well what Fiorello was proposing to do spectacularly.[63]

Just a short while back, a City College professor had applied for an exemption from the city's prohibition on municipal workers holding multiple positions. He wanted to serve as a consultant to the Department of Welfare. The mayor turned him down. "There is no one who cannot be replaced," FH asserted. "That includes everybody in the City of New York from the Mayor down." But he did not mean it, at least not the last part.[64]

The *New York Times* echoed his own words and suggested that La Guardia choose New York and let others get defense off the ground. Raymond Moley wrote in *Newsweek* that "every consideration of public interest required La Guardia to focus on his duties in New York City." But Fiorello entertained no doubts. He charged ahead. "I am rushing for a meeting with the U.S.-Canadian Joint Defense Board," he wrote to Burlingham. "Am speaking in Philadelphia tonight and will return to Washington. Monday here [New York], Tuesday and Wednesday, Boston. Thursday, here. Friday, Baltimore, and Saturday Columbus . . . most of next week in Washington."

He would fly to Washington early Tuesday morning for three days of work and return to Gotham on Thursday nights unless there was a cabinet meeting, in which case he would stay in the capital for Friday. The mayor insisted that he was just putting in a little overtime, but clearly, as he undertook the colossal job of gearing up the nation for defense preparations, La Guardia no longer thought of the mayoralty as a 24-hour-a-day job. Pictures showing a man with huge black circles around his eyes only hint at the price he paid for his grueling schedule.[65]

La Guardia threw himself into his directorship with the doggedness of a man still trying to prove himself. He wanted 50 million gas masks for the entire population of the Atlantic, Pacific, and Gulf coasts. He planned a force of United States Guards to protect vulnerable railroad beds, water sources, and national defense plants around the clock, pulled together emergency plans for the states, recruited fire and air raid wardens, studied evacuation plans and defenses for cities, and initiated lessons in defending against industrial and chemical warfare. He advised the president on what types of airplanes he should purchase, studied proposed changes in Social Security, and mediated between the government and disaffected blacks who complained about discrimination in defense industries. To forestall a threatened march on Washington of tens of thousands of blacks bent on publicizing economic discrimination, La Guardia, in his position as "Protector of Morale," pulled together representatives from industry, labor, the black community, and government to "come in and thrash it out right then and there" at the White House. He was making more than fifty speeches a month and was "positively swollen with importance," wrote Rexford Tugwell.[66]

By midsummer, however, Bernard Baruch confided to Harold Ickes that La Guardia was getting in the president's hair. In his own department he was mixing into the tiniest details and finding it hard to work with anyone. He had run New York without delegating power and he was doing the same thing at OCD, only now he was scampering about forty-eight states instead of five boroughs. "He is too spectacular to keep his feet on the ground," said Baruch. Instead of coordinating regional defense groups through governors as originally called for, La Guardia irritated the state executives by placing his own appointees into their states. La Guardia was inflating the appointment to the size of his counterpart in England, who was one of the most influential figures in the government, but bombs were not dropping on American cities to invest civilian defense with a sense of driven urgency. In the United States the mock bombing raids and full-dress rescue drills were more laughable than sobering. Here La Guardia was running around the nation crying about impending attacks, spending freely, and screaming about awareness and readiness, but so long as there was no war it all smacked of scare tactics and manufactured crises.[67]

Americans were just too confident that a mainland attack was an unlikely possibility to take his hyperactivity seriously. Hospitals around the country were tired of this loud little man ordering them to spend hours planning for emergencies and set aside materials when they needed their equipment now. It was an impossible task, serving as a professional Cassandra, building dungeons in the air, alarming the public. His demand for a $70 million home defense program struck many as excessive. Without the terrifying impetus of war, the emergency remained too remote for the pent-up energies and the immediacy that he brought to it. The president, said Baruch, took rueful comfort in the fact that at least he had not brought La Guardia into the cabinet.[68]

La Guardia's sense that action in itself was important resulted in half-baked programs that were announced with little or no planning. He asked the FBI to provide uniform national training for police, but an internal memorandum to J. Edgar Hoover noted that the OCD director had not the faintest idea of *what* he wanted the police to be trained in. "The Mayor . . . needs guidance in this regard very badly." He defined no clear limits for his own responsibilities, so that one day he was planning recreation and health facilities in training camps and on the next he was writing the introduction to booklets describing the duties of air raid wardens. Even when he did have an idea worth trumpeting, his shrill voice had become so common that few paid it much heed.[69]

The other half of his OCD job, that of setting up a propaganda bureau, continued to lag. FBI, OSS, and OCD all bickered about how to divide internal surveillance and propaganda. Finally, La Guardia, in what was no doubt intended as a shrewd move, took Eleanor Roosevelt as a codirector to handle precisely this part of the job. He hoped that this would raise OCD's visibility as well as the level of presidential interest in its work.[70]

The pairing proved less than felicitous. The two were as different in their backgrounds as could be. She approached politics with an air of patrician saintliness, as an arena for doing good works; she expected good manners from associates. La Guardia viewed politics as a profession, and dismissed the rules of etiquette with his favorite term, "lousy." He used ideas to bring results, she respected them and made dainty little constructions of them. And she did not have any special influence on her husband.

Perhaps all of this could have been worked out. There was enough mutual respect at first, but La Guardia was forced to establish policy and manage OCD while doing other things. He did not have the time to sit and discuss, only to make rapid-fire decisions and move on. He did not have time because he had decided to run for mayor again in 1941.

---

3. He Deserved to Win But He Deserved the Slap

T HE driven Flower could not discipline himself into a single job. Unwilling to give up the mayoralty, he added to his burdens by seeking an unprecedented third term in city hall. In July of 1941 La Guardia accepted a draft from reformers, renegade Democrats, and a corps of long-suffering Republicans. With daughter Jean at his side, La Guardia piously announced that he would really have preferred not to run but he could not ignore the call of the electorate. Then he recounted his accomplishments and attacked the tired bogeyman of "boss rule."

At first the usual group threatened to join the opposition, but they had no one else to go to. "C.C., I shouldn't do this for the son-of-a-bitch," Tom Dewey told Charles Burlingham, "but we're going to give him the endorsement again!" Even Robert Moses delivered his blessing, such as it was. He offered "no brief for the Mayor's bad manners," twitted him for "his excursions into the far capital, where they give him nothing but the husks and leavings," and pronounced delusive the notion that politics could operate without parties; RM even poked fun at the mayor's habit of rushing to fires, taking space that might be better occupied by a hook and ladder. Despite these failings and "his cussedness toward those whose support is indispensable in critical times," Moses declared La Guardia the best mayor in memory.[71]

Democrats, rejecting Adolf Berle's recommendation that they nominate La Guardia, selected Brooklyn's mob-busting district attorney, William O'Dwyer. Except for charging that the administration had pressured municipal workers and relief recipients to gather signatures for the mayor and that La Guardia had suppressed a report on the influence of Communists in the Welfare Department, the Democrat was reduced to rehashing previous campaigns: The real estate tax was too high; the welfare department had too many radicals; anti-Semitic street speakers should be cleared away; mayoral protege Vito Marcantonio was a Communist; and La Guardia was ignoring the city for his ambitions in Washington.[72]

For his part, the mayor offered voters the politics of reform nostalgia, thumping the bosses and recalling the marvelous days of the crusade against corruption. He reinforced his ethnic constituencies, reminded labor that he was an old friend, and trumpeted his closeness with the White House. When the president needed an important job done, ran the line, he did not turn to Ed Flynn. And he put on the old show:

> In his opening campaign speech [reported *Time* magazine] little Fiorello tossed away his prepared manuscript, grabbed off his horn rimmed glasses and used them alternately as a cutlass, a rapier, a back scratcher, a wand. . . . he touched his toes imitating a football player's kickoff, spat on an imaginary apple and polished it on his sleeve. He told the audience that his extra work came out of him and not out of the city. He ridiculed critics who complain of his Washington visits: "I saw the city needed this. . . . The bankers wanted to charge me 6%, but I could

get the money in Washington for 3%. So wham! (He ducked his head, took a track runner's on-your-mark position, dashed madly across the stage, pulled up puffing, but triumphant.) So, away to Washington I go again."[73]

Friends rallied round. "I don't know of any Mayor of any city, . . ." wrote Hugh Johnson, "whose record can challenge . . . [La Guardia's] in excellence, prudence, courage, despisal of partisan influence in his job, fiscal soundness, unremitting work and energy, an expert's knowledge of every aspect of his responsibility. . . . They don't combine in any one man but once in a blue moon." La Guardia flayed old foes, recalled the warmth of old relationships, and toward the end of the campaign unveiled his own magical tin box. Just before the election, he discovered a budget surplus and proposed a cut in sales taxes.[74]

O'Dwyer was not able to capture a real honest-to-goodness issue with a net, and bad news kept coming. After the mayor hinted that he could use some help, his friends asked the president to lend a hand. "Please tell Skipper from me," came a message from C.C. Burlingham, "rare opportunity for statement that in present emergency honest efficient smooth running city government should be continued regardless of state politics." The very next day, Roosevelt announced before a press conference that he had no intention of taking sides in the New York City election. Then he went on to express the "opinion" that La Guardia had given the city the "most honest . . . most efficient municipal government of any," thereby cutting O'Dwyer off at the knees. Fiorello responded with a one-word telegram: *"Merci,"* as the presidential endorsement sent his popularity soaring.[75]

The campaign was going very well, but La Guardia was never one to coast or leave well enough alone. Unlike the president, Herbert Lehman had taken the not unusual step of endorsing his party's candidate. Nevertheless, he did it so gingerly and took such care to give Fiorello his proper due and avoid offending that it was weak tea indeed. The unkindest thing that he had to say about the incumbent was that FH was no superman and could not be expected to do two superhuman jobs well. He also added, correctly, that La Guardia had left the impression when he took over OCD that he would be giving up the mayoralty. With its emphasis on the need for a two-party system, the entire speech could be read as an apology for not supporting La Guardia.

But La Guardia did not see it that way. He reacted as if he had heard a different speech. Without mentioning the governor by name, he left no doubt about whom he meant when he shot back: "When you are once in a political organization . . . [y]ou have got to do what the political bosses tell you to. A politican always remains a politician." Berle released an equally biting statement regretting Lehman's willingness to "lend his name to reestablish the tin box politicians. . . ."[76]

Earlier in the year New York State Comptroller Morris Tremaine of Buffalo had died, and the governor appointed ALP member Joseph O'Leary to fill the position. The state attorney general challenged the appointment, arguing that a special election was required to fill the office. The state court of appeals, with Justice Irving Lehman presiding, ruled against the attorney general. In all of this, La Guardia sensed something nefarious. "Who's looney now—Lehman or Flynn or both? Boy oh boy, have I got them groggy." Except that after he started to recount his version of what had happened, many thought that it was the mayor who was groggy. He suggested that Lehman had initially appointed O'Leary as a favor to the bosses to strengthen the O'Dwyer ticket. Then, the governor, regretting the appointment, had the attorney general call for an election, only to change his mind again and command his brother's court to throw out that determination. "You have heard of goniffs [Yiddish for thieves] stealing from goniffs. Well now you are hearing of doublecrossers doublecrossing the doublecrossers." Lehman punched himself in the chin and "knocked himself out politically," he announced with delight.[77]

Lehman flushed with anger and hit back.

> The Mayor not only in this campaign, but for a long time since in his capacity as Chief Executive of the City has abused and vilified everyone who opposed him or criticized him. "Thief," "double crosser," "crook," "bum" are among the milder of the Mayor's epithets. Most people . . . have no desire to compete with him in intemperate abuse and so they have permitted themselves to be intimidated into silence. But I cannot be intimidated. . . . New Yorkers are sick and tired of Mr. La Guardia's unbridled tongue.

When the Mayor persisted, Lehman denounced him for a "shameless and scurrilous attack . . . on the highest court in our state." Everything Lehman said was true. His brother was honorable, and few besides La Guardia under a full head of steam would have dreamed that the governor would become involved in so convoluted a scheme as he charged.[78]

This single episode dominated the last few weeks of the campaign. Suddenly La Guardia himself became the chief issue. Few quarreled with his accomplishments but many feared that he was losing control over what had always been a volatile set of emotions. James Farley took the opportunity to remark that he was not surprised that the president had kept La Guardia out of the cabinet, for the mayor had neither the stability nor gentlemanly instincts nor the poise or dignity to hold national office.

Even those less partisan were asking whether La Guardia was still capable of leadership, or had the overwork, lack of vacation and rest, and frustration worn away his good sense? His gratuitous insults were increasingly bitter and contemptible. Passing a vegetable stand displaying fresh cabbages, he picked one up and smiled at it, commenting "My opponent's head."[79]

His attack on Lehman proved costly. Polls showed a drop in his support following this incident. Berle wrote that the "town has been full of this [issue] ever since." In Jewish districts over a period of five days the mayor's popularity rating plummeted fifteen percentage points. New Yorkers were becoming tired of politics with the volume turned up. La Guardia managed to make a close contest of what had been a sure victory.[80]

On November 4 New Yorkers went to the polls and decided, in Rexford Tugwell's words, that "La Guardia, absurd and childish was better than scoundrels and wasters." It was the first time in the history of the modern city that a mayor had been reelected to a third term; it was also the closest contest since 1904. New Yorkers still wanted La Guardia but they had also delivered a message. As Herbert Bayard Swope wrote to Roosevelt: "The vote was a commendation of his record and, at the same time, a rebuke for his intemperateness and his sometimes arrogant assumption of all that is virtuous. He deserved to win," Swope confided, "but he deserved the slap."[81]

Oswald Garrison Villard, the liberal editor of the *Nation*, searched for the right words to impress upon Fiorello the meaning of this message. He wrote a letter appealing to the mayor to "come back to New York. . . . I know you say that you have not neglected the business of the City, but you have, and if I am wrong in that, you certainly have affronted many of your supporters who are of the belief that the City of New York needs a full time Mayor." Villard was happy that the OCD job was not going well. Maybe that would make FH give it up. The only way La Guardia would make a national name for himself was by making a "tremendous success and a continuing success of the job you now hold."

Villard was right. New York was too important to be placed on automatic pilot. The city's finances were edging close to trouble again, and the taxes on real estate were not keeping pace with expenses. The coming war would place further strain on hundreds of thousands of New Yorkers. Harlem, Villard reminded Fiorello, was still a festering sore. There was crime and there was poverty, and the mayor's attention was off elsewhere.

Newspapers, friends, and common New Yorkers echoed this call for Fiorello to come home again, to take to heart the interests of his constituents and grab hold of himself before his ambition wore away his right to their support and affection. New Yorkers wanted to know whether Fiorello La Guardia still dreamed, as he had told an interviewer two years before, only of what his city might be tomorrow, or was he more concerned with where he would be tomorrow?[82]

4. I Am to Give Up the Double Life

H IS reelection by a cautionary margin and his own conviction that the job would be hell drained La Guardia's triumph of any personal sense of joy and accomplishment. Following the election La Guardia went directly to work. It had become a tradition with him not to celebrate. He had made a fetish of taking his victories in low key and it was a welcome step at first, but he sorely needed some celebration and personal uplift. Now more than ever, he needed to take pleasure in triumph. That he did not, and that he poured his energies into a task he could not master, was a form of self-torment that was immeasurably damaging. While no one could question the hours and the dedication, the infectious exuberance that La Guardia used to bring to his work was absent. He was doing dutiful labor.

Embarrassing slipups persisted in OCD operations. Fiorello stuck his nose where it was decidedly unwelcome, suggesting that ministers throughout the country make defense the major theme of their sermons on "Freedom Sunday." Oblivious to his intrusion into forbidden territory, he composed a "canned" homily that he asked preachers to use as a model for their prayers and talks. The Reverend John Haynes Holmes, who not more than five months before had showered La Guardia with excessive praise, now assailed him for his presumption in attempting to "goose-step the priests, ministers and rabbis of this country." The editor of a religious publication remarked that "Hitler and Goebbels never went further." In the rush to achieve his ends he was losing sight of the proper means; it was a difficulty with which New Yorkers had become all too familiar.

A campaign to collect scrap aluminum resulted in huge piles of shiny metal occupying village greens and city parks, and freight cars crammed to the top with pots and pans. Unfortunately, no plans had been made for the next step of smelting this material down. Similar difficulties made plain the lack of planning and follow-through that plagued the operations.[83]

La Guardia had brought Eleanor Roosevelt in as codirector, expecting the president's wife to handle morale and bring extra clout to the operations, but La Guardia never intended to make her his equal. Over the years La Guardia had received letters from Mrs. Roosevelt inquiring about the treatment of blacks in the city or intervening on behalf of aggrieved workers. In tones that might easily be read as patronizing, Fiorello would try to explain why things were not always as they appeared. The tone did not change much after Mrs. FDR became his codirector. At times he treated her like a secretary, having her open the mail and make little comments for him to review. At other times he sent her on errands or asked her

500

to handle the dull details. "I soon found that every activity which Mayor La Guardia did not want in his part of the program," Eleanor Roosevelt later recalled, "was thrust in my division."[84]

She complained that she worked very hard, at times through the night, but could not get La Guardia to stand still for a minute to discuss policy with him. He was always hastening off to stage some dramatic defense tableau or to his duties in New York. What was even more troublesome was that the entire operation was filed under the big black Stetson that he wore; decisions were taken on the run, unilaterally, with little thought given to systematic policy.

Personal differences between the codirectors further strained their relationship. One day Eleanor invited her colleague to a luncheon at her New York City apartment. As they completed the talks, the mayor delivered his compliments to the hostess: "My wife never asks me where have I been, nor whom I saw, nor what I did, but she always asks me what I have had to eat. Today I can truthfully say I did not have too much!"

Mrs. Roosevelt brought her own baggage to OCD in a way La Guardia had not anticipated. It seemed that every time the First Lady got behind a particular program or appointee, a core of conservative congressmen would rip into OCD, finding it easier to rag Eleanor than Franklin. La Guardia did not hide his frustration at being saddled with this extra burden, ungallantly disclaiming any responsibility for the personnel that Eleanor brought into OCD. By winter, Congress signaled its loss of confidence in the codirectors by transferring disbursement authority over a $100 million authorization for air raid defense from La Guardia-Roosevelt to the secretary of state.[85]

In November 1941 La Guardia warned national leaders to focus on the threat of attack from the Far East, but he issued so many pessimistic reports that he was ignored. This time he turned out to be right. The shock of Pearl Harbor temporarily halted the criticism. All the scare talk of bombs, emergencies, and defense was now proven correct. Because he had been so insistent there was a civilian defense operation prepared to operate immediately.

The December 7 attack put OCD on solid footing, and despite the grimness, which he did not minimize, La Guardia was exhilarated by being put to the real test. The president too appeared to his wife as more serene than he had been in a long time; the die had finally been cast, all ambiguity had been swept away by the surprise attack, and the orders crackled with the excitement of momentous decisions being made cleanly. "All necessary . . . measures have been taken," La Guardia advised the commander in chief. "On my own, I am issuing orders for all Japanese subjects to remain in their homes until their status is determined by the Federal Government. . . . I am closing a Japanese Club in order to prevent congregating of Japanese subjects. . . . I am going to pep it up."[86]

He went on the radio to advise New Yorkers about measures to secure the city, and offering a balanced presentation of the grave dangers facing America at war. But his bitterness at having been dismissed as a Chicken Little whose sky was never going to fall surfaced in a churlish, vindictive sentence. He assured "all persons who have been sneering and jeering at defense activities, and even those who have been objecting to them and placing obstacles in their path, that we will protect them now. But we expect their cooperation and there will be no fooling." Within a few hours an emergency control board dispatched guards to protect essential areas, implemented contingency plans, and confined Japanese nationals to their homes.[87]

Leaving Newbold Morris to serve as acting mayor, La Guardia dashed off for Washington, dictated a memorandum for the president about seizing enemy marine vessels docked in U.S. harbors, and picked up the First Lady to fly to the West Coast to take charge of defense needs in the nation's most vulnerable region. In midair the pilot received a report that San Francisco was being bombed by the Japanese. Mrs. Roosevelt awakened La Guardia with the news just before the plane was to land for a refueling stop—"he put his head out of the curtains, looking for all the world like a Kewpie"—and he immediately ordered her to call Washington to check the report. "If it is true we will go direct to San Francisco." Despite their differences, she could not help but be impressed with his reckless pursuit of the trouble spot. "One could be exasperated with him at times," she would recall, "but one had to admire his real integrity and courage." The report turned out to be groundless and the plane continued to Los Angeles.

As they landed, the mayor bolted from the plane to check on the firefighting equipment—which had become a pet project of his—and on the general state of defense preparedness. "His complete . . . lack of fear had an effect on everyone," Mrs. Roosevelt remembered. He reorganized the local fire departments, pulled together doctors into emergency teams, ordered a shipment of medical supplies, and did much to lift the morale of a shocked and scared populace. He urged the president to level with the people. "We might as well have the truth as have it seep through in continuous messages from Tokio and Berlin."[88]

All were impressed with his energy and decisiveness, but Mrs. Roosevelt closes her description of these few days with an important doubt. How much of this work was in vain because not enough had been done before? "I did not know and never have known how much all our plans, his and mine, really helped since so much of our equipment was lacking that they could not do the things that were considered essential." More systematic planning in the preceding months, she suggested, would have counted for more than all the courage and comfort that they could now offer.[89]

For one week the demands for La Guardia to resign OCD ceased, but while he was out of New York the air raid sirens had gone off unexpectedly three times in two days, the last time during rush hour, throwing the city into chaos. Many of the emergency procedures failed to work. Increasingly impatient New Yorkers were demanding that their roving OCD mayor come back to work on his own city before tinkering with defense in Sandusky.

OCD too needed a full-time head. "Temperamental civilian leaders, however politically gifted," wrote the New York *World Telegram*, "are not always the best . . . in the stress of war peril. Nerves don't calm nerves." A few days later the *Telegram* was more emphatic: "The situation does not call for a dizzy show off of one man juggling with multiple jobs. . . . How can the Mayor be blind to it?" With its accustomed air of authority the *New York Times* offered a definitive conclusion: "the Office of Civilian Defense and the office of Mayor of New York [have] ceased suddenly, definitely and irrevocably to be two offices that could be filled completely by a single man."[90]

Then, just before the New Year, the mayor put on another display of poor judgment and bullying that demonstrated the damaging effect of his multiple responsibilities. William Fellowes Morgan, one of La Guardia's original distinguished appointees, had accomplished a great deal as city markets commissioner, getting rid of rackets, bringing the pushcarts off the streets under roofed central markets, and pioneering in the areas of consumer education and information. The well-disposed Morgan was one of the most diffident of La Guardia's commissioners. He had tolerated the mayor's habit of appointing markets department personnel without consulting or even informing him because the appointments were generally good. But the appointees were no longer uniformly good, or politically impartial. After the 1941 election La Guardia had sent over three new appointees, at least one of whom was being rewarded for loyal work during the campaign. Morgan tried to bring his objections to the mayor, but he was repeatedly told that La Guardia was either out of town or too busy.

The final break came over an unpaid volunteer, Mrs. Preston Davie, whom Morgan had enlisted in the city's conservation efforts. La Guardia's civil defense associates wanted someone else, and the mayor ordered Morgan to fire the respected woman reformer. Morgan refused. The mayor just kept screaming hysterically, "Fire that dame, fire that dame." The long-suffering commissioner, finally fed up, resigned.[91]

It was, all agreed, a serious loss to the city. Morgan sadly commented in parting that FH was just too preoccupied to run the city. "The unfortunate thing about it all is that the Mayor is so darned busy with other matters that he hasn't got the time to sit down and talk things over with his commissioners." La Guardia, refusing to acknowledge any difficulties, dismissed questions about the affair with the statement "*È finita la commedia*." But Morgan was not finished. He revealed to the press the pressure that had been brought upon him to make spoils appointments. "You will have to appoint Lynch," one staffer had told him. "The Mayor is under political obligation to him. He did good work in the last campaign."

An angry La Guardia retaliated by announcing that irregularities had been uncovered in the markets department (only later did he admit that the trivial issue was whether a tenant of the Bronx Terminal Market had illegally plugged into city electrical lines, and whether Morgan had known about this), and he was therefore dispatching Investigations Commissioner Herlands to probe the Department of Markets. "Am I glad I am your friend," Charles Burlingham chided La Guardia. "I should not like to be investigated *dum vivo* or *post mortem*." The mayor's practice of closing unpleasant debates with a visit from the investigations commissioner, scolded the *Times*, was "a bit of cheap drama . . . an ironic commentary on the gratitude of public officials."[92]

That so fine and loyal a commissioner should be forced into so unseemly an exchange to get the mayor's ear confirmed many in their misgivings about his two jobs. The *Herald Tribune*, perhaps La Guardia's most consistent supporter, called the Morgan affair an alarming example of "the deterioration of municipal rule." To assume that La Guardia could continue to run New York while bouncing around the country, it wrote, was a "tragic absurdity." Just a bit over a month after the mayor was reelected to a historic third term, the taste of victory had long left him. "I have suffered too much during the last six months," he was saying, "absorbing the criticism, the abuse, the sneers and jeers. . . ." He was despondent and feeling sorry for himself.

Increasingly, the question that New Yorkers were asking was whether they were the ones who deserved the pity. In a blistering New Year's Day address over the municipal radio station WNYC, La Guardia smeared his tormentors as "Japs" or "friends of Japs." Continuing the unfortunate habit of assigning the worst motives to those who disagreed with him, the bowed mayor lashed back at the "two-by-four editors," "swivel chair scribes," and "liars" who refused to admit the great job that he had accomplished in Washington. OCD was "magnificently organized." New York, he assured its citizens, would be attacked. "The war will come to . . . our residential districts." And then New Yorkers would appreciate their unique advantage of having a mayor who was head of OCD.[93]

But nasty problems kept cropping up. "I had heard," J. Edgar Hoover reported in an internal memorandum to FBI officials, "that Mrs. Roosevelt and the Mayor had a terrific feud; that he had discharged certain of her employees and she had promptly rehired them." The press kept up its drumbeat criticism, describing La Guardia as too overwrought, overworked, and overtired to do both jobs. La Guardia's executive secretary, Lester Stone, devised a cynical scheme to flood the press with favorable stories and pictures, coopt critics by appointing them to advisory boards, and move OCD offices to New York. But as the city hall staff circled the wagons, it became plain even to La Guardia that his days at OCD were numbered. Early in January columnists Robert Allen and Drew Pearson reported in their "Washington Go Round" column that the skids were being greased for Fiorello.[94]

On January 10, 1942, the president appointed Dean James Landis of the Harvard Law School as OCD executive director, to administer the office under La Guardia. "I suppose a decision will have to be made," La Guardia said a few days later, adding wistfully that he hoped he still had a good grasp on the situation in New York City. Having finally realized his situation, La Guardia eased himself into the inevitable. At a New York University alumni dinner he remarked, "Sin does not pay—I am about to give up the double life." On February 10 La Guardia resigned as OCD chief, making way for James Landis to assume the post of full-time director. Mrs. Roosevelt sent a gracious note expressing her thanks "for letting me organize a part of the work in which you did not believe."[95]

Friends and editorial writers praised the decision. "Believe it or not," wrote Charles Burlingham, "I feel a little shy about saying anything to you about your resignation." But his wise friend congratulated him on making a decision that he would have preferred him to make on December 8, when war broke out and OCD became a full-time job. Perhaps understandably, too few acknowledged the real contribution he had made. In the early days, when Americans preferred not to think about defense, he hectored and threatened and cajoled to extract from the United States at least a rudimentary civil defense operation so that when war came emergency plans were in place and a system for protecting vital areas had been developed.[96]

To an extent few could imagine, it had indeed all come out of him. In order to bring warning, he had deprived himself of the comforts of family, rest, vacation, and the normal hectic life of governing the nation's most challenging metropolis. He had done his best in a cause that he believed in; his mistake had been to try to do too much and to think that only he could do it. William Fellowes Morgan, ever the gentleman, and sincerely well-meaning, suggested that La Guardia's nerves were "shot to pieces" and that he take a vacation. "When you come back, forgive and forget." He knew only too well the mayor's vindictive disposition, especially when he was all pumped up for battle. La Guardia desperately needed that rest if he was to start fresh and leave the resentments of this searing business behind.[97]

On the heels of the OCD fiasco, however, came a series of setbacks that prevented La Guardia from recovering the steady footing he so sorely needed. Throughout the thirties periodic charges and investigations of the city's Welfare Department disclosed an active group of Communists working there. In itself this was not illegal, although it sometimes proved embarrassing for the mayor, like the time that newspapers reported that Miss Sylvia Angeloff, the accused killer of Leon Trotsky, was being suspended from her position as a home relief investigator because she was being held in Mexico on murder charges. Now came serious new allegations that the department was dominated by Communists who were doing far more than holding discussions on dialectical materialism. Former welfare workers charged that powerful Communist supervisors controlled promotions, radicalized clients, and pressured subordinates into joining the party and contributing to its coffers. They testified that those who resigned from the CP received poor ratings and were hounded from their positions. Supreme Court Justice Lloyd Church reported that his own investigation revealed active communist rabble-rousing among the welfare employees.[98]

In the past La Guardia had dismissed such charges. He was no longer able to do that. Instead Commissioner Hodson launched a sweeping investigation of his own department. Every official with a vote in promotions, demotions, transfers, or dismissals was examined under oath to determine whether political prejudices had influenced personnel policies. Investigators scrutinized Board of Elections files going back five years, studied copies of leaflets that had been distributed in welfare offices, and checked into all complaints, even those reported anonymously. The chief investigator who led this probe reports today that his findings were startling. Of some 20,000 employees in the department, an estimated 12,000 were found to belong to the Communist party. "But," adds the investigator,

> we also discovered that damn few of them were actually Communists. They joined the CP to have a social life, to be greeted at the office by the others. . . . Otherwise you were ostracized. Hardly any of them *knew* about communism or cared anything about it. . . . It was the equivalent of the old Tammany district leaders. You got advanced or better assignments if you were a member than if you weren't. There wasn't a Stalinist-Leninist quality to it [their political commitments].

The results became moot, however, with Hitler's invasion of the Soviet Union. It made allies of the United States and the Soviet Union and changed the Soviet line to one of cooperation with the liberal democracies, robbing the Red hunt of its intensity. La Guardia ordered the investigation killed, and in 1945, as the administration was clearing out its papers, the raw data of the investigation was destroyed. "I thought, my gosh, so few of these people were Communists and I had so many names and memoranda in the files that I—destroyed all of the files on this communist examination," the investigator recalls.[99]

Attention next turned to the close of the Paul Kern affair. While La Guardia was still directing both New York City and OCD, a county reform bill eliminating the offices of borough registrar and sheriff together with their staffs (a piece of business that La Guardia had advocated since 1933) was passed in November, increasing the population of unemployed Democrats. State Democrats tried to maneuver their displaced compatriots onto civil service lists without the benefit of competitive examinations. Embattled commission president Paul Kern scotched the transfers. To Kern's amazement, La Guardia overruled him on four individuals who were close to Democratic boss Ed Flynn, who had managed Roosevelt's presidential campaign. If FH was ever to get back to Washington he needed all the help he could muster, and Kern could not avoid the suspicion that he was mustering.

Kern tried to explain his disagreements to the mayor, who was still in Washington at this point, only to be told that La Guardia was too busy with war work for his trivialities. Stung by the mayor's disregard, Kern attacked his old patron for his newfound sensitivity to the plight of jobless Democrats and refused to approve payroll checks for the disputed four. The unpaid officials then secured a court order

506

commanding release of their salaries. When the Civil Service Commission resolved to appeal the decision, the mayor directed city corporation counsel William Chanler to refuse to carry the appeal.[100]

The commission next took legal action against the corporation counsel. The mayor was trying to salvage as much dignity as he could while retiring from OCD, and here his own crew was staging a pitiful version of city hall follies, with Kern attacking the corporation counsel as a "politically minded lawyer . . . who supported Ed Flynn's candidate for Mayor against La Guardia in 1933." Impatient almost to the point of violence, La Guardia, just before departing for Washington on February 6 for his last two days at OCD, suspended the entire Civil Service Commission for "insubordination." Tammany immediately declared itself "overjoyed" with the mayor's decision. Bronx Democratic councilman Joseph Kinsley predicted "dancing in the streets." The investigations commissioner, by now, for all purposes, the mayor's personal liege, served the suspensions and sealed the premises to "conduct an investigation." The *Times* lamented another "unhappy display of irascibility."[101]

Kern responded with a lethal public volley at the man who had brought him into politics. He attacked La Guardia for surrounding himself with "fawning sycophants" who feared to voice an opinion. What had become of the old times, the pained Kern asked, when "you did not send me messages by reporters. You called me up in the morning and at night in all hours when you wanted me to work?" La Guardia had become more interested in La Guardia, declared Kern, than in reform. It was all politics, ambition, and hot temper now. Sinister political deals had driven out the regard for fairness and merit that fusion had battled so hard to achieve. On the "hollowest of pretexts" the mayor suspended officials, denounced respected judges, "compiled unspeakably vulgar notes to newspaper men," and referred to his own commissioners on the steps of city hall as "asses." The unscrupulous political slickers who were once his sworn enemies have become his favored constituents. Those now "dancing in the streets" were "the Christian Front who attacked [the Civil Service Commission] because we allowed Jews in the Police Department, the Camorra of crooks who sold political jobs in the old days," and those who were in politics for the money they could make. It was with individuals such as these that La Guardia's reputation was keeping company. "Your old friends," he taunted, "are gone with the snows of yesteryear."[102]

At public hearings Kern arraigned Fiorello for allowing a historic opportunity for urban reform to descend into a "strange interlude between two regimes of bossdom and piracy." Brimming with feelings of personal and political betrayal, Kern looked La Guardia in the eye and told him that "the same stiletto that you are now sticking in our backs will be stuck in yours by [your] sycophants." Then Kern detailed specific charges of mayoral efforts to rerate civil service exam papers and tampering with the merit system. The most spectacular accusation concerned Democratic boss Ed Flynn. Kern claimed that twenty-seven city-paid laborers and a few thousand Belgian granite blocks belonging to the city were used for Flynn's Lake Mahopac summer home. For four months, said Kern, the mayor and his investigations commissioner—who had been only too happy to move precipitously against such fusion stalwarts as Alfred Rheinstein, William Fellowes Morgan, Fire Commissioner McElligott, and Paul Kern himself—had ignored this information until Kern forced his hand. Subpoenas for Flynn and others were sitting on Kern's desk ready for delivery on the morning of his suspension. Why was La Guardia connected with Flynn? The former commission president intimated that Flynn had gotten to La Guardia by offering to support him for the Democratic Senate nomination.[103]

The charge that La Guardia was so duplicitous, so "sinister," was shocking. Nothing in his past suggested such a weakness, and many indeed disbelieved it. La Guardia was called to testify before a Bronx grand jury on the case and the decision was favorable, but only by the narrowest of hair-splits. The jury found that the work on the Flynn estate had indeed been illegal but that the prosecution had failed to establish that Flynn had ordered it. The Bronx politico was cleared, and for a man of Ed Flynn's background that was as good as gold, but for La Guardia, who aspired to a higher political standard, it was poor company for his reputation to keep. The narrow basis of the decision left the impression that in coveting a national position La Guardia had thrown himself in with a fast political bunch and that these power brokers had claimed a piece of his soul with their implicit promises and explicit deals.

Civil service reform, La Guardia had once said, was the one reform for which he wanted to be remembered. It would be his legacy, a municipal civil service based on merit and objective selection, the spawning ground for a scientific politics. It would banish forever the spectacle of the tin box brigade, the shame of a civil service that owed their allegiance not to the people but to a boss, or to the mayor who happened to appoint them. That was in the days when his ambition was still to be the best mayor New York ever had.

5. What Has Happened to La Guardia?

NEW Yorkers were asking each other what had happened to their mayor. The *New Republic* ran a piece by George Britt asking, "What Has Happened to La Guardia?" Just six months after his unprecedented third-term victory, Britt wrote, he was certain that La Guardia could not win an election in the city that he had saved from bankruptcy and led into modernity. The strongest reform groups, the City Club, the Women's City Club, the League of Women Voters, the City Affairs Committee, the Citizens Union, the United Neighborhood Houses, all complained about his behavior. They were chagrined by his crude language, abuse of commissioners, and personal use of the Investigations Commission. During the first eight years there had been scattered episodes, but now it seemed that the daily administration of government was conducted by mayoral tantrum. Tired, uninterested in his responsibilities, and eyeing opportunities elsewhere, he was a dangerously irritable and distracted man. The liberals had come to him during the campaign because they had no choice. Now they were hurt and afraid of his contempt.[104]

He surprised even nonreformers with his casual attitudes about police violence. When an FBI agent suggested that use of the third degree against blacks in the South was wrong, La Guardia affably disagreed. "He thought it was a splendid thing to beat up those particularly guilty of sex violations." Of course he did not think that those who were arrested for minor offenses should be brutalized but "the tough babies he thinks need a good working over."[105]

It did not concern him that the discretion was left in the hands of arresting police officers, the same police whose hands he had tied during labor confrontations in his earlier years for fear of their overreaction. His tenure in office had worn down the healthy distrust of government that is at the heart of liberal guarantees. He favored efficiency over freedom now. The same impatience with civil liberties that allowed him to condone the beating of suspects led him to unilaterally order city employees to work a seven-day week, without discussions or negotiations. That this imposed hardships for those who for personal reasons or requirements of religious conviction could not follow such a schedule concerned him not at all.[106]

His acute inability to abide differing views surfaced most obviously in his relationship with the press. In the past he had won attention for himself and the issues he sought to publicize, offering in return easy access and colorful copy. This relationship was doomed from the outset because he tended to view the press as an adjunct of his administration, the information arm of his crusade for good government. His friendship with reporters and his good intentions, he thought, entitled him to special consideration. He expected publishers who supported him to cast their stories with positive care. Editors who had supported fusion he assumed to be La Guardia men. And falling into the pit dug for every ambitious leader, he equated himself with his cause. The fact that intelligent persons, well-meaning though they may be, can disagree was something La Guardia never fully appreciated. Single-minded, impatient, fierce-willed, he found the notion of "fair criticism" an oxymoron, and ultimately took it all personally.

Testy relations between a free press and political leaders was not new. George Washington had said that he would rather be in his grave than continue to suffer the insults of a press corps that denounced him in such exaggerated terms "as could be applied to a Nero, a notorious defaulter, or even a common pickpocket." But,

509

as the *New York Times* asserted in a thoughtful editorial: "one of the occupational hazards of public office is to be misunderstood and misrepresented," and criticized. The press were no longer uniform in their praise, and because he was stung by their criticism he attacked their integrity.[107]

When publisher William Baumrucker, Jr., asked for an "unbiased opinion" about the afternoon daily *PM* in order to promote the paper, Fiorello wrote back: "*PM* started off with a good idea. . . . Today it is lousy. . . . worthy of the old days of yellow journalism"; not quite the blurb they had sought. He responded to a similar request from *Time* magazine with: "*Time* is . . . pretty good . . . [and] can be very accurate when it wants to be. It can be very ornery and lousy if the boss tells it to on any particular subject." The *Sun* he characterized as a "filthy sheet," unsolicited.[108]

He had legitimate gripes. He had seen too many reporters write stories by boiling down press releases. Most stories about him repeated the same few superficial facts and offered no larger insight into his motivation than that he was short, Latin, and excitable. He tired easily of such adjectives as swarthy, squat, and diminutive. He saw through the journalists who focused on his colorful activities and his hard work as an alternative to doing the real job of analyzing his programs and the new processes that he brought into municipal government.

A few months before taking office as mayor, La Guardia had told a symposium of reporters and editors at the Columbia University School of Journalism that they were to blame for allowing their newspapers to become promoters rather than informers. Instead of fulfilling their responsibilities as tough adversaries they had served as shills for the bankers and the corporations, failing to carry out their purpose as society's skeptics and investigators. For their easy relationship with politicians and business leaders he assigned them partial blame for the Depression.

But once in office he tolerated precious little of the press's insistent curiosity. Just two months after being sworn in, in a fit of pique at a reporter's persistent questioning, he placed a curb on press interviews, requiring questions to be submitted in writing. Within a few more months he was badgering publishers about unfair reports in their papers. At times an infuriated La Guardia could put on a display of kindergarten tantrums. Paul Crowell, the *New York Times* city hall reporter, recalled the time that the infuriated mayor snatched a notebook from the hands of a stunned journalist, threw it to the floor, and jumped up and down on the offending pad. When Peter Kihss of the *World Telegram* persisted in questioning La Guardia about the appointment of Jimmy Walker to his labor post, he made the mistake of doing it on the steps of city hall. The mayor grabbed his arm, shouting in a rage, "I'm going to throw you right down the steps," if he did not stop his pestering. But it was the *Herald Tribune*'s Robert Donovan who was the only member of the fourth estate to wrest an apology from the mayor, after his face was scratched by a car door that La Guardia slammed in his face.[109]

He barred offensive reporters from city hall conferences, abused others, complained regularly to editors, and when all else failed called them "pimps," "punks," unethical liars," or "lobbygow." He also threatened libel suits to quiet contentious critics. Veteran city hall reporter William Conklin disclosed that La Guardia got "some newspapermen fired, had others transferred from City Hall, and intimidated a good many into reluctance to tell the whole truth about him." "Make no mistake about it," wrote John Hennessey Walker, "there is scarcely a man in the [city hall press] corps who doesn't fear La Guardia's power of reprisal."[110]

La Guardia left OCD with such rancor toward the fourth estate that he stopped speaking to news reporters. Let the newspapermen "learn the ethics of their profession," he commanded, before they came to interview him. As an afterthought he added that he would be willing to discuss policy with sports writers, music critics, or woman's page reporters, anyone but the offensive crew that knew him. Mary Draggioth, the *Post*'s women's page editor, took advantage of the offer and pronounced the rumpled executive "a lovely mayor." But the Wilting Flower soon tired of explaining fiscal policy to football experts and fashion page savants. He was left to muse on the imperfectibility of the press, something that as a young man he had granted as the necessary price of democracy. So downgraded did the city hall assignment become that five of the city's most important newspapers no longer assigned a full-time reporter to the place.[111]

He fell into the self-serving habit of arguing that unfavorable portrayals of himself undermined public confidence in the job that he was trying to do. Putting it that way transformed fighting for his own reputation into a cause higher than himself. It also marked real changes in his view of the press. Before taking office he had told the Columbia University symposium that newspapers were too meek, too submissive to advertisers. They did not probe deeply enough. Now La Guardia was demanding that his statements be reported without comment or interpretations—news reporting by official communique. By denying journalists access to himself and his commissioners, he limited them to accepting handouts and rewriting press releases. He managed to create a tighter monopoly on news than any Tammany boss had ever dreamed of.

Mark the change. Now Fiorello was writing to the *advertisers* complaining to them about articles that were "false," "vicious," and "close to subversive." "I am appealing to you," he wrote to Jack Straus, president of Macy's, because we had another case of sabotaging. . . . Fortunately several big advertisers were present . . . and were able to stop a deliberate plan to destroy confidence even at the expense of the morale of the business of New York City." The saboteurs that the mayor was complaining of were the New York newspapers, "the *Times* in particular!" and he was relying on the advertisers to keep the newspapers honest! His earlier good humor worn down to a grimace, he refused an invitation to the annual Inner Circle dinner that he usually attended to celebrate with the New York City press corps.[112]

He had in the past taken pride in afflicting the comfortable, in guaranteeing free speech, regardless of the discomfort it caused, in protecting unpopular opinions, not because he agreed with them, but because free speech was critical for maintaining civic integrity. Now he had a new ambition, to operate in a world where orders were orders, where city councils did not make pesky investigations, where his word was more important than civil liberties, where press critics were properly muzzled. He was tired of the restraints and consciously emplaced barriers of democratic government.

CHAPTER 14

The Personal Mayoralty

1. The Radio Mayor

I N 1942 the La Guardias finally moved out of their East Harlem tenement. From the mid-thirties the city legislature had bandied about the idea of an official mayoral residence, but the plebian La Guardia had repeatedly rejected all such efforts in his behalf. His Honor's secretary explained, "No one so devoted to public service, and with such an unselfish attitude toward his task as Mayor La Guardia would want to encourage such a home for himself." But now he relented. Marie La Guardia and her friends went to work scrubbing the floors of the renovated eighteenth-century Gracie Mansion overlooking the East River, and in May New York's first family moved out of the tenement that had been their home since the late 1920s. Typically, Mrs. La Guardia was left to supervise the move while Fiorello was in Canada on war-related business.

The mayor also got a new car, a small coupe with a green body and a white top. The Fiorellomobile had fire engine-type emergency lights, with a red sign flashing "Mayor" on top and five stars painted on its hood, one more than permitted a full general in the army. Luminous blackout paint on the front and back bumpers allowed easy identification in an emergency.[1]

As his own interest in the mayoral office waned, La Guardia kept adding to its trappings, trying to chase the emptiness and boredom that placed his mayoralty in eclipse. But nothing so recharged La Guardia and expanded the influence of his third-term mayoralty so much as the regular Sunday radio broadcasts that he initiated early in 1942.

After Pearl Harbor La Guardia had gone on the air to reassure the public and discuss defense planning. The response to his broadcasts was very positive, quite different from the constant barrage of criticism carried in the press. This convinced La Guardia that the press was to blame for the bad image of his work at OCD. No matter how honest or effective a job he did, they always found some way to present it in negative terms. Reporters with little more expertise than the ability to type a grammatical sentence were passing judgment on officials who had to act swiftly in the midst of the most dire national emergency. He was tired of their prying questions and their corrosive skepticism. If not for the journalists the people would respect their leaders more. He resolved to clear a more direct path to the public, for whom he retained a genuine affection, by cutting out the middlemen journalists, for whom he did not. "I have . . . learned," he remarked, "that important public questions must be presented impartially and the only way I know of doing that—if you get what I mean—is by word of mouth."

On January 18, 1942, he initiated a series of Sunday "Talks to the People" on municipal radio station WNYC, a free-form combination of fireside chat and cracker-barrel hour. For the rest of his mayoralty, La Guardia's Sunday programs, opening with the Marine Hymn and the mayor's favorite salutation, "Patience and fortitude," attracted as many as 2 million listeners tuning in to their mayor's opinions on politics and life.[2]

———

From a report on defense-related plans and current war strategies, La Guardia segues into matters of immediate concern. "Ladies," he says, in his unmistakable tenor, "I want to ask you a favor, I want you please to wear your rubbers when you go out in this weather. If you don't . . . you may slip and fall . . . and hurt yourselves. Then we'll have to take care of you and we don't like to ask our doctors and nurses to take care of any more patients. . . . So won't you please be sensible and wear your rubbers? . . . Now about fish," the chief executive continues, "you should take advantage of the low prices this week and buy fish. . . ."[3]

From such advice, delivered in fatherly tones, he drops into another mood. Chin taut and fist pounding on the desk before him, the riled magistrate turns to the subject of the "no good thieving, chiseling tinhorns." These are the snakes in his city, the gamblers, loan sharks, and black marketeers whom he delights in naming and threatening. "Cut it out," he screams into the microphone as he gives the name of a loan shark. "Cut it out right now. That sort of business don't go in New York. Not while I'm Mayor. Get me?" Or "Oh I've got to give a little notice now. Certain firms manufacturing stirrup pumps have raised their prices from eight to twenty dollars. . . . Cut it out. If you don't I'll tell [Office of Price Administration director] Leon Henderson. The two of us will get after you."[4]

On some Sundays the mayor instructed on national economics, on others he spoke about city planning or war strategy, and even about corruption that had been uncovered in his administration. Commissioners were appointed, civil servants berated, children entertained, and New Yorkers informed in a show that absorbed the mayor's mulitfaceted predilection for minding the business of his citizens. He would gather information for his programs from commissioners' reports, news clips, citizen's letters, federal announcements, food lists, Marie's recipe book, or Eric's classroom, and he would guard some bit of news with all the jealousy of a cub reporter protecting an exclusive. And the following day the newspapers would run from three to seven separate stories spawned by the mayor's half hour.

The experts said that his voice was all wrong, rising to a harsh squeak at odd moments. His feverish demeanor and earthy syntax contrasted with the polished style of conventional radio announcers. Under stress he mashed his pronunciation and did violence to the king's grammar, and there was little pattern to his stream-of-consciousness presentation. But while others counted themselves successful on the ability to sell a can of soup or the right brand of soap, La Guardia influenced what people ate, thought, wore, knew, and did through his weekly half hour. Caught up in the intimacy of the medium, he would speak into the microphone as if there were only a few close buddies before him. "I told you [before the 1941 election] that I would not run. Oh, I sometimes feel I should have stuck to that decision. . . . Well, now I don't know as I should have said that." Sometimes it came as a shock to him that the city was listening.[5]

A few months into the program, Fiorello became involved in a controversy that showed how far the new intimacy crossed old barriers. La Guardia read a letter from young George, complaining that his father gambled away his weekly pay at a local store, leaving the family destitute. The mayor promised over the air that he would send the police to the store and clean it out. "You just keep me informed." Then he added an invitation to "other little boys" who see their fathers gambling to "please let me know," promising, "I won't tell anybody that you told me, but I'll send the police." The idea of asking boys to send in evidence against their fathers horrified civil libertarians. "The Communists were the first to set children against their parents," James Marshall, president of the Board of Education, wrote the mayor, accusingly. When La Guardia saw what he said in print, it sounded so different from what he had meant to say that he denied it: "I did not ask any boys to peach on their fathers. Whoever said that is a dirty, lousy, stinking, putrid liar."[6]

But he did say that and much more. The radio brought La Guardia into the homes and lives of the citizens, breaking traditional barriers between municipal government and its citizens. On Easter Sunday 1943 La Guardia delivered a full sermon, preceded by music from Wagner's *Parsifal* and followed by selections from Handel's *Messiah*, praying for a divinely wrought peace wherein "nations will not exploit nations, nor will any nation be in want." On a winter Sunday he broadcast an appeal to sixteen-year-old Kenneth Doukas, who had disappeared after receiving an unsatisfactory report card from his high school. "When your dad went away, he told you that you were to be the man of the house. He's coming home in a few days on furlough and you must be home when he gets there."[7]

During these years of shortage and rationing, the people came to rely on La Guardia to keep them informed about supplies of coal, fuel, food, and even shoe leather. After La Guardia hinted at shoe rationing on one of the brodcasts—he advised his listeners to keep off of their feet—anxious New Yorkers piled into Lower East Side shoe stores to stock up, causing a near riot. He led consumers through the maze of rationing rules, scarce goods, and inflated prices. "Hello housewives. . . . Remember what I told you last Sunday about snap beans? Remember? They were asking fifty-four cents a pound and I told you to stop buying snap beans and the price'd come down—and you did, and it did. Look we got them down to seventeen cents Saturday. . . ." He suggested substitutes for regular staples, dictating recipes for a new vegetable, a little-known fish, or a new cut of meat. He championed "oxtail ragout," "Jerusalem artichokes," and B-grade eggs with brown shells—"Well you don't eat the shells, do you?" Conserve. Turn off lights. Do not waste heat. Save fats, he admonished. World War I was lost because of a shortage of fats; just do not use the same oils for fish and meat. And don't waste bread. "There is such a thing as bread pudding." (CCB chided Fiorello for setting a poor example after he spied the huge city hall chandelier burning on a sunny morning; and perhaps Fiorello could do without the fancy engraved official stationery? The mayor turned off the lights, but kept the heavy paper.)[8]

Before long, Sunday with the mayor was attracting the highest ratings of any radio program in the city, leading opponents to attack WNYC, the municipal radio station that presented the program, as the "Mayor's personal plaything . . . [to] disseminate his own personal and political views." They threatened to strike WNYC's appropriation from the budget. La Guardia smiled back that if the elected officials in their wisdom boarded up WNYC, he would find a way to carry on his dialogue with New Yorkers. On cue, the Coty Corporation offered $1000 a week to sponsor the program, and more than 1800 letters came into city hall in support of the broadcasts. The Board of Estimate sheepishly dropped the matter, and Fiorello continued to use his bully pulpit unimpeded.[9]

When real estate interests announced a hefty rent increase, he broadcast statistics demonstrating that there were practically no apartment vacancies, resulting in the highest return on property investments in years. He turned to the *New York Times* classified, and "lo and behold," ads were offering apartment houses for sale, guaranteeing net profits of 20 and 30 percent. These fellows were doing very well, he told his audience of apartment dwellers. They had no business raising rents, "and I'm going to tell them down in Washington that I think so. . . ." And lo and behold, the Office of Rent Administration saw it precisely that way! To restaurants that would not cooperate on "meatless" days, he said: "You think you're smart, but you're going to get what's coming to you. Get me?" Barbers who charged sailors $2.20 and more for a haircut were asked, "What in the world do you do to them for $2.20. Now cut it out. . . ."[10]

Gambling attracted his special attention. He would announce names and addresses, ordering Police Commissioner Lewis Valentine to "run these two out of town, will you Lew," over the air. When he heard that gamblers used the phone booths at Yankee Stadium to call in their bets, he ordered the doors ripped off the booths so that police could overhear the conversations. After he learned that Madison Square Garden basketball fans were calling New Jersey numbers to place bets, he disclosed the numbers. "Take your pencil. Here are some of the tinhorn telephone numbers. . . . Are you listening, New Jersey? Are you listening Mr. Attorney General of New Jersey? . . . PAssaic 3-2590, PAssaic 3-1043, PAssaic 2-9333, LInden 2-3763. . . ." When a new ban was slapped on race gambling, he warned: "I do not know what the firms of Chiselers, *Gonovim* [Yiddish] & *Imbroglioni* [Italian], unincorporated, are going to do, but we are going to watch. If you try any monkey business, we will grab you by the back of the neck and the seat of the pants and kick you out, do you hear?"[11]

Discovering that Western Union transmitted race track information, La Guardia delivered a plain message to the company: "Now Mr. Western Union let me tell you this, I think the law should compel refusal to take messages from gamblers and chiselers and tinhorns and touts, and also should prohibit transmitting . . . information of plugs trotting or creeping around a track in Havana or Tijuana." It did not, but he had found a law that he thought might sustain a prosecution. "I am going to try it." And if Western Union continued to transmit such data, "I am going to ask the police to . . . hold responsible the management of the company who gets the profit from these messages. . . ." The company agreed to cooperate.[12]

A man entangled in debt from betting losses wrote that he was going crazy trying to repay his gambling debts while keeping his family fed. He could no longer take the pressure. La Guardia was right, these tinhorns were evil. He saw no way of escaping them but to take his life. Fiorello read the entire letter over the air and then bent into the microphone to say in his most soothing fatherly tones: "Don't do it. Come in to see me. I am sure that out of seven and a half million people there will be some that I can call in to help you out. You have your wife and your children and your God. You must not do it."[13]

The papers criticized him for his zealousness and his intrusions into such protected precincts as the family, but many of his critics, old friends, and liberals, missed an equally important point. Children as well as many common New Yorkers needed a warm government hand to hold, someone in government to report their problems to. Having cleaned out many of the bosses and their ward heelers, the reformers had not replaced the friendly local complaint bureau that the political club had been with anything nearly as efficient or intimate. Citizens wanted some sense that the government could be reached, could be talked to without having to stand on line before a forbidding bureaucracy. Invariably New Yorkers today remember La Guardia as the mayor who spoke on the radio because it meant so much to them to have such an accessible mayor, whose voice, feelings, and family they got to know from his years on WNYC, and who advised them about where to shop, what to cook, how to raise children, and how to deal with these difficult times.

2. The Ethnic Battlefield

L A Guardia had warned that the war would come to New York City and now
it did, only not quite in the way that he had predicted. The war threatened its
damage not in the form of planes strafing the residential districts but by in-
flaming emotions in ethnic communities and dividing the city's diverse population,
confronting La Guardia with issues that put both his personal principles and political
dexterity to the test.

Reporters demanded to know if La Guardia, as the most visible Italian politician in a nation at war with Mussolini, would consider returning the World War
I medals that he had been awarded by Italy. No, the shrewd old Major replied, he
would hold onto the awards that he had received in 1919 for his bombing missions,
adding: "Italy was a nation then. It is only a colony of Germany now. Of course
the people of Italy will get rid of Mussolini." This is the way he dealt with the
problem for the rest of the war, treating Mussolini as an aberration of the true
Italian spirit. "No one can tell me that the Italian people were made to goose step
in back of any dictator," he would insist.[14]

Nonetheless, La Guardia was aware that many in the Italian community held
the Fascist dictator in higher regard than he, and he worked with the FBI and local
police to root out Italian fifth column activity in New York and assisted Washington
in its efforts to quash suspected sedition. La Guardia visited Italian communities
around the country to dispel Fascist sentiments and "guide Italian American public
opinion." The United States, he would tell his compatriots, deserved their undivided
loyalty. Here was the "true Italy," the nation that had given them refuge and
opportunity, where the "sons of the *Santa Maria* mixed with the sons of the *Half
Moon* and the *Mayflower*."[15]

Concerned that Generoso Pope's Italian-language newspapers openly supported Mussolini, Assistant Secretary of State Adolf Berle consulted La Guardia
about what to do. Fiorello dismissed the publisher as a *cullo di cavallo* [horse's
ass] to Berle, but he brought the subject of Pope's split loyalties and Fascist backing
to the FBI. He told special agent B. E. Sackett that he was prepared to warn Pope
personally that he had better be more discriminating about what he published. To
make the message clear, La Guardia was going to "ask Mr. Hugh McQuillian of
the Internal Revenue Service here to initiate an income tax investigation of Pope
and question Pope in a frank effort to intimidate him. . . ." La Guardia suggested
that Sackett keep up the pressure by putting Pope through a rough grilling. When
the FBI hesitated, fearing that such action might backfire, La Guardia secured

presidential approval for the investigation himself. By 1941 publisher Pope was mincing his Fascist sentiments, at least in the English-language sections of his papers.[16]

"Do you realize," one correspondent asked the mayor, "what a wonderful moral effect you would achieve if you spoke over the radio to the people of Italy, and told them how the Italians who do not live in Italy feel about this war?" In fact, by the summer of 1942, when this letter reached La Guardia, he was already doing precisely this, beaming weekly shortwave programs, titled "Mayor La Guardia Calling Rome," over the ocean. The fifteen-minute segments began with the words "This is your friend La Guardia speaking" and proceeded to take aim at Mussolini and his German allies. La Guardia reminded his listeners of their glorious past and called upon them to despise the slavemaster Hitler and fight for their dignity. In speeches designed to "create . . . trouble and incite . . . to riot," he urged Italians to lay down their tools and weapons and free themselves of "this fascist gang." In a widely publicized appeal, La Guardia asked King Victor Emmanuel III "NOT TO SACRIFICE [ITALY'S] SONS FOR HITLER. . . . I APPEAL TO YOU LET US STAND FOR PEACE AND FREEDOM AS WE DID IN NINETEEN EIGHTEEN."[17]

The Office of War Information reported in October of 1943 that La Guardia's weekly talks were the most popular of all American programs broadcast to Italy. Anti-Fascists risked their lives to listen to the New York mayor. When the town of Torre Annunziata was liberated by the Fifth Army, the *New York Times* described how a young man who had been jailed by the Fascists for listening to La Guardia's broadcasts was hailed as a hero. "Yes, yes, . . ." the townsfolk told reporters about the broadcasts. "They were a great help to our morale . . . helping us understand that the Americans realized our plight." By the end of the war there was talk of La Guardia being appointed a general in Italy, and an American GI wrote to city hall, "Everybody speaks of your coming over as a certainty" and "a blessing."[18]

La Guardia did everything in his power to help the anti-Fascists. When appeals reached him from Italy asking for food and other necessities, he lobbied the State Department to round up the necessary assistance. Late in 1942, as U.S. bombers strafed Italian cities, he implored Roosevelt to declare Rome an open city and save it from destruction. The distant son also petitioned the White House on behalf of the American Italians who wanted to send remittances to their relatives in the occupied territories, asked the navy to distribute clothes, medicines, and supplies to residents in liberated areas, and kept tabs on Allied treatment of Italian civilians during the occupation.[19]

Once the Fascists fell, he insisted on a generous and swift rehabilitation policy, demanding that Italy be accorded the full privileges of such allies as Belgium, Holland, and Poland. Pressing the point rather strongly on behalf of a nation that only a short while back had been an enemy, La Guardia offended Americans who were less devoted to Italy's interests. The *Pittsburgh Press* denounced his special pleading on behalf of a nation that had stuck "the dagger into the back of its neighbor. The Italians," the newspaper continued,

> were happy—and very brave—on that day. So much for the criminal background of Italy—her slaughter of helpless Ethiopians, her practice warfare against the Spanish and her ghoulish sneak punch against dying France.
>
> The Italian people yelled gleefully and loudly to show their approval of all these things. They were hot stuff while pounding those who were helpless.[20]

But La Guardia refused to be daunted by the ridicule or threats of a backlash from Italy's enemies. He was a loyal and committed friend whose support rested on more than practical political grounds. When the State Department did not move as quickly as he wanted in providing assistance programs, he did not hesitate to tell his overseas audience that his government had done them wrong.

> It is now over two years that we have been talking every week.
>
> We suggested that Mussolini should be kicked out. You have done so.
>
> We advised breaking relations with the Nazis. You have done so.
>
> We declared that you should reject Fascism. You have done so.
>
> We declared the hope that your troops would be fighting alongside ours against the Nazis. You are doing so.
>
> What are we waiting for?[21]

If La Guardia's regard for Italy made him a loyal son and an outspoken advocate, his response to the crises facing New York's Jews was more complicated. He understood the anxieties of the Jews well. His symbolic audacities had often lifted their spirits at a time when they had few real friends. When the State Department apprised Fiorello of German government fears for its property and nationals in New York City, the mayor created an all-Jewish detail of police under Captain Max Finkelstein, president of the Shomrin Society (the department's Jewish fraternal organization), to protect the German consul, embassy staff, and assorted Teutonic dignitaries. The move cheered beleaguered Jews and infuriated the Nazis, who compared La Guardia to a gorilla.[22]

While La Guardia insisted on permitting the German-American Bund to hold a public meeting, he managed to cripple the Fritz Kuhn-directed group by directing his investigations commissioner to study the group's records. By the time William Herlands was through, Kuhn was jailed for embezzlement. But anti-Jewish feeling in the city was not limited to the crude nazism of Fritz Kuhn and his Bund. Historian David Wyman has counted more than 100 anti-Jewish organizations that brought Jew-hatred to a dangerous boil in these years. Perhaps the best known of these organizations was the one led by the "golden-voiced radio priest" Charles Coughlin, who attracted a large Catholic following by playing heavily on economic fears and religious resentments.

The gospel of hate made easy headway all across the United States. In one midwestern city, hoodlums ripped the shirt off a Jewish boy and painted a Star of David with the word "Jude" on his chest. In Boston, Jewish schoolboys were severely beaten by their classmates. In 1940 Joseph E. McWilliams, campaigning for a Manhattan congressional seat, announced enthusiastically, "I am the anti-Jewish candidate for Congress." He was defeated, but others no less biased won seats in the national legislature. Mississippi's John Rankin was only the most rabid of the congressional haters to flourish in the hothouse atmosphere of international turmoil. His colleague, Montana's Jacob Thorkelson, attributed to the Jews a fantastic invisible government that linked global banking operations with an international Communist conspiracy.

A Protestant clergyman, Dr. L. M. Birkhead, traveling throughout the midwest found vicious anti-Jewish attitudes rampant, even in the "best circles." And Fritz Kuhn's Bund was estimated to have 25,000 followers, with perhaps 8000 of them full-fledged Bund troopers. In 1939 Kuhn packed 20,000 sympathizers into Madison Square Garden to praise Hitler, denounce Roosevelt, and cheer Charles Coughlin. When journalist Dorothy Thompson laughed after a speaker attributed the moral superiority of the assembled to the purity of their white Christian lineage, she was beaten.[23]

The worst examples of anti-Semitism took place in La Guardia's New York. Ronald Bayor reports in his perceptive study of New York's *Neighbors in Conflict* that Jewish communities "were raked by constant anti-semitic vandalism." This is a New York unrecognizable from any of La Guardia's speeches and broadcasts that touted unity and the Immigrant City as exemplar of American pluralism; it was a New York in which one journal feared that Jews were no longer safe on the streets.

With the tacit support of some church leaders, lower-class toughs took to heart Father Charles Coughlin's anti-Jewish rabble-rousing and fashioned an organization to preserve the nation and the "Christian social order upon which it was founded." This "Christian Front"—in the main drawn from the Irish Catholic population—launched a program of overt anti-Jewish intimidation that resulted in stabbings, sluggings, and random violence. In such mixed ethnic neighborhoods as Washington Heights and the South Bronx, the Front launched boycotts of Jewish merchants, carried out an "employ Christians only" campaign, and harassed Jews

521

on the streets. Front-led youths barged in on services shouting, "Kill the Jews," desecrated almost every synagogue in Washington Heights, vandalized Jewish-owned businesses, abused the elderly, and attacked the young. When residents reported incidents to the local police, their complaints were dismissed with the comment: "Ah the boys are just playing."[24]

Jews were puzzled by the unfolding events. They had great respect for La Guardia's fairness. He had spoken feelingly about the depredations of the Nazis. All the more had they expected that he would do something to control the local hooliganism and employ the police to protect them. They were surprised and hurt when he did nothing.

Clearly there are certain rights that even dangerous people have in a democracy. And only a few were calling for the Christian Front to be closed down, or for its streetside orators to be shut up. But when brash teenagers shouted into the faces of elderly Jewish men and women, "Kill the Kikes," more than free speech was involved. This was not the republic of civic virtue and citizen happiness that La Guardia had so often promised.[25]

The *Nation* printed a thoughtful consideration of the problem, admitting that "the road is choked with the skeletons of unsuccessful precedents and the shapes of dangerous possibilities" in dealing with these issues. Without minimizing the philosophical and practical difficulties in identifying the limits of free speech, the *Nation* thought that the mayor, practiced in making hard pragmatic decisions, must deal with the problem, especially the neglect of the police.[26]

James Wechsler, writing in the same magazine, went further, accusing the police of open sympathy for the Coughlin movement. "You people have gone too far," Wechsler quoted a police officer saying to a man he was dragging into the stationhouse, "and we are going to stop you. . . . When the time comes I'll resign from the force and we'll settle the question our way." The accused man had been guilty of carrying a placard denouncing Charles Coughlin![27]

Wechsler's article detailed similar incidents illustrating the dilemma of a diverse city whose public guardians were making no effort to hide their own bigotry. What was the mayor prepared to do about this problem? the *Nation* demanded to know. Such police had to be watched carefully; certainly they should not be the watchers.

> There is no need for us to tell Mayor La Guardia or Commissioner Valentine how. . . . They are past masters of the art of switching recreant patrolmen who live in the Bronx to lonely beats in Far Rockaway; demotions are a powerful argument; and there is always expulsion for cause. There is no doubt in the world that under reactionary administrations such procedures are utilized to the hilt. They must be used now with cause by a liberal administration for the safety of the city.[28]

The mayor's response was uncharacteristically pat: "The police have rendered excellent service and have exerted the proper kind of restraint."[29]

There was room for disagreement. Joseph Schwartz, a twenty-six-year-old Brooklyn man, passed a "Christian Mobilizers" street rally where the speaker was proclaiming that the only good Jews were to be found in cemeteries. Schwartz shouted back that he was a good Jew and still alive. Patrolman James Cavanaugh, assigned to guard the peace, pounced on the offending Schwartz and arrested him for creating a disturbance. Asked in court to testify whether the facts in the case were as described, the policeman admitted that he had arrested the man unjustly, but, the cop sputtered, he had only been acting on the orders of his captain, Michael McCarron.

The magistrate hearing the case was incredulous "that things of this kind can occur in the streets of this city!" Others thought that this case might convince the mayor that there was a problem in his police department and that he could no longer hide behind platitudes about free speech. But La Guardia did little more than send advisers to attend Christian Front meetings and report back to him.[30]

In a letter to the editor of the *New York Times*, Owen Taylor complained of having written fifteen letters about prejudiced police enforcement to various officials, including the mayor, without receiving a single reply. Those who did hear from La Guardia were not much more satisfied. "This report is typical of the exaggerated accounts circulated from some quarters," La Guardia wrote to Isadore Fried, who asked for closer attention to the activities of anti-Semitic groups.[31]

But on January 14, 1940, the FBI arrested eighteen New Yorkers on charges of conspiring to bomb the *Jewish Daily Forward*, the *Daily Worker*, a Brooklyn theater that showed Russian-made films, a number of Jewish businesses, and selected Jewish neighborhoods. In the midst of the havoc that the conspirators anticipated from their handiwork, they planned to assassinate Jewish congressmen, hoping thereby to set off a nationwide uprising of anti-Semitic forces. Too fantastic to be taken seriously, this plot nonetheless shook Jews with an example of the extremes to which the fevered ideas of local Christian Fronters could lead.[32]

Only after these charges disclosed how dangerous the Front could be did La Guardia finally order Commissioner Herlands to investigate police membership in the Christian Front. Police were instructed to complete anonymously a single questionnaire asking whether they were members of the Christian Front or any "subversive, Communist, bund or fascist club or organization." This limited investigation nonetheless produced the sort of barbed controversy that La Guardia had feared. The journal of the Brooklyn Catholic diocese, the *Brooklyn Tablet*, demanded to know why the Christian Front was being maligned. "Yes, he may say . . . that some of the members of this organization are anti-semitic. Well what of it? Just what law was violated?"

The *Tablet* suggested that La Guardia was too solicitous of Jewish opinion.

"Let anyone be associated, directly or indirectly, with any movement or person which is reported to cherish dislike of some Jews then the Mayor and his whole spy system are turned loose on them." The journal denounced the questionnaire as "infamous, demoralizing, insulting, unAmerican, anti-Christian, and little less than a slander on all Christians." Still, more than 400 police answered that they had been members of the Front.[33]

It was not until three years later, just before Herlands released an "Investigative Report on Anti-Semitism in New York City" detailing police laxity and ineffectualness in dealing with anti-Semitism, that Commissioner Valentine took steps to combat anti-Semitic vandalism and the desecration of synagogues. La Guardia was asked whether he was responsible for the new orders, but he avoided a direct answer. In Massachusetts, revelations of police negligence had resulted in the resignation of the police commissioner. In New York, La Guardia was still trying to distance himself from the thorny issue.[34]

As head of OCD La Guardia had been concerned with internal morale. He developed a long list of goals ranging from gas masks for babies to controlling the movement of enemy aliens, but while anti-Semitism in the United States reached the highest levels in history—just "slightly below the boiling point," wrote sociologist David Reisman—and surveys taken between 1938 and 1945 revealed that about 15 percent of Americans supported an anti-Jewish campaign in the United States and another 20 to 25 percent sympathized with such a movement, La Guardia ignored this explosive internal issue.[35]

By 1944 New York's Jewish community was wrapped up in more immediate concerns, the destruction of millions of their brethren in Europe. Early in 1937, before the gas chambers had even been conceived and fascism had not yet become associated with a murderous anti-Semitism, La Guardia refused to comment on Mussolini's order commanding Italy's Jewish population to cease criticizing Hitler. In 1943 the problem was far more acute. Jews were being gassed by Nazis and La Guardia was no longer brushing off questions. He proposed that the United Nations serve notice on the slaughterers that they would be held to account. At this point such threats were, of course, irrelevant, although they made good copy. The more critical issue involved how to make room for those Jews who could still be saved and funneling assistance to them. On this matter La Guardia spoke with calculated ambivalence: "We cannot tell others to take in the doomed while we keep our own door closed. While we consider emigration and colonization, however, we must realize that taking the Jews and others out of terrorist controlled lands is not really the solution. The rights of Jews and other minorities must be made safe in every country in the world."[36]

A few weeks later La Guardia testified before Congress in favor of creating a commission to "save the Jewish people of Europe from extinction at the hands of Nazi Germany." Then he called upon the United States to open immigration *"in the same proportion that it asked other countries to do so."* But America was not asking anybody to open doors and therefore, according to La Guardia's formula, had no moral responsibility to open its own.[37]

David Wyman's relentless indictment of American inaction while Hitler systematically destroyed European Jewry argues that Franklin Roosevelt's policy during the holocaust amounted to an abandonment of the Jews. He sums up a critical difference in motivation between Hitler and the Allies in two simple sentences. "To kill the Jews the Nazis were willing to weaken their capacity to fight the war," committing crucial supplies and manpower to the extermination program. "The U.S. and its allies were willing to attempt almost nothing to save them." While authenticated information about the extermination of European Jewry reached the public in November 1942, the United States did nothing for fourteen months, and then only the fear of a "nasty scandal over its rescue policies" thrust the administration toward involvement, but only at minimal levels, and in view of what could still have been accomplished, in a way that was scandalously inadequate.[38]

La Guardia was not Roosevelt, neither in terms of the president's steely aloofness from this issue nor in terms of his potential for making a difference. But his city did have the largest concentration of Jews in the world, and although he did not think of himself as a Jew, his estranged sister was still in Europe and he was aware that she had been taken away by the Nazis. Throughout his career he had made his own unequivocal hatred of the haters clear. Throughout the terrible crisis, he was one of a handful of non-Jews who consistently voiced concern, attended rallies, stoked liberal consciences, and appealed for attention. If Fiorello La Guardia is to be criticized for not doing all he could, it is not because others did more. It is because his own past suggested that a fully engaged Fiorello could have done more. To do more, given the obstacles, would have required, in David Wyman's words, "an unquenchable sense of urgency." And what La Guardia did was to stop at the limits of reasonable action.

He had gone further in behalf of other causes earlier in his life. If there was ever a time when the semicolon boys and the comma-pushers in the State Department should have been held to account it was now, when they were using every possible technicality to create "paper walls" to keep refugees out. From mid-1940 to mid-1941, when refugee emigration was still feasible, administrative red tape was used to delay and limit immigration. Careful calculations suggest that this translates into 25,000 lives that could have been saved in that one year alone. During the following three and one-half years that the United States was at war with Germany only 21,000 refugees were permitted into the country. This represents no more than 10 percent of the number eligible under relevant laws. This would have been cause enough to have the old Fiorello burning the wires with fiery phone calls and telegrams, lashing the bureaucrats for their racist barbarity.[39]

During the twenties he had taken on the armed forces establishment. He had ample reason to do it again. Jewish groups made repeated appeals to the War Department imploring the generals to bomb the crematoria and the railroads that transported the thousands of doomed persons to their final destination. The War Department rejected these demands, claiming that such sorties would divert essential air power from operations that were part of overall Allied strategy. Yet in this very period Americans were carrying out massive bombing raids no more than fifty miles from Auschwitz. Twice bombers struck within five miles of the gas chambers and inexplicably failed to try to knock them out of operation. One can imagine the bristling congressman of the twenties drenching the army in righteous contumely. What better time for this man whom Arthur Mann described as a "Fighter Against His Times" to blaze forth with "his explosive resentment against the power and cruelty, the stupidity and arrogance of Anglo-Saxon America."[40]

But he had grown politically cautious. He still had his dreams about Washington and he would not pressure FDR or challenge him on the issue of rescue. He peppered the president with many ideas, on Latin America, the treatment of Italians, military strategy, European propaganda, and a host of other issues that had nothing to do with New York City, but not on the holocaust, arguably the most momentous historical event of his time.

He did more than most—more than many Jews, perhaps including Rabbi Stephen Wise, who hesitated to use his own good connections with the White House to force action—but the uncalculating passion that had ignited his social conscience earlier had now been tamped by a shrewder politics and a wartime sensitivity to rocking the boat.

---

3. The Race Quandary in New York

O N civil rights for blacks La Guardia stood well ahead of contemporary American society; his words at the very least reflected where he thought his heart should be. He believed in the fair treatment of New Yorkers, regardless of color, appointed blacks to important positions in the city, and made symbolic sorties against prejudice. He signed petitions demanding the hiring of blacks in defense industries and attacked employment agencies that blatantly discriminated against non-Anglo-Saxons. Once, when Eleanor Roosevelt wrote to him on behalf of an unemployed black, the mayor wrote back that of course he would help the young subject of Mrs. Roosevelt's appeal, but his heart would continue to ache for those who remained unemployed and unchampioned, and in 1942 he signed a public appeal to her husband to eliminate discrimination in the armed forces. When Franklin Roosevelt, somewhat less committed to civil rights than his wife, asked Fiorello to help forestall a threatened March on Washington by disillusioned blacks, La Guardia used the opportunity to extract from the president a promise to meet face-to-face with black leaders and establish a Fair Employment Practices Commission. In the total picture, La Guardia was one of the most sincere advocates of Negro rights in public life.[41]

Once the FEPC was established, A. Philip Randolph, the widely respected black labor leader, urged Roosevelt to make La Guardia its chairman, this while FH was still mayor, director of OCD, and chairman of the U.S.-Canadian Joint Defense Commission. Randolph felt confident that an overworked and harried La Guardia was still the most effective individual to trust with the issue of racial fairness. Walter White, head of the NAACP, told the president that "La Guardia's standing among colored people and his reputation for getting things done, make it imperative that he be named Chairman." Roosevelt, following his own policy of entrusting civil rights issues to southern advisers, decided instead on Mark Etheridge, the liberal editor of the Louisville *Courier Journal*.[42]

Despite the Depression, despite the disproportionate unemployment, prejudice, police problems, and decrepit housing, New York's black population had grown by 40 percent during La Guardia's tenure. Between 1930 and 1940 more than 145,000 blacks settled within the five boroughs, bringing Gotham's total Negro population to half a million. The rhetoric of equality came easily to La Guardia, but he had also made tangible progress. Blacks who had been in the city since the beginning of the fusion administration could point to such solid achievements as the Harlem River Houses, the Central Harlem Center, a new wing at Harlem Hospital, and two additional public schools, all reflecting La Guardia's palpable interest in servicing the black families of upper Manhattan. Black doctors and nurses were brought into city hospitals, and more blacks were put to work in transit, relief, police, and other services, while La Guardia made a point of spreading these appointments around the city and not limiting them to black neighborhoods.[43]

Like other liberals, La Guardia wanted to believe that race was irrelevant, but Harlem's high crime rates, massive unemployment, and pervasive social malaise proved that, one way or another, race mattered. With attitudes fixed in traditional values that looked to a stable home as the benchmark of a decent environment, he could not understand, much less excuse, common-law marriages, illegitimacy, drinking, gambling, and loose control over the activities of juveniles. An added wrinkle complicated his ideas on the race issue. Many of the plain New Yorkers whose cause he championed were biased against blacks. They were not prejudiced in the same way as some of the southern bigots who participated in lynch mobs and straight-out violence, but rather in a way that was more insidious. They would deny blacks a job, refuse to live near them, view them as inferior human beings, and deny their children equal opportunities. As mayor, La Guardia worked with such people, understood them, did not think that they were necessarily evil, and sometimes compromised with them.[44]

The shortage of good housing plagued every major older city in the country. This was what had brought La Guardia and many of his fellow mayors flocking to the federal public housing programs. But by 1943 it was clear to even the most visionary housing reformer that Washington was not going to build enough housing to make much of a difference. La Guardia turned to creating interest, among private investors, in a version of the "philanthropy and 5 percent" projects of the progressive era that resulted in low-rent tenements for the poor and moderate profits for the well-intentioned developers who put them up.

In June 1943 he initialed an agreement with the Metropolitan Life Insurance Company for the development of a $40 to $50 million "quasi-public" low-rent housing complex for 30,000 tenants on the Lower East Side of Manhattan to be known as Stuyvesant Town, assigning to the company responsibility for clearing and rehabilitating the area and managing the buildings once they were built. In signing this agreement the city chose to ignore Metropolitan's record of persistent discrimination against blacks. With more than 100,000 insurance policies sold in Harlem alone, Metropolitan categorically refused to hire blacks, not in Harlem, and not elsewhere, period. And Metropolitan followed a policy of residential segregation in its apartments. In this regard, Metropolitan chairman Frederick Eckers wrote in a letter of understanding with the city, "We shall rent apartments to applicants solely on the basis of the standard which must govern a fiduciary's prudent investment in the particular neighborhood. . . ." In plain English, given the company's record, this meant that Stuyvesant Town would be all white.[45]

The contract with Metropolitan wounded many blacks in a way that La Guardia had not anticipated. He had been as true a friend as they had in government, and it hurt to see their own dignity being dealt away in a dispassionate balancing of municipal needs. Certain things they had hoped were nonnegotiable. "Can it be, Mr. Mayor," cried a disillusioned housewife, "that you of all people, are approving . . . discrimination?" Others looked at the implied restrictive covenant and responded more in anger than in sorrow. One Harlem resident, tired of hearing about the war that seemed to have gobbled up all of La Guardia's available idealism, said that Harlem's boys were going to come home from overseas to find "Hitler's policies right here in dear old New York." Despite his practice of consulting blacks on issues of interest to them, the mayor was too busy now to discuss Stuyvesant Town, fearing that such discussions might sidetrack the project. La Guardia did append a pro forma letter disapproving of discriminatory tenant selection. The point, however, was that such control had been dealt over to Metropolitan by the agreements.[46]

Established black leaders did not question the mayor's commitment, but a newer group, symbolized by the dynamic minister Adam Clayton Powell, Jr., was less deferential. Here were two men, Powell and La Guardia, whose instincts were

528

so similar. As a brash young man on the make, Fiorello La Guardia had spoken with a disdain for the establishment and a snarling contempt for the comfortable that easily matched Powell's. But now they were meeting at different points in their lives. The young Powell, ambitious to become a leader of the Harlem community, where he had grown up as the privileged son of a respected minister, articulated the anger and resentment of his community. La Guardia had created as good an administration as he could, and the status quo in municipal affairs no longer offended him. He had come to respect his own successes within the established order. His ambitions had carried this son of immigrants to the edge of the White House. Pretty good country, this America! Now the nation was in the midst of a global battle for its own future. He held little sympathy for those who attacked it.

But many in Harlem viewed things differently. They did not see the war as the most important issue on the contemporary agenda. "What is the Negro expected to defend?" a black man from Brooklyn asked Franklin Roosevelt. Weren't they too black to go to America's beaches, eat in its restaurants, attend its schools, work in its factories, and therefore to die on its battlefields? Malcolm X had a last name in 1942 (Little) when he got his "Greetings" from Uncle Sam, instructing him to report for the armed services. He dressed in a zoot suit, brushed his hair into a "bush of conk," and told the inducting officers that his ambition for the moment was to go down south and hunt "crackers." "I don't like goin' over there fightin' for the white man," remarked a young Harlem resident. And he probably liked it even less when he was sent to the deep south for training and dispatched to battle in a segregated army. It did not help soothe feelings when the Red Cross announced that it would not accept blood plasma from blacks. The simple gab of a cab driver best sums up the depths of black resentment: "One thing you've got to give those Japs, they showed the white man that a brown hand could handle a plane and a machine gun too."[47]

Adam Powell also worried about other things besides the war. The massive northward migration of tens of thousands of southern blacks had made a bad situation horrible, and the Depression made it unbearable. Unemployment, slum housing, poor health, and low education levels combined to produce a grim picture. Improvements would come by hitting hard at the best targets, and Powell was prepared to do the hitting. As leader of the Greater New York Coordinating Committee for Employment he pressured for jobs and flirted with all who promised help, including the Communists. He liked to say that he respected the "guy who was nationally a Democrat, locally a Republican, theoretically a Socialist, but practically a Communist."[48]

A charismatic speaker, Powell, with the help of a "People's Committee" that he put together, became at the age of thirty-three the first black elected to the New York City Council. The committee, initially a grass roots organization for community betterment, attacked the La Guardia administration for its inattention to Harlem's needs, launching a "Double V" campaign that called for victory overseas against the dictators and victory over the racist administration at home. The committee's comparison of his government with the Fascists embittered La Guardia, and he refused to work with it or its charismatic leader. Powell could not have cared less about the man he now dismissed as a burned-out progressive. "The Mayor," Powell said in May of 1942, "is one of the most pathetic figures on the current American scene."[49]

That scene was gashed in the spring of 1943 by some of the ugliest race riots in American history. Black communities in such cities as Beaumont, Mobile, Los Angeles, and Detroit flared into open disorder. The worst of these disturbances, the Detroit riot of June 21, resulted in thirty-four deaths, mostly blacks killed by police. Another 700 were injured, and property damage ran into the millions. "The long expected riot," Walter White said, "had come."

After the Detroit disorder, Adam Clayton Powell, Jr., wired La Guardia warning of local tensions and demanding that the mayor meet with a biracial committee to discuss the issues. When La Guardia ignored Powell's invitation, the young minister warned that the combination of a weak mayor and irresponsible police had caused a riot in Detroit, and New York with its "prima donna" mayor and racist police could expect no better. "Get rid of your inferiority complex," Powell ordered La Guardia, and then commanded his community to prepare to defend itself.[50]

La Guardia resolved to fashion his own plans with the cooperation of more moderate black leaders. As soon as the Detroit riot broke out he broadcast a thoughtful address imploring citizens to keep cool and avoid the "snakes" bent on fomenting trouble. "Above all have an understanding of the other fellow's problems. . . . We have faults of our own, all of us, without being subjected to instigation or provocation of people who are not friends and do not love our country." He assured blacks that "if any white man provokes or instigates assaults against a Negro group, I will protect the Negro group and prosecute the white man." And he pleaded for patience. "We must not forget that in New York City we still have the aftermath of prejudice, racial hatred and exploitation that has existed in many parts of the country. I want to assure the people of this city that with just a bit of cooperation and understanding . . . we are able to cope with any situation."[51]

Two New York City policemen, one black and one white, were dispatched to Detroit to gather firsthand observations, and the mayor asked Walter White for a report on the NAACP chief's perceptions as well. On June 28 La Guardia brought together an interracial group to study Detroit's mistakes and lay plans to avoid them. City hall carefully tracked incidents that might explode into racial strife and announced a Unity Movement, asking citizens to take a pledge to guard against provocation and resist "every attempt to set me against my fellow New Yorker." At La Guardia's urging, Walter White corresponded with blacks in Harlem and Brooklyn to "see that our people so conduct themselves during the next few critical weeks and months," that despite their justifiable complaints they give "no cause for racial friction."

If trouble was to come, White pleaded, let it be started by "our enemies." Police Commissioner Valentine agreed to appoint more black police officers, new housing projects were announced, and the mayor scurried about doing what he could to show good faith.

La Guardia also developed careful ground rules for police restraint if disorder should break out. Although they were expected to protect property, police were ordered to use deadly force only to defend against physical harm. Bars would be closed, guns in sports and pawn shops guarded, traffic diverted around trouble spots, and passengers of public conveyances protected. Tear gas would be used only as a last resort.[52]

And it happened anyway.

As another hot summer weekend came to a close on Sunday evening, August 1, 1943, Marjorie Polite checked into a hotel in Harlem. Dissatisfied with her accommodations, Miss Polite demanded a refund and was checking out when she started arguing with the elevator operator, demanding the return of a dollar tip she had left him. Patrolman James Collins, on duty inside the hotel, tried to calm the irate woman, but when she began shouting and cursing at him, he arrested her for disorderly conduct. Witnessing the event were Mrs. Florine Roberts and her son, Private Robert Bandy. They insisted that the policeman release Polite. The offical report contended that Roberts and Bandy started beating the policeman over the head with his own nightstick before they took off down the block, whereupon Officer Collins drew his revolver and shot at the escaping pair. Private Bandy's account differed in several important particulars. He claimed that he interceded only after the policeman began abusing Miss Polite and that the angry cop threw his nightstick at him. Bandy said that he had caught the stick and started running. Collins then shot him. The wounds were superficial.[53]

It took but a few minutes for garbled news to reach the Harlem streets. A black soldier who had been protecting his mother had been shot—some said killed—by a white cop. Crowds began to gather, feeding each other's anger. At one point more than 3000 massed in front of Harlem's twenty-eighth police precinct. By 10:30 the noise of breaking glass and disorderly looters rang through the streets. Vandals destroyed what the looters missed, and then came the arsonists, filling the Harlem night with flames and chaos. "R," an anonymous eighteen-year-old interviewed by the *Amsterdam News*, was one of the looters. He had dropped out of school to have some fun, and this was fun. He felt no emotion at the pain of the evening; he wanted only to get some loot and make a simple statement: "Do not," he warned, "attempt to fuck with me." Others quickly took up the spirit. "A," who had never broken the law before and would later write La Guardia a contrite letter of regret for her involvement, joined the riot, handing stolen merchandise out of a store to passing youths.[54]

La Guardia was informed of the incident at about 9:00 P.M. He immediately rushed up to the twenty-eighth precinct with his police and fire commissioners and converted the station house into an emergency command post patrolled by a detachment of army infantry. Then he went out to tour the riot area, rapping out orders and screaming at the crowds to go back home. Police who finished their shifts were held on duty. Reinforcements were brought in, and volunteers, mostly blacks, were deputized to patrol the streets. Within less than an hour more than 5000 police flooded the district, guards were placed on all subways traveling through Harlem, and neighboring precincts were held on reserve. La Guardia went on radio to correct rumors and offer assurances that life and property would be protected. Black luminaries toured the streets in sound trucks to reinforce the mayor's appeals.

"Shame has come to our city and sorrow to the large number of our fellow citizens . . . who live in Harlem," La Guardia said in his third broadcast of the day. He would make five in all, directing his comments primarily to the black community, blaming the riot on hoodlums and pleading with the others to cooperate with the authorities. From Sunday night until Tuesday morning La Guardia was in tireless control. Avoiding angry words, he advised New Yorkers of restrictions that he was putting into place to seal off the area, and of the special plans for the flow of essential food and medical supplies. Gradually over the next week, curfews were lifted, the number of police was reduced to normal, stores were opened, and Harlem cooled down. But before order was restored, 6 persons, all blacks, were dead, and 185 others were injured. Estimates for damage ranged upwards of $5 million.[55]

All agreed that La Guardia had done a superb job containing the worst disorder in Harlem's history while protecting area residents. Even Adam Clayton Powell, Jr., offered praise for the mayor's "wise and effective" leadership. The police had avoided the indiscriminate shooting and "willful inefficiency" (in Walter White's words) that had marked the Detroit experience and had led Roy Wilkins to charge that the police there used the riot as an excuse to "murder Negroes. . . . in cold blood."[56]

Ten days after order was restored La Guardia inaugurated his own alternative to the "Double V" campaign that had emphasized black anger. His five-part series of radio programs, dedicated to "Unity at Home and Victory Abroad," included promises of meaningful progress. In a stiff letter to the Metropolitan Insurance Company he warned that he would oppose with all powers at his disposal the practice of discrimination in the selection of tenants for Stuyvesant Town. He also created a Mayor's Committee on Unity under Charles Evans Hughes to study the root causes of prejudice, discrimination, and exploitation. He envisioned an authoritative city institution that would carry out a permanent investigation of American race relations and issue periodic reports based on its research. (One of the Unity Committee's early studies was on baseball's "color line.") Whether La

Guardia believed that such a committee could actually influence public policy, however, is doubtful.[57]

———

Two months after the Harlem disturbance a Brooklyn grand jury delivered a broad finding criticizing the mayor for failing to halt another neighborhood's decline into a racial slum. Wartime migration from the South had brought many black families to Brooklyn in search of housing. As poor Negroes, consigned to low-paying jobs by prejudice and inadequate education, jammed into the neighborhood, "hundreds of formerly very fine one-family homes . . . [were taken over] by 3 to 8 families with only one bathroom. . . . Oftentimes," reported the grand jury, "a bed will be shared by two or more persons over a 24 hour period. . . . [O]ne person will be entitled to use the bed from 6 in the morning to 6 at night, and the other from 6 at night to 6 in the morning." Packs of unattended youths roamed the streets, cursing and assaulting passersby with sharpened penknives. Children were harassed on their way home from school, and churches cut evening services because parishoners were afraid to attend; others closed their doors entirely. "Only recently," noted the Grand Jury, a fourteen-year-old and some friends had pounced on a sailor for no apparent reason and stabbed him to death. As middle-class whites fled to other neighborhoods, concluded the grand jury, Brooklyn's old Bedford Stuyvesant neighborhood, "at one time one of the finest residential sections of this borough," and still filled with stately homes and prominent brownstones, was dying right under the mayor's nose.

The grand jury held the mayor responsible for committing an "appallingly insufficient number of patrolmen" to the problem. On his first day in office in 1934, La Guardia had marched over to police headquarters to warn all cops that the custom of writing off areas of the city as beyond police control was ended. "I have been told that Fulton street is considered the deadline for crooks. That deadline is now removed," he had said. The 1943 grand jury suggested that there were new "deadlines" where prostitution and crime were being ignored. Commissioner Valentine said as much in his grand jury testimony, when he admitted that he was powerless to control Bed-Stuy's flagrant delinquency.[58]

The problem was exquisitely difficult. Between offering police—whose own racial attitudes could not be ignored—a free hand, which could precipitate a riot, and holding them back, which gave citizens the impression that crime was sanctioned on their streets, there were few sure options. La Guardia was stuck. "Let's be more frank about it," he said. This was not a question of police policy, in which case it would be possible to simply order a crackdown and mussing up, as he had with gangsters. "This is the Negro problem we are talking about. . . . When a neighborhood changes its complexion . . . there is bound to be trouble. . . ."

Accusing the administration of "confessing anarchy, the grand jury pro-

533

nounced its verdict in oracular tones: "The Grand Jury does not consider it any excuse whatsoever for the Mayor to say that he can do nothing. No part of the City of New York should be regarded as dangerous or unsafe to live in." There was no race problem, only a crime problem. The grand jury made a series of essentially irrelevant recommendations: Increase the colored state guard, require a permit to carry a knife, keep people from congregating in front of bars, tighten relief inspections, promote supervised recreation and special classroom activities to inculcate good behavior, instruct adolescent court to mete out stiffer sentences, increase the staff of the Juvenile Delinquency Bureau, interrupt radio programs at nine o'clock in the evening to ask parents where their children were at this hour. They recommended additional police, the use of the National Guard, and the canceling of such festivities as Mardi Gras, which often lead to boisterous and sometimes uncontrollable mobs. Let the mayor give this problem the same vigorous attention that he gave to the problem of tinhorn gamblers. Just enforce the laws and everybody will be happy, most of all law-abiding Negroes.[59]

But grand juries were in the position of prescribing actions without having to weigh consequences. They were dissolved before any of their prescriptions were implemented. Then it was left for city officials to reap the whirlwind. Juries did not have to be concerned with the possibility that a policeman might arrest the wrong person or be excessively tough on a youth, and then have the city erupt into a deadly riot.

What was La Guardia to do? Come down hard on an angry black community weighed down with a conscious sense of oppression and take the chance that this would set off a citywide explosion, or suffer the disaffection of law-abiding citizens who did not want to tolerate different rules for different circumstances? He had no solutions, only problems.

Here he was with one foot out the door and both eyes on a federal prize, and the grand jury was demanding easy solutions to the intractable problems of race, poverty, and crime. La Guardia hit back, denouncing the grand jurors as "crackpots" and "publicity seekers." They were shooting fish in a barrel, and he was tired of being the fish. He was being held to impossible standards and denounced for "misconduct" and inciting the criminal element by those who looked at the city one street at a time. He could not do that. The kind of ham-fisted response that the jury demanded threatened more harm than protection. The "contained" Harlem riot had resulted in millions in damage, several deaths and many injuries, and a terrible setback for race relations. Could La Guardia afford to chance another riot that would be exponentially more destructive, through insensitive crackdowns? It was the quandary of modern urban race relations that urban mayors would come to know intimately in the 1960s.[60]

Like them he fell into the trap of believing that a safe lie was better than the dangerous truth. He supposed that given time he could paint a new reality, and if no one disturbed his delicate castle in the air the entire city would be able to move in. New Yorkers would get along because he would convince them that they *were* getting along. It was rather an audacious hope that he would be able to fix the way 7 million people thought. And then along came *Collier's* magazine in its September 23, 1944, edition and published an article entitled "Harlem: Dense and Dangerous," emphasizing the neighborhood's evil corners, dangerous avenues, and hardened youth who strutted the streets with zip guns and "a knife that could have sheared off the leg of an elephant." Here, wrote the author, William Davenport, was a race riot ready to happen. Almost anything could set it off and probably would.

This all too realistic article upset the fragile fictions that La Guardia had been constructing. Presenting Negro communities in such bad light that whites would harden their prejudices and blacks would despair all the more threatened the unsteady peace of his city. He was furious and demanded a retraction. No longer was the old champion of free speech saying correct the root problem instead of its description. Some problems he now wanted unreported.[61]

The publisher asked La Guardia to write a rebuttal article, which he did, titling it "Harlem: Homelike and Hopeful." But *Collier's* editor Henry La Cossit ultimately rejected the statistics-studded puff piece. La Guardia's unpublished manuscript provides an interesting perspective on the race issue, tracing the problem back to slavery and the failure to wipe out the remnants of that institution's sad legacy. La Guardia emphasized that the "problem" was a national one, and no city had the resources to solve it alone, but New York had done its best, and precisely because it built new housing and provided assistance to the needy, it attracted blacks from all over the country, where such improvements were not even contemplated.[62]

La Guardia wrote that "Negroes [were] going through a bad period," much as other groups had suffered their own difficult periods of adaptation. Italians, Fiorello pointed out, had a particularly hard adjustment in the early years of the century because their numbers included kidnappers, dope pushers, and assorted other unsavory characters who gave the rest of the group a bad name. Instead of protesting reports about these embarrassing activities, La Guardia said, "I suggested that the thing to do was to clean house, to cooperate with the authorities, to provide help for the families in need, to encourage better attendance in schools, to point the finger of scorn to those of the same blood who would bring disgrace on the overwhelming majority of hard working, honest people."

Fine people in the black community were making similar suggestions, he added. "Frankly I would say that at times the number of arrests in precincts . . . inhabited by Negroes are rather high in comparison with others. . . . Sure Harlem loves to dance, and so do other people. . . . I admit there are too many saloons and liquor places in Harlem. . . ." La Guardia was torn between the fact of disproportionate criminality and the degree to which he felt this should be excused by objective conditions of deprivation. But, he continued, the city was doing its best to provide services and educate the young. New York's contribution to solving the problem, La Guardia declared too optimistically, was its willingness to treat all of its citizens equally.

It would take several decades for the spotlight to turn back to such cities as New York and put the lie to La Guardia's smug pronouncement that "if the rest of the country will treat the Negroes as we do in New York . . . [we] will not have a Negro problem in our country." He kept up the positive patter, and he believed much of it, but the problem was bigger than he imagined, and perhaps that is why he, like every other mayor before and after, responded to racial problems when they became too dangerous to ignore, but offered no direct programs to solve them.[63]

4. The Japanese

L A Guardia had come into office as a progressive reformer who valued process and respected the safeguards of democracy. He brought with him a broad open agenda and a commitment to strengthening government's ability to address the challenge of urban modernization and integrity. But now he was developing policy in a very personal way, depending on secrecy and manipulation to secure his ends. Liberalism had fixed the outlines of his philosophy in 1933; it no longer did. Nor was he following an agenda; he was reacting to crises as they came up, and as he saw fit. It is no accident that the major themes of his later years are personal rather than programmatic ones and that they were frequently overshadowed by his ambition to leave the mayoralty for offices that he thought more worthy of him.

War unleashed in La Guardia some of his own darkest racial prejudices and demonstrated shocking blind spots. His abandonment of process in favor of personal whim is glaringly evident in his treatment of the Japanese in this time of war, and it surprised his good friend and fellow progressive Harold Ickes.

On December 22, 1941, while he was serving as director of OCD, La Guardia broadcast a radio address to remind Americans that "it is the policy of our government that so long as aliens in this country conduct themselves in accordance with the law, they need fear no interference in the normal pursuits of life." Some employers were discharging German and Italian aliens, and La Guardia reminded his listeners that this was unwise and unfair: "We cannot hold law abiding Germans and Italians in this country responsible for what is happening in Europe." Any vigilantism or bias aimed at these people violated our national principles.[64]

La Guardia pointedly kept the Japanese out of these concerns. Not only did he not mention them in his address, he did not intend for his words to apply to them. He defended the policy of detaining the Japanese in special centers, as did many other American progressives, but he went even further. By 1944 it had become clear that the detained Japanese represented no threat, and national authorities began relocating these Japanese around the country. Before sending several hundred of the recently freed Japanese to New York, Harold Ickes took pains to explain that these were entirely innocent people, United States citizens entitled to all rights and privileges of citizenship.

But La Guardia sent a fevered protest to Ickes, calling it "manifestly unfair" for the government to "turn these people loose" and to "force them on New York City." Ickes was shocked by La Guardia's response. In a confidential letter he begged his old colleague to consider the effect of his protests. Such words from so prominent a progressive, Ickes wrote, presented a "disastrous" example "and would almost surely be used as a propaganda device in convincing other Oriental nations that the U.S. is conducting a racial war." La Guardia refused to reconsider. He had the police department run checks on each of the Japanese that settled in the city and demanded that the army, navy, and other agencies in Washington prevent "these alien enemies [!]" from roaming around his city unimpeded.[65]

Finally, sadly, Ickes let him have it. He expressed his public dismay that "of all people, the Mayor of New York City," who had "fought long and vigorously for racial equality," would join the "strange fife and drum corps . . . playing the discordant anthem of racial discrimination" against "homeless and blameless victims of a wartime military decision."[66]

But La Guardia's war anger at the Japanese overwhelmed whatever liberalism he may have felt. He could excuse the Italians, he was one of them. As the Civil Liberties Union said, "Large numbers of persons of Italian . . . extraction have been living peaceably among us and their national origin had properly not been held a bar in the midst of war to even the holding of high public office." But Japanese treachery had been so great that La Guardia could not contain his racial feelings. When the Australian government sought a vote of confidence in their handling of an attempted breakout of Japanese prisoners in September, which resulted in Aussie guards killing 200 Japanese prisoners of war, La Guardia wired back:

NO DOUBT AS TO WHAT HAPPENED AS WELL AS RESTRAINT OF AUS-
TRALIAN GUARDS. [AUSTRALIAN] PREMIER CURTIN'S STATEMENT OF
COURSE WILL BE ACCEPTED BY THE CIVILIZED WORLD AS AGAINST ANY-
THING THE DECEITFUL JAP MONKEYS WILL SAY. IN ALL LIKELIHOOD

FAIR AND HUMANE TREATMENT OF THE AUSTRALIANS COULD NOT BE
APPRECIATED ACCORDING TO JAPANESE STANDARD AND WAS CONSTRUED
BY THEM AS A SIGN OF WEAKNESS. . . .

WHEN MONKEY GETS NAUGHTY, HE SHOULD NOT BE SURPRISED IF HE
RUNS UP AGAINST AUSTRALIAN BAYONET.[67]

Such talk fit no principle of liberalism. It was the talk of a man wholly
engulfed by the mood of war, and by the racism that he had fought so strenuously
in other contexts.

CHAPTER 15

. . . To Pay for All You Have with All You Are

1. I Want to Be Part of It

WARTIME spending had brought recovery to many cities. But New York drew only bitter consequences from the war: Its population was fragmented, its mayor was preoccupied, and its light industry could not exploit the open-fisted programs for defense spending. Moreover, as federal budget dollars were allocated to defense, they were withdrawn from relief and public works of the type that had sustained the city during the thirties. As a result, there were 50,000 more persons unemployed in New York in 1942 than in the Depression year of 1939. Conditions were so bad that state officials appealed to upstate military contractors to hire New York's unemployed, and Paul McNutt, chairman of the War Powers Board, advised New Yorkers seeking jobs to leave the city. Just a few years before, housing had been in dangerously short supply; now more than 75,000 apartments stood vacant and the market was glutted with private homes.[1]

La Guardia had come into office facing desperate unemployment and a budget crisis. His fresh energies and new policies helped solve that crisis, but he was older, more tired and distracted now. How much of this job could he still do? many wondered. In fact, the answer was, quite a good part of it. The president was still committed to helping his insistent friend. Roosevelt ordered the War Production Board, the War Manpower Commission, the Office of Price Administration, and the Treasury secretary to confer with the mayor about "the use of plant and man-power facilities in New York City," and over the next few months Washington designed a massive affirmative action program for the metropolis. Between July and October, 12 percent of all navy contracts were assigned to New York firms.

539

By November the War Manpower Commission estimated that more than 200,000 people had been put to work in the city. And it was "Fiorello," Roosevelt told David K. Niles, who deserved much of the credit when by the end of 1943 New York newspapers trumpeted full employment.[2]

The rounds of crises were becoming wearisome, however. La Guardia took little joy even in his accomplishments, as criticism kept focusing on his short temper and authoritarian strain. His old crew continued to depart, like musicians performing the Farewell Symphony. Commissioners McElligott, Morgan, and Kern departed, followed by Dr. John L. Rice's resignation as commissioner of health. The chairman of the Housing Authority, Gerard Swope, left to fill a war post in Washington. Budget director Kenneth Dayton went off to work on foreign relief and rehabilitation and city corporation counselor, William Chanler, accepted a lieutenant colonel's commission. Brooklyn District Attorney O'Dwyer, the man Fiorello had defeated in the last election, went to Italy as an army major. La Guardia badly wanted to be part of the war too. When Burlingham asked point-blank if he was sick of his job, Fiorello answered, "Yes." He had taken it the third time "Because . . . you asked me to." And now he wanted to be relieved to join the other men and battle for good old democracy.[3]

La Guardia had been thinking of an army appointment for some time. Shortly after he left OCD in the spring of 1942, La Guardia told a friend that his World War I experience in "bombing, defense, politic[s] economic[s], and the avoiding of mistakes and delays and red tape" could all be put to proper use in the army, adding, "I never did like politics." Fiorello wrote Burlingham that he had absorbed much punishment from "small and selfish men, without complaint." He admired Roosevelt for the job he had done. "I burned all my bridges ahead of me for him. I shall continue to give him my utmost support during this war." And he wanted very much to serve in the armed forces.[4]

The president was soon looking for a military position for La Guardia. Roosevelt had appointed a coordinator to smooth the relationship between occupying forces and the local civilian population in Algiers and Morocco, and he told Fiorello that he was thinking of sending him to do the same job in his beloved Italy once the North was occupied. Fiorello was interested, but looking the gift horse deep in the mouth, he made it clear to the president that he would accept only a military position, he was not interested in working as a civilian under the State Department. "I don't mind getting killed in action," he wrote to Lieutenant General Stanley D. Embrick of the Joint Chiefs, "but I would hate to be hung by the enemy." The position must be "entirely military. . . ."[5]

The idea was passed on to Allied European Commander, General Dwight D. Eisenhower, who at first hesitated to "complicate my staff problems" by bringing the New York mayor into his command in the midst of the battle of Tunisia. He did agree, however, that La Guardia could eventually be of assistance directing a separate staff operation over nonmilitary American activities in the war area. Choosing to inform La Guardia only about the good news, Major General George Strong secretly advised Fiorello to begin "preparing to take over just as soon as the present phase of the Tunisia campaign is completed."[6]

A few weeks later, on January 3, 1943, La Guardia was in Washington attending to "some odds and ends" on behalf of New York when the president nominated Edward Flynn for ambassador to Australia. The Bronx boss had qualifications, of a sort: "Australia," Flynn wrote in his memoirs, "is nearly fifty per cent Irish Catholic and I am of that faith and people." The Senate, however, remained skeptical and, when it received the nomination on January 8, questioned the president's effort to make a diplomat of the Bronx politician, especially after the papers recalled the recent controversy over city-owned Belgian blocks used to pave Flynn's country home.[7]

For three days in January the Senate Committee on Foreign Relations heard testimony on Flynn's checkered political past, including several charges of misconduct. Then the committee called on Fiorello La Guardia, a proven expert on political bosses, to testify about the paving blocks episode and on Flynn's general fitness for a diplomatic post. With the appointment very much in doubt, La Guardia could easily kill the chances of one of the most powerful machine politicians in his city.

Spectators crowded the hearing room anticipating Fiorello's revenge. All morning they waited, but by noon he had not arrived, and as a recess was announced some speculated about the mayor's recent reticence in matters sensitive to the president. Finally, at 2:02 P.M. La Guardia strode in, walked to the front of the hearing room, and was sworn in. The crowd leaned forward, aware that La Guardia had more than Flynn's fitness for service in the Outback to consider. Between fidelity to his own past as a boss-slayer and his desire to please Roosevelt, La Guardia was sufficiently squeezed to make the scene interesting.

The mayor was asked if he wished to make a statement. "No," he answered, he awaited the pleasure of the committee. The next question was about the paving blocks, and the mayor allowed that although he had heard about the claims, he lacked firsthand information. Commissioner Herlands had handled the investigation and passed his findings on to the district attorney and the Bronx borough president's office. Members of the committee were a bit taken aback by the distance the mayor was placing between himself and the case, and by his new diffidence on the subject of bosses. Well, did the mayor think that "crooked and corrupt" individuals should be appointed to represent the United States? Calculating the effect of every word, La Guardia again avoided a direct answer. "Your question answers itself," he replied.

The next question left him less room. Had he not referred to Mr. Flynn in just such terms? "Now look here," he said, making a great show of bringing his temper under control. He and Flynn had been enemies a long time and they had called each other many things. La Guardia had "licked" Flynn every time they confronted each other politically and there was a great deal of enmity between them. "Because of the bitterness . . . and my prejudice against him, I cannot qualify as an opinion witness." With that the mayor's nine minutes of testimony ended. La Guardia had done very well indeed in controlling the damage that the situation could have brought him. He had avoided hurting Roosevelt and he had done so without having to support Flynn (whose nomination was eventually withdrawn by the president).[8]

As American forces pushed their way through North Africa and toward Italy, La Guardia reminded Roosevelt of their earlier discussions. "My dear Chief," La Guardia scrawled to Roosevelt in his own writing on February 3, 1943, shortly after the president returned from his Casablanca conference with Winston Churchill, "I still believe that Genl Eisenhower can *not* get along without me and am awaiting your order (but as a soldier). . . . Let me know. . . . *Con Amore*, Fiorello."[9]

"Clearly New York is about to lose a Mayor and the army is about to gain an officer," reported the *Herald Tribune*. Mitzi Somach, having long forgiven the mayor for her bad treatment, forwarded a gift of general's stars for the new soldier's shirt collars and assured him that now that he was in it, the war could not last too long. Congratulations flooded into city hall. La Guardia just kept his fingers crossed. "Dear Harry," he wrote to his friend Hopkins on March 17, "writing this by hand as I do not want office to know until last minute. . . . I saw the Chief yesterday and I am so happy that I can be of service to my country. . . . I expect to get my medical exam—next week—The Chief indicated I could be commissioned right after I finish the Executive Budget in early April." The letter glows with La Guardia's anticipation of working with Eisenhower and the chance to be "really useful . . . besides cleaning the streets of NYC."[10]

For all of his desire to join the military and leave politics behind, La Guardia had no intention of giving up the powers he already held. In Albany a bill titled "Absence from office for Military Duty" was put into the hopper and quickly passed by the legislators, who assumed that it dealt with technical issues of little interest to them or their constituents. The bill did not mention New York City at all. Only after they passed the artfully drawn measure did the legislators learn that by the device of referring to a previous section this bill applied exclusively to the downstate metropolis, and that they had approved sweeping changes in New York City's line of succession, permitting La Guardia to leave the country without resigning his office. So sweeping a law, chock-full of concealed provisions, had not been enacted since the days when Robert Moses was drafting legislation in Albany.

Under normal circumstances, once a mayor left city hall for another position, the office was declared vacant and filled briefly by the president of the City Council as acting mayor until a special election could be held for a permanent replacement. The new measure allowed La Guardia to accept an army commission, appoint a temporary successor, and return to office at any time before the next election. In the past, when the president of the City Council became acting mayor, he brought his own three votes on the Board of Estimate with him and the former mayor's votes simply disappeared, but a sleeper provision in the new law empowered La Guardia to designate a deputy mayor who would vote in his stead on the Board of Estimate. Under this provision the acting mayor held executive authority while the deputy mayor cast the absent mayor's three votes on the Board of Estimate. The practical effect of this "gem" of a self-serving law, then, was that La Guardia could go off to shoot Germans and feed Italy and all the while control New York City through a puppet deputy mayor. The bill contained another twist. All emergency war legislation like this bill was supposed to carry a one-year expiration date. Reuben Lazarus, who crafted the law, took care to leave off the one-year termination formula. Democratic leaders who helped pass the law were described as "stunned" once it was explained to them (among other things the bill guaranteed a Republican successor to Newbold Morris if the City Council president should also go into the army).[11]

Something had happened to La Guardia's relationship to his office. Once he had thought of it as a trust. Now he viewed it as a private possession, something for him to pass around or keep at his own pleasure. Reformers, even among his own inner circle, assailed this piece of legislative legerdemain as "a vicious departure from our democratic form of government." And those who still held to the idea of fusion and progressive government felt betrayed. "What right have you," an old Washington acquaintance demanded,

> to throw back the greatest City—back into the arms of Tammany? You have been trusted and upheld almost miraculously. . . . You are the only man alive who can handle affairs in New York City. . . . Don't let the glamor and glimmer delude you. There's heroism in standing the abuse, the pestering, the boredom of your long term in New York City. . . . That's a bigger thing to consider than *how* you can *brigadier* anywhere on earth.
>
> Consider well before you just drop the world's greatest problem child at the most dangerous period of its life back into the lap of corrupt politics.[12]

Walter White of the NAACP told La Guardia that he fervently hoped that "like Mark Twain's death," the news of La Guardia's leaving was greatly exaggerated. "Running a City like New York is as great a contribution to the war effort, and perhaps more important than almost any other job outside the President's." The *New York Times*, suggesting that the city would happily "lend-lease" the mayor for a couple of weeks, reminded him that his "front line trench is right here in the five boroughs." But it was Burlingham who stated it plain: "What is this political streptococcus that is biting you? Are you sick of your job? Well why did you take it?'' Like the excellent lawyer that he was, Burlingham delivered his point simply, tellingly: ''you owe it to this City to stay right here and do your job.''[13]

But even Burlingham could not talk La Guardia into being happy with his job, and by the end of March the papers were reporting La Guardia's appointment as a brigadier general to serve as an administrator in North Africa and Italy after a planned invasion. The Associated Press announced that La Guardia had already made his choice of three aides (Albert Spalding, Louis Adamic, and Ugo Carusi). In Washington, Stephen Early, the president's secretary, told the press: ''All indications point to service in the Army for the Mayor. . . . It is being worked out.'' La Guardia himself bantered with the city hall press corps about his imminent departure for the far climes.[14]

New York's best men continued to try to reason with La Guardia not to shirk his obligation to the city. Burlingham wrote Samuel Seabury: ''I cannot hurrah for FH's warlike spirit. It is infantile and shows no true sense of proportion,'' and encouraged the old fusioners to reason with the mayor, but they got nowhere. Burlingham then took the situation into his own hands, writing Secretary of War Henry L. Stimson that he thought that the appointment was a bad idea. Paul Windels, Samuel Seabury, and the other ''mammoths of civic righteousness'' added their own objections. Stimson, dreading the task of controlling La Guardia while he served as a distant proconsul, required little prodding to tell the president that he was unwilling to work with La Guardia.[15]

Felix Frankfurter shared his doubts directly with the president, telling Roosevelt that a ''quixotic and incalculable'' La Guardia was not what was needed overseas. Others warned Roosevelt to consider Fiorello's ''fiery provocative presence.'' And Congress too was critical. The chairman of the powerful Committee to Investigate the National Defense Program, Senator Harry S Truman, bluntly objected to military commissions for presidential favorites. La Guardia had no business seeking appointment as a brigadier general, said Truman. Governing New York City was responsibility enough for any man.[16]

The president had not expected such opposition. He had just recently suffered the embarrassing rejection of Ed Flynn's nomination and he was in no mood for another public fight over an appointment that promised to be no less rancorous. The president's resolve was further eroded when General Eisenhower voiced reservations and Secretary Stimson and General George C. Marshall recommended to Roosevelt that he keep La Guardia in New York.

On April 6, 1943, Roosevelt responded to a planted press conference question about the mayor of New York City, denying that there were plans to make La Guardia a brigadier general. The following day Secretary of War Stimson announced that while the mayor had patriotically offered his services to the War Department, no position in the army could be found to match his potential usefulness in New York City.[17]

La Guardia, who was in Washington anticipating more welcome news, gamely told reporters that he would go back to New York to don his "street cleaner's uniform" and lead his own little army. But he was devastated. For the past three years he had based his plans and hopes on Roosevelt. His presidential hopes had disappeared with FDR's third campaign; still he had served as the good soldier, even after the vice presidency could not be worked out. After talk of a cabinet position he passed up chances for the Senate and the State House, but no Washington post materialized. OCD had been a curse. Then he was assured of appointment as a brigadier general and now the president had let him down rather ungently. It was a harsh descent, and the ruinous self-pity that La Guardia had usually been able to avoid overwhelmed him now.

It prevented him from acknowledging the real sympathy most New Yorkers felt for his embarrassment. It also stopped him from focusing his energies on the city. He had extended the hand of humane government, but with new priorities the federal government was cutting back on the vast programs for relief, unemployment, and public construction. The per capita cost of municipal government was sky-rocketing, with New York's figures at the highest levels in the nation. Taxation was driving away business, and the wartime boom was passing New York by. These were all serious issues, worthy of La Guardia's full energies. Charles Burlingham put together a list of these new problems to show La Guardia the challenges that still required his experienced hand. Fiorello began scribbling some answers about what he had already done in these areas, but then gave up. "I am reconciled to getting credit in history and reward in Heaven," he wrote. And then, as he better understood what his friend was trying to do, he closed his comments with "Lots of love, C.C. I still like & love you! Fiorello."[18]

He was unhappy, and he had cleared out everyone with the nerve to try to stop him from committing the mistakes that unhappy individuals tend to make. "I know what you need, though you will laugh me to scorn," Burlingham had written to him. The prescription was simple: periodic vacations to refresh himself physically and mentally and "somebody near you who will say as Paul Windels used to say to you, 'Don't.' Like Roosevelt you are almost completely surrounded by yes men. Yours," the astute counselor wrote, "are made by fear, his by charm." But while Roosevelt had a Stimson who would speak his mind forthrightly, the city administration had only one Moses, and he was a "a wild man, and his comebacks are very much like your own."[19]

La Guardia's erratic emotional state produced episodes of dismaying willfulness. He refused to respond to a Transit Workers Union complaint about unfair labor practices, resulting in New York's censure by the War Labor Board for failing to bargain in good faith. La Guardia then tried to bully public representative Wayne L. Morse, who had rendered the decision, by threatening to go to the president and his friends in labor. Morse paid the disturbing threats no mind, but for the people of New York their excitable mayor's frequent outbursts were becoming difficult to ignore. Shortly after this incident, La Guardia attacked the Board of Education because it refused to appoint his choice, a man named Mark Starr, as director of adult education. Advisers pleaded with him to keep out of board business as the charter intended. Instead, he became involved in another mudslinging match. So unbridled were La Guardia's tactics that eventually even Starr denounced him for trying to bring the board to rough heel. You must "restore your badly shattered reputation," wrote Burlingham sadly.[20]

The hard skepticism of his early days had turned into a brittle insistence on his will as the only legitimate way. La Guardia fell into believing that the world was filled with demons, whether the press, Secretary Stimson, Senator Truman, the Board of Education, or a host of others bent on hurting him. The fact that his friends were critical and his reputation sliding he took as a sign that he was the last honest man. Not one of his speeches, or even of his private writings, indicates his entertaining the possibility that he might be wrong. He could stop the chorus of opposition, he told Burlingham, by "ignoring inefficiency . . . [and] waste . . . ," by tolerating corruption and political deals. He had been trained in one-dimensional opposition. Every opponent was Tammany or a grafter. Only now it was the reformers and fusionists who were Tammany. "Frankly C.C, . . ." he wrote, "I am getting sick and tired of the whole thing. If people like you cannot understand and instead of giving aid and help, continue to listen to gossip and spread it and directly, or indirectly heap abuse, then let the thing go back to Tammany."[21]

La Guardia's frequent absences to lobby for preferment in Washington or to carry out presidential errands left Newbold Morris with the reins, but Morris did not have La Guardia's equipment. Petty corruption crept into the administration through the cracks of La Guardia's disinterest. When he was in town, the Little Flower relied even more than ever on his own opinions and ideas, bypassing his commissioners. By 1943 New York progressives were prepared to make an open break with the most successful reform politician in the city's history.

The reform plaint "What has happened to La Guardia" became: "We must not allow La Guardia to destroy the gains for which we fought." Roger Baldwin and the Reverend John Haynes Holmes composed a detailed *j'accuse* on behalf of the American Civil Liberties Union and sent it to other reform leaders, soliciting their signatures for a public rebuke of La Guardia. While acknowledging his unparalleled achievements, the petition's signatories cited his "summary methods," "dictatorial shortcuts," and a "pattern of control widely condemned." His means, they complained, were a high price to pay for his considerable achievements, "for the precedents established by extra-legal measures may be used for bad ends by your successors. As Judge Gaynor, your predecessor, remarked years ago, 'Good men in good times should not set precedents for bad men in bad times.' "[22]

Their bill of particulars was long and growing: He had cut budgets to bend independent agencies to his will, paralyzed his own administrators with fear, and tampered with the autonomy of the City Planning Commission. The petition decried his high-handed dismissal of civil service commissioners, encouragement of police violence, and arbitrary seizing of lurid magazines on the dubious grounds that "the Constitution and laws of the state do not apply to plain smut and filth" and that "trials take too much time and advertise obscenity." His custom of publicizing over the radio the names of figures whom the mayor identified as known gamblers, but who had not been tried in a court, indicated a chilling disregard for civil liberties, and his obstinate rejection of municipal unions represented a retreat from earlier commitments. The disappointed reform petitioners listed other specific criticisms, closing their letter with an appeal:

> We advance only a single proposition, that in your efforts for public
> education, for a cleaner, better more moral and law abiding community,
> and in your dealings with city employees, you desist from arbitrary and
> lawless short-cuts which defy established rights. The temptation to do
> good, as you see it, by extra-legal means—natural doubtless to a man
> of your temperament—will we hope, be resisted in the interest of the
> larger democratic purposes which you have so long professed to serve."

La Guardia wanted to forestall this painful indictment by his former supporters, but he would not accept their criticism. He sent a mimeographed note to all recipients of the original letter, dismissing the charges as giving "comfort to the racketeers and gamblers . . . and producers of salacious and immoral stage productions."[23]

Lewis Gannett was one of the men who received the petition. He wrote La Guardia that he was just reading the "indictment of your administration sent out by the Civil Liberties Union and trying to put into words just why I didn't want to sign it, when your reply arrived. . . . Its deny-it-all tone almost made me want to sign." He was only fooling himself, Gannett told Fiorello if he dismissed the petition. There was a lot of truth in it.

Attorney Albert Bard also refused to sign the letter. He did not want to attack the mayor so publicly, but he wanted La Guardia to know that he agreed with each point in the petition and added his own *cri de coeur*. What had once been a wonderfully accessible mayor had declined into an irascible, unpredictable, distracted leader whose attention had drifted from the people who needed him. "There exist many grounds for disappointment," wrote Bard. "They seem to arise in part out of insufficiently guarded personal defects."[24]

"Of course I refused to sign the letter," wrote CCB. But even this good and loyal friend did so on personal grounds. "The Mayor should not be wounded publicly, especially now when the war had laid such a heavy burden on him."

Another friend who would not sign, Fannie Hurst, suggested that La Guardia meet with the disaffected reformers and, to her surprise, he agreed. But while the meeting aired some of the differences, it changed no minds. La Guardia insisted that they could not understand: "It is quite different to be in this seat. . . ." He was wrong. They understood that, but what *he* failed to appreciate was that precisely for that reason he was expected to treat power with more restraint. No meeting could bridge so vast a divide. In February 1944 the ACLU issued its letter marking publicly the final break between La Guardia and his reform supporters.[25]

As the number of his supporters declined, his old enemies took the opportunity to attack. The City Council's Hart Committee launched another investigation of the Mayor, merrily subpoenaing commissioners, bringing mistakes under the microscope, and poking into every ethical crevice it could find. (La Guardia predictably retaliated by setting his own investigations commissioner on the trail of the investigating councilmen.) The Hart Committee found no smoking guns, but there were sufficient peccadillos to give pause, especially to those who recalled the old La Guardia who had fired civil servants for the merest of ethical infractions.

The panel noted that millionaire sanitation commissioner, William Carey, served as a director on the boards of several major corporations, in violation of charter provisions that prohibited officeholders from private business connections. Carey, who followed the practice in his private businesses of offering generous fringe benefits to his employees, had taken it upon himself to do the same in the municipal service. He hatched a well-intentioned plan to build a vacation resort for the city's sanitation men. Sanita Hills, as it was called, was originally to be built with WPA labor, but when federal funding ran out, Carey completed the resort in the Taconic Hills by using city employees and materials. No one doubted Carey's good intentions in setting up the 1140-acre resort where a sanitation worker could bring a family of six on vacation for $20 a week, and Carey assured the committee that he had intended all along to pay the city back from the proceeds of the annual departmental baseball games.[26]

But the baseball team itself was another problem. Some (who recalled the story of the scowmen/baseball players from the Al Smith, Jr., investigation—and it was hard to pin the label of Tammany on all of them) had their doubts about a department creating its own baseball team while the city was curbing essential expenditures, especially after they learned the true cost of this team. The Sanitation Nine consisted of nineteen civil service employees and a manager who played nineteen games against police, fire, army, navy, and college teams. During their seven-month season the men practiced for five and one-half hours a day, when they were excused from all sanitation work. Following the season they each went away for a paid one-month vacation, and the team star was granted a bonus of several hundred dollars to send his family to Florida.

But this was not the entire story. Investigators learned that hundreds of additional workers spent thousands of hours selling tickets to the games during their regular work hours. For the five years between 1938 and 1943 the city in effect paid $2,660,531 to sell $1 million in tickets, of which no more than $85,000 actually went for the stated purpose of assisting distressed sanitation workers. Confronted with this information, Carey replied to a councilman's comment that public officials must fit their operations to the city charter by saying, "Well let them fix up their City Charter to fit the public official."[27]

La Guardia's attitude precisely! Commissioner Herlands, whose own status had declined pitiably to that of house apologist, launched a parallel investigation to support Carey, dismissing the violations as technical ones, "honest mistakes" committed in good faith. With all the proper intentions, La Guardia's administration was doing precisely what the civil liberties reformers had feared, allowing good men in good times to set awful precedents for bad men in other times. A $3 million baseball team was not a tin box brigade, but a millionaire commissioner who thought that the charter ought to be tailored to his sense of the public good, no matter how frivolous, and a mayor who no longer railed at this sort of insensitivity represented a sad decline from the heyday of La Guardian reform.[28]

Little wonder that Stanley Isaacs, "the conscience of fusion," notified La Guardia that the minority members of the City Council were no longer bound to support a man who himself "varies in loyalty to himself and the things he used to stand for." They would no longer accept his word on the budget, on allocation formulae, or even on the findings presented by his commissioner of investigations. For half a dozen years, Isaacs told a Citizens Union gathering, La Guardia had given New York the finest administration ever seen in city hall, "but now it has slumped, retrograded." La Guardia made another of his snappy comments regarding the council. "If they disagree with me I understand it. If they agree with me, I appreciate it. If they abuse me I take it. And I still believe in democracy." These quotable little statements, colorful and interesting at first, had now become an empty habit, a style of speech all surface shine with nothing underneath. This lover of democracy was pining in the worst way to go off and order men around in the ultimate badge of power, a military uniform.[29]

And he continued to hound Roosevelt to get him out.

"Dear Chief," he wrote almost pathetically on June 6, 1943, "Soldier La Guardia reports to the C[ommander] in C[hief] that he awaits orders. He believes General Eisenhower needs him now more than ever." Burlingham could do nothing but muse that "Patriotism is not only the last refuge of a scoundrel but a substitute for common sense."[30]

Roosevelt was still sympathetic. In April, Secretary of War Stimson had told La Guardia that he could make more of a difference in the United States as a civilian than as a "make-believe general." Roosevelt was furious when he found out about the insensitive way that Stimson spoke to La Guardia and sent his war secretary a letter that Roosevelt biographer James MacGregor Burns calls "the stiffest he . . . ever sent a senior Cabinet member." But while Stimson tried to placate the president's displeasure at the way La Guardia was treated, he would not relax his opposition to bringing the fiery Flower into his department. And every time the president brought up La Guardia's name to another of his executives, there was always an excuse for not being able to use him.[31]

After a while even La Guardia understood what was happening. This brave, proud man was reduced to wearing his disappointment on his sleeve. In a letter to Roosevelt he asked for a favor, taking pains to point out that it was not for himself. "I am asking although I vowed never to ask for anything after the raw deal I got." But by June La Guardia was lobbying for his swagger stick again. "If in World War I," wrote *Survey* editor Paul Kellog, "why not in World War II," wondering if La Guardia might be used in Italy. Eleanor Roosevelt carried the message to Secretary Stimson, who suggested that she take up the issue with the State Department. "Should I now send to Mr. Hull?" Eleanor queried. "Yes," responded the president.[32]

Hull was noncommittal. FDR asked the secretary of the navy, James Forrestal, if he had use for Fiorello, but Forrestal thought not. Perhaps he should go off to the Philippines and administer the islands after they were taken. Roosevelt informed Stimson of Forrestal's suggestion to make La Guardia a brigadier general and send him to the Pacific islands as an advisor to the civilian administration: "What do you think of this? I do not think that you and I can still say that he must remain as Mayor of New York." Stimson, however, would not hear of it. Plans for the Philippines, he told FDR, called for the "lightest control over the civilian population consistent with the military operation," and he noted drily, "I rather doubt that the Mayor fits into this picture"; his "vigorous personality" might upset the entire plan. If James Forrestal was the one who expressed interest in La Guardia's military future, Stimson told the president, let him take him into the navy.[33]

A year later La Guardia was still pining for the epaulets. "I am still out of the army," he wrote an acquaintance in the service in Asia. "But I haven't given up hope yet. Certainly would like to go. . . . I want to be part of it."[34]

---

2. No More Strategies, Only Tactics

R OBERT Moses saw the mayor in the midst of war, a conflicted man "uncertain as to whether to be a national, an international or a local character, whether to be a legislator whose every act is privileged or an executive who must be responsible tomorrow for everything he does today, whether to be a conservative or a radical, an artist or a tough boss, a broad minded cosmopolitan or an uncompromising reformer.'' La Guardia had been New York's best mayor, but frustrated ambition was taking a vast toll. La Guardia stopped listening to the press, to friends, even to Burlingham. Information flowed only one way. His weekly radio shows, full of concern for the citizenry and colorful outbursts at tinhorns and chiselers, were a poor substitute for critical dialogue. Few officials could match his intuitive grasp of city government, but by closing himself off from criticism La Guardia became brittle and remote, and isolation reinforced his least attractive tendencies for willfulness.[35]

Self-indulgence hardened into an ungenerous arrogance and incivility. His powers of outrage, which in the past aimed at redressing social imbalances and skewering uncaring officials, declined into orneriness, into the pleasures of finding fault and harping on the failures of others. The refreshing iconoclasm that had made his progressivism so human had long since become an irrepresible irritability. He aimed at easy targets, highlighting the inevitable mess of war-disrupted Washington, where decisions were often taken on the run. His old diatribes had been focused by a social agenda, the new ones seemed the random crotchets of an aging politician firing at anyone falling between his gunsights. Only Roosevelt was spared his tongue, and this just barely. ''Our poor President,'' La Guardia wrote to a friend in the fall of 1943, ''is just overburdened with responsibilities of war, and I fear some of the fakers are putting it over on him. . . . OPA . . . is in a mess and Manpower rapidly getting there.'' The complaints multiplied: OPA was poorly managed, rationing was inequitable, New York was being shortchanged, the food pipeline was all fouled up, the disposal of surplus materials was a scandal. It made him a difficult person to have around. The Little Flower had become the prime whiner of the home front.[36]

With his opportunities limited to New York, the open national vision that he had displayed in the past shriveled into the provincialism of the local official. He became a special pleader for the city in ways that were sometimes unattractive and even unfair. During a blackout La Guardia decided that spectators at a Polo Grounds baseball game did not have to extinguish their cigarettes. The Germans would find the place even if it was all dark, he winked, dismissing in one irresponsible remark the entire premise of blackout drills. Had any municipal official done this while he was at OCD, La Guardia would have seriously pursued charges of treason.

As soon as the selective service system was established there was La Guardia tearing it apart for its ''lack of vision.'' Then this fan of the universal draft turned around and demanded that members of New York's uniformed services be exempted from service. Police, firemen, even sanitation men, the mayor argued, were too important for the city's safety to be drafted.[37]

When New York's night clubs and restaurants, the joy palaces that La Guardia had so often attacked in the past, pleaded that a new national policy of midnight curfews would hurt business, the mayor announced on radio: ''I have caused my own survey to be made and I have come to the conclusion that unless we adjust the situation to meet local conditions . . . it will defeat its very own purpose. . . . I think I have diagnosed it pretty well." Then he countermanded the federal order. "So now we will allow one hour tolerance after midnight." A disappointed Charles Burlingham chided, "You have set yourself up as superior to the federal government and encourage other cities to follow your example of defiance." Burlingham wished that La Guardia would retract his ill-conceived policy, but he did not expect it. "*Peccavi* [I have erred] isn't in your vocabulary." Other cities were outraged; even New Yorkers denounced La Guardia's "indefensible lawlessness."[38]

In the summer of 1945, Fabio Scinia wrote from Pozzonti, Italy, that an American sailor, Frederick Brooks, had seduced his daughter, and he asked La Guardia to bring the sailor to justice. Fiorello was touched by the father's sadness and leaned on the navy to take "proper action." Months after this unusual intrusion, the sailor was placed under arrest and shipped back to Italy to stand trial. The press and veterans groups tore into La Guardia, and his own City Council censured him for prejudging an American fighting man on the word of an enemy civilian. This was not the first time, one newspaper suggested, that an American soldier had pursued a foreign girl during war.[39]

But La Guardia did not see it that way. If he kept any of his original brilliance as a unique political leader, it was in his true feeling for the "little guy," and whether it was a shamed father, renters who wanted their living costs controlled, workers who borrowed from loan sharks, or housewives abused by the food industry, he continued to make their fight his own. When a National Association of Manufacturers spokesman objected to Vice President Henry Wallace's characterization of the war as a fight to ease the lot of the needy, declaring that the war was not about providing "a quart of milk for every Hottentot, or a TVA on the Danube, or free governmental handouts for a free Utopia," La Guardia pounced, merrily lancing the narrow men of assured comfort. Perhaps a businessman would not understand, he declared, but there were things more important than self-interest, and "a quart of milk to every Hottentot" was part of the noble purpose for which the war was being fought. His faith in the need to do good for the people remained firm.[40]

One afternoon three representatives of a Soviet commercial delegation visited La Guardia at city hall. He welcomed them in his frayed suit with its baggy knees. The delegates were in their striped trousers with formal coats. He looked at them and at his own suit. "Gentlemen," he said, "I represent the proletariat." It was his saving grace. His radio talks were concerned with how much they paid for butter, how they fed their families, helping them avoid the pitfalls of gambling, loan sharking, and unfair businesses; their every penny was important to him. He worried over their health and how they raised their children. And he pursued unmercifully those who took unfair advantage of them. The genuine hope that New Yorkers would be happy and be good, that they would have a life easier, better, healthier, more cultured than they had had before, continued to motivate him.[41]

La Guardia had long before rejected the notion that the higher culture was reserved for the rich and wellborn, while the poor could entertain themselves with cheap amusements, with wrestling matches and jazz concerts. He had come by his love of music honestly, without any pretension, and it gave him great pleasure throughout his life. This thing of beauty he wanted to make available to all New Yorkers at reasonable cost. Despite the turmoil overseas it was important for New York to develop a City Center for the Performing Arts, he said, to secure "the flame of art . . . and to hold until the younger generation lay down their arms and come back, the beautiful, spiritual and happy things in life."

The City Center, which he established, offered opera, classical theater, and the New York Philharmonic under the baton of Leopold Stokowski, all at prices from a quarter to a dollar. The shirtleeved audiences who flocked to the productions—"Dubinsky's garment workers and Curran's seamen"—filled the velvet-cushioned seats to hear Tchaikovsky and Gershwin, more than justifying his enthusiasm for the project.[42]

Like the construction of La Guardia airport, this venture's every detail absorbed him. He coached Gertrude Lawrence on her lines, carefully reviewed John Golden's proposal for an institute for promising actors, persuaded Marc Connelly to accept a role in *Our Town*, and read some of the plays that were considered for production. When it came to a ballet company for the center, however, he was reluctant; it was difficult for him to see art in young men who "leap around the stage in white tights, exhibiting their crotches." Before the year was over the proletarian theater had become so popular that Broadway was complaining about the competition.[43]

Having made some effort to pay the working class's fiddler, he turned his attention to paying its medical bills. La Guardia was stunned to learn from a survey that the most common cause of city employee indebtedness was health-related expenses. Since his congressional days Fiorello had supported a bill for national health insurance, but he realized that it was unrealistic to expect a federal health bill during the war. New York City would have to lead the way. La Guardia created a committee to develop a plan for city-sponsored group medical insurance in April of 1943. The indigent, he told the committee, could get the best medical care in the world free in the municipal hospitals. The rich could get it anywhere they chose. But those with moderate income were limited to the level of care they could pay for. Concern for the cost of medical attention forced many to delay such care until it was unavoidable, and then they fell into heavy debt. Nearly 30 percent of all small loans in the city went for medical bills.[44]

The mayor's innovative health insurance plan, HIP, offered to make available for those earning less than $5000 a year the most comprehensive system of medical, surgical, and hospital protection in the United States, with at least half of the cost of the program borne by the employer. Ten years before, the American Medical Association had rejected community health insurance as "Communism, Socialism and incitement to riot." This time the representatives of the five New York County medical societies still voted against the proposal. They argued that the $5000 earnings ceiling for applicants should be cut, and they offered other objections based on the possible loss in income to physicians. The Little Flower had managed to convert the scare of Red medicine into a haggle over price! Delayed a bit in getting off the ground, HIP began operations in March of 1947 and by the end of that year had enrolled more than 110,000 members.[45]

Clearly, he could still summon the visions of municipal improvement that had motivated him in the thirties: "Taken in all it is a great city. . . . a mighty city. One has to absorb a great deal of abuse, but, it is worthwhile. Sometimes you get so discouraged at the end of the day, you say, 'Oh what is the use?' But you look around and you see the playgrounds and the different parkways, you see these health centers and you see these happy healthy children. Oh! I will tell you it is worthwhile, but it does require a great deal of patience and fortitude."[46]

In some areas, however, his vision, and the progressive confidence that supported it, had dimmed. La Guardia had brought with him into office a strong faith in city planning. In the 1930s he had criticized unguided urban growth as a remnant of primitive laissez faire thinking. When New York's 1936 charter, calling for a strong City Planning Commission, passed, La Guardia appointed FDR brain truster Rexford Tugwell to head the CPC and shape the city's future to the lineaments of a rational system of social, political, economic, and aesthetic goals. But while La Guardia was happy to place Tugwell in such a powerful office when he anticipated leaving the city for Washington, he viewed this all differently after he was forced to remain in the city and contend with an independent Planning Commission.[47]

Tugwell's long-term goal was to steer city development toward stability instead of growth. He wanted to intersperse generous "green belts" between residential areas to add beauty and a sense of human scale to the massive metropolis. After devoting more than a year and a half to dividing the city into residential, manufacturing, and other sectors, the CPC designed detailed land-use maps. Such a plan for shaping the city's next decade, with its limitations on building and development, naturally raised strong objections among real estate and commercial groups. Only a fully committed La Guardia could clear the way for Tugwell's plans, but he was far from committed, criticizing Tugwell for being impractical and unrealistic. And without La Guardia's support the administrative departments did not fall in line with the policies that Tugwell needed to bring his master plan alive.[48]

Fed up with his impossible job, and with La Guardia's tepid support, Tugwell accepted a White House offer to go off and govern Puerto Rico. Eighteen months of finely detailed work toward a rational plan for future city development went with him. The new commission appointed in 1942 threw out the plans that Tugwell had painstakingly constructed, limiting itself to imposing restrictions on building heights and residential concentrations.[49]

La Guardia's fading support for city planning was more than matched by a declining commitment to fiscal prudence. When he assumed office amidst the fiscal crisis of the early 1930s, La Guardia promised that his successor would not have to face "the bankrupt and financially disorganized condition that I found when I assumed office. . . ." He counted as one of his signal achievements the creation of a stable and rational fiscal policy. "I took the City over when it was bankrupt," he recalled in an interview; "it is now financially sound." But it wasn't.

I "like your emphasis on the economy of abundance and full employment," Henry Wallace cheered in a letter to La Guardia in 1944. But the economy of abundance was expensive, and throughout his tenure La Guardia failed to confront openly the budget implications of a progressive urban policy.[50]

La Guardia prefaced the presentation of his 1939–1940 budget to the City Council with a frank prediction: "This budget was conceived in despair, developed in agony. . . . This condition will become increasingly more difficult unless a permanent and constructive new financial policy is determined and made possible." La Guardia thought that he would not be running for mayor again, so he candidly explained that growing municipal government would come up inevitably against budget limits. "I feel it is my duty to sound the warning that unless this matter of finance is given consideration, a real crisis will be reached around 1944 or 1945." To balance the 1940–1941 budget, he withdrew funds from police and fire pension allocations and diverted salaries from unfilled civil service positions.

Even before he decided to run for mayor again, La Guardia was employing questionable accounting schemes to cover the services that he had introduced, and Comptroller Joseph McGoldrick was dismissing deficits as "entirely a bookkeeping transaction," as he switched current expenses from tax levy funds to bonded debt. This business of passing on to future generations the price of current government was just the sort of thing La Guardia had criticized when he came into office. And the fiscal manipulations went further as La Guardia reallocated dedicated tax levies so that a rent occupancy tax meant to subsidize low-cost housing was diverted to general funds, and the sales tax, passed expressly for the purpose of providing relief, was also used for general operating expenses.[51]

To increase city receipts without raising taxes, the administration jacked up property assessments, which created a larger tax base to support the high budgets.

This tactic not only hurt real estate owners but also led to abandonment, even on posh Fifth Avenue. "Never in the history of the world has so much private wealth been concentrated on a single street," observed *Fortune* magazine. But by 1940 upper Fifth Avenue was pocked with more than thirty empty houses with their windows boarded up. The single largest factor in this abandonment, reported an investigator, was the high assessments on property.[52]

Meanwhile, citizens groups were demanding a cut in the sales tax. As late as May 1941 La Guardia would not hear of such a cut, despite a rise in employment, mounting tax receipts, and declining relief expenses. Suddenly, in the autumn, after La Guardia decided to run for mayor again, he himself proposed a 50 percent cut to go into effect four days before the election. The proposal prompted Assemblyman Louis Cohen to declare that he did not trust the mayor "as far as I can throw a piano."[53]

"The City faces a crisis in its fiscal affairs," the Citizens Budget Commission announced shortly after the 1941 election, detailing the price that the city was paying for its modern, caring government. In fifteen years annual city expenditures, exclusive of emergency unemployment relief, had grown three times more rapidly than the city population, while the debt multiplied five and half times population growth. Over and above a 210 percent increase in federal and state contributions, city expenditures advanced by more than 40 percent, while gross bonded debt doubled. Rather than accept this as the price of good intentions and large government, La Guardia used every possible fiscal artifice to hide the full cost of his progressive urban policies. During the war, La Guardia took advantage of the forced savings produced by the war economy (supply shortages prevented some expenditures that had already been approved and budgeted, and the draft pulled a large number of civil servants off the salary rolls) to camouflage growing municipal costs. Then he still overspent. Came the end of the year, when the city was behind in its receipts, and McGoldrick would roll over its bills to the next year's budget. *Brooklyn Eagle* columnist William Heffernan referred to the camouflaged budget as the "final stage of a municipal rake's progress . . . the gimme philosophy raised to the nth degree," the legacy of a "government that has spent without discretion and taxed without care. . . ."[54]

In one of its periodic reviews of city finances, Lazard Freres & Co. expressed concern over "a lack of proper retrenchment in expenditures for both current and capital purposes." More significantly, the audit hinted at a troubling difference between Tammany fiscal problems and those of the fusion regime. Tammany budgets, full of waste and mismanagement, could be squeezed down by an honest administration. But under fusion, expenditures were not bloated by corruption or inefficiency, they reflected the real costs of a liberal government's expanded services. By 1941 the Citizens Budget Commission was warning that La Guardia's great gifts to the city rested upon an "insubstantial fiscal foundation."[55]

The city paid the price of its progressive convictions in other ways as well.

Its emphasis on humane safety and welfare requirements in the workplace and its pro-labor tilt raised the cost of doing business in New York City. And a growing number of firms refused to pay the price of virtue. Deciding that they could not be both profitable and good, some companies departed for warmer climes, laissez faire governments, fewer restrictive regulations, and alluring tax breaks.

The exodus of businesses so threatened the future of the city that for a long time La Guardia refused to acknowledge it. Informed by industry leaders and by the New York Board of Trade that "one industry after another" was leaving the city, the mayor denied that any but dishonest businessmen would leave New York. Such reports, he bellowed, were "cheap propaganda . . . cowardly despicable, . . . a malicious, deliberate lie, and the people who make it know that it is a lie, and anyone who passes it on must know that it is a lie." But it wasn't a lie, and in his heart La Guardia knew that. He knew that the price of a humane city was often lower profits, and that businessmen often sought profits above all else.[56]

He denied that businesses were leaving the city and he denied that his budgets were growing. But the reformers, his old friends, were on to him, and when they publicized his evasions he started calling his critics names, telling Nicholas Murray Butler that the Citizens Budget Commission analysis of his budget was "unfair, inaccurate and captious . . . without regard for the public interest." They had gotten used to his bad-mouthing. He proceeded in an eighteen-page letter to rip apart CBC statements with a flair for technical objections that would have done the most artful "semi-colon boys" proud. They responded with a twenty-page retort hitting back point for point.[57]

What emerged from the colloquy was how little La Guardia was willing to make the tough fiscal decisions on the transit fare, on pensions, on salaries, on curbing such insistent men as Robert Moses who threatened at every turn to use his considerable public relations skill to turn the mothers loose. In 1942 La Guardia did cut the parks budget, and Moses yelped as if mortally wounded. He flooded the press with reports showing that the parks would soon be stripped by invading Goths and Vandals unless the money he demanded was forthcoming. Waving press clippings about violence in the parks, telling one and all that more cuts would mean more rapes, muggings, and deaths and the rapid deterioration of the magnificent system he had created, Moses showed what it would take to win smaller parks budgets.[58]

There were other places where cuts could have been made. La Guardia was proud of expanding the city hospital system, but it was uneconomic. Comptroller Joseph McGoldrick reported that it cost $6.37 a day to maintain a patient in a city-operated hospital while the city paid voluntary hospitals $3.25 a day to care for charity cases. It cost the city $3.12 extra per person to treat patients in its own hospitals! With more than 2600 beds unfilled in private hospitals, La Guardia was planning new construction and additional expenditures of more than $20 million a year. The cost of police protection in New York was the most expensive in the

557

nation. Chicago paid $5.41 per capita, Philadelphia $5.89, Detroit $6.20, and Los Angeles $4.52, while the price of La Guardia's Finest came to $7.91 per person. Fire protection was equally high-priced. Reported per capita costs for major fire departments ranged from $2.45 in Chicago to $2.80 in Philadelphia, $2.82 in Detroit, and $3.56 in Los Angeles. In New York the rate was $4.56. Welfare was even more extravagantly different. New York's figure stood at $18.99 while Chicago spent only $8.11 and Detroit $5.29.[59]

Equally troubling was the chaotic condition of city pension funds. Originally established to protect loyal workers against penniless old age, pensions had become a golden annuity for the well-heeled as well as the needy, beckoning civil servants to retire on half and three-quarters pay after twenty years and take jobs in private industry. Not only had the pensions become a disincentive to longevity, they had no sound actuarial underpinnings. Retirees were paid from current departmental budgets. A wave of retirements could force a department into huge payments to nonproductive labor, paralyzing its ability to perform regular functions. Civil service personnel had learned to take particular advantage of the provision awarding pensions as a fraction of the last earned salary, piling up overtime during their last year of employment. With no reserve to cover these huge pension obligations, the entire fiscal structure of the city was at risk. Yet La Guardia avoided addressing the problem for fear of a damaging confrontation with uniformed civil servants.

What burdened the budget even more was the newly unified transit system. When the private companies operated the system they had complained that the 5-cent fare was driving the system bankrupt. Now the albatross was hung around the municipality's neck. Each year labor costs rose and expenditures on expansion, renovation, and maintenance climbed while the fare box continued to return its fixed amount. By 1944 the transit deficit exceeded $40 million annually. According to one report, New Yorkers had paid close to $400 million to offset transit deficits alone since 1932. Each ride cost the city 2 to 3 cents, with the subsidies squeezed out of the same budget that paid for hospitals, police, and schools. A committee headed by La Guardia's former confidant and corporation counsel, Paul Windels, characterized the transit budget as the "shabby practice of illegal extortion from people who can't help themselves."[60]

Transit was so hopelessly uneconomic that no one expected it to break even or to do a decent job. "I wish," Charles Burlingham wrote to Fiorello, "you would send . . . the Comptroller, the President of the Council and every member of the Council to take a ride on the Subway at 5 p.m. any weekday. It is like going to sea. The only difference is that ships pitch as well as roll and the Subway cars only roll. . . . The tracks are bad and the wheels are bad, and it is very dangerous." Even La Guardia admitted that the condition of the rolling stock was run-down, and that the system suffered from delays, discomfort, overcrowding, and impaired safety. As for the bottom line, it was crimson, and yet La Guardia was unwilling to raise the fare.[61]

Despite all this, La Guardia wanted to end his third term with a *beau geste*, to reward the municipal workers, who "had been loyal to their appointed tasks in spite of the many temptations of higher wages and who have conscientiously rendered the many services enjoyed by the residents of this city." Let the real estate interests complain; let the merchants complain; he larded his final budget with bonuses and wage increases. It had taken twelve years, but he was now convinced that there were more important things than a balanced budget.[62]

The Citizens Budget Commission blasted him for failing to "exercise caution, prudence and economy," squandering war-related savings, and tying the city to a level of expenditure that normal times would not support. The last La Guardia budget for 1946, the report continued, was drawn "solely with an eye to the present hour" and avoided any steps to prepare the city for the great costs that would come inevitably after the war. More than 20,000 civil servants were due to come back from the armed forces. The city would have to find $20 million to pay their salaries and the new bonuses. Another $10 million was needed for maintenance that had been deferred. The fire and police departments were well below prewar levels. The transit deficit would swallow $50 million, and a much-needed rehabilitation of the system could run another $145 million. Little of the prudent, economy-minded urban strategist of 1934 could be found in La Guardia's 1946 budget. There was no strategy, only tactics.[63]

The problem extended beyond fiscal issues. The American Institute of Architects reported in 1944 that New York was a city in eclipse. Its office district, docks, terminals, warehouses, and housing were all declining. The traffic alone was so badly tangled that it promoted "premature obsolescence." The nondescript master plan, the one put together by the post-Tugwell CPC, had failed to tackle the problem.[64]

Governor Thomas E. Dewey's Hanes Committee was equally blunt in its criticism, projecting enormous budget burdens, expanding blight, high taxes, and declines in such critical industries as the women's garment trades and the printing industry. The report, directed by former Treasury undersecretary John W. Hanes, called attention to the alarming flight of industry to younger cities, concluding that the number of "ghost neighborhoods" in the city was growing, and "ghost cities," the study said pointedly, "are made up of ghost neighborhoods."[65]

La Guardia's interest in New York's day-to-day problems had long since been dulled, but large issues continued to arouse his leadership impulses, and he saw no larger challenge than planning for a postwar future to avoid just these calamities. Those who were writing his city's obituary did not long detain him. New York was far more resilient, he believed, than they knew. It was still the manufacturing, commercial, and financial capital of the nation as well as its most important port. Admittedly, the number of its factories might decline, but its primary resource was its human capital, its creative people, intellectuals, artists, managers, investment theorists, and financial leaders. And La Guardia had designs for these gifted New

559

Yorkers. Their special expertise would make his City of Tomorrow into the culture and trade capital of the world. La Guardia's New York, gibed the *New York Post*, still overflowed with "milk and parkways."[66]

That was a deceptively simple way of putting an idea that was occupying more and more of La Guardia's thoughts: preparing to resume the progressive national relationship between Washington and the cities once the war ended. New Deal dollars had made La Guardia's New York the most innovative city in the nation. The war now absorbed these dollars and that imagination, but La Guardia was already laying plans. He had cautioned New Yorkers to prepare for war early; now he was preparing them for peace. Some morning the war would end, billions in defense contracts would be canceled, millions of war-related jobs would suddenly disappear, and the United States would be tested to maintain prosperity without conscription and military contracts. La Guardia wanted to guarantee that programs would be ready to soak up the millions of suddenly unemployed and that the cities would continue to serve as agents of Washington's welfare and public works programs. "I tell you now," he wrote Senator Claude Pepper in 1942, "that unless we are ready and know exactly what to do after the war, all the effort, all the sacrifice, all the loss of life will not have been worth while. Hell will break loose and it will take generations to recover."[67]

He knew what he wanted to do after the war, to continue the agenda for growth that had helped bring New York out of the Depression. He drew up fully detailed engineering and architectural plans for a $1.25 billion program of postwar public improvements, with new traffic arteries, a modernized waterfront, school construction, water purification and sewage disposal plants, neighborhood reconstruction, street, road, and transit improvements and maintenance. Literally hundreds of projects came off the drawing boards, with all the preliminary work complete on more than a quarter of them. Projects were planned to eventually absorb the labor of 250,000 returning veterans and war workers in the New York area alone.[68]

There was a critical flaw in all of these plans, however. The New Deal, for all of its lack of coherence, represented a central strategy, or at least it cohered around a strategic goal: using federal programs to achieve economic recovery. This goal validated its new departures. What La Guardia was trying to do was supply plans that would absorb postwar federal spending, but he tied it to no larger economic strategy. If the government was to spend heavily in good times as well as bad, when would it square its deficits, and what would determine its spending priorities? If one of the chief ends of planning is to lay out a future agenda, another is to match goals with resources, to accept a reasonable sense of limit. La Guardia spoke with abandon about billion-dollar-plus programs, but he failed to analyze the real impact of the decade of government largesse on his city. He neglected to appreciate the true cost of more such programs and to accept the fact that New York had reached the limit of its ability to absorb such expensive gifts.

In La Guardia's mind New York was still the growing, expanding, unlimited independent city of old. But New York had become critically addicted to federal assistance, not only for the big projects but even for the small ones. As war forced Washington to divert its expenditures from the city, the extent of this dependency was apparent in the city's disrepair and in its inability to maintain the spanking new infrastructure its rich Uncle Sam had provided.

The city's physical plant had simply grown beyond its own ability to care for it. "How are we to . . . groom the gift horse sent by our wealthy governmental relations?" the American Society of Landscape Architects had asked even before the war. The answer then had been to have Moses draw up a plan and send La Guardia down to Washington for more money. But that money was no longer coming, and despite La Guardia's frenetic postwar planning, there was no reason to think that it would flow permanently. Much of this money was specifically for make-work projects that would be rolled back in normal times anyway, and much of this money was won through the unusual personal relationship between La Guardia and Roosevelt. But that too would pass. And with all of his postwar planning, La Guardia laid no plans to set New York on a solid fiscal footing.[69]

Rexford Tugwell considered La Guardia one of the few men of his generation of true presidential mettle. He thought that La Guardia brought rare gifts to his office as mayor of the largest, most complex metropolis in the world. But he also noted that La Guardia's successor was stunned by the mess he inherited, by the gaps he left in his last budget, gaps of tens of millions of dollars that had to be filled very quickly. Parks, parkways, pools, and recreational facilities were in disarray. Garbage lined the streets, and the schools were too crowded to hold all of the city's children. "The whole of the City machinery," observed Tugwell, "was breaking down from sheer lack of funds." By raising the city's level of indebtedness, concluded Tugwell, "he had pledged [New Yorkers] to the bankers, permanently increased the cost of their utilities, and made municipal bankruptcy inevitable." Progressive municipal government had come at a high price indeed.[70]

And New York was headed for a trap. Unless the federal government resumed its deep-pocketed support, the city would soon stand as a vast agglomeration of rusted steel and crumbling brick, a reprise of Shelley's "Ozymandias":

"My name is Ozymandias, King of Kings
look on my works ye mighty and despair!"
Nothing beside remains. Round the decay
of that colossal wreck, boundless and bare,
The lone and level sands stretch far away.

561

3. Gemma

THE war that had led to his public break with reformers and repeated humiliation in the press also touched La Guardia in ways few appreciated. He had a sister in a German concentration camp.

Early in the spring of 1944, after Germany abandoned its policy of peaceful domination of Hungary, it dumped the premier and replaced him with the head of the local Nazi organization. Immediately thereafter, Gemma La Guardia Gluck's Jewish husband, Herman Gluck, was dismissed from his position with the Budapest Central Bank. The Glucks had lived comfortably in an attractive section of the Hungarian capital. Their home boasted a servant and a fine collection of books and musical instruments. But one day in May, this middle-class comfort was rashly disturbed as SS guards barged in and started clearing bookshelves and emptying furniture drawers into a huge pile at the center of the living room. No part of the apartment was left unsearched. Later Gemma heard that officials, having discovered her famous overseas relative, thought that she might be hiding a prohibited transmitter to receive his broadcasts.[71]

The next slide into the forbidding soullessness of Nazi occupation came on June 7, 1944, when four armed Nazi storm troopers burst into the Gluck home and arrested the sixty-four-year-old Gemma for questioning. Though much older than his wife, and much weaker, Herman insisted on going along. They never went home again. They were taken to the Mauthausen concentration camp, where Gemma was separated from her husband. She writes in her memoirs that high Nazi officials, having discovered her relationship to Fiorello, decided to spare her for possible "political" use, and had her sent to the forced labor camp in Ravensbruck.[72]

In the succeeding eleven months Gemma became ill and demoralized, losing almost fifty pounds. She feared every day for herself, for what might have happened to her husband, and also for her daughter's family. (Daughter Yolanda had given birth to a son, Richard, a few months before the Glucks had been imprisoned, and she and her husband, Erno Denes, had moved in with the Glucks.) By early spring Gemma was certain that her time for the lethal "showers" had come. She began to scream hysterically, as so many others did, but in her case it reminded someone that she could be more valuable in these fading weeks of the Nazi Reich as a bargaining chip than as another corpse.

Shortly after Gemma's own arrest, Yolanda and Erno Denes and their five-month-old baby had also been led away. In April of 1945 Gemma learned that Yolanda was in Ravensbruck with a sickly infant and that the Nazis had decided to transport the three of them to Berlin to be exchanged for prisoners. No such exchange ever took place. Instead they were locked in the basement of Kaiserdam prison, from where they experienced the terrifying fall of Nazi Berlin to the Russians.[73]

The Red Cross had kept La Guardia informed about his sister's imprisonment and her situation at Ravensbruck. But in April, when Gemma was removed to Berlin, Fiorello feared the worst, writing sadly to the woman who had taught them both when they were army brats out west that he had lost track of Gemma. It was a month before he was able to pick up her trail again when he learned that his sister had been liberated in the Russian attack upon the capital.[74]

Gemma was without her husband and had two individuals dependent on her. She needed help, and all she had right now was her brother's name. She used it to win respect, decent treatment, special allotments from the Americans, and access to newspaper reporters who were searching for stories. From these stories Fiorello discovered her whereabouts and arranged to send her money. He also asked Red Cross officials to search for the missing husbands. In the letters he sent to Gemma he suggested to his sister that she keep the publicity down, but she was finding it too useful to give it up. Indeed, her minor celebrity won for her an opportunity in July to speak to her brother over restricted transatlantic phone lines when Katherine Craven of the Mutual Broadcasting Network interviewed her for American radio. After the interview Mutual offered Gemma and Fiorello a private channel to exchange a few words.

"Hello sister," the mayor said in his direct manner.

"Oh, Fiorello is it really you? I can't believe it!" gushed Gemma.

Briskly clearing away the emotions, he asked Gemma to tell him "what you want me to do and I will do it."

She wanted help finding the missing men (only later was it learned that they had both been killed) and to arrange for them all to come to the United States. He would do his best, he told her, but it would take time. Her daughter and baby Richard were not citizens. They would have to wait for a visa. He promised to do everything that he could properly do, but he would not use improper influence to push her ahead of others.[75]

Over the next few months Gemma kept her brother informed about the conditions and her suffering. "We are like beggars," she wrote, describing "the soul suffering . . . the cruelties of these beasts," impressing upon Fiorello the need to move quickly. But he could offer only faint reassurance: "Your situation is extremely difficult. . . . The publicity which you obtained and the fact that I might be known, makes it all the more difficult. But let me repeat your case is the same as that of hundreds of thousands of displaced people." At the same time, as recently released private letters between Gemma and Fiorello demonstrate, while Fiorello sounded more dutiful than driven, he did everything in his power to assist his sister. He wrote to the State Department, immigration authorities, local consuls, foreign ambassadors, military officials, and a host of others to bring Gemma and her family into the United States. Every month Fiorello wired Gemma $150, which went a long way in Europe to meeting all of her material needs, and he took care of all other costs.[76]

When she tried to hurry things on her own, Fiorello often found that her efforts only obstructed his, and he could be pointed in getting his message across. "I think you displayed a little impatience in your letter to Mr. Carroll. By the way, he was killed in an automobile accident a few days ago." He repeatedly asked her to avoid publicity. So long as she did this, he would be able to reach up to the highest channels for gentle assistance. He would deliver a letter through General Eisenhower, send cash through the president of the Red Cross and the State Department, or appeal for a visa to the Special Projects Division. When American doors were temporarily closed, he arranged short-term asylum in Denmark and backed his sister's visa application with an affidavit offering his annual income as insurance against the refugees' becoming public charges.[77]

Still it was not before mid-February 1947 that they were able to secure visas, and it was April before La Guardia wrote his friend E. J. McCormack of the Moore McCormack Shipping Lines asking for passage for his sister on the first available ship out of Copenhagen. McCormack passed on La Guardia's request with his own note: "This is a MUST," and room was promptly found for the three passengers. Fiorello asked for the bill, writing to his friend, "I am quite sure that my sister did not pay the passage."[78]

Later, in recalling the events of this difficult time, Gemma thought that her brother was "unsentimental, brisk and businesslike" in his dealings with her. But there was good reason for his reticence. He trusted Gemma's discretion very little, and the less he wrote to her the better off both of them would be. Finally, in April of 1947 Fiorello wrote Gemma that all plans were complete. Again he warned her not to complicate matters "with a lot of talk." All she was to do "is to show your documents, get your steamship tickets, and . . . get on the ship the day it sails. Do not show off during the passage." They arrived in May, and Fiorello made plans to find a modest home for them, provide for little Richard's education, and try to make them all comfortable.[79]

Gemma's account of her brother's assistance, with its undertone of dissatisfaction, leaves the impression that Fiorello was more interested in helping humanity in the abstract than in focusing on the specific needs of his own family. It is a distinctly unfair implication. La Guardia did all he could and more, but he did it in uncharacteristically low tones, without the splash and drama that could have threatened the success of his efforts. What Gemma hints at is that Fiorello never really demonstrated the kind of emotion that one would expect under the circumstances. But then that was the way he behaved toward his own wife and children. From the time his first wife, Thea, had died, he related to people with a reserve that would protect him if they turned on him, died on him, or disappointed him.

This emotional buffer prevented him from the joyous highs that others could experience in their relationships, and it protected him from the depressed lows when, as had often happened in his career, he had to turn against individuals who had been close to him.

4. The Insurgent Era Passes

"I COULD wish," La Guardia wrote Lieutenant T. H. Johnson in 1943, more reflectively than usual, "for some sort of study of the eternal verities. . . . I sometimes think that what America needs as much as a five cent cigar is a clear sighted philosopher." Ruefully he concluded that the idealistic dreams of the progressives had not yielded the shining new world that he had hoped for. "Our generation," he told a group of students, "is responsible to history for two devastating, unnecessary world wars." Later, after he left office, La Guardia spoke even more remorsefully about his own misguided hopes: "When I was a younger man I helped my country make one of the most serious mistakes in its history." During the twenties he had opposed a peacetime army as a provocation to war. He and his colleagues in Congress had "chucked out" the War Department's request for the compulsory training of 500,000 men. The army was chopped to 200,000, and in the following year this figure was sliced in half. "And the rest," wrote La Guardia pensively, "is history."[80]

His era and its assumptions were passing. Al Smith died. Wendell Willkie, who had taken La Guardia's harsh attacks with grace and repaid them with a warm mayoral endorsement in 1941, also passed from the scene. The men of his generation were retiring and dying. It was the death of Senator George Norris, with whom his name was joined on a piece of landmark congressional legislation and whom he revered as the soul of progressivism, that touched him most deeply. La Guardia told his radio audience that the senator's death on September 2, 1944, profoundly saddened him, not only for the passing of a progressive tribune but also for the dispiriting way in which Norris had been abandoned in his lifetime. The last time he ran for the Senate, young voters, unfamiliar with his earlier work, did not vote for him and older ones simply forgot about him. After Norris's defeat, Fiorello asked President Roosevelt to appoint the Nebraskan to an honorific post that would keep him in the Washington that he loved and served so loyally, but "I guess it skipped the President's mind. . . ." Tears rolling down his cheeks, La Guardia told his radio audience: "Some will say, well he lived to a ripe old age, but I can't help feeling that the Senator was unhappy. You see he was an insurgent and the life of an insurgent in American politics is an unhappy one. . . .'' Wiping the tears from his eyes, La Guardia closed the program with words to his own wife: "I'm coming home early this afternoon, Marie. I don't think I can work much today."[81]

La Guardia was tired. The passing of friends, his failure to win appointment to the army, the growing rift between himself and liberal reformers, the intractability of New York's budget crisis, and his sense of being unappreciated and unjustly maligned all combined to make a sad, bent man. He was troubled about his sister, Gemma, and concerned about the way his son, Eric, was developing. Many of the young men who had surrounded Fiorello, his surrogate sons, were no longer around. Some were in the service; others, like Paul Kern, had long before broken with him. The most recent to leave was William Herlands, the loyal, many said subservient, investigations commissioner, outraged by La Guardia's acceptance of Police Commissioner Valentine's exoneration of a patrolman charged with anti-Semitism.[82]

The job seemed to grow more difficult and less rewarding daily. "There is not much glamor to it, but heart-breaking work—just hard labor," he complained. Except for postwar planning, there were no large ideas; only a lot of bickering and ingratitude. "Damn it, that makes me good and sore," he grumbled to the publisher of the *Herald Tribune*. The newspapers took note of city government only when they could splash some spectacular failure across the front pages. "The mayor is abused all during the year," he muttered, turning nostalgic for his days as a congressman. "I'd rather be a third rate congressman from a third rate district," he told friends in the House of Representatives, "than a first rate mayor of a first rate city."[83]

He drew momentary respite from pomp and ceremony. When he first came into office, La Guardia had scorned meaningless ceremony as an impediment to the real work of governing; now the ephemeral symbols of the affection of the crowd came to mean very much to him. Every major war hero seemed to pass through New York City for the purpose of having confetti rained upon him and favoring the mayor with a ride among cheering throngs. Nothing reflected more the sense of being cheated of fulfillment than his rapture from riding the sidecars of the famous.

Late in June the largest and most enthusiastic crowd in New York history turned out to welcome the heroic leader of the European victory, Dwight David Eisenhower. Four million people lined thirty-seven miles of city streets cramming fire escapes and windows to offer tribute. A General Electric noise meter registered the equivalent of 3000 simultaneous peals of thunder along the route. For the

566

moment, La Guardia submerged his own disappointments in paying homage to the man and the uniform.

This rousing welcome was followed by a 2 million-person welcome for the hero of French resistance, Charles de Gaulle, who offered the spectacle of bending his tall frame almost double to kiss La Guardia on the cheek while presenting him with the Grand Cross of the Legion of Honor. A beaming Fiorello responded by eloquently praising Paris and New York as "two great cities of art and beauty and happiness . . . constant reminder[s] to the entire world that free people too can build and build permanently, can create the thing of beauty, can dedicate their lives to make life sweeter and happier." Two weeks later the city shone its spotlight on the courageous survivor of Bataan, Corregidor, and more than three years as a war prisoner, General Jonathan Mayhew Wainwright. Another tumultuous crowd assembled less than a month later to roar their gratitude before the admiral of the fleet, Chester W. Nimitz, for spearheading the conquest of Japan. Then came the leader of the "Flying Tigers," Claire Chennault. In October the president of the United States came calling, the first time in history that a sitting president paid his respects to a New York City mayor at city hall.[84]

Few missed the ticking of clocks as the celebrations proceeded through the summer. The mayor's third term was coming to an end in 1945. It was time again to think of what to do next. At age sixty-three politicians still thought of their futures. What would he do in 1945?

The political landscape had changed. Before the war he had predicted a political shake-up that would re-form parties along ideological lines. But the war had blocked any fundamental redefinition and the national mood did not favor any new departures right now. The entire world was being remapped; change enough there. No need for new parties.

Even if he could take another four years in office, there was no guarantee that he could be reelected. The 1941 contest had been close enough and the list of his supporters had dwindled. His party, the ALP, was irreparably split between liberals and a more left-leaning faction headed by Marcantonio. When La Guardia refused to repudiate Marc and his Communist supporters, David Dubinsky and Alex Rose barred any Liberal endorsement for him, with Rose saying:

> When we speak of an honest administration we don't mean honest in dollar only. We mean intellectual honesty, political honesty and emotional sincerity. When we speak of a nonpartisan administration, we don't mean a one man rule which completely ignores public opinion or is annoyed by the instruments of our democracy which gives expression

to that opinion. We mean a truly nonpartisan administration . . . which serves the best interests of all of its citizens.[85]

But as the election drew nearer, the reformers became frightened of a New York City politics without him. They had looked around and there was no one nearly as good as La Guardia. He was the old shoe of fusion politics, well worn, torn at the edges, but comfortable and familiar. As president of the Citizens Budget Commission, Nicholas Murray Butler had tussled with La Guardia often. In February he called for La Guardia's reelection. Oswald Garrison Villard had served on the Harlem riot committee and criticized the mayor vehemently over La Guardia's failure to take strong action against police racism. In the summer of 1945 he wrote La Guardia a letter that began by reasserting his reservations about the police and ended by imploring La Guardia to consider a fourth term.

> The truth is that the failings of your temperament have antagonized multitudes of people . . . so that they were relieved when you announced that you would not run again. Now, however, the situation has changed so much that they are turning back and would sincerely welcome your heading a third ticket. . . . I sincerely hope that you will consent to run again and shall do everything possible to further your candidacy.

Samuel Seabury also fell in line, circulating a letter signed by forty-five Republicans urging the party to back good government and renominate the present administration for another term. This time Republican leaders reacted swiftly, unanimously blocking any nomination for La Guardia.[86]

On April 12, 1945, Franklin Roosevelt died. "Centuries and centuries from now," La Guardia said simply of his friend and liberal colleague, "people [will] know [that] Franklin Roosevelt loved humanity." If La Guardia had entertained any hopes for help with his candidacy from the White House, they were buried with FDR. The new president, Harry S Truman, and La Guardia quite simply did not like each other.[87]

La Guardia's weak position was signaled by Comptroller Joseph D. McGoldrick, the fusion workhorse of earlier days, who took the step no reformer had dared take before, advertising his own availability for the mayoralty after publicly disagreeing with La Guardia on the budget and other issues. The move put pressure on La Guardia to make his own plans known.[88]

On May 6 La Guardia, with his family around him, prepared to go on the air with his Sunday radio program. Just before the broadcast began he turned to them, asking, "Okay?" Each replied in turn, "Okay." After some words about the impending end of war, La Guardia took some pleasure in having driven everybody a bit mad by delaying his decision about his candidacy.

It has been so amusing to observe the panorama of the past few months. This panorama of politicians, yes panorama of scheming and conniving. To do what. To join forces to destroy a good administration. Of course, it is always difficult for gentry of that kind to get together. Erickson and Costello, and the rest of the racketeers, perhaps, have not yet agreed. But have they not been confused? Have you seen all the maneuvering? Yes, and some very high officials holding certain offices who are not supposed to be in politics have been braintrusting in some of this conniving and conspiracy. Of course I knew all along.

Then he made his announcement: "I am not going to run for Mayor this year."[89]

There were strong reasons for his retirement from city hall. He had not even one party behind him, and the office no longer interested or excited him. But La Guardia did not offer these as his reasons for the decision, masking any regret with false bravado: "I can be reelected this fall without the nomination of any regular party. . . ." He echoed Al Smith: "I can run on a laundry ticket and beat these political bums any time." His retirement had nothing to do with any budget problems, he said. It was unrelated to the changed situation in the White House. He just did not want to grow stale in office; he did not want to lose the edge of anger and outrage that fueled his integrity; he feared becoming indifferent, smug, too bossy ("they tell me I am inclined that way at times"). "Yes my friends you gave me a job and I did it."

For those who had come in with him but parted ways—Comptroller McGoldrick perhaps?—the mayor suggested that they read the twenty-seventh chapter of Matthew, "and I will contribute the fifth verse for their individual guidance." The reference is to Judas: "And he cast down the pieces of silver in the temple and departed and went and hanged himself." It was a sad, silly, troubling broadcast, especially for those who remembered a different La Guardia.[90]

His friends and a good number of New Yorkers who had grown up knowing only one mayor wrote their regrets, but La Guardia was exhausted and he could not win. It must have been painful for him to read results of a straw poll on mayoralty candidates reporting that James J. Walker led the pack with 38 percent, followed by 30 percent for William O'Dwyer, the Democratic front-runner, and only 25 percent for La Guardia. The insurgent era was passing. Postwar America embraced other voices and other agendas.[91]

Perhaps the moment was on May 7, 1945. The beloved New Deal president had died less than a month before and soldiers were still killing each other in the Pacific. But the news of war's end in Europe threw New Yorkers into a frenzied celebration. La Guardia stood off to the side, offended by the mindlessness of the revelers, who were more taken with celebrating than with the cause of the celebrating. Finally, he could not stand the emptiness of it all. There was still a war going on in Japan. Men were dying "at this very moment," he called out with unusual emotion to the crowd at Times Square. It was La Guardia of 1929 again calling upon a people bent on release to be sober and serious. He would join the festive celebrations, especially as the heroes trooped through the city to collect their honors. But his style of government was pitched to a different time and a different sensibility. He felt deeply for the poor and the needy, and he had been so comforting and effective to the huge population displaced by the Depression. But he had little to offer postwar boom America bent on each making his own. He had emphasized old values, but as Americans made ready to break free of the restrictions that depression and war had placed upon them, his demand for attention to the poor and the hurt sounded less appealing, especially as they would be a small minority again.[92]

"What am I proudest of?" La Guardia said to John Gunther. "That I raised the standard of municipal government everywhere in this country, by raising it in New York and so proving it could be raised." There he was favoring rent control, while free enterprisers were preparing to charge what an undersupplied market would bear for apartments. The go-go spirit of the postwar period was more tolerant of sharp dealing, political friendships, and payoffs. America was ready to take off again and its citizens were prepared to fuel the takeoff with a boomtown tolerance. After a while integrity stops being an issue. How many remembered the rogue's gallery of crooked politicians and tin boxes that La Guardia had helped make a thing of the past?[93]

La Guardia told New Yorkers that he was withdrawing with an easy heart, leaving behind a long list of competent men to succeed him. But the truth was that he had prepared no successor. Two fusion candidates seemed genuinely interested, Newbold Morris and Joseph McGoldrick. Of the two, Morris was less likely to win. In 1941 Fiorello had explained to George Baehr his reservations about Newbold Morris: He was too "aristocratic" and talked like a "boy scout." As late as June, when he was asked if he intended to run, Morris glanced nervously in the direction of the mayor and, lacking any signal, delivered the kind of stiff-lipped response that forecast his political fortunes: "My mind," he confessed, "has not crystallized on that." McGoldrick had made his own decisions and went out to try to build a political base. La Guardia should have backed McGoldrick, who was a superior candidate to Morris, but he could not tolerate his independence. He took McGoldrick's interest in higher office as a personal affront and retaliated by scaring off any support for the professorial reformer. "La Guardia will knock McGoldrick's head off if we nominate him for mayor," said one fusionist.[94]

Meanwhile, the two parties went about their business of nominating his successor without reference to La Guardia, glad that he was out of the picture. The

Democrats nominated William O'Dwyer again, and the Republicans raided the opposition for a "fusion" candidate, nominating a loyal machine Democrat, Judge Jonah J. Goldstein. The ALP fell in behind O'Dwyer, while its anti-Communist wing, reconstituted as the Liberal party, backed Goldstein. Burlingham thought that La Guardia's proper role in the campaign was to support "the anti-Democratic ticket, whatever it is," but Fiorello would not be pinned down, issuing Delphic proclamations that "I will support only an honorable man."[95]

It took La Guardia until August to decide that this meant Newbold Morris on a new political ticket. To many fusionists this was another of the mayor's splenetic little games, toward no constructive purpose. The Citizens Union berated this "irrational and solitary caprice" in trying to bury fusion now that it could no longer serve his purposes. Even friends suggested that La Guardia was supporting Morris in order to split fusion and return the Democrats with their racketeers and tin boxes, to place his own three terms in lustrous relief, and to ensure the historical justification that he craved.[96]

Morris liked to think that La Guardia "put his whole heart and soul into the fight," but the fact is that his heart and soul were tired. Aside from saddling the new party with its inelegant "No Deal Party" label and making several speeches, La Guardia did not do much. He had little respect for quixotic campaigns, and there was none more doomed than this one, which lacked money, organization, and a strong candidate.[97]

The election generated little excitement. Registration fell to the lowest level since Walker's days, and in a sad commentary about the short life of the La Guardia legacy, New York was turned over to William O'Dwyer, the man he had compared unfavorably to a cabbage, a representative of the party that La Guardia had repeatedly tarred with charges of corruption and dishonesty. There hovered about O'Dwyer dismaying charges that despite his career as a cop, judge, lawyer, and DA, he seemed intent on ignoring mob kingpins Albert Anastasia and Joe Adonis, at least professionally. As Brooklyn DA he had appointed James Moran to be chief clerk of his office, despite Moran's connection with underworld figures. There were other troubling shadows: the disappearance of certain records damaging to Albert Anastasia that a police sergeant swore were removed on Moran's orders; the mysterious death of Abe (Kid Twist) Reles, who plunged to his death out of a sixth-story window while being held under O'Dwyer's protective custody, thereby quashing a "perfect murder case" against Anastasia. O'Dwyer's preelection visit to Frank Costello's apartment and the subsequent involvement of the Mafia boss in soliciting funds for O'Dwyer's campaign were equally disturbing.

Withal, the Democrat was elected by a 700,000-vote plurality, the largest margin of victory in New York history to that time, sweeping in with him a Democratic comptroller, City Council president, and four borough presidents.[98]

Fusion fell on its face in this election and reformers blamed La Guardia. They thought he should have groomed a successor and built a party around his principles.

Rexford Tugwell argued that "La Guardia should have . . . concentrated on building a machine in opposition to the bosses." But there was no party of the bosses. That was a campaign device for La Guardia to use against opponents to dramatize his politics of integrity. The big bad bogeymen were always one election away from extermination when he ran. Even in 1945 he would say: "Four more years of nonpolitical, nonpartisan, honest efficient municipal government will destroy political control of this city forever. . . . Political bosses cannot survive on decency, honesty. . . ." But apparently they had survived three terms of his own leadership![99]

If Emerson divided politics into a party of the past and a party of the future, Democrats and Republicans did not. Both had a good part of the past and a bit of the future in their platforms, and then for the rest it came to individual candidates. Politics had become more and less than parties. The automatic assumptions of the past, with their knee-jerk loyalties, were going the way of the horse and buggy. The bosses of the 1940s were not the bosses of the 1930s, much less were they the same Tammany group.

As for the notion of a political leader choosing a successor, it is as misleading as it is interesting. "In a democracy," La Guardia once said, "a public official cannot designate his crown prince." One would have to search long for a powerful American leader who groomed a successor, other than a family member, as in the case of the Longs or the Kennedys. Preparing a successor requires passing power to others, and powerful leaders do not like to do that while they still are in power.

There were capable reformers who could have developed into strong political figures, but rather than build them up, La Guardia resented them. He was more worried about having a successor too soon than about having a proper one after he retired. FDR did not groom a successor either. He did not even keep one vice president for more than a single term, and he so little trusted the man who finally did take over that Truman did not know the status of atomic bomb research in the United States. When Nelson Rockefeller left the office of governor of the State of New York after a long tenure as a powerful chief executive, he turned the office over to little-known and less-remembered Malcolm Wilson. Richard Daley, perhaps the most powerful machine mayor in recent times, did not leave behind anyone of comparable power in Chicago, and La Guardia did not even love politics, much less respect it. He constantly degraded it as a profession and did not want his children to get involved in it. He saw that the one party to which he did give his commitment, the ALP, tore itself apart in factional jealousies and personality clashes.[100]

It was folly to think that La Guardian reform could be made permanent. With victory in the war and returning prosperity, with the cold war mentality and the fears that led to HUAC excesses, with the mood of Taft-Hartley replacing that of Norris-La Guardia, with the rise of a new conservativism, the era of insurgency and underdog politics was passing. His strident political voice was as out of place as it was in the twenties when Jimmy Walker owned New York.

Does fusion have any meaning beyond a temporary coalition of the disaffected? Fusion governments are a piece of many parts, a combination of political and civic groups pressed together by the starkest of necessities, the fear that they will all go sinking in the same leaky boat unless they find a good patch. By their exigent nature they are held together by the most transient of bonds, the emergency of the instant. They lack cohesion, discipline, and organization, attempting to substitute for these with principles drawn thin by the nature of coalition government. La Guardia himself was ambivalent about a permanent Fusion party. On the one hand, he thought that a government could be drawn together from nonpolitical experts. On the other, he knew better than anyone the cunning alignments that kept a party in power. Many times he said that he could not work with starry-eyed reformers who had no sense of power. He needed realists who reached for ideals. He needed people with one foot firmly planted on the ground and the other stepping off for the sky. What did fusion have to do with that beyond bringing together good-government forces, outsiders, political puritans, and partisan anti-Democrats to throw out the rascals?

La Guardia had lent cohesion to the fusion effort by hitching it to his own progressive reform agenda, but he left no party legacy, no structure, no institutional fusion or urban reform movement. It had been a great flashing star that tore across the firmament for its moment. It shone so because the sky was so dark, and because it had an enormous energy and a huge tail of followers, but it was a product of time and place. Depression had made Americans a nation of underdogs, and for that brief instant the round, outspoken, gritty, and intensely proud mayor perfectly reflected their needs and demands in a pragmatic reformism. After the moment passed, it left behind the legacy of a modern city but effected little permanent structural change in elective politics. Fifteen years after La Guardia had left office, Robert Wagner was still making votes out of fighting the bosses.

5. Farewell

FH refused to fade out of power quietly. Before leaving office he announced plans for a World Trade Center where buyers from all over the world would do business. To a correspondent who chided him for his imperial attitude he wrote back, "Just give me a chance won't you?—A young fellow trying to make good. The first 40 years in office, you know are the hardest." He still filled his days to the brim and snapped off decisions with a confident crackle.[101]

His car radio still honed in on all disaster news, and likely as not the mayor would rush off to a fire or some other mishap to shout his directions. After all, it was still his city and these were his people in trouble. Who knew better than he how to help them? And there were some spectacular disasters. The most noteworthy occurred on a Saturday morning, July 29, 1945, when an army bomber, its field of vision obscured by a heavy fog, crashed into the Empire State Building, 900 feet above street level. The plane hung in dramatic suspension between the seventy-eighth and seventy-ninth floors as fire broke out all around. La Guardia rushed to the scene and climbed to the top floors to supervise the rescue operation. Only the fact that this was a weekend kept the list of casualties to thirteen.

He wrestled with the budget, although he knew that its ultimate fate would be in O'Dwyer's hands. Still at the watch, he refused to change his style just because he was going to leave in a few months. John Dos Passos made one of those ritual "Day With . . ." visits to city hall and found a still-energetic La Guardia bounding up the steps two at a time. Like other visiting journalists, Dos Passos was impressed with the three secretaries working simultaneously as the mayor dictated rapid-fire answers to correspondence. Determined to the end to keep telephone distractions to a minimum, Fiorello still refused to have a phone on his desk; the few calls that he took were answered in a separate cubicle away from his workplace. Officials were still dismissed in midsentence, after La Guardia heard enough of what they had to say and arrived at his conclusion about what to do next. The round of decisions, advice, plans, and meetings still amounted to a daunting display of helmsmanship. Individuals glided through for two- and three-minute spells, sandwiched between aides, city officials, and community representatives. Some were granted longer sessions, as much as ten minutes. The tone remained sharp, businesslike, and often suspicious: "Are you sure they are unemployable. . . . I want to save every cent I can, to be ready when the time comes"; or admonishing: "Be alert on this one won't you please"; or outright disbelieving: "Is this on the level"; or simply angry: "It's just an outrage to play politics with that. Cheap bastards."[102]

Before he retired there was a bit more heartbreak in some shabby treatment from the White House. To celebrate their liberation, French authorities in 1945 invited La Guardia to a postwar Bastille Day celebration along with leading municipal figures from around the world. La Guardia was pleased by the recognition. From his own government, which had not found a fit place for him in the war service, he now made only a modest request, that the purpose of his trip be filled out with an official role as a representative of the United States. Displaying a clumsy insensitivity, President Truman, who had helped frustrate La Guardia's hopes of overseas appointment before, laughed heartily when a reporter asked if La Guardia was going to get to go in uniform. No, said Truman, adding gratuitously that the mayor's trip would be in a strictly "personal capacity." Whether he feared that La Guardia would make some unauthorized statement or something else, Truman's denial of even this modest recognition was undeserved. The president's waspishness hurt Fiorello. "This private citizen La Guardia that they're talking about in Washington—I don't know what he is going to do, but La Guardia the Mayor, is staying right here in New York."[103]

But he could still stage an episode to disarm the hardest-hearted and demonstrate the deft touch that won him a special place in the hearts of his constituents.

To Fiorello La Guardia newspaper comic strips were a serious business. Former alderman Murray W. Stand learned that one day when he accompanied the mayor on a ride downtown. Stand was already frazzled, having been up all night in order not to miss the 6:00 A.M. appointment. He got into the car, where the mayor had spread out his newspapers, and uttered some remarks about the weather.

"Keep quiet!" barked Fiorello.

Stand waited a few minutes until the silence unnerved him and tried again.

"Damn it, didn't I tell you to keep quiet?" growled the mayor.

A few minutes later Stand again attempted to make some conversation. This time La Guardia slammed his papers to the floor and glaring at his companion said: "Will you keep quiet? I don't want any conversation until I'm all through with Dick Tracy, Little Orphan Annie and the Gumps. *Now* will you keep quiet?"[104]

It was natural then that the strips should figure in an episode for which perhaps more than anything else La Guardia would be remembered. Right in the midst of his pinky-wrestle with the president over traveling to Paris, a strike stopped the delivery of daily papers in New York, turning the mayor's thoughts to the melancholy impact on boys and girls who were denied their favorite comics. As His Honor later wrote to an appreciative parent, "I felt that the children should not be deprived of them due to a squabble among the adults." In shirtsleeves on a hot, humid Sunday in July, La Guardia, perspiration running down his forehead, was completing his broadcast from city hall when his voice turned soft and called gently to the children in his audience to "gather around and I will tell you about Dick Tracy today." There followed a breathless rendering of the detective's adventures, the mayor filling the role of each of the characters with appropriate voice and gestures. Then, over the air, he called out to WNYC program director Morris Novik, "Morris, every afternoon . . . I want a program . . . so long as the papers are not being delivered, of the funnies for the children."[105]

The next week, with five newsreel cameras grinding away, La Guardia pulled out the comics, again offering an inspired reading of Detective Tracy's adventures. Delivering his lines with gusto, La Guardia improvised his own moral for his listeners. The $50,000 mentioned in the comic strip he said, was "dirty money," and dirty money brought nothing but woe and disgrace to its possesors. Forty years later, fifty- and sixty-year-old New Yorkers get a glint in their eye recalling La Guardia. "He was a great mayor. He read the comics on the air. He was special."[106]

But a goodly number of New Yorkers found themselves agreeing with the message and rejecting the medium. "I agree with almost all of your Sunday talks," wrote one citizen, "[but] your attitude to put it mildly, rubs me the wrong way. I . . . [am] tempted to tell you to go to the Devil. . . . You were elected Mayor not divinely appointed." There was more than a little truth in the criticism. Until his last days as mayor, the unfortunate habit of assigning the worst motives to those who disagreed with him continued to yield ugly episodes of petty vindictiveness.[107]

When Frank E. Karelsen, a respected attorney, resigned as chairman of the Board of Education's Committee on Human Relations, he leveled a parting blast charging school officials with "administrative bankruptcy" and indicting the system for overcrowded, disorderly, and "chaotic" conditions. La Guardia himself had made many of the same criticisms, but he refused to take it from others, especially as he prepared to tidy up his record for the history books. In a late October Sunday broadcast he hit back, running Karelsen over with a steamroller of innuendo. Then he asked the new investigations commissioner, Louis Yavner, to probe Karelsen's connection to "the boys on the inside." Fifteen members of the city investigative staff worked day and night for six weeks to learn all they could about this man who had the temerity to criticize the school system. Seventy witnesses were examined, more than 1500 pages of testimony were assembled, and more than 3000 pages of records studied. "My job was really to destroy Karelsen," recalls a former investigator, "and I set out to do it." The report concluded that "frictions, factions, falsehoods, prejudices, jealousies and spites, clashes of issues and personalities, charges and countercharges, plots and counterplots" characterized Karelsen's leadership of the committee. Karelsen's own charges were dismissed as "largely a series of demagogic phrases and political catchwords."[108]

La Guardia's continued excesses hinted at how dangerous he could be. Fortunately, most of the time he did not allow himself this sort of joyride on an opponent's reputation. Despite the strongest tendencies toward abuse of power, he limited himself generally to its proper use for the benefit of those who needed it. It was perhaps his greatest unsung personal accomplishment, but it was getting away from him. More than anyone supposed, the Karelsen case showed why it was time for a change.

———

While he joked about his impending unemployment and broadcast an appeal to his good friends in the real estate business to help him find a home in the Riverdale section of the Bronx, it was soon clear that La Guardia was going to be quite busy once he left city hall. First there was talk again of an overseas appointment, as ambassador to Italy perhaps, or as head of United Nations Relief activities there. There were rumors of a position with the Conference of Mayors, maybe a run for the Senate, or for the House—"I honestly do feel that my forty years experience in public office has given me something that I could contribute as a Representative in Congress," he wrote to Edward R. Welks, dean of St. Paul's Cathedral.[109]

In the meantime, he made sure there was bread on the family table, negotiating a book contract, writing Lynn Carrick of Lippincott's, "The offer I have from Doubleday is much better . . . and . . . Alfred Knopf says he has a priority." But when the other offers did not pan out he wrote again: "I saw a couple of agents. They all make me tired. You wrote me. I wrote you. We met. We talked. You made a definite offer." A deal was struck: a $10,000 advance, and the assistance of two researchers as well as a writer, M. R. Werner.[110]

But it was his radio shows and newspaper punditry that promised to make La Guardia comfortable in his old age. He signed a contract for more than $50,000 a year to broadcast a local program on Sunday afternoons. *Liberty* magazine bought another program to be beamed to some 200 stations over the ABC network for $2500 a week. The afternoon daily *P.M.* took Fiorello on as a columnist, and the Sachs Furniture Company asked La Guardia to write a feature, titled "Under the Hat," on news issues that would be inserted in the company's regular newspaper advertising. In all of these contracts Fiorello insisted that he be uncensored and allowed to speak about any topic that caught his attention. He hired a staff of six to help him with his "thinking, writing, and talking" and rented office space at 30 Rockefeller Center.[111]

Louis Yavner walked into city hall late the night before La Guardia's last day in office to gather up some of his belongings, and he found La Guardia there alone typing letters. It led him to ponder the ironies of power. It comes in with a host of fellow travelers, it fades away in isolation. The mayor was alone, quietly undergoing the transformation from the most powerful man in the city to a private citizen.

The time for the final broadcast came, and with a clean desk before him for the first time in twelve years, La Guardia vowed that he would avoid hostile comments. He summed up his own accomplishment over the three terms of office by saying proudly that under his administration "the City government has acquired a soul." And he had a last word for those men who could not keep their minds off the ponies: "Put $2 on the wife, $2 on the oldest boy and $2 on the little girl. I guarantee you will win. . . . Go out and buy something. . . . You will make them happy. That is the way to wean yourself of this terrible, terrible habit." To a boy who sent in 18 cents to cover the cost of a light bulb that he had filched from a park lamp and signed his letter a "City Ruffian," he said: "Don't call yourself a ruffian again. You are a good boy." He closed his broadcast with a poem that included the line "Give me the power to labor for mankind."[112]

He wrote letters to families of those officials who had died while in office, and he sent recordings of their speeches along with his personal words of gratitude.

Then he walked down the long stairway from city hall to the street. Harry, the city hall peddler who in fair weather and foul would stand in front of the city hall to greet the mayor as he stepped from his car, came forward to say "Goodbye. I hope I'll be seeing you again." Almost inaudibly Fiorello replied, "I'll be around."[113]

CHAPTER 16

A Fighter Again

1. A Faded Hope

IN January 1946 President Truman sent La Guardia to Brazil as a special emissary. The Little Flower dazzled the Latin Americans with his big hats, down-to-earth speeches, and broad gestures of friendship. After he returned to New York he settled into a new office with a full schedule of writing and broadcasting. For the first time in his life he was making a very handsome living. "Fear not those radicals who make good money," quipped the *New York Times*.[1]

It did not take La Guardia long to offend in his new profession. His first column for *P.M.* attacked the curmudgeonly conservative publisher of the *Daily News*, Joseph Medill Patterson, as a mean, bigoted hater bent on stirring prejudices, who "would gleefully [have] been singing *Deutschland Über Alles*" had the United States not gone to war. Within a few weeks several newspapers were refusing to carry his Sachs pieces for fear of libel suits. He responded in proven La Guardia fashion. "I am not writing news. I am giving my opinion, and I am going to nail every lie wherever I see it. Get me?"[2]

After a few more weeks *Liberty* magazine, the sponsor of his network broadcast, canceled his contract over his blasting one powerful interest after another, many of whom were valued advertisers. He seemed bent even more than before on proving that he could still discomfit the interests while drawing a rich man's salary. "I have lost my 'Liberty,'" snapped La Guardia, "but I retain my soul."[3]

And then he was offered a job equal to his ambitions, to feed the world's hungry and help rebuild the devastated regions of war-torn Europe. As early as January 1943 La Guardia had spoken of America's need to plan not only for her own return to a normal peacetime economy but also for the displaced survivors who would be crowding Europe's devastated streets. "The moment that firing ceases

579

we will have a great deal to do in getting food and medical supplies to millions and millions of people. We must all contribute. . . . We must see that millions of little children get as much of their childhood as is humanly possible. . . . We must provide for these children at once in all countries, even in the countries of our enemies."[4]

The situation following the war was desperate. War-torn areas were overrun by stateless people for whom no one claimed responsibility. Poland, Hungary, Greece, Italy, Austria, and Yugoslavia were skirting famine and widespread disaster. Political and economic dislocation threatened the entire continent. It was a Europe that Winston Churchill later described as a "rubble heap, a charnel house, a breeding ground of pestilence and hate," with millions of distressed folk seeking food, clothing, and shelter.

In March of 1946, as a private citizen, La Guardia appealed on his radio program for Americans to cut back on their own consumption to aid the starving millions of Europe and the Far East. No private charity could accomplish this emergency relief effort; it was the responsibility of the United States government to gather food and distribute it to the needy around the world through the United Nations. "President Truman, you just have got to do it. Never mind the pressure groups. Cast the politicians on the water, but do it when the tide is going out, so that they will not find you later." He described the United Nations as a "tremendous influence for good, for right, for justice, for peace, along with world leadership. . . ."[5]

Three months after La Guardia's retirement from office, President Truman threw his challenge back at him by asking Fiorello to replace the heavily discouraged Herbert Lehman as director general of the United Nations Relief and Rehabilitation Administration. UNRRA's forty-eight nations were committed to the rehabilitation and reconstruction of invaded nations and to providing emergency food relief for millions of displaced persons. Each country that was not invaded during the war contributed 1 percent of its national income to a fund that eventually reached $4 million.

"I was just getting the office organized," Elsie Fisher, La Guardia's sister-in-law and office manager, recalls. The former mayor was settling into some comfortable earnings and the easy life of a pundit and commentator. UNRRA offered $15,000 a year, a long shot at the most intractable problems of the time, months of grueling fifteen-hour days traveling through the most devastated regions on the globe, and a firsthand look at the world's weakened, wasted, and dispirited. Miss Fisher, fearing the worst, turned to her brother-in-law: "You're not going to take it, are you?"

"He said 'No.' "

She knew better. "Of course he was going to take it."

He had grown old on fourteen- to eighteen-hour days, wrestling with the significant political issues of his day, and now he was being offered the chance to do important work again. Of course he was going to do it. He took the post, turned back the salary, and flew to Washington. Substituting world hunger for Tammany, he had a new enemy at which to tilt. The challenge of feeding the homeless and shaping an enduring peace with international generosity absorbed him as no $150,000 salary could. (Besides he would do the writing and radio broadcasting too!) He had fought, worked, and lived abroad. He knew the terrain, and his sympathies were broad enough to take in all of the people who needed help. He was off to command his "army of mercy" in feeding the world![6]

He took off immediately for the midwest to ask American farmers to open their granaries. "We can plant wheat every year, but people . . . starving die only once." He told the farmers that peace was costly, "but it creates; it protects. A war is greater in its cost, but it destroys; it devastates. I won't be here again, but those suffering people will be here again, if you do not do your job. . . ."[7]

Herbert Lehman later confided that La Guardia's UNRRA appointment made him apprehensive. He thought that the ambition-fired Flower was too political, too connected, to stand up to the cold warriors of the State Department who wanted to make UNRRA an arm of American foreign policy. La Guardia had wanted to be Roosevelt's general; now he would serve as Truman's quartermaster, feeding nations onto our side against Russia.[8]

He was wrong.

The misery that La Guardia confronted in the ruined European villages and cities that he had known as a teen overwhelmed him. "I thought I had seen some pretty hard and difficult situations but there is nothing I have been through . . . where so many people were facing death through starvation." He could not view the world from the vantage point of Foggy Bottom after seeing it through the eyes of the miserable villagers and bombing victims, the displaced persons and the concentration camp survivors. The suffering engaged him more than the politics.[9]

Accompanied by his old sidekick Frank "Cheech" Giordano, he toured the war-torn regions of Egypt, Yugoslavia, Poland, Russia, Italy, Greece, Germany, and Austria, making quick judgments about food allocations, walking among the people, becoming familiar with their suffering, and feeling their pain. His long days did not end until he made his reports and ordered food and supplies for the regions he had inspected. Streets were named for him, he claimed awards by the armful, and in Seoul, Korea, the first child born in a displaced persons camp was named Lee Mi Wah, Little Flower. In Italy he was welcomed on a sunny July day by a tumultuous crowd gathered in his honor. Later, as he toured an orphans home, he was given a collection of children's art and essays, one of which was titled "à Fiorello La Guardia Nostro Amato Protettore (our Beloved Protector)." In the Villagio de Fanciullo in Rome he visited the "shoeshine boys," street urchins who had survived the war by scraping through on petty thievery, begging, and digging through street scraps. These young survivors claimed a special place in his heart. To support a number of similar homes for these "dead end kids," La Guardia and several American journalists pledged the reprint rights from their newspaper columns to a special assistance fund.[10]

La Guardia's trip to Morocco quite simply startled him. The poor were *so* poor, while the rich exploited them mercilessly. From Egypt he wrote, "I HAVE NEVER SEEN SUCH ABJECT POVERTY ALONGSIDE OF SUCH OSTENTATIOUS SPLENDOR EASY LIVING AND WEALTH." In Greece a man gave young Eric La Guardia, who accompanied his father for part of the trip, 100 billion drachmas. Fiorello thought this too generous until he learned it was all worth less than 2 cents. Inflation was destroying Europe's economic base, causing massive hardship throughout the continent.[11]

Then he came to Germany. Most Americans were just now learning the extent of German barbarism during the war from survivor and journalist accounts, and the United States adopted a policy of limiting Germany's industrial output and dividing her into separate occupation zones. But La Guardia discovered the State Department and the army quietly carrying out a lenient and rapid rehabilitation and merging the military sectors, casting Germany in the role of defender of Western Europe against Stalinist expansionism. In the shadow of the death camps, Germany was being dressed up into a proper ally. General Lucius Clay, commander of the American Occupation Zone in Germany, was assigning Germans to administrative duties, even in the Jewish quarters. "In the event of another war," General Clay asserted with no trace of irony, "the Germans would probably be the only Continental peoples upon whom we could rely." He echoed the sympathies of his colleague, General George Patton, who had said earlier that "the only decent people left in Europe were the Germans."[12]

This facile rehabilitation of the immediate past enemy outraged La Guardia. He could not trust the Nazi generation that had made war on the world and carried out its own racial extermination policies. "Not even a toy pistol should be permitted to be owned or seen by any supporter of the former Nazi government." To offset Russia with Nazis, he wrote, represented a medicine far worse than the disease. "I notice an inclination on the part of some . . . to have great sympathy for these rascals . . . and also to absorb . . . the attitude toward the very people that these brutes oppressed." The millions of deaths and awful destruction must not be forgotten, and they belonged on Germany's account. "Now you will understand," La Guardia said, at the end of his piece on Germany, "why some of the countries in Eastern Europe," are so insistent on security.[13]

Encountering the all too plain evidence of mass murder, he called it the "blackest page in all history. . . . I cannot help but think what a great contribution the people of this country might have made to civilization, to humanity and to the world. Instead they have brought ruin and devastation." He concluded: "It would be unsafe . . . to accept this nation among peace-loving nations for many many years to come. The mistake of 1919 must not be repeated." Tolerance would be better used toward our past allies than toward our recent enemies.

"Say what you will about denazification, this generation in Germany is of the ilk, of the same blood, of the same mentality. They were part of it. . . . They do not seem to regret the misery and ruin they created. . . . Had they won there would have been no mercy. I cannot help talking feelingly on the subject. I visited the places of destruction. . . . I have visited Lidice [a town in Czechoslovakia where the entire male population was murdered, the children taken and distributed to Nazi families, the women shipped to death camps, and the town razed]. . . . Every blade of grass seems to cry to heaven in protest." He also visited Poland, where the devastation stunned him even more."[14]

La Guardia paid particular attention to the Jewish survivors. Approximately 850,000 homeless refugees, "the most pathetic and difficult problem facing the world today," were wandering among those who had murdered their friends and families. Regarding these people there had been too many resolutions with confounding "whereas"es and elegantly worded debates that all added up to excuses for inaction. But if he found the politicians mealy-mouthed and insensitive, he judged the military administration of the displaced persons camps criminal. Others had already reported on the strange affinity between the military occupiers and the former Nazi population, but La Guardia was astounded by what the military was doing. "I think it is simply outrageous," he complained to General Joseph T. McNarney, commanding general of the American sector of occupied Germany, "to have armed Germans police in the immediate neighborhood of D.P. camps, occupied by persecuted Jews." The day before, La Guardia wrote General McNarney, one of these Aryan police brutally slaughtered an "unarmed defenseless Jew." Conducting his own investigation, La Guardia learned that American forces had covered up for the German and spirited him out of the region to spare him the justice he deserved. He would tolerate none of this. When a British lieutenant general assigned to UNRRA disregarded warnings about anti-Jewish statements and ridiculed the testimony of Jewish escapees from Poland about terrifying pogroms, La Guardia removed him immediately.[15]

The real solution, La Guardia insisted, was to accept responsibility for these displaced populations and for the United States to bring its share of perhaps 150,000 refugees into the country. "They have a right to live. Here we have an opportunity to demonstrate that finally a wicked world has learned the lesson. . . ."[16]

La Guardia was back to the old fight with Americans of pinched vision, advocating the cause of the displaced and the wounded. National boundaries, whether geographic or ideological, were pushed aside to clear the path for UNRRA assistance. He proposed international arrangements to move surplus materials and workers across national borders. "I am not a diplomat," La Guardia had warned upon accepting the UNRRA post, "so from this point on protocol is off." International free enterprise he attacked as outdated and ineffective in the face of massive global need. The grain exchanges where speculators played the market on food especially attracted his ire. "If you do what is needed," he said to President Truman, "You *will* interfere and will put every dabbling grain exchange out of business. . . ." Reading these words today, one might conclude a bit too much; La Guardia had nothing against free enterprise, except for the suffering that he saw.[17]

Professional diplomats had argued for tying aid to a compatible foreign policy, but La Guardia rejected "food diplomacy" as an ineffective way to buy friends and pressure enemies. As La Guardia traveled the camps and disaster regions, he met with leaders in each of the countries he visited who invariably expressed their admiration for him and for the United States, while making their best pitch for UNRRA assistance. The poverty and obvious suffering that he saw swept all skepticism aside, disposing him to generous assistance. He accepted what he was told, often uncritically. In Czechoslovakia, Poland, and Russia he reported ("I have been told by the highest officials . . .") finding significant progress and amity toward the United States. In the midst of such suffering he wanted to believe the best, and he did, whether it was that free and open elections would be held in Poland, or that no foreign influence was felt in Czechoslovakia, or that the Russian economy was "clicking" in Byelorussia. The tough, calculating La Guardia of New York politics became a trusting crusader for nonpolitical foreign aid, insisting that Americans heed the imperious call of a stricken humanity and provide food without calculating political balances.[18]

Critics cried that he had grown muddleheaded with his plans for a "worldwide WPA" and a global boondoggle. But La Guardia reminded his countrymen that America had been revolutionary once too, and it had given the established monarchies the jitters; "we were spunky." La Guardia refused to join the cold warriors. He had a certain affinity for collective farming, for planned economies, and for government-directed progress. Nor would he dismiss out of hand the possibility that communism might be of value to impoverished Eastern Europeans. He criticized the knee-jerk opposition to anything faintly Red. Better to accept the idea of a sophisticated pluralist world where Russians could be Communist, England could have a king, and the United States could elect politicians from Tammany. "We must not, and we must not permit others to gang up against Russia. . . ."[19]

He rejected Winston Churchill's coded call for a "concert of English speaking peoples" as a dangerously parochial return to the old politics of power blocs and alliances. "We have had enough of that. . . . Let us stop talking cynically about the next war and think sincerely about future peace," and he asked Americans to heed Franklin Roosevelt's plan for an international relief effort instead of a unilateral American program. With liberals like Henry A. Wallace he shared the willingness to trust Russia enough to meet in mutually respectful negotiation. Those who insisted on "talk[ing] tough," he warned, were dividing the world prematurely, before peace had been given its chance.[20]

In July of 1946 Secretary of Commerce Henry Wallace handed President Truman a memorandum outlining the recent provocative steps that the administration had taken: a $13 billion allocation for a peacetime army and navy, atomic weapons testing on Bikini Island and continued production of A-bombs, the placing of heavy weaponry in Latin America, continued production of fighter bombers, and the equipping of air bases around the world. "How would it look to us if Russia had the atomic bomb and we did not, if Russia had ten thousand-mile bombers and air bases within a thousand miles of our coast lines and we did not?" Wallace warned that a policy aiming for superior force would trigger a race for weaponry. Such a race for deterrence was itself the largest danger. He called instead for a gamble on Russian goodwill. For his efforts the commerce secretary's resignation was accepted.[21]

La Guardia's reaction reflected his own sadness at the fading hope for enduring peace. He called the controversial Wallace a "casualty of peace. The target of every hatred. A true Christian whose bruised cheeks will never heal. A man who knows how to love, but refuses to learn to hate. Just a humble little man who has lived the Sermon on the Mount—bigger than any man in his Party."[22]

The State Department had never accepted UNRRA's underlying assumption of plain humanitarian aid with no strings, and as the Soviets spread their sphere of influence through Eastern Europe, the United States responded with a broad policy of global containment, linking foreign aid—both military and food relief—to strategic goals. As international tensions mounted, UNRRA came under intense American fire for distributing much of its relief aid to Soviet bloc nations who, critics charged, squirreled away their own funds to build armies while throwing their starving populations on the international dole. It was not merely that UNRRA was off on some idealistic binge, Undersecretary of State Dean Acheson explained; it was rather that UNRRA assistance was saving the Red governments of Europe from the consequences of their antidemocratic policies:

> The governments of countries loudest in their demand for relief have preferred to carry out a political and economic revolution at the risk of starving their own people. Instead of centering their efforts on recovery and reconstruction . . . they have impaired the production of Europe's agricultural surplus areas. . . . [Through] nationalization, economic control and currency inflation, coupled with a liquidation of the former managerial class . . . they have produced mass unemployment, black markets and hoarding by the peasants of what little they produce.[23]

La Guardia responded by attacking the emerging "Truman Doctrine" for transforming aid into a political weapon. "You can't go to them with a piece of bread in one hand and a ballot in the other," he cried. "It is reminiscent," he told a United Nations Assembly in November, "of the old days of politics . . . in my town, when the poor in the district were given a basket of food on Christmas and during the winter a bag of coal or two,'' and then ordered to vote the ticket. He told Louis Adamic that he was afraid of where this would lead. ''Where can it get us? Another war? Doesn't make sense.'' You cannot run international relations with the heart of a pawnbroker, he cried, bargaining for allies while the surviving masses ''die second deaths''[24]

He was an American patriot who willingly would have fought on the battlefield for his country, but now he stood before the world organization and defied his president, criticizing his nation for being stingy, narrow-minded, and wrong. Through personal pleas, in confidential letters, and over the radio, he tried to compel an understanding that without trust the next decade would be an international hell. As UN delegates met in Lake Success, New York, to decide UNRRA's fate, La Guardia moved his offices from Washington to wage a last battle to extend UNRRA's life beyond its expiration date of December 1946. But the hope quickly faded as Americans adopted an aggressive anti-Soviet policy. The *New York Daily News* criticized UNRRA as ''the greatest single scandal ever perpetrated in the name of the American people.'' Americans, declared the newspaper, were tired of following the pipe dreams of ''world savers'' and La Guardia types who were lending aid and comfort to the enemy. The State Department too saw a world divided between ''us'' and ''them,'' with La Guardia on the wrong side.''[25]

''That is the old fashioned imperialist way,'' stormed La Guardia. If we wanted ''to lick communism,'' do it by ''making democracy work, by proving to the world that people can live properly and decently.'' But his point of view was quickly disappearing. Even La Guardia could not explain to the satisfaction of the American people why they should contribute 72 percent of UNRRA's budget and see the bulk of its aid going to pro-Soviet governments. He could thunder that ''bread diplomacy'' was ''plain ordinary old time power politics that has produced war after war,'' but he failed to persuade them in a conflicted world to place their faith in Russia's good intentions. And he could not explain to them why the United States should unilaterally foreswear the use of a powerful weapon like foreign aid when the Soviet Union would not agree to international on-site atomic inspection to prevent the spread of nuclear weapons. When two army C-47s were gunned down over Yugoslavia in the summer, critics raged that through UNRRA Americans had paid the bulk of Tito's $500 million food relief bill and this was what it had bought them.[26]

In the end he was back to fighting against his times. While statesmen spoke of descending iron curtains and presidents adopted policies of containment, he pleaded for ''One World'' and a moral foreign policy based on a willingness to understand and cooperate. But as the two major powers pulled apart, La Guardia's dream to feed, clothe, and assist the tens of millions of needy for the humanitarian good of it was shattered. He tried to keep UNRRA alive, but Americans were tired of what they perceived as one-sided gestures.[27]

He fulfilled the predictions of those who had both opposed and supported his appointment: He recognized no master when it came to the public interest but his soul. But that soul was weary, and the defeat of his herculean efforts took its toll. He gave up the office to allow another to preside over the liquidation of UNRRA, announcing that "the need still continues."

The bitter spectacle of UNRRA's defeat seemed to age La Guardia much beyond his years. He was haggard, tired, and weak. His cheeks sagged, his color was pallid, and his eyes looked hollow as he scolded that the abandonment of international principles "is wrong . . . morally wrong; it is wicked."[28]

———— —

On February 21, 1947, England informed the U.S. State Department that London could no longer afford to subsidize Greece, which had traditionally been a British client state, or to support Turkey. The situation in both countries was dire. In Greece, Communist-led guerillas were poised in the north to fight the monarchist forces. If Greece and Turkey fell, American officials were certain that other nations in the region would be undermined. President Truman asked Congress for $400 million to assist the embattled pair under a broad doctrine of responsibility for shielding non-Communist nations from leftist insurgencies.

Here, thundered La Guardia, was precisely what he had been warning about. The Greek government was a dictatorship headed by a king, and Turkey had played a treacherous game in the recent war, yet the new policy of containment was forcing the United States to cozy up to this odd couple of tyrannical regimes. If Russia was intervening, he pleaded, let the United Nations handle it. It had been created for just that purpose.[29]

A policy of foreign aid aimed at quelling the spread of Communist ideology, he warned, would embroil the United States all over the world, often on the wrong side, and at great cost. After Greece and Turkey absorbed billions, he predicted, the United States would find that it was holding a tiger by the tail, propping up corrupt police states against the will of the masses. "Training the Greek Army to shoot a few communists," he said bitterly, "will not solve the problems of Greece." And then when the Greeks stopped killing each other and came to their senses, both sides would resent America for the carnage and destruction that it had financed. Fighting communism no matter where it developed, he feared, was destined to be expensive, unpopular, and ultimately would "stimulate communism and not strangle it." The United States, he said, must not become the country of the past, when it had the resources and vision to be the country of the future. "This is 1947. We have had two world wars. . . . the good old days of dollar diplomacy and banana republics and exploitation by American capital in South American countries are over, and the quicker some of the big boys with money learn this, the better it will be for themselves as well as for the country."[30]

587

He feared also the effect of a reflexive anticommunism on the rights of Americans. He had lived through a Red scare after World War I and he knew how insidiously fear corrodes the tolerance of a people for their own liberties. All it took nowadays to kill some plan or idea, he complained, was to brand it Communist. "It is getting so now that a husband can divorce his wife if he charges that he found her in bed reading the *Daily Worker*." His outspoken opposition to the Red-baiters and cold warriors won for La Guardia a place on the Office of Army Intelligence and Security's "Subversive Annex."[31]

But few were listening to the old man. Increasingly he was dismissed as out of sorts, out of touch with the times. In the old days he could share his gripes with the president and his advisers. But the times were different now. And many were prepared to ignore his old shrill voice.

2. Incorruptible as the Sun

FIORELLO La Guardia's political career had been lifted high by a wave of national liberalism brought on by the Depression. During the twenties he had been a progressive at odds with the dominant conservatism of the times, a representative of East Harlem who had attended to the underside of American prosperity and triumphalism, speaking for the poor and the foreign-born when they were still a minority. So blistering were his attacks on the interests, insisting that laissez faire was an excuse for ignoring those least able to take care of themselves, that some labeled him a Socialist. While his rhetoric was radical, it supported no ideological program. His political stands were based on moral indignation against corruption, unfairness, and the optimism-drunk spirit of permanent prosperity. In Congress he was frozen off important committees for his irregularity, and at election time he was always looking for a party of convenience to run with. Ironically, by 1932, when his ideas did achieve some prominence as a result of economic catastrophe, he was buried in the New Deal landslide.

The story of his mayoralty is the story of a fundamentally altered America. Experiment, New Deals, and the progressive spirit of moderate reform that La Guardia so forcefully represented in the twenties became the conventional politics of the thirties, thrusting him into a leading role. Ascending to power in dispirited times, he refreshed the faith of the people in their political institutions while moving forward on a broad agenda that laid the foundations of the modern metropolis. Breaking Tammany's hold, making urban politics clean and challenging, La Guardia attracted to it some of the best men and women of his time; for the first time in a generation, individuals felt that the city could be changed for the better through their efforts. His breadth of character and his ability to balance a combustible righteousness with a keen political craft lifted urban politics to new levels of possibility. Max Weber thought that the art of politics was the "knowledge of influencing men . . . of holding in one's hands a nerve fiber of historically important events. . . ." By marshaling the forces of municipal government to address the transforming public issues of his times, La Guardia demonstrated the ability of politics to instruct, provide care, and fix a palpable sense of the common good. He made political integrity a civic habit, and by example he taught what dreams a committed honest leader could accomplish.[32]

La Guardia's leadership made so many uncomfortable because until the very end no one could say with certainty whether the ultimate goal was personal power or public service. In the best of politicians—or at least the most effective ones— these two aims, theoretically so distinct, are inseparably entwined: personal rule in the service of transcendent public purpose. Felix Frankfurter did not fail to criticize and even fear La Guardia, but in the end he thought that the Little Flower had "translated the complicated conduct of [New York] City's vast government into warm significance for every man, woman and child."[33]

La Guardia himself created the pat images of him that survive: the diminutive, barrel-shaped mayor pouring all of his feeling into a creative reading of "Dick Tracy" for the kids; the determined La Guardia smashing slot machines with a sledgehammer to rid his New York of tinhorns; the chief magistrate's bulky figure swathed in a fireman's raincoat directing firefighters at a dawn blaze. These and hundreds of similar images of La Guardia symbolize a style of personal government that pushed democratic power to the limits of its authority through charisma and skill. Political mastery requires imposing one's will and vision on a community, shaping its contradictory and opposed elements into a harmonious, peaceful, and effectively operating unit. Without this there is no leadership. But democratic leadership requires in addition the ability to communicate goals and convince the public of their desirability. It requires the ability to hold the devotion of the people. La Guardia's colorful language and theatricality allowed him to shape fresh perceptions: dramatic action with the intent of parable.

He cast away the old ideas of municipal government to meet the challenge of depression, pervasive political corruption, *and* modern times. Robert Moses, a man not given to easy praise, said about the man he sometimes referred to as that "dago bastard," "Only those who recall the cynicism of the late Twenties and early Thirties and remember how low the City's morale had fallen can gauge what this man did to lift us up and to attract to New York the lost respect of the nation." He brought experience and skills and toughness, achieving a degree of control over New York's complex urban machinery that remains unsurpassed.[34]

Before La Guardia, the metropolis was a congeries of antiquated boroughs;

a city haphazardly administered with parsimonious social and health services, no public housing, decaying parks, and inadequate bridges; a city in which it was said every department had its price and its contact person for graft. Under La Guardia the city built itself anew, throwing bridges over the waters and digging tunnels under them, erecting new reservoirs, sewer systems, parks, highways, schools, hospitals, health centers, swimming pools, and super air terminals. For the first time New York offered its poor public housing, its working class a unified transit system, and its artists and musicians special training and subsidies. The outdated charter of 1898 was replaced by a fresh compact that centralized municipal powers.

La Guardia came into office with an idea, and to an extent few would have dared imagine, he achieved it. He made New York a modern city, an honest city, a humane city, a city that got out from under the thumb of the state to develop its own relationship with Washington. He wanted New Yorkers to be happy (though sometimes he seemed more involved with making them good), to live with a sense of ease and security, to be rid of debt, to inhabit decent quarters and raise healthy children. Walter Lippmann once said that La Guardia took the human sympathy, which had been the abiding strength of Tammany, and infused it into the tradition of good government.[35]

La Guardia led not only New York City but all the other cities in the country in forging a new relationship with the federal government. As president of the United States Conference of Mayors from 1935 to 1945 he fashioned the lineaments of this new partnership. As mayor of New York, in great favor with the New Deal, he won for his city a richly disproportionate share of federal funds, while insisting on as much local autonomy as possible.

So comprehensively did he reform the city that his successors still address the agenda that he defined for them and continue to insist in their campaigns that they are the true heirs of a man who died more than forty years ago.

The rise of the modern city was not an unmixed blessing, and La Guardia's achievement was not without its serious shortcomings. New York's new infrastructure testified to its mayor's ability to bargain better than any other municipal leader in behalf of his city. But it was built in unusual times with federal funds. Before he even left office this cash had already stopped flowing as freely as it once had. Would New Yorkers be able to revert back to a smaller, less expensive government? He led a campaign to unify mass transit, but he failed to meet the challenge of the 5-cent fare, and he offered no solution to the problem of negotiating contracts with politically effective unions. La Guardia often burned the candle at both ends, extending government bureacracy at the same time that he demanded personal service to the citizens of the metropolis. His furious tirades against the bureaucrats obscured the fact, but a society growing ever more complex could not provide the benefits he planned without rational systems of mass service, without, in other words, depersonalized bureacracy. His power, cultivated over three terms and reinforced by his special relationship with the people and the remarkable extent to which he established an expectation of ruthless integrity, made it possible for him to press the bureaucrats into a rarely gifted municipal service (even La Guardia, however, could not handle the police). He had created a wonderful paradox: a huge expanding bureacracy with a furious, tireless, incorruptible human heart beating at its core. But when he left office he took that heart with him, and New York City lost the leader who kept whipping it on to higher achievement. After him this vast service factory lost its center, becoming a brittle, impersonal, municipal work force.

He did not understand the paradox, nor did he appreciate the element of leadership that requires planning not only for future roadways and parks but also for future mayors. Abetted by a crisis that disposed people to tolerate powerful leadership, he created an office that no other individual could fill. It was a mayoralty of a piece with its times, with the presidency of Franklin Roosevelt, with the quest for honest leadership to replace Tammany, with a population made pliant and liberal by widespread suffering and the crashing of economic icons.

Complex, endlessly fascinating, La Guardia was a fiercely ambitious man who aspired greatly, but his hunger for federal office led to his frustration and made him a deeply disappointed man. Yet his personality was so large and instinct for public service so powerful that he directed the Office of Civilian Defense, chaired the U.S.-Canadian Joint Permanent Defense Board, and furiously lobbied for a generalship, all while he was still mayor. And then he turned to the task of feeding the world's needy, while trying to stave off the cold war. That he failed in some of his goals and showed the frailties of powerful men is no surprise. That he refreshed his times with the conviction that the world could be changed, that he achieved so generous a portion of his personal hopes to lead an important life and make a vast difference in public affairs is the important theme.

But before he died Americans passed into another political cycle. And there he was fighting again. His political life was a massive consistency stretched out over as inconsistent a period in American life as it has passed through in its history.

———

Over the year since he left the mayoralty La Guardia had aged a great deal. Those who saw him early in 1947 saw a startlingly decayed man, grimmer, grayer, with a disturbingly hollow look. He was still practicing the soft art of communication, demanding attention to injustice. He continued to write, to speak on public issues, and to raise large sums of money for the causes he favored. But his health was failing. The magnificent spirit pushed forward; he remained involved in public issues, testifying before Congress, meeting with progressives, agonizing over the shape of foreign policy, proposing new ideas and fresh approaches.

His serious addresses were full of insight about the future problems of a changing society and a restless, ruthless demand for social justice. What the free market could not arrange he demanded that the government try to correct by placing the state between the individual and extreme hardship. It was the old La Guardia, but the sharp words were dulled by a growing pain and a spreading illness. He campaigned for a program of federal health insurance, a plan for dealing with technological unemployment, a national welfare system that would protect progressive localities like New York from being inundated by the nation's needy.

By the spring he was in and out of the hospital with abdominal pains. He would leave the hospital to fly out west to raise money for a favorite cause and return a few days later for more hospital observations and tests. Then he would check out for a few broadcasts. But he kept returning. He told his audience that the good doctors at Mt. Sinai hospital had punctured and probed and tested but so far they could only tell him what was not wrong with him. But "there's so much to be done in these days," he said, "and gosh I want to do it if I possibly can." He collected a bushel of awards and decorations from the nations that he had helped through UNRRA. The One World Committee selected him for its Around the World Award. But he was growing weaker, suffering "hellish pains."[36]

Dr. George Baehr told Fiorello that he had a stone blocking the pancreas and that he would lose a lot of weight before the stone would pass. It would take some time, and there would be pain, but surgery was too dangerous. La Guardia told his doctor that he would probably be dead before the cure worked. But there was no stone. He had cancer of the pancreas and it had spread.[37]

He plugged on with his autobiography, his column, and his radio broadcasts. He packed off Eric for a Texas summer, continued his campaign against the "big shots" and the cold warriors. On June 15 he told his listeners that he was "back in the repair shop. In all likelihood I will not be able to broadcast next week. I doubt very much I'll be able to even crawl to a microphone, but I'll keep you informed." And when he could not, he invited others to take the microphone in the sunroom of his home. He could hardly sit up, but he would still make suggestions for guests. Newbold Morris took over the airwaves one Sunday, and he was fifteen minutes into the program, which La Guardia was monitoring upstairs by a small radio near his bed, when he suddenly heard a thumping overhead followed by a thin voice crying, "Put more hell in it, Newbold, put more hell in it." When Robert Moses came up to Fiorello's Riverdale home, the old La Guardia nemesis "was shocked at the change in him. He was in bed so shrunken, so chapfallen and yet so spunky. . . . I felt like crying. It was a battle not even the most courageous fighter could win."[38]

La Guardia had never allowed such odds to scare him before. He kept up as best he could, writing officials with plans and advice and challenging their ideas. In July Adolf Berle came by for a visit. La Guardia still overflowed with plans and indignation. They talked of the need to mobilize progressive sentiment, a subject he pursued with Jack Kroll, director of the CIO's political action arm. "We must all get together," he wrote on September 9. "There is a deliberate and determined effort to revert back! The struggle is on. . . . I do so want to help in the big job ahead.''[39]

A few days later Newbold Morris drove up with Judge Learned Hand and his wife, who were Morris's in-laws. Morris rang at the door. There was no answer so he opened the door and went in. He heard groans coming from an upstairs room and went there. A shrunken La Guardia was curled up on a sofa.

''Is that you, Newbold?'' he called out in a trembling voice. ''What time is it?''

Morris told him.

''Oh my,'' he groaned. ''It's another fifteen minutes before I can take another shot of morphine.''

The pain was unbearable, and Morris turned to leave.

''Don't go,'' Fiorello pleaded.

Morris explained that his in-laws were outside.

''Bring them in.''

La Guardia braced himself and stood up to greet Judge and Mrs. Hand. With a smile on his face he stuck out his hand, exclaiming, ''I'm glad to meet an honest judge.'' He launched into a tirade about those who were burying the United Nations and the humanitarian ideal in international affairs. For fifteen minutes he spoke of the issues that were his life. Then he saluted the guests and nodded farewell.[40]

On September 16 La Guardia collapsed into a coma. Four days later the long, lonely fight was over. On September 20 at 7:22 A.M. the dynamic, greathearted little man with the explosive energy succumbed to pancreatic cancer. ''He was as incorruptible as the sun,'' President Harry Truman wrote in a telegram to Mrs. La Guardia. ''The greatest mayor in the history of New York is dead,'' mourned Samuel Seabury. ''A splendid product of our democracy,'' Secretary of State George Marshall called him, while Rabbi Stephen Wise described Fiorello as a ''builder of standards for urban government,'' passionately committed to making life ''better, finer, gladder for all . . . in his beloved city,'' and Harold Ickes said that ''no one in his generation did more for the underpriviledged or strove harder for justice and fair dealing.'' But it was the common people of the city whose plain tribute showed how much he had meant to them.[41]

On the following day, September 21, showgirls in stage makeup, workers with lunch pails, cabdrivers, mothers, barmaids, children, street cleaners, school-teachers, and transit workers, blacks, whites, Jews, and Christians, 45,000 in all, stood silently for hours to file past his coffin to offer a prayer, touch his lips, or simply say a private good-bye. An elderly man stopped for an extra second, sobbing a few words in Italian. A tailor recalled how Congressman La Guardia had intervened to bring his mother out of Russia. A Negro woman placed a single rose into the casket. It was a fitting reminder that to Fiorello La Guardia, political institutions were only worthwhile so long as they could be used to help the people.

The following day, after a service at the Cathedral of St. John the Divine, he was buried at Woodlawn Cemetery.

And when they opened his black box in the bank there was a total of $8000 dollars in war bonds; that and a mortgaged house in Riverdale and his political legacy was what he left behind.[42]

He had built modern New York, provided relief in heroic proportions, and clasped his city to Washington in a way that changed the history of American cities forever. He was honest. He cared. He knew no friend when the public interest was to be served. He set standards of integrity that few even dared to consider, and he gave New York City as good a government as it ever had.

Notes

Abbreviations

CCBP	Charles C. Burlingham Papers, Harvard University Law School Library
FDR	Franklin D. Roosevelt
FDRP	Franklin D. Roosevelt Papers, Franklin D. Roosevelt Presidential Library, Hyde Park, New York
FHL	Fiorello H. La Guardia
LAGA	Fiorello H. La Guardia Archives, Fiorello H. La Guardia Community College, Queens, New York
NYMA	New York City Municipal Archives, La Guardia Papers
NYPL	New York Public Library, La Guardia Papers

Unless otherwise stated, all newspapers cited are from New York City (e.g., *"Times"* is *New York Times*).

The New York Municipal Archives were in the process of reorganizing and microfilming the Fiorello H. La Guardia Mayoral Papers while the research for this book was in progress. Some boxes referred to in these notes—those numbered below 3114—will eventually be renumbered. Researchers wishing to determine the new location of these materials can do so by consulting the index available at the New York Municipal Archives.

Thousands of articles from New York City newspapers dealing with LaGuardia's terms in Congress and as mayor are conveniently collected in scrapbooks at the New York Municipal Archives. Because the scrapbooks do not indicate from what page an article was clipped, I have not been able to provide them for most of these notes, but all newspapers articles cited without page numbers can be found in chronological order in the FHL Scrapbooks or by consulting the *New York Times Index* for material from that newspaper.

Chapter 1

1. Watertown *Times*, November 18, 1933; September 20, 26, 1947; Scrapbooks, LAGA.

2. Lydio Tomasi, *The Italian American Family* (Staten Island, New York: Center for Migration Studies, 1972); Denis Mack-Smith, *A History of Sicily* (New York: Viking, 1968).

3. Arthur Mann, *La Guardia: A Fighter Against His Times, 1882–1933* (Philadelphia: J. B. Lippincott, 1959), 24–25.

4. Mann, *La Guardia*, 25.

5. Charlotte Adams, "Italian Life in New York," *Harper's Monthly* 62 (April 1881): 676–684.

6. FHL to Bruce Chapman, February 18, 1944, Box 2704, NYMA; *Times*, July 1, 1906; Caroline Ware, *Greenwich Village, 1920–1930: A Comment on American Civilization in the Post-War Years* (New York: Octagon, 1977), 9; John S. Billings, *Vital Statistics of New York City and Brooklyn for Six Years Ending May 31, 1890* (U.S. Census Office: 1890), 119–120; FHL's Birth Certificate, December 11, 1882, New York County Clerk Birth Records, NYMA.

7. John A. Garraty, *The American Nation* (Fifth edition, New York: Harper & Row, 1983), 521.

8. *Times*, December 12, 1882.

9. Jacob Riis, *How the Other Half Lives: Studies Among the Tenements of New York* (New York: Scribner, 1890), 18–19.

10. Lowell Limpus and Burr W. Leyson, *This Man La Guardia* (New York: E. P. Dutton, 1938), 22; Gemma La Guardia Gluck, *My Story* (New York: D. McKay Co., 1961), 3–20.

11. *A Brief History of the Eleventh U. S. Infantry* (Fort Benjamin Harrison, Indiana: 1926); Wayne Andrews, ed., *Autobiography of Theodore Roosevelt* (New York: Scribner, 1958), 58–59.

12. Gluck, *My Story*, 4–5.

13. FHL to Ralph Cooke, July 19, 1940, Box 2704, NYMA; Watertown *Times*, November 18, 1933. See also reprint of article of September 9, 1890, in Watertown *Times*, September 9, 1940, Box 2703, NYMA.

14. See Watertown *Times*, November 18, 1933, August 20, 1937, and clippings in Boxes 2703 and 2704, NYMA, and *Herald Tribune*, June 30, 1938. The Watertown *Times* reprinted stories dating from La Guardia's Sackett's Harbor days throughout the thirties.

15. Kitty Jo Parker Nelson, "Prescott: A Sketch of a Frontier Capital, 1863–1900," *Arizona* 4 (Winter 1963): 17–21; *Arizona: A State Guide* (New York: Hastings House, 1940), 18–24, 237.

16. *Arizona: A State Guide*, 236.

17. Limpus and Leyson, *La Guardia*, 19–20; *Times*, October 5, 1938; New York *Post*, "Lyons Den," September 22, 1947.

18. Lawrence Elliott, *Little Flower: The Life and Times of Fiorello La Guardia* (New York: Morrow, 1983), 30.

19. Gluck, *My Story*, 5; Mann, *La Guardia*, 27.

20. FHL, *The Making of an Insurgent, An Autobiography, 1882–1919* (Philadelphia: J. B. Lippincott, 1948), 20–21; Gluck, *My Story*, 8.

21. Photographs of the La Guardia family, LAGA; Gluck, *My Story*, 5.

22. Limpus and Leyson, *La Guardia*, 20.

23. Gluck, *My Story*, 3–4; Mann, *La Guardia*, 32.

24. Nelson, "Prescott," 17–36; FHL, *Autobiography*, 25.

25. Gluck, *My Story*, 13–14; Louis Rittenberg, "La Guardia Pays Tribute to His Mother," *American Hebrew and Jewish Tribune* (January 12, 1934): 183; M. R. Werner, "La Guardia" (unpublished manuscript, FDR Presidential Library, Hyde Park, n.d.), 2.

26. Charles Barnes, *The Longshoreman* (New York: 1915), 9; Humbert Nelli, *The Business of Crime* (New York: Oxford University Press, 1978), 70–85; FHL, *Autobiography*, 27–28.

27. FHL, *Autobiography*, 27.

28. Michael Gibson, *The American Indian: From Colonial Times to the Present* (New York: G. P. Putnam's Sons, 1974), 354.

29. Walter L. Williams, "United States Indian Policy and the Debate Over Philippine Annexation: Implications for the Origins of American Imperialism," *Journal of American History* 66 (1980): 812–813; WPA, *Arizona*, 30; Jay Wagoner, *Arizona Territory 1863–1912* (Tucson: University of Arizona Press, 1970), 125–126, 142, 144, 148–157 (see 154 for an example of a crooked agent); Werner, "La Guardia," 6.

30. FHL, *Autobiography*, 23.

31. FHL to A. E. Bacon, June 17, 1940, Box 2706, NYMA; FHL to FDR, April 20, 1940, Box 3757, NYMA.

32. Andrew F. Rolle, *The Immigrant Upraised: Italian Adventurers and Colonists in an Expanding America* (Norman: University of Oklahoma Press, 1968), 151, 155; Sidney Lens, *The Labor Wars* (Garden City, New Jersey: 1973), 38.

33. Mann, *La Guardia*, 31–32.

34. Mann, *La Guardia*, 30; FHL, *Autobiography*, 20.

35. Limpus and Leyson, *La Guardia*, 21.

36. *Times*, October 5, 1938; Watertown *Times*, November 18, 1933, August 20, 1937; Watertown *News*, May 16, 1944, Box 2704, NYMA.

37. Thomas G. Paterson et al., *American Foreign Policy* (second edition, Lexington, Massachusetts: D. C. Heath, 1983), volume I, 195–197.

38. Harold U. Faulkner, *Politics, Reform, and Expansion: 1890–1900* (New York: Harper & Row, 1959), 227–231; Phillip Knightley, *The First Casualty: From the Crimea to Vietnam: The War Correspondent as Hero, Propagandist, and Myth Maker* (New York: Harcourt Brace Jovanovich, 1975), 56.

39. John A. Garraty, *The American Nation*, (Fifth edition, New York: Harper & Row, 1983), 549; Paterson, *Foreign Policy*, I, 200–203. See Paterson's bibliography (p. 212) for works on the Spanish-American War.

40. Wagoner, *Arizona Territory*, 341–344; FHL, *Autobiography*, 31–32; Paterson, *Foreign Policy*, I, 203.

41. Gluck, *My Story*, 6–8; FHL to Major Henry W. Webb, February 15, 1944, Box 2704, NYMA; Mann, *La Guardia*, 32.

42. Garraty, *American Nation*, 551; Mann, *La Guardia*, 33; Elliott, *Little Flower*, 37; Werner, "La Guardia," 8–9.

43. Theodore Roosevelt, *Autobiography*, xi, 12, 44, 79–80; Elliott, *Little Flower*, 38; Wagoner, *Arizona Territory*, 345.

44. Roosevelt, *Autobiography*, 138; FHL, *Autobiography*, 33.

45. Mann, *La Guardia*, 33; Gluck, *My Story*, 8–9.

46. FHL, *Autobiography*, 34; William Manners, *Patience and Fortitude: Fiorello La Guardia* (New York: Harcourt Brace Jovanovich, 1976), 16–17.

47. Manners, *La Guardia*, 16–17; Mann, *La Guardia*, 36.

48. FHL, *Autobiography*, 37.

49. FHL, *Autobiography*, 45–53.

50. Mann, *La Guardia*, 35; Elliott, *Little Flower*, 42; Jay Franklin, *La Guardia: A Biography* (New York: Modern Age Books, 1937), 18–19.

51. FHL, *Autobiography*, 53–55.

52. FHL, *Autobiography*, 53–55; Byron Uhl to FHL, October 13, 1916, in FHL's Personnel File from the Bureau of Immigration and Naturalization, Record Group 85, file 7-2098, National Archives.

53. FHL, *Autobiography*, 58–60.

54. Mann, *La Guardia*, 34; FHL, *Autobiography*, 33.

55. Mann, *La Guardia*, 39–41.

56. Mann, *La Guardia*, 40–41.

57. FHL, *Autobiography*, 60; Gluck, *My Story*, 10–11; Mann, *La Guardia*, 41.

58. FHL to Sra. Lydia de La Guardia Bueno, May 26, 1943, Box 2704, NYMA.

59. Henry Adams, *The Education of Henry Adams*, Ernest Samuels, ed. (Boston: Houghton Mifflin, 1973), 499–500.

60. Theodore Dreiser, *The Color of a Great City* (New York: Boni and Liveright, 1923), 5–7; FHL, transcript of interview with M. R. Werner, February 13, 1947, p. 2, Box 2525, NYMA.

61. FHL, *Autobiography*, 30; Mann, *La Guardia*, 43–44.

62. FHL to Frederick C. Tanner, September 11, 1911, Tanner Collection, Columbia University; various records from FHL's personnel file, including his Personal Question Sheet, are in Bureau of Immigration and Naturalization, Record Group 35, File 7-2098, National Archives; Werner, Notes on FHL's Ellis Island Period, February 13, 1947, Box 2525, NYMA; FHL, *Autobiography*, 62–63.

63. FHL interview with M. R. Werner, February 13, 1947, p. 4, Box 2525, NYMA.

64. FHL interview with M. R. Werner, p. 5. Felix Frankfurter, *Fiorello La Guardia, Address on the Occasion of the Fiorello La Guardia Memorial Dedication Ceremony at the La Guardia Houses, Rutgers Place and Clinton Street, September 20, 1957* (n.p.: n.d. [pamphlet at LAGA]), 1.

65. FHL, *Autobiography*, 69; FHL interview with M. R. Werner, p. 6.

66. FHL, interview with M. R. Werner, p. 7; FHL, *Autobiography*, 70–71; Mann, *La Guardia*, 45.

67. FHL, *Autobiography*, 74.

68. FHL to Robert Watchorn, April 17, 1909; Efficiency Report, June 12, 1909; Watchorn to Daniel J. Keefe, April 19, 1909; Letter of Recommendation #13810, all from Bureau of Immigration and Naturalization, Record Group 35, File 7-2098, National Archives.

69. Mann, *La Guardia*, 46, 341; Limpus and Leyson, *La Guardia*, 28.

70. FHL interview with M. R. Werner, pp. 3–4; FHL, *Autobiography*, 77–80; FHL to William Williams, November 29, 1910, Record Group 35, File 7-2098, Bureau of Immigration and Naturalization.

71. Mann, *La Guardia*, 47.

72. Mann, *La Guardia*, 47–48; Eugene Canudo, interview with author, June 13, 1983.

73. FHL, *Autobiography*, 81, 91, 80.

74. Mann, *La Guardia*, 49.

75. Robert Caro, *The Power Broker: Robert Moses and the Fall of New York* (New York: Vintage, 1974), 55.

76. Ronald Steel, *Walter Lippmann and the American Century* (New York: Vintage, 1981), 21–23.

77. Mann, *La Guardia*, 49.

78. Mann, *La Guardia*, 55.

79. Mann, *La Guardia*, 49–57.

80. Elliott, *Little Flower*, 63; FHL, *Autobiography*, 96–97; "Memoirs of Jacob Panken," *Amalgamated Clothing Workers of America Local 25 Fiftieth Anniversary Pamphlet* (pamphlet at Taminent Library, New York University), 37.

81. Mann, *La Guardia*, 58; Moses Rischin, *The Promised City: New York's Jews, 1870–1914* (Cambridge: Harvard University Press, 1962), 255; FHL, *Autobiography*, 96–98. See also New York *Call*, March 3, 4, 6, 7, 8, 12, 1913.

82. FHL, *Autobiography*, 102; FHL to Frederick Tanner, September 11, 1911, Tanner Collection, Columbia University; William L. Riordan, *Plunkitt of Tammany Hall* (New York: Alfred A. Knopf, 1948), 25; Thomas M. Henderson, *Tammany Hall and the New Immigrants* (New York: Arno Press, 1976), 7–8.

83. Henderson, *Tammany*, 42–43.

84. FHL, *Autobiography*, 102; Lincoln Steffens, *Shame of the Cities* (New York: McClure, 1904); Arthur and Lila Weinberg, eds., *The Muckrakers* (New York: Simon & Schuster, 1961).

85. FHL, *Autobiography*, 102; Riordan, *Plunkitt*, 45.

86. Mann, *La Guardia*, 50–51; Irving Howe, *World of Our Fathers: The Journey of the East European Jews to America and the Life They Found and Made* (New York: Simon & Schuster, 1976), 372; Frederick C. Tanner to Samuel Koenig, September 15, 1911, Tanner Papers, Columbia University.

87. FHL to Tanner, September 11, September 25, 1911, Tanner to FHL, September 27, 1911, FHL to Tanner, October 2, 1911, Tanner Papers, Columbia University.

88. FHL to Tanner, July 16, 1914, Tanner Papers, Columbia University; Mann, *La Guardia*, 53.

89. FHL to Tanner, August 13, 1913, Tanner Papers, Columbia University.

90. Mann, *La Guardia*, 52–53.

91. FHL, *Autobiography*, 103.

92. Limpus and Leyson, *La Guardia*, 30–31; FHL, *Autobiography*, 103; Mann, *La Guardia*, 61.

93. FHL to Tanner, July 16, 1914, Tanner Papers, Columbia University.

94. Mann, *La Guardia*, 61–63; FHL, *Autobiography*, 103.

95. FHL, *Autobiography*, 104.

96. FHL, *Autobiography*, 104; Mann, *La Guardia*, 62.

97. Mann, *La Guardia*, 62–63.

98. Mann, *La Guardia*, 63–64; FHL, *Autobiography*, 105.

99. FHL, *Autobiography*, 106–109.

100. FHL, *Autobiography*, 109.

101. FHL, *Autobiography*, 109–112.

102. FHL, *Autobiography*, 112–113.

103. *World*, January 4, 1919; Limpus and Leyson, *La Guardia*, 29, 44; Elliott, *Little Flower*, 75.

104. Mann, *La Guardia*, 65; FHL, *Autobiography*, 119–120.

105. Mann, *La Guardia*, 66; FHL, *Autobiography*, 120, 91.

106. FHL to Harry Andrews, May 6, 1947, Box 2522, NYMA; FHL, *Autobiography*, 120–122; Mann, *La Guardia*, 66–67.

107. FHL, *Autobiography*, 124.

108. Mann, *La Guardia*, 68–69.

109. Limpus and Leyson, *La Guardia*, 37; Riordan, *Plunkitt*, 50; FHL, *Autobiography*, 122.

110. FHL, *Autobiography*, 125–126; Mann, *La Guardia*, 70–71.

111. Mann, *La Guardia*, 65, 72; FHL, *Autobiography*, 127, 133.

Chapter 2

1. Arthur Link, *Woodrow Wilson and the Progressive Era* (New York: Harper & Brothers, 1954), 81.

2. John M. Blum, *Woodrow Wilson and the Politics of Morality* (Boston: Little, Brown, 1956), 9; Link, *Woodrow Wilson*, 176; David P. Thelen, *Robert M. La Follette and the Insurgent Spirit* (Boston: Little, Brown, 1976), 133–134.

3. Howard Zinn, *La Guardia in Congress* (Ithaca: Cornell University Press, 1959), 12–13; Arthur Mann, *La Guardia: A Fighter Against His Times, 1882–1933* (Philadelphia: J. B. Lippincott, 1959), 74.

4. FHL, *The Making of An Insurgent, An Autobiography*, (Philadelphia: J. B. Lippincott, 1948), 136; Zinn, *La Guardia*, 1, 11–13; Lowell Limpus and Burr W. Leyson, *This Man La Guardia*, (New York: E. P. Dutton, 1938), 40–41.

5. Link, *Wilson*, 276; Ronald Steel, *Walter Lippmann and the American Century* (Boston: Little, Brown, 1980), 106; Louis Filler, *The President Speaks* (New York: Putnam, 1964), 125–126; Thelen, *La Follette*, 126–140 (quote 134–135).

6. FHL, *Autobiography*, 116, 131, 140–141; Zinn, *La Guardia*, 14–15; Mann, *La Guardia*, 76; Limpus and Leyson, *La Guardia*, 42.

7. *Congressional Record* 55 (April 3, 1917): 168; Zinn, *La Guardia*, 15; Mann, *La Guardia*, 75.

8. Zinn, *La Guardia*, 18; Mann, *La Guardia*, 80–81; FHL, *Autobiography*, 145.

9. *Congressional Record* 55 (April 18, 1917): 805, Appendix, 108.

10. Zinn, *La Guardia*, 22; Limpus and Leyson, *La Guardia*, 42–43.

11. Zinn, *La Guardia*, 19–20.

12. Zinn, *La Guardia*, 19–20.

13. Zinn, *La Guardia*, 20; Zechariah Chafe, *Free Speech in the United States* (Cambridge: Harvard University Press, 1941), 107; Steel, *Lippmann*, 124; *Congressional Record* 55 (May 2, 1917): 1700.

14. Zinn, *La Guardia*, 24–25.

15. Limpus and Leyson, *La Guardia*, 46–47; *Congressional Record* 55 (June 7, 21, 1917): 3085, 4054.

16. Eric Goldman, *Rendezvous with Destiny* (New York: Knopf, 1952), 259; M. R. Werner, "La Guardia" (unpublished manuscript, FDR Library, Hyde Park, n.d.), 56.

17. Zinn, *La Guardia*, 23, Mann, *La Guardia*, 79.

18. Zinn, *La Guardia*, 22, 80.

19. Lawrence Elliott, *Little Flower: The Life and Times of Fiorello La Guardia* (New York: Morrow, 1983), 84.

20. *Congressional Record* 55 (1917), 4501, 4920, 3690–3691.

21. Mann, *La Guardia*, 77.

22. FHL, *Autobiography*, 118–119, 161.

23. Limpus and Leyson, *La Guardia*, 49; Mann, *La Guardia*, 82.

24. Frederick C. Tanner to FHL, November 12, 1917, Tanner Papers, Columbia University; Mann, *La Guardia*, 76.

25. Mann, *La Guardia*, 84.

26. Mann, *La Guardia*, 84; Elliott, *Little Flower*, 88.

27. Mann, *La Guardia*, 85.

28. Thomas G. Paterson et al., *American Foreign Policy* (Second ed., Lexington, Massachusetts: D. C. Heath, 1983), volume II, 279; Ernest Cuneo, *Life With Fiorello* (New York: Macmillan, 1955), 119; Limpus and Leyson, *La Guardia*, 54–56.

29. A. D. Farquar to FHL, December 4, 1933, Box 2703, NYMA. This box contains many letters from Foggiani.

30. FHL, *Autobiography*, 166.

31. Mann, *La Guardia*, 85.

32. Albert Spalding, *Rise to Follow: An Autobiography* (New York: Holt and Company, 1943), 231–232, 214; Elliott, *Little Flower*, 87, 97.

33. Mann, *La Guardia*, 86, 90, 93; FHL, *Autobiography*, 179–181.

34. Spalding, *Rise to Follow*, 253–254; Steel, *American Century*, 147.

35. Mann, *La Guardia*, 89; FHL, *Autobiography*, 184–185; Jay Franklin [John

Franklin Carter], *La Guardia: A Biography* (New York: Modern Age Books, 1937), 64; Elliott, *Little Flower*, 92–93.

36. Cuneo, *Fiorello*, 117 (quote); Elliott, *Little Flower*, 93; Spalding, *Rise to Follow*, 254 (quote); Mann, *La Guardia*, 89–90; Franklin, *La Guardia*, 44; *Times*, January 20, February 4, 1918.

37. Arthur M. Schlesinger, Jr., *The Crisis of the Old Order*, Vol. 1 of *The Age of Roosevelt* (Boston: Houghton Mifflin, 1957), 356; Mann, *La Guardia*, 90; *Times*, January 20, February 4, 1918; *Giornale d'Italia* quoted in "A Violinist and a Congressman," *Literary Digest* (July 13, 1918): 27; FHL, *Autobiography*, 185.

38. Mann, *La Guardia*, 91.

39. Mann, *La Guardia*, 86–87; Spalding, *Rise to Follow*, 232.

40. FHL, *Autobiography*, 175–176; Mann, *La Guardia*, 87.

41. Limpus and Leyson, *La Guardia*, 60.

42. Mann, *La Guardia*, 88, 346–347.

43. Spalding, *Rise to Follow*, 233–235, 253; FHL, *Autobiography*, 191–192.

44. Spalding, *Rise to Follow*, 237.

45. Spalding, *Rise to Follow*, 242.

46. Sandy Hand quoted in Elliott, *Little Flower*, 90.

47. Elliott, *Little Flower*, 90–91; Mann, *La Guardia*, 88; FHL, *Autobiography*, 191; Limpus and Leyson, *La Guardia*, 60–61; O. B. Kiel to Col. Wilson Davidson, October 11, 1938, Box 2703, NYMA.

48. Elliott, *Little Flower*, 94; Mann, *La Guardia*, 93; FHL, *Autobiography*, 188.

49. Limpus and Leyson, *La Guardia*, 69; Mann, *La Guardia*, 91–92.

50. Mann, *La Guardia*, 93; FHL to Mrs. Paul Durbin, June 18, 1940; FHL to John Rankin, June 10, 1940; Rankin to FHL, June 11, 1940; FHL to Durbin, June 10, 1940; Durbin to FHL, February 27, 1940, all in Box 2704, NYMA.

51. FHL to Frederick C. Tanner, September 11, 1917, Tanner Papers, Columbia University.

52. Mann, *La Guardia*, 93–95; Zinn, *La Guardia*, 27; Limpus and Leyson, *La Guardia*, 73.

53. Tanner to FHL, November 12, 1917; FHL to Tanner, September 12, 1918; Tanner Papers, Columbia University; Mann, *La Guardia*, 94.

54. Murphy and *Financial America* quoted in Zinn, *La Guardia*, 28.

55. Mann, *La Guardia*, 94.

56. Mann, *La Guardia*, 95.

57. Mann, *La Guardia*, 96.

58. FHL to Harry Andrews quoted in Limpus and Leyson, *La Guardia*, 64; *Tribune*, November 6, 1918; Zinn, *La Guardia*, 30–31.

59. Mann, *La Guardia*, 99; Limpus and Leyson, *La Guardia*, 78; Elliott, *Little Flower*, 101. Several years later in 1926, Congressman La Guardia received a letter from Nearing, who was studying the use of black strikebreakers in coal mines. La Guardia offered Nearing every assistance he could in obtaining information and helping with the study. Nearing to FHL, April 2, 1928; FHL to Nearing, April 20, 1928, Box 2522, NYMA.

60. *Times* quoted in Limpus and Leyson, *La Guardia*, 72; *Tribune* quoted in Zinn, *La Guardia*, 29.

61. Zinn, *La Guardia*, 33.

62. *Tribune* March 9, 1919; Mann, *La Guardia*, 100; Limpus and Leyson, *La Guardia*, 29.

63. Rochester *Post Express* quoted in Thomas G. Paterson et al., *American Foreign Policy* (Second edition Lexington, Massachusetts: D. C. Heath, 1983), volume II, 280; William E. Leuchtenburg, *The Perils of Prosperity, 1914–1932* (Chicago: University of Chicago Press, 1958), 36–37.

64. Frederick Lewis Allen, *Only Yesterday: An Informal History of the Nineteen-Twenties* (New York: Harper and Brothers, 1931), 23–24; Leuchtenburg, *Perils*, 50; Paterson, *American Foreign Policy*, II, 282; Mann, *La Guardia*, 106.

65. Mann, *La Guardia*, 108; Zinn, *La Guardia*, 41. The New York *Evening Journal* reported that "Mr. La Guardia is the recognized authority in the House on Italian affairs," adding that the congressman felt that Wilson had "blundered" on Fiume. *Evening Journal*, June 21, 1919. See also *Evening Sun*, May 13, 1919.

66. FHL, *Autobiography*, 212–213; M. R. Werner, "La Guardia," 102; *Jewish Daily Forward*, May 22, 1919; Zinn, *La Guardia*, 35; Limpus and Leyson, *La Guardia*, 95; Mann, *La Guardia*, 105; Elliott, *Little Flower*, 104.

67. FHL, *Autobiography*, 205–206; Limpus and Leyson, *La Guardia*, 86–87; Werner, "La Guardia," 93.

68. FHL, "Why I *Now* Believe in Universal Military Training," *Reader's Digest* (April 1947): 81–84.

69. Steel, *Lippmann*, 155; Link, "The Failure of Progressivism," Richard M. Abrams and Lawrence W. Levine, eds., *The Shaping of Twentieth Century America* (Second edition Boston: Little, Brown, 1971), 224.

70. Russell Nye, *Midwestern Progressive Politics* (East Lansing: Michigan State University, 1959), 298.

71. Steel, *Lippmann*, 215–218; Arthur Link, "What Happened to the Progressive Movement in the 1920s?" *American Historical Review*, LXIV (July 1959): 833–851.

72. *Bronx Home News*, March 1, 1921.

73. Limpus and Leyson, *La Guardia*, 44; Werner, "La Guardia," 92–94; Mann, *La Guardia*, 101; Zinn, *La Guardia*, 21.

74. Zinn, *La Guardia*, 39, 35–36; Elliott, *Little Flower*, 104.

75. *Congressional Record* 55 (May 16, June 15, 1917): 2424, 3697; Mann, *La Guardia*, 102.

76. Troy *Observer*, June 29, 1919; Houston *Post*, July 4, 1919; Elliott, *Little Flower*, 102; FHL, *Autobiography*, 203; Zinn, *La Guardia*, 38.

77. Troy *Observer*, June 29, 1919.

78. FHL, *Autobiography*, 214–215.

79. Zinn, *La Guardia*, 166.

80. Werner, "La Guardia," 109.

81. John D. Buenker, *Urban Liberalism and Progressive Reform* (New York: Scribner, 1973), 41. For Smith see Oscar Handlin, *Al Smith and His America* (Boston: Little, Brown, 1958); Paula Eldot, *Governor Al Smith: The Politician as Reformer* (New York: Garland, 1983); Richard O'Connor, *The First Hurrah: A Biography of Alfred E. Smith* (New York: Putnam, 1970).

82. Robert Caro, *The Power Broker: Robert Moses and the Fall of New York* (New York: Vintage, 1974), 118; J. J. Huthmacher, *Senator Robert F. Wagner and the Rise of Urban Liberalism* (New York: Atheneum, 1971), 13; Schlesinger, *Crisis of the Old Order*, 96–97.

83. Caro, *Power Broker*, 123–135.

84. Paul Windels interview, Columbia University Oral History Collection, 55–56; Mann, *La Guardia*, 110; Zinn, *La Guardia*, 48.

85. Windels interview, 55–56; Limpus and Leyson, *La Guardia*, 95–100; Elliott, *Little Flower*, 107.

86. Elliott, *Little Flower*, 107; Windels interview, 56, 59; Werner, "La Guardia," 112–115; Mann, *La Guardia*, 114–115.

87. Mann, *La Guardia*, 115–116; Franklin, *La Guardia*, 54; Brooklyn *Citizen*, January 4, 1921.

88. Mann, *La Guardia*, 117–119.

89. Werner, "La Guardia," 126–127; Limpus and Leyson, *La Guardia*, 109 (both quotations).

90. Mann, *La Guardia*, 121–122; Werner, "La Guardia," 147; William R. Conklin, "The Mayor Flings in His Hat," *New York Times Magazine* (July 18, 1937): 2; New York *World*, June 22, 1920, quoted by Werner, "La Guardia," 129–130; William Manners, *Patience and Fortitude: Fiorello La Guardia* (New York: Harcourt Brace Jovanovich, 1976), 86.

91. Manners, *La Guardia*, 87; see also 1921 newspaper clippings from the La Guardia Scrapbooks, LAGA.

92. Alexander Callow, *The Tweed Ring* (New York: Oxford, 1966), 198–206.

93. Franklin, *La Guardia*, 55; Brooklyn *Standard Union*, December 18, 1921, La Guardia Clippings Folder, Box 2603, NYMA; Limpus and Leyson, *La Guardia*, 104–107; Mann, *La Guardia*, 122–123.

94. Brooklyn *Standard Union*, July 3, 1921, La Guardia Clippings Folder, Box 2603, NYMA.

95. Brooklyn *Standard Union*, July 3, 1921, La Guardia Clippings Folder, Box 2603, NYMA; Limpus and Leyson, *La Guardia*, 114–115.

96. Press releases, March 27, 1920 and April 7, 1920, Microfilm Reel 46, FHL Papers, NYPL; Werner, "La Guardia," 143–146; Limpus and Leyson, *La Guardia*, 118.

97. *Post*, March 12, 1920, La Guardia Clippings Folder, Box 2603, NYMA.

98. *Times*, March 1, 1921.

99. Leuchtenburg, *Perils of Prosperity*, 66; Chafee, *Free Speech*, 269–282; *Times*, March 1, 1921.

100. *Times*, March 1, 1921; Mann, *La Guardia*, 126.

101. Mann, *La Guardia*, 125.

102. *Herald*, November 11, 1921; *Times*, November 11, 1921; Al Smith, *Up To Now* (New York: Viking, 1929), 236–237; Mann, *La Guardia*, 125–128; Elliott, *Little Flower*, 107.

103. New York *Call*, February 27, 1921, Box 2603, NYMA; Mann, *La Guardia*, 126–129; John F. Hylan to Voters, August 27, 1925, Box A-20, John F. Hylan Correspondence, Citizens Union Collection, Columbia University.

104. *Times*, March 1, 1921; see also the papers in the file labeled "Politics," Box 2521, NYMA.

105. *Herald*, June 7, 1921; Mann, *La Guardia*, 130.

106. Bronx *Home News*, February 24, 1921, Box 2603, NYMA.

107. Mann, *La Guardia*, 136–139; Brooklyn *Standard Union*, June 7, 1921, Box 2603, NYMA.

108. Werner, "La Guardia," 151; Mann, *La Guardia*, 126, 131; Brooklyn *Eagle*, June 15, 1921, Box 2601, NYMA; FHL Press Release, July 1, 1921, Roll 46, FHL Papers, NYPL.

109. Quotations from Werner, "La Guardia," 152; *Williamsburgh Press*, July 16, 1921; Bensonhurst *Progress*, June 24, 1921; *Globe*, August 29, 1921, all in Box 2603, NYMA.

110. *Post*, September 25, 1921; *Times*, September 24, 1921; Limpus and Leyson, *La Guardia*, 125–126; Mann, *La Guardia*, 135.

111. See assorted campaign materials in Box 2521, NYMA.

112. *Herald, Times*, and *Sun*, October 11, 1921; *Tribune*, October 5, 1921.

113. *Tribune*, October 28, 1921.

114. Mann, *La Guardia*, 139; Werner, "La Guardia," 96.

115. Limpus and Leyson, *La Guardia*, 127–129; *Herald*, December 10, 1921; *Mail*, December 9, 1921; *Globe*, December 2, 1921; *Daily News*, December 10, 1921; Franklin, *La Guardia*, 58; Werner, "La Guardia," 168–169.

116. Caro, *Power Broker*, 136; Elliott, *Little Flower*, 121.

117. *Times*, October 10, 1921; Limpus and Leyson, *La Guardia*, 129; *Journal*, November 10, 1921.

Chapter 3

1. Lowell Limpus and Burr W. Leyson, *This Man La Guardia* (New York: E. P. Dutton, 1938), 129; Charles C. Burlingham interview, Columbia University Oral History Collection, 37; George Baehr interview, February 6, 1976, Lawrence Elliott Collection, LAGA.

2. M. R. Werner, "La Guardia" (unpublished manuscript, FDR Library, Hyde Park), 34–36; Helen Harris, interview with the author, October 25, 1983; Elsie Fisher, interview with the author, March 14, 1983.

3. Marc Siegel, "Father, The Third Party, and the Mayor," *New Yorker* (September 18, 1948), 71.

4. *Evening Mail*, December 19, 1921, Box 2603, NYMA.

5. Lawrence Elliott, *Little Flower: The Life and Times of Fiorello La Guardia* (New York: Morrow, 1983), 123; Barbara Sapinsky to the author, May 18, 1982.

6. Limpus and Leyson, *La Guardia*, 132–133.

7. Thomas M. Henderson, *Immigrants, Tammany, and New York: The Progressive Years* (New York: Arno, 1976), 288–289; Limpus and Leyson, *La Guardia*, 132.

8. Frank Luther Mott, *American Journalism: A History*, (Third ed., New York: Macmillan, 1962), 546–560, 596–600; FHL to Duff Gilfond, July 27, 1929, Miscellaneous Manuscripts, Columbia University.

9. Limpus and Leyson, *La Guardia*, 132; *Evening Mail*, May 3, 1922; Brooklyn *Standard Union*, May 10, 1922; *Times*, May 8, 1922.

10. Arthur Mann, *La Guardia: A Fighter Against His Times, 1882–1933* (Philadelphia: J. B. Lippincott, 1959), 145.

11. W. A. Swanberg, *Citizen Hearst* (New York: Scribner, 1961), 327–333; Al Smith, *Up To Now* (New York: Viking, 1929), 233.

12. "Proposed Planks for the Republican State Platform," Box 2522, NYMA; *Times* quoted in Howard Zinn, *La Guardia in Congress* (Ithaca: Cornell University Press, 1959), 61.

13. *The Harlemite*, November 1921; FHL, "Old Ideas and the New School of Politics," Draft of New York *Journal* article, Box 2521, NYMA.

14. FHL, "Economic Problems are the Issues of the Present," and "Is the Most Important Provision in the Peace Treaty Forgotten?" Drafts of New York *Journal* articles, Box 2521, NYMA.

15. FHL, "Injunctions," "Platform and Injunctions," and "Government Pay," Drafts of New York *Journal* articles, Box 2521, NYMA; FHL to Charity Organization Society, June 19, 1917, and reply, Charity Organization Society Collection, Columbia University.

16. Charles A. Beard, *The Economic Interpretation of the Constitution* (New York: Macmillan, 1913); FHL, "Play for Children—Pay for Women," "Old Ideas and the New School of Politics," and "Constitutional Limitations Should Be Construed in the Light of Changed Times and Changed Conditions," Drafts of New York *Journal* articles, Box 2521, NYMA.

17. FHL, "More Casualties From the Front," "Who Is Your County Committeeman," "State Conventions," "Figures Speak Louder Than Words," "Protecting the Ballot," "Reorganization of State Government (Less Talk—More Action)," "Good Roads and Use of Canals Necessary to Reduce the Cost of Living," "Literacy Test for New Voters," Drafts of New York *Journal* articles, Box 2521, NYMA.

18. FHL, "Food," "Happy, Healthy Childhood," Drafts of New York *Journal* articles, Box 2521, NYMA.

19. FHL, "New York the City Beautiful—The Home of Happiness," Drafts of New York *Journal* articles, Box 2521, NYMA.

20. *Times* quoted in Mann, *La Guardia*, 147; FHL, "Food," Drafts of New York *Journal* articles, Box 2521, NYMA.

21. Limpus and Leyson, *La Guardia*, 133; Mann, *La Guardia*, 150; Siegel, "Father and the Mayor," 64–71. *The Harlemite*, East Harlem's Italo-American newspaper, had begun touting "the Major" for the local congressional seat nearly a year earlier while mentioning rumors that he might try for the governor's mansion. *Harlemite*, November 19, 1921; *Times* quoted in Zinn, *La Guardia*, 62.

22. Mann, *La Guardia*, 151–152 (quote); Zinn, *La Guardia*, 63; *World*, October 1, 1922.

23. *World*, October 1, 1922; Limpus and Leyson, *La Guardia*, 139.

24. Limpus and Leyson, *La Guardia*, 139; Mann, *La Guardia*, 153.

25. Limpus and Leyson, *La Guardia*, 142.

26. Limpus and Leyson, *La Guardia*, 143–145.

27. Limpus and Leyson, *La Guardia*, 142–146, 157; Werner, "La Guardia," 176–177.

28. Mann, *La Guardia*, 158; Limpus and Leyson, *La Guardia*, 141, 146 (quote); Zinn, *La Guardia*, 65.

29. Press Release of Speech Before the Institutional Synagogue, December 10, 1922, Box 2521, NYMA. See also *Times*, December 11, 1922.

30. William E. Leuchtenburg, *The Perils of Prosperity, 1914–1932* (Chicago: University of Chicago Press, 1958), 121–122; Arthur M. Schlesinger, Jr., *The Crisis of the Old Order*, Vol. 1 of *The Age of Roosevelt* (Boston: Houghton Mifflin, 1957), 20, 101; John Dos Passos, *U.S.A.* (Boston: Houghton Mifflin, 1937), 367–368.

31. FHL, "La Follette Sees It Through," "The Sick Old Man of Europe," Drafts of New York *Journal* articles, Box 2521, NYMA; Mann, *La Guardia*, 161, 165; Belle C. La Follette and Fola La Follette, *Robert M. La Follette*, 2 vols. (New York: Macmillan, 1953), II, 1066–1067; Press Release of Speech Before the Institutional Synagogue, December 10, 1922, Box 2521, NYMA.

32. Press Release of Speech Before the Institutional Synagogue, December 10, 1922, Box 2521, NYMA.

33. Press Release of Speech Before the Institutional Synagogue, December 10, 1922, Box 2521, NYMA.

34. Mann, *La Guardia*, 163; Limpus and Leyson, *La Guardia*, 149–153.

35. Limpus and Leyson, *La Guardia*, 155.

36. FHL to John Q. Tilson, March 3, 1923, Box 2522, NYMA.

37. Schlesinger, *Crisis*, 50–51; Leuchtenburg, *Perils*, 81; Paul Carter, *Another Part of the Twenties* (New York: Columbia University Press, 1983), 167–179.

38. Leuchtenburg, *Perils*, 89–90, 110.

39. Leuchtenburg, *Perils*, 95–97.

40. Leuchtenburg, *Perils*, 97, 190, and see pages 98–103 for a discussion of Coolidge's relationship with businessmen.

41. Limpus and Leyson, *La Guardia*, 158.

42. David P. Thelen, *Robert M. La Follette and the Insurgent Spirit* (Boston: Little, Brown, 1976), 156; Frederick Lewis Allen, *Only Yesterday: An Informal History of the Nineteen-Twenties* (New York: Harper and Brothers, 1931), 133.

43. Eric Goldman, *Rendezvous with Destiny: A History of Modern American Reform* (New York: Knopf, 1952), 310; Paul Carter, *The Twenties in America* (New York: T. Y. Crowell, 1975), 51.

44. FHL, "Bonus," and "Bonus Issue Still Alive," Drafts of New York *Journal* articles, Box 2521, NYMA.

45. Limpus and Leyson, *La Guardia*, 176–177; Mann, *La Guardia*, 169.

46. Brooklyn *Eagle* quoted in Zinn, *La Guardia*, 74; Jay Franklin [John Franklin Carter], *La Guardia: A Biography* (New York: Modern Age Books, 1937), 71.

47. Schlesinger, *Crisis*, 95, 98–100; Leuchtenburg, *Perils*, 133; Mann, *La Guardia*, 170.

48. Mann, *La Guardia*, 169; Leuchtenburg, *Perils*, 132–136; Schlesinger, *Crisis*, 101.

49. Ronald Steel, *Walter Lippmann and the American Century* (Boston: Little, Brown, 1980), 225.

50. *Times* quoted in Mann, *La Guardia*, 171–172; Siegel, "Father and the Mayor," 64–71. See also Norman Thomas to FHL, October 19, 1925, Box 2521, NYMA; Mann, *La Guardia*, 173; Harry Fleischman, *Norman Thomas: A Biography* (New York: Norton, 1964), 101; Limpus and Leyson, *La Guardia*, 181.

51. FHL to La Follette, September 2, 1924, La Follette Family Papers, Library of Congress; Limpus and Leyson, *La Guardia*, 183.

52. Thelen, *Robert M. La Follette*, 185; FHL to Nelson, September 6, 1924, La Follette Family Papers, Library of Congress.

53. Zinn, *La Guardia*, 82–83; Leuchtenburg, *Perils*, 127, 134–135; Goldman, *Rendezvous with Destiny*, 298; Fleischman, *Norman Thomas*, 102.

54. Goldman, *Rendezvous with Destiny*, 315; FHL to Nelson, April 25, 1925, La Guardia Papers, NYPL.

55. Siegel, "Father and the Mayor," 65; Limpus and Leyson, *La Guardia*, 186–189. On the meaning of "Ghibboni" see E. R. Canudo to Arthur Mann, August 26 and September 4, 1957, LAGA.

56. Limpus and Leyson, *La Guardia*, 184, 188; Siegel, "Father and the Mayor," 70; Mann, *La Guardia*, 180.

57. Limpus and Leyson, *La Guardia*, 191; Mann, *La Guardia*, 181; Elliott, *Little Flower*, 123.

58. Zinn, *La Guardia*, 158–159; Ray Tucker, *Sons of Wild Jackass* (Boston: L. C. Page, 1932), 376.

59. Schlesinger, *Crisis*, 60.

60. F. Scott Fitzgerald, "Echoes of the Jazz Age," in Loren Baritz, ed., *The Culture of the Twenties* (Indianapolis: Bobbs-Merrill, 1970), 414; Mencken quoted in Goldman, *Rendezvous with Destiny*, 317.

61. Walter Lippmann, *A Preface of Morals* (New York: Macmillan; 1929), 6–7; Leuchtenburg, *Perils*, 221; Joseph Wood Krutch, "The Modern Temper," in Baritz, ed., *Culture of the Twenties*, 355–371, quotes on 368, 370.

62. Thorstein Veblen, "Dementia Praecox," in Baritz, ed., *Culture of the Twenties*, 35; Paula Fass, *The Damned and the Beautiful* (New York: Oxford University Press, 1977), 327–328.

63. FHL, "Tony Goes to Congress" (unpublished manuscript, n.d., LAGA).

64. Ernest Cuneo, *Life With Fiorello* (New York: Macmillan, 1955), 111–112.

65. Cuneo, *Life With Fiorello*, 65–66, 93; FHL, "Measuring Candidates," Drafts of New York *Journal* articles, Box 2521, NYMA. On the suffrage amendment, La Guardia shared with other reformers the fear that it would undermine social welfare legislation that protected women from the most exploitative abuses of industry. See

Lydia E. Sayer to FHL, November 12, 1923, and FHL to Sayer, November 19, 1923, Box 2522, NYMA.

66. Mann, *La Guardia*, 235; Irving Bernstein, *The Lean Years: A History of the American Worker, 1920–1933* (Boston: Houghton Mifflin, 1960). For charge that La Guardia was not radical enough, see Ben Howe to FHL, July 8, 1922, Box 2521, NYMA.

67. Limpus and Leyson, *La Guardia*, 194; Cuneo, *Life With Fiorello*, 26. See Box 2724, NYMA, for La Guardia on prohibition.

68. Limpus and Leyson, *La Guardia*, 93.

69. Limpus and Leyson, *La Guardia*, 94–95; *Tribune*, July 8 and 9, 1919; FHL to E. J. D. Larson, May 7, 1929; "High Spots in Congressman La Guardia's Argument in Favor of Modification of Existing Enforcement Laws," both in Box 2742, NYMA.

70. W. L. Jones to FHL, February 10, 1930, FHL to Jones, February 10, 1930, Box 2742, NYMA.

71. Limpus and Leyson, *La Guardia*, 167, 198–199, 248.

72. Prohibition correspondence is in Box 2742, NYMA; Limpus and Leyson, *La Guardia*, 249, 194, 200; *World*, October 1, 1922; Werner, "La Guardia," 263–275.

73. Herbert Asbury, "The Noble Experiment of Izzy and Moe," 47, in Isabel Leighton, *The Aspirin Age* (New York: Simon & Schuster, 1949); Tucker, *Jackass*, 380; Limpus and Leyson, *La Guardia*, 238; Elliott, *Little Flower*, 153.

74. Elliott, *Little Flower*, 153; Tucker, *Jackass*, 379; Werner, "La Guardia," 254–255; Limpus and Leyson, *La Guardia*, 202–203; Mann, *La Guardia*, 202–203.

75. Elliott, *Little Flower*, 152–153; Mann, *La Guardia*, 203; "High Spots in Congressman La Guardia's Argument in Favor of Modification of Existing Enforcement Laws," Box 2742, NYMA.

76. Limpus and Leyson, *La Guardia*, 278–279; Zinn, *La Guardia*, 156; Leuchtenburg, *Perils*, 214; FHL to Charles Tuttle, April 3, 1929, Box 2742, NYMA; Mann, *La Guardia*, 206.

77. Humbert Nelli, *The Italians of Chicago* (New York: Oxford University Press, 1970), 211–212. Nelli says prohibition produced the "Golden Age of organized crime."

78. FHL, "Statement on Prohibition, January 21, 1930," Box 2742, NYMA.

79. Unidentified newspaper clipping dated September 26, 1930, La Guardia Scrapbooks, LAGA. See also announcement from La Guardia office, March 2, 1932, Box 2742, NYMA.

80. FHL to D. H. Blair, August 23, 1924, Microfilm Roll 11, NYPL.

81. Henry May, *The End of American Innocence* (New York: Knopf, 1959), 7; John Tomisch, *A Genteel Endeavor: American Culture and Politics in the Gilded Age* (Stanford: Stanford University Press, 1971).

82. Leuchtenburg, *Perils*, 205–206.

83. Goldman, *Rendezvous with Destiny*, 299

84. Bourne quoted in Baritz, *Culture of the Twenties*, 283. On Bourne, see Bruce Clayton, *Forgotten Prophet: The Life of Randolph Bourne* (Baton Rouge: Louisiana State University Press, 1985).

85. Mann, *La Guardia*, 188; FHL to Louis Post, June 9, 1917; Post to FHL, June 7, 1917; FHL to Anthony Caminetti, May 24, 1917; Post to FHL, May 28, 1917, Bureau of Immigration and Naturalization, Record Group 85, File 7-2098, National Archives.

86. Elliott, *Little Flower*, 140.

87. Elliott, *Little Flower*, 140–141; Press Release on Planned Deportation of Russian Immigrants, March 24, 1923, Box 2522, NYMA.

88. La Guardia file, Library of the Masons; Cuneo, *Life With Fiorello*, 82–83; *Congressional Record* 65 (April 8, 1924): 5886.

89. Leuchtenburg, *Perils*, 82; Steel, *Lippmann*, 229.

90. Zinn, *La Guardia*, 101; Cuneo, *Life With Fiorello*, 107.

91. Dos Passos quoted in Leuchtenburg, *Perils*, 83.

92. Limpus and Leyson, *La Guardia*, 250.

93. Carter, *The Twenties in America*, 95; John Higham, *Strangers in the Land: Patterns of American Nativism, 1860–1925* (New Brunswick: Rutgers University Press, 1955), 155–156, 271–273.

94. William S. Bernard, "A History of United States Immigration Policy," in Stephen Thernstrom et al., *Immigration* (Cambridge: Harvard University Press, 1982), 97.

95. FHL, "Immigration," Drafts of New York *Journal* articles, Box 2521, NYMA; Werner, "La Guardia," 180.

96. FHL, "Immigration," and "Naturalization," Drafts of New York *Journal* articles, Box 2521, NYMA; Zinn, *La Guardia*, 88; *Evening Mail*, July 17, 1923.

97. FHL, "Immigration," Drafts of New York *Journal* articles, Box 2521, NYMA.

98. Mann, *La Guardia*, 190–192; Zinn, *La Guardia*, 89–90.

99. Higham, *Strangers*, 318; FHL to "Prisco," March 14, 1928; FHL to Dr. Leopold Vaccarello, September 26, 1928; J. J. Davis to FHL, June 21 and 29, 1928; FHL to Davis, June 26 and July 3, 1928, all in Box 2522, NYMA; Limpus and Leyson, *La Guardia*, 263.

100. FHL, "Immigration" and "Naturalization," Drafts of New York *Journal* articles, Box 2521, NYMA; Leroy Ashby, *The Spearless Leader: Senator Borah and the Progressive Movement* (Chicago: University of Illinois Press, 1972), 248; Zinn, *La Guardia*, 90, 93.

101. "American Citizenship and European Titles," Drafts of New York *Journal* articles, Box 2521, NYMA; Mann, *La Guardia*, 197.

102. Mann, *La Guardia*, 199.

103. Arthur Link and Bruce Catton, *The American Epoch* (Fourth edition, New York: Knopf, 1980), 177; Preston Hubbard, *The Origins of the TVA* (Nashville: Vanderbilt University Press, 1961), passim; Carter, *The Twenties in America*, 7.

104. Leuchtenburg, *Perils*, 13, 175–176, 186–188; Goldman, *Rendezvous with Destiny*, 288; Stephan Thernstrom, *A History of the American People* (New York: Harcourt Brace Jovanovich, 1984), 589. See also Keith Sward, *The Legend of Henry Ford* (New York: Rinehart, 1948).

105. Hubbard, *Origins of TVA*, 34–46, 76, 90.

106. Hubbard, *Origins of TVA*, 118–120; Zinn, *La Guardia*, 124; Press Release on Henry Ford Offer, Box 2525, NYMA; Mann, *La Guardia*, 218; *World*, March 3, 1924.

107. R. Noble Esty to FHL, March 7, 1924, and FHL to Esty, March 8, 1924, Box 2526, NYMA.

108. Hubbard, *Origins of TVA*, 144.

109. Zinn, *La Guardia*, 129.

110. Werner, "La Guardia," 198; Mann, *La Guardia*, 220; Zinn, *La Guardia*, 131–134; Hubbard, *Origins of TVA*, 252–253.

111. Link and Catton, *American Epoch*, 177–178.

112. Zinn, *La Guardia*, 149, 210, 150; Limpus and Leyson, *La Guardia*, 256; Mann, *La Guardia*, 209.

113. Zinn, *La Guardia*, 210, 150–152; Mann, *La Guardia*, 209; Duff Gilfond, "La Guardia of Harlem," *American Mercury* 11 (June 1927): 158; Brooklyn *Times*, June 28, 1923.

114. Press Release on Gold Star Mothers, December 7, 1925, Box 2525, NYMA; E. M. H. Guedry to FHL, June 17, 1932, Box 2525, NYMA; Limpus and Leyson, *La Guardia*, 192.

115. Bernstein, *Lean Years*, 360; FHL, "The Government Must Act," *The Nation* 126 (April 4, 1928): 378–379; Mann, *La Guardia*, 216; Limpus and Leyson, *La Guardia*, 257; Werner, "La Guardia," 286–291. See Box 2522, NYMA, for more on the coal issue.

116. Werner, "La Guardia," 229–230; Zinn, *La Guardia*, 141; Elliott, *Little Flower*, 157.

117. FHL to William Jardine, September 21, 1925; Jardine to FHL, October 6 and 21, 1925, Box 2521, NYMA; Limpus and Leyson, *La Guardia*, 211–212; Elliott, *Little Flower*, 158; Zinn, *La Guardia*, 143; Mann, *La Guardia*, 212.

118. See Box 2522, NYMA; Zinn, *La Guardia*, 144.

119. Werner, "La Guardia," 278; Limpus and Leyson, *La Guardia*, 253–255; Mann, *La Guardia*, 229.

120. Leuchtenburg, *Perils*, 137.

121. Gilfond, "La Guardia," 155.

122. Mann, *La Guardia*, 208; Limpus and Leyson, *La Guardia*, 206; Zinn, *La Guardia*, 162.

123. Zinn, *La Guardia*, 164.

124. Mann, *La Guardia*, 324, 228; *Post Office Clerk* (January 1933), in 1931–1933 Scrapbook, LAGA; Limpus and Leyson, *La Guardia*, 254; Werner, "La Guardia," 314, 242–244; Cuneo, *Life With Fiorello*, 123.

125. Zinn, *La Guardia*, 152; FHL, "Progressives—Past, Present, and Future" (circulated 1933), 4, LAGA; Zinn, *La Guardia*, 157.

126. Brandes quoted in Van Wyck Brooks's introduction to Randolph Bourne, *The History of a Literary Radical* (New York: Russell, 1956), 8.

Chapter 4

1. Robert A. Caro, *The Power Broker: Robert Moses and the Fall of New York* (New York: Knopf, 1974), 393; W. P. A., Mayor's Committee on City Planning, East Harlem Study, Project No. 165-97-6037, (1937), LAGA.

2. Gerald Meyer, "Vito Marcantonio: A Successful New York City Radical Politician" (Ph.D. dissertation, City University of New York, 1984), 8–10; Jeffrey Gurock, *When Harlem Was Jewish* (New York: Columbia University Press, 1978), 28; Leonard Covello, *The Social Background of the Italo-American School Child* (Leiden: E. J. Brill, 1967); *West Harlem and East Harlem Population Compiled by the Welfare Council of New York City Based on U.S. Census Data* (Washington: U.S. Department of Commerce, 1940); Thomas Kessner, "New Yorkers in Prosperity and Depression: A Preliminary Reconnaissance," in Diane Ravitch and Ronald Goodenow, eds., *Educating an Urban People: The New York Experience* (New York: Teacher's College Press, 1981), 95–97.

3. *West Harlem and East Harlem Population Compiled by the Welfare Council of New York City Based on U.S. Census Data*; E. Warburg, "Data Regarding the Jewish Population in the Area from 92nd to 122nd Streets Between Fifth Avenue and the East River" (Typescript, Covello Collection, Balch Institute, Philadelphia).

4. Robert E. Park and Herbert A. Miller, *Old World Traits Transplanted* (New York, 1921), 146–147; George E. Pozzetta, "The Italians of New York" (Ph.D. dissertation, University of North Carolina, 1971), 102–107; Meyer, "Marcantonio," 2; Richard Gambino, *Blood of My Blood* (Garden City: Doubleday, 1974).

5. Federal Writers' Project, *Italians of New York* (New York: Random House, 1938), 52–58, 97, 123–124; Arthur Mann, *La Guardia: A Fighter Against His Times, 1882–1933* (Philadelphia: J. B. Lippincott, 1959), 253; M. R. Werner, "La Guardia" (unpublished manuscript, FDR Library, Hyde Park), 222.

6. Mann, *La Guardia*, 253–254.

7. Alan Cassels, "Fascism for Export: Italy and the United States in the Twenties," *American Historical Review* 69 (1964): 710; Cuneo, *Life With Fiorello*, 129; Mann, *La Guardia*, 252, 254.

8. Mann, *La Guardia*, 255.

9. FHL to L. C. Andrews, May 2, 1927, Box 2742, NYMA; Mann, *La Guardia*, 249; Limpus and Leyson, *La Guardia*, 264.

10. Zinn, *La Guardia*, 118; Mann, *La Guardia*, 246; H. M. Towner to FHL, Confidential and Personal, April 16, 1928; FHL to Jose Soto [Speaker of the House of San Juan], January 28, 1929, Box 2522, NYMA.

11. FHL to Edward Sanders [secretary to the president], September 15, 1928, Box 2522, NYMA; Limpus and Leyson, *La Guardia*, 267; Mann, *La Guardia*, 247. On Puerto Rican support for La Guardia see also Anthony Cinao to FHL, n.d. [1929], Box 2522, NYMA.

12. John T. Doyle to FHL, May 16, 1929; FHL to Doyle, May 21, 1929, Box 2524, NYMA; Mann, *La Guardia*, 233.

13. On Marcantonio see Alan Schaeffer, *Vito Marcantonio: Radical in Congress* (Syracuse: Syracuse University Press, 1966); Salvatore La Gumina, *Vito Marcantonio, The People's Politician* (Dubuque: Kendall/Hall, 1969); Meyer, "Marcantonio," cited above; *Italians of New York*, 105–106.

14. Limpus and Leyson, *La Guardia*, 232; Mann, *La Guardia*, 242; Werner, "La Guardia," 209; Meyer, "Marcantonio," 23–26.

15. Werner, "La Guardia," 218–219; interview with Mrs. Marcantonio cited in Zinn, *La Guardia*, 248; Mann, *La Guardia*, 240.

16. Limpus and Leyson, *La Guardia*, 264; Werner, "La Guardia," 219–220.

17. Mann, *La Guardia*, 240.

18. Cuneo, *Life With Fiorello*, 161–162, 165.

19. Cuneo, *Life With Fiorello*, 4–10.

20. Cuneo, *Life With Fiorello*, x–xi; Edmund Palmieri, interview with the author, November 9, 1982.

21. Ray Ginger, *Altgeld's America* (New York: Funk and Wagnalls, 1958), 1.

22. Cuneo, *Life With Fiorello*, 163–164.

23. Cuneo, *Life With Fiorello*, 170–171, 174–175.

24. Werner, "La Guardia," 211–212; Mann, *La Guardia*, 244.

25. Cuneo, *Life With Fiorello*, 20.

26. Cuneo, *Life With Fiorello*, 107–108 See Box 2522, NYMA, for La Guardia and community affairs; microfilm rolls 1–10, La Guardia Collection, NYPL, for complaints handled by La Guardia's district office.

27. Cuneo, *Life With Fiorello*, 109–110.

28. Morris Diamond to FHL, April 8, 1944, Box 2703, NYMA.

29. Cuneo, *Life With Fiorello*, 110–111.

30. Mann, *La Guardia*, 233–235.

31. Mann, *La Guardia*, 233.

32. Limpus and Leyson, *La Guardia*, 219.

33. Samuel Gnasso to FHL, January 19, 1932, FHL to Gnasso, January 25, 1932, Box 2525, NYMA; Limpus and Leyson, *La Guardia*, 171–172.

34. Cuneo, *Life With Fiorello*, 141.

35. FHL to Hugh Flaherty, November 22, 1925, Box 2521, NYMA.

36. Limpus and Leyson, *La Guardia*, 220; Zinn, *La Guardia*, 162; Mann, *La Guardia*, 263.

37. "Congressman F. H. La Guardia States That He Will Not Be a Candidate for Mayor in 1925," Box 2521, NYMA.

38. Mann, *La Guardia*, 268.

39. FHL to John Q. Tilson, March 3, 1923, Box 2522, NYMA; Zinn, *La Guardia*, 167; FHL to S. Koenig, April 2, 1927; S. Koenig to FHL April 5, 1927, Box 2522, NYMA.

40. *World*, April 20, 1920, quoted in Werner, "La Guardia," 149; Zinn, *La Guardia*, 169; Ray Tucker, *Sons of Wild Jackass* (Boston: L. C. Page, 1932), 374, 378; Zinn, *La Guardia*, 78, 170.

41. Werner, "La Guardia," 250; Duff Gilfond, "La Guardia of Harlem," *American Mercury* 11 (June 1927): 153; Jay Franklin [John Franklin Carter], *La Guardia: A Biography* (New York: Modern Age, 1937), 77; Tucker, *Jackass*, 395; Mann, *La Guardia*, 261.

42. FHL to Gauvreau, August 27, 1928, quoted in Zinn, *La Guardia*, 272.

43. Eric F. Goldman, *Rendezvous with Destiny: A History of Modern American Reform* (New York: Knopf, 1952), 315; Zinn, *La Guardia*, 166; Leuchtenburg, *Perils*, 153; Gilfond, "La Guardia," 153–154; Limpus and Leyson, *La Guardia*, 168.

44. Limpus and Leyson, *La Guardia*, 90.

45. Gilfond, "La Guardia," 152–158; Tucker, *Jackass*, 378; Marie La Guardia interview, Columbia University Oral History Collection, 9–12.

46. *Congressional Record* 70 (February 4, 1929): 2768–2770; Marie La Guardia

interview, Columbia University Oral History Collection, 9–12; Limpus and Leyson, *La Guardia*, 190–191, 159–160.

47. *Congressional Record* 70 (February 4, 1929): 2767–2770.

48. Tucker, *Jackass*, 371; Oswald Garrison Villard to Alfred Artyn Gross, October 29, 1928, Villard Papers, Harvard University.

49. Tucker, *Jackass*, 398; Limpus and Leyson, *La Guardia*, 150.

50. Limpus and Leyson, *La Guardia*, 268.

51. FHL to Oswald Garrison Villard, November 15, 1928, Villard Papers, Harvard University.

52. Marie La Guardia, interview with the author, March 14, 1983; Elsie Fisher, interview with the author, March 14, 1983.

53. Maurice Postley, interview with the author, June 16, 1983.

54. Limpus and Leyson, *La Guardia*, 273–274.

55. Mann, *La Guardia*, 237.

56. Marie La Guardia, interview with the author, March 14, 1983.

57. Mann, *La Guardia*, 237.

58. Tucker, *Jackass*, 396; William Manners, *Patience and Fortitude: Fiorello La Guardia, A Biography* (New York: Harcourt, Brace, 1976), 112.

59. Elsie Fisher, interview with the author, March 14, 1983.

60. Bayrd Still, *Mirror for Gotham* (New York: University Press, 1956), 297.

61. Still, *Mirror*, 258, 297–299, 260.

62. Still, *Mirror*, 263–266.

63. Still, *Mirror*, 260–261, 274–275, 296–297.

64. Still, *Mirror*, 278.

65. Gene Fowler, *Beau James: The Life and Times of Jimmy Walker* (New York: Viking, 1949), 34–45.

66. Fowler, *Beau James*, 54; Charles Garrett, *The La Guardia Years: Machine and Reform Politics in New York City* (New Brunswick: Rutgers University Press, 1961), 53.

67. Edward Robb Ellis, *Epic of New York* (New York: Coward-McCann, 1966), 523–525; Garrett, *The La Guardia Years*, 84; Fowler, *Beau James*, 166–167, 172–173, 229, 164.

68. Fowler, *Beau James*, 183–185.

69. Louis J. Gribetz and Joseph Kaye, *Jimmie Walker: The Story of a Personality* (New York: Dial Press, 1932), 244–246; Fowler, *Beau James*, 226, 219; George Walsh, *Gentleman Jimmy Walker* (New York: Praeger, 1974), 146–147.

70. Fowler, *Beau James*, 164; Garrett, *The La Guardia Years*, 54; Lawrence Elliott, *Little Flower: The Life and Times of Fiorello La Guardia* (New York: Morrow, 1983), 164.

71. Fowler, *Beau James*, 191, 197, 212–215, 167–168; Walsh, *Gentleman Jimmy Walker*, 68, 110, 321–322; Ellis, *Epic of New York*, 526; Gribetz and Kaye, *Jimmie Walker*, 249.

72. Fowler, *Beau James*, 243–245; Werner, "La Guardia," 328–329.

73. Mann, *La Guardia*, 269; FHL to Oswald G. Villard, May 2 and 31, 1929, Villard to FHL, May 27, 1929, Villard Papers, Harvard University; Franklin, *La Guardia*, 84; John Bakeless, "New York, The Nation's Prodigal: The City of Glorious Graft," *The Forum*

(October, 1929): 599–611; M. R. Werner, "Fiorello's Finest Hour," *American Heritage* 12 (October 1961): 41.

74. *New Yorker* quoted in Elliott, *Little Flower*, 163; Werner, "Fiorello's Finest Hour," 40.

75. Zinn, *La Guardia*, 171; Werner, "Fiorello's Finest Hour," 41; Ed Flynn, *You're The Boss* (New York: Viking, 1947), 55.

76. Werner, "Fiorello's Finest Hour," 41; Franklin, *La Guardia*, 85; Harry Fleischman, *Norman Thomas: A Biography* (New York: Norton, 1964), 120.

77. Fowler, *Beau James*, 245–246.

78. Werner, "Fiorello's Finest Hour," 107; Mann, *La Guardia*, 274; Fleischman, *Thomas*, 120.

79. Werner, "La Guardia," 349–351; Franklin, *La Guardia*, 83; Limpus and Leyson, *La Guardia*, 287; Mann, *La Guardia*, 271; and materials in file marked "Mayoralty Campaign 1929," Box 2522, NYMA.

80. Mann, *La Guardia*, 277.

81. Fowler, *Beau James*, 246, 230; Franklin, *La Guardia*, 86.

82. Mann, *La Guardia*, 272; Walsh, *Gentleman Jimmy Walker*, 172–173; Fowler, *Beau James*, 225.

83. Fowler, *Beau James*, 222–226; Walsh, *Gentleman Jimmy Walker*, 171; "A Murdered Rothstein Is Political Dynamite," *Literary Digest* (October 19, 1929): 61–71; Werner, "Fiorello's Finest Hour," 108; Franklin, *La Guardia*, 86.

84. Frank Freidel, *The Triumph*, Vol. 3 of *Franklin D. Roosevelt* (Boston: Little, Brown, 1956), 92; Zinn, *La Guardia*, 173.

85. Fowler, *Beau James*, 256; Werner, "La Guardia," 371; Mann, *La Guardia*, 278; Werner, "Fiorello's Finest Hour," 110–111.

86. Limpus and Leyson, *La Guardia*, 291–292, 295; Zinn, *La Guardia*, 174; Mann, *La Guardia*, 278.

Chapter 5

1. John Kenneth Galbraith, *The Great Crash, 1929* (Boston: Houghton Mifflin, 1955), 79.

2. Irving Bernstein, *The Lean Years: A History of the American Worker, 1920–1933* (Boston: Houghton Mifflin, 1960), 251.

3. William E. Leuchtenburg, *The Perils of Prosperity, 1914–1932* (Chicago: University of Chicago Press, 1958), 245–247; Edward R. Ellis, *A Nation in Torment: The Great American Depression, 1929–1939* (New York: Capricorn, 1971), 57; Galbraith, *Great Crash*, 179–192.

4. National Bureau for Economic Research, *Recent Economic Changes in the United States*, 2 vols. (New York: McGraw-Hill, 1929), II, 862–910; Galbraith, *Great Crash*, 150–151; Leuchtenburg, *Perils*, 244.

5. Leuchtenburg, *Perils*, 260; Edward R. Ellis, *Epic of New York City* (New York: Coward-McCann, 1966), 532.

6. Ellis, *Epic of New York*, 532.

7. Carolyn Bird, *The Invisible Scar* (New York: D. McKay, 1966), 24–25, 34; Ellis, *Nation in Torment*, 126, 130.

8. Bird, *Invisible Scar*, 26; Ellis, *Nation in Torment*, 126–127.

9. Bird, *Invisible Scar*, 27, 29, 34; Leuchtenburg, *Perils*, 249; Ellis, *Nation in Torment*, 130–131.

10. Leuchtenburg, *Perils*, 251.

11. Arthur M. Schlesinger, Jr., *The Crisis of the Old Order*, Vol. 1 of *The Age of Roosevelt* (Boston: Houghton Mifflin, 1957), 169; Bernstein, *The Lean Years*, 190–191, 229–239.

12. John A. Garraty, *The American Nation* (Fifth edition, New York: Harper & Row, 1983), 649.

13. Ellis, *Nation in Torment*, 236.

14. Ellis, *Nation in Torment*, 154–155, 242; Leuchtenburg, *Perils*, 253; Bird, *Invisible Scar*, 27.

15. Ellis, *Epic of New York*, 532–533.

16. Schlesinger, *Crisis of the Old Order*, 457; Lowell Limpus and Burr W. Leyson, *This Man La Guardia* (New York: E. P. Dutton, 1938), 255.

17. Bernstein, *The Lean Years*, 261; Schlesinger, *Crisis of the Old Order*, 457.

18. FHL, "New York the City Beautiful—The Home of Happiness," Drafts of New York *Journal* articles, Box 2521, NYMA.

19. Limpus and Leyson, *La Guardia*, 299–300.

20. J. Joseph Huthmacher, *Senator Robert F. Wagner and the Rise of Urban Liberalism* (New York: Atheneum, 1971), 75; Ellis, *Nation in Torment*, 195; Leuchtenburg, *Perils*, 264; Schlesinger, *Crisis of the Old Order*, 165.

21. Huthmacher, *Wagner*, 77, 67, 73; Schlesinger, *Crisis of the Old Order*, 169, 188.

22. Bernstein, *The Lean Years*, 263–266, 270; Huthmacher, *Wagner*, 59, 63–71. On La Guardia's belief in the need for such statistics, see FHL to Leo Wohrman, March 10, 1930, Roll 8, FHL Papers, NYPL.

23. Limpus and Leyson, *La Guardia*, 324; Tucker, *Jackass*, 384; FHL to John Andrews, February 5, 1932, Roll 8, NYPL; *Congressional Record* 73 (December 16, 1930): 894; (December 8, 1931): 87; (February 17, 1931): 5240–5241; FHL Press Release, June 23, 1930, Box 2528, NYMA; Zinn, *La Guardia*, 179.

24. Bernstein, *The Lean Years*, 311, 273–274, 285; Zinn, *La Guardia*, 188.

25. *Times* quoted in Zinn, *La Guardia*, 244.

26. FHL to G. Norris, March 10, 1931, Box 2527, NYMA.

27. M. R. Werner, "La Guardia" (unpublished manuscript, FDR Library, Hyde Park), 415; FHL, "Statement in Favor of Unemployment Insurance," transcript of radio speech, Box 2528, NYMA.

28. FHL to J. J. Morse, June 17, 1931, FHL to Thomas Wrigley, June 19, 1931, Box 2524, NYMA.

29. FHL to G. Norris, March 10, 1931, Box 2527, NYMA; FHL, "Statement in

Favor of Unemployment Insurance," transcript of radio speech, Box 2528, NYMA; Leuchtenburg, *Perils*, 250; *Congressional Record* 74 (December 21, 1931): 1033–1036, quoted in Zinn, *La Guardia*, 197–198, 252.

30. Werner, "La Guardia," 423–424; FHL, "Statement in Favor of Unemployment Insurance," transcript of radio speech, Box 2528, NYMA.

31. Zinn, *La Guardia*, 198, 186–187, 190; Clipping of Washington dispatch in FHL to C. W. Ervin, March 19, 1943, Box 2703, NYMA; Werner, "La Guardia," 427.

32. Werner, "La Guardia," 437–438.

33. FHL to J. J. Morse, June 17, 1931, Box 2524, NYMA; FHL, Speech on Hoover and the Veto of Relief, n.d. [1932], Box 2527, NYMA; FHL "The Inside on the Banking Investigations," *Liberty* (May 13, 1933): 9; Werner, "La Guardia," 437, 439; Zinn, *La Guardia*, 209; Mann, *La Guardia*, 303.

34. FHL "The Inside on the Banking Investigations, Part II" *Liberty* (May 20, 1933): 22.

35. Galbraith, *Great Crash*, 151–159.

36. FHL, "The Inside on the Banking Investigations," *Liberty* (May 13, 1933): 6–7, 9–10.

37. FHL, "The Inside on the Banking Investigations," 10; Zinn, *La Guardia*, 216–217.

38. Zinn, *La Guardia*, 208; Cuneo, *Life With Fiorello*, 20–21; Galbraith, *Great Crash*, 165–169; Ellis, *Nation in Torment*, 69.

39. Leuchtenburg, *Perils*, 259.

40. Page Smith, *America Enters the World: A People's History of the Progressive Era and World War I* (New York: McGraw-Hill, 1985), 1010; Zinn, *La Guardia*, 213–224.

41. Zinn, *La Guardia*, 199.

42. Galbraith, *Great Crash*, 142, 188; Werner, "La Guardia," 456; Eliott, *Little Flower*, 177.

43. Cuneo, *Life With Fiorello*, 53–56; Zinn, *La Guardia*, 219–220; Werner, "La Guardia," 430.

44. Werner, "La Guardia," 461–462; Zinn, *La Guardia*, 221; Cuneo, *Life With Fiorello*, 44–45; Jay Franklin [John Franklin Carter], *La Guardia: A Biography* (New York: Modern Age, 1937), 94; "La Guardia Plan for Increased Federal Revenues," n.d., Box 2524; FHL, "Taxation, Lobbying, and the Freedom of the Air," transcript of radio address on NBC, January 27, 1932, Box 2524, NYMA.

45. Zinn, *La Guardia*, 225–226 (Sandusky *Register*); Werner, "La Guardia," 365, 457 (Washington *Star*), 467 (Chicago *Tribune*), 469. See also Chicago *Tribune*, March 25, 1932 in FHL Scrapbook, LAGA.

46. Zinn, *La Guardia*, 222–224, 226; Cuneo, *Life With Fiorello*, 46.

47. Werner, "La Guardia," 458, 470, 472, 474.

48. *American Observer*, May 11, 1932; *Evening Journal*, March 24, 1932; Chicago *Tribune*, March 25, 1932, all in FHL Scrapbooks, LAGA.

49. Werner, "La Guardia," 441; FHL to William Harris, April 15, 1932, Box 2524, NYMA.

50. *Congressional Record*, Appendix, 74 (June 7, 1932): 12763–12764; Werner, "La Guardia," 529; *Congressional Record* 74 (May 31, 1932): 2056; *Congressional Record* 74

(April 14, 1932): 8225–8229. The Congressional questionnaire can be found in Box 2524, NYMA.

51. Cuneo, *Life With Fiorello*, 39.

52. Cuneo, *Life With Fiorello*, 39; Zinn, *La Guardia*, 215–216; Mann, *La Guardia*, 306; Bud Armstrong to FHL, December 28, 1932; E. Schaefer to FHL, n.d., both in Box 2525, NYMA. For other letters to La Guardia on the mortgage situation, see Roll 7, FHL Papers, NYPL, and Box 2527, NYMA.

53. Leuchtenburg, *Perils*, 261–262; *Business Week*, October 7, 1931, quoted in David A. Shannon, ed., *The Great Depression* (Englewood Cliffs, New Jersey: Prentice-Hall, 1963), 12.

54. Werner, "La Guardia," 434–435.

55. Werner, "La Guardia," 490; Zinn, *La Guardia*, 201–202.

56. Werner, "La Guardia," 490–491, 493; Zinn, *La Guardia*, 204; Mann, *La Guardia*, 312; Folder marked "Relief," Box 2527, NYMA.

57. Zinn, *La Guardia*, 205; Werner, "La Guardia," 494.

58. Zinn, *La Guardia*, 204, FHL, "The Price of Coal This Winter," and "Bonus," Drafts of New York *Journal* articles, Box 2521, NYMA; Zinn, *La Guardia*, 205; Ellis, *Nation in Torment*, 163.

59. Cuneo, *Life With Fiorello*, 86–88; Mann, *La Guardia*, 308; Zinn, *La Guardia*, 205; John D. Hicks, *Republican Ascendancy, 1921–1933* (New York: Harper & Brothers, 1960), 275, 309, 374–375; Leuchtenburg, *Perils*, 262–263; Ellis, *Nation in Torment*, 178; Werner, "La Guardia," 481.

60. Limpus and Leyson, *La Guardia*, 29; Mann, *La Guardia*, 257; Zinn, *La Guardia*, 145–149.

61. FHL speech in House of Representatives quoted in clipping enclosed in William R. Vallance to FHL, April 26, 1932, Roll 8, NYPL. On job retraining see Lewis Sampson to FHL, February 15, 1932, Roll 4, NYPL.

62. Werner, "La Guardia," 219; FHL to Edward F. McGrady, July 15, 1931, Roll 8, NYPL.

63. Sam Squibb to FHL, December 15, 1932, Box 2526, NYMA; FHL to Patrick Boland, August 2 and 4, 1931, John Burke to FHL, January 10, 1932, FHL to Willis Johnson, June 23, 1932, Roll 8, NYPL. See also FHL to Hugh Frayne, June 29, 1931, and on Roll 8, letter to Bricklayers, Plasterers, and Masons International Union (July 23, 1931); M. Bertinelli to FHL, July 30, 1931; S. Hillman to FHL, February 3, 1932; FHL to G. Cutler, May 2, 1931; A. Bellows to FHL, February 14, 1932; Roll 8, NYPL.

64. Marie La Guardia interview, Columbia University Oral History Collection, 19.

65. Marie La Guardia interview, Columbia University Oral History Collection, 21; Bernstein, *The Lean Years*, 392.

66. Bernstein, *The Lean Years*, 191–196; Melvin Segal, *The Norris La Guardia Act* (Washington: American Council on Public Affairs, n.d.), 1.

67. Bernstein, *The Lean Years*, 196; Cuneo, *Life With Fiorello*, ix; Smith, *America Enters the World*, 1028.

68. FHL, "Injuctions," Drafts of New York *Journal* articles, Box 2521, NYMA; Zinn, *La Guardia*, 227, 334.

69. Bernstein, *The Lean Years*, 399–413.

70. A. P. Randolph to FHL, May 12, 1932, Roll 8, NYPL; H. Bennett to FHL, July 5, 1932, Roll 4, NYPL. For instances in which La Guardia sought to make sure that Norris-La Guardia was being properly enforced, see FHL to H. Bennett, July 20, 1932 and Van Bittner to FHL, July 19, 1932, both on Roll 4, NYPL; Robert F. Mathews to FHL, November 4, 1932, Roll 8, NYPL.

71. Norris to FHL, April 12 and 23, 1932, Box 2524, NYMA; Werner, "La Guardia," 443–448. Correspondence between Norris and La Guardia is scarce, but for more on La Guardia's views on Norris-La Guardia see material on labor in Roll 8, NYPL. Joseph G. Rayback, *A History of American Labor* (New York: Macmillan, 1967), 319–320 and Bernstein, *The Lean Years*, 390–413, discuss the Norris-La Guardia Act.

72. Mann, *La Guardia*, 289; Zinn, *La Guardia*, 263; Marie La Guardia interview, Columbia University Oral History Collection, 17–19; Cuneo, *Life With Fiorello*, x–xi.

73. T. K. Carskadon, "New York's Fighting Mayor," *Current History* 43 (January 1936): 353–358; Marie La Guardia interview, Columbia University Oral History Collection, 17–18; FHL to [?] Panza, September 24, 1932, Roll 2, NYPL; Limpus and Leyson, *La Guardia*, 320.

74. Zinn, *La Guardia*, 254.

75. Limpus and Leyson, *La Guardia*, 339–341; Werner, "La Guardia," 420.

76. Zinn, *La Guardia*, 235–236; letter to FHL signed "Republican," n.d., Box 2525, NYMA.

77. FHL to Edward Keating, July 24, 1929, Roll 1, NYPL; FHL to Congressman William Kopp, August 12, 1931, Box 2525, NYMA; Zinn, *La Guardia*, 238; *Times*, May 21, 1931.

78. Limpus and Leyson, *La Guardia*, 318, 332–335, 339; Werner, "La Guardia," 406–409; Detroit *Free Press*, September 25, 1932, on Roll 2, NYPL; FHL to W. Newton, May 8, 1931; W. W. Phelps to FHL, October 10, 1931; FHL to L. Millowitz, October 20, 1931; L. Millowitz to FHL, September 28, 1931; FHL to J. Shafroth, May 8, 1931; J. Shafroth to FHL, May 9, 1931, all on Roll 8, NYPL. On the investigations of the judges, see material in Box 2526, NYMA.

79. Werner, "La Guardia," 416; Limpus and Leyson, *La Guardia*, 336, 290–291; FHL to L. R. de Steigner, May 5, 1931, Roll 8, NYPL.

80. FHL to Hugh Frayne, July 1, 1931, Roll 8, NYPL; A. P. Randolph to FHL, August 15 and 20, December 5, 1931, May 16, September 26, 1932; FHL to Randolph, August 25, September 21, November 27, 1931, April 23, July 5, 1932, all on Roll 8, NYPL. For more on Randolph's relationship with La Guardia, see Werner, "La Guardia," 502.

81. Werner, "La Guardia," 525. The list of bills introduced by La Guardia in the 72nd Congress is at LAGA.

82. Ronald Steel, *Walter Lippmann and the American Century* (New York: Random House, 1981), 286.

83. See letters on Rolls 3–9, NYPL, and in Boxes 2522, 2525, 2527, and 2528, NYMA.

84. Typescript of NBC address, January 31, 1933, Box 2523, NYMA.

85. Clipping of Pittsburgh *Press*, May 20, 1932, LAGA; *The Nation* 136 (January

4, 1933): 7; Zinn, *La Guardia*, 246; FHL to V. Marcantonio, July 13, 1932, FHL to N. Saldiveri, July 20, 1932, FHL to David Halpern, August 16, 1932, FHL to Arcolo Corleone, September 16, 1932, all on Roll 4, NYPL.

86. Cuneo, *Life With Fiorello*, 148; Zinn, *La Guardia*, 246; Limpus and Leyson, *La Guardia*, 329; Mann, *La Guardia*, 314–319.

87. Werner, "La Guardia," 507.

88. Panza to FHL, September 23, 1932, FHL to Panza, September 24, 1932, Roll 2, NYPL.

89. *World Telegram*, October 21, 1932; Werner, "La Guardia," 506; FHL to Harry Watts, October 27, 1932, Roll 3, NYPL; FHL to J. Engel, October 26, 1932, Roll 2, NYPL; *Evening Journal*, October 21, 1932; FHL to J. R. Valles (on Puerto Rican community), December 12, 1932, Roll 3, NYPL; Mann, *La Guardia*, 313–319; A. P. Randolph to FHL, n. d. [1932], Box 2526, NYMA.

90. Cuneo, *Life With Fiorello*, 166; Washington *Post*, January 8, 1933, Washington *Herald*, January 8, 1933, LAGA scrapbook; Werner, "La Guardia," 510–514.

91. FHL to Harry Hall, February 3, 1933; P. McWilliams to FHL, January 11, 1933; Nicola Mafia to FHL, January 10, 1933, all on Roll 3, NYPL; Limpus and Leyson, *La Guardia*, 351–353; Mann, *La Guardia*, 320; FHL to Gilfond, November 16, 1932, General Ms. Collection, Columbia University; FHL to M. J. Weeker, November 14, 1932; FHL to Abraham Krakauer, November 14, 1932, both Roll 3, NYPL.

92. Robert H. LaFollette to FHL, February 20, 1933, Box 2526, NYMA; W. Green to FHL, November 11, 1932, Roll 2, NYPL; Limpus and Leyson, *La Guardia*, 352–353; Werner, "La Guardia," 514.

93. A. E. Tenga to FHL, September 28, 1932, FHL to Frank Tufaro, February 1, 1933, Roll 3, NYPL; Zinn, *La Guardia*, 251. Also see Dominic Felitti to FHL, December 7, 1932; S. Appel to FHL, October 26, December 7, 1932; FHL to Frank Kidde, December 9, 1932 (on helping get kosher food for a public assistance kitchen); FHL to Frank Kidde, December 28, 1932 (on getting the maximum emergency federal allotments); FHL to V. Marcantonio, January 11, 1933; Frank Kidde to FHL, January 25, 1933, all in Box 2527, NYMA. On pleas for jobs, Luigi Valenti to FHL, October 27, 1932, and FHL to Valenti, October 28, 1932, Roll 3, NYPL; Ramon Rosario to FHL, September 7, 1932, Roll 2, NYPL; FHL to Catherine Sanders, January 18, 1933, Roll 3, NYPL; Murray Lasky to FHL, August 5, 1933, Roll 3, NYPL; FHL to Emergency Home Relief Bureau, January 5, 1933, Roll 3, NYPL. Many other similar letters can be found on Roll 3, NYPL.

94. Zinn, *La Guardia*, 253–255; San Francisco *Examiner*, February 4, 1933, and Wilkes-Barre *Record*, February 4, 1933, both in clipping collection, LAGA; *Times*, December 27, 1932 quoted in Zinn, *La Guardia*, 254.

95. Marie La Guardia interview, Columbia University Oral History Collection, 23–25; FHL to Louis M. Howe, February 28, 1933, FDRP, FDR Library, Hyde Park; Schlesinger, *Crisis of the Old Order*, 192–193, 263–264, 309; Frank Freidel, *The Triumph*, Vol. 3 of *Franklin D. Roosevelt* (Boston: Little, Brown, 1956); Mann, *La Guardia*, 323–324; Zinn, *La Guardia*, 255; Drew Lewis and Rob Allen, "Hydraulic Press," undated clipping [1933], LAGA; William R. Watkins to FHL, June 30, 1932, Roll 4, NYPL; Address on NBC radio by William Hard, January 31, 1933, FHL to Norman Coetz, January 28, 1933,

FHL to M. S. Ruckeyser, February 21, 1933, all in Box 2523, NYMA; Washington *News*, January 11, 1933, clippings file, LAGA.

96. "U.S. Pays for Marines' Crime," *Labor* (January 24, 1933), in clippings file, LAGA; Werner, "La Guardia," 522–523; *The Nation* 136 (March 8, 1933): 246.

97. Mann, *La Guardia*, 329; Werner, "La Guardia," 515–517; Limpus and Leyson, *La Guardia*, 356.

Chapter 6

1. Edward R. Ellis, *Epic of New York City* (New York: Coward-McCann, 1966), 524; Gene Fowler, *Beau James: The Life and Times of Jimmy Walker* (New York: Viking, 1949), 256–257.

2. Fowler, *Beau James*, 259; George Walsh, *Gentleman Jimmy Walker: Mayor of the Jazz Age* (New York: Praeger, 1974), 210, 214; Robert A. Caro, *The Power Broker: Robert Moses and the Fall of New York* (New York: Vintage, 1974), 323; Lillian Brandt, *An Impressionistic View of the Winter of 1930–31 in New York City* (New York: Welfare Council of New York City, 1932), 6–8; *Times*, November 28, 1930, quoted in B. Blumberg, "The W. P. A. in New York City" (Ph.D. dissertation, Columbia University, 1974), 1; Irving Bernstein, *The Lean Years: A History of the American Worker, 1920–1933* (Boston: Houghton Mifflin, 1960), 293–295.

3. William E. Leuchtenburg, *The Perils of Prosperity, 1914–1932* (Chicago: University of Chicago Press, 1958), 256; Edward R. Ellis, *A Nation in Torment: The Great American Depression, 1929–1939* (New York: Capricorn, 1971), 229–230; Bayrd Still, *Mirror for Gotham: New York as Seen By Contemporaries from Dutch Days to the Present* (New York: University Press, 1956), 300, 319.

4. Ellis, *Nation in Torment*, 214, 535; Harry Fleischman, *Norman Thomas: A Biography* (New York: Norton, 1964), 126; Leuchtenburg, *Perils*, 262.

5. Bernstein, *The Lean Years*, 427–428; Ellis, *Nation in Torment*, 136, 139; Walsh, *Gentleman Jimmy Walker*, 212; Police Department Press Release, April 21, 1930, Box 2524, NYMA; H. A. Swain to FHL, May 10, 1930, and FHL to Representative George Schneider, May 9, 1930, both Box 2524, NYMA; Lowell Limpus and Burr W. Leyson, *This Man La Guardia* (New York: E. P. Dutton, 1938), 323; Walter Goodman, *The Committee: The Extraordinary Career of the House Committee on Un-American Activities* (New York: Farrar, Straus & Giroux, 1968), 6; Howard Zinn, *La Guardia in Congress* (Ithaca: Cornell University Press, 1959), 234–235. Box 2524, NYMA, contains a file on the charge that Communists led the aborted march, and the discovery by the New York *Graphic* that this claim was untrue.

6. Brandt, *Impressionistic View*, 8–10; Fowler, *Beau James*, 259; Leuchtenburg, *Perils*, 251; *Times*, January 18, 20, 24, 25, 28, April 28, June 19, June 20, 1931.

7. *Times*, February 11, September 6, 15, 1931; Herbert Mitgang, *The Man Who*

Rode the Tiger: The Life and Times of Judge Samuel Seabury (Philadelphia: J. B. Lippincott, 1963), 169; Walsh, *Gentleman Jimmy Walker*, 223–224.

8. *Population Growth of New York City By Districts, 1910–1948* (New York: Consolidated Edison Industrial and Economic Development Department, 1948), Table 1; Walter Laidlaw, *Population of the City of New York, 1890–1930* (New York: Cities Census Committee, 1932), 236; Robert H. Armstrong and Homer Hoyt, *Decentralization in New York City* (Chicago: 1941), 71, 120. In 1930 Manhattan contained 26.9% of the city's population, Brooklyn 36.9%, the Bronx 18.3%, Queens 15.6%, and Staten Island 2.3%.

9. Still, *Mirror*, 269–271, 213–214; Laidlaw, *Population of New York City*, 247, 275, 289.

10. Thomas Adams, et al, *The Building of New York City*, Vol. 2 of *Regional Plan of New York and Its Environs* (New York: 1931), 36.

11. Gilbert Osofsky, *Harlem: The Making of a Ghetto* (New York: Harper & Row, 1966), 127; *Fourteenth Census of the United States Taken in the Year 1920* (Washington: Government Printing Office, 1921–1923), III, 691; Ira Rosenwaike, *Population History of New York City* (Syracuse: Syracuse University Press, 1972), 121; Cheryl Greenberg, "Community and Crisis: Black Harlem in the Great Depression" (Ph.D. dissertation, Columbia University, 1987), 2, 12.

12. "The Making of Harlem," *Survey Graphic* (1925): 635, quoted in Greenberg, "Harlem," 1; Osofsky, *Harlem*, 138; Mark Naison, *Communists in Harlem During the Depression* (Urbana: University of Illinois Press, 1983), 32; Greenberg, "Harlem," 16, 20.

13. *U.S. Census, 1930*, I, 732, 1130–1146; Gladys L. Palmer and Katherine D. Wood, *Urban Workers on Relief* (Washington, 1933), I: 6, II: 266; Osofsky, *Harlem*, 152–153; Greenberg, "Harlem," 32–34.

14. Osofsky, *Harlem*, 147; Greenberg, "Harlem," 61–63, 68.

15. Clifton Hood, "Underground Politics: A History of Mass Transit in New York City Since 1904" (Ph.D. dissertation, Columbia University, 1986), 243–310; *Times*, January 28, 1934; FHL to "Fellow Republicans," March 26, 1923, Box 2522, NYMA; Transportation section, Postley Collection, LAGA [Maurice Postley collected information about the various departments in the city government for La Guardia's use during campaigns. They provide convenient information on all aspects of the city's government before La Guardia]; Department of Docks section, Postley Collection, LAGA; Caro, *The Power Broker*, 330–331.

16. John Bakeless, "New York, The Nation's Prodigal: The City of Glorious Graft," *The Forum* (October 1928); 599; Regional Plan Association, *From Plan to Reality* (New York: 1933), 88–90.

17. Regional Plan Association, *From Plan to Reality*, 17; *Highlights of the La Guardia Administration* (New York: Citizens' Committee for the Reelection of La Guardia, McGoldrick, and Morris, 1941), 7; Caro, *The Power Broker*, 331–336; "Robert Or I'll Resign Moses," *Fortune* (June 1938): 70–79.

18. *The Fusion Hand Book* (New York: Fusion Campaign Headquarters, 1933), 55; Caro, *The Power Broker*, 331–336.

19. Caro, *The Power Broker*, 339.

20. *Fusion Handbook*, 121; Jacob Riis, *How the Other Half Lives* (1890; reprint ed., New York: Hill and Wang, 1957), 199–203.

21. *Fusion Handbook*, 45–47, 123–125; Paul Blanshard, *Investigating City Government* (New York: New York City Department of Investigations, 1937), 132–133.

22. *Fusion Handbook*, 45–47; Civil Service section, Postley Collection, LAGA.

23. *Fusion Handbook*, 46–47; *Times*, May 18, 1932.

24. *Fusion Handbook*, 54 (*World Telegram* quote), 57 (*American* quote).

25. Department of Sanitation section, Postley Collection, LAGA; *Regional Plan for New York and Environs*, I, 90.

26. Health and Hospitals Department section, Postley Collection, LAGA; *Highlights*, 14; Rebeccah Rankin, ed., *New York Advancing: World's Fair Edition*, (New York: Municipal Reference Library, 1939), 58.

27. Blanshard, *Investigating City Government*, 30–34.

28. *Highlights*, 17.

29. Lowell Limpus, *Honest Cop: The Dramatic Life Story of Lewis J. Valentine* (New York: E. P. Dutton, 1939), 55, 113–124, 128, 150; Blanshard, *Investigating City Government*, 12–13, 85.

30. Frederick Shaw, *The History of the New York City Legislature* (New York: Columbia University Press, 1954), 8–10; Garrett, *The La Guardia Years*, 86.

31. Shaw, *New York City Legislature*, 14, 16–20, 24, 28–29; Bakeless, "New York, The Nation's Prodigal," 608.

32. Shaw, *New York City Legislature*, 78, 31.

33. *Regional Plan*, II, 587–588.

34. Excerpted in *The Voter's Digest: A Biography of Good Government* (New York: Citizens' Committee for the Reelection of La Guardia, McGoldrick, and Morris, 1941), 63.

35. Bernstein, *The Lean Years*, 295.

36. Bernstein, *The Lean Years*, 292–293; William Bremner, *Depression Winters: New York Social Workers and the New Deal* (Philadelphia: Temple University Press, 1984), 66–69; Dominic O'Keefe, "The History of Work Relief in New York City" (Ph.D. dissertation, New York University, 1978), 220–223.

37. Bernstein, *The Lean Years*, 457; Bremner, *Depression Winters*, 64–65; Zinn, *La Guardia*, 196.

38. Bremner, *Depression Winters*, 64–65; Bernstein, *The Lean Years*, 459–460.

39. Ronald H. Bayor, *Neighbors in Conflict: The Irish, Germans, Jews, and Italians of New York City, 1929–1941* (Baltimore: Johns Hopkins University Press, 1978), 25; Brandt, *Impressionistic View*, 35; Blumberg, "W. P. A. in New York City," 15; Henry Pringle, "Tammany Hall Inc.," *Atlantic Monthly* (October 1932), reprinted in *Voter's Digest* (October 1941): 19–21; Mitgang, *Seabury*, 228; Shaw, *New York City Legislature*, 149.

40. Bremner, *Depression Winters*, 120–121; Mitgang, *Seabury*. 228.

41. *Times*, October 22, 1931; Shaw, *New York City Legislature*, 143–144.

42. *Times*, January 24, 29, May 24, October 11, November 24, 1931.

43. *Times*, August 16, 26, 1931, January 17, October 4, 1932.

44. *Times*, January 20, 1932.

45. *Times*, January 11, 18, 1932.

46. *Fusion Handbook*, 24.

47. *Times*, September 21, 1932.

48. *Times*, October 17, 18, 23, November 1, 1932.

49. "Events Preceding Bankers Agreement," n.d., LAGA; *Times*, December 3, December 5, December 8, 30, 1932.

50. Werner, "La Guardia," 351, 379; Arthur Mann, *La Guardia: A Fighter Against His Times, 1882–1933* (Philadelphia: J. B. Lippincott, 1959), 276–277.

51. Garrett, *The La Guardia Years*, 65; Mitgang, *Seabury*, 167; Arthur Mann, *La Guardia Comes to Power: The Mayoral Election of 1933* (Philadelphia: Lippincott, 1965), 45; *Voter's Digest*, 64–65; Mitgang, *Seabury*, 168–169.

52. Blanshard, *Investigating City Government*, 53–54; *World*, February 8, 1931 (quote); Garrett, *The La Guardia Years*, 66.

53. Godkin quoted in Mitgang, *Seabury*, 157.

54. Mitgang, *Seabury*, xix, 7, 27–30, 33, 57 (quote); Mann, *La Guardia Comes to Power*, 38–42.

55. Mitgang, *Seabury*, 70, 75.

56. Mitgang, *Seabury*, 116–118, 122.

57. Mitgang, *Seabury*, 148–152, 157.

58. Mitgang, *Seabury*, 176, 171.

59. Garrett, *The La Guardia Years*, 69.

60. Mitgang, *Seabury*, 180–185; Mann, *La Guardia Comes to Power*, 58.

61. Mitgang, *Seabury*, 189, 195.

62. Seabury speech, February 16, 1932, quoted in *Fusion Handbook*, 92.

63. Garrett, *The La Guardia Years*, 65–68; Mitgang, *Seabury*, 212–215.

64. Mitgang, *Seabury*, 219–231; Mann, *La Guardia Comes to Power*, 51–53.

65. *Times*, March 17, 1932; Mitgang, *Seabury*, 232–234.

66. Mitgang, *Seabury*, 234–236.

67. Mann, *La Guardia Comes to Power*, 54; Mitgang, *Seabury*, 238–239.

68. Mitgang, *Seabury*, 240–241.

69. Mitgang, *Seabury*, 241–242; Garrett, *The La Guardia Years*, 74–75, 77; *Times*, June 2, August 6, 1932.

70. *The Nation* quoted in Mitgang, *Seabury*, 243.

Chapter 7

1. John Gunther, *Inside USA* (New York: Harper, 1946), 596.

2. *Times*, March 31, 1932.

3. *Times*, March 31 (quote), May 4, 5, 6, 8, 1932; Charles Garrett, *The La Guardia Years, Machine and Reform Politics in New York City* (New Brunswick: Rutgers University Press, 1961), 74–75.

4. *Times*, May 12, 1932; Herbert Mitgang, *The Man Who Rode the Tiger: The Life and Times of Judge Samuel Seabury* (Philadelphia: J. B. Lippincott, 1963), 249–252.

5. Mitgang, *Seabury*, 252–253.

6. Louis Gribetz and Joseph Kaye, *Jimmie Walker: The Story of a Personality* (New

York: Dial Press, 1932), 298–299, 306; Mitgang, *Seabury*, 254–255; *Times*, May 26, 27, September 2, 1932. Gribetz and Kaye's account is an apologia for Walker.

7. Mitgang, *Seabury*, 255–256, 261–263, 279; Gribetz and Kaye, *Walker*, 300; Bernard Bellush, *FDR as Governor of New York* (New York: Columbia University Press, 1955), 159–164.

8. Mitgang, *Seabury*, 283–285, 291, 295–299; *Times*, August 11, 13, 14, 16, 17, 18, 1932; Gene Fowler, *Beau James: The Life and Times of Jimmy Walker* (New York: Viking, 1949), 326–327, 226; Frank Friedel, *The Triumph*, Vol. 3 of *Franklin Roosevelt* (Boston: Little, Brown, 1956), 336.

9. Paul Blanshard, *Investigating City Government* (New York: 1937), 35–41, 66, 85, 106–107, 124–127; Bryce quoted in P. W. Wilson, "Can New York Afford Tammany Hall," *Review of Reviews* (October 1933), reprinted in *Voter's Digest: A Biography of Good Government* (New York: Citizens Committee for the Reelection of La Guardia, McGoldrick and Morris, 1941), 7; George Creel, "The Tammany Take," *Collier's* (February 18, 1933) reprinted in *Voter's Digest*, 40.

10. Arthur Mann, *La Guardia Comes to Power: The Mayoral Election of 1933* (Philadelphia: Lippincott, 1965), 115; *Times*, September 1, 2 (quote), 4, 1932. On his mayoralty see *Times*, March 6, September 5, 7, 11, 17, November 1, 17, December 4, 1932, September 30, 1933; George Walsh, *Gentleman Jimmy Walker: Mayor of the Jazz Age* (New York: Praeger, 1974), 330.

11. *Times*, January 26, 1932.

12. Ed Flynn, *You're The Boss* (New York: Viking, 1947), 142–144; *Times*, September 13, 22, 23; *Times*, September 30, October 1, 7, 1932.

13. *Times*, November 3, 9, 10, 1932.

14. Grenville Vernon to FHL, April 8, 1932, LAGA; [?] *Times-Journal*, April 15, 1935, FHL Scrapbook, NYMA.

15. *Times*, February 21, March 10, 1933; FHL to M. E. Gilfond, April 11, 1933, General ms. collection, Columbia University; W. H. Allen to FHL, August 5, 1933, Roll 3, NYPL; Mann, *La Guardia Comes to Power*, 65 (quote).

16. FHL to O. G. Villard, November 22, 1932, Villard Papers, Harvard University; *"What Are You Going To Do About It?" Appeal Made to the City of New York by F. H. La Guardia at Town Hall, November 28, 1932*, NYMA; Leone Pecoraro to FHL, January 29, 1933, Roll 3, NYPL; Garrett, *The La Guardia Years*, 95; *Times*, December 5, 6, 1932.

17. Mann, *La Guardia Comes To Power*, 69; *Times*, November 18, 19, 20, December 21 (McKee's break with Tammany), 1932.

18. Garrett, *The La Guardia Years*, 95–96; Mann, *La Guardia Comes to Power*, 75–78; *Times*, April 3, 1933.

19. Mann, *La Guardia Comes to Power*, 74; Lawrence Elliott, *Little Flower: The Life and Times of Fiorello La Guardia* (New York: Morrow, 1983), 195; *Times*, May 11, 1933.

20. Mann, *La Guardia Comes to Power*, 79; *Times*, May 20, 1933; Transcript of FHL radio address at Broadway Temple, May 21, 1933, LAGA.

21. Marie La Guardia interview, Columbia University Oral History Collection, 28; Mitgang, *Seabury*, 317; Mann, *La Guardia Comes to Power*, 74–76; Stanley Isaacs interview, Columbia University Oral History Collection, 72.

22. Newbold Morris, *Let the Chips Fall: My Battles Against Corruption* (New York: Appleton-Century-Crofts, 1955), 85–88; Mann, *La Guardia Comes to Power*, 77, 79.

23. Mann, *La Guardia Comes To Power*, 69.

24. Mann, *La Guardia Comes to Power*, 79–82; Nathan Straus interview, Columbia University Oral History Collection, 76.

25. Mann, *La Guardia Comes to Power*, 80.

26. Robert A. Caro, *The Power Broker: Robert Moses and the Fall of New York* (New York: Vintage, 1974), 348–354; Mitgang, *Seabury*, 3, 318; *Times*, July 12, 1933.

27. Caro, *The Power Broker*, 352–353, 357; Mann, *La Guardia Comes To Power*, 83; Mitgang, *Seabury*, 318; *Times*, July 27, 1933.

28. Henry Bruere to C. C. Burlingham, July 27, 1933, quoted in Frank Vos, "La Guardia and Burlingham: A Study of Political Friendship and Personal Influence" (M.A. Thesis, Columbia University, 1983), 16.

29. Mann, *La Guardia Comes To Power*, 84; Paul Windels interview, Columbia University Oral History Collection, Appendix, 22; *Times*, July 28, 1933; *Herald-Tribune* quoted in Vos, "Burlingham," 18.

30. R. Fulton Cutting to C. C. Burlingham, August 1, 1933, quoted in Vos, "Burlingham," 17; Charles C. Burlingham, *Nomination of Fiorello H. La Guardia for Mayor of the City of New York in 1933* (n.p.: 1943), 2; *Times*, July 29, 1933; Mann, *La Guardia Comes To Power*, 84 (quote).

31. *Times*, September 30, October 1, 1933; C. C. Burlingham to Emory Bruckner, August 15, 1933, CCBP; Caro, *The Power Broker*, 356.

32. Kenneth Dayton to C. C. Burlingham, August 1, 1932; Burlingham to Geoffrey Parsons, August 2, 1932, CCBP; *Herald-Tribune*, August 3, 1933, quoted in Vos, "Burlingham," 20.

33. Mann, *La Guardia Comes To Power*, 86.

34. Charles Tuttle interview, Columbia University Oral History Collection, 85–88; Windels interview, Columbia University Oral History Collection, Appendix, 22; Mann, *La Guardia Comes To Power*, 86–87; Mitgang, *Seabury*, 319 (all quotes).

35. Mitgang, *Seabury*, 312; C. C. Burlingham to B. Burritt, August 9, 1933, CCBP.

36. *The Fusion Handbook* (New York: Campaign Headquarters, 1933), 132–150; Garrett, *The La Guardia Years*, 96.

37. C. C. Burlingham to Felix Frankfurter, November 8, 1933, CCBP; Garrett, *The La Guardia Years*, 107; *Times*, September 8, 1933; Mann, *La Guardia Comes To Power*, 108–109 for a list of FHL's supporters.

38. Johnson quoted in "Fusion Baits the Tiger in New York," *Literary Digest* (September 2, 1933): 7; Mann, *La Guardia Comes To Power*, 90–91; Elliott, *Little Flower*, 198. See also *Times*, April 12, 23, May 10, July 28, September 26, October 10, November 22, 1933.

39. Garrett, *The La Guardia Years*, 103; Mann, *La Guardia Comes To Power*, 90–91; *Times*, April 12, 1933 (police quote).

40. *New Republic* (November 8, 1933): 346–347; Mann, *La Guardia Comes To Power*, 94.

41. Flynn, *You're The Boss*, 148; *Times*, September 22, 30, 1933; Windels interview,

Columbia University Oral History Collection, Appendix, 19; James Farley interview, Columbia University Oral History Collection, 145.

42. *Fusion Handbook*, 81; *World-Telegram*, September 25, 1933; Flynn, *You're The Boss*, 149.

43. *Times*, September 20, 23, 24, 26, 1933; Edward A. Balzar to FDR, n.d., PPF 1376, FDR to C. C. Burlingham, October 4, 1933, PSF Burlingham, both in FDRP; Mann, *La Guardia Comes To Power*, 95.

44. Flynn, *You're The Boss*, 150; Garrett, *The La Guardia Years*, 106; *Times*, September 17, 1933; Mann, *La Guardia Comes To Power*, 91–96, 104–105 (quotes), 109 (*Nation* quote).

45. Mann, *La Guardia Comes To Power*, 103; Burlingham quoted by Vos, "Burlingham," 23.

46. Garrett, *The La Guardia Years*, 109–111; *Times*, October 22, 1933.

47. Both Berle to FDR letters quoted in Beatrice Bishop Berle and Travis B. Jacobs, eds., *Navigating the Rapids, 1918–1941; From the Papers of Adolf Berle* (New York: Harcourt Brace Jovanovich, 1973), 88–89; Mann, *La Guardia Comes To Power*, 105.

48. Windels interview, Columbia University Oral History Collection, Appendix, 19–20; Flynn, *You're The Boss*, 151.

49. Mann, *La Guardia Comes To Power*, 111–113; *Times*, October 11, 13, 1933; Windels interview, Columbia University Oral History Collection, Appendix, 15; Mitgang, *Seabury*, 321.

50. Mitgang, *Seabury*, 321; *Times*, October 15, 1933.

51. Windels interview, Columbia University Oral History Collection, Appendix, 15–16; *Times*, October 15, 1932; Mann, *La Guardia Comes To Power*, 114.

52. Mann, *La Guardia Comes To Power*, 29; Lowell Limpus and Burr W. Leyson, *This Man La Guardia* (New York: E. P. Dutton, 1938), 368–369.

53. Mann, *La Guardia Comes To Power*, 114; Garrett, *The La Guardia Years*, 112.

54. Berle and Jacobs, *Navigating the Rapids*, 89; Flynn, *You're The Boss*, 152–153; Caro, *The Power Broker*, 357–358; Mann, *La Guardia Comes To Power*, 117.

55. Bea Blanchard, interview with the author, July 7, 1982; Mann, *La Guardia Comes To Power*, 102–104; C. C. Burlingham to Thomas M. Debevoise, October 26, 1933; C. C. Burlingham to F. Frankfurter, November 8, 1933, CCBP. See also C. C. Burlingham to Tom [Lamont], October 5, 1933, cited in Vos, "Burlingham," 24; C. C. Burlingham to Felix Warburg, October 26, 1933, CCBP.

56. Richard Knaust to FHL, October 7, 1933, Roll 3, NYPL; *Times*, October 5, 1933; Stanley Kreutzer, interview with the author, October 27, 1982; Louis Yavner, interview with the author, November 23, 1982; Mann, *La Guardia Comes To Power*, 99, 102; Garrett, *The La Guardia Years*, 110; Daniel Bell, "Crime as an American Way of Life," *Antioch Review* 13 (Summer 1953): 149; Flynn, *You're The Boss*, 153.

57. Mitgang, *Seabury*, 324; Mann, *La Guardia Comes To Power*, 118.

58. Mann, *La Guardia Comes To Power*, 106.

59. Mann, *La Guardia Comes To Power*, 120.

60. Garrett, *The La Guardia Years*, 113; Mann, *La Guardia Comes To Power*, 111, 121; *Times*, November 8, 28, 1933.

61. *Times*, October 14, 15 (in Little Italy), 1933; Mann, *La Guardia Comes To Power*, 123–159 (quote 135).

62. C. C. Burlingham to F. Frankfurter, November 8, 1933, CCBP

Chapter 8

1. August Heckscher, *When La Guardia Was Mayor: New York's Legendary Years* (New York: W. W. Norton & Co., 1978), 15; *Newsweek* (January 6, 1934): 34 (quote); *Times*, January 8, 1934.

2. *Herald-Tribune*, January 1, 1934.

3. Alan Brinkley, *Voices of Protest: Huey Long, Father Coughlin, and the Great Depression* (New York: Vintage, 1982), 32, 9, 26–27.

4. Irving Ben Cooper, interview with the author, June 17, 1983.

5. C. C. Burlingham to Felix Frankfurter, November 29, December 6, 1933, CCBP; *Times*, November 14, December 29 (quote), 1933; *News*, November 14, 1933; Lowell Limpus and Burr W. Leyson, *This Man La Guardia* (New York: E. P. Dutton, 1938), 377.

6. Arthur Mann, "When La Guardia Took Over," *New York Times Magazine* (January 2, 1966): 22; *Times*, November 9, December 26, 31, 1933.

7. Henry Graff, "The Kind of Mayor La Guardia Was," *New York Times Magazine* (October 22, 1961): 48; *Times, Herald-Tribune, World-Telegram*, January 2, 1934.

8. *Herald-Tribune*, January 6, 1934; *Times*, January 2, 1934; Heckscher, *La Guardia*, 18.

9. Robert Moses, "La Guardia: A Salute and a Memoir," *New York Times Magazine* (September 8, 1957): 18–19; Heckscher, *La Guardia*, 18; Lawrence Elliott, *Little Flower: The Life and Times of Fiorello La Guardia* (New York: Morrow, 1983), 207.

10. Transcript of January 1, 1934 radio speech, Box 2585, NYMA.

11. *Herald-Tribune, Times, News*, January 2, 1934.

12. "A Plan for Cities in Financial Distress," *Literary Digest* 116 (October 28, 1933): 38; *Post*, January 3, 1934; *Times*, February 15, 1933.

13. *Fusion Handbook* (New York: Campaign Headquarters, 1933), 26; *Times*, June 12, September 1, 1933.

14. *Times*, September 29, 1933.

15. *Times*, October 4, 1933.

16. *Times*, November 16, 1933.

17. *Times*, January 25, 1934; Leonard Chalmers, "The Crucial Test of La Guardia's First Hundred Days: The Emergency Economy Bill," *New York Historical Society Quarterly* 57 (1973): 239–240.

18. William L. Leuchtenburg, *Franklin D. Roosevelt and The New Deal* (New York: Harper & Row, 1963), 45; *Times*, December 29, 1933.

19. *World-Telegram*, January 2, 1934.

20. *Mirror, Post*, January 3, 1934.

21. Charles Garrett, *The La Guardia Years, Machine and Reform Politics in New York City* (New Brunswick: Rutgers University Press, 1961), 143; *Times*, November 16, 1933; Herbert Lehman interview, Columbia University Oral History Collection, 616; Albany *Times-Union*, January 2, 1934.

22. Brooklyn *Times-Union*, January 6, 1934; *World-Telegram*, January 5, 1934; *Times*, January 7, 1934; Brinkley, *Voices of Protest*, 78, 121.

23. Herbert H. Lehman to FHL, January 5, 1934, FHL to Lehman, January 7, 1934, Lehman Papers, Columbia University; Lehman interview, Columbia University Oral History Collection, 615–628.

24. *World-Telegram*, Brooklyn *Times-Union*, January 6, 1934; FHL to Lehman, January 7, 1934, Lehman Papers, Columbia University; *Times* on La Guardia's letter quoted in Heckscher, *La Guardia*, 40; *American*, January 10, 1934.

25. Lehman interview, Columbia University Oral History Collection, 528, 565, 603; Allan Nevins, *Herbert H. Lehman and His Era* (New York: Scribner, 1963), 148; FHL to Lehman, January 10, 1934, Lehman Papers, Columbia University; Robert P. Ingalls, *Herbert H. Lehman and New York's Little New Deal* (New York: New York University Press, 1975), 40; *American*, January 21, 1934; *Times*, January 20, 1934; C. C. Burlingham to F. Frankfurter, January 10, 1934, CCBP.

26. *World-Telegram*, February 1, 1934; *Times*, January 25, 1934; *News*, January 26, 1934; Teacher Joint Committee advertisement in *Herald-Tribune*, February 12, 1934; Chalmers, "Emergency Bill," 245.

27. *Times*, February 15, 1934 (quote); Chalmers, "Emergency Bill," 246.

28. FHL, "Rebalancing the 1934 Budget," text of radio speech, Box 2585, NYMA (quote); *Times*, January 19, February 2, 15, 16, 18, 1934; *Mirror*, February 17, 1934. The La Guardia administration's case for the bill is in A. A. Berle's January 28, 1934, speech in Box 2556, NYMA, and in La Guardia's speech before the legislature, in *Times*, January 25, 1934.

29. *Times*, February 2, 9 (editorial), 15, 1934; editorials on defeat of the bill in *Herald-Tribune, Evening Journal, Mirror*, February 16, 1934; *Sun*, February 27, 1934, Albany *Times-Union*, March 1, 1934.

30. Elliott, *Little Flower*, 208; FHL to M. W. Bray, March 12, 1934, Box 2556, NYMA; *News*, March 2, 1934; *Herald-Tribune*, January 28, 1934 (quote).

31. *Herald-Tribune*, February 2, March 6, 7, 1934.

32. *Herald-Tribune*, March 8, 1934.

33. Chalmers, "Emergency Bill," 247; *News*, March 8, 1934.

34. *Herald-Tribune*, March 18, 1934, and other city newspapers of the same date (concerning pressure from FDR); Albany *Times-Union*, March 27, 1934; *Times*, March 28, 1934.

35. Paul Windels interview, Columbia University Oral History Collection, 95; *Times*, March 29, 1934.

36. *Times*, March 30, 31, April 1, 3, 6, 1934; *Herald-Tribune, News*, March 31, 1934.

37. *Times*, April 6 (quote), 17, 1934; Brooklyn *Eagle, World-Telegram*, May 4, 1934.

38. *Herald-Tribune*, April 11, 1934; *Times*, April 6, 1934; Garrett, *The La Guardia Years*, 145.

39. *Times*, April 6, 17, May 14, 15, August 23, September 30, November 18, 27, 1934.

40. *Times*, December 6, 1934.

41. *Times*, December 11, 1934.

42. *Times*, July 7, 10, 11 (quote), 20, 1934; A. A. Berle, Jr., to FDR, April 23, 1934 (quote), McIntyre to FDR, July 20, 1934, PPF 1306, FDRP-HP; Berle to FDR, July 25, 1934, Adolf A. Berle, Jr., Papers, FDR Library Hyde Park.

43. *Times*, May 15, July 13, 15, August 1, November 30, December 6, 15, 1934; Garrett, *The La Guardia Years*, 145.

44. FHL, "New York Must Clean House," *Liberty* (January 20, 1934): 36–39.

45. *Times* quoted in Heckscher, *La Guardia*, 18; *Times*, January 4, 1934.

46. *Times*, January 3–30, 1934 (quotes from January 3, 4, and 16); *World-Telegram*, February 1, 1934.

47. *World-Telegram*, February 1, 1934; S. J. Woolf, "A Full Day on the Job With the Mayor," *New York Times Magazine* (January 14, 1934): 4.

48. Newbold Morris, *Let the Chips Fall: My Battles Against Corruption* (New York: Appleton-Century-Crofts, 1955), 118; Leonard Chalmers, "Fiorello La Guardia: Paterfamilias at City Hall; An Appraisal," *New York History* 71 (April 1975): 212–213; Woolf, "A Full Day," 13.

49. Chalmers, "Paterfamilias," 212; on FHL carrying a gun see *Times*, February 28, 1935.

50. FHL to Clement Stone, May 7, 1935, Box 2706, NYMA; William Fellowes Morgan, "From Confusion to Fusion: My Eight Years as New York's Commissioner of Markets" (typed manuscript, Lawrence Elliott Collection, LAGA), 26.

51. Limpus and Leyson, *La Guardia*, 384.

52. Limpus and Leyson, *La Guardia*, 380; Woolf, "Full Day," 5; Harold Seidman, *Investigating Municipal Administration: A Study of the New York City Department of Investigation* (New York: Institute of Public Administration, 1941), 109.

53. Rogers quoted in Arthur M. Schlesinger, Jr., *The Coming of the New Deal*, Vol. 2 of *The Age of Roosevelt* (Boston: Houghton Mifflin, 1957–1960), 13; Pegler in *Herald-Tribune*, February 17, 1934.

54. Woolf, "A Full Day," 4–5.

55. Heckscher, *La Guardia*, 48; Lowell Limpus, *Honest Cop, Lewis J. Valentine; Being a Chronicle of the Commissioner's Thirty-Six Years in the New York Police Department* (New York: E. P. Dutton, 1939), 156–157; *Times* and *Herald-Tribune*, December 17, 1933.

56. Heckscher, *La Guardia*, 48; Morgan, "From Confusion to Fusion," 6, 23.

57. Elliott, *Little Flower*, 209; *Times* and *Herald-Tribune*, December 14, 1933.

58. A. A. Berle to FHL, December 12, 1933, in *Times*, December 14, 1933.

59. *Times*, January 9, 1934 (quote); Wallace S. Sayre and Henry Kaufman, *Governing New York City* (New York: Russell Sage Foundation, 1960), 265.

60. William P. Brown, "The Political and Administrative Leadership of Fiorello H. La Guardia as Mayor of the City of New York, 1934–1941" (Ph.D. dissertation, New York University, 1960), 23–25.

61. Limpus and Leyson, *La Guardia*, 378; *Times*, January 2, 1934; Brown, "La Guardia," 23–24.

62. *Times*, December 6, 14, 1933.

63. Anna L. Strauss interview, Columbia University Oral History Collection, 92 (quote); *Times*, January 15, 1934; Goldwater quoted in Jerold Auerbach, "A New Deal For New York City, Fiorello La Guardia: 1934–1937" (Master's Essay, Columbia University, 1959), 29; Felix Frankfurter to C. C. Burlingham, January 15, 1934, CCBP; Theodore J. Lowi, *At the Pleasure of the Mayor: Patronage and Power in New York City, 1898–1958* (New York: Free Press, 1964), 60, 62.

64. Mann, "When La Guardia Took Over," 23.

65. Elliott, *Little Flower*, 209 (quote); *Times*, March 22, April 6, 1934; *American*, April 6, 1934; Brooklyn *Eagle*, March 21, 1934; J. Marshall, "La Guardia" (unpublished manuscript in the possession of the author, n.d.), 3; Limpus and Leyson, *La Guardia*, 377.

66. Frankel quoted in Brown, "La Guardia," 319; Felix Frankfurter to C. C. Burlingham, January 15, 1934, CCBP; Ernest Cuneo, *Life With Fiorello* (New York: Macmillan, 1955), xi.

67. Chalmers, "Paterfamilias," 215–216 (first two quotes); *Herald-Tribune* (quote) and *News* (rug), November 18, 1933; Eric F. Goldman, *Rendezvous with Destiny: A History of Modern American Reform* (New York: Knopf, 1952), 344.

68. Brown, "La Guardia," 64.

69. *Times*, January 2, 1934; FHL to Paul Windels, January 2, 1934, Box 659, NYMA; Brown, "La Guardia," 63–64 (quote).

70. Brown, "La Guardia," 137–138; *Times*, May 25, 1935.

71. Brown, "La Guardia," 44; Garrett, *The La Guardia Years*, 139.

72. Brooklyn *Eagle*, March 3, 1941; Chalmers, "Paterfamilias," 217.

73. Paul Blanshard, *Investigating City Government* (New York: 1937), 7 (on origins of his department); *Herald-Tribune*, January 6, 1934; *American* and *Journal*, March 21, 1934; *Times*, January 19, 1934, May 29, 1935; Press Releases, February 24 and 28, 1934, Box 659, NYMA; Brooklyn *Eagle* and *Journal*, March 2, 1934.

74. Blanshard, *Investigating City Government*, passim; Garrett, *The La Guardia Years*, 137; Auerbach, "La Guardia," 31–40.

75. *World-Telegram*, December 24, 1935; *Times*, January 25, 1934.

76. *Times*, March 28, 1934; *American*, March 18, 1934; *Sun*, March 8, 1934; Garrett, *The La Guardia Years*, 163.

77. Chalmers, "Paterfamilias," 216; *Times*, November 28, 1935.

78. Brown, "La Guardia," 62; FHL to William Hodson, December 22, 1936, Box 32, NYMA.

79. FHL to K. Dayton, July 11, 1938, Box 3199, NYMA; FHL to W. F. Morgan, August 20, 1936, in Brown, "La Guardia," 70.

80. FHL to J. McElligot, February 27, 1940, and FHL to A. McCormick, both quoted in Brown, "La Guardia," 70–71; Chalmers, "Paterfamilias," 219.

81. FHL to L. Valentine, July 7, 1936, Box 59, NYMA; Brown, "La Guardia," 71; E. Palmieri, interview with the author, November 9, 1982.

82. "Schedule of Meetings of Mayor's Department Heads," Box 14, NYMA; Goodhue Livingston, interview with the author, November 12, 1982; FHL to L. Valen-

tine, May 3, 1937, Box 82, NYMA; E. Palmieri, interview with the author, November 9, 1982.

83. *Herald-Tribune*, April 28, 1935.

84. Brown, "La Guardia," 82–84; FHL to S. Goldwater, January 14, 1934, in Brown, "La Guardia," 83–84; *Times*, September 19, 1935; Elliott, *Little Flower*, 213 (snow); Morgan, "Confusion to Fusion," 14 (hara-kiri).

85. I. B. Cooper, interview with the author, June 17, 1983; FHL to W. Hodson, January 21, 1939, quoted in Brown, "La Guardia," 69.

86. *Sun*, August 19, 1935; *Times*, August 21, 1935.

87. Anna L. Strauss interview, Columbia University Oral History Collection, 91; Woolf, "A Full Day," passim; Anna Clark, interview with the author, November 4, 1982; C. C. Burlingham interview, Columbia University Oral History Collection, 35.

88. Morgan, "Confusion to Fusion," Appendix, 9; Garrett, *The La Guardia Years*, 130.

89. Rexford G. Tugwell Diary, May 22, 1940, FDR Library, Hyde Park; *Sun*, November 21, 1934; B. Blanshard, interview with the author, July 7, 1982; Will Maslow, interview with the author, June 1982; Garrett, *The La Guardia Years*, 123.

90. Morgan, "Confusion to Fusion," Appendix; E. Palmieri, interview with the author, November 9, 1982.

91. Moses, "La Guardia," 116; F. Bloustein, interview with the author, May 3, 1983.

92. P. Windels to FHL, September 23, 1935, quoted in Brown, "La Guardia," 77; Chalmers, "Paterfamilias," 221.

93. FHL to Paul Kern, December 28, 1939, FHL to A. McCormick, and FHL to All Commissioners, January 24, 1934, all quoted in Brown, 73–74, 76.

94. Marshall, "La Guardia," 5; Garrett, *The La Guardia Years*, 131.

95. Edward I. Koch, *Mayor* (New York: Simon & Schuster, 1984), 55; Brown, "La Guardia," 84.

96. FHL to W. Carey, February 11, 1937, quoted in Brown, "La Guardia," 61; La Guardia quoted in *Times*, March 2, 1934; Auerbach, "La Guardia," 85; Lowi, *At The Pleasure of the Mayor*, 203.

97. C. C. Burlingham to FHL, February 16, 19, 1934, CCBP; Brown, "La Guardia," 90–128.

98. *Times*, February 12, 1935; Brown, "La Guardia," 99, 109; Garrett, *The La Guardia Years*, 134.

99. *Times*, June 6, 16, 1934; J. Finnegan to FHL, FHL to Finnegan, both September 11, 1934, quoted in Brown, "La Guardia," 106–107, 110.

100. Brown, "La Guardia," 111, 98; *Times*, September 10, 1935; Garrett, *The La Guardia Years*, 136.

101. *Times*, July 23, 1935 (quote); Brown, "La Guardia," 120–123, 125 (quote), 132 (quote), 140 (quote); B. Blanshard, interview with the author, July 7, 1982 (on firing adulterous employees).

102. Woolf, "A Full Day," 5.

103. Ronald Bayor, *Neighbors in Conflict: The Irish, Germans, Jews, and Italians of New York City: 1929–1941* (Baltimore: Johns Hopkins University Press), 30–32.

104. Bayor, *Neighbors in Conflict*, 39.

105. Bayor, *Neighbors in Conflict*, 39 (quote); *Times*, May 25, 1934, June 25, August 25, 1936; Warren Moscow, *Politics in the Empire State* (New York: Knopf, 1948), 126.

106. Robert A. Caro, *The Power Broker: Robert Moses and the Fall of New York* (New York: Vintage, 1974), 712; Bayor, *Neighbors in Conflict*, 41–44; Garrett, *The La Guardia Years*, 305–307; Alan Block, *East Side, West Side: Organizing Crime in New York, 1930–1950* (Cardiff: University College Cardiff Press, 1980), 242–244; Craig Thompson and Allen Raymond, *Gang Rule in New York City: The Story of a Lawless Era* (New York: Dial Press, 1940), 382.

107. E. Palmieri, interview with the author, November 9, 1982; James Marshall, interview with the author, December 2, 1982.

108. Moses, "La Guardia," 116; Brown, "La Guardia," 59 (quote), 316–317; Garrett, *The La Guardia Years*, 121 (quote).

109. Marshall, "Confusion to Fusion," 13; Felix Frankfurter, *Fiorello La Guardia, Address on the Occasion of the Fiorello La Guardia Memorial Dedication Ceremony at the La Guardia Houses, Rutgers Place and Clinton Street, September 20, 1957* (n.p., n.d.), 4.

110. Mann, "When La Guardia Took Over," 47; Cuneo, *Life With Fiorello*, 194–195.

111. C. C. Burlingham to FHL, September 25, 1934, CCBP.

Chapter 9

1. Mark Gelfand, *A Nation of Cities: The Federal Government and Urban America, 1933–1965* (New York: Oxford University Press, 1975), 5–6, 22–23; Newbold Morris, *Let the Chips Fall: My Battles Against Corruption* (New York: Appleton-Century-Crofts, 1955), 97.

2. Gelfand, *A Nation of Cities*, 24, 54–55.

3. Howard Chudacoff, *Evolution of American Urban Society*, (Second edition, Englewood Cliffs, New Jersey: Prentice-Hall, 1981), 238; Arthur M. Schlesinger, Jr., *The Coming of the New Deal*, Vol. 2 of *The Age of Roosevelt* (Boston: Houghton Mifflin, 1957–1960), 264–265.

4. William E. Leuchtenburg, *Franklin D. Roosevelt and the New Deal* (New York: Harper & Row, 1963), 120; Chudacoff, *Evolution of American Urban Society*, 239; Edward R. Ellis, *Nation in Torment: The Great American Depression, 1929–1939* (New York: Coward McCann, 1970), 490.

5. Schlesinger, *Coming of the New Deal*, 268 (quote); *Times, American*, November 11, 1933; Joseph Verdicchio, "New Deal Work Relief and New York City: 1933–1938," (Ph.D. dissertation, New York University, 1980), 6–80; William A. Wallace to FHL, November 12, 1933, Box 2716, NYMA.

6. *Times*, November 29, 1933 (also editorial in *Times* of September 15, 1933, on New York City's past difficulties obtaining funds in Washington); FHL to Robert Moses,

November 16, 1933, Moses Papers, NYPL; *The Secret Diary of Harold Ickes*, Vol. I (New York: Simon & Schuster, 1953), 126.

7. Gelfand, *A Nation of Cities*, 28; Adolf A. Berle, Jr., to FDR, January 9, 1934, FDR Library, Hyde Park.

8. *World-Telegram*, November 29, 1933; *Times*, November 30, 1933; Verdicchio, "New Deal and New York City," 107.

9. *Times*, November 23, 1933; Ellis, *Nation in Torment*, 500.

10. Barbara Blumberg, *The New Deal and the Unemployed: The View From New York City* (Lewisburg: Bucknell University Press, 1979), 32; Verdicchio, "New Deal and New York City," 104.

11. *Times*, February 1, 1934, quoted in Verdicchio, "New Deal and New York City," 115.

12. Roger Biles, *Big City Boss in Depression and War* (DeKalb: Northern Illinois University Press, 1984), 77; Charles Trout, *Boston: The Great Depression and the New Deal* (New York: Oxford University Press, 1977), 148–151; *Times*, April 21, 1936; Verdicchio, "New Deal and New York City," 115–117. See also Walter DeLamater to FHL, January 7, 1934, FHL to DeLamater, January 20, 27, 1934, Box 2626, NYMA.

13. Hickok and Gellhorn quoted in Schlesinger, *Coming of the New Deal*, 272.

14. Schlesinger, *Coming of the New Deal*, 274–275.

15. *Times*, September 25, 1933, January 22 (FHL speech), 31, February 4, 5, 10, March 12, August 23, 1934.

16. *Times*, March 30, 1934.

17. Leuchtenburg, *FDR*, 122; *Times*, August 30, September 23, 1934.

18. *Times*, August 23 (quote), 1934, July 23 (quote), 1936; New York *Daily Worker*, July 24, 1939; *Herald-Tribune*, April 19, 1940; August Heckscher, *When La Guardia Was Mayor: New York's Legendary Years* (New York: W. W. Norton & Co., 1978), 62 (quote).

19. *Times*, August 23, 1934; John F. Hylan to FHL, September 15, 1934, Box 659, NYMA.

20. Fay in Bayrd Still, *Mirror for Gotham: New York as Seen by Contemporaries from Dutch Days to the Present* (New York: University Press, 1956), 297; Robert A. Caro, *Power Broker: Robert Moses and the Fall of New York* (New York: Vintage, 1974), 358 (quote); *Times*, November 30 (quote), 1933; Heckscher, *La Guardia*, 68 (quote).

21. Jay Franklin, *La Guardia: A Biography* (New York: Modern Age, 1937), 114; Caro, *Power Broker*, 359.

22. Caro, *Power Broker*, 171–240, 360 (quotes).

23. *Herald-Tribune*, January 7, 1934 (quote); Caro, *Power Broker*, 362.

24. *World-Telegram*, December 14, 1934; Caro, *Power Broker*, 368, 371.

25. Caro, *Power Broker*, 371 (quote), on Orchard Beach, 363–368; *World-Telegram*, December 14, 1934; *Times*, February 28, 1934.

26. Caro, *Power Broker*, 361, 386–388, 447–448; *Times*, January 14, 16, February 4, 1934; Nathan Barkan (the lone Tammany man left on the commission) to Harold Ickes, January 16, 1934, Box 24, NYMA; Paul Windels interview, Columbia University Oral History Collection, Appendix, 14.

27. FHL to R. Moses, December 19, 1934, and Moses to FHL, January 2, 1934, both quoted in William P. Brown, "The Political and Administrative Leadership of Fiorello

H. La Guardia as Mayor of the City of New York, 1934–1941'' (Ph.D. dissertation, New York University, 1960), 72; Caro, *Power Broker*, 447.

28. Lawrence Elliott, *Little Flower: The Life and Times of Fiorello La Guardia* (New York: Morrow, 1983), 215–216; Caro, *Power Broker*, 448.

29. Caro, *Power Broker*, 390–397; Marshall Berman, *All That Is Solid Melts Into Air: The Experience of Modernity* (New York: Simon & Schuster, 1982), 299–302.

30. Caro, *Power Broker*, 287–298 (quote 290).

31. *Times*, February 16, 1934.

32. Caro, *Power Broker*, 426; Press Release, January 30, 1934, Box 659, NYMA.

33. *Secret Diary of Harold Ickes*, I, 148–149.

34. Caro, *Power Broker*, 427; A. A. Berle to FDR, March 1, 1934, Personal File 1306, FDRP-HP; FDR to Berle, March 2, 1934, Berle Papers, FDR Library, Hyde Park.

35. A. A. Berle to FDR, March 15, 1934, Personal File 1306, FDRP-HP; *Secret Diary of Harold Ickes*, I, 229.

36. Verdicchio, ''New Deal and New York City,'' 159–161; FHL to Ickes, August 2, 1934, Box 2547, NYMA (on West Side Highway); *Times*, May 17, 20, November 18, 1934 (on other grants); Caro, *Power Broker*, 372.

37. *Times*, August 10, 1934.

38. *World-Telegram*, December 14, 1934.

39. *World-Telegram*, December 14, 1934; Caro, *Power Broker*, 372–374, 376–378.

40. *Times*, November 30, 1934; Caro, *Power Broker*, 383; Brooklyn *Times-Union*, March 2, 1934.

41. Caro, *Power Broker*, 413; C. C. Burlingham to FHL, April 16, 1934, January 10, 1935, CCBP.

42. *Secret Diary of Harold Ickes*, I, 229, 267.

43. C. C. Burlingham to FHL, April 16, 1934, CCBP.

44. *World-Telegram*, January 30, 1935; *Times*, January 4, 1935; Caro, *Power Broker*, 430; *Secret Diary of Harold Ickes*, I, 267.

45. *Times*, December 31, 1934 (FHL's building plans).

46. *Times*, January 4, 1935; *Secret Diary of Harold Ickes*, I, 268.

47. *Times*, January 5, 1934.

48. C. C. Burlingham to FHL, FHL to Burlingham, January 4, 1935, Burlingham to Felix Frankfurter, January 9, 1935, CCBP; *Times*, January 5, 1934 (quote).

49. *Times*, January 14, 1935; various editorials quoted in Caro, *Power Broker*, 432–433.

50. *Secret Diary of Harold Ickes*, I, 268–269.

51. C. C. Burlingham to Louis Howe quoted in Burlingham to Frankfurter, January 9, 1935, CCBP; *Herald-Tribune*, January 6, 8, 12, 1935; *Times*, January 11, 1935.

52. *Secret Diary of Harold Ickes*, I, 269, 277 (and *Times*, February 10, 11, 12, 1935, for the new loans and grants mentioned by FDR).

53. *Times*, January 16 (quote), 17, 19, February 1 (quote), 1935. On the rumor that Moses would resign see *Times* and Brooklyn *Eagle*, January 19, 1935.

54. C. C. Burlingham to FHL February 14, 1935, CCBP; Caro, *Power Broker*, 436–437; *Times*, February 3, 1935.

55. Leuchtenburg, *FDR and the New Deal*, 216–217; *Secret Diary of Harold Ickes*, I, 290–291; *Times*, March 7, 1935; Caro, *Power Broker*, 438 (quote).

56. *Times*, February 24, 1935; *Secret Diary of Harold Ickes*, I, 308, 317; FHL to FDR, February 23, 1935, Personal File 1376, FDRP-HP.

57. *Times*, March 1, 1935.

58. FHL to FDR, February 23, 1935, Personal File 1376, FDRP-HP.

59. Copy of Ickes letter in *Times*, March 12, 1935; *Secret Diary of Harold Ickes*, I, 317.

60. *Times*, March 12, 1935; C. C. Burlingham to FDR, March 18, 1935, CCBP.

61. *Times*, June 29 (quote), July 1, 2, 3, 4, 1935.

62. *Times*, July 4 (quote), 6, 11 (quote), 1935; Marie La Guardia interview, Columbia University Oral History Collection, 34–35.

63. *Times*, July 13, 1936; *Secret Diary of Harold Ickes*, I, 623, 637.

64. Peter Marcuse, "Public Housing in the United States in the 1930s: The Case in New York City" (paper delivered at Conference on Public Housing in New York, Columbia University, October 12–13, 1984), 1 (quote), 9, 29.

65. Langdon Post, "memorandum on a Comprehensive Housing Program," January 18, 1935, New York City Housing Authority (NYCHA) Papers, LAGA.

66. *News*, November 28, 1933.

67. Kenneth T. Jackson, *Crabgrass Frontier: The Suburbanization of the United States* (New York: Oxford University Press, 1985), 191–193 (quote 193).

68. Jacob Riis quoted in PWA, *Williamsburg Houses: A Case History of Housing* (Washington: U.S. Government Printing Office, 1937), unnumbered back page; NYCHA, *First Houses* (New York: NYCHA, 1935), 9.

69. *First Houses*, 9–13; "Facts Divulged by the Delinquency Survey of Slum Areas Completed Under the Direction of the Tenement House Department" (quote), and Langdon Post, Press Release on Slum Survey, July 30, 1934, both in NYCHA Papers, LAGA.

70. Jackson, *Crabgrass Frontier*, 362 n. 13; Joel Schwartz, "A Road Not Taken: The District Rehabilitation Idea and the New York City Housing Authority in the 1930s" (paper delivered at Conference on Housing in New York, Columbia University, October 12–13, 1984), 9–10; Heckscher quoted in *American*, December 29, 1933.

71. *News*, February 20 (quote), March 13, 1934; *Times*, February 20, March 6, April 9, 1934; Anthony Jackson, *A Place Called Home: A History of Low Cost Housing in Manhattan* (Cambridge: M.I.T. Press, 1976), 209–211.

72. *Times*, April 9, 1934 (quote); NYCHA, *The Failure of Housing Regulation* (New York: NYCHA, 1936), 13–15; NYCHA, *Must We Have Slums?* (New York: NYCHA, 1937), 14, 16 (quote).

73. NYCHA, *Failure of Housing Regulation*, 15; NYCHA, *First Houses*, 13 (quote); *Times*, December 4, 1935 (quote); PWA, *Williamsburg Houses*, 12–13.

74. Ickes to FHL, January 3, 1934, quoted in "Report to Fiorello H. La Guardia on the Progress of the New York City Housing Authority and Its Relationship to the Housing Division of the PWA in Washington," June 27, 1937, NYCHA Papers, LAGA; Arnold H. Diamond, "The New York City Housing Authority: A Study in Public Corporations" (Ph.D. dissertation, Columbia University, 1954), 3–6.

75. NYCHA, *First Houses*, 15; Diamond, "New York City Housing Authority," 5.

76. *Herald-Tribune*, March 3, 1934; Tenement House Department Press Release, June 17, 1934, NYCHA Papers, LAGA; NYCHA, *First Houses*, 20.

77. Langdon Post, internal memo, April 3, 1934, Frederick L. Ackerman, memo to NYCHA, March 27, 1934, both in General Correspondence, NYCHA Papers, LAGA; Memorandum #2 to Housing Division of the PWA and the PWA Emergency Housing Corporation from the NYCHA, March 28, 1934; Ackerman quoted in L. Post to FHL, "Relations of the Authority with the PWA," October 5, 1934, NYCHA Papers, LAGA.

78. Rev. E. B. Moore, "Much Ado About Housing," *Saturday Evening Post* (June 10, 1939): 25; NYCHA, *Must We Have Slums*, 10; L. Post memo to FHL on dealings with PWA during first six months of his administration, June 13, 1934, NYCHA Papers, LAGA. See also Charles Abrams's report, "The Significance and Importance of the Plan Proposed by the NYCHA for the Development and Construction of the Low Cost Housing Projects in NYC," July 19, 1934, NYCHA Papers, LAGA.

79. Abrams, "Significance of NYCHA Plan," 1; L. Post memo to FHL, "Relations of the Authority with the PWA," June 28, 1934; "Confidential Report of Washington Trip, June 20–21"; "Statement of L. W. Post," June 23, 1934; Ickes arguments cited in "Memo on July 20 Meeting Between Post and Ickes," July 25, 1934; Ickes to O. G. Villard, July 3, 1934 (copy sent to M. K. Simkovitch), all in NYCHA Papers, LAGA.

80. Norbert Brown, "Confusion Attends the New York Housing Program," *Real Estate Record and Builder's Guide* (July 14, 1934): 4; FHL to H. Ickes, June 25, 1934, Box 2571, NYMA.

81. H. Ickes to O. G. Villard, July 3, 1934 (copy), NYCHA Papers, LAGA; FHL to Ickes, July 5, 6 (quote), 1934, Box 2571, NYMA.

82. "Memo on July 20 Meeting Between Post and Ickes," July 25, 1934; "Confidential Memo for the Mayor for Interview with the President on September 5, 1934," September 5, 1934, NYCHA Papers, LAGA.

83. L. Post to FHL, "Relations of the Authority with the PWA," October 5, 1934, NYCHA Papers, LAGA; *Times*, September 11, October 12, 13, 1934.

84. Peter Marcuse, "The Beginnings of Public Housing in New York," *Journal of Urban History* 12 (1986): 356–360.

85. Langdon Post, *The Challenge of Housing* (New York: Farrar and Rinehart, 1938), 181; NYCHA, *First Houses*, 20–25.

86. Jackson, *Crabgrass Frontier*, 222.

87. NYCHA, *Toward the End to Be Achieved: The New York City Housing Authority, Its History in Outline* (New York: NYCHA, 1937), 14–15; Muller vs. NYCHA (1936) 270 N. Y. 333 1 N. E. (2d) 153, quoted in Diamond, "New York City Housing Authority," 6–7, and NYCHA, *First Houses*, 22–23; *Times*, April 13, 1935.

88. John F. St. George, "An Analysis of the City's Astor Housing Project," *Real Estate Record and Builder's Guide* (May 4, 1935): 4.

89. *Times*, November 24, 1935; NYCHA, *First Houses*, 26–28; Marcuse, "Public Housing in New York," 356.

90. Diamond, "New York City Housing Authority," 73–74, 256; NYCHA, *First Houses*, 31; Marcuse, "Public Housing in New York," 363–364.

91. *Times*, December 4, 1935.

92. *Times*, February 7, 8 (quote), May 2 (quote), 1935.

93. *Times*, May 15, June 7 (quote), 13, 1935; *American*, June 7, 1935; *World-Telegram*, June 6, 1935.

94. NYCHA, *Must We Have Slums*, 9 (quote); FHL to L. Post, October 15, 1934, NYCHA Papers, LAGA; PWA, *Williamsburg Houses*, 20, 24.

95. Norbert Brown, "Williamsburg: A Case Study of Federal Apartment Houses," *Real Estate Record and Builder's Guide* (March 5, 1938): 11, 15–16; PWA, *Williamsburg Houses*, 28; NYCHA, *Toward the End to Be Achieved*, 13 (quote).

96. Post quoted in NYCHA, *Eight Reasons for Public Housing* (New York: NYCHA, 1937), 14.

97. Marcuse, "Public Housing in New York," 369–370; Marcuse, "Public Housing in the United States," 20–21 (quote); NYCHA, *Must We Have Slums*, 9–11; *Times*, May 23 ("just crazy"), November 24, 1935; Schwartz, "A Road Not Taken," 23–24 (quote); NYCHA, *Toward the End to Be Achieved*, 11–12.

98. Langdon Post, "Memorandum on a Comprehensive Housing Program," January 18, 1935, sent to FDR with L. Post to FDR, January 21, 1935, NYCHA Papers, LAGA.

99. Rosalie Genevro, "Site Selection and the New York City Housing Authority, 1934–1939," *Journal of Urban History* 12 (1986): 338–341; Gelfand, *Nation of Cities*, 132 (quote).

100. Leuchtenburg, *FDR and the New Deal*, 134, 88–89; *Secret Diary of Harold Ickes*, I, 207 (quote), 480, 488; Gelfand, *Nation of Cities*, 61; Jackson, *A Place Called Home*, 219.

101. FHL quoted in *Times*, February 14, 1935 in Jerold Auerbach, "A New Deal For New York City, Fiorello La Guardia: 1934–1937" (M. A. Thesis, Columbia University, 1959), 46; Nathan Straus, "Low Cost Housing Here and Abroad, Report to Mayor La Guardia by Nathan Straus, Special Housing Commissioner," 36–37, NYCHA Papers, LAGA; *Times*, October 21, 1935 (for FHL on Straus's report).

102. Blumberg, *New Deal*, 38–39; FHL in United States Conference of Mayors, *Proceedings* (1935): 247.

103. Hopkins quoted in Blumberg, *New Deal*, 41; FHL quoted in Albany *Times-Union*, April 30, 1935.

104. *Times*, October 29, 1940; Albany *Times-Union*, June 28, 1935.

105. *Times*, February 12, 1935.

106. *Herald-Tribune*, July 20, 1935 (quotes); *Times*, July 21, 1935.

107. Heckscher, *La Guardia*, 83; *Times*, May 30, 1935; *American*, May 30, 1935.

108. United States Conference of Mayors, *Proceedings* (1935): 248; FDR to FHL, June 12, 1935, charges against FHL quoted in Salvatore A. Cotillo to FDR, July 1, 1935, both in Personal File 1376, FDRP-HP; FDR to FHL, June 10, 1935, FHL to FDR, June 12, 1935 (quote), both in Box 2573, NYMA; *Times*, June 1–3, July 2, 1935; Brooklyn *Eagle*, June 2, 1935; *News*, June 1, 1935.

109. *Times*, April 12 (quote), 1935; United States Conference of Mayors, *Proceedings* (1935): 249.

110. Gelfand, *Nation of Cities*, 47–48 (quotes); United States Conference of Mayors, *Proceedings* (1935): 248; *Times*, May 8, 24, July 23, 1935.

111. *Sun*, November 20, 1935 (on Conference of Mayors); Blumberg, *New Deal*, 48–49.

112. *Times*, June 25, 1935; Blumberg, *New Deal*, 50–57 (quote 55).

113. Blumberg, *New Deal*, 58–59; *Times*, August 5, September 10, 1935; *Herald-Tribune*, September 3, 1935; *News* and *Journal*, September 10, 1935 (quotes from September 10 newspapers).

114. FHL to Commissioners of All City Departments, September 20, 1935, Box 15, NYMA.

115. S. J. Woolf, "Mayor Two Years and Still Optimistic," *New York Times Magazine* (January 5, 1936): 22; Henry Graff, "The Kind of Mayor La Guardia Was," *New York Times Magazine* (October 22, 1961): 46; Hopkins quoted in Auerbach, "La Guardia," 43.

Chapter 10

1. E. Palmieri, interview with the author, November 9, 1982; *Sun*, November 3, 1936; Jay Franklin [John Franklin Carter], *La Guardia: A Biography* (New York: Modern Age, 1937), 123; Robert A. Caro, *The Power Broker: Robert Moses and the Fall of New York* (New York: Vintage, 1974), 444.

2. Leo Carrillo to Lester Stone, June 29, July 3, 1937, Box 2706, NYMA; *Sun*, March 2, 1935; *Times*, March 20, 1935; Franklin, *La Guardia*, 126.

3. *American*, January 30, 1935 (truck strike); *News* and *Mirror*, February 19, 1935 (elevator operator strike); *Times*, March 23, July 2, 1935 (waiters' strike); *Post*, January 24, 1936, and *Herald-Tribune*, January 28, 1936 (both on garment workers strike); *Times*, February 22, 1934 (hotel employees strike); Charles Garrett, *The La Guardia Years, Machine and Reform Politics in New York City* (New Brunswick: Rutgers University Press, 1961), 122. For the charge that La Guardia's sympathy for strikers fomented labor unrest in New York, see *Sun*, April 26, 1935.

4. *Times*, April 19, 21, 26, 29, May 3, 15, June 7, July 8–10, 1934 (milk); *The Nation* (January 16, 1935): 61; *World-Telegram*, December 23, 1935 (quote); *Times*, December 20, 29, 1936 (alligator), December 22, 1936 (gun).

5. FHL to P. Windels, FHL to L. Valentine, both Wednesday [November 13, 1935], Box 32; FHL to Herbert Lehman, November 15, 1935, Box 2703, NYMA.

6. *Times*, January 22 (judges), December 7–8 (doctors), 1934, December 31, 1935 (flag); C. C. Burlingham to FHL, October 22, 1934, October 5, 1935, FHL to Burlingham, October 22, 1934, October 5, 1935, FHL to William L. Ransom, October 4, 1935, CCBP.

7. *Times*, March 29, April 1, May 14, 18, August 3, 15, 1935; Memo from J. Pasciutti to FHL, "Fire Hose Bids," March 25, 1947, LAGA; C. C. Burlingham to FHL, April 15, 1935, CCBP.

8. *Times*, March 4 (magazines), October 14 (slot machines), 1934, May 12 (drunk drivers), May 17 (sanitation), 1935, May 10 (insurance), July 26 (pollution), August 6 (slot machines), 1936.

9. *Herald-Tribune*, July 24, 1936; E. Cuneo to FHL, April 4, 1934, FHL to Cuneo, April 5, 1934, Box 2675, NYMA.

10. *Herald-Tribune*, December 21, 1935; *Journal*, December 19, 1935; *Times*, June 1 (markets), December 20, 1935.

11. *Times* and *Herald-Tribune*, September 15, 29, 30, November 3, 1935; William F. Morgan, untitled recollections of La Guardia, L. Elliott Collection, LAGA.

12. Ira Hirschmann, interview with the author, January 13, 1983; Ernest Cuneo, *Life With Fiorello* (New York: Macmillan, 1955), 198; *Times*, August 15, 1934.

13. FHL to John Erskine, September 20, 1934, Erskine Collection, Columbia University; *Herald-Tribune*, January 16, 1935; *Times*, January 16, June 27, 1935, January 7, February 15, May 19, 1936; Jerold S. Auerbach, "A New Deal For New York City, Fiorello La Guardia: 1934–1937" (M.A. Thesis, Columbia University, 1959), 77.

14. Brooklyn *Eagle*, January 20, 1935; *Herald-Tribune*, February 15, 1936; *Times*, January 26, 1936.

15. *Times*, December 24, 1935 (delinquency), March 31 (circus), July 14 (tuition), October 10–11 (movies), 1936; Newbold Morris, *Let the Chips Fall: My Battles Against Corruption* (New York: Appleton-Century-Crofts, 1955), 117.

16. *Times*, January 3 (second quote), June 26, 1935, March 12 (third quote), 1936, February 17 (first quote), 1937; *Herald-Tribune*, January 18, 1935; Franklin, *La Guardia*, 125–127 (last quote).

17. *Times*, July 14 (quote), 15, 1936; Morris, *Let the Chips Fall*, 118 (quote); A. G. Hays to FHL, January 14, 1938, FHL to Hays, January 15, 1938, Box 2701, NYMA.

18. C. C. Burlingham to FHL, January 4, 1937, CCBP; S. J. Woolf, "Mayor Two Years and Still Optimistic," *New York Times Magazine* (January 5, 1936): 9; *Times*, December 22, 1936; William Seabrook, "Wild Bull of Manhattan," *American Magazine* (April 1937): 17.

19. Brooklyn *Citizen*, April 4, 1934; *Times*, April 2, 1934, June 25–26 (boundary dispute), June 27 (quote), August 16 ("Communing with the Mayor at the Summer City Hall"), 1936; *Herald-Tribune*, April 5, 1934; Brooklyn *Times-Union*, April 4 (quote), 1934, on reel 19, NYPL.

20. Morris, *Let the Chips Fall*, 118–119 (quote); *Times*, June 20, 1936.

21. FHL to Andrew Somers, August 24, 1936 (quote), Box 2703, NYMA; M. DeSerio to FHL, n.d. [1934], Reel 19, NYPL; Seabrook, "Wild Bull," 107.

22. Seabrook, "Wild Bull," 18.

23. Woolf, "Mayor Two Years," 9 (quotes); *Times*, March 21, 1934 (quote); "few compensations" quote was part of the standard response to letters praising La Guardia's administration and can be found throughout reel 19, NYPL, and the "General" and "Miscellaneous" Correspondence, NYMA.

24. *Nation* (January 16, 1935): 61.

25. Stanley Isaacs interview, Columbia University Oral History Collection, 78; S. J. Woolf, "General O'Ryan Outlines a New Police Deal," *New York Times Magazine* (February 4, 1934): 9; *Times*, January 23, 1934 (quotes).

26. *Times*, April 1, 13, June 23, 1934; FHL to J. O'Ryan, May 5, Box 17, NYMA.

27. FHL to J. O'Ryan, January 4, 1934, Box 17, NYMA; Lowell Limpus, *Honest*

Cop, Lewis J. Valentine; Being a Chronicle of the Commissioner's Thirty-Six Years in the New York Police Department (New York: E. P. Dutton, 1939), 149–159.

28. Cuneo, *Life With Fiorello*, 60 (quote); Humbert Nelli, *The Business of Crime* (New York: Oxford University Press, 1978), 230; Garrett, *The La Guardia Years*, 160–163; various letters in Box 4112, NYMA; Craig Thompson and Allen Raymond, *Gang Rule in New York City: The Story of a Lawless Era* (New York: Dial Press, 1940), 189.

29. *Herald-Tribune*, February 15, 17 (quotes from Jurovaty case), March 11, April 13, 1934; *Times*, January 14, February 15, 27, April 3, May 2, 22, 1934.

30. *Herald-Tribune*, March 11, 1934; *Times*, March 15, 1934 (both on Radio City); *World-Telegram*, October 13, 1934 (sledgehammer); materials on slot machines in Box 3514, NYMA; Garrett, *The La Guardia Years*, 160; Nelli, *Business of Crime*, 223–224; Thompson and Raymond, *Gang Rule in New York City*, 382, 392–393.

31. *American*, March 2, 1934; Limpus, *Honest Cop*, 171; *Times*, January 2 (quote), March 19 (quote), June 28 (uniform changes), 1934; FHL to J. O'Ryan, January 27, 29, March 21, 1934, Box 17, NYMA.

32. *Times*, March 28, 1933.

33. C. C. Burlingham to FHL, February 6, 1934, CCBP; *Times*, February 5, 1934; March 23, 24 (quote), 1934.

34. *Times*, February 6, 8, March 11, 1934.

35. *Times*, March 24 ("Chicago"), 25, April 10 (other quotes), 1934.

36. *Herald-Tribune*, March 23, 1934; *Times*, March 23, April 10, 1934; *Evening Journal*, March 23, 1934.

37. *Times*, April 10 (quote), 11, 12 (Grand Jury quote), 13, 1934.

38. *World-Telegram*, December 11, 1934 ("Fusion's First Year"); *Times*, March 18, 1934.

39. Louis Waldman to FHL, July 28, 30, 1934, Reel 19, NYPL ("rifle squad"); *Times*, August 1 (quote), 4 (quote), 16, 21, 22, 23, 25 (quote), 26, 1934.

40. Limpus, *Honest Cop*, 173; *World-Telegram*, November 12, 1934.

41. *Herald-Tribune*, November 9, 1933; *Sun*, September 25, 1935.

42. *Times* and *Sun*, April 30, 1934.

43. Limpus, *Honest Cop*, 178–181; FHL to C. C. Burlingham, November 28, 1934, CCBP.

44. Limpus, *Honest Cop*, 178–181; Burlingham to FHL, November 28, 1934, CCBP; O. G. Villard to FHL, November 27, 1934, Villard Papers, Harvard University.

45. FHL to C. C. Burlingham, November 28, 1934, Burlingham to FHL, November 30, 1934, CCBP; Brooklyn *Citizen*, January 21, 1935; *Times*, January 27, 1935.

46. *Post*, January 23, 1935; *Times*, January 23 (quote), February 1 (quote), October 20, December 3, 1935; Brooklyn *Citizen*, February 2, 1935 ("sentimentality"); *Herald-Tribune*, January 29, 1935; *Journal*, December 2 (quote), 1935.

47. Martin A. Gosch and Richard Hammer, *The Last Testament of Lucky Luciano* (Boston: Little, Brown, 1974), 43–44, 74, 81. This book, supposedly Luciano's autobiography as told to Gosch, was published under a cloud of mystery. The publishers claimed to have tapes proving that the book contained Luciano's actual words, but these assertions later proved to be false. Since Gosch was dead by the time it was published, he could not

be questioned either. Most reviewers doubted that these could actually be Luciano's own words and suggested that the book should be treated as Gosch's account of Luciano's recollections. I have made use of it only when its assertions can be substantiated with other sources.

48. Nelli, *Business of Crime*, 173–174; Lippmann quoted in Francis Ianni and Elizabeth Reuss-Ianni, *Crime Society: Organized Crime and Corruption in America* (New York: New American Library, 1976), 162–163, 167.

49. Gosch and Hammer, *Last Testament of Lucky Luciano*, 101 (quote), 133–136, 146–147; Nelli, *Business of Crime*, 199, 219, 223, 227, 244 (quote).

50. Garrett, *The La Guardia Years*, 158; Alan Block, *East Side, West Side: Organizing Crime in New York, 1930–1950* (Cardiff: University College Cardiff Press, 1980), 154–155; Nelli, *Business of Crime*, 227; Thompson and Raymond, *Gang Rule in New York City*, 337.

51. Paul Blanshard, *Investigating City Government* (New York: 1937), 7–8; Block, *East Side, West Side*, 65.

52. *Times*, March 1, 1935.

53. Morris, *Let the Chips Fall*, 120; William F. Morgan, "From Confusion to Fusion" (unpublished manuscript, L. Elliott Collection, LAGA), 15; *Herald-Tribune*, December 23, 1935; *Times*, December 22–25, 29, 1935; *World-Telegram*, December 21, 1935; *Mirror*, December 22 (quote), 1935; Brooklyn *Eagle*, December 24, 1935.

54. *World-Telegram*, December 19, 1935; Gosch and Hammer, *Last Testament of Lucky Luciano*, 264.

55. *Times*, July 11, 1935, January 17, February 22, August 12, November 22, December 6, 1936. Also see *Times*, December 3, 1935, for La Guardia's debate with Chicago officials over which city was more racket-ridden. The title of S. J. Woolf's "The Mayor Trains Guns on Rackets," *New York Times Magazine* (December 6, 1936): 3, suggests that La Guardia had not accomplished much by the end of 1936.

56. Garrett, *The La Guardia Years*, 160; *Times*, April 27, 1937; Reports on pinball machines in Boxes 3283 and 3514, NYMA.

57. Limpus, *Honest Cop*, 194; *Times*, February 28, July 31, August 23, 1935, January 17, April 1, and September 9, 1936 on various shake-ups.

58. *Times*, October 8, 1936; Rebecca Rankin, ed., *New York Advancing: An Accounting to the Citizens by the Departments and Boroughs of the City of New York, 1934–1935* (New York: 1936), 159 (quote).

59. FHL to L. Valentine, August 18, 1936, Box 59, NYMA. See also "Disgusted Sergeant" to FHL, November 3, 1935, FHL to Valentine (re: "Disgusted Sergeant"), November 3, 1935, Valentine to FHL, January 28, 1936, Box 41, NYMA, and other complaints about the police forwarded by FHL to Valentine in this box. Though La Guardia wrote Valentine that "it strikes me as if 'Disgusted Sergeant' knows what he is talking about," Valentine reported, as usual, that no evidence could be found to substantiate his claims.

60. FHL to L. Valentine, November 23, 1936, Box 59, NYMA.

61. Limpus, *Honest Cop*, 224–234; FHL to L. Valentine, July 8, August 10 (quote), 1937, Valentine to FHL, August 5, 1937, Box 2675, NYMA.

62. Gosch and Hammer, *Last Testament of Lucky Luciano*, 178–179.

63. *Times*, June 25, 30, 1935, January 5, 1936; Block, *East Side, West Side*, 72–74, 134, 155–157.

64. Nelli, *Business of Crime*, 234; Block, *East Side, West Side*, 144–147; miscellaneous materials, Boxes 3163 and 4112, NYMA.

65. *Times*, January 5, 1936; Block, *East Side, West Side*, 69–70; materials in Box 4112, NYMA; *Time* (February 1, 1937): 6; *Newsweek* (March 6, 1939): 5; *Saturday Evening Post* (October 30, 1937): 19; miscellaneous materials, Boxes 3580, 4112, NYMA; Burton Turkus and Sid Feder, *Murder, Inc., The Story of "The Syndicate"* (New York: Farrar, Straus, and Young, 1941), 360–362; Thompson and Raymond, *Gang Rule in New York City*, 381–383.

66. *Times*, November 1, 1938.

67. *Times*, November 12, 1935; Limpus, *Honest Cop*, 227.

68. Limpus, *Honest Cop*, 210–212, 216, 225–226 (quote), 231; Block, *East Side, West Side*, 77–80 (quote); FHL to L. Valentine, March 16, 1936, Box 51, NYMA. See also Anonymous to FHL, September 9, 1936, Box 59, NYMA, for the charge that political connections determined promotions among the police in Brooklyn.

69. Block, *East Side, West Side*, 75–86; *Times*, October 3, 4, 11, 15, 30, 1938.

70. Block, *East Side, West Side*, 84–123.

71. Garrett, *The La Guardia Years*, 162 (quote); August Heckscher, *When La Guardia Was Mayor: New York's Legendary Years* (New York: W. W. Norton & Co., 1978), 104.

72. *Herald-Tribune* and *Times*, March 20, 21, 1935; *The Complete Report of Mayor La Guardia's Commission on the Harlem Riot of March 19, 1935* (New York: Arno Press, 1969), 7–8 (quotes). Box 2550, NYMA, file 193 contains police reports and letters from the community on the riot, files 194 and 195 contain the report of the mayoral commission and letters in response, and file 196 contains the responses of city and state officials to the report.

73. *Report on the Harlem Riot*, 10 (quote); *Times*, March 20, 1935; Young Communist League handbill in Box 2550, NYMA.

74. *Herald-Tribune*, March 20, 1935; *Report on the Harlem Riot*, 7–8 (quote); *Times*, March 21, 1935 (quote).

75. *Times*, March 21, 1935.

76. *Times*, March 21 (including *Worker* headline), 22, 1935.

77. *Herald-Tribune*, March 22, 1935; *Times*, March 21, 1935.

78. *Amsterdam News*, undated clipping, Box 5, NYPL; *Times*, May 25, 1934; Adam Clayton Powell, Jr., to FHL, May 25, 1934, FHL to John H. Delaney [Chairman of the Board of Transportation], June 23, 1934, Box 2550, NYMA.

79. *Times*, September 8, 1934 ("slumming").

80. Edward Boyle to FHL, and L. B. Dunham to FHL, both June 15, 1934, Box 659, NYMA (Boyle's report is in same box).

81. *Times*, September 16, 1935; Dominic J. Capeci, *The Harlem Riot of 1943* (Philadelphia: Temple University Press, 1977), 38.

82. Fragment of Harlem Survey, n.d. [completed in the early part of La Guardia's first term], Box 2550, NYMA; Capeci, *Harlem Riot*, 35–36; *Times*, May 12, 1935 (quote); Mark Naison, *Communists in Harlem During the Depression* (Urbana: University of Illinois Press, 1983), 105–106; *Report on the Harlem Riot*, 50–52, 59–62.

83. *Report on the Harlem Riot*, 39; Capeci, *Harlem Riot*, 37.

84. *Report on the Harlem Riot*, 32–33 (quote), 40–41; Charles Johnson, "Black Workers in the City," *Survey Graphic* 6 (March, 1925): 719; Capeci, *Harlem Riot*, 35–36 (quote).

85. Capeci, *Harlem Riot*, 42; *Herald-Tribune*, March 18, 1934; Lowell Limpus, *Honest Cop*, 168–169. There is also material on this incident in file 197, Box 2550, NYMA.

86. Fragment of Harlem Survey, n.d., Box 2550, NYMA; Capeci, *Harlem Riot*, 41; Limpus, *Honest Cop*, 195, 244, 255; *Report on the Harlem Riot*, 113–116 (quote), 118–121.

87. *Report on the Harlem Riot*, 14 (quote), 23; Capeci, *Harlem Riot*, 41; *Times*, August 10, 1935, April 21, 1936. One member of the commission, Reverend William McCann, condemned the "orgy of police baiting" at the commission's public hearings and refused to sign the report.

88. *Report on the Harlem Riot*, 14; *Times*, April 8, 1935 (quote).

89. *Times*, March 21, 1935; *Herald-Tribune*, March 21, 26, 1935; Capeci, *Harlem Riot*, 4–5.

90. Heckscher, *La Guardia*, 137, 94; *Report on the Harlem Riot*, 75–76; *Times*, May 7, 1936.

91. *Times*, August 10, 1935; *Report on the Harlem Riot*, 120.

92. Capeci, *Harlem Riot*, 6.

93. *Times*, June 25, July 1, 1936 (on construction jobs for blacks), May 25, 1934, July 16, 1936 (on appointing blacks to office).

94. C. C. Burlingham to FHL, June 13, 1935, CCBP; *Times*, September 6, 1935 (quote), September 3, 1936 (quote); Capeci, *Harlem Riot*, 7–8.

95. *Times*, July 16, 1935, May 7 (quote), June 25, 1936 (*Amsterdam News* quote); Walter White to FHL, December 5, 1940, Box 2693, NYMA, cited in Capeci, *Harlem Riot*, 8.

Chapter 11

1. George L. Ritchie, "La Guardia: Manhattan Messiah," *American Mercury* 38 (1936): 142.

2. *Sun*, November 3, 1935.

3. *Sun*, July 21, 1935; Ritchie, "La Guardia," 147; Paul Windels interview, Columbia University Oral History Collection, 110.

4. B. Blanshard, interview with the author, July 7, 1982; Will Maslow, interview with the author, June 25, 1982; *Times*, October 24, 1935, for FHL's jealousy of Blanshard.

5. Ritchie, "La Guardia," 150.

6. "Writer Views Dictatorship of La Guardia," unlabeled newspaper clipping [*Sun*?] dated January 6, 1934, FHL Scrapbooks, NYMA; *Sun*, July 21, 1935 (quote); Lawrence Elliott, *Little Flower: The Life and Times of Fiorello La Guardia* (New York: Morrow, 1983), 222 (quote).

7. *Times* quoted in Jay Franklin, *LaGuardia: A Biography* (New York: Modern Age, 1937), 118.

8. Ritchie, "La Guardia," 143 (quote); Elliott, *Little Flower*, 222; *Times*, May 3 (burlesque), 7 and 8 (left-winger), 1937; *Herald-Tribune*, June 19, 1937 (burlesque).

9. *Times*, October 19, 1934 (quote); Ritchie, "La Guardia," 142–151; *Post* quoted in August Heckscher, *When La Guardia Was Mayor: New York's Legendary Years* (New York: W. W. Norton, 1978), 112.

10. *Sun*, February 17, 1937; Ritchie, "La Guardia," 149 (quote).

11. *Sun*, May 26, 1936.

12. *Times*, April 15, 1934, January 9, 13, April 1, 2, 1935 (all on ineligibles); *Times*, March 23, 1935; *Journal*, March 22, 1935 (on pay raises).

13. *Times*, March 23, 1935; *Journal*, March 22–24, 1935.

14. *Times*, March 27, 1935; Robert Moses, "La Guardia: A Salute and a Memoir," *New York Times Magazine* (September 8, 1957): 116.

15. *Times*, April 3, 1935.

16. *Journal*, April 2, 1935.

17. *Journal* (quotes) and *Times*, April 3, 1935; Heckscher, *La Guardia*, 125 (quote).

18. *Times*, September 8, 1935; *Journal*, April 8, 1935 (Knauth quotes).

19. Heckscher, *La Guardia*, 122.

20. Barbara Blumberg, *The New Deal and the Unemployed: The View From New York City* (Lewisburg: Bucknell University Press, 1979), 89–90, 94; Heckscher, *La Guardia*, 122, 125.

21. Heckscher, *La Guardia*, 124–125 (quote); *Times*, April 4, 15, 25, 1936.

22. Blumberg, *New Deal*, 103–106; *Herald-Tribune*, April 25, 1937 (quote); William H. Allen, *Why Tammanies Revive: La Guardia's Mis-Guard* (New York: New York Institute for Public Service, 1947), 48–49; O'Ryan quoted in Ritchie, "La Guardia," 148; *Times*, April 26, 1937.

23. *Times*, December 3, 1936; Blumberg, *New Deal*, 105, 108.

24. Harvey Klehr, *The Heyday of American Communism: The Depression Decade* (New York: Basic Books, 1984), 266 (quote); on the Red Squad see Box 3705, NYMA, and *Times*, April 30, June 19, 1934; *Herald-Tribune*, January 8, 1935 (quote); "How to Make a Riot," *New Republic* (June 27, 1934): 178–179 (quotes); *American*, March 30, 1934 (quote).

25. Ritchie, "La Guardia," 142 (quote); *American*, April 6, 1936; Allen, *Why Tammanies Revive*, 43; Brooklyn *Times-Union*, February 18, 1936 (quote); *Times*, December 9, 17, 27, 1935.

26. *News*, March 23, 1935; *Times*, April 14, 1937.

27. *Times*, October 17, 1935 (quote), April 4, 1937 (editorial); Richard H. Rovere, "Vito Marcantonio: Machine Politician, New Style," *Harper's Monthly* (April 1944): 394 (quote); Klehr, *Heyday of American Communism*, 293–294; Lowell Limpus, *Honest Cop, Lewis J. Valentine; Being a Chronicle of the Commissioner's Thirty-Six Years in the New York Police Department* (New York: E. P. Dutton, 1939), 236 (quote); FHL to Valentine, February 18, 1936, Box 59, NYMA.

28. *Times*, August 24, 1936; Paul Blanshard, *Investigating City Government* (New York: 1937), 153–160; Allen, *Why Tammanies Revive*, 100.

29. *Times*, August 24, 1936.

30. *Times*, November 26, 1938; Allen, *Why Tammanies Revive*, 59–62.

31. Rebeccah Rankin, *New York Advancing: A Scientific Approach to Municipal Government* (New York 1936), 1; *Times*, June 21, 1936 on police brutality continuing "unabated;" Allen, *Why Tammanies Revive*, 59–62.

32. *Times*, May 24, November 1, 3, 1936, May 11, 1937; Allen, *Why Tammanies Revive*, 58.

33. Ritchie, "La Guardia," 142 (quote); *Times*, August 24, September 15, October 3, 1936.

34. *Herald-Tribune*, September 4, 1935.

35. *Times*, October 2, 1935, January 13 (quote), June 6 (Citizens Budget Commission letter), 1937; *Journal*, March 26, 1935; Brooklyn *Citizen*, March 28, 1935. Allen's charges are elaborated in *Why Tammanies Revive*, 70–79. Allen also filed a petition with Governor Lehman to remove La Guardia from office for the inequitable assessments. See *Times*, August 27, 1937. The petition itself can be found in the L. Elliott Collection, LAGA.

36. *Times*, March 27 (quote), April 5, 1935, May 11, July 1, September 7, 19, October 3, 4, November 19, 1937; Brooklyn *Times-Union*, March 17, 1935.

37. Allen, *Why Tammanies Revive*, 60–61.

38. *Sun*, May 16, 1935, February 18, 1936 (on FHL's excessive spending).

39. Mumford quoted in Mark Gelfand, *A Nation of Cities: The Federal Government and Urban America, 1933–1965* (New York: Oxford University Press, 1975), 132–133; Wright quoted in Alexander Klein, ed., *The Empire City* (New York: Rinehart, 1955), 433–435.

40. Ritchie, "La Guardia," 151.

41. Low quoted in John Palmer Gavit, "La Guardia: Portrait of a Mayor," *Survey Graphic* 25 (January 1936): 8; George L. Ritchie, "La Guardia," *American Mercury* 38 (1936): 142.

42. Charles Garrett, *The La Guardia Years, Machine and Reform Politics in New York City* (New Brunswick: Rutgers University Press, 1961), 256–257; Lowell Limpus and Burr W. Leyson, *This Man La Guardia* (New York: E. P. Dutton 1938), 396–397; Jay Franklin, *La Guardia: A Biography* (New York: Modern Age, 1937), 119; *Sun*, November 13, 1935 (quote).

43. *Sun*, November 6, 13, 1935.

44. *Herald-Tribune*, November 22, 1935; *World-Telegram*, November 23, 1935. See also *Herald-Tribune, Times*, and *Post*, November 6, 1935, for election results.

45. *Times*, July 10, 16, 17, 18, September 19, 1936; John Gunther, *Inside USA* (New York: Harper Brothers, 1951), 591.

46. Clifton Hood, "Underground Politics: A History of Mass Transit in New York City Since 1904" (Ph.D. dissertation, Columbia University, 1986), 322–323 (quote); Memo from Stephen Early to FDR, July 18, 1936, PPF 1376, FDRP-HP; Beatrice Bishop Berle and Travis B. Jacobs, eds., *Navigating the Rapids, 1918–1941; From the Papers of Adolf Berle* (New York: Harcourt Brace Jovanovich, 1973), 126; *Times*, August 6, September 14, 1935, November 24, 1936.

47. *Herald-Tribune*, January 23, 1936 (quote).

48. Materials in file 5, Box 32, NYMA; Allen, *Why Tammanies Revive*, 17, and

passim; *Sun*, November 6, 1935 (quote); *Times*, January 26, 1937. See also *Times*, January 10 (Republicans and patronage), March 10, 19, March 20–22, April 5, 1934.

49. Allen, *Why Tammanies Revive*, 17.

50. C. Belous to FHL, October 28, 1935, Box 2703, NYMA.

51. Belous to Stanley Howe, January 4, 1937, Box 2703, NYMA; Ben Howe to FHL, November 15, 1934, Reel 17, NYPL. See also Charles Belous, *Faith in Fusion* (New York: Vantage Press, 1951).

52. Allen, *Why Tammanies Revive*, 16; *Times*, May 24, 1935; Leonard Chalmers, "Fiorello La Guardia: Paterfamilias at City Hall; An Appraisal," *New York History* 71 (April 1975): 223.

53. Franklin, *La Guardia*, 119; *Times*, July 31, 1935 (quote); *Sun*, July 30, 1935.

54. Kenneth A. Waltzer, "The American Labor Party: Third Party Politics in New Deal-Cold War New York, 1936–1954" (Ph.D. dissertation, Harvard University, 1978), 146; *Times*, May 7, 1937.

55. FHL to John C. Parker, March 11, 1935, Box 3615, NYMA; *Times*, February 15, 1936; FHL to FDR, October 18, 1937, OF 407b, FDRP-HP.

56. *Times*, September 4, 1934, April 3, June 7, 1937.

57. Waltzer, "American Labor Party," 152; C. C. Burlingham to FHL, February 16, 1934, April 30, 1935, April 11, 1936, May 5, 14, 1937, CCBP Stanley Howe to FHL, February 24, 1937, Box 2678, NYMA; A. A. Berle to FHL, November 10, 1937, Berle Papers, FDR Library, Hyde Park.

58. Ronald Bayor, *Neighbors in Conflict: The Irish, Germans, Jews, and Italians of New York City: 1929–1941* (Baltimore: Johns Hopkins University Press), 26–39, 56; *Fortune* Magazine, *Jews In America* (New York: 1936), 34; Memo to Staff of Jewish Book, Federal Writer's Project Collection, Box 3631, NYMA.

59. Bayor, *Neighbors in Conflict*, 29; Windels interview, Columbia University Oral History Collection, Appendix, 9.

60. *Times*, June 6, 1933; FHL, "Hitler A Menace to World Peace," draft of newspaper article [1933], LAGA.

61. *Times*, July 24, 25, 1935; *Herald-Tribune*, July 25, 28, 1935.

62. *Mirror*, July 25, 1935; *Herald-Tribune*, April 26, 1937.

63. Press Release, November 14, 1935, Box 2704, NYMA.

64. FHL to W. A. Brown, May 3, 1937, Box 2675, NYMA; Dov Fisch, "The Libel Trial of Robert Edward Edmonson: 1936–1938," *American Jewish History* 71 (September 1981): 79–102; *Times*, June 9, 1936.

65. *Times*, March 4, 5, 1937; *Herald-Tribune*, March 5, 1937; Heckscher, *La Guardia*, 163; *News*, March 7, 1937; *Secret Diary of Harold Ickes*, 3 Vols. (New York: Simon & Schuster, 1953–1954), II, 89–90.

66. *Times*, March 6, 9, 13, 1937; Heckscher, *La Guardia*, 163 (quote); letters to FHL in Boxes 739 and 2546, NYMA; *Sun* and *Herald-Tribune*, April 14, 15, 1937; Henry Morgenthau Diary, March 5, 1937, Morgenthau Papers, FDR Library, Hyde Park; M. R. Werner, "Fiorello H. La Guardia: An Intimate Portrait," *New Republic* (September 29, 1947), 13 (quote).

67. *Times*, March 6, 16, 1937; *American Hebrew* (May 7, 1937): 1189.

68. *News*, October 4, 1935; *Afro American Week*, October 26, 1935; *World-Tele-*

gram, December 12, 16, 1935; *Times*, December 14 (quote), 15 (quote), 1935; *Herald-Tribune*, December 16, 1935 (quote).

69. *Times*, December 14, 1935; Heckscher, *La Guardia*, 162.

70. Smith quoted in Citizens Charter Campaign Committee Press Release, September 4, 1936, Box 3408, NYMA; Jerold S. Auerbach, "A New Deal for New York City, Fiorello La Guardia: 1934–1937" (M. A. Thesis Columbia University, 1959), 57–58.

71. Frederick Shaw, *The History of the New York City Legislature* (New York: Columbia University Press, 1954), 153–157; Auerbach, "La Guardia," 59, 68; *Times*, January 14, 1935.

72. Auerbach, "La Guardia," 69 (quotes); William C. Chadbourne to FHL, November 5, 1936, and other materials relating to the charter, Box 3408, NYMA.

73. Franklin, *LaGuardia*, 145; *Times*, May 20, 1935, April 16, 1936; London *Express* quoted in William L. Leuchtenburg, *Franklin D. Roosevelt and The New Deal* (New York: Harper & Row, 1963), 145; *Post*, December 17, 1935; FHL, "What Will the Progressives Do in the Presidential Election?" undated speech in Box 2706, NYMA, reprinted in *Liberty* (April, 1936).

74. Leuchtenburg, *FDR and the New Deal*, 150, 156, 184; Arthur M. Schlesinger, Jr., *The Coming of the New Deal*, Vol. 2 of *The Age of Roosevelt* (Boston: Houghton Mifflin, 1957–1960), 567–569.

75. Leuchtenburg, *FDR and the New Deal*, 184, 178.

76. *Times*, September 3, 1934, September 11, 1936; Berle, *Navigating the Rapids*, 111.

77. Warren Moscow, *Politics in the Empire State* (New York: Knopf, 1948), 102–105; Lorraine Colville, "A Comparison and Evaluation of the Organization and Techniques of the Major Political Parties in New York City and the Reaction of the Electorate to the Organizations, 1929–1949" (Ph.D. dissertation, New York University, 1954), 144.

78. James Farley interview, Columbia University Oral History Collection, 362–363; Waltzer, "American Labor Party," 132; *Times*, September 3, 1936; Colville, "Political Parties in New York City," 148.

79. FHL to Missey Le Hand, October 29, 1936, Stephen Early to FHL, October 30, 1936, Personal File 1376, FDRP-HP; Rexford G. Tugwell, *The Art of Politics, as Practiced by Three Great Americans: Franklin Delano Roosevelt, Luis Munoz Marin, and Fiorello H. La Guardia* (Garden City: Doubleday, 1958), 112–115.

80. Adolf A. Berle Diary, April 13, 1937, Berle Papers, FDR Library, Hyde Park; Berle, *Navigating the Rapids*, 121 (includes quote and Berle to FHL, February 4, 1937); *Times*, December 27, 1936.

81. Waltzer, "American Labor Party," 114, 147.

82. Waltzer, "American Labor Party," 147–148, 115–117 (quotes).

83. *Times*, February 15, 1937; *Sun*, November 6, 1935 (quote); FHL to Robert McC. Marsh, July 19, 1937 (quote), Box 2706, NYMA; Moscow, *Politics in New York*, 107 (quote).

84. Paul Windels interview, Columbia University Oral History Collection, Appendix, 7; *Times*, February 7, March 11, June 9, 1937; *Sun*, February 10, 1937; unlabeled newspaper clipping, dated February 17, 1937, FHL scrapbook, NYMA; FHL to Robert McC. Marsh, July 19, 1937, Box 2706, NYMA.

85. Limpus and Leyson, *La Guardia*, 406; K. Simpson to C. C. Burlingham, August 17, 1937, CCBP.

86. Berle, *Navigating the Rapids*, 128; Heckscher, *La Guardia*, 170; Limpus and Leyson, *La Guardia*, 406; *Times*, July 24, 26, 27, 1937.

87. Franklin, *La Guardia*, 151–152 (quote); Berle, *Navigating the Rapids*, 125; FHL to Robert McC. Marsh, July 19, 1937, Box 2706, NYMA; Heckscher, *La Guardia*, 165 (quote); *Times*, March 2, 1937.

88. Robert A. Caro, *The Power Broker: Robert Moses and the Fall of New York* (New York: Vintage, 1974), 471; *Times*, February 1, 1935, March 15, 1936; *Herald-Tribune* and *World Telegram*, March 13, 1936.

89. Caro, *The Power Broker*, 450; *Times*, July 23, 26, 1936; Heckscher, *La Guardia*, 135.

90. *Times*, February 13, April 7, 1937; Caro, *The Power Broker*, 450–452; Heckscher, *La Guardia*, 167; Berle, *Navigating the Rapids*, 126–128.

91. M. Hobson to Goodhue Livingston, April 17, 1937, Hylda Goldsmith to Livingston, April 4, 1937, Lawrence Ellman to Livingston, April 2, 1937, Lindley Vinton to Livingston, April 15, 1937, Chester Braman to Livingston, April 1, 1937, Livingston Collection, LAGA; Franklin, *La Guardia*, 140; Lincoln Cromwell to C. C. Burlingham, July 23, 1937, CCBP.

92. Windels interview, Columbia University Oral History Collection, 86–88; Limpus and Leyson, *La Guardia*, 406–409.

93. Windels interview, Columbia University Oral History Collection, Appendix, 7; *Sun*, June 19, 1937; *Times*, January 1, 2, 1937.

94. *Secret Diary of Harold Ickes*, II, 162–163.

95. *Secret Diary of Harold Ickes*, II, 163; William P. Vogel, "What Did the New York Election Prove," *Common Sense* (December 1937): 15; Heckscher, *La Guardia*, 171; Limpus and Leyson, *La Guardia*, 411–412.

96. See Box 4113, NYMA, for the reports by each department detailing their accomplishments during La Guardia's first term; *Times*, September 14, 1937 (quote); Irish Committee for La Guardia in Box 2705, NYMA; Robert Moses, "La Guardia: A Salute and a Memoir," *New York Times Magazine* (September 8, 1957):18.

97. John Gunther, *Inside USA* (New York: Harper and Brothers, 1946), 590; *Times*, October 5, 1937; on not reappointing Jews to office, see article in Yiddish entitled "Sensational Facts: Why Has La Guardia Not Halted the Nazis in New York," Box 4121, NYMA, and Ronald Bayor, *Neighbors in Conflict: The Irish, Germans, Jews, and Italians of New York City: 1929–1941* (Baltimore: Johns Hopkins University Press), 135–136.

98. Berle, *Navigating the Rapids*, 145; material on Nazi parades in Box 2564, NYMA; Bayor, *Neighbors in Conflict*, 136; *Times*, October 31, November 1, 1937; F. Frankfurter to C. C. Burlingham, November 17, 1936, Burlingham to FHL, May 14, 1937, CCBP.

99. *Times*, October 5, 1937; James Gerard to FDR, October 6, 1937, PPF 1306, FDRP-HP; William P. Vogel, "What Did the New York Election Prove," *Common Sense* (December, 1937): 15. The *News* provided each camp with space on its editorial page from October 11 to election day to debate the issues and sling mud in whatever form they wished.

One La Guardia column (October 22, 1937) showed a pack of swine feeding at a trough with the caption "As It Was And As They Hope It Will Be Again."

100. *Times*, May 27, 1937; Allen, *Why Tammanies Revive*, 27 (quote), 50. The "lessons on city government" can be found almost daily beginning in *Times*, October 15, 1937; on the Communist endorsement see *Times*, February 8, July 5, August 27, October 1, 1937; for Mahoney quotations on FHL as Communist see Waltzer, "American Labor Party," 116, *Times*, September 29, October 24–26, 29, 1937, *News*, October 26, 1937.

101. *Times*, September 14, 1937.

102. Berle, *Navigating the Rapids*, 126; Farley, *Jim Farley's Story*, 102; J. Farley interview, Columbia University Oral History Collection, 147, 362; *Secret Diary of Harold Ickes*, II, 233, 243, 252; *Times*, October 24, 1937 (quote); Raymond Moley, *The First New Deal* (New York: Harcourt, Brace, and World, 1966), 359–362.

103. Ritchie, "La Guardia," 144; *New Republic* (August 18, 1937): 37; *Post*, October 29, 1937.

104. James Gerard to FDR, October 6, 1937 (quote), FDRP-HP; *Times*, July 10, 1937 (on FHL victory will make him presidential contender); Paul Windels interview, Columbia University Oral History Collection, 89–91; George Britt, "The Fiery Little Flower," *Collier's* (March 11, 1939): 17; Goodhue Livingston, interview with the author, November 12, 1982.

105. Limpus and Leyson, *La Guardia*, 102; *Times*, November 3, 1937; Berle, *Navigating the Rapids*, 145 (quote); *Secret Diary of Harold Ickes*, II, 271.

Chapter 12

1. *Times*, November 3, 1937; James Farley, *Jim Farley's Story: The Roosevelt Years* (New York: Whittlesey House, 1948), 102; Robert Moses, "La Guardia: A Salute and a Memoir," *New York Times Magazine* (September 8, 1957): 17.

2. S. J. Woolf, "City Hall Dynamo," *New York Times Magazine* (July 17, 1937): 15; *Times*, December 26, 1935.

3. *Times*, November 27, 1935; *World-Telegram*, December 2, 1935; *Herald-Tribune*, November 22, 1935.

4. A. G. Newmeyer to FHL, July 28, 1937, FHL to Newmeyer, July 29, 1937, Box 2675, NYMA.

5. *Times*, July 20, November 7 (quote), 8, 1937, May 3, 1938; William P. Vogel, "What Did New York's Election Prove?" *Common Sense* (December 1937): 13–17; William R. Conklin, "A Wider Horizon for La Guardia," *New York Times Magazine* (August 28, 1938): 6, 18 (quote).

6. George Britt, "Fiery Little Flower," *Collier's* (March 11, 1939): 17; Rexford Tugwell, *The Art of Politics, as Practiced by Three Great Americans: Franklin Delano Roosevelt, Luis Munoz Marin, and Fiorello H. La Guardia* (Garden City: Doubleday, 1958), 99; FHL to Edward Schwerin, October 7, 1941, Box 2675, NYMA.

7. Woolf, "City Hall Dynamo," 15; *Times*, November 10, 16, 1935; FHL to S. Tilden Levy, August 11, 1939, Box 2675, NYMA.

8. *Times*, December 21, 1938 (attack), August 7, 1940 (bomb crew); John J. White to FHL, August 23, 1938, FHL to White, August 26, 1938, Box 2703; Mrs. Louis Dreyfuss to FHL, December 20, 1938, Box 2675; FHL to Edward J. Nuolo, January 18, 1944 (quote), Box 2704, NYMA.

9. William Conklin, "The Mayor Again Flings in His Hat," *New York Times Magazine* (July 18, 1937): 8; *Secret Diary of Harold Ickes*, 3 Vols. (New York: Simon & Schuster, 1953–1954), II, 233; [David Lilienthal], *The Journals of David Lilienthal*, 7 Vols. (New York: Harper & Row, 1964), I, 56–71.

10. Beatrice Bishop Berle and Travis B. Jacobs, eds., *Navigating the Rapids, 1918–1941; From the Papers of Adolf Berle* (New York: Harcourt Brace Jovanovich, 1973), 136; *Secret Diary of Harold Ickes*, II, 404; C. B. Yorke to FHL, December 20, 1937, Box 2703, NYMA.

11. *Times*, April 27, 1938, editorial.

12. *Atlantic Monthly* (January 1938): 55–63; *Movie and Radio Guide* (August 3, 1940): 34–35, 43; White in *Herald-Tribune*, June 30, 1938; *Newsweek* (November 15, 1937); *Time* (August 2, 1937); Conklin, "Wider Horizon for La Guardia," 6, 18; Conklin, "Mayor Again Flings in His Hat," 8; Woolf, "City Hall Dynamo," 15, 23.

13. *Times*, April 20, 1940; Samuel Seabury to FHL, June 19, 1940, Box 3521, NYMA; C. C. Burlingham to FHL, June 14, 1940, CCBP. Features included Carl Schriftgiesser, "Portrait of a Mayor: Fiorello La Guardia," *Atlantic Monthly* (January 1938): 55–63; George Britt, "Fiery Little Flower," *Collier's* (March 11, 1939): 17; William Saybrook, "Wild Bull of Manhattan," *American Magazine* (April 1937): 16–17, 107–111; John Chamberlain, "Mayor La Guardia," *Yale Review* (September 1939): 11–26; T. R. Carskadon, "New York's Fighting Mayor," *Current History* (January 1936); Jack Alexander, "A Day With La Guardia," *New Yorker* (October 16, 1937): 42; William Moulton Marston, "The Furiousest Man," *Esquire* (March 1936).

14. "S.R.O. at City Hall," *New York Times Magazine* (November 31, 1938): 8, 19; FHL to Henry H. Curran, December 7, 1939, CCBP.

15. C. C. Burlingham to FHL, November 9, 1937, CCBP; Berle, *Navigating the Rapids*, 158.

16. Heckscher, *La Guardia*, 188; C. C. Burlingham to FHL, November 9, 1937, CCBP; A. A. Berle to FHL, November 10, 1937, Berle Papers, FDR Library, Hyde Park.

17. August Heckscher, *When La Guardia Was Mayor: New York's Legendary Years* (New York: W. W. Norton, 1978), 201; *Times*, February 20, March 1, 1938.

18. *Times*, November 9 (quote), 19, 23, 24, December 3 (quote), 1937; FHL to L. Post, December 1, 1937, Post to FHL, December 2, 1937, Box 22, NYMA.

19. NYCHA, *Must We Have Slums* (New York: NYCHA, 1937), 13–15; *Times*, December 9, 1936; Anthony Jackson, *A Place Called Home: A History of Low Cost Housing in Manhattan* (Cambridge: M.I.T. Press, 1976), 221.

20. FHL to Henry Barklie McKee, December 7, 1936, Miscellaneous Manuscripts, Columbia University; L. Post to FDR, March 13, June 13, 1936, Chairman's File, NYCHA Papers, LAGA; FHL to Post, December 18 (quote), 1936, FHL to Ickes, April 13, 1936 (quote), Box 3673, NYMA.

21. Joseph A. Spencer, "Tenant Organization and Housing Reform: The Citywide Tenants Council, 1936–1943," in *Community Organization for Urban Social Change* (Westport, Connecticut: Greenwood Press, 1981), 138 (for tenant opposition to La Guardia); Joel Schwartz, "A Road Not Taken: The District Rehabilitation Idea and the New York City Housing Authority in the 1930s" (paper delivered at Conference on Public Housing in New York, Columbia University, October 12–13, 1984), 23 (on Post raising tenant expectations); FHL to L. Post, February 7, March 29, 1937, Commissioner's files, NYCHA Papers, LAGA; *Secret Diary of Harold Ickes*, II, 215; Ickes to FHL quoted in Jerold S. Auerbach, "A New Deal For New York City, Fiorello La Guardia: 1934–1937" (M.A. Thesis, Columbia University, 1959), 50.

22. *Times*, November 23, 24, December 1–3, 9–10, 12, 18, 21, 1937.

23. Jackson, *A Place Called Home*, 226 (quote); *Times*, December 7, 10, 15, 1937; Alfred Rheinstein to Robert Moses, September 7, 1938 (quote), NYCHA Papers, LAGA; Langdon Post, *The Challenge of Housing* (New York: Farrar and Rinehart, 1938), 213.

24. *Times*, September 14, 1940; Jackson, *A Place Called Home*, 235; figures for NYCHA construction accomplishments in Edmund B. Butler to FHL, January 4, 1943, NYCHA Papers, LAGA.

25. *Times*, November 25, 1934 (quote), October 19, 1935; Albany *Times-Union*, November 18, 1933.

26. *Times*, December 7, 1934; Florence Teets, "The Little Flower's Folly," *Pegasus* (October 1954): 2; FHL to William H. Howes, October 21, 23, November 24, 1936, Harlee Branch to FHL, November 2, 1936, FHL to Branch, November 4, 1936, Box 3756, NYMA; H. I. Brock, "Governor's Island Hears New Alarums," *New York Times Magazine* (April 15, 1934): 6, 11; *Herald-Tribune*, August 25, December 13, 1935, March 2, July 9, 1936, all on La Guardia's pleas to the post office.

27. *Times*, December 5, 1934, January 6, April 30, 1935; *American*, January 6, 1935; *Journal*, September 20, 1935; *Herald-Tribune*, May 1, 1935.

28. "City Problems of the South," *Proceedings of the Southern Regional Conference of the United States Conference of Mayors* (March 8–9, 1940): 7.

29. Teets, "The Little Flower's Folly," 3–7; Heckscher, *La Guardia*, 253; *Time* (September 20, 1937): 37–38; FHL to FDR, September 13, 1939, Box 3756, NYMA.

30. *Times*, November 3, 1939 (naming it "La Guardia Field"), February 9, 1940 (undercutting Newark airport); Teets, "The Little Flower's Folly," 4; Lawrence Elliott, *Little Flower: The Life and Times of Fiorello La Guardia* (New York: Morrow, 1983), 234; Oklahoma City *Times*, November 15, 1939, Box 3373, NYMA; Heckscher, *La Guardia*, 254.

31. Teets, "The Little Flower's Folly," 10–12; *Times*, February 22, 1939; *Sun*, October 4, 1939; Elliott, *Little Flower*, 234.

32. Michael Hare, "Why Have a Fair," Papers of the 1939/40 New York World's Fair Corporation, NYPL (quote); Joseph P. Cusker, "The World of Tomorrow: Science, Culture, and Community at the New York World's Fair, 1939–1940," in *The Dawn of a New Day: The New York World's Fair, 1939–1940* (Exhibition Catalog, Helen A. Harrison, guest curator, New York: The Queens Museum, 1980): 4; Lewis Mumford, "Address at the Dinner Meeting of Progressives in the Arts," December 11, 1935, World's Fair Papers, NYPL.

33. *The Great Gatsby* quoted in Marshall Berman, *All That Is Solid Melts Into Air: The Experience of Modernity* (New York: Simon & Schuster, 1982), 303–304; Warren Susman, ed., *Culture and Commitment, 1929–1945* (New York: Braziller, 1973), 296.

34. Robert Kohn, "Social Ideas in a World's Fair," in Susman, *Culture and Commitment*, 298; Warren Susman, *Culture As History: The Transformation of American Society in the Twentieth Century* (New York: Pantheon, 1984), 214.

35. *Times*, June 3, 1938, April 4, May 5, 1939; *Post*, December 28, 1938.

36. Cusker, "The World of Tomorrow," 4, 14.

37. C. C. Burlingham to FHL, May 2, 1939, CCBP; Susman, *Culture As History*, 223–225; Wendt quoted in Cusker, "The World of Tomorrow," 131.

38. Bruce Bliven, "Gone Tomorrow," *New Republic* (May 17, 1939): 42; Burlingham to FHL, May 2, 1939, CCBP; Susman, *Culture As History*, 223–225.

39. Marie La Guardia interview, Columbia University Oral History Collection; Marie La Guardia and Elsie Fisher, interview with the author, March 14, 1983; *Herald-Tribune*, July 10, 1935.

40. *Times*, March 27, 1939; FHL to Bruce Reynolds, April 12, 1943, Box 2704, NYMA; William Fellowes Morgan to Arthur Mann, January 6, 1958, LAGA; Britt, "Fiery Little Flower," 17; S. Wise to FHL, August 27, 1935, Reel 21, NYPL; Anna Clark, interview with the author, November 4, 1982; Louis Yavner, interview with the author, November 23, 1982; Helen Harris, interview with the author, October 25, 1983.

41. Robert A. Caro, *The Power Broker: Robert Moses and the Fall of New York* (New York: Vintage, 1974), 452; August Heckscher, *When La Guardia Was Mayor: New York's Legendary Years* (New York: W. W. Norton, 1978), 113; FHL to Marie La Guardia, April 30, 1941, Mrs. J. N. Gardner to FHL, April 18, 1941, LAGA.

42. Marie La Guardia and Elsie Fisher, interview with the author, March 14, 1983; *Secret Diary of Harold Ickes*, III, 47; S. J. Woolf, "Mayor Two Years and Still Optimistic," *New York Times Magazine* (January 5, 1936): 9.

43. *Times*, September 29, 1943; *Secret Diary of Harold Ickes*, II, 86; Elsie Fisher, interview with the author, March 21, August 10, 1983.

44. See Box 78, File 2, NYMA, for correspondence with Modern Age Books and legal advice that FHL's libel case against them would be weak.

45. Jean La Guardia, "Father Fiorello" (unpublished manuscript, LAGA, n.d.), 3; *Secret Diary of Harold Ickes*, III, 47.

46. Elsie Fisher, interviews with the author, July 23, August 10, 1983; *Times*, August 28, 1938; Eleanor Roosevelt, "My Day," unlabeled newspaper clipping, August 29, 1938, FHL scrapbook, NYMA.

47. FHL to C. C. Burlingham, July 22, 1939, CCBP; *Times*, July 28, 1938, March 11, 1939; J. La Guardia, "Father Fiorello," 5; FHL to Thomas J. Scannell, January 25, 1939, Box 2703, FHL to Bruce Reynolds, April 12, 1943, Box 2704, NYMA.

48. Conklin, "Mayor Flings in His Hat," 9; J. La Guardia, "Father Fiorello," 4; John D. Rockefeller III to FHL, December 28, 1936, FHL to Rockefeller, January 4, 1937, Box 2675, NYMA; Elsie Fisher, interview with the author, March 14, 1983; Helen Harris, interview with the author, October 25, 1983.

49. Conklin, "Mayor Flings in His Hat," 9 (quote); *Times*, December 22, 1936, May 1, 1938 (quote).

50. FHL to I. N. McCrary, March 31, June 7, 11, 1947, LAGA.

51. FHL to Eric La Guardia, June 12, 1946 (including quoted comment written on the carbon copy), A. Ornstein to FHL, December 26, 1946, Ornstein to Eric La Guardia, September 19, 1946, LAGA; original drawing entitled "The Dreamer and the Doer," LAGA; Marie La Guardia and Elsie Fisher, interview with the author, March 14, 1983. Fiorello wanted Eric to become a doctor or a scientist, and to avoid politics.

52. Ralph Gillette to FHL, February 8, 1935, Box 2543, NYMA; Elsie Fisher, interview with the author, August 10, 1983.

53. Elsie Fisher, interview with the author, August 10, 1983; Press Release Concerning Mayor's "Jewishness," January 5, 1934, Box 2704, NYMA; Louis Rittenberg, "Mayor La Guardia Pays Tribute to Mother," *American Hebrew and Jewish Tribune* (January 12, 1934): 183, 196; Heckscher, *La Guardia*, 118–119.

54. FHL to Paul Moss, October 7, 1936, Box 2675, NYMA; Tugwell, *Art of Politics*, 222.

55. Elsie Fisher, interview with the author, March 14, 1983; Britt, "Fiery Little Flower," 17; Helen Harris, interview with the author, October 25, 1983; Ira Hirschmann, interview with the author, January 13, 1983; Joey Adams, transcript of interview, Lawrence Elliott Collection, LAGA.

56. FHL to Edward N. La Corte, November 19, 1936, Box 2675, FHL to Irving Lehman, May 5, 1939, Box 2703, NYMA; C. C. Burlingham interview, Columbia University Oral History Collection, 34; Goodhue Livingston, interview with the author, November 12, 1982.

57. Burlingham to Seabury, May 24, 1940, CCBP; Frank Voss, "La Guardia and Burlingham: A Study of Political Friendship and Personal Influence" (M. A. thesis, Columbia University, 1983), 3–5.

58. Voss, "La Guardia and Burlingham," 3–5; FHL to Burlingham, June 3, 1937, CCBP; Goodhue Livingston, interview with the author, November 12, 1982.

59. Burlingham to F. Frankfurter, January 10, 1934, Burlingham to FHL, November 20, 1934, February 19, 1936, March 12, July 20, 1938, CCBP.

60. Burlingham to FHL, December 22, 1935, Stanley Howe to FHL, December 19, 1939, FHL to Burlingham, February 1, 1940, CCBP.

61. FHL to Burlingham, July 22, December 16, 1939, September 19, 1940, CCBP.

62. FHL to Burlingham, July 23, August 23, 1938, CCBP.

63. FHL to Burlingham, July 31, August 7, 1938, CCBP.

64. FHL to Burlingham, July 3, 22, 1939, CCBP.

65. *Times*, February 2, 1938; Heckscher, *La Guardia*, 197; Berle, *Navigating the Rapids*, 307.

66. Berle, *Navigating the Rapids*, 307.

67. See for example FHL to Burlingham, January 18, 1940, CCBP.

68. R. Moses to FHL, August 29, 1938, Box 35, NYMA; Moses to A. Rheinstein, November 18, 22, 1938, July 1, 7, September 18, 1939, Rheinstein to Moses, November 21, 1938, NYCHA Papers, LAGA.

69. Caro, *The Power Broker*, 611–612; *Times*, November 24, 25, 1938, June 24, 1939.

70. Berman, *All That Is Solid*, 305–306; Caro, *The Power Broker*, 615–621.

71. Elliott, *Little Flower*, 215; Berman, *All That Is Solid*, 301.

72. Caro, *The Power Broker*, 688, 607, 641–644; *Times*, October 12, 1938.

73. Caro, *The Power Broker*, 641, 658, 662, 668; Berman, *All That Is Solid*, 304.

74. Caro, *The Power Broker*, 666–668, 672; C. C. Burlingham to FDR, April 10, October 24, 1939, PPF 1169, FDRP-HP; William Chadbourne to Edwin Watson April 18, 1939, CCBP.

75. Caro, *The Power Broker*, 673–674; Edwin Watson to FDR, May 18, 1939, Personal File 1376, FDRP-HP; *Times*, July 18, 1939.

76. FHL to C. C. Burlingham, July 22, 1939, CCBP; Moses, "La Guardia," 116; Berle, *Navigating the Rapids*, 267.

77. "Robert Or I'll Resign Moses," *Fortune* (June 1938): 72; Caro, *The Power Broker*, 641, 674–676; *Times*, January 23, 1940.

78. Clifton Hood, "Underground Politics: A History of Mass Transit in New York City Since 1904" (Ph.D. dissertation, Columbia University, 1986), 260–261.

79. Harold Phelps Stokes, "Subway Unification: A New York Effort Begins," *Times*, January 28, 1934 (section XI); Hood, "Underground Politics," 332–335, 347; *Times*, January 7, 1934.

80. Hood, "Underground Politics," 354–355; Charles Garrett, *The La Guardia Years, Machine and Reform Politics in New York City* (New Brunswick: Rutgers University Press, 1961), 210–218; Arthur W. McMahon, "The New York City Transit System: Public Ownership, Civil Service, and Collective Bargaining," *Political Science Quarterly* 56 (June 1941): 161–190.

81. McMahon, "The New York City Transit System," 173, 182; Joshua Freeman, "The Transport Workers Union in New York City, 1933–1948" (Ph.D. dissertation, Rutgers University, 1983), 34–35.

82. FHL to FDR, March 28, 1940, FDR to FHL, March 3, 1940, PPF 1376, FDRP-HP; *World Telegram*, April 10, 1941.

83. *Secret Diary of Harold Ickes*, II, 252; *Times*, November 22, 1937, June 26, 1938, February 21, 1939; Conklin, "Wider Horizon for La Guardia," 6; A. A. Berle Diary, November 8, 1937, May 3, 1938, A. A. Berle to FDR, April 26, May 3, 1938, Berle Papers, FDR Library, Hyde Park; Berle, *Navigating the Rapids*, 173–175.

84. Berle, *Navigating the Rapids*, 173, 175; Berle to FDR, May 3, 1938, Berle Papers, FDR Library, Hyde Park; *Times*, April 30, 1938 (quote), March 26, 1939 (quote).

85. Britt, "Fiery Little Flower," 47; John Chamberlain, "Mayor La Guardia," *Yale Review* (September 1939): 26.

86. William Walsh, letter to the author, [1983]; FHL to FDR, February 1, 1938, PPF 1376, FDRP-HP; *Times*, October 4, 1938.

87. FHL to William S. Murray, October 20, 1938, Box 2703, NYMA; A. A. Berle Diary, November 1, 1938, Berle Papers, FDR Library, Hyde Park.

88. Arthur Krock, "A Good Samaritan in Politics," *Times*, October 25, 1938; *Times*, November 4, 5, 7, 1938.

89. *Times*, October 4, November 20–21, 1938; Heckscher, *La Guardia*, 244; FHL to Missy Le Hand, April 11, 1938, PPF 1376, FDRP-HP.

90. *Times*, December 3, 15, 1937, January 28, April 23, September 10, 1938; FHL, "Balancing the Population," *Survey Graphic* (January 1938): 15; Jay Franklin, *La Guardia: A Biography* (New York: Modern Age, 1937), 159.

91. *Times*, September 15, 24, 1938; Lowell Limpus and Burr W. Leyson, *This Man La Guardia* (New York: E. P. Dutton, 1938), 417.

92. *Secret Diary of Harold Ickes*, II, 464, 523, 545; *Times*, September 25, 1938; Franklin, *La Guardia*, 159–160.

93. *Times*, March 17, 1939; Newbold Morris, *Let the Chips Fall: My Battles Against Corruption* (New York: Appleton-Century-Crofts, 1955), 133–136; Heckscher, *La Guardia*, 211–212.

94. *Times*, April 4, September 25, 1938; Arthur Schlesinger, Jr., *The Politics of Upheaval*, Vol. 3 of *The Age of Roosevelt* (Boston: Houghton Mifflin, 1960), 56.

95. *Times*, September 10, 19, October 28, 1938; Helen Harris, interview with the author, October 25, 1983.

96. Berle, *Navigating the Rapids*, 150–151, 194, 216, 288; *Secret Diary of Harold Ickes*, II, 257; R. Tugwell Diary, February 13, 1940, Tugwell Papers, FDR Library, Hyde Park.

97. Susman, *Culture As History*, 226–229.

98. FHL to Nicholas Roerich, April 13, 1930 (quote), Roll 6, NYPL. On South America see FHL's letters to Secretary of State Frank B. Kellog in Box 2522, NYMA, and in the "Foreign Policy File," Roll 6, NYPL; *Times*, March 11, 1936; FHL to FDR, February 1, 1938 (quote), FDRP-HP; Simon W. Gerson, "What Happened to La Guardia," *New Masses* (October 22, 1940): 6 (quote).

99. *Times*, November 3, 1938 (quote); H. Lehman to FHL, November 14, 1938, FHL to Lehman, November 15, 1938 (quote), Box 3679, NYMA.

100. John A. Garraty, *The American Nation*, (Fifth ed., New York: Harper & Row, 1983): 685–686; Mary Beth Norton, et al., *A People and a Nation* (Boston: Houghton Mifflin, 1987), 777.

101. *Times*, February 20 (Little Rock), March 17 (West Coast), April 3 ("cooties"), 1939; Sumner Welles to FDR, March 20, 1939, PPF 3000, FHL to Cordell Hull, September 5, 1939, Personal File 1376, FDRP-HP; Drew Pearson, "Washington Merry Go Round" in *Mirror*, September 28, 1939; A. A. Berle Diary, April 11, 1938, Berle Papers, FDR Library, Hyde Park.

102. Cordell Hull, *The Memoirs of Cordell Hull*, 2 Vols. (New York: Macmillan, 1948), I, 855–859; Berle, *Navigating the Rapids*, 308.

103. R. Tugwell Diary, April 26, 1940, FDR Library, Hyde Park; Tugwell, *Art of Politics*, 141; Berle, *Navigating the Rapids*, 194, 234, 265–266. Hull, *Memoirs*, I, 859–860, speaks of FDR making up his mind to run by July 3, 1940.

104. *Times*, January 30 (quote), May 2, 1940; *International Herald-Tribune*, December 24, 1939; *Secret Diary of Harold Ickes*, III, 203.

Chapter 13

1. *Sunday Star*, February 4, 1940.

2. *Times*, October 5, 1939 (quote), May 2, September 6 (quote), 19, November 1, 1940. See also Simon W. Gerson, "What Happened to La Guardia?" *New Masses* (October 22, 1940): 6; *The Secret Diary of Harold Ickes*, 3 Vols. (New York: Simon & Schuster, 1953–1954), II, 655; *Daily Worker*, May 3, 1940.

3. C. C. Burlingham to FHL, July 16, 1939, CCBP; "Whither Little Flower," *Friday* (May 3, 1940), a long piece full of charges that La Guardia was buckling under pressure from the rich and powerful, in La Guardia File, New York City Municipal Reference Library.

4. Rexford Tugwell Diary, September 20, 1940, Tugwell Papers, FDR Library, Hyde Park.

5. A. Rheinstein to Nathan Straus, June 23, 1938, Rheinstein to FHL, June 24, 1938, FHL to Rheinstein, January 20, 23, 1939, Chairman's File, NYCHA Papers, LAGA; Rosalie Genevro, "Site Selection and the New York City Housing Authority, 1934–1939," *Journal of Urban History* 12 (1986): 334–352.

6. A. Rheinstein to FHL, October 3, 1939, Chairman's File, NYCHA Papers, LAGA; *Times*, October 9, 10, 1939.

7. *Mirror*, October 10, 1939; *Times*, October 13, 1939; *Secret Diary of Harold Ickes*, III, 47, 92.

8. Quoted by Sidney Hook in review of *The Collected Papers of Bertrand Russell*, in *New York Times Book Review* (January 29, 1984): 7–8. See also Ronald Clark, *Bertrand Russell and His World* (New York: Thames and Hudson, 1981).

9. Bertrand Russell, *Marriage and Morals* (Garden City: Garden City Publishing, 1929), 48, 63, 165–166, 230; Bertrand Russell, *Education and the Good Life* (New York: Boni and Liveright, 1927), 220–221; August Heckscher, *When La Guardia Was Mayor: New York's Legendary Years* (New York: W. W. Norton, 1978), 269; FHL to Ordway Tead, March 5, 1940, Box 2582, NYMA; C. C. Burlingham to FHL, March 25, 1940, CCBP.

10. Ronald Clark, *The Life of Bertrand Russell* (New York: Knopf, 1976), 471–472; copy of court decision in Box 2582, NYMA; Burlingham to FHL, May 17, 1940, CCBP.

11. George Counts, John Dewey, Sidney Hook, and Horace Kallen to FHL, April 2, 1940, John Dewey to FHL, April 6, 1940, Box 2582, NYMA; *Times*, April 6, 7, 1940; Burlingham to FHL, April 18, 1940, quoted in Heckscher, *La Guardia*, 273.

12. Rexford Tugwell, *The Art of Politics, as Practiced by Three Great Americans: Franklin Delano Roosevelt, Luis Munoz Marin, and Fiorello H. La Guardia* (Garden City: Doubleday, 1958), 97; "Whither Little Flower," *Friday* (May 3, 1940), La Guardia file, New York Municpal Reference Library; *Daily Worker* May 3, 1940; R. Tugwell Diary, April 26, 1940, Tugwell Papers, FDR Library, Hyde Park.

13. *Times*, September 26 (quote), December 25, 1940; Brooklyn *Eagle*, August 19, 1940; *Daily Worker*, September 26, 1940.

14. James Marshall, interview with the author, December 2, 1982; Louis Yavner, interviews with the author, November 23, 1982, January 27, 1983, May 3, 1983; Morris R. Cohen to C. C. Burlingham, January 7, 1941, CCBP.

15. Harold Seidman, interview with the author, November 24, 1983; Louis Yavner, interviews with the author November 23, 1982, January 27, 1983, May 3, 1983 (quote); Paul Windels interview, Columbia University Oral History Collection, 107 ff.; Charles Garrett, *The La Guardia Years, Machine and Reform Politics in New York City* (New Brunswick: Rutgers University Press, 1961), 281.

16. Harold Seidman, interview with the author, November 24, 1983.

17. The investigator who told the author this story insisted on anonymity.

18. FHL to Joseph M. Patterson, April 5, 1939, Box 2704, NYMA; C. C. Burlingham to FHL, July 26, 1939, CCBP.

19. A. A. Berle Diary, April 30, 1940, Berle Papers, FDR Library, Hyde Park; Geoffrey Parsons to Burlingham, December 11, 1939, CCBP.

20. Burlingham to FHL, May 16, 1940, FHL to Burlingham, Burlingham to FHL, both May 17, 1940, G. Baehr to Burlingham, G. Baehr to FHL, FHL to Burlingham, FHL to Burlingham, all May 18, 1940, CCBP.

21. *Times*, April 30, 1940; R. Tugwell Diary, April 17, 1940, Tugwell Papers, FDR Library, Hyde Park; Beatrice Bishop Berle and Travis B. Jacobs, eds., *Navigating the Rapids, 1918–1941; From the Papers of Adolf Berle* (New York: Harcourt Brace Jovanovich, 1973), 308, 274.

22. William L. Leuchtenburg, *Franklin D. Roosevelt and The New Deal* (New York: Harper & Row, 1963), 302, 312.

23. FHL to C. C. Burlingham, June 25, 1940, CCBP; FHL to FDR, July 18, 1940, Personal File 1376, FDRP-HP; Gerson, "What Happened to La Guardia," 6; *Secret Diary of Harold Ickes*, II, 321; *Times*, September 13, 1940.

24. C. C. Burlingham Interview, Columbia University Oral History Collection, 38; FDR to FHL, June 15, 1940, Box 2675, NYMA.

25. *Times*, September 12 (quote), October 14 (boodle quote), November 2, 1940.

26. E. M. Watson to FDR, October 1, 1940, Personal File 1376, FDRP-HP; *Secret Diary of Harold Ickes*, III, 300; *Times*, September 15, November 2 (quote), 1940; Windels interview, Columbia University Oral History Collection, 22.

27. *Times*, October 22, November 2, 1940.

28. *Secret Diary of Harold Ickes*, III, 181; R. Tugwell Diary, 49, 69, 78, 163, FDR Library, Hyde Park; Heckscher, *La Guardia*, 277.

29. Leuchtenburg, *FDR and the New Deal*, 321, 324; FHL to William Allen White, December 26, 1940, Box 2675, NYMA.

30. *Times*, December 20, 1940; Heckscher, *La Guardia*, 288; C. C. Burlingham to FHL, December 5, 1940, CCBP.

31. R. Tugwell Diary, June 16, 1940 (quote), Tugwell Papers, FDR Library, Hyde Park.

32. *World-Telegram*, September 22, 1947; FHL to Marvin McIntyre, December 22,

1938 (quote), FDR to FHL, January 17, March 11, 1941, FDR to [J. Farley], April 25, 1941 (quote), Edwin W. Watson to FHL, July 14, December 19, 1939, May 22, July 13, 1940, FHL to Watson, July 11, November 18, December 23, 1940, January 21, 1941, FHL to FDR, June 28, 1940, PPF 1376, FDRP-HP; FHL to FDR, July 11, 1940, Box 2675, NYMA.

33. See various letters to FDR recommending La Guardia dated July 5, November 10, 11, 23, 25, 26, 27, 28, 1940, Official File 15a; May 21, June 3, September 18, December 24, 1940, May 21, 1941, O. B. Kiel to FDR, August 21, 1940, Official File 25a, FDRP-HP.

34. Berle, *Navigating the Rapids*, 347.

35. *Times*, August 27, 1940.

36. Frederick Davenport to FDR, December 17, 1940, FDR to Davenport, December 19, 1940, Personal File 1376, FDRP-HP; *Secret Diary of Harold Ickes*, III, 398; *News*, January 11, 1941.

37. R. Tugwell Diary, 97, 152, Tugwell Papers, FDR Library, Hyde Park.

38. *Times*, April 23, 1941; C. C. Burlingham to S. Seabury, May 24, 1940, Burlingham to FHL, January 22, 1941, CCBP; Burlingham interview, Columbia University Oral History Collection, 38.

39. Tugwell Diary, December 24, 1940, January 30, February 6, 1941, and p. 152, Tugwell Papers, FDR Library, Hyde Park.

40. *New Republic* (January 27, 1941): 115; A. A. Berle to FDR, May 20, 1940, PSF "Dept. of State," Box 94, FDRP-HP.

41. *News*, January 11, 1941; Lehman interview, Columbia University Oral History Collection, 675–677; Allan Nevins, *Herbert H. Lehman and His Era* (New York: Scribner, 1963), 215; *Secret Diary of Harold Ickes*, III, 186.

42. Tugwell, *Art of Politics*, 75.

43. Berle, *Navigating the Rapids*, 354, 358.

44. *Times*, December 22, 1939 (quote), December 20, 1940; C. C. Burlingham to FHL, August 3, 1939, CCBP.

45. *Mirror*, November 13, 1938; *Times*, June 21, October 23, 1941, May 9, 1940.

46. Garrett, *The La Guardia Years*, 135–136; *World-Telegram*, May 23, 1939 (quote); Press Release, May 23, 1939, Chairman's Files, NYCHA Papers, LAGA.

47. Robert A. Caro, *The Power Broker: Robert Moses and the Fall of New York* (New York: Vintage, 1974), 472–473; *Times*, November 21, 1939.

48. *Times*, May 8, 9, July 25, October 11, December 24, 1940, January 1, October 15 (final report), 1941.

49. *Times*, January 1, May 3, October 15, 1941; FHL to Philip McCook, November 5, 1941, Box 2703, NYMA.

50. *Times*, January 21, February 6, March 15, April 12, May 30, June 28 (editorial), 1941.

51. *Times*, June 27, October 15, 1941.

52. *Times*, March 30, 1941.

53. *Times*, April 20, 1941.

54. *Times*, April 20, 1941.

55. FDR to FHL, January 29, 1941, FDRP-HP; FHL, "Presidential Address," United States Conference of Mayors, *Proceedings* (1940): 4–5; Heckscher, *La Guardia*, 280–281.

56. St. Louis *Star-Times*, February 20, 1941 (quote); *Herald-Tribune*, February 23, 1941; *Sun*, February 25, 1941 (quote); *Post*, February 11, 1941. At another time, O'Brien made anti-Semitic comments that La Guardia also regretted. See Maurice Rappaport to FHL, October 13, 1938, FHL to Rappaport, October 24, 1938, Box 2675, NYMA.

57. FHL to FDR, April 11, 1941, James H. Rowe to FDR, April 21, 1941, FDR to FHL, April 22, 1941, PPF 1376 and PSF "La Guardia," FDRP-HP; *Times*, January 9–11, 1941.

58. Wayne Coy to FDR, April 9, 1941, OF 4422; E. M. Watson to FDR, April 21, 1941, PSF "La Guardia," FDRP-HP.

59. FHL to FDR, April 25, 1941, Box 4221, NYMA.

60. *Times*, May 15, 1947; P. E. Foxworth to Director [J. Edgar Hoover], May 24, 1940, Personal and Confidential, FBI file 66-5424-1-179X FOIA 237648.

61. FHL to FDR, April 25, 1941, Box 4221, NYMA; *Secret Diary of Harold Ickes*, III, 519; E. M. Watson to FDR, May 6, 1941, PPF 8101, FDRP-HP.

62. Executive Order 8757, OF 4422, FDRP-HP; "The Office of Civilian Defense," Box 4221, NYMA; Ernest K. Lindley, "La Guardia and the Civilian Defense Program," Washington *Post*," May 25, 1941.

63. Ickes to FDR, May 22, 1941, OF 4422, FDRP-HP; *Secret Diary of Harold Ickes*, III, 518.

64. FHL to William Hodson, July 17, 1939, Box 3593, NYMA.

65. *Time* and *Newsweek* in Heckscher, *La Guardia*, 298–299; FHL to Burlingham, May 28, 1941, CCBP; Arthur Krock column in *Times*, May 22, 1941.

66. *Times*, July 2, 1941; Memo for the Director [J. Edgar Hoover], July 16, 1941, FBI file 66-8700-23-6; FHL to FDR, July 3, 1941, OF 4422, FDRP-HP; *Secret Diary of Harold Ickes*, III, 584; E. Watson to FDR, June 14, 1941, PPF 1376, FDRP-HP; *Time*, (October 27, 1941): 29; R. Tugwell Diary, July 3, 1941, Tugwell Papers, FDR Library, Hyde Park.

67. *Secret Diary of Harold Ickes*, III, 572; *Times*, September 25, 1941.

68. *Times*, September 3, October 10, 1941; "Director of the Budget" to FDR, September 5, 1941, OF 4422, FDRP-HP; *Secret Diary of Harold Ickes*, III, 572.

69. Edward A. Tamm to Director [Hoover], August 8, 1941, FBI file 1-49-X7; J. Edgar Hoover to B. R. Sackett, August 10, 1941, FBI file 66-8700-56-61; Heckscher, *La Guardia*, 299; FHL to Col. Franklin D'Olier, Confidential, November 8, 1941, Box 4221, NYMA.

70. *Secret Diary of Harold Ickes*, III, 601; Informal Minutes of Interdepartmental Intelligence Conference, Confidential and Secret, September 3, 1941, FBI file 66-8603-261X.

71. *Times*, August 20, 1941; R. A. Lazarus interview, Columbia University Oral History Collection, 206; *Herald-Tribune*, September 16, 1941.

72. *Times*, January 23, September 20, October 21, 22, 30, 1941.

73. *Time*, (October 27, 1942): 23.

74. Hugh Johnson in *World-Telegram*, October 21, 1941; *Times*, October 8, 1941.

75. E. Watson to FDR, October 14, 1941, OF 4422; David H. Morris to FDR, October 22, 1941, PPF "La Guardia"; C. C. Burlingham to FDR, October 23, 1941, Memorandum for Press Conference, [October 24, 1941], FHL to FDR, October 24, 1941, PPF 1376; B. Lindsey to FDR, October 28, 1941, PPF 2083, FDRP-HP; *News*, November 4, 1941.

76. *World-Telegram*, October 28, 1941; Herbert H. Lehman interview, Columbia University Oral History Collection, 677; *Times*, October 22, 1941; Press Release, November 1, 1941, Berle Papers, FDR Library, Hyde Park.

77. *Post* and *World-Telegram*, October 28, 1941.

78. Herbert Lehman, Press Statement, October 28, 1941, Lehman Papers, Columbia University; C. C. Burlingham to FHL, July 26, 1939, CCBP.

79. *Times*, October 29, 1941.

80. A. A. Berle Diary, November 3, 1941, Berle Papers, FDR Library, Hyde Park; *News*, November 3, 1941.

81. Tugwell, *Art of Politics*, 102; H. B. Swope to FDR, November 5, 1941, OF 331, FDRP-HP.

82. O. G. Villard to FHL, November 10, 1941, Villard Papers, Harvard University; S. J. Woolf, "City Hall Dynamo," *New York Times Magazine* (September 17, 1939): 15, 23.

83. *Herald-Tribune*, November 9, 16 (metal), 1941; Boston *Herald*, November 17, 1941.

84. Eleanor Roosevelt, *This I Remember* (New York: Harper & Row, 1949), 240.

85. E. Roosevelt to FHL, October 24, 1941, E. Roosevelt Papers, FDR Library, Hyde Park; E. Roosevelt, *This I Remember*, 231–232, 240; *Times*, November 26, 1941.

86. E. Roosevelt, *This I Remember*, 231–232; FHL to FDR, December 7, 1941, OF 4422, FDRP-HP.

87. *Times*, December 8, 1941.

88. FHL to FDR, December 8, 1941, Department of State file FW858.85/168; E. Roosevelt, *This I Remember*, 236–237; *World-Telegram*, September 22, 1947; FHL to FDR, December 12, 1941, OF 4422, FDRP-HP.

89. E. Roosevelt, *This I Remember*, 237–238 (quote); *World-Telegram*, September 22, 1947; *Times*, December 15, 1941.

90. *Herald-Tribune*, December 12, 1941 (editorial); *World-Telegram*, December 26 (quote), 29 (quote), 1941 (editorials); *Times*, December 11, 16, 20, 24, 1941, January 3, 1942 (editorial, quote).

91. *Times*, December 29, 1941, January 3, 1942 (quote).

92. *Times*, December 28 (editorial), 30, 1941, January 3, 26, 27 (editorial), 1942; C. C. Burlingham to FHL, January 27, 1942, CCBP.

93. *Times*, December 30, 1941 (editorial), January 2, 3, 8, 1942; *Herald-Tribune*, December 29, 1941 (editorial).

94. J. Edgar Hoover to staff, January 2, 1942, ["informational memo," no file number] FBI Papers; Lester Stone to FHL, [January 1942], Box 3298, NYMA; *PM*, January 5, 1942.

95. Heckscher, *La Guardia*, 324; *Herald-Tribune*, February 3, 1942; E. Roosevelt to FHL, February 18, 1942, E. Roosevelt Papers, FDR Library, Hyde Park.

96. C. C. Burlingham to FHL, February 13, 1942, CCBP.

97. Heckscher, *La Guardia*, 324.

98. *Times*, September 12, 1940, March 3, 1942.

99. Louis Yavner interview with the author, May 3, 1983.

100. *Times*, October 29, 1941, February 10 (editorial), December 28, 1942.

101. *Times*, February 6, 7, 9, 10 (editorial), 1942.

102. Heckscher, *La Guardia*, 327; *Times*, February 10, 17, 1942.

103. *World-Telegram*, April 1, 1942; *Sun*, March 30, 1942.

104. George Britt, "What Has Happened to La Guardia," *New Republic* (March 9, 1942).

105. Memo for the Director [Hoover], August 2, 1939, FBI file 62-52569-2.

106. *Times*, January 15, 1942.

107. *Times*, April 8, 1942 (editorial).

108. FHL to William Baumricker, April 25, 1941, FHL to Eric Hodgins, October 27, 1942, Box 3438, NYMA; *Times*, July 12, 1939.

109. *Times*, March 25, 1933, March 11, 1934, December 30, 1984 (Obituary of Peter Kihss); various letters from FHL to Roy Howard, Reel 17, NYPL; Garrett, *The La Guardia Years*, 124; John Hennessey Walker, "The Men Who Cover the Mayor," *PM* (September 13, 1942): 4.

110. Walker, "The Men Who Cover the Mayor," 4; John G. Rogers, "The Terrific Mr. La Guardia," *American Mercury* (February, 1944): 149–156; Brooklyn *Eagle*, February 27, 1935; William Conklin, "Fearless Fiorello," *Saturday Evening Post* (September 16, 1941): 72; Erich Brandes to FHL, May 28, 1945, Box 3437, NYMA.

111. *Herald-Tribune*, February 3, 1942; Walker, "The Men Who Cover the Mayor," 4 (quote); Heckscher, *La Guardia*, 337 (quote).

112. *Times*, March 25, 1933; FHL to Jack Strauss, August 10, 1942, Box 3437, NYMA; Heckscher, *La Guardia*, 336.

Chapter 14

1. "Secretary to the Mayor" to J. J. Coogan, June 8, 1935, Box 3524, NYMA; *Times*, December 6, 1941, March 8, April 14 (car), May 27, 28, 1942.

2. S. J. Woolf, "The Mayor Talks About Our Town," *New York Times Magazine* (September 30, 1945): 52 (quote); Lowell Limpus and Burr W. Leyson, *This Man La Guardia* (New York: E. P. Dutton, 1938), 170; John K. Hutchens, "His Honor the Radio Showman," *New York Times Magazine* (July 16, 1944): 14, 41.

3. Amy Porter, "Butch Says Cut It Out," *Collier's* (April 28, 1945): 23.

4. Porter, "Butch Says Cut It Out," 23; Transcript of Radio Broadcast, April 22, 1942, LAGA.

5. Transcript of Radio Broadcast, March 15, 1942, LAGA. See also folder 2, Box 3295, NYMA.

6. Transcript of Radio Broadcast, September 13, 1942, LAGA; FHL to Victor Ridder, September 23, 1942, Box 3438, NYMA.

7. *Times*, December 7, 1942, April 26, 1943.

8. Hutchens, "His Honor the Radio Showman," 14; Harrisburg *Patriot*, August 8, 1945 (quote); August Heckscher, *When La Guardia Was Mayor: New York's Legendary Years* (New York: W. W. Norton, 1978), 339 (quote); Kenneth Dayton to C. C. Burlingham, July 22, 1942, CCBP.

9. Porter, "Butch Says Cut It Out," 43; *Times*, May 15, 1944; Transcript of Radio Broadcast, April 12, 1942, LAGA.

10. Porter, "Butch Says Cut It Out," 44.

11. Porter, "Butch Says Cut It Out," 44; Transcript of Radio Broadcasts, April 12, 1942, LAGA; *Times*, March 12, 1945.

12. Transcript of Radio Broadcast, December 31, 1944, LAGA.

13. Transcript of Radio Broadcast, September 20, 1942, LAGA.

14. *Times*, October 21, 1942; *Sun*, June 18, 1940.

15. J. E. Hoover to Special Agent in Charge, June 11, 1940, FBI file 66-5423-1-179; B. E. Sackett to [Hoover], August 15, 1940, FBI file 61-7602-607; A. A. Berle to FHL, April 19, 1939, June 1, 1940, Berle Papers, FDR Library, Hyde Park; *World-Telegram*, October 12, 1939.

16. Ronald Bayor, *Neighbors in Conflict: The Irish, Germans, Jews, and Italians of New York City: 1929–1941* (Baltimore: Johns Hopkins University Press), 120; A. A. Berle to FHL, June 2, 1940, FHL to Berle, June 9, 1940, Berle Papers, FDR Library, Hyde Park; B. E. Sackett to [Hoover], June 18, 1940, FBI file 61-7602-553; J. E. Hoover to Henry Morgenthau, July 2, 1940, FBI file 65-1482-25; P. E. Foxworth to J. E. Hoover, August 7, 1941, FBI file 62-63892-57.

17. A. M. Travers to FHL, July 28, 1942, Box 3394, NYMA; P. E. Foxworth to Hoover, August 7, 1941, FBI file 62-63892-57; *Times*, October 26, 1942; FHL to Fred B. Bates, September 4, 1942, Box 3395, NYMA; Transcript of Radio Broadcast, July 18, 1943, Box 3395, NYMA; FHL to Victor Emmanuel III, May 9, 1940, Box 3394, NYMA. See Box 3394, NYMA, for other information on these broadcasts.

18. Maurice English to FHL, December 3, 1943, Natalie Murray to FHL, September 2, 1942, [American GI] to FHL, October 11, 1944, Box 3395, NYMA; *Times*, September 2, October 29 (quote), 1942, October 3, 1943 (quote), October 11, 1944.

19. FHL to FDR, December 27, 1942, FDR to FHL, December 30, 1942, FDRP-HP; FHL to FDR, November 1, December 31, 1943, FDR to FHL, January 1, 1944, Box 4069; FHL to Emory Land, January 24, 1944, Box 4068, NYMA.

20. *Times*, April 5, 1945; Pittsburgh *Press*, April 23, 1945.

21. Transcript of Radio Broadcast, [late 1943 or early 1944], Box 3394, NYMA.

22. *Times*, November 11, 17, 1938, November 3, 1941; Victor Ridder to Betty Cohen, November 4, 1943, Box 2706, NYMA; Richard B. Henderson, *Maury Maverick: A Political Biography* (Austin: University of Texas Press, 1970), 195.

23. *Journal*, March 2, 1939; Bayor, *Neighbors in Conflict*, 140; David Wyman, *The Abandonment of the Jews: America and the Holocaust, 1941–1945* (New York: Pantheon, 1984), 10, 13–14; David Wyman, *Paper Walls: America and the Refugee Crisis, 1938–1941* (Amherst: University of Massachusetts Press, 1968), 10, 14–15.

24. Bayor, *Neighbors in Conflict*, 99–100, 150, 155–156, 160–161; Wyman, *Abandonment*, 10. *The Commonweal* (September 1, 1939): 428–429 contains a firsthand account of a Front meeting.

25. *Jewish Examiner*, September 18, 1939; *Sun*, September 15, 1939; Goodhue Livingston, interview with the author, November 12, 1982; Goodhue Livingston, "Reminiscence," *Hampton Tradition* 4 (July 1983): 14.

26. *Nation* (July 22, 1939): 87; *Times*, July 21, 1939.

27. *Nation* (July 22, 1939): 92–97.

28. *Nation* (July 22, 1939): 87, 92–97.

29. *Times*, July 21, 1939.

30. *Jewish Examiner*, September 18, 1939; *Sun*, September 15, 1939; police reports on the Front in NYMA Boxes 3702, 3703, 3705; Livingston, "Reminiscence," 14.

31. *Times*, January 11, 1940; FHL to Isadore Fried, November 13, 1939, Box 3411, NYMA.

32. Bayor, *Neighbors in Conflict*, 102–103.

33. Brooklyn *Tablet*, February 17, 1940; *Times*, February 10, 14, 15, 1940.

34. *Times*, January 3, 11, 12, 1944; Brooklyn *Tablet*, February 17, 1940; Wyman, *Abandonment*, 11.

35. Wyman, *Abandonment*, 9–11, 15.

36. *Times*, July 26, 1943.

37. *Times*, November 25, 1943.

38. Wyman, *Abandonment*, xvi, 5.

39. Wyman, *Abandonment*, vii, xiv; Wyman, *Paper Walls*, 211.

40. Arthur Mann, *La Guardia: A Fighter Against His Times, 1882–1933* (Philadelphia: J. B. Lippincott, 1959), 226.

41. *Times*, August 8, 1938, August 16, December 28, 1939, May 7, 1941, February 1, June 23, 1942 (on jobs for blacks), April 2, 1941, May 10, 1942 (on employment agencies), March 2, 1939 (on Anderson); Dominic J. Capeci, Jr., "Fiorello H. La Guardia and the Harlem 'Crime Wave' of 1941," *New York Historical Society Quarterly* 64 (January, 1980): 7–29; FHL to E. Roosevelt, July 17, 1936, E. Roosevelt Papers, Stephen Early to Wayne Coy, June 6, 1941, OF 4422; E. M. Watson to FDR, June 14, 1941, OF 4025; FHL to FDR, August 10, 1942, PPF 1376, FDRP-HP; *Times*, May 30, 1942 (on discrimination in armed forces); Dominic J. Capeci, Jr., *The Harlem Riot of 1943* (Philadelphia: Temple University Press, 1977), 11.

42. A. Philip Randolph to FDR, July 14, 1941, OF 4422, FDR Papers; Capeci, *Harlem Riot*, 11.

43. *Times*, January 22, 1942; Capeci, *Harlem Riot*, 8–9, 32.

44. Capeci, "La Guardia and the Harlem 'Crime Wave' of 1941," 27–29; Capeci, *Harlem Riot*, 15.

45. Capeci, *Harlem Riot*, 13, 140–141; Frederick Eckers to FHL, July 26, 1943, Box 3650, NYMA.

46. Capeci, *Harlem Riot*, 14; FHL to Eckers, July 31, 1943, Box 3650, NYMA.

47. Capeci, *Harlem Riot*, 49–52.

48. Capeci, *Harlem Riot*, 21, 35.

49. Capeci, *Harlem Riot*, 23–27 (quote 27).

50. Capeci, *Harlem Riot*, 70, 72–74.

51. Capeci, *Harlem Riot*, 82; Transcript of Radio Broadcast, June 22, 1943, Box 2550, NYMA.

52. Capeci, *Harlem Riot*, 84, 86–87, 118.

53. Heckscher, *La Guardia*, 357; Capeci, *Harlem Riot*, 100. Box 2550, NYMA also contains much valuable information on the outbreak of the riot.

54. Capeci, *Harlem Riot*, 127–128.

55. Walter F. White, *A Man Called White* (New York: Viking, 1948), 102–104 (quote 104); Capeci, *Harlem Riot*, 104.

56. Capeci, *Harlem Riot*, 117.

57. F. Eckers to FHL, August 16, 1943, Box 3650, NYMA; *Times*, August 12, 1945. See also E. Roosevelt to FHL, August 4, 1943, FHL to E. Roosevelt, August 6, 7, October 27, December 11, 1943, PPF 1688, E. Roosevelt Papers, FDR Library, Hyde Park.

58. "Presentment of the August 1943 Grand Jury of Kings County in the Investigation of Crime and Disorderly Conditions of the Bedford Stuyvesant Area of Brooklyn," 2–3, Box 3384, NYMA; *Times*, January 2, 1934 (on "deadline").

59. "Presentment of the August 1943 Grand Jury of Kings County in the Investigation of Crime and Disorderly Conditions of the Bedford Stuyvesant Area of Brooklyn," 4–5, Box 3384, NYMA.

60. "Presentment of the August 1943 Grand Jury of Kings County in the Investigation of Crime and Disorderly Conditions of the Bedford Stuyvesant Area of Brooklyn," 5, Box 3384, NYMA. The mayor replied to the presentment in a point-by-point response. See "Application for an Order Expunging from the Record a Certain 'Presentment' Made by the August 1943 Grand Jury of Kings County," Box 3385, NYMA. For other criticism of the presentment, see "Judge Sobel Flays Presentment," Brooklyn *Eagle*, December 6, 1943. Despite all excuses, the central point of the jury's presentment—that Bedford Stuyvesant was becoming a dangerous slum—was undeniable. See also "Presentment of the July 1943 Grand Jury of Kings County, City and State of New York, Term Extended for the Purpose of Investigating the Adequacy of Police Protection in the County of Kings, City and State of New York," Box 3385, NYMA, which charged La Guardia with allowing the Brooklyn police force to become depleted.

61. William Davenport, "Harlem: Dense and Dangerous," *Collier's* (September 23, 1944): 11–13, 92; La Guardia's rebuttal, "Harlem: Homelike and Hopeful," which *Collier's* never printed, can be found in Box 2550, NYMA, or in Capeci, "Fiorello H. La Guardia and the American Dream: A Document," *Italiana Americana* 4 (1978), 2 ff.

62. FHL, "Harlem: Homelike and Hopeful," 2, 7.

63. FHL, "Harlem: Homelike and Hopeful," 7, 9, 17, Box 2550, NYMA; Capeci, "La Guardia and the American Dream," 11.

64. FHL, *Non-Citizen Americans in the War Emergency* (New York: American Committee for the Protection of the Foreign Born, 1942, transcript of December 22, 1941 Radio Broadcast), 7–9.

65. FHL to H. Ickes, April 11, 1944, Ickes to FHL, Confidential, April 22, 1944, Box 4069, NYMA; *Times*, April 27, 1944; FHL to W. R. Monroe, April 25, 1944, Box 4069, NYMA (calling American citizens of Japanese extraction "aliens").

66. *Times*, April 28, 1944.

67. *Times*, April 28, 1944; FHL to Lindsey Clinch, September 8, 1944, Box 3517, NYMA.

Chapter 15

1. Dominic J. Capeci, *The Harlem Riot of 1943* (Philadelphia: Temple University Press, 1977), 61–62; August Heckscher, *When La Guardia Was Mayor: New York's Legendary Years* (New York: W. W. Norton., 1978), 340; *Times*, July 18, 1942, April 12, 1943.

2. Capeci, *Harlem Riot of 1943*, 62–62.

3. *Times*, January 24, April 28, July 10, November 30, December 13, 1942; FHL to C. C. Burlingham, March 17, 1943, CCBP.

4. FHL to Emil Ludwig, March 22, 1942, Box 4221, NYMA; FHL to C. C. Burlingham, April 25, 1942, CCBP; FDR to Steven Early, May 2, 1942, PPF 1376, FDRP-HP.

5. FHL to Stanley D. Embrick, November 19, 1943, Box 3646, NYMA.

6. George Strong to FHL, December 7, 1942, LAGA.

7. *Times*, March 27, 1941 (quote), January 3, 1943; Edward J. Flynn, *You're the Boss* (New York: Viking, 1947), 188; Heckscher, *La Guardia*, 348.

8. *Times*, January 24, 1943; Flynn, *You're the Boss*, 190–191.

9. Robert H. Ferrel, *American Diplomacy, A History* (New York: Norton, 1975), 589; FHL to FDR, February 3, 1943, PPF 1376, FDRP-HP.

10. *Herald-Tribune* quoted in Heckscher, *La Guardia*, 351; *Times*, March 4, 1943; FHL to Lowell Thomas, March 1, 1943, Morry Luxembourg to FHL, March 29, 1943, Box 2562, NYMA; FHL to Harry Hopkins, March 17, 1943, Box 161, Hopkins Papers, FDR Library, Hyde Park.

11. *Times*, March 3, 4, 5, 1943; Rexford Tugwell, *The Art of Politics, as Practiced by Three Great Americans: Franklin Delano Roosevelt, Luis Munoz Marin, and Fiorello H. La Guardia* (Garden City: Doubleday, 1958), 110.

12. *Times*, April 8, 1943; W. N. Guthrie to FHL, April 2, 1943, Box 2562, NYMA.

13. Walter White to FHL, March 30, 1943, Box 2550, NYMA; *Times*, April 8, 1943; C. C. Burlingham to FHL, March 15, 1943, CCBP.

14. *Times*, March 28, 1943.

15. C. C. Burlingham to Samuel Seabury, March 31, 1943, CCBP; Paul Windels interview, Columbia University Oral History Collection, Appendix, 8; Tugwell, *Art of Politics*, 110.

16. Bruce Allen Murphy, *The Brandeis/Frankfurter Connection: The Secret Political Activities of Two Supreme Court Justices* (New York: Oxford University Press, 1982), 196; C. C. Burlingham interview, Columbia University Oral History Collection, 38; *Times*, April 4, 1943.

17. James MacGregor Burns, *Roosevelt: The Soldier of Freedom* (New York: Harcourt Brace Jovanovich, 1970), 491–492; *Times*, April 7, 1943.

18. *Mirror*, April 9, 1943; handwritten note from FHL written on C. C. Burlingham to FHL, April 13, 1943, CCBP.

19. Burlingham to FHL, November 9, 1942, CCBP.

20. Wayne L. Morse to FHL, December 30, 1942, Box 4070, NYMA; J. Marshall, "Life with La Guardia" (manuscript in author's posession), 4; *Times*, April 12, 30, May 12, 19, 21, 1943; FHL to Burlingham, May 14, 1943, Burlingham to FHL, April 6, 13, 1943, CCBP.

21. FHL to Burlingham, May 14, 1943, CCBP.

22. All quotations from Roger Baldwin et al. to FHL (draft), September 18, 1943, Box 4066, NYMA. The final version of the letter, dated February 8, 1944, can also be found in this location.

23. Roger Baldwin et al. to FHL (draft), September 18, 1943; FHL unaddressed draft letter, September 18, 1943, Box 4066, NYMA.

24. Lewis Gannett to FHL, September 22, 1943, Albert Bard to FHL, September 21, 1943, Box 3416, NYMA.

25. C. C. Burlingham to J. H. Holmes, September 24, 1943, CCBP; Fannie Hurst to FHL, September 20, 1943, FHL to Lewis Gannett, September 23, 1943, Box 3614, NYMA.

26. *Times*, October 19, 25, 28, December 16, 1943.

27. *Times*, October 19 (quote), November 11, December 16, 1943.

28. *Times*, November 21, December 16, 1943.

29. Charles Garrett, *The La Guardia Years, Machine and Reform Politics in New York City* (New Brunswick: Rutgers University Press, 1961), 290; *Times*, December 19, 1943.

30. FHL to FDR, June 6, 1943, PPF "Hyde Park," FDRP-HP; C. C. Burlingham to Elinore M. Herrick, n.d., CCBP.

31. Burns, *Roosevelt: The Soldier of Freedom*, 492.

32. FHL to FDR, May 13, 1944, PPF "La Guardia," FDRP-HP; Henry L. Stimson to E. Roosevelt, June 20, 1944, Box 913, E. Roosevelt Papers, FDR Library, Hyde Park; William Manners, *Patience and Fortitude: Fiorello La Guardia* (New York: Harcourt Brace Jovanovich, 1976), 262.

33. James V. Forrestal to FDR, August 26, 1944, FDR to Stimson, September 4, 1944, PPF "La Guardia," FDRP-HP; FHL to C. C. Burlingham, July 17, 1944, Burlingham to FHL, October 3, 1944, CCBP; Stimson to FDR, September 7, 1944, PPF "La Guardia," FDRP-HP; Drew Pearson, "Washington Merry Go Round," *Mirror*, September 28, 1944.

34. "GGT" to FDR, October 11, 1944, FDR to Stimson, September 29, 1944, FDR to H. Hopkins, October 17, 1944, PPF "La Guardia," FDRP-HP; *Times*, September 30, October 18, 27, 1944; FHL to FDR, October 18, 1944, L. Elliott Collection, LAGA; Drew Pearson, "Washington Merry Go Round," Washington *Post*, October 14, 1944; FHL to Cal Tinney, November 13, 1944, Box 3647, NYMA.

35. Robert Moses, "What's the Matter with New York," *New York Times Magazine* (August 1, 1943): 29.

36. FHL to Richard Neuberger, September 8, 1943, Box 3376, NYMA; *Times*, October 23, 1945.

37. *Times*, May 5, 1941, July 9, 1942.

38. Transcript of Radio Broadcast, March 18, 1945, LAGA; C. C. Burlingham to FHL, March 26, 1945, CCBP; James Byrnes to FHL, n.d., Box 3446; Alfred Knopf to FHL, March 19, 1945, Box 3447, NYMA; Heckscher, *La Guardia*, 392–394.

39. FHL to Mrs. Frederick Brooks, March 7, 1945, Box 3397, NYMA; Heckscher, *La Guardia*, 392; *Times*, March 8, 13, 14, April 25, May 2, 1945.

40. *Times*, September 26, November 1, 1943, February 24, September 1, 1944.

41. *Post*, July 23, 1947.

42. *Times*, July 23, December 11, 12 (quote), 1943; Heckscher, *La Guardia*, 367 (quote); Newbold Morris, *Let the Chips Fall: My Battles Against Corruption* (New York: Appleton-Century-Crofts, 1955), 162–167.

43. Heckscher, *La Guardia*, 368; FHL to John Golden, March 6, 1944, Box 3518, NYMA.

44. Heckscher, *La Guardia*, 376; FHL to Editors of *Fortune*, November 3, 1944, Box 3544, FHL to Paul V. McNutt, May 4, 1944, Box 3543, NYMA; *Times*, April 23, 1943; "Notes of a Meeting of City Committee to Study Plan to Provide Medical Service for People in Moderate Income Group, Box 3542, NYMA; St. Louis *Post-Dispatch*, October 29, 1944.

45. *Times*, May 1, 1944; FHL to McNutt, May 4, 1944, Box 3543, FHL to Editors of *Fortune*, November 3, 1944, Box 3544, NYMA; Dr. George Baehr, interview with L. Elliott, February 6, 1976, LAGA; St. Louis *Post-Dispatch*, October 29, 1944; Garrett, *The La Guardia Years*, 198.

46. *Times*, March 27, 1944.

47. S. J. Woolf, "Planning the City of Tomorrow," *New York Times Magazine* (June 18, 1939): 7, 15.

48. Rexford Tugwell, Diary, April 16, 26, 1940, Tugwell Papers, FDR Library, Hyde Park.

49. *Times*, February 12, 1942.

50. *Times*, April 1, 1939; S. J. Woolf, "The Mayor Talks About Our Town," *New York Times Magazine* (September 30, 1945): 14, 52; Henry A. Wallace to FHL, August 16, 1944, Box 60, Wallace Papers, FDR Library, Hyde Park.

51. FHL quoted in Citizens Budget Commission, *Annual Report* (1940): 8–9; *Times*, February 4, 5, 28 (quote), 1938.

52. Citizens Budget Commission, *Annual Report* (1942): 6; "Death and Taxes," *Fortune Magazine* (July 1939): 80.

53. *Times*, October 8, 11, 1941; Citizens Budget Commission, *Annual Report* (1941): 10–11.

54. Citizens Budget Commission, *Annual Report* (1942): 7–9, (1945): 7; Brooklyn *Eagle*, March 27, 1942.

55. *Times*, April 21, 1941.

56. FHL to Percy Magnus, September 2, 1938, Box 3570, NYMA; *Times*, February 10, 1940, July 18, 1942, April 12, September 19, 1943.

57. FHL to N. Butler, June 9, 1939, FHL to P. Grimm, January 5, 28, 1940, Grimm to FHL, February 7, 1940, Box 3411, NYMA.

58. *Times*, April 3, 1942.

59. Citizens Budget Commission, *Annual Report* (1944): 14; *Times*, June 3, 1943.

60. Citizens Budget Commission, *Annual Report* (1944): 39–41; *Times*, March 4, 1944.

61. C. C. Burlingham to FHL, March 31, 1945, CCBP; transcript of Radio Broadcast, March 25, 1945, LAGA.

62. *Times*, April 2, 1945.

63. *Report on the Executive Budget by the Citizens Budget Commission Inc.* (New York: Citizens Budget Commission, 1945); Citizens Budget Commission, *Annual Report* (1945): 5–10.

64. *Times*, July 9, 1944.

65. *Times*, April 12, 1943; Heckscher, *La Guardia*, 374 (quote).

66. *Times*, February 6, September 19, 1943; *Post* quoted in Heckscher, *La Guardia*, 375.

67. FHL to Claude Pepper, June 4, 1942, Box 3571, NYMA; *Times*, August 20, 1945; FHL, "Perspective on Postwar Planning," *New York University Conferences of the Institute on Postwar Reconstruction*, Third Series (February 23, 1944). For a full discussion of FHL's postwar plans for New York City, see the transcript of his August 13, 1944 radio broadcast, LAGA.

68. "New York Opens Its Post War Exhibit," *The American City* (May 1944): 5; FHL, "Vast Public Works Program Essential to Full Time Production," *The American City* (September 1945): 101; *Times*, December 20, 1940. See also FHL to FDR, February 9, 1943, Box 3571, NYMA; FDR to FHL, September 23, 1943, OF 129, FDRP-HP; Henry A. Wallace to FHL, August 16, 1944, Box 60, Wallace Papers, FDR Library, Hyde Park.

69. Heckscher, *La Guardia*, 372.

70. Citizens Budget Commission, *Annual Report* (1945): 9; Tugwell, *Art of Politics*, 28–30.

71. A. A. Berle to FHL, April 14, 1941, FHL to A. A. Berle, July 8, 1941, LAGA; Gemma La Guardia Gluck, *My Story* (New York: D. McKay, 1961), 16–22.

72. Gemma La Guardia Gluck to FHL, July 15, September 11, 1945, LAGA; Gluck, *My Story*, x; *Times*, February 5, 1945.

73. Gluck, *My Story*, 73–82, 109.

74. FHL to Lynne Stockton, June 15, 1945, Box 2704, NYMA; *Times*, July 5, 1945.

75. *Times*, May 4, July 5, 11, 1945; Gluck, *My Story*, 100.

76. FHL to G. Gluck, October 31, 1945, LAGA.

77. FHL to Gluck, October 31, 1945; FHL to Dwight D. Eisenhower, January 7, 1946; Harvey Gibson to FHL, September 12, 17, October 31, 1945; FHL to James W. Riddelberger, June 1, 1946; Albert Clattenburg, Jr., to FHL, June 6, 1946; FHL to Henrik de Kauffmann, December 20, 1945; "Affidavit for Application for Quota Visas for Yolanda Denes and her Infant Son Richard, June 1946," LAGA.

78. FHL to G. J. Haering, February 17, 1947; FHL to Howard K. Travers, Chief of Visa Division, February 7, 1947; FHL to E. J. McCormack, April 15, May 14, 1947; L. E. Archer to V. H. Moller, April 15, 1947, LAGA.

79. Gluck, *My Story*, 114; records indicating monthly remittances of $150 for

Gemma in Gemma La Guardia Gluck file, LAGA. See also FHL to Gluck, September 11, 1945, LAGA; FHL to Gluck, April 19, 1947, Elsie Fisher to Gluck, June 2, 1947, LAGA; Gluck, *My Story*, 114–115.

80. FHL to T. H. Johnson, September 12, 1943, Box 3376, NYMA; *Times*, June 23, 1943; FHL, "Why I Now Believe in Universal Military Training," *Reader's Digest* (April 1947): 1–2.

81. *Times*, September 4, 1944.

82. *Times*, February 7, 1944.

83. FHL to Ogden Reid, April 4, 1945, Box 3438, NYMA; *Times*, January 13, 1943, January 2, 1944.

84. *Times*, June 20, August 28, September 14, October 10, 28, 1945.

85. *Times*, March 16, 24, 1945; Kenneth A. Waltzer, "The American Labor Party: Third Party Politics in New Deal-Cold War New York, 1936–1954" (Ph.D. dissertation, Harvard University, 1978), 308. For Republican determination to block La Guardia from seeking a fourth term, see *Times*, November 10, 1944, January 2, February 28, 1945.

86. *Times*, February 13, April 21, 22, 1945; O. G. Villard to FHL, July 27, 1945, FHL to Villard, July 30, 1945, Villard Papers, Harvard University.

87. FHL, "Remarks on the Death of Franklin Roosevelt," April 12, 1945, LAGA; *Times*, April 14, 1945.

88. *Times*, April 25, 28, 1945.

89. FHL to Samuel Seabury, May 1, 1945, Box 4148, NYMA; *Times*, May 7, 1945.

90. *Times*, May 7, 1945.

91. C. C. Burlingham to FHL, December 15, 1945, CCBP; FHL to Harold Ickes, May 31, 1945, Box 4148, NYMA; *Times*, May 22, 1945.

92. Heckscher, *La Guardia*, 394.

93. John Gunther, *Inside USA* (New York: Harper, 1951), 622.

94. George Baehr interview, Columbia University Oral History Collection, 125–127; *Times*, June 4, 1945.

95. C. C. Burlingham to FHL, June 4, 1945 (quote), CCBP; Heckscher, *La Guardia*, 398.

96. Heckscher, *La Guardia*, 399; Garrett, *The La Guardia Years*, 296.

97. Morris, *Let the Chips Fall*, 209.

98. Robert A. Caro, *The Power Broker: Robert Moses and the Fall of New York* (New York: Vintage, 1974), 756; Gunther, *Inside USA*, 589–595; Alan Block, *East Side, West Side: Organizing Crime in New York, 1930–1950* (Cardiff: University College Cardiff Press, 1980), 98–124.

99. Tugwell, *Art of Politics*, 27; *Times*, October 17, 1945.

100. Morris, *Let the Chips Fall*, 204; Tugwell, *Art of Politics*, 255.

101. Woolf, "Mayor Talks About Our Town," 14; FHL to Robert Bloom, January 30, 1945, Box 2659, NYMA.

102. Heckscher, *La Guardia*, 404; John Dos Passos, "Everybody Knows the Mayor," *Liberty* (May 5, 1945): 20–21, 58, 78.

103. *Times*, June 7, July 6, 16, 1945.

104. William Conkin, "Fiery Fiorello," *Saturday Evening Post* (September 16, 1941): 72.

105. FHL to Harry Spengler, August 20, 1945, Box 2703, NYMA; Transcript of Radio Broadcast, July 1, 1945, LAGA.

106. Transcript of Radio Broadcast, July 8, 1945, LAGA.

107. Robert Bloom to FHL, January 21, 1945, Box 2659, NYMA.

108. *Times*, October 28, 29, December 21, 1945; Louis Yavner, interviews with the author, November 23, 1982, January 27, May 3, 1983.

109. *Times*, July 26, August 23, 29, 1945; FHL to Edward Welks, November 5, 1944, Box 2706, NYMA.

110. FHL to Lynn Carrick, October 3, 31, 1945, Carrick to FHL, September 20, 26, October 10, 25, December 4, 1945, March 14, 1946, LAGA.

111. *Times*, December 3, 7, 16, 17, 30, 31, 1945.

112. Lawrence Elliott, *Little Flower: The Life and Times of Fiorello La Guardia* (New York: Morrow, 1983), 11; *Times*, December 31, 1945; Transcript of Radio Broadcast, December 30, 1945, LAGA.

113. Newbold Morris, Transcript of Radio Broadcast, September 21, 1947, LAGA; *Times*, September 23, 1947.

Chapter 16

1. *Times*, January 11, 30, 1946; Adolf Berle to James Byrnes, February 4, 1946, Department of State files.

2. FHL, "How the *Daily News* Creates Dissension," *PM*, January 6, 1946; *Times*, February 15, 1946 for censored Sachs ad; *Post*, March 7, 1946 for article judged libelous by the *Times* and therefore rejected.

3. *PM*, December 20, 1946; editorial signed by Paul Hunter, publisher, in *Liberty* (May 18, 1946): 3; Edward Maher to O. F. Lever, June 11, 1946, LAGA; "Statement by F. H. La Guardia, May 29, 1946," LAGA; "La Guardia Cracks Back at His Critics," *PM*, June 2, 1946.

4. FHL, "A New Peace for a New Era," *Free World* (January 1943): 23.

5. Robert H. Ferrel, *American Diplomacy, A History* (New York: Norton, 1975), 632; Transcripts of ABC Radio Broadcasts, March 3, 10, 1946, LAGA.

6. Elsie Fisher, interview with the author, March 14, 1983.

7. Newbold Morris, *Let the Chips Fall: My Battles Against Corruption* (New York: Appleton-Century-Crofts, 1955), 211; *Times*, November 12, 1946. See also materials in Boxes 4520, 4521, and 4573, NYMA.

8. Herbert Lehman interview, Columbia University Oral History Collection, 757, 763–764.

9. Ira Hirschmann, "Bread Diplomacy: The Story of La Guardia's Last Great Fight," (unpublished manuscript, n.d., LAGA), 4.

10. Bella Rodman, *Fiorello La Guardia* (New York: Hill and Wang, 1962), 232–233; *Times*, May 18, 1946; See file of letters from Seymour (Sid) Kline to Rome *Daily American* and to FHL, March 20, April 1, 11, September 21, 29, 1946, Jack L. Begon to FHL, January 28, April 11, 1946, *News: Official Organ of American Relief for Italy* (December 1946): 2, LAGA; Elsie Fisher, interview with the author, March 14, 1983. See also drawings and letters from Italian children to FHL, LAGA.

11. FHL, "La Guardia in Europe: Inflation's Terrors," *PM*, July 28, 1946.

12. Stephen Ambrose, *Rise to Globalism* (Baltimore: Penguin, 1971), 125–127; Martin Blumenson, ed., *The Patton Papers, 1940–1945* (Boston: Houghton Mifflin, 1972–1974), 755.

13. Transcripts of WJZ Radio Broadcasts, August 14, 21, 1946, LAGA.

14. Transcripts of WJZ Radio Broadcasts, August 7, 14, 28, 1946, LAGA.

15. FHL, "Address on Displaced Persons" (delivered October 29, 1946 at the *Herald-Tribune* Forum on Current Problems), LAGA; *Times*, August 20, September 12, 1946; FHL, Address to the United Nations, September 18, 1946, LAGA; Leonard Dinnerstein, *America and the Survivors of the Holocaust* (New York: Columbia University Press, 1982), 110; FHL to General Joseph McNarney, August 4, 1946, letter in the possession of Cecile Fields, Miami, copy in the possession of the author.

16. FHL, "Address on Displaced Persons," LAGA; *Times*, September 12, 1946.

17. Unidentified clipping, March 30, 1946, in UNRRA clippings collection, LAGA; "La Guardia: Pool World Food Surplus," *PM*, August 25, 1946; Transcript of WJZ Radio Broadcast, September 11, 1946, LAGA; Rodman, *La Guardia*, 233; C. H. Conway to FHL, April 29, 1946, LAGA.

18. FHL quoted on "An Oath of Devotion," LAGA 1988 Calendar; Hirschmann, "Bread Diplomacy," 4; "La Guardia: America's Chance to Lead the World," *PM*, July 21, 1946; Transcripts of WJZ Radio Broadcasts, August 26, September 1, 1946, LAGA; "La Guardia: Report on Russia," *PM*, September 1, 1946; "La Guardia: Soviet Collective Farms," *PM*, September 8, 1946.

19. "Intelligence Report," Navy Department, Office of Chief of Naval Operations, July 24, 1947; "La Guardia: America's Chance to Lead the World," *PM*, July 21, 1946; Transcript of ABC Radio Broadcast, March 10, 1946, LAGA.

20. Transcripts of Radio Broadcasts, March 10 (ABC), September 11 (WJZ), 1946, LAGA.

21. Thomas G. Paterson, ed., *Major Problems in American Foreign Policy* (Lexington, Massachusetts: Heath, 1978), vol. II, 302; Henry A. Wallace, "The Path to Peace with Russia," *New Republic* 115 (1946): 401–406.

22. FHL memo for *Time*, September 21, 1946, FHL Personal Files, LAGA.

23. *Herald-Tribune*, December 9, 1946.

24. I. F. Stone, "La Guardia," *PM*, September 22, 1947; Louis Adamic, "My Friend Cvyetko," *Trends and Issues* (October–December 1947), in scrapbook, LAGA; Hirschmann, "Bread Diplomacy," 4, 7.

25. Joseph Lilly, "La Guardia," *The Nation* 165 (October 4, 1947): 337; *News*, December 10, 1946; *Times*, November 12, 1946.

26. I. F. Stone, "La Guardia," *PM*, September 22, 1947; *Times*, August 12, 1946; *Herald-Tribune*, November 12, 1946.

27. *Times*, November 11, 13, 14, 1946; *Herald-Tribune*, November 12, 1946.

28. FHL to Learned Hand, November 13, 1946, Hand Papers, Harvard University Law School Library; FHL, "Proposal For a United Nations Emergency Food Fund," UNRRA speech, November 11, 1946, LAGA (quote); Hirschmann, "Bread Diplomacy," 15.

29. Ambrose, *Rise to Globalism*, 131–133; Transcript of Mutual Network Radio Broadcast, April 19, 1947. See also Mutual broadcasts of March 15, 29, April 5, 12, May 10, 1947, and broadcast over WJZ of March 16, 1947, LAGA.

30. Transcripts of Mutual Network Radio Broadcasts, March 29, April 12, 16, 1947; FHL, untitled draft of article on "Contemporary Issues Regarding Foreign Affairs," 1–2, 7. This article was solicited by Clifton Fadiman for a new magazine called *'47, The Magazine of the Year*. See Fadiman to FHL, May 22, 23, 27, August 13, 27, September 8, 1947, FHL to Fadiman June 9, 10, August 20, 1947, LAGA.

31. FHL, "Contemporary Issues Regarding Foreign Affairs," 1.

32. H. H. Gerth and C. Wright Mills, *From Max Weber: Essays in Sociology* (New York: Oxford University Press, 1946), 115.

33. Felix Frankfurter, *Fiorello La Guardia, Address on the Occasion of the Fiorello La Guardia Memorial Dedication Ceremony at the La Guardia Houses, Rutgers Place and Clinton Street, September 20, 1957* (pamphlet at LAGA), 4–5.

34. Robert Moses, "La Guardia: A Salute and a Memoir," *New York Times Magazine* (September 8, 1957): 17.

35. Oakland *Daily News*, November 4, 1937.

36. *Times*, April 16, 1947; *Sun* and *World-Telegram*, April 15, 24, 1947; Transcript of WJZ Radio Broadcast, April 27, 1947; C. C. Burlingham interview, Columbia University Oral History Collection, 39.

37. G. Baehr, interview with L. Elliott, February 6, 1976, LAGA; *World-Telegram*, September 25, 1947; Baehr to FHL, August 21, 1947, CCBP.

38. Transcript of WJZ Radio Broadcast, June 15, 1947; FHL to Howard Cullman, August 12, 1947, LAGA; Morris, *Let the Chips Fall*, 213; Newbold Morris, "The Most Unforgettable Character I've Ever Met," *Reader's Digest* 76 (June 1960): 115; Moses, "La Guardia: A Salute and a Memoir," 118.

39. FHL to Stanley Isaacs, July 30, August 21, 26, 1947; FHL's secretary to Isaacs, August 29, 1947; FHL to Cullman, August 21, 1947; FHL to Jack Kroll, September 9, 1947, LAGA; Beatrice Bishop Berle and Travis B. Jacobs, eds., *Navigating the Rapids, 1918–1941; From the Papers of Adolf Berle* (New York: Harcourt Brace Jovanovich, 1973), 578.

40. Morris, "The Most Unforgettable Character," 116; C. C. Burlingham interview, Columbia University Oral History Collection, 39; Morris, *Let the Chips Fall*, 213.

41. Various New York newspaper clippings in LAGA, September 17–21, 1947; Truman quoted in *Time* (September 29, 1947): 28.

42. Morris, *Let the Chips Fall*, 213.

Index